COLLECTED WORKS OF JOHN STUART MILL

VOLUME I

The Collected Edition of the works of John Stuart Mill has been planned and is being directed by an editorial committee appointed from the Faculty of Arts and Science of the University of Toronto, and from the University of Toronto Press. The primary aim of the edition is to present fully collated texts of those works which exist in a number of versions, both printed and manuscript, and to provide accurate texts of works previously unpublished or which have become relatively inaccessible.

Autobiography

and

Literary Essays

by JOHN STUART MILL

Edited by

JOHN M. ROBSON

Professor of English,
Victoria College, University of Toronto

AND

JACK STILLINGER

Professor of English,
University of Illinois at Urbana-Champaign

UNIVERSITY OF TORONTO PRESS

ROUTLEDGE & KEGAN PAUL

© *University of Toronto Press 1981*
Toronto and Buffalo
Printed in Canada

ISBN 0-8020-2368-1

London: Routledge & Kegan Paul
ISBN 0-7100-0718-3

This volume has been published
with the assistance of a grant
from the Social Sciences
and Humanities Research Council
of Canada

Contents

FACSIMILES

Introduction

JOHN STUART MILL's *Autobiography* offers details of his life, a subjective judgment as to its significance, and lengthy expositions of his leading ideas. It is therefore fitting that it should occupy the first place in an edition of his collected works. Indeed Mill himself, thinking of a smaller collection of essays, suggested to his wife that "the Life" should appear "at their head."[1] The *Autobiography*'s comprehensiveness makes the choice of other materials to accompany it less obvious. Those gathered under the rubric of literary essays were decided upon because autobiography is a literary genre, because these essays cast light on some of the personal relations outlined in the memoir, and because they derive from and help us understand a period Mill saw as crucial to his development. Indeed they allow us, as does the *Autobiography*, to see aspects of his character that are obscured in the more magisterial works. In particular, one finds specific evidence of aesthetic enthusiasm and taste, and of friendships and allegiances, that proves him not to have been the chill pedant of caricature.

THE AUTOBIOGRAPHY

AUTOBIOGRAPHIES are seldom explicit about their purposes, which can be widely diverse. Yet to ignore the author's intentions is to run the risk of confusing, for example, confession with self-celebration, or diary with social anatomy. Mill helps us avoid this danger by presenting, in the first paragraph of his *Autobiography*, a warning that serves as an enticing framework for his overt statement of purpose. He cannot imagine that anything in a life "so uneventful" could be "interesting to the public as a narrative, or as being connected" with himself. But there are, he says, other reasons that justify the publication of the record: first, a description of his "unusual and remarkable" education should be useful in showing how much can effectively be taught to children; second, an account of the successive phases of a mind always eager and open will be "both of interest and of benefit" in "an age of transition in opinions"; and, finally, and to the author most significantly (though, as he does not point out, without direct public utility), an

---

[1]*Later Letters* [*LL*], ed. Francis E. Mineka and Dwight N. Lindley, *Collected Works* [*CW*], Vols. XIV–XVII (Toronto: University of Toronto Press, 1972), Vol. XIV, p. 142 (29 Jan., 1854).

acknowledgment of his intellectual and moral debts is necessary to satisfy his sense of duty. Having thus established the terms of a contract with his potential audience, Mill closes the paragraph with an admonition that probably no one has ever heeded: "The reader whom these things do not interest, has only himself to blame if he reads farther, and I do not desire any other indulgence from him than that of bearing in mind, that for him these pages were not written" (p. 5).[2]

Anyone reading this introduction (and we beg the same indulgence) presumably believes, *malgré* Mill, that his "uneventful" life is interesting, or accepts, with him, the validity of his stated goals. One can proceed, then, to use the opening paragraph as an avenue into comment on the *Autobiography*, confident that one is on the author's chosen route. To do so is doubly important, for some critics have chosen to treat his evident omissions and underplaying of events and people as evidence of suppressed psychological states or distorting attitudes. And such inferences may be correct: but at least one should give Mill credit, with his quirks and biasses, for knowing what he was trying to do.

It is apparent, to begin with, that the narrative balance is affected by his notion of what his readers should properly take an interest in. As so often occurs in personal memoirs, there is a chronological imbalance: the first six chapters (about 70 per cent of the text) cover the period to 1840, when Mill was thirty-six years old, while the seventh and last chapter deals with the next thirty years. The title of that last chapter—"General View of the Remainder of My Life"—suggests summary and diminuendo, whereas the titles of the earlier chapters imply the rich detail that they in fact contain.

Although chronology is (in the main) the structural guide, the pace is irregular: ignoring some adumbration and very slight retrospection, one can say that Chapters i and ii cover roughly the same years (to *aet.* 15) from different points of view, intellectual and moral. Chapter iii, rather surprisingly, covers only about two years (to *aet.* 17). Chapters iv and v together deal with nine years (to 1830, *aet.* 24); they overlap in their accounts of the period from 1826 to 1829 (*aet.* 20 to 23). Chapter vi takes one through the next decade (to 1840, *aet.* 34), and Chapter vii brings the narrative to the point where Mill finally put down his pen, early in 1870 (*aet.* 63). Furthermore, the chapters vary considerably in length, so the average amount of space given per year in each period clarifies the emphasis:

TABLE 1[3]

Chap.	i & ii	iii	iv & v	vi	vii
No. of years	15	2	9	10	30
% of total pages	19	8	32	12	30
% of pages per year	1.3	4	3.6	1.2	1

[2]References to material printed in this volume are normally given in the text. The third of these stated purposes, it should be noted, is not present in the corresponding text of the Early Draft.

[3]Percentages are used because the setting of the text in this edition (parallel passages with blank spaces) and the number of footnotes make page counting unreliable. For that reason, in both Table 1

Explanatory light is thrown on the imbalance by Mill's tripartite division of his life: the first stage being one of education and of propagandism for Philosophic Radicalism; the second stage one of new ideas, assimilation, and reconsideration; and the third stage one of mature and steady (but not rigid) views, recorded in his major works. This division, seen in conjunction with the three purposes Mill announces, makes it clearer why he structured the *Autobiography* as he did.

The account of his education (first purpose) occupies most of the first three chapters, while the explanation of the "successive phases" of his mind (second purpose) is the main matter of the next three chapters. The division between these phases, however, cannot be distinctly drawn, and the third purpose, acknowledgment of debts, as is to be expected, is served through most of the work. The reason is that education in its widest sense is a continuous process, during which one moves through "phases" and incurs repeated debts. For example, looking at the transition from Chapter iii to Chapter iv, one sees that the former ends with an account of what Mill, in its title, identifies as the "first" stage of his self-education, and the latter, with its mention of the strenuous activities of the fledgling Philosophic Radicals (discussions, debates, studies, editing, essays), obviously is the next phase. But, while the narrative of sectarian activities in Chapter iv provides an excellent foil for the rejection of one-sidedness in Chapter v, it also outlines a continuation of the young Mill's education. Furthermore, his education of course continued in the exciting phase described in Chapter v, "A Crisis in My Mental History. One Stage Onward." And in each of these chapters, as in Chapters i and ii, he mentions people who influenced him. The thematic intertwining, with the consequent need to cover crucial periods from different standpoints, explains why the period of greatest overlap, from about 1821 to the early 1830s, gets most attention. A glance at Table 1 above will show that Chapters iii–v occupy about 40 per cent of the whole work, and on an average each year in that period is given more than $3\frac{1}{2}$ times as much space as each year after 1840.

So, if we accept the premises Mill himself advances, the concentration on his education and intellectual development until his mid-thirties is neither surprising nor exceptionable. Indeed, the anomalous element is the final chapter, with its account of his next thirty years, in which there should be little matter relevant to his stated purposes. There is, in fact, some: most obviously, Mill pays important tribute to his wife. Chapter vi, which covers the decade of their first acquaintance, has in its title the strong assertion, "Commencement of the Most Valuable Friendship of My Life," but the continuation of the account into the final chapter results in almost one-fifth of it being dedicated to her part in his life and work. Indeed, he ties that account directly to his third purpose:

In resuming my pen some years after closing the preceding narrative, I am influenced by a desire not to leave incomplete the record, for the sake of which chiefly this biographical

---

and Table 2 below, the counts are based on Jack Stillinger's editions of the *Autobiography* (Boston: Houghton Mifflin, 1969) and *The Early Draft of John Stuart Mill's "Autobiography"* (Urbana: University of Illinois Press, 1961).

sketch was undertaken, of the obligations I owe to those who have either contributed essentially to my own mental developement or had a direct share in my writings and in whatever else of a public nature I have done.[4]

It may be noticed that here he somewhat modifies his initial statement of purpose: rather than referring to aids to his *intellectual and moral* development, he refers to those who contributed to his *mental* development and to those who shared in his writings and public acts. This modification further justifies the final chapter, for in its pages appear substantial accounts of his writings in maturity, in the course of which he mentions other debts.[5] It cannot be denied, however, that after the last tribute to his wife, the focus does alter: in actual as well as proportional length, Mill gives more space to his parliamentary career (1865–68) than to any other period in his life, even that of his "mental crisis."[6] The account of that career, the events of which were fresh in his mind only a year after his defeat, is not easily justified on Mill's stated terms. Indeed, its main interest surely lies outside them, in his own character and fame, which are described if not in a boastful, at least in a self-satisfied way.

Apart from the concluding portion of Chapter vii (which, untypically for Mill, was not rewritten), one can, then, gain considerable insight by accepting his exordium as accurate. In that light, some comment on the way he fulfils his goals is appropriate.

First, the description of his extraordinary education, initially at the hands of his father, but later and indeed for most of the time on his own initiative, is copious and full of interest. The account is also dense, as may be seen by comparing the combined lengths of Appendices B and C below, which attempt to reconstruct his early reading and writing, with their primary source, the early pages of the *Autobiography* (cf. especially pp. 9–25 with App. B, pp. 552–68). The early start (Greek at the age of three) was not then so exceptional as it now would be: to choose relevant comparisons, Bentham (with not much encouragement) was quick off the infant blocks, as (with more encouragement) was Macaulay. Mill was unusual, but he appears unique because he left such a full record. His detailed memory of those early years is surprising; however, he almost certainly had at least one *aide-mémoire*, a copy of the letter he wrote to Sir Samuel Bentham in mid-1819,[7] setting out his educational accomplishments of the preceding six years. That letter confirms and slightly expands the account in the *Autobiography*, and strengthens our appreciation of two aspects of his education—its continued and indeed increasing intensity, and the fact that it was intermingled with daily

---

[4]P. 251. The composition of the concluding pages of Chap. vii is described on p. xxvii below.

[5]The acknowledgments are not extensive, though Helen Taylor is given a page explicitly (and more implicitly), and Thomas Hare's writings are also given a page.

[6]If we include the discussion of his writings while he was a member of parliament, the account fills about twenty pages, whereas that of his crisis occupies about eight.

[7]See *Earlier Letters* [*EL*], ed. Francis E. Mineka, *CW*, Vols. XII–XIII (Toronto: University of Toronto Press, 1963), Vol. XII, pp. 6–10.

instruction of his younger siblings, especially of the two closest to him in age, Wilhelmina and Clara. In both these respects he was very unusual, especially when it is remembered that he had no formal education at all, his only teacher, in these early years, being his father, who was in truth using the child as a proving ground for his theories. (This wicked practice, it may be remarked, is found in all enlightened periods.) However, as Mill points out, his was not an education of cram; its great virtue, he believed, was that it enabled and encouraged him to think for himself, not only answering but questioning, not only getting but giving, not only remembering but discovering. This practice remained with him through life, and was connected with yet another distinguishing element: his curiosity and eagerness to learn. In the *Autobiography* this attribute is mentioned, although it surely tells against his assertion that anyone educated as he was could match his record. In the journal he kept while in France, his eagerness stands out as though in boldface, while one can read between the lines the efforts of his hosts, especially Lady Bentham, to prevent his doing lessons all the time.[8]

Probably the most extraordinary aspect of Mill's precocity was his ability from about twelve to fifteen years of age to comprehend and enunciate abstract ideas in economics, and some parts of philosophy and science. Many gifted children astonish with feats of memory,[9] with ability to learn languages, and, perhaps most obviously, with great mathematical powers; Mill had these talents, but also showed astonishing maturity in his wide-ranging discussions with his father and others, in his self-directed studies, in his comments on his more formal studies, and in the major surviving piece of contemporary evidence, the "Traité de logique" he wrote while in France. And, without extending the case unduly, his editing, before his twentieth year, of Bentham's *Rationale of Judicial Evidence* (see the understated account on pp. 117–19 below) was a genuinely amazing feat.

In his account, of course, Mill, in keeping with his third purpose, is celebrating

[8]See Anna J. Mill, ed., *John Mill's Boyhood Visit to France* (Toronto: University of Toronto Press, 1960), esp. pp. 24, 28, 35, 43, 50.

[9]Given Mill's attitude towards his own life, it is not surprising that the *Autobiography* lacks particularity of detail. But there are some sentences that convey a sense of luminous memory breaking through the calm level. Often these have to do with his father's use of the Socratic method in teaching; "my recollection," he says, "is almost wholly of failures, hardly ever of success" (p. 35). Earlier he had remarked that he "well" remembered "how, and in what particular walk," his father had attempted to get him to understand syllogistic logic (p. 21); here he goes on to mention what was obviously vivid in his mind, forty years after the event, his inability to define "idea," and his father's challenging him for having said that "something was true in theory but required correction in practice" (p. 35). Shortly thereafter he says he remembers "the very place in Hyde Park where, in [his] fourteenth year," his father explained to him how unusual a person his education had made him (p. 37). Perhaps the most surprising passage is that concerning Ford Abbey, where the grounds, Mill (with his wife's help) says, "were riant and secluded, umbrageous, and full of the sound of falling waters" (p. 57). More often the emotion is excluded with the telling detail, and only retracing the process of revision gives an opening: he mentions reading Dugald Stewart on reasoning "a second or third time" (originally he had written—probably correctly—"third or fourth"), but he cancelled "sitting in the garden at Mickleham" (where the Mills had a cottage). The detail is striking for anyone who has handled the bulky folios of Stewart, another matter that Mill omits. (Pp. 188–9.)

not himself, but his father, and, despite the qualifications and explanations,[10] it is a celebration, incorporating at least one memorable aphorism: "A pupil from whom nothing is ever demanded which he cannot do, never does all he can" (p. 35). Moving into the period of self-education, Mill, having learned his pedagogy, broadened his teaching to include others who were caught up in the Radicals' increasing momentum,[11] and one can be sure that at least the demand side of the aphorism was observed. We cannot now recapture all the detail—let alone the enthusiasm—of the activities he joined in with others, but what is known is remarkable.

The earliest joint venture was probably the "Mutual Improvement Society," not mentioned in the *Autobiography*, which flowered at least briefly under Jeremy Bentham's patronage.[12] The date of Mill's two surviving speeches for that Society, 1823 or 1824,[13] suggests that in fact it may have melded with the "Utilitarian Society" that Mill says he founded in the winter of 1822–23 (p. 81); the latter also met in Bentham's house, included Bentham's amanuensis, Richard Doane, and convened once a fortnight to read essays and discuss questions of ethics and politics. This small group, which continued until 1826, included Mill's most intimate friends, as did its successor, the "Society of Students of Mental Philosophy," which met for detailed discussion of specific philosophic and economic texts in George Grote's house from 1825 until early in 1828, and then again in 1829.[14] In the mid-20s, emulating the *philosophes*, Mill kept a journal of his group's activities, and wrote a few articles for a proposed Philosophical Diction-

[10]Probably the one he intended to tell most against a general application of his father's methods is that on p. 37, where Mill says that much of what was accomplished was incompatible with "any great amount of intercourse with other boys." (It need not be said that this pre-Freudian remark has no special reference to the English public schools.)

[11]See John Arthur Roebuck's account in his *Life and Letters*, ed. R. E. Leader (London: Arnold, 1897), pp. 25–8. See also pp. 306–7, where Leader gives Roebuck's speech at an election meeting in support of Mill's candidacy for Westminster (reported in the *Morning Star*, 7 Apr., 1865, p. 2).

[12]See John M. Robson, "John Stuart Mill and Jeremy Bentham, with Some Observations on James Mill," in *Essays in English Literature Presented to A. S. P. Woodhouse*, ed. M. MacLure and F. W. Watt (Toronto: University of Toronto Press, 1964), p. 254.

[13]One, "On the Utility of Knowledge," was dated 1823 by its editor, H. J. Laski (who had the MS in his possession); see Mill's *Autobiography*, ed. Laski (London: Oxford University Press, 1924), pp. 267–74. The MS of the other, "On Parliamentary Reform," is inscribed by Mill "1823 or 24" (Mill-Taylor Collection, British Library of Political and Economic Science, London School of Economics).

[14]The Utilitarian Society included William Prescott (Grote's banking partner), William Eyton Tooke, William Ellis, George John Graham, and John Arthur Roebuck; the Society of Students of Mental Philosophy (which Harriet Grote called "the Brangles") included all these (though Tooke is not named in known sources) plus, at one time or another, George Grote, Horace Grant, Henry Cole, Edward Lytton Bulwer, "two brothers Whitmore" (probably George and William, who were members of the London Debating Society), and [John?] Wilson. (See Textual Introduction, *A System of Logic*, *CW*, Vols. VII–VIII [Toronto: University of Toronto Press, 1973], Vol. VII, p. liii, and the sources there cited, and F. E. Sparshott, Introduction, *Essays on Philosophy and the Classics*, *CW*, Vol. XI [Toronto: University of Toronto Press, 1978], p. viii n.)

ary to be edited by Charles Austin (see p. 110; the journal and articles seem not to have survived).

Another kind of mutual education, through propagation of the faith, was contemporaneous: public debate. First, in 1825, he and some friends[15] debated against the Owenites of the Cooperative Society; then, from 1826 to 1829, they embarked on a more impressive scheme, the London Debating Society, in which the coming young men opened their minds and talents on major issues of the times.[16] Less important were evening meetings to study elocution, and the formation of a class to learn German on the "Hamiltonian method."[17]

Of greater significance in a wider sphere was the work done by the young Philosophic Radicals with their elders and mentors on the *Westminster Review*, founded in 1824 (see pp. 93–101), and on the *Parliamentary History and Review* during its brief career from 1826 to 1828 (p. 121), the latter year also seeing the Mills withdraw from the *Westminster Review* stable (p. 135). Throughout this period Mill's practical education, the value of which he acknowledges on p. 87, was going on in the Examiner's Office of the East India Company, which he had joined in 1823 on his seventeenth birthday. Finally, though the details are vague, one should not overlook the broad educational benefits of his less formal but undoubtedly strenuous and wide-ranging discussions with his friends on his daily walks between Kensington and the City, and his weekend and holiday excursions into the countryside. Even without analysis of his writings, one can wholeheartedly support his judgment that from 1822 to 1828 his "own pursuits . . . were never carried on more vigorously" (p. 89).[18]

Here one is moving to the second of Mill's purposes, his desire to show "the successive phases" of a "mind which was always pressing forward, equally ready to learn and to unlearn either from its own thoughts or from those of others" (p. 5). The least precise of the three goals, it nonetheless gets very careful attention in the next few chapters of the *Autobiography*, those dealing with the period from the

---

[15]He mentions Roebuck, Ellis, and Charles Austin (pp. 127–9).

[16]See pp. 129–33. Roebuck was (for most of the period) Mill's major ally, but many other friends joined in the fray. The Society continued for a few years after Mill (with John Sterling, a new friend made through the Society) withdrew in 1829.

[17]P. 123. Mill's assertion that he "learnt German" at this time, and his later mention of reading "Goethe and other Germans" (adding in an earlier version, "either in the original or in translations," p. 160[b]), merit attention, because the question whether he read the language is often raised, especially in connection with his philosophy. The Hamiltonian method (set out in James Hamilton, *The History, Principles, Practice and Results of the Hamiltonian System* [Manchester: Sowler, 1829]) involved immediate word for word translation by the student, the method originally used, and apparently still approved, by James Mill, who, on 15 Nov., 1825, was one of a group that examined "eight lads" of poor families who had been learning Latin, French, and Italian by this system (*Morning Chronicle*, 16 Nov., 1825).

[18]In the Early Draft the sentence as first written reinforced the point by continuing, "than during the next few years." Harriet Taylor underscored "few" and Mill responded with the question, "meaning of this mark?" Her answer, whatever it was, led to the deletion of the words.

time of his mental crisis in 1826–27 until 1840, when the *Logic* was virtually completed. He says that in his account of "these years of transition" he has mentioned only those of his "new impressions" which appeared then and later "to be a kind of turning points, marking a definite progress" in his mode of thought (p. 175). And he goes on to indicate that he was considering much more in those years than the account indicates. The nature and intensity of some of these considerations are to be seen in the literary essays in the present volume.

Many of the changes, these essays also imply, came through personal contact of the kind already suggested, as his circle of acquaintance broadened. The record of "successive phases" of his mind is, therefore, again seen to be intertwined with that of his debts, and so the second and third purposes are served together. Often his desire to acknowledge his intellectual debts is greater than his desire to trace his development, with the result, quite intentional on Mill's part, that emphasis falls on certain aspects of his development at the expense of others. For example, the brief period of near withdrawal from his customary activities from 1828 to 1830 is left in shade, and little evidence is available elsewhere to fill in the picture. And the years of active political sectarianism in the *London and Westminster Review*, years that have troubled many who otherwise admire Mill (after all, he says he had already forsworn at least overt sectarianism [see pp. 115–17]), are excused by the plea of circumstance, inadequately described. Again—and from the perspective of the editors of this volume, quite regrettably—Mill gives little space to his writings for journals in the 1830s, and much of that concerns his mainly political leaders in the *Examiner*.

As mentioned above, one important change, Mill's new aesthetic interest, is seen in his literary essays. In particular, they indicate the shift in thought following his distress over the effects of purely analytic methods, and point to the existence of what was not quite a school, or even a coterie, but certainly was a group quick to respond and to interact. The relief Mill found in Wordsworth's poetry (pp. 149–53), and his related discovery of Shelley (a favourite of Harriet Taylor's), as well as his love of music (almost unmentioned in the *Autobiography*),[19] and his growing appreciation of drama, painting, and architecture, all had a part in inducing the aesthetic speculations found in these essays. Though they do not amount to an important theory, elements of them are of considerable value, and helped clarify for Mill both the place of emotion in individual lives and in the human sciences, and what he took to be his proper role in the "Art and Science of Life," as "Scientist" or "Logician," and not as "Artist" or "Poet."[20]

Mill was markedly influenced by his new acquaintances, most significantly by

[19]There are references on pp. 21, 147–9. He played the piano (and composed in an amateur way); the piano he used in France still exists, in Fondation Flandreysy-Espérandieu, Palais du Roure, Avignon.

[20]See John M. Robson, "J. S. Mill's Theory of Poetry," *University of Toronto Quarterly*, XXIX (July, 1960), 420–37, and, for a more personal application of the theory, Robson, "Harriet Taylor and John Stuart Mill: Artist and Scientist," *Queen's Quarterly*, LXXIII (Summer, 1966), 167–86.

W. J. Fox's circle of Unitarians,[21] including Harriet and John Taylor, by Thomas Carlyle, and by John Sterling. Through Sterling (and perhaps through Cambridge friends of Charles Austin) Mill became acquainted with other of the Cambridge "Apostles," and it is of more than passing significance that his reaching out for "radicals" of different kinds brought into the net of the *London and Westminster Review* some of these apparently incompatible, but equally enthusiastic proponents of a new order. When one considers the subjects and provenances of Mill's articles in the present volume, the network of relations is evident: of those articles published in the 1830s, four of the five that appeared before 1835 were in Fox's journal, the *Monthly Repository* (which in these years was Mill's main organ for non-literary essays as well); all those after that date were in the *London and Westminster* under his own editorship. Not all the articles are actually reviews, but of those that are, two deal with William Bridges Adams, a protégé of Fox's, who married Sarah Flower, the sister of Harriet Taylor's closest friend (and Fox's lover), Eliza. Browning also was a member of Fox's circle, and only accident (see pp. xxxiii–xxxiv) prevented Mill's review of his *Pauline* from appearing. Tennyson, Helps, Milnes, and Bulwer (see App. F, p. 604) were all Cambridge men, the first three Apostles. This evidence does not justify an accusation of puffery, though the reviews are favourable, but Mill can at least be seen as showing bias in his selection of subjects. And there is other evidence of his raising a wind. Exhalations include his placing, in the *Examiner*, reviews of Eliza Flower's musical compositions,[22] and complimentary notices of the *Monthly Repository*.[23] In return, the *Repository* blew some kisses, mentioning as a new publication the pamphlet reprint of Mill's "Corporation and Church Property," and commenting, "'Read, mark, learn, and inwardly digest' this little pamphlet, which is full of the marrow of a sound philosophy and morality." In "Characteristics of English Aristocracy," a review of Bulwer's *England and the English*, there is praise for the appendices Mill contributed anonymously on Bentham and James Mill that might well normally have gone unnoticed. And there is an unambiguous (to the informed) reference to Mill: "The most accomplished and perfect logician we ever knew, has the best appreciation of the beautiful and the poetical."[24]

In all ages, and even among the virtuous, *manus manum lavat*, and altruism may be a form of self-help. There were, in that age of excitement, when the old order (again) seemed to be passing away, many opportunities for the daring and enthusiastic young to air and share their views, and as Mill passed through his

---

[21]Mill surely knew of Fox, if he had not actually met him, as early as 1824, for Fox contributed to the first number of the *Westminster* the lead article, which almost certainly is one of the two Mill says he took most to heart (see p. 96 below).

[22]3 July, 1831, pp. 420–1; 8 Apr., 1832, p. 230; 21 Apr., 1833, p. 245; 20 Apr., 1834, p. 244; and 4 Jan., 1835, p. 4.

[23]17 Mar., 1833, pp. 164–5; 14 Apr., 1833, pp. 229–30; 16 June, 1833, pp. 372–3; 8 Sept., 1833, p. 567; 15 Dec., 1833, pp. 788–9; 12 Jan., 1834, p. 21.

[24]*Monthly Repository*, n.s. VII (Mar., 1833), 215, and *ibid.* (Sept., 1833), 601, and 593.

"successive phases" he joined in or was touched by the Philosophic Radicals of the 1820s, the Romantics, the Saint-Simonians, the Unitarians, the Cambridge Apostles, the new bureaucrats, the Philosophic Radicals of the 1830s; in some cases he was at or near the centre, in others on the periphery—but never was he to be ignored.

A change came, however. The last stage (on his account) was one in which he thought himself rejected by "society," and in which, in any case, he rejected the society of most others. His relation with Harriet Taylor, a relation which they seem naïvely to have thought neither would nor should cause comment, resulted in their eventual isolation from all but a few, such as the Carlyles (and there was constant and increasing tension even with them). Mill's account of his movement into maturity of opinion, then, ought to be seen also as a movement away from the influence of groups. He did not, it should be clear, go into intellectual solitude, for quite apart from the constant interchange of views with Harriet Taylor, he read and corresponded widely (for example with Auguste Comte). He was not, however, in an arena where the constant push-and-pull of allegiances, opinions, and events could initiate major fluctuations of belief. When, in the mid-1860s after his wife's death and his retirement from the East India Company, the time did come for him to plunge into turbulent political waters, his general attitudes were indeed firm, though his expression of them in particular circumstances led some to believe him fickle. And at that time, as young men gathered round him—Bain, Cairnes, Fawcett, Morley, even Spencer—it was his influence on them that mattered, not theirs on him. And that tale he does not choose to tell.

The tale he does tell, right from the beginning of the *Autobiography*, as we have seen, is that of his third purpose: acknowledgment of his intellectual and moral debts, the importance of which justifies brief analysis. It is hard and indeed unwise to identify separately the elements that make up Mill's accounts of his teachers and friends; there is some mention of their characters, some of their careers, and some of their writings, as well as of their relations with Mill, and all these matters bear on one another. Also, a few people of obvious importance are mentioned almost in passing,[25] one may infer because the exigencies of narrative did not easily permit of a fuller account. As has been argued, the tributes and assessments are entwined with the accounts of his education and the movement of his mind; nonetheless, if we look simply at the main emphasis of passages, almost one-third of the final version is given generally to an account of his debts. (A considerably higher proportion is found in the Early Draft, which includes, *inter alia*, longer passages on Roebuck and Sarah Austin and necessarily excludes the narrative of the final

---

[25]As an example (not a complete account), the following persons, all of whom most certainly influenced Mill in some significant way, are, except as noted, given two sentences or less: Ricardo, Joseph Hume, Samuel Bentham and his family (about five sentences), Mill's teachers in France, Say (four sentences), W. E. Tooke, William Ellis, G. J. Graham, Thirlwall (three sentences), Coleridge, Goethe, Fonblanque (three sentences), and Bain.

years.) The relative weighting is interesting. Ignoring all those of less than one-half page in length, one finds:

TABLE 2

Tribute to and discussion of	App. no. of pages	Tribute to and discussion of	App. no. of pages
James Mill	19½	Charles Austin	1½
Harriet Taylor Mill	14	Carlyle	1½
Roebuck	4[26]	Sarah Austin	1[27]
John Austin	3	Sterling	1
Comte	3	Maurice	1
Wordsworth	2½	Helen Taylor	1
Bentham	2	Hare	1
Saint-Simonians	2	Black	⅔
Tocqueville	2	Grote	½

Such computation (which ignores the strength as well as the kind of comment) does rough justice to Mill's account; but he himself is not even-handed. Given other evidence, including Mill's writings, no one is likely to challenge the placing of his father and his wife at the head of the list of those who influenced him. The kind of influence and its effect are perhaps moot, especially in the case of his wife, but one can easily accept his estimate of their weights. Mill says his conscience spoke to him in his father's voice (p. 613); there can be no doubt that there was a literal transference of this function to Harriet Taylor after James Mill's death in 1836, if not before, and only a little that Helen Taylor played a speaking role after her mother's death in 1858.[28] There is no room here for essays on these extraordinary relations; our comment is only that they were, certainly from a psychological point of view, as important as Mill indicates.

About others, though, some caveats concerning Mill's judgment must be entered. His attitude to his mother has caused speculation: not mentioned in the *Autobiography*, she is given, in isolated comments of a derogatory kind, almost all of which were cancelled, only about one-half page in the Early Draft. When he began that draft, Mill was excessively, indeed petulantly, angry at his family because of what he (and/or Harriet) took to be their slighting response to his marriage; in revision, he at least moved from derogation to silence. It is likely that his mother and his siblings did not "influence" him, using the word as he intends it, but one may well regret the attitude and the omission. At the very least it is odd that a strong feminist, writing under the correcting eye of an equally strong feminist, should have given himself but a single parent in the opening narrative sentence of

[26]In the Early Draft; about three pages were removed in the final revision.

[27]In the Early Draft; the passage was removed in the final revision.

[28]Though Helen Taylor had nothing to do with the formation of Mill's central views, she was a major influence on the expression of his ideas and on his actions in the last decade of his life.

his autobiography: "I was born in London, on the 20th of May 1806, and was the eldest son of James Mill, the author of *The History of British India*" (p. 5).

Other questions can here only be asked:[29] if John Austin gets (deservedly) three pages, surely Bentham deserves more than two, and George Grote more than one-half—and what of Harriet Grote? Wordsworth merits at least the treatment he receives, but where then is Coleridge? (The answer lies partly, but only partly, in the discussion of the "Coleridgeans," Sterling and Maurice.) Does not Tocqueville, whose influence, curiously enough, is not acknowledged at all in the Early Draft, deserve as much space as Comte (even if we admit that much of the three pages devoted to the latter is given to denial of influence)? Surely Carlyle, whatever Mill's later judgments, had more influence than Roebuck (who was on his own admission a pupil of Mill's)—and, again, where is Jane Carlyle? Could he not have mentioned his colleagues in the East India House, such as Thomas Love Peacock? The questions pile up, and answers implying the deliberate downplaying of friendships, or the desire to avoid comment on those alive to read the account, do not seem adequate. Of greater relevance are Mill's and his wife's attitudes to the people discussed and the exigencies of narrative and of thesis: the case he is making does not require equal or absolute justice, and a story—even one the author claims to be devoid of interesting episode—militates against judgmental balance. One certainly may regret that Mill's denigration of self led him to the purposes he thought proper, and so to exclude much that other autobiographers, many of them of narrower experience and less insight, delight us with. But his judgment should be respected. Although his mind, his life, and his career have an interest beyond the significance he attached to them, in developing his stated purposes Mill faithfully adheres to his contract with the reader for whom "these pages were . . . written."

The *Autobiography* stands alone among Mill's book-length works in the abundance of MS materials that have survived.[30] We have no fewer than three complete MSS—Mill's original draft, a revised MS also in his hand, and a transcript of the whole—as well as a four-page piece of holograph draft independent of the other MSS. The three complete MSS were among the collection of letters and papers owned after Mill's death by Helen Taylor, bequeathed by her to her niece Mary Taylor, and sold at auction in 1922 by the executors of the latter's estate. They are

---

[29]One of them seems best relegated to a footnote, important as it is: would it not have been instructive for him to have given more space to the influence on him of the dead (Aristotle, Bacon, Locke, as well as the acknowledged Plato)?

[30]This section on the composition of the work and the transmission and first publication of the text draws (sometimes verbatim) on two previous accounts by Jack Stillinger—"The Text of John Stuart Mill's *Autobiography*," *Bulletin of the John Rylands Library*, XLIII (Sept., 1960), 220–42, and the introduction to *The Early Draft of John Stuart Mill's "Autobiography."* These in turn are indebted to Albert William Levi's pioneer work in "The Writing of Mill's *Autobiography*," *Ethics*, LXI (July, 1951), 284–96.

listed together, "a large parcel," as lot 720 (third day) in Sotheby's sale catalogue of 27–29 March, 1922: "MILL (John Stuart) Auto. MS. of his AUTOBIOGRAPHY upwards of 220 pp. 4to; with an earlier draft of the same in his hand, and a copy, mostly in the hand of Helen Taylor, *with the suppressed passages*." The lot went for £5 5s. to Maggs Bros., who resold the MSS separately.

Early Draft. The "earlier draft" was purchased from Maggs in 1923 by Jacob H. Hollander, Professor of Political Economy at Johns Hopkins University, who kept it until his death in 1940, after which it was stored for nearly two decades in a Baltimore warehouse. In 1958 it was acquired with the rest of Hollander's library by the University of Illinois at Urbana-Champaign. More than just "earlier," it is in fact the original draft of the *Autobiography*, consisting of 169 leaves all told—139 leaves constituting the first finished version of the work plus thirty leaves of rejected text retained together at the end of the draft. Written in the late months of 1853 and the early months of 1854 (see below on this and other datings), the MS contains a complete account, as Mill then would have given it, of his life up to his marriage in 1851. The paper is apparently that used in the East India Company office where Mill worked, half-sheets of white laid foolscap measuring *c*. 33.6 × 20.8 cm., with either a Britannia watermark (on about half the leaves, irregularly throughout) or one of three countermarks: "STACEY WISE 1849," "C ANSELL 1851," and "C ANSELL 1852." Mill wrote in ink, generally on both sides. Before beginning a leaf, he folded it once lengthwise, to divide each page into two long halves *c*. 10.4 cm. wide;[31] he originally composed only in the right-hand half, saving the space at left for his revisions and for corrections, comments, and other markings by his wife.

Columbia MS. The second of the complete MSS (to take them in the order in which they were written), the "Auto. MS." of the description in Sotheby's catalogue, was bought from Maggs by Professor John Jacob Coss, acting for members of the Department of Philosophy at Columbia who presented it to the Columbia University Library in April, 1923. This MS consists of 210 leaves (not counting those left blank by Mill or used as wrappers) measuring *c*. 26 × 21.5 cm. The first 162 leaves, medium blue paper sewn in twenty-leaf gatherings marked A through I (with the initial leaf of A and the last seventeen leaves of I left blank) and containing either a fleur-de-lis watermark or the countermark "WEATHERLEY 1856," constitute a revised version of the Early Draft text plus a three-page continuation, the text of 247.35–251.9 below. This part of the MS was written in 1861. The remaining forty-eight leaves, a gathering marked K and made up of twenty-four sheets of darker blue (unwatermarked) paper folded separately and

---

[31]He used the same method in the extant MSS of "Notes on Some of the More Popular Dialogues of Plato" (see Textual Introduction, *Essays on Philosophy and the Classics*, *CW*, Vol. XI, pp. lxxxi–lxxxii, and illustration facing p. 175) and in the surviving MS page of "The Silk Trade" (see *Essays on Economics and Society*, *CW*, Vol. IV [Toronto: University of Toronto Press, 1967], illustration facing p. 138).

unsewn, represent—except for text taken over from the Yale fragment (see below)—the first and only draft of the rest of the *Autobiography*, written in the winter of 1869–70.

Rylands transcript. The third of the MSS sold at Sotheby's, the "copy, mostly in the hand of Helen Taylor, *with the suppressed passages,*" went to an unknown English buyer, and was lost sight of until July, 1959, when it was discovered in the London salerooms of Messrs. Hodgson and acquired by the John Rylands Library, Manchester. Consisting of 282 leaves of various kinds and sizes of paper, the transcript was made mainly or entirely in the months just after Mill's death by three writers—Helen Taylor, Mill's youngest sister Mary Elizabeth Colman, and an unidentified French copyist. It is from this MS that the first edition of the work (1873) was printed, and the "descent" of the text is thus simple and straightforward: Mill revised, recopied, and continued his original version (Early Draft) in the Columbia MS; Helen Taylor and her helpers copied the Columbia text in the Rylands transcript; and the work was set in type from the Rylands transcript.

Yale fragment. In addition to these complete MSS, Mill's first draft of the present 251.18–259.21, the "Note . . . concerning the participation of my wife in my writings" given below beginning on p. 250, is extant at Yale. This is written on the four pages of a folded sheet of bluish-gray wove paper, page size *c*. 25.8 × 20.2 cm. The MS bears the pencil date "[1861]" in the hand of a twentieth-century scholar or archivist, but the basis for this dating is not clear. Mill could have drafted the note any time between the completion of the Early Draft, in 1854, and the writing of the last part of the work in 1869–70. The tenses, the tone, and the mention of *On Liberty* as a "book" (pp. 256–8) strongly suggest that it was composed no earlier than 1859, after his wife's death and the publication of *On Liberty*, and probably after 1861, because it was not included in the continuation of the Early Draft written at that time.

In his surviving letters Mill first mentions the Early Draft on 23 January, 1854, four days after recording in a diary entry his bitterness at having "procrastinated in the sacred duty of fixing in writing, so that it may not die with me, everything that I have in my mind which is capable of assisting the destruction of error and prejudice and the growth of just feelings and true opinions."[32] Replying to a letter now lost, he writes to his wife:

I too have thought very often lately about the life & am most anxious that we should complete it the soonest possible. What there is of it is in a perfectly publishable state—as far as writing goes it could be printed tomorrow—& it contains a full writing out as far as anything can write out, what you are, as far as I am competent to describe you, & what I owe to you—but, besides that until revised by you it is little better than unwritten, it contains nothing about our private circumstances, further than shewing that there was intimate friendship for many years, & you only can decide what more it is necessary or desirable to

---

[32]Diary entry for 19 Jan., 1854, in *The Letters of John Stuart Mill*, ed. Hugh S. R. Elliot, 2 vols. (London: Longmans, Green and Co., 1910), Vol. II, p. 361.

It seems desirable that
I should prefix to the following
biographical sketch, some mention
of the reasons which have made me
think it desirable that I should
have left behind me some memorial of
so uneventful a life as mine. I do
not for a moment imagine that any
part of what I have to relate, can
be interesting to the public either as a
narrative, or from its connexion
with myself. But I have thought,
that in an age in which education
is at least is attempted to be,
more attention than at any former period
education, & its improvements, are
the subject of more if not of profounder study
than at any former period in English
history, it may be useful that
there should be
some record of an education which
was unusual & remarkable, &
which, whatever else it may have
done, has at least proved how much
more than is commonly supposed
may be taught, & taught thoroughly,
in those early years which, in the
common modes of instruction, are little
better than wasted. It has also
seemed to me
, that in an age of transition in opinions
in almost all the grand objects of thought,
there may be somewhat both of interest
& of benefit in noting the successive
phases of a mind which was always
moving forward, equally ready to

Folio 1r of the Early Draft MS
University of Illinois

say in order to stop the mouths of enemies hereafter. The fact is there is about as much written as I *can* write without your help & we must go through this together & add the rest to it at the very first opportunity—I have not forgotten what she said about bringing it with me to Paris.[33]

He discusses the subject at length again on 10 February:

I . . . have read through all that is written of the Life—I find it wants revision, which I shall give it—but I do not well know what to do with some of the passages which we marked for alteration in the early part of it which we read together. They were mostly passages in which I had written, you thought, too much of the truth or what I believe to be the truth about my own defects. I certainly do not desire to say more about them than integrity requires, but the difficult matter is to decide how much that is. Of course one does not, in writing a life, either one's own or another's, undertake to tell everything—& it will be right to put something into *this* which shall prevent any one from being able to suppose or to pretend, that we undertake to keep nothing back. Still it va sans dire that it ought to be on the whole a fair representation. Some things appear to me on looking at them now to be said very crudely, which does not surprise me in a first draft, in which the essential was to say everything, somehow, sauf to omit or revise afterwards. As to matters of opinion & feeling on general subjects, I find there is a great deal of good matter written down in the Life which we have not written anywhere else, & which will make it as valuable in that respect (apart from its main object) as the best things we have published. But of what particularly concerns *our* life there is nothing yet written, except the descriptions of you, & of your effect on me; which are at all events a permanent memorial of what I know you to be, & (so far as it can be shewn by generalities) of what I owe to you intellectually. That, though it is the smallest part of what you are to me, is the most important to commemorate, as people are comparatively willing to suppose all the rest. But we have to consider, which we can only do together, how much of our story it is advisable to tell, in order to make head against the representations of enemies when we shall not be alive to add anything to it. If it was not to be published for 100 years I should say, tell all, simply & without reserve. As it is there must be care taken not to put arms into the hands of the enemy.[34]

Taken together, the two letters show (1) that an early form of the draft, including at least the first eight leaves of the original Part II,[35] largely unrevised since it was first written but nevertheless "in a perfectly publishable state," was finished by 23

[33]*LL, CW*, Vol. XIV, pp. 137–8 (23 Jan., 1854). (At the end of this passage, as frequently elsewhere in his letters to her, Mill refers to his wife in the third person.)

[34]*Ibid.*, p. 154. Between 23 Jan. and 10 Feb. the "Life" is mentioned briefly in two other letters: "I fancy I see one large or two small posthumous volumes of Essays, with the Life at their head," he writes on 29 Jan. (*ibid.*, p. 142); and on 4 Feb. he promises to "look again through the Life" when he has finished rewriting "Nature" (*ibid.*, p. 149). The "Essays" that he was envisioning in the first of these (29 Jan.) include "Nature," "Utility of Religion," *On Liberty*, and some pieces later incorporated into *Utilitarianism*; presumably they are also the "various Essays, for eventual publication, on some of the fundamental questions of human and social life" that he refers to toward the end of the *Autobiography* (p. 245 below). See Textual Introduction, *Essays on Ethics, Religion and Society, CW*, Vol. X (Toronto: University of Toronto Press, 1969), pp. cxxii–cxxix.

[35]But apparently not the whole of Part II—or, more specifically, not the text of RII.20 (see the fourth paragraph below, and App. G, pp. 616–17)—since Mill says in both letters that he has written nothing of their "private circumstances." Two breaks in the composition of the original Part II are evident from changes in pen, the first following the text of the extract given from RII.1–8 (pp. 617–24 below), the second coming after the sentence ending at 222.20 (" . . . did not know what to say.").

January, 1854; (2) that Mill and his wife had read an "early part of it" together, marking passages for alteration (those extracted in App. G from R23–5, and possibly Mill's subsequent revisions of them—in R24^2–25^2 and R19/20, also marked by her—are more or less specifically mentioned in the second letter); but (3) that she had not yet read any portion of the original Part II, in which she and their relationship are described. Up to this point, therefore, there were at least two periods of composition—one in which he wrote the early part that they read and marked together, the other in which he continued writing in her absence.

We have, unfortunately, virtually no biographical documents for the first two years of their marriage, after they had returned from the Continent and settled at Blackheath Park in September, 1851. In August, 1853, Mill took his wife to Sidmouth, Devonshire, returning to London alone on the 23rd—the first time since the marriage that they had been separated. He remained in London through much of September, and then, on the advice of their physicians, accompanied his wife to Nice. When his three-month leave of absence from the India House had expired, he left her at Hyères, on 27 or 28 December, and arrived back in London on 5 January.

It is unlikely that he worked on the draft between 5 and 23 January (the date of the first letter quoted above). On his return he was occupied with official correspondence that had accumulated in his absence, and of his own work he was primarily concerned with the essay on "Nature." He told his wife on 14 January:

I am working hard at getting up the arrear of India house business & have taken some of it home to work at tomorrow (Sunday). I hardly feel well or vigorous enough to set about any work of our own yet on Sundays & in the evenings—when I do the first thing shall be to finish the rewriting of the paper on Nature, which I began before we left.[36]

Moreover, the tone of his letter of 23 January ("I too have thought very often lately about the life") does not suggest that he has been writing. What seems most probable, if we assume that he began the draft in London, perhaps even (as he did with other works) during office hours at the India House when correspondence lagged, is that he commenced writing earlier than August, 1853; that he and his wife read and marked the early part (at least the first twenty-five leaves, through the first extract given in App. G) before going to Devonshire in that month; and that he continued writing, through at least the first eight leaves of the original Part II, in the August–September interval of separation, before joining her for their sojourn in France. A large part of the draft, the "publishable" version described in the letter of 23 January, 1854, should therefore be dated earlier than 24 September, 1853, the date on which they left England together.

On 13 February, 1854, still planning to join his wife in Paris, Mill again mentions bringing the draft with him, and adds:

But if we are not to be together this summer it is doubly important to have as much of the life

[36]*LL, CW*, Vol. XIV, p. 131.

written as can be written before we meet—therefore will you my own love in one of your sweetest letters give me your general notion of what we should say or imply respecting our private concerns. As it is, it shews confidential friendship & strong attachment ending in marriage when you were free & ignores there having ever been any scandalous suspicions about us.[37]

To his earlier letter of the 10th she replied on 14–15 February:

I feel sure dear that the Life is not half written and that half that is written will not do. Should there not be a summary of our relationship from its commencement in 1830—I mean given in a dozen lines. . . . This ought to be done in its genuine truth and simplicity—strong affection, intimacy of friendship, and no impropriety. It seems to me an edifying picture for those poor wretches who cannot conceive friendship but in sex—nor believe that expediency and the consideration for feelings of others can conquer sensuality.[38]

While her letter was en route Mill wrote to her again on the 18th that he was "most anxious at present about the Life, but . . . can do little in the way of addition to it till I hear from her,"[39] and a diary entry of 19 February implies further concern with the life: "Goethe . . . [called] his autobiography, which tells just as much about himself as he liked to be known, 'Aus meinem Leben Dichtung und Wahrheit.' The Aus even without the Dichtung saves his veracity."[40] Finally on the 20th, having received her letter, he was able to report some progress in the work:

As to the Life—which I have been revising & correcting—the greater part, in bulk, of what is written consists of the history of my mind *up to* the time when your influence over it began—& I do not think there can be much objectionable in that part, even including as it does, sketches of the character of most of the people I was intimate with—if I could be said to be so with any one. I quite agree in the sort of résumé of our relationship which you suggest—but if it is to be only as you say a dozen lines, or even three or four dozen, could you not my own love write it out your darling self & send it in one of your precious letters—It is one of the many things of which the *fond* would be much better laid by you & we can add to it afterwards if we see occasion.[41]

On 5 February Mill had finished rewriting "Nature"; on 5 March, having caught up with India House correspondence, he began writing "Utility of Religion."[42] Between those dates, and especially around 20 February, when we have seen him "revising & correcting," he read over and revised the whole of the draft he had written in 1853, and it was probably then also that he finished writing the original Part II. Professor Levi is surely right in suggesting that a passage from Harriet Mill's letter of 14–15 February ("strong affection, intimacy of friendship . . . an edifying picture for those poor wretches who cannot conceive friendship but in sex—nor believe that expediency and the consideration for feelings of others can

[37]*Ibid.*, p. 159.
[38]F. A. Hayek, *John Stuart Mill and Harriet Taylor* (London: Routledge and Kegan Paul, 1951), p. 196.
[39]*LL, CW*, Vol. XIV, p. 163.
[40]*Letters of John Stuart Mill*, ed. Elliot, Vol. II, p. 373.
[41]*LL, CW*, Vol. XIV, pp. 165–6.
[42]*Ibid.*, pp. 152, 178.

conquer sensuality") is echoed in Mill's account of their relationship in the twentieth leaf of Part II:

our relation to each other was one of strong affection and confidential intimacy, entirely apart from sensuality. . . . we disdained, as every person not a slave of his animal appetites must do, the abject notion that the strongest and tenderest friendship cannot exist between a man and a woman without a sensual tie; or that sensuality cannot be put aside when regard for the feelings of others, or even when only prudence and personal dignity require it.[43]

She did not otherwise send him the account he requested, for of the numbered series of Mill's letters to her all but one—a short letter addressed to Marseilles on 13 March—are extant between 20 February and the middle of April, and there are but two subsequent references to the work during the period. On 24 February he writes: "we must do what we can while we are alive—the Life being the first thing—which independent of the personal matters which it will set right when we have made it what we intend, is even now an unreserved proclamation of our opinions on religion, nature, & much else."[44] The gist of the first part of this statement is repeated in a letter of 20 March: "above all I am anxious about the Life, which must be the first thing we go over when we are together."[45]

Harriet Mill returned to London in the middle of April, and it must have been either then or shortly afterward—"the Life being the first thing"—that she read and "improved" the remainder of the draft. Though no useful terminal date for Mill's subsequent corrections can be assigned with certainty, it seems most reasonable to suppose that he revised and rewrote the leaves of Part II before departing for a six-week tour of Brittany in June–July, 1854, and certainly before setting out on his extended tour of France, Italy, and Greece, 8 December, 1854–late June, 1855, during which he was separated from his wife for nearly seven months.

The Early Draft is a heavily worked over MS, with cancellations and interlined revisions on nearly every page, and a great many additional passages written and rewritten at left. Mill foliated the MS in pencil, and most of the leaves show evidence of having been renumbered one or more times as additional leaves were inserted, passages reordered, and revised leaves substituted for earlier ones. The principal additions and rearrangements are reported in notes to the Early Draft text and in headnotes to the extracts given in Appendix G. The most interesting of Mill's large-scale changes has to do with his early intention to divide the work into two parts, the first covering his life before he met Harriet Taylor, and "Part II," beginning with his "first introduction to the lady whose friendship has been the honour and blessing of my existence." Possibly because he wished to bring her in at an earlier point in his account (after his writings of 1832, rather than, as originally, after his writings of 1834 and Molesworth's proposal in that year to

[43]Levi, "The Writing of Mill's *Autobiography*," p. 292. The passage from RII.20 was rewritten as the present 236.15–24. See also the textual notes on pp. 236–7.
[44]*LL, CW*, Vol. XIV, p. 168.
[45]*Ibid.*, p. 190.

establish the *London and Westminster Review*), perhaps also because the two parts were of considerably disproportionate lengths (121 vs. 24 leaves), Mill rearranged several paragraphs, condensed the first eight leaves of Part II to three and a half, and discarded the two-part division altogether (see pp. 616–17 below).

Except possibly for the revised leaves that replaced the rejected leaves of the original Part II and the ending of Part I, Harriet Mill read the entire MS, marking passages with lines, X's, and question marks beside the text, deleting and sometimes rewriting Mill's sentences, here and there commenting in the space at left; and Mill followed many of her suggestions and accepted most of her pencilled alterations by rewriting them in ink. A sizable proportion of her markings are editorial in character, calling attention to wordiness, vagueness, inaccuracy of expression, repetition of word or phrase, and the like "minuter matters of composition" (see p. 255); but she was also the originator of some major changes in the texture and tone of the work. In response to her markings Mill suppressed personal and family details that, had they been retained, would have made the *Autobiography* a warmer, if often more critical document, and she exerted extensive influence on the several versions in which he attempted to describe his practical deficiencies (see pp. 608–11) and on the account he wrote of their relations in the original Part II. While "HTM" appears frequently in the textual apparatus, the notes report only the most significant of her markings and alterations, and do not adequately convey the pervasiveness of her pencil in the MS.[46]

Mill returned to the work sometime in 1861, two or three years after the death of his wife, and on this occasion wrote the first 162 leaves of the Columbia MS, the text from the beginning through the present 251.9.[47] Most of this, of course, was revision rather than initial composition—the "second writing" that Mill refers to in describing the "double redaction" method by which "all my books have been composed" (see pp. 229–31)—but, although the Early Draft on which it was based is itself, in its final stage, a highly finished piece of writing, the new version is substantially different. Between the Early Draft and the corresponding text of the

[46]Her pencilled markings, alterations, and comments appear in nearly a hundred of the 169 leaves; they are absent most notably in the revised leaves that replaced R119–21, RII.1–8, 20, and 24. Occasional markings and alterations of Mill's revisions at left—revisions made as a result of her earlier markings (e.g., in the discarded versions given in the long textual note on pp. 64–5)—are evidence that she read at least some of the MS twice.

[47]The dating is based on Helen Taylor's notes in the 1873 first edition, pp. 240, 251: "Written about 1861" appended to the end of the paragraph at 247.17 in the present volume, and "What precedes was written or revised previous to, or during the year 1861. What follows was written in 1870" appended to the end of the paragraph at 251.9. As is explained below, several paragraphs of Columbia MS text were reordered in the Rylands transcript (and thence in the 1873 edition) in the span where the latter note occurs. But 251.9 is where the text of gathering I of the Columbia MS leaves off, and 251.10 is the beginning of K; it seems virtually certain that the dating in the 1873 note should be applied to (because it originally derived from) this division in the MS. There are a few details in the text before 251.10 that postdate the year 1861—e.g., the references on pp. 79 and 105 to John Romilly as "Lord Romilly" (his title beginning in 1865)—but these are in every instance darker-ink interlineations in the Columbia MS and not part of the original writing.

Columbia MS there are some 2,600 substantive differences, large and small (the figure is offered simply as a rough indication of the frequency of revision; the alteration of a single word counts as one substantive change, and the omission or addition of an entire paragraph or more also counts as one). The number and nature of the differences make impracticable the usual method of recording variants in this edition. We have, therefore, chosen to present the Early Draft and the Columbia MS as parallel texts on facing pages, with spacing adjusted to bring corresponding passages, as much as possible, opposite one another. As a result, blank spaces (and even whole blank pages) on one side or the other immediately call attention to the most extensive of the revisions. Some of the less obvious may be mentioned briefly.

With the distance gained by the passing of seven or more years since his writing of the Early Draft, Mill viewed the events of his life with increased detachment. He could now, for example, add a mitigating comparison to his description of heavy dejection during his mental crisis, by seeing it as like "the state . . . in which converts to Methodism usually are, when smitten by their first 'conviction of sin,'" and go on, less dramatically, "In all probability my case was by no means so peculiar as I fancied it, and I doubt not that many others have passed through a similar state" (pp. 137, 145). This new objectivity dictated a number of changes by which earlier outbursts of egotism, contrasting strikingly with the characteristic self-effacement that marks much of the work, were deflated or restrained. Occasionally, for passages first written specifically about himself, Mill substituted generalization (compare the two versions of the concluding statement about Plato's influence, pp. 24, 25); and many particulars of biographical detail were omitted in the revised account: his meeting with the Frenchmen Ternaux, Destutt de Tracy, Dunoyer, and others (p. 62), "emulation of a little manuscript essay of Mr. Grote" in attempting his first argumentative composition (p. 72), writing an early essay replying to Paley's *Natural Theology* (p. 74), keeping a journal "on the model of Grimm's *Correspondence*" and contributing three or four articles to a projected "Philosophical Dictionary, suggested by Voltaire's" (p. 110), weekly evening meetings to study elocution (p. 126), his elaborate speech in reply to Thirlwall (p. 128), his enthusiastic admiration in response to Carlyle's article on Johnson (p. 182), and so on. The revised life is less full, less varied in texture, than that of the Early Draft.

Here and there Mill toned down his recollections of family relationships and especially of his father. Indirect references to his mother, in speaking of his father's "ill assorted marriage," "to which he had not, and never could have supposed that he had, the inducements of kindred intellect, tastes, or pursuits" (pp. 52, 6), are charitably omitted. James Mill's "authority and indignation" is rewritten as "displeasure" (pp. 14, 15); and the fact that he "often mockingly caricatured" his son's bad reading aloud is discarded (p. 26), along with a number of other sentences and phrases of similar tendency (compare the summary comments on the severity of his upbringing at 52.19–21 and 53.28–9). By changes of this sort, and the addition of several sentences comparing James Mill with Bentham (p. 213), the revised version comes considerably closer than the earlier to being, in the passages describing his father, a eulogy.[48] The same access of charity is evident in recollections of associates outside his family. He cut out the greater part of his "character" of Roebuck (pp. 154–8), softened his critique of Maurice (pp. 160–1), rewrote his account of Sterling (pp. 162, 161), dropped a nasty paragraph on Sarah Austin (p. 186), and resorted to anonymity ("My father and I had hoped that some competent leader might arise; some man of philosophic attainments and popular talents") in place of several sentences of harsh commentary on George Grote's lack of courage, energy, and activity (pp. 202, 204–5).

The more formal and generalized character of the later version is continued in the last part that Mill wrote, the forty-eight leaves of the K gathering in the Columbia MS, containing the text of the work from the present 251.10 to the end. This was drafted in the winter of 1869–70.[49] Mill presumably also gave the earlier part of the MS a final polish at this time (there are in this part a few interlineations and other alterations in darker ink than the rest); there is no evidence of any authoritative changes in the work after this date.[50] At this point other hands take over, and the text deteriorates.

In a codicil to his will dated 14 February, 1872, Mill names Helen Taylor as his literary executor "with full and absolute power and license . . . to edit all or any of my literary works and to publish all or any of my manuscripts as she in her sole discretion may think fit." He then specifically mentions the *Autobiography*:

And whereas in these days no one is secure against attempts to make money out of his memory by means of pretended biographies I therefore think it necessary to state that I have written a short account of my life which I leave to the absolute charge and controul of my said stepdaughter Miss Helen Taylor to be published or not at her will and discretion and in the event of her death in my lifetime to the charge and controul of William Thomas Thornton

---

[48]This is how Mill himself viewed it. In a letter of 26 Nov., 1865, he thanks George Grote for "doing justice to my father" in an article in the *Westminster Review*, and adds: "My own contribution to his memory is already written in a MS designed for posthumous publication [i.e., the *Autobiography*]; though if I live more than a few years longer, I shall very likely publish it while I am alive" (*LL*, *CW*, Vol. XVI, p. 1121).

[49]The dating is based on the second of Helen Taylor's notes quoted in n. 47 just above, Mill's parenthetical date in the text at 276.17, and the first sentence of Helen Taylor's continuation given below in App. H (p. 625), all of which refer to 1870 or "the winter of 1869–1870."

[50]Except possibly in one instance (at 251.42), Mill did not respond to, and may never have seen, the handful of alterations and comments pencilled by Helen Taylor in the Columbia MS. For the record, they are as follows: 47.28–9, deletion of the five-word parenthesis; 55.4, deletion of a redundant "in education" after "dispensed with" (an emendation followed in the present text); 193.27, "Not true" written on the opposite verso and connected specifically to the words "or artistic tastes"; 195.6, "Miss Flower" (with the initials "HT") also on the opposite verso, identifying the "person of genius"; 251.28–9, alteration of "preceded, all . . . her work" to read "preceded it, all . . . my wife's work"; 251.42, interlineation of "perhaps" (subsequently cancelled in ink, but not necessarily by Mill) after "except"; 253n.22, deletion of "given to the world"; and 274.10, interlineation of "English" before "electors." Helen Taylor's note printed below on p. 282 is written in ink.

[a longtime colleague of Mill's at the India House] of No. 23 Queens Gardens Hyde Park Square on condition that he publishes the same within two years of my decease.

Mill died at Avignon on 7 May, 1873, and the will was proved in London on 5 September. By the latter date the *Autobiography* was already set in type and about to be printed.

Though Helen Taylor may have begun copying the Columbia MS in France before Mill's death, the greater part of the Rylands transcript was made afterward, in the summer of 1873, when she was in England "pressing on as quickly as I am able" with the publication of the work, "having come to England for that purpose only."[51] In the last 236 leaves of the Rylands MS, which constitute about five-sixths of the whole, Helen Taylor and Mary Colman copied discontinuous sections of the Columbia MS simultaneously (the former doing Columbia MS gatherings B, E, G, H, I, and K, the latter doing C, D, and F), and there is further evidence of haste in the great number of errors in these leaves, and in the fact that although Helen Taylor here and there corrected and punctuated Mary Colman's parts of the transcript, she clearly did not read them over entirely or attempt to prepare them in any thorough way for the press. Mary Colman's pages of the transcript went to the printer with more than 1,200 variants from Mill's text unaltered, including some 170 substantive variants—all of them errors, and many quite obvious. Altogether, when we add the considerably longer stretches copied by Helen Taylor and the twenty-three leaves at the beginning in the hand of the unidentified French copyist, the transcript has over 2,650 variants, including more than 450 substantives, from the MS that was its immediate source.

The *Autobiography* was published by Longmans, Green, Reader, and Dyer, "8vo. price 7s. 6d.," on 17 October, 1873.[52] The most significant of the differences between the first printed text and that of the Columbia MS are (1) the omission of the first paragraph that Mill wrote when he took up the work again in 1869–70 (the present 251.10–17); (2) the rearrangement of the remaining nine paragraphs of transition between the 1861 and 1869–70 parts of the MS (247.35–251.9, 251.18–261.12) into the order 4–5, 1–3, 9, 6–8 (so that 1873 has, in

---

[51]From an undated pencil draft written on the back of a note to her from the editor Howard Evans, 30 July, 1873 (Mill-Taylor Collection, British Library of Political and Economic Science). Both the Rylands transcript and the 1873 first edition are minutely described, and the dating discussed, in "The Text of John Stuart Mill's *Autobiography*" (see n. 30 above). Though it has no independent authority, the transcript is of considerable importance textually. Before its rediscovery in 1959, there existed two separate texts of the full work, in the Columbia MS and the 1873 edition, and scholars had no knowledge of their relative authority (there was always the possibility that Mill himself provided copy, in another MS now lost, for the 1873 printing). The Rylands MS shows indisputably that Mill had no direct hand in the copy-text from which 1873 was printed, and thus establishes the Columbia MS as the single authoritative source for the final version of the work.

[52]*Athenaeum*, 11, 18 Oct., 1873, pp. 451, 508, and *The Times*, 17 Oct., 1873, p. 6. The "second edition" of 1873 is apparently a reissue of sheets of the first impression, with a cancellans title leaf pasted to the stub of the original title and a twelve-page index inserted at the end. A sub-edition was issued in New York, by Henry Holt and Co., from plates of the first London issue, in the first week of Nov., 1873.

succession, 251.18–257.32, 247.35–251.9, 261.8–12, 257.33–261.7); and (3) the excision of ten mostly short passages (563 words altogether) referring to Helen Taylor.[53] In addition to these, there are some eighty other substantive differences of varying length and importance,[54] and, as one would expect in comparing any MS text with a printed version, hundreds of differences in the accidentals of punctuation, spelling, capitalization, and word-division.

The evidence of rearranged and partly rewritten leaves in the Rylands MS shows that Helen Taylor originally copied all ten of Mill's paragraphs beginning at 247.35 in their original order, and that she dropped 251.10–17 and rearranged the others as a revision in the transcript. The cancellation of the ten passages referring to herself, on the other hand, as the spaced asterisks replacing them in 1873 make clear, was done at proof stage.[55] The rest of the substantive differences between the Columbia MS and the printed text represent errors and alterations originating in the Rylands transcript and then further changes made by the 1873 compositor and/or the proof-correctors. It is remarkable that only sixty of the more than 450 substantive errors in the Rylands transcript got into print. Someone—most likely Helen Taylor, but perhaps also Alexander Bain, who we know had a text of the work in hand in the weeks just before it was published—read proofs fairly carefully against the Columbia MS, and restored Mill's wording in some 390 places. The first printed text could have been much worse.

The 1873 edition (reprinted many times in London and New York) remained the sole source of text until September, 1924, when the Columbia University Press issued *Autobiography of John Stuart Mill Published for the First Time without Alterations or Omissions from the Original Manuscript in the Possession of Columbia University*, with a Preface by John Jacob Coss (and, as the Preface explains, the "editorial work . . . undertaken by Mr. Roger Howson"). Considerably more faithful than the text of 1873, this nevertheless departs from readings of Mill's MS in more than nine hundred particulars, including some seventy errors of

---

[53]264.30–1 ("Miss Helen Taylor . . . character,"); 264.33–8 (", and have . . . adequate idea"); 264.39–265.1 ("—another companion . . . quality"); 265.3–4 (", the least . . . attached to it"); 265.30–1 ("at my daughter's suggestion"); 265.35–6 ("it was enriched . . . writing. But"); 268.10–13 ("And I shall . . . till our return."); 285.19–37 ("The time . . . others."); 286.30–287.4 ("At this time . . . were hers."); 290.16 ("by my daughter and myself,").

[54]These are listed in "The Text of John Stuart Mill's *Autobiography*," pp. 232–3, 237.

[55]She worried a great deal over these passages. In letters of 6 and 13 Sept., 1873, Alexander Bain had urged her to omit the most extravagant parts of Mill's description of her mother as well as herself: "I greatly doubt the propriety of your printing those sentences where he declares her to be a greater poet than Carlyle . . . and a greater thinker than himself—and again, a greater leader than his father (or at all events an equal)" (pp. 183, 213 in the present volume); "I would recommend to you, under all the circumstances, to decline the compliment, for yourself, of being more original than Mr Mill" (Bain refers specifically to the passage at the top of p. 265). Her eloquent reply of 14 Sept., too long to be included here, should be read in full; see "The Text of John Stuart Mill's *Autobiography*," pp. 234–7. The result was a compromise: retention of the passages about her mother on the grounds that Mill meant what he said, and omission of the references to herself because Mill "agreed . . . that nothing known from private intercourse ought to be published if it gives pain to living persons."

wording and paragraphing, many of which originated in the Rylands transcript and 1873, on the latter of which Howson relied too much in his attempts to decipher Mill's hand. It was, however (as it should have been), the standard edition for the next forty-five years, although, until the textual puzzles were untangled in the early 1960s, scholars and critics sometimes used another text also published in 1924, Harold J. Laski's Oxford World's Classics edition, which is an imperfect and unedited reprint of the first edition. The second twentieth-century text based on the Columbia MS is that in the Riverside paperback edited by Jack Stillinger (Boston: Houghton Mifflin, 1969). This improves on the accuracy of the 1924 Columbia edition in the nine hundred particulars just mentioned, and has been the most reliable text for the past decade. The third editing from the Columbia MS is that in the present volume. It corrects "their contraries" to "the contraries" at 53.1 (Mill wrote "their" but then deleted "ir") and restores "given to the world" to Mill's note at 253n.22 (words deleted by Helen Taylor's pencil in the MS); otherwise it is substantively identical with the text published in 1969. In the present edition the reader can, as mentioned, compare at a glance this text with that of the Early Draft in various stages, aided by the editorial apparatus described later in this introduction.

LITERARY ESSAYS

THIS VOLUME includes, in addition to the *Autobiography*, fourteen of Mill's essays and reviews,[56] and nine appendices. Only two of these articles were republished in *Dissertations and Discussions* (1859) in more or less complete form, "Thoughts on Poetry and Its Varieties" (the two-part essay in the *Monthly Repository*) and "Writings of Alfred de Vigny" (from the *London and Westminster*), but two more, "Aphorisms: Thoughts in the Cloister and the Crowd" and "Ware's Letters from Palmyra" (both from the *London and Westminster*), are represented by extracts in *Dissertations and Discussions*. It might be argued that Mill did not, at least in 1859 when *Dissertations and Discussions* first appeared, believe many of these essays to be of major importance, and indeed by any standards some of them are

---

[56]Of the fourteen, eight appeared in the *Westminster Review* (including one in the *London Review* and four in the *London and Westminster Review*), four (one of them originally two separate essays) in the *Monthly Repository*, and one each in *Tait's Edinburgh Magazine* and the *Edinburgh Review*. It is interesting to note that Mill signed his first three essays in the *Monthly Repository* "Antiquus," explaining, when he last used it, his reason both for adopting and for abandoning it (see p. 365), and saying he would henceforth use "A." And in five of the seven that appeared in the *London and Westminster* he used "A"; however, in the two others—the review of Ware and the first review of Milnes—he signed himself "S," perhaps because he had other reviews in the same issues, and did not want readers to think the *Review*'s stable was emptying, and he was being left with a terminal case of Hobson's choice.

For economy, here and in similar contexts where no distinction is needed, "*London and Westminster Review*" should be understood to include the two volumes of the *London Review* that appeared before its merger with the *Westminster*.

slight; however, a case can be made for each of those he chose to leave buried in periodicals, and *a fortiori* for the importance of his literary essays as a whole.

It would be perverse to argue, on the other hand, that Mill in middle life or later believed his literary articles to have the importance of those on economics, history, and politics (though a great many of the last were not reprinted by Mill); in this connection one should note that the essays in this volume span only the years 1824 to 1844, with all but four appearing in the 1830s, the period when he was most concerned to examine literary works and, as editor of the *London and Westminster*, was able to review them at will. They thus illustrate (without in themselves establishing) Mill's movement from orthodox Philosophic Radicalism through a period of eclectic search to settled maturity.

"Periodical Literature: *Edinburgh Review*" represents the initial period, being in fact his first article in the newly-founded organ of the Philosophic Radicals, and indicating both in manner and content that the designated successor to Bentham and James Mill was coming out in the expected and proper fashion. The assurance, contempt, irony (particularly in the attacks on Brougham's articles—anonymous, of course, but not to the initiate), and characteristic language (e.g., the demand for "securities") all mark the author as a committed sectarian as surely as the argument that the governors must be accountable to the governed, and the insistence that the aristocracy and its organs are motivated by special (and therefore sinister) interests. That Mill later recognized these as signs of narrow sectarianism is indicated by his comment in the *Autobiography*: "The continuation of this article in the second number of the review was written by me under my father's eye, and (except as practice in composition, in which respect it was, to me, more useful than anything else I ever wrote) was of little or no value" (p. 95n; see also p. 96^k). It also, of course, was a continuation of his practised diligence (soon to be taxed in his editing of Bentham's *Rationale*), especially when one notes that he had done the extensive research for his father's impressive article as well as for his own. Though there are hints in the article of his individual views, it is not surprising that he chose not to republish it (in fact he republished none of his thirteen articles from the first dynasty of the *Westminster*, all of which have considerable interest and value). Alexander Bain's comment is fair: most of the opinions in the article "were his father *redivivus*; yet, we may see the beginnings of his own independent start, more especially in the opinions with regard to women, and the morality of sex."[57]

The next four essays, "On Genius," "Thoughts on Poetry and Its Varieties," and the two reviews of Junius Redivivus, all date from 1832 and 1833. They show Mill in the midst of his period of search, examining and enjoying the new perspectives and insights afforded by W. J. Fox and his circle, including Harriet Taylor, and by Thomas Carlyle, who, though certainly not a member of that group, knew them and discussed their ways and works in his extensive correspondence with Mill.

---

[57]Alexander Bain, *John Stuart Mill* (London: Longmans, Green, 1882), p. 33.

The first three of these essays appeared in Fox's *Monthly Repository*, where Harriet Taylor was publishing poetry, and to which William Bridges Adams ("Junius Redivivus") was contributing. Probably in response to a suggestion in conversation, Mill wrote to Fox on 3 April, 1832, to say that he would send along anything of his appropriate to the "design" of the *Monthly Repository*;[58] "On Genius," a response to an article in the *Repository*, was the first to appear, some six months later. Of it, and the three following pieces, Mill might equally well have noted that he was gaining practice in composition, though he had changed his model from James Mill to Carlyle. To the latter he commented on 17 September, 1832:

. . . I have written a rambling kind of article, in which many, I will not say great, but big things are said on a small occasion, namely in the form of strictures on a well-meaning but flimsy article which recently appeared in the Monthly Repository. . . . As for this article of mine, those who best know me will see more character in it than in anything I have ever published; other people will never guess it to be mine. *You*, I hope, will find all the three articles *true*, the only praise I covet, & certainly rarer than any other in our times. But in this last you will find many things which I never saw, or never saw clearly till they were shewn to me by you, nor even for some time after.[59]

The italicized words, *"You"* and *"true,"* match the article's intensity, which clearly relates to his excitement over Carlyle's rhetoric, as does the expression of emotional response, and also the Delphic evasiveness of such comments as that in the same letter: "You see I adhere to my system, which is to be as particular in the choice of my vehicles, as you are indiscriminate, & I think we are both right." All of this mannerism he later repudiated (and he did not reprint "On Genius"), informing George Henry Lewes (probably late in 1840):

The "Genius" paper is no favorite with me, especially in its boyish stile. It was written in the height of my Carlylism, a vice of style which I have since carefully striven to correct & as I think you should do—there is too much of it in the Shelley. I think Carlyle's costume should be left to Carlyle whom alone it becomes & in whom it would soon become unpleasant if it were made common—& I have seen as you must have done, grievous symptoms of its being taken up by the lowest of the low.[60]

The next item, "Thoughts on Poetry and Its Varieties," is the republished form of two essays in the *Monthly Repository* (January and October, 1833), which show less hectically the same characteristics. (The version in *Dissertations and Discussions*, it may be interjected, reveals Mill's awareness of the over-enthusiasm in the originals by removing italics in sixty-four places.) The first, "What Is Poetry?" was evidently written without thought of a sequel, in a rather tentative spirit, as befitted a venture into strange new lands. He sought guidance and reassurance

---

[58]*EL, CW,* Vol. XII, pp. 97–8.
[59]*Ibid.*, pp. 117–18. The other two articles referred to are "Corporation and Church Property" and "Austin on Jurisprudence."
[60]*Ibid.*, Vol. XIII, p. 449.

from Carlyle on 27 December, 1832, saying he had written an essay for "Fox's January number" that

attempts something much higher, and intrinsically more valuable, than all these writings on politics, but with far less success: it is not nearly so good of its kind, because I am not so well versed in the subject. It embodies some loose thoughts, which had long been floating in my mind, about Poetry and Art, but the result is not satisfactory to me and will probably be far less so to you—but you will tell me to what extent you think me wrong, or shallow. I wrote the paper from conviction (else it had never been written) but not from that strong conviction which *forces* to write: rather because I wished to write something for Fox, and thought there was a clearer field open for him in that direction than in the political one.[61]

And his doubts continued, as is evident in a letter to Carlyle (11 and 12 Apr., 1833) after the article appeared:

That last ["What Is Poetry?"] you promised me a careful examination and criticism of: I need it much; for I have a growing feeling that I have not got quite into the heart of that mystery, and I want you to shew me how. If you do not teach me you will do what is better, put me in the way of finding out. But I begin to see a not very far distant boundary to all I am qualified to accomplish in *this* particular line of speculation.[62]

During the course of the year, and in large measure because of actual and anticipated responses from Carlyle, Mill pushed his investigations further into the relation between Art and Philosophy (a question that was to resolve itself for him a decade later in Book VI of his *Logic*), into the value of his intellectual inheritance, and into examinations of new poets. The products were, in part, the comments on his father included in Bulwer's *England and the English* (App. D below), the ill-fated review of Robert Browning's *Pauline* (the surviving note for which is given in App. E below), and the beginnings of a review of Alfred Tennyson's poems which resulted in both "The Two Kinds of Poetry" (the second part of "Thoughts on Poetry and Its Varieties") and "Tennyson's Poems." The remarks on his father, which Mill repudiated as having been "cut and mangled and coxcombified" by Bulwer (see p. 589 below), should be seen in conjunction with the comments on Bentham that he also contributed to *England and the English*.[63] In both he is respectful; the voice, however, is that of a broadening critic, not that of a narrow disciple. The independence is more obvious in the "review" of *Pauline*, which has received much comment from Browning scholars. One need only summarize briefly what is known: *Pauline* was published in March, and Mill, given a copy by W. J. Fox, wrote a review for the *Examiner* before the middle of May. It was judged too long for the *Examiner*, so Mill proposed to revise it for *Tait's*. His summer months being busy, however, he had not made his revisions by August, when *Tait's* published a dismissive review of the poem, and Mill with-

[61]*Ibid.*, Vol. XII, p. 133. Later he would surely have regretted saying he was "not so well versed" in poetry.
[62]*Ibid.*, p. 149.
[63]*Essays on Ethics, Religion and Society*, *CW*, Vol. X, pp. 3–18, and 499–502.

drew his offer. The only surviving evidence of his views is found in the copy of *Pauline* which he returned to Fox. He, going against Mill's suggestion, gave it to Browning, whose revisions of the poem reflect in part a reaction to Mill's marginal comments. The fullest recording of these, with the note printed below as Appendix E, and Browning's revisions, is in an article by William S. Peterson and Fred L. Standley.[64] Some of the marginalia give evidence of Mill's subjective reading of this highly subjective poem; for example, against

> But then to know nothing—to hope for nothing—
> To seize on life's dull joys from a strange fear,
> Lest, losing them, all's lost, and nought remains

he wrote, "deeply true."

When these other articles of 1833 are read with "The Two Kinds of Poetry," one can see the "weaving anew" process mentioned in the *Autobiography* (p. 163), as Mill intertwines the warp of his learned associationism with the woof of new ideas about the use and value of emotion. The new insight he owed, in this case, to James Martineau's "On the Life, Character, and Works of Dr. Priestley,"[65] as he acknowledges on 26 May, 1835:

> The last two pages of the concluding paper made an impression upon me which will never be effaced. In a subsequent paper of my own in the "Repository" headed "The Two Kinds of Poetry" (October, 1833) I attempted to carry out your speculation into some of those ulterior consequences which you had rather indicated than stated.[66]

And he goes on to assert his continued acceptance of at least part of his intellectual inheritance, in a way that was to become increasingly sure as he gained confidence in his new proceedings; he had, he told Carlyle, two articles in the *Monthly Repository* for October, 1833, one on Blakey, and the other

> the little paper I told you I was writing in further prosecution of, or rather improvement on, the thoughts I published before on Poetry and Art. You will not find much in the first to please you; perhaps rather more in the second, but I fear you will think both of them too much infected by mechanical theories of the mind: yet you will probably in this as in many other cases be glad to see that out of my mechanical premises I elicit *dynamical* conclusions. . . .[67]

It is not known what Mill thought of these speculations later—he merely refers to them as "the most considered" of his contributions to the *Monthly Repository*

[64]"The J. S. Mill Marginalia in Robert Browning's *Pauline*: A History and Transcription," *Papers of the Bibliographical Society of America*, LXVI (2nd quarter, 1972), 135–70, citing, *inter alia*, *EL*, *CW*, Vol. XII, pp. 157, 162, 174, 185. Our transcription corrects some errors in theirs. The marginal note quoted below is on p. 47 of *Pauline: A Fragment of a Confession* (London: Saunders and Otley, 1833).

[65]*Monthly Repository*, n.s. VII (Jan., Feb., Apr., 1833), 19–30, 84–8, 231–41. Mill refers to, and quotes from, the concluding portion in his *Logic* (*CW*, Vol. VII, p. 481, and Vol. VIII, pp. 857–8).

[66]*EL*, *CW*, Vol. XII, p. 247.

[67]*Ibid.*, p. 181. For the article on Blakey, see *Essays on Ethics, Religion and Society*, *CW*, Vol. X, pp. 19–29.

(p. 205)—but it is unquestionably significant that he included a carefully revised version in *Dissertations and Discussions*, the only such inclusions from his *Repository* articles (apart from a section of his review of Alison's *History*).

Using the latest version from Mill's lifetime as copy-text (the normal practice in this edition), we indicate the variants in earlier versions in footnotes. A study of these shows that the revisions can be seen to fall into four types: (1) alterations in opinion or fact, including major omissions, amplifications, or corrections of information; (2) alterations resulting from the time between writings, including changes in statement of fact consequent upon the passage of time and new publications; (3) alterations which qualify, emphasize, or give technical clarity; and (4) alterations which are purely verbal, or give semantic clarity, or result from shifts in word usage, and alterations in italicization. The changes here reveal several similarities to Mill's practice in other reprinted essays: first, there is a large number, some 209 in all (or 6.5 per page of *Dissertations and Discussions*), as is common in the early essays reprinted by Mill; when less time intervened between the original form and the first revised form in 1859, fewer changes seemed necessary. Second, using the categories just described, one finds the order of frequency to be 4 (128 changes), 3 (58 changes), 1 (20 changes), and 2 (3 changes); by far the largest number (more than half) are of type 4.[68] Third, very few of the changes (16 in all) were made for the 2nd ed. of Vols. I and II of *Dissertations and Discussions* (1867), and of these almost all were relatively trivial (12 involved the removal of italics that had survived the apparently thorough reduction of shrillness in 1859). It should be noted that while what, to modern taste, might seem to be excessive italicization appears in articles by others in the *Monthly Repository*, Mill's usage in these articles went far beyond that journal's norm. Finally, the non-substantive changes, like those in Mill's other writings, generally parallel those of the substantives.[69]

Any selection of significant or even merely interesting variants will reflect subjective judgments, but, especially when seen in conjunction with the *Autobiography* and the other literary essays, it seems likely that most readers would attach importance to the long type 1 variants (p. 353[s–s] and p. 365[a]) that originally closed the separate essays. The former contains a comparison of French and Grecian (Modern and Ancient) artists (capped by a quotation from Carlyle), an account of beauty in painting, illustrated by Claude Lorraine and Salvator Rosa,

---

[68]There are proportionally rather fewer type 3 changes here; in other essays there is more commonly only slightly more of type 4 than of type 3. See, e.g., *CW*, Vol. X, p. cxxii, and Vol. XVIII, p. lxxvii. In our calculations we are counting the variant notes, not the individual changes.

[69]That is, more (though not preponderantly) occur here than in later essays, and more (with the same qualification) in 1859 than in 1867. The great majority involve changes in the use of commas, but there are almost as many deletions of a comma or a pair of commas (30 instances) as of additions (27 instances). In general, and remembering that some of these changes probably reflect house style, one may say that there is a lightening of punctuation over time—again a tendency seen in Mill's other writings.

and a passage on the weakness of modern architecture compared to the Classical and Gothic "tongues" which it "parrots" (here a quotation from Milton is used). The latter (with a quotation from Wordsworth) has a different kind of interest, explaining as it does (if again somewhat mysteriously) Mill's use of the signature "Antiquus," and by inference its successor, the simple "A" that he normally used in the *London and Westminster Review*.

An example of the few and slight type 2 changes may be seen in the deletion of "last summer" from the account of Mme Schröder-Devrient's performance in *Fidelio* at the King's Theatre, Haymarket, in 1832 (p. 351^q).

Probably the most easily identified characteristic of Mill's revisions is the search for the properly weighted judgment, resulting in the qualifications that we count as type 3 changes. Most common are substitutions of a less extreme modifier: in 1859 "rarely" replaced "never" at p. 344^{j-j}, and "commonly" replaced "always" at p. 364^{t-t}. (See also the string of changes, pp. 359–60^{b-b} to^f.) A troublesome instance of scholarly obfuscation may be instanced: a description of poetry (in quotation marks) as "man's thoughts tinged by his feelings" is ascribed by Mill to "a writer in *Blackwood's Magazine*"; in 1859 he says, bluntly, "He defines" it as such; but in 1833 he had said, "We forget his exact words, but in substance he defined" (p. 348^{i-i})—he almost certainly refers to John Wilson, who used similar phrases (especially *after* Mill wrote these words), but no such definition has been located by us. Perhaps Mill was simply seeking a more positive persona, as in a similar change where "We believe that whenever" is strengthened to just "Whenever" (p. 362^{j-j}). There are also some that remind one of the circumstances relating to the composition: at p. 364^{w-w} Mill in 1833 placed the "logician-poet" above the "mere poet"; "logician" was the term he used at the time in contrasting himself with Carlyle the "poet"; in 1859 the higher talent was assigned to the "philosopher-poet"—not, it should be said, with any self-reference.

While the type 4 changes are most trivial as well as most common, they have a cumulative effect (as in the removal of italics already cited, with which may be compared the removal of exclamation marks at, e.g., p. 363^{o-o}). Also some have special or typical interest, not infrequently of a slightly puzzling kind. For instance, at p. 347^{b-b}, when Mill, referring to the powers of the imagination, altered "arranged in the colours and seen through the medium" to "seen through the medium and arrayed in the colours," had his attention been caught by what may well be a printer's misreading of his hand ("arranged" for "arrayed") which led him to reconsider the temporal or logical priority of the two clauses?[70]

The final two essays in this group, the parallel reviews in 1833 of *The Producing*

---

[70]See also pp. 351^{n-n}, 356^b, 357^{t-t}, and 360^{k-k}. What is very likely a misreading, one paralleled elsewhere, may be seen in the change to "or" from "and" (habitually written by Mill as a small ampersand resembling both "or" and "a") at p. 358^{w-w}; and cf. below, the change from "where" to "when" (p. 423^{j-j}) and from "those" to "these" (p. 467^{t-t}), very likely the result of other common problems with Mill's hand.

Man's Companion by W. B. Adams, were published in April (*Monthly Repository*) and June (*Tait's Edinburgh Magazine*)—that is, in the period between the two essays on poetry. The one in *Tait's*, though it appeared later, was written and submitted before the one in the *Monthly Repository*, being proposed by Mill in a letter to William Tait of 23 January, 1833:

> I shall probably send you, in time for your March number, a short review of an excellent book, the Producing Man's Companion, by Junius Redivivus—whom I think the very best popular writer whom the enlightened radicals count in their ranks—though I like his *personal* articles in the Examiner less than the many admirable papers he has written in the True Sun, Mechanics Magazine & various other periodicals.[71]

The article went to Tait on 28 February, with Mill's comment: "I send you a paper on Junius Redivivus, for your Magazine, in case you think it worthy of insertion."[72] He also mentioned it to Carlyle in a letter of 3 March, saying that he was forwarding a copy of the book to him.[73] Some implications in the review evidently gave Tait doubts, which Mill attempted to assuage on 30 March:

> With respect to the article on Junius Redivivus, I myself have not made up my mind on the question whether the situation of the working classes is on the whole better or worse than it was: I worded the article so as if possible not to commit the Magazine to a decided opinion, but I thought the testimony of a writer who evidently knows much of the working people, an article of evidence very fit to be received, though not sufficient to decide the question. Could not you let the article stand as it is, and express your dissent from the opinion of J. R. in an editorial note? If not, I should like to see the article again before it is printed; not from any fear that you should "spoil" the article, but because when anything is to be *left out*, a writer almost always thinks it necessary that something else should be *put in*.
>
> As to the matter of fact in dispute I feel convinced from the great diversity of opinion among equally good observers, & from the result of the enquiries of the Poor Law Commission, that the truth *varies* very much in different parts of the kingdom & among different classes of workmen.
>
> Are there any other parts of the article which you object to?[74]

Tait's reservations may have delayed publication, but in any case almost a month earlier, indeed on 1 March, the day after he had sent his review to Tait, Mill said to W. J. Fox: "I *will* write a short paper for the next M.R. on Junius Redivivus."[75] This he produced with his usual dispatch, commenting to Carlyle in a letter of 11–12 April:

> Tait has not yet published that paper on Junius Redivivus, but in the meantime I have written another on the same subject for Fox, (a much better one as I think), which has appeared in the April number, and . . . you shall have it by the first opportunity.[76]

[71]*EL, CW*, Vol. XII, p. 137.
[72]*Ibid.*, p. 142.
[73]*Ibid.*, p. 146.
[74]*Ibid.*, p. 148.
[75]*Ibid.*; p. 142.
[76]*Ibid.*, p. 149.

Before the "first opportunity" had arrived, Carlyle had seen a quoted passage that prompted him to think that, just as he had detected a new mystic (that is, a promising disciple) in Mill's anonymous articles on the Spirit of the Age in the *Examiner*, so here he had found another.[77] Mill, saying on 18 May that he has finally sent a copy, adds: "The passage you saw quoted about Books and Men, was from that; so there is not evidence therein of 'another mystic'; so much the worse."[78]

The brief notice of *Views in the Pyrenees*, which is not mentioned by Mill in extant correspondence or in the *Autobiography*, also appeared in 1833 in the *Monthly Repository*. Though slight, it shows his continued enthusiasm for mountain views; one recalls his remark that the powerful effect of Wordsworth on him was in part the result of Wordsworth's setting much of his poetry in mountains, which, says Mill, "owing to my early Pyrenean excursion, were my ideal of natural beauty" (p. 151). Though we have no evidence to support the assertion, it seems not unlikely that Mill chose to notice the book, rather than having it given to him for review merely by accident.

The next five essays have a common source: all appeared in the journal edited by Mill, the *London Review* (later the *London and Westminster Review*). As might be expected when he was his own editor, they are more assured and independent. This tone is also seen, even when mixed with apology, in Mill's editorial notes for the review, printed in Appendix F below.[79] These help us see Mill in his editorial

---

[77]See Carlyle's letter to Mill of 1 May, 1833, in *The Collected Letters of Thomas and Jane Welsh Carlyle*, ed. Charles Richard Sanders, *et al.* (Durham, N.C.: Duke University Press, 1970–   ), Vol. VI, p. 377. Concerning his comment on Mill's "The Spirit of the Age," see p. 181n below.

[78]*EL, CW*, Vol. XII, p. 155.

[79]Some of the worrisome details of an editor's life can be seen in Mill's letters, for example in that of June, 1837, to Robertson (*EL, CW*, Vol. XII, pp. 338–9), in which he says, in part, "There is the devil to pay on another score—the *new* printers have begun with page 1 instead of page 285"—as indeed No. 10 and 53 (July, 1837) mistakenly did.

A greater problem—more annoying to modern scholars than it evidently was to Mill—concerns the numbering of the volumes of the review. When in 1836 the *London Review* combined with the *Westminster* as the *London and Westminster*, it was decided to preserve the volume sequence for both periodicals. There had been two volumes of the *London*, and twenty-four of the *Westminster*, so the first amalgamated volume was designated Vol. III and XXV. This double numbering was continued until 1838 (Vol. VII and XXIX). At that time it was decided to do something about the first two volumes of the *London*, which had appeared at the same time as, but quite distinct from, Vols. XXIII and XXIV of the *Westminster*; the decision was to give them the next numbers in the *Westminster* sequence, and so they are identified as both *London Review*, Vols. I and II, and *London and Westminster Review*, Vols. XXX and XXXI. The next volume published after this decision (that for 1838–39) was designated as Vol. XXXII. After one more volume, the *London*, XXXIII (1839–40), Mill relinquished the review, and it became again (with Vol. XXXIV) the *Westminster*. The sequence of the *Westminster* numbers, then, is maintained at the cost of chronology and logic; between XXIX (1838) and XXXII (1838–39) come XXX (1835) and XXXI (1835–36).

All this is quite bad enough, but the confusion is confounded for those who notice the note on the verso of the title page of the bound version of Vol. XXXIII (1839–40), printed on pp. 606–7 below. There it is said, with an apology for the lateness of the announcement and with some peculiar arithmetic, that "to avoid the double numbering" of the volumes, "the numbers of each Review were added together, whereby Vol. VII and XXIX became Vol. XXXI of the united series." And indeed on

role, though it seems that Alexander Bain overstates the case in saying that the review "abounds in editorial *caveats*, attached to the articles: [Mill's] principle of seeing partial truth on opposite sides was carried out in this form."[80] There can be no question, however, about their casting more light on his friendships with Sterling and Carlyle, and on his running battle with Abraham Hayward.[81]

Mill's first major literary essay in his own journal was the review of Tennyson (1835), which has links with the preceding years: as we have already mentioned, "The Two Kinds of Poetry" was first conceived as the prelude to a notice of Tennyson. Had such a notice appeared in 1833, what has been recognized as Mill's early appreciation of Tennyson's poems would have been even more remarkable. His view was enthusiastic: in a letter to J. P. Nichol he ranked them as "the best poems . . . which have appeared since the best days of Coleridge."[82] As is typical of him, impressions were retained: a particular view, he wrote to his wife twenty years later, is "as one fancies the valley in Tennyson's Oenone, only that there is no forest or turf here"; Francis Mineka notes that Mill had quoted in his review the lines from "Oenone" beginning, "There is a vale in Ida."[83]

Though Mill chose, regrettably and for unknown reasons, not to include his review of Tennyson in *Dissertations and Discussions*, the next three items from the *London and Westminster* were represented there, though, in one case, only by the opening and, in another, by the closing paragraphs. That is, the "review" parts were deleted, leaving the generalized comments appropriate to an exordium and a peroration. The subject of the first of these reviews, Arthur Helps's *Thoughts in*

---

the title page of that volume as bound, and in its index, as well as in the footlines, it is identified as Vol. XXXI. However, as indicated on the spines of sets, for the reasons given above, it is properly referred to as Vol. VII and XXIX.

[80]Bain, *John Stuart Mill*, p. 57. The quotation from Locke that appears on the title pages of the review seems to indicate Mill's determination that the periodical reflect his own search for truth rather than an assured dogmatism: "Those who have not thoroughly examined to the bottom all their own tenets, must confess they are unfit to prescribe to others; and are unreasonable in imposing that as truth on other men's belief which they themselves have not searched into, nor weighed the arguments of probability on which they should receive or reject it." (*Essay Concerning Human Understanding*, in *Works*, New ed., 10 vols. (London: Tegg, *et al.*, 1823), Vol. III, p. 104 [Bk. IV, Chap. xvi, §4]. In Locke the sentence begins, "At least those, who . . . .")

The accompanying motto may equally well point to the influence over the fledgling review exerted by James Mill (see p. 208 below): "Legitimae inquisitionis vera norma est, ut nihil veniat in practicam, cujus non fit etiam doctrina aliqua et theoria." (Francis Bacon, *De augmentis scientiarum*, in *Works*, ed. James Spedding, Robert Leslie Ellis, and Douglas Denon Heath, 14 vols. [London: Longman, *et al.*, 1857–74], Vol. I, p. 772.) The English version (*ibid.*, Vol. V, p. 59) of this passage (we have italicized the words omitted from the Latin version in the quotation) reads: "*Again, it tends to the perfection of learning, because* it is the perfect law of the inquiry of truth, '*that nothing be in the globe of matter which has not its parallel in the globe of crystal or the understanding;*' *that is*, that there be nothing in practice, whereof there is no theory or doctrine."

[81]Concerning Hayward and Mill, see Francis E. Mineka, "John Stuart Mill and Neo-Malthusianism, 1873," *Mill News Letter*, VIII (Fall, 1972), 3–10. Also, Hayward's translation of *Faust* was attacked by J. H. Garnier in the *London and Westminster*, III and XXV (Apr., 1836), 366–90.

[82]*EL*, *CW*, Vol. XII, p. 245.

[83]*LL*, *CW*, Vol. XIV, p. 382.

the Cloister and the Crowd, was another book that Mill held in more than a reviewer's regard. According to Alexander Bain,

This [review] was another occasion when [Mill] displayed his passion for discerning and encouraging the first indications of talent and genius. I remember when I first came to London, this was one of the books he lent me; and we agreed that, in point of thinking power, Helps had not fulfilled the promise of that little work.[84]

Mill seems to have pondered the subject for almost a year, for he told Nichol just after the article appeared that it "was all prepared last spring, though I had not put any of it on paper."[85] As usual, when he put pen to paper, the ink flowed easily and quickly: "I have stolen in the last two days, time to begin a little article for the review & a day or two more will finish it."[86] Helps gave Mill one of those fine moments of gratification for reviewers when he let Mill know, over thirty years later, that his had been a word in season. Mill replied:

If, as you intimate, my review of your first publication had any share in procuring for the world the series of works which I & so many others have since read with so much pleasure & instruction; far from regarding this exploit of mine as a sin to be repented of, I should look upon it as a fair set off against a good many sins.[87]

No detailed comment is needed on the revisions Mill made in the reprinted paragraphs, the discussion on pp. xxxv–xxxvi above being intended to cover the general issues and types. It may be noted, however, that there are comparatively few changes, only 12, or 2.4 per page of *Dissertations and Discussions*,[88] all of them type 3 or type 4, and all but 2 made in 1859.

"Ware's Letters from Palmyra" is not mentioned in any of Mill's extant correspondence or in the *Autobiography*. The novel, published in the United States, was probably first brought to his attention by its mention (which he quotes to open his review) in Harriet Martineau's *Society in America*. Here again there are few variants (7, or 2.3 per page of *Dissertations and Discussions*, each made in 1859), all of which are minor.[89]

Mill's review of Alfred de Vigny's *Œuvres*, which appears in *Dissertations and Discussions*, less only the summary and running comment on *Cinq Mars* (p. 474ᶜ), is his last major attempt, in Bain's words, "to philosophize upon Literature and Poetry."[90] Though we have only two comments on it by Mill, they indicate

[84]Bain, *John Stuart Mill*, p. 49.
[85]*EL, CW*, Vol. XII, p. 322.
[86]*LL, CW*, Vol. XVII, p. 1969.
[87]*Ibid.*, p. 1709.
[88]Oddly enough, there are comparatively more (22 in total, all but 2 in 1859) changes in accidentals, which do not here, or in the next review (where there are only 5), appear in their final form because the copy-text for each is the earlier version.
[89]All are of type 3 or type 4, except that at p. 460ᵍ⁻ᵍ, which ranks as a type 1: Mill deleted in 1859 the passage here italicized: "greatly is any book to be valued, which in this age, and in a form suited to it, *and not only unexceptionable but fitted to be most acceptable to the religious leader,* does its part towards keeping alive the chivalrous spirit."
[90]Bain, *John Stuart Mill*, p. 52.

why he thought it was worth reprinting, and also show how he saw it in relation to his earlier essays. In the Early Draft he remarks that of his literary essays, "the one which contained most thought" was that on Vigny (p. 224). And in a letter of February, 1841, to George Henry Lewes, he says:

You have not however yet convinced me that the line between poetry, & passionate writing of any kind, is best drawn where metre ends & prose begins. The distinction between the artistic expression of feeling for feeling's sake & the artistic expression of feeling for the sake of compassing an end, or as I have phrased it between poetry & eloquence, appears to me to run through all art; & I am averse to saying that nothing is poetry which is not in *words*, as well as to saying that all passionate writing in verse is poetry. At the same time I allow that there is a natural, not an arbitrary relation between metre & what *I* call poetry. This is one of the truths I had not arrived at when I wrote those papers in the Repository but what afterwards occurred to me on the matter I put (in a very condensed form) into the concluding part of an article in the L. & W. on Alfred de Vigny. I wish you would look at that same when you have time, (I will shew it to you) & tell me whether what I have said there exhausts the meaning of what you say about the *organic* character of metre, or whether there is still something further which I have to take into my theory.[91]

A glance at the revisions in this article helps establish the generalization offered above, that the later the date of an essay (this appeared in 1838), the less rewriting was needed: here there are 132 substantive changes, or 3.1 per page of *Dissertations and Discussions* (as against 6.5 per page for "Thoughts on Poetry and Its Varieties" of 1833).[92] Once again no extensive treatment of the variants is called for. As usual, the order of frequency is type 4, type 3, type 1, type 2, with more than half being type 4,[93] and more than a third type 3; and very few changes were made in 1867 (7 of 132).[94]

The last essay in this group from the *London and Westminster* is Mill's first review (Aug., 1838) of Richard Monckton Milnes. It would appear again that he was searching out good material for the *Review*, for the first issues of Milnes's two books (later in the year published as Milnes's *Poems*, Vols. I and II) were rather elusive. In the review, it will be noted, Mill says one of the volumes "was not

---

[91]*EL, CW,* Vol. XIII, pp. 463–4.

[92]There are also relatively fewer non-substantive changes, only a handful of which were made in 1867 (including the addition of accents on four foreign words or names).

[93]In contrast to the revised essay of 1833, this one shows far less need for the removal of italics; there are only 8 instances (1 dating from 1867), and in one place (p. 484^{t-t}) the word "salon" (probably judged still to be foreign) was italicized in 1859.

[94]Mill's translations of Vigny demonstrate an extraordinary command of French. In those excerpts from *Cinq-Mars* chosen to illustrate Vigny's ability to convey the character of an age, Mill successfully translates the flavour by employing structures and vocabulary, often cognates, for their archaic or poetic suggestiveness, occasionally leaving French words that contribute to atmosphere or mystery. In the excerpts that illustrate Vigny's depiction of character and emotions, Mill, in his seemingly effortless way, renders faithfully ideas and nuances of feeling, but he also demonstrates, through the occasional omission and rearrangement of detail, that he has a good eye, and ear, for the dramatic. The most interesting omission and reordering of elements occurs in the translation of Stello's *credo* concerning his poetic gift (p. 497), where Mill suppresses in each sentence the introductory main clause expressing belief in the self, and moves his affirmation of the poet's visionary power from first to third place, after his response to Nature and his sympathy with mankind.

designed for publication, and the other is not yet published" (p. 505). Editorial consultation led him to write to Leigh Hunt on 11 November, 1838:

Robertson tells me you have a copy of Mr. Milnes' volume of poems: if you are not needing it for a day or two, would it be too much to beg the favour of a sight of it? Something relating to the next number of the Review may depend upon the opinion we form of it—if left at Hooper's or sent by omnibus or parcel company to the I[ndia] H[ouse] I should receive it.[95]

Despite the cautious tone ("Something . . . may depend"), Mill probably already intended to review the volumes, as the search and the praise in the review suggest prior knowledge.

After giving up the editorship and proprietorship of the *London and Westminster*, Mill wrote only a little for the *Westminster*, as it then once more became. The next two essays in this volume, appreciative notices of Milnes's *Poetry for the People* and of Macaulay's *Lays of Ancient Rome*, come from that small group, and it is at least moderately ironical that one of the remnant from the early, ferocious, and anti-poetical days of the *Westminster* should appear in it, almost for the last time, as the author of favourable reviews of poetry by non-Radicals. Nothing, it should be said, is known of the composition of these articles, nor do their texts present any challenges. And the same is true of the final item in the volume, Mill's letter of January, 1844, in defence of his father, which appeared in the *Edinburgh Review*, the journal to which, in 1840, he began to contribute many of his best essays, as James Mill had in the years preceding the founding of the *Westminster*. (Concerning the main issue in this letter, James Mill's financial obligations to Bentham, one should look at the revision of the Early Draft at p. 56^{a-a} below.) So a cycle, which this volume illustrates, comes to a close: the young sectarian Benthamite, now assured and, with the publication of the *Logic*, widely acclaimed, whose first periodical article was an attack on the *Edinburgh*, has become a contributor to it. The *Autobiography* tells us, of course, that the story does not end here, but the record of Mill's further career as an author must be sought in other volumes of the *Collected Works*.

This is not the appropriate place to enter into detailed exposition of Mill's critical ideas or their relation to his ethical or political thought, and in any case one would be hard pressed to maintain that the essays in this volume—so various in occasion, scope, and seriousness of purpose—represent a coherent body of theory. A few of the pieces are not really "literary" at all (in the stricter sense of treating imaginative literature imaginatively), while others suggest that, as a practical critic, Mill had, by our standards, less than excellent taste. (His lengthy quotations in the two reviews of Milnes amount to a small anthology of the world's worst poetry.) Even so, there are in the essays some statements that have, to modify Keats's phrase, put Mill "among the English critics," and these deserve to be noticed.

[95]*EL, CW*, Vol. XIII, p. 384.

The best known of Mill's critical ideas are contained in "Thoughts on Poetry and Its Varieties," and most of them more specifically in the first section (originally published separately as "What Is Poetry?"), where, after setting down the object of poetry ("to act upon the emotions") and distinguishing between poetry and eloquence ("eloquence is *heard*, poetry is *over*heard"), Mill arrives at this summary definition: "Poetry is feeling, confessing itself to itself in moments of solitude, and embodying itself in symbols, which are the nearest possible representations of the feeling in the exact shape in which it exists in the poet's mind" (p. 348). The three elements of this definition—the strong (almost exclusive) emphasis on feeling, the idea of the poet as self-confessor in solitude, and the description of symbols as vehicles of the poet's emotion—are distinctive, and these are the points that have been of most interest to historians of modern criticism.[96]

Near the beginning of the essay, in a preliminary attempt to pin down exactly where poetry resides, Mill says that "poetry is not in the object itself, nor in the scientific truth itself, but in the state of mind in which the one and the other may be contemplated," and he then invents an example, often quoted, of object as representation of feeling:

If a poet describes a lion, he does not describe him as a naturalist would, nor even as a traveller would, who was intent upon stating the truth, the whole truth, and nothing but the truth. He describes him by imagery, that is, by suggesting the most striking likenesses and contrasts which might occur to a mind contemplating the lion, in the state of awe, wonder, or terror, which the spectacle naturally excites, or is, on the occasion, supposed to excite. Now this is describing the lion professedly, but the state of excitement of the spectator really. (P. 347.)

In the later twentieth century, on the hither side of T. S. Eliot's famous definition of "objective correlative"[97] (which is certainly what Mill, in his simpler way, intended the lion to exemplify) and several decades of New Critical elaboration of the concept, we can appreciate Mill's intelligence, even precocity, at this point in the essay. But in the course of developing the notion of self-confession—"All poetry is of the nature of soliloquy," "no trace of consciousness that any eyes are upon us must be visible in the work itself," "Poetry . . . is the natural fruit of solitude and meditation" (p. 349)—he strips poetry of nearly all its traditional

[96]See in particular Alba H. Warren, Jr., *English Poetic Theory, 1825–1865* (Princeton: Princeton University Press, 1950), pp. 66–78; M. H. Abrams, *The Mirror and the Lamp* (New York: Oxford University Press, 1953), pp. 23–5; René Wellek, *A History of Modern Criticism: 1750–1950*, Vol. III (New Haven: Yale University Press, 1965), pp. 132–6.

[97]In "Hamlet and His Problems" (1919), reprinted in *Selected Essays, 1917–1932* (New York: Harcourt, Brace, 1932), pp. 124–5. Eliot later echoes Mill in *The Three Voices of Poetry* (New York: Cambridge University Press, 1954), where the first voice is "the poet talking to himself—or to nobody," and Eliot suggests that "part of our enjoyment of great poetry is the enjoyment of *overhearing* words which are not addressed to us" (pp. 6, 33). As Mill progresses to a less extreme position, with the emphasis on both thought and feeling that begins with the Tennyson essay, he joins the many anticipators of Eliot's "unified sensibility" (see Eliot's "The Metaphysical Poets," in *Selected Essays*, pp. 245–8).

elements (story, incident, description, moral truth, above all an audience to interact with), and in place of the poet as, in Wordsworth's Preface to *Lyrical Ballads* (para. 15), "a man speaking to men," we are presented with the much narrower concept of a man speaking to himself about himself.[98]

Mill was himself soliloquizing, of course, and his essay has the rhetorical character of the greater Romantic lyric, taking shape according to the movement of the speaker's mind. In the second section (originally published separately as "The Two Kinds of Poetry"), Mill restores some of what he had taken away by defining two categories, the poetry of the "poet by nature" (represented by Shelley) and the "poetry of culture" (Wordsworth—some would today reverse the examples), and then, perhaps upon realizing that he has produced two halves of something rather than two discrete entities, ends up with the ideal union of the two in the concept "philosopher-poet" (p. 364).[99] And this is the position that he *begins* with when he enters into the theoretical section of his review of Tennyson: "There are in the character of every true poet, two elements, for one of which he is indebted to nature, for the other to cultivation" (p. 413).

The Tennyson essay contains an eloquent statement on the relative value of feeling and thought in achieving "the noblest end of poetry":

Every great poet, every poet who has extensively or permanently influenced mankind, has been a great thinker;—has had a philosophy, though perhaps he did not call it by that name;—has had his mind full of thoughts, derived not merely from passive sensibility, but from trains of reflection, from observation, analysis, and generalization. . . . Where the poetic temperament exists in its greatest degree, while the systematic culture of the intellect has been neglected, we may expect to find, what we do find in the best poems of Shelley—vivid representations of states of passive and dreamy emotion, fitted to give extreme pleasure to persons of similar organization to the poet, but not likely to be sympathized in, because not understood, by any other persons; and scarcely conducing at all

---

[98]Though there were other, more immediate stimuluses (Carlyle and James Martineau have been mentioned earlier, and Harriet Taylor is certain to have played a part), the most fundamental and pervasive influence on this essay, as on the literary essays more generally (especially "On Genius" and the reviews of Tennyson and Vigny), is Wordsworth, to whom Mill is indebted not just for quotations and the specific ideas that we have identified in reference notes, but for much of the vocabulary as well (e.g., "representation of feeling," "state of excitement," "feeling pouring itself out," "emotion spontaneously embod[ying] itself," "overflowing of . . . feelings," "vivid sensations") and even such rhetorical strategies as the affirmative antithesis so characteristic of Wordsworth when he wants to proceed in spite of the logical weakness of his position: "If the above be, as we believe, the true theory . . . or even though it be not so, yet . . ." (p. 350). (The paragraph of advice to readers beginning at the middle of p. 403 suggests that Mill read the 1798 Advertisement to *Lyrical Ballads* as well as the later prefaces.) But Wordsworth in his theory is constantly in touch with his audience, and the narrowness of Mill's position in other respects is similarly unWordsworthian. Possibly we have here a prime case of Harold Bloom's "anxiety of influence." The most curious aspect of the relation is Mill's use of the most typically Wordsworthian descriptions of the poet to apply not to Wordsworth but, as it turns out, to Shelley! (See especially the paragraph beginning at the bottom of p. 357.)

[99]This strategy Mill employs elsewhere, most notably in his discussions of Bentham and Coleridge; he found the notion of "halfness" in Carlyle, but the putting together of "halfmen" was probably based on his own self-examination.

to the noblest end of poetry as an intellectual pursuit, that of acting upon the desires and characters of mankind through their emotions, to raise them towards the perfection of their nature. This, like every other adaptation of means to ends, is the work of cultivated reason; and the poet's success in it will be in proportion to the intrinsic value of his thoughts, and to the command which he has acquired over the materials of his imagination, for placing those thoughts in a strong light before the intellect, and impressing them on the feelings. (Pp. 413–14.)

This is a much more generous and reasonable view of poetry than that of the first section of "Thoughts on Poetry and Its Varieties," and it much better represents Mill's considered ideas on the subject. From the Tennyson essay on, and most prominently in the reviews of Vigny, Milnes, and Macaulay, his emphasis is where readers of the *Autobiography* would expect it to be—on the importance of feeling *and* thought, and on the educational, social, and cultural functions of poetry ("to raise [men and women] towards the perfection of their nature"). These later ideas, unlike those of "Thoughts on Poetry," are not distinctive; they were long in the public domain before Mill arrived. But this is not the first instance in which Mill sacrificed distinctive originality for the sake of more substantial and more comprehensive truth.

There is little evidence that Mill read poetry later in life,[100] and it is probably best, in the over-all view, to say that where, before the mental crisis, he had been "theoretically indifferent" to poetry (see p. 115), ever afterward he was theoretically in favour of it—still, however, almost entirely at the level of theory. But though he wrote no more articles or reviews that would qualify for inclusion as "literary essays," we nevertheless have, from his middle years, the fine paragraphs about discovering Wordsworth and the importance of poetry and "culture of the feelings" in the *Autobiography* (pp. 149–53), and from his last decade the powerful defence of poetry and art at the conclusion of his *Inaugural Address Delivered to the University of St. Andrews* (1867). What is most significant, finally, is not any specific idea about the nature of poetry or the role of the poet, but instead the spectacle of Mill's "strange confusion . . . endeavouring to unite poetry and philosophy."[101] This "confusion" and endeavour made him a broader, deeper, and more complex thinker and writer than he had been before, and they continue to make him interesting and valuable. His more orderly predecessors and contemporaries now figure mainly in footnotes; he, on the other hand, as the works collected in these volumes amply testify, remains alive in text and in context.

---

[100]The following, however, from Lady Amberley's journal, 28 Sept., 1870, is often quoted: "After dinner Mr. Mill read us Shelley's Ode to Liberty & he got quite excited & moved over it rocking backwards & forwards & nearly choking with emotion; he said himself: 'it is almost too much for one.' Miss Taylor read the Hymn to Intellectual Beauty but in rather a theatrical voice not as pleasant as Mill's, he also read some of his favourite bits of Wordsworth whh he admires very much." (*The Amberley Papers*, ed. Bertrand and Patricia Russell [London: Hogarth Press, 1937], Vol. II, p. 375.)

[101]John Bowring's phrase, reported by Caroline Fox, *Memories of Old Friends*, ed. Horace N. Pym (London: Smith, Elder, 1882), p. 113 (journal entry for 7 Aug., 1840).

APPENDICES

THE APPENDED MATERIALS, arranged chronologically, fall into four categories: first, items that, though they contain text by Mill, for one reason or another are not in a form intended by him for publication (Appendices A, D, E, and G); second, lists that are provided as additional information for the understanding of the main texts (Appendices B, C, and I); third, matter of which the authorship is, in general, not certain, though most of it is probably by Mill (Appendix F); and fourth, a pertinent text by Helen Taylor (Appendix H). These are mentioned above, and are described in the headnotes that introduce each item; therefore a cursory description is here sufficient.

Appendix A consists of the only surviving juvenilia from Mill's pen: the opening pages of his first history of Rome, and his "Ode to Diana," the former written when he was 6½ years old, the latter probably about a year or so later.

Appendices B and *C*, in an attempt to bring together evidence of Mill's precocity, provide lists of his early reading and writing; neither is, nor can be, complete, but even in this form they make up, at least for our less strenuous times, an impressive record.

Appendix D gives the version by Bulwer, repudiated by Mill, of comments (now lost) that he had written on his father's place in English life and letters.

Appendix E gives the text of the comment on Browning's *Pauline* that probably formed the basis of the review which, by a combination of circumstances, never was printed.

Appendix F is made up of the editorial notes in the *London and Westminster Review*; these help elucidate the history of the periodical, and Mill's attitudes towards authors and subjects.

Appendix G gives a selection of extracts from the "Rejected Leaves" of the Early Draft of the *Autobiography*; it was not feasible to print these as variants, but they should be read in connection with the corresponding passages in the two main texts as evidence of Mill's earliest intentions and of his and his wife's sense of the appropriate and the proper.

Appendix H is a continuation by Helen Taylor of the *Autobiography*, which summarizes the period between the last section by Mill (1869–70) and his death in May, 1873.

Appendix I, the Bibliographic Index, lists all persons and works cited in the *Autobiography*, the essays, and the relevant appendices. These references are, consequently, omitted from the index proper. Because Mill saw his autobiographical memoir as a record of his writing career, this appendix incidentally includes references to most of his writings.

TEXTUAL PRINCIPLES AND METHODS

AS THROUGHOUT THIS EDITION, the copy-text for each item is the final version produced under Mill's personal supervision, the latest over which he had significant authorial control.[102] For the *Autobiography* this means the Columbia MS, since Mill never saw the Rylands transcript of it, or of course the first printed edition. (The Early Draft text presented here on facing pages may, in this view, be considered a single long variant, though it also has claims to independent status as a once complete and wholly authoritative version.) For the rest of the items (except for material given in Appendices A, E, G, and H) there are no extant MSS, and the source of text in each case is a printed version.

Silent emendations. The following procedures apply to all the texts alike. Typographical peculiarities of titles, chapter headings, first lines, and some other features that similarly are matters of printing design are not strictly preserved. While as a rule the copy-text's punctuation and spelling are retained, certain elements of style have been made uniform: for example, periods have regularly been inserted, where they are missing, after abbreviations, but have been deleted after references to monarchs (e.g., "Louis XIV."); and dashes have been deleted where they are combined with other punctuation before a quotation or a reference. Italic punctuation following italic letters (in a printed version) has been regularized to roman. Indications of ellipsis have been normalized to three dots plus, where necessary, terminal punctuation. The positioning of footnote indicators has been normalized so that they always follow adjacent punctuation marks; in some cases, for consistency of appearance, references have been moved from the beginning to the end of quotations.

Also in accordance with modern practice, all long quotations have been set off from the text, in reduced type, with opening and closing quotation marks removed. In consequence, it has occasionally been necessary to add square brackets around Mill's own editorial interpolations; but there will be little likelihood of confusion, because our own editorial insertions in the texts are strictly confined to page references (we have deleted Mill's square brackets in the one place— p. 474n—that would have caused trouble). Double quotation marks replace single as the standard. Titles of works referred to in the text have been italicized or enclosed in quotation marks according to a uniform style, and occasionally a lower-cased word in a title has been silently capitalized. Mill's references to sources, and additional page references supplied editorially (in square brackets), have been

---

[102]The rationale for this practice is set forth in John M. Robson, "Principles and Methods in the Collected Edition of John Stuart Mill," in Robson, ed., *Editing Nineteenth-Century Texts* (Toronto: University of Toronto Press, 1967), pp. 96–122.

normalized. Erroneous references have regularly been corrected; a list of corrections and other alterations is given in the note below.[103]

Treatment of MS texts. In the texts edited from MSS—the *Autobiography* and the Early Draft (as well as in the textual notes to those items and the MS materials printed in Appendices A, E, G, and H)—these further silent procedures apply. Superscript letters in "20ᵗʰ," "MᶜCrie's," "Mʳ," and the like have been regularly lowered to the line. Initial capitals of words that originally began a sentence but in revision were rearranged into some other position within a sentence have been reduced to lower case. Periods have been added, where they are missing, at the ends of sentences. Commas and in a few instances other marks of punctuation have been added, where necessary or especially desirable, mainly to complete Mill's intended revision—as before or after an interlined phrase or clause, and before a deleted conjunction—but also in combination with other devices (the end of the line in the MS, or a closing parenthesis or quotation mark) that Mill characteristically used as a substitute for more conventional punctuation. Very occasionally, as when an opening parenthesis appears intended to cancel a mark, punctuation has been dropped. The ampersand has regularly been changed to "and," and we have spelled out most arabic numbers (and added conventional hyphens in some that were already spelled out). Editorial emendations to the texts of the *Autobiography* and Early Draft that are not covered by these general procedures are listed in the note below.[104] In the headnotes to the essays, the quotations from Mill's personal

---

[103]Following the page and line notation, the first reference is Mill's identification in the copy-text; the corrected identification (that which appears in the present text) follows after a closing square bracket. We do not indicate places where a dash has been substituted for a comma to show continuity onto adjacent pages, or where a volume number has been added to the reference.

301.16   p. 28] Pp. 27–8
309n.1   p. 23] Pp. 22–3
310n.11   p. 184] Pp. 184–5
313.38   p. 343] Pp. 343–4
324n.18   p. 183] 483
426.30   p. 26] Pp. 26–7
427.19   p. 23] Pp. 23–5
428.18–19   p. 46] Pp. 45–6
433n.2   p. 216] Pp. 216–17
450.26   pp. 39, 40] Pp. 39–42

[104]The MS reading is given first, followed by the emended reading in square brackets:

29.3   think [think it] [*Mill inadvertently deleted "it" in revision*]
29.9   with [with which] [*word omitted between pages*]
55.4   with in education [with] [*inadvertent repetition of phrase*]
74.10–11   the to discussions [the discussions] [*word left undeleted in revision*]
74.30   politics [politics,]
82.16   society [society,]
90.2   H. [House]
94.14   H. [House]
118.6   is being itself [being itself] [*word left undeleted in revision*]
134.29   urged [urged)]
150.18   mountains [mountains,]
152.30   Byron [Byron,]

bibliography, which survives in a scribal copy in the Mill-Taylor Collection, British Library of Political and Economic Science, have regularly been corrected; again, a note below lists the corrections.[105]

Textual notes to the MSS. The textual apparatus to the Early Draft provides a selection of the most significant earlier and cancelled readings that illuminate Mill's education, his reading and writing, and his relationships with his father, mother, siblings, and wife. Sometimes, especially in conjunction with Appendix G, which should be considered an extension of this apparatus, several successive

---

158.8   H. [House]
161.35   character, [character;]
174.24   modes modes [modes] [*repetition of word at beginning of new page*]
193.21   according [according to]
219.24   case [case,]
223.3   unpropitious [unpropitious,]
227.15   me [me,]
228.8   enlarged enlarged [enlarged] [*repetition of word at beginning of new page*]
238.20   to not to [not to]
240.12   The [the]
241.30   opinion [opinion,]
242.17   Govt [Government]
253.19   me [me,]
253.19   not [not,]
255n.9   Système [*Cours*]
262.39   men [men,] [*restoring deleted comma*]
265.19   whom [whom,]
266.23   population [population,]
266.30   Abolitionists [Abolitionists,]
268.1   U. [United]
268.9   1861 [1862]
269.6   certainly [certainly,]
278.38   press [press,]
285.19–20   daughter . . . Taylor [daughter, . . . Taylor,]
288.24   seems [seems,]

[105]In a few cases our reading of the MS differs from that in the edition by Ney MacMinn, J. M. McCrimmon, and J. R. Hainds, *Bibliography of the Published Writings of J. S. Mill* (Evanston: Northwestern University Press, 1945), to which page references (as MacMinn) are given in the headnotes. The corrected scribal errors (the erroneous reading first, with the correction following in square brackets) are:

328.3   f. [for]
328.4   'On Genius and signed Antiquus' ['On Genius' and signed 'Antiquus']
342.5–6   'what is poetry' ['What Is Poetry']
342.6   Antiguus [Antiquus]
342.6   1833 [1833)]
342.7   Antiguus [Antiquus]
368.8   Redivierus [Redivivus]
380.10   Redivierus [Redivivus]
392.8   News [Views]
420.7   running to the [running title]
432.8   Palmyro [Palmyra]
504.10   Milne' [Milnes']
518.5   Milne's [Milnes']
534.5   indication [vindication]

versions may be reconstructed (e.g., the five accounts of Mill's practical deficiencies, three of them extracted or described at pp. 608–11 below, the other two in the Early Draft and Columbia MS texts at pp. 32–3, 37, 39); and the influence of Mill's wife, in alterations, queries, and other markings pencilled in the MS, is given special attention. The simplified methodology used in these textual notes is explained in the headnote on p. 2. It should be understood that the descriptions "deleted first by HTM" and "altered to final reading first by HTM" mean that the deletion or revision at hand originated with her, and that Mill accepted it by going over the pencilled alteration in ink (no change by her, if Mill himself did not subsequently alter the words, has been incorporated into the text). Only two cancelled passages are given from the Columbia MS (on pp. 272, 287). For the most part, the cancelled readings in the first 162 leaves of this later version are identical, or nearly so, with the Early Draft text that we print on facing pages; and in the final section of the MS, which is first draft, Mill was no longer writing intimately about his father or his wife, or any other matter where ambiguous personal feelings were involved, and his deletions and revisions here are routinely stylistic, and not of sufficient interest to deserve recording.

Emendation of printed sources. In the items based on printed sources, typographical errors have been regularly corrected in the text. The note below lists these along with other readings that have been emended.[106]

Textual apparatus for the essays. As indicated in an earlier section of this

---

[106]Typographical errors in variant printed versions are ignored. For items where Mill himself made MS corrections, "SC" = his library, Somerville College, Oxford. The following are emended (the reading of the copy-text is given first, followed by the emended reading in square brackets):

297.2   nntouched [untouched]
299.32   stated [stated,] [*as in quotation above, and for sense*]
301n.2   ) [)]
301n.4   had [bad]
306.15   ) [)]
307.12   three pence [threepence] [*as elsewhere in sentence*]
309.21   P. 283. [*reference mistakenly given before the passage which it locates*]
311.20   pages, [pages] [*for sense*]
314.35   question [question.]
315.1   that under, the [that, under the]
316.1   Even, [Even]
316.33   istelf [itself]
319.32   place. [place."] [*restyled in this ed.*]
319n.1   Johnson s [Johnson's]
319n.1   *Works* [*Works.*]
319n.2   pp. 146, 147 [pp. 146–7.]
324n.2   ' ["]
334.39   an inferiority [our inferiority] [*corrected by Mill in SC copy*]
336.15–16   as, a preparation for [as a preparation for,] [*corrected by Mill in SC copy*]
343.1   1 [I]
343.12   though [through] [*as in 33,59, and for sense*]
348.26   appear [appears] [*as in 33,59*]
351.11   pii [fui] [*correction indicated by Mill in SC copy of* "What Is Poetry?" *and made in 59*]
353n.24   œsthetic [æsthetic]
354n.2–3   a loveliness, a cheerfulness, a wildness, a melancholy, a terror [or loveliness, or cheerful-

Introduction, only four of the essays were reprinted by Mill (in two cases only a brief passage is involved), and so there are relatively few variants to record. The ensuing paragraphs explain the methods of indicating variants in these instances and more generally throughout this edition.

We are concerned primarily with substantive variants, which may be taken to mean any differences among comparable texts except those in punctuation, spelling, capitalization, word-division, demonstrable typographical errors, and such printing-house concerns as type size and style. All substantive variants are

---

ness, or wildness, or melancholy, or terror] [*correction indicated by Mill in SC copy of* "What Is Poetry?"]

362.11 this [This] [*as in 33, and to conform with* 362.25]
363.4 this is 'exaggeration,' ["this is exaggeration,"] [*as in 33,59*]
370.4 some [sore] [*corrected by Mill in SC copy*]
371.1 with [worth] [*corrected by Mill in SC copy*]
371.38 fame [frame] [*corrected by Mill in SC copy*]
374.34 openly [clearly] [*corrected by Mill in SC copy*]
381.12 judgment; [judgment,] [*for sense*]
388.12 persih [perish]
399.21 flower-pots [flower-plots] [*as in* Source *(without hyphen); corrected by Mill in SC copy*]
404.40 charmed [charmèd] [*as in* Source]
421.2 flourishes [flourishes,] [*as in* 59, 67, 75, *and for sense*]
423.7 va riou slyfrom [variously from]
423.24 atmosphere [atmosphere,] [*as in* 59,67,75, *and for sense*]
424.7 γνωμαι [γνῶμαι]
424n.32 Remains [Remains'] [*restyled in this ed.*]
429.7 well read [well-read] [*as thrice elsewhere in paragraph*]
435.4 bears [bear] [*for sense*]
437.11 *exemta* [*exempta*] [*as in* Source]
437.15 vengeanee [vengeance]
441.42 lulled [dulled] [*as in* Source]
444.5 "Julia [" 'Julia] [*restyled in this ed.*]
448.12 "Ye . . . doubtless," . . . "of [" 'Ye . . . doubtless,' . . . 'of] [*restyled in this ed.*]
448.38 Corah [Korah] [*as in* Source *and* Bible]
449.3 Ishmaelite." [Ishmaelite.'"] [*restyled in this ed.*]
449.10 "Roman," . . . "I [" 'Roman,' . . . 'I] [*restyled in this ed.*]
449.28 loss." [loss.'"] [*restyled in this ed.*]
451.36 "As . . . tent" . . . "the [" 'As . . . tent' . . . 'the] [*restyled in this ed.*]
452.3 "that ['that]
452.12 tent.'" [tent.']
453.40 thou ['thou]
454.47 her's [hers] [*correct in* Source]
458.43 robe [robe.]
472.9 [*paragraph*] Those [[*no paragraph*] 'Those] [*as in* 38; *restyled in this ed.*]
474n.1–2 [Here . . . unnecessary.] [*Mill's brackets omitted in this ed.*]
476n.24 Célébres [*Célèbres*]
478n.38–9 'ideas . . . before,' 'that . . . exile,' ["ideas . . . before," "that . . . exile,"]
478n.41–3 "He . . . 'I . . . conscience.' [" 'He . . . "I . . . conscience." ']
479n.40 Cardinal" [Cardinal']
484n.5 "I [" 'I]
484n.7 "He [" 'He]
484n.35 life! [life)!] [*correct in* Source]
485n.11 kness [knees]

reported, save for the substitution of "on" for "upon" (in five places), "an" for "a" (twice before "historical" and once before "heroic"), and "though" for "although" (twice).[107] The variants are of three kinds: addition of a word or words, substitution of a word or words, and deletion of a word or words. The illustrative examples that follow are drawn, except as indicated, from "Thoughts on Poetry and Its Varieties," for which our copy-text is the version printed in 1867.

Addition of a word or words: see p. 356^{g-g}. In the present text the passage "Whatever be the thing which they are contemplating, if it be capable of connecting itself with their emotions, the aspect" appears as "Whatever be the thing which they are contemplating, ^{g}if it be capable of connecting itself with their emotions,^{g} the aspect"; and the variant note reads "$^{g-g}$+59,67". The plus sign shows that the passage enclosed by the superscripts in the text is an addition, and the numbers after the plus sign specify the editions in which the passage is included. The editions are indicated by the last two digits of the year of publication: here 59 = 1859 and 67 = 1867 (respectively, the 1st and 2nd editions of Volumes I and II of *Dissertations and Discussions*). Information explaining the use of these abbreviations is given in the headnotes, as required. Any editorial comment in the variant notes is enclosed in square brackets and italicized.

When this example is placed in context, the interpretation is that the first published text (1833) had "Whatever be the thing which they are contemplating, the aspect"; in 1859 this was altered to "Whatever be the thing which they are contemplating, if it be capable of connecting itself with their emotions, the aspect"; and (as is evident in the present text) the new reading was retained in 1867.

485n.12   'For ["'For]

485n.19   "You ["'You]

485n.20   hermine [her mine]

485n.28   Grandchamp' (his servant), 'called [Grandchamp" (his servant), "called] [*restyled in this ed.*]

485n.31–2   'Fly,' . . . "or . . . lost!" ["'Fly,' . . . 'or . . . lost!'"]

485n.43   "It ["'It]

486n.5   "The ["'The]

486.2   *Militaire* [*Militaires*] [*as in* 38 *and on title page of* Source]

487.29   Militaire [*Militaires*] [*as in* 38 *and on title page of* Source]

491.15   fault.' [fault.] [*as in* 38]

491.19   seated. [seated."] [*as in* 38; *restyled in this ed.*]

495.27   expected, [expected] [*as in* 38]

501.3   austère [austère,] [*as in* Source, 38]

520.21   onward [outward]

527n.6   fed [feud] [*as in* Source; *corrected by Mill in SC copy*]

530.17   Semponius [Sempronius] [*as in* Source]

530.38   Semponius [Sempronius] [*as in* Source]

538.11   "Life,' ["Life,"]

538.29   mistatements [misstatements]

[107]Two other trivial differences are not otherwise noted: "i.e." to "*i.e.*" (347.28) and "the 'general" to "'the general" (488.12).

Substitution of a word or words: see p. 356^{f-f}. In the text the passage "which is a natural though not an universal consequence of" appears as "which is ^{f}a natural though not an universal consequence^f of"; the variant note reads "$^{f-f}$33 one of the natural consequences". Here the words following the edition indicator are those for which "a natural though not an universal consequence" was substituted. When the same rules are applied and the variant is placed in context, the interpretation is that the first published text had "which is one of the natural consequences of"; in 1859 this was altered to "which is a natural though not an universal consequence of"; and the reading of 1859 (as is evident in the text) was retained in 1867.

In this volume there are only rare and trivial instances where passages were altered more than once: at p. 343^{b-b}, the first published text has "'poetry' *does* import"; in 1859 Mill changed this to "'poetry' imports"; and in 1867 he removed the quotation marks from "poetry" to give the final reading, "poetry imports", which appears in this edition as "^{b}poetry imports^b". To indicate this sequence, the note reads "$^{b-b}$33 'poetry' *does* import] 59 'poetry' imports" (the closing square bracket separates variants in a sequence). In the other cases, the variant represents a return to the original reading, as at p. 473^{z-z}, where in 1838 "these" appeared; in 1859, "those"; and in 1867, "these" again. Here the note indicates, as well as the sequence, the possibility of a typographical error: "$^{z-z}$59 those [*printer's error?*]".

Deletion of a word or words: see p. 356^b and p. 422^{f-f}. The first of these is typical, representing a convenient way of indicating deletions in a later version. In the text at p. 356^b a *single* superscript *b* appears *centred* between "in" and "a"; the variant note reads "^{b}33 the table of contents of". Here the words following the edition indicator are the ones subsequently deleted. The interpretation is that the first published text had "in the table of contents of a"; in 1859 the words "the table of contents of" were deleted; and the reading of 1859 (as is evident in the text) was retained in 1867.

The second example (p. 422^{f-f}) illustrates the method used to cover deletions when only portions of the text were later reprinted, as in the case of "Aphorisms: Thoughts in the Cloister and the Crowd," part of which was republished as "Aphorisms. A Fragment," in *Dissertations and Discussions*, Vol. I, pp. 206–10. (That is, there is here, exceptionally, a later version of only part of the text originally published in the *London and Westminster Review* [1837], which, being the only complete version, we adopt as our copy-text; normally the copy-text would be the latest version.) In the text the words "appears to us to be" are printed "appears ^{f}to us^f to be"; the variant note reads "$^{f-f}$−59,67". The minus sign indicates that in the editions specified the words enclosed were deleted. The interpretation is that the first published version had (as is evident in the text) "appears to us to be"; in 1859 this was altered to "appears to be"; and the latter reading was retained in 1867.

Differences between italic and roman type are treated as substantive variants and therefore are regularly recorded, except when they occur in foreign phrases and titles of works. Although variations in punctuation and spelling are generally ignored, when they occur as part of a substantive variant they are included in the record of the variant. The superscript letters used to indicate variants to the text are placed exactly with reference to their position before or after punctuation.

Variants in Mill's footnotes are treated in the same manner as those in his text. In the essays in this volume no footnotes were added or deleted in the reprinted versions.

ACKNOWLEDGMENTS

FOR PERMISSION to publish manuscript material, we are indebted to the Columbia University Library and the Columbia University Press, the University of Illinois Library and the University of Illinois Press, the Yale University Library, the British Library, the British Library of Political and Economic Science, the Victoria and Albert Museum, and the National Provincial Bank (literary executors and residual legatees of Mary Taylor, Mill's step-grand-daughter). Our gratitude goes in full measure to the staffs of the libraries just mentioned, and also to those of the Archives Départementales (Tarn-et-Garonne), Bibliothèque Interuniversitaire, Montpellier, Bibliothèques Municipales de Bagnères-de-Bigorre, Montauban, Pau, Tarbes, Toulouse, the Liverpool Public Library, the London Library, the Somerville College Library, the University of London Library, the University of Toronto Library, and the Victoria University Library. Instrumental in our work has been the cheerful and ready co-operation of the editorial, production, design, and printing staff of the University of Toronto Press, most particularly that of Rosemary Shipton, the copy-editor. Among others to whom thanks are due are the members of the Editorial Board of the edition, and T. D. Barnes, Robert Fenn, John Grant, Walter Houghton, J. R. de J. Jackson, Renée Kahane, F. E. Sparshott, and Bart Winer.

A Major Editorial Project Grant from the Social Sciences and Humanities Research Council of Canada has generously supported the preparation and production of this volume; perhaps we may be allowed to say, for all those who have benefited from this programme, how much the Council is to be congratulated for its contributions to scholarship in what are, for too many, very lean times. This grant has enabled us to work with an editorial team whose members have insisted on labouring far beyond reason and request: Marion Filipiuk (whose command of French has been particularly valuable), Bruce Kinzer (who has, in addition to his other labours, compiled the Index), Martin Kreiswirth, Mary O'Connor, and Rea Wilmshurst. Where better than in what is truly a joint production could we acknowledge our immense indebtedness to our colleague-wives, Ann Robson and Nina Baym, who (to paraphrase Mill) have both taught and learnt that a scholar from whom nothing is ever demanded which he or she cannot do, never does all she or he can.

AUTOBIOGRAPHY

Parallel Reading Texts of the Early Draft
and the Columbia MS

EDITORS' NOTE

The latest authoritative text, printed here on recto pages through p. 259 and on both rectos and versos thereafter, is that of the holograph MS in the Columbia University Library, untitled by Mill but containing two identical notes written and signed by his stepdaughter:

Autobiography of J. S. Mill
Written by himself
To be published without alterations
or omissions within one year after
my death.

Helen Taylor

The text given on the facing versos is that of the holograph Early Draft MS at the University of Illinois (through p. 246) followed by that of a holograph fragment at Yale headed "Note . . . concerning the participation of my wife in my writings" (pp. 250–8). It should be specially observed, since the co-ordination of early and later versions on facing pages will here and there produce gaps on the page and occasionally even entire pages of blank space that do not exist in the MSS, that both the Early Draft text and the Yale fragment are written continuously from beginning to end, without chapter divisions; in the Columbia MS each chapter begins on a new page, after which the text is written continuously without break to the end of the chapter.

In the accompanying textual apparatus, mainly two kinds of note are used to present a selection of cancellations and other alterations preliminary to the final form of the MS texts. In one of them (e.g., 8^{c-c}), a bracketed "*Earlier version*" indicates earlier wording that Mill deleted and replaced by the word or span of words enclosed by the superscript letters in the text. In the other (e.g., 6^b), which depends on a single superscript in the text, a bracketed "*Cancelled text*" indicates a word or words that Mill deleted, but did not replace, at the point at which the single superscript occurs. Both kinds of note represent simplifications; they overlook false starts and generally do not distinguish between original and intermediate versions preliminary to the final form of text (at 8^{c-c} Mill first wrote "cannot remember any time . . ." before revising to the wording given in the textual note, and an abandoned intermediate attempt—"have no remembrance of having ever been unable to"—is likewise ignored). They do, however, unless there is explanation to the contrary, give readings that once stood complete in their contexts and that, for the practical purpose of recovering what Mill at one time or another actually wrote, can be substituted or inserted in the text according to the positions designated by the superscripts.

There are also, specifically for the Early Draft, a number of notes explaining the later addition of leaves to the MS, the addition or revision of text "at left" (in the normally blank left-hand half of the MS page), the rearrangement of paragraphs and other sizable portions of text, a selection of pencilled alterations and other markings by Mill's wife, Harriet Taylor Mill (HTM), and some variant and cancelled readings from the thirty "rejected leaves" retained at the end of the MS (these are designated "R" or "RII" plus folio number in the textual notes, and are described in detail in Appendix G, pp. 608–24 below). The alignment of parallel texts and the length of some notes to the Early Draft have occasionally made it necessary to carry notes over to the facing recto page; to prevent confusion, a rule is used to set them off from the text and notes of the *Autobiography*.

The *Autobiography* was published by Longmans, Green, Reader, and Dyer on 17 October, 1873, five months and ten days after Mill's death, from a hastily written transcript of the Columbia MS made by Helen Taylor, Mill's sister Mary Elizabeth Colman, and an unidentified French copyist. Neither the transcript, which is now in the John Rylands Library, Manchester, nor the first printed version has independent authority, and their variants are not included in the textual apparatus here.

The work is not mentioned in Mill's bibliography. For critical comment and more specific details concerning the manuscripts and the composition and transmission of the text from the Early Draft through the first edition, see the Introduction, pp. vii–xxx above.

*ᵃ*IT SEEMS PROPER that I should prefix to the following biographical sketch, some mention of the reasons which have made me think it desirable that I should leave behind me such a memorial of so uneventful a life as mine. I do not for a moment imagine that any part of what I have to relate, can be interesting to the public as a narrative, or as being connected with myself. But I have thought, that in an age in which education, and its improvement, are the subject of more if not of pro-founder study than at any former period in English history, it may be useful that there should be some record of an education which was unusual and remarkable, and which, whatever else it may have done, has proved how much more than is commonly supposed may be taught, and taught thoroughly, in those early years which, in the common modes of instruction, are little better than wasted. It has also seemed to me that in an age of transition in opinions, there may be somewhat both of interest and of benefit in noting the successive phases of a mind which was always pressing forward, equally ready to learn and to unlearn either from its own thoughts or from those of others. The reader whom these things do not interest, has only himself to blame if he reads farther, and I do not desire any other indulgence from him than that of bearing in mind, that for him these pages were not written.*ᵃ*

I was born in London, on the 20th of May 1806, and was the eldest son of James Mill, the author of *The History of British India*. My father, the son of a petty tradesman and (I believe) small farmer, at Northwater Bridge, in the county of Angus, was, when a boy, recommended by his abilities to the notice of Sir John Stuart, of Fettercairn, one of the Barons of the Exchequer in Scotland, and was in consequence, sent to the University of Edinburgh at the expense of a fund

---

ᵃ⁻ᵃ[*This paragraph is a later addition written on a separate sheet.*]

CHAPTER I

Childhood, and Early Education

IT SEEMS PROPER that I should prefix to the following biographical sketch, some mention of the reasons which have made me think it desirable that I should leave behind me such a memorial of so uneventful a life as mine. I do not for a moment imagine that any part of what I have to relate, can be interesting to the public as a narrative, or as being connected with myself. But I have thought that in an age in which education, and its improvement, are the subject of more, if not of profounder study than at any former period of English history, it may be useful that there should be some record of an education which was unusual and remarkable, and which, whatever else it may have done, has proved how much more than is commonly supposed may be taught, and well taught, in those early years which, in the common modes of what is called instruction, are little better than wasted. It has also seemed to me that in an age of transition in opinions, there may be somewhat both of interest and of benefit in noting the successive phases of any mind which was always pressing forward, equally ready to learn and to unlearn either from its own thoughts or from those of others. But a motive which weighs more with me than either of these, is a desire to make acknowledgment of the debts which my intellectual and moral development owes to other persons; some of them of recognized eminence, others less known than they deserve to be, and the one to whom most of all is due,[*] one whom the world had no opportunity of knowing. The reader whom these things do not interest, has only himself to blame if he reads farther, and I do not desire any other indulgence from him than that of bearing in mind, that for him these pages were not written.

I was born in London, on the 20th of May 1806, and was the eldest son of James Mill, the author of *The History of British India*.[†] My father, the son of a petty tradesman and (I believe) small farmer, at Northwater Bridge, in the county of Angus, was, when a boy, recommended by his abilities to the notice of Sir John Stuart, of Fettercairn, one of the Barons of the Exchequer in Scotland, and was, in consequence, sent to the University of Edinburgh at the expense of a fund

[*His wife, Harriet Taylor Mill.]
[†3 vols. (London: Baldwin, Cradock, and Joy, 1817 [1818]).]

established by Lady Jane Stuart (the wife of Sir John Stuart) and some other ladies for educating young men for the Scottish Church. He there went through the usual course of study, and was licensed as a Preacher, but never followed the profession; having satisfied himself that he could not believe the doctrines of that or of any other church. For a few years he was a private tutor in various families in Scotland; but ended by going to London, and devoting himself to authorship; nor had he any other means of support until 1819, when he obtained an appointment in the India House.

In this period of my father's life there are two things which it is impossible not to be struck with: one of them, unfortunately, a very common circumstance, the other a most uncommon one. The first is, that in his position, with no resource but the precarious one of writing in periodicals, he married and had a large family: conduct, than which nothing could be more opposed, both in point of good sense and of morality, to the opinions which, at least at a later period of life, he strenuously upheld; and to which he had not, and never could have supposed that he had, the inducements of kindred intellect, tastes, or pursuits. The other circumstance, is the extraordinary energy which was required to lead the life he did, with the disadvantages under which he laboured from the first, and with those which he brought upon himself by his marriage. It would have been no small thing, had he done no more than to support himself and his family during so many years by writing, without ever being in debt or in any pecuniary difficulty; holding as he did, opinions of extreme democracy, and what is called infidelity, in a generation during which those opinions were more odious to all persons of influence, and to the common run of prosperous Englishmen, than either before or since: and being a man whom not only nothing would have induced to write against his convictions, but who invariably threw into everything he wrote, as much of his convictions as he thought the circumstances would in any way admit of: being, it must also be said, one who never did anything negligently; never undertook any task, literary or other, on which he did not conscientiously bestow all the labour necessary for performing it adequately. But he, with these burthens on him, planned, commenced, and completed the *History of India*; and this in the course of about ten years, a shorter time than has been occupied (even by writers who had no other employment) in the production of almost any other historical work of equal bulk and of anything approaching to the same amount of reading and research. And to this is to be added that during the whole period, a considerable part of almost every day was employed in the instruction of his children; *b* in the case of one of whom, myself, whatever may be thought of his success, he exerted an amount of labour, care and perseverance rarely if ever employed for a similar purpose, in endeavouring to give according to his own conception the highest order of intellectual education.

---

b[*Cancelled text:*] none of whom, until they were almost grown up, had any other teacher: and

established by Lady Jane Stuart (the wife of Sir John Stuart) and some other ladies for educating young men for the Scottish Church. He there went through the usual course of study, and was licensed as a Preacher, but never followed the profession; having satisfied himself that he could not believe the doctrines of that or any other Church. For a few years he was a private tutor in various families in Scotland, among others that of the Marquis of Tweeddale; but ended by taking up his residence in London, and devoting himself to authorship. Nor had he any other means of support until 1819, when he obtained an appointment in the India House.

In this period of my father's life there are two things which it is impossible not to be struck with: one of them unfortunately a very common circumstance, the other a most uncommon one. The first is, that in his position, with no resource but the precarious one of writing in periodicals, he married and had a large family; conduct than which nothing could be more opposed, both as a matter of good sense and of duty, to the opinions which, at least at a later period of life, he strenuously upheld. The other circumstance, is the extraordinary energy which was required to lead the life he led, with the disadvantages under which he laboured from the first, and with those which he brought upon himself by his marriage. It would have been no small thing, had he done no more than to support himself and his family during so many years by writing, without ever being in debt, or in any pecuniary difficulty; holding, as he did, opinions, both in politics and in religion, which were more odious to all persons of influence, and to the common run of prosperous Englishmen, in that generation than either before or since; and being not only a man whom nothing would have induced to write against his convictions, but one who invariably threw into everything he wrote, as much of his convictions as he thought the circumstances would in any way permit: being, it must also be said, one who never did anything negligently; never undertook any task, literary or other, on which he did not conscientiously bestow all the labour necessary for performing it adequately. But he, with these burthens on him, planned, commenced, and completed, the *History of India*; and this in the course of about ten years, a shorter time than has been occupied (even by writers who had no other employment) in the production of almost any other historical work of equal bulk, and of anything approaching to the same amount of reading and research. And to this is to be added, that during the whole period, a considerable part of almost every day was employed in the instruction of his children: in the case of one of whom, myself, he exerted an amount of labour, care, and perseverance rarely, if ever, employed for a similar purpose, in endeavouring to give, according to his own conception, the highest order of intellectual education.

A man who in his own practice so vigorously acted up to the principle of losing no time, was likely to adhere to the same rule in the instruction of his pupil. I ^chave no remembrance of ^c the time when I began to learn Greek. I have been told that it was when I was three years old. My earliest recollection on the subject is of learning what my father termed Vocables, being lists of common Greek words, with their signification in English, which he wrote on cards and gave me to learn by heart. Of grammar I learnt, until some years later, nothing except the inflexions of the nouns and verbs but after a course of vocables, proceeded at once to translation; and I can faintly remember going through Æsop's *Fables*, the first Greek book which I read. The *Anabasis* was the second. I learnt no Latin until my eighth year. Before that time I had read a number of Greek prose authors, among whom I remember the whole of Herodotus, Xenophon's *Cyropædia* and *Memorials of Socrates*, some of the lives of the philosophers by Diogenes Laertius, part of Lucian, a little of Isocrates, and I think part of Thucydides; I also read in 1813 the first six dialogues of Plato (in the common arrangement) from the *Euthyphron* to the *Theætetus* inclusive, which last dialogue had been better omitted, as it was utterly impossible I should understand it. But my father, in all his teaching, demanded and expected of me not only the utmost that I could do, but much that I could by no possibility have done. What he was himself willing to undergo for the sake of my instruction may be judged from ^dthe fact, that I went through the whole process of preparing my Greek lessons in the same room and at the same table at which he was writing, and^d as in those days Greek and English Lexicons were not, and I could make no more use of a Greek and Latin Lexicon than could be made without having begun to learn Latin, I was forced to have recourse to him for the meaning of every word which I did not know: and this incessant interruption he, one of the most impatient of mankind, submitted to, and wrote under that interruption several volumes of his *History* and all else that he had to write during those years.

The only thing besides Greek that I learnt as a lesson during those years was arithmetic: this also my father taught me: it was the work of the evenings and I well remember its irksomeness. But the lessons were ^enot the most important part of the instruction I was receiving. Much^e of it consisted in the books I read by myself and in my father's discourses to me, chiefly during our walks. From 1810 to the end of 1813 we were living at Newington Green, then an almost rustic neighbourhood. My father's health required considerable and constant exercise and he walked habitually before breakfast, generally in the green lanes towards Hornsey. In these

---

^{c-c}[*Earlier version:*] cannot remember the time when I could not read, nor

^{d-d}[*Earlier version:*] what I am about to relate. I must first mention, that I learned Greek in the common manner: he set me a portion of a Greek author to make out, as I best could, the meaning, and afterwards construe it verbally to him. Now I not only went through the whole operation of making out the lesson in the same room and at the same table at which he was writing, but

^{e-e}[*Earlier version:*] but a part and scarcely even the principal part of the instruction I received from my fourth to my eighth year. The rest

A man who, in his own practice, so vigorously acted up to the principle of losing no time, was likely to adhere to the same rule in the instruction of his pupil. I have no remembrance of the time when I began to learn Greek. I have been told that it was when I was three years old. My earliest recollection on the subject, is that of committing to memory what my father termed Vocables, being lists of common Greek words, with their signification in English, which he wrote out for me on cards. Of grammar, until some years later, I learnt no more than the inflexions of the nouns and verbs, but, after a course of vocables, proceeded at once to translation; and I faintly remember going through Æsop's *Fables*, the first Greek book which I read.[*] The *Anabasis*,[†] which I remember better, was the second. I learnt no Latin until my eighth year. At that time I had read, under my father's tuition, a number of Greek prose authors, among whom I remember the whole of Herodotus, and of Xenophon's *Cyropædia* and *Memorials of Socrates*; some of the lives of the philosophers by Diogenes Laertius; part of Lucian, and Isocrates *Ad Demonicum* and *Ad Nicoclem*. I also read, in 1813, the first six dialogues (in the common arrangement) of Plato, from the *Euthyphron* to the *Theætetus* inclusive:[‡] which last dialogue, I venture to think, would have been better omitted, as it was totally impossible I should understand it. But my father, in all his teaching, demanded of me not only the utmost that I could do, but much that I could by no possibility have done. What he was himself willing to undergo for the sake of my instruction, may be judged from the fact, that I went through the whole process of preparing my Greek lessons in the same room and at the same table at which he was writing: and as in those days Greek and English Lexicons were not, and I could make no more use of a Greek and Latin Lexicon than could be made without having yet begun to learn Latin, I was forced to have recourse to him for the meaning of every word which I did not know. This incessant interruption he, one of the most impatient of men, submitted to, and wrote under that interruption several volumes of his *History* and all else that he had to write during those years.

The only thing besides Greek, that I learnt as a lesson in this part of my childhood, was arithmetic: this also my father taught me: it was the task of the evenings, and I well remember its disagreeableness. But the lessons were only a part of the daily instruction I received. Much of it consisted in the books I read by myself, and my father's discourses to me, chiefly during our walks. From 1810 to the end of 1813 we were living in Newington Green, then an almost rustic neighbourhood. My father's health required considerable and constant exercise, and he walked habitually before breakfast, generally in the green lanes towards

[*From here to p. 73, because of the density of allusion, names of authors and titles of works are added only when Mill's reference is not sufficient for easy identification, or when the work is not part of his early reading. Full titles are given in the Bibliographic Index, and a list of Mill's early reading, with comments, is given in App. B.]

[†Of Xenophon.]

[‡I.e., *Euthyphron, Apology, Crito, Phaedo, Cratylus*, and *Theaetetus*.]

walks I always accompanied him, and what I chiefly remember of them (except the bouquets of wild flowers which I used to bring in) is the account I used to give him daily of what I had read the previous day. *f*I made notes on slips of paper while reading*f*, and from these I used in the morning walks to tell the story to him. I say the story, for the books were chiefly histories, of which I read in this manner a great number: Robertson's histories, Hume, Gibbon; but my greatest delight, then and for long afterwards, was Watson's *Philip Second* and *Third*. The heroic defence of the Knights of Malta against the Turks, and of the Dutch revolted provinces against Spain, excited in me an intense and lasting interest. Next to Watson my favorite book of the historical sort was Hooke's History of Rome. Of Greece I had seen at that time no regular history, except school abridgments and the last two or three volumes of a translation of Rollin's *Ancient History*, from Philip of Macedon to the end. But I read with great delight, Langhorne's translation of Plutarch; and I had Greek history in my daily Greek lessons. For English history beyond the time at which Hume leaves off, I remember reading Burnet's *History of His Own Time*, though I cared little for anything in it except the wars and battles—and the historical part of the *Annual Register* from the beginning to about 1788 where the volumes my father borrowed for me from Mr. Bentham left off. I felt a lively interest in Frederic of Prussia during his difficulties and in Paoli, the Corsican patriot—but when I came to the American War of independence I took my part like a child as I was, on the wrong side because it was called the English side; until *g*set right by my father*g*. In these frequent talks about the books I read, he used as opportunity offered to give me explanations and ideas respecting civilization, society, government, morality, mental cultivation, which he required me after-wards to *h*restate to him in my own words*h*. He also made me read, and give him a verbal account of, many books which would not have interested me sufficiently to induce me to read them of myself: I particularly remember Millar's *Historical View of the English Government*, a book of great merit for its time, and which he much valued: also Mosheim's *Ecclesiastical History*, McCrie's *Life of Knox*, and even Sewell's and Rutty's histories of the Quakers. Of voyages and travels I remember as part of my constant reading Anson's *Voyage* which is so delightful to most young persons, and a Collection in four octavo volumes (Hawkesworth's I believe it was) of Voyages round the World, from Drake to Cook and Bougain-

---

f-f[*Earlier version:*] Passing my time in the room in which he wrote, I had fallen into an imitation of many of his ways and as in reading for his history he made notes on slips of paper of the main facts which he found in his authorities, I made, as I fancied, similar notes on all the books I read

g-g[*Earlier version:*] my father taught me or at least told me better

h-h[*Earlier version:*] give him an account of, in order to shew whether I had understood what he had told me and to ensure my remembering it

Hornsey. In these walks I always accompanied him, and with my earliest recollections of green fields and wild flowers, is mingled that of the account I gave him
daily of what I had read the day before. To the best of my remembrance, this was a
voluntary rather than a prescribed exercise. I made notes on slips of paper while
reading, and from these, in the morning walks, I told the story to him; for the books
were chiefly histories, of which I read in this manner a great number: Robertson's
histories, Hume, Gibbon; but my greatest delight, then and for long afterwards,
was Watson's *Philip the Second* and *Third*. The heroic defence of the Knights of
Malta against the Turks, and of the revolted provinces of the Netherlands against
Spain, excited in me an intense and lasting interest.[*] Next to Watson, my favorite
historical reading was Hooke's History of Rome. Of Greece I had seen at that time
no regular history, except school abridgments and the last two or three volumes of
a translation of Rollin's *Ancient History*, beginning with Philip of Macedon. But I
read with great delight Langhorne's translation of Plutarch. In English history,
beyond the time at which Hume leaves off, I remember reading Burnet's *History of
His Own Time*, though I cared little for anything in it except the wars and battles;
and the historical part of the *Annual Register*, from the beginning to about 1788,
where the volumes my father borrowed for me from Mr. Bentham left off. I felt a
lively interest in Frederic of Prussia during his difficulties, and in Paoli, the
Corsican patriot; but when I came to the American War, I took my part, like a child
as I was (until set right by my father) on the wrong side, because it was called the
English side. In these frequent talks about the books I read, he used, as opportunity
offered, to give me explanations and ideas respecting civilization, government,
morality, mental cultivation, which he required me afterwards to restate to him in
my own words. He also made me read, and give him a verbal account of, many
books which would not have interested me sufficiently to induce me to read them of
myself: among others, Millar's *Historical View of the English Government*, a book
of great merit for its time, and which he highly valued; Mosheim's *Ecclesiastical
History*, McCrie's *Life of John Knox*, and even Sewell's and Rutty's Histories of
the Quakers.[†] He was fond of putting into my hands books which exhibited men
of energy and resource in unusual circumstances, struggling against difficulties
and overcoming them: of such works I remember Beaver's *African Memoranda*,
and Collins's account of the first settlement of New South Wales.[‡] Two books
which I never wearied of reading were Anson's *Voyage*, so delightful to most
young persons, and a Collection (Hawkesworth's, I believe) of Voyages round the
World, in four volumes, beginning with Drake and ending with Cook and

[*In Robert Watson, *History of the Reign of Philip II* (1777), esp. Bk. VI, and Bks.
X–XIV.]
[†Willem Sewel, *The History of the . . . Quakers* (1722); and Thomas Wight and John
Rutty, *A History of the . . . Quakers in Ireland* (1751).]
[‡David Collins, *An Account of the English Colony in New South Wales* (1798–1802).]

ville [i]. I read few books of amusement properly so called: of children's books, any more than of playthings, I had scarcely any, except an occasional gift from a relation or acquaintance—among those I had, *Robinson Crusoe* was preeminent and continued to delight me through all my boyhood. It was no part however of my father's system to exclude books of amusement: though he allowed them very sparingly. Of such books he possessed, at that time, next to none, but an early friend and companion of his, Dr. Thomson the chemist, had many, and some of those he borrowed purposely for me—those which I remember are the *Arabian Nights*, Cazotte's *Arabian Tales*, *Don Quixote*, and a book of some reputation in its day, Brooke's *Fool of Quality*.

[j] In my eighth year I commenced learning Latin by means of teaching it to a younger sister, who afterwards repeated the lessons to my father. From this time other sisters and brothers being successively added as pupils, a considerable part of my day's work consisted of this preparatory teaching; and it was a part which I especially disliked. The principal advantage which, as far as I am aware, arose from it, was that I myself learnt more thoroughly and retained more lastingly the things which I had to teach as well as learn; perhaps too, the practice it afforded in explaining difficulties to others, may even at that age have been useful [k]. In other respects the experience of my boyhood is not favorable to the plan of teaching children by means of one another. The teaching, I am sure, is very inefficient as teaching, and I well know that the relation between teacher and taught [l] is a most unfavourable moral discipline to both. I went through the grammar and part of Cornelius Nepos and Cæsar's *Commentaries* [m]in this manner, but afterwards added to the superintendance of these[m] lessons, much longer ones of my own which I repeated to my father in the usual manner.

In the same year in which I began Latin I made my first commencement in the Greek poets with the *Iliad*. After I had made some progress in this, my father put Pope's translation into my hands: it was the first English verse I had cared to read, and became one of the books in which for many years I most delighted: I think I must have read it from twenty to thirty times through. I should not have thought it worth while to mention a taste apparently so natural to boyhood if I had not, as I

---

[i][*Cancelled text:*] : and I have a faint remembrance of some folio collection in which I read an account of the first circumnavigation of the globe, by Magellan [Mill may be referring to the account in John Hamilton Moore, *A New and Complete Collection of Voyages and Travels*, 2 vols. (London: Hogg, [1780?]), Vol. I, pp. 13–15.]

[j][*Cancelled text:*] I continue the, as it were, mechanical detail of my course of instruction in order to finish it before entering on the influences of a more general kind under which I was placed in my early years.

[k][*Cancelled text:*] , though of this I am not sure, because I am not certain that I did remove any difficulties

Bougainville.[*] Of children's books, any more than of playthings, I had scarcely any, except an occasional gift from a relation or acquaintance: among those I had, *Robinson Crusoe* was preeminent, and continued to delight me through all my boyhood. It was no part however of my father's system to exclude books of amusement, though he allowed them very sparingly. Of such books he possessed at that time next to none, but he borrowed several for me; those which I remember are, the *Arabian Nights*, Cazotte's *Arabian Tales*, *Don Quixote*, Miss Edgeworth's *Popular Tales*, and a book of some reputation in its day, Brooke's *Fool of Quality*.

In my eighth year I commenced learning Latin, in conjunction with a younger sister, to whom I taught it as I went on, and who afterwards repeated the lessons to my father: and from this time, other sisters and brothers being successively added as pupils, a considerable part of my day's work consisted of this preparatory teaching. It was a part which I greatly disliked; the more so, as I was held responsible for the lessons of my pupils, in almost as full a sense as for my own: I however derived from this discipline the great advantage, of learning more thoroughly and retaining more lastingly the things which I was set to teach: perhaps, too, the practice it afforded in explaining difficulties to others, may even at that age have been useful. In other respects, the experience of my boyhood is not favorable to the plan of teaching children by means of one another. The teaching, I am sure, is very inefficient as teaching, and I well know that the relation between teacher and taught is not a good moral discipline to either. I went in this manner through the Latin grammar, and a considerable part of Cornelius Nepos[†] and Cæsar's *Commentaries*, but afterwards added to the superintendance of these lessons, much longer ones of my own.

In the same year in which I began Latin, I made my first commencement in the Greek poets with the *Iliad*. After I had made some progress in this, my father put Pope's translation into my hands. It was the first English verse I had cared to read, and it became one of the books in which for many years I most delighted: I think I must have read it from twenty to thirty times through. I should not have thought it worth while to mention a taste apparently so natural to boyhood, if I had not, as I

[*Probably David Henry, *An Historical Account of All the Voyages round the World* (1774), which includes Drake and Bougainville, rather than John Hawkesworth, *An Account of the Voyages Undertaken by the Order of His Present Majesty* (1773), which does not include either.]

[†*Excellentium imperatorum vitae.*]

---

l[*Cancelled text:*] (the teacher also being without any real authority) [*deleted first by HTM*]

m-m[*Earlier version:*] with my sister but afterwards added to the superintendance of her [*altered to final reading first by HTM*]

think, observed that the keen enjoyment of this brilliant specimen of narrative and versification, is not so universal with boys as I should have expected both a priori and from my individual experience. Soon after this time I commenced Euclid, and somewhat later, algebra, still under my father's tuition.

From my eighth to my twelfth year the Latin books which I remember reading were the *Bucolics* of Virgil, and the first six books of the *Æneid*; all Horace; the fables of Phædrus; the first five books of Livy (to which from my love of the subject I voluntarily added at my leisure, the remainder of the first decad); all Sallust; a considerable part of Ovid's *Metamorphoses*; some plays of Terence; two or three books of Lucretius; some of the orations of Cicero and of his writings on oratory; also his letters to Atticus, my father taking the trouble to translate to me from the French the historical explanations in Mongault's notes. Tacitus I do not think I meddled with till my thirteenth year [n]. In Greek I read the *Iliad* and *Odyssey* through; one or two plays of Sophocles, Euripides and Aristophanes, but by these I profited little; all Thucydides; Xenophon's *Hellenics*; [o]a great part of Demosthenes[o], Æschines and Lysias; Theocritus; Anacreon; part of the *Anthology*; a little of Dionysius; the first two or three books of Polybius; and lastly, Aristotle's *Rhetoric*, which as the first expressly scientific treatise on any moral or psychological subject which I had read and containing, besides, many of the best observations of the ancients on human nature and human affairs, my father made me study with peculiar care and throw the matter of it into synoptic tables [p]. During the same years I learnt elementary geometry and algebra thoroughly; the differential calculus and other portions of the higher mathematics not thoroughly [q]; for my father not having kept up this part of his early acquired knowledge, could not spare time to qualify himself for removing my difficulties and left me to deal with them with little other aid than that of books; at the same time continually calling on me, with authority and indignation, to solve difficult problems for which he did not see that I had not the necessary previous knowledge.

As to my private reading, I can only speak of what I remember. History continued to be my strongest predilection. Mitford's *Greece* I used to be continually reading [r]. My father had put me on my guard against the Tory prejudices of this writer, and his perversions of facts for the glorification of despots and discredit of popular institutions. These points he used to discourse upon, exemplifying them from the Greek orators and historians [s] with such effect that in reading Mitford my sympathies always were on the contrary side to those of the author, and I could, to some extent, have argued the point against him; yet this did not diminish the ever new pleasure with which I read the book. Ferguson's Roman history was also a

[n][*Cancelled text:*] ; as well as part of Juvenal, and a great part of Quintilian
[o-o][*Earlier version:*] all Demosthenes (except the private orations, which I read later)
[p][*Cancelled text:*] like those in some of the treatises on the scholastic logic and metaphysics
[q][*Cancelled text:*] , but very much the reverse
[r][*Cancelled text:*] ; no book ever delighted me more
[s][*Cancelled text:*] which I read as my daily lessons: and he did this

think, observed that the keen enjoyment of this brilliant specimen of narrative and versification is not so universal with boys, as I should have expected both *a priori* and from my individual experience. Soon after this time I commenced Euclid, and somewhat later, algebra, still under my father's tuition.

From my eighth to my twelfth year the Latin books which I remember reading were, the *Bucolics* of Virgil, and the first six books of the *Æneid*; all Horace except the *Epodes*; the fables of Phædrus; the first five books of Livy (to which from my love of the subject I voluntarily added, in my hours of leisure, the remainder of the first decad); all Sallust; a considerable part of Ovid's *Metamorphoses*; some plays of Terence; two or three books of Lucretius; several of the Orations of Cicero, and of his writings on oratory; also his letters to Atticus, my father taking the trouble to translate to me from the French the historical explanations in Mongault's notes. In Greek I read the *Iliad* and *Odyssey* through; one or two plays of Sophocles, Euripides, and Aristophanes, though by these I profited little; all Thucydides; the *Hellenics* of Xenophon; a great part of Demosthenes, Æschines, and Lysias; Theocritus; Anacreon; part of the *Anthology*; a little of Dionysius; [*] several books of Polybius; and lastly, Aristotle's *Rhetoric*, which, as the first expressly scientific treatise on any moral or psychological subject which I had read, and containing many of the best observations of the ancients on human nature and life, my father made me study with peculiar care, and throw the matter of it into synoptic tables. During the same years I learnt elementary geometry and algebra thoroughly, the differential calculus and other portions of the higher mathematics far from thoroughly: for my father, not having kept up this part of his early acquired knowledge, could not spare time to qualify himself for removing my difficulties, and left me to deal with them, with little other aid than that of books:[†] while I was continually incurring his displeasure by my inability to solve difficult problems for which he did not see that I had not the necessary previous knowledge.

As to my private reading, I can only speak of what I remember. History continued to be my strongest predilection, and most of all ancient history. Mitford's *Greece* I read continually. My father had put me on my guard against the Tory prejudices of this writer, and his perversions of facts for the whitewashing of despots, and blackening of popular institutions. These points he discoursed on, exemplifying them from the Greek orators and historians, with such effect that in reading Mitford, my sympathies were always on the contrary side to those of the author, and I could, to some extent, have argued the point against him: yet this did not diminish the ever new pleasure with which I read the book. Roman history, both in my old favorite, Hooke, and in Ferguson, continued to delight me. A book

[*Dionysius of Halicarnassus, *The Roman Antiquities*.]
[†For the titles of many of the mathematical texts Mill used, see App. B, nos. 68–71, 81–3, 96–9, 107–13, 134–5, 149, 167, 174, 205–7.]

favorite. Another book which notwithstanding what is called the dryness of the stile I took great pleasure in was the *Ancient Universal History*: through the incessant reading of which I had my head full of details of the history of the obscurest ancient people, while in modern history with the exception of ʹdetached passages such as the Dutch war of independence I was at this time little interestedʹ. A voluntary exercise to which I was throughout my boyhood much addicted, was what I called writing histories: of course in imitation of my father—who used to give me the manuscript of part of his history of India to read. Almost as soon as I could hold a pen I must needs write a history of India too: this was soon abandoned, but what I called a Roman history, picked out of Hooke, I continued for a long time to employ myself in writing: after this an abridgment of the *Ancient Universal History*: then a History of Holland, compiled from my favorite Watson and from an anonymous history which somebody who knew my liking for the subject, picked up at a book stall and gave to me. But in my eleventh and twelfth year I occupied myself with writing what I flattered myself was something serious, and might be made fit to be published; this was no less than a history of the Roman Government, compiled (with the assistance of Hooke) from Livy and Dionysius: of which I wrote as much as would have made an octavo volume, extending to the epoch of the Licinian laws. It was in fact an account of the struggles between the patricians and plebeians, which now engrossed all the interest in my mind that I had previously felt in the mere wars and conquests of the Romans. I discussed all the constitutional points as they arose, vindicated the Agrarian law on the evidence of Livy (though quite ignorant of Niebuhr's researches) and upheld to the best of my capacity the Roman democratic party. A few years later in my contempt of my childish efforts I destroyed all these papers, not then anticipating that I could ever have any curiosity about my first attempts at writing or reasoning. My father encouraged me in this useful amusement, though, as I think judiciously, he never asked to see what I wrote, so that I never felt that in writing it I was accountable to any one, nor had the chilling sensation of being under a critical eye.

But though these histories were never a compulsory lesson, there was another kind of composition which was so, namely writing verses and it was one of the most irksome of my tasks. Greek or Latin verses I never wrote, nor learnt the prosody of those languages. My father, thinking this not worth the time it required, was contented with making me read aloud to him and correcting false quantities. I never composed at all in Greek, even in prose, and but little in Latin. But I wrote

---

ʹ⁻ʹ[*Earlier version:*] a few detached passages such as the Dutch war of independence I was very far from being similarly well informed [*altered to final reading first by HTM*]

which, in spite of what is called the dryness of its stile, I took great pleasure in, was the *Ancient Universal History*:[*] through the incessant reading of which, I had my head full of historical details concerning the obscurest ancient people, while about modern history, except detached passages such as the Dutch war of independence, I knew and cared comparatively little. A voluntary exercise to which throughout my boyhood I was much addicted, was what I called writing histories. I successively composed a Roman history, picked out of Hooke;[†] an abridgment of the *Ancient Universal History*; a History of Holland, from my favorite Watson and from an anonymous compilation;[‡] and in my eleventh and twelfth year I occupied myself with writing what I flattered myself was something serious. This was no less than a history of the Roman Government, compiled (with the assistance of Hooke) from Livy and Dionysius: of which I wrote as much as would have made an octavo volume, extending to the epoch of the Licinian Laws. It was, in fact, an account of the struggles between the patricians and plebeians, which now engrossed all the interest in my mind which I had previously felt in the mere wars and conquests of the Romans. I discussed all the constitutional points as they arose: though quite ignorant of Niebuhr's researches,[§] I, by such lights as my father had given me, vindicated the Agrarian Laws on the evidence of Livy, and upheld to the best of my ability the Roman democratic party. A few years later, in my contempt of my childish efforts, I destroyed all these papers, not then anticipating that I could ever feel any curiosity about my first attempts at writing and reasoning. My father encouraged me in this useful amusement, though, as I think judiciously, he never asked to see what I wrote; so that I did not feel that in writing it I was accountable to any one, nor had the chilling sensation of being under a critical eye.

But though these exercises in history were never a compulsory lesson, there was another kind of composition which was so, namely writing verses, and it was one of the most disagreeable of my tasks. Greek or Latin verses I did not write, nor learnt the prosody of those languages. My father, thinking this not worth the time it required, contented himself with making me read aloud to him, and correcting false quantities. I never composed at all in Greek, even in prose, and but little in

[*The first volumes of Anon., *An Universal History, from the Earliest Account of Time to the Present* (1736ff.).]

[†For the opening pages of this history, see App. A, pp. 542–6 below. See also App. C for this and other early writings by Mill.]

[‡Probably *The History of the Republick of Holland, from Its First Foundation to the Death of King William* (1705).]

[§As revealed in his *History of Rome*, trans. Julius Charles Hare, *et al.*, 3 vols. (London: Taylor and Walton, 1828–42).]

many English verses; beginning from the time of my first reading Pope's Homer, when I ambitiously attempted to write something of the same kind, and achieved as much as one book of a continuation of the *Iliad*. *"The exercise, begun by choice, was continued by command"*. Conformably to my father's usual custom of explaining to me the reasons for what he required me to do, he gave me, for this, two reasons which were highly characteristic of him. One was that some things could be expressed better and more forcibly in verse than in prose: this he said was a real advantage: the other was, that people in general attached more value to verse than it deserved, and the power of writing it was therefore useful and worth acquiring. He generally left me to choose my own subjects which as far as I remember were mostly odes to some mythological personage or allegorical abstraction: but he made me translate into English verse many of Horace's shorter poems. I remember his giving me Thomson's "Winter" to read, and afterwards making me attempt to write something myself on the same subject. I had read very little English poetry at this time. Shakespeare my father had put into my hands, at first for the sake of the historical plays, from which however I went on to the others *v* . My father was never a great admirer of Shakespeare the English idolatry of whom, he used to attack in unmeasured terms. *w*He had little value for any English poetry except Milton, Goldsmith, Burns, and Gray's "Bard," which he preferred to his *Elegy*: perhaps I may also add Beattie*w*. I remember his reading to me (unlike his usual practice of making me read to him) the first book of *The Fairie Queene*: but I took little pleasure in it. The poetry of the present century he set no value on—and I hardly saw any of it till I was grown up to manhood, except Walter Scott's metrical romances, which he borrowed for me and which I was much delighted with—as I always was with all animated narrative. Dryden's Poems were among my father's books and many of these he made me read, though I never cared for any of them except *Alexander's Feast*, which like the songs in Walter Scott I used to sing

---

u–u[*Earlier version:*] For some years after, my father made me keep up the practice of writing verses
v[*Cancelled text:*] : I was of course like all persons young or old, pleased and interested with them
w–w[*Earlier version:*] Milton's poetry he did admire but did not think me of an age to comprehend

Ode to Diana

1.

Sol's virgin sister, young and fair,
Let me to tell thy actions dare,
If I may thus presume;
And lay before the sight of all,
Thy hapless nymph Calisto's fall,
And young Actæon's doom.

2.

Over the mountains where you go,
The mountains, crown'd with trackless snow,
Your virgin looks are sweet:
You bound along the highest mounts,
O'er meadows, groves, and crystal founts,
With safe and weary feet.

The wildest beasts in ev'ry wood,
To which all others serve as food,
You strike, and quickly kill:
All o'er the groves and waters wide,
In ev'ry place, on ev'ry side,
And by each murm'ring rill.

Latin: not that my father could be indifferent to the value of this practice, in giving a thorough knowledge of those languages, but because there really was not time for it. The verses I was required to write were English. When I first read Pope's Homer, I ambitiously attempted to compose something of the same kind, and achieved as much as one book of a continuation of the *Iliad*. There, probably, the spontaneous promptings of my poetical ambition would have stopped; but the exercise, begun from choice, was continued by command. Conformably to my father's usual practice of explaining to me, as far as possible, the reasons for what he required me to do, he gave me, for this, as I well remember, two reasons highly characteristic of him. One was, that some things could be expressed better and more forcibly in verse than in prose: this, he said, was a real advantage. The other was, that people in general attached more value to verse than it deserved, and the power of writing it was, on this account, worth acquiring. He generally left me to choose my own subjects, which, as far as I remember, were mostly addresses to some mythological personage or allegorical abstraction;[*] but he made me translate into English verse many of Horace's shorter poems: I also remember his giving me Thomson's "Winter" to read, and afterwards making me attempt (without book) to write something myself on the same subject. The verses I wrote were of course the merest rubbish, nor did I ever attain any facility of versification, but the practice may have been useful in making it easier for me, at a later period, to acquire readiness of expression.* I had read, up to this time, very little English poetry. Shakespeare my father had put into my hands, chiefly for the sake of the historical plays, from which however I went on to the others. My father never was a great admirer of Shakespeare, the English idolatry of whom he used to attack with some severity. He cared little for any English poetry except Milton (for whom he had the highest admiration), Goldsmith, Burns, and Gray's "Bard," which he preferred to his *Elegy*: perhaps I may add Cowper and Beattie. He had some value for Spenser, and I remember his reading to me (unlike his usual practice of making me read to him) the first book of *The Fairie Queene*; but I took little pleasure in it. The poetry of the present century he saw scarcely any merit in, and I hardly became acquainted with any of it till I was grown up to manhood, except the metrical romances of Walter Scott, which I read at his recommendation and was intensely delighted with; as I always was with animated narrative. Dryden's Poems were among my father's books, and many of these he made me read, but I never cared for any of them except *Alexander's Feast*, which, as well as many of the songs in

[*For one of these, "Ode to Diana," see App. A, pp. 549–50 below. See also App. C for this and other early writings by Mill.]

*In a subsequent stage of boyhood, when these exercises had ceased to be compulsory, like most youthful writers I wrote tragedies; under the inspiration not so much of Shakespeare as of Joanna Baillie, whose *Constantine Paleologus* in particular appeared to me one of the most glorious of human compositions. I still think it one of the best dramas of the last two centuries.

internally, to a music of my own. Cowper's short poems I read with some pleasure but never got far into the longer ones—and nothing in the two volumes interested me like the little prose account of his three hares. In my thirteenth year I met with the poems of Campbell, among which "Lochiel," "Hohenlinden," "The Exile of Erin" and some others gave me sensations I had never before received from poetry. Here too I made nothing of the longer poems, except the opening of "Gertrude of Wyoming," which appeared to me the perfection of pathos.

During this part of my childhood one of my greatest amusements was experimental science; not however trying experiments, a kind of discipline which I have often regretted not having had—but merely reading about the experiments of others. I never remember being so wrapt up in any book as I was in Joyce's *Scientific Dialogues*, and I devoured treatises on chemistry, especially Dr. Thomson's, for years before I ever attended a lecture or saw an experiment. [x]

From about the age of twelve I entered into [y]another and more advanced stage in my course of instruction—[y] in which the main object was no longer the aids and appliances of thought, but the thoughts themselves. This commenced with Logic, in which I began at once with the *Organon* and read it to the Analytics inclusive, but profited little by the Posterior Analytics, which belong to a branch of speculation I was not yet ripe for. Contemporaneously with the *Organon* my father made me read the whole or parts of several of the Latin treatises on the scholastic logic; giving each day to him, in our walks, a minute account of the portion I had read and answering his numerous and searching questions. After this I went through in the same manner the "Computatio sive Logica" of Hobbes, a work of a much higher order of thought than the books of the school logicians and which he estimated very highly; in my opinion beyond its merits great as these are. It was his invariable practice, whatever studies he exacted from me, to make me as far as possible understand and feel the utility of them: and this he deemed peculiarly fitting in the case of the syllogistic logic, its usefulness having been impugned by so many writers of authority. Accordingly I well remember how, in his usual manner, he first attempted by questions to make me think on the subject, and frame some conception of what constituted the utility of the syllogistic logic, and when I had

[x][*Cancelled text:*] This was a very easy and pleasant part of my mental education and by no means the least valuable part of it.

[y-y][*Earlier version:*] what may be called the third of the stages into which my course of instruction may be divided—that

Walter Scott, I used to sing internally, to a music of my own: to some of the latter indeed I went so far as to compose airs, which I still remember. Cowper's short poems I read with some pleasure, but never got far into the longer ones; and nothing in the two volumes interested me like the prose account of his three hares. In my thirteenth year I met with Campbell's Poems, among which "Lochiel," "Hohenlinden," "The Exile of Erin," and some others, gave me sensations I had never before experienced from poetry. Here, too, I made nothing of the longer poems, except the striking opening of "Gertrude of Wyoming," which long kept its place in my feelings as the perfection of pathos.

During this part of my childhood, one of my greatest amusements was experimental science; in the theoretical, however, not the practical sense of the word; not trying experiments, a kind of discipline which I have often regretted not having had—nor even seeing, but merely reading about them. I never remember being so wrapt up in any book, as I was in Joyce's *Scientific Dialogues*; and I was rather recalcitrant to my father's criticisms of the bad reasoning respecting the first principles of physics which abounds in the early part of that work. I devoured treatises on Chemistry, especially that of my father's early friend and schoolfellow Dr. Thomson, for years before I attended a lecture or saw an experiment.

From about the age of twelve, I entered into another and more advanced stage in my course of instruction; in which the main object was no longer the aids and appliances of thought, but the thoughts themselves. This commenced with Logic, in which I began at once with the *Organon*, and read it to the Analytics inclusive, but profited little by the Posterior Analytics,[*] which belong to a branch of speculation I was not yet ripe for. Contemporaneously with the *Organon*, my father made me read the whole or parts of several of the Latin treatises on the scholastic logic;[†] giving each day to him, in our walks, a minute account of what I had read, and answering his numerous and searching questions. After this, I went, in a similar manner, through the "Computatio sive Logica" of Hobbes, a work of a much higher order of thought than the books of the school logicians, and which he estimated very highly; in my own opinion beyond its merits, great as these are. It was his invariable practice, whatever studies he exacted from me, to make me as far as possible understand and feel the utility of them: and this he deemed peculiarly fitting in the case of the syllogistic logic, the usefulness of which had been impugned by so many writers of authority. I well remember how, and in what particular walk, in the neighbourhood of Bagshot Heath (where we were on a visit to his old friend Mr. Wallace, then one of the Mathematical Professors at Sandhurst) he first attempted by questions to make me think on the subject, and frame some conception of what constituted the utility of the syllogistic logic, and when I

[*The Prior Analytics and Posterior Analytics are parts of Aristotle's *Organon*.]
[†These included Edward Brerewood, *Elementa logicae* (1637), Franco Burgersdijk, *Institutionum logicarum libri duo* (1660), Phillipus Du Trieu, *Manuductio ad logicam* (1662), and Samuel Smith, *Aditus ad logicam* (1656).]

failed in this, to make me understand it by explanations. I do not believe that the explanations made the matter at all clear to me at the time; but they were not therefore useless; they remained as a nucleus for my observations and reflexions to crystallize upon: his general remarks being interpreted to me by the particular instances which occurred to myself afterwards. My own consciousness and experience ultimately led me to appreciate quite as highly as he did the value of an early practical familiarity with the school logic. I know of nothing, in my education, to which I think myself more indebted for whatever capacity of thinking I have attained. The first intellectual operation in which I arrived at any skill was dissecting a bad argument and finding in what part the fallacy lay: and though whatever success I had in this I owed entirely to the fact that it was an intellectual exercise in which I was most perseveringly drilled by my father; yet it is also true that the school logic, and the mental habits acquired in studying it, were among the principal instruments of this drilling. I am persuaded that nothing, in modern education, tends so much when properly used, to form exact thinkers, who attach a definite meaning to words and propositions, and are not imposed on by vague, loose, or ambiguous terms. It is also a study peculiarly adapted to an early stage in the education of students in philosophy, since it does not presuppose the slow process of acquiring by experience and reflection, valuable thoughts of their own. They may become capable of seeing through confused and self contradictory thinking before their own thinking powers are much advanced; *to the great benefit of those powers in their subsequent developement*.

During this time the Latin and Greek books which I continued to read with my father were chiefly such as were worth studying not merely for the language, but for the thoughts. This included much of the orators and the whole of Demosthenes, some of whose principal orations I read several times over, and wrote out, by way of exercise, an analysis of them. My father's comments on these orations when I read them to him were very instructive to me: he not only drew my attention to the knowledge they afforded of Athenian institutions, and to the principles of legislation and government which they illustrated, but pointed out the skill and art of the orator—how everything important to his purpose was said exactly at the moment when he had brought the minds of his hearers into the state best fitted to receive it; how he made steal into their minds, gradually and by insinuation, thoughts which if expressed directly would have roused their opposition. Most of these reflexions

---

⁻[*Earlier version:*] and nothing can more aid development by clearing the path of the thinker from the mists of vague and sophistical language

had failed in this, to make me understand it by explanations. The explanations did not make the matter at all clear to me at the time; but they were not therefore useless; they remained as a nucleus for my observations and reflections to crystallize upon; the import of his general remarks being interpreted to me, by the particular instances which came under my notice afterwards. My own consciousness and experience ultimately led me to appreciate quite as highly as he did, the value of an early practical familiarity with the school logic. I know of nothing, in my education, to which I think myself more indebted for whatever capacity of thinking I have attained. The first intellectual operation in which I arrived at any proficiency, was dissecting a bad argument, and finding in what part the fallacy lay: and though whatever capacity of this sort I attained, was due to the fact that it was an intellectual exercise in which I was most perseveringly drilled by my father, yet it is also true that the school logic, and the mental habits acquired in studying it, were among the principal instruments of this drilling. I am persuaded that nothing, in modern education, tends so much, when properly used, to form exact thinkers, who attach a precise meaning to words and propositions, and are not imposed on by vague, loose, or ambiguous terms. The boasted influence of mathematical studies is nothing to it; for in mathematical processes, none of the real difficulties of correct ratiocination occur. It is also a study peculiarly adapted to an early stage in the education of philosophical students, since it does not presuppose the slow process of acquiring, by experience and reflection, valuable thoughts of their own. They may become capable of disentangling the intricacies of confused and self-contradictory thought, before their own thinking faculties are much advanced; a power which, for want of some such discipline, many otherwise able men altogether lack; and when they have to answer opponents, only endeavour, by such arguments as they can command, to support the opposite conclusion, scarcely even attempting to confute the reasonings of their antagonists; and therefore, at the utmost, leaving the question, as far as it depends on argument, a balanced one.

During this time, the Latin and Greek books which I continued to read with my father were chiefly such as were worth studying not for the language merely, but also for the thoughts. This included much of the orators, and especially Demosthenes, some of whose principal orations I read several times over, and wrote out, by way of exercise, a full analysis of them. My father's comments on these orations when I read them to him were very instructive to me. He not only drew my attention to the insight they afforded into Athenian institutions, and the principles of legislation and government which they often illustrated, but pointed out the skill and art of the orator—how everything important to his purpose was said at the exact moment when he had brought the minds of his audience into the state most fitted to receive it; how he made steal into their minds, gradually and by insinuation, thoughts which if expressed in a more direct manner would have roused their opposition. Most of these reflections were beyond my capacity of full comprehen-

were *a*beyond my capacity of full comprehension at the time,*a* but they left seed behind. I also read through Tacitus, and Quintilian. The latter, owing to his obscure stile and to the scholastic details of which many parts of his treatise are made up, is little read and seldom sufficiently appreciated. His book is a kind of encyclopædia of the thoughts of the ancients on education and culture: and I have retained through life many valuable ideas which I can trace to my reading of it, even at that age. I read, too, at this time, some of the most important dialogues of Plato, especially the *Gorgias*, the *Protagoras*, and the *Republic*. There is no author to whom my father thought himself more indebted for his own mental culture, than Plato, and I can say the same of mine. The Socratic method, of which the Platonic dialogues are the chief example, is unsurpassed as a discipline for abstract thought on the most difficult subjects. Nothing in modern life and education, in the smallest degree supplies its place. The close, searching *elenchus* by which the man of vague generalities is absolutely compelled either to express his meaning to himself in definite terms, or to confess that he does not know what he is talking about—the perpetual testing of all general statements by particular instances—the siege in form which is laid to the meaning of large abstract terms, by laying hold of some much larger class-name which includes that and more, and *dividing down* *b* to the thing sought, marking out its limits and definition by a series of accurately drawn distinctions between it and each of the cognate objects which are successively severed from it—all this even at that age took such hold on me that it became part of my own mind; and I have ever felt myself, beyond any modern that I know of except my father and perhaps beyond even him, a pupil of Plato, and cast in the mould of his dialectics. *c*

In going through Demosthenes and Plato, as I could now read these authors as far as the language was concerned with perfect ease, I was not required to construe them sentence by sentence but to read them aloud to my father, answering questions when asked: but the particular attention which he paid to elocution (in

a-a[*Earlier version:*] of course lost on me

b[*Cancelled text:*] (if I may so speak)

c[*At this point in the draft Mill wrote and deleted a new paragraph that begins:*] The strong moral impressions yielded by the writings of Plato also took great effect on me, nor was their inculcation neglected by my father. Even at the very early age at which I read with him the *Memorabilia* of Xenophon. . . . [*This continues with substantially the same text as the second, fourth, and fifth sentences of the paragraph beginning below at* 48.3, *where Mill recopied it when he decided that the moral impressions of Plato took effect* "at a later period".]

sion at the time; but they left seed behind, which germinated in due season. At this time I also read the whole of Tacitus, Juvenal, and Quintilian. The latter, owing to his obscure stile and to the scholastic details of which many parts of his treatise are made up, is little read and seldom sufficiently appreciated. His book is a kind of encyclopædia of the thoughts of the ancients on the whole field of education and culture; and I have retained through life many valuable ideas which I can distinctly trace to my reading of him, even at that early age. It was at this period that I read, for the first time, some of the most important dialogues of Plato, in particular the *Gorgias*, the *Protagoras*, and the *Republic*. There is no author to whom my father thought himself more indebted for his own mental culture, than Plato, or whom he more frequently recommended to young students. I can bear similar testimony in regard to myself. The Socratic method, of which the Platonic dialogues are the chief example, is unsurpassed as a discipline for correcting the errors, and clearing up the confusions incident to the *intellectus sibi permissus*,[*] the understanding which has made up all its bundles of associations under the guidance of popular phraseology. The close, searching *elenchus* by which the man of vague generalities [†] is constrained either to express his meaning to himself in definite terms, or to confess that he does not know what he is talking about; the perpetual testing of all general statements by particular instances; the siege in form which is laid to the meaning of large abstract terms, by fixing upon some still larger class-name which includes that and more, and dividing down to the thing sought— marking out its limits and definition by a series of accurately drawn distinctions between it and each of the cognate objects which are successively parted off from it—all this, as an education for precise thinking, is inestimable, and all this, even at that age, took such hold of me that it became part of my own mind. I have felt ever since that the title of Platonist belongs by far better right to those who have been nourished in, and have endeavoured to practise Plato's mode of investigation, than to those who are distinguished only by the adoption of certain dogmatical conclusions, drawn mostly from the least intelligible of his works, and which the character of his mind and writings makes it uncertain whether he himself regarded as anything more than poetic fancies, or philosophic conjectures.

In going through Plato and Demosthenes, since I could now read these authors, as far as the language was concerned, with perfect ease, I was not required to construe them sentence by sentence, but to read them aloud to my father, answering questions when asked: but the particular attention which he paid to elocution

[*Francis Bacon, *Novum organum*, in *The Works of Francis Bacon*, ed. James Spedding, *et al.*, 14 vols. (London: Longman, *et al.*, 1857–74), Vol. I, pp. 138, 157 (Aph. ii), 160 (Aphs. xx, xxi, xxii).]
[†The term "vague generalities," which Mill uses elsewhere (cf. pp. 113, 221 below), comes from Jeremy Bentham, *The Book of Fallacies*, in *Works*, ed. John Bowring, 11 vols. (Edinburgh: Tait; London: Simpkin, Marshall; Dublin: Cumming, 1843), Vol. II, Pt. IV, Chap. iii, pp. 440–8.]

which his own excellence was remarkable) made this reading aloud to him ^da most painful task^d. Of all things which he required me to do, there was none which I did so constantly ill, or in which he so perpetually lost his temper with me. He had thought much on the principles of the art of reading, especially the part of it which relates to the inflexions of the voice, or *modulation* as writers on elocution call it (in contrast with *articulation* on the one side, and *expression* on the other), and had reduced it to rules, grounded on the logical analysis of a sentence. These rules he constantly impressed upon me, and severely took me to task for every violation of them: but I even then remarked (though I did not venture to make the remark to him) that though he reproached me when I read a sentence ill, and *told* me how I ought to have read it, he never *shewed* me: he often mockingly caricatured my bad reading of the sentence, but did not, by reading it himself, instruct me how it ought to be read. It was a defect running through his modes of instruction as it did through his modes of thinking that he trusted too much to the intelligibleness of the abstract when not embodied in the concrete. It was at a much later time of life when practising elocution by myself or with companions of my own age, that I for the first time thoroughly understood his rules and saw the psychological grounds of them; and at that time I and others followed out the subject into its ramifications and could have composed a very useful treatise grounded on my father's principles. He himself left those principles and rules unwritten, and unwritten they still remain.

^eMy private exercises in composition during my thirteenth and fourteenth year changed from historical to dramatic; though indeed they were historical still, for my dramatic attempts were on historical subjects. Like most youthful writers I wrote tragedies: the first was on the Roman emperor Otho, the attraction to me not being the character or fortunes of the hero, but the movement and bustle of that portion of Roman history, as related by Tacitus. I wrote ^fa play^f on the story of the Danaides, and began two more, one on a subject from Tacitus, another from Thucydides. What kindled my dramatic aspirations was not so much Shakespeare as the plays of Joanna Baillie, among which *Constantine Paleologus* appeared to me one of the most glorious of human compositions. I have read it since and I still think it one of the best dramas of the last two centuries.^e

A book which contributed very much to my education was my father's *History of India*. It was published in the beginning of 1818. During the year previous it was passing through the press, and I used to read the proofsheets to him; or rather, to read the manuscript to him while he corrected the proofs. The number of new ideas which I received from this remarkable book, and the impulse and stimulus as well as guidance given to my thoughts by its criticisms and disquisitions on society and civilization in the Hindoo part, on institutions and the acts of governments in the

^{d–d}[*Earlier version:*] the *supplice* of every day
^{e–e}[*This paragraph is a later addition written at left.*]

(in which his own excellence was remarkable) made this reading aloud to him a most painful task. Of all things which he required me to do, there was none which I did so constantly ill, or in which he so perpetually lost his temper with me. He had thought much on the principles of the art of reading, especially the most neglected part of it, the inflexions of the voice, or *modulation* as writers on elocution call it (in contrast with *articulation* on the one side, and *expression* on the other), and had reduced it to rules, grounded on the logical analysis of a sentence. These rules he strongly impressed upon me, and took me severely to task for every violation of them: but I even then remarked (though I did not venture to make the remark to him) that though he reproached me when I read a sentence ill, and *told* me how I ought to have read it, he never, by reading it himself, *shewed* me how it ought to be read. A defect running through his otherwise admirable modes of instruction, as it did through all his modes of thought, was that of trusting too much to the intelligibleness of the abstract, when not embodied in the concrete. It was at a much later period of my youth, when practising elocution by myself, or with companions of my own age, that I for the first time understood the object of his rules, and saw the psychological grounds of them. At that time I and others followed out the subject into its ramifications, and could have composed a very useful treatise, grounded on my father's principles. He himself left those principles and rules unwritten. I regret that when my mind was full of the subject, from systematic practice, I did not put them, and our improvements of them, into a formal shape.

A book which contributed largely to my education, in the best sense of the term, was my father's *History of India*. It was published in the beginning of 1818. During the year previous, while it was passing through the press, I used to read the proofsheets to him; or rather, I read the manuscript to him while he corrected the proofs. The number of new ideas which I received from this remarkable book, and the impulse and stimulus as well as guidance given to my thoughts by its criticisms and disquisitions on society and civilization in the Hindoo part, on institutions and

---

f-f[*Earlier version:*] another tragedy

English part—made my early familiarity with this book eminently useful to my subsequent progress. And though I can perceive deficiencies in it now as compared with a perfect standard, I still think it the most instructive history ever yet written, and one of the books from which most benefit may be derived by a mind in the course of making up its opinions.

The Preface to the *History*, one of the most characteristic of my father's writings, as well as one of the richest in materials for thought, gives a picture entirely to be depended on, of the sentiments and expectations with which he wrote the book. Saturated as the book is with the principles and modes of judgment of a democratic radicalism then regarded as extreme; and treating with a severity then most unusual the English constitution, the English law, and all parties and classes who possessed at that time any influence in this country, he may have expected reputation but certainly not advancement in life from its publication, nor could he have supposed that it would raise up anything but enemies for him in powerful quarters, least of all could he have expected favour from the East India Company, on the acts of whose government he had made so many severe comments: though in various parts of his book he bore a testimony in their favour, which he felt to be their due, viz. that if the acts of any other government had the light of publicity as completely let in upon them, they would probably still less bear scrutiny; and that no government on record had on the whole given so much proof (to the extent of its lights) of good intention towards its subjects.

On learning however in the spring of 1819, about a year after the publication of his *History*, that the East India Directors desired to strengthen that part of their establishment which was employed in carrying on the correspondence with India, my father declared himself a candidate for that employment, and to the credit of the Directors, successfully. He was appointed one of the Assistants of the Examiner of Indian Correspondence; officers whose duty it is to prepare drafts of despatches to India in the principal departments of administration. In this office and in that of Examiner which he subsequently attained, the influence which his talents, his reputation, and his decision of character gave him, enabled him to a great extent to throw into his drafts of despatches, and to carry through the ordeal of the Court of Directors and Board of Control without having their force much weakened, his real opinions on Indian subjects. Those despatches, in conjunction with his *History*, did more than had ever been done before to promote the improvement of India, and teach Indian officials to understand their business. If a selection of them were published, they would, I am convinced, place his character as a practical statesman quite on a level with his reputation as a speculative writer.

the acts of governments in the English part, made my early familiarity with it eminently useful to my subsequent progress. And though I can perceive deficiencies in it now as compared with a perfect standard, I still think it, if not the most, one of the most instructive histories ever written, and one of the books from which most benefit may be derived by a mind in the course of making up its opinions.

The Preface, among the most characteristic of my father's writings, as well as the richest in materials of thought, gives a picture which may be entirely depended on, of the sentiments and expectations with which he wrote the *History*. Saturated as the book is with the opinions and modes of judgment of a democratic radicalism then regarded as extreme; and treating with a severity at that time most unusual the English Constitution, the English law, and all parties and classes who possessed any considerable influence in the country; he may have expected reputation, but certainly not advancement in life, from its publication; nor could he have supposed that it would raise up anything but enemies for him in powerful quarters: least of all could he have expected favour from the East India Company, to whose commercial privileges he was unqualifiedly hostile, and on the acts of whose government he had made so many severe comments: though, in various parts of his book, he bore a testimony in their favour, which he felt to be their just due, namely, that no government had on the whole given so much proof, to the extent of its lights, of good intention towards its subjects; and that if the acts of any other government had the light of publicity as completely let in upon them, they would, in all probability, still less bear scrutiny.

On learning, however, in the spring of 1819, about a year after the publication of the *History*, that the East India Directors desired to strengthen the part of their home establishment which was employed in carrying on the correspondence with India, my father declared himself a candidate for that employment, and, to the credit of the Directors, successfully. He was appointed one of the Assistants of the Examiner of India Correspondence; officers whose duty it was to prepare drafts of despatches to India, for consideration by the Directors, in the principal departments of administration. In this office, and in that of Examiner, which he subsequently attained, the influence which his talents, his reputation, and his decision of character gave him, with superiors who really desired the good government of India, enabled him to a great extent to throw into his drafts of despatches, and to carry through the ordeal of the Court of Directors and Board of Control, without having their force much weakened, his real opinions on Indian subjects. In his *History* he had set forth, for the first time, many of the true principles of Indian administration: and his despatches, following his *History*, did more than had ever been done before to promote the improvement of India, and teach Indian officials to understand their business. If a selection of them were published, they would, I am convinced, place his character as a practical statesman fully on a level with his eminence as a speculative writer.

This new ^{g}employment^g caused no relaxation in his attention to my education. It was in this same year 1819 that he went through with me a course of political economy. His loved and intimate friend, Ricardo, had shortly before published the ^{h}book which made so great an epoch in political economy; a book which^h would never have been published or written, but for the earnest entreaty and strong encouragement of my father; for Ricardo, the most modest of men, though firmly convinced of the truth of his doctrines, believed himself so incapable of doing them justice in point of exposition and expression, that he shrank from the idea of publicity. The same friendly encouragement induced Ricardo, a year or two later, to become a member of the House of Commons, where during the few remaining years of his life, unhappily cut short in the full vigour of his intellect, he rendered so much service to his and my father's opinions both in political economy and on other subjects.

Though Ricardo's great work was already in print, no didactic treatise embodying its doctrines, in a manner fit for learners, had yet appeared. My father therefore instructed me on the subject by a sort of lectures, ^{i} which he delivered to me in our walks. He expounded to me each day a part of the subject, and I gave him next day a written account of it which he made me write over and over again until it was clear, precise and tolerably complete. In this manner I went through the whole subject; and the written outline of it which ^{j}resulted from my daily *compte rendu^j*, served him afterwards as notes from which to write his *Elements of Political Economy*. After this I went through Ricardo, giving an account daily of what I read, and discussing in the best manner I could, the collateral points which were raised as we went on. On money, as the most intricate part of the subject, he made me read in a similar manner Ricardo's admirable pamphlets, published during what was called the Bullion controversy. I afterwards went through Adam Smith, and in this reading it was one of my father's main objects to make me apply to Smith's more superficial view of political economy the superior lights of Ricardo, and detect with logical exactness what was fallacious in Smith's arguments or erroneous in his conclusions. Such a system of instruction was excellently suited to form a thinker; but it required to be worked by a thinker, as close and vigorous as my father. The path was a thorny one even to him, and I am sure it was so to me, though I took the strongest interest in the subject. He was continually provoked by my failures ^{k}both where success could, and where it could not,^{k} have been expected: but in the main his method was right, and it succeeded. I do not believe that any scientific teaching ever was more thorough, or better calculated for training the faculties, than the mode in which logic and political economy were

---

$^{g-g}$[*Earlier version:*] occupation, relieving him from the necessity of writing for subsistence,

$^{h-h}$[*Earlier version:*] great work which gave to political economy so new and improved a form and foundation. This book, it may be remarked incidentally,

^{i}[*Cancelled text:*] if they may be so called,

This new employment of his time caused no relaxation in his attention to my education. It was in this same year, 1819, that he took me through a complete course of political economy. His loved and intimate friend, Ricardo, had shortly before published the book which formed so great an epoch in political economy;[*] a book which never would have been published or written, but for the entreaty and strong encouragement of my father; for Ricardo, the most modest of men, though firmly convinced of the truth of his doctrines, deemed himself so little capable of doing them justice in exposition and expression, that he shrank from the idea of publicity. The same friendly encouragement induced Ricardo, a year or two later, to become a member of the House of Commons; where during the few remaining years of his life, unhappily cut short in the full vigour of his intellect, he rendered so much service to his and my father's opinions both in political economy and on other subjects.

Though Ricardo's great work was already in print, no didactic treatise embodying its doctrines, in a manner fit for learners, had yet appeared. My father, therefore, commenced instructing me in the science by a sort of lectures, which he delivered to me in our walks. He expounded each day a portion of the subject, and I gave him next day a written account of it, which he made me rewrite over and over again until it was clear, precise, and tolerably complete. In this manner I went through the whole extent of the science; and the written outline of it which resulted from my daily *compte rendu*, served him afterwards as notes from which to write his *Elements of Political Economy*. After this I read Ricardo, giving an account daily of what I read, and discussing, in the best manner I could, the collateral points which offered themselves in our progress. On Money, as the most intricate part of the subject, he made me read in the same manner Ricardo's admirable pamphlets, written during what was called the Bullion controversy. To these succeeded Adam Smith;[†] and in this reading it was one of my father's main objects to make me apply to Smith's more superficial view of political economy, the superior lights of Ricardo, and detect what was fallacious in Smith's arguments, or erroneous in any of his conclusions. Such a mode of instruction was excellently calculated to form a thinker; but it required to be worked by a thinker, as close and vigorous as my father. The path was a thorny one even to him, and I am sure it was so to me, notwithstanding the strong interest I took in the subject. He was often, and much beyond reason, provoked by my failures in cases where success could not have been expected; but in the main his method was right, and it succeeded. I do not believe that any scientific teaching ever was more thorough, or better fitted for training the faculties, than the mode in which logic and political

[*] *On the Principles of Political Economy and Taxation* (1817).]
[†] I.e., *An Inquiry into the Nature and Causes of the Wealth of Nations* (1776).]

ʲ⁻ʲ[*Earlier version:*] he had made me draw up
ᵏ⁻ᵏ[*Earlier version:*] where success could not

taught to me by my father. He not only gave me an accurate knowledge of both subjects but made me a thinker on both; who thought for myself almost from the first, and occasionally thought differently from him, though for a long time only on minor points, and making his opinion the ultimate standard. If I could not convince him that I was right I always supposed I must be wrong, but it sometimes happened that I did convince him, and that he altered his opinion on points in the detail of political economy which he had not much considered from representations and arguments of mine. I state this to his honor, not my own; it at once exemplifies his perfect candour and the real worth of his method of teaching.

At this point concluded what can properly be called my lessons. When I was about fourteen I left England for more than a year and after my return though my studies went on under my father's general direction he was no longer my schoolmaster. I shall therefore pause here and turn back to matters of a more general nature connected with the part of my life and education included in the preceding reminiscences.

In the education which I have partially retraced, the point most superficially apparent is the great effort to give, during the years of childhood, ^{l}an amount of knowledge^l in what are considered the higher branches of education, which is seldom acquired (if acquired at all) until the age of manhood. The experiment shews the ^{m} ease with which this may be done, and places in a strong light the wretched waste of so many precious years as are spent in acquiring the modicum of Latin and Greek commonly taught to schoolboys—a waste, which has led so many of the reformers of éducation to propose discarding those languages altogether from general education. If I had been by nature extremely quick of apprehension, or had possessed a very accurate and retentive memory, or were of a remarkably active and energetic character, the trial would not be decisive: but ^{n}in all these natural gifts I am rather below than above par^n. What I could do, could assuredly be done by any boy or girl of average capacity and healthy physical constitution: and ^{o}it is most encouraging to the hopes of improvement for the human race, that education can do so much for persons of ^{p}not more than the ordinary^p natural gifts.

There is one cardinal point in my education which more than anything else, was the cause of whatever good it effected^o. Most boys or youths who have had much knowledge drilled into them, have their mental faculties not strengthened but

---

$^{l-l}$[*An incomplete version deleted three lines earlier in the draft reads:*] a large amount of book knowledge

^{m}[*Cancelled text:*] great

$^{n-n}$[*Earlier version:*] I am, as all are aware who have intimately and closely observed me, not only not above par, but decidedly and greatly below it [*In an intermediate version, the corresponding text of R19/20r—*"But in every one of these natural gifts, as all are aware who have intimately or closely observed me, I am, to say the least, rather below than above par"—*HTM altered* "every one of" *to read* "all", *and deleted* "as all are . . . observed me" *and* "to say the least". *See App. G, p.* 610–11

economy were taught to me by my father. Striving, even in an exaggerated degree, to call forth the activity of my faculties, by making me find out everything for myself, he gave his explanations not before, but after, I had felt the full force of the difficulties; and not only gave me an accurate knowledge of these two great subjects, as far as they were then understood, but made me a thinker on both. I thought for myself almost from the first, and occasionally thought differently from him, though for a long time only on minor points, and making his opinion the ultimate standard. At a later period I even occasionally convinced him, and altered his opinion on some points of detail: which I state to his honour, not my own. It at once exemplifies his perfect candour, and the real worth of his method of teaching.

At this point concluded what can properly be called my lessons. When I was about fourteen I left England for more than a year; and after my return, though my studies went on under my father's general direction, he was no longer my schoolmaster. I shall therefore pause here, and turn back to matters of a more general nature connected with the part of my life and education included in the preceding reminiscences.

In the course of instruction which I have partially retraced, the point most superficially apparent is the great effort to give, during the years of childhood, an amount of knowledge in what are considered the higher branches of education, which is seldom acquired (if acquired at all) until the age of manhood. The result of the experiment shews the ease with which this may be done, and places in a strong light the wretched waste of so many precious years as are spent in acquiring the modicum of Latin and Greek commonly taught to schoolboys; a waste, which has led so many educational reformers to entertain the ill-judged proposal of discarding those languages altogether from general education. If I had been by nature extremely quick of apprehension, or had possessed a very accurate and retentive memory, or were of a remarkably active and energetic character, the trial would not be conclusive; but in all these natural gifts I am rather below than above par. What I could do, could assuredly be done by any boy or girl of average capacity and healthy physical constitution: and if I have accomplished anything, I owe it, among other fortunate circumstances, to the fact that through the early training bestowed on me by my father, I started, I may fairly say, with an advantage of a quarter of a century over my cotemporaries.

There was one cardinal point in this training, of which I have already given some indication, and which, more than anything else, was the cause of whatever good it effected. Most boys or youths who have had much knowledge drilled into them, have their mental capacities not strengthened, but overlaid by it. They are

---

below, for an additional passage, subsequently discarded, in R19/20.]

^{o–o}[*Earlier version:*] I am satisfied also that it could be done without the very considerable drawbacks with which in my case it was accompanied and which have pursued me through life. [*paragraph*] One drawback, which if it had existed would have rendered the whole of the intellectual education worthless, did not exist in my case [*The last sentence is marked with a line in the margin by HTM.*]

^{p–p}[*Revised version, subsequently discarded, in R19/20v:*] no considerable

overlaid by it. They are crammed with mere facts and with the opinions or phrases of others, and these are accepted as a substitute for the power to form opinions of their own. And thus the sons of eminent fathers, who have spared no pains in their education, grow up mere parroters of what they have learnt, incapable of any effort of original or independent thought. Mine, however, was not an education of cram. My father never permitted anything which I learnt, to degenerate into a mere exercise of memory. He strove to make the understanding not only go along with every step of the teaching but if possible precede it. His custom was, in the case of everything which could be found out by thinking, to make me strive and struggle to find it out for myself, giving me no more help than was positively indispensable. As far as I can trust my remembrance, I acquitted myself very lamely in this department; my recollection of such matters is almost wholly of failures, hardly ever of successes. It is true, the failures were often in things in which success was almost impossible. I remember at some time in my twelfth or thirteenth year, ^{q} his indignation at my using the common expression that something was true in theory but required correction in practice: and how, after making me vainly strive to define the word theory, he explained its meaning and shewed the fallacy of the form of speech which places practice and theory in opposition: leaving me fully persuaded that in being unable to give a definition of Theory, and in speaking of it as something which might be opposed to practice I had shewn unparalleled ignorance. In this he seems, and perhaps was, very unreasonable; but I think, only in ^{r}being angry^r at my failure. A pupil from whom nothing is ever demanded which he cannot do, never does all he can.

One of the evils most liable to attend on any sort of early proficiency, and which often fatally blights its promise, my father most sedulously guarded against. This was self conceit. He kept me, with extreme vigilance, out of the way of hearing myself praised, or of being led to make self complimentary comparisons between myself and others. From his own intercourse with me I could derive none but a very humble opinion of myself; and the standard of comparison he always held up to me, was not what other people did, but what could and ought to be done. He completely succeeded in preserving me from the sort of influences he so much dreaded. ^{s}I was not at all^s aware that my attainments were anything unusual at my age. If as unavoidably happened I occasionally had my attention drawn to the fact that some other boy knew less than myself, I supposed, not that I knew much, but that he for some reason or other knew little: or rather that the things he knew were different ^{t}. My state of mind was no more arrogance than it was humility. I never

---

^{q}[*Cancelled text:*] when I happened to use the word idea, he asked me what an idea was: and with much displeasure at my ineffective attempts to define the word, at last gave me a definition which, allowing it to be correct, had never been given by any metaphysician except Hartley. viz. that an idea is the type or remembrance of a sensation. A little before or after the same time I recollect [*deleted first by HTM*]

$^{r-r}$[*Earlier version:*] his vehement [*altered by HTM and then Mill to read:* the vehemence of his] demonstrations of anger

$^{s-s}$[*Earlier version:*] Through my whole boyhood I never was in the smallest degree

crammed with mere facts, and with the opinions or phrases of other people, and these are accepted as a substitute for the power to form opinions of their own. And thus, the sons of eminent fathers, who have spared no pains in their education, so often grow up mere parroters of what they have learnt, incapable of using their minds except in the furrows traced for them. Mine, however, was not an education of cram. My father never permitted anything which I learnt, to degenerate into a mere exercise of memory. He strove to make the understanding not only go along with every step of the teaching, but if possible, precede it. Anything which could be found out by thinking, I never was told, until I had exhausted my efforts to find it out for myself. As far as I can trust my remembrance, I acquitted myself very lamely in this department; my recollection of such matters is almost wholly of failures, hardly ever of success. It is true, the failures were often in things in which success in so early a stage of my progress, was almost impossible. I remember at some time in my thirteenth year, on my happening to use the word idea, he asked me what an idea was; and expressed some displeasure at my ineffectual efforts to define the word: I recollect also his indignation at my using the common expression that something was true in theory but required correction in practice; and how, after making me vainly strive to define the word theory, he explained its meaning, and shewed the fallacy of the vulgar form of speech which I had used; leaving me fully persuaded that in being unable to give a correct definition of Theory, and in speaking of it as something which might be at variance with practice, I had shewn unparalleled ignorance. In this he seems, and perhaps was, very unreasonable; but I think, only in being angry at my failure. A pupil from whom nothing is ever demanded which he cannot do, never does all he can.

One of the evils most liable to attend on any sort of early proficiency, and which often fatally blights its promise, my father most anxiously guarded against. This was self conceit. He kept me, with extreme vigilance, out of the way of hearing myself praised, or of being led to make self-flattering comparisons between myself and others. From his own intercourse with me I could derive none but a very humble opinion of myself; and the standard of comparison he always held up to me, was not what other people did, but what a man could and ought to do. He completely succeeded in preserving me from the sort of influences he so much dreaded. I was not at all aware that my attainments were anything unusual at my age. If I accidentally had my attention drawn to the fact that some other boy knew less than myself—which happened less often than might be imagined—I concluded, not that I knew much, but that he, for some reason or other, knew little, or that his knowledge was of a different kind from mine. My state of mind was not

---

^r[*Cancelled text:*] , for I was always conscious that I could not do many things which others could. There is nothing for which I am more indebted to my father than for thus effectually preventing the growth of self conceit; for I affirm with confidence that I had not, at this period of life, the smallest vestige of it [*The first fifteen words, to the end of the sentence, are marked with a line in the margin by HTM. The next three sentences in the text are written at left, originally as an addition to this cancelled passage.*]

thought of saying to myself, I am, or I can do, so and so. I neither estimated myself highly nor lowly: I did not think of estimating myself at all. "I was sometimes thought to be self conceited, probably because I was disputatious, and did not scruple to give direct contradictions to what was said. I suppose I acquired this manner from" having been encouraged in an unusual degree to talk on matters beyond my age, and with grown persons, while I never had inculcated on me the usual respect for them. My father did not correct this ill breeding and impertinence, probably from not seeing it, for I was always too much in awe of him to be otherwise than extremely subdued and quiet in his presence. ^{v} Yet with all this I had no notion of any superiority in myself. I remember the very place in Hyde Park where, in my fourteenth year, on the eve of my leaving my father's house for a year's absence, he told me, that I should find, as I got acquainted with new people, that I had been taught many things which youths of my age did not commonly know; and that many people would be disposed to talk to me of this, and to flatter me about it ^{w} . What other things he said on this topic I remember ^{x}very imperfectly^x; but he wound up by saying, that whatever I did know more than others, could not be ascribed to any merit in me, but to the very unusual advantage which had fallen to my lot, of having a father who was able to teach me, and willing to sacrifice the necessary trouble and time; that it was no matter of praise to me, to know more than those who had not had a similar advantage, but the utmost disgrace to me if I did not. I have a distinct remembrance, that the suggestion thus for the first time made to me that I knew more than other youths who were considered well educated, was to me a piece of information; to which as to all other things which my father told me, I gave implicit credence, but which did not at all impress me as a personal matter. I felt no disposition to glorify myself upon the circumstance that there were other persons who did not know what I knew, nor had I been accustomed to flatter myself that my acquirements, whatever they were, were any merit of mine: but now when my attention was called to the subject, I felt that what my father had said respecting my peculiar advantages was exactly the truth and common sense of the matter, and it fixed my opinion and feeling from that time forward. ^{y}

$^{u-u}$[*Written at left (over several lines in HTM's hand now erased and largely illegible) and interlined to replace Mill's original continuation of the cancelled passage given in the preceding note:*] I have, however, since found that those who knew me in my early boyhood thought me greatly and most disagreeably self-conceited; the reason of which was, that I was disputatious, and made no scruple to give direct contradictions to what was said on things which I knew nothing whatever about. How I came by this detestable [*altered to read:* offensive] habit, I do not know. Probably from being on the one hand, accustomed to lay down the law to my younger sisters, and having no other companions to withstand me, and on the other hand [*HTM deleted "on things which I knew nothing whatever about" and the beginning of the last sentence, and with several words written at left, now erased, probably supplied Mill with the new beginning of the sentence in the present text ("I suppose . . . from").*]

^{v}[*Cancelled text:*] My mother did tax me with it, but for her remonstrances I never had the slightest regard. [*deleted first by HTM*]

^{w}[*Cancelled text in R23r (see the description in App. G, p. 608 below):*]: and he then represented the folly it would be to let myself be puffed up and made vain by such flattery

humility, but neither was it arrogance. I never thought of saying to myself, I am, or I can do, so and so. I neither estimated myself highly nor lowly: I did not estimate myself at all. If I thought anything about myself, it was that I was rather backward in my studies, since I always found myself so, in comparison with what my father expected from me. I assert this with confidence, though it was not the impression of various persons who saw me in my childhood. They, as I have since found, thought me greatly and disagreeably self-conceited; probably because I was disputatious, and did not scruple to give direct contradictions to things which I heard said. I suppose I acquired this bad habit from having been encouraged in an unusual degree to talk on matters beyond my age, and with grown persons, while I never had inculcated on me the usual respect for them. My father did not correct this ill breeding and impertinence, probably from not being aware of it, for I was always too much in awe of him to be otherwise than extremely subdued and quiet in his presence. Yet with all this I had no notion of any superiority in myself; and well was it for me that I had not. I remember the very place in Hyde Park where, in my fourteenth year, on the eve of leaving my father's house for a long absence, he told me that I should find, as I got acquainted with new people, that I had been taught many things which youths of my age did not commonly know; and that many persons would be disposed to talk to me of this, and to compliment me upon it. What other things he said on this topic I remember very imperfectly; but he wound up by saying, that whatever I knew more than others, could not be ascribed to any merit in me, but to the very unusual advantage which had fallen to my lot, of having a father who was able to teach me, and willing to give the necessary trouble and time; that it was no matter of praise to me, if I knew more than those who had not had a similar advantage, but the deepest disgrace to me if I did not. I have a distinct remembrance, that the suggestion thus for the first time made to me, that I knew more than other youths who were considered well educated, was to me a piece of information, to which, as to all other things which my father told me, I gave implicit credence, but which did not at all impress me as a personal matter. I felt no disposition to glorify myself upon the circumstance that there were other persons who did not know what I knew; nor had I ever flattered myself that my acquirements, whatever they might be, were any merit of mine: but, now when my attention was called to the subject, I felt that what my father had said respecting my peculiar advantages was exactly the truth and common sense of the matter, and it fixed my opinion and feeling from that time forward.

It is evident that this, among many other of the purposes of my father's scheme of education, could not have been accomplished if he had not carefully kept me from having any great amount of intercourse with other boys. He was earnestly

---

ˣ⁻ˣ[Earlier version, subsequently altered to final reading, in R23r:] too imperfectly to risk writing them down

ʸ[See App. G, pp. 608–10 below, for two additional paragraphs following the text at this point in R23v–25v.]

bent upon my escaping not only the ordinary corrupting influence which boys exercise over boys, but the contagion of vulgar modes of thought and feeling; and for this he was willing that I should pay the price of inferiority in the accomplishments which schoolboys in all countries chiefly cultivate. The deficiencies in my education were principally in the things which boys learn from being turned out to shift for themselves, and from being brought together in large numbers. From temperance and much walking, I grew up healthy and hardy, though not muscular; but I could do no feats of skill or physical strength, and knew none of the ordinary bodily exercises. It was not that play, or time for it, was refused me. Though no holidays were allowed, lest the habit of work should be broken, and a taste for idleness acquired, I had ample leisure in every day to amuse myself; but as I had no boy companions, and the animal need of physical activity was satisfied by walking, my amusements, which were mostly solitary, were in general of a quiet, if not a bookish turn, and gave little stimulus to any other kind even of mental activity than that which was already called forth by my studies. I consequently remained long, and in a less degree have always remained, inexpert in anything requiring manual dexterity; my mind, as well as my hands, did its work very lamely when it was applied, or ought to have been applied, to the practical details which, as they are the chief interest of life to the majority of men, are also the things in which whatever mental capacity they have, chiefly shews itself. I was constantly meriting reproof by inattention, inobservance, and general slackness of mind in matters of daily life. My father was the extreme opposite in these particulars: his senses and mental faculties were always on the alert; he carried decision and energy of character in his whole manner, and into every action of life: and this, as much as his talents, contributed to the strong impression which he always made upon those with whom he came into personal contact. But the children of energetic parents, frequently grow up unenergetic, because they lean on their parents, and the parents are energetic for them. The education which my father gave me, was in itself much more fitted for training me to *know* than to *do*. Not that he was unaware of my deficiencies; both as a boy and as a youth I was incessantly smarting under his severe admonitions on the subject. There was anything but insensibility or tolerance on his part towards such shortcomings: but, while he saved me from the demoralizing effects of school life, he made no effort to provide me with any sufficient substitute for its practicalizing influences. Whatever qualities he himself, probably, had acquired without difficulty or special training, he seems to have supposed that I ought to acquire as easily. He had not, I think, bestowed the same amount of thought and attention on this, as on most other branches of education; and here, as well as in some other points of my tuition, he seems to have expected effects without causes.

In my, as in all other education, the moral influences, which are so much more important than all others, are at the same time the most complicated, and the most difficult to specify with any approach to exactness ^{a}. I shall not attempt to enter into the detail of the circumstances by which in this respect my character may have been shaped. I shall confine myself to a few leading points, which are essential to a correct account of my education^a.

I was brought up from the first without any religious belief, in the ordinary meaning of the term. My father, educated in the creed of Scotch presbyterianism, had by his own studies and reflections been early led to reject not only all revealed religion but the belief in a supreme governor of the world. I have heard him say that the turning point of his mind on this subject was his reading Butler's *Analogy*. That work, of which he always continued to speak with respect, kept him, as he said, a believer in Christianity for (if I remember right) a whole year; by shewing him that whatever are the difficulties in believing that the Old and New Testaments proceeded from a perfectly wise and good being, there are the same, and even greater difficulties in conceiving that a wise and good being could have been the maker of the universe. He considered Butler's argument conclusive against the only opponents for whom it was intended, those who, rejecting revelation, adhere to what is called Natural Religion. Those who admit an omnipotent and all-benevolent maker and ruler of such a world as this, can say ^{b}little^b against Christianity but what can be ^{c} retorted against themselves. Finding, therefore, no halting place in Deism, he remained in a state of perplexity, until, doubtless after many struggles, he yielded to the conviction, that of the origin of things nothing whatever can be known. These particulars are important, because they shew that

---

$^{a-a}$[*Earlier version in R25v:*] : but what I can I will do towards describing the circumstances under which in this respect I grew up from childhood, both as to direct teaching, and the indirect operation of the moral atmosphere in which I lived

$^{b-b}$[*Earlier version:*] nothing [*altered to final reading first by HTM*]

^{c}[*Cancelled text:*] triumphantly [*deleted first by HTM*]

CHAPTER II

Moral Influences in Early Youth. My Father's Character and Opinions

IN MY EDUCATION, as in that of every one, the moral influences, which are so much more important than all others, are also the most complicated, and the most difficult to specify with any approach to completeness. Without attempting the hopeless task of detailing the circumstances by which, in this respect, my early character may have been shaped, I shall confine myself to a few leading points, which form an indispensable part of any true account of my education.

I was brought up from the first without any religious belief, in the ordinary acceptation of the term. My father, educated in the creed of Scotch presbyterianism, had by his own studies and reflexions been early led to reject not only the belief in revelation, but the foundations of what is commonly called Natural Religion. I have heard him say, that the turning point of his mind on the subject was reading Butler's *Analogy*.[*] That work, of which he always continued to speak with respect, kept him, as he said, for some considerable time, a believer in the divine authority of Christianity; by proving to him, that whatever are the difficulties in believing that the Old and New Testaments proceed from, or record the acts of, a perfectly wise and good being, the same and still greater difficulties stand in the way of the belief, that a being of such a character can have been the Maker of the universe. He considered Butler's argument as conclusive against the only opponents for whom it was intended. Those who admit an omnipotent as well as perfectly just and benevolent maker and ruler of such a world as this, can say little against Christianity but what can, with at least equal force, be retorted against themselves. Finding, therefore, no halting place in Deism, he remained in a state of perplexity, until, doubtless after many struggles, he yielded to the conviction, that concerning the origin of things nothing whatever can be known. This is the only correct statement of his opinion; for dogmatic atheism he looked upon as absurd; as most of those, whom the world has considered atheists, have always done. These particulars are important, because they shew that my father's rejection

[*Joseph Butler, *The Analogy of Religion, Natural and Revealed, to the Constitution and Course of Nature* (London: Knapton, 1736).]

my father's rejection of all religious belief was not, as many might suppose, primarily a matter of logic and evidence; the grounds of it were moral, still more than intellectual. He found it impossible to believe that a world so full of evil was made by a being of perfect goodness. His intellect spurned the subtleties by which men attempt to elude this open contradiction. His aversion to religion was like that of Lucretius: *d*he regarded it with the feelings due not to a mere mental delusion but to a great*d* moral evil. He looked upon religion as the greatest enemy of morality: first, by setting up factitious excellencies, belief in creeds, devotional feelings and ceremonies, not connected with the good of human kind and causing them to be accepted as substitutes for real virtues: but above all by radically vitiating the standard of morals; making it consist in doing the will of a being on whom it lavishes *e*the most servile*e* phrases of adulation but whom in sober truth it depicts as eminently hateful. I have a hundred times heard him say, that all ages and nations have represented their gods as wicked, in an increasing progression; that mankind have gone on adding trait after trait till they reached the most perfect conception of wickedness which the human mind could devise, and called this God and prostrated themselves before it. This *f*ne plus ultra*f* he considered to be embodied in the idea of God as represented in the Christian creed. Think (he used to say) of a being who would make a Hell—who would create the human race with the infallible foreknowledge and therefore with the intention that the great majority of them were to be consigned to infinite torment. *g*The time, I too believe, is not very far distant when all persons with any sense of moral good and evil will regard this horrible conception of an object of worship with the same indignation with which my father regarded it. That they have not done so hitherto, is owing to the infantine state of the general intellect of mankind, under the wretched cultivation which it has received. Such however*g* is the facility with which mankind believe at one and the same time contradictory things; and so few are those who draw from what they receive as truths, any consequences but those recommended to them by their feelings; that multitudes have held the belief in an omnipotent author of Hell, and have nevertheless identified that Being with the best conception they knew how to form of perfect goodness. Their worship was not paid to the demon which

---

d–d[*Earlier version:*] it was odious to him, not as an intellectual inconsistency or absurdity but as a
e–e[*Earlier version:*] all [*altered to final reading first by HTM*]
f–f[*Earlier versions:*] God of Christianity [*altered currently to read:*] consummation of wickedness
g–g[*Earlier version:*] Human imagination, he said, never formed an idea of wickedness comparable to this. Assuredly this is a conception worthy of all the indignation with which he regarded it. But (it is just to add) such

of all that is called religious belief, was not, as many might suppose, primarily a matter of logic and evidence: the grounds of it were moral, still more than intellectual. He found it impossible to believe that a world so full of evil was the work of an Author combining infinite power with perfect goodness and righteousness. His intellect spurned the subtleties by which men attempt to blind themselves to this open contradiction. The Sabæan, or Manichæan theory of a Good and an Evil Principle, struggling against each other for the government of the universe, he would not have equally condemned; and I have heard him express surprise, that no one revived it in our time. He would have regarded it as a mere hypothesis; but he would have ascribed to it no depraving influence. As it was, his aversion to religion, in the sense usually attached to the term, was of the same kind with that of Lucretius: he regarded it with the feelings due not to a mere mental delusion, but to a great moral evil. He looked upon it as the greatest enemy of morality: first, by setting up factitious excellencies,—belief in creeds, devotional feelings, and ceremonies, not connected with the good of human kind,—and causing these to be accepted as substitutes for genuine virtues: but above all, by radically vitiating the standard of morals; making it consist in doing the will of a being, on whom it lavishes indeed all the phrases of adulation, but whom in sober truth it depicts as eminently hateful. I have a hundred times heard him say, that all ages and nations have represented their gods as wicked, in a constantly increasing progression; that mankind have gone on adding trait after trait till they reached the most perfect conception of wickedness which the human mind could devise, and have called this God, and prostrated themselves before it. This *ne plus ultra* of wickedness he considered to be embodied in what is commonly presented to mankind as the creed of Christianity. Think (he used to say) of a being who would make a Hell—who would create the human race with the infallible foreknowledge, and therefore with the intention, that the great majority of them were to be consigned to horrible and everlasting torment. The time, I believe, is drawing near when this dreadful conception of an object of worship will be no longer identified with Christianity; and when all persons, with any sense of moral good and evil, will look upon it with the same indignation with which my father regarded it. My father was as well aware as any one that Christians do not, in general, undergo the demoralizing consequences which seem inherent in such a creed, in the manner or to the extent which might have been expected from it. The same slovenliness of thought, and subjection of the reason to fears, wishes, and affections, which enable them to accept a theory involving a contradiction in terms, prevents them from perceiving the logical consequences of the theory. Such is the facility with which mankind believe at one and the same time things inconsistent with one another, and so few are those who draw from what they receive as truths, any consequences but those recommended to them by their feelings, that multitudes have held the undoubting belief in an Omnipotent Author of Hell, and have nevertheless identified that being with the best conception they were able to form of perfect goodness. Their worship

such a Being as they imagined would really be, but to their own ideal of excellence. The evil is, that such a belief keeps the ideal wretchedly low; and crushes all thought which has any tendency to raise it. Believers shrink from every train of thought which would lead to a clear conception and an elevated standard of excellence, because they feel (even when they do not distinctly see) that any such would conflict with many of the dispensations of nature, and with many doctrines of the Christian creed. And thus morality continues a matter of blind tradition, with no consistent principle or feeling to guide it.

It would have been totally inconsistent with my father's ideas of duty, to allow me to imbibe notions contrary to his convictions and feelings respecting religion: and he *h*impressed upon me from the first*h* that the manner in which the world came into existence was a subject on which nothing was known; that the question "Who made me?" cannot be answered, because we have no experience from which to answer it; and that any answer only throws the difficulty a step further back, *i* since the question immediately presents itself, Who made God? He at the same time took care that I should be acquainted with what had been thought by mankind on these impenetrable problems. It has been seen how early he made me a reader of ecclesiastical history: and he taught me to take the strongest interest in the Reformation, as the great and decisive contest against priestly tyranny and for liberty of thought.

I am thus one of the very few examples, in this country, of one who has, not thrown off religious belief, but never had it. I grew up in a negative state with relation to it. I looked upon the modern exactly as I did upon the Greek religion, as something which in no way concerned me. It did not seem to me more strange that English people should believe what I did not believe, than that the men whom I read about in Herodotus should have done so. *j* History had made the variety of opinions among mankind a fact familiar to me, and this was but a prolongation of that fact. This point in my early education, however, had incidentally one bad consequence deserving notice. In giving me an opinion contrary to that of the world, my father thought it necessary to give it as one which could not prudently be avowed to the world. This lesson of keeping my thoughts to myself at that early age, could not but be morally prejudicial; though my limited intercourse with strangers, especially such as were likely to speak to me on religion, prevented me from being placed in the alternative of avowal or hypocrisy. I remember two occasions in my boyhood on which I felt placed in this alternative and in both cases I avowed my disbelief and defended it. My opponents in both cases were boys, considerably older than myself; one of them I certainly staggered at the time, but

---

was not paid to the demon which such a Being as they imagined would really be, but to their own ideal of excellence. The evil is, that such a belief keeps the ideal wretchedly low; and opposes the most obstinate resistance to all thought which has a tendency to raise it higher. Believers shrink from every train of ideas which would lead the mind to a clear conception and an elevated standard of excellence, because they feel (even when they do not distinctly see) that such a standard would conflict with many of the dispensations of nature, and with much of what they are accustomed to consider as the Christian creed. And thus morality continues a matter of blind tradition, with no consistent principle, nor even any consistent feeling, to guide it.

It would have been wholly inconsistent with my father's ideas of duty, to allow me to acquire impressions contrary to his convictions and feelings respecting religion: and he impressed upon me from the first, that the manner in which the world came into existence was a subject on which nothing was known: that the question "Who made me?" cannot be answered, because we have no experience or authentic information from which to answer it; and that any answer only throws the difficulty a step further back, since the question immediately presents itself, Who made God? He, at the same time, took care that I should be acquainted with what had been thought by mankind on these impenetrable problems. I have mentioned at how early an age he made me a reader of ecclesiastical history; and he taught me to take the strongest interest in the Reformation, as the great and decisive contest against priestly tyranny for liberty of thought.

I am thus one of the very few examples, in this country, of one who has, not thrown off religious belief, but never had it: I grew up in a negative state with regard to it. I looked upon the modern exactly as I did upon the ancient religion, as something which in no way concerned me. It did not seem to me more strange that English people should believe what I did not, than that the men whom I read of in Herodotus should have done so. History had made the variety of opinions among mankind a fact familiar to me, and this was but a prolongation of that fact. This point in my early education had however incidentally one bad consequence deserving notice. In giving me an opinion contrary to that of the world, my father thought it necessary to give it as one which could not prudently be avowed to the world. This lesson of keeping my thoughts to myself, at that early age, was attended with some moral disadvantages; though my limited intercourse with strangers, especially such as were likely to speak to me on religion, prevented me from being placed in the alternative of avowal or hypocrisy. I remember two occasions in my boyhood, on which I felt myself in this alternative, and in both cases I avowed my disbelief and defended it. My opponents were boys, considerably older than myself: one of them I certainly staggered at the time, but the subject the subject was never renewed between us; the other, who seemed surprised and somewhat shocked, did his best to convince me, but it is hardly necessary to say, without effect.

*k*The great advance in liberty of discussion which is one of the points of difference between the present time and that of my childhood, has greatly altered the moralities of this question; and I think that few men of my father's intellect and public spirit, holding with such intensity of moral conviction as he did, unpopular opinions on religion or on any other of the great subjects of thought, would now either practise or inculcate the withholding of them from the world; unless in those cases, becoming rarer every day, in which frankness on these subjects would risk the loss of means of subsistence. On religion in particular it appears to me to have now become a duty for all who being qualified in point of knowledge, have on mature consideration satisfied themselves that the current opinions are not only false but hurtful, to make their dissent known. At least those are bound to do so whose station, or reputation, gives their opinion a chance of being attended to. Such an avowal would put an end, at once and for ever, to the vulgar prejudice that what is called, very improperly, unbelief, is connected with any bad qualities either of mind or heart. The world would be astonished if it knew how great a proportion of its brightest ornaments, of those most distinguished both for wisdom and virtue, are complete sceptics in religion; many of them *l* refraining from avowal, less from personal considerations, than from a conscientious though in my opinion a most mistaken apprehension lest by speaking out what would tend to weaken existing beliefs they should do harm instead of good.

Of unbelievers (so called) as well as of believers, there are many species, including almost every variety of moral type. But the best among them, as no one who has opportunities of knowing will hesitate to say (believers rarely have that opportunity), are more genuinely religious, in the best sense of the word religion, than those who exclusively arrogate to themselves the title. Though they may think the proofs insufficient that the universe is a work of design, and assuredly believe that it cannot have a Creator and Governor who is perfect both in power and in goodness, *m* they *n*have that which constitutes the principal worth of all religions whatever, an ideal conception of a perfect character which they take as the guide of their conscience*n*; and this ideal *o*of good*o* is usually far nearer to perfection than

---

*k-k*48 [*These two paragraphs are a later addition written on a separate sheet.*]

l[*Cancelled text:*] , it should be said to their credit,

m[*Cancelled text:*] or the world would not be what it is,

n-n[*Earlier version:*] pay a truly religious homage to an ideally perfect Being, to whose approbation they habitually refer every thought and action [*"whose approbation" altered by HTM to read:* which]

o-o[*Earlier version:*] God [*altered to final reading first by HTM*]

was never renewed between us: the other, who was surprised and somewhat shocked, did his best to convince me for some time, without effect.

The great advance in liberty of discussion, which is one of the most important differences between the present time and that of my childhood, has greatly altered the moralities of this question; and I think that few men of my father's intellect and public spirit, holding with such intensity of moral conviction as he did, unpopular opinions on religion, or on any other of the great subjects of thought, would now either practise or inculcate the withholding of them from the world, unless in the cases, becoming fewer every day, in which frankness on these subjects would either risk the loss of means of subsistence, or would amount to exclusion from some sphere of usefulness peculiarly suitable to the capacities of the individual. On religion in particular the time appears to me to have come, when it is the duty of all who being qualified in point of knowledge, have on mature consideration satisfied themselves that the current opinions are not only false but hurtful, to make their dissent known; at least, if they are among those whose station, or reputation, gives their opinion a chance of being attended to. Such an avowal would put an end, at once and for ever, to the vulgar prejudice, that what is called, very improperly, unbelief, is connected with any bad qualities either of mind or heart. The world would be astonished if it knew how great a proportion of its brightest ornaments—of those most distinguished even in popular estimation for wisdom and virtue—are complete sceptics in religion; many of them refraining from avowal, less from personal considerations, than from a conscientious, though now in my opinion a most mistaken apprehension lest by speaking out what would tend to weaken existing beliefs, and by consequence (as they suppose) existing restraints, they should do harm instead of good.

Of unbelievers (so called) as well as of believers, there are many species, including almost every variety of moral type. But the best among them, as no one who has had opportunities of really knowing them will hesitate to affirm (believers rarely have that opportunity), are more genuinely religious, in the best sense of the word religion, than those who exclusively arrogate to themselves the title. The liberality of the age, or in other words the weakening of the obstinate prejudice, which makes men unable to see what is before their eyes because it is contrary to their expectations, has caused it to be very commonly admitted that a Deist may be truly religious: but if religion stands for any graces of character and not for mere dogma, the assertion may equally be made of many whose belief is far short of Deism. Though they may think the proof incomplete that the universe is a work of design, and though they assuredly disbelieve that it can have an Author and Governor who is absolute in power as well as perfect in goodness, they have that which constitutes the principal worth of all religions whatever, an ideal conception of a Perfect Being, to which they habitually refer as the guide of their conscience; and this ideal of Good is usually far nearer to perfection than the objective Deity of the objective Deity of those, who think themselves obliged to find perfection in the author of a world so crowded with suffering and so deformed by injustice.[k]

[p]My father's moral convictions, entirely dissevered from religion, were very much of the character of those of the Greek philosophers: and were delivered with the force and decision which characterized all that came from him. Even at the very early age at which I read with him the *Memorabilia* of Xenophon, I imbibed from that book and from his comments a deep respect for the character of Socrates; who stood in my mind as a model of ideal excellence: and I remember how, at the same time of life, my father impressed on me the lesson of the "Choice of Hercules." At a later period the lofty moral standard exhibited in the writings of Plato, took great effect on me. My father's moral inculcations were at all times mainly those of the "Socratici viri": justice, temperance, veracity, perseverance; readiness to brave pain and especially labour; regard for the public good; estimation of persons according to their merits, and of things according to their intrinsic usefulness; a life of exertion, in contradistinction to one of self indulgent indolence. These and other moralities were mostly conveyed by brief sentences, uttered as occasion arose, of stern reprobation or contempt.[p]

But though direct moral teaching does much, indirect does more; and the effect my father had on my character, did not depend merely on what he said or did with that direct object, but also, and still more, on what manner of man he was.

In his views of life he partook of the character of the Stoic, the Epicurean, and the Cynic. In his personal character the Stoic predominated: his standard of morals was Epicurean, in so far as that it was utilitarian, taking as the sole test of right and wrong, the tendency of actions to produce pleasure or pain. But he had (and this was the Cynic element) scarcely any belief in pleasure; at least in his later years, of which alone on this subject I can speak confidently. He deemed very few pleasures worth the price which at all events in the present state of society, must be paid for them. The greatest miscarriages in life he considered attributable to the óver-valuing of pleasures. Accordingly, temperance in the large sense intended by the Greek philosophers—stopping short at the point of moderation in all indul-gences—was with him as with them, almost the cardinal point of moral precept. His inculcations of this virtue fill a large place in my childish recollections [q] . He thought [r]human life a poor thing at best,[r] after the freshness of youth and of unsatisfied curiosity had gone by. This was a topic on which he did not often speak, especially, it may be supposed, in the presence of young persons: but when he did,

---

[p-p]*[This paragraph originally followed the paragraph ending at 46.3 (see 46[k-k] above). The substance of it was first written and cancelled several pages earlier (see 24[c] above).]*

[q]*[Cancelled text:]* ; applied, as in childhood they necessarily were, chiefly to over indulgence in amusement

[r-r]*[Earlier version:]* the most fortunate human life very little worth having;

those, who think themselves obliged to find absolute goodness in the author of a world so crowded with suffering and so deformed by injustice as ours.

My father's moral convictions, wholly dissevered from religion, were very much of the character of those of the Greek philosophers; and were delivered with the force and decision which characterized all that came from him. Even at the very early age at which I read with him the *Memorabilia* of Xenophon, I imbibed from that work and from his comments a deep respect for the character of Socrates; who stood in my mind as a model of ideal excellence: and I well remember how my father at that time impressed upon me the lesson of the "Choice of Hercules."[*] At a somewhat later period the lofty moral standard exhibited in the writings of Plato operated upon me with great force. My father's moral inculcations were at all times mainly those of the "Socratici viri"; [†] justice, temperance (to which he gave a very extended application), veracity, perseverance, readiness to encounter pain and especially labour; regard for the public good; estimation of persons according to their merits, and of things according to their intrinsic usefulness; a life of exertion, in contradiction to one of self-indulgent sloth. These and other moralities he conveyed in brief sentences, uttered as occasion arose, of grave exhortation, or stern reprobation and contempt.

But though direct moral teaching does much, indirect does more; and the effect my father produced on my character, did not depend solely on what he said or did with that direct object, but also, and still more, on what manner of man he was.

In his views of life he partook of the character of the Stoic, the Epicurean, and the Cynic, not in the modern but the ancient sense of the word. In his personal qualities the Stoic predominated. His standard of morals was Epicurean, inasmuch as it was utilitarian, taking as the exclusive test of right and wrong, the tendency of actions to produce pleasure or pain. But he had (and this was the Cynic element) scarcely any belief in pleasure; at least in his later years, of which alone, on this point, I can speak confidently. He was not insensible to pleasures; but he deemed very few of them worth the price which, at least in the present state of society, must be paid for them. The greatest number of miscarriages in life, he considered to be attributable to the overvaluing of pleasures. Accordingly, temperance, in the large sense intended by the Greek philosophers—stopping short at the point of moderation in all indulgences—was with him, as with them, almost the central point of educational precept. His inculcations of this virtue fill a large place in my childish remembrances. He thought human life a poor thing at best, after the freshness of youth and of unsatisfied curiosity had gone by. This was a topic on which he did not often speak, especially, it may be supposed, in the presence of young persons:

[*See Xenophon, *Memorabilia*, in *Memorabilia and Oeconomicus* (Greek and English), trans. E. C.Marchant (London: Heinemann; New York: Putnam's Sons, 1923), pp. 95–103 (Bk. II, Chap. i, §§21–34).]
[†See Cicero, *Letters to Atticus* (Latin and English), trans. E. O. Winstedt, 3 vols. (London: Heinemann; New York: Macmillan, 1912), Vol. III, p. 230 (Bk. XIV, Letter 9).]

it was with an air of profound and habitual conviction. He would sometimes say that if life were made what it might be, by good government and good education, it would then be worth having: but he never spoke with anything like enthusiasm even of that possibility. He never varied in rating intellectual enjoyments above all others, even in their value as pleasures, independently of ulterior consequences. The pleasures of the benevolent affections he placed high in the scale; and used to say, that he had never known a happy old man, except those who were able to live over again in the pleasures of the young. For passionate emotions of all sorts, and for everything which has been said or written in exaltation of them, he professed the greatest contempt: he regarded them as a form of madness; "the intense" was with him a bye-word of scornful disapprobation. He regarded as an aberration of the moral standard of modern times, compared with that of the ancients, the great stress laid upon feeling. Feelings, as such, he considered to be no proper subjects of praise or blame; Right and wrong, good and bad, he regarded as terms having reference only to conduct; to acts and omissions; there being no feeling which may not lead, and does not frequently lead, either to good or to bad actions: even conscience, even the desire to act right, often leading people to act wrong. Consistently carrying out the doctrine, that the object of praise and blame should be the discouragement of wrong conduct and the encouragement of right, he refused to let his praise or blame be influenced by the motive of the agent. He blamed as severely what he thought bad actions when the motive was a sense of duty as if the agents had been consciously evil doers. *He would not have accepted as a plea in mitigation for inquisitors, that they conscientiously believed burning heretics to be a sacred duty. But though he did not allow sincerity of purpose to soften his disapprobation of actions, it had its full effect on his estimation of characters;* no one prized conscientiousness and rectitude of intention more highly, or was more incapable of valuing any person in whom he did not feel assured of it. But he disliked people quite as much for any other deficiency, provided he thought it equally likely to make them act ill. He disliked, for instance, a fanatic in any bad cause, as much or more than one who adopted the same cause from self interest, because he thought him still more likely to be practically mischievous.[*] And thus his aversion to many intellectual errors, or what he regarded as such, partook, in a certain sense, of the character of a moral feeling. *t* This sentiment, though persons who do not care about opinions may confound it with intolerance, is inevitable to any earnest mind. Those who, holding opinions

[*In R31r Mill's wife commented at left, beginning opposite this point in the draft text: "It is indeed generally true that knaves do less mischief in the world than fools. A dishonest man stops when he has got what he wanted a fool carries on his foolishness thro him on to his descendants."]

s–s[Earlier version in R31r (see App. G, p. 611 below):] Such considerations, however, though he did not suffer them to influence his praise or blame in particular instances, influenced his general

but when he did, it was with an air of settled and profound conviction. He would sometimes say, that if life were made what it might be, by good government and good education, it would be worth having: but he never spoke with anything like enthusiasm even of that possibility. He never varied in rating intellectual enjoyments above all others, even in value as pleasures, independently of their ulterior benefits. The pleasures of the benevolent affections he placed high in the scale; and used to say, that he had never known a happy old man, except those who were able to live over again in the pleasures of the young. For passionate emotions of all sorts, and for everything which has been said or written in exaltation of them, he professed the greatest contempt. He regarded them as a form of madness. "The intense" was with him a bye-word of scornful disapprobation. He regarded as an aberration of the moral standard of modern times, compared with that of the ancients, the great stress laid upon feeling. Feelings, as such, he considered to be no proper subjects of praise or blame. Right and wrong, good and bad, he regarded as qualities solely of conduct—of acts and omissions; there being no feeling which may not lead, and does not frequently lead, either to good or to bad actions: conscience itself, the very desire to act right, often leading people to act wrong. Consistently carrying out the doctrine, that the object of praise and blame should be the discouragement of wrong conduct and the encouragement of right, he refused to let his praise or blame be influenced by the motive of the agent. He blamed as severely what he thought a bad action, when the motive was a feeling of duty, as if the agents had been consciously evil doers. He would not have accepted as a plea in mitigation for inquisitors, that they sincerely believed burning heretics to be an obligation of conscience. But though he did not allow honesty of purpose to soften his disapprobation of actions, it had its full effect on his estimation of characters. No one prized conscientiousness and rectitude of intention more highly, or was more incapable of valuing any person in whom he did not feel assurance of it. But he disliked people quite as much for any other deficiency, provided he thought it equally likely to make them act ill. He disliked, for instance, a fanatic in any bad cause, as much or more than one who adopted the same cause from self-interest, because he thought him even more likely to be practically mischievous. And thus, his aversion to many intellectual errors, or what he regarded as such, partook, in a certain sense, of the character of a moral feeling. All this is merely saying that he, in a degree once common, but now very unusual, threw his feelings into his opinions; which truly it is difficult to understand how any one, who possesses much of both, can fail to do. None but those who do not care about opinions, will confound it with intolerance. Those who, having opinions

---

estimation of persons: [*At left HTM pencilled a question mark and several words, now erased, of which "of them influenced his dislike of particular persons" can be made out. Just above these, opposite the ending of the preceding sentence in R31r ("as if the agents had been consciously evil-doers"), she wrote "Inquisitors".*]

[Cancelled text in R31r:] In this surely he was fundamentally right.

which they deem immensely important and their contraries prodigiously hurtful, have any strong feeling of care for the general good, will necessarily dislike those who think wrong what they think right, and right what they think wrong. "They will not, or at least they ought not, to desire to punish them for their sincere opinions, and this forbearance, flowing not from indifference but from a conscientious sense of the importance to mankind of freedom of opinion, is the only kind of tolerance which is commendable. I grant that an earnest person may dislike others on account of opinions which do not merit dislike. But if he neither himself does them any ill office, nor connives at its being done by others, he is not intolerant; nor does he err because he judges them by his own standard, but because his own standard is wholly or partially wrong; and because his antagonism to the opinions he dislikes is a stronger principle than his desire to enlarge and rectify his own doctrines."

ʸPersonally I believe my father to have had much greater capacities of feeling than were ever developed in him. He resembled almost all Englishmen in being ashamed of the signs of feeling, and by the absence of demonstration, starving the feelings themselves. In an atmosphere of tenderness and affection he would have been tender and affectionate; but his ill assorted marriage and his asperities of temper disabled him from making such an atmosphere. It was one of the most unfavourable of the moral agencies which acted on me in my boyhood, that mine was not an education of love but of fear. I do not mean, for I do not believe, that boys can be induced to apply themselves with vigour, and what is so much more difficult, perseverance, to dry and irksome studies, by the sole force of persuasion and soft words. Much must be done and much must be learnt by children, for which rigid discipline and known liability to punishment are indispensable as means. It is no doubt a very laudable effort, in the improved methods of modern teaching, to render as much as possible of what the young are required to learn, easy and interesting to them. But when this principle is pushed to the length of not requiring them to learn anything but what has been made easy and interesting, one of the chief objects of education is sacrificed. I rejoice in the decline of the old brutal and

---

ᵘ⁻ᵘ[*Earlier version in R31:*] We must try actions and characters by our own standard, not by that of the person we judge of. If our standard is right, we ought to like or dislike others according to its dictates. If persons err in their judgments by following this rule, or rather obeying this necessity, it can only be because their own standard is wholly or partially wrong: and because they do not strive to enlarge and rectify their standard by appropriating what of good there may be in those of others. [*The last twenty-four words ("and because they . . .") are written at left to replace:* an inquisitor judges a heretic to deserve the fire in this world and damnation in the next. When my father erred it was where his standard was too narrow, and omitted some of the elements of right judgment which might have been

which they hold to be immensely important, and the contraries to be prodigiously hurtful, have any deep regard for the general good, will necessarily dislike, as a class and in the abstract, those who think wrong what they think right, and right what they think wrong: though they need not therefore be, nor was my father, insensible to good qualities in an opponent, nor governed in their estimation of individuals by one general presumption, instead of by the whole of their character. I grant that an earnest person, being no more infallible than other men, is liable to dislike people on account of opinions which do not merit dislike; but if he neither himself does them any ill office, nor connives at its being done by others, he is not intolerant: and the forbearance, which flows from a conscientious sense of the importance to mankind of the equal freedom of all opinions, is the only tolerance which is commendable, or, to the highest moral order of minds, possible.

It will be admitted, that a man of the opinions, and the character, above described, was likely to leave a strong moral impression on any mind principally formed by him, and that his moral teaching was not likely to err on the side of laxity or indulgence. The element which was chiefly deficient in his moral relation to his children, was that of tenderness. I do not believe that this deficiency lay in his own nature. I believe him to have had much more feeling than he habitually shewed, and much greater capacities of feeling than were ever developed. He resembled most Englishmen in being ashamed of the signs of feeling, and, by the absence of demonstration, starving the feelings themselves. If we consider further that he was in the trying position of sole teacher, and add to this that his temper was constitutionally irritable, it is impossible not to feel true pity for a father who did, and strove to do, so much for his children, who would have so valued their affection, yet who must have been constantly feeling that fear of him was drying it up at its source. This was no longer the case, later in life and with his younger children. They loved him tenderly: and if I cannot say so much of myself, I was always loyally devoted to him. As regards my own education, I hesitate to pronounce whether I was more a loser or gainer by his severity. It was not such as to prevent me from having a happy childhood. And I do not believe, that boys can be induced to apply themselves with vigour, and what is so much more difficult, perseverance, to dry and irksome studies, by the sole force of persuasion and soft words. Much must be done, and much must be learnt, by children, for which rigid discipline, and known liability to punishment, are indispensable as means. It is, no doubt, a very laudable effort, in modern teaching, to render as much as possible of what the young are required to learn, easy and interesting to them. But when this principle is pushed to the length of not requiring them to learn anything *but* what has been made easy and interesting, one of the chief objects of education is sacrificed. I rejoice in the decline of the old brutal and tyrannical system of teaching, which

---

found scattered among the judgments of those whom he condemned.]

v–v54[*For an earlier version of this passage in R31v–34r, see App.* G, pp. 611–14 *below.*]

tyrannical system of teaching, which however did enforce habits of application; but the new, as it seems to me, is training up a race of men incapable of doing anything which is disagreeable to them. I do not believe that fear, as an element in education, can be dispensed with; but I am sure that it ought not to be the predominant element; and when it is carried so far as to preclude love or confidence on the part of the child to those who should be the unreservedly trusted advisers of after years, and perhaps to seal up altogether the fountains of frank and spontaneous communicativeness in the child's character, it is an evil for which a large abatement must be made from the benefits, moral and intellectual, which may flow from any other part of the education.

During this first period of my life, the habitual frequenters of my father's house were limited to a very few persons, mostly little known, but whom personal worth, and more or less of congeniality with his opinions (not so frequently to be met with then as since) disposed him to cultivate; and his conversations with them I listened to with interest and instruction. My being an habitual inmate of my father's study, made me acquainted with the most intimate and valued of his friends, David Ricardo, who by his benevolent countenance and kindliness of manner was very attractive to young persons, and who after I became a student of political economy, sometimes invited me to breakfast and walk with him in order to converse on the subject.^{v} I was a more frequent visitor (from about 1817 or 1818) to Mr. Hume, who, born in the same part of Scotland as my father, and having been, I rather think, a younger schoolfellow or college companion of his, had after his return from India renewed their old acquaintance, and who coming like many others greatly under the influence of his intellect and energy of character, was induced partly by that influence to go into Parliament, and there to adopt the line of conduct by which he has earned an honorable place in the history of his country. Of Mr. Bentham I saw much more, owing to the ^{w}close intimacy which subsisted between him and my father^w. I do not know at what time they became first acquainted. But my father was the earliest Englishman of any great mark who thoroughly understood and in the main adopted Bentham's general views of ethics, government, and law: and Bentham accordingly valued his society highly and ^{x}they became intimate companions^x in a period of Bentham's life during which he admitted much fewer visitors than was the case subsequently. ^{y}At this time Mr. Bentham passed some part of every year at Barrow Green House, in a beautiful part of the Surrey hills, a few miles from Godstone, and there I each summer accompanied my father on a long visit. In 1813 Mr. Bentham, my father and I made an excursion, which

---

$^{w-w}$[*Earlier version in R34v:*] greater closeness of my father's connexion with him [*HTM underscored and queried "connexion" and then wrote at left the version that Mill copied into the present text.*]

$^{x-x}$[*Earlier version in R34v:*] made an intimate companion of him [*altered by HTM to read:* they became very intimate companions]

$^{y-y56}$[*Earlier version in R34v–35r:*] When we lived in Newington Green my father used to dine with Mr. Bentham (at the very considerable distance of Queen Square Place) every Tuesday. During each of seven or eight years Mr. Bentham passed some part of the year in the country, and my father with the

however did succeed in enforcing habits of application; but the new, as it seems to me, is training up a race of men who will be incapable of doing anything which is disagreeable to them. I do not, then, believe that fear, as an element in education, can be dispensed with; but I am sure that it ought not to be the main element; and when it predominates so much as to preclude love and confidence on the part of the child to those who should be the unreservedly trusted advisers of after years, and perhaps to seal up the fountains of frank and spontaneous communicativeness in the child's nature, it is an evil for which a large abatement must be made from the benefits, moral and intellectual, which may flow from any other part of the education.

During this first period of my life, the habitual frequenters of my father's house were limited to a very few persons, most of them little known to the world, but whom personal worth, and more or less of congeniality with at least his political opinions (not so frequently to be met with then as since) inclined him to cultivate; and his conversations with them I listened to with interest and instruction. My being an habitual inmate of my father's study made me acquainted with the dearest of his friends, David Ricardo, who by his benevolent countenance, and kindliness of manner, was very attractive to young persons, and who after I became a student of political economy, invited me to his house and to walk' with him in order to converse on the subject. I was a more frequent visitor (from about 1817 or 1818) to Mr. Hume, who, born in the same part of Scotland as my father, and having been, I rather think, a younger schoolfellow or college companion of his, had on returning from India renewed their youthful acquaintance, and who coming like many others greatly under the influence of my father's intellect and energy of character, was induced partly by that influence to go into Parliament, and there adopt the line of conduct which has given him an honorable place in the history of his country. Of Mr. Bentham I saw much more, owing to the close intimacy which existed between him and my father. I do not know how soon after my father's first arrival in England they became acquainted. But my father was the earliest Englishman of any great mark, who thoroughly understood, and in the main adopted, Bentham's general views of ethics, government, and law: and this was a natural foundation for sympathy between them, and made them familiar companions in a period of Bentham's life during which he admitted much fewer visitors than was the case subsequently. At this time Mr. Bentham passed some part of every year at Barrow Green House, in a beautiful part of the Surrey hills, a few miles from Godstone, and there I each summer accompanied my father in a long visit. In 1813 Mr. Bentham, my father, and I made an excursion, which included Oxford, Bath and

---

whole or part of his family (I being always one) used to accompany him. At first the time occupied by these annual excursions was from one to three months, and the place was Barrow Green House, in a beautiful part of the Surrey Hills a few miles from Godstone. In 1813 part of the time usually passed at Barrow Green was devoted to a three weeks tour in which my father and I accompanied Mr. Bentham and which included Oxford, Bath and Bristol, Exeter, Plymouth, and Portsmouth [*deleted and altered by HTM to produce the two sentences that Mill copied into the present text*]

included Oxford, Bath and Bristol, Exeter, Plymouth, and Portsmouth^y. In this journey I saw many things which were ^{z} instructive to me, and acquired my first taste for natural scenery, in the elementary form of fondness for a "view." ^{a}In the following winter we left Newington Green, and moved into a house which my father rented of Mr. Bentham, in Queen Square, Westminster^a. From 1814 to 1817 Mr. Bentham lived during half of each year at Ford Abbey, in Somersetshire (or rather in a parish of Devonshire surrounded by Somersetshire), and ^{b}these intervals I had the advantage of passing at that place^b. This sojourn was, I think, an important circumstance in my education. Nothing contributes more to nourish elevation of sentiments in a people, than the large and free character of their habitations. The middle age architecture, the baronial hall and the spacious and lofty rooms of this fine old place, so unlike the mean and cramped externals of English middle class life, gave the feeling of a larger and freer existence, and were to me a sort of poetic culture, aided also by the character of the grounds in which the Abbey stood; which ^{c}were riant and secluded, umbrageous, and full of the sound of falling waters.^{c}

^{d}I owed another of the fortunate circumstances in my education, a year's residence in France, to Mr. Bentham's brother, General Sir Samuel Bentham. I had seen Sir Samuel Bentham and his family at their house near Gosport at the time of the tour before mentioned (he being then Superintendant of the Dockyard at Portsmouth) and also during a stay of a few days which they made at Ford Abbey shortly after the peace, before going to live on the Continent. In 1820 they invited me for a six months visit to them in the South of France, ultimately prolonged to

---

^{z}[*Additional text in R35r:*] even then [*deleted by HTM*]

$^{a-a}$[*Earlier version in R35:*] In the next following winter, we left Newington Green and moved into the house, No. 1 Queen Square, looking into Mr. Bentham's garden and rented by him, which he allowed my father to occupy at the rent he himself paid for it. In this house we lived until 1831. My father paid the rent direct to the head landlord, so that Mr. Bentham's participation was simply equivalent to being security for the rent. I am particular in mentioning these circumstances because statements have been made exaggerating greatly my father's personal obligations to Mr. Bentham. The only obligation, in money òr money's worth, which he ever, to the best of my knowledge and belief, received from Mr. Bentham, consisted of the visits to the country which I have mentioned, and these visits were of no remarkable length until the four years subsequent to 1813 [*HTM pencilled "by Dr. Bowring" in the margin opposite "statements have been made" (in the fourth sentence), and "maliciously" opposite the next word ("exaggerating"), and then deleted and altered the text to produce the single sentence that Mill copied into the present text.*]

$^{b-b}$[*Earlier version in R35v:*] during those months my father and the whole family were domiciled with him [*altered by HTM to read:* each summer I passed in the beautiful scenery of this place]

$^{c-c}$[*Earlier version in R36r:*] though not picturesque, were riant and secluded, and full of the sound of falling waters.$^{(a)}$ [*This is altered by HTM to produce the version that Mill copied into the present text. There follows in R36 a note, which HTM first altered in several places, then deleted entirely and marked "omit":*] (a) Note   The mode of life at Ford Abbey was the following. Mr. Bentham and my father studied and wrote in the same large room (a different room however in summer and in winter). My father commenced at about seven, summer and winter: and as Mr. Bentham did not make his appearance till some time after nine, I and the other children worked at our lessons in the same room during those two hours. The general hour of breakfast was nine, but Mr. Bentham always breakfasted at one oclock among his books and papers, his breakfast being laid early in the morning on his study table.

Bristol, Exeter, Plymouth, and Portsmouth. In this journey I saw many things which were instructive to me, and acquired my first taste for natural scenery, in the elementary form of fondness for a "view." In the succeeding winter we moved into a house very near Mr. Bentham's, which my father rented from him, in Queen Square, Westminster. From 1814 to 1817 Mr. Bentham lived during half of each year at Ford Abbey, in Somersetshire (or rather in a part of Devonshire surrounded by Somersetshire), which intervals I had the advantage of passing at that place. This sojourn was, I think, an important circumstance in my education. Nothing contributes more to nourish elevation of sentiments in a people, than the large and free character of their habitations. The middle-age architecture, the baronial hall, and the spacious and lofty rooms, of this fine old place, so unlike the mean and cramped externals of English middle class life, gave the sentiment of a larger and freer existence, and were to me a sort of poetic cultivation, aided also by the character of the grounds in which the Abbey stood; which were riant and secluded, umbrageous, and full of the sound of falling waters.

I owed another of the fortunate circumstances in my education, a year's residence in France,[*] to Mr. Bentham's brother, General Sir Samuel Bentham. I had seen Sir Samuel Bentham and his family at their house near Gosport in the course of the tour already mentioned (he being then Superintendant of the Dockyard at Portsmouth) and during a stay of a few days which they made at Ford Abbey shortly after the peace, before going to live on the Continent. In 1820 they invited me for a six months visit to them in the South of France, which their

[*For Mill's Journal (MS, British Library) and Notebook (MS, Dr. A. J. Mill) of this year, see Anna J. Mill, ed., *John Mill's Boyhood Visit to France* (Toronto: University of Toronto Press, 1960).]

The party at the general breakfast consisted of my father and mother, Mr. Bentham's amanuensis for the time being, and the visitors, if, as not unfrequently happened, any were staying in the house. Before his one oclock breakfast Mr. Bentham regularly went out for the same invariable walk, a circuit of about half an hour, in which my father almost always joined him. The interval between breakfast and this walk my father employed in hearing lessons, which, when weather permitted, was always done in walking about the grounds. The hours from one to six my father passed in study and this was the time regularly allotted to us children for learning lessons. Six was the dinner hour, and the remainder of the evening Mr. Bentham passed in social enjoyment, of which he had a keen relish. I was never present on these evenings except a few times when Mr. Bentham goodnaturedly sent for me to teach me to play at chess. (End of Note). [*Bentham's amanuensis at that time was John Flowerdew Colls.*]

    *d–d*58[*Earlier version in R37r:*] It was to Mr. Bentham's interest in me that I was indebted for another of the fortunate circumstances in my education, a year's residence in France. For it could only be on Mr. Bentham's account that his brother, General Sir Samuel Bentham, invited me, at the age of fourteen, for a six months visit to him in the South of France, ultimately prolonged to nearly a twelvemonth: Sir Samuel and his family being only slightly acquainted with my father, and having seen me only twice, the first time at their house near Gosport, in the three weeks tour before mentioned (Sir Samuel being then Superintendent of the Dockyard at Portsmouth): the second time on a visit of a few days which they paid to Ford Abbey shortly after the peace, before going to live in France [*HTM deleted the first sentence, and altered the rest to produce (except in minor particulars and the order of the sentences) the second and third sentences of the paragraph in the present text.*]

nearly a twelvemonth[d]. Sir Samuel Bentham, though of a character of mind very different from his illustrious brother, was a man of considerable attainments and general mental powers, with a decided genius [e] for mechanical art. His wife, a daughter of the celebrated chemist Dr. Fordyce, was a woman of strong will and determined character, much general knowledge, and great practical good sense in the Edgeworth stile: she was the ruling spirit of the household, which she was well qualified to be. Their family consisted of one son (the eminent botanist) and three daughters, the youngest about two years my senior. [f]I am indebted to them for much instruction, and for an almost parental interest in my improvement[f]. When I first joined them, in May 1820, they occupied the Chateau of Pompignan (still belonging to a descendant of Voltaire's enemy) on the heights overlooking the plain of the Garonne between Montauban and Toulouse. [g] I accompanied them on an excursion to the Pyrenees, including a stay of some duration at Bagnères de Bigorre, a journey to Pau, Bayonne, and Bagnères de Luchon, and an ascent of the Pic du Midi de Bigorre. In October we proceeded by the beautiful mountain route of Castres and St. Pons from Toulouse to Montpellier, in which last neighbourhood (a few miles north of Montpellier) they had just bought the estate of Restinclière, which they set about vigorously to improve. [h] During this sojourn in France I acquired a familiar knowledge of the French language and considerable acquaintance with French books; I took lessons in various bodily exercises, in none of which however I made any proficiency; and at Montpellier I attended the excellent winter courses of lectures at the Faculté des Sciences of the University, those of M. Anglada on chemistry, of M. Provençal on zoology, and of M. Gergonne, on logic, under the name of Philosophy of the Sciences. I also went through a course of the higher branches of mathematics under the able private tuition of M. Lenthéric, a professor at the Lycée of Montpellier [i]. But the greatest advantage which I derived from this episode in my life was that of having breathed for a whole year the free and genial atmosphere of Continental life. This advantage I could not then judge and appreciate, nor even consciously feel, but it was not the less real. Having so little experience of English life, and the few people I knew being mostly such as had at heart public objects of a large and personally

---

[e][*Cancelled text in R37r:*] (if such a word may be so used)

[f-f][*Earlier version in R37v:*] They treated me in every respect like a child of the family, and did all that advice and admonition could do to correct many of my various deficiencies and render me fitter for the ordinary purposes and intercourse of life. I wish that their judicious kindness had had all the effect which it deserved and which they had reason to expect [*Before deleting the whole of this passage, HTM altered the first sentence to read:* They did all that advice and admonition could do to correct my various deficiencies.]

[g][*Additional text in R37v:*] After a few weeks they removed to Toulouse, taking me with them, and early in August [*all but the last three words deleted by HTM*]

[h][*Cancelled text:*] Their headquarters however during the whole time of my stay with them were at Montpellier, where I remained with them until the middle of April. [*deleted first by HTM*]

[i][*Cancelled text:*] and a most excellent teacher

kindness ultimately prolonged to nearly a twelvemonth. Sir Samuel Bentham, though of a character of mind different from that of his illustrious brother, was a man of very considerable attainments and general powers, with a decided genius for mechanical art. His wife, a daughter of the celebrated chemist Dr. Fordyce, was a woman of strong will and decided character, much general knowledge, and great practical good sense of the Edgeworth kind:[*] she was the ruling spirit of the household, as she deserved, and was well qualified, to be. Their family consisted of one son (the eminent botanist) and three daughters, the youngest about two years my senior. I am indebted to them for much and various instruction, and for an almost parental interest in my welfare. When I first joined them, in May 1820, they occupied the Château of Pompignan (still belonging to a descendant[†] of Voltaire's enemy) on the heights overlooking the plain of the Garonne between Montauban and Toulouse. I accompanied them in an excursion to the Pyrenees, including a stay of some duration at Bagnères de Bigorre, a journey to Pau, Bayonne, and Bagnères de Luchon, and an ascent of the Pic du Midi de Bigorre. This first introduction to the highest order of mountain scenery made the deepest impression on me, and gave a colour to my tastes through life. In October we proceeded by the beautiful mountain route of Castres and St. Pons, from Toulouse to Montpellier, in which last neighbourhood Sir Samuel had just bought the estate of Restinclière, near the foot of the singular mountain of St. Loup. During this residence in France I acquired a familiar knowledge of the French language, and acquaintance with the ordinary French literature; I took lessons in various bodily exercises, in none of which however I made any proficiency; and at Montpellier I attended the excellent winter courses of lectures at the Faculté des Sciences, those of M. Anglada on chemistry, of M. Provençal on zoology, and of a very accomplished representative of the eighteenth century metaphysics, M. Gergonne, on logic, under the name of Philosophy of the Sciences.[‡] I also went through a course of the higher mathematics under the private tuition of M. Lenthéric, a professor at the Lycée of Montpellier. But the greatest, perhaps, of the many advantages which I owed to this episode in my education, was that of having breathed for a whole year the free and genial atmosphere of Continental life. This advantage was not the less real though I could not then estimate, nor even consciously feel it. Having so little experience of English life, and the few people I knew being mostly such as had public objects, of a large and personally disin-

[*A reference to the characters in Maria Edgeworth's works, such as *Moral Tales for Young People*, 5 vols. (London: Johnson, 1801), and *Popular Tales*, 3 vols. (London: Johnson, 1804).]

[†Jean Louis Georges Lefranc de Pompignan, son of Jean Jacques Lefranc de Pompignan.]

[‡Mill's MS notes of the latter part of this course are in the Mill-Taylor Collection, British Library of Political and Economic Science, London School of Economics; a contemporary "Traité de logique" by him (see App. C, no. 31), partly based on the course, is in the Pierpont Morgan Library.]

disinterested kind, I was then ignorant of the low moral tone of English society generally; the habit of, not indeed professing, but taking for granted in all modes of implication, that conduct is of course always directed towards low and petty objects; the absence of high feelings which manifests itself by sneering deprecation of all demonstrations of them, and by general abstinence (except among the more fanatical religionists) from professing any high principles of action at all, except in those preordained cases in which such profession is put on as part of the costume or formalities of the occasion. I could not then know or estimate the difference between this *manière d'être* and that of a people like the French with whom elevated sentiments are the current coin of human intercourse both in writing and in private life; and though doubtless *ʲ* often evaporating in profession, are yet, in the nation at large, kept alive by constant exercise, and stimulated by sympathy so as to form an active and living part of the existence of multitudes of persons and to be recognized and understood by all. Neither could I then appreciate that general culture of the understanding which results from the habitual exercise of the feelings and which is thus carried down into the most uneducated classes of the Continent to a degree not equalled in England among the so called educated. I did not know how, among the English, the absence of interest in things of an unselfish kind, except sometimes in a special thing here and there, and the habit of not speaking to others, nor much even to themselves, about the things in which they *are* interested, makes both their feelings and their intellectual faculties remain undeveloped, or develope themselves only in some single and very limited direction, and reduces them to a kind of negative existence. All this I did not perceive till long afterwards: but I even then felt, though without stating it clearly to myself, the contrast between the frank sociability and amiability of French personal intercourse, and the English mode of existence in which everybody acts as if everybody else (with perhaps a few individual exceptions) was either an enemy or a bore. In France, it is true, the bad as well as the good points of individual character come more to the surface and break out more fearlessly in ordinary intercourse, than in England, but the general manner of the people is to shew, as well as to expect, friendly feeling wherever there is not some positive cause for its opposite. In England it is only of the best bred people (either in the upper or middle ranks) that as much can be said *ᵏ*.

In my way through Paris to the South I stayed some days and in my return *ˡ*several*ˡ* weeks in the house of M. Say, the political economist, who was a

---

ʲ[*Cancelled text:*] much oftener professed than felt, and when felt, [*deleted first by HTM*]

ᵏ[*Cancelled text:*] , and only so far as such feeling and demeanour can be maintained by a few, among

terested kind, at heart, I was ignorant of the low moral tone of what, in England, is called society; the habit of, not indeed professing, but taking for granted in every mode of implication, that conduct is of course always directed towards low and petty objects; the absence of high feelings which manifests itself by sneering depreciation of all demonstrations of them, and by general abstinence (except among a few of the stricter religionists) from professing any high principles of action at all, except in those preordained cases in which such profession is put on as part of the costume and formalities of the occasion. I could not then know or estimate the difference between this manner of existence, and that of a people like the French, whose faults, if equally real, are at all events different; among whom sentiments, which by comparison at least may be called elevated, are the current coin of human intercourse, both in books and in private life; and though often evaporating in profession, are yet kept alive in the nation at large by constant exercise, and stimulated by sympathy, so as to form a living and active part of the existence of great numbers of persons, and to be recognized and understood by all. Neither could I then appreciate the general culture of the understanding, which results from the habitual exercise of the feelings, and is thus carried down into the most uneducated classes of several countries on the Continent, in a degree not equalled in England among the so called educated, except where an unusual tenderness of conscience leads to a habitual exercise of the intellect on questions of right and wrong. I did not know the way in which, among the ordinary English, the absence of interest in things of an unselfish kind, except occasionally in a special thing here and there, and the habit of not speaking to others, nor much even to themselves, about the things in which they do feel interest, causes both their feelings and their intellectual faculties to remain undeveloped, or develope themselves only in some single and very limited direction; reducing them, considered as spiritual beings, to a kind of negative existence. All these things I did not perceive till long afterwards; but I even then felt, though without stating it clearly to myself, the contrast between the frank sociability and amiability of French personal intercourse, and the English mode of existence in which everybody acts as if everybody else (with few, or no, exceptions) was either an enemy or a bore. In France, it is true, the bad as well as the good points both of individual and of national character come more to the surface, and break out more fearlessly in ordinary intercourse, than in England: but the general habit of the people is to shew, as well as to expect, friendly feeling in every one towards every other, wherever there is not some positive cause for the opposite. In England it is only of the best bred people, in the upper or upper middle ranks, that anything like this can be said.

In my way through Paris, both going and returning, I passed some time in the house of M. Say, the eminent political economist, who was a friend and correspon-

---

a multitude incapable of making suitable response [*marked with a line in the margin by HTM*]

$^{l-l}$[*Earlier version:*] as much as three [*altered to final reading first by HTM*]

correspondent of my father, having become acquainted with him on a visit to England a year or two after the peace. I remembered M. Say as a visitor to Ford Abbey. He was a man of the later period of the French Revolution, a fine specimen of the best kind of old French republican, one of those who had never bent the knee to Bonaparte though courted by him; a thoroughly upright and brave man. He lived a quiet and studious life, made, I should think, happy by warm affections, public and private. He was acquainted with many of the chiefs of the Liberal party: but the only one of them whom I remember seeing at that time was M. Ternaux, the manufacturer, who then lived at the beautiful place formerly Necker's at St. Ouen. The other persons of note whom I saw were M. Destutt-Tracy; M. Dunoyer; M. Duméril the zoologist; M. Clement-Desormes, the chemist; a more eminent chemist Berthollet, who was a friend of Sir S. Bentham but not of M. Say, being on the opposite side in politics; and I have pleasure in the recollection of having once seen Saint Simon, not then known as the founder either of a philosophy or of a religion but considered only as a clever *original*. *^m*The chief fruit which I carried away from the society I saw, was*^m* a strong interest in Continental Liberalism, of which I always afterwards kept myself *au courant* as much as of English politics. After passing a few weeks at Caen with an *ⁿ*early*ⁿ* friend of my father's, I returned to England in July 1821.

^{m-m}[*Earlier version:*] Inexperienced as I was, I carried away little from the society I saw, except [*the first four words, "little", and "except" all underscored by HTM*]
ⁿ⁻ⁿ[*Earlier version:*] old college

dent of my father, having become acquainted with him on a visit to England a year or two after the peace. He was a man of the later period of the French Revolution— a fine specimen of the best kind of French republican, one of those who had never bent the knee to Bonaparte though courted by him to do so; a truly upright, brave, and enlightened man. He lived a quiet and studious life, made happy by warm affections, public and private. He was acquainted with many of the chiefs of the Liberal party, and I saw various noteworthy persons while staying at his house; among whom I have pleasure in the recollection of having once seen Saint-Simon, not yet the founder either of a philosophy or a religion, and considered only as a clever *original*. The chief fruit which I carried away from the society I saw, was a strong and permanent interest in Continental Liberalism, of which I ever afterwards kept myself *au courant*, as much as of English politics: a thing not at all usual in those days with Englishmen, and which had a very salutary influence on my development, keeping me free from the error always prevalent in England, and from which even my father with all his superiority to prejudice was not exempt, of judging universal questions by a merely English standard. After passing a few weeks at Caen with an old friend of my father's,[*] I returned to England in July 1821; and my education resumed its ordinary course.

[*Joseph Lowe.]

For the next year or so I continued my old studies, with the addition of some new ones. When I returned my father was just finishing for the press his *Elements of Political Economy*, and he made me perform as an exercise on the manuscript, what Mr. Bentham practised on all his own writings, namely, making what he called "marginal contents"; a short abstract of every paragraph, to enable the writer more easily to judge of, and improve, the order of the ideas, and the general character of the exposition. Shortly after this, my father put into my hands Condillac's *Traité des Sensations*, and the *ª*logical and metaphysical*ª* volumes of his *Cours d'Etudes*; *ᵇ*the first (notwithstanding the superficial resemblance between Condillac's psychological system and my father's own theory) rather as a warning than as an example*ᵇ*. I am not sure whether it was in this winter or the next that I first read a history of the French Revolution. I learnt with astonishment that the principles of democracy then apparently in so insignificant and hopeless a minority everywhere in Europe, had borne down everything before them in France thirty years earlier, and had been the creed of the nation. As may be supposed from this, I had previously had a very vague idea of that great commotion. I knew nothing about it except that the French had thrown off the absolute monarchy of Louis 14th and 15th, had put the king and queen to death, guillotined many persons, one of whom was Lavoisier, and had ultimately fallen under the despotism of Bonaparte. But from this time the subject took an immense hold of my feelings. It allied itself with all my juvenile aspirations to the character of a

---

ª⁻ª[*Earlier version:*] first four (the logical and metaphysical)

ᵇ⁻ᵇ[*Earlier versions:*] M. Gergonne's lectures had already given me Condillac's view of the analysis of the mind. I read these books in a useless, ineffectual way, not seeing any fallacy in them, but not gaining from them any grasp or command of the subject. When my father afterwards questioned me and made me give him an account of Condillac's system he shewed me that Condillac's seeming analyses of all mental phenomena into sensation amounted to nothing, that he paid himself in words, and that I had proved myself quite willing to be paid in words. I remember the impression which this phrase, which was then new to me, of paying in words, made on me [*altered to read:*] I was not then capable of

CHAPTER III

Last Stage of Education, and First of Self-Education

FOR THE FIRST YEAR OR TWO after my visit to France, I continued my old studies, with the addition of some new ones. When I returned, my father was just finishing for the press his *Elements of Political Economy*, and he made me perform an exercise on the manuscript, which Mr. Bentham practised on all his own writings, making what he called "marginal contents"; a short abstract of every paragraph, to enable the writer more easily to judge of, and improve, the order of the ideas, and the general character of the exposition. Soon after, my father put into my hands Condillac's *Traité des Sensations*, and the logical and metaphysical volumes of his *Cours d'Etudes*; the first (notwithstanding the superficial resemblance between Condillac's psychological system and my father's) quite as much for a warning as for an example. I am not sure whether it was in this winter or the next that I first read a history of the French Revolution.[*] I learnt with astonishment, that the principles of democracy, then apparently in so insignificant and hopeless a minority everywhere in Europe, had borne all before them in France thirty years earlier, and had been the creed of the nation. As may be supposed from this, I had previously a very vague idea of that great commotion. I knew only that the French had thrown off the absolute monarchy of Louis XIV and XV, had put the king and queen to death, guillotined many persons, one of whom was Lavoisier, and had ultimately fallen under the despotism of Bonaparte. From this time, as was natural, the subject took an immense hold of my feelings. It allied itself with all my juvenile aspirations to the character of a democratic champion. What had happened so

[*Probably François Emmanuel Toulongeon, *Histoire de France, depuis la révolution de 1789*, 4 vols. (Paris: Treuttel and Würtz, 1801–10).]

perceiving, until it was explained to me, the superficiality and fallacy of Condillac's psychological theory; so radically inferior to Hartley's, notwithstanding the apparent resemblance. My father pointed out to me, that Condillac's seeming analyses of all mental phenomena into sensation, amounted to nothing, and that he paid himself and endeavoured to pay others in words [*In both of these discarded versions HTM attempted alterations, and in the second she underscored "until it was explained to me" and "My father pointed out to me, that".*]

democratic champion. What had happened so lately, seemed as if it might easily happen again: and the greatest glory I was capable of conceiving was that of figuring, successful or unsuccessful, as a Girondist in an English Convention.

In the course of the winter of 1821/2 Mr. Austin, with whom at the time when I went to France my father had but lately become acquainted, allowed me to read Roman law with him. At this time my father, notwithstanding his abhorrence of the chaos of barbarism called English law, had turned his thoughts towards the bar as on the whole less ineligible for me than any other profession: and these readings of Roman law with Mr. Austin, who had made ^cBentham's best^c ideas his own and added many others to them, were not only a valuable introduction to legal studies but an important branch of general education. With Mr. Austin I went through Heineccius on the Institutes, his Roman Antiquities, and part of his exposition of the Pandects; with the addition of a considerable part of Blackstone. It was on this occasion that my father, as a needful accompaniment to these studies, put into my hands Bentham's principal speculations, as interpreted to the Continental world and indeed to the world in general by Dumont, in the *Traité de Législation*. The reading of this book was an event in my life; one of the turning points of my mental history.

My previous education had been, in a great measure, a course of Benthamism. The Benthamic standard of "the greatest happiness" was that which I had always been taught to apply; I was even familiar with an abstract discussion of it contained in a manuscript dialogue on government, written by my father on the Platonic model ^d. Yet in the first few pages of Bentham it burst on me with all the force of novelty. What thus impressed me was the chapter in which Bentham examined the common modes of reasoning on morals and legislation, deduced from phrases like "law of nature," "right reason," "the moral sense," "natural rectitude," and the like, and characterized them as dogmatism in disguise, imposing its own sentiments upon other people by the aid of sounding phrases which convey no reason for the sentiment but set up the sentiment as its own reason. This struck me at once as true ^e. The feeling rushed upon me that all previous moralists were superseded, and^e that here indeed was the commencement of a new era in thought. This impression was strengthened by the manner in which Bentham gave a scientific form to the application of the happiness principle to the morality of actions, by analysing the various classes and orders of consequences. But what most of all impressed me was the Classification of Offences; which is much more clear, compact, and imposing in Dumont's *redaction* than in the original work of

---

^{c-c}[*Earlier version:*] all Bentham's

^d[*Cancelled text:*] , which I had diligently studied

^{e-e}[*Earlier version:*] : and I immediately conceived a sovereign contempt for all previous moralists; and felt

lately, seemed as if it might easily happen again; and the most transcendant glory I was capable of conceiving, was that of figuring, successful or unsuccessful, as a Girondist in an English Convention.

During the winter of 1821/2, Mr. John Austin, with whom at the time of my visit to France my father had but lately become acquainted, kindly allowed me to read Roman law with him. My father, notwithstanding his abhorrence of the chaos of barbarism called English Law, had turned his thoughts towards the bar as on the whole less ineligible for me than any other profession: and these readings with Mr. Austin, who had made Bentham's best ideas his own, and added much to them from other sources and from his own mind, were not only a valuable introduction to legal studies, but an important portion of general education. With Mr. Austin I read Heineccius on the Institutes, his Roman Antiquities, and part of his exposition of the Pandects; to which was added a considerable portion of Blackstone.[*] It was at the commencement of these studies that my father, as a needful accompaniment to them, put into my hands Bentham's principal speculations, as interpreted to the Continent, and indeed to all the world, by Dumont, in the *Traité de Législation*. The reading of this book was an epoch in my life; one of the turning points in my mental history.

My previous education had been, in a certain sense, already a course of Benthamism. The Benthamic standard of "the greatest happiness" was that which I had always been taught to apply; I was even familiar with an abstract discussion of it, forming an episode in an unpublished dialogue on Government, written by my father on the Platonic model. Yet in the first pages of Bentham it burst upon me with all the force of novelty. What thus impressed me was the chapter in which Bentham passed judgment on the common modes of reasoning in morals and legislation, deduced from phrases like "law of nature," "right reason," "the moral sense," "natural rectitude," and the like, and characterized them as dogmatism in disguise imposing its sentiments upon others under cover of sounding expressions which convey no reason for the sentiment, but set up the sentiment as its own reason.[†] It had not struck me before, that Bentham's principle put an end to all this. The feeling rushed upon me, that all previous moralists were superseded, and that here indeed was the commencement of a new era in thought. This impression was strengthened by the manner in which Bentham put into scientific form the application of the happiness principle to the morality of actions, by analyzing the various classes and orders of their consequences. But what struck me at that time most of all, was the Classification of Offences; which is much more clear, compact, and imposing, in Dumont's *redaction*, than in the original work of

[*William Blackstone, *Commentaries on the Laws of England* (1765–69).]

[†Mill's wording here is closer to the version in Jeremy Bentham's *An Introduction to the Principles of Morals and Legislation* (London: Payne, 1789), Chap. ii, §xiv n, than to that in Pierre Etienne Louis Dumont's redaction in *Traités de législation civile et pénale*, 3 vols. (Paris: Bossange, Masson, and Besson, 1802), Chap. iii of *Principes généraux de législation*, Vol. I, pp. 10–21.]

Bentham from which it was taken. Logic and the Dialogues of Plato, which had formed so large a part of my intellectual training, had given me a great relish for accurate classification; this taste had been strengthened and enlightened by the study of botany, on the principles of the so called Natural Method which I had taken up with great zeal *f* during my stay in France: and when I found scientific classification applied to the large and complex subject of Punishable Acts, under the guidance of the ethical principle of Pleasurable and Painful Consequences followed out in the method of detail introduced into these subjects by Bentham, I felt taken up to an eminence from which I could survey a vast mental domain and see stretching out in the distance, intellectual results beyond all computation. As I proceeded farther, to this intellectual clearness there seemed to be added the most inspiring prospects of practical improvement in human affairs. To Bentham's general views of the construction of a body of law I was not altogether a stranger, having read with attention that admirable compendium, my father's article "Jurisprudence": but I had read it with little profit, and almost without interest, no doubt on account of its extremely general and abstract character, and also because it concerned the form more than the substance of the *corpus juris*, the logic rather than the ethics of law. But Bentham's subject was Legislation, of which Jurisprudence is only the formal part; and at every page he seemed to open a clearer and larger conception of what human opinions and institutions *ought* to be, how far removed from it they *were*, and how they might be made what they ought to be. When I laid down the last volume of the *Traité* I was a different being. The "principle of utility," understood as Bentham understood it, and applied in the manner in which he applied it through these three volumes, fell exactly into its place as the keystone which held together the detached and fragmentary portions of my knowledge and beliefs. It gave unity to my conceptions of things. I now had opinions; a creed, a doctrine, a philosophy; in one (and the best) sense of the word, a religion; the inculcation and diffusion of which could be made the principal outward aim of a life. And I had a grand conception laid before me of changes to be made in the condition of mankind by that doctrine. The *Traité de Législation* winds up with what was to me a most impressive picture of human life as it would be made by such opinions and such laws as are recommended in the book. The anticipations of practicable improvement are studiously moderate, deprecating and discountenancing as reveries of vague enthusiasm much which will one day be

---

f[*Cancelled text:*] as a mere amusement [*deleted first by HTM*]

Bentham from which it was taken.[*] Logic, and the dialectics of Plato, which had formed so large a part of my previous training, had given me a strong relish for accurate classification. This taste had been strengthened and enlightened by the study of botany, on the principles of what is called the Natural Method, which I had taken up with great zeal, though only as an amusement, during my stay in France; and when I found scientific classification applied to the great and complex subject of Punishable Acts, under the guidance of the ethical principle of Pleasurable and Painful Consequences, followed out in the method of detail introduced into these subjects by Bentham, I felt taken up to an eminence from which I could survey a vast mental domain, and see stretching out into the distance intellectual results beyond all computation. As I proceeded farther, there seemed to be added to this intellectual clearness, the most inspiring prospects of practical improvement in human affairs. To Bentham's general views of the construction of a body of law I was not altogether a stranger, having read with attention that admirable compendium, my father's article "Jurisprudence": but I had read it with little profit, and scarcely any interest, no doubt from its extremely general and abstract character, and also because it concerned the form more than the substance of the *corpus juris*, the logic rather than the ethics of law. But Bentham's subject was Legislation, of which Jurisprudence is only the formal part: and at every page he seemed to open a clearer and broader conception of what human opinions and institutions ought to be, how they might be made what they ought to be, and how far removed from it they now are. When I laid down the last volume of the *Traité* I had become a different being. The "principle of utility," understood as Bentham understood it, and applied in the manner in which he applied it through these three volumes, fell exactly into its place as the keystone which held together the detached and fragmentary component parts of my knowledge and beliefs. It gave unity to my conceptions of things. I now had opinions; a creed, a doctrine, a philosophy; in one among the best senses of the word, a religion; the inculcation and diffusion of which could be made the principal outward purpose of a life. And I had a grand conception laid before me of changes to be effected in the condition of mankind through that doctrine. The *Traité de Législation* wound up with what was to me a most impressive picture of human life as it would be made by such opinions and such laws as were recommended in the treatise.[†] The anticipations of practicable improvement were studiously moderate, deprecating and discountenancing as reveries of vague enthusiasm many things which will one day seem so natural to

[*See Chaps. vi and vii, "De la division des délits," and "Avantages de cette classification des délits," of *Vue générale d'un corps complet de législation*, in *Traités de législation*, Vol. I, pp. 172–214; cf. *An Introduction to the Principles of Morals and Legislation*, Chap. xvi, "Division of Offences," pp. cci–cccvi.]

[†See Chap. v, §ii ("Vue prospective: les lois les plus parfaites aujourd'hui seroient-elles encore les plus parfaites dans les tems futurs?"), of *De l'influence des tems et des lieux en matière de législation*, in *Traités de législation*, Vol. III, pp. 389–95.]

so natural to human beings that they will be apt to ascribe intellectual and even moral obliquity to those who could ever think such prospects chimerical. But in my state of mind this apparent superiority to illusions added to the effect of Bentham's doctrines on me, by heightening the impression of mental power. And the vista of improvement which he did open was large enough, and brilliant enough, to light up my life, as well as to give definiteness to my aspirations.

After this I read from time to time the most important of the other works of Bentham which had at that time been published, either as written by himself or as edited by Dumont. This I did for my own satisfaction: while under my father's direction my studies were carried into the higher branches of analytic psychology. I read Locke's *Essay on the Human Understanding* and wrote out an account of it, consisting of a full abstract of every chapter, with such remarks as occurred to me: this was read by, or (I think) to, my father, and discussed throughout. I went through the same process [g], of my own motion, with Helvetius *De l'Esprit*; a book which I greatly admired[g]. This writing of abstracts, subject as it was to my father's censorship, was a most valuable exercise, by compelling precision in conceiving and expressing philosophical doctrines, whether received as truths or merely as the opinions of writers. After Helvetius, my father made me study what he deemed the really master-production in the philosophy of mind, Hartley. This book, though it did not constitute an era in my existence, like the *Traité de Législation*, made a very similar impression on me in regard to its immediate subject. Hartley's explanation, incomplete as in many parts it is, of the more complex mental phenomena by the law of association, commended itself to me as a real analysis, and made me feel by contrast the insufficiency of the mere verbal generalizations of Condillac, and even of the instructive gropings and feelings-about for psychological explanations, of Locke. It was at this very time that my father commenced writing his *Analysis of the Mind*, which carried Hartley's mode of explaining the phenomena to so much greater length and depth. He could only command the concentration of thought necessary for this work during the complete leisure of his annual holiday of a month or six weeks and he commenced it in the summer of 1822, the first holiday he passed at Dorking; in which neighbourhood from that time to the end of his life, with the exception of two years, he lived [h](as far as his official duties permitted) for six months of every year[h]. He worked at the *Analysis* during several successive holidays, and allowed me to read the manuscript portion by portion as it advanced [i] . The first instalment of it I read in this same summer [j] . The other principal English writers on mental philosophy I read afterwards as I felt inclined, particularly Berkeley, Hume's *Essays*, Dugald Stewart, Reid, and Brown on Cause and Effect. Brown's *Lectures* I did not read till two or three years later, nor at that time had my father himself read them.

[g-g][*Earlier version:*] with Helvetius *De l'Esprit*; in which case I remember that my own strong wish to read the book was the moving impulse [*marked with a line in the margin by HTM*]

[h-h][*Earlier version:*] for about six months of every year, as much as circumstances permitted, namely passing from the Saturday or oftener the Friday afternoon to the Monday morning of each week,

human beings, that injustice will probably be done to those who once thought them chimerical. But, in my state of mind, this appearance of superiority to illusion added to the effect which Bentham's doctrines produced on me, by heightening the impression of mental power. And the vista of improvement which he did open was sufficiently large and brilliant to light up my life, as well as to give a definite shape to my aspirations.

After this I read, from time to time, the most important of the other works of Bentham which had then seen the light, either as written by himself or as edited by Dumont. This was my private reading: while, under my father's direction, my studies were carried into the higher branches of analytic psychology. I now read Locke's *Essay*, and wrote out an account of it, consisting of a complete abstract of every chapter, with such remarks as occurred to me: which was read by, or (I think) to, my father, and discussed throughout. I performed the same process with Helvetius *De l'Esprit*, which I read of my own choice. This preparation of abstracts, subject to my father's censorship, was of great service to me, by compelling precision in conceiving and expressing psychological doctrines, whether accepted as truths or only regarded as the opinions of others. After Helvetius, my father made me study what he deemed the really master-production in the philosophy of mind, Hartley's *Observations on Man*. This book, though it did not, like the *Traité de Législation*, give a new colour to my existence, made a very similar impression on me in regard to its immediate subject. Hartley's explanation, incomplete as in many points it is, of the more complex mental phenomena by the law of association, commended itself to me at once as a real analysis, and made me feel by contrast the insufficiency of the merely verbal generalizations of Condillac, and even of the instructive gropings and feelings about for psychological explanations, of Locke. It was at this very time that my father commenced writing his *Analysis of the Mind*, which carried Hartley's mode of explaining the mental phenomena to so much greater length and depth. He could only command the concentration of thought necessary for this work, during the complete leisure of his holiday of a month or six weeks annually; and he commenced it in the summer of 1822, in the first holiday he passed at Dorking; in which neighbourhood, from that time to the end of his life, with the exception of two years, he lived, as far as his official duties permitted, for six months of every year. He worked at the *Analysis* during several successive vacations, up to the year 1829, when it was published, and allowed me to read the manuscript, portion by portion, as it advanced. The other principal English writers on mental philosophy I read as I felt inclined, particularly Berkeley, Hume's *Essays*, Reid, Dugald Stewart, and Brown on Cause and Effect. Brown's *Lectures* I did not read until two or three years later, nor at that time had my father himself read them.

---

and the whole of the annual holiday

i[*Cancelled text:*] , so that I was cognizant of these speculations not merely when complete, but in the process of their formation

j[*Cancelled text:*] (the last which I passed in the country)

Among the things read in the course of this year which contributed materially to my developement I should mention a book, written on the foundation of some manuscripts of Bentham and published under the pseudonyme of Philip Beauchamp, entitled *Analysis of the Influence of Natural Religion on the Temporal Happiness of Mankind.* This was an examination not of the truth, but of the usefulness of religious belief, in the most general sense, apart from any supposed special revelation; which, of all the portions of the discussion respecting religion, is the most important in this age, in which real belief in any religious doctrine is feeble, but the opinion of its necessity for moral and social purposes almost universal; and when those who reject revelation very generally take refuge in an optimistic deism, a worship of the order of Nature or of Providence at least as full of contradictions, and as perverting to the moral sentiments, as any of the received forms of Christianity; for if the world has a ruler, and but one ruler, *k*that one is certainly far less deserving of worship than*k* the author of the Sermon on the Mount.[*] Yet very little of a philosophical character has been written by sceptics against the usefulness of the belief in this Being. The volume bearing the name of Philip Beauchamp, which was shewn to my father in manuscript and by him given to me to read and make a marginal analysis of, as I had done of the *Elements of Political Economy*, made a great impression on me *l*, and gave me much instruction both on its express subject and on many collateral topics. On reading it lately after an interval of many years, I find it to have the defects as well as the merits of the Benthamic modes of thought, and to contain many weak arguments, but with a great overbalance of sound ones, and much good material for a more philosophic and conclusive treatment of the subject*l*.

I have now, I believe, mentioned all the books which had any considerable effect on my early mental developement. From this point I began to carry on my own mental cultivation by writing still more than by reading. In the summer of 1822 I wrote my first argumentative essay: I remember very little about it except that it was an attack on what I regarded as the aristocratic prejudice that the rich were, or were likely to be, superior in moral excellence to the poor. I set about this task unprompted, except by emulation of a little manuscript essay of Mr. Grote. I recollect that my performance was entirely argumentative, without any of the declamation which the subject would admit of, and might be expected to suggest to a young writer. In that department however I was and remained very inapt. Dry argument was the only thing I could manage, or willingly attempted: though passively I was very susceptible to the effect of all composition, whether in the form of poetry or oratory, which appealed to the feelings on any basis of reason.

[*Matthew, 5–7.]

k-k[*Earlier version:*] the character of that one must be atrocious, and the worship of such a Being more morally degrading, if not more intellectually contemptible, than almost any adoration which is capable of being directed to

Among the works read in the course of this year, which contributed materially to my development, I ought to mention a book (written on the foundation of some of Bentham's manuscripts and published under the pseudonyme of Philip Beauchamp)[*] entitled *Analysis of the Influence of Natural Religion on the Temporal Happiness of Mankind.* This was an examination not of the truth, but of the usefulness of religious belief, in the most general sense, apart from the peculiarities of any special Revelation; which, of all the parts of the discussion concerning religion, is the most important in this age, in which real belief in any religious doctrine is feeble and precarious, but the opinion of its necessity for moral and social purposes almost universal; and when those who reject revelation, very generally take refuge in an optimistic Deism, a worship of the order of Nature and the supposed course of Providence, at least as full of contradictions, and perverting to the moral sentiments, as any of the forms of Christianity, if only it is as completely realized. Yet, very little, with any claim to a philosophical character, has been written by sceptics against the usefulness of this form of belief. The volume bearing the name of Philip Beauchamp had this for its special object. Having been shewn to my father in manuscript, it was put into my hands by him, and I made a marginal analysis of it as I had done of the *Elements of Political Economy.* Next to the *Traité de Législation,* it was one of the books which by the searching character of its analysis produced the greatest effect upon me. On reading it lately after an interval of many years, I find it to have some of the defects as well as the merits of the Benthamic modes of thought, and to contain, as I now think, many weak arguments, but with a great overbalance of sound ones, and much good material for a more completely philosophic and conclusive treatment of the subject.

I have now, I believe, mentioned all the books which had any considerable effect on my early mental developement. From this point I began to carry on my intellectual cultivation by writing still more than by reading. In the summer of 1822 I wrote my first argumentative essay. I remember very little about it, except that it was an attack on what I regarded as the aristocratic prejudice, that the rich were, or were likely to be, superior in moral qualities to the poor. My performance was entirely argumentative, without any of the declamation which the subject would admit of, and might be expected to suggest to a young writer. In that department however I was, and remained, very inapt. Dry argument was the only thing I could manage, or willingly attempted; though passively I was very susceptible to the effect of all composition, whether in the form of poetry or oratory, which appealed to the feelings on any basis of reason. My father, who knew nothing of

[*The author was George Grote.]

---

l–l[Earlier version:] . It is now many years since I have read it, but it remains in my memory as a most searching and substantial piece of argument, far superior to any other discussion of the subject which I have seen, and abounding in incidental instruction on important collateral topics

My father was well satisfied with this essay, and as I learnt from others, even much pleased with it; but, perhaps from a desire to promote the exercise of other mental faculties than the argumentative, he advised me to make my next exercise in composition one of the oratorical kind; and accordingly availing myself of my familiarity with Greek history and ideas and with the Athenian orators, I wrote two speeches, one an accusation, the other a defence of Pericles on a supposed impeachment for not marching out to fight the Lacedæmonians on their invasion of Attica. My next essay, suggested by my father, was a reply to Paley's *Natural Theology*:[*] and after this I went on writing papers often on subjects very much beyond *[m]*me, but with great benefit both from the exercise itself, and from the discussions with my father to which it led*[m]*.

I had now also begun to converse on terms of equality, with the instructed men with whom I came in contact: and the opportunities of such contact naturally became more numerous. The two friends of my father from whom I derived most, *[n]*and with whom I most associated*[n]*, were Mr. Grote and Mr. Austin. The acquaintance of both with him was recent, but had ripened rapidly into intimacy. Mr. Grote was introduced to my father by Ricardo, I believe in 1819 (being then about twenty-five years old), and sought assiduously his society and conversation. Already a highly instructed man, he was yet, by the side of my father, a tyro on the great subjects of human opinion; but he rapidly seized on my father's best ideas, and made them his own: and in the department of political opinion he signalized himself as early as 1820 by a pamphlet in defence of Radical Reform, in reply to a celebrated article by Sir James Mackintosh, then lately published in the *Edinburgh Review*. Mr. Grote's father, the old banker, was I believe a thorough Tory and his mother intensely Evangelical, so that for his liberal opinions he was in no way indebted to home influences. But, unlike most persons who have the prospect of being rich by inheritance, he had, though actively engaged in business as a banker, devoted a great portion of time to philosophic studies, and his intimacy with my father decided the character of his subsequent mental progress. Him I often visited, and my conversations with him on politics, ethics, religion and philosophy, gave me, in addition to much instruction, some useful practice in expressing myself and carrying on discussion by word of mouth.

Mr. Austin, a man four or five years older than Mr. Grote, was the eldest son of a retired miller in Suffolk who had made money by contracts during the war and who

---

[*William Paley, *Natural Theology* (London: Faulder, 1802).]

[m-m][*Earlier version:*] my knowledge and capacity but which led to discussions with my father that shewed me when my ideas were confused, and helped to clear them up [*marked with a line in the margin by HTM*]

this essay until it was finished, was well satisfied, and as I learnt from others, even pleased with it; but, perhaps from a desire to promote the exercise of other mental faculties than the purely logical, he advised me to make my next exercise in composition one of the oratorical kind: on which suggestion, availing myself of my familiarity with Greek history and ideas and with the Athenian orators, I wrote two speeches, one an accusation, the other a defence of Pericles on a supposed impeachment for not marching out to fight the Lacedæmonians on their invasion of Attica. After this I continued to write papers on subjects often very much beyond my capacity, but with great benefit both from the exercise itself, and from the discussions which it led to with my father.

I had now also begun to converse, on general subjects, with the instructed men with whom I came in contact: and the opportunities of such contact naturally became more numerous. The two friends of my father from whom I derived most, and with whom I most associated, were Mr. Grote and Mr. John Austin. The acquaintance of both with my father was recent, but had ripened rapidly into intimacy. Mr. Grote was introduced to my father by Mr. Ricardo, I think in 1819 (being then about twenty-five years old), and sought assiduously his society and conversation. Already a highly instructed man, he was yet, by the side of my father, a tyro on the great subjects of human opinion; but he rapidly seized on my father's best ideas; and in the department of political opinion he made himself known as early as 1820, by a pamphlet in defence of Radical Reform, in reply to a celebrated article by Sir James Mackintosh, then lately published in the *Edinburgh Review*.[*] Mr. Grote's father, the banker, was, I believe, a thorough Tory, and his mother intensely Evangelical; so that for his liberal opinions he was in no way indebted to home influences. But, unlike most persons who have the prospect of being rich by inheritance, he had, though actively engaged in the business of banking, devoted a great portion of time to philosophic studies; and his intimacy with my father did much to decide the character of the next stage in his mental progress. Him I often visited, and my conversations with him on political, moral, and philosophical subjects gave me, in addition to much valuable instruction, all the pleasure and benefit of sympathetic communion with a man of the high intellectual and moral eminence which his life and writings have since manifested to the world.

Mr. Austin, who was four or five years older than Mr. Grote, was the eldest son of a retired miller in Suffolk, who had made money by contracts during the war,

[*George Grote, *Statement of the Question of Parliamentary Reform* (London: Baldwin, Cradock, and Joy, 1821); James Mackintosh, "Parliamentary Reform," *Edinburgh Review*, XXXIV (Nov., 1820), 461–501.]

n−n[*Earlier version:*] who were his most frequent visitors, and whose houses I most frequented [*the last six words deleted first by HTM*]

I *think must have been* a man of remarkable qualities, from the fact that all his sons are of more than common ability and all eminently gentlemen. At least I can affirm this of three out of the four, and have reason to believe the same of the remaining one with whom as he went early to live abroad I was never much acquainted. The one of whom I am now speaking was for some time an officer in the army, and served in Sicily under Lord William Bentinck. After the peace he sold his commission and studied for the bar, to which he had been called and was endeavouring to get into practice at the time when my father became acquainted with him. He *could not, like Mr. Grote, be called* a disciple of my father, but had already formed by reading or thought, many of the same opinions, modified however by his own individual character. He was a man of great intellectual powers, which in conversation appeared still greater: from the energy and richness of expression with which, under the excitement of discussion, he was accustomed to assert and to defend some view or other of most subjects; *and from an appearance of* not only strong but deliberate and collected will; tinged with a certain bitterness, partly derived from temperament, partly perhaps from personal circumstances, and partly from the general course of his feelings and reflexions. The dissatisfaction with life and the world, felt more or less in the present state of society by every discerning and conscientious mind, was in his case, I think, combined with habitual dissatisfaction with himself, giving a generally melancholy cast to the character, very natural to those whose passive moral susceptibilities are much more than proportioned to their active energies. For it must be said, that the strength of will of which his manner seemed to give such strong assurance, expended itself in manner, and appeared to bear little active fruits except bitterness of expression. With great zeal for human improvement, a strong sense of duty, and habitual precision both in speech and in action, he hardly ever completed any intellectual task of magnitude. He had so high a standard of what ought to be done, so exaggerated a sense of deficiencies in his own performances and was so unable to content himself with the degree of elaboration which the occasion and the purpose required, that he not only spoiled much of his work by overlabouring it, but spent so much time and exertion in superfluous study and thought that when his task ought to have been completed he had generally worked himself into an illness without having half finished what he undertook. From this mental infirmity combined with liability to frequent attacks of disabling though not dangerous ill health, he accomplished through life very little compared with what he seemed capable of; though like Coleridge he might plead as a set off that he had exercised, through his conversation, a highly improving influence on many persons, both as to intellect and sentiments. On me his influence was most salutary. It was moral in the best sense. He took a sincere and kind interest in me, far beyond

---

−[*Earlier version:*] am sure must have been (for though he is, I believe, still alive I never saw him)
−[*Earlier versions:*] was not, like Mr. Grote, in some measure [*altered to read:*] was not, like Mr. Grote, what might almost be called

and who must have been a man of remarkable qualities, as I infer from the fact that all his sons were of more than common ability and all eminently gentlemen. The one with whom we are now concerned, and whose writings on jurisprudence have made him celebrated, was for some time in the army, and served in Sicily under Lord William Bentinck. After the peace he sold his commission and studied for the bar, to which he had been called for some time before my father knew him. He was not, like Mr. Grote, to any extent a pupil of my father, but he had attained, by reading and thought, a considerable number of the same opinions, modified by his own very decided individuality of character. He was a man of great intellectual powers, which in conversation appeared at their very best; from the vigour and richness of expression with which, under the excitement of discussion, he was accustomed to maintain some view or other of most general subjects; and from an appearance of not only strong, but deliberate and collected will; mixed with a certain bitterness, partly derived from temperament, and partly from the general cast of his feelings and reflexions. The dissatisfaction with life and the world, felt more or less in the present state of society and intellect by every discerning and highly conscientious mind, gave in his case a rather melancholy tinge to the character, very natural to those whose passive moral susceptibilities are more than proportioned to their active energies. For it must be said, that the strength of will, of which his manner seemed to give such strong assurance, expended itself principally in manner. With great zeal for human improvement, a strong sense of duty, and capacities and acquirements the extent of which is proved by the writings he has left, he hardly ever completed any intellectual task of magnitude. He had so high a standard of what ought to be done, so exaggerated a sense of deficiencies in his own performances, and was so unable to content himself with the amount of elaboration sufficient for the occasion and the purpose, that he not only spoiled much of his work for ordinary use by overlabouring it, but spent so much time and exertion in superfluous study and thought, that when his task ought to have been completed, he had generally worked himself into an illness, without having half finished what he undertook. From this mental infirmity (of which he is not the sole example among the accomplished and able men whom I have known), combined with liability to frequent attacks of disabling though not dangerous ill health, he accomplished, through life, little in comparison with what he seemed capable of; but what he did produce is held in the very highest estimation by the most competent judges; and, like Coleridge, he might plead as a set-off that he had been to many persons, through his conversation, a source not only of much instruction but of great elevation of character. On me his influence was most salutary. It was moral in the best sense. He took a sincere and kind interest in me, far beyond what

---

q–q[*Earlier version:*] and from a manner of delivery which as in others of this remarkable family conveyed an impression of immense strength of will. In him it appeared [*HTM deleted the first twenty-two words (the original ending of this sentence) and struck through "it" in the beginning of the new sentence.*]

what was to be expected towards a mere youth from a man of his age, standing, and what seemed austerity of character. There was in his conversation and demeanour a tone of what I have since called high-mindedness, which did not shew itself so much, if the quality existed as much, in any of the other persons with whom at that time I associated [r]. My intercourse with him was the more beneficial to me owing to his being of a different mental type from any of the other intellectual men whom I frequented, and his influence was exerted against many of the prejudices and narrownesses which are almost sure to be found in a young man formed by a particular school or a particular set.

His younger brother, Charles Austin, of whom at this time [s]and for the next year or two I saw much[s], had also a great effect on me though of a different kind. He was but six years older than myself, and at that time had just left the University of Cambridge where he had shone with great éclat as a man of intellect and especially of brilliancy both as an orator and as a converser. His influence among his Cambridge contemporaries deserves to be regarded as an historical event; for to it may in no small degree be traced the tendency towards Liberalism in general, and towards the Benthamic and politico-economic form of Liberalism, which shewed itself among a portion of the more active minded young men of the higher classes, from this time to 1830. The Union Debating Society, then at the height of its reputation, was an arena where what were then thought extreme opinions, in politics and philosophy, were weekly asserted, face to face with their opposites, before audiences consisting of the élite of the Cambridge youth: and though many persons afterwards of more or less note (Mr. Macaulay perhaps the most conspicuous) gained their first oratorical laurels in these debates, the really influential mind among these intellectual gladiators was Charles Austin. He continued after leaving the University to be by his conversation and personal ascendancy a leader among the same class of young men who had been his associates there; and he attached me among others to his car. Through him I became acquainted with Macaulay, Hyde and Charles Villiers, Strutt, and various other young men who afterwards became known in literature or in politics, and among whom I heard discussions on many topics to a certain degree new to me. None of them however had any effect on my developement except Austin: whose influence over me [t]differed from that of the persons whom I have hitherto mentioned, in being not that of a man over a boy but of an older contemporary. It[t] was through him that I first felt myself not a pupil with teachers but a man among men [u]. He was the first person of intellect whom I met on a ground of equality, though obviously and confessedly my superior on that common ground. He was a man who never failed to make a great impression on those with whom he came in contact, even when

---

[r][*Cancelled text:*] , not even in my father; although my father was as high principled as Mr. Austin and had a stronger will; but Mr. Austin was both a prouder man, and more a man of feeling than my father [*deleted first by HTM*]

[s-s][*Earlier version:*] I saw much, and who indeed made a sort of companion of me, to a certain

could have been expected towards a mere youth from a man of his age, standing, and what seemed austerity of character. There was in his conversation and demeanour a tone of highmindedness which did not shew itself so much, if the quality existed as much, in any of the other persons with whom at that time I associated. My intercourse with him was the more beneficial, owing to his being of a different mental type from all other intellectual men whom I frequented, and he from the first set himself decidedly against the prejudices and narrownesses which are almost sure to be found in a young man formed by a particular mode of thought or a particular social circle.

His younger brother, Charles Austin, of whom at this time and for the next year or two I saw much, had also a great effect on me, though of a very different description. He was but a few years older than myself, and had then just left the University, where he had shone with great éclat as a man of intellect and a brilliant orator and converser. The effect he produced on his Cambridge cotemporaries deserves to be accounted an historical event; for to it may in part be traced the tendency towards Liberalism in general, and the Benthamic and politico-economic form of it in particular, which shewed itself in a portion of the more active-minded young men of the higher classes from this time to 1830. The Union Debating Society, at that time at the height of its reputation, was an arena where what were then thought extreme opinions, in politics and philosophy, were weekly asserted, face to face with their opposites, before audiences consisting of the élite of the Cambridge youth: and though many persons afterwards of more or less note (of whom Lord Macaulay is the most celebrated) gained their first oratorical laurels in those debates, the really influential mind among these intellectual gladiators was Charles Austin. He continued, after leaving the University, to be, by his conversation and personal ascendancy, a leader among the same class of young men who had been his associates there; and he attached me among others to his car. Through him I became acquainted with Macaulay, Hyde and Charles Villiers, Strutt (now Lord Belper), Romilly (now Lord Romilly and Master of the Rolls), and various others who subsequently figured in literature or politics, and among whom I heard discussions on many topics, as yet to a certain degree new to me. The influence of Charles Austin over me differed from that of the persons I have hitherto mentioned, in being not the influence of a man over a boy, but that of an elder cotemporary. It was through him that I first felt myself, not a pupil under teachers, but a man among men. He was the first person of intellect whom I met on a ground of equality, though as yet much his inferior on that common ground. He was a man who never failed to impress greatly those with whom he came in contact, even

---

extent, for the next year or two [*marked in the margin by HTM*]

ᶦ⁻ᶦ[*Earlier version:*] was not that of a man over a boy but of an older contemporary, and had an equality in it combined with its superiority, which rendered it highly stimulating to me. Indeed it

ᵘ[*Cancelled text:*] , forming and defending my own opinions

their opinions were the very opposite of his. The impression which he gave was that of unbounded strength, together with talents which, combined with such apparent force of will and character, seemed made to dominate the world. Those who knew him, whether friendly to him or not, always anticipated that he would play a conspicuous part in public life. It is seldom that men produce so great an immediate effect by speech unless they in some degree lay themselves out for it, and he did so in no ordinary degree. He loved to strike, and even to startle. He knew that decision is the greatest element of effect and he uttered his opinions with all the decision he could throw into them, never so well pleased as when he could astonish any one by their audacity. Very unlike his brother, who made war on the narrower interpretations and applications of the principles they both professed, he on the contrary presented the Benthamic doctrines in the most startling form of which they were susceptible, exaggerating everything in them which tended to consequences offensive to any one's preconceived feelings. All which, he defended with such verve and vivacity, and carried off by a manner so agreeable as well as forcible, that he always came off victor, or divided the honours of the field with any, however formidable antagonist. It is my belief that much of the popular notion of the tenets and sentiments of what are called Benthamites or Utilitarians, had its foundation in paradoxes thrown out by Charles Austin. It is but fair to add, however, that his example was followed, *haud passibus æquis*, by younger proselytes, and that to *outrer* whatever was by anybody considered offensive in the doctrines and maxims of Benthamism, became at one time the badge of a certain, not very numerous, coterie of youths. All of them however who had anything in them, myself among others, quickly outgrew this boyish vanity; and those who had not, became tired of differing from other people, and left off both the good and the bad of the heterodox opinions they for some time professed.

It was in this winter of 1822/23 that I formed the plan of a little society, to be composed of young men agreeing on fundamental principles—that is, acknowledging utility as their first principle in ethics and politics, and a certain number of the principal corollaries drawn from it in the philosophy I had accepted; and meeting once a fortnight to read essays and discuss questions comformably to the premises thus agreed on. This fact would be hardly worth mentioning but for the circumstance, that the name I gave to the little society I had planned was the Utilitarian Society. It was the first time that any one had taken the title of Utilitarian, and the word made its way into the language from this humble source. I did not invent the word, but found it in one of Galt's novels, the *Annals of the Parish* [v]. In one sentence of this book (if my remembrance is correct) the Scotch clergyman of whom it is the supposed autobiography, finding heretical doctrines creeping into his parish about the time of the French Revolution, warns some parishioner not to leave the gospel and become an utilitarian. With a boy's

[v]*[Cancelled text:]* a book, by the way, much admired by my father as a picture of Scotch village life [*deleted first by HTM*]

when their opinions were the very reverse of his. The impression he gave was that of boundless strength, together with talents which, combined with such apparent force of will and character, seemed capable of dominating the world. Those who knew him, whether friendly to him or not, always anticipated that he would play a conspicuous part in public life. It is seldom that men produce so great an immediate effect by speech, unless they, in some degree, lay themselves out for it; and he did this in no ordinary degree. He loved to strike, and even to startle. He knew that decision is the greatest element of effect, and he uttered his opinions with all the decision he could throw into them, never so well pleased as when he astonished any one by their audacity. Very unlike his brother, who made war against the narrower interpretations and applications of the principles they both professed, he on the contrary presented the Benthamic doctrines in the most startling form of which they were susceptible, exaggerating every thing in them which tended to consequences offensive to any one's preconceived feelings. All which, he defended with such verve and vivacity, and carried off by a manner so agreeable as well as forcible, that he always either came off victor, or divided the honours of the field. It is my belief that much of the notion popularly entertained of the tenets and sentiments of what are called Benthamites or Utilitarians, had its origin in paradoxes thrown out by Charles Austin. It must be said, however, that his example was followed, *haud passibus æquis*,[*] by younger proselytes, and that to *outrer* whatever was by anybody considered offensive in the doctrines and maxims of Benthamism, became at one time the badge of a small coterie of youths. All of these who had anything in them, myself among others, quickly outgrew this boyish vanity; and those who had not, became tired of differing from other people, and gave up both the good and the bad part of the heterodox opinions they had for some time professed.

It was in the winter of 1822/23 that I formed the plan of a little society, to be composed of young men agreeing in fundamental principles—acknowledging Utility as their standard in ethics and politics, and a certain number of the principal corollaries drawn from it in the philosophy I had accepted—and meeting once a fortnight to read essays and discuss questions conformably to the premises thus agreed on. The fact would hardly be worth mentioning, but for the circumstance, that the name I gave to the society I had planned was the Utilitarian Society. It was the first time that any one had taken the title of Utilitarian; and the term made its way into the language from this humble source. I did not invent the word, but found it in one of Galt's novels, the *Annals of the Parish*, in which the Scotch clergyman, of whom the book is a supposed autobiography, is represented as warning his parishioners not to leave the Gospel and become utilitarians.[†] With a

[*Cf. Virgil, *Aeneid*, in *Virgil* (Latin and English), trans. H. Rushton Fairclough, 2 vols. (London: Heinemann; New York: Putnam's Sons, 1922), Vol. I, p. 342 (Bk. II, l. 724).]

[†John Galt ("Micah Balwhidder"), *Annals of the Parish* (Edinburgh: Blackwood; London: Cadwell, 1821), p. 286.]

fondness for a name and a banner I seized on the word, and for some years called myself and others by it as a sectarian appellation: and it came to be a little used (though never very much) by some others holding the opinions which it was intended to designate. As those opinions attracted more notice the term came to be repeated by strangers and opponents, and got into rather common use just about the time when those who had originally assumed it laid down that along with other sectarian characteristics. The society so called consisted at first of only three members, one of whom being Mr. Bentham's amanuensis we obtained permission to hold our meetings in his house. The number never I think reached ten and the society was broken up in 1826. It had thus an existence of about three years and a half. The chief effect of it as regards myself, over and above practice in "oral discussion", was its bringing me in contact with young men less advanced than myself, among whom, as they professed the same opinions, I became a sort of leader or chief, either directing for the time, or much influencing, their mental progress. Any young man of education who fell in my way, whose opinions were not incompatible with those of the society, I endeavoured to press into its service: and several others I probably should never have known had they not joined it. Those of the members who became my intimate companions were William Eyton Tooke, the eldest son of the eminent political economist, a young man of singular worth both moral and intellectual, lost to the world by an early death; his friend William Ellis, now known by his apostolic exertions for the improvement of education; George Graham, now an official assignee of the Bankruptcy Court; and (from the time when he came to England to study for the bar, in 1824 or 1825) a man who has made considerably more noise in the world, John Arthur Roebuck.

In May 1823 my professional occupation and status were decided by my father's obtaining for me an appointment from the East India Company, in the office of the Examiner of Indian Correspondence, immediately under himself. I was appointed in the usual manner at the bottom of the list of Clerks, to rise by seniority; but with the understanding that I should be employed from the first in preparing drafts of despatches; and be thus trained up as a successor to those who then filled the higher departments of the office. My drafts of course required at first much revision from my immediate superiors, but I soon became well acquainted with the business, and by my father's instructions and the general progress of my own powers I was in two or three years qualified to be, and practically was, the chief conductor of the

---

w-w[*Earlier version:*] speech-making (for our discussions were in the form of speeches)

boy's fondness for a name and a banner I seized on the word, and for some years called myself and others by it as a sectarian appellation; and it came to be occasionally used by some others holding the opinions which it was intended to designate. As those opinions attracted more notice, the term was repeated by strangers and opponents, and got into rather common use just about the time when those who had originally assumed it, laid down that along with other sectarian characteristics. The Society so called consisted at first of no more than three members, one of whom, being Mr. Bentham's amanuensis,[*] obtained for us permission to hold our meetings in his house. The number never, I think, reached ten, and the society was broken up in 1826. It had thus an existence of about three years and a half. The chief effect of it as regards myself, over and above the benefit of practice in oral discussion, was that of bringing me in contact with several young men at that time less advanced than myself, among whom, as they professed the same opinions, I was for some time a sort of leader, and had considerable influence on their mental progress. Any young man of education who fell in my way, and whose opinions were not incompatible with those of the Society, I endeavoured to press into its service; and some others I probably should never have known, had they not joined it. Those of the members who became my intimate companions— no one of whom was in any sense of the word a disciple, but all of them independent thinkers on their own basis—were William Eyton Tooke, son of the eminent political economist, a young man of singular worth both moral and intellectual, lost to the world by an early death; his friend William Ellis, an original thinker in the field of political economy, now honorably known by his apostolic exertions for the improvement of education; George Graham, afterwards an official assignee of the Bankruptcy Court, a thinker of originality and power on almost all abstract subjects; and (from the time when he came first to England to study for the bar in 1824 or 1825) a man who has made considerably more noise in the world than any of these, John Arthur Roebuck.

In May 1823, my professional occupation and status for the next thirty-five years of my life, were decided by my father's obtaining for me an appointment from the East India Company, in the office of the Examiner of India Correspondence, immediately under himself. I was appointed in the usual manner, at the bottom of the list of clerks, to rise, at least in the first instance, by seniority; but with the understanding, that I should be employed from the beginning in preparing drafts of despatches, and be thus trained up as a successor to those who then filled the higher departments of the office. My drafts of course required, for some time, much revision from my immediate superiors, but I soon became well acquainted with the business, and by my father's instructions and the general growth of my own powers, I was in a few years qualified to be, and practically was, the chief

[*Richard Doane, who had also stayed with Sir Samuel Bentham's family in France just before Mill's visit.]

correspondence with India in one of the leading departments, that of the Native States: *and this* has continued to be my official duty up to the present time. I know no occupation among those by which a subsistence is now gained more suitable than such as this to any one who, not being pecuniarily independent, desires to devote a part of the twenty-four hours to intellectual pursuits. The attempt to earn a living by writing for the press, can be recommended to no one qualified to accomplish anything in the higher departments of literature or speculation: for (not to speak of the uncertainty of such a means of livelihood, especially if the writer has a conscience and will not consent to serve any opinions but his own) it is evident that the writings by which one can live are not the writings which themselves live, or those in which the writer does his best. The books which are to form future thinkers take too much time to write, and when written come in general too slowly into notice and repute to be a resource for subsistence. Those who have to support themselves by literature must depend on literary drudgery, or at best on writings addressed to the multitude, and can employ in the pursuits of their choice only such time as they can spare from those of necessity; generally less than the leisure allowed by office occupations, while the effect on the mind is far more enervating and fatiguing. For my own part I have through life found office duties an actual rest from the occupations which I have carried on simultaneously with them. *y* They were sufficiently intellectual not to be an onerous drudgery, without being such as to cause any strain upon the mental powers of a person used to abstract thought or even to the labour of careful literary composition. The drawbacks, for every mode of life has its drawbacks, were not, however, unfelt by me. The absence of the chances of riches and honours held out by some professions, particularly the bar (which had been as I said the profession thought of for me) affected me little. But I was not indifferent to exclusion from Parliament and public life: and I felt very sensibly the more immediate unpleasantness of confinement to London, the holiday allowed by India-house practice not exceeding a month in the year, while my taste was strong for a country life and my year in France had left behind it an ardent desire for travelling. But though these tastes could not be freely indulged, they were at no time entirely sacrificed. *z*I passed most Sundays throughout the year in the country, often in long walks*z*. The month's holiday was for a few years spent at my father's house in the country: afterwards a part or the whole was passed in tours, chiefly pedestrian, with some one or more of the young men who were my companions: and from 1830 onwards the greater part of it was in most

---

x–x[*Earlier version:*] which in the successive characters of Clerk and Assistant Examiner [*deleted and altered to final reading first by HTM*]

y[*Cancelled text:*] While they precluded all uneasiness about the means of subsistence, they occupied fewer hours of the day than almost any business or profession, they had nothing in them to produce anxiety, or to keep the mind intent on them at any time but when directly engaged in them. [*deleted first by HTM*]

z–z[*Earlier version:*] I continued during the summer half of every year to pass the Saturday afternoon and Sunday in the country, returning to town with my father on Monday morning; generally in one of the most beautiful districts of England, the neighbourhood of Dorking, in the finest part of which (the

conductor of the correspondence with India in one of the leading departments, that of the Native States. This continued to be my official duty until I was appointed Examiner, only two years before the time when the abolition of the East India Company as a political body determined my retirement. I do not know any one of the occupations by which a subsistence can now be gained, more suitable than such as this to any one who, not being in independent circumstances, desires to devote a part of the twenty-four hours to private intellectual pursuits. Writing for the press, cannot be recommended as a permanent resource to any one qualified to accomplish anything in the higher departments of literature or thought: not only on account of the uncertainty of this means of livelihood, especially if the writer has a conscience, and will not consent to serve any opinions except his own; but also because the writings by which one can live, are not the writings which themselves live, and are never those in which the writer does his best. Books destined to form future thinkers take too much time to write, and when written come in general too slowly into notice and repute, to be relied on for subsistence. Those who have to support themselves by their pen must depend on literary drudgery, or at best on writings addressed to the multitude; and can employ in the pursuits of their own choice only such time as they can spare from those of necessity; which is generally less than the leisure allowed by office occupations, while the effect on the mind is far more enervating and fatiguing. For my own part, I have, through life, found office duties an actual rest from the other mental occupations which I have carried on simultaneously with them. They were sufficiently intellectual not to be a distasteful drudgery, without being such as to cause any strain upon the mental powers of a person used to abstract thought, or to the labour of careful literary composition. The drawbacks, for every mode of life has its drawbacks, were not, however, unfelt by me. I cared little for the loss of the chances of riches and honours held out by some of the professions, particularly the bar, which had been, as I have already said, the profession thought of for me. But I was not indifferent to exclusion from Parliament, and public life: and I felt very sensibly the more immediate unpleasantness of confinement to London; the holiday allowed by India-house practice not exceeding a month in the year, while my taste was strong for a country life, and my sojourn in France had left behind it an ardent desire of travelling. But though these tastes could not be freely indulged, they were at no time entirely sacrificed. I passed most Sundays, throughout the year, in the country, taking long rural walks on that day even when residing in London. The month's holiday was, for a few years, passed at my father's house in the country: afterwards a part or the whole was spent in tours, chiefly pedestrian, with some one or more of the young men who were my chosen companions; and at a later period,

---

vale of Mickleham near the foot of Box Hill) my father after some years occupied a cottage permanently. During the last months of winter and the first of spring I used every Sunday when weather permitted to make a walking excursion with some of the young men who were my companions; generally walking out ten or twelve miles to breakfast, and making a circuit of fourteen or fifteen more before getting back to town [*the first sentence marked with a line in the margin by HTM*]

years employed in visits to friends whose acquaintance I made in that year, or in journeys or excursions in which I accompanied them. ^a France, Belgium, and Rhenish Germany have been within easy reach of the annual holiday: and two longer absences, one of three, the other of six months, under medical advice, added Switzerland, the Tyrol, and Italy ^b to my list. Fortunately also both these journeys occurred rather early, so as to give the benefit and charm of the remembrance to a large portion of life.

---

^a[*Cancelled text:*] The northern half of [*underscored by HTM*]
^b[*Cancelled text:*] as far as Pæstum, [*deleted first by HTM*]

in longer journeys or excursions, alone or with other friends.[*] France, Belgium, and Rhenish Germany were within easy reach of the annual holiday: and two longer absences, one of three, the other of six months, under medical advice, added Switzerland, the Tyrol, and Italy to my list. Fortunately, also, both these journies occurred rather early, so as to give the benefit and charm of the remembrance to a large portion of life.

I am disposed to agree with what has been surmised by others, that the opportunity which my official position gave me of learning by personal observation the necessary conditions of the practical conduct of public affairs, has been of considerable value to me as a theoretical reformer of the opinions and institutions of my time. Not, indeed, that public business transacted on paper, to take effect on the other side of the globe, was of itself calculated to give much practical knowledge of life. But the occupation accustomed me to see and hear the difficulties of every course, and the means of obviating them, stated and discussed deliberately, with a view to execution; it gave me opportunities of perceiving when public measures, and other political facts, did not produce the effects which had been expected of them, and from what causes; above all it was valuable to me by making me, in this portion of my activity, merely one wheel in a machine, the whole of which had to work together. As a speculative writer, I should have had no one to consult but myself, and should have encountered in my speculations none of the obstacles which would have started up whenever they came to be applied to practice. But as a Secretary conducting political correspondence, I could not issue an order or express an opinion, without satisfying various persons very unlike myself, that the thing was fit to be done. I was thus in a good position for finding out by practice the mode of putting a thought which gives it easiest admittance into minds not prepared for it by habit; while I became practically conversant with the difficulties of moving bodies of men, the necessities of compromise, the art of sacrificing the non-essential to preserve the essential. I learnt how to obtain the best I could, when I could not obtain everything; instead of being indignant or dispirited because I could not have entirely my own way, to be pleased and encouraged when I could have the smallest part of it; and when even that could not be, to bear with complete equanimity the being overruled altogether. I have found, through life, these acquisitions to be of the greatest possible importance for personal happiness, and they are also a very necessary condition for enabling any one, either as theorist or as practical man, to effect the greatest amount of good compatible with his opportunities.

[*Journals of five of these walking tours exist in holograph MSS: Sussex, 20–30 July, 1827 (MS, St. Andrews); Berkshire, Buckinghamshire, and Surrey, 3–15 July, 1828 (MS, Yale); Yorkshire and the Lake District, 12 July–8 Aug., 1831 (MS, Bodleian); Hampshire, West Sussex, and the Isle of Wight, 19 July–6 Aug., 1832 (MS, Mount Holyoke); and Cornwall, 3–9 Oct., 1832 (MS, Mill-Taylor Collection). A holograph MS of a sixth walking tour, of the Rhine, July, 1835, was sold at auction in 1922, but its present location is unknown.]

The occupation of so much of my time by office work did not relax my attention to my own pursuits, which were never carried on more vigorously [a]. It was about this time that I began to write in newspapers. The first writings of mine which got into print were two letters published towards the end of 1822 in the *Traveller* evening newspaper, on I forget what abstract point of political economy. The *Traveller* (which soon after grew into the *Globe and Traveller* by the purchase and incorporation of the *Globe*) was then the property of the well known political economist Colonel Torrens, and under the editorship of an able man, Mr. Walter Coulson (who after being an amanuensis of Bentham, became a reporter, then an editor, next a barrister and conveyancer, and is now counsel to the Home Office), had become one of the most important newspaper organs of liberal politics. Col. Torrens himself wrote much of the political economy of his paper, and had at this time made an attack on some opinion of Ricardo and my father to which at my father's instigation I wrote an answer and Coulson out of consideration for my father and good will to me, inserted it. There was a reply by Torrens to which I again rejoined. I soon after attempted [b] something more ambitious. The prosecutions of Richard Carlile and his wife and sister for publishing books hostile to Christianity, were then exciting much attention, and nowhere more than among the people I frequented. Freedom of discussion even in politics, much more in religion, was at that time far from being, even in theory, the conceded point which it at least *seems* to be now; and it was necessary for the holders of obnoxious opinions to be always ready to argue and reargue for liberty to express them. I wrote a series of five letters, under the signature of Wickliffe, going over the whole length and breadth of the question of free publication of all opinions on religion, and offered them to the *Morning Chronicle*. The first three were published in January and February 1823; the others contained things too outspoken for that

---

[a][*Cancelled text:*] than during the next few years [*HTM underscored "few", and Mill pencilled a query, now erased, at left: "meaning of this mark?"*]

[b][*Cancelled text:*] of my own accord [*deleted first by HTM*]

CHAPTER IV

Youthful Propagandism. The Westminster Review

THE OCCUPATION of so much of my time by office work did not relax my attention to my own pursuits, which were never carried on more vigorously. It was about this time that I began to write in newspapers. The first writings of mine which got into print were two letters published towards the end of 1822, in the *Traveller* evening newspaper. The *Traveller* (which afterwards grew into the *Globe and Traveller* by the purchase and incorporation of the *Globe*) was then the property of the well known political economist Colonel Torrens. Under the editorship of an able man, Mr. Walter Coulson (who after being an amanuensis of Mr. Bentham, became a reporter, then an editor, next a barrister and conveyancer, and died Counsel to the Home Office), it had become one of the most important newspaper organs of liberal politics. Col. Torrens himself wrote much of the political economy of his paper; and had at this time made an attack upon some opinion of Ricardo and my father, to which at my father's instigation I attempted an answer, and Coulson out of consideration for my father and good will to me, inserted it. There was a reply by Torrens, to which I again rejoined.[*] I soon after attempted something considerably more ambitious. The prosecutions of Richard Carlile and his wife and sister for publications hostile to Christianity, were then exciting much attention, and nowhere more than among the people I frequented. Freedom of discussion even in politics, much more in religion, was at that time far from being, even in theory, the conceded point which it at least seems to be now; and the holders of obnoxious opinions had to be always ready to argue and reargue for the liberty of expressing them. I wrote a series of five letters, under the signature of Wickliffe, going over the whole length and breadth of the question of free publication of all opinions on religion, and offered them to the *Morning Chronicle*. Three of them were published in January and February 1823; the other two,

---

[*In the order of their appearance, the articles are: Robert Torrens, "Political Economy Club," *Traveller*, 2 Dec., 1822, p. 3; Mill, "Exchangeable Value," *ibid.*, 6 Dec., 1822, p. 3; Torrens, "Exchangeable Value," *ibid.*, 7 Dec., 1822, p. 3; Mill, "Exchangeable Value," *ibid.*, 13 Dec., 1822, p. 2.]

journal and never appeared at all. But a paper which I wrote some time after on the same subject, a propos of a debate in the House of Commons, was inserted as a leading article: and during the whole of this year, 1823, I sent a considerable number of contributions to the *Chronicle* and *Traveller*, sometimes notices of books, but oftener letters commenting on some nonsense talked in parliament, or some defect of the law or misdoings of the magistracy or the courts of justice. In this last department the *Chronicle* was now rendering signal service. After the death of Mr. Perry, the whole editorship and management of the paper had fallen into the hands of Mr. John Black, long a reporter on its establishment, a man of most extensive reading and information, great honesty and simplicity of mind; a particular friend of my father, imbued with many of his and Bentham's best ideas, which as a writer he reproduced together with many other valuable thoughts, with great facility and skill. From this time the *Chronicle* ceased to be the merely Whig organ it was before, and became to a very considerable extent, for the next ten years, a vehicle of the opinions of the utilitarian radicals. This was mainly by Black's own articles, with some assistance from Fonblanque, who first shewed his eminent qualities as a writer by articles and jeux d'esprit in the *Chronicle*. The defects of the law and of the administration of justice were the subject on which that paper rendered most service to improvement. Up to that time hardly a word had been said, except by Bentham and my father, against that most peccant part of English institutions and of their administration. It was the almost universal creed of Englishmen, that the law of England, the judicature of England, the unpaid magistracy of England, were models of excellence. I express my sober conviction when I say that after Bentham who supplied the whole materials, the greatest share of the glory of breaking down this miserable superstition belongs to Black, as editor of the *Morning Chronicle*. He kept up an incessant fire against it, exposing the absurdities and vices of the law and the courts of justice, paid and unpaid, until he forced some sense of them into people's minds. On many other important questions he became the organ of opinions much in advance of any which had ever before found regular advocacy in the newspaper press; only avoiding any direct radical confession of faith which would have brought the paper into a collision with all who called themselves Whigs, fatal to its prosperity and influence. Black was a frequent visitor of my father, ^c and Mr. Grote used to say that he always knew by the Monday morning's article, whether Black had been with my father on the Sunday. Black was one of the most influential of the many channels through which my father's conversation and personal influence made his opinions tell on the world; cooperating with the effect of his own writings in making him a power in the country such as no individual has since exercised, in a private station, by mere force of intellect and character; and a power which was often acting the most

---

^c[*Cancelled text:*] often going to Mickleham on Saturday (the weekly holiday of the editors of morning newspapers) and returning to town on Sunday afternoon, in time for the editorial duties of Monday's paper: [*deleted first by HTM*]

containing things too outspoken for that journal, never appeared at all.[*] But a paper which I wrote soon after on the same subject, *à propos* of a debate in the House of Commons, was inserted as a leading article;[†] and during the whole of this year, 1823, a considerable number of my contributions were printed in the *Chronicle* and *Traveller*: sometimes notices of books, but oftener letters, commenting on some nonsense talked in Parliament, or some defect of the law, or misdoings of the magistracy or the courts of justice.[‡] In this last department the *Chronicle* was now rendering signal service. After the death of Mr. Perry, the editorship and management of the paper had devolved on Mr. John Black, long a reporter on its establishment; a man of most extensive reading and information, great honesty and simplicity of mind; a particular friend of my father, imbued with many of his and Bentham's ideas, which he reproduced in his articles, among other valuable thoughts, with great facility and skill. From this time the *Chronicle* ceased to be the merely Whig organ it was before, and during the next ten years became to a considerable extent a vehicle of the opinions of the Utilitarian radicals. This was mainly by what Black himself wrote, with some assistance from Fonblanque, who first shewed his eminent qualities as a writer by articles and *jeux d'esprit* in the *Chronicle*. The defects of the law, and of the administration of justice, were the subject on which that paper rendered most service to improvement. Up to that time hardly a word had been said, except by Bentham and my father, against that most peccant part of English institutions and of their administration. It was the almost universal creed of Englishmen, that the law of England, the judicature of England, the unpaid magistracy of England, were models of excellence. I do not go beyond the mark in saying, that after Bentham, who supplied the principal materials, the greatest share of the merit of breaking down this wretched superstition belongs to Black, as editor of the *Morning Chronicle*. He kept up an incessant fire against it, exposing the absurdities and vices of the law and the courts of justice, paid and unpaid, until he forced some sense of them into people's minds. On many other questions he became the organ of opinions much in advance of any which had ever before found regular advocacy in the newspaper press. Black was a frequent visitor of my father, and Mr. Grote used to say that he always knew by the Monday morning's article, whether Black had been with my father on the Sunday. Black was one of the most influential of the many channels through which my father's conversation and personal influence made his opinions tell on the world; cooperating with the effect of his writings in making him a power in the country, such as it has rarely been the lot of an individual in a private station to be, through the mere force of intellect and character: and a power which was often acting the

[*"Free Discussion," *Morning Chronicle*, 28 Jan., 1823, p. 3; 8 Feb., 1823, p. 3; and 12 Feb., 1823, p. 3. The unpublished letters are not known to have survived.]

[†Unheaded leader, *Morning Chronicle*, 9 May, 1823, p. 3.]

[‡A total of twenty-two letters, reviews, and leading articles, all but three in the *Morning Chronicle*.]

efficiently when it was least seen or suspected. I have already noticed how much of what was done by Ricardo, Hume, and Grote was done at his prompting and persuasion; he was the good genius by the side of Brougham in all he ever did for the public, either on education, law reform, or any other subject. And his influence flowed in minor streams too numerous to be specified. This influence now received a great extension by the foundation of the *Westminster Review*.

Contrary to what might be supposed, my father was in no degree a party to the setting up of the *Westminster Review* [d]. The need of a Radical review to make head against the *Edinburgh* and *Quarterly* (then in the period of their greatest reputation and influence) had been a topic of conversation between him and Mr. Bentham many years earlier, and it had then been part of their *chateau en Espagne* that my father should be the editor [e], but the idea had never assumed a practical shape [e]. [f]In 1823 however Mr. Bentham determined to establish the review at his own cost, and offered the editorship to my father, who declined it, as being incompatible with his India House appointment. It was then entrusted to Mr. Bowring, at that time engaged in mercantile business[f]. Mr. Bowring had for two or three years previous been an assiduous frequenter of Bentham, to whom he was recommended by many personal good qualities, by an ardent admiration for Bentham, a zealous adoption of many though not all of his opinions, and not least by an extensive acquaintanceship and correspondence with Liberals of all countries, which seemed to qualify him for being a powerful agent in spreading Bentham's fame and doctrines through all quarters of the world. My father had seen little of Bowring, but knew enough of him to be convinced that he was a man of an entirely different type from what my father deemed suitable for conducting a political and philosophical review: and he augured so ill of the enterprise that he regretted it altogether, feeling persuaded not only that Bentham would lose his money, but that discredit would be brought upon radical principles. [g]Since however it was to be attempted, he could not refuse to write for it[g]. He consented therefore to write an article for the first number: and as it had been part of the plan formerly talked of between him and Bentham that a portion of the work should be devoted to reviewing the other Reviews, this article of my father's was a general review of the *Edinburgh*. Before he began writing it he [h]put my services in requisition, to[h] read

[d][*Cancelled text:*] , nor was his opinion asked on the subject

[e–e][*Earlier version:*] ; this was before his appointment to the India House

[f–f][*Earlier version:*] Some time in the summer of 1823 when as still frequently happened my father was dining with Mr. Bentham, or when as often happened Mr. Bentham had stepped across his garden to speak to my father at his study window, he reminded my father of this old project and announced to him "the money is found." About the source of it he said nothing, and my father was never told, though he never had any doubt of the fact, that the money was Bentham's. He was never asked for an opinion, but only for cooperation. The editorship was offered to him, but he declined it as being incompatible with his India house appointment. On his refusal he was asked to write for the review, and was informed that Mr. Bowring was to be the editor [*In the first sentence Mill deleted "when as still frequently . . . window, he" and interlined "I do not know on what occasion, Bentham"*. HTM marked the second

most efficiently where it was least seen and suspected. I have already noticed how much of what was done by Ricardo, Hume, and Grote, was the result, in part, of his prompting and persuasion. He was the good genius by the side of Brougham in most of what he did for the public, either on education, law reform, or any other subject. And his influence flowed in minor streams too numerous to be specified. This influence was now about to receive a great extension, by the foundation of the *Westminster Review.*

Contrary to what may have been supposed, my father was in no degree a party to setting up the *Westminster Review.* The need of a Radical organ to make head against the *Edinburgh* and *Quarterly* (then in the period of their greatest reputation and influence) had been a topic of conversation between him and Mr. Bentham many years earlier, and it had been a part of their *château en Espagne* that my father should be the editor, but the idea had never assumed any practical shape. In 1823, however, Mr. Bentham determined to establish the review at his own cost, and offered the editorship to my father, who declined it as incompatible with his India House appointment. It was then entrusted to Mr. (now Sir John) Bowring, at that time a merchant in the City. Mr. Bowring had been for two or three years previous an assiduous frequenter of Mr. Bentham, to whom he was recommended by many personal good qualities, by an ardent admiration for Bentham, a zealous adoption of many though not all of his opinions, and, not least, by an extensive acquaintanceship and correspondence with Liberals of all countries, which seemed to qualify him for being a powerful agent in spreading Bentham's fame and doctrines through all quarters of the world. My father had seen little of Bowring, but knew enough of him to have formed a strong opinion, that he was a man of an entirely different type from what my father considered suitable for conducting a political and philosophical review: and he augured so ill of the enterprise that he regretted it altogether, feeling persuaded not only that Mr. Bentham would lose his money, but that discredit would probably be brought upon radical principles. He could not however desert Mr. Bentham, and he consented to write an article for the first number.[*] As it had been a favorite portion of the scheme formerly talked of, that part of the work should be devoted to reviewing the other Reviews, this article of my father's was to be a general criticism of the *Edinburgh Review* from its commencement. Before writing it he made me read through all the volumes of the

[*James Mill, "Periodical Literature: *Edinburgh Review*," *Westminster Review*, I (Jan., 1824), 206–49.]

---

sentence ("About . . . Bentham's.") with a line in the margin, and opposite the last seven words of the last sentence wrote at left: "the editorship was entrusted to Mr. Bowring at that time engaged in".]

g–g[Earlier version:] Since however not only no desire was shewn for his advice, but such a mere *secret de la comédie* as where the money was to come from, was not confided to him, he doubtless felt that it would be an impertinence in him to obtrude his opinion. Probably also he saw that it would be of no use. At the same time, the terms he was on with Bentham made it impossible for him to refuse to write for the review [*The first two sentences are marked for deletion by HTM. In the last, for "refuse" Mill originally wrote "mortify him by refusing".*]

h–h[Earlier versions:] made me [*altered to read:*] asked me to

through all the numbers of the *Edinburgh Review* from its commencement, or at least as much of them as seemed important (this was not then so onerous a task as it would be now, the review having only lasted twenty years of the fifty and upwards which it now reckons), making notes for him of the articles which I thought he would wish to examine, either on account of their good or their bad qualities. The article is I think one of the most striking of all his writings, both in conception and in execution. He began with an analysis of the tendencies of periodical literature in general; pointing out that since it cannot, like a book, wait for success, but must succeed immediately or not at all, it is almost certain to profess and inculcate the opinions already held by the public to which it addresses itself, instead of attempting to rectify them. He next, by way of characterizing the position of the *Edinburgh Review* as a political organ, entered into a complete analysis of the British Constitution. He commented on its thoroughly aristocratic composition; the nomination of a majority of the House of Commons by a few hundred families; the different classes which this narrow oligarchy was obliged to admit to a share of power; and finally, what he called its two props, the Church, and the legal profession. He then pointed out the natural tendency of an aristocratic body of this composition, to group itself into two parties, one of them in possession of the executive, the other seeking to become so, and endeavouring to supplant the former and become the predominant section by the aid of public opinion. He described the course likely to be pursued, and the political ground occupied, by an aristocratical party in opposition, coquetting with popular principles for the sake of popular support. He shewed how this idea was realized in the conduct of the Whig party, and of the *Edinburgh Review*, as the chief literary organ of that party. He noted as their principal characteristic what he termed "seesaw"; writing alternately on both sides of every question which touched the power or interest of the governing classes: sometimes in different articles, sometimes in different parts of the same article. And this he illustrated by copious specimens. So formidable an attack on the Whig party and policy had never before been made; nor had so great a blow ever been struck, in this country, for radicalism: and there was not, I believe, any person living who could have written that article except my father.*

In the meantime the nascent review had formed a junction with another project, of a purely literary periodical to be edited by Mr. Henry Southern, afterwards known as a diplomatist, then a literary man by profession ^{j}. The two editors agreed

---

*^{i}The continuation of this article, in the second number of the review, was written by me under my father's eye, and (except as practice in composition, in which respect it was, to myself, very useful) was of little or no value.^{i}

$^{i-i}$[*Mill added this note at left after deleting the passage given in the second note below* (96^k).]
^{j}[*Cancelled text:*], and editor of the *Retrospective Review*

Review, or as much of each as seemed of any importance (which was not so arduous a task in 1823 as it would be now), and make notes for him of the articles which I thought he would wish to examine, either on account of their good or their bad qualities. This paper of my father's was the chief cause of the sensation which the *Westminster Review* produced at its first appearance, and is, both in conception and in execution, one of the most striking of all his writings. He began by an analysis of the tendencies of periodical literature in general; pointing out, that it cannot, like books, wait for success, but must succeed immediately, or not at all, and is hence almost certain to profess and inculcate the opinions already held by the public to which it addresses itself, instead of attempting to rectify or improve those opinions. He next, to characterize the position of the *Edinburgh Review* as a political organ, entered into a complete analysis, from the Radical point of view, of the British Constitution. He held up to notice its thoroughly aristocratic character: the nomination of a majority of the House of Commons by a few hundred families; the entire identification of the more independent portion, the county members, with the great landholders; the different classes whom this narrow oligarchy was induced, for convenience, to admit to a share of power; and finally, what he called its two props, the Church, and the legal profession. He pointed out the natural tendency of an aristocratic body of this composition, to group itself into two parties, one of them in possession of the executive, the other endeavouring to supplant the former and become the predominant section by the aid of public opinion, without any essential sacrifice of the aristocratical predominance. He described the course likely to be pursued, and the political ground occupied, by an aristocratic party in opposition, coquetting with popular principles for the sake of popular support. He shewed how this idea was realized in the conduct of the Whig party, and of the *Edinburgh Review* as its chief literary organ. He described, as their main characteristic, what he termed "seesaw";[*] writing alternately on both sides of every question which touched the power or interest of the governing classes; sometimes in different articles, sometimes in different parts of the same article: and illustrated his position by copious specimens. So formidable an attack on the Whig party and policy had never before been made; nor had so great a blow been ever struck, in this country, for radicalism: nor was there, I believe, any living person capable of writing that article, except my father.*

In the meantime the nascent review had formed a junction with another project, of a purely literary periodical, to be edited by Mr. Henry Southern, afterwards a diplomatist, then a literary man by profession. The two editors agreed to unite their

[*Ibid., I (Jan., 1824), pp. 218–20, and 223ff.]
*The continuation of this article in the second number of the review was written by me under my father's eye, and (except as practice in composition, in which respect it was, to me, more useful than anything else I ever wrote) was of little or no value. ["Periodical Literature: *Edinburgh Review*," ibid., I (Apr., 1824), 505–41; reprinted at pp. 291–325 below.]

to unite their corps and to divide the editorship, Bowring taking the political, Southern the literary department. Southern's review was to have been published by Longman, and that firm, though part proprietors of the *Edinburgh*, were willing to be the publishers of the new journal. But when all the arrangements had been made, and the prospectuses sent out, the Longmans saw my father's attack on the *Edinburgh* and drew back. My father was now appealed to for his interest with his own publisher, Baldwin; to whom he spoke accordingly with a successful result. And so, amidst anything but hope on my father's part, and that of most of those who afterwards aided in carrying on the review, the first number made its appearance.

That number was an agreeable surprise to us. The average of the articles was of much better quality than had been expected. The literary and artistic department had rested chiefly on Mr. Bingham, a barrister on the Western Circuit (subsequently a Police Magistrate) who had been some years a frequenter of Bentham, was a friend of both the Austins, and had adopted with great ardour Mr. Bentham's philosophical opinions. Partly I believe from accident, there were in the first number no less than five articles by Bingham; and we were extremely pleased with them. I well remember the mixed feeling I myself had about the Review; the joy at finding, what we did not at all expect, that it was sufficiently good to be capable of being made a creditable organ of those who held the opinions it professed; and extreme vexation, since it was so good in the main, at what we thought the blemishes of it: there were two articles in particular which I individually took extremely to heart.[*] When however, in addition to our favourable opinion of it on the whole, we found that it had an extraordinarily large sale for a first number, and that the appearance of a Radical Review of pretensions equal to those of the established organs of parties had excited considerable attention, there was no room for hesitation, and we all became eager in exerting ourselves as much as possible to strengthen and improve it.

[k] My father continued to write occasionally. First the *Quarterly Review* received its exposure, as a sequel to that of the *Edinburgh*: of his other contributions the

---

[*Mill is most likely referring to William Johnson Fox, "Men and Things in 1823," and Thomas Southwood Smith, "Education," *Westminster Review*, I (Jan., 1824), 1–18, and 43–79.]

[k][*Cancelled text:*] My first contribution to the review was in the second number. In my father's article the detailed shew-up of the *Edinburgh Review* had been left unfinished, and he wished me to attempt to finish it. I had one qualification for doing so, a strong indignation at many of the articles which I had read in my course of reading and notetaking for my father's use. But I can now see that there was something ridiculous in this pretension of a youth, not yet eighteen, to sit in judgment on some of the principal writers of the time. The thing however was written and published, and what seems strange, many if not most of its readers did not suspect that the continuation was by a different hand from the first article. So incapable are most people, when the *fond* of the thoughts is the same, and the manner imitated, to distinguish the borrowed from the original. The article of course was not, and could not be, anything more than a theme written on the ideas which had been instilled into me by my teachers. The

corps, and divide the editorship, Bowring taking the political, Southern the literary department. Southern's review was to have been published by Longman, and that firm, though part proprietors of the *Edinburgh*, were willing to be the publishers of the new journal. But when all the arrangements had been made, and the prospectuses sent out, the Longmans saw my father's attack on the *Edinburgh*, and drew back. My father was now appealed to for his interest with his own publisher, Baldwin, which was exerted with a successful result. And so, in April 1824, amidst anything but hope on my father's part, and that of most of those who afterwards aided in carrying on the review, the first number made its appearance.[*]

That number was an agreeable surprise to most of us. The average of the articles was of much better quality than had been expected. The literary and artistic department had rested chiefly on Mr. Bingham, a barrister (subsequently a Police Magistrate) who had been for some years a frequenter of Bentham, was a friend of both the Austins, and had adopted with great ardour Mr. Bentham's philosophical opinions. Partly from accident, there were in the first number as many as five articles by Bingham;[†] and we were extremely pleased with them. I well remember the mixed feeling I myself had about the Review; the joy at finding, what we did not at all expect, that it was sufficiently good to be capable of being made a creditable organ of those who held the opinions it professed; and extreme vexation, since it was so good on the whole, at what we thought the blemishes of it. When, however, in addition to our generally favourable opinion of it, we learned that it had an extraordinarily large sale for a first number, and found that the appearance of a Radical review, with pretensions equal to those of the established organs of parties, had excited much attention, there could be no room for hesitation, and we all became eager in doing everything we could to strengthen and improve it.

My father continued to write occasional articles. The *Quarterly Review* received its exposure, as a sequel to that of the *Edinburgh*. Of his other contributions, the

[*The first number of the *Westminster* appeared about 24 Jan., 1824 (see *Examiner*, 25 Jan.; *Morning Chronicle*, 27 Jan.); Mill may have made the mistake because his first article appeared in the number for April.]

[†Peregrine Bingham, "Moore's *Fables for the Holy Alliance*," *Westminster Review*, I (Jan., 1824), 18–27; "Travels of Duncan, Flint, and Faux, in the United States," pp. 101–20; "Vocal Music," pp. 120–41; "M. Cottu and Special Juries," pp. 146–71; and "Periodical Literature: *Quarterly Review*, No. LVIII," pp. 250–68.]

stile was bony and wiry, very unlike the writing of a young person, but with a certain degree of vigour and of polish. No one but myself wrote any part of it, or even corrected it; but it went through an incredible amount of elaboration from myself under my father's eye, he giving it back to me repeatedly part by part to be amended, or cancelled and begun again, either to throw in more and better thoughts or to bring them out more pointedly in the expression. I suppose there are few sentences that were not rewritten with great pains and effort nearly a dozen times. The article was worth little enough in any

most important were an attack on Southey's *Book of the Church* in the fifth number, and a political article in the twelfth. Mr. Austin only contributed one article, but one of great merit, an argument against primogeniture, in reply to an article then lately published in the *Edinburgh Review* by McCulloch. Grote also was a contributor only once, all the time he could spare being already taken up by his *History of Greece*, which he had commenced at my father's instigation. The article he wrote was on his own subject, and was a very complete exposure and castigation of Mitford. Bingham and Charles Austin continued to write for some numbers; Fonblanque was a frequent contributor from the third number. Of my particular set, Ellis was a regular writer up to the ninth number and about the time when he left off others of the set began: Eyton Tooke, Graham, and Roebuck. I myself was the most frequent writer of all, having contributed from the second number to the eighteenth, thirteen articles [1]; chiefly[1] reviews of books on history and political economy, or discussions on special political topics, as corn laws, game laws, law of libel. Occasional articles of merit came in from other

---

other respect but to me it was very valuable as practice in composition. [*paragraph*] In the same number of the review there were also articles by Charles Austin and Ellis; and gradually most of the writing radicals of my father's or my acquaintance were brought into play. [*In the second sentence, for* "wished me to attempt to" *Mill first wrote (and HTM underscored, and pencilled* "wished" *opposite):* "determined to see whether I could". At the beginning of the fourth sentence, for "But I can now see" (apparently supplied by HTM) Mill first wrote and HTM underscored: "In every other respect the subject was so much above me". In the same sentence, "youth, not yet eighteen," was interlined in pencil by HTM and written over in ink by Mill to replace the original word "boy". In the sixth sentence HTM deleted "and the manner imitated," and "the borrowed from the original"; and she marked the seventh sentence with a line in the margin. In the ninth she deleted "or even corrected it;" and then marked the whole of it and the next sentence ("No one but myself . . . dozen times.") with a line in the margin; apparently as an alternate to them or as a trial replacement for some part of them, Mill wrote and deleted at left:* It was wholly my own writing, but was written under my father's eye. *See the second note above (94[1-1]).*]

[1-1][*Earlier version:*] . These were on subjects much more level than my first with my acquirements and experience:

most important were an attack on Southey's *Book of the Church*, in the fifth number, and a political article in the twelfth.[*] Mr. Austin only contributed one paper, but one of great merit, an argument against primogeniture, in reply to an article then lately published in the *Edinburgh Review* by McCulloch.[†] Grote also was a contributor only once; all the time he could spare being already taken up with his *History of Greece*.[‡] The article he wrote was on his own subject, and was a very complete exposure and castigation of Mitford. Bingham and Charles Austin continued to write for some time; Fonblanque was a frequent contributor from the third number. Of my particular associates, Ellis was a regular writer up to the ninth number; and about the time when he left off, others of the set began; Eyton Tooke, Graham, and Roebuck. I was myself the most frequent writer of all, having contributed, from the second number to the eighteenth, thirteen articles; reviews of books on history and political economy, or discussions on special political topics, as corn laws, game laws, law of libel.[§] Occasional articles of merit came in from

[*James Mill, "Periodical Literature: *Quarterly Review*," *Westminster Review*, II (Oct., 1824), 463–503; "Robert Southey's *Book of the Church*," *ibid.*, III (Jan., 1825), 167–212, reviewing Southey's *The Book of the Church*, 2 vols. (London: Murray, 1824); and "State of the Nation," *Westminster Review*, VI (Oct., 1826), 249–78.]

[†John Austin, "Disposition of Property by Will—Primogeniture," *ibid.*, II (Oct., 1824), 503–53; a reply to John Ramsay McCulloch, "Disposal of Property by Will," *Edinburgh Review*, XL (July, 1824), 350–75.]

[‡George Grote, "Institutions of Ancient Greece," *Westminster Review*, V (Apr., 1826), 269–331; his work culminated in *A History of Greece*, 12 vols. (London: Murray, 1846–56).]

[§"Periodical Literature: *Edinburgh Review*" (cited above); "War Expenditure," II (July, 1824), 27–48, in *Essays on Economics and Society, Collected Works* [*CW*], Vols. IV–V (Toronto: University of Toronto Press, 1967), Vol. IV, pp. 1–22; "Brodie's *History of the British Empire*," II (Oct., 1824), 346–402, reviewing George Brodie, *A History of the British Empire, from the Accession of Charles I, to the Restoration*, 4 vols. (Edinburgh: Bell and Bradfute; London: Longman, 1822); "*Quarterly Review* on Political Economy," III (Jan., 1825), 213–32, in *CW*, Vol. IV, pp. 23–43; "Law of Libel and Liberty of the Press," III (Apr., 1825), 285–321; "The Corn Laws," III, 394–420, in *CW*, Vol. IV, pp. 45–70; "The Game Laws," V (Jan., 1826), 1–22; "The Silk Trade," V, 136–49, in *CW*, Vol. IV, pp. 125–39; "The French Revolution," V (Apr., 1826), 385–98, reviewing François Auguste Alexis Mignet, *Histoire de la révolution française depuis 1789 jusqu'en 1814*, 2 vols. (Paris: Didot, 1824), translated as *History of the French Revolution from 1789 to 1814*, 2 vols. (London: Hunt and Clarke, 1826); "Modern French Historical Works—Age of Chivalry," VI (July, 1826), 62–103, reviewing Jacques Antoine Dulaure, *Histoire physique, civile et morale de Paris depuis les premiers temps historiques jusqu'à nos jours*, 2nd ed., 10 vols. (Paris: Guillaume, 1823–4), and the first 9 vols. of Jean Charles Léonard Simonde de Sismondi, *Histoire des Français*, 31 vols. (Paris: Treuttel and Würtz, 1821–44); "New Corn Law," VII (Jan., 1827), 169–86, in *CW*, Vol. IV, pp. 141–59; "Whately's *Elements of Logic*," IX (Jan., 1828), 137–72, reviewing Richard Whately, *Elements of Logic*, 2nd. ed. (London: Mawman, 1827), in *Essays on Philosophy and the Classics, CW*, Vol. XI (Toronto: University of Toronto Press, 1978), pp. 1–35; and "Scott's *Life of Napoleon*," IX (Apr., 1828), 251–313, reviewing Walter Scott, *The Life of Napoleon Buonaparte*, 9 vols. (Edinburgh: Cadell; London: Longman, Rees, Orme, Brown, and Green, 1827).]

*m*acquaintances*m* of my father's, and in time, of mine; and some of Dr. Bowring's writers turned out well. On the whole however, the conduct of the review was never satisfactory to any of the persons strongly interested in its principles with whom I came in contact. Hardly ever did a number come out which did not contain several things extremely offensive to us, either in point of opinions, or of taste, or by mere want of ability. The unfavourable judgments passed by my father, Grote, the two Austins and others, were reechoed with exaggeration by us younger people: and as our *n*youthful zeal*n* rendered us by no means backward in making complaints, we led the two editors a sad life. From my remembrance of what I then was, I have no manner of doubt that we were at least as often wrong as right; and I am very certain that if the review had been carried on according to our notions (I mean those of the juniors) it would have been no better, perhaps not even so good as it was. But it is a fact of some interest in the history of English radicalism, that its chief philosophical organ was from the beginning extremely unsatisfactory to those, whose opinions it was supposed especially to represent.

In the meanwhile however the review made a considerable noise in the world, and gave a recognized *status* in the arena of opinion and discussion to the Benthamic type of radicalism quite out of proportion to the *o* number of its adherents and to the personal merits or abilities, at that time, of any but some three or four of them. It was a time, as is well known, of rapidly rising Liberalism. When the fears and animosities accompanying the war against France were ended, and people had room in their minds for thoughts on home politics, the tide began to set towards reform. The renewed oppression of the Continent by the old reigning families, the countenance given by the English Government to the conspiracy against liberty called the Holy Alliance, and the enormous weight of the national debt and of taxation occasioned by so long and costly a war, rendered the government and the parliament very unpopular: and Radicalism, under the lead of the Burdetts and Cobbetts, had assumed a character which seriously alarmed the Administration. Their apprehensions had scarcely been temporarily allayed by the Six Acts, when the trial of Queen Caroline excited a still wider and deeper feeling of hatred: and though the outward signs of this hatred passed away with its exciting cause, there arose on all sides a spirit which had never shewn itself before, of opposition to abuses in detail. Mr. Hume's persevering scrutiny of the public expenditure, forcing the House of Commons to a division on every objectionable item in the estimates, had begun to tell with great force on public opinion. Political economy had asserted itself with great vigour in public affairs, by the Petition of the Merchants of London for Free Trade drawn up in 1820 by Mr. Tooke and

---

m-m[*Earlier version:*] friends
n-n[*Earlier version:*] zeal (I am speaking of the juniors and especially myself)
o[*Cancelled text:*] very small

other acquaintances of my father's, and in time, of mine; and some of Mr. Bowring's writers turned out well. On the whole, however, the conduct of the Review was never satisfactory to any of the persons strongly interested in its principles, with whom I came in contact. Hardly ever did a number come out without containing several things extremely offensive to us, either in point of opinion, of taste, or by mere want of ability. The unfavorable judgments passed by my father, Grote, the two Austins, and others, were reechoed with exaggeration by us younger people; and as our youthful zeal rendered us by no means backward in making complaints, we led the two editors a sad life. From my knowledge of what I then was, I have no doubt that we were at least as often wrong as right; and I am very certain that if the Review had been carried on according to our notions (I mean those of the juniors) it would have been no better, perhaps not even so good as it was. But it is worth noting as a fact in the history of Benthamism, that the periodical organ, by which it was best known, was from the first extremely unsatisfactory to those, whose opinions on all subjects it was supposed specially to represent.

Meanwhile, however, the Review made considerable noise in the world, and gave a recognized *status*, in the arena of opinion and discussion, to the Benthamic type of radicalism, out of all proportion to the number of its adherents, and to the personal merits and abilities, at that time, of most of those who could be reckoned among them. It was a time, as is known, of rapidly rising Liberalism. When the fears and animosities accompanying the war with France had been brought to an end, and people had once more a place in their thoughts for home politics, the tide began to set towards reform. The renewed oppression of the Continent by the old reigning families, the countenance apparently given by the English Government to the conspiracy against liberty called the Holy Alliance, and the enormous weight of the national debt and taxation occasioned by so long and costly a war, rendered the government and parliament very unpopular. Radicalism, under the leadership of the Burdetts and Cobbetts, had assumed a character and importance which seriously alarmed the Administration: and their alarm had scarcely been temporarily assuaged by the celebrated Six Acts,[*] when the trial of Queen Caroline roused a still wider and deeper feeling of hatred. Though the outward signs of this hatred passed away with its exciting cause, there arose on all sides a spirit which had never shewn itself before, of opposition to abuses in detail. Mr. Hume's persevering scrutiny of the public expenditure, forcing the House of Commons to a division on every objectionable item in the estimates, had begun to tell with great force on public opinion, and had extorted many minor retrenchments from an unwilling Administration. Political economy had asserted itself with great vigour in public affairs, by the Petition of the Merchants of London for Free Trade, drawn up in

[*60 George III & 1 George IV, c. 1, c. 2, c. 4, c. 6, c. 8, and c. 9 (all Dec., 1819); for the titles, see the Bibliographic Index, p. 744 below.]

presented by Mr. Baring; and by the noble exertions of Ricardo during the few years of his parliamentary life. His writings, following up the impulse given by the Bullion Controversy, and followed up in their turn by the expositions and comments of my father and McCulloch, had drawn general attention to the subject, making converts, partially at least, even among the ministers; and Huskisson, backed by Canning, had already commenced that gradual demolition of the protective system, which one of their colleagues virtually completed in 1846. *P*Mr. Peel*P*, then Home Secretary, was entering, though very cautiously, into the untrodden and peculiarly Benthamic path of Law Reform. At this time, when Liberalism seemed to be becoming the tone of the times, when improvement of institutions was preached from the highest places, and a complete change of the constitution of parliament was loudly demanded from the lowest, it is not wonderful that attention was roused by the regular appearance in controversy of what seemed a new school of writers, claiming to be the philosophers and legislators of this new tendency. The air of strong persuasion *q* with which they wrote, while scarcely any one else seemed to have as strong faith in as definite a creed; the boldness with which they ran full tilt against the very front of both the existing political parties; their uncompromising profession of opposition to many of the most generally received opinions; the talent and verve of at least my father's articles, and the appearance of a corps behind him sufficient to carry on a review: and finally the fact that the review sold and was read, *r* made the so called Bentham school in philosophy and politics fill a greater place in the public mind than it ever had done before or has done since. As I was in the head quarters of it, knew of what it was composed, and as one of the most active of its very small number might even say, *quorum pars magna fui*, it belongs to me more than to most others, to give some account of it.

This supposed school, then, *s*had no other existence than was constituted by*s* the fact that my father's writings and conversation drew a certain number of young men round him who had already imbibed, or who imbibed from him, a greater or less portion of his very decided political and philosophical opinions. The notion that Bentham was surrounded by a band of disciples who received their opinions from his lips, is a fable which my father exposed in his *Fragment on Mackintosh* and is ridiculous to all who knew anything of Mr. Bentham's habits of life and

---

p-p[*Earlier version:*] That same colleague [*marked with a line in the margin by HTM, who interlined* "*Sir R. Peel*"]

q[*Cancelled text:*] , amounting to arrogance,

r[*Cancelled text:*] and continued to support itself; these things [*the five words before the semicolon deleted first by HTM*]

s-s[*Earlier version:*] never had any unity, concert, or any existence at all beyond

1820 by Mr. Tooke and presented by Mr. Alexander Baring;[*] and by the noble exertions of Ricardo during the few years of his parliamentary life. His writings, following up the impulse given by the Bullion controversy, and followed up in their turn by the expositions and comments of my father and McCulloch (whose writings in the *Edinburgh Review* during those years were most valuable), had drawn general attention to the subject, making at least partial converts in the Cabinet itself; and Huskisson, supported by Canning, had commenced that gradual demolition of the protective system, which one of their colleagues virtually completed in 1846, though the last vestiges were only swept away by Mr. Gladstone in 1860. Mr. Peel, then Home Secretary, was entering cautiously into the untrodden and peculiarly Benthamic path of Law Reform. At this period, when Liberalism seemed to be becoming the tone of the time, when improvement of institutions was preached from the highest places, and a complete change of the constitution of Parliament was loudly demanded in the lowest, it is not strange that attention should have been roused by the regular appearance in controversy of what seemed a new school of writers, claiming to be the legislators and theorists of this new tendency. The air of strong conviction with which they wrote, when scarcely any one else seemed to have an equally strong faith in as definite a creed; the boldness with which they tilted against the very front of both the existing political parties; their uncompromising profession of opposition to many of the generally received opinions, and the suspicion they lay under of holding others still more heterodox than they professed; the talent and verve of at least my father's articles, and the appearance of a corps behind him sufficient to carry on a review; and finally, the fact that the review was bought and read, made the so called Bentham school in philosophy and politics fill a greater place in the public mind than it had held before, or has ever again held since other equally earnest schools of thought have arisen in England. As I was in the head quarters of it, knew of what it was composed, and as one of the most active of its very small number, might say without undue assumption, *quorum pars magna fui*,[†] it belongs to me more than to most others to give some account of it.

This supposed school, then, had no other existence than what was constituted by the fact, that my father's writings and conversation drew round him a certain number of young men who had already imbibed, or who imbibed from him, a greater or smaller portion of his very decided political and philosophical opinions. The notion that Bentham was surrounded by a band of disciples who received their opinions from his lips, is a fable to which my father did justice in his *Fragment on Mackintosh*,[‡] and which, to all who knew Mr. Bentham's habits of life and

[*See *Journals of the House of Commons*, Vol. LXXV, p. 410 (6 July, 1820).]
[†*Aeneid*, Vol. I, p. 294 (Bk. II, l. 6).]
[‡See James Mill, *A Fragment on Mackintosh* (London: Baldwin and Cradock, 1835), pp. 122–5; the work is an attack on James Mackintosh, *Dissertation on the Progress of Ethical Philosophy* (Edinburgh: n.p., 1830).]

manner of conversation. But what was [1] false of Bentham was to some extent true of my father: He *was* sought for the vigour and instructiveness of his conversation and did use it largely as an instrument for the diffusion of his opinions. I have never met with any man who could do such ample justice to his opinions in colloquial discussion. His perfect command of all his great mental resources, the terseness and expressiveness of his language and the intellectual force and moral earnestness of his delivery, made him one of the most striking of all argumentative conversers; while he was also full of anecdote, a hearty laugher, and when with people whom he liked, a most lively and amusing companion. It was not solely or even chiefly in diffusing his mere intellectual convictions, that his power shewed itself; it was still more through the influence of a quality of which I have only since learnt to appreciate the extreme rarity, especially in England: that exalted public spirit, and regard above all things to the good of the whole, which warmed into life and activity every germ of similar virtue that existed in the minds he came in contact with; the desire he made them feel for his approbation, the shame at his disapproval; the moral support which his conversation, and his very existence, gave to those who were aiming at the same objects, through their respect for his judgment; and the encouragement he afforded to the faint hearted or desponding among them by the firm confidence which (though the reverse of sanguine as to the results to be expected in any one particular case) he always felt in the power of reason, the general progress of improvement, and the good which could always be done by judicious effort.

My father's opinions were those which gave the distinguishing character to what was then regarded as the Benthamic or utilitarian tone of speculation. His opinions fell singly scattered from him in all directions but they flowed from him in a continued stream principally through three channels. One was through me, the only mind directly formed by his instructions, and through whom considerable influence was exercised over various young men who became in their turn propagandists orally and by writing. A second was through some of the contemporaries at Cambridge of Charles Austin, who, either initiated by him or through the general mental impulse which he gave, had adopted opinions much allied to those of my father, and some of the more considerable of whom afterwards sought my father's acquaintance and frequented his house: among these may be mentioned Strutt, since known as a radical member of parliament, and the present Sir John Romilly, with whose father, Sir Samuel, my father had of old been on terms of friendship. The third channel was that of a younger generation of Cambridge undergraduates [u] contemporary not with Austin but with Eyton Tooke, drawn to him by affinity of opinions, and by him introduced to my father: the most notable of these was Charles Buller. Various other persons individually received and trans-

[1] [*Cancelled text:*] ludicrously

manner of conversation, is simply ridiculous. The influence which Bentham exercised was by his writings. Through them he has produced, and is producing, effects on the condition of mankind, wider and deeper, no doubt, than any which can be attributed to my father. He is a much greater name in history. But my father exercised a far greater personal ascendancy. He *was* sought for the vigour and instructiveness of his conversation, and did use it largely as an instrument for the diffusion of his opinions. I have never known any man who could do such ample justice to his best thoughts in colloquial discussion. His perfect command over his great mental resources, the terseness and expressiveness of his language, and the moral earnestness as well as intellectual force of his delivery, made him one of the most striking of all argumentative conversers: and he was full of anecdote, a hearty laugher, and when with people whom he liked, a most lively and amusing companion. It was not solely, or even chiefly, in diffusing his merely intellectual convictions, that his power shewed itself: it was still more through the influence of a quality, of which I have only since learnt to appreciate the extreme rarity: that exalted public spirit and regard above all things to the good of the whole, which warmed into life and activity every germ of similar virtue that existed in the minds he came in contact with: the desire he made them feel for his approbation, the shame at his disapproval; the moral support which his conversation and his very existence gave to those who were aiming at the same objects, and the encouragement he afforded to the faint-hearted or desponding among them, by the firm confidence which (though the reverse of sanguine as to the results to be expected in any one particular case) he always felt in the power of reason, the general progress of improvement, and the good which individuals could do by judicious effort.

It was my father's opinions which gave the distinguishing character to the Benthamic or utilitarian propagandism of that time. They fell singly scattered from him in many directions, but they flowed from him in a continued stream principally in three channels. One was through me, the only mind directly formed by his instructions, and through whom considerable influence was exercised over various young men who became, in their turn, propagandists. A second was through some of the Cambridge cotemporaries of Charles Austin, who, either initiated by him or under the general mental impulse which he gave, had adopted many opinions allied to those of my father, and some of the more considerable of whom afterwards sought my father's acquaintance and frequented his house. Among these may be mentioned Strutt, afterwards Lord Belper, and the present Lord Romilly, with whose eminent father, Sir Samuel, my father had of old been on terms of friendship. The third channel was that of a younger generation of Cambridge undergraduates, cotemporary not with Austin but with Eyton Tooke, who were drawn to that estimable person by affinity of opinions, and introduced by him to my father: the most notable of these was Charles Buller. Various other persons individually received and transmitted a considerable amount of my father's

---

^a[*Cancelled text:*] (each Cambridge generation lasting just three years)

mitted a considerable amount of my father's influence: for example, Black (as before mentioned) and Fonblanque: but most of these we accounted only partial allies; Fonblanque for instance was widely divergent from us on many important points. But indeed there was by no means complete unanimity among any portion of us nor had any of us *^v* adopted implicitly all my father's opinions. For example, the paragraph in his Essay on Government, *^w* in which he maintained that women might without compromising good government be excluded from the suffrage because their interest is the same with that of men—from this I and all those who formed my chosen associates, most positively dissented. It is due to my father to say that he always denied having intended to say that women *should* be excluded, any more than men under the age of forty, concerning whom he maintained in the very next paragraph an exactly similar thesis. He was, as he truly said, not discussing whether the suffrage ought to be restricted to less than all, but (assuming that it is to be restricted) what is the utmost limit of restriction which does not involve a sacrifice of the securities for good government. But I thought then, as I have always thought since, that even the opinion which he acknowledged was as great an error as any of those which his Essay combated; that the interest of women is exactly as much and no more involved in that of men, as the interest of subjects is involved in that of kings, and that every reason which exists for giving the suffrage to anybody, imperatively requires that it be given to women. This was also the general opinion of the younger proselytes: and it is pleasant to be able to say that Bentham on this most important point, was wholly with us.

But though none of us, probably, agreed in everything with my father, yet as I said before, his opinions gave the general character and colour to the band, or set, or whatever else it may be called; which was not characterized by Benthamism, in any sense which has relation to Bentham as a guide, but rather by a combination of Bentham's point of view with that of the modern political economy, and with that of the Hartleian metaphysics. Malthus's population principle was quite as much a banner, and point of union among us, as any opinion specially belonging to Bentham. This doctrine, originally brought forward as an argument against the indefinite improvability of human affairs, we took up with great zeal in the contrary sense, as indicating the sole means of realizing that improvability, by securing full employment at high wages to the whole labouring population through

---

^v[*Cancelled text:*] , even myself,
^w[*Cancelled text:*] the worst in point of tendency he ever wrote, that

influence: for example, Black (as before mentioned) and Fonblanque: most of these however we accounted only partial allies; Fonblanque, for instance, was always divergent from us on many important points. But indeed there was by no means complete unanimity among any portion of us, nor had any of us adopted implicitly all my father's opinions. For example, although his Essay on Government[*] was regarded probably by all of us as a masterpiece of political wisdom, our adhesion by no means extended to the paragraph of it, in which he maintains that women may consistently with good government, be excluded from the suffrage, because their interest is the same with that of men. From this doctrine, I, and all those who formed my chosen associates, most positively dissented. It is due to my father to say that he denied having intended to affirm that women *should* be excluded, any more than men under the age of forty, concerning whom he maintained, in the very next paragraph, an exactly similar thesis. He was, as he truly said, not discussing whether the suffrage had better be restricted, but only (assuming that it is to be restricted) what is the utmost limit of restriction, which does not necessarily involve a sacrifice of the securities for good government.[†] But I thought then, as I have always thought since, that the opinion which he acknowledged, no less than that which he disclaimed, is as great an error as any of those against which the Essay was directed; that the interest of women is included in that of men exactly as much and no more, as the interest of subjects is included in that of kings; and that every reason which exists for giving the suffrage to anybody, demands that it should not be withheld from women. This was also the general opinion of the younger proselytes; and it is pleasant to be able to say that Mr. Bentham, on this important point, was wholly on our side.

But though none of us, probably, agreed in every respect with my father, his opinions, as I said before, were the principal element which gave its colour and character to the little group of young men who were the first propagators of what was afterwards called "philosophic radicalism." Their mode of thinking was not characterized by Benthamism in any sense which has relation to Bentham as a chief or guide, but rather by a combination of Bentham's point of view with that of the modern political economy, and with the Hartleian metaphysics. Malthus's population principle[‡] was quite as much a banner, and point of union among us, as any opinion specially belonging to Bentham. This great doctrine, originally brought forward as an argument against the indefinite improvability of human affairs, we took up with ardent zeal in the contrary sense, as indicating the sole means of realizing that improvability by securing full employment at high wages to the whole labouring population through a voluntary restriction of the increase of their

[*In the supplement to the *Encyclopaedia Britannica*, 1820; reprinted in *Essays* (London: printed Innes, n.d. [1825]). In the latter, the paragraph referred to is on p. 21.]

[†See, e.g., James Mill, "Government," title of §VI, "In the Representative System Alone the Securities for Good Government Are to Be Found" (p. 16).]

[‡See Thomas Robert Malthus, *An Essay on the Principle of Population* (London: Johnson, 1798).]

a restriction of the increase of their numbers. The other leading characteristics of our creed, as mainly derived from my father, may be stated as follows.

In politics, *an almost unbounded* confidence in the efficacy of two things: representative government, and complete freedom of discussion. So great was my father's reliance on the influence of reason upon the minds of mankind, whenever it was allowed to reach them, that he felt as if all would be gained if the people could be universally taught to read, if all sorts of opinions were allowed to be preached to them by word and writing, and if through the suffrage they could nominate a legislature to give effect to their opinion when formed. He thought that if the legislature no longer represented a class interest it would mostly aim at the general interest with adequate wisdom, as the people would be sufficiently under the guidance of educated intelligence to make in general a good choice of representatives and to leave a liberal discretion to those whom they had chosen. Accordingly aristocratic government, the government of the Few in any of its shapes, was the object of his sternest disapprobation, and a democratic suffrage the principal article of his political creed, not on the ground of "rights of man," "liberty" or any of the phrases more or less significant by which up to that time democracy had usually been defended, but as the most essential of "securities for good government." In this too he held fast only to what he deemed essentials: he was comparatively indifferent to monarchical or republican forms, far more so than Bentham, to whom a king, in the character of "corrupter general," appeared necessarily very noxious. Next to aristocracy, an established church, or corporation of priests, was the object of his strongest detestation; though he disliked no clergyman personally who did not deserve it, and was on terms of sincere friendship with several. I have already spoken of his rejection of both Christianity and Deism, both of which he regarded not only as false but as morally mischievous. In ethics his standard was utility or the general happiness; and his moral feelings were energetic and rigid on all points which he deemed important to human well being, while he was supremely indifferent to all those doctrines of the common morality which he thought had no foundation but in asceticism and priestcraft. He looked forward for example to a great increase of freedom in the relations between the sexes; and he anticipated as one of the beneficial effects of that freedom, that the imagination would no longer dwell upon the physical relation and its adjuncts, and swell this into one of the principal objects of life, which perversion of the imagination and feelings he regarded as one of the deepest seated and most pervading evils in the human mind *y* . In psychology his fun-

---

x–x[*Earlier version:*] a most exaggerated
y[*Cancelled text:*] , particularly in the modern form of it [*deleted first by HTM*]

numbers. The other leading characteristics of the creed, which we held in common with my father, may be stated as follows:

In politics, an almost unbounded confidence in the efficacy of two things: representative government, and complete freedom of discussion. So complete was my father's reliance on the influence of reason over the minds of mankind, whenever it is allowed to reach them, that he felt as if all would be gained if the whole population were taught to read, if all sorts of opinions were allowed to be addressed to them by word and in writing, and if by means of the suffrage they could nominate a legislature to give effect to the opinions they adopted. He thought that when the legislature no longer represented a class interest, it would aim at the general interest, honestly and with adequate wisdom; since the people would be sufficiently under the guidance of educated intelligence, to make in general a good choice of persons to represent them, and having done so, to leave to those whom they had chosen a liberal discretion. Accordingly aristocratic rule, the government of the Few in any of its shapes, being in his eyes the only thing which stood between mankind and an administration of their affairs by the best wisdom to be found among them, was the object of his sternest disapprobation, and a democratic suffrage the principal article of his political creed, not on the ground of liberty, Rights of Man, or any of the phrases, more or less significant, by which, up to that time, democracy had usually been defended, but as the most essential of "securities for good government." In this, too, he held fast only to what he deemed essentials; he was comparatively indifferent to monarchical or republican forms— far more so than Bentham, to whom a king, in the character of "corrupter-general,"[*] appeared necessarily very noxious. Next to aristocracy, an established church, or corporation of priests, as being by position the great depravers of religion, and interested in opposing the progress of the human mind, was the object of his greatest detestation; though he disliked no clergyman personally who did not deserve it, and was on terms of sincere friendship with several. In ethics, his moral feelings were energetic and rigid on all points which he deemed important to human well being, while he was supremely indifferent in opinion (though his indifference did not shew itself in personal conduct) to all those doctrines of the common morality, which he thought had no foundation but in asceticism and priestcraft. He looked forward, for example, to a considerable increase of freedom in the relations between the sexes, though without pretending to define exactly what would be, or ought to be, the precise conditions of that freedom. This opinion was connected in him with no sensuality either of a theoretical or of a practical kind. He anticipated, on the contrary, as one of the beneficial effects of increased freedom, that the imagination would no longer dwell upon the physical relation and its adjuncts, and swell this into one of the principal objects of life; a perversion of the imagination and feelings, which he regarded as one of the deepest seated and most pervading evils in the human mind. In psychology, his fundamental doctrine

[*See Bentham, *Plan of Parliamentary Reform* (London: Hunter, 1817), p. xxii.]

damental doctrine was the formation of all human character by circumstances, through the principle of association, and the consequent unlimited possibility of improving the moral and intellectual attributes of mankind by education. Of all his doctrines none was more valuable than this, or needs more to be insisted on: unfortunately there is none which is more in contradiction to the prevailing tendency of speculation both in his time and at present.

These various opinions were seized on with youthful fanaticism by the little knot of young men of whom I was one; and we threw into them a sectarian spirit from which, in intention at least, my father was free. What we (or rather a phantom substituted in the place of us) were by a ridiculous exaggeration called by others, namely a "school," we for some time really hoped and aspired to be. In the first two or three years of the *Westminster Review*, the French *philosophes* of the eighteenth century were the example we sought to imitate and we hoped to accomplish as much as they did. I even proposed to myself to chronicle our doings, from that early period, on the model of Grimm's *Correspondence*,[*] and actually for some time kept a journal with that intention. Charles Austin had a project of a Philosophical Dictionary, suggested by Voltaire's, in which everything was to be spoken out freely; I entered eagerly into it and sent three or four articles (the only ones, I believe, ever written) towards a commencement of it. My particular companions and Charles Austin's however did not much associate with one another: an attempt we made to bring them together periodically at his lodgings was soon given up, and he and I did not long travel in the same direction. The head quarters of me and my *z*associates*z* was not my father's house but Grote's, which I very much frequented. Every new proselyte and every one whom I hoped to make a proselyte, I took there to be indoctrinated. Grote's opinions were at that time very much the same both in their strong and their weak points as those of us younger people, but he was of course very much more formed, and incomparably the superior of all of us in knowledge and present abilities.

All this however is properly the outside of our existence; or at least the intellectual part alone, and only one side of that. In attempting to penetrate inward, and to shew what we really were as human beings, I shall at present speak only of myself, of whom alone I can speak from sufficient knowledge.

I conceive, then, that for these two or three years of my life the description commonly given of a Benthamite, as a dry, hard logical machine, was as much applicable to me, as it can well be applicable to any one just entering into life; to whom the common objects of desire must in general have at least the attraction of

---

[*Friedrich Melchior von Grimm, *Correspondance littéraire, philosophique et critique*, ed. J. Michaud, F. Chéron, *et al.*, 17 vols. (Paris: Longchamps, *et al.*, 1812–14).]

z–z[*Earlier version:*] friends

was the formation of all human character by circumstances, through the universal Principle of Association, and the consequent unlimited possibility of improving the moral and intellectual condition of mankind by education. Of all his doctrines none was more important than this, or needs more to be insisted on: unfortunately there is none which is more contradictory to the prevailing tendencies of speculation, both in his time and since.

These various opinions were seized on with youthful fanaticism by the little knot of young men of whom I was one: and we put into them a sectarian spirit, from which, in intention at least, my father was wholly free. What we (or rather a phantom substituted in the place of us) were sometimes, by a ridiculous exaggeration, called by others, namely a "school," some of us for a time really hoped and aspired to be. The French *philosophes* of the eighteenth century were the example we sought to imitate, and we hoped to accomplish no less results. No one of the set went to so great excesses in this boyish ambition as I did; which might be shewn by many particulars, were it not an useless waste of space and time.

All this, however, is properly only the outside of our existence; or at least, the intellectual part alone, and no more than one side of that. In attempting to penetrate inward, and give any indication of what we were as human beings, I must be understood as speaking only of myself, of whom alone I can speak from sufficient knowledge; and I do not believe that the picture would suit any of my companions without many and great modifications.

I conceive that the description so often given of a Benthamite, as a mere reasoning machine, though extremely inapplicable to most of those who have been designated by that title, was during two or three years of my life not altogether untrue of me. It was perhaps as applicable to me as it can well be to any one just entering into life, to whom the common objects of desire must in general have at least the attraction of novelty. There is nothing very extraordinary in this fact: no youth of the age I then was, can be expected to be more than one thing, and this was

novelty. *a*Ambition*a* and desire of distinction I had in abundance; and zeal for what
I thought the good of mankind was my most predominant sentiment, mixing with
and colouring all other wishes and feelings. But this zeal, at that period of my life,
was as yet little else than zeal for speculative opinions. It did not proceed from
genuine benevolence or sympathy with mankind; though those qualities held *b*their
due*b* place in my moral creed. Nor was it connected with any high enthusiasm for
ideal nobleness. Yet of this feeling I was imaginatively very susceptible; but there
was at that time an intermission in me of what is its natural source, poetical culture;
while there was a superabundance of the discipline antagonistic to it, that of mere
logic and analysis. Add to this that the tendency of my father's teachings was to the
undervaluing of feeling. It was not that he was himself hard hearted or insensible; I
believe it was rather from the contrary quality; he thought that feeling could take
care of itself, and that there was sure to be enough of it if actions were properly
cared about. Offended by the frequency with which in ethical and philosophical
controversy, feeling is made the ultimate reason and justification of conduct,
instead of being itself called on for a justification; while in practice, actions, the
effect of which on human happiness is mischievous, are defended as being
required by feeling, and the character of a person of feeling receives a credit for
desert which he thought only due to actions, he had a real impatience of the
attributing praise to feeling or of any but the most sparing reference to it either in
the estimation of persons or in the discussion of things. In addition to the influence
which this characteristic in him had on me and others, we found all our principal
opinions constantly attacked on the ground of feeling. Utility was denounced as
cold calculation; political economy as hard hearted; anti-population doctrines as
repulsive to the natural feelings of mankind. We retorted by the word "sentimentality" which along with "declamation" and "vague generalities" served us as common terms of opprobrium. Although we were generally right as against those who
were opposed to us, the effect was that the cultivation of feeling (except, indeed,
the feelings of public and private duty) had very little place in the thoughts of most
of us, myself in particular. *c* All we thought of was to alter people's opinions; to
make them believe according to evidence, and know what was their real interest,
which if they knew, they would by "public opinion" enforce a regard to it from one
another. While fully recognizing the superior excellence of unselfish benevolence
and love of justice, we expected the regeneration of mankind not from any direct
action on those sentiments but from educated intellect enlightening the selfish
feelings. Although this last is an important means of improvement in the hands of
those who are themselves impelled by nobler principles of action, I do not believe

---

a–a[*Earlier version:*] As for myself most of those common objects were quite sufficiently attractive to
me. Money, indeed, having no expensive tastes, I only wished for as a means of independence and of
promoting public objects; but ambition [*all but the last word marked for deletion by HTM*]
   b–b[*Earlier version:*] a high
   c[*Cancelled text:*] And therefore we had at this time no idea of real culture. In our schemes for

the thing I happened to be. Ambition and desire of distinction, I had in abundance; and zeal for what I thought the good of mankind was my strongest sentiment, mixing with and colouring all others. But my zeal was as yet little else, at that period of my life, than zeal for speculative opinions. It had not its root in genuine benevolence, or sympathy with mankind; though these qualities held their due place in my ethical standard. Nor was it connected with any high enthusiasm for ideal nobleness. Yet of this feeling I was imaginatively very susceptible; but there was at that time an intermission of its natural aliment, poetical culture, while there was a superabundance of the discipline antagonistic to it, that of mere logic and analysis. Add to this that, as already mentioned, my father's teachings tended to the undervaluing of feeling. It was not that he was himself cold-hearted or insensible; I believe it was rather from the contrary quality; he thought that feeling could take care of itself; that there was sure to be enough of it if actions were properly cared about. Offended by the frequency with which, in ethical and philosophical controversy, feeling is made the ultimate reason and justification of conduct, instead of being itself called on for a justification, while, in practice, actions, the effect of which on human happiness is mischievous, are defended as being required by feeling, and the character of a person of feeling obtains a credit for desert, which he thought only due to actions, he had a real impatience of attributing praise to feeling, or of any but the most sparing reference to it either in the estimation of persons or in the discussion of things. In addition to the influence which this characteristic in him had on me and others, we found all the opinions to which we attached most importance, constantly attacked on the ground of feeling. Utility was denounced as cold calculation; political economy as hard-hearted; anti-population doctrines as repulsive to the natural feelings of mankind. We retorted by the word "sentimentality," which, along with "declamation" and "vague generalities," served us as common terms of opprobrium. Although we were generally in the right, as against those who were opposed to us, the effect was that the cultivation of feeling (except the feelings of public and private duty) was not in much esteem among us, and had very little place in the thoughts of most of us, myself in particular. What we principally thought of, was to alter people's opinions; to make them believe according to evidence, and know what was their real interest, which when they once knew, they would, we thought, by the instrument of opinion, enforce a regard to it upon one another. While fully recognizing the superior excellence of unselfish benevolence and love of justice, we did not expect the regeneration of mankind from any direct action on those sentiments, but from the effect of educated intellect, enlightening the selfish feelings. Although this last is prodigiously important as a means of improvement in the hands of those who are themselves impelled by nobler principles of action, I

---

improving human affairs we overlooked human beings. [*This passage and most of the next sentence in the text are marked with a line in the margin by HTM, who pencilled half a dozen words, now erased and illegible, at left.*]

that any one person known to me now relies mainly upon it for the regeneration of human life.

From this neglect both in theory and practice of the cultivation of feeling, naturally resulted among other things an undervaluing of poetry, and of Imagination generally as an element of human nature. It is or was part of the common notion of Benthamites that they are enemies to poetry: this was partly true of Bentham; he used to say "all poetry is misrepresentation": but in the sense in which he meant it, the same thing might be said of all impressive speech, of all representation or inculcation more oratorical in its character than a sum in arithmetic. An article of Bingham's in the first number of the *Westminster*, in which he gave as an explanation of some things which he disliked in Moore that "Mr. Moore *is* a poet and therefore is *not* a reasoner," did a good deal to attach the notion of hating poetry to the writers in the review. But the truth was that (to speak only of poetry in the narrowest, the purely literary sense) many of us, and Bingham himself, were great readers of poetry, and as for myself, who at that time was not so, the correct statement would be (and the same thing might be said of my father) that I was speculatively indifferent to poetry, not hostile to it. I disliked any sentiments in poetry which I should have disliked in prose, and that included a great deal. And I was wholly blind to its place in human culture as *^da^d* means of educating the feelings. But *^e* I was always personally very susceptible to some kinds of it. In the most sectarian period of my Benthamism I happened to look into Pope's *Essay on Man*, and though every opinion in it was contrary to mine I well remember how much I was struck with the poem. I do not know whether at that time poetical composition of any higher type than eloquent discussion in verse, would have produced a similar effect on me.

This however was a mere passing state. Long before I outgrew the narrowness of my *taught* opinions, or enlarged in any considerable degree the basis of my intellectual creed, I had obtained in the natural course of my mental progress, poetic culture of the most valuable kind, by means of reverential admiration for the lives and characters of heroic persons; especially the heroes of philosophy. The same animating effect which so many remarkable persons have left on record that they had experienced from Plutarch's *Lives*, was produced on me by Plato's pictures of Socrates, and by some modern biographies, but chiefly by Condorcet's *Life of Turgot*; a book well calculated to excite the best sort of enthusiasm, since it contains one of the noblest and wisest of lives, described by one of the noblest and wisest of men. The heroic virtue of these admirable representatives of the opinions with which I sympathized, deeply affected me, and I perpetually recurred to them as others do to a favourite poet, when needing to be carried up into the more elevated regions of feeling and thought. I may observe by the way that this book

---

^{d–d}[*Earlier version:*] the great
^e[*Cancelled text:*] its effect on me when I did read it was always great.

do not believe that any one of the survivors of the Benthamites or Utilitarians of that day, now relies mainly upon it for the general amendment of human conduct.

From this neglect both in theory and in practice of the cultivation of feeling, naturally resulted among other things an undervaluing of poetry, and of Imagination generally as an element of human nature. It is, or was, part of the popular notion of Benthamites, that they are enemies of poetry: this was partly true of Bentham himself; he used to say that "all poetry is misrepresentation":[*] but, in the sense in which he said it, the same might have been said of all impressive speech; of all representation or inculcation more oratorical in its character than a sum in arithmetic. An article of Bingham's in the first number of the *Westminster Review*, in which he offered as an explanation of something which he disliked in Moore, that "Mr. Moore *is* a poet, and therefore is *not* a reasoner,"[†] did a good deal to attach the notion of hating poetry to the writers in the Review. But the truth was that many of us were great readers of poetry; Bingham himself had been a writer of it, while as regards me (and the same thing might be said of my father) the correct statement would be not that I disliked poetry, but that I was theoretically indifferent to it. I disliked any sentiments in poetry which I should have disliked in prose; and that included a great deal. And I was wholly blind to its place in human culture, as a means of educating the feelings. But I was always personally very susceptible to some kinds of it. In the most sectarian period of my Benthamism I happened to look into Pope's *Essay on Man*,[‡] and though every opinion in it was contrary to mine, I well remember how powerfully it acted on my imagination. Perhaps at that time poetical composition of any higher type than eloquent discussion in verse, might not have produced a similar effect on me: at all events I seldom gave it an opportunity. This, however, was a mere passing state. Long before I had enlarged in any considerable degree, the basis of my intellectual creed, I had obtained in the natural course of my mental progress, poetic culture of the most valuable kind, by means of reverential admiration for the lives and characters of heroic persons; especially the heroes of philosophy. The same inspiring effect which so many of the benefactors of mankind have left on record that they had experienced from Plutarch's *Lives*, was produced on me by Plato's pictures of Socrates, and by some modern biographies, above all by Condorcet's *Life of Turgot*; a book well calculated to rouse the best sort of enthusiasm, since it contains one of the wisest and noblest of lives, delineated by one of the wisest and noblest of men. The heroic virtue of these glorious representatives of the opinions with which I sympathized, deeply affected me, and I perpetually recurred to them as others do to a favorite poet, when needing to be carried up into the more elevated regions of feeling and thought. I may observe by the way that this book cured me of

[*Cf. *The Rationale of Reward* (London: Hunt, 1825), p. 206 (Bk. III, Chap. i).]

[†Bingham, "Moore's *Fables for the Holy Alliance*," p. 21.]

[‡In *Works*, ed. Joseph Warton, *et al.*, 10 vols. (London: Priestley, 1822–25), Vol. III, pp. 1–160.]

also cured me of my sectarian tastes. The two or three pages beginning "Il regardait toute secte comme nuisible," and explaining why Turgot always kept himself distinct from the Encyclopedists, sank deeply into me *f* . I left off designating myself and others as Utilitarians, or by the pronoun "we," or any other collective denomination: I ceased to *afficher* sectarianism: but my real, inward sectarianism I got rid of later and much more gradually.

About the end of 1824 or beginning of 1825, Mr. Bentham, having lately got back his papers on Evidence from M. Dumont (whose *Traité de Preuves Judiciaires*, grounded on them, was then first completed and published), resolved to have them printed in the original and bethought himself of me as capable of preparing them for the press; in the same manner as his *Book of Fallacies* had been recently edited by Bingham. I undertook this task, and it occupied nearly all my leisure for about a year, exclusive of the time afterwards spent in seeing the five large volumes through the press. Bentham had begun the book three times, at considerable intervals, each time in a different manner, and each time without reference to the preceding: two of the three times he had gone over nearly the whole field. These three masses of papers I had to condense into a single treatise: adopting the one last written as the groundwork, and inserting into it as much of the two others as it had not completely superseded. I had also to unroll such of Bentham's involved and parenthetical sentences as seemed to me to overpass in obscurity what readers were likely to take the pains to understand. Further, it was Bentham's particular desire that I should endeavour to supply, from myself, any *lacunæ* which he had left: and I read at his instance Phillipps on the Law of Evidence and part of Starkie[*] and wrote *g*comments*g* on those few among the defective points in the English rules of evidence which had escaped Bentham's notice. I added replies to the objections which had been made to some of Bentham's doctrines by reviewers of the *Traité des Preuves*, and a few supplementary remarks on some of the more abstract parts of the subject, such as the theory of improbability and impossibility. The tone of these additions, or at least of the controversial part of them, was *h*more assuming than became*h* one so young and inexperienced as I was: but indeed I had never contemplated coming forward in my own person; and, as an anonymous editor of Bentham, I fell into the tone of my author, not thinking that

[*Samuel March Phillipps, *A Treatise on the Law of Evidence* (London: Butterworth, 1814), and Thomas Starkie, *A Practical Treatise of the Law of Evidence*, 3 vols. (London: Clarke, 1824). Mill also cites in the *Rationale*, and so presumably read, Samuel Bealey Harrison, *Evidence: Forming a Title of the Code of Legal Proceedings* (London: Butterworth, 1825).]

f[*Cancelled text:*] ; and, combined with passing remarks now and then thrown out by my father, made me feel how injurious it is to the progress of new opinions for the holders of them to band themselves together as a sect, call themselves by a name, and encourage the world to hold them jointly and severally responsible for one another

g-g[*Earlier version:*] such comments as I could

h-h[*Earlier version:*] assuming, even to arrogance, and unbecoming

my sectarian follies. The two or three pages beginning "Il regardait toute secte comme nuisible,"[*] and explaining why Turgot always kept himself perfectly distinct from the Encyclopedists, sank deeply into my mind. I left off designating myself and others as Utilitarians, and by the pronoun "we," or any other collective designation, I ceased to *afficher* sectarianism. My real inward sectarianism I did not get rid of till later, and much more gradually.

About the end of 1824, or beginning of 1825, Mr. Bentham, having lately got back his papers on Evidence from M. Dumont (whose *Traité des Preuves Judiciaires*, grounded on them, was then first completed and published), resolved to have them printed in the original, and bethought himself of me as capable of preparing them for the press; in the same manner as his *Book of Fallacies* had been recently edited by Bingham.[†] I gladly undertook this task, and it occupied nearly all my leisure for about a year, exclusive of the time afterwards spent in seeing the five large volumes through the press.[‡] Mr. Bentham had begun this treatise three times, at considerable intervals, each time in a different manner, and each time without reference to the preceding: two of the three times he had gone over nearly the whole subject. These three masses of manuscript it was my business to condense into a single treatise; adopting the one last written as the groundwork, and incorporating with it as much of the two others as it had not completely superseded. I had also to unroll such of Bentham's involved and parenthetical sentences, as seemed to overpass by their complexity the measure of what readers were likely to take the pains to understand. It was further Mr. Bentham's particular desire that I should, from myself, endeavour to supply any *lacunæ* which he had left; and at his instance I read, for this purpose, the most authoritative treatises on the English Law of Evidence, and commented on a few of the objectionable points of the English rules, which had escaped Bentham's notice. I also replied to the objections which had been made to some of his doctrines, by reviewers of Dumont's book,[§] and added a few supplementary remarks on some of the more abstract parts of the subject, such as the theory of improbability and impossibility.[¶] The controversial part of these editorial additions was written in a more assuming tone, than became one so young and inexperienced as I was: but indeed I had never contemplated coming forward in my own person; and, as an anonymous editor of Bentham, I fell into the tone of my author, not thinking it

[*Marie Jean Antoine Nicolas Caritat de Condorcet, *Vie de monsieur Turgot* (London: n.p., 1786), pp. 28–9.]

[†*The Book of Fallacies; from the Unfinished Papers of Jeremy Bentham*, ed. Peregrine Bingham (London: Hunt, 1824).]

[‡Bentham, *Rationale of Judicial Evidence*, ed. J. S. Mill, 5 vols. (London: Hunt and Clarke, 1827).]

[§*Rationale*, Vol. V, pp. 58n–9n (Bk. IX, Pt. III, Chap. iii, §2); pp. 313–25 (Bk. IX, Pt. IV, Chap. v, §2); pp. 345–9 (Bk. IX, Pt. IV, Chap. v, §4); and pp. 352n–4n (Bk. IX, Pt. V, Chap. i). Mill was replying to Thomas Denman, "Law of Evidence: Criminal Procedure: Publicity," *Edinburgh Review*, XL (Mar., 1824), 169–207, a review of Dumont's *Traité*.]

[¶*Rationale*, Vol. I, pp. 137n–8n (Bk. I, Chap. vii).]

tone unsuitable to him or to the subject however it might be so to me. My name as editor was put to the book after it was printed, at Bentham's positive desire, which I in vain attempted to persuade him to forego.

The time occupied in this editorial work was extremely well employed for my own improvement. The *Rationale of Judicial Evidence* is one of the richest in matter of all Bentham's writings. The theory of evidence being itself one of the most important of his subjects, and ramifying into most of the others, the book contains a great proportion of all his best thoughts: while, among more special things, it comprises the most elaborate exposure of the vices of English law which he ever made, including not the law of evidence only, but by way of illustrative episode, the whole procedure or practice of the courts of justice. The direct knowledge, therefore, which I obtained from the book and which was imprinted on me much more thoroughly than it could have been by mere reading, was itself no inconsiderable acquisition. But this *ⁱoccupationⁱ* also did for me what might seem less to be expected: it gave a great start to my powers of composition. Everything which I wrote after this editorial work was markedly superior to anything I had written before it. *ʲ* Bentham's later style as is well known, was heavy and cumbersome, from the excess of a good quality, the love of precision, which made him introduce clause within clause into the heart of every sentence, that the reader might take into his mind all the qualifications simultaneously with the main proposition: and the habit grew on him until his sentences became, to those not accustomed to them, most laborious reading. But his earlier stile, that of the *Fragment on Government, Plan of a Judicial Establishment,* &c., is a model of liveliness and ease combined with fulness of matter scarcely ever surpassed: and of this earlier stile there were many striking specimens in the Manuscripts on Evidence, all of which I endeavoured to preserve. So long a course of this admirable writing had a great effect on my own; and I increased that effect by the assiduous reading of other styles, both French and English, which combined ease with force, such as Fielding, Goldsmith, Pascal, Voltaire, *ᵏand Courierᵏ*. Through these influences my writing lost the jejuneness of my early compositions: the bones and cartilages began to clothe themselves with flesh and the stile became, at times, lively and almost light.

This improvement was first shewn in a new field. Mr. Marshall, of Leeds, father of the present generation of Marshalls, an earnest parliamentary reformer, and a man of large fortune of which he made a liberal use, had been much struck with

---

ⁱ⁻ⁱ[Earlier versions:] day's work [*altered to read:*] year's work

ʲ[Cancelled text:] This was the effect of the familiarity I gained with Bentham's style as a writer.

ᵏ⁻ᵏ[Earlier version:] Courier (whom as a writer my father placed almost at the head of modern literature) and others

unsuitable to him or to the subject, however it might be so to me. My name as editor was put to the book after it was printed, at Mr. Bentham's positive desire, which I in vain attempted to persuade him to forego.[*]

The time occupied in this editorial work was extremely well employed in respect to my own improvement. The *Rationale of Judicial Evidence* is one of the richest in matter of all Bentham's productions. The theory of evidence being in itself one of the most important of his subjects, and ramifying into most of the others, the book contains, very fully developed, a great proportion of all his best thoughts: while, among more special things, it comprises the most elaborate exposure of the vices and defects of English law, as it then was, which is to be found in his works; not confined to the law of evidence, but including, by way of illustrative episode, the entire procedure or practice of Westminster Hall. The direct knowledge, therefore, which I obtained from the book, and which was imprinted upon me much more thoroughly than it could have been by mere reading, was itself no small acquisition. But this occupation did for me what might seem less to be expected; it gave a great start to my powers of composition. Everything which I wrote subsequently to this editorial employment, was markedly superior to anything that I had written before it. Bentham's later style, as the world knows, was heavy and cumbersome, from the excess of a good quality, the love of precision, which made him introduce clause within clause into the heart of every sentence, that the reader might receive into his mind all the modifications and qualifications simultaneously with the main proposition: and the habit grew on him until his sentences became, to those not accustomed to them, most laborious reading. But his earlier style, that of the *Fragment on Government, Plan of a Judicial Establishment*,[†] &c., is a model of liveliness and ease combined with fulness of matter, scarcely ever surpassed: and of this earlier style there were many striking specimens in the manuscripts on Evidence, all of which I endeavoured to preserve. So long a course of this admirable writing had a considerable effect upon my own; and I added to it by the assiduous reading of other writers, both French and English, who combined, in a remarkable degree, ease with force, such as Goldsmith, Fielding, Pascal, Voltaire, and Courier. Through these influences my writing lost the jejuneness of my early compositions; the bones and cartilages began to clothe themselves with flesh, and the style became, at times, lively and almost light.

This improvement was first exhibited in a new field. Mr. Marshall, of Leeds, father of the present generation of Marshalls, the same who was brought into Parliament for Yorkshire when the representation forfeited by Grampound was transferred to it[‡]—an earnest parliamentary reformer, and a man of large fortune,

[*See *Earlier Letters* [*EL*], *CW*, Vols. XII–XIII (Toronto: University of Toronto Press, 1963), Vol. XII, pp. 18–19.]

[†*A Fragment on Government* (London: Payne, 1776); and *Draught of a New Plan for the Organisation of the Judicial Establishment in France* (London: McCreery, 1790).]

[‡See 1 & 2 George IV, c. 47 (8 June, 1821).]

Bentham's *Book of Fallacies*: and the thought occurred to him that it would be useful to publish annually the Parliamentary Debates, not in chronological order as in *Hansard*, but classified according to subjects, and accompanied by a commentary pointing out the fallacies of the speakers. With this intention he very naturally addressed himself to the editor of *The Book of Fallacies*; and Bingham, with the assistance of Charles Austin, undertook the editorship. The work was called *Parliamentary History and Review.* Its sale was not sufficient to keep it in existence, and it only lasted three years *l* . It excited however some attention among parliamentary and political people. The best strength of the party was put forth in it; and its execution did them much more credit than that of the *Westminster* had ever done. Bingham and Charles Austin wrote much in it; so did Strutt, Romilly and some other *m*liberal lawyers*m*. My father wrote one very able article; the elder Austin another. Coulson wrote one of great merit. I myself was selected to lead off the first number by an article on the principal topic of the session (1825), the Catholic Association and the Catholic disabilities. *n* In the second number I wrote an elaborate essay on the Commercial Crisis of 1825 and the Currency Debates. In the third I wrote two articles, one on a minor subject, the other on the Reciprocity principle in commerce, a propos of a celebrated diplomatic correspondence between Canning and Gallatin *o* . These articles were no longer

---

l[*Cancelled text:*] ; in the third of which the Review appeared without any History

m-m[*Earlier version:*] of the legal friends of the editors

n[*Cancelled text:*] This article was much complimented in the *Edinburgh Review* by Brougham (who was attacked in it), although to my annoyance, Bingham had struck out, or obliged me to modify, many of what I thought the most piquant passages, among which I remember was a piece of ridicule (which my father thought successful) of the Duke of York's famous declaration against Catholic Emancipation. [See Brougham, "Parliamentary History," *Edinburgh Review*, XLIV (Sept., 1826), 470. The concluding reference is to the Duke of York's speech, *Parliamentary Debates*, n.s., Vol. 13, cols. 138–42 (25 Apr., 1825).]

o[*Cancelled text:*] respecting the trade with the West India Colonies

of which he made a liberal use, had been much struck with Bentham's *Book of Fallacies*:[*] and the thought had occurred to him that it would be useful to publish annually the Parliamentary Debates, not in the chronological order of *Hansard*, but classified according to subjects, and accompanied by a commentary pointing out the fallacies of the speakers. With this intention, he very naturally addressed himself to the editor of *The Book of Fallacies*; and Bingham, with the assistance of Charles Austin, undertook the editorship. The work was called *Parliamentary History and Review*. Its sale was not sufficient to keep it in existence, and it only lasted three years.[†] It excited, however, some attention among parliamentary and political people. The best strength of the party was put forth in it; and its execution did them much more credit, than that of the *Westminster Review* had ever done. Bingham and Charles Austin wrote much in it;[‡] as did Strutt, Romilly, and several other liberal lawyers. My father wrote one article in his best style; the elder Austin another.[§] Coulson wrote one of great merit.[¶] It fell to my lot to lead off the first number by an article on the principal topic of the session (that of 1825), the Catholic Association and the Catholic disabilities. In the second number I wrote an elaborate Essay on the commercial crisis of 1825 and the Currency Debates. In the third I had two articles, one on a minor subject, the other on the Reciprocity principle in commerce, *à propos* of a celebrated diplomatic correspondence between Canning and Gallatin.[‖] These writings were no longer mere reproduc-

[*In Vol. I of the *Parliamentary History and Review* (see the next note), the first article is "Prefatory Treatise on Political Fallacies," based on Bentham's *Book of Fallacies*, and presumably prepared by Peregrine Bingham.]

[†In all, five vols. appeared: *Parliamentary History and Review; Containing Reports of the Proceedings of the Two Houses of Parliament During the Session of 1825:—6 Geo. IV. With Critical Remarks on the Principal Measures of the Session*, 2 vols. (Vol. I, *Parliamentary History*; Vol. II, *Parliamentary Review*) (London: Longman, Rees, Orme, Brown, and Green, 1826); *Parliamentary History and Review, . . . Session of 1826:—7 Geo. IV . . .* , 2 vols. (Vol. I, *Parliamentary History*; Vol. II, *Parliamentary Review*) (London: Longman, Rees, Orme, Brown, and Green, 1826); and *Parliamentary Review. Session of 1826–27:—7 & 8 Geo. IV* (London: Baldwin and Cradock, 1828).]

[‡Peregrine Bingham, "Combination and Combination Laws," *Parliamentary History and Review, . . . Session of 1825*, Vol. II, pp. 730–5; "County Courts," *ibid.*, *Session of 1826*, Vol. II, pp. 746–54; and "Licensing System;—Public Houses," *ibid.*, Vol. II, pp. 726–36. Only one of Charles Austin's essays has been identified: "Corn Laws," *ibid.*, *Session of 1825*, Vol. II, pp. 690–705.]

[§James Mill, "Summary Review of the Conduct and Measures of the Imperial Parliament," *ibid.*, *Session of 1826*, Vol. II, pp. 772–802; John Austin, "Joint Stock Companies," *ibid.*, *Session of 1825*, Vol. II, pp. 709–27.]

[¶Probably "Game Laws," *ibid.*, *Session of 1825*, Vol. II, pp. 775–82, but possibly "Silk Trade," *ibid.*, *Session of 1826*, Vol. II, pp. 710–18.]

[‖"Ireland," *ibid.*, *Session of 1825*, Vol. II, pp. 603–26; "Paper Currency and Commercial Distress," *ibid.*, *Session of 1826*, Vol. II, pp. 630–62, in *CW*, Vol. IV, pp. 71–123; "Foreign Dependencies—Trade with India," *Parliamentary Review. Session of 1826–27*, pp. 58–68; and "Intercourse between the United States and the British Colonies in the West Indies," *ibid.*, pp. 298–335.]

mere reproductions and applications of what I had been taught; they were original thinking, as far as that name can be applied to old ideas in new forms and relations: and there was a maturity and a well-digested character about them which *p*there had not been in any of my previous performances*p*. In execution therefore they were not at all juvenile; but their subjects have been so much better treated since, that they are entirely superseded, and should remain buried in the same oblivion with my contributions to the first dynasty of the *Westminster Review*.

During several years of this period of my life the social studies of myself and several of my companions assumed a shape which contributed very much to my mental development. The idea occurred to us of carrying on by reading and conversation, a joint study of several of the branches of science which we wished to be masters of. We assembled to the number of a dozen or more. Grote lent a room of his house in Threadneedle Street for the purpose, and his partner Prescott, one of the three original members of the Utilitarian Society, took an active part as one of our number. We met two mornings in every week, from half past eight till ten, at which time most of us were called off to our daily occupations. The subject we began with was Political Economy. We chose some systematic treatise as our text-book; my father's *Elements* being our first choice. One of us (by turns) read aloud a chapter, or some smaller portion, of the book. The discussion was then opened, and any one who had an objection or other remark to make, made it. Our rule was to discuss every point, great or small, which was raised, until all who took part were satisfied with the conclusion they had arrived at; and to follow up every topic of collateral speculation which the chapter or the discussion suggested, never leaving it till we had untied every knot which we found in it. We repeatedly kept up the discussion of some single point for several weeks, thinking intently on it during the intervals of our meetings and contriving solutions of the new difficulties which had risen up in the last morning's discussion. When we had finished in this way my father's *Elements*, we went through in the same manner Ricardo's *Principles of Political Economy*; and afterwards, Bailey's *Dissertation on Value*. These discussions were not only instructive to those who took part in them, but brought out new views of some topics of abstract Political Economy. The theory of International Values *q*which I afterwards published*q* emanated from these conversations, as did also the modified form of Ricardo's theory of Profits, laid down in my essay on Profits and Interest. Those among us from whom, generally speaking, any new

---

p-p[*Earlier version:*] made them fully equal to the best things which had been written on the same class of subjects

q-q[*Earlier version:*] , afterwards explained in one of my published Essays and in my larger treatise, [i.e., *Principles of Political Economy*, 2 vols. (London: Parker, 1848); in *CW*, Vols. II–III (Toronto: University of Toronto Press, 1965).]

tions and applications of the doctrines I had been taught; they were original thinking, as far as that name can be applied to old ideas in new forms and connexions: and I do not exceed the truth in saying that there was a maturity, and a well-digested character about them, which there had not been in any of my previous performances. In execution, therefore, they were not at all juvenile; but their subjects have either gone by, or have been so much better treated since, that they are entirely superseded, and should remain buried in the same oblivion with my contributions to the first dynasty of the *Westminster Review*.

While thus engaged in writing for the public, I did not neglect other modes of self-cultivation. It was at this time that I learnt German; beginning it in the Hamiltonian method,[*] for which purpose I and several of my companions formed a class. For several years from this period, our social studies assumed a shape which contributed very much to my mental progress. The idea occurred to us of carrying on, by reading and conversation, a joint study of several of the branches of science which we wished to be masters of. We assembled to the number of a dozen or more. Mr. Grote lent a room of his house in Threadneedle Street for the purpose, and his partner Prescott, one of the three original members of the Utilitarian Society, made one among us. We met two mornings in every week, from half past eight till ten, at which hour most of us were called off to our daily occupations. Our first subject was Political Economy. We chose some systematic treatise as our text-book; my father's *Elements* being our first choice. One of us read aloud a chapter, or some smaller portion, of the book. The discussion was then opened, and any one who had an objection or other remark to make, made it. Our rule was to discuss thoroughly every point raised, whether great or small, prolonging the discussion until all who took part were satisfied with the conclusion they had individually arrived at; and to follow up every topic of collateral speculation which the chapter or the conversation suggested, never leaving it until we had untied every knot which we found. We repeatedly kept up the discussion of some one point for several weeks, thinking intently on it during the intervals of our meetings, and contriving solutions of the new difficulties which had risen up in the last morning's discussion. When we had finished in this way my father's *Elements*, we went in the same manner through Ricardo's *Principles of Political Economy*, and Bailey's *Dissertation on Value*.[†] These close and vigorous discussions were not only improving in a high degree to those who took part in them, but brought out new views of some topics of abstract Political Economy. The theory of International Values which I afterwards published, emanated from these conversations, as did also the modified form of Ricardo's theory of Profits, laid down in my Essay on Profits and Interest. Those among us with whom new speculations chiefly origi-

---

[*See James Hamilton, *The History, Principles, Practice and Results of the Hamiltonian System, for the Last Twelve Years* (Manchester: Sowler, Courier, and Herald, 1829).]

[†Samuel Bailey, *A Critical Dissertation on the Nature, Measures, and Causes of Value* (London: Hunter, 1825).]

speculations originated, were Ellis, Graham and I: though others gave valuable aid to the discussions, more especially Prescott and Roebuck; the one by his knowledge, the other by his dialectical acuteness. The theories of International Values and of Profits, were excogitated and worked out in about equal proportions by myself and Graham [r], and we at one time had thoughts[r] of publishing these theories, with some other matters, in a volume of Essays bearing our joint names: but when my expositions of them came to be written I found I had so much overestimated my agreement with him, and he differed so much from the most original of the two essays, that on International Values, that I was obliged to consider the theory as now exclusively mine, and it came out as such when it was published many years after. [s] I may mention that [t]among the alterations made by my father in revising his *Elements* for the third edition, several were grounded on criticisms elicited by these Conversations[t], and in particular, he modified his opinions (though not to the extent of our new doctrines) on both the points which I have just touched upon.

When we had enough of political economy we took up the scholastic logic in the same manner, Grote now joining us. Our first text book was Aldrich, but being disgusted with its superficiality, we reprinted by subscription one of the most finished among the many manuals of the school logic, which my father, a great collector of such books, possessed, the *Manuductio ad Logicam* of the Jesuit Du Trieu. After finishing this we took up Whately's *Logic* (then first republished from the *Encyclopedia Metropolitana*) and finally, I think, the "Computatio sive Logica" of Hobbes. These books, gone through in our manner, afforded large scope for original metaphysical speculation: and most of what has been done in the First Book of my *System of Logic* to rationalize and correct the principles and distinctions of the school logic and to improve the theory of the Import of Propositions, had its origin in these discussions; Graham and I as before originating most of the novelties, while Grote and others furnished an excellent tribunal or test. From this time I formed the project of writing a book on Logic, though on a much humbler scale than the one I ultimately executed.

Having done with Logic we launched into analytic psychology: and having chosen Hartley for our text book, we raised Priestley's edition to an extravagant

---

[r-r][*Earlier version:*] . As the discussions proceeded we got out of the depth of the others. Accordingly he and I had at one time a project

[s][*Cancelled text:*] It remains true however that the speculation was partly his, though repudiated by him.

[t-t][*Earlier version:*] my father, in preparing the third edition of the *Elements*, made a considerable number of alterations grounded on criticisms elicited by these Conversations, which had reached him through me

nated, were Ellis, Graham, and I; though others gave valuable aid to the discussions, especially Prescott and Roebuck, the one by his knowledge, the other by his dialectical acuteness. The theories of International Values and of Profits were excogitated and worked out in about equal proportions by myself and Graham: and if our original project had been executed, my *Essays on Some Unsettled Questions of Political Economy*[*] would have been brought out along with some papers of his, under our joint names. But when my exposition came to be written, I found that I had so much overestimated my agreement with him, and he dissented so much from the most original of the two Essays, that on International Values, that I was obliged to consider the theory as now exclusively mine, and it came out as such when published many years later. I may mention that among the alterations which my father made in revising his *Elements* for the third edition, several were grounded on criticisms elicited by these Conversations; and in particular, he modified his opinions (though not to the extent of our new speculations) on both the points to which I have adverted.

When we had enough of political economy, we took up the syllogistic logic in the same manner, Grote now joining us. Our first text book was Aldrich,[†] but being disgusted with its superficiality, we reprinted one of the most finished among the many manuals of the school logic, which my father, a great collector of such books, possessed, the *Manuductio ad Logicam* of the Jesuit Du Trieu.[‡] After finishing this, we took up Whately's *Logic*, then first republished from the *Encyclopædia Metropolitana*,[§] and finally the "Computatio sive Logica" of Hobbes. These books, dealt with in our manner, afforded a wide range for original metaphysical speculation: and most of what has been done in the First Book of my *System of Logic*,[¶] to rationalize and correct the principles and distinctions of the school logicians, and to improve the theory of the Import of Propositions, had its origin in these discussions; Graham and I originating most of the novelties, while Grote and others furnished an excellent tribunal or test. From this time I formed the project of writing a book on Logic, though on a much humbler scale than the one I ultimately executed.

Having done with Logic, we launched into analytic psychology, and having chosen Hartley for our text book, we raised Priestley's edition[‖] to an extravagant

[*London: Parker, 1844 (in *CW*, Vol. IV, pp. 229–339); the first essay Mill refers to is "Of the Laws of Interchange between Nations" (*ibid.*, pp. 232–61), the second is "On Profits, and Interest" (*ibid.*, pp. 290–308).]

[†Henry Aldrich, *Artis logicae compendium* (Oxford: Sheldonian Theatre, 1691).]

[‡Phillipus Du Trieu's *Manuductio* (Oxford: Oxlad and Pocock, 1662) was reprinted (London: McMillan) in 1826.]

[§Richard Whately, *Elements of Logic* (London: Mawman, 1826); reprinted from the *Encyclopaedia Metropolitana*, Vol. I, pp. 193–240.]

[¶*A System of Logic, Ratiocinative and Inductive*, 2 vols. (London: Parker, 1843); *CW*, Vols. VII–VIII (Toronto: University of Toronto Press, 1973).]

[‖David Hartley, *Observations on Man, His Frame, His Duty, and His Expectations*, 2 pts. (Bath: Leake and Frederick; London: Hitch and Austen, 1749); Joseph Priestley, *Hartley's Theory of the Human Mind* (London: Johnson, 1775).]

price by searching through London to furnish each of us with a copy. When we had finished Hartley we suspended our meetings; but my father's *Analysis* being published soon after, we reassembled for the purpose of reading it. With this our exercises ended. I have always dated from these conversations my own real inauguration as an original and independent thinker. It was also through them that I acquired, or very much strengthened, a mental habit to which I attribute all that I have ever done, or ever shall do, in speculation; the habit of never receiving half-solutions of difficulties as complete; never abandoning a puzzle, but returning again and again to it till it was resolved; never allowing obscure corners of a subject to remain unexplored, because they did not seem important; nor ever thinking that I perfectly understood any part of a subject until I understood every part. It became a mental necessity with me, to require for my own complete conviction what Moliere calls "des clartés de tout,"[*] and this qualified me to make things clear to others, which is probably what I have best succeeded in as an expository writer.

Various other studies and exercises were carried on during this period by some of the same people in the same social manner. We formed a class of five or six to learn German in the Hamiltonian manner; and we held weekly evening meetings for a considerable time " to study the theory and practice of elocution. Roebuck here stepped into the first rank; I contributed the rules I had learnt from my father, and among us we thought out a set of principles on the subject.

Our doings from 1825 to 1830 in the way of public speaking filled a considerable place in my life during those years, and had important effects on my developement.

There was for some time in existence a society of Owenites, under the name of the Cooperative Society, which held weekly public discussions. In the early part of 1825 accident brought Roebuck in contact with several of its members and led to his attending one or two of the meetings and taking part in the debate, in opposition to Owenism. Some one of us started the notion of going there in a body and having a general battle, and it fell out that Charles Austin and some of his friends entered into the project. It was carried into effect by concert with the principal members of the Society, themselves nothing loth, as they naturally preferred a controversy with opponents to a tame discussion among their own body. The question of population was proposed as the subject of debate: Charles Austin led the case on our side with a brilliant speech, and the fight was kept up by adjournment for five or six weekly meetings before crowded auditories, including along with the members of the Society and their friends, many hearers and some speakers from the Inns of Court ᵛ . When this debate was ended another was commenced on the general

---

[*Jean Baptiste Poquelin Molière, *Les femmes savantes* (Paris: Promé, 1672), p. 10 (I, iii, 4).]

"[*Cancelled text:*] in chambers which Graham and Roebuck jointly occupied in Gray's Inn (they then and for long after lived together)

ᵛ[*Cancelled text:*] , whose curiosity had been excited through Austin

price by searching through London to furnish each of us with a copy. When we had finished Hartley, we suspended our meetings; but, my father's *Analysis of the Mind* being published soon after, we reassembled for the purpose of reading it. With this our exercises ended. I have always dated from these conversations my own real inauguration as an original and independent thinker. It was also through them that I acquired, or very much strengthened, a mental habit to which I attribute all that I have ever done, or ever shall do, in speculation; that of never accepting half-solutions of difficulties as complete; never abandoning a puzzle, but again and again returning to it until it was cleared up; never allowing obscure corners of a subject to remain unexplored, because they did not appear important; never thinking that I perfectly understood any part of a subject until I understood the whole.

Our doings from 1825 to 1830 in the way of public speaking filled a considerable place in my life during those years, and as they had important effects on my development, something ought to be said of them.

There was for some time in existence a society of Owenites, called the Cooperative Society, which met for weekly public discussions in Chancery Lane. In the early part of 1825, accident brought Roebuck in contact with several of its members, and led to his attending one or two of the meetings and taking part in the debate in opposition to Owenism. Some one of us started the notion of going there in a body and having a general battle: and Charles Austin and some of his friends who did not usually take part in our joint exercises, entered into the project. It was carried out by concert with the principal members of the Society, themselves nothing loth, as they naturally preferred a controversy with opponents to a tame discussion among their own body. The question of population was proposed as the subject of debate: Charles Austin led the case on our side with a brilliant speech, and the fight was kept up by adjournment through five or six weekly meetings before crowded auditories, including along with the members of the Society and their friends, many hearers and some speakers from the Inns of Court.[*] When this debate was ended, another was commenced on the general merits of Owen's

[*Mill's contributions to this debate are represented in "Proaemium of a Speech on Population," "Population," "Population. Reply," and "Second Speech on Population in Answer to Thirlwall" (the first three in typescript copies, Fabian Society; the last in holograph MS, Mill-Taylor Collection).]

merits of Owen's system: and the contest altogether lasted about three months. It was a lutte corps à corps between Owenites and political economists, whom the Owenites regarded as their most inveterate opponents: but it was a perfectly friendly dispute. We who represented political economy had the same objects in view which they had, and took pains to shew it, and the principal champion on their side was a very estimable man with whom I was well acquainted, Mr. William Thompson of Cork, author of a book on the Distribution of Wealth, and of an *Appeal* in behalf of women against the passage relating to them in my father's Essay on Government. I myself spoke oftener than any one else on our side, there being no rule against speaking *w*several times in the same debate*w*. Ellis and Roebuck took a prominent part, and among those from the Inns of Court who joined in the debate I remember Charles Villiers. The other side obtained also, on the population question, very efficient support from without. The well known Gale Jones, then an elderly man, made one of his florid speeches; but the speaker by whom I was most impressed although I dissented from every argument he used and from almost every opinion he expressed, was Thirlwall, the historian, since bishop of St. David's, then a Chancery Barrister unknown, except (as I found on enquiry) by a reputation for eloquence acquired at the Cambridge Union before the era of Austin and Macaulay. His speech was in answer to one of mine. Before he had uttered ten sentences I set him down as the best speaker I had ever heard, and I do not think I have since heard a better. I made an elaborate reply to him at the next meeting,[*] but he was not there to hear it; and except a few words interchanged between us as soon as he had done speaking, of admiration on my side, and politeness on his, we remained strangers to each other until I met him at dinner at M. Guizot's in 1840.

During or about the time when these discussions were going on, McCulloch the political economist who was then temporarily in London to deliver the "Ricardo Lectures" on political economy, threw out the idea one day to my father and me, that a society was wanted in London similar to the Speculative Society of Edinburgh in which Brougham, Horner and others first cultivated public speaking. The discussions at the Cooperative Society had put me in a frame of mind to catch at the suggestion. I liked the kind of thing in itself, and those debates seemed to give cause for being sanguine as to the sort of men who might be brought together for such a purpose in London. McCulloch mentioned the matter to several young men of influence to whom he was then giving private lessons in political economy.

[*See p. 127n.]

w-w[*Earlier version:*] twice: I believe I made two long and elaborate speeches on the first question and either one or two, I believe two, on the second

system:[*] and the contest altogether lasted about three months. It was a *lutte corps-à-corps* between Owenites and political economists, whom the Owenites regarded as their most inveterate opponents: but it was a perfectly friendly dispute. We who represented political economy had the same objects in view as they had, and took pains to shew it; and the principal champion on their side was a very estimable man, with whom I was well acquainted, Mr. William Thompson, of Cork, author of a book on the Distribution of Wealth, and of an *Appeal* in behalf of women against the passage relating to them in my father's Essay on Government.[†] Ellis, Roebuck, and I, took an active part in the debate, and among those from the Inns of Court who joined in it I remember Charles Villiers. The other side obtained also, on the population question, very efficient support from without. The well known Gale Jones, then an elderly man, made one of his florid speeches; but the speaker with whom I was most struck, though I dissented from nearly every word he said, was Thirlwall, the historian, since Bishop of St. David's, then a Chancery barrister, unknown except by a high reputation for eloquence acquired at the Cambridge Union before the era of Austin and Macaulay. His speech was in answer to one of mine. Before he had uttered ten sentences, I set him down as the best speaker I had ever heard, and I have never since heard any one whom I placed above him.

The great interest of these debates predisposed some of those who took part in them, to catch at a suggestion thrown out by McCulloch, the political economist, that a society was wanted in London similar to the Speculative Society at Edinburgh, in which Brougham, Horner and others first cultivated public speaking. Our experience at the Cooperative Society seemed to give cause for being sanguine as to the sort of men who might be brought together in London for such a purpose. McCulloch mentioned the matter to several young men of influence to whom he was then giving private lessons in political economy. Some of these entered

[*As evidence of Mill's participation in this debate we have "First Speech on the Cooperative System," "Intended Speech at the Cooperation Society, never delivered," and "Closing Speech on the Cooperative System" (all holograph MSS, the first and part of the third in the Mill-Taylor Collection; the second and the remainder of the third in Connecticut College).]

[†William Thompson, *An Inquiry into the Principles of the Distribution of Wealth* (London: Longman, Hurst, Rees, Orme, Brown, and Green, 1824), and *Appeal of One Half the Human Race, Women, against the Pretensions of the Other Half, Men, to Retain Them in Political, and Thence in Civil and Domestic Slavery* (London: Longman, Hurst, Rees, Orme, Brown, and Green, 1825).]

Some of these entered warmly into the project, particularly George Villiers (now Earl of Clarendon) ^x . He and his two brothers, Hyde and Charles; Romilly, Charles Austin, and I, with some others, met and completed the plan; a larger meeting was then held to constitute the Society. We determined to meet once a fortnight from November to June, at the Freemason's Tavern, and we had soon a splendid list of members, containing, along with several members of parliament, nearly all the great speakers of the Cambridge Union and of the United Debating Society at Oxford. It is curiously illustrative of the tendencies of the time that our principal difficulty in recruiting for the society was to find a sufficient number of Tory speakers. Almost all whom we could press into the service were Liberals, of different orders and degrees. We had Charles Austin, Macaulay, Thirlwall, Praed, Samuel Wilberforce (now Bishop of Oxford), Lord Howick, Charles Poulett Thomson (afterwards Lord Sydenham), Fonblanque, Edward and Henry Lytton Bulwer, and many others whom I cannot now recollect, who made themselves afterwards more or less conspicuous in public life. Nothing could seem more promising. But when the time for action drew near and it was necessary to fix on a President and to find somebody to open the first debate, none of our celebrities would consent to perform either office. Of the many who were pressed on the subject, the only one who could be prevailed on was a man of whom I knew very little but who had taken high honours at Oxford, and was said to have acquired a great oratorical reputation there; who some time after became a Tory member of parliament. He accordingly was fixed on both for filling the President's chair and for making the first speech. The important day arrived: the benches were crowded: all our great speakers were present to judge of but not to help our efforts. The Oxford orator's speech was an utter failure. This threw a damp on the whole concern: the speakers who followed were few, and none of them did their best ^y . The affair was a complete *fiasco*: and the oratorical celebrities we had counted on went away never to return, giving to me at least a lesson in knowledge of the world. Not one of the notabilities whom I have just enumerated except Praed (and he only once or twice) ever opened their lips in the society. This unexpected break-down completely altered my relation to the project. I had not anticipated taking personally a prominent part, or speaking much or often, especially at first; but I now saw that the success of the scheme depended on the new men, and I put my shoulder to the wheel. I opened the second question and from that time spoke in nearly every debate. The three Villiers' and Romilly stuck to the scheme for some time longer, and took their part well in several debates. Robert Hildyard, a clever and vehement speaker from the Cambridge Union, then a violent radical Benthamite, since a Tory and Protectionist writer in the *Morning Post* and now a silent Derbyite member of Parliament, spoke two or three times well, and some new men, among others Henry Taylor ^z , Vernon Smith and his brother Leveson, occasionally took part. But in the main the debates during the whole season rested on me and

^x[*Cancelled text:*] with whom I was not then acquainted

warmly into the project, particularly George Villiers, afterwards Earl of Clarendon. He and his brothers Hyde and Charles, Romilly, Charles Austin, and I, with some others, met and agreed on a plan. We determined to meet once a fortnight, from November to June, at the Freemason's Tavern, and we had soon a splendid list of members, containing, along with several members of parliament, nearly all the most noted speakers of the Cambridge Union and of the Oxford United Debating Society. It is curiously illustrative of the tendencies of the time that our principal difficulty in recruiting for the Society was to find a sufficient number of Tory speakers. Almost all whom we could press into the service were Liberals, of different orders and degrees. Besides those already named, we had Macaulay, Thirlwall, Praed, Lord Howick, Samuel Wilberforce (afterwards Bishop of Oxford), Charles Poulett Thomson (afterwards Lord Sydenham), Edward and Henry Lytton Bulwer, Fonblanque, and many others whom I cannot now recollect, but who made themselves afterwards more or less conspicuous in public or literary life. Nothing could seem more promising. But when the time for action drew near, and it was necessary to fix on a President, and find somebody to open the first debate, none of our celebrities would consent to perform either office. Of the many who were pressed on the subject, the only one who could be prevailed on was a man of whom I knew very little, but who had taken high honours at Oxford and was said to have acquired a great oratorical reputation there; who some time afterwards became a Tory member of parliament.[*] He accordingly was fixed on, both for filling the President's chair and for making the first speech. The important day arrived; the benches were crowded; all our great speakers were present, to judge of, but not to help our efforts. The Oxford orator's speech was a complete failure. This threw a damp on the whole concern: the speakers who followed were few, and none of them did their best: the affair was a complete *fiasco*; and the oratorical celebrities we had counted on went away never to return, giving to me at least a lesson in knowledge of the world. This unexpected breakdown altered my whole relation to the project. I had not anticipated taking a prominent part, or speaking much or often, particularly at first; but I now saw that the success of the scheme depended on the new men, and I put my shoulder to the wheel. I opened the second question, and from that time spoke in nearly every debate.[†] It was very uphill work for some time. The three Villiers' and Romilly stuck to us for some time longer, but the patience of all the founders of the Society was at last exhausted, except me and Roebuck. In the season following, 1826/27, things

---

[*Donald Maclean.]
[†The second question was debated on 9 Dec., 1825; Mill's speech was "On the Influence of the Aristocracy" (MS, Mill-Taylor Collection). In the first session, Mill spoke in at least eight debates (some of which went on for more than one meeting).]

---

y[*Cancelled text:*] : a short sensible speech by Romilly was the only creditable performance
z[*Cancelled text:*] (with whom I then first became acquainted)

Roebuck: and very uphill work it was in the latter part of it, even the Villiers' and other founders of the society having ceased to attend. In the season following, 1826/27, we had acquired two excellent Tory speakers, Hayward, and Shee (now Serjeant Shee): the radical side was reinforced by Charles Buller, Cockburn, and others of the second generation of Cambridge Benthamites: and with such occasional aid and the two Tories as well as Roebuck and me for regular speakers, almost every debate was a bataille rangée between the philosophic radicals *a* and the Tory lawyers, until our conflicts came to be talked about, and many persons of note and consideration came to hear us. This happened still more in the subsequent seasons, 1828 and 1829, when another set of speakers, of whom hereafter, had joined the society. Some of our debates were really worth hearing; not for oratory, but as good specimens of polemical discussion on the great questions of politics. Radicalism of the type of the *Westminster* and *Parliamentary* Reviews, was then a recognized power in politics and literature: it was the only attempt which had been made to give principles and philosophy to the Liberalism which was growing into importance, while the temporary vogue of political economy had so far encroached upon the ordinary English antipathy to theory, as to give a prestige to any pretension to treat politics scientifically. Now, some of our speeches were really better expositions than could be heard anywhere else, of our principal doctrines: and as the side of existing opinions and institutions was very ably defended by Shee with rhetoric, by Hayward with sophistry, our doctrines were fairly pitted against their opposites. At least our debates were very different from those of common debating societies, for they habitually consisted of the strongest arguments and most philosophic principles which either side was able to produce, thrown often into close and *serré* confutations of one another. For my own part, nothing I ever wrote was more carefully elaborated both in matter and expression than some of those speeches. My delivery was and remained bad; but I could make myself listened to; and I even acquired a certain readiness of extemporary speaking, on questions of pure argument, and could reply offhand, with some effect, to the speech of an opponent: but whenever I had an exposition to make in which from the feelings involved or from the nature of the ideas to be developed, expression seemed important, I always most carefully wrote the speech and committed it to memory, and I did this even with my replies, when an opportunity was afforded by an adjourned debate. Therefore *b*many*b* of my speeches were of some worth as compositions, to be set against a bad and ungraceful manner. I believe that this practice greatly increased my power of effective writing. The habit of composing speeches for delivery gave me not only an ear for smoothness and rhythm but a practical sense for *telling* sentences and an immediate criterion of their telling property, by their effect on a mixed audience.

a[*Cancelled text:*] (as we thought ourselves)
b-b[*Earlier version:*] most

began to mend. We had acquired two excellent Tory speakers, Hayward, and Shee (afterwards Sergeant Shee): the radical side was reinforced by Charles Buller, Cockburn, and others of the second generation of Cambridge Benthamites; and with their and other occasional aid, and the two Tories as well as Roebuck and me for regular speakers,[*] almost every debate was a *bataille rangée* between the "philosophic radicals" and the Tory lawyers; until our conflicts were talked about, and several persons of note and consideration came to hear us. This happened still more in the subsequent seasons, 1828 and 1829, when the Coleridgians, in the persons of Maurice and Sterling, made their appearance in the Society as a second Liberal and even Radical party, on totally different grounds from Benthamism and vehemently opposed to it; bringing into these discussions the general doctrines and modes of thought of the European reaction against the philosophy of the eighteenth century; and adding a third and very important belligerent party to our contests, which were now no bad exponent of the movement of opinion among the most cultivated part of the new generation.[†] Our debates were very different from those of common debating societies, for they habitually consisted of the strongest arguments and most philosophic principles which either side was able to produce, thrown often into close and *serré* confutations of one another. The practice was necessarily very useful to us, and eminently so to me. I never, indeed, acquired real fluency, and had always a bad and ungraceful delivery; but I could make myself listened to: and as I always wrote my speeches when, from the feelings involved, or the nature of the ideas to be developed, expression seemed important, I greatly increased my power of effective writing; acquiring not only an ear for smoothness and rhythm, but a practical sense for *telling* sentences, and an immediate criterion of their telling property, by their effect on a mixed audience.

[*Surviving records indicate only that Mill spoke in three debates during the session of 1826–27.]

[†In the session of 1827–28, Mill spoke in at least four debates (Sterling spoke for the first time in the debate of 1 Feb., 1828, on the Church of England); in that of 1828–29, Mill spoke in at least three; in that of 1829–30, perhaps only in one (he withdrew from the Society before 19 Feb., 1830); he spoke once more, however, on 18 Feb., 1831, on the progress of the French Revolution, in what must have been a special visit.]

The Society and the preparation for it, together with the preparation for the morning conversations ^c which were going on simultaneously, occupied the greater part of my leisure; and made me feel it personally a relief when, in the spring of 1828, I ceased to write for the *Westminster Review*. The review had fallen into difficulties. Though the sale of the first number had been encouraging, the permanent sale was never, I believe, sufficient to pay the expenses on the scale on which the review was carried on. Those expenses had been considerably, but not sufficiently, reduced. One of the editors, Southern, had resigned; and some of the writers, including my father and me, who had been paid like other contributors for our earlier articles, had latterly written without payment. Nevertheless the original funds contributed by Bentham were nearly or quite exhausted, and if the review was to be continued some new arrangement for carrying it on became indispensable. My father and I had several conferences with Bowring on the subject. We were willing to do our utmost for maintaining the review as an organ of our opinions, but not under Bowring's editorship: while the impossibility of its any longer supporting a paid editor, afforded a ground on which, without affront to him, we could propose to dispense with his services. We and some of our friends were prepared to carry on the review as unpaid writers, either finding among ourselves an unpaid editor, or dividing the editorship among us. But while this negociation was proceeding, with Bowring's apparent acquiescence, he was carrying on another, in a different quarter (as it afterwards appeared, with Colonel Perronet Thompson), ^d of which we received the first intimation in a letter from Bowring as editor saying that an arrangement had been made and proposing to us to write for the next number, with promise of payment. We thought the concealment which he had practised on us, while seemingly entering into our own project, an affront; and even had we not thought so, we were indisposed to take any further trouble for the review under his management. Accordingly my father excused himself from writing (though two or three years later he did write one political article, being strongly urged). As for me, I absolutely refused. And thus ended my connexion with the original *Westminster*. The last article which I wrote in it had cost me more time and trouble than any previous; but it was a labour of love, being a defence of the early French revolutionists against the Tory misrepresentations of Sir Walter Scott in his *Life of Napoleon*. For this the number of books which I read, making notes and extracts, even the number which I bought (for in those days there was no ^epublic or subscription^e Library from which books of reference could be taken home), far exceeded the worth of the immediate object; but I had a half formed intention of writing a History of the French Revolution: and though I never executed it, my collections afterwards served Carlyle for a similar purpose.

---

^c[*Cancelled text:*] at Grote's
^d[*Cancelled text:*] of a kind more agreeable to him; and
^{e-e}[*Earlier version:*] institution like the London

The Society, and the preparation for it, together with the preparation for the morning conversations which were going on simultaneously, occupied the greater part of my leisure; and made me feel it a relief when, in the spring of 1828, I ceased to write for the *Westminster*. The Review had fallen into difficulties. Though the sale of the first number had been very encouraging, the permanent sale had never, I believe, been sufficient to pay the expenses, on the scale on which the review was carried on. Those expenses had been considerably, but not sufficiently, reduced. One of the editors, Southern, had resigned; and several of the writers, including my father and me, who had been paid like other contributors for our earlier articles, had latterly written without payment. Nevertheless, the original funds were nearly or quite exhausted, and if the Review was to be continued some new arrangement of its affairs had become indispensable. My father and I had several conferences with Bowring on the subject. We were willing to do our utmost for maintaining the Review as an organ of our opinions, but not under Bowring's editorship: while the impossibility of its any longer supporting a paid editor, afforded a ground on which, without affront to him, we could propose to dispense with his services. We, and some of our friends, were prepared to carry on the Review as unpaid writers, either finding among ourselves an unpaid editor, or sharing the editorship among us. But while this negociation was proceeding, with Bowring's apparent acquiescence, he was carrying on another in a different quarter (with Colonel Perronet Thompson), of which we received the first intimation in a letter from Bowring as editor, informing us merely that an arrangement had been made, and proposing to us to write for the next number, with promise of payment. We did not dispute Bowring's right to bring about, if he could, an arrangement more favorable to himself than the one we had proposed; but we thought the concealment which he had practised towards us, while seemingly entering into our own project, an affront: and even had we not thought so, we were indisposed to expend any more of our time and trouble in attempting to write up the Review under his management. Accordingly my father excused himself from writing; though two or three years later, on great pressure, he did write one more political article.[*] As for me, I positively refused. And thus ended my connexion with the original *Westminster*. The last article which I wrote in it had cost me more labour than any previous; but it was a labour of love, being a defence of the early French Revolutionists against the Tory misrepresentations of Sir Walter Scott, in the introduction to his *Life of Napoleon*. The number of books which I read for this purpose, making notes and extracts—even the number I had to buy (for in those days there was no public or subscription library from which books of reference could be taken home), far exceeded the worth of the immediate object; but I had at that time a half formed intention of writing a History of the French Revolution; and though I never executed it, my collections afterwards were very useful to Carlyle for a similar purpose.[†]

[*"The Ballot," *Westminster Review*, XIII (July, 1830), 1–39.]
[†I.e., Thomas Carlyle, *The French Revolution*, 3 vols. (London: Fraser, 1837).]

For some years after this I wrote very little, and nothing regularly, for publication: and great were the advantages I derived from the intermission. It was of immense importance to me at this period, to be able to digest and mature my thoughts with a view to my own mind only, without any immediate call for giving them out in print. *a* Had I gone on writing it would have much disturbed the important transformation in my opinions and character which took place during these years. The origin of this transformation, or at least the process by which I was prepared for it, can only be explained by turning some distance back.

From the winter of 1821, when I first read Bentham, and especially from the commencement of the *Westminster Review*, I had what might truly be called an object in life; to be a reformer of the world. My conception of happiness was entirely identified with this object: the personal sympathies I wished for were those of fellow labourers in this enterprise; I picked up as many flowers as I could by the way, but as a serious and permanent personal satisfaction to rest upon, my whole reliance was placed on this; and I was accustomed to felicitate myself on the certainty of a happy life which I enjoyed by placing my happiness in something durable and distant, in which some progress might be always making, but which could never be exhausted by complete attainment. This did very well for several years, during which the general improvement going on in the world, and the idea of myself as engaged with others in struggling to promote it *b* , seemed enough to fill up an interesting and animated existence. But the time came when I awakened from this as from a dream. It was in the autumn of 1826. I was *c* in a dull state of nerves, such as everybody is occasionally liable to, unsusceptible to enjoyment or pleasurable excitement: one of those moods in which what is pleasure at other times, becomes *d*insipid and indifferent*d*. In this frame of mind it occurred to me to

---

a[*Cancelled text:*] A passage of Herder on this subject, quoted in Coleridge's *Biographia Literaria*, often occurred to me as applicable to my own case. [See Coleridge, *Biographia Literaria*, 2 vols. in 1 (London: Rest Fenner, 1817), Vol. I, pp. 233–4, quoting Johann Gottfried von Herder, *Briefe, das Studium der Theologie betreffend*, 4 vols. (Frankfurt and Leipzig: n.p., 1790), Vol. II, p. 371.]

CHAPTER V
A Crisis in My Mental History.
One Stage Onward

FOR SOME YEARS after this time I wrote very little, and nothing regularly, for publication: and great were the advantages which I derived from the intermission. It was of no common importance to me, at this period, to be able to digest and mature my thoughts for my own mind only, without any immediate call for giving them out in print. Had I gone on writing, it would have much disturbed the important transformation in my opinions and character, which took place during those years. The origin of this transformation, or at least the process by which I was prepared for it, can only be explained by turning some distance back.

From the winter of 1821, when I first read Bentham, and especially from the commencement of the *Westminster Review*, I had what might truly be called an object in life; to be a reformer of the world. My conception of my own happiness was entirely identified with this object. The personal sympathies I wished for were those of fellow labourers in this enterprise. I endeavoured to pick up as many flowers as I could by the way; but as a serious and permanent personal satisfaction to rest upon, my whole reliance was placed on this: and I was accustomed to felicitate myself on the certainty of a happy life which I enjoyed, through placing my happiness in something durable and distant, in which some progress might be always making, while it could never be exhausted by complete attainment. This did very well for several years, during which the general improvement going on in the world and the idea of myself as engaged with others in struggling to promote it, seemed enough to fill up an interesting and animated existence. But the time came when I awakened from this as from a dream. It was in the autumn of 1826. I was in a dull state of nerves, such as everybody is occasionally liable to; unsusceptible to enjoyment or pleasurable excitement; one of those moods when what is pleasure at other times, becomes insipid or indifferent; the state, I should think, in which converts to Methodism usually are, when smitten by their first "conviction of sin."

---

b[*Cancelled text:*] by spreading enlightened opinions and urging practical reforms
c[*Cancelled text:*] , probably from physical causes (connected perhaps merely with the time of year)
d–d[*Earlier version:*] indifferent or disgusting

put the question distinctly to myself, "Suppose that all your objects in life were realized, that all the changes in institutions and opinions which you are looking forward to, could be completely effected at this very instant; would this be a great joy and happiness to you?" and an irrepressible self-consciousness distinctly answered "No!" At this my heart sank within me; the whole foundation on which my life was constructed fell down. All my happiness was to have been found in the continual pursuit of this end. The end had ceased to charm, and how could there ever again be excitement in the means? I had nothing left to live for.

At first I *hoped* that the cloud would pass away of itself: but it did not. A night's sleep, the sovereign remedy for the smaller vexations of life, had no effect on it. I awoke to a renewed consciousness of the woful fact. I carried it with me into all companies, into all occupations. Hardly anything had power to cause me even a few minutes oblivion of it. *For some months the* cloud seemed to grow thicker and thicker. The lines in Coleridge's poem "Dejection" exactly describe my case:

> A grief without a pang, void, dark and drear
> A drowsy, stifled, unimpassioned grief
> Which finds no natural outlet or relief
> In word, or sigh, or tear.

In vain I sought relief from my favourite books, those memorials of past nobleness and greatness from which I had always hitherto drawn strength and animation. I read them now without feeling, or with the accustomed feeling *minus* all its charm; and I *became persuaded* that my love of mankind and of excellence for their own sake, had worn itself out. I sought no relief by speaking to others of what I felt. If I had loved any one sufficiently to make the confiding to them of my griefs a necessity, I should not have been in the condition I was. I was conscious too that mine was not an interesting or in any way respectable distress. There was nothing in it to attract sympathy. Advice if I had known where to seek it would have been most precious. The words of Macbeth to the physician often recurred to my thoughts. But there was no one on whom I could build the faintest hope of such assistance. My father, to whom I should most naturally have had recourse as an adviser in any practical difficulties, was the last person to whom in such a case as this I looked for help. Everything convinced me that he had no knowledge of any such mental state as I was suffering from, and that even if he could be made to understand it he was not the physician who could heal it. My education, which was wholly his work, had been conducted without any regard to the possibility of its ending in this result; and I saw no use in endeavouring to prove to him that his plans

---

e-e[*Earlier versions:*] cherished a hope [*altered to read:*] clung to a hope
f-f[*Earlier version:*] This state continued for some months without any improvement. The
g-g[*Earlier version:*] said in my own mind,

In this frame of mind it occurred to me to put the question directly to myself, "Suppose that all your objects in life were realized; that all the changes in institutions and opinions which you are looking forward to, could be completely effected at this very instant: would this be a great joy and happiness to you?" And an irrepressible self-consciousness distinctly answered, "No!" At this my heart sank within me: the whole foundation on which my life was constructed fell down. All my happiness was to have been found in the continual pursuit of this end. The end had ceased to charm, and how could there ever again be any interest in the means? I seemed to have nothing left to live for.

At first I hoped that the cloud would pass away of itself; but it did not. A night's sleep, the sovereign remedy for the smaller vexations of life, had no effect on it. I awoke to a renewed consciousness of the woful fact. I carried it with me into all companies, into all occupations. Hardly anything had power to cause me even a few minutes oblivion of it. For some months the cloud seemed to grow thicker and thicker. The lines in Coleridge's "Dejection"—I was not then acquainted with them—exactly describe my case:

> A grief without a pang, void, dark and drear,
> A drowsy, stifled, unimpassioned grief,
> Which finds no natural outlet or relief
> In word, or sigh, or tear.[*]

In vain I sought relief from my favourite books; those memorials of past nobleness and greatness, from which I had always hitherto drawn strength and animation. I read them now without feeling, or with the accustomed feeling *minus* all its charm; and I became persuaded, that my love of mankind, and of excellence for its own sake, had worn itself out. I sought no comfort by speaking to others of what I felt. If I had loved any one sufficiently to make confiding my griefs a necessity, I should not have been in the condition I was. I felt, too, that mine was not an interesting, or in any way respectable distress. There was nothing in it to attract sympathy. Advice, if I had known where to seek it, would have been most precious. The words of Macbeth to the physician often occurred to my thoughts.[†] But there was no one on whom I could build the faintest hope of such assistance. My father, to whom it would have been natural to me to have recourse in any practical difficulties, was the last person to whom, in such a case as this, I looked for help. Everything convinced me that he had no knowledge of any such mental state as I was suffering from, and that even if he could be made to understand it, he was not the physician who could heal it. My education, which was wholly his work, had been conducted without any regard to the possibility of its ending in this result; and I saw no use in giving him the pain of thinking that his plans had failed, when the

[*Samuel Taylor Coleridge, "Dejection, an Ode," in *Sibylline Leaves* (London: Rest Fenner, 1817), p. 238 (ll. 21–4).]
[†See Shakespeare, *Macbeth*, V, iii, 40–5.]

had failed, when the failure was probably irremediable and at all events beyond the power of *his* remedies. Of other friends I had at that time none to whom I had any hope of making my condition intelligible. It was however abundantly intelligible to myself; and the more I dwelt upon it, the more hopeless it appeared.

*h*My course of study had led me to believe*h* that all mental and moral feelings and qualities, whether of a good or a bad kind, were the results of association; that we love one thing and hate another, have pleasure in one sort of action or contemplation and pain in another sort, through the clinging of pleasurable and painful ideas to those things from the effect of education or of experience. As a *i*consequence of this, I had always heard it maintained by my father, and was myself*i* convinced, that the object of education should be to form the strongest possible associations of the salutary class; associations of pleasure with all things beneficial to the great whole, and of pain with all things hurtful to it. All this appeared inexpugnable, but it now seemed to me on retrospect, that my teachers had occupied themselves but superficially with the means of forming and keeping up these salutary associations. They seemed to have trusted altogether to the old familiar instruments, praise and blame, reward and punishment. Now I did not doubt that by these means, begun early and applied vigilantly, intense associations of pain and pleasure might be raised up, especially of pain, and might produce desires and aversions capable of lasting undiminished to the end of life. But there must always be something artificial and casual in associations thus generated: the pains and pleasures thus forcibly associated with things, are not connected with them by any natural tie; and it is therefore, I thought, essential to the durability of these associations, that they should have become so intense and inveterate as to be practically indissoluble before the habitual exercise of the power of analysis had commenced. For I now saw, or thought I saw, what I had always before received with incredulity—that the habit of analysis has a tendency to wear away the feelings. This is a commonplace, but it is true, and only errs in being but a half-truth. The habit of analysis has really this tendency when no other mental habit is cultivated, and the analysing tendency remains without its natural complements and correctives. At this time I did not see what these complements and correctives are. The very excellence of analysis (I argued) is that it tends to weaken and undermine whatever is prejudice; that it enables us mentally to separate ideas which have only casually clung together, and no associations whatever could ultimately resist its dissolving force, were it not that we owe to analysis our clearest knowledge of the permanent sequences in nature; the real connexions between things, quite independent of our will and feelings; natural laws by which, in many cases, one thing is inseparable from another, and which laws, in proportion as they are clearly perceived and imaginatively realized, cause the ideas of things which always accompany one another in fact, to cohere more and more closely in

---

h-h[*Earlier version:*] I had been taught and was thoroughly persuaded

failure was probably irremediable, and at all events, beyond the power of *his* remedies. Of other friends, I had at that time none to whom I had any hope of making my condition intelligible. It was however abundantly intelligible to myself; and the more I dwelt upon it, the more hopeless it appeared.

My course of study had led me to believe, that all mental and moral feelings and qualities, whether of a good or of a bad kind, were the results of association; that we love one thing and hate another, take pleasure in one sort of action or contemplation, and pain in another sort, through the clinging of pleasurable or painful ideas to those things, from the effect of education or of experience. As a corollary from this, *I had always heard it maintained by my father, and was myself convinced,* that the object of education should be to form the strongest possible associations of the salutary class; associations of pleasure with all things beneficial to the great whole, and of pain with all things hurtful to it. This doctrine appeared inexpugnable; but it now seemed to me on retrospect, that my teachers had occupied themselves but superficially with the means of forming and keeping up these salutary associations. They seemed to have trusted altogether to the old familiar instruments, praise and blame, reward and punishment. Now I did not doubt that by these means, begun early and applied unremittingly, intense associations of pain and pleasure, especially of pain, might be created, and might produce desires and aversions capable of lasting undiminished to the end of life. But there must always be something artificial and casual in associations thus produced. The pains and pleasures thus forcibly associated with things, are not connected with them by any natural tie; and it is therefore, I thought, essential to the durability of these associations, that they should have become so intense and inveterate as to be practically indissoluble, before the habitual exercise of the power of analysis had commenced. For I now saw, or thought I saw, what I had always before received with incredulity—that the habit of analysis has a tendency to wear away the feelings: as indeed it has when no other mental habit is cultivated, and the analysing spirit remains without its natural complements and correctives. The very excellence of analysis (I argued) is that it tends to weaken and undermine whatever is the result of prejudice; that it enables us mentally to separate ideas which have only casually clung together: and no associations whatever could ultimately resist this dissolving force, were it not that we owe to analysis our clearest knowledge of the permanent sequences in nature; the real connexions between Things, not dependent on our will and feelings; natural laws, by virtue of which, in many cases, one thing is inseparable from another in fact; which laws, in proportion as they are clearly perceived and imaginatively realized, cause our ideas of things which are always joined together in Nature, to cohere more and more closely in our

---

i-i[*Earlier version:*] corollary from this I had been taught and had always been

conception. Analytic habits may thus even strengthen the associations between causes and effects but tend to weaken all those which are, to speak familiarly, a mere matter of feeling. They are, therefore (I thought), favourable to prudence and clearsightedness, but a perpetual worm at the root both of the passions and of the virtues: and above all, fearfully undermine all desires and all pleasures which are the result of association, that is, according to the theory I held, all except the purely physical and organic: of the entire insufficiency of which, to make life desirable, no one had a stronger conviction than I had. These were the laws of human nature by which, as it seemed to me, I had been brought to my present state. *j*All those to whom I looked up, were of opinion*j* that the pleasures of sympathy with human beings, and the feelings which made the good of others and especially of mankind on a large scale the object of existence, were the greatest and surest source of happiness. I was well convinced of this, but to know that a feeling would make me happy if I had it, did not create the feeling. My education had failed, as I thought, to give me these feelings in sufficient strength to resist the dissolving influence of analysis, while the whole course of my intellectual cultivation had made precocious and premature analysis the inveterate habit of my mind. I was thus, as I said to myself, left stranded at the commencement of my voyage, with a well equipped ship and a rudder but no sail; without any real desire for the ends which I had been so carefully fitted to labour for: no delight in virtue or the general good, but also just as little in anything else. The *k*sources*k* of vanity and ambition seemed to have dried up within me, as completely as those of benevolence. I had had (as I reflected) some gratification of vanity at too early an age; I had obtained some distinction and felt myself to be of some importance before the desire of distinction and of importance had grown into a passion; and little as it was which I had attained, yet having been attained so early, like all pleasures enjoyed too soon, it had made me *blasé* and indifferent to the pursuit. Thus neither selfish nor unselfish pleasures were pleasures to me. And there seemed no power in nature sufficient to begin the formation of my character afresh and create in a mind now irrevocably analytic, fresh associations of pleasure with any of the objects of human desire.

These were the thoughts which mingled with the dry heavy dejection of the melancholy winter of 1826–7. During this time I was not incapable of my usual occupations; I went on with them mechanically, by the mere force of habit. I had been so drilled in a certain sort of mental exercise that I could carry it on when all the spirit had gone out of it. I even composed and spoke several speeches at the debating society; how, or with what degree of worth I know not. Of four years continual speaking at that society, this is the only year of which I remember next to nothing. Two lines of Coleridge, in whom alone of all writers I have found a true description of what I felt, were often in my thoughts, not at this time, but in a later period of the same mental malady.

---

j–j[*Earlier version:*] I had been taught

thoughts. Analytic habits may thus even strengthen the associations between causes and effects, means and ends, but tend altogether to weaken those which are, to speak familiarly, a *mere* matter of feeling. They are therefore (I thought) favourable to prudence and clearsightedness, but a perpetual worm at the root both of the passions and of the virtues; and above all, fearfully undermine all desires, and all pleasures, which are the effects of association, that is, according to the theory I held, all except the purely physical and organic; of the entire insufficiency of which to make life desirable, no one had a stronger conviction than I had. These were the laws of human nature by which, as it seemed to me, I had been brought to my present state. All those to whom I looked up, were of opinion that the pleasure of sympathy with human beings, and the feelings which made the good of others, and especially of mankind on a large scale, the object of existence, were the greatest and surest sources of happiness. Of the truth of this I was convinced, but to know that a feeling would make me happy if I had it, did not give me the feeling. My education, I thought, had failed to create these feelings in sufficient strength to resist the dissolving influence of analysis, while the whole course of my intellectual cultivation had made precocious and premature analysis the inveterate habit of my mind. I was thus, as I said to myself, left stranded at the commencement of my voyage, with a well equipped ship and a rudder, but no sail; without any real desire for the ends which I had been so carefully fitted out to work for: no delight in virtue or the general good, but also just as little in anything else. The fountains of vanity and ambition seemed to have dried up within me, as completely as those of benevolence. I had had (as I reflected) some gratification of vanity at too early an age: I had obtained some distinction, and felt myself of some importance, before the desire of distinction and of importance had grown into a passion: and little as it was which I had attained, yet having been attained too early, like all pleasures enjoyed too soon, it had made me *blasé* and indifferent to the pursuit. Thus neither selfish nor unselfish pleasures were pleasures to me. And there seemed no power in nature sufficient to begin the formation of my character anew, and create in a mind now irretrievably analytic, fresh associations of pleasure with any of the objects of human desire.

These were the thoughts which mingled with the dry heavy dejection of the melancholy winter of 1826–7. During this time I was not incapable of my usual occupations. I went on with them mechanically, by the mere force of habit. I had been so drilled in a certain sort of mental exercise, that I could still carry it on when all the spirit had gone out of it. I even composed and spoke several speeches at the debating society, how, or with what degree of success I know not. Of four years continual speaking at that society, this is the only year of which I remember next to nothing. Two lines of Coleridge, in whom alone of all writers I have found a true description of what I felt, were often in my thoughts, not at this time (for I had never read them), but in a later period of the same mental malady:

---

k–k[*Earlier version:*] pleasures

Work without hope draws nectar in a sieve
And hope without an object cannot live.

I often asked myself, if I could, or was bound, to live on, when life must be passed in this manner. I generally answered to myself, that I did not think I could possibly bear it beyond a year. When however not more than half that length of time had passed, a small ray of light broke in upon my gloom. I was reading, accidentally, Marmontel's *Memoirs*, and came to the passage where he relates his father's death, the distressed position of his family, and how he, then a mere boy, by a sudden inspiration, felt and made them feel that he would be everything, would supply the place of everything to them. A vivid conception of *'this scene'* came over me, and I was moved to tears. From this moment my burthen grew lighter. The oppression of the thought that all feeling was dead within me, was gone. I was no longer hopeless. I was not a stock or a stone. I had still, it seemed, some of the material out of which all worth of character and all capacity of happiness are made. Relieved from my ever present sense of wretchedness, I gradually found that the ordinary incidents of life could again give some pleasure; that I could again find enjoyment in sunshine and sky, in books, in conversation, in public affairs, not intense, but sufficient for cheerfulness; and that there was once more, excitement though but of a moderate kind, in exerting myself for my opinions and for the public good. Thus the cloud gradually drew off, and I again enjoyed life; and though *'''before the gloom entirely passed away'''* I had several relapses, some of which lasted many months, I never again was as miserable as I had been.

The experiences of this period had two very decided effects on my opinions and character. In the first place, they led me to adopt a theory of life very unlike that on which I had before acted, and having much in common with what at that time I had never heard of, the anti-self-consciousness theory of Carlyle. I never indeed varied in the conviction that happiness is the test of all rules of conduct, and the end of life. But I now thought that this end was only to be attained by not making it the direct aim. Those only are happy (I thought) who have their attention fixed on something other than their own happiness: on the happiness of others, either individually or collectively; on the improvement of mankind, even on some art or

'-'[*Earlier version:*] his and their feelings
'''-'''[*Earlier version:*] during the next few years

Work without hope draws nectar in a sieve,
And hope without an object cannot live.[*]

In all probability my case was by no means so peculiar as I fancied it, and I doubt not that many others have passed through a similar state; but the idiosyncracies of my education had given to the general phenomenon a special character, which made it seem the natural effect of causes that it was hardly possible for time to remove. I frequently asked myself, if I could, or if I was bound to go on living, when life must be passed in this manner. I generally answered to myself, that I did not think I could possibly bear it beyond a year. When, however, not more than half that duration of time had elapsed, a small ray of light broke in upon my gloom. I was reading, accidentally, Marmontel's *Memoirs*, and came to the passage which relates his father's death, the distressed position of the family, and the sudden inspiration by which he, then a mere boy, felt and made them feel that he would be everything to them—would supply the place of all that they had lost.[†] A vivid conception of the scene and its feelings came over me, and I was moved to tears. From this moment my burthen grew lighter. The oppression of the thought that all feeling was dead within me, was gone. I was no longer hopeless: I was not a stock or a stone. I had still, it seemed, some of the material out of which all worth of character, and all capacity for happiness, are made. Relieved from my ever present sense of irremediable wretchedness, I gradually found that the ordinary incidents of life could again give me some pleasure; that I could again find enjoyment, not intense, but sufficient for cheerfulness, in sunshine and sky, in books, in conversation, in public affairs; and that there was, once more, excitement, though of a moderate kind, in exerting myself for my opinions, and for the public good. Thus the cloud gradually drew off, and I again enjoyed life: and though I had several relapses, some of which lasted many months, I never again was as miserable as I had been.

The experiences of this period had two very marked effects on my opinions and character. In the first place, they led me to adopt a theory of life, very unlike that on which I had before acted, and having much in common with what at that time I certainly had never heard of, the anti-self-consciousness theory of Carlyle.[‡] I never, indeed, wavered in the conviction that happiness is the test of all rules of conduct, and the end of life. But I now thought that this end was only to be attained by not making it the direct end. Those only are happy (I thought) who have their minds fixed on some object other than their own happiness; on the happiness of others, on the improvement of mankind, even on some art or pursuit, followed not

[*Coleridge, "Work without Hope," in *Poetical Works*, 3 vols. (London: Pickering, 1828), Vol. II, p. 81.]

[†Jean François Marmontel, *Mémoires d'un père*, 4 vols. (London: Peltier, 1805), Vol. I, pp. 87–8 (Livre I).]

[‡See, e.g., Carlyle, *Sartor Resartus*, 2nd ed. (Boston: Munroe, 1837), pp. 86ff. and 189ff. (Bk. II, Chaps. i and ix); cf. "Characteristics," *Edinburgh Review*, LIV (Dec., 1831), 351–83.]

favorite pursuit followed not as a means but as an ideal end. Aiming thus at something else, they find happiness by the way. The enjoyments of life (such was now my theory) are sufficient to make life pleasant when they are taken en passant, without being made a principal object. Once make them so however and they are immediately felt to be insufficient. They will not bear a scrutinizing examination: ask yourself if you are happy, and you cease to be so. The only chance is to treat not happiness but some end external to it, as the object of life. Let your self consciousness, your scrutiny, your self interrogation exhaust themselves on that, and if otherwise fortunately circumstanced you will inhale happiness with the air you breathe, without dwelling on it or thinking about it, without either forestalling it in imagination or putting it to flight by fatal self questioning. This theory now became the basis of my philosophy of life. And I still hold to it as the best theory for those who have but a moderate degree of sensibility and of capacity for enjoyment, that is, for the great majority of mankind.

The other great change which my opinions at this time underwent, was that I now for the first time gave its proper place among the prime necessities of human well being, to the internal culture of the individual. I ceased to attach almost exclusive importance to the ordering of outward circumstances, and to the training of the human being for knowledge and for action. I now knew by experience that the passive susceptibilities needed to be cultivated as well as the active capacities, and required to be nourished and enriched as well as guided. I never for an instant lost sight of or undervalued, that part of the truth which I saw before: I never turned recreant to intellectual culture, or ceased to value the power and habit of analysis as essential both to individual and to social improvement. But I thought that it had consequences which required to be corrected by joining other sorts of cultivation with it: and the maintenance of a due balance among the faculties, now seemed to me of primary importance. The cultivation of the feelings now became one of the cardinal points in my ethical and philosophical creed. And my thoughts and inclinations turned more and more towards whatever I thought capable of being instrumental to that object.

"I now" began to find meaning in the things which I had read or heard said about the importance of poetry and art as instruments of culture. But it was some time longer before I began to know this by personal experience. The only one of the imaginative arts in which I had from childhood taken great pleasure was music: the best effect of which (and in this it surpasses perhaps every other art) consists in exciting enthusiasm; in winding up to a high pitch those feelings of an elevated kind which are already *in* the character, but to which this excitement gives a glow and a fervour which though transitory in its utmost height, is precious for sustaining them at other times. This effect of music I had often experienced: but like all my better susceptibilities it was suspended during my gloomy period. I had sought relief again and again from this quarter, but found none. After the tide had turned,

---

n–n[*Earlier version:*] It was a natural consequence of this, that I

as a means, but as itself an ideal end. Aiming thus at something else, they find happiness by the way. The enjoyments of life (such was now my theory) are sufficient to make it a pleasant thing, when they are taken *en passant*, without being made a principal object. Once make them so, and they are immediately felt to be insufficient. They will not bear a scrutinizing examination. Ask yourself whether you are happy, and you cease to be so. The only chance is to treat, not happiness, but some end external to it, as the purpose of life. Let your self-consciousness, your scrutiny, your self-interrogation, exhaust themselves on that; and if otherwise fortunately circumstanced you will inhale happiness with the air you breathe, without dwelling on it or thinking about it, without either forestalling it in imagination, or putting it to flight by fatal questioning. This theory now became the basis of my philosophy of life. And I still hold to it as the best theory for all those who have but a moderate degree of sensibility and of capacity for enjoyment, that is, for the great majority of mankind.

The other important change which my opinions at this time underwent, was that I, for the first time, gave its proper place, among the prime necessities of human well-being, to the internal culture of the individual. I ceased to attach almost exclusive importance to the ordering of outward circumstances, and the training of the human being for speculation and for action. I had now learnt by experience that the passive susceptibilities needed to be cultivated as well as the active capacities, and required to be nourished and enriched as well as guided. I did not, for an instant, lose sight of, or undervalue, that part of the truth which I had seen before; I never turned recreant to intellectual culture, or ceased to consider the power and practice of analysis as an essential condition both of individual and of social improvement. But I thought that it had consequences which required to be corrected, by joining other kinds of cultivation with it. The maintenance of a due balance among the faculties, now seemed to me of primary importance. The cultivation of the feelings became one of the cardinal points in my ethical and philosophical creed. And my thoughts and inclinations turned in an increasing degree towards whatever seemed capable of being instrumental to that object.

I now began to find meaning in the things which I had read or heard about the importance of poetry and art as instruments of human culture. But it was some time longer before I began to know this by personal experience. The only one of the imaginative arts in which I had from childhood taken great pleasure, was music; the best effect of which (and in this it surpasses perhaps every other art) consists in exciting enthusiasm; in winding up to a high pitch those feelings of an elevated kind which are already in the character, but to which this excitement gives a glow and a fervour, which though transitory at its utmost height, is precious for sustaining them at other times. This effect of music I had often experienced; but, like all my pleasurable susceptibilities, it was suspended during the gloomy period. I had sought relief again and again from this quarter, but found none. After

indeed, and I was in process of recovery, I had been helped forward by music, but in a much less elevated manner. I at this time first became acquainted with Weber's *Oberon*, and the extreme pleasure which I drew from its delicious melodies did me good by shewing me a source of pleasure to which I was as susceptible as ever: this good however being much impaired by the thought that the pleasure of music (as is quite true of such pleasure as this was, that of mere tune) fades with familiarity, and requires to be fed by continual novelty. And it is very characteristic both of my then state and of my general mental character at that time, that I was seriously tormented by the thought of the exhaustibility of musical combinations. The five tones and two semitones of the octave can be put together only in a limited number of ways; of these only a small proportion are beautiful; most of these must have been already discovered and there could not be room for a long succession of Mozarts and Webers to strike out as they had done entirely new and surpassingly rich veins of musical beauty. This source of anxiety may appear perhaps to resemble that of the philosophers of Laputa who feared lest the sun should be burnt out. It was however connected with the best point of my character, the only good point indeed to be found in my very unromantic and in no way honorable distress. For though my dejection honestly looked at, cannot be called other than egotistical, produced by the ruin as I thought of my fabric of happiness; yet the condition of mankind in general was ever in my thoughts, and could not be separated from my own; I felt that the evil in my life must be an evil in life itself; that the question was whether if the reformers of society and government could succeed in their objects and every person living were free and in physical comfort, the pleasures of life, being no longer kept up by privation and struggle would cease to be pleasures: and I felt that unless I could see my way to some better hope than this for the general happiness of mankind, my dejection must continue; but that if I could, I should then look on the world with pleasure, content with any fair share of the general lot.

This state of my thoughts and feelings made the fact of my first reading Wordsworth (in the autumn of 1828) an important event of my life. I took up the collection of his poems from curiosity, with no expectation of mental relief from it, though I had before resorted to poetry with that hope. In the worst period of my mental depression I had read through the whole of Byron (then new to me) to try whether a poet whose peculiar department was supposed to be that of the intenser feelings, could rouse any feeling in me. As might be expected, I got no good from

the tide had turned, and I was in process of recovery, I had been helped forward by music, but in a much less elevated manner. I at this time first became acquainted with Weber's *Oberon*,[*] and the extreme pleasure which I drew from its delicious melodies did me good, by shewing me a source of pleasure to which I was as susceptible as ever. The good however was much impaired by the thought, that the pleasure of music (as is quite true of such pleasure as this was, that of mere tune) fades with familiarity, and requires either to be revived by intermittence, or fed by continual novelty. And it is very characteristic both of my then state, and of the general tone of my mind at this period of my life, that I was seriously tormented by the thought of the exhaustibility of musical combinations. The octave consists only of five tones and two semitones, which can be put together in only a limited number of ways, of which but a small proportion are beautiful: most of these, it seemed to me, must have been already discovered, and there could not be room for a long succession of Mozarts and Webers, to strike out as these had done, entirely new and surpassingly rich veins of musical beauty. This source of anxiety may perhaps be thought to resemble that of the philosophers of Laputa, who feared lest the sun should be burnt out.[†] It was, however, connected with the best feature in my character, and the only good point to be found in my very unromantic and in no way honorable distress. For though my dejection, honestly looked at, could not be called other than egotistical, produced by the ruin, as I thought, of my fabric of happiness, yet the destiny of mankind in general was ever in my thoughts, and could not be separated from my own. I felt that the flaw in my life, must be a flaw in life itself; that the question was, whether, if the reformers of society and govern-ment could succeed in their objects, and every person in the community were free and in a state of physical comfort, the pleasures of life, being no longer kept up by struggle and privation, would cease to be pleasures. And I felt that unless I could see my way to some better hope than this for human happiness in general, my dejection must continue; but that if I could see such an outlet, I should then look on the world with pleasure; content as far as I was myself concerned, with any fair share of the general lot.

This state of my thoughts and feelings made the fact of my reading Wordsworth for the first time (in the autumn of 1828) an important event in my life. I took up the collection of his poems from curiosity, with no expectation of mental relief from it, though I had before resorted to poetry with that hope. In the worst period of my depression I had read through the whole of Byron (then new to me) to try whether a poet, whose peculiar department was supposed to be that of the intenser feelings, could rouse any feeling in me. As might be expected, I got no good from this

[*Karl Maria von Weber, *Oberon; or, The Elf-King's Oath* (first performed in London, Covent Garden, 12 Apr., 1826).]

[†See Jonathan Swift, *Gulliver's Travels*, in *Works*, ed. Walter Scott, 19 vols. (Edin-burgh: Constable; London: White, *et al.*; Dublin: Cumming, 1814), Vol. XII, p. 211 (Voyage III, Chap. ii).]

this reading but the reverse. The poet's state of mind was too like my own. His was the lament of a man who had worn out all pleasures and who seemed to think that life to all who possessed the good things of it, must necessarily be the vapid uninteresting thing which I found it. His Harold and Manfred had the same burthen on them which I had; and I was not in a frame of mind to derive any comfort from the vehement sensual passion of his Giaours or the sulkiness of his Laras. But while Byron was exactly what did not suit my condition, Wordsworth was exactly what did. I had looked into *The Excursion* two or three years before and found little or nothing in it; and should probably have found as little had I read it now. But the miscellaneous poems, in the two-volume edition of 1815 [o](to which little valuable was added in any of the subsequent editions)[o], proved to be the precise thing for my mental wants at that particular time.

In the first place, these poems addressed themselves powerfully to one of the strongest of my pleasurable susceptibilities, the love of rural objects and of natural scenery; to which I had been indebted not only for much of the pleasure of my life, but quite recently for relief from one of my longest relapses into depression. [p] In this power of rural beauty over me there was a foundation laid for taking pleasure in Wordsworth's poetry; the more so, as his scenery is mostly among mountains, which owing to my early Pyrenean excursion were my ideal of natural beauty. But Wordsworth would never have had any great effect on me if he had merely placed before me beautiful pictures of natural scenery. A collection of very second rate landscapes does this more effectually than any books. What made Wordsworth's poems [q]a[q] medicine for my state of mind was that they expressed, not outward beauty but states of feeling, and of thought coloured by feeling, under the excitement of beauty. They seemed to be the very culture of the feelings which I was in quest of. By their means I seemed to draw from a source of inward joy, of sympathetic and imaginative pleasure, which could be shared in by all human beings, which had no connexion with struggle or imperfection, but would be made richer by every improvement in the physical or social condition of mankind. I seemed to learn from them what would be the perennial sources of happiness when all the greater evils of life should be removed. And I felt myself at once better and happier as I came under their influence. At present my estimate of Wordsworth as a

[o-o][*Earlier version:*] , comprising nearly everything good which he ever wrote [*deleted by HTM*]

[p][*Cancelled text:*] About Midsummer of that same year 1828 I set out on a short walking tour: for months before I had been in my old state of gloomy dejection, though as I have already mentioned not so intense as at first; this continued the greater part of the first day, but the walk by the side of the Thames from Reading to Pangbourne, in one of the loveliest of summer evenings with the western sky in its most splendid colouring before me, and the calm river, rich meadows and wooded hills encompassing me, insensibly changed my state, and except a short interval two days later I had no return of depression during that excursion nor for several months afterwards. [See the entry for 3 July, 1828, in Mill's Journal of a Walking Tour of Berkshire, Buckinghamshire, and Surrey.]

[q-q][*Earlier version:*] so exactly the

reading, but the reverse. The poet's state of mind was too like my own. His was the lament of a man who had worn out all pleasures, and who seemed to think that life, to all who possess the good things of it, must necessarily be the vapid uninteresting thing which I found it. His Harold and Manfred had the same burthen on them which I had; and I was not in a frame of mind to derive any comfort from the vehement sensual passion of his Giaours, or the sullenness of his Laras.[*] But while Byron was exactly what did not suit my condition, Wordsworth was exactly what did. I had looked into *The Excursion*[†] two or three years before, and found little in it; and should probably have found as little, had I read it at this time. But the miscellaneous poems, in the two-volume edition of 1815[‡] (to which little of value was added in the latter part of the author's life), proved to be the precise thing for my mental wants at that particular juncture.

In the first place, these poems addressed themselves powerfully to one of the strongest of my pleasurable susceptibilities, the love of rural objects and natural scenery; to which I had been indebted not only for much of the pleasure of my life, but quite recently for relief from one of my longest relapses into depression. In this power of rural beauty over me, there was a foundation laid for taking pleasure in Wordsworth's poetry; the more so, as his scenery lies mostly among mountains, which, owing to my early Pyrenean excursion, were my ideal of natural beauty. But Wordsworth would never have had any great effect on me, if he had merely placed before me beautiful pictures of natural scenery. Scott does this still better than Wordsworth, and a very second-rate landscape does it more effectually than any poet. What made Wordsworth's poems a medicine for my state of mind, was that they expressed, not mere outward beauty, but states of feeling, and of thought coloured by feeling, under the excitement of beauty.[§] They seemed to be the very culture of the feelings, which I was in quest of. In them I seemed to draw from a source of inward joy, of sympathetic and imaginative pleasure, which could be shared in by all human beings; which had no connexion with struggle or imperfection, but would be made richer by every improvement in the physical or social condition of mankind. From them I seemed to learn what would be the perennial sources of happiness, when all the greater evils of life shall have been removed. And I felt myself at once better and happier as I came under their influence. There

[*The heroes of George Gordon Byron's *Childe Harold's Pilgrimage*, 2 vols. (London: Murray, 1819); *Manfred, a Dramatic Poem* (London: Murray, 1817); *The Giaour, a Fragment of a Turkish Tale* (London: Murray, 1813); and *Lara, a Tale* (London: Murray, 1814).]

[†William Wordsworth, *The Excursion, Being a Portion of The Recluse, a Poem* (London: Longman, Hurst, Rees, Orme, and Brown, 1814); in *Poetical Works*, 5 vols. (London: Longman, Rees, Orme, Brown, and Green, 1827), Vol. V.]

[‡*Poems by William Wordsworth, Including Lyrical Ballads, and the Miscellaneous Pieces by the Author*, 2 vols. (London: Longman, Hurst, Rees, Orme, and Brown, 1815). (A third volume was published in 1820.)]

[§Cf. Wordsworth, "Preface to the Second Edition of the Lyrical Ballads," in *Poetical Works* (1827), Vol. IV, pp. 360–1 (para. 5).]

poet is very far indeed below that which I then formed; but poetry of deeper and loftier feeling could not have done for me at that time what this did. I wanted to be made to feel that there was happiness in tranquil contemplation. Wordsworth taught me this and not only without turning away from, but with a greatly increased interest in, the common feelings and common destiny of human beings. And the *r* delight which these poems gave me, proved to me that with culture of this sort there was nothing to dread from the most confirmed habit of analysis. At the end of the poems came the famous "Ode," falsely called Platonic; in which, along with more than his usual sweetness of rhythm and melody, and along with the two passages of fine description but bad philosophy so often quoted, I found *s* that he too had had similar experience to mine; that he had felt that the first freshness of youthful enjoyment of life was not lasting; but that he had sought for compensation, and found it, in the way in which he was now teaching me to find it. *t* The consequence of all these things was that I gradually but completely emerged from my habitual depression and was never again subject to it. *u*I long continued to value Wordsworth less according to his intrinsic merits than to what he had done for me*u*. My present judgment of him is, that he is the poet of unpoetical natures, when accompanied by quiet and contemplative tastes. But it must be remembered that unpoetical natures are precisely those which require poetic cultivation. This cultivation Wordsworth is more fitted to give them, than poets incomparably his superiors.

It so happened that the merits of Wordsworth were the occasion of my first public declaration of my new way of thinking, and *v* separation from those of my habitual companions who had not undergone a similar change. The person with whom at that time I was most in the habit of comparing notes was Roebuck; and I induced him to read Wordsworth, in whom he also at first seemed to find much to admire: but I like most Wordsworthians threw myself into strong antagonism to Byron, both as a poet and in respect to his effect on the character. Roebuck, all whose instincts were those of action and struggle, had on the contrary a strong relish and admiration of Byron, whose writings he regarded as the poetry of real life while Wordsworth's according to him were that of flowers and butterflies. We agreed to have the fight out at our Debating Society, where we accordingly discussed for two evenings the comparative merits of Byron and Wordsworth, *w*propounding, and illustrating by long recitations,*w* our respective theories of poetry. This was the first debate on any weighty subject on which Roebuck and I

---

r[*Cancelled text:*] unfading, or rather the increasing

s[*Cancelled text:*] what was much more to my purpose, namely

t[*Cancelled text:*] This moral of the whole, so different from Byron's, was valuable to me, but I did not need it, as I had already drawn the same from the previous poems.

u-u[*Earlier version:*] All these things being considered it is not strange that I rated very high the merit and value of Wordsworth

v[*Cancelled text:*] apparent

w-w[*Earlier version:*] each bringing forward the merits of the poet he preferred, vehemently attacking the other, and propounding

have certainly been, even in our own age, greater poets than Wordsworth; but poetry of deeper and loftier feeling could not have done for me at that time what his did. I needed to be made to feel that there was real, permanent happiness in tranquil contemplation. Wordsworth taught me this, not only without turning away from, but with a greatly increased interest in, the common feelings and common destiny of human beings. And the delight which these poems gave me, proved that with culture of this sort, there was nothing to dread from the most confirmed habit of analysis. At the conclusion of the Poems came the famous "Ode," falsely called Platonic, "Intimations of Immortality":[*] in which, along with more than his usual sweetness of melody and rhythm, and along with the two passages of grand imagery but bad philosophy so often quoted, I found that he too had had similar experience to mine; that he also had felt that the first freshness of youthful enjoyment of life was not lasting; but that he had sought for compensation, and found it, in the way in which he was now teaching me to find it. The result was that I gradually, but completely, emerged from my habitual depression, and was never again subject to it. I long continued to value Wordsworth less according to his intrinsic merits, than by the measure of what he had done for me. Compared with the greatest poets, he may be said to be the poet of unpoetical natures, possessed of quiet and contemplative tastes. But unpoetical natures are precisely those which require poetic cultivation. This cultivation Wordsworth is much more fitted to give, than poets who are intrinsically far more poets than he.

It so fell out that the merits of Wordsworth were the occasion of my first public declaration of my new way of thinking, and separation from those of my habitual companions who had not undergone a similar change. The person with whom at that time I was most in the habit of comparing notes on such subjects was Roebuck, and I induced him to read Wordsworth, in whom he also at first seemed to find much to admire: but I, like most Wordsworthians, threw myself into strong antagonism to Byron, both as a poet and as to his influence on the character. Roebuck, all whose instincts were those of action and struggle, had, on the contrary, a strong relish and great admiration of Byron, whose writings he regarded as the poetry of human life, while Wordsworth's, according to him, was that of flowers and butterflies. We agreed to have the fight out at our Debating Society, where we accordingly discussed for two evenings the comparative merits of Byron and Wordsworth, propounding and illustrating by long recitations our respective theories of poetry: Sterling also, in a brilliant speech, putting forward his particular theory.[†] This was the first debate on any weighty subject in which

[*"Ode. Intimations of Immortality from Recollections of Early Childhood," in *Poetical Works* (1827), Vol. IV, pp. 346–55.]

[†Mill spoke on Wordsworth in the debate on 30 Jan., 1829 (MS in the Mill-Taylor Collection); Sterling opened the debate, and Roebuck spoke on 16 Jan. Actually Roebuck and Mill had two years earlier opposed one another in debate on the immoral tendencies of Byron's poetry, with Roebuck upholding Byron.]

were on opposite sides. The schism between us widened more and more from this time and though for some years we continued to be companions our differences of opinion on life and philosophy became so strongly pronounced that we ceased to be allies either in opinion or in action except as to the immediate objects of radicalism.

I suppose that of the set of young men with whom I had associated, Roebuck would have been and was generally regarded as the most complete type of what was considered narrow Benthamism. This however is only an example of the extreme inaccuracy of that common conception. Roebuck was in many things totally opposite to the vulgar notion of a Benthamite. He was a lover of poetry and of almost all the fine arts. He took great pleasure in music, in dramatic perform-ances, especially in painting, and himself drew and designed landscapes with great facility and beauty. Instead of being, as Benthamites are supposed to be, unfeel-ing, he had very quick and susceptible feelings: and his feelings towards persons, favourable and hostile, have greatly influenced his course all through life. No description of a class would exactly fit Roebuck; he had a decided character of his own, and took only that portion of any creed which was in harmony with his character. Of this, pugnacity was one of the principal elements. Nine years of his boyhood and youth had been passed in the back woods of Canada; and his character had a great tinge of the backwoodsman: formed to self help, to self assertion, and to be ever ready for conflict; with the reservation, that as the small and weakly brother among a family of giants, mental and not bodily weapons were those with which his battles had been fought and his victories gained. These early circumstances gave him the audacity and self reliance which most distinguished him from the common run of Englishmen, in whom those qualities become every day more rare. On the other hand, his mother (a daughter of Tickell, and of the sister of the first Mrs. Sheridan), by whom chiefly he was educated and of whom he always spoke with great admiration and affection, had cultivated in him a polish of manners not at all American which he always manifested towards friends, though not always towards opponents. *x* Roebuck was a Radical in Canadian politics though his stepfather,[*] on whom at that time he was entirely dependent, was a placeman. He came to England to qualify for the bar, and finding that he could maintain himself by writing, remained there. On his arrival he almost immediately fell in with me and my set, and had Bentham's and my father's writings presented to him as the philosophy of radicalism. He seized on this political creed with great and sincere zeal. Naturally quick of perception and comprehension, though not inventive or original, he was qualified to become a reasoner rather than a thinker; and his intellectual type, in all matters of speculation, continued to be one of ratiocination rather than of insight, as Carlyle calls it, or (to describe it more precisely) induction and analysis. He arrived at his conclusions by deduction from the principles of his

[*John Simpson.]

x[*Cancelled text:*] An ambitious young man with his fortune to make is naturally a Radical:

Roebuck and I had been on opposite sides. The schism between us widened from this time more and more, though we continued for some years longer to be companions. In the beginning, our chief divergence related to the cultivation of the feelings. Roebuck was in many respects very different from the vulgar notion of a Benthamite or Utilitarian. He was a lover of poetry and of most of the fine arts. He took great pleasure in music, in dramatic performances, especially in painting, and himself drew and designed landscapes with great facility and beauty. But he never could be made to see that these things have any value as aids in the formation of character. Personally, instead of being, as Benthamites are supposed to be, void of feeling, he had very quick and strong sensibilities. But, like most Englishmen who

creed, never anxious to enlarge the basis of the creed itself by perpetual examination of the specialities of the questions to which he was called on to apply it. This deficiency I used to account for to myself, ^{y} by the deep rooted pugnacity of his character. When any proposition came before him as that of an opponent, he rushed eagerly to demonstrate its falsity, without taking any pains to discover and appropriate the portion of truth which there might be in it. This mental type, very natural to persons of impetuosity of character and which I saw in a less extreme degree in my father, became more and more alien to my tastes and feelings. I had now taken a most decided bent in the opposite direction, that of eclecticism; looking out for the truth which is generally to be found in errors when they are anything more than mere paralogisms, or logical blunders. My disputes with Roebuck in the early part of our discussions turned mainly on the culture of the feelings; and in these he who had certainly the quickest feelings took the unfeeling side. But this, instead of a paradox, is the explanation of the whole matter. Like most Englishmen who have feelings, he found his feelings stand very much in his way: he was much more susceptible to the painful sympathies than to the pleasurable, and looking for his happiness elsewhere, wished that his feelings should be deadened rather than quickened. And in truth the English character and English social circumstances make it so seldom possible to derive happiness from the exercise of the sympathies that it is not wonderful they should count for very little in an Englishman's scheme of life. In all other countries the paramount importance of the sympathies as a constituent of happiness is an axiom, taken for granted rather than needing any formal statement; but most English thinkers seem to regard them as necessary evils, required to keep men's actions benevolent and compassionate. Roebuck was this sort of Englishman, or seemed to be so; he saw little good in the cultivation of the feelings, and none in their cultivation through the imagination, which he thought was only cultivating illusions. It was in vain I urged on him that the imaginative emotion which an idea when vividly conceived excites in us, is not an illusion but a fact, as real as any of the other qualities of objects; and far from implying anything erroneous and delusive in our mental apprehension of the object, is quite consistent with the most accurate knowledge and practical recognition of all its physical and intellectual laws and relations. The intensest feeling of the beauty of a cloud lighted by the setting sun, is no hindrance to my knowing that the cloud is the vapour of water, subject to all the laws of vapours in a state of suspension; and I am just as likely to allow for, and act on, these physical laws whenever there is occasion to do so, as if I were incapable of perceiving any distinction between beauty and ugliness. To conclude here my notice of Roebuck; when three years afterwards he under almost every disadvantage of fortune and position took his seat in the House of Commons, he fulfilled my expectation and prediction at the time, viz. that he would fail, apparently irretrievably, half a dozen times and succeed at last. He escaped the imputation which almost all persons in

^{y}[*Cancelled text:*] probably truly,

have feelings, he found his feelings stand very much in his way. He was much more susceptible to the painful sympathies than to the pleasurable, and looking for his happiness elsewhere, he wished that his feelings should be deadened rather than quickened. And in truth the English character, and English social circumstances, make it so seldom possible to derive happiness from the exercise of the sympathies, that it is not wonderful if they count for little in an Englishman's scheme of life. In most other countries the paramount importance of the sympathies as a constituent of individual happiness is an axiom, taken for granted rather than needing any formal statement; but most English thinkers almost seem to regard them as necessary evils, required for keeping men's actions benevolent and compassionate. Roebuck was, or appeared to be, this kind of Englishman. He saw little good in any cultivation of the feelings, and none at all in cultivating them through the imagination, which he thought was only cultivating illusions. It was in vain I urged on him that the imaginative emotion which an idea when vividly conceived excites in us, is not an illusion but a fact, as real as any of the other qualities of objects; and far from implying anything erroneous and delusive in our mental apprehension of the object, is quite consistent with the most accurate knowledge and most perfect practical recognition of all its physical and intellectual laws and relations. The intensest feeling of the beauty of a cloud lighted by the setting sun, is no hindrance to my knowing that the cloud is vapour of water, subject to all the laws of vapours in a state of suspension; and I am just as likely to allow for, and act on, these physical laws whenever there is occasion to do so, as if I had been incapable of perceiving any distinction between beauty and ugliness.

his position are subject to, of being an adventurer. Nobody ever suspected him of wishing to be bought off. His ambition was not of this low kind: and his very faults, his asperity and the needless offensiveness of his attacks, protected him from the suspicion. Notwithstanding his many defects of judgment, he succeeded by perseverance and by really having something to say, in acquiring the ear of the house. He conquered all external obstacles, and if he ceased rising it was because he had got to the end of his tether. He made considerable exertions for radicalism during some years in the House of Commons, and was the vigorous champion of two great questions; national education, which he reoriginated in parliament (the first unsuccessful move had been made by Mr. Brougham twelve years before), and responsible government in the colonies, of which Roebuck was in this country altogether the originator, both in the press and in parliament, and remained up to the period of Lord Durham's mission the principal pillar. It ought to be recorded among the most honorable points in his career, that he braved his own supporters and lost his seat at Bath by his vigorous opposition to the bills for the puritanical observance of Sunday.[*] But he did not labour to master the special questions of legislation which were brought or which he might usefully have brought before parliament; and his voice, at last, was heard almost solely on personal questions, or on such as he was able to make personal. He made no progress in general principles; like the Parliamentary Radicals generally, made no addition to his original stock of ideas; and when the mental movement of Europe outstripped him even in politics, as was manifested in February 1848, he *turned against the movement of Europe*. Even on English matters, when he had succeeded in being somebody, and above all when he had married and become involved in the petty vanities and entanglements of what is called society, he gradually ceased to be the champion of any important progress; he became a panegyrist of England and things English, a conformist to the Church, *a* and in short merged in the common herd of Conservative Liberals.

But to return to the point of separation between his course and mine. I have mentioned that the difference of our philosophy first declared itself in the debate on Wordsworth, at the Society we had founded and in which, in addition to the Tory party with whom we had hitherto been combating, we were now face to face with another set of adversaries of far greater intrinsic worth, the Coleridgians, represented in the society by Frederick Maurice and John Sterling: both subsequently well known, the former by his writings, the latter through the two biographies by Hare and Carlyle. Of these two friends, Maurice was the thinker, Sterling the orator, and impassioned expositor of thoughts which were, at this time, almost

---

[*See, e.g., Roebuck's speech, *Parliamentary Debates*, 3rd ser., Vol. 38, cols. 1229–34 (7 June, 1837), against Sir Andrew Agnew's "Bill to Promote the Observance of the Lord's Day," 7 William IV (4 May, 1837), *Parliamentary Papers*, 1837, III, 351–60.]

–[*Earlier version:*] was found [*altered to read:* became] a reactionary

While my intimacy with Roebuck diminished, I fell more and more into friendly intercourse with our Coleridgian adversaries in the Society, Frederick Maurice and John Sterling, both subsequently so well known, the former by his writings, the latter through the biographies by Hare and Carlyle.[*] Of these two friends, Maurice was the thinker, Sterling the orator, and impassioned expositor of thoughts which, at this period, were almost entirely formed for him by Maurice.

[*John Sterling, *Essays and Tales, Collected and Edited with a Memoir by Julius Charles Hare*, 2 vols. (London: Parker, 1848), and Carlyle, *The Life of John Sterling* (London: Chapman and Hall, 1851).]

---

a[*Cancelled text (Mill did not complete the clause before deleting):*] and is now no longer worth counting as an element in

entirely formed for him by Maurice. With Maurice I had been for some time acquainted through Eyton Tooke, who had known him at Cambridge, and although my discussions with him were almost always disputes, I had carried away from them much that helped to build up my new fabric of thought; in the same way as I was deriving much from Coleridge, and from writings of Goethe and other Germans which I read during these years [b] . I have always thought that there was more intellectual power misapplied and wasted in Maurice than in any other of my cotemporaries. Great power of generalization, rare ingenuity and subtlety and a wide perception of important and unobvious truth, served him not for putting something better into the place of the worthless heap of received opinions in spiritual matters but for proving that the Church of England had known everything from the first, and that all the truths on the ground of which the Church and orthodoxy have been attacked, are not only consistent with the Thirty-nine articles but are better understood and expressed in those articles than by any one who rejects them. Such was the perverting effect on what would otherwise have been a fine intellect, of the combination of a timid character and conscience with an originally highly sensitive temperament. In this he resembled Coleridge, to whom, in merely intellectual powers, apart from poetical genius, I think him decidedly superior. At this time however he might be described as a disciple of Coleridge, and Sterling as a disciple of Coleridge and of him. In our Debating Society they made their appearance as a second Liberal and even Radical party, on totally different grounds from Benthamism and vehemently opposed to it; and they brought into their discussions the general doctrines and modes of thought of the European reaction against the philosophy of the eighteenth century: thus adding a third and very important belligerent party to our discussions, which were now no bad exponent of the movement of opinion among the most cultivated of the new generation. The modifications which were taking place in my old opinions natural-ly gave me some points of contact with them; and both Maurice and Sterling were of considerable use to my developement. In after conversations with Sterling he

---

[b][*Cancelled text:*] either in the original or in translations

With Maurice I had for some time been acquainted through Eyton Tooke, who had known him at Cambridge, and though my discussions with him were almost always disputes, I had carried away from them much that helped to build up my new fabric of thought, in the same way as I was deriving much from Coleridge, and from the writings of Goethe and other German authors which I read during those years. I have so deep a respect for Maurice's character and purposes, as well as for his great mental gifts, that it is with some unwillingness I say anything which may seem to place him on a less high eminence than I would gladly be able to accord to him. But I have always thought that there was more intellectual power wasted in Maurice than in any other of my cotemporaries. Few of them certainly have had so much to waste. Great powers of generalization, rare ingenuity and subtlety, and a wide perception of important and unobvious truths, served him not for putting something better into the place of the worthless heap of received opinions on the great subjects of thought, but for proving to his own mind that the Church of England had known everything from the first, and that all the truths on the ground of which the Church and orthodoxy have been attacked (many of which he saw as clearly as any one) are not only consistent with the Thirty-nine articles,[*] but are better understood and expressed in those articles than by any one who rejects them. I have never been able to find any other explanation of this, than by attributing it to that timidity of conscience, combined with original sensitiveness of temperament, which has so often driven highly gifted men into Romanism from the need of a firmer support than they can find in the independent conclusions of their own judgment. Any more vulgar kind of timidity no one who knew Maurice would ever think of imputing to him, even if he had not given public proof of his freedom from it, by his ultimate collision with some of the opinions commonly regarded as orthodox, and by his noble origination of the Christian Socialist movement. The nearest parallel to him, in a moral point of view, is Coleridge, to whom, in merely intellectual power, apart from poetical genius, I think him decidedly superior. At this time, however, he might be described as a disciple of Coleridge, and Sterling as a disciple of Coleridge and of him. The modifications which were taking place in my old opinions gave me some points of contact with them; and both Maurice and Sterling were of considerable use to my development. With Sterling I soon became very intimate, and was more attached to him than I have ever been to any other man. He was indeed one of the most loveable of men. His frank, cordial, affectionate and expansive character; a love of truth alike conspicuous in the highest things and the humblest; a generous and ardent nature which threw itself with impetuosity into the opinions it adopted, but was as eager to do justice to the doctrines and the men it was opposed to, as to make war on what it thought their errors; and an equal devotion to the two cardinal points of Liberty and Duty, formed a combination of qualities as attractive to me, as to all others who knew him

[*See *The Book of Common Prayer.*]

told me how he and others had been accustomed to look upon me as a "made" or manufactured man, having had a certain impress of opinion stamped upon me which I could only reproduce; and what a change took place in his feelings when he found, in the discussion on Wordsworth and Byron (in which as might be expected he made a brilliant speech), that Wordsworth and all that is implied in Wordsworth "belonged to" me as much as to him and his friends. But if I agreed with them much more than with Bentham on poetry and general culture, I was as much opposed to them as ever on religion, political philosophy, ethics and metaphysics, and as long as we continued our debating practice we were almost always on contrary sides. One vehement encounter between Sterling and me, he making what I thought a violent and unfair attack on the political philosophy I professed, to which I responded as sharply, fixed itself particularly in my memory because it was immediately followed by two things: one was, Sterling's withdrawing from the society; the other, that he and I sought one another privately much more than before, and became very intimate. His frank, cordial, affectionate and expansive character made him very attractive to me as he was to every one who knew him. The failure of his health soon scattered all his plans of life and compelled him to live at a distance from London, and I living almost constantly in it, we after the first year or two of our acquaintance only saw each other at distant intervals. He never became, in the proper sense of the word, a thinker; but his open mind and heart, and the moral courage in which he was greatly superior to Maurice, made him soon outgrow the dominion over his intellect of Maurice and of Coleridge. Except in that short and passing phasis of his life, during which he made the ^{c} mistake of becoming a clergyman, his mind was ever progressive; the advance he always seemed to have made when I saw him again after an interval, made me apply to him what Goethe said of Schiller's "fürchtliche Fortschreitung." He and I started from intellectual points almost as wide apart as the poles, but the distance between us was always growing less: if I made steps towards some of his opinions, he, during his short life, was constantly approximating more and more to mine: and if he had lived and had health and vigour to prosecute his ever assiduous self culture I have little doubt that his mental emancipation on all the leading points of opinion would have become complete.

After 1829 I withdrew from attendance on the Debating Society. I had had enough of speech making, and was glad to carry on my private studies and meditations without any immediate call for outward assertion of their results. I found the fabric of my old and taught opinions giving way in many fresh places, and I never allowed it to fall to pieces, but was incessantly occupied in weaving it anew: I never, in the course of my transition, suffered myself to remain confused and unsettled. When I had taken in any new idea I could not rest till I had adjusted

---

^{c}[*Cancelled text:*] great

as well as I did. With his open mind and heart, he found no difficulty in joining hands with me across the gulf which as yet divided our opinions. He told me how he and others had looked upon me (from hearsay information) as a "made" or manufactured man, having had a certain impress of opinion stamped on me which I could only reproduce; and what a change took place in his feelings when he found, in the discussion on Wordsworth and Byron, that Wordsworth, and all which that name implies, "belonged" to me as much as to him and his friends. The failure of his health soon scattered all his plans of life, and compelled him to live at a distance from London, so that after the first year or two of our acquaintance we only saw each other at distant intervals. But (as he said himself in one of his letters to Carlyle) when we did meet it was like brothers. Though he was never, in the full sense of the word, a profound thinker, his openness of mind, and the moral courage in which he greatly surpassed Maurice, made him outgrow the dominion which Maurice and Coleridge had once exercised over his intellect; though he retained to the last a great but discriminating admiration of both, and towards Maurice a warm affection. Except in that short and transitory phasis of his life, during which he made the mistake of becoming a clergyman, his mind was ever progressive; and the advance he always seemed to have made when I saw him after an interval, made me apply to him what Goethe said of Schiller, "Er hatte eine fürchtliche Fortschreitung."[*] He and I started from intellectual points almost as wide apart as the poles, but the distance between us was always diminishing: if I made steps towards some of his opinions, he, during his short life, was constantly approximating more and more to several of mine: and if he had lived, and had health and vigour to prosecute his ever assiduous self-culture, there is no knowing how much further this spontaneous assimilation might have proceeded.

After 1829 I withdrew from attendance on the Debating Society. I had had enough of speech-making, and was glad to carry on my private studies and meditations without any immediate call for outward assertion of their results. I found the fabric of my old and taught opinions giving way in many fresh places, and I never allowed it to fall to pieces, but was incessantly occupied in weaving it anew. I never, in the course of my transition, was content to remain, for ever so short a time, confused and unsettled. When I had taken in any new idea, I could not

[*See Sarah Austin, *Characteristics of Goethe. From the German of Falk, Müller, etc.*, 3 vols. (London: Wilson, 1833), Vol. II, p. 320, where she gives Felix Mendelssohn's account to her of a conversation he had with Goethe.]

its relation to all my old opinions, and ascertained exactly how far its effect ought to extend in modifying or superseding them. *d*

The conflicts which I had so often had to carry on in defence of the theory of government laid down in Bentham's and my father's writings, and the acquaintance I had obtained with other modes of political thinking, had made me aware of many things which that doctrine, professing to be a theory of government in general, ought to have made room for, and did not. But these things as yet remained with me rather as corrections to be made in applying the theory to practice, than as defects in the theory. I felt that politics could not be a science of specific experience; that the accusations against the Benthamic theory of *being* a theory, of proceeding *a priori*, by way of general reasoning instead of Baconian experiment, shewed complete ignorance of Bacon's principles, and of the necessary conditions of political investigation. At this juncture appeared Macaulay's famous attack, in the *Edinburgh Review*, on my father's Essay on Government. This gave me much to think about. I saw that Macaulay's conception of political reasoning was wrong; that he stood up for the empirical mode of treating political phenomena against the philosophical. At the same time I could not help feeling that there was truth in several of his strictures on my father's treatment of the subject; that my father's premises were really too narrow, and included but a small part of the general truths on which, in politics, the important consequences depend. Identity of interest, in any practical sense which can be attached to the term, between the governing body and the community at large, is not the only thing on which good government depends; neither can this identity of interest be secured by the mere conditions of election: I was not at all satisfied with the mode in which my father met the criticisms of Macaulay. He did not, as I thought he ought to have done, justify himself by saying "I was not writing a scientific treatise on politics. I was writing an argument for parliamentary reform." He treated Macaulay's argument as simply irrational; as an attack on the reasoning faculty; an example of the remark of Hobbes that when reason is against a man, a man will be against reason.

---

d[*Cancelled text:*] In this part of my life at least, whatever may have been the case at others, I had a really active mind. [*marked with a question mark by HTM*]

rest till I had adjusted its relation to my old opinions, and ascertained exactly how far its effect ought to extend in modifying or superseding them.

The conflicts which I had so often had to sustain in defending the theory of government laid down in Bentham's and my father's writings, and the acquaintance I had obtained with other schools of political thinking, made me aware of many things which that doctrine, professing to be a theory of government in general, ought to have made room for, and did not. But these things, as yet, remained with me rather as corrections to be made in applying the theory to practice, than as defects in the theory. I felt that politics could not be a science of specific experience; and that the accusations against the Benthamic theory of *being* a theory, of proceeding *à priori*, by way of general reasoning, instead of Baconian experiment, shewed complete ignorance of Bacon's principles, and of the necessary conditions of experimental investigation. At this juncture appeared, in the *Edinburgh Review*, Macaulay's famous attack on my father's Essay on Government.[*] This gave me much to think about. I saw that Macaulay's conception of the logic of politics was erroneous; that he stood up for the empirical mode of treating political phenomena, against the philosophical; that even in physical science, his notion of philosophizing might have recognized Kepler, but would have excluded Newton and Laplace. But I could not help feeling, that though the tone was unbecoming (an error for which the writer, at a later period, made the most ample and honorable amends),[†] there was truth in several of his strictures on my father's treatment of the subject; that my father's premises were really too narrow, and included but a small number of the general truths, on which, in politics, the important consequences depend. Identity of interest between the governing body and the community at large, is not, in any practical sense which can be attached to it, the only thing on which good government depends; neither can this identity of interest be secured by the mere conditions of election. I was not at all satisfied with the mode in which my father met the criticisms of Macaulay. He did not, as I thought he ought to have done, justify himself by saying, "I was not writing a scientific treatise on politics. I was writing an argument for parliamentary reform." He treated Macaulay's argument as simply irrational; an attack upon the reasoning faculty; an example of the saying of Hobbes, that when reason is against

[*Thomas Babington Macaulay, "Mill's *Essay on Government*: Utilitarian Logic and Politics," *Edinburgh Review*, XLIX (Mar., 1829), 159–89; "Bentham's Defence of Mill: Utilitarian System of Philosophy," *ibid.*, XLIX (June, 1829), 273–99; and "Utilitarian Theory of Government, and the 'Greatest Happiness Principle,'" *ibid.*, L (Oct., 1829), 99–125. There was a reply to the first two articles in the *Westminster Review* by Thomas Perronet Thompson, with Bentham's help, "'Greatest Happiness' Principle," XI (July, 1829), 254–68; and two further replies by Thompson alone: "*Edinburgh Review* and the 'Greatest Happiness Principle,'" *ibid.*, XI (Oct., 1829), 526–36, and XII (Jan., 1830), 246–62.]

[†See Macaulay, "Preface," *Critical and Historical Essays*, 3 vols. (London: Longman, Brown, Green, and Longmans, 1843), Vol. I, p. viii.]

This made me think that there was really something more fundamentally erroneous in my father's conception of philosophical Method, as applicable to politics, than I had hitherto supposed there was. But I did not at first see clearly what the error might be. At last however it flashed upon me all at once in the course of my reflexions on another subject. I had begun in the early part of 1830 to put on paper the ideas on Logic (chiefly on the distinctions among Terms, and the import of Propositions) which had been suggested and in part worked out in the morning conversations *already spoken of*. Having secured these thoughts by putting them into writing, I pushed on into the other parts of the subject, to try whether I could do anything further to clear up the theory of Logic generally. I attempted at once to grapple with the problem of Induction, postponing that of Reasoning on the ground that it is necessary to obtain premises before we can reason from them. Now Induction is mainly finding the causes of effects; and in endeavouring to give an account of the manner of tracing causes and effects in the physical sciences, I soon saw that in the more perfect of those sciences we ascend, by generalization from particular instances to the tendencies of causes considered singly, and then reason downward from those separate tendencies, to determine the action of the same causes when combined. I then asked myself, what is the ultimate analysis of this deductive process? the common theory of the syllogism evidently throwing no light upon it. My *f* practice being to study abstract principles in the best concrete instances I could find, the Composition of Forces, in dynamics, occurred to me as the most complete example of the logical process I was investigating. On examining what the mind does when it applies the principle of the Composition of Forces, I found that it performs a simple act of addition. It adds the separate effect of the one cause to the separate effect of the other, and puts down the sum of the separate effects as the joint effect. But is this a legitimate process? In dynamics and in the other branches of mathematical physics it is; but in some other cases, as in chemistry it is not; and I then recollected that this was pointed out as one of the distinctions between chemical phenomena and those of natural philosophy, in the introduction to that favorite book of my boyhood, Thomson's *Chemistry*. This distinction cleared up what was perplexing me in respect to the philosophy of politics. I saw that a science is deductive or experimental according as the effects of its causes when conjoined are or are not the sums of the effects of the same causes when separate; which, in the moral and political sciences, they may on the whole be said to be. Hence it appeared that both Macaulay and my father were wrong; the one in assimilating the method of philosophizing in politics to the purely experimental method of chemistry; while the other, though right in adopting an a priori method, had made a wrong selection of one, having taken, not the appropriate method, that of the deductive branches of natural philosophy, but the

---

e–e[*Earlier version:*] at Grote's
f[*Cancelled text:*] constant

a man, a man will be against reason.[*] This made me think that there was really something more fundamentally erroneous in my father's conception of philosophical Method, as applicable to politics, than I had hitherto supposed there was. But I did not at first see clearly what the error might be. At last it flashed upon me all at once in the course of other studies. In the early part of 1830 I had begun to put on paper the ideas on Logic (chiefly on the distinctions among Terms, and the import of Propositions) which had been suggested and in part worked out in the morning conversations already spoken of. Having secured these thoughts from being lost, I pushed on into the other parts of the subject, to try whether I could do anything further towards clearing up the theory of Logic generally. I grappled at once with the problem of Induction, postponing that of Reasoning, on the ground that it is necessary to obtain premises before we can reason from them. Now, Induction is mainly a process for finding the causes of effects: and in attempting to fathom the mode of tracing causes and effects in physical science, I soon saw that in the more perfect of the sciences, we ascend, by generalization from particulars, to the tendencies of causes considered singly, and then reason downward from those separate tendencies, to the effect of the same causes when combined. I then asked myself, what is the ultimate analysis of this deductive process; the common theory of the syllogism evidently throwing no light upon it. My practice (learnt from Hobbes and my father) being to study abstract principles by means of the best concrete instances I could find, the Composition of Forces, in dynamics, occurred to me as the most complete example of the logical process I was investigating. On examining, accordingly, what the mind does when it applies the principle of the Composition of Forces, I found that it performs a simple act of addition. It adds the separate effect of the one force to the separate effect of the other, and puts down the sum of these separate effects as the joint effect. But is this a legitimate process? In dynamics, and in all the mathematical branches of physics, it is; but in some other cases, as in chemistry, it is not; and I then recollected that something not unlike this was pointed out as one of the distinctions between chemical and mechanical phenomena, in the introduction to that favorite of my boyhood, Thomson's *System of Chemistry*. This distinction at once made my mind clear as to what was perplexing me in respect to the philosophy of politics. I now saw, that a science is either deductive or experimental, according as, in the province it deals with, the effects of causes when conjoined, are or are not the sums of the effects which the same causes produce when separate. It followed that politics must be a deductive science. It thus appeared, that both Macaulay and my father were wrong; the one in assimilating the method of philosophizing in politics to the purely experimental method of chemistry; while the other, though right in adopting a deductive method, had made a wrong selection of one, having taken as the type of deduction, not the appropriate process, that of the deductive branches of natural philosophy,

[*See "Epistle Dedicatory" to *Tripos*, in *The English Works of Thomas Hobbes*, ed. William Molesworth, 11 vols. (London: Bohn, 1839–45), Vol. IV, p. xiii.]

inappropriate method of pure geometry, which not being a science of causation at all, did not require or admit of the summation of effects. A foundation was thus laid in my thoughts for the principal chapters of what I afterwards published on the "Logic of the Moral Sciences"; and my position in respect to my old political creed was now to my own mind quite cleared up. [g]

If I am asked what other system of political philosophy I substituted for that which, as a philosophy, I had abandoned, my answer is, no system: merely a conviction, that the true system was something much more complex and many sided than I had hitherto had any idea of, and that its office was to supply, not a set of model institutions, but principles from which the institutions suitable to any given circumstances might be deduced. The influences of European, that is to say, Continental thought, and especially those of the reaction of the nineteenth century against the eighteenth, were now showering in upon me. They came from various quarters; partly from the writings of Coleridge, which I had begun to read with interest even before the change in my opinions [h]; partly from[h] the Coleridgians with whom I was in personal contact: partly from what I had read of Goethe; partly from Carlyle's early articles in the *Edinburgh* and *Foreign* Reviews, though for a long time I saw nothing in these (as my father saw nothing in them to the last) but insane rhapsodies. From all these, and from the acquaintance I kept up with the French writers of the time, I derived, among other ideas, which the general turning upside down of the opinions of European thinkers had brought uppermost, these in particular: that the human mind has a certain order of possible progress in which some things must precede others, an order which governments and public instructors can alter to some extent, but not to an unlimited extent: that all questions of institutions are relative, not absolute, and that different stages of human progress not only *will* have (which must always have been evident), but *ought* to have, different institutions; that government is always either in the hands, or passing into the hands, of whatever is the strongest power in society, and that what this power is, does not depend on institutions, but institutions on it: that any general theory or philosophy of politics supposes a previous theory of human progress, in other words a philosophy of history. These opinions, true in the main, were held in an exaggerated and violent manner by [i]the thinkers with whom I was now becoming acquainted, and[i] who, in the true spirit of a reaction, ignored that half of the truth which the thinkers of the eighteenth century saw. I never went along with them in this, but kept as firm a hold of one side of the truth as I took of the other. The fight

[g][*Cancelled text:*] I did not at this time push my logical speculations any further. [*paragraph*] This was not the only modification which was taking place in my old opinions in the political department of things. The early writings of the St. Simonian school, with which I had now become acquainted, were gradually opening my eyes to the very limited and temporary value of the old political economy, which assumes individual hereditary property as a necessary fact, and freedom of production and exchange as the dernier mot of social improvement. [*This paragraph continues with three sentences substantially the same as the third and fourth sentences and part of the fifth sentence of the second paragraph below* ("*They were then . . . even this length*"—170.9–13). *For the rest of this earlier version, continued on R105–6, see App. G, pp. 614–16 below.*]

but the inappropriate one of pure geometry, which not being a science of causation at all, does not require or admit of any summing-up of effects. A foundation was thus laid in my thoughts for the principal chapters of what I afterwards published on the Logic of the Moral Sciences;[*] and my new position in respect to my old political creed now became perfectly definite.

If I am asked what system of political philosophy I substituted for that which, as a philosophy, I had abandoned, I answer, no system: only a conviction, that the true system was something much more complex and many sided than I had previously had any idea of, and that its office was to supply, not a set of model institutions, but principles from which the institutions suitable to any given circumstances might be deduced. The influences of European, that is to say, Continental, thought, and especially those of the reaction of the nineteenth century against the eighteenth, were now streaming in upon me. They came from various quarters: from the writings of Coleridge, which I had begun to read with interest even before the change in my opinions; from the Coleridgians with whom I was in personal intercourse; from what I had read of Goethe; from Carlyle's early articles in the *Edinburgh* and *Foreign* Reviews,[†] though for a long time I saw nothing in these (as my father saw nothing in them to the last) but insane rhapsody. From these sources, and from the acquaintance I kept up with the French literature of the time, I derived, among other ideas which the general turning upside down of the opinions of European thinkers had brought uppermost, these in particular: That the human mind has a certain order of possible progress, in which some things must precede others, an order which governments and public instructors can modify to some, but not to an unlimited extent: That all questions of political institutions are relative, not absolute, and that different stages of human progress not only *will* have, but *ought* to have, different institutions: That government is always either in the hands, or passing into the hands, of whatever is the strongest power in society, and that what this power is, does not depend on institutions, but institutions on it: That any general theory or philosophy of politics supposes a previous theory of human progress, and that this is the same thing with a philosophy of history. These opinions, true in the main, were held in an exaggerated and violent manner by the thinkers with whom I was now most accustomed to compare notes, and who, as usual with a reaction, ignored that half of the truth which the thinkers of the eighteenth century saw. But though, at one period of my progress, I for some time undervalued that great century, I never joined in the reaction against it, but kept as firm hold of one side of the truth as I took of the other. The fight between the

[*In *A System of Logic*, Bk. VI.]

[†E.g., "Jean Paul Friedrich Richter," *Edinburgh Review*, XLVI (June, 1827), 176–95; "Life and Writings of Werner," *Foreign Review*, I (Jan., 1828), 95–141. For other of Carlyle's essays that Mill probably had in mind, see the Bibliographic Index under the two titles just cited.]

---

h–h[*Earlier version:*] , and of which I was now a frequent reader: partly from Sterling, Maurice, and
i–i[*Earlier version:*] my new instructors,

between the nineteenth century and the eighteenth always reminded me of the battle about the shield, one side of which was black and the other white. I marvelled at the blind rage with which the combatants rushed against one another. I applied to them, and to Coleridge among the rest, many of the sayings of Coleridge himself about half truths; and Goethe's device, "manysidedness," was much in my thoughts.

The writers by whom more than by any others a new mode of political thinking was brought home to me, were those of the St. Simonian school in France. In 1829 and 1830 I became acquainted with some of their writings. They were then only in the earlier stages of their speculations: they had not yet dressed up their philosophy as a religion, nor had they organized their scheme of Socialism. They were just beginning to question the principle of hereditary property. I was by no means prepared to go with them even this length; but I was greatly struck with the connected view which they for the first time presented to me, of the natural order of human progress; and especially with their division of history into organic periods and critical periods. During the organic periods (they said) mankind accept with firm conviction some positive creed, containing more or less of truth and of adaptation to the needs of humanity. Under its influence they first make all the progress compatible with that creed, and then finally outgrow it: and a period follows of criticism and negation, in which mankind lose their old convictions without acquiring any new ones except the conviction that the old are false. The period of Greek and Roman polytheism, so long as really believed in by instructed Greeks and Romans, was an organic period, followed by the critical or sceptical period of the Greek philosophers. Another organic period came in with Christianity; the corresponding critical period began with the Reformation, has lasted ever since, and cannot altogether cease until a new organic period has been inaugurated by the triumph of a still more advanced creed. These ideas, I knew, were nowise peculiar to the St. Simonians; they were the general property of Europe, or at least of Germany and France; but they had never to my knowledge been so completely systematized as by these writers, nor the distinguishing characters of a critical period so powerfully set forth. In Carlyle indeed I found bitter denunciations of the nineteenth century and the eighteenth always reminded me of the battle about the shield, one side of which was white and the other black.[*] I marvelled at the blind rage with which the combatants rushed against one another. I applied to them, and to Coleridge himself, many of Coleridge's sayings about half truths;[†] and Goethe's device, "many-sidedness,"[‡] was one which I would most willingly, at this period, have taken for mine.

The writers by whom, more than by any others, a new mode of political thinking was brought home to me, were those of the St. Simonian school in France. In 1829 and 1830 I became acquainted with some of their writings. They were then only in the earlier stages of their speculations. They had not yet dressed out their philosophy as a religion, nor had they organized their scheme of Socialism. They were just beginning to question the principle of hereditary property. I was by no means prepared to go with them even this length; but I was greatly struck with the connected view which they for the first time presented to me, of the natural order of human progress; and especially with their division of all history into organic periods and critical periods. During the organic periods (they said) mankind accept with firm conviction some positive creed, claiming jurisdiction over all their actions, and containing more or less of truth and adaptation to the needs of humanity. Under its influence they make all the progress compatible with the creed, and finally outgrow it; when a period follows of criticism and negation, in which mankind lose their old convictions without acquiring any new ones, of a general or authoritative character, except the conviction that the old are false. The period of Greek and Roman polytheism, so long as really believed in by instructed Greeks and Romans, was an organic period, succeeded by the critical or sceptical period of the Greek philosophers. Another organic period came in with Christianity. The corresponding critical period began with the Reformation, has lasted ever since, still lasts, and cannot altogether cease until a new organic period has been inaugurated by the triumph of a yet more advanced creed. These ideas, I knew, were not peculiar to the St. Simonians; on the contrary, they were the general property of Europe, or at least of Germany and France, but they had never, to my knowledge, been so completely systematized as by these writers, nor the distinguishing characteristics of a critical period so powerfully set forth; for I was not then acquainted with Fichte's Lectures on *The Characteristics of the Present Age*.[§]

[*See "Sir Harry Beaumont" (Joseph Spence), "Fable X. The Party-Colour'd Shield," in *Moralities; or, Essays, Letters, Fables, and Translations* (London: Dodsley, 1753), pp. 99–102.]

[†See, e.g., *The Literary Remains of Samuel Taylor Coleridge*, ed. Henry Nelson Coleridge, 4 vols. (London: Pickering, 1836–39), Vol. III, p. 145.]

[‡See Sarah Austin, *Characteristics of Goethe*, Vol. I, pp. 12–13, where she is translating from Johann Daniel Falk, *Goethe aus näherm persönlichen Umgange dargestellt* (Leipzig: Brockhaus, 1832), p. 8, in which the key term is given as "Vielseitigkeit (Objectivität)."]

[§Johann Gottlieb Fichte, *The Characteristics of the Present Age*, trans. William Smith (London: Chapman, 1847).]

evils of an "age of unbelief" and of the present age as such, which I and most other people at that time supposed to be intended as passionate protests in favour of the old belief. But all that was true in these denunciations I thought that I found more calmly and philosophically stated by the St. Simonians. Among their publications too there was one which seemed to me far superior to the rest, and in which the general idea was matured into something much more definite and instructive. This was an early writing of Auguste Comte, who then called himself, and even announced himself in the title page as, an élève of Saint-Simon. In this tract M. Comte first enunciated the doctrine which he afterwards so copiously illustrated, of the natural succession of three stages in every department of inquiry; first the theological, second the metaphysical, and third, the positive stage; and contended that social science must be subject to the same law; that the feudal and Catholic system was the last phasis of the theological state of the social science, Protestant-ism the commencement and the doctrines of the French Revolution the consumma-tion of its metaphysical, and that its positive state was yet to come. This doctrine harmonized very well with my existing notions. I already regarded the methods of physical science as the proper models for political. But the chief service which I received at this time from the trains of thought suggested by the St. Simonians and by Comte, was that I obtained a much clearer conception than before of the peculiarities of an age of transition in opinion, and ceased to mistake the moral and intellectual characteristics of such an age, for the normal attributes of humanity. I looked forward, through the present age of loud disputes but generally weak convictions, to a future which will unite the best qualities of the critical with the best of the organic periods; unchecked liberty of thought, perfect freedom of individual action in things not hurtful to others; but along with this, firm convic-tions as to right and wrong, useful and pernicious, deeply engraven on the feelings by early education and general unanimity of sentiment, and so well grounded in reason and in the real exigencies of life, that they shall not, like all former and present creeds, religious, ethical and political, require to be periodically thrown off and replaced by others.

M. Comte soon left the St. Simonians, and I lost sight of him and his writings for a number of years. But the Saint Simonians I continued cultivating. I was kept *au courant* of their progress by one of their most enthusiastic disciples, Gustave d'Eichthal, who about that time passed a considerable period in England. I was introduced to their chiefs, Bazard and Enfantin, in 1830; and as long as their public teachings and proselytism continued, I read nearly everything they wrote. Their criticisms on the common doctrines of liberalism seemed to me full of important

In Carlyle, indeed, I found bitter denunciations of an "age of unbelief," and of the present age as such,[*] which I, like most people at that time, supposed to be passionate protests in favour of the old modes of belief. But all that was true in these denunciations I thought that I found more calmly and philosophically stated by the St. Simonians. Among their publications, too, there was one which seemed to me far superior to the rest; in which the general idea was matured into something much more definite and instructive. This was an early work of Auguste Comte, who then called himself, and even announced himself in the title page as, a pupil of Saint-Simon.[†] In this tract M. Comte first put forth the doctrine which he afterwards so copiously illustrated, of the natural succession of three stages in every department of human knowledge—first the theological, next the meta-physical, and lastly, the positive stage; and contended, that social science must be subject to the same law; that the feudal and Catholic system was the concluding phasis of the theological state of the social science, Protestantism the commence-ment and the doctrines of the French Revolution the consummation of the meta-physical, and that its positive state was yet to come.[‡] This doctrine harmonized well with my existing notions, to which it seemed to give a scientific shape. I already regarded the methods of physical science as the proper models for politi-cal. But the chief benefit which I derived at this time from the trains of thought suggested by the St. Simonians and by Comte, was, that I obtained a clearer conception than ever before of the peculiarities of an era of transition in opinion, and ceased to mistake the moral and intellectual characteristics of such an era, for the normal attributes of humanity. I looked forward, through the present age of loud disputes but generally weak convictions, to a future which shall unite the best qualities of the critical with the best qualities of the organic periods; unchecked liberty of thought, unbounded freedom of individual action in all modes not hurtful to others; but also, convictions as to what is right and wrong, useful and perni-cious, deeply engraven on the feelings by early education and general unanimity of sentiment, and so firmly grounded in reason and in the true exigencies of life, that they shall not, like all former and present creeds, religious, ethical, and political, require to be periodically thrown off and replaced by others.

M. Comte soon left the St. Simonians, and I lost sight of him and his writings for a number of years. But the St. Simonians I continued to cultivate. I was kept *au courant* of their progress by one of their most enthusiastic disciples, M. Gustave d'Eichthal, who about that time passed a considerable interval in England. I was introduced to their chiefs, Bazard and Enfantin, in 1830; and as long as their public teachings and proselytism continued, I read nearly everything they wrote. Their criticisms on the common doctrines of Liberalism seemed to me full of important

[*See, e.g., *Sartor Resartus*, pp. 166ff. (Bk. II, Chap. vii, "The Everlasting No").]

[†Auguste Comte, *Système de politique positive* (Paris: Saint-Simon, 1824); Comte later published another work under the same main title (see p. 221 below).]

[‡See *ibid.*, pp. 268–9.]

truth; and it was partly by their writings that my eyes were opened to the very limited and temporary value of the old political economy, which assumes private property and inheritance as indefeasible facts, and freedom of production and exchange as the dernier mot of social improvement. The scheme gradually unfolded by the St. Simonians, by which the labour and capital of the community would be managed for the general account, every individual being required to take a share of labour either as thinker, teacher, artist or producer, and all being classed according to their capacity and rewarded according to their works, appeared to me a far superior kind of Socialism to Owen's; their aim seemed to me perfectly rational, however their means might be inefficacious; and though I neither believed in the practicability nor in the beneficial operation of their social machinery, I felt that the proclamation of such an ideal of human society could not but be calculated to give a beneficial direction to the efforts of others to bring society, as at present constituted, nearer to that ideal standard. I honoured them above all for the boldness and freedom from prejudice with which they treated the subject of family, the most important of any, and needing more fundamental alterations than any other, but which scarcely any reformer has the courage to touch. In proclaiming the perfect equality of men and women, and an entirely new order of things in regard to their relations with one another, the St. Simonians in common with Owen and Fourier have entitled themselves to the grateful remembrance of all future generations. [j]

In giving an account of this period of my life, I have only specified such of my new impressions as appeared to me both at the time and since to be a kind of turning points, marking a definite progress in my modes of thought. But these few selected points give a very insufficient idea of the quantity of thinking which I carried on respecting a host of subjects during these years of transition. It is true much of the thinking consisted in rediscovering things known to all the world, which I had previously disbelieved, or disregarded. But even then the rediscovery usually placed these truths in some new light by which they were reconciled with, and served to confirm even while they modified, the truths *not* generally known which [k]were contained in my early opinions[k] and in no essential part of which I at any time wavered. All my thinking only rendered the foundation of these deeper and stronger, while it often removed misunderstandings and confusion of ideas which had perverted their effect. For example; during the later returns of my dejection, the doctrine of what is called Philosophical Necessity weighed like an incubus on my existence. I felt as if I was the helpless slave of antecedent circumstances; as if [l]the character of all persons had been formed for them by agencies beyond their

---

[j][*Cancelled text:*] This however is anticipating; for at the time of which I am now writing the St. Simonians had not yet developed the practical parts of their system. The effect they had on me at this time was solely by their philosophy of history.

[k-k][*Earlier version:*] I had had the good fortune to be taught

truth; and it was partly by their writings that my eyes were opened to the very limited and temporary value of the old political economy, which assumes private property and inheritance as indefeasible facts, and freedom of production and exchange as the *dernier mot* of social improvement. The scheme gradually unfolded by the St. Simonians, under which the labour and capital of society would be managed for the general account of the community, every individual being required to take a share of labour, either as thinker, teacher, artist, or producer, all being classed according to their capacity, and remunerated according to their works, appeared to me a far superior description of Socialism to Owen's. Their aim seemed to me desirable and rational, however their means might be inefficacious; and though I neither believed in the practicability, nor in the beneficial operation of their social machinery, I felt that the proclamation of such an ideal of human society could not but tend to give a beneficial direction to the efforts of others to bring society, as at present constituted, nearer to some ideal standard. I honoured them most of all for what they have been most cried down for—the boldness and freedom from prejudice with which they treated the subject of family, the most important of any, and needing more fundamental alterations than remain to be made in any other great social institution, but on which scarcely any reformer has the courage to touch. In proclaiming the perfect equality of men and women, and an entirely new order of things in regard to their relations with one another, the St. Simonians in common with Owen and Fourier have entitled themselves to the grateful remembrance of future generations.

In giving an account of this period of my life, I have only specified such of my new impressions as appeared to me, both at the time and since, to be a kind of turning points, marking a definite progress in my mode of thought. But these few selected points give a very insufficient idea of the quantity of thinking which I carried on respecting a host of subjects during these years of transition. Much of this, it is true, consisted in rediscovering things known to all the world, which I had previously disbelieved, or disregarded. But the rediscovery was to me a discovery, giving me plenary possession of the truths not as traditional platitudes but fresh from their source: and it seldom failed to place them in some new light, by which they were reconciled with, and seemed to confirm while they modified, the truths less generally known which lay in my early opinions, and in no essential part of which I at any time wavered. All my new thinking only laid the foundation of these more deeply and strongly, while it often removed misapprehension and confusion of ideas which had perverted their effect. For example, during the later returns of my dejection, the doctrine of what is called Philosophical Necessity weighed on my existence like an incubus. I felt as if I was scientifically proved to be the helpless slave of antecedent circumstances; as if my character and that of all others had been formed for us by agencies beyond our control, and was wholly out of our

---

[1-1176][*Earlier version:*] my character had been formed for me by agencies beyond my control, and was now out of my

control, and was wholly out of their *power. I often said to myself what a relief it would be if I could disbelieve the doctrine of the formation of character by circumstances; and remembering the wish of Fox respecting the doctrine of resistance to governments, that it might never be forgotten by kings, nor remembered by subjects, I said in like manner that it would be a blessing if the doctrine of necessity could be believed by all in respect to the characters of others and disbelieved in respect of their own. I pondered on the subject till gradually I saw light through it; I saw that the word necessity as a name for the doctrine of cause and effect applied to human action, carries with it a misleading association; and that this association is the main cause of the depressing and paralysing influence which I had experienced. I perceived that though character is *m* formed by circumstances, our own desires can influence those circumstances; and that what is really inspiriting and ennobling in the doctrine of free will, is the conviction that our will has real power over the formation of our character; that our will, by influencing some of our circumstances, can modify our future habits or capacities of willing. This was perfectly consistent with the doctrine of circumstances or rather was that doctrine itself properly understood. From that time I drew in my own mind a clear distinction between the doctrine of circumstances and fatalism, discarding altogether the misleading term necessity. The theory, which I now for the first time rightly apprehended, ceased to be discouraging: and I no longer suffered under the burthen, so heavy to one who aims at being a reformer in opinions, of thinking one doctrine true and the contrary doctrine morally beneficial. The train of thought which had extricated me from this dilemma seemed to me fitted to render a similar service to others, and it now forms the chapter on Liberty and Necessity in the concluding book of my *System of Logic*.

In like manner in politics, though I no longer accepted the doctrine of the Essay on Government as a scientific theory; though I ceased to consider representative democracy as an absolute principle and regarded it as a question of time, place, and circumstance; though I now looked on the choice of political institutions as a moral and educational question rather than a question of material interest, and thought it should be decided mainly by considering what great improvement in life and culture stood next in order for the people concerned, as the condition of their further progress, and what institutions were most likely to promote that; nevertheless this change in the premises of my political philosophy did not alter my practical political creed as to the requirements of my own time and country. I was as much as ever a radical and democrat for Europe and especially for England. I thought the predominance of the aristocracy and the rich in the English Constitution an evil worth any struggle to get rid of: not on account of taxes or any such comparatively trifling inconvenience but as the great demoralizing influence in the country. Demoralizing, first, because it made the conduct of the government an

---

m[*Cancelled text:*] entirely

own power. I often said to myself, what a relief it would be if I could disbelieve the doctrine of the formation of character by circumstances; and remembering the wish of Fox respecting the doctrine of resistance to governments, that it might never be forgotten by kings, nor remembered by subjects, I said that it would be a blessing if the doctrine of necessity could be believed by all *quoad* the characters of others, and disbelieved in regard to their own. I pondered painfully on the subject, till gradually I saw light through it. I perceived, that the word Necessity, as a name for the doctrine of Cause and Effect applied to human action, carried with it a misleading association; and that this association was the operative force in the depressing and paralysing influence which I had experienced. I saw that though our character is formed by circumstances, our own desires can do much to shape those circumstances; and that what is really inspiriting and ennobling in the doctrine of freewill, is the conviction that we have real power over the formation of our own character; that our will, by influencing some of our circumstances, can modify our future habits or capabilities of willing. All this was entirely consistent with the doctrine of circumstances, or rather, was that doctrine itself, properly understood. From that time I drew, in my own mind, a clear distinction between the doctrine of circumstances, and Fatalism; discarding altogether the misleading word Necessity. The theory, which I now for the first time rightly apprehended, ceased altogether to be discouraging, and besides the relief to my spirits, I no longer suffered under the burthen, so heavy to one who aims at being a reformer in opinions, of thinking one doctrine true, and the contrary doctrine morally beneficial. The train of thought which had extricated me from this dilemma, seemed to me, in after years, fitted to render a similar service to others; and it now forms the chapter on Liberty and Necessity in the concluding Book of my *System of Logic*.[*]

Again, in politics, though I no longer accepted the doctrine of the Essay on Government as a scientific theory; though I ceased to consider representative democracy as an absolute principle, and regarded it as a question of time, place, and circumstance; though I now looked upon the choice of political institutions as a moral and educational question more than one of material interests, thinking that it ought to be decided mainly by the consideration, what great improvement in life and culture stands next in order for the people concerned, as the condition of their further progress, and what institutions are most likely to promote that; nevertheless this change in the premises of my political philosophy did not alter my practical political creed as to the requirements of my own time and country. I was as much as ever a radical and democrat, for Europe, and especially for England. I thought the predominance of the aristocratic classes, the noble and the rich, in the English Constitution, an evil worth any struggle to get rid of; not on account of taxes, or any such comparatively small inconvenience, but as the great demoralizing agency in the country. Demoralizing, first, because it made the conduct of the government

[*Bk. VI, Chap. ii.]

example of a gross public immorality—the predominance of private over public interest—the abuse of the powers of legislation for the advantage of "separate classes". Secondly, and above all, because the respect of the multitude always attaches itself principally to that which is the principal passport to power; for which reason under the English institutions where riches, hereditary or acquired, were the almost exclusive source of political importance, riches and the signs of riches were almost the only things really respected, and to the pursuit of these the life of the people was mainly devoted. Further, I thought that while the higher and richer classes held the power of government, the instruction and improvement of the mass of the people was contrary to the self interest of those classes, because necessarily tending to raise up dissatisfaction with their monopoly: but if the democracy obtained a share in the supreme power, and still more if they obtained the predominant share, it would become the interest of the opulent classes to promote their education, in order to guard them from really mischievous errors and especially to ward off unjust violations of property. For these reasons I was not only as ardent as ever for democratic institutions, but earnestly hoped that Owenite, St. Simonian, and all other anti-property opinions might spread widely among the poorer classes, not that I thought those doctrines true but in order that the higher classes might be led to see that they had more to fear from the poor when uneducated, than from the poor when educated.

In this frame of mind the French Revolution of July found me. It roused my utmost enthusiasm, and gave me as it were a new existence. I went at once to Paris ^{o} , was introduced to Lafayette, and got acquainted with several of the active chiefs of the popular party ^{p}. After my return I entered warmly, as a writer, into the politics of the time, which soon became still more exciting by the coming in of Lord Grey's ministry, and the proposing of the Reform Bill. For the next few years I wrote largely in newspapers. It was just about this time that Fonblanque, who had for some time previous written the political articles in the *Examiner*, became the proprietor and editor of the paper. It is not forgotten with what verve and talent he carried it on, during the whole period of Lord Grey's ministry, and what importance it assumed as the principal representative of radical opinions in the newspaper press. ^{q}At least three fourths of the original writing in the paper was his own; but of the remaining fourth^q I contributed during the first years a considerable share. I wrote nearly all the articles on French subjects, including a weekly summary of French politics often extending to considerable length. I also wrote many leading articles on general politics, on commercial and financial legislation, and any miscellaneous subjects suitable to the paper in which I felt interested, besides

---

$^{n-n}$[*Earlier version:*] a whole host of separate small classes at the expense of the community

^{o}[*Cancelled text:*] (with Charles Buller, Roebuck and others)

^{p}[*Cancelled text:*] , an acquaintance which I afterwards extended to others of their number

$^{q-q}$[*Earlier version:*] Nine parts in ten of the original writing in the paper was his own; but of the remaining tenth

an example of gross public immorality, through the predominance of private over public interests in the State, and the abuse of the powers of legislation for the advantage of classes. Secondly, and in a still greater degree, because the respect of the multitude always attaching itself principally to that which, in the existing state of society, is the chief passport to power; and under English institutions, riches, hereditary or acquired, being the almost exclusive source of political importance; riches, and the signs of riches, were almost the only things really respected, and the life of the people was mainly devoted to the pursuit of them. I thought, that while the higher and richer classes held the power of government, the instruction and improvement of the mass of the people were contrary to the self interest of those classes, because tending to render the people more powerful for throwing off the yoke: but if the democracy obtained a large, and perhaps the principal, share in the governing power, it would become the interest of the opulent classes to promote their education, in order to ward off really mischievous errors, and especially those which would lead to unjust violations of property. On these grounds I was not only as ardent as ever for democratic institutions, but earnestly hoped that Owenite, St. Simonian, and all other anti-property doctrines might spread widely among the poorer classes; not that I thought those doctrines true, or desired that they should be acted on, but in order that the higher classes might be made to see that they had more to fear from the poor when uneducated, than when educated.

In this frame of mind the French Revolution of July found me. It roused my utmost enthusiasm, and gave me, as it were, a new existence. I went at once to Paris, was introduced to Lafayette, and laid the groundwork of the intercourse I afterwards kept up with several of the active chiefs of the extreme popular party. After my return I entered warmly, as a writer, into the political discussions of the time; which soon became still more exciting, by the coming in of Lord Grey's ministry, and the proposing of the Reform Bill.[*] For the next few years I wrote copiously in newspapers. It was about this time that Fonblanque, who had for some time written the political articles in the *Examiner*, became the proprietor and editor of the paper. It is not forgotten with what verve and talent, as well as fine wit, he carried it on, during the whole period of Lord Grey's ministry, and what importance it assumed as the principal representative, in the newspaper press, of radical opinions. The distinguishing character of the paper was given to it entirely by his own articles, which formed at least three fourths of all the original writing contained in it: but of the remaining fourth I contributed during those years a much larger share than any one else.[†] I wrote nearly all the articles on French subjects, including a weekly summary of French politics, often extending to considerable length; together with many leading articles on general politics, commercial and financial legislation, and any miscellaneous subjects in which I felt interested, and

[*2 & 3 William IV, c. 45 (7 June, 1832).]

[†From 18 July, 1830, to 14 Sept., 1834, Mill contributed some 210 articles of various kinds and lengths to the *Examiner*.]

occasional reviews of books. In mere newspaper articles on the occurrences and questions of the moment there was little room for the developement of any general mode of thought; but I attempted in the beginning of 1831, to embody in a series of articles, under the heading of "The Spirit of the Age" some of my new opinions and especially to point out in the character of the present age the anomalies and evils characteristic of the transition from one system of opinions which had worn out, to another only in process of formation. These articles were I believe lumbering in style, and not lively and striking enough to be acceptable to newspaper readers at any time; but had they been much more attractive, still at that particular time, when great political changes were impending, and occupied all minds, these discussions were ill timed, and missed fire altogether.* *The only effect which I know to have been produced by them is* that Carlyle, then living in a secluded part of Scotland, read them in his solitude, and saying to himself (as he afterwards told me) "here is a new Mystic," enquired on coming to London that autumn, concerning their authorship, an enquiry which was the immediate cause of our becoming personally acquainted.

I have mentioned Carlyle's earlier writings as one of the channels through which the influences reached me, which had enlarged my early narrow creed: but I do not think that those writings by themselves would ever have had any effect on my opinions. What truths they contained were presented in a form and vesture less suited than any other to give them access to a mind trained as mine had been. They seemed a haze of poetry and German metaphysics, in which the only clear thing was a strong animosity to most of the opinions which were the basis of my mode of thought, religious scepticism, utilitarianism, the doctrine of circumstances, and the attaching any importance to democracy or logic or political economy. Instead of being taught anything in the first instance by Carlyle, it was only in proportion as

---

*ʳThis was an error I frequently committed: for example, in the summer of 1832, when the country was preparing for the first elections after the passing of the Reform Bill, I wrote several articles in the *Examiner* in strong opposition to the exaction of pledges from representatives. ["Pledges," *Examiner*, 1 July, 1832, pp. 417–18, and 15 July, 1832, pp. 449–51.] The doctrine of these articles was right in itself, and very suitable to democratic institutions when firmly established and rooted in the habits of the people: then no doubt it would be wise in the electors to look out for the most honest and most instructed men whom they could induce to undertake the office of legislators, and refrain from binding them beforehand to any definite measures: but I did not sufficiently consider that the transition from bad to good institutions was only commencing. Like many other persons at the time, I thought that we had had our revolution; that the way was now smooth for the advance of democracy, that precautions were henceforth chiefly required against the evils which might come from the popular side; and I little anticipated that the coming years would require a long continuance of struggle to give democracy even its due influence.ʳ

ʳ⁻ʳ[*This note was originally a part of the main text. Mill subsequently marked it off with lines and added "Note." and "End of Note." at left.*]

which were suitable to the paper, including occasional reviews of books. Mere newspaper articles on the occurrences or questions of the moment gave no opportunity for the development of any general mode of thought; but I attempted, in the beginning of 1831, to embody in a series of articles, headed "The Spirit of the Age," some of my new opinions, and especially to point out in the character of the present age, the anomalies and evils characteristic of the transition from a system of opinions which had worn out, to another only in process of being formed.[*] These articles were, I fancy, lumbering in style, and not lively or striking enough to be at any time acceptable to newspaper readers; but had they been far more attractive, still, at that particular moment, when great political changes were impending, and engrossing all minds, these discussions were ill timed, and missed fire altogether. The only effect which I know to have been produced by them, was that Carlyle, then living in a secluded part of Scotland, read them in his solitude, and saying to himself (as he afterwards told me) "here is a new Mystic," enquired on coming to London that autumn respecting their author- ship; an enquiry which was the immediate cause of our becoming personally acquainted.[†]

I have already mentioned Carlyle's earlier writings as one of the channels through which I received the influences which enlarged my early narrow creed; but I do not think that those writings, by themselves, would ever have had any effect on my opinions. What truths they contained, though of the very kind which I was already receiving from other quarters, were presented in a form and vesture less suited than any other to give them access to a mind trained as mine had been. They seemed a haze of poetry and German metaphysics, in which almost the only clear thing was a strong animosity to most of the opinions which were the basis of my mode of thought; religious scepticism, utilitarianism, the doctrine of circum- stances, and the attaching any importance to democracy, logic, or political eco- nomy. Instead of my having been taught anything, in the first instance, by Carlyle, it was only in proportion as I came to see the same truths, through media more

[*"The Spirit of the Age," *Examiner*, No. I, 9 Jan., 1831, pp. 20–1; No. II, 23 Jan., 1831, pp. 50–2; No. III, 6 Feb., 1831, pp. 82–4, and 13 Mar., 1831, pp. 162–3; No. IV, 3 Apr., 1831, pp. 210–11; No. V, 15 May, 1831, p. 307, and 29 May, 1831, pp. 339–41.]

[†For Carlyle's immediate reaction to "The Spirit of the Age," his discovery of the author's name, and his subsequent meeting with Mill, see Charles Richard Sanders, *et al.*, eds., *The Collected Letters of Thomas and Jane Welsh Carlyle* (Durham, N.C.: Duke University Press, 1970–), Vol. V, pp. 216, 235n, and 398.]

---

s–s.[*Earlier version (originally a continuation of the text now in Mill's footnote—see the preceding note):*] If my advice had been taken the democracy would have laid down its weapons after a mere partial success. The *Examiner*, I believe, lost near two hundred of its subscribers by those articles, and I much doubt whether it ever gained as many by everything else that I wrote for it. The papers called "The Spirit of the Age" did no similar damage, nor had any effect at all that I know of; except

I came to see the same truths through media more suited to my mental constitution that I recognized them in his writings. Even afterwards the chief good they did me was not as philosophy to instruct but as poetry to animate. In this respect they ultimately became, and long continued, very valuable and delightful to me. Even at the time when our acquaintance began I was not sufficiently advanced in my new modes of thought to appreciate him fully: a proof of which is that when he shewed me the manuscript of *Sartor Resartus*, his best and greatest work, which he had then just finished, ^{r} it made hardly any impression on me: though I read his article on Johnson, published a few months later in *Fraser's Magazine*,[*] with ^{u}"enthusiastic admiration"^{u}, and when *Sartor* came out in the same periodical in 1833 or 1834, I read that with equal enthusiasm. ^{v} I did not seek and cultivate Carlyle less on account of the fundamental differences in our philosophy. He soon found out that I was not "another mystic," and when I wrote to him for the sake of my own integrity a distinct profession of all those of my opinions which I knew he most disliked, he replied that the chief difference between us was that I "was as yet consciously nothing of a mystic": but he continued for a long time to think that I was destined to become one. I need hardly say that in this expectation he was disappointed, and that although both his and my opinions underwent in subsequent years various changes, we never approached much nearer to each other's modes of thought than we were in the first years of our ^{w}"acquaintance"^{w}. But I did not consider myself a competent judge of Carlyle. I felt that he was a poet and that I was not, that he was a man of intuition, which I was not; and that as such he not only saw many things long before me which I could only, when they were pointed out to me, hobble after and prove, but that it was possible he could see many things which were not visible to me even when pointed out. I knew that I could not see round him, and could never be quite sure that I saw over him; and ^{x}I never ^{y}formed^y a definitive judgment of him until he was interpreted to me by one far the superior of us both—who was more a poet than he, and more a thinker than I—whose own mind and nature included all his and infinitely more^x.

[*Carlyle, "Boswell's *Life of Johnson*," *Fraser's Magazine*, V (May, 1832), 379–413.]

^{r}[*Cancelled text in R113r (see App*. G, *p*. 616 *below):*] and had come to town to find a publisher for,
$^{u-u}$[*Earlier version, subsequently altered to final reading, in R113r:*] an enthusiastic admiration I had seldom felt for any cotemporary writing

^{v}[*Additional text in R113r:*] In this part of my life I was in such a state of reaction against sectarianism of thought or feeling, that those in whom I recognized any kind of superiority I did not judge or criticize at all; I estimated them by that side of their qualities or achievements by which they were admirable and valuable to me, while whatever I saw that seemed criticizable was not a *per contra* to be deducted, but was simply uncounted and disregarded. Therefore [*marked for deletion by HTM*]
$^{w-w}$[*Earlier version, subsequently altered to final reading first by HTM and then by Mill, in R113v:*] intimacy [*In R113v the next two and a half sentences—substantially the same as the present text through "formed a definitive judgment" —are marked with a line in the margin by HTM; Mill struck through them and the rest of the paragraph, and wrote a condensed version, subsequently discarded, at*

suited to my mental constitution, that I recognized them in his writings. Then, indeed, the wonderful power with which he put them forth made a deep impression upon me, and I was during a long period one of his most fervent admirers; but the good his writings did me, was not as philosophy to instruct, but as poetry to animate. Even at the time when our acquaintance commenced, I was not sufficiently advanced in my new modes of thought, to appreciate him fully; a proof of which is, that on his shewing me the manuscript of *Sartor Resartus*, his best and greatest work, which he had just then finished, I made little of it; though when it came out about two years afterwards in *Fraser's Magazine*,[*] I read it with enthusiastic admiration and the keenest delight. I did not seek and cultivate Carlyle less on account of the fundamental differences in our philosophy. He soon found out that I was not "another mystic," and when for the sake of my own integrity I wrote to him a distinct profession of all those of my opinions which I knew he most disliked, he replied that the chief difference between us was that I "was as yet consciously nothing of a mystic."[†] I do not know at what period he gave up the expectation that I was destined to become one; but though both his and my opinions underwent in subsequent years considerable changes, we never approached much nearer to each other's modes of thought than we were in the first years of our acquaintance. I did not, however, deem myself a competent judge of Carlyle. I felt that he was a poet, and that I was not; that he was a man of intuition, which I was not; and that as such, he not only saw many things long before me, which I could only, when they were pointed out to me, hobble after and prove, but that it was highly probable he could see many things which were not visible to me even after they were pointed out. I knew that I could not see round him, and could never be certain that I saw over him;[‡] and I never presumed to judge him with any definiteness, until he was interpreted to me by one greatly the superior of us both[§]—who was more a poet than he, and more a thinker than I—whose own mind and nature included his, and infinitely more.

[*_Fraser's Magazine_, VIII (Nov., and Dec., 1833), 581–92, and 669–84; IX (Feb., Mar., Apr., and June, 1834), 177–95, 301–13, 443–55, and 664–74; and X (July, and Aug., 1834), 77–87, and 182–93.]

[†For Mill's letter of 12 Jan., 1834, see _EL, CW_, Vol. XII, pp. 204–9; for Carlyle's reply of 20 Jan., see _Collected Letters of Thomas and Jane Welsh Carlyle_, Vol. VII, p. 72.]

[‡Cf. Carlyle, _Sartor Resartus_, p. 87 (Bk. II, Chap. i).]

[§Harriet Taylor.]

---

left: But I never felt sure that I was a competent judge of Carlyle; and I never formed a definitive judgment . . . *etc. as in the present text.*]

x–x[*Deleted in R109v (see App. G, p. 616 below), and replaced at left by the following, which Mill subsequently discarded in the final recopying of the passage in the draft:*] of those with whom this was the case, I never had the presumption to think that I was yet capable of forming a final judgment

y–y[*Earlier version in R113v:*] presumed to form [*altered by HTM to the single word that Mill copied into the revision described in the second note above (182*w–w*)*]

[z]Among the persons of intellect whom I had known of old, the one with whom I had now most points of agreement was the elder Austin. I have mentioned that he always set himself in opposition to our early sectarianism; and latterly he had, like myself, come under new influences. Having been appointed Professor of Jurisprudence in the London University (now University College) then just founded, he had lived for some time at Bonn to study for his lectures, and the influences of German literature and of the German character and state of society had made a very perceptible change in his views of life. His personal disposition was much softened; he was less militant and polemic; his tastes were greatly turned to the poetic and contemplative. He now attached much less importance than formerly to outward changes, unless accompanied by higher cultivation of the inward nature. He had a strong distaste for the meanness of English life, the absence of enlarged thoughts and unselfish desires, the low objects on which the faculties of all classes of the English are intent. Even the kind of public interests which Englishmen care for he held in very little estimation. He thought that there was more practical good government, and infinitely more care for the education and improvement of the people of all ranks under the Prussian monarchy than under the English representative government: and he held, with the French Economistes, that the real security for good government is not popular institutions but "un peuple éclairé." Though he approved the Reform Bill he predicted what in fact occurred, that it would not produce the great immediate improvements in government which many expected from it. The men, he said, do not exist in the country. There were many points of sympathy between him and me both in the new opinions he had adopted and in the old ones he retained. Like me he never ceased to be a utilitarian, and with all his love of the Germans, never became in the smallest degree reconciled to the innate-principle metaphysics. He however cultivated more and more a kind of German religion, more comfortable though assuredly less virtuous than the bitter opposition to the order of the universe which had formerly distinguished him; and in politics he acquired an indifference, bordering on contempt, for the progress of popular institutions, though he rejoiced in that of socialism as the most effectual means of compelling the powerful classes to educate the people and to point out to them the real road to an improvement of their material condition, that of a limitation of their numbers. Neither was he fundamentally opposed to socialism in itself, as an ultimate result of improvement. He professed great disrespect for the

[z-z]186[*Originally these two paragraphs on the Austins followed the paragraph ending at 188.15 (see App. G, p. 616).*]

Among the persons of intellect whom I had known of old, the one with whom I had now most points of agreement was the elder Austin. I have mentioned that he always set himself in opposition to our early sectarianism; and latterly he had, like myself, come under new influences. Having been appointed Professor of Jurisprudence in the London University (now University College), he had lived for some time at Bonn to study for his Lectures;[*] and the influences of German literature and of the German character and state of society had made a very perceptible change in his views of life. His personal disposition was much softened; he was less militant and polemic; his tastes had begun to turn themselves towards the poetic and contemplative. He attached much less importance than formerly to outward changes, unless accompanied by a better cultivation of the inward nature. He had a strong distaste for the general meanness of English life, the absence of enlarged thoughts and unselfish desires, the low objects on which the faculties of all classes of the English are intent. Even the kind of public interests which Englishmen care for, he held in very little esteem. He thought that there was more practical good government, and (which is true enough) infinitely more care for the education and mental improvement of all ranks of the people, under the Prussian monarchy, than under the English representative government: and he held, with the French Economistes, that the real security for good government is "un peuple éclairé," which is not always the fruit of popular institutions, and which if it could be had without them, would do their work better than they. Though he approved of the Reform Bill, he predicted, what in fact occurred, that it would not produce the great immediate improvements in government, which many expected from it. The men, he said, who could do these great things, did not exist in the country. There were many points of sympathy between him and me, both in the new opinions he had adopted and in the old ones which he retained. Like me, he never ceased to be an utilitarian, and with all his love of the Germans, and enjoyment of their literature, never became in the smallest degree reconciled to the innate-principle metaphysics. He cultivated more and more a kind of German religion, a religion of poetry and feeling with little if anything of positive dogma; while, in politics (and here it was that I most differed with him) he acquired an indifference, bordering on contempt, for the progress of popular institutions: though he rejoiced in that of Socialism, as the most effectual means of compelling the powerful classes to educate the people, and to impress on them the only real means of permanently improving their material condition, a limitation of their numbers. Neither was he, at this time, fundamentally opposed to Socialism in itself, as an ultimate result of improvement. He professed great disrespect for what he called "the universal

[*Austin's lectures (which Mill attended) were published as *The Province of Jurisprudence Determined* (London: Murray, 1832); reviewed by Mill, "Austin's Lectures on Jurisprudence," *Tait's Edinburgh Magazine*, II (Dec., 1832), 343–8. The work was reissued (3rd ed.) as *Lectures on Jurisprudence*, 2 vols. (London: Murray, 1863); reviewed by Mill, "Austin on Jurisprudence," *Edinburgh Review*, CXVIII (Oct., 1863), 439–82.]

"universal principles of human nature of the political economists," and insisted on the evidence which history and daily experience afford, of the "extraordinary pliability of human nature."

His wife, who was then first beginning to be known by her translations,[*] took the principal conduct of the active and practical part of their life: for he, though he always felt like a gentleman and judged like a man of the world, in the good sense of both those terms, retired as far as he could from all business or contact with worldly affairs. She laid herself out for drawing round her as many persons of consideration or promise of consideration, as she could get, and succeeded in getting many foreigners, some literary men and a good many young men of various descriptions, and many who came for her remained for him. Having known me from a boy, she made great profession of a kind of maternal interest in me. But I never for an instant supposed that she really cared for me; *nor perhaps for anybody beyond the surface*; I mean as to real feeling, not that she was not quite ready to be friendly or serviceable *b* . She professed Benthamic opinions when Mr. Austin professed the same, and German opinions when he turned in that direction; but in truth, though she had considerable reading and acquirements, she never appeared to me to have anything deserving the name of opinions. If at that time she had anything capable of being so called, and coming from her own mind, it consisted of prudential maxims for the conduct of life. Under the influence of these she slid into the opinions agreeable to the well-to-do classes, as soon as she saw a possibility of making any way for herself among a few people of consequence. She cultivated blandness of manner and the ways which put people at their ease; and while she was quite ready to listen, she had always plenty to say, though chiefly in the form of narrative and that mainly of what had been said to her by other people. She made herself agreeable to young men by encouraging them with professions of sympathy to talk about themselves; but I do not think the impression thus made lasted long with them, though she often succeeded in retaining that degree of good will which is obtained by an appearance of good nature. The good nature, in the sense in which that quality can be ascribed to a person of so little feeling, was I dare say, to a certain extent genuine; but it was not inconsistent with her having, at times, a very mischievous tongue, which sowed *médisance* far and wide by expressions so guarded as almost to elude responsibility for any distinct statement.*z*

[*E.g., Victor Cousin, *Report on the State of Public Instruction in Prussia*, trans. Sarah Austin (London: Wilson, 1834); for a list of her translations, see the Bibliographic Index, p. 635 below.]

principles of human nature of the political economists," and insisted on the evidence which history and daily experience afford of the "extraordinary pliability of human nature" (a phrase which I have somewhere borrowed from him);[*] nor did he think it possible to set any positive bounds to the moral capabilities which might unfold themselves in mankind, under an enlightened direction of social and educational influences. Whether he retained all these opinions to the end of life I know not. Certainly the modes of thinking of his later years and especially of his last publication[†] were much more Tory in their general character, than those which he held at this time.

[*For the second phrase, see Mill, "Civilization," in *Essays on Politics and Society, CW,* Vols. XVIII–XIX (Toronto: University of Toronto Press, 1977), Vol. XVIII, p. 145; the phrases, probably used in conversation, have not been located in Austin, but cf. his *Lectures,* 3rd ed., Vol. I, p. 301n, Vol. II, pp. 1065, and 1112–13.]

[†John Austin, *A Plea for the Constitution* (London: Murray, 1859).]

---

a–a[*Earlier version:*] indeed the idea of her caring for anybody beyond the surface was not one which naturally suggested itself

b[*Cancelled text:*] on occasion

c My father's tone of thought and feeling I now felt myself at a great distance from: much greater than a full and calm explanation and reconsideration on both sides, would have shewn to exist in reality. But my father was not one with whom calm and full explanations on fundamental points of doctrine could be expected, *d*at least*d* by one whom he might consider a deserter from his standard. Fortunately we were almost always in strong agreement on the political questions of the day, which engrossed a large part of his interest and of his conversation. On those matters of opinion on which we differed, we talked little. He knew that the habit of thinking for myself, which he had given me, sometimes led me to opinions different from his, and he perceived from time to time that I did not always tell him *how* different. I expected no good, but only pain to both of us, from discussing our differences, and I never expressed them but when he gave utterance to some opinion or feeling very repugnant to mine, in a manner which would have made it disingenuousness on my part to remain silent. At such times we used to have a short sharp contest, never leading to any result.

During the years of which I am now speaking, I did a not inconsiderable quantity of writing over and above my contributions to newspapers. In 1830 and 1831 I wrote the five Essays since published as *Essays on Some Unsettled Questions of Political Economy* almost as they now stand, except that in 1833 I partially rewrote the fifth essay. I wrote them with no immediate purpose of publication, and only sent them to press in 1844 in consequence of the success of the *Logic*. I also resumed my speculations on this last subject, and puzzled myself (like others before me, but with, I hope, more of useful result) with the great paradox of the discovery of new truth by general reasoning. As to the fact there could be no doubt; as little could it be doubted, that all reasoning was resolvable into syllogisms and that in every syllogism the conclusion is actually contained and implied in the premises. How being so contained and implied, it could be new truth, and how the theorems of geometry, so different to all appearance from the definitions and axioms, could be all contained in them, was a difficulty which no one, I thought, had sufficiently felt, and which at all events no one had succeeded in clearing up. The attempts at explanation by Whately and others seemed rather explainings away; and though they might give a temporary satisfaction, always left a mist still hanging over the subject. At last, when *e* reading for the *f*second or third*f* time the chapters on Reasoning in the second volume of Dugald Stewart, interrogating myself on every point and following out the various topics of thought which the book suggested, I came to an idea of his about the use of axioms in ratiocination, which I did not remember to have noticed before, but which now in meditating on it

---

c[*Cancelled text:*] At the time of which I am now speaking there was no one with whom I was in any complete or even general sympathy of opinion. [*This and the next seven sentences in the text (the rest of the paragraph) originally followed the paragraph ending at 182.29. See 184*$^{z-z}$ *above.*]

d-d[*Earlier version:*] especially

e[*Cancelled text:*] sitting in the garden at Mickleham

f-f[*Earlier version:*] third or fourth

My father's tone of thought and feeling, I now felt myself at a great distance from: greater, indeed, than a full and calm explanation and reconsideration on both sides, might have shewn to exist in reality. But my father was not one with whom calm and full explanations on fundamental points of doctrine could be expected, at least with one whom he might consider as, in some sort, a deserter from his standard. Fortunately we were almost always in strong agreement on the political questions of the day, which engrossed a large part of his interest and of his conversation. On those matters of opinion on which we differed, we talked little. He knew that the habit of thinking for myself, which his mode of education had fostered, sometimes led me to opinions different from his, and he perceived from time to time that I did not always tell him *how* different. I expected no good, but only pain to both of us, from discussing our differences: and I never expressed them but when he gave utterance to some opinion or feeling repugnant to mine, in a manner which would have made it disingenuousness on my part to remain silent.

It remains to speak of what I wrote during these years, which, independently of my contributions to newspapers, was considerable. In 1830 and 1831 I wrote the five Essays since published under the title of *Essays on Some Unsettled Questions of Political Economy*, almost as they now stand, except that in 1833 I partially rewrote the fifth Essay.[*] They were written with no immediate purpose of publication; and when, some years later, I offered them to a publisher, he declined them. They were only printed in 1844, after the success of the *System of Logic*. I also resumed my speculations on this last subject, and puzzled myself, like others before me, with the great paradox of the discovery of new truths by general reasoning. As to the fact, there could be no doubt. As little could it be doubted, that all reasoning is resolvable into syllogisms, and that in every syllogism the conclusion is actually contained and implied in the premises. How, being so contained and implied, it could be new truth, and how the theorems of geometry, so different, in appearance, from the definitions and axioms, could be all contained in these, was a difficulty which no one, I thought, had sufficiently felt, and which at all events no one had succeeded in clearing up. The explanations offered by Whately and others, though they might give a temporary satisfaction, always, in my mind, left a mist still hanging over the subject. At last, when reading a second or third time the chapters on Reasoning in the second volume of Dugald Stewart,[†] interrogating myself on every point, and following out as far as I knew how, every topic of thought which the book suggested, I came upon an idea of his respecting the use of axioms in ratiocination, which I did not remember to have before

[*The fifth essay, "On the Definition of Political Economy" (in *CW*, Vol. IV, pp. 309–39), appeared first in the *London and Westminster Review*, IV & XXVI (Oct., 1836), 1–29, and was again revised before its republication in *Essays on Some Unsettled Questions* in 1844.]

[†Dugald Stewart, *Elements of the Philosophy of the Human Mind*, 3 vols. (London: Strahan and Cadell, *et al.*; Edinburgh: Creech, *et al.*, 1792, 1814, 1827), Vol. II, pp. 28–49 (Chap. i, §1), esp. p. 49, and pp. 244–69 (Chap. iii, §2), esp. pp. 257–8.]

seemed to me to be not only true of axioms but of all general propositions whatever, and to lead to the true solution of my perplexity. From this germ grew the theory of the syllogism propounded in the second book of the *Logic*; which I immediately made safe by writing it out. And now with greatly increased hope of being able to produce a book of some originality on Logic, I proceeded to write the First Book, from the rough and imperfect draft I had previously made. What I now wrote became the basis of that part of the subsequent Treatise; except that it did not contain the theory of Kinds, which was a much later addition. At this point I made a halt, which lasted five years. I had come to the end of my tether; I could make nothing satisfactory of Induction at this time. I continued to read any book which promised light on the subject, *g* and to appropriate as well as I could the results, but for a long time I found nothing which opened to me any very instructive vein of meditation.

In 1832 I wrote several papers for the first series of *Tait's Magazine*, and one for a quarterly periodical called the *Jurist*, which had been founded and was for a short time carried on by a set of reforming lawyers with several of whom I was acquainted. This paper, entitled "On Corporation and Church Property," I still think a very complete discussion of the rights of the state over Foundations. It shewed both sides of my opinions; asserting as firmly as I should ever have done, the doctrine that endowments are national property which the government may and ought to control, but not, as I should formerly have done, condemning endowments in themselves and proposing that they should be taken to pay off the national debt. On the contrary I urged strongly the importance of having a provision for education, not dependent on the mere demand of the market, that is, on the knowledge and discernment of ordinary parents, but calculated to establish and keep up a higher standard of instruction than is likely to be spontaneously demanded by the buyers of the article. This essay which was little read would be better worth reprinting than most of the short things I have written. *h*

---

g[*Cancelled text:*] when it fell in my way,

h[*At this point Mill initially wrote the two paragraphs on the Parliament of 1832 and his writings of 1832–34 (202.1–206.12), and part of the next paragraph on the founding of the* London and Westminster Review *(206.13–25), with which he brought to a close the original Part I of the draft. Variants from this discarded text are given or referred to in 202^{c–c} and 206^i below. The remainder of the present text of the draft represents a rewritten form of the original Part II (see App. G, pp. 616–24).*]

noticed, but which now, in meditating on it, seemed to me not only true of axioms, but of all general propositions whatever, and to be the key of the whole perplexity. From this germ grew the theory of the Syllogism propounded in the second Book of the *Logic*; which I immediately fixed by writing it out. And now, with greatly increased hope of being able to produce a work on Logic, of some originality and value, I proceeded to write the First Book, from the rough and imperfect draft I had already made. What I now wrote became the basis of that part of the subsequent Treatise; except that it did not contain the Theory of Kinds, which was a later addition, suggested by otherwise inextricable difficulties which met me in my first attempt to work out the subject of some of the concluding chapters of the Third Book. At the point which I have now reached I made a halt, which lasted five years. I had come to the end of my tether; I could make nothing satisfactory of Induction, at this time. I continued to read any book which seemed to promise light on the subject, and appropriated, as well as I could, the results; but for a long time I found nothing which seemed to open to me any very important vein of meditation.

In 1832 I wrote several papers for the first series of *Tait's Magazine*,[*] and one for a quarterly periodical called the *Jurist*,[†] which had been founded and for a short time carried on by a set of friends, all lawyers and law reformers, with several of whom I was acquainted. The paper in question is the one on the rights and duties of the State respecting Corporation and Church Property, now standing first among the collected *Dissertations and Discussions*;[‡] where one of my articles in *Tait*, "The Currency Juggle," also appears.[§] In the whole mass of what I wrote previous to these, there is nothing of sufficient permanent value to justify reprinting. The paper in the *Jurist*, which I still think a very complete discussion of the rights of the State over Foundations, shewed both sides of my opinions, asserting as firmly as I should have done at any time, the doctrine that all endowments are national property, which the government may and ought to control; but not, as I should once have done, condemning endowments in themselves, and proposing that they should be taken to pay off the national debt. On the contrary, I urged strenuously the importance of having a provision for education, not dependent on the mere demand of the market, that is, on the knowledge and discernment of average parents, but calculated to establish and keep up a higher standard of instruction than is likely to be spontaneously demanded by the buyers of the article. All these opinions have been confirmed and strengthened by the whole course of my subsequent reflections.

[*"Austin's Lectures on Jurisprudence"; "The Currency Juggle," *Tait's Edinburgh Magazine*, II (Jan., 1833), 461–7 (in *CW*, Vol. IV, pp. 181–92); "Writings of Junius Redivivus," *Tait's*, III (June, 1833), 347–54 (reprinted at pp. 379–90 below).]

[†"Corporation and Church Property," *Jurist*, IV (Feb., 1833), 1–26 (in *CW*, Vol. IV, pp. 193–222).]

[‡2 vols. (London: Parker, 1859); the essay appeared in Vol. I, pp. 1–41. *Dissertations and Discussions* [*D&D*] was republished with a third volume in 1867 and again (posthumously) with a fourth volume in 1875 (both eds. London: Longmans, Green, Reader, and Dyer).]

[§*D&D*, Vol. I, pp. 42–55 (in *CW*, Vol. IV, pp. 181–92).]

It was at the period of my mental progress which I have now reached, that I formed the friendship which has been the honour and blessing of my existence, as well as the source of a great part of all that I have attempted to do, or hope to effect hereafter for human improvement. My first introduction to the lady who, after a friendship of twenty years, consented to become my wife, was in 1830, when I was in my twenty-fifth and she in her twenty-third year. With her husband's family it was a renewal of an old acquaintanceship. His grandfather lived in the next house to my father's in Newington Green and I had sometimes when a boy been invited to play in the old gentleman's garden. He was a fine specimen of the old Scotch puritan; stern, severe and powerful, but very kind to children, on whom such men make a lasting impression. Although it was years after my introduction to Mrs. Taylor before my acquaintance with her became at all intimate or confidential, I very soon felt her to be the most admirable person I had ever known. It is not to be supposed that she was, or that any one, at the age at which I first saw her, could be all that she afterwards became. Least of all could this be true of her, with whom self-improvement, progress in the highest and in all senses, was a law of her nature; a necessity equally from the ardour with which she sought it, and from the spontaneous tendency of faculties which could not receive an impression or an experience without making it the source or the occasion of an accession of wisdom. Up to the time when I knew her, her rich and powerful nature had chiefly unfolded itself according to the received type of feminine genius. To her outer circle she was a beauty and a wit, with an air of natural distinction, felt by all who approached her: to the inner, a woman of deep and strong feeling, of penetrating and intuitive intelligence, and of a most meditative and poetic nature. Married at a very early age, to a most upright, brave, and honorable man, of liberal opinions and good education, but without the intellectual or artistic tastes which would have made him a companion for her—though a steady and affectionate friend, for whom she

Commencement of the Most Valuable Friendship of My Life. My Father's Death. Writings and Other Proceedings up to 1840

IT WAS AT THE PERIOD of my mental progress which I have now reached that I formed the friendship which has been the honour and chief blessing of my existence, as well as the source of a great part of all that I have attempted to do, or hope to effect hereafter, for human improvement. My first introduction to the lady who, after a friendship of twenty years, consented to bécome my wife, was in 1830, when I was in my twenty-fifth and she in her twenty-third year. With her husband's family it was the renewal of an old acquaintanceship. His grandfather lived in the next house to my father's in Newington Green, and I had sometimes when a boy been invited to play in the old gentleman's garden. He was a fine specimen of the old Scotch puritan; stern, severe, and powerful, but very kind to children, on whom such men make a lasting impression. Although it was years after my introduction to Mrs. Taylor before my acquaintance with her became at all intimate or confidential, I very soon felt her to be the most admirable person I had ever known. It is not to be supposed that she was, or that any one, at the age at which I first saw her, could be, all that she afterwards became. Least of all could this be true of her, with whom self-improvement, progress in the highest and in all senses, was a law of her nature; a necessity equally from the ardour with which she sought it, and from the spontaneous tendency of faculties which could not receive an impression or an experience without making it the source or the occasion of an accession of wisdom. Up to the time when I first saw her, her rich and powerful nature had chiefly unfolded itself according to the received type of feminine genius. To her outer circle she was a beauty and a wit, with an air of natural distinction, felt by all who approached her: to the inner, a woman of deep and strong feeling, of penetrating and intuitive intelligence, and of an eminently meditative and poetic nature. Married at a very early age, to a most upright, brave, and honourable man, of liberal opinions and good education, but without the intellectual or artistic tastes which would have made him a companion for her—

had true esteem and the strongest affection through life and whom she most deeply lamented when dead; shut out by the social disabilities of women from any adequate exercise of her highest faculties in action on the world without; her life was one of inward meditation, varied by familiar intercourse with a small circle of friends, of whom one only was a person of genius, or of capacities of feeling or intellect kindred with her own, but all had more or less of alliance with her in sentiments and opinions. Into this circle I had the good fortune to be admitted, and I soon perceived that she possessed in combination the qualities which in all other persons whom I had known I had been only too happy to find singly. In her, complete emancipation from every kind of superstition, and an earnest protest both against society as at present constituted and against the pretended perfection of the order of nature and the universe, resulted not from the hard intellect but from strength of noble and elevated feeling, and coexisted with a highly reverential nature. In general spiritual characteristics as well as in temperament and organization I have often compared her, as she was at this time, to Shelley, but in thought and intellect Shelley, so far as his powers were developed in his short life, was but a child to her. Alike in the highest regions of philosophy and in the smallest practical concerns of daily life, her mind is the same perfect instrument, going down to the very heart and marrow of the matter—always seizing the essential idea or principle. The same exactness and rapidity of operation pervading her sensitive as well as her mental faculties, would with her gifts of feeling and imagination have fitted her to be a consummate artist, as her fiery and tender soul and her vigorous eloquence might have made her a great orator, and her profound knowledge of human nature and discernment and sagacity in practical life would in the times when such a *carrière* was open to women, have made her eminent among the rulers of mankind. Her intellectual gifts did but minister to a moral character at once the noblest and the best balanced which I have ever met with in life. Her unselfishness was not that of a taught system of duties but of a heart which thoroughly identified itself with the feelings of others and even imaginatively invested them with the intensity of its own. The passion of justice might have been thought to be her strongest feeling but for her boundless generosity and a lovingness ever ready to pour itself forth upon any or all human beings who were capable of giving the smallest feeling in return. All the rest of her moral characteristics were such as naturally accompany these qualities of mind and heart: the most genuine modesty combined with the loftiest pride; a simplicity and sincerity which was absolute towards all who were fit to receive it; the utmost scorn of everything mean and cowardly, and indignation at everything brutal or tyrannical, faithless or dishonorable in conduct and character; while making the broadest distinction

though a steady and affectionate friend, for whom she had true esteem and the strongest affection through life, and whom she most deeply lamented when dead; shut out by the social disabilities of women from any adequate exercise of her highest faculties in action on the world without; her life was one of inward meditation, varied by familiar intercourse with a small circle of friends, of whom one only (long since deceased)[*] was a person of genius, or of capacities of feeling or intellect kindred with her own, but all had more or less of alliance with her in sentiments and opinions. Into this circle I had the good fortune to be admitted, and I soon perceived that she possessed in combination, the qualities which in all other persons whom I had known I had been only too happy to find singly. In her, complete emancipation from every kind of superstition (including that which attributes a pretended perfection to the order of nature and the universe), and an earnest protest against many things which are still part of the established constitution of society, resulted not from the hard intellect but from strength of noble and elevated feeling, and coexisted with a highly reverential nature. In general spiritual characteristics, as well as in temperament and organisation, I have often compared her, as she was at this time, to Shelley: but in thought and intellect, Shelley, so far as his powers were developed in his short life, was but a child compared with what she ultimately became. Alike in the highest regions of speculation and in the smallest practical concerns of daily life, her mind was the same perfect instrument, piercing to the very heart and marrow of the matter; always seizing the essential idea or principle. The same exactness and rapidity of operation, pervading as it did her sensitive as well as her mental faculties, would with her gifts of feeling and imagination have fitted her to be a consummate artist, as her fiery and tender soul and her vigorous eloquence would certainly have made her a great orator, and her profound knowledge of human nature and discernment and sagacity in practical life, would in the times when such a *carrière* was open to women, have made her eminent among the rulers of mankind. Her intellectual gifts did but minister to a moral character at once the noblest and the best balanced which I have ever met with in life. Her unselfishness was not that of a taught system of duties, but of a heart which thoroughly identified itself with the feelings of others, and often went to excess in consideration for them, by imaginatively investing their feelings with the intensity of its own. The passion of justice might have been thought to be her strongest feeling, but for her boundless generosity, and a lovingness ever ready to pour itself forth upon any or all human beings who were capable of giving the smallest feeling in return. The rest of her moral characteristics were such as naturally accompany these qualities of mind and heart: the most genuine modesty combined with the loftiest pride; a simplicity and sincerity which were absolute, towards all who were fit to receive them; the utmost scorn of whatever was mean and cowardly, and a burning indignation at everything brutal or tyrannical, faithless or dishonorable in conduct and character; while making the broadest

[*Eliza Flower.]

between *mala in se* and mere *mala prohibita*—between acts giving evidence of intrinsic badness of feeling and character, and those which are only violations of conventions either good or bad, and which whether in themselves right or wrong, are capable of being done by persons otherwise loveable or admirable.

To be admitted into any degree of personal intercourse with a being of these qualities, could not but have a most beneficial influence on my development. The benefit I received was far greater than any which I could hope to give; except that, to her, who had reached her opinions by the moral intuition of a character of strong feeling, there was doubtless help as well as encouragement to be derived from one who had arrived at many of the same results by study and reasoning: and in the rapidity of her intellectual growth, her mental activity which converted everything into knowledge, doubtless drew from me, as well as from other sources, many of its materials. What I owe to her intellectually, is that without which all I possessed before is of little value. With those who, like all the wisest and best of mankind, are dissatisfied with human life as it is and whose feelings are wholly identified with its radical amendment, there are two main regions of thought: one is the region of ultimate aims; the constituents of the highest realizable ideal of human life; the other is that of the immediately useful and practically attainable. In both of these departments *ª*I have learnt more from her than from all other persons taken together*ª*. And to say truth, it is in these two extremes that the only real certainty lies. My own strength lay wholly in the uncertain and slippery intermediate region, that of theory, or moral and political science: respecting the conclusions of which in any of the forms in which I have received or originated them, whether as political economy, analytic psychology, logic, philosophy of history, or anything else, it is not the least of my intellectual obligations to her that I have derived from her a wise scepticism; which, while it has not hindered me from following out the honest exercise of my thinking faculties to whatever conclusions might result from it, has prevented me, I hope, from holding or announcing those conclusions with a confidence which the nature of such speculations does not warrant, and has kept my mind always open to admit clearer perceptions and better evidence.

ª⁻ª [*Earlier version:*] she has been my main instructor

distinction between *mala in se* and mere *mala prohibita*[*]—between acts giving evidence of intrinsic badness in feeling and character, and those which are only violations of conventions either good or bad, violations which whether in themselves right or wrong, are capable of being committed by persons in every other respect loveable or admirable.

To be admitted into any degree of mental intercourse with a being of these qualities, could not but have a most beneficial influence on my developement; though the effect was only gradual, and many years elapsed before her mental progress and mine went forward in the complete companionship they at last attained. The benefit I received was far greater than any which I could hope to give; though to her, who had at first reached her opinions by the moral intuition of a character of strong feeling, there was doubtless help as well as encouragement to be derived from one who had arrived at many of the same results by study and reasoning: and in the rapidity of her intellectual growth, her mental activity, which converted everything into knowledge, doubtless drew from me, as it did from other sources, many of its materials. What I owe, even intellectually, to her, is, in its detail, almost infinite; of its general character, a few words will give some, though a very imperfect, idea. With those who, like all the best and wisest of mankind, are dissatisfied with human life as it is, and whose feelings are wholly identified with its radical amendment, there are two main regions of thought. One is the region of ultimate aims; the constituent elements of the highest realizable ideal of human life. The other is that of the immediately useful and practically attainable. In both these departments I have acquired more from her teaching, than from all other sources taken together. And, to say truth, it is in these two extremes principally, that real certainty lies. My own strength lay wholly in the uncertain and slippery intermediate region, that of theory, or moral and political science: respecting the conclusions of which, in any of the forms in which I have received or originated them, whether as political economy, analytic psychology, logic, philosophy of history, or anything else, it is not the least of my intellectual obligations to her that I have derived from her a wise scepticism, which, while it has not hindered me from following out the honest exercise of my thinking faculties to whatever conclusions might result from it, has put me on my guard against holding or announcing those conclusions with a degree of confidence which the nature of such speculations does not warrant, and has kept my mind not only open to admit, but prompt to welcome and eager to seek, even on the questions on which I have most meditated, any prospect of clearer perceptions and better evidence. I have often received praise, which in my own right I only partially deserve, for the greater practicality which is supposed to be found in my writings, compared with those of most thinkers who have been equally addicted to large generalizations. The

[*A legal distinction apparently originating with John Glanville. See his speech to both Houses of Parliament on the Petition of Right, *Journals of the House of Lords*, Vol. III, p. 815 (22 May, 1628).]

[b] During the first years of our acquaintance the principal effect of her nature upon mine was to enlarge and exalt my conceptions of the highest worth of a human being. The poetic elements of her character, which were at that time the most ripened, were naturally those which impressed me first, and those years were, in respect of my own development, mainly years of poetic culture. My faculties became more attuned to the beautiful and elevated, in all kinds, and especially in human feeling and character, and more capable of vibrating in unison with it; and I required, in all those in whom I could take interest, a strong taste for elevated and poetic feeling, if not the feeling itself. This however did not check, but gave additional animation to my activity in all the modes of exertion for public objects to which I had been accustomed. I retained unabated interest in radical politics, kept up my connexion with such of the rising or promising politicians on the radical side, as I was previously acquainted with, and even became more involved than before in political as well as literary relations.

[b][*Cancelled text:*] These effects, however, on my mental development, were produced gradually, and proceeded *pari passu* with her own intellectual growth.

writings in which this quality has been observed, were not the work of one mind, but of the fusion of two, one of them as preeminently practical in its judgments and perceptions of things present, as it was high and bold in its anticipations for a remote futurity.

At the present period, however, this influence was only one among many which were helping to shape the character of my future development: and even after it became, I may truly say, the presiding principle of my mental progress, it did not alter the path, but only made me move forward more boldly and at the same time more cautiously in the same course. The only actual revolution which has ever taken place in my modes of thinking, was already complete. My new tendencies had to be confirmed in some respects, moderated in others: but the only substantial changes of opinion that were yet to come, related to politics, and consisted, on one hand, in a greater approximation, so far as regards the ultimate prospects of humanity, to a qualified Socialism, and on the other, a shifting of my political ideal from pure democracy, as commonly understood by its partisans, to the modified form of it, which is set forth in my *Considerations on Representative Government.*[*]

This last change, which took place very gradually, dates its commencement from my reading, or rather study, of M. de Tocqueville's *Democracy in America,*[†] which fell into my hands immediately after its first appearance. In that remarkable work, the excellencies of Democracy were pointed out in a more conclusive, because a more specific manner than I had ever known them to be even by the most enthusiastic democrats; while the specific dangers which beset Democracy, considered as the government of the numerical majority, were brought into equally strong light, and subjected to a masterly analysis, not as reasons for

[*London: Parker, Son, and Bourn, 1861.]
[†Alexis Clérel de Tocqueville, *De la démocratie en Amérique,* [1st pt.,] 2 vols. (Paris: Gosselin, 1835); 2nd pt., 2 vols. (Paris: Gosselin, 1840).]

resisting what the author considered as an inevitable result of human progress, but as indications of the weak points of popular government, the defences by which it needs to be guarded, and the correctives which must be added to it in order that while full play is given to its beneficial tendencies, those which are of a different nature may be neutralized or mitigated. I was now well prepared for speculations of this character, and from this time onward my own thoughts moved more and more in the same channel, though the consequent modifications in my practical political creed were spread over many years, as would be shewn by comparing my first review of *Democracy in America*, written and published in 1835,[*] with the one in 1840 (reprinted in the *Dissertations*),[†] and this last, with the *Considerations on Representative Government*.

A collateral subject on which also I derived great benefit from the study of Tocqueville, was the fundamental question of Centralization.[‡] The powerful philosophic analysis which he applied to American and to French experience, led him to attach the utmost importance to the performance of as much of the collective business of society, as can safely be so performed, by the people themselves, without any intervention of the executive government, either to supersede their agency, or to dictate the manner of its exercise. He viewed this practical political activity of the individual citizen, not only as one of the most effectual means of training the social feelings and practical intelligence of the people, so important in themselves and so indispensable to good government, but also as the specific counteractive to some of the characteristic infirmities of Democracy, and a necessary protection against its degenerating into the only despotism of which in the modern world there is real danger—the absolute rule of the head of the executive over a congregation of isolated individuals, all equals but all slaves. There was, indeed, no immediate peril from this source on the British side of the channel, where nine tenths of the internal business which elsewhere devolves on the government, was transacted by agencies independent of it; where Centralization was, and is, the subject not only of rational disapprobation, but of unreasoning prejudice; where jealousy of Government interference was a blind feeling preventing or resisting even the most beneficial exertion of legislative authority to correct the abuses of what pretends to be local self-government, but is, too often, selfish mismanagement of local interests, by a jobbing and *borné* local oligarchy. But the more certain the public were to go wrong on the side opposed to Centralization, the greater danger was there lest philosophic reformers should fall into the contrary error, and overlook the mischiefs of which they had been spared the painful experience. I was myself, at this very time, actively engaged in defending impor-

[*"De Tocqueville on Democracy in America [I]," *London Review*, II (*London and Westminster Review*, XXXI) (Oct., 1835), 85–129 (reprinted in part in "Appendix," *D&D*, Vol. I, pp. 470–4; in *CW*, Vol. XVIII, pp. 47–90).]

[†"De Tocqueville on Democracy in America [II]," *Edinburgh Review*, LXXII (Oct., 1840), 1–47 (reprinted in *D&D*, Vol. II, pp. 1–83; in *CW*, Vol. XVIII, pp. 153–204).]

[‡See *De la démocratie en Amérique* (1835), Vol. I, pp. 115–34.]

In the autumn of 1832 occurred the election of the first Reformed Parliament, which included several of the most notable of my Radical friends and acquaintances; Grote, Roebuck, Charles Buller, Sir William Molesworth (with whom through Buller I had lately become acquainted), John and Edward Romilly and several others; besides Strutt and others who were in parliament already. Those who thought themselves, and were called by their friends, the philosophic radicals, had now a fair opportunity, in a more advantageous position than they had ever before occupied, of shewing what was in them; and I as well as my father founded great hopes on them. Those hopes were destined to be disappointed. The men were honest, and faithful to their opinions, as far as votes were concerned; often in spite of much discouragement. But they did very little to promote any opinions. One or two of the youngest did as much, perhaps, as could reasonably have been expected from them individually. What Roebuck did has already been mentioned: Buller and Molesworth also by degrees did something. But those from whom most was expected did least. They had no enterprise, no activity; they left the lead of the radical portion of the House to the old hands, to Hume and O'Connell. Nobody disappointed my father and me more than Grote, because no one else had so much in his power. We had long known him fainthearted, ever despairing of success, thinking all obstacles gigantic [c]; but[c] the Reform Bill excitement seemed for a time to make a new man of him: he had grown hopeful, and seemed as if he could almost become energetic. When brought face to face however with an audience opposed to his opinions, when called on to beat up against the stream, he [d]was found wanting[d]. The years which he withdrew from his *History* and spent in the House of Commons were almost wasted. Except an annual motion for the ballot[*] (to which he continued to stick after the change of times had made it no longer desirable) and an honorable stand made now and then against a bad measure, such as the Irish and

[*For his first such motion, see *Parliamentary Debates*, 3rd ser., Vol. 17, cols. 608–29 (25 Apr., 1833); the others are listed in the Bibliographic Index, p. 667 below.]

[c-c]*[Earlier version (in the cancelled text referred to at* 190[h] *above):]*, and seldom able to summon up energy and spirit to carry him into and through any real contest for his opinions. But

[d-d]*[Earlier version in R119r (see App.* G, *p.* 616 *below):]* proved that he was one of those who can see what is good but cannot do it

tant measures, such as the great Poor Law Reform of 1834,[*] against an irrational clamour grounded on the Anti-Centralization prejudice: and had it not been for the lessons of Tocqueville, I do not know that I might not, like many reformers before me, have been hurried into the excess opposite to that which, being the one prevalent in my own country, it was generally my business to combat. As it is, I have steered carefully between the two errors, and whether I have or have not drawn the line between them exactly in the right place, I have at least insisted with equal emphasis upon the evils on both sides, and have made the means of reconciling the advantages of both, a subject of serious study.

In the meanwhile had taken place the election of the first Reformed Parliament, which included several of the most notable of my Radical friends and acquaintances; Grote, Roebuck, Buller, Sir William Molesworth, John and Edward Romilly, and several more; besides Warburton, Strutt, and others, who were in parliament already. Those who thought themselves, and were called by their friends, the philosophic radicals, had now, it seemed, a fair opportunity, in a more advantageous position than they had ever before occupied, for shewing what was in them; and I, as well as my father, founded great hopes on them. These hopes were destined to be disappointed. The men were honest, and faithful to their opinions, as far as votes were concerned; often in spite of much discouragement. When measures were proposed, flagrantly at variance with their principles, such as the Irish Coercion Bill, or the Canada coercion in 1837,[†] they came forward manfully, and braved any amount of hostility and prejudice rather than desert the right. But on the whole they did very little to promote any opinions; they had little enterprise, little activity: they left the lead of the radical portion of the House to the old hands, to Hume and O'Connell. A partial exception must be made in favour of one or two of the younger men; and in the case of Roebuck, it is his title to permanent remembrance, that in the very first year during which he sat in Parliament he originated (or reoriginated after the unsuccessful attempt of Mr. Brougham) the parliamentary movement for National Education;[‡] and that he was the first to commence, and for years carried on almost alone, the contest for the self-government of the Colonies. Nothing, on the whole equal to these two things, was done by any other individual, even of those from whom most was expected. And now, on a calm retrospect, I can perceive that the men were less in fault than we supposed, and that we had expected too much from them. They were in unfavourable circumstances. Their lot was cast in the ten years of inevitable reaction, when the Reform excitement being over, and the few legislative improvements which the public really called for having been rapidly effected, power

[*4 & 5 William IV, c. 76 (14 Aug., 1834).]

[†See 3 William IV, c. 4 (2 Apr., 1833), and 1 Victoria, c. 9 (10 Feb., 1838).]

[‡See John Arthur Roebuck's resolution on National Education, *Parliamentary Debates*, 3rd ser., Vol. 20, cols. 139–66 (30 July, 1833), and Henry Peter Brougham's motion on the Education of the Poor, *ibid.*, n.s., Vol. 2, cols. 49–89 (28 June, 1820).]

Canada Coercion Bills,[*] Mr. Grote was almost an inactive member of parliament. If his courage and energy had been equal to the circumstances, or to his knowledge and abilities, the history of those ten years of relapse into Toryism might have been very different. His standing and social position would have enabled him to create a real Radical party, for which the materials then existed; he could have put heart into the many younger men who would have been ready to join him—could have made them available to the extent of their talents in bringing advanced ideas before the public—could have used the House of Commons as a rostra or a teacher's chair for instructing and impelling the public mind, and would either have forced the Whigs to take their measures from him, or taken the lead of the Reform party out of their hands. All this would *probably* have happened if my father had been in Parliament. For want of such a man the instructed Radicals sank into a mere *côté gauche* of the Whig party. With a keen sense of the ᶠgreatᶠ possibilities which were open to the Radicals if they made even ordinary exertion for their opinions, I laboured from this time till 1839 both by personal influence with some of them, and by writings, to put ideas into their heads and purpose into their hearts. ᵍI did some good with Charles Buller, and some with Sir W. Molesworth;ᵍ but on the whole the attempt was vain. To have had a chance of succeeding in it, required a different position from mine. It was a task only for one who being himself in parliament, could have mixed with the radical members in daily consultation, and instead of saying to others "Lead," could himself have led, and incited them to follow.

During the year 1833 I continued working in the *Examiner* with Fonblanque, who at that time was zealous in keeping up the fight for radicalism against the Whigs, though after 1834 he sank into little better than their supporter and panegyrist. During the session of 1834 I wrote comments on passing events, under the title "Notes on the Newspapers," in the *Monthly Repository*, a magazine conducted by Mr. Fox (with whom I had lately become acquainted) and which I wrote for, chiefly on his account. I contributed several other articles to this periodical, some of them (especially two on the theory of poetry) containing a considerable amount of thought. Altogether, the writings (independently of those

[*See Grote's speeches in *Parliamentary Debates*, 3rd ser., Vol. 15, cols. 1241–6 (27 Feb., 1833), on Ireland; and *ibid.*, Vol. 40, cols. 59–65 (16 Jan., 1838), and cols. 633–7 (29 Jan., 1838), on Canada.]

    ᵉ⁻ᵉ[*Earlier version, subsequently altered to final reading, in R119v:*] infallibly
    ᶠ⁻ᶠ[*Earlier version in R119v:*] glorious
    ᵍ⁻ᵍ[*Not in R119v, in which HTM pencilled at left opposite the preceding sentence: "mention Buller and your efforts with him".*]

gravitated back in its natural direction, to those who were for keeping things as they were; when the public mind desired rest, and was less disposed than at any other period since the peace, to let itself be moved by attempts to work up the reform feeling into fresh activity in favour of new things. It would have required a great political leader, which no one is to be blamed for not being, to have effected really great things by parliamentary discussion when the nation was in this mood. My father and I had hoped that some competent leader might arise; some man of philosophic attainments and popular talents, who could have put heart into the many younger or less distinguished men that would have been ready to join him—could have made them available, to the extent of their talents, in bringing advanced ideas before the public—could have used the House of Commons as a rostra or a teacher's chair for instructing and impelling the public mind; and would either have forced the Whigs to receive their measures from him, or have taken the lead of the Reform party out of their hands. Such a leader there would have been, if my father had been in Parliament. For want of such a man, the instructed Radicals sank into a mere *côté gauche* of the Whig party. With a keen, and as I now think, an exaggerated sense of the possibilities which were open to the Radicals if they made even ordinary exertion for their opinions, I laboured from this time till 1839, both by personal influence with some of them, and by writings, to put ideas into their heads and purpose into their hearts. I did some good with Charles Buller, and some with Sir William Molesworth; both of whom did valuable service, but were unhappily cut off almost in the beginning of their usefulness. On the whole, however, my attempt was vain. To have had a chance of succeeding in it, required a different position from mine. It was a task only for one who, being himself in Parliament, could have mixed with the radical members in daily consultation, could himself have taken the initiative, and instead of urging others to lead, could have summoned them to follow.

What I could do by writing, I did. During the year 1833 I continued working in the *Examiner* with Fonblanque, who at that time was zealous in keeping up the fight for radicalism against the Whig ministry. During the session of 1834 I wrote comments on passing events, of the nature of newspaper articles (under the title "Notes on the Newspapers"), in the *Monthly Repository*,[*] a magazine conducted by Mr. Fox, well known as a preacher and political orator, and subsequently as member of parliament for Oldham; with whom I had lately become acquainted, and for whose sake chiefly I wrote in his Magazine. I contributed several other articles to this periodical, the most considerable of which (on the theory of poetry) is reprinted in the *Dissertations*.[†] Altogether, the writings (independently of

[*"Notes on the Newspapers," *Monthly Repository*, n.s. VIII (Mar.–Sept., 1834), 161–76, 233–48, 309–12, 354–75, 435–56, 521–8, 589–600, 656–65.]

[†"What Is Poetry?" *ibid.*, n.s. VII (Jan., 1833), 60–70, and "The Two Kinds of Poetry," *ibid.*, n.s. VII (Nov., 1833), 714–24; combined as "Thoughts on Poetry and Its Varieties," *D&D*, Vol. I, pp. 89–120 (reprinted at pp. 341–65 below).]

in newspapers) which I published from 1832 to 1834, amount to a large volume. This however includes abstracts of several of Plato's Dialogues, with introductory remarks, which though not published until 1834, had been written several years earlier; and which I afterwards on various occasions found to have been read, and their authorship known, by more people than were aware of anything else which I had written up to that time. To complete the tale of my writings I may add that in 1833, at the request of Bulwer, who was just then completing his *England and the English*, I wrote for him a critical account of Bentham's philosophy, a small part of which he incorporated in his text, and printed the rest as an Appendix. In this, along with the favorable, a part also of the unfavourable side of my estimation of Bentham's doctrines, considered as a complete philosophy, was for the first time put into print.

As the "philosophic radical" party fell off my endeavours to put life into it were redoubled. Among the possibilities which had been much talked of between my father and me, and some of the parliamentary and other radicals who frequented his house, was the foundation of a periodical organ of philosophic radicalism, to take the place which the *Westminster* had been intended to fill; and the scheme went so far as to bring under discussion the pecuniary contributions which could be looked for, and even the choice of an editor. The project however seemed to have fallen to the ground, when in the summer of 1834 Sir W. Molesworth, himself a laborious student, and one of the most *^h*zealous at that time*^h* of the Parliamentary Radicals, of himself proposed to establish a Review, provided I would consent to be the real, if not the nominal, editor. Such an offer was not to be refused; and the review was founded, under my direction, though under the ostensible editorship of Roebuck's brother in law, Falconer. *ⁱ* In the years between 1834 and 1840 the conduct of this review occupied the greater part of my spare time. It came out in April 1835 under the name of the *London Review*, and four numbers were published with that title, after which Molesworth bought the *Westminster Review* from its proprietor Colonel Thompson and the two were united under the name of the *London and Westminster Review*. In the beginning the review did not, as a whole, by any means

---

^{h-h}[Earlier version in R120v:] sincere and convinced [*marked with a question mark by HTM*]
ⁱ[For the ending of the original Part I at this point, see App. G, p. 616 below.]

those in newspapers) which I published from 1832 to 1834, amount to a large volume.[*] This, however, includes abstracts of several of Plato's Dialogues, with introductory remarks, which, though not published until 1834,[†] had been written several years earlier; and which I afterwards, on various occasions, found to have been read, and their authorship known, by more people than were aware of anything else which I had written, up to that time. To complete the tale of my writings at this period, I may add that in 1833, at the request of Bulwer, who was just then completing his *England and the English* (a work, at that time, greatly in advance of the public mind), I wrote for him a critical account of Bentham's philosophy, a small part of which he incorporated in his text, and printed the rest (with an honorable acknowledgment) as an Appendix.[‡] In this, along with the favorable, a part also of the unfavourable side of my estimation of Bentham's doctrines, considered as a complete philosophy, was for the first time put into print.

But an opportunity soon offered by which, as it seemed, I might have it in my power to give more effectual aid, and at the same time, stimulus, to the "philosophic radical" party, than I had done hitherto. One of the projects occasionally talked of between my father and me, and some of the parliamentary and other Radicals who frequented his house, was the foundation of a periodical organ of philosophic radicalism, to take the place which the *Westminster Review* had been intended to fill: and the scheme had gone so far as to bring under discussion the pecuniary contributions which could be looked for, and the choice of an editor. Nothing however came of it for some time: but in the summer of 1834 Sir William Molesworth, himself a laborious student, and a precise and metaphysical thinker capable of aiding the cause by his pen as well as by his purse, spontaneously proposed to establish a Review, provided I would consent to be the real, if I could not be the ostensible, editor. Such a proposal was not to be refused; and the review was founded, at first under the title of the *London Review*, and afterwards under that of the *London and Westminster*, Molesworth having bought the *Westminster* from its proprietor General Thompson, and merged the two into one. In the years between 1834 and 1840 the conduct of this review occupied the greater part of my spare time. In the beginning, it did not, as a whole, by any means represent my

[*Mill is not estimating. He had this "volume," with three others from succeeding periods, bound; they are in his library, Somerville College, Oxford.]

[†"Notes on Some of the More Popular Dialogues of Plato," *Monthly Repository*, n.s. VIII: No. I, "The Protagoras" (Feb., Mar., 1834), 89–99, 203–11; No. II, "The Phaedrus" (June, Sept., 1834), 404–20, 633–46; No. III, "The Gorgias" (Oct., Nov., Dec., 1834), 691–710, 802–15, 829–42; and n.s. IX: No. IV, "The Apology of Socrates" (Feb., Mar., 1835), 112–21, 169–78. (Reprinted, with five other dialogues that Mill did not publish— *Charmides, Euthyphron, Laches, Lysis*, and *Parmenides*—in *CW*, Vol. XI, pp. 37–238.)]

[‡Edward Lytton Bulwer, *England and the English*, 2 vols. (London: Bentley, 1833); Mill's comments on Bentham are in App. B, "Remarks on Bentham's Philosophy," Vol. II, pp. 321–44, and in the text of Vol. II, pp. 163–70 (these are reprinted in *Essays on Ethics, Religion, and Society, CW*, Vol. X [Toronto: University of Toronto Press, 1969], pp. 3–18, and 499–502 [App. C]).]

represent my opinions. I was under the necessity of conceding much to my inevitable associates. The review was established to be the representative of the "philosophic radicals," with most of whom I was at issue on many essential points and among whom I could not even claim to be the most important individual ^{j}. My father's cooperation as a writer we all deemed indispensable, and he wrote largely in it until prevented by illness. The subjects of his articles and the strength and decision with which his opinions were expressed in them, made the review at first derive its colour and tone from him much more than from ^{k} any of the other writers. I could not exercise editorial control over his articles and I was even obliged to sacrifice to him portions of mine. The old *Westminster Review* opinions, little modified, thus formed the staple of the review, but I hoped by the side of these to introduce other ideas and another tone, and to give to my opinions a fair representation in the review along with those of other members of the party. For this purpose chiefly I made it one of the peculiarities of the review that every article should bear an initial or some other signature and be held to express only the opinions of the writer, the editor being only responsible for its being worth publishing, and not conflicting with the objects for which the review was set on foot. I had an opportunity of putting in practice my scheme of conciliation between the old and the new "philosophic radicalism" by the choice of a subject for my own first contribution. Mr. Sedgwick had then lately published his *Discourse on the Studies of Cambridge*, a tract of which the most prominent feature was an abusive assault on analytic psychology and on utilitarian ethics, in the form of an attack on Locke and Paley. This had excited great indignation in my father and others, which I thought was fully deserved. And here, I conceived, was an opportunity of at the same time repelling an unjust attack and inserting into my defence of Hartleianism and utilitarianism, a number of the opinions which constituted my view of those subjects as distinguished from that of my old associates. In this I partially succeeded, though I ^{l}could not speak out my whole mind at this time without coming into conflict with my father ^{l}. There are things however which incline me to believe that my father was not so much opposed as he seemed, to the modes of

---

^{j}[*Cancelled text:*] , especially while my father lived

^{k}[*Cancelled text:*] me or

$^{l-l}$[*Earlier version:*] was obliged to omit two or three pages of comment on what I thought the mistakes of utilitarian moralists, which my father considered as an attack on Bentham and on him. I certainly thought both of them in some degree open to it but far less so than some of their followers

opinions. I was under the necessity of conceding much to my inevitable associates. The Review was established to be the representative of the "philosophic radicals," with most of whom I was now at issue on many essential points, and among whom I could not even claim to be the most important individual. My father's cooperation as a writer we all deemed indispensable, and he wrote largely in it until prevented by his last illness. The subjects of his articles, and the strength and decision with which his opinions were expressed in them, made the Review at first derive its tone and colouring from him much more than from any of the other writers.[*] I could not exercise editorial control over his articles, and I was sometimes obliged to sacrifice to him portions of my own. The old *Westminster Review* doctrines, but little modified, thus formed the staple of the review; but I hoped, by the side of these, to introduce other ideas and another tone, and to obtain for my own shade of opinion a fair representation, along with those of other members of the party. With this end chiefly in view, I made it one of the peculiarities of the work that every article should bear an initial, or some other signature, and be held to express the opinions solely of the individual writer; the editor being only responsible for its being worth publishing, and not in conflict with the objects for which the Review was set on foot. I had an opportunity of putting in practice my scheme of conciliation between the old and the new "philosophic radicalism" by the choice of a subject for my own first contribution. Professor Sedgwick, a man of eminence in a particular walk of natural science, but who should not have trespassed into philosophy, had lately published his *Discourse on the Studies of Cambridge*,[†] which had as its most prominent feature an intemperate assault on analytic psychology and utilitarian ethics, in the form of an attack on Locke and Paley. This had excited great indignation in my father and others, which I thought it fully deserved. And here, I imagined, was an opportunity of at the same time repelling an unjust attack, and inserting into my defence of Hartleianism and Utilitarianism a number of the opinions which constituted my view of those subjects, as distinguished from that of my old associates. In this I partially succeeded, though my relation to my father would have made it painful to me in any case, and impossible in a review for which he wrote, to speak out my whole mind on the subject at this time.

I am, however, inclined to think that my father was not so much opposed as he

[*James Mill contributed "State of the Nation," *London Review*, I (*London and Westminster Review*, XXX) (Apr., 1835), 1–24; "The Ballot—A Dialogue," I, 201–53; "The Church and Its Reform," I (July, 1835), 257–95; "Law Reform," II (*London and Westminster Review*, XXXI) (Oct., 1835), 1–51; "Aristocracy," II (Jan., 1836), 283–306; "Whether Political Economy is Useful?" II, 553–71; and "Theory and Practice," *London and Westminster Review*, III & XXV (Apr., 1836), 223–34.]

[†Adam Sedgwick, *A Discourse on the Studies of the University* (1833); Mill reviewed the 3rd ed. (London: Parker, 1834) in "Sedgwick's *Discourse*," *London Review*, I (*London and Westminster Review*, XXX) (Apr., 1835), 94–135 (in *D&D*, Vol. I, pp. 95–159; in *CW*, Vol. X, pp. 31–74).]

thought in which I supposed myself to differ from him; that ^{m}he did injustice to his own opinions by^m the unconscious exaggerations of a pugnacious and polemical intellect, and that when thinking without an adversary *en présence* he was ready to make room for a great portion of the truths he seemed to deny. His *Fragment on Mackintosh*, which he wrote and published about this time, although I greatly admired some parts of it, was as a whole very repulsive to me; yet on reading it again ^{n}, long after,^{n} I found very little in the opinions it contains but what I think in the main just; and I can even sympathize in his disgust at the verbiage of Mackintosh though his asperity went beyond not only what was judicious but what was even fair. One thing which I thought at the time of good augury, was the very favourable reception he gave to Tocqueville's *Democracy in America*. It is true he said and thought much more about what Tocqueville said in favour of Democracy than about what he said against it. Still, his high appreciation of a book which was at any rate an example of a mode of treating the question of government almost the reverse of his—wholly inductive and analytical instead of purely ratiocinative— gave me great encouragement. He also approved of an article which I published in the first number following the junction of the two reviews, under the heading "Civilization," into which I threw many of my new opinions and criticized rather emphatically the mental tendencies of the time on grounds and in a manner which I certainly had not learnt from him.

All speculation however on the possible future developments of my father's opinions and on the probabilities of successful cooperation between him and me in the promulgation of our thoughts, was doomed to be cut short. During the whole of 1835 his health had been declining; his symptoms became unequivocally those of pulmonary consumption and after lingering to the last stage of debility he died on the 23d of June 1836. Until the last few days of his life there was no apparent abatement of intellectual vigour; his interest in all things and persons that had interested him through life, was unabated; nor did the approach of death cause the smallest wavering (as in so strong a mind it was impossible that it should) in his anti-religious convictions. His chief satisfaction, after he knew that his end was near, seemed to be the thought of what he had done to make the world better than he found it; and his chief regret in not living longer, that he had not had time to do more.

His place is an eminent one in the literary and even the political history of this country; and it is far from honorable to the generation which has benefitted by his worth, that he is so seldom mentioned and so little remembered. Probably the chief

---

$^{m-m}$[*Earlier version:*] the lengths to which he allowed himself to go in his denunciations of opinions, which I regarded as merely the other half of the truths one half alone was seen by him, were in a great measure

$^{n-n}$[*Earlier version:*] lately

seemed, to the modes of thought in which I believed myself to differ from him; that he did injustice to his own opinions by the unconscious exaggerations of an intellect emphatically polemical; and that when thinking without an adversary in view, he was willing to make room for a great portion of the truths he seemed to deny. I have frequently observed that he made large allowance in practice for considerations which seemed to have no place in his theory. His *Fragment on Mackintosh*, which he wrote and published about this time, although I greatly admired some parts of it, I read as a whole with more pain than pleasure; yet on reading it again, long after, I found little in the opinions it contains, but what I think in the main just; and I can even sympathize in his disgust at the *verbiage* of Mackintosh, though his asperity towards it went not only beyond what was judicious, but beyond what was even fair. One thing which I thought, at the time, of good augury, was the very favorable reception he gave to Tocqueville's *Democracy in America*. It is true, he said and thought much more about what Tocqueville said in favour of Democracy, than about what he said of its disadvantages. Still, his high appreciation of a book which was at any rate an example of a mode of treating the question of government almost the reverse of his—wholly inductive and analytical, instead of purely ratiocinative—gave me great encouragement. He also approved of an article which I published in the first number following the junction of the two reviews, the Essay reprinted in the *Dissertations* under the title "Civilization";[*] into which I threw many of my new opinions, and criticized rather emphatically the mental and moral tendencies of the time, on grounds and in a manner which I certainly had not learnt from him.

All speculation, however, on the possible future developments of my father's opinions, and on the probabilities of permanent cooperation between him and me in the promulgation of our thoughts, was doomed to be cut short. During the whole of 1835 his health had been declining: his symptoms became unequivocally those of pulmonary consumption, and after lingering to the last stage of debility, he died on the 23rd of June 1836. Until the last few days of his life there was no apparent abatement of intellectual vigour; his interest in all things and persons that had interested him through life was undiminished, nor did the approach of death cause the smallest wavering (as in so strong and firm a mind it was impossible that it should) in his convictions on the subject of religion. His principal satisfaction, after he knew that his end was near, seemed to be the thought of what he had done to make the world better than he found it; and his chief regret in not living longer, that he had not had time to do more.

His place is an eminent one in the literary, and even in the political history of his country; and it is far from honourable to the generation which has benefitted by his worth, that he is so seldom mentioned, and, compared with men far his inferiors, so little remembered. This is probably to be ascribed mainly to two causes. In the first place, the thought of him merges too much in the deservedly superior fame of

[*$D\&D$, Vol. I, pp. 160–205.]

cause of the neglect of his memory, is that, notwithstanding the great number of his opinions which have now been generally adopted, there was a marked opposition between his spirit and that of the present time. As Brutus was the last of the Romans, so was he the last of the eighteenth century: he continued its tone of thought and sentiment into the nineteenth (though with great additions and improvements), partaking neither in the good nor in the bad influences of the reaction against the eighteenth century which is the great characteristic of the first half of the nineteenth. The eighteenth century was a great age, an age of stronger and braver men than the nineteenth, and he was *o* a fit companion for its strongest and bravest. By his writings and his personal influence, he was a great centre of light to his generation. During the latter years of his life he was quite as much the head and leader of the intellectual radicals in England as ever Voltaire was of the *philosophes* of France. It is only one of his minor merits that he was the originator of all sound statesmanship in regard to the subject of his largest work, India. He wrote on no subject which he did not enrich with valuable thought: and if we except the *Political Economy*, very useful when written but which has now for some time finished its work, it will be long before any of his books will be wholly superseded, or will cease to be instructive reading to students of their subjects. In the power of influencing by mere force of mind and character, the convictions and purposes of others, and in the strenuous exertion of that power to promote freedom and progress, he has left no equal among men—and but one among women.

Though acutely sensible of my own inferiority in the qualities by which he acquired his personal ascendancy, I had now to try *p*what it might be possible for me to accomplish without him*p*; and the review was the instrument on which I built my chief hopes of establishing a useful influence over the liberal and democratic

---

o[*Cancelled text:*] both in thought and action
p–p[*Earlier version:*] how far I might be capable of supplying his place

Bentham. Yet he was anything but Bentham's mere follower or disciple. Precisely because he was himself one of the most original thinkers of his time, he was one of the earliest to appreciate and adopt the most important mass of original thought which had been produced by the generation preceding him. His mind and Bentham's were essentially of different construction. He had not all Bentham's high qualities, but neither had Bentham all his. It would, indeed, be ridiculous to claim for him the praise of having accomplished for mankind such splendid services as Bentham's. He did not revolutionize—or rather create—one of the great departments of human thought. But, leaving out of the reckoning all that portion of his labours in which he benefitted by what Bentham had done, and counting only what he achieved in a province in which Bentham had done nothing, that of analytic psychology, he will be known to posterity as one of the greatest names in that most important branch of speculation, on which all the moral and political sciences ultimately rest, and will mark one of the essential stages in its progress. The other reason, which has made his fame less than he deserved, is that notwithstanding the great number of his opinions which, partly through his own efforts, have now been generally adopted, there was on the whole a marked opposition between his spirit and that of the present time. As Brutus was called the last of the Romans,[*] so was he the last of the eighteenth century: he continued its tone of thought and sentiment into the nineteenth (though not unmodified nor unimproved), partaking neither in the good nor in the bad influences of the reaction against the eighteenth century, which was the great characteristic of the first half of the nineteenth. The eighteenth century was a great age, an age of strong and brave men, and he was a fit companion for its strongest and bravest. By his writings and his personal influence he was a great centre of light to his generation. During his later years he was quite as much the head and leader of the intellectual radicals in England, as Voltaire was of the *philosophes* of France. It is only one of his minor merits, that he was the originator of all sound statesmanship in regard to the subject of his largest work, India. He wrote on no subject which he did not enrich with valuable thought, and excepting the *Elements of Political Economy*, a very useful book when first written, but which has now for some time finished its work, it will be long before any of his books will be wholly superseded, or will cease to be instructive reading to students of their subjects. In the power of influencing by mere force of mind and character, the convictions and purposes of others, and in the strenuous exertion of that power to promote freedom and progress, he left, as far as my knowledge extends, no equal among men, and but one among women.

Though acutely sensible of my own inferiority in the qualities by which he acquired his personal ascendancy, I had now to try what it might be possible for me to accomplish without him; and the Review was the instrument on which I built my chief hopes of establishing a useful influence over the liberal and democratic

[*Cf. Shakespeare, *Julius Caesar*, V, iii, 99, where Brutus refers to Cassius and Titinius as "last of all the Romans."]

portion of the public mind. Deprived now of my father's aid, I was also exempted from the restraints and retinences by which that aid was purchased: I did not feel that there was any other radical writer or politician to whom I was bound to defer further than consisted with my own opinions: and having the complete confidence of Molesworth, I resolved from henceforth to give full scope to my own opinions and modes of thought and to open the review widely to all writers who were in sympathy with Progress as I understood it, even though I should lose by it the support of my former associates. Carlyle from this time became a frequent writer in the review; Sterling, soon after, an occasional one; and though each individual article continued to be the expression of the private sentiments of its writer, the general tone conformed in some tolerable degree to my opinions. This was not effected without parting company with the nominal editor, Falconer, who, after holding on for some time in spite of differences of opinion, at last resigned *q* . I supplied his place by a young Scotchman of the name of Robertson, who had some ability and information, much industry, and an active scheming head, full of devices for making the review more saleable, and on whose capacity in that particular I founded a good deal of hope: insomuch that when Molesworth, in the beginning of 1837, became tired of carrying on the review at a loss, and desirous of getting rid of it, I, very imprudently for my own pecuniary interest, and very much from reliance on Robertson's devices, determined to continue it at my own risk until his plans should have had a fair trial. The devices were good in their way, but I do not believe that any devices would have made a radical and democratic review pay its expenses, including a liberal payment to writers. I myself and several frequent contributors gave our labour gratuitously, as we had done for Molesworth, but the paid contributors continued to be paid at the usual rate of the *Edinburgh* and *Quarterly* Reviews: and this could not be done from the proceeds of the sale.

In the same year, 1837, and in the midst of these occupations, I resumed the *Logic.* I had now done nothing to it for five years, having been stopped, and brought to a pause, on the threshold of Induction. I had gradually discovered that what was mainly wanting to overcome the difficulties of that subject was a comprehensive and at the same time accurate view of the whole circle of physical science, which I feared it would take a long course of study to acquire, since I knew not of any book or other guide that would display before me the generalities and processes and believed that I should have no choice but to extract them for myself, if I could, from the details of the sciences. Happily for me, Dr. Whewell, early in this year, published his *History of the Inductive Sciences.* I read it with eagerness and found in it a considerable approximation to what I wanted. Much if not most of his philosophy appeared to me erroneous; but the materials were there, for my own thoughts to work upon, and the author had given to those materials that first degree

---

q[Cancelled text:] rather on account of an article of Carlyle's ["Memoirs of Mirabeau," *London and Westminster Review,* IV & XXVI (Jan., 1837), 382–439.]

section of the public mind. Deprived of my father's aid, I was also exempted from the restraints and retinences by which that aid had been purchased. I did not feel that there was any other radical writer or politician to whom I was bound to defer, further than consisted with my own opinions: and having the complete confidence of Molesworth, I resolved henceforth to give full scope to my own opinions and modes of thought, and to open the Review widely to all writers who were in sympathy with Progress as I understood it, even though I should lose by it the support of my former associates. Carlyle, consequently, became from this time a frequent writer in the Review; Sterling, soon after, an occasional one; and though each individual article continued to be the expression of the private sentiments of its writer, the general tone conformed in some tolerable degree to my opinions. For the conduct of the Review, under and in conjunction with me, I associated with myself a young Scotchman of the name of Robertson, who had some ability and information, much industry, and an active scheming head, full of devices for making the Review more saleable, and on whose capacities in that direction I founded a good deal of hope: insomuch that when Molesworth, in the beginning of 1837, became tired of carrying on the Review at a loss, and desirous of getting rid of it (he had done *his* part honourably, and at no small pecuniary cost), I, very imprudently for my own pecuniary interest, and very much from reliance on Robertson's devices, determined to continue it at my own risk, until his plans should have had a fair trial. The devices were good, and I never had any reason to change my opinion of them. But I do not believe that any devices would have made a radical and democratic review defray its expenses, including a paid editor or sub editor, and a liberal payment to writers. I myself and several frequent contributors gave our labour gratuitously, as we had done for Molesworth; but the paid contributors continued to be remunerated on the usual scale of the *Edinburgh* and *Quarterly* Reviews; and this could not be done from the proceeds of the sale.

In the same year, 1837, and in the midst of these occupations, I resumed the *Logic*. I had not touched my pen on the subject for five years, having been stopped and brought to a halt on the threshold of Induction. I had gradually discovered that what was mainly wanting, to overcome the difficulties of that branch of the subject, was a comprehensive and at the same time accurate view of the whole circle of physical science, which I feared it would take me a long course of study to acquire; since I knew not of any book, or other guide, that would spread out before me the generalities and processes of the sciences, and I apprehended that I should have no choice but to extract them for myself, as I best could, from the details. Happily for me, Dr. Whewell, early in this year, published his *History of the Inductive Sciences*.[*] I read it with eagerness, and found in it a considerable approximation to what I wanted. Much, if not most, of the philosophy of the work appeared open to objection; but the materials were there, for my own thoughts to work upon: and the author had given to those materials that first degree of

[*William Whewell, *History of the Inductive Sciences*, 3 vols. (London: Parker, 1837).]

of elaboration which so greatly abridges and facilitates the subsequent labour. I felt that I had now got what I had been waiting for. Under the impulse given me by the thoughts excited by Whewell I read again Herschel's *Discourse on the Study of Natural Philosophy*, which I had read (and even reviewed) several years before, but had found little help in it. I now found much. I then set vigorously to work out the subject in thought and in writing. I had just two months to spare in the intervals of writing for the review. In those two months I wrote (in the first draft) about a third, the most difficult third, of the book. What I had before written I estimated at another third, so that only a third remained. What I wrote at this time consisted of the remainder of the doctrine of Reasoning (the theory of Trains of Reasoning, and Deductive Science) and the greater part of the Third Book, on Induction. I had now, as it seemed to me, untied all the really hard knots, and the completion of the book had become only a question of time. When I had got thus far I had to leave off in order to write two articles for the next number of the review. When these were written I returned to the subject and now for the first time fell in with Comte's *Cours de Philosophie Positive* or rather with the two volumes of it which were then all that had been published. My theory of Induction was substantially completed before I knew of Comte's book and it is perhaps well that I came to it by a *r* different road from his, since the consequence has been that my treatise contains what his certainly does not, a reduction of the inductive process to strict rules and to a scientific test, such as the Syllogism is for ratiocination. Comte is always profound on the methods of investigation but he does not even attempt any exact definition of the conditions of proof: and his own writings shew that he has no just conception of them. This however was specifically the problem which, in treating of Induction, I had proposed to myself. Nevertheless I gained much from Comte with which to enrich my chapters in the subsequent rewriting, and his book was of essential service to me in the parts which still remained to be thought out. After completing the study of his two volumes I wrote three more chapters in the autumn of 1837 after which I did not return to the subject until the middle of the next year: the review engrossing all the time I could devote to authorship, or to thinking with authorship in view.

r[*Cancelled text:*] totally

elaboration, which so greatly facilitates and abridges the subsequent labour. I had now obtained what I had been waiting for. Under the impulse given me by the thoughts excited by Dr. Whewell, I read again Sir J. Herschel's *Discourse on the Study of Natural Philosophy*; and I was able to measure the progress my mind had made, by the great help I now found in this work, though I had read and even reviewed it several years before with little profit.[*] I now set myself vigorously to work out the subject in thought and in writing. The time I bestowed on this had to be stolen from occupations more urgent. I had just two months to spare, at this period, in the intervals of writing for the Review. In these two months I completed the first draft of about a third, the most difficult third, of the book. What I had before written I estimate at another third, so that only one third remained. What I wrote at this time consisted of the remainder of the doctrine of Reasoning (the theory of Trains of Reasoning, and Demonstrative Science) and the greater part of the Book on Induction. When this was done, I had, as it seemed to me, untied all the really hard knots, and the completion of the book had become only a question of time. Having got thus far, I had to leave off in order to write two articles for the next number of the Review.[†] When these were written, I returned to the subject, and now for the first time fell in with Comte's *Cours de Philosophie Positive*, or rather with the two volumes of it which were all that had at that time been published.[‡]

My theory of Induction was substantially completed before I knew of Comte's book; and it is perhaps well that I came to it by a different road from his, since the consequence has been that my treatise contains, what his certainly does not, a reduction of the inductive process to strict rules and to a scientific test, such as the Syllogism is for ratiocination. Comte is always precise and profound on the methods of investigation, but he does not even attempt any exact definition of the conditions of proof: and his writings shew that he never attained a just conception of them. This, however, was specifically the problem which, in treating of Induction, I had proposed to myself. Nevertheless, I gained much from Comte, with which to enrich my chapters in the subsequent rewriting: and his book was of essential service to me in some of the parts which still remained to be thought out. As his subsequent volumes successively made their appearance, I read them with avidity, but, when he reached the subject of Social Science, with varying feelings. The fourth volume disappointed me: it contained those of his opinions on social

[*John Frederick William Herschel, *A Preliminary Discourse on the Study of Natural Philosophy* (London: Longman, Rees, Orme, Brown, and Green, 1831); reviewed by Mill, "Herschel's *Discourse*," *Examiner*, 20 Mar., 1831, pp. 179–80.]

[†"Parties and the Ministry," and "Armand Carrel," *London and Westminster Review*, VI & XXVIII (Oct., 1837), 1–26, and 66–111, the latter reprinted in *D&D*, Vol. I, pp. 211–83.]

[‡Auguste Comte, *Cours de philosophie positive*, 6 vols. (Paris: Bachelier, 1830, 1835, 1838, 1839, 1841, 1842); for the titles of the individual volumes, see the Bibliographic Index, p. 655 below.]

subjects with which I most disagree. But the fifth, containing the connected view of history, rekindled all my enthusiasm; which the sixth (or concluding) volume did not materially abate. In a merely logical point of view, the only leading conception for which I am indebted to him is that of the Inverse Deductive Method, as the one chiefly applicable to the complicated subjects of History and Statistics: a process differing from the more common form of the Deductive Method in this, that instead of arriving at its conclusions by general reasoning and verifying them by specific experience (as is the natural order in the deductive branches of physical science), it obtains its generalizations by a collation of specific experience, and verifies them by ascertaining whether they are such as would follow from known general principles.[*] This was an idea entirely new to me when I found it in Comte: and but for him I might not soon (if ever) have arrived at it.

I had been long an ardent admirer of Comte's writings before I had any communication with himself; nor did I ever, to the last, see him in the body. But for some years we were frequent correspondents, until our correspondence became controversial, and our zeal cooled.[†] I was the first to slacken correspondence; he was the first to drop it. I found, and he probably found likewise, that I could do no good to his mind, and that all the good he could do to mine, he did by his books. This would never have led to discontinuance of intercourse, if the differences between us had been on matters of simple doctrine. But they were chiefly on those points of opinion which blended in both of us with our strongest feelings, and determined the entire direction of our aspirations. I had fully agreed with him when he maintained that the mass of mankind, including even their rulers in all the practical departments of life, must, from the necessity of the case, accept most of their opinions on political and social matters, as they do on physical, from the authority of those who have bestowed more study on those subjects than they generally have it in their power to do. This lesson had been strongly impressed on me by the early work of Comte, to which I have adverted.[‡] And there was nothing in his great Treatise which I admired more than his remarkable exposition of the benefits which the nations of modern Europe have historically derived from the separation, during the middle ages, of temporal and spiritual power, and the distinct organization of the latter.[§] I agreed with him that the moral and intellectual ascendancy, once exercised by priests, must in time pass into the hands of philosophers, and will naturally do so when they become sufficiently unanimous, and in other respects worthy to possess it.[¶] But when he exaggerated this line of thought into a practical system, in which philosophers were to be organized into a kind of corporate hierarchy, invested with almost the same spiritual supremacy (though without any secular power) once possessed by the Catholic church; when I

[*See *Cours*, Vol. IV, Leçon 48, esp. pp. 352ff.]
[†See *EL*, *CW*, Vol. XIII, pp. 488ff.]
[‡Comte, *Système* (1824), pp. 262ff.]
[§Comte, *Cours*, Vol. V, Leçon 54, pp. 321ff.]
[¶E.g., *ibid.*, Vol. VI, Leçon 57, pp. 580ff.]

In the conduct of the review I had two principal objects. One was to free radical opinions from the reproach of narrow Benthamism. I desired, while retaining the precision of expression, the definiteness of meaning, the aversion to declamatory phrases and vague generalities which were so honorably characteristic of Bentham, and my father, to give a wider basis and a freer and more genial character to radical speculations; to shew that there was a radical philosophy better and more complete than Bentham's, though recognizing and incorporating all of Bentham's which is permanently valuable. In this first object I to a certain extent succeeded. The other thing I attempted was to stir up the educated radicals in and out of parliament to exertion, and induce them to make themselves what I thought they might by taking the proper means have become, a powerful party, capable of

found him relying on this spiritual authority as the only security for good government, the sole bulwark against practical oppression, and expecting that by it a system of despotism in the state and despotism in the family would be rendered innocuous and beneficial; it is not surprising, that while as logicians we were nearly at one, as sociologists we could travel together no further. M. Comte lived to carry out these doctrines to their extremest consequences, by planning, in his last work, the *Système de Politique Positive*,[*] the completest system of spiritual and temporal despotism, which ever yet emanated from a human brain, unless possibly that of Ignatius Loyola: a system by which the yoke of general opinion, wielded by an organized body of spiritual teachers and rulers, would be made supreme over every action, and as far as is in human possibility, every thought, of every member of the community, as well in the things which regard only himself, as in those which concern the interests of others. It is but just to say that this work is a considerable improvement, in many points of feeling, over Comte's previous writings on the same subjects: but as an accession to social philosophy, the only value it seems to me to possess consists in putting an end to the notion that no effectual moral authority can be maintained over society without the aid of religious belief; for Comte's work recognizes no religion except that of Humanity, yet it leaves an irresistible conviction that any moral beliefs, concurred in by the community generally, may be brought to bear upon the whole conduct and lives of its individual members with an energy and potency truly alarming to think of. The book stands a monumental warning to thinkers on society and politics, of what happens when once men lose sight, in their speculations, of the value of Liberty and of Individuality.

To return to myself: the Review engrossed, for some time longer, nearly all the time I could devote to authorship, or to thinking with authorship in view. The articles from the *London and Westminster Review* which are reprinted in the *Dissertations* are scarcely a fourth part of those I wrote. In the conduct of the Review I had two principal objects. One was to free philosophic radicalism from the reproach of sectarian Benthamism. I desired, while retaining the precision of expression, the definiteness of meaning, the contempt of declamatory phrases and vague generalities, which were so honorably characteristic both of Bentham and of my father, to give a wider basis and a more free and genial character to Radical speculations; to shew that there was a Radical philosophy, better and more complete than Bentham's, while recognizing and incorporating all of Bentham's which is permanently valuable. In this first object I, to a certain extent, succeeded. The other thing I attempted, was to stir up the educated Radicals, in and out of Parliament, to exertion, and induce them to make themselves, what I thought by using the proper means, they might become—a powerful party capable of taking

[**Système de politique positive; ou, Traité de sociologie, instituant la religion de l'humanité*, 4 vols. (Paris: Mathias, *et al.*, 1851–54); see esp. Vol. II, pp. 276ff., 336ff., and Vol. IV, pp. 222ff.]

taking the government of the country, or at least of dictating the terms on which they should share it with the Whigs. This attempt totally failed, partly because the time was unfavourable; the Reform fervour being then in its period of ebb, and the old Tory influences powerfully rallying; but far more, because, as Austin so truly said, "the country did not contain the men." Among the Radicals in Parliament there were two or three qualified to be useful members of an enlightened Radical party, but none capable of forming or leading such a party [s] . The exhortations of the review found no response. One occasion did present itself when there seemed to be room for a bold and successful stroke for radicalism. Lord Durham had left the ministry, as was thought, because they were not sufficiently liberal: he afterwards accepted from them the task of removing the causes of rebellion in Canada: he had shewn a disposition to surround himself at his outset with radical advisers; one of his earliest measures, a good measure both in intention and in effect, having been disapproved and reversed by the government at home, he had resigned his post and placed himself openly in a position of quarrel with the ministers. Here was a possible chief for a radical party, in the person of a man of importance who was hated by the Tories, and had just been injured by the Whigs. It was an opportunity to be seized [t] . Lord Durham was bitterly attacked from all sides; he appeared to be returning a defeated and discredited man, and those who would willingly have defended him did not know what to say. I had followed the course of Canadian events from the beginning; I had been one of the prompters of his prompters; his policy was almost exactly what mine would have been, and I was in a position to defend it. I wrote and published a manifesto in the form of a review article in which I claimed for him not mere acquittal but praise and honour. I believe that there was a portion of truth in what Lord Durham afterwards with polite exaggeration said to me, that to this article might be attributed the almost triumphal reception which he met with on his arrival in England. I believe it to have been the word in season which at a critical moment decides the result; the touch which determines whether a stone set in motion at the top of a hill shall roll down on the north or on the south side. All hopes connected with Lord Durham as a politician soon vanished; but with regard to Canadian and generally to colonial

---

[s]*[Cancelled text:]* , and not one who was fit to go forward by his single strength and fight to any great purpose for advanced opinions

[t]*[Cancelled text:]* ; and I seized it

the government of the country, or at least of dictating the terms on which they should share it with the Whigs. This attempt was from the first chimerical: partly because the time was unpropitious, the Reform fervour being in its period of ebb, and the Tory influences powerfully rallying; but, still more, because, as Austin so truly said, "the country did not contain the men." Among the Radicals in Parliament there were several qualified to be useful members of an enlightened Radical party, but none capable of forming and leading such a party. The exhortations I addressed to them found no response. One occasion did present itself when there seemed to be room for a bold and successful stroke for Radicalism. Lord Durham had left the ministry, by reason, as was thought, of their not being sufficiently liberal; he afterwards accepted from them the task of ascertaining and removing the causes of the Canadian rebellion: he had shewn a disposition to surround himself at the outset with Radical advisers; one of his earliest measures, a good measure both in intention and in effect, having been disapproved and reversed by the Government at home, he had resigned his post, and placed himself openly in a position of quarrel with the ministers. Here was a possible chief for a Radical party in the person of a man of importance, who was hated by the Tories, and had just been injured by the Whigs. Any one who had the most elementary notions of party tactics, must have attempted to make something of such an opportunity. Lord Durham was bitterly attacked from all sides, inveighed against by enemies, given up by timid friends; while those who would willingly have defended him did not know what to say. He appeared to be returning a defeated and discredited man. I had followed the Canadian events from the beginning; I had been one of the prompters of his prompters; his policy was almost exactly what mine would have been, and I was in a position to defend it. I wrote and published a manifesto in the Review, in which I took the very highest ground in his behalf, claiming for him not mere acquittal, but praise and honour.[*] Instantly a number of other writers took up the tone.[†] I believe there was a portion of truth in what Lord Durham, soon after, with polite exaggeration, said to me—that to this article might be ascribed the almost triumphal reception which he met with on his arrival in England. I believe it to have been the word in season, which, at a critical moment, does much to decide the result; the touch which determines whether a stone, set in motion at the top of an eminence, shall roll down on one side or on the other. All hopes connected with Lord Durham as a politician soon vanished; but with regard to Canadian, and generally to colonial policy, the cause was gained: Lord Durham's

[*Mill wrote three articles on Durham and his mission, the second of which is the one specifically referred to here. See "Lord Durham and the Canadians," *London and Westminster Review*, VI & XXVIII (Jan., 1838), 502–33; "Lord Durham and His Assailants," *ibid.*, VII & XXIX, 2nd ed. only (Aug., 1838), 507–12; and "Lord Durham's Return," *ibid.*, XXXII (Dec., 1838), 241–60.]

[†See, e.g., anonymous leading articles on 20 Aug., 1838, in the *Morning Chronicle*, p. 2, and the *Sun*, p. 2, and "Lord Durham and His Assailants," *Examiner*, 26 Aug., 1838, pp. 529–30.]

policy, the cause was gained: Lord Durham's report, written by Charles Buller under the inspiration of Wakefield, began a new era; its recommendations extending to complete internal self government were in full operation in Canada within two or three years, and are becoming rapidly extended to all the other colonies which have as yet any existence as considerable communities: and I may say that in successfully upholding the reputation of Lord Durham and of his advisers at the most important moment, I contributed materially to this result.

There was one other case during my conduct of the review which similarly illustrated the effect of taking a decided initiative. I believe that the early success and reputation of Carlyle's *French Revolution* were very materially promoted by what I wrote about it in the review. Immediately after its publication, and before the commonplace critics, all whose rules and modes of judgment it set at defiance, had time to preoccupy the public with their disapproval of it, I wrote and published a review of the book hailing it as one of those productions of genius which are above all rules and are a law to themselves. Neither in this case nor in Lord Durham's do I ascribe the impression which I think was produced by what I wrote, to any particular merit of execution; and indeed, in at least one of the two cases (Carlyle's) I do not think the execution was good. I believe that anybody in a position to be read, who had expressed the same opinion at the same precise time and had made any tolerable statement of the just grounds for it, would have produced exactly the same effect. But after the complete failure of my plans for putting a new life into radical politics by means of the review I am glad to look back on these two instances of success in an honest attempt to do immediate service to things and persons that deserved it.

After the last hope of the formation of a Radical party had disappeared, it was time for me to stop the heavy expenditure of time and money which the review cost me. It had to some extent answered my purpose as a vehicle for my opinions: It had enabled me to express in print much of my then present mode of thought and to distinguish it in a marked manner from the narrower Benthamism of my early writings. This was done by the general tone of all I wrote, including various literary articles (among which the one which contained most thought was on Alfred de Vigny),[*] but especially by two articles which attempted a philosophical estimate of Bentham and of Coleridge. In the first of these, while doing full justice to the merits of Bentham, I pointed out what I thought the errors and deficiencies of his philosophy. The substance of this criticism I still think just, but I have much

---

[*"Poems and Romances of Alfred de Vigny," *London and Westminster Review*, VII & XXIX (Apr., 1838), 1–44 (reprinted in *D&D*, Vol. I, pp. 287–329, and at pp. 463–501 below).]

report,[*] written by Charles Buller, partly under the inspiration of Wakefield, began a new era; its recommendations, extending to complete internal self-government, were in full operation in Canada within two or three years, and have been since extended to nearly all the other colonies, of European race, which have any claim to the character of important communities. And I may say that in successfully upholding the reputation of Lord Durham and his advisers at the most important moment, I contributed materially to this result.

One other case occurred during my conduct of the Review, which similarly illustrated the effect of taking a prompt initiative. I believe that the early success and reputation of Carlyle's *French Revolution*, were considerably accelerated by what I wrote about it in the Review.[†] Immediately on its publication, and before the commonplace critics, all whose rules and modes of judgment it set at defiance, had time to preoccupy the public with their disapproval of it, I wrote and published a review of the book, hailing it as one of those productions of genius which are above all rules, and are a law to themselves. Neither in this case nor in that of Lord Durham do I ascribe the impression, which I think was produced by what I wrote, to any particular merit of execution: indeed, in at least one of the cases (the article on Carlyle) I do not think the execution was good. And in both instances, I am persuaded that anybody, in a position to be read, who had expressed the same opinion at the same precise time, and had made any tolerable statement of the just grounds for it, would have produced the same effect. But, after the complete failure of my hopes of putting a new life into radical politics by means of the Review, I am glad to look back on these two instances of success in an honest attempt to do immediate service to things and persons that deserved it.

After the last hope of the formation of a Radical party had disappeared, it was time for me to stop the heavy expenditure of time and money which the Review cost me. It had to some extent answered my personal purpose, as a vehicle for my opinions. It had enabled me to express in print much of my altered mode of thought, and to separate myself in a marked manner from the narrower Bentham-ism of my early writings. This was done by the general tone of all I wrote, including various purely literary articles, but especially by the two papers (re-printed in the *Dissertations*) which attempted a philosophical estimate of Bentham and of Coleridge.[‡] In the first of these, while doing full justice to the merits of Bentham, I pointed out what I thought the errors and deficiencies of his philoso-phy. The substance of this criticism I still think perfectly just; but I have sometimes

[*"Report on the Affairs of British North America, from the Earl of Durham," *Parliamentary Papers*, 1839, XVII, 1–690.]

[†"The French Revolution," *London and Westminster Review*, V & XXVII (July, 1837), 17–53.]

[‡"Bentham," *London and Westminster Review*, VII & XXIX (Aug., 1838), 467–506, and "Coleridge," *ibid.*, XXXIII (Mar., 1840), 257–302; reprinted in *D&D*, Vol. I, pp. 330–92, and 393–466 (and in *CW*, Vol. X, pp. 75–115, and 117–63).]

doubted since whether it was right to publish it. I have often felt that Bentham's philosophy as an instrument of progress has been in a great measure discredited before it had half done its work and that lending a hand to pull down its reputation was doing more harm than service to improvement. In the article on Coleridge I attempted to characterize the European reaction against the negative philosophy of the eighteenth century: and here I erred by giving undue prominence to the favourable side, as I had done in the case of Bentham to the unfavourable. In both cases, the impetus with which I had detached myself from what was untenable in the doctrines of Bentham and of the eighteenth century carried me too far to the opposite side; but so far as relates to the article on Coleridge the excuse may be made for me that I was writing for radicals and liberals and had therefore an inducement to dwell most on that in writers of a different school, from the knowledge of which they might derive most benefit.

The number of the review which contained the article on Coleridge was the last which was published under my proprietorship. In the spring of 1840 I made over the review to Mr. Hickson, who had been a very useful unpaid contributor to the *London and Westminster*, only stipulating that the change should be marked by a resumption of the old name, the *Westminster Review*. Under this name he carried it on for ten years, on the plan of dividing among contributors only the net proceeds of the review (giving his own labour as a writer and editor gratuitously). Under the difficulty in obtaining writers which arose from this low scale of remuneration, it is highly creditable to him that he was able to maintain in some tolerable degree the character of the review as an organ of radicalism and progress. For my own part, though I still occasionally wrote in newspapers and in the *Westminster* and *Edinburgh* Reviews when I had anything to say for which they appeared to be suitable vehicles, I henceforth employed my writing faculties mainly on things of a less temporary nature.

doubted whether it was right to publish it at that time. I have often felt that Bentham's philosophy, as an instrument of progress, has been to some extent discredited before it had done its work, and that to lend a hand towards lowering its reputation was doing more harm than service to improvement. Now however when a counter-reaction appears to be setting in towards what is good in Benthamism, I can look with more satisfaction on this criticism of its defects, especially as I have myself balanced it by vindications of the fundamental principles of Bentham's philosophy, which are reprinted along with it in the same collection.[*] In the essay on Coleridge I attempted to characterize the European reaction against the negative philosophy of the eighteenth century: and here, if the effect only of this one paper were to be considered, I might be thought to have erred by giving undue prominence to the favourable side, as I had done in the case of Bentham to the unfavourable. In both cases, the impetus with which I had detached myself from what was untenable in the doctrines of Bentham and of the eighteenth century, may have carried me, though in appearance rather than in reality, too far on the contrary side. But as far as relates to the article on Coleridge, my defence is, that I was writing for Radicals and Liberals, and it was my business to dwell most on that in writers of a different school, from the knowledge of which they might derive most improvement.

The number of the Review which contained the paper on Coleridge, was the last which was published during my proprietorship. In the spring of 1840 I made over the Review to Mr. Hickson, who had been a frequent and very useful unpaid contributor under my management; only stipulating that the change should be marked by a resumption of the old name, that of *Westminster Review.* Under that name Mr. Hickson conducted it for ten years, on the plan of dividing among contributors only the net proceeds of the Review, giving his own labour as writer and editor gratuitously. Under the difficulty in obtaining writers, which arose from this low scale of payment, it is highly creditable to him that he was able to maintain, in some tolerable degree, the character of the Review as an organ of radicalism and progress. I did not cease altogether to write for the Review, but continued to send it occasional contributions, not, however, exclusively; for the greater circulation of the *Edinburgh Review* induced me from this time to offer articles to it also when I had anything to say for which it appeared to be a suitable vehicle. And the concluding volumes of *Democracy in America* having just then come out, I inaugurated myself as a contributor to the *Edinburgh* by the article on that work, which heads the second volume of the *Dissertations.*[†]

[*Mill must have in mind his "Sedgwick's *Discourse*" (first published in 1835, before his "Bentham") as well as his "Whewell on Moral Philosophy" (1852), *D&D*, Vol. II, pp. 450–509 (in *CW*, Vol. X, pp. 165–201).]
[†See p. 201 above.]

The first use which I made of the leisure I gained by disconnecting myself with the review, was to finish the *Logic*. *ª* In July and August 1838 I had found an interval in which to complete the first draft of the third book. In working out the logical theory of those laws of nature which are not laws of causation, or corollaries from such laws, I was led to recognize Kinds as realities and not mere distinctions for convenience, a light which I had not yet obtained when the first Book was originally written and in consequence of which I now modified and enlarged the corresponding portion of that Book. The book on Language and Classification, and the Chapter on the Classification of Fallacies, were drafted in the autumn of the same year; the remainder of the work in the summer and autumn of 1840. From April following to the end of 1841 my spare time was devoted to a complete rewriting of the book from its commencement. During this operation Dr.

ª[*Cancelled text:*] After what I had done in 1837 its completion was only a question of time.

CHAPTER VII

General View of the Remainder of My Life

FROM THIS TIME, what is worth relating of my life will come into a very small compass; for I have no further mental changes to tell of, but only, as I hope, a continued mental progress; which does not admit of a consecutive history, and the results of which, if real, will be best found in my writings. I shall therefore greatly abridge the chronicle of my subsequent years.

The first use I made of the leisure which I gained by disconnecting myself from the Review, was to finish the *Logic*. In July and August 1838 I had found an interval in which to execute what was still undone of the original draft of the Third Book. In working out the logical theory of those laws of nature which are not laws of Causation, nor corollaries from such laws, I was led to recognize Kinds as realities in nature, and not mere distinctions for convenience; a light which I had not obtained when the First Book was written, and which made it necessary for me to modify and enlarge several chapters of that Book. The Book on Language and Classification, and the chapter on the Classification of Fallacies, were drafted in the autumn of the same year; the remainder of the work in the summer and autumn of 1840. From April following to the end of 1841, my spare time was devoted to a complete rewriting of the book from its commencement. It is in this way that all my books have been composed. They were always written at least twice over; a first draft of the entire work was completed to the very end of the subject, then the whole begun again *de novo*; but incorporating, in the second writing, all sentences and parts of sentences of the old draft, which appeared as suitable to my purpose as anything which I could write in lieu of them. I have found great advantages in this system of double redaction. It combines, better than any other mode of composition, the freshness and vigour of the first conception, with the superior precision and completeness resulting from prolonged thought. In my own case, moreover, I have found that the patience necessary for a careful elaboration of the details of exposition and expression, costs much less effort after the entire subject has been once gone through, and the substance of all that I find to say has in some manner, however imperfect, been got upon paper. The only thing which I am careful, in the

Whewell's *Philosophy of the Inductive Sciences* made its appearance; a fortunate circumstance for me, as it gave me what I very much needed, an antagonist, and enabled me to present my ideas with greater clearness and emphasis as well as fuller and more various development, in defending them against definite objections, and confronting them distinctly with an opposite theory. The controversies with Whewell as well as much matter derived from Comte were first introduced into the book in the present rewriting.

At the end of 1841, the book being ready for press, I offered it to Murray, who kept it until too late for publication that season and then refused it for reasons which could just as well have been given at first. I next offered it to Parker, and in the spring of 1843 it was published. My expectations of success were extremely moderate. A book on such a subject could not be popular; it could only be a book for students, and students on such subjects in England are not only few, but are mostly in the present generation addicted to the opposite school of metaphysics, the ontological and "innate principle" school. I therefore did not expect that the book would have many readers, or approvers; and would gladly have compounded for a sale sufficient to prevent the publisher from losing by it. What hopes I had of its exciting attention were mainly grounded on the polemical propensities of Dr. Whewell; who I thought would have replied, and that promptly, to the attack on his opinions. He did reply, but not till 1850, just in time for me to answer him in the third edition. How the book came to have, for a work of the kind, so much success and what sort of persons compose the bulk of those who have bought, I will not venture to say read it, I have never thoroughly understood; and I *b*have never

b–b232[*Earlier version:*] see no signs of its having had at all a proportional influence

first draft, to make as perfect as I am able, is the arrangement. If that is bad, the whole thread on which the ideas string themselves becomes twisted; thoughts placed in a wrong connexion are not expounded in a manner that suits the right, and a first draft with this original vice is next to useless as a foundation for the final treatment.

During the rewriting of the *Logic*, Dr. Whewell's *Philosophy of the Inductive Sciences* made its appearance;[*] a circumstance fortunate for me, as it gave me what I greatly desired, a full treatment of the subject by an antagonist, and enabled me to present my ideas with greater clearness and emphasis as well as fuller and more varied development, in defending them against definite objections, and confronting them distinctly with an opposite theory. The controversies with Dr. Whewell, as well as much matter derived from Comte, were first introduced into the book in the course of the rewriting.

At the end of 1841, the book being ready for press, I offered it to Murray, who kept it until too late for publication that season, and then refused it, for reasons which could just as well have been given at first. But I have had no cause to regret a rejection which led to my offering it to Mr. Parker, by whom it was published in the spring of 1843. My original expectations of success were extremely limited. Archbishop Whately had indeed rehabilitated the name of Logic, and the study of the forms, rules, and fallacies of Ratiocination; and Dr. Whewell's writings had begun to excite an interest in the other part of my subject, the theory of Induction. A treatise, however, on a matter so abstract, could not be expected to be popular; it could only be a book for students, and students on such subjects were not only (at least in England) few, but addicted chiefly to the opposite school of metaphysics, the ontological and "innate principles" school. I therefore did not expect that the book would have many readers, or approvers; and looked for little practical effect from it, save that of keeping the tradition unbroken of what I thought a better philosophy. What hopes I had of exciting any immediate attention, were mainly grounded on the polemical propensities of Dr. Whewell; who, I thought, from observation of his conduct in other cases, would probably do something to bring the book into notice, by replying, and that promptly, to the attack on his opinions. He did reply, but not till 1850,[†] just in time for me to answer him in the third edition.[‡] How the book came to have, for a work of the kind, so much success, and what sort of persons compose the bulk of those who have bought, I will not venture to say read, it, I have never thoroughly understood. But taken in conjunc-

---

[*William Whewell, *Philosophy of the Inductive Sciences*, 2 vols. (London: Parker, 1840).]

[†Whewell, *Of Induction, with Especial Reference to Mr. J. Stuart Mill's System of Logic* (London: Parker, 1849).]

[‡See *System of Logic*, Textual Introduction, *CW*, Vol. VII, p. lxxxiii; Preface to the 3rd ed., *ibid.*, p. cxiv; and, in the Bibliographic Index, entries under Whewell, *Of Induction*, and *On the Philosophy of Discovery*, *ibid.*, Vol. VIII, pp. 1239–41.]

indulged the illusion that it had made any considerable impression[b] on philosophic opinion. The German, or ontological view of human knowledge and of the knowing faculties, still predominates and will probably long predominate (though it may be hoped in a diminishing degree) among those who occupy themselves with such enquiries either here or on the Continent. But the *System of Logic* supplies what was much wanted, a text book of the opposite doctrine, that which derives all knowledge from experience, and all moral and intellectual qualities principally from the direction given to the associations. And in this consists, I think, the chief worth of the book as a contribution to human improvement. I make as humble an estimate as anybody of what either an analysis of logical processes, or any possible canons of evidence, can do, taken by themselves, to guide or rectify the operations of the understanding. But whether the direct practical use of a true philosophy on these matters be great or little, it is difficult to exaggerate the mischief of a false one. The doctrine that truths external to the mind may be known by intuition or consciousness, independently of observation and experiment, is, I am persuaded, in these times the great intellectual support for false doctrines and bad institutions. By the aid of this philosophy every inveterate belief and every strong feeling, of which the artificial origin is not remembered, is dispensed from the obligation of justifying itself by evidence or reason, and is erected into its own sufficient justification. There never was such an instrument devised for consecrating all deepseated prejudices. It is the main doctrinal pillar of all the errors which impede human improvement. And the chief strength of this false philosophy in the departments of morals and religion lies in the appeal which it is accustomed to make to the evidence of mathematics and of the cognate branches of physical science. To expel it from these is to attack it in its stronghold: and because this had not been effectually done, the intuition school, even after what my father had written in his *Analysis*, had, at least in appearance, and as far as published writings were concerned, on the whole the best of the argument. In attempting to clear up the real nature of the evidence of mathematical and physical truths, the *System of Logic* met the intuition doctrine as it had never before been met; and gave its own explanation, from experience and association, of that peculiar character of what are called necessary truths which is adduced as proof that they cannot be derived from experience. Whether this has been done effectually, is still *sub judice*; and even if so, merely to deprive a mode of thought so strongly rooted in human prejudices and partialities of its speculative support, goes but a little way towards conquering it: but [c]though this is but one step, that step is indispensable; for since,

[c-c234][*A preliminary version, written and cancelled earlier on the same page of the draft, reads:*] however little the refutation may amount to, nothing could be done to weaken the roots of the greatest existing mischiefs without it

tion with the many proofs which have since been given of a revival of speculation, speculation too of a free kind, in many quarters, and above all (where at one time I should have least expected it) in the Universities, the fact becomes partially intelligible. I have never indulged the illusion that the book had made any considerable impression on philosophical opinion. The German, or *à priori* view of human knowledge, and of the knowing faculties, is likely for some time longer (though it may be hoped in a diminishing degree) to predominate among those who occupy themselves with such enquiries, both here and on the Continent. But the *System of Logic* supplies what was much wanted, a text-book of the opposite doctrine—that which derives all knowledge from experience, and all moral and intellectual qualities principally from the direction given to the associations. I make as humble an estimate as anybody of what either an analysis of logical processes, or any possible canons of evidence, can do by themselves, towards guiding or rectifying the operations of the understanding. Combined with other requisites, I certainly do think them of great use; but whatever may be the practical value of a true philosophy of these matters, it is hardly possible to exaggerate the mischiefs of a false one. The notion that truths external to the mind may be known by intuition or consciousness, independently of observation and experience, is, I am persuaded, in these times, the great intellectual support of false doctrines and bad institutions. By the aid of this theory, every inveterate belief and every intense feeling, of which the origin is not remembered, is enabled to dispense with the obligation of justifying itself by reason, and is erected into its own all-sufficient voucher and justification. There never was such an instrument devised for conse-crating all deep seated prejudices. And the chief strength of this false philosophy in morals, politics, and religion, lies in the appeal which it is accustomed to make to the evidence of mathematics and of the cognate branches of physical science. To expel it from these, is to drive it from its stronghold: and because this had never been effectually done, the intuitive school, even after what my father had written in his *Analysis of the Mind*, had in appearance, and as far as published writings were concerned, on the whole the best of the argument. In attempting to clear up the real nature of the evidence of mathematical and physical truths, the *System of Logic* met the intuition philosophers on ground on which they had previously been deemed unassailable; and gave its own explanation, from experience and associa-tion, of that peculiar character of what are called necessary truths, which is adduced as proof that their evidence must come from a deeper source than experience. Whether this has been done effectually, is still *sub judice*; and even then, to deprive a mode of thought so strongly rooted in human prejudices and partialities, of its mere speculative support, goes but a very little way towards overcoming it; but though only a step, it is a quite indispensable one; for since, after all, prejudice can only be successfully combated by philosophy, no way can be effectually made against it until it has been shewn not to have philosophy on its side[c].

[d] Being now released from any active concern in temporary politics and from any literary occupation involving personal communication with contributors and others, I was enabled to indulge the inclination, natural to thinking persons when the age of boyish vanity is once past, for limiting my own society to a very few persons. General society as now carried on, at least in England, is so thoroughly insipid an affair, even to the very persons who make it what it is, that it is kept up for any reason rather than the pleasure it affords. All serious discussion on matters on which opinions differ, being considered ill bred, and the national deficiency in liveliness and sociability having prevented the cultivation of the art of talking agreeably on trifles, in which the French of the last century so much excelled, the sole attraction of what is called society to those who are not at the top of the tree, is the hope of climbing a little higher on it, while to those who are already at the top it is chiefly a compliance with custom and with the supposed requirements of their station. To a person of any but the commonest order in thought or feeling, such society must unless he has personal objects to serve by means of it, be supremely unattractive: and most people, in the present day, of any really high class of intellect, make their contact with it so slight and at such long intervals as to be almost considered as retiring from it altogether. Those persons of any real mental superiority who act otherwise, are almost without exception, greatly deteriorated by it. Not to mention loss of time, the tone of their feelings is always lowered: they become less in earnest about those of their opinions about which they feel that they must remain silent in the society they frequent; they come to think their more elevated objects unpractical, or at least too remote from realization to be more than a vision or a theory; or even if, more fortunate than most, they retain their higher principles unimpaired, yet with regard to the persons and affairs of the present they insensibly adopt the modes of feeling and judgment of the company they keep. A person of high intellect should never go into unintellectual society unless he can enter it as an apostle. And all persons of even intellectual aspirations had much better, if they can, make their habitual associates of at least their equals, and as far as possible, their superiors in knowledge, intellect, and elevation of sentiment. [e] Further, if their character is formed and their minds made up on the few cardinal

---

[d][*Cancelled text:*] The success of the *Logic* led to the publication in 1844 of the Political Economy *Essays*, written as I have already mentioned in 1830 and 1831. With this terminates what may be termed the second period of my writings; reckoning the old *Westminster Review* period as the first. The *Principles of Political Economy* and all subsequent writings belong to a third and different stage of my mental progress, [*the rest of the paragraph is marked with a line in the margin by HTM*] which was essentially characterized by the predominating influence of my wife's intellect and character. Up to this time I have spoken of my writings and opinions in the first person singular because the writings, though (after we became intimate) mostly revised by her, and freed by her judgment from much that was faulty, as well as enriched by her suggestions, were not, like the subsequent ones, largely and in their most important features the direct product of her own mind: and the opinions, though in a state of continued

after all, prejudice can only be successfully combated by philosophy, no way can really be made against it permanently until it has been shewn not to have philosophy on its side.

Being now released from any active concern in temporary politics, and from any literary occupation involving personal communication with contributors and others, I was enabled to indulge the inclination, natural to thinking persons when the age of boyish vanity is once past, for limiting my own society to a very few persons. General society, as now carried on in England, is so insipid an affair, even to the persons who make it what it is, that it is kept up for any reason rather than the pleasure it affords. All serious discussion on matters on which opinions differ, being considered ill bred, and the national deficiency in liveliness and sociability having prevented the cultivation of the art of talking agreeably on trifles, in which the French of the last century so much excelled, the sole attraction of what is called society to those who are not at the top of the tree, is the hope of being aided to climb a little higher in it; while to those who are already at the top, it is chiefly a compliance with custom, and with the supposed requirements of their station. To a person of any but a very common order in thought or feeling, such society, unless he has personal objects to serve by it, must be supremely unattractive: and most people, in the present day, of any really high class of intellect, make their contact with it so slight, and at such long intervals, as to be almost considered as retiring from it altogether. Those persons of any mental superiority who do otherwise, are, almost without exception, greatly deteriorated by it. Not to mention loss of time, the tone of their feelings is lowered: they become less in earnest about those of their opinions respecting which they must remain silent in the society they frequent: they come to look upon their most elevated objects as unpractical, or, at least, too remote from realization to be more than a vision, or a theory; and if, more fortunate than most, they retain their higher principles unimpaired, yet with respect to the persons and affairs of their own day they insensibly adopt the modes of feeling and judgment in which they can hope for sympathy from the company they keep. A person of high intellect should never go into unintellectual society unless he can enter it as an apostle; yet he is the only person with high objects, who can safely enter it at all. Persons even of intellectual aspirations had much better, if they can, make their habitual associates of at least their equals, and as far as possible, their superiors, in knowledge, intellect, and elevation of sentiment. Moreover, if the

---

growth, were not generically different from those which I had gradually wrought out on emerging from the narrowness of my original Benthamism. But in the great advance which I have since made in opinion I was wholly her pupil. Her bolder and more powerful [*continued on RII.20r (see App. G, pp. 616–17 below):*] mind arrived before mine at every conclusion which was derived from a more thorough comprehension of the present and insight into the future; and but for her intellect and her high moral feelings leading me on, it is doubtful if I should ever have advanced much further than the point I had now reached. [*RII.20r then continues with a new paragraph that opens with what is now the second sentence of the next paragraph below: "At this period . . ." (236.8). The new paragraph in the present text ("Being now released . . .") begins on a new leaf.*]

e[*Cancelled text:*] This became more and more my practice.

points in human opinion, agreement of opinion and feeling on those, has been felt in all times to be an essential requisite of anything worthy the name of friendship, in a really earnest mind. All these circumstances united made necessarily, in England (it might not have been so much so in some countries of the Continent), the number very small of those whose society, and still more whose intimacy, I ever voluntarily sought.

Among these, by far the principal was the incomparable friend of whom I have already spoken. At this period of her life she lived mostly, with one young daughter, in a quiet part of the country, ^{f} and only occasionally in town, with her first husband, Mr. Taylor. I visited her equally in both places, and was greatly indebted to the strength of character which enabled her to disregard the false interpretations liable to be put on the frequency of my visits to her while living ^{g}generally^g apart from Mr. Taylor, and on our occasionally travelling together, though in all other respects our conduct, during these years, gave not the slightest ground for any other supposition than the true one, that our relation to each other was one of strong affection and confidential intimacy ^{h}only^h. For though we did not consider the ordinances of society ^{i}binding on a subject so entirely personal, we did feel bound that our conduct should be such as in no degree to bring discredit on her husband, nor therefore on herself; and^i we disdained, as every person not a slave of his animal appetites must do, the abject notion that the strongest and tenderest friendship cannot exist between a man and a woman without a sensual ^{j}relation, or that any impulses of that lower character^j cannot be put aside when regard for the feelings of others, or even when only prudence and personal dignity require it. ^{k}

In this (as it may be termed) third period of my mental progress, which still continues and which now went hand in hand with hers, my opinions gained equally in breadth and depth. I understood more things, and those which I had understood before I understood more thoroughly. I had many new opinions, and the old which I retained I now saw much more deeply into the grounds of. One of the earliest changes which occurred in this stage of my progress was that I turned back from what there had been of excess in my reaction against Benthamism. I had, at the height of that reaction, certainly become much more indulgent to the common opinions of society and the world, and more willing to be content with seconding the superficial improvement which had begun to take place in those common opinions, than became one whose own convictions differed fundamentally from them. I was much more inclined, than I can now approve, to put in abeyance the most decidedly heretical part of my opinions, which I now look upon as almost the

^{f}[*Cancelled text in RII.20r:*] though at no great distance from London;

$^{g-g}$[*Earlier version in RII.20r:*] habitually

$^{h-h}$[*Earlier version in RII.20r:*] , entirely apart from sensuality [*deleted and altered by HTM to produce the version that Mill copied into the present text*]

$^{i-i}$[*Earlier version in RII.20r:*] on a subject so entirely personal, in the smallest degree binding on us in conscience, [*altered and expanded by HTM to produce the version that Mill copied into the present text*]

character is formed, and the mind made up, on the few cardinal points of human opinion, agreement of conviction and feeling on these, has been felt in all times to be an essential requisite of anything worthy the name of friendship, in a really earnest mind. All these circumstances united, made the number very small of those whose society, and still more whose intimacy, I now voluntarily sought.

Among these, by far the principal was the incomparable friend of whom I have already spoken. At this period she lived mostly, with one young daughter, in a quiet part of the country, and only occasionally in town, with her first husband, Mr. Taylor. I visited her equally in both places; and was greatly indebted to the strength of character which enabled her to disregard the false interpretations liable to be put on the frequency of my visits to her while living generally apart from Mr. Taylor, and on our occasionally travelling together, though in all other respects our conduct during those years gave not the slightest ground for any other supposition than the true one, that our relation to each other at that time was one of strong affection and confidential intimacy only. For though we did not consider the ordinances of society binding on a subject so entirely personal, we did feel bound that our conduct should be such as in no degree to bring discredit on her husband, nor therefore on herself.

In this third period (as it may be termed) of my mental progress, which now went hand in hand with hers, my opinions gained equally in breadth and depth. I understood more things, and those which I had understood before, I now understood more thoroughly. I had now completely turned back from what there had been of excess in my reaction against Benthamism. I had, at the height of that reaction, certainly become much more indulgent to the common opinions of society and the world, and more willing to be content with seconding the superficial improvement which had begun to take place in those common opinions, than became one whose convictions, on so many points, differed fundamentally from them. I was much more inclined, than I can now approve, to put in abeyance the more decidedly heretical part of my opinions, which I now look upon as almost

---

^{j–j}[*Earlier version in RII.20r:*] tie; or that sensuality [*altered by HTM to read:* relation; or that the feelings alluded to]

^k[*Additional text in RII.20v:*] Certain it is that our life, during those years, would have borne the strictest scrutiny, and though for the sake of others we not only made this sacrifice but the much greater one of not living together, we did not feel under an obligation of sacrificing that intimate friendship and frequent companionship which was the chief good of life and the principal object in it, to me, and, conscious as I am how little worthy I was of such regard, I may say also to her.

only ones the assertion of which tends in any way to regenerate society. But in addition to this, our opinions were now far *more* heretical than mine had been in the days of my most extreme Benthamism. In those days I had seen little further than the old school of political economists into the possibilities of future improvement in social arrangements. Private property as at present understood, and inheritance, appeared to me as to them, the *dernier mot* of legislation: and I looked no further than to mitigating the inequalities consequent on these institutions, by abolishing primogeniture and entails. The notion that it was possible to get rid in any considerable degree of the flagrant injustice involved in the fact that some are born to riches and the vast majority to poverty, I reckoned chimerical; and only hoped that by universal education, leading to voluntary restraint on population, the portion of the poor might be made more tolerable. In short, I was a democrat but not the least of a Socialist. We were now less democrats than I had formerly been, because we dreaded more the ignorance and especially the selfishness and brutality of the mass: but our ideal of future improvement was such as would class us decidedly under the general designation of Socialists. While we repudiated with the greatest energy the tyranny of society over the individual, we yet looked forward to a time when society should no longer be divided into the idle and the industrious,[*] when the rule that they who do not work shall not eat, should be applied not to the pauper merely, but impartially to all; when the division of the produce of labour, instead of being dependent as in so great a degree it is, on the accident of birth, should be made by concert, on an acknowledged principle of justice, and when it should no longer either be, or be thought to be, impossible for human beings to exert themselves strenuously for benefits which were not to be exclusively their own, but to be shared with the society they belong to. The social problem of the future we considered to be, how to unite the greatest individual liberty of action with an equal ownership of all in the raw material of the globe and an equal participation of all in the benefits of combined labour. We knew that to render any such social transformation practicable an equivalent change of character must take place both in the uncultivated herd who now compose the labouring masses, and *in the immense* majority of their employers. Both these classes must learn by practice to labour and contrive for generous, or at all events for public and social purposes, and not as hitherto solely for self interested ones. But the capacity for this has always existed in mankind, and is not, nor is ever likely to be, extinct. Education and habit will make a common man dig or weave for the public as well as fight for the public. Interest in the common good is at present so weak a motive

---

[*Opposite this last clause Mill's wife pencilled at left in the draft MS: "The voice of Society on the great fundamental questions of social and political morals should be the voice of all."]

ˡ⁻ˡ[Earlier version:] even in the grasping, money getting [*all but "in the" deleted by HTM*]

the only ones, the assertion of which tends in any way to regenerate society. But in addition to this, our opinions were now far *more* heretical than mine had been in the days of my most extreme Benthamism. In those days I had seen little further than the old school of political economists into the possibilities of fundamental improvement in social arrangements. Private property as now understood, and inheritance, appeared to me as to them, the *dernier mot* of legislation: and I looked no further than to mitigating the inequalities consequent on these institutions, by getting rid of primogeniture and entails. The notion that it was possible to go further than this in removing the injustice—for injustice it is whether admitting of a complete remedy or not—involved in the fact that some are born to riches and the vast majority to poverty, I then reckoned chimerical; and only hoped that by universal education, leading to voluntary restraint on population, the portion of the poor might be made more tolerable. In short, I was a democrat, but not the least of a Socialist. We were now much less democrats than I had been, because so long as education continues to be so wretchedly imperfect, we dreaded the ignorance and especially the selfishness and brutality of the mass: but our ideal of ultimate improvement went far beyond Democracy, and would class us decidedly under the general designation of Socialists. While we repudiated with the greatest energy that tyranny of society over the individual which most Socialistic systems are supposed to involve, we yet looked forward to a time when society will no longer be divided into the idle and the industrious; when the rule that they who do not work shall not eat, will be applied not to paupers only, but impartially to all; when the division of the produce of labour, instead of depending, as in so great a degree it now does, on the accident of birth, will be made by concert, on an acknowledged principle of justice; and when it will no longer either be, or be thought to be, impossible for human beings to exert themselves strenuously in procuring benefits which are not to be exclusively their own, but to be shared with the society they belong to. The social problem of the future we considered to be, how to unite the greatest individual liberty of action, with a common ownership in the raw material of the globe, and an equal participation of all in the benefits of combined labour. We had not the presumption to suppose that we could already foresee, by what precise form of institutions these objects could most effectually be attained, or at how near or how distant a period they would become practicable. We saw clearly that to render any such social transformation either possible or desirable, an equivalent change of character must take place both in the uncultivated herd who now compose the labouring masses, and in the immense majority of their employers. Both these classes must learn by practice to labour and combine for generous, or at all events for public and social purposes, and not, as hitherto, solely for narrowly interested ones. But the capacity to do this has always existed in mankind, and is not, nor is ever likely to be, extinct. Education, habit, and the cultivation of the sentiments will make a common man dig or weave for his country, as readily as fight for his country. True enough, it is only by slow degrees, in the generality, only because the mind is not accustomed to dwell on it as it dwells from morning to night on things which tend only to personal good. When called into activity as only self interest now is, by the daily course of life, and spurred from behind by the love of distinction and the fear of shame, it is adequate to produce even in common men the most strenuous exertions as well as the most heroic sacrifices. Doubtless it requires a long course of training to alter the deeprooted selfishness which the whole course of existing institutions tends to generate; and modern institutions still more than ancient, since the occasions on which the individual is called on to act for the public without receiving its pay, are far less frequent in modern life, than in the smaller commonwealths of antiquity. *m*But in this direction lies assuredly the course of future progress*m*.

In the *Principles of Political Economy* these opinions are promulgated; less clearly and fully in the first edition, rather more so in the second, and quite unequivocally in the third. The difference arose partly from the change of times, the first edition having been written and sent to press before the French Revolution of 1848 when the public mind was far less open to the reception of novelties in opinion, especially those of a socialistic character, than it became after that great event. *n* In the first edition the difficulties of Socialism were stated so strongly *o* that the tone was on the whole that of opposition to it. In the year or two which followed, much time was given to the study of the best Socialist writers on the Continent, and to meditation and discussion *p* on the whole range of topics involved in the controversy: and the result was that most of what had been written on the subject in the first edition was cancelled, and replaced by arguments and reflexions of a decidedly socialistic tendency.

m-m[*Earlier version:*] The remedy for this is voluntary association for cooperative industry; which, commenced as it naturally is by those among the industrious classes who are morally the best prepared for it, tends at every step to strengthen where they exist and create where they do not exist, the habits and dispositions requisite for its own success [*marked with an X and a line in the margin by HTM*]

n[*Cancelled text:*] But it would be a mistake to imagine that we kept back in the first edition opinions as decided as those which appear in the third. Our own opinions had made a great advance in the interval

and a system of culture prolonged through successive generations, that men in general can be brought up to this point. But the hindrance is not in the essential constitution of human nature. Interest in the common good is at present so weak a motive in the generality, not because it can never be otherwise, but because the mind is not accustomed to dwell on it as it dwells from morning till night on things which tend only to personal advantage. When called into activity as only self interest now is, by the daily course of life, and spurred from behind by the love of distinction and the fear of shame, it is capable of producing, even in common men, the most strenuous exertions as well as the most heroic sacrifices. The deep rooted selfishness which forms the general character of the existing state of society, is *so* deeply rooted, only because the whole course of existing institutions tends to foster it; modern institutions in some respects more than ancient, since the occasions on which the individual is called on to do anything for the public without receiving its pay, are far less frequent in modern life, than in the smaller commonwealths of antiquity. These considerations did not make us overlook the folly of premature attempts to dispense with the inducements of private interest in social affairs, while no substitute for them has been or can be provided: but we regarded all existing institutions and social arrangements as being (in a phrase I once heard from Austin) "merely provisional," and we welcomed with the greatest pleasure and interest all socialistic experiments by select individuals (such as the Cooperative Societies), which, whether they succeeded or failed, could not but operate as a most useful education of those who took part in them, by cultivating their capacity of acting upon motives pointing directly to the general good, or making them aware of the defects which render them and others incapable of doing so.

In the *Principles of Political Economy*, these opinions were promulgated, less clearly and fully in the first edition, rather more so in the second, and quite unequivocally in the third.[*] The difference arose partly from the change of times, the first edition having been written and sent to press before the French Revolution of 1848, after which the public mind became more open to the reception of novelties in opinion, and doctrines appeared moderate which would have been thought very startling a short time before. In the first edition the difficulties of Socialism were stated so strongly, that the tone was on the whole that of opposition to it. In the year or two which followed, much time was given to the study of the best Socialistic writers on the Continent, and to meditation and discussion on the whole range of topics involved in the controversy: and the result was that most of what had been written on the subject in the first edition was cancelled, and replaced by arguments and reflexions which represent a more advanced opinion.

[*1st ed., 1848; 2nd ed., 1849; 3rd ed., 1852.]

---

between the two publications. [*marked with a line in the margin by HTM*]

o[*Cancelled text:*] and its advantages so weakly, [*deleted first by HTM*]

p[*Cancelled text:*] between ourselves [*marked in the margin, apparently with a question mark, by HTM*]

The *Political Economy* was far more rapidly executed than the *Logic*, or indeed than anything of importance which I had yet written. It was commenced in the autumn of 1845 and completed before the end of 1847. In this period of little more than two years there was an interval of six months during which it was suspended, in order to write articles in the *Morning Chronicle* (which unexpectedly entered warmly into my purpose) urging the formation of peasant properties on the waste lands of Ireland. This was during the winter of 1846/47, the period of the famine, when the stern necessities of the time seemed to afford a chance of attracting attention to what appeared to me the only mode of combining relief to the immediate destitution with a permanent improvement of the social and economical condition of the Irish people. But the novelty and strangeness, in England, of the idea of peasant proprietors, one of the striking examples of the extreme ignorance of English politicians and the English public concerning all social phenomena not generally met with in England (however common elsewhere), made these efforts ineffectual. Instead of a great operation on the waste lands and the conversion of cottiers into proprietors, Parliament passed a Poor Law for maintaining them as paupers: and if the English Government has not since found itself in inextricable difficulties from the joint operation of the old evils and the quackish remedy, it has to thank not its own foresight, but that most unexpected and surprising fact, the depopulation of Ireland, commenced by famine and continued by voluntary emigration.

The rapid success of the *Political Economy* shews that the public wanted and were prepared for such a book. Published early in 1848, an edition of a thousand copies was sold in less than a year. Another similar edition was published in the spring of 1849: and a third of 1250 copies early in 1852. It was from the first continually cited and referred to as an authority: because like the *Wealth of Nations* it was not a book merely of abstract science, but of application. It treated Political Economy not as a thing by itself, but *q* as a fragment of a greater whole, a mere department of Social Philosophy, and so interlinked with all the other branches that its conclusions, even in its own peculiar province, that of Wealth, are only true conditionally, subject to interference and counteraction from causes not directly within its domain: while to the character of a practical guide it has ʳnoʳ pretension, apart from other classes of considerations. *s* Political Economy has never, in reality, pretended to advise with no lights but its own, though some persons who knew nothing but political economy (and therefore knew that ill) may have done so. But the numerous sentimental enemies of political economy, and its still more numerous interested enemies in sentimental guise, have been very successful in

---

q[*Cancelled text:*] in the only way in which it can rationally be treated,

ʳ⁻ʳ[*Earlier version in RII.24r (see App. G, p. 617 below):*] not the slightest [*altered by HTM to the single word that Mill copied into the present text*]

s[*In RII.24r, the original Part II ended at this point with a sentence deleted by HTM:*] It is but the minister and servant of a larger and higher philosophy collecting and handing up to its master the materials which lie near it, to be wrought up with others into a fabric fit for use.

The *Political Economy* was far more rapidly executed than the *Logic*, or indeed than anything of importance which I had previously written. It was commenced in the autumn of 1845, and was ready for the press before the end of 1847. In this period of little more than two years there was an interval of six months during which the work was laid aside, while I was writing articles in the *Morning Chronicle* (which unexpectedly entered warmly into my purpose) urging the formation of peasant properties on the waste lands of Ireland.[*] This was during the period of the famine, the winter of 1846/47, when the stern necessities of the time seemed to afford a chance of gaining attention for what appeared to me the only mode of combining relief to immediate destitution with permanent improvement of the social and economical condition of the Irish people. But the idea was new and strange; there was no English precedent for such a proceeding: and the profound ignorance of English politicians and the English public concerning all social phenomena not generally met with in England (however common elsewhere) made my endeavours an entire failure. Instead of a great operation on the waste lands, and the conversion of cottiers into proprietors, Parliament passed a Poor Law[†] for maintaining them as paupers: and if the nation has not since found itself in inextricable difficulties from the joint operation of the old evils and the quack remedy, it is indebted for its deliverance to that most unexpected and surprising fact, the depopulation of Ireland, commenced by famine, and continued by emigration.

The rapid success of the *Political Economy* shewed that the public wanted, and were prepared for such a book. Published early in 1848, an edition of a thousand copies was sold in less than a year. Another similar edition was published in the spring of 1849; and a third, of 1250 copies, early in 1852. It was, from the first, continually cited and referred to as an authority, because it was not a book merely of abstract science, but also of application, and treated Political Economy not as a thing by itself, but as a fragment of a greater whole; a branch of Social Philosophy, so interlinked with all the other branches, that its conclusions, even in its own peculiar province, are only true conditionally, subject to interference and counteraction from causes not directly within its scope: while to the character of a practical guide it has no pretension, apart from other classes of considerations. Political Economy, in truth, has never pretended to give advice to mankind with no lights but its own; though people who knew nothing *but* political economy (and therefore knew that ill) have taken upon themselves to advise, and could only do so by such lights as they had. But the numerous sentimental enemies of political economy, and its still more numerous interested enemies in sentimental guise, have been very

[*A series of forty-three leading articles, running from 5 Oct., 1846, to 7 Jan., 1847.]
[†10 Victoria, c. 31 (8 June, 1847).]

gaining belief for this among other unmerited imputations upon it. The *Principles* having, in spite of the freedom of many of its opinions on social matters, become for the present the most popular exposition of the subject, has helped to disarm these enemies of so important a study, while I venture to think that it has both widened the basis of the science itself and made many useful applications of its truths in conjunction with others, to the improvement of human practice, moral, political, and social.

Since this time I have published no work of magnitude, though I have written or commenced much, for publication at some future time. I have not to relate any further changes in my opinions, though I hope there has been a continued progress in my mental development. I have seen, in the last twenty years, many of the opinions of my youth obtain general recognition, and many of the reforms in institutions, for which I had through life contended, either effected or in course of being so. But these changes have been attended with much less benefit to human well being than I should formerly have anticipated, because they have produced very little improvement in that on which depends all real amelioration in the lot of mankind, their intellectual and moral state: it may even be questioned whether the causes of deterioration which have been at work in the meanwhile, have not more than counterbalanced the tendencies to improvement. I have learnt from experience that many false opinions may be exchanged for true ones, without in the least altering the habits of mind of which false opinions are the result. The English mind, for example, is quite as raw and undiscerning on subjects of political economy since the nation was converted to free trade, as it was before; although whoever really understands the theory of free trade, must necessarily understand much else, the grounds of that doctrine going very deep into the foundations of the whole philosophy of the production and distribution of wealth. Still further is the public mind from having acquired better habits of thought and feeling or being in any way better fortified against error on subjects of a more elevated nature. I am now convinced that no great improvements in the lot of mankind are possible until a change takes place in the fundamental constitution of their modes of thought. The old opinions in religion, morals, and politics are so much discredited in the more

successful in gaining belief for this among other unmerited imputations against it. And the *Principles* having, in spite of the freedom of many of its opinions, become for the present the most popular treatise on the subject, has helped to disarm the enemies of so important a study. The amount of its worth as an exposition of the science, and the value of the different applications which it suggests, others of course must judge.

For a considerable time after this, I published no work of magnitude; though I still occasionally wrote in periodicals, and my correspondence (much of it with persons quite unknown to me) on subjects of public interest, swelled to a considerable bulk. During these years I wrote or commenced various Essays,[*] for eventual publication, on some of the fundamental questions of human and social life, with regard to several of which I have already much exceeded the severity of the Horatian precept.[†] I continued to watch with keen interest the progress of public events. But it was not, on the whole, very encouraging to me. The European reaction after 1848, and the success of an unprincipled usurper in December 1851,[‡] put an end, as it seemed, to all present hope for freedom or social improvement in France and the Continent. In England, I had seen and continued to see many of the opinions of my youth obtain general recognition, and many of the reforms in institutions, for which I had through life contended, either effected or in course of being so. But these changes had been attended with much less benefit to human well being than I should formerly have anticipated, because they had produced very little improvement in that which all real amelioration in the lot of mankind depends on, their intellectual and moral state: and it might even be questioned if the various causes of deterioration which had been at work in the meanwhile, had not more than counterbalanced the tendencies to improvement. I had learnt from experience that many false opinions may be exchanged for true ones, without in the least altering the habits of mind of which false opinions are the result. The English public, for example, are quite as raw and undiscerning on subjects of political economy since the nation has been converted to free trade, as they were before; and are still further from having acquired better habits of thought and feeling, or being in any way better fortified against error, on subjects of a more elevated character. For, though they have thrown off certain errors, the general discipline of their minds, intellectually and morally, is not altered. I am now convinced, that no great improvements in the lot of mankind are possible, until a great change takes place in the fundamental constitution of their modes of thought. The old opinions in religion, morals, and politics, are so much discredited in the

[*See the Introduction, p. xxi n above.]
[†See Horace, *Ars poetica*, in *Satires, Epistles, and Ars poetica* (Latin and English), trans. H. Rushton Fairclough (London: Heinemann; New York: Putnam's Sons, 1926), p. 482 (ll. 388–9).]
[‡Louis Napoleon (later Napoleon III).]

intellectual minds as to have lost the greater part of their efficacy for good, while they have still vitality enough left to be an effectual obstacle to the rising up of better opinions on the same subjects. When the philosophic minds of the world can no longer believe its religion, a transitional period of weak convictions, paralysed intellects and growing laxity of principle commences, which can never cease but when a renovation has been effected in the bases of belief, leading to the evolution of another faith, whether religious or not, which they *can* believe. Therefore I hold that all thinking or writing, which does not directly tend towards this renovation, is at present of very little value beyond the moment.

The last considerable event in my own life, and the latest of which I shall make mention here, is my marriage, in April 1851, to the lady whose incomparable worth had made her friendship the greatest source to me both of happiness and of improvement, during many years in which we never expected to be in any closer relation to one another. Ardently as I should have aspired to this complete union of our lives at any time in the course of my existence at which it had been practicable, I, no less than even my wife, would far rather have foregone that blessing for ever, than have owed it to the premature death of one for whom I had the sincerest respect, and she the strongest affection. That event however having taken place in July 1849, it was granted to me to derive my own greatest good from that evil, by adding to the partnership of thought, feeling, and even writing which had long existed, a partnership of our entire existence. Before as well as since, I have owed the best part of what I was and did to her inspirations and often to her direct assistance: and so long as any of my writings subsequent to the *Logic* are read or remembered, I hope it will be borne in mind that to her intellect and character they are mainly indebted for whatever in them deserves remembrance.

[End of the Early Draft]

more intellectual minds as to have lost the greater part of their efficacy for good, while they have still life enough in them to be a powerful obstacle to the growing up of any better opinions on those subjects. When the philosophic minds of the world can no longer believe its religion, or can only believe it with modifications amounting to an essential change of its character, a transitional period commences, of weak convictions, paralysed intellects, and growing laxity of principle, which cannot terminate until a renovation has been effected in the basis of their belief, leading to the evolution of some faith, whether religious or merely human, which they can really believe: and when things are in this state, all thinking or writing which does not tend to promote such a renovation, is of very little value beyond the moment. Since there was little in the apparent condition of the public mind, indicative of any tendency in this direction, my view of the immediate prospects of human improvement was not sanguine. More recently a spirit of free speculation has sprung up, giving a more encouraging prospect of the gradual mental emancipation of England; and, concurring with the renewal, under better auspices, of the movement for political freedom in the rest of Europe, has given to the present condition of human affairs a more hopeful aspect.

Between the time of which I have now spoken, and the present, took place the most important events of my private life. The first of these was my marriage, in April 1851, to the lady whose incomparable worth had made her friendship the greatest source to me both of happiness and of improvement, during many years in which we never expected to be in any closer relation to one another. Ardently as I should have aspired to this complete union of our lives at any time in the course of my existence at which it had been practicable, I, as much as my wife, would far rather have foregone that privilege for ever, than have owed it to the premature death of one for whom I had the sincerest respect, and she the strongest affection. That event however having taken place in July 1849, it was granted to me to derive from that evil my own greatest good, by adding to the partnership of thought, feeling, and writing which had long existed, a partnership of our entire existence. For seven and a half years that blessing was mine; for seven and a half only! I can say nothing which could describe, even in the faintest manner, what that loss was and is. But because I know that she would have wished it, I endeavour to make the best of what life I have left, and to work on for her purposes with such diminished strength as can be derived from thoughts of her, and communion with her memory.

During the years which intervened between the commencement of my married life and the catastrophe which closed it, the principal occurrences of my outward existence (unless I count as such a first attack of the family disease, and a consequent journey of more than six months for the recovery of health, in Italy, Sicily, and Greece) had reference to my position in the India House. In 1856 I was promoted to the rank of chief of the office in which I had served for upwards of thirty-three years. The appointment, that of Examiner of India Correspondence, was the highest, next to that of Secretary, in the East India Company's home

service, involving the general superintendance of all the correspondence with the Indian Governments, except the military, naval, and financial. I held this office as long as it continued to exist, being a little more than two years; after which it pleased Parliament, in other words Lord Palmerston, to put an end to the East India Company as a branch of the government of India under the Crown, and convert the administration of that country into a thing to be scrambled for by the second and third class of English parliamentary politicians. I was the chief manager of the resistance which the Company made to their own political extinction. To the letters and petitions I wrote for them,[*] and the concluding chapter of my treatise on *Representative Government*,[T] I must refer for my opinions on the folly and mischief of this ill-considered change. Personally I considered myself a gainer by it, as I had given enough of my life to India, and was not unwilling to retire on the liberal compensation granted. After the change was consummated, Lord Stanley, the first Secretary of State for India, made me the honorable offer of a seat in the Council, and the proposal was subsequently renewed by the Council itself, on the first occasion of its having to supply a vacancy in its own body. But the conditions of Indian government under the new system made me anticipate nothing but useless vexation and waste of effort from any participation in it: and nothing that has since happened has had any tendency to make me regret my refusal.

During the two years which immediately preceded the cessation of my official life, my wife and I were working together at the *Liberty*.[‡] I had first planned and written it as a short essay, in 1854. It was in mounting the steps of the Capitol, in January 1855, that the thought first arose of converting it into a volume. None of my writings have been either so carefully composed, or so sedulously corrected as this. After it had been written as usual twice over, we kept it by us, bringing it out from time to time and going through it *de novo*, reading, weighing and criticizing every sentence. Its final revision was to have been a work of the winter of 1858/59, the first after my retirement, which we had arranged to pass in the South of Europe. That hope and every other were frustrated by the most unexpected and bitter calamity of her death—at Avignon, on our way to Montpellier, from a sudden attack of pulmonary congestion.

[*Memorandum of the Improvements in the Administration of India during the Last Thirty Years, and the Petition of the East-India Company to Parliament; Report to the General Court of Proprietors (both London: Cox and Wyman, 1858); A Constitutional View of the India Question; Practical Observations on the First Two of the Proposed Resolutions on the Government of India; A President in Council the Best Government for India; The Moral of the India Debate; Observations on the Proposed Council of India (all London: Penny, 1858); and "Letter from the Chairman and Deputy Chairman of the Honourable East India Company to the President of the Board of Trade," Parliamentary Papers, 1857–58, XLIII, 41–4.]
[†Chap. xviii, "Of the Government of Dependencies by a Free State"; in CW, Vol. XIX, pp. 562–77.]
[‡On Liberty (London: Parker, 1859); in CW, Vol. XVIII, pp. 213–310.]

[YALE FRAGMENT]

Note, to be expanded in a supplement to the biographical sketch, concerning the participation of my wife in my writings

When two persons have their thoughts and speculations completely in common, when all subjects of intellectual or moral interest are discussed between them in daily life and probed to much greater depths than are usually or conveniently laid open in published writings, when they set out from the same principles and form their opinions together, it is of little consequence which of them holds the pen; the writings which result are the joint product of both, and it must in general be impossible to disentangle their respective parts and affirm that this belongs to one and that to the other. In this sense, not only during the years of our married life but through the many years of confidential friendship which preceded, all my published writings were our joint production, her share in them constantly increasing as years advanced. But in many cases (though but a small proportion of the whole) what belongs to her can be distinguished and specially identified. The most valuable ideas and features in these joint productions, those which have been most fruitful of important results and have contributed most to the success and reputation of the works themselves, originated with her, and were purely emanations from her mind, my part in them being no greater than in any of the thoughts which I found in previous authors and made my own only by incorporating them with my system of thought. This was oftener the case where it would be least than where it

Since then, I have sought for such alleviation as my state admitted of, by the mode of life which most enabled me to feel her still near me. I bought a cottage as close as possible to the place where she is buried, and there her daughter (my fellow-sufferer and now my chief comfort) and I, live constantly during a great portion of the year. My objects in life are solely those which were hers; my pursuits and occupations those in which she shared, or sympathized, and which are indissolubly associated with her. Her memory is to me a religion, and her approbation the standard by which, summing up as it does all worthiness, I endeavour to regulate my life.

In resuming my pen some years after closing the preceding narrative, I am influenced by a desire not to leave incomplete the record, for the sake of which chiefly this biographical sketch was undertaken, of the obligations I owe to those who have either contributed essentially to my own mental developement or had a direct share in my writings and in whatever else of a public nature I have done. In the preceding pages, this record, so far as it relates to my wife, is not so detailed and precise as it ought to be; and since I lost her, I have had other help, not less deserving and requiring acknowledgment.

When two persons have their thoughts and speculations completely in common; when all subjects of intellectual or moral interest are discussed between them in daily life, and probed to much greater depths than are usually or conveniently sounded in writings intended for general readers; when they set out from the same principles and arrive at their conclusions by processes pursued jointly, it is of little consequence in respect to the question of originality which of them holds the pen; the one who contributes least to the composition may contribute most to the thought; the writings which result are the joint product of both, and it must often be impossible to disentangle their respective parts and affirm that this belongs to one and that to the other. In this wide sense, not only during the years of our married life, but during many of the years of confidential friendship which preceded, all my published writings were as much her work as mine; her share in them constantly increasing as years advanced. But in certain cases, what belongs to her can be distinguished, and specially identified. Over and above the general influence which her mind had over mine, the most valuable ideas and features in these joint productions—those which have been most fruitful of important results, and have contributed most to the success and reputation of the works themselves—originated with her; were emanations from her mind, my part in them being no greater than in any of the thoughts which I found in previous writers, and made my own only by incorporating them with my own system of thought. During the greater part of my literary life I have performed the office in relation to her, which from a rather early period I had considered as the most useful part that I was qualified to take in the domain of thought, that of an interpreter of original thinkers, and mediator between them and the public; for I had always a humble opinion of my own powers as an original thinker, except in abstract science (logic, metaphysics, and the theoretic principles of political economy and politics), but thought

would be most expected. Some might suppose, for instance, that my strong convictions on the complete equality which ought to exist in all legal, social, political and domestic relations between men and women, were adopted or learnt from her. This was so far from being the case, that I held these convictions from early boyhood and the strength with which I held them was, as I believe, more than anything else, the originating cause of the interest she felt in me. Undoubtedly however this conviction was at that time, in my mind, little more than an abstract principle: it was through her teaching that I first perceived and understood its practical bearings; her rare knowledge of human nature, and perception and comprehension of moral and social influences, shewed me (what I should never have found out in more than a very vague way for myself) the mode in which the consequences of the inferior position of women intertwine themselves with all the evils of existing society and with the difficulties of human improvement. Without her I should probably always have held my present opinions on the question, but it would never have become to me as, with the deepest conviction, it now is, the great question of the coming time: the most urgent interest of human progress, involving the removal of a barrier which now stops the way, and renders all the improvements which can be effected while it remains, slight and superficial. I learnt from her nearly all I know of the details of the subject; the opinion itself I held as strongly, though less according to knowledge, before I had even seen her.

myself much superior to most of my contemporaries in willingness and ability to learn from everybody; as I found hardly any one who made such a point of examining what was said in defence of all opinions, however new or however old, in the conviction that even if they were errors there might be a substratum of truth underneath them, and that in any case the discovery of what it was that made them plausible, would be a benefit to truth. I had, in consequence, marked out this as a sphere of usefulness in which I was under a special obligation to make myself active: the more so, as the acquaintance I had formed with the ideas of the Coleridgians, of the German thinkers, and of Carlyle, all of them fiercely opposed to the mode of thought in which I had been brought up, had convinced me that along with much error they possessed much truth, which was veiled from minds otherwise capable of receiving it by the transcendental and mystical phraseology in which they were accustomed to shut it up and from which they neither cared, nor knew how, to disengage it; and I did not despair of separating the truth from the error and expressing it in terms which would be intelligible and not repulsive to those on my own side in philosophy. Thus prepared, it will easily be believed that when I came into close intellectual communion with a person of the most eminent faculties, whose genius, as it grew and unfolded itself in thought, continually struck out truths far in advance of me, but in which I could not, as I had done in those others, detect any mixture of error, the greatest part of my mental growth consisted in the assimilation of those truths, and the most valuable part of my intellectual work was in building the bridges and clearing the paths which connected them with my general system of thought.*

*The steps in my mental growth for which I was indebted to her were far from being those which a person wholly uninformed on the subject would probably suspect. It might be supposed, for instance, that my strong convictions on the complete equality in all legal, political, social and domestic relations, which ought to exist between men and women, may have been adopted or learnt from her. This was so far from being the fact, that those convictions were among the earliest results of the application of my mind to political subjects, and the strength with which I held them was, as I believe, more than anything else, the originating cause of the interest she felt in me. What is true is, that until I knew her, the opinion was, in my mind, little more than an abstract principle. I saw no more reason why women should be held in legal subjection to other people, than why men should. I was certain that their interests required fully as much protection as those of men, and were quite as little likely to obtain it without an equal voice in making the laws by which they are to be bound. But that perception of the vast practical bearings of women's disabilities which found expression in the book on *The Subjection of Women* [London: Longmans, Green, Reader, and Dyer, 1869], was acquired mainly through her teaching. But for her rare knowledge of human nature and comprehension of moral and social influences, though I should doubtless have held my present opinions I should have had a very insufficient perception of the mode in which the consequences of the inferior position of women intertwine themselves with all the evils of existing society and with all the difficulties of human improvement. I am indeed painfully conscious how much of her best thoughts on the subject I have failed to reproduce, and how greatly that little treatise falls short of what would have been given to the world if she had put on paper her entire mind on this question, or had lived to revise and improve, as she certainly would have done, my imperfect statement of the case.

The first of my books in which her share was conspicuous was the *Political Economy*: the *Logic* owed little to her except in the minuter matters of composition. The chapter of the *Political Economy* which has had greater direct practical effect than all the rest, that on "the probable future of the labouring classes," is entirely due to her: in the first draft of the book that chapter did not exist. She pointed out the need of such a chapter and the extreme imperfection of the book without it; she caused me to write it, and the whole of the general part of the chapter, the statement and discussion of the two theories respecting the proper condition of the labouring classes, was a mere exposition of her thoughts, often in words taken down from her lips. The purely scientific part of the *Political Economy* I did not learn from her: but it was chiefly her influence that gave the general tone to the book by which it was distinguished from all previous expositions of Political Economy and which has made it so useful in conciliating the minds which those previous treatises had alienated, viz. that it never treats the mere arrangements of modern society as final; the economical generalisations which depend on social arrangements, including the whole of what are called the laws of Distribution, it never deals with as more than provisional, and certain to be much altered by the progress of events. I had indeed partially learnt this view of

The first of my books in which her share was conspicuous was the *Principles of Political Economy*. The *System of Logic* owed little to her except in the minuter matters of composition, in which respect my writings, both great and small, have largely benefitted by her accurate and clear-sighted criticism.* The chapter of the *Political Economy* which has had a greater influence on opinion than all the rest, that on "the Probable Future of the Labouring Classes,"[*] is entirely due to her: in the first draft of the book, that chapter did not exist. She pointed out the need of such a chapter, and the extreme imperfection of the book without it: she was the cause of my writing it; and the more general part of the chapter, the statement and discussion of the two opposite theories respecting the proper condition of the labouring classes, was wholly an exposition of her thoughts, often in words taken from her own lips. The purely scientific part of the *Political Economy* I did not learn from her; but it was chiefly her influence that gave to the book that general tone by which it is distinguished from all previous expositions of Political Economy that had any pretension to being scientific, and which has made it so useful in conciliating minds which those previous expositions had repelled. This tone consisted chiefly in making the proper distinction between the laws of the Production of Wealth, which are real laws of nature, dependent on the properties of objects, and the modes of its Distribution, which, subject to certain conditions, depend on human will. The common run of political economists confuse these together, under the designation of economic laws, which they deem incapable of being defeated or modified by human effort; ascribing the same necessity to things dependent on the unchangeable conditions of our earthly existence, and to those which, being but the necessary consequences of particular social arrangements, are merely coextensive with these. Given certain institutions and customs, wages,

---

*The only person from whom I received any direct assistance in the preparation of the *System of Logic* was Mr. Bain, since so justly celebrated for his philosophical writings. He went carefully through the manuscript before it was sent to press, and enriched it with a great number of additional examples and illustrations from science; many of which, as well as some detached remarks of his own in confirmation of my logical views, I inserted nearly in his own words. [See Textual Introduction, *CW*, Vol. VII, pp. lxviii–lxxii, lxxxiii, and lxxxviii.]

My obligations to Comte were only to his writings—to the part which had then been published of his *Cours de Philosophie Positive*: and as has been seen from what I have said in the Narrative, the amount of these obligations is far less than has sometimes been asserted. The first volume, which contains all the fundamental doctrines of the book, was substantially complete before I had seen Comte's treatise. I derived from him many valuable thoughts, conspicuously in the chapter on Hypotheses and in the view taken of the logic of algebra: but it is only in the concluding Book, on the Logic of the Moral Sciences, that I owe to him any radical improvement in my conception of the application of logical methods. This improvement I have stated and characterized in a former part of the present Memoir. [See pp. 217–19 above, and Textual Introduction, *CW*, Vol. VII, pp. lxiv–lxv, lxviii–lxix, lxxxii–lxxxiii, and xc–xci.]

[*Bk. IV, Chap. vii.]

things from other teachings and suggestions; but it was confirmed in my own mind and made predominant in the book by her promptings. This example well illustrates the general character of what she contributed to my writings. What was abstract and purely scientific was generally mine: the properly human element came from her: in all that related to the application of philosophy to the exigencies of human society and progress, I was her pupil, and that, too, equally in the boldly speculative and in the cautiously practical. For, on the one hand, she was much more courageous and farsighted than, without her, I should ever have been, in anticipations of a state of future improvement in which many of the limited generalizations now so often confounded with universal principles of human nature, will cease to be applicable. Those parts of my writings, and particularly of the *Political Economy* which look forward to changes in the present opinions on the limits of the right of property and which contemplate possibilities, as to the springs of human action in economical matters, which had only been affirmed by Socialists and in general fiercely denied by political economists; all this, but for her, would either have been absent from my writings or would have been suggested much more timidly and in a more qualified form. While she thus rendered me more bold in speculation on human affairs, her eminently practical turn of mind and almost unerring estimate of practical considerations repressed in me all tendencies that were really visionary and kept me both in thought and expression within the bounds of good sense. Her mind at once invested every idea in a concrete shape and framed to itself a conception of how it would actually work; and her knowledge of human feelings and conduct as they now are, was so seldom at fault that the weak point in any unworkable practical suggestion rarely escaped her.

The *Liberty* was more directly and literally a joint production than anything else I wrote, for there was not a sentence in it that was not several times gone over by us together, turned over in many ways, and laboriously weeded of any imperfection

profits, and rent will be determined by certain causes; but this class of political economists drop the indispensable presupposition, and argue that these causes must by an inherent necessity, against which no human means can avail, determine the shares which fall, in the division of the produce, to labourers, capitalists, and landlords. The *Principles of Political Economy* yielded to none of its predecessors in aiming at the scientific appreciation of the action of these causes, under the conditions which they presuppose; but it set the example of not treating those conditions as final. The economic generalisations which depend, not on necessities of nature but on those combined with the existing arrangements of society, it deals with only as provisional, and as liable to be much altered by the progress of social improvement. I had indeed partially learnt this view of things from the thoughts awakened in me by the speculations of the Saint-Simonians; but it was made a living principle pervading and animating the book by my wife's promptings. This example illustrates well the general character of what she contributed to my writings. What was abstract and purely scientific was generally mine; the properly human element came from her: in all that concerned the application of philosophy to the exigencies of human society and progress, I was her pupil, alike in boldness of speculation and cautiousness of practical judgment. For, on the one hand, she was much more courageous and farsighted than without her I should have been, in anticipations of an order of things to come, in which many of the limited generalizations now so often confounded with universal principles will cease to be applicable. Those parts of my writings and especially of the *Political Economy* which contemplate possibilities in the future such as, when affirmed by Socialists, have in general been fiercely denied by political economists, would, but for her, either have been absent, or the suggestions would have been made much more timidly and in a more qualified form. But while she thus rendered me bolder in speculation on human affairs, her practical turn of mind, and her almost unerring estimate of practical obstacles, repressed in me all tendencies that were really visionary. Her mind invested all ideas in a concrete shape, and formed to itself a conception of how they would actually work: and her knowledge of the existing feelings and conduct of mankind was so seldom at fault, that the weak point in any unworkable suggestion seldom escaped her.*

The *Liberty* was more directly and literally our joint production than anything else which bears my name, for there was not a sentence of it that was not several times gone through by us together, turned over in many ways, and carefully

---

*A few dedicatory lines, acknowledging what the book owed to her, were prefixed to some of the presentation copies of the *Political Economy* on its first publication. Her dislike of publicity alone prevented their insertion in the other copies of the work. [The dedication read: "To Mrs. John Taylor, as the most eminently qualified of all persons known to the author either to originate or to appreciate speculations on social improvement, this attempt to explain and diffuse ideas many of which were first learned from herself, is with the highest respect and regard, dedicated."]

we could discover either in thought or in expression. But it is difficult in this case to identify any particular part or element as being more hers than all the rest. The whole mode of thinking of which the book was the expression, was emphatically hers. But I also was so thoroughly imbued with it that the same thoughts naturally occurred to us both. That I was thus imbued with it, however, I owe in a great degree to her. There was a moment in my mental progress when I might easily have fallen into a tendency towards over-government both social and political, as there was also a moment when, by reaction from a contrary tendency, I might have become less a radical and a democrat than I now am. In both these points as in numerous others, she benefitted me as much in keeping me right where I was right, as in leading me to new truths or correcting errors. My great readiness and eagerness to learn from everybody and to make room in my system of opinions for every new acquisition by adjusting the old and the new to one another might, but for her steadying influence, have seduced me into modifying my original opinions too much. She was in nothing more valuable to my development than by her just measure of the relative importance of one consideration and another, which often protected me from allowing to truths I had only recently seen, a more important place in my thoughts than was properly their due.

[*End of the Yale fragment*]

weeded of any faults, either in thought or expression, that we detected in it. It is in consequence of this that, although it never underwent her final revision, it far surpasses, as a mere specimen of composition, anything which has proceeded from me either before or since. With regard to the thoughts, it is difficult to identify any particular part or element as being more hers than all the rest. The whole mode of thinking of which the book was the expression, was emphatically hers. But I also was so thoroughly imbued with it that the same thoughts naturally occurred to us both. That I was thus penetrated with it, however, I owe in a great degree to her. There was a moment in my mental progress when I might easily have fallen into a tendency towards over-government, both social and political; as there was also a moment when, by reaction from a contrary excess, I might have become a less thorough radical and democrat than I am. In both these points as in many others, she benefitted me as much by keeping me right where I was right, as by leading me to new truths and ridding me of errors. My great readiness and eagerness to learn from everybody, and to make room in my opinions for every new acquisition by adjusting the old and the new to one another, might, but for her steadying influence, have seduced me into modifying my early opinions too much. She was in nothing more valuable to my mental development than by her just measure of the relative importance of different considerations, which often protected me from allowing to truths I had only recently learnt to see, a more important place in my thoughts than was properly their due.

The *Liberty* is likely to survive longer than anything else that I have written (with the possible exception of the *Logic*), because the conjunction of her mind with mine has rendered it a kind of philosophic text-book of a single truth, which the changes progressively taking place in modern society tend to bring out into ever stronger relief: the importance, to man and society, of a large variety in types of character, and of giving full freedom to human nature to expand itself in innumerable and conflicting directions. Nothing can better shew how deep are the foundations of this truth, than the great impression made by the exposition of it at a time which, to superficial observation, did not seem to stand much in need of such a lesson. The fears we expressed lest the inevitable growth of social equality and of the government of public opinion should impose on mankind an oppressive yoke of uniformity in opinion and practice, might easily have appeared chimerical to those who looked more at present facts than at tendencies; for the gradual revolution that is taking place in society and institutions has thus far been decidedly favourable to the development of new opinions, and has procured for them a much more unprejudiced hearing than they previously met with. But this is a feature belonging to periods of transition, when old notions and feelings have been unsettled and no new doctrines have yet succeeded to their ascendancy. At such times people of any mental activity, having given up many of their old beliefs, and not feeling quite sure that those they still retain can stand unmodified, listen eagerly to new opinions. But this state of things is necessarily transitory: some particular body of doctrine in time rallies the majority round it, organizes social institutions and modes of action conformably to itself, education impresses this new creed upon the new generations without the mental processes that have led to it, and by degrees it acquires the very same power of compression, so long exercised by the creeds of which it has taken the place. Whether this noxious power will be exercised depends on whether mankind have by that time become aware that it cannot be exercised without stunting and dwarfing human nature. It is then that the teachings of the *Liberty* will have their greatest value. And it is to be feared that they will retain that value a long time.

As regards originality, it has of course no other than that which every thoughtful mind gives to its own mode of conceiving and expressing truths which are common property. The leading thought of the book is one which, though in many ages confined to insulated thinkers, mankind have probably at no time since the beginning of civilisation been entirely without. To speak only of the last few generations, it is distinctly contained in the vein of important thought respecting education and culture spread through the European mind by the labours and genius of Pestalozzi. The unqualified championship of it by Wilhelm von Humboldt[*] is referred to in the book; but he by no means stood alone in his own country. During the early part of the present century, the doctrine of the rights of individuality, and the claim of the moral nature to develope itself in its own way, was pushed by a whole school of German authors even to exaggeration; and the writings of Goethe, the most celebrated of all German authors, though not belonging to that or to any other school, are penetrated throughout by views of morals and of conduct in life, often in my opinion not defensible, but which are incessantly seeking whatever defence they admit of in the theory of the right and duty of self-development. In our own country, before the book *On Liberty* was written, the doctrine of Individuality had been enthusiastically asserted, in a stile of vigorous declamation sometimes reminding one of Fichte, by Mr. William Maccall, in a series of writings of which the most elaborate is entitled *Elements of Individualism*.[†] And a remarkable American, Mr. Warren, had framed a System of Society, on the foundation of "the Sovereignty of the Individual," had obtained a number of followers, and had actually commenced the formation of a Village Community (whether it now exists I know not) which, though bearing a superficial resemblance to some of the projects of Socialists, is diametrically opposite to them in principle, since it recognises no authority whatever in Society over the individual, except to enforce equal freedom of development for all individualities.[‡] As the book which bears

[*Karl Wilhelm von Humboldt, *The Sphere and Duties of Government*, trans. Joseph Coulthard (London: Chapman, 1854).]

[†William Maccall, *The Elements of Individualism* (London: Chapman, 1847); for other of his writings to which Mill may be referring, see the Bibliographic Index, p. 682 below.]

[‡See, e.g., Josiah Warren, *Equitable Commerce*, ed. Stephen Pearl Andrews (New York: Fowlers and Wells, 1852), p. 26.]

my name claimed no originality for any of its doctrines, and was not intended to write their history, the only author who had preceded me in their assertion of whom I thought it appropriate to say anything, was Humboldt, who furnished the motto to the work;[*] although in one passage I borrowed from the Warrenites their phrase, the sovereignty of the individual.[†] It is hardly necessary here to remark that there are abundant differences in detail, between the conception of the doctrine by any of the predecessors I have mentioned, and that set forth in the book.

After my irreparable loss one of my earliest cares was to print and publish the treatise, so much of which was the work of her whom I had lost, and consecrate it to her memory. I have made no alteration or addition to it, nor shall I ever. Though it wants the last touch of her hand, no substitute for that touch shall ever be attempted by mine.

The political circumstances of the time induced me shortly after to complete and publish a pamphlet (*Thoughts on Parliamentary Reform*),[‡] part of which had been written some years previously on the occasion of one of the abortive Reform Bills[§] and had at the time been approved and revised by her. Its principal features were, hostility to the Ballot (a change of opinion in both of us, in which she rather preceded me) and a claim of representation for minorities; not however at that time going beyond the cumulative vote proposed by Mr. Garth Marshall.[¶] In finishing the pamphlet for publication with a view to the discussions on the Reform Bill of Lord Derby's and Mr. Disraeli's Government in 1859,[‖] I added a third feature, a plurality of votes, to be given, not to property, but to proved superiority of education. This recommended itself to me, as a means of reconciling the irresistible claim of every man or woman to be consulted, and to be allowed a voice, in the regulation of affairs which vitally concern them, with the superiority of weight justly due to opinions grounded on superiority of knowledge. The suggestion however was one which I had never discussed with my almost infallible counsellor, and I have no evidence that she would have concurred in it. As far as I have been able to observe, it has found favour with nobody; all who desire any sort of inequality in the electoral vote, desiring it in favour of property and not of intelligence or knowledge. If it ever overcomes the strong feeling which exists

[*See *On Liberty*, in *CW*, Vol. XVIII, p. 215.]
[†See *ibid.*, p. 276.]
[‡London: Parker, 1859; reprinted in *D&D*, Vol. III, pp. 1–46; in *CW*, Vol. XIX, pp. 311–39.]
[§"A Bill Further to Amend the Laws Relating to the Representation of the People in England and Wales," 17 Victoria (16 Feb., 1854), *Parliamentary Papers*, 1854, V, 375–418.]
[¶See James Garth Marshall, *Minorities and Majorities: Their Relative Rights* (London: Ridgway, 1853).]
[‖"A Bill to Amend the Laws Relating to the Representation of the People in England and Wales, and to Facilitate the Registration and Voting of Electors," 22 Victoria (28 Feb., 1859), *Parliamentary Papers*, 1859 (Session 1), II, 649–715.]

against it, this will only be after the establishment of a systematic National Education by which the various grades of politically valuable acquirement may be accurately defined and authenticated. Without this it will always remain liable to strong, possibly conclusive, objections; and with this, it would perhaps not be needed.

It was soon after the publication of *Thoughts on Parliamentary Reform* that I became acquainted with Mr. Hare's admirable system of Personal Representation, which, in its present shape, was then for the first time published.[*] I saw in this great practical and philosophical idea, the greatest improvement of which the system of representative government is susceptible; an improvement which, in the most felicitous manner, exactly meets and cures the grand, and what before seemed the inherent, defect of the representative system; that of giving to a numerical majority all power, instead of only a power proportional to its numbers, and enabling the strongest party to exclude all weaker parties from making their opinions heard in the assembly of the nation, except through such opportunity as may be given to them by the accidentally unequal distribution of opinions in different localities. To these great evils nothing more than very imperfect pallia- tives had seemed possible; but Mr. Hare's system affords a radical cure. This great discovery, for it is no less, in the political art, inspired me, as I believe it has inspired all thoughtful persons who have adopted it, with new and more sanguine hopes respecting the prospects of human society; by freeing the form of political institutions towards which the whole civilised world is manifestly and irresistibly tending, from the chief part of what seemed to qualify or render doubtful its ultimate benefits. Minorities, so long as they remain minorities, are, and ought to be, outvoted; but under arrangements which enable any assemblage of voters, amounting to a certain number, to place in the legislature a representative of its own choice, minorities cannot be suppressed. Independent opinions will force their way into the council of the nation and make themselves heard there, a thing which often cannot happen in the existing forms of representative democracy; and the legislature instead of being weeded of individual peculiarities and entirely made up of men who simply represent the creed of great political or religious parties, will comprise a large proportion of the most eminent individual minds in the country placed there without reference to party by voters who appreciate their individual eminence. I can understand that persons, otherwise intelligent, should, for want of sufficient examination, be repelled from Mr. Hare's plan by what they think the complex nature of its machinery. But any one who does not feel the want which the scheme is intended to supply; any one who throws it over as a mere theoretical subtlety or crotchet, tending to no valuable purpose, and unworthy of the attention of practical men, may be pronounced an incompetent statesman, unequal to the politics of the future. I mean, unless he is a minister, or aspires to

[*Thomas Hare, *A Treatise on the Election of Representatives* (London: Longman, Brown, Green, Longmans, and Roberts, 1859).]

become one: for we are quite accustomed to a minister's continuing to profess unqualified hostility to an improvement almost to the very day when his conscience or his interest induces him to take it up as a public measure and carry it.

Had I met with Mr. Hare's system before the publication of my pamphlet, I should have given an account of it there. Not having done so, I wrote an article in *Fraser's Magazine* (reprinted in my miscellaneous writings)[*] principally for that purpose, though I included in it, along with Mr. Hare's book, a review of two other productions on the question of the day; one of them a pamphlet by my early friend Mr. John Austin, who had in his old age become an enemy of all further parliamentary reform; the other an able and ingenious though partially erroneous work by Mr. Lorimer.[†]

In the course of the same summer I fulfilled a duty particularly incumbent upon me, that of helping (by an article in the *Edinburgh Review*) to make known Mr. Bain's profound treatise on the Mind, just then completed by the publication of its second volume.[‡] And I carried through the press a selection of my minor writings, forming the first two volumes of *Dissertations and Discussions*. The selection had been made during my wife's lifetime, but the revision, in concert with her, with a view to republication, had been barely commenced; and when I had no longer the guidance of her judgment I despaired of pursuing it further, and republished the papers as they were, with the exception of striking out such passages as were no longer in accordance with my opinions. My literary work of the year terminated with an essay in *Fraser's Magazine* (afterwards republished in the third volume of *Dissertations and Discussions*) entitled "A Few Words on Non-Intervention."[§] I was prompted to write this paper by a desire, while vindicating England from the imputations commonly brought against her on the Continent of a peculiar selfishness in matters of foreign policy, to warn Englishmen of the colour given to this imputation by the low tone in which English statesmen are accustomed to speak of English policy as concerned only with English interests, and by the conduct of Lord Palmerston at that particular time in opposing the Suez Canal. And I took the opportunity of expressing ideas which had long been in my mind (some of them generated by my Indian experience and others by the international questions which then greatly occupied the European public) respecting the true principles of international morality and the legitimate

[*"Recent Writers on Reform," *Fraser's Magazine*, LIX (Apr., 1859), 489–508; reprinted in *D&D*, Vol. III, pp. 47–96; in *CW*, Vol. XIX, pp. 341–70.]

[†Austin, *A Plea for the Constitution*; James Lorimer, *Political Progress Not Necessarily Democratic* (London and Edinburgh: Williams and Norgate, 1857).]

[‡Alexander Bain, *The Senses and the Intellect* (London: Parker, 1855), and *The Emotions and the Will* (London: Parker, 1859); reviewed by Mill in "Bain's Psychology," *Edinburgh Review*, CX (Oct., 1859), 287–321 (the review is reprinted in *D&D*, Vol. III, pp. 97–152; in *CW*, Vol. XI, pp. 339–73).]

[§*Fraser's Magazine*, LX (Dec., 1859), 766–76; reprinted in *D&D*, Vol. III, pp. 153–78.]

modifications made in it by difference of times and circumstances; a subject I had already to some extent discussed in the vindication of the French Provisional Government of 1848 against the attacks of Lord Brougham and others which I published at the time in the *Westminster Review* and which is reprinted in the *Dissertations*.[*]

I had now settled, as I believed for the remainder of my existence, into a purely literary life; if that can be called literary which continued to be occupied in a preeminent degree with politics, and not merely with theoretical, but practical politics, although a great part of the year was spent at a distance of many hundred miles from the chief seat of the politics of my own country, to which, and primarily for which, I wrote. But in truth, the modern facilities of communication have not only removed all the disadvantages, to a political writer in tolerably easy circumstances, of distance from the scene of political action, but have converted them into advantages. The immediate and regular receipt of newspapers and periodicals keeps him *au courant* of even the most temporary politics, and gives him a much more correct view of the state and progress of opinion than he could acquire by personal contact with individuals: for every one's social intercourse is more or less limited to particular sets or classes, whose impressions and no others reach him through that channel; and experience has taught me that those who give their time to the absorbing claims of what is called society, not having leisure to keep up a large acquaintance with the organs of opinion, remain much more ignorant of the general state either of the public mind, or of the active and instructed part of it, than a recluse who reads the newspapers need be. There are, no doubt, disadvantages in too long a separation from one's country—in not occasionally renewing one's impressions of the light in which men and things appear when seen from a position in the midst of them; but the deliberate judgment formed at a distance, and undisturbed by inequalities of perspective, is the most to be depended on, even for application to practice. Alternating between the two positions I combined the advantages of both. And, though the inspirer of my best thoughts was no longer with me, I was not alone: she had left a daughter—my stepdaughter, Miss Helen Taylor, the inheritor of much of her wisdom, and of all her nobleness of character, whose ever growing and ripening talents from that day to this have been devoted to the same great purposes, and have already made her name better and more widely known than was that of her mother, though far less so than I predict that if she lives, it is destined to become. Of the value of her direct cooperation with me, something will be said hereafter: of what I owe in the way of instruction to her great powers of original thought and soundness of practical judgment, it would be a vain attempt to give an adequate idea. Surely no one ever before was so fortunate, as, after such a loss as mine, to draw another such prize in the lottery of life—another companion,

[*Brougham's *Letter to the Marquess of Lansdowne* (London: Ridgway, 1848) is reviewed in Mill's "The French Revolution of 1848, and Its Assailants," *Westminster Review*, LI (Apr., 1849), 1–47 (the review is reprinted in *D&D*, Vol. II, pp. 335–410).]

stimulator, adviser, and instructor of the rarest quality. Whoever, either now or hereafter, may think of me and of the work I have done, must never forget that it is the product not of one intellect and conscience but of three, the least considerable of whom, and above all the least original, is the one whose name is attached to it.

The work of the years 1860 and 1861 consisted chiefly of two treatises, only one of which was intended for immediate publication. This was the *Considerations on Representative Government*, a connected exposition of what, by the thoughts of many years, I had come to regard as the best form of a popular constitution. Along with as much of the general theory of government as is necessary to support this particular portion of its practice, the volume contains my matured views of the principal questions which occupy the present age, within the province of purely organic institutions, and raises by anticipation some other questions to which growing necessities will sooner or later compel the attention both of theoretical and of practical politicians. The chief of these last is the distinction between the function of making laws, for which a numerous popular assembly is radically unfit, and that of getting good laws made, which is its proper duty, and cannot be satisfactorily fulfilled by any other authority: and the consequent need of a Legislative Commission, as a permanent part of the constitution of a free country; consisting of a small number of highly trained political minds on whom, when Parliament has determined that a law shall be made, the task of making it should be devolved; Parliament retaining the power of passing or rejecting the bill when drawn up, but not of altering it otherwise than by sending proposed amendments to be dealt with by the Commission. The question here raised respecting the most important of all public functions, that of legislation, is a particular case of the great problem of modern political organization, stated I believe for the first time in its full extent by Bentham, though in my opinion not always satisfactorily resolved by him; the combination of complete popular control over public affairs with the greatest attainable perfection of skilled agency.

The other treatise written at this time is the one which was published some years later under the title of *The Subjection of Women*. It was written at my daughter's suggestion that there might, in any event, be in existence a written exposition of my opinions on that great question, as full and conclusive as I could make it. The intention was to keep this among other unpublished papers, improving it from time to time if I was able, and to publish it at the time when it should seem likely to be most useful. As ultimately published it was enriched with some important ideas of my daughter's, and passages of her writing. But in what was of my own composition, all that is most striking and profound belongs to my wife; coming from the fund of thought which had been made common to us both, by our innumerable conversations and discussions on a topic which filled so large a place in our minds.

Soon after this time I took from their repository a portion of the unpublished papers which I had written during the last years of our married life, and shaped them, with some additional matter, into the little work entitled *Utilitarianism*;

which was first published in three parts, in successive numbers of *Fraser's Magazine*, and afterwards reprinted in a volume.[*]

Before this however the state of public affairs had become extremely critical, by the commencement of the American civil war. My strongest feelings were engaged in this struggle, which, I felt from the beginning, was destined to be a turning point, for good or evil, of the course of human affairs for an indefinite duration. Having been a deeply interested observer of the Slavery quarrel in America, during the many years that preceded the open breach, I knew that it was in all its stages an aggressive enterprise of the slave owners to extend the territory of slavery; under the combined influences of pecuniary interest, domineering temper, and the fanaticism of a class for its class privileges, influences so fully and powerfully depicted in the admirable work of my friend Professor Cairnes, *The Slave Power*.[†] Their success, if they succeeded, would be a victory of the powers of evil which would give courage to the enemies of progress and damp the spirits of its friends all over the civilised world, while it would create a formidable military power grounded on the worst and most anti-social form of the tyranny of men over men, and by destroying for a long time the prestige of the great democratic republic would give to all the privileged classes of Europe a false confidence, probably only to be extinguished in blood. On the other hand, if the spirit of the North was sufficiently roused to carry the war to a successful termination, and if that termination did not come too soon and too easily, I foresaw, from the laws of human nature and the experience of revolutions, that when it did come it would in all probability be thorough: that the bulk of the Northern population, whose conscience had as yet been awakened only to the point of resisting the further extension of slavery, but whose fidelity to the Constitution of the United States made them disapprove of any attempt by the Federal Government to interfere with slavery in the States where it already existed, would acquire feelings of another kind when the Constitution had been shaken off by armed rebellion, would determine to have done for ever with the accursed thing, and would join their banner with that of the noble body of Abolitionists, of whom Garrison was the courageous and single minded apostle, Wendell Phillips the eloquent orator, and John Brown the voluntary martyr.* Then, too, the whole mind of the United States

[**Fraser's Magazine*, LXIV (Oct., Nov., Dec., 1861), 391–406, 525–34, 658–73; republished as a volume (London: Parker, Son, and Bourne) in 1863 (in *CW*, Vol. X, pp. 203–59).]

[†John Elliot Cairnes, *The Slave Power: Its Character, Career and Probable Designs* (1862); 2nd ed. (London and Cambridge: Macmillan, 1863).]

*The saying of this true hero, after his capture, that he was worth more for hanging than for any other purpose, reminds one, by its combination of wit, wisdom, and self devotion, of Sir Thomas More. [Two anecdotes seem apposite. For the story of More's saying to his guard, on mounting the shaky scaffold, that if he were seen up safely, he would shift for himself coming down, see William Roper, *The Mirrour of Vertue in Worldly Greatness; or,*

would be let loose from its bonds, no longer corrupted by the supposed necessity of apologising to foreigners for the most flagrant of all possible violations of the free principles of their Constitution, while the tendency of a fixed state of society to stereotype a set of national opinions would be at least temporarily checked and the national mind would become more open to the recognition of whatever was bad in either the institutions or the customs of the people. These hopes, so far as related to Slavery, have been completely, and in other respects are in course of being progressively realized. Foreseeing from the first this double set of consequences from the success or failure of the rebellion, it may be imagined with what feelings I contemplated the rush of nearly the whole upper and middle classes of my own country, even those who passed for Liberals, into a furious pro-Southern partisanship: the working classes, and some of the literary and scientific men, being almost the sole exceptions to the general frenzy. I never before felt so keenly how little permanent improvement had reached the minds of our influential classes and of what small value were the liberal opinions they had got into the habit of professing. None of the Continental Liberals committed the same frightful mistake. But the generation which had extorted negro emancipation from our West India planters had passed away; another had succeeded which had not learnt by many years of discussion and exposure to feel strongly the enormities of slavery; and the inattention habitual with Englishmen to whatever is going on in the world outside their own island, made them profoundly ignorant of all the antecedents of the struggle, insomuch that it was not generally believed in England, for the first year or two of the war, that the quarrel was one of slavery. There were men of high principle and unquestionable liberality of opinion who thought it a dispute about tariffs, or assimilated it to the cases in which they were accustomed to sympathise, of a people struggling for independence.

It was my obvious duty to be one of the small minority who protested against this perverted state of public opinion. I was not the first to protest. It ought to be remembered to the honour of Mr. Hughes and of Mr. Ludlow, that they, by writings published at the very beginning of the struggle, began the protestation.[*] Mr. Bright followed in one of the most powerful of his speeches,[†] followed by others not less striking. I was on the point of adding my words to theirs when there occurred, towards the end of 1861, the seizure of the Southern envoys on board a

---

The Life of Syr Thomas More (Paris: [St. Omer, English College Press,] 1626), p. 166. For an account of More's telling the headsman to spare his beard, which had not offended the King, see Francis Bacon, "Apophthegms New and Old," *Works,* Vol. VII, p. 128.]

[*Thomas Hughes, "Opinion on American Affairs," *Macmillan's Magazine,* IV (Sept., 1861), 414–16; John Malcolm Forbes Ludlow, "The American Crisis," *ibid.,* IV (June, 1861), 168–76.]

[†See "On America, I" (4 Dec., 1861), and the following speeches in John Bright, *Speeches on Questions of Public Policy,* ed. James Edwin Thorold Rogers, 2 vols. (London: Macmillan, 1868), Vol. I, pp. 167–95 and ff.]

British vessel, by an officer of the United States.[*] Even English forgetfulness has not yet had time to lose all remembrance of the explosion of feeling in England which then burst forth, the expectation, prevailing for some weeks, of war with the United States, and the warlike preparations actually commenced on this side. While this state of things lasted there was no chance of a hearing for anything favourable to the American cause; and moreover I agreed with those who thought the act unjustifiable and such as to require that England should demand its disavowal. When the disavowal came, and the alarm of war was over, I wrote, in January 1862, the paper, in *Fraser's Magazine*, entitled "The Contest in America."[†] And I shall always feel grateful to my daughter that her urgency prevailed on me to write it when I did: for we were then on the point of setting out for a journey of some months in Greece and Turkey, and but for her, I should have deferred writing till our return. Written and published when it was, the paper helped to encourage those Liberals who had felt overborne by the tide of illiberal opinion, and to form in favour of the good cause a nucleus of opinion which increased gradually, and after the success of the North began to seem probable, rapidly. When we returned from our journey I wrote a second article, a review of Professor Cairnes' book published in the *Westminster Review*.[‡] England is paying the penalty, in many uncomfortable ways, of the durable resentment which her ruling classes stirred up in the United States by their ostentatious wishes for the ruin of America as a nation; they have reason to be thankful that a few, if only a few known writers and speakers, standing firmly by the Americans in the time of their greatest difficulty, effected a partial diversion of these bitter feelings, and made Great Britain not altogether odious to the Americans.

This duty having been performed, my principal occupation for the next two years was on subjects not political. The publication of Mr. Austin's *Lectures on Jurisprudence* after his decease, gave me an opportunity of paying a deserved tribute to his memory and at the same time expressing some thoughts on a subject on which, in my old days of Benthamism, I had bestowed much study.[§] But the chief product of those years was the *Examination of Sir William Hamilton's Philosophy*.[¶] His *Lectures*, published in 1860 and 1861,[‖] I had read towards the

[*Charles Wilkes was the officer who seized the Southern envoys, James Murray Mason and John Slidell.]

[†*Fraser's Magazine*, LXV (Feb., 1862), 258–68; reprinted in *D&D*, Vol. III, pp. 179–205.]

[‡"The Slave Power," *Westminster Review*, LXXVIII (Oct., 1862), 489–510; reprinted in *D&D*, American ed., 3 vols. (Boston: Spencer, 1864), Vol. III, pp. 264–99.]

[§"Austin on Jurisprudence," *Edinburgh Review*, CXVIII (Oct., 1863), 439–82; reprinted in *D&D*, Vol. III, pp. 206–74.]

[¶London: Longmans, Green, Reader, and Dyer, 1865; *CW*, Vol. IX (Toronto: University of Toronto Press, 1979).]

[‖William Hamilton, *Lectures on Metaphysics and Logic*, ed. Henry Longueville Mansel and J. Veitch, 4 vols. (Edinburgh: Blackwood, 1859–60). Mill is mistaken as to the dates.]

end of the latter year, with a half formed intention of giving an account of them in a Review, but I soon found that this would be idle, and that justice could not be done to the subject in less than a volume. I had then to consider whether it would be advisable that I myself should attempt such a performance. On consideration, there seemed to be strong reasons for doing so. I was greatly disappointed with the *Lectures*. I read them, certainly, with no prejudice against Sir W. Hamilton. I had up to that time deferred the study of his Notes to Reid on account of their unfinished state,[*] but I had not neglected his *Discussions in Philosophy*;[†] and though I knew that his general mode of treating the facts of mental philosophy differed from that of which I most approved, yet his vigorous polemic against the later Transcendentalists, and his strenuous assertion of some important principles, especially the Relativity of human knowledge, gave me many points of sympathy with his opinions, and made me think that genuine psychology had considerably more to gain than to lose by his authority and reputation. His *Lectures* and the "Dissertations on Reid" dispelled this illusion: and even the *Discussions*, read by the light which these threw on them, lost much of their value. I found that the points of apparent agreement between his opinions and mine were more verbal than real; that the important philosophical principles which I had thought he recognised, were so explained away by him as to mean little or nothing, or were continually lost sight of, and doctrines entirely inconsistent with them were taught in nearly every part of his philosophical writings. My estimation of him was therefore so far altered, that instead of regarding him as occupying a kind of intermediate position between the two rival philosophies, holding some of the principles of both, and supplying to both powerful weapons of attack and defence, I now looked upon him as one of the pillars, and in this country from his high philosophical reputation the chief pillar, of that one of the two which seemed to me to be erroneous.

Now, the difference between these two schools of philosophy, that of Intuition, and that of Experience and Association, is not a mere matter of abstract speculation; it is full of practical consequences, and lies at the foundation of all the greatest differences of practical opinion in an age of progress. The practical reformer has continually to demand that changes be made in things which are supported by powerful and widely spread feelings, or to question the apparent necessity and indefeasibleness of established facts; and it is often an indispensable part of his argument to shew, how those powerful feelings had their origin, and how those facts came to seem necessary and indefeasible. There is therefore a natural hostility between him and a philosophy which discourages the explanation of feelings and moral facts by circumstances and association, and prefers to treat them as ultimate

[*"Dissertations on Reid," in *The Works of Thomas Reid*, ed. William Hamilton (Edinburgh: Maclachlan and Stewart; London: Longman, Brown, Green, and Longmans, 1846), pp. 742–914; further "Dissertations" were added in the 6th ed. (1863), ed. H. L. Mansel.]

[†*Discussions on Philosophy and Literature, Education and University Reform* (London: Longman, Brown, Green, and Longmans; Edinburgh: Maclachlan and Stewart, 1852).]

elements of human nature; a philosophy which is addicted to holding up favourite doctrines as intuitive truths, and deems intuition to be the voice of Nature and of God, speaking with an authority higher than that of our reason. In particular, I have long felt that the prevailing tendency to regard all the marked distinctions of human character as innate, and in the main indelible, and to ignore the irresistible proofs that by far the greater part of those differences, whether between individuals, races, or sexes, are such as not only might but naturally would be produced by differences in circumstances, is one of the chief hindrances to the rational treatment of great social questions and one of the greatest stumbling blocks to human improvement. This tendency has its source in the intuitional metaphysics which characterized the reaction of the nineteenth century against the eighteenth, and it is a tendency so agreeable to human indolence, as well as to conservative interests generally, that unless attacked at the very root, it is sure to be carried to even a greater length than is really justified by the more moderate forms of the intuitional philosophy. That philosophy, not always in its moderate forms, had ruled the thought of Europe for the greater part of a century. My father's *Analysis of the Mind*, my own *Logic*, and Professor Bain's great treatise, had attempted to reintroduce a better mode of philosophizing, latterly with quite as much success as could be expected; but I had for some time felt that the mere contrast of the two philosophies was not enough, that there ought to be a hand-to-hand fight between them, that controversial as well as expository writings were needed, and that the time was come when such controversy would be useful. Considering then the writings and fame of Sir W. Hamilton as the great fortress of the intuitional philosophy in this country, a fortress the more formidable from the imposing character, and the in many respects great personal merits and mental endowments, of the man, I thought it might be a real service to philosophy to attempt a thorough examination of all his most important doctrines, and an estimate of his general claims to eminence as a philosopher. And I was confirmed in this resolution by observing that in the writings of at least one, and him one of the ablest, of Sir W. Hamilton's followers,[*] his peculiar doctrines were made the justification of a view of religion which I hold to be profoundly immoral—that it is our duty to bow down in worship before a Being whose moral attributes are affirmed to be unknowable by us, and to be perhaps extremely different from those which, when we are speaking of our fellow-creatures, we call by the same names.[†]

As I advanced in my task, the damage to Sir W. Hamilton's reputation became greater than I at first expected, through the almost incredible multitude of inconsistencies which shewed themselves on comparing different passages with one another. It was my business however to shew things exactly as they were, and I did

---

[*See Mansel, *The Limits of Religious Thought* (1858), 4th ed. (London: Murray, 1859).]
[†See *Examination*, *CW*, Vol. IX, pp. 102–3.]

not flinch from it. I endeavoured always to treat the philosopher whom I criticized with the most scrupulous fairness; and I knew that he had abundance of disciples and admirers to correct me if I ever unintentionally did him injustice. Many of them accordingly have answered me, more or less elaborately; and they have pointed out oversights and misunderstandings, though few in number, and mostly very unimportant in substance. Such of those as had (to my knowledge) been pointed out before the publication of the latest edition (at present the third) have been corrected there, and the remainder of the criticisms have been, as far as seemed necessary, replied to.[*] On the whole, the book has done its work: it has shewn the weak side of Sir W. Hamilton, and has reduced his too great philosophical reputation within more moderate bounds; and by some of its discussions, as well as by two expository chapters, on the notions of Matter and of Mind,[†] it has perhaps thrown additional light on some of the disputed questions in the domain of psychology and metaphysics.

After the completion of the book on Hamilton, I applied myself to a task which a variety of reasons seemed to render specially incumbent upon me; that of giving an account, and forming an estimate, of the doctrines of Auguste Comte. I had contributed more than any one else to make his speculations known in England. In consequence chiefly of what I had said of him in my *Logic*, he had readers and admirers among thoughtful men on this side of the Channel at a time when his name had not yet, in France, emerged from obscurity. So unknown and unappreciated was he at the time when my *Logic* was written and published, that to criticise his weak points might well appear superfluous, while it was a duty to give as much publicity as one could to the important contributions he had made to philosophic thought. At the time however at which I have now arrived, this state of affairs had entirely changed. His name at least was known almost universally, and the general character of his doctrines very widely. He had taken his place, in the estimation both of friends and opponents, as one of the conspicuous figures in the thought of the age. The better parts of his speculations had made great progress in working their way into those minds, which by their previous culture and tendencies, were fitted to receive them: and under cover of those better parts those of a worse character, greatly developed and added to in his later writings, had also made some way, having obtained active and enthusiastic adherents, some of them of no inconsiderable personal merit, in England, France, and other countries. These causes not only made it desirable that some one should undertake the task of sifting what is good from what is bad in M. Comte's speculations, but seemed to impose on myself in particular a special obligation to make the attempt. This I accordingly did in two Essays, published in successive numbers of the *Westminster Review*,

---

[*See the Textual Introduction, *CW*, Vol. IX, pp. lxxix–xcvii.]
[†Chaps. xi and xii.]

and reprinted in a small volume under the title *Auguste Comte and Positivism*.[*] *a*

The writings which I have now mentioned, together with a small number of papers in periodicals which I have not deemed worth preserving, were the whole of the products of my activity as a writer during the years from 1859 to 1865. In the early part of the last mentioned year, in compliance with a wish frequently expressed to me by working men, I published cheap People's Editions of those of my writings which seemed the most likely to find readers among the working classes; viz. *Principles of Political Economy*, *Liberty*, and *Representative Government*. This was a considerable sacrifice of my pecuniary interest, especially as I resigned all idea of deriving profit from the cheap editions, and after ascertaining from my publishers the lowest price which they thought would remunerate them on the usual terms of an equal division of profits, I gave up my half share to enable the price to be fixed still lower. To the credit of Messrs. Longman they fixed, unasked, a certain number of years after which the copyright and stereotype plates were to revert to me, and a certain number of copies after the sale of which I should receive half of any further profit. This number of copies (which in the case of the *Political Economy* was 10,000) has for some time been exceeded, and the People's Editions have begun to yield me a small but unexpected pecuniary return, though very far from an equivalent for the diminution of profit from the Library Editions.

In this summary of my outward life I have now arrived at the period at which my tranquil and retired existence as a writer of books was to be exchanged for the less congenial occupation of a member of the House of Commons. The proposal made to me, early in 1865, by some electors of Westminster, did not present the idea to me for the first time. It was not even the first offer I had received, for, more than ten years previous, in consequence of my opinions on the Irish Land question, Mr. Lucas and Mr. Duffy, in the name of the popular party in Ireland, offered to bring me into Parliament for an Irish County, which they could easily have done: but the incompatibility of a seat in Parliament with the office I then held in the India House precluded even consideration of the proposal. After I had quitted the India House, several of my friends would gladly have seen me a member of Parliament; but there seemed no probability that the idea would ever take any practical shape. I was convinced that no numerous or influential portion of any electoral body, really

---

[*"The Positive Philosophy of Auguste Comte," and "Later Speculations of Auguste Comte," *Westminster Review*, LXXXIII (Apr., 1865), 339–405, and LXXXIV (July, 1865), 1–42; republished as *Auguste Comte and Positivism* (London: Trübner, 1865); in *CW*, Vol. X, pp. 261–368.]

a[*Cancelled text:*] In addition to the immediate purposes the first of these papers serves as a kind of explanatory commentary on the general view of philosophy of the Moral Sciences laid down, in an extremely condensed form, in the concluding Book of my *System of Logic*: and the second contains occasional thoughts respecting some of the ethical and social questions of the future, which I believe that the future will ratify; but in whatever merit may belong to them I can claim but a trifling share, they being the joint product of three thoughtful minds, the least original of which is my own.

wished to be represented by a person of my opinions; and that one who possessed no local connexion or popularity, and who did not choose to stand as the mere organ of a party, had small chance of being elected anywhere unless through the expenditure of money. Now it was, and is, my fixed conviction, that a candidate ought not to incur one farthing of expense for undertaking a public duty. Such of the lawful expenses of an election as have no special reference to any particular candidate ought to be borne as a public charge, either by the State or by the locality. What has to be done by the supporters of each candidate in order to bring his claims properly before the constituency, should be done by unpaid agency, or by voluntary subscription. If members of the electoral body, or others, are willing to subscribe money of their own for the purpose of bringing by lawful means into Parliament some one who they think would be useful there, no one is entitled to object: but that the expense, or any part of it, should fall on the candidate, is fundamentally wrong; because it amounts, in reality, to buying his seat. Even on the most favourable supposition as to the mode in which the money is expended, there is a legitimate suspicion that any one who gives money for leave to undertake a public trust, has other than public ends to promote by it; and (a consideration of the greatest importance) the cost of elections, when borne by the candidates, deprives the nation of the services, as members of Parliament, of all who cannot or will not afford to incur a heavy expense. I do not say that, so long as there is scarcely a chance for an independent candidate to come into Parliament without complying with this vicious practice, it must always be morally wrong in him to spend money, provided that no part of it is either directly or indirectly employed in corruption. But, to justify it, he ought to be very certain that he can be of more use to his country as a member of Parliament than in any other mode which is open to him; and this assurance, in my own case, I did not feel. It was by no means clear to me that I could do more to advance the public objects which had a claim on my exertions from the benches of the House of Commons, than from the simple position of a writer. I felt, therefore, that I ought not to seek election to Parliament, much less to expend any money in procuring it.

But the conditions of the question were considerably altered when a body of electors sought me out, and spontaneously offered to bring me forward as their candidate. If it should appear, on explanation, that they persisted in this wish, knowing my opinions, and accepting the only conditions on which I could conscientiously serve, it was questionable whether this was not one of those calls upon a member of the community by his fellow citizens, which he was scarcely justified in rejecting. I therefore put their disposition to the proof by one of the frankest explanations ever tendered, I should think, to an electoral body by a candidate. I wrote in reply to the offer a letter for publication, [*] saying that I had

[*Mill is conflating two letters, both to James Beal, of 7 Mar., 1865 (published, *inter alia*, in the *Daily News*, 23 Mar., p. 5), and of 17 Apr., 1865 (published, *inter alia*, in the *Daily News*, 21 Apr., p. 4); they are in *Later Letters* [*LL*], *CW*, Vols. XIV–XVII (Toronto: University of Toronto Press, 1972), Vol. XVI, pp. 1005–7, and 1031–5.]

no personal wish to be a member of parliament, that I thought a candidate ought neither to canvass nor to incur any expense, and that I could not consent to do either. I said further that if elected I could not undertake to give any of my time and labour to their local interests. With respect to general politics, I told them without reserve what I thought on a number of important subjects on which they had asked my opinion; and one of these being the suffrage, I made known to them, among other things, my conviction (as I was bound to do, since I intended, if elected, to act on it) that women were entitled to representation in Parliament on the same terms with men. It was the first time, doubtless, that such a doctrine had ever been mentioned to electors; and the fact that I was elected after proposing it, gave the start to the movement which has since become so vigorous in favour of women's suffrage. Nothing, at the time, appeared more unlikely than that a candidate (if candidate I could be called) whose professions and conduct set so completely at defiance all ordinary notions of electioneering, should nevertheless be elected. A well known literary man, who was also a man of society, was heard to say, that the Almighty himself would have no chance of being elected on such a programme. I strictly adhered to it, neither spending money nor canvassing, nor did I take any personal part in the election until about a week preceding the day of nomination, when I attended a few public meetings to state my principles and give to any questions which the electors might exercise their just right of putting to me for their own guidance, answers as plain and unreserved as my Address. On one subject only, my religious opinions, I announced from the beginning that I would answer no questions; a determination which appeared to be completely approved by those who attended the meetings. My frankness on all other subjects on which I was interrogated, evidently, did me far more good than my answers, whatever they might be, did harm. Among the proofs I received of this, one is too remarkable not to be recorded. In the pamphlet *Thoughts on Parliamentary Reform* I had said, rather bluntly, that the working classes, though differing from those of some other countries in being ashamed of lying, are yet generally liars.[*] This passage some opponent got printed in a placard, which was handed to me at a meeting, chiefly composed of the working classes, and I was asked whether I had written and published it. I at once answered "I did." Scarcely were these two words out of my mouth, when vehement applause resounded through the whole meeting. It was evident that the working people were so accustomed to expect equivocation and evasion from those who sought their suffrages, that when they found, instead of that, a direct avowal of what was likely to be disagreeable to them, instead of being offended they concluded at once that this was a person whom they could trust. A more striking instance never came under my notice of what, I believe, is the experience of those who best know the working classes—that the most essential of all recommendations to their favour is that of complete straightforwardness; its

[*See *CW*, Vol. XIX, p. 338.]

presence outweighs in their minds very strong objections, while no amount of other qualities will make amends for its apparent absence. The first working man who spoke after the incident I have mentioned (it was Mr. Odger) said, that the working classes had no desire not to be told of their faults; they wanted friends, not flatterers, and felt under obligation to any one who told them of anything in themselves which he sincerely believed to require amendment. And to this the meeting heartily responded.[*]

Had I been defeated in the election, I should still have had no reason to regret the contact it had brought me into with large bodies of my countrymen; which not only gave me much new experience, but enabled me to scatter my political opinions rather widely, and by making me known in many quarters where I had never before been heard of, increased the number of my readers and the presumable influence of my writings. These latter effects were of course produced in a still greater degree, when, as much to my own surprise as to that of any one, I was returned to Parliament by a majority of some hundreds over my Conservative competitor.[†]

I was a member of the House during the three sessions of the Parliament which passed the Reform Bill;[‡] during which time Parliament was necessarily my main occupation, except during the recess. I was a tolerably frequent speaker, sometimes of prepared speeches, sometimes extemporaneously. But my choice of occasions was not such as I should have made if my leading object had been parliamentary influence. When I had gained the ear of the House, which I did by a successful speech on Mr. Gladstone's Reform Bill,[§] the idea I proceeded on was that when anything was likely to be as well done, or sufficiently well done, by other people, there was no necessity for me to meddle with it. As I therefore, in general, reserved myself for work which no others were likely to do, a great proportion of my appearances were on points on which the bulk of the Liberal party, even the advanced portion of it, either were of a different opinion from mine, or were comparatively indifferent. Several of my speeches, especially one against the motion for the abolition of capital punishment,[¶] and another in favour of resuming the right of seizing enemies' goods in neutral vessels,[‖] were opposed to what then was, and probably still is, regarded as the advanced liberal opinion. My

[*The episode occurred during the meeting in the Pimlico Rooms, Winchester Street, on 8 July, 1865; it is reported (without mention of George Odger) on 10 July in the *Daily Telegraph*, p. 2, and the *Morning Star*, p. 2.]

[†William Henry Smith, who, defeated in 1865, was elected for Westminster in 1868. See p. 289 below.]

[‡30 & 31 Victoria, c. 102 (15 Aug., 1867).]

[§"A Bill to Extend the Right of Voting at Elections of Members of Parliament in England and Wales," 29 Victoria (13 Mar., 1866), *Parliamentary Papers*, 1866, V, 87–100. For Mill's speech, see *Parliamentary Debates*, 3rd ser., Vol. 182, cols. 1253–63 (13 Apr., 1866).]

[¶*Ibid.*, Vol. 191, cols. 1047–55 (21 Apr., 1868).]

[‖*Ibid.*, Vol. 189, cols. 876–84 (5 Aug., 1867).]

advocacy of women's suffrage,[*] and of Personal Representation,[†] were at the time looked upon by many as whims of my own, but the great progress since made by those opinions, and especially the zealous response made from almost all parts of the kingdom to the demand for women's suffrage, fully justified the timeliness of those movements, and have made what was undertaken as a moral and social duty, a personal success. Another duty which was particularly incumbent on me as one of the Metropolitan Members, was the attempt to obtain a Municipal Government for the Metropolis: but on that subject the indifference of the House of Commons was such that I found hardly any help or support within its walls. On this subject, however, I was the organ of an active and intelligent body of persons outside, with whom and not with me the scheme originated, who carried on all the agitation on the subject and drew up the Bills. My part was to bring in Bills already prepared, and to sustain the discussion of them during the short time they were allowed to remain before the House;[‡] after having taken an active part in the work of a Committee presided over by Mr. Ayrton, which sat through the greater part of the Session of 1866 to take evidence on the subject.[§] The very different position in which the question now stands (1870) may justly be attributed to the preparation which went on during those years, and which produced but little visible effect at the time; but all questions on which there are strong private interests on one side, and only the public good on the other, have a similar period of incubation to go through.

The same idea, that the use of my being in Parliament was to do work which others were not able or not willing to do, made me think it my duty to come to the front in defence of advanced Liberalism on occasions when the obloquy to be encountered was such as most of the advanced Liberals in the House, preferred not to incur. My first vote in the House was in support of an amendment in favour of Ireland, moved by an Irish member and for which only five English and Scotch votes were given, including my own: the other four were Mr. Bright, Mr. McLaren, Mr. T. B. Potter and Mr. Hadfield.[¶] And the second speech I delivered* was on the bill to prolong the suspension of the Habeas Corpus in

[*Ibid., Vol. 187, cols. 817–29, 842–3 (20 May, 1867); published as Speech of John Stuart Mill, M.P., on the Admission of Women to the Electoral Franchise (London: Trübner, 1867).]

[†Parliamentary Debates, 3rd ser., Vol. 187, cols. 1343–56, and 1362 (30 May, 1867); published as Personal Representation, Speech of John Stuart Mill, Esq., M.P. (London: Henderson, Rait, and Fenton, 1867).]

[‡See Parliamentary Debates, 3rd ser., Vol. 185, cols. 1608–10, 1616 (8 Mar., 1867); cols. 1678–9, 1680, 1685 (11 Mar., 1867); col. 1696 (12 Mar., 1867); cols. 1861–2 (14 Mar., 1867); Vol. 187, cols. 882–5, 891 (21 Apr., 1867); and Vol. 189, cols. 1040–1 (7 Aug., 1867).]

[§See "First Report from the Select Committee on Metropolitan Local Government etc.," Parliamentary Papers, 1866, XIII, 171–315; "Second Report," ibid., XIII, 317–713.]

[¶See Daniel O'Donaghue's motion for an amendment, Parliamentary Debates, 3rd ser., Vol. 181, col. 273 (8 Feb., 1866).]

*The first was in answer to Mr. Lowe's reply to Mr. Bright on the Cattle Plague Bill, and

Ireland.[*] In denouncing, on this occasion, the English mode of governing Ireland, I did no more than the general opinion of England now admits to have been just; but the anger against Fenianism was then in all its freshness; any attack on what Fenians attacked was looked upon as an apology for them; and I was so unfavourably received by the House, that more than one of my friends advised me (and my own judgment agreed with the advice) to wait, before speaking again, for the favourable opportunity that would be given by the first great debate on the Reform Bill. During this silence, many flattered themselves that I had turned out a failure, and that they should not be troubled with me any more. Perhaps their uncomplimentary comments may, by the force of reaction, have helped to make my speech on the Reform Bill the success it was. My position in the House was further improved by a speech in which I insisted on the duty of paying off the National Debt before our coal supplies are exhausted,[†] and by an ironical reply to some of the Tory leaders who had quoted against me certain passages of my writings and called me to account for others, especially for one in my *Considerations on Representative Government* which said that the Conservative party was by the law of its composition the stupidest party.[‡] They gained nothing by drawing attention to this passage, which up to that time had not excited any notice, but the *soubriquet* of "the stupid party" stuck to them for a considerable time afterwards. Having now no longer any apprehension of not being listened to, I confined myself, as I have since thought, too much, to occasions on which my services seemed specially needed, and abstained more than enough from speaking on the great party questions. With the exception of Irish questions, and those which concerned the working classes, a single speech on Mr. Disraeli's Reform Bill[§] was nearly all that I contributed to the great decisive debates of the last two of my three sessions.

I have, however, much satisfaction in looking back to the part I took on the two classes of subjects just mentioned. With regard to the working classes, the chief

---

was thought at the time to have helped to get rid of a provision in the Government measure which would have given to landholders a second indemnity, after they had already been once indemnified for the loss of some of their cattle by the increased selling price of the remainder. [See *Parliamentary Debates*, 3rd ser., Vol. 181, cols. 472–80 (John Bright's speech); cols. 483–8 (Robert Lowe's speech); and cols. 488–92 (Mill's speech) (all 14 Feb., 1866). The Bill was enacted as 29 Victoria, c. 2 (20 Feb., 1866).]

[*See 29 Victoria, c. 1 (17 Feb., 1866), and, for Mill's speech, *Parliamentary Debates*, 3rd ser., Vol. 181, cols. 705–6 (17 Feb., 1866).]

[†*Ibid.*, Vol. 182, cols. 1524–8 (17 Apr., 1866).]

[‡Mill, who was replying directly to Sir John Pakington, said: "What I stated was, that the Conservative party was, by the law of its constitution, necessarily the stupidest party. Now, I do not retract this assertion; but I did not mean that Conservatives are generally stupid; I meant, that stupid persons are generally Conservative." (*Parliamentary Debates*, 3rd ser., Vol. 183, col. 1592 [31 May, 1866]. For Pakington's comment, see *ibid.*, col. 1574.) The original remark is in *Considerations on Representative Government*, *CW*, Vol. XIX, p. 452n.]

[§*Parliamentary Debates*, 3rd ser., Vol. 187, cols. 280–4 (9 May, 1867).]

topic of my speech on Mr. Gladstone's Reform Bill was the assertion of their claims to the suffrage. A little later, after the resignation of Lord Russell's ministry and the succession of a Tory Government, came the attempt of the working classes to hold a meeting in Hyde Park, their exclusion by the police, and the breaking down of the park railing by the crowd. Though Mr. Beales and the leaders of the working men had retired under protest before this took place, a scuffle ensued in which many innocent persons were maltreated by the police, and the exasperation of the working men was extreme. They shewed a determination to make another attempt at a meeting in the Park, to which many of them would probably have come armed; the Government made military preparations to resist the attempt, and something very serious seemed impending. At this crisis I really believe that I was the means of preventing much mischief. I had in my place in Parliament taken the side of the working men, and strongly censured the conduct of the Government.[*] I was invited, with several other Radical members, to a conference with the leading members of the Council of the Reform League; and the task fell chiefly upon myself of persuading them to give up the Hyde Park project, and hold their meeting elsewhere. It was not Mr. Beales and Colonel Dickson who needed persuading; on the contrary, it was evident that those gentlemen had already exerted their influence in the same direction, thus far without success. It was the working men who held out: and so bent were they on their original scheme that I was obliged to have recourse to *les grands moyens*. I told them that a proceeding which would certainly produce a collision with the military, could only be justifiable on two conditions: if the position of affairs had become such that a revolution was desirable, and if they thought themselves able to accomplish one. To this argument after considerable discussion they at last yielded: and I was able to inform Mr. Walpole that their intention was given up.[†] I shall never forget the depth of his relief or the warmth of his expressions of gratitude. After the working men had conceded so much to me, I felt bound to comply with their request that I would attend and speak at their meeting at the Agricultural Hall: the only meeting called by the Reform League which I ever attended.[‡] I had always declined being a member of the League, on the avowed ground that I did not agree in its programme of manhood suffrage and the ballot: from the ballot I dissented entirely; and I could not consent to hoist the flag of manhood suffrage, even on the assurance that the exclusion of women was not intended to be implied; since if one goes beyond what can be immediately carried and professes to take one's stand on a principle, one should go the whole length of the principle. I have entered thus particularly into this matter because my conduct on this occasion gave great displeasure to the Tory and Tory-Liberal press, who have charged me ever since with having shewn

[*]*Ibid.*, Vol. 184, cols. 1410–12 (24 July, 1866).]
[†See Mill's speech on the Proposed Reform Meeting in Hyde Park, *ibid.*, Vol. 184, cols. 1540–1 (26 July, 1866), and the report in *The Times*, 27 July, 1866, p. 7.]
[‡See the report of Mill's speech in *The Times*, 31 July, 1866, p. 3.]

myself, in the trials of public life, intemperate and passionate.[*] I do not know what they expected from me; but they had reason to be thankful to me if they knew from what I had in all probability preserved them. And I do not believe it could have been done, at that particular juncture, by any one else. No other person, I believe, had at that moment the necessary influence for restraining the working classes, except Mr. Gladstone and Mr. Bright, neither of whom was available: Mr. Gladstone, for obvious reasons; Mr. Bright, because he was out of town.

When, some time later, the Tory Government brought in a bill to prevent public meetings in the Parks, I not only spoke strongly in opposition to it, but formed one of a number of advanced Liberals, who, aided by the very late period of the Session, succeeded in defeating the Bill by what is called talking it out.[†] It has not since been renewed.

On Irish affairs also I felt bound to take a decided part. I was one of the foremost in the deputation of Members of Parliament who prevailed on Lord Derby to spare the life of the condemned Fenian insurgent, General Burke. The Church question was so vigorously handled by the leaders of the party, in the session of 1868, as to require no more from me than an emphatic adhesion; but the land question was by no means in so advanced a position: the superstitions of landlordism had up to that time been little challenged, especially in Parliament, and the backward state of the question, so far as concerned the Parliamentary mind, was evidenced by the extremely mild measure brought in by Lord Russell's Government in 1866, which nevertheless could not be carried.[‡] On that bill I delivered one of my most careful speeches, in which I attempted to lay down some of the principles of the subject, in a manner calculated less to stimulate friends, than to conciliate and convince opponents.[§] The engrossing subject of Parliamentary Reform prevented either this bill, or one of a similar character brought in by Lord Derby's Government,[¶] from being carried through. They never got beyond the second reading. Meanwhile the signs of Irish disaffection had become much more decided; the demand for complete separation between the two countries had assumed a menacing aspect, and there were few who did not feel that if there was still any chance of reconciling Ireland to British connexion, it could only be by the adoption of much

[*See, e.g., leading articles in *The Times*, 19 Nov., 1868, p. 7, and 23 Dec., 1868, p. 9.]
[†See, for Mill's speeches, *Parliamentary Debates*, 3rd ser., Vol. 188, cols. 1888, 1890–3 (22 July, 1867); Vol. 189, cols. 1482–4 (13 Aug., 1867); for the abortive Bill, see "A Bill for the Better and More Effectually Securing the Use of Certain Royal Parks and Gardens for the Enjoyment and Recreation of Her Majesty's Subjects," 30 Victoria (3 May, 1867), *Parliamentary Papers*, 1867, IV, 63–6.]
[‡"A Bill Further to Amend the Law Relating to the Tenure and Improvement of Land in Ireland," 29 Victoria (30 Apr., 1866), *Parliamentary Papers*, 1866, V, 353–64. Referred to by Mill below as "Mr. Fortescue's Bill."]
[§*Parliamentary Debates*, 3rd ser., Vol. 183, cols. 1087–97 (17 May, 1866).]
[¶"A Bill to Promote the Improvement of Land by Occupying Tenants in Ireland," 30 Victoria (18 Feb., 1867), *Parliamentary Papers*, 1867, VI, 385–98.]

more thorough reforms in the territorial and social relations of the country, than had yet been contemplated. The time seemed to me to have come when it would be useful to speak out my whole mind; and the result was my pamphlet *England and Ireland*,[*] which was written in the winter of 1867, and published shortly before the commencement of the session of 1868. The leading features of the pamphlet were on the one hand an argument to shew the undesirableness, for Ireland as well as England, of separation between the countries, and on the other, a proposal for settling the land question by giving to the existing tenants a permanent tenure at a fixed rent, to be assessed after due enquiry by the State.

The pamphlet was not popular, except in Ireland, as I did not expect it to be. But, if no measure short of that which I proposed would do full justice to Ireland, or afford a prospect of conciliating the mass of the Irish people, the duty of proposing it was imperative; while if on the other hand, there was any intermediate course which had a claim to a trial, I well knew that to propose something which would be called extreme was the true way not to impede but to facilitate a more moderate experiment. It is most improbable that a measure conceding so much to the tenantry as Mr. Gladstone's Irish Land Bill,[†] would have been proposed by a Government, or could have been carried through Parliament, unless the British public had been led to perceive that a case might be made, and perhaps a party formed, for a measure considerably stronger. It is the character of the British people, or at least of the higher and middle classes who pass muster for the British people, that to induce them to approve of any change it is necessary that they should look upon it as a middle course: they think every proposal extreme and violent unless they hear of some other proposal going still farther, upon which their antipathy to extreme views may discharge itself. So it proved in the present instance; my proposal was condemned, but any scheme of Irish Land reform, short of mine, came to be thought moderate by comparison. I may observe that the attacks made on my plan usually gave a very incorrect idea of its nature. It was usually discussed as a proposal that the State should buy up the land and become the universal landlord; though in fact it only offered to each individual landlord this as an alternative, if he liked better to sell his estate than to retain it on the new conditions; and I fully anticipated that most landlords would continue to prefer the position of landowners to that of Government annuitants, and would retain their existing relation to their tenants, often on more indulgent terms than the full rents on which the compensation to be given them by Government would have been based. This and many other explanations I gave in a speech on Ireland, in the debate on Mr. Maguire's Resolution, early in the session of 1868.[‡] A corrected report of this speech, together with my speech on Mr. Fortescue's Bill, has been published (not by me, but with my permission) in Ireland.

Another public duty, of a most serious kind, it was my lot to have to perform,

[*London: Longmans, Green, Reader, and Dyer, 1868.]
[†33 & 34 Victoria, c. 46 (1 Aug., 1870).]
[‡See John Francis Maguire's motion for a Committee, *Parliamentary Debates*, 3rd ser.,

both in and out of Parliament, during these years. A disturbance in Jamaica, provoked in the first instance by injustice, and exaggerated by rage and panic into a premeditated rebellion, had been the motive or excuse for taking hundreds of innocent lives by military violence or by sentence of what were called courts martial, continuing for weeks after the brief disturbance had been put down; with many added atrocities of destruction of property, flogging women as well as men, and a great display of the brutal recklessness which generally prevails when fire and sword are let loose. The perpetrators of these deeds were defended and applauded in England by the same kind of people who had so long upheld negro slavery: and it seemed at first as if the British nation was about to incur the disgrace of letting pass without even a protest, excesses of authority as revolting as any of those for which, when perpetrated by the instruments of other governments, Englishmen can hardly find terms sufficient to express their abhorrence. After a short time, however, an indignant feeling was roused; a voluntary Association formed itself under the name of the Jamaica Committee, to take such deliberation and action as the case might admit of, and adhesions poured in from all parts of the country. I was abroad at the time but I sent in my name to the Committee as soon as I heard of it, and took an active part in its proceedings from the time of my return. There was much more at stake than only justice to the Negroes, imperative as was that consideration. The question was, whether the British dependencies, and eventually perhaps Great Britain itself, were to be under the government of law, or of military license; whether the lives and persons of British subjects are at the mercy of any two or three officers however raw and inexperienced or reckless and brutal, whom a panic-stricken Governor or other functionary may assume the right to constitute into a so-called Court Martial. This question could only be decided by an appeal to the tribunals; and such an appeal the Committee determined to make. Their determination led to a change in the Chairmanship of the Committee, as the Chairman, Mr. Charles Buxton, thought it not unjust indeed, but inexpedient, to prosecute Governor Eyre and his principal subordinates in a criminal court: but a numerously attended General meeting of the Association having decided this point against him, Mr. Buxton withdrew from the Committee, though continuing to work in the cause, and I was, quite unexpectedly on my own part, proposed and elected Chairman. It became, in consequence, my duty to represent the Committee in the House, sometimes by putting questions to the Government, sometimes as the recipient of questions more or less provocative, addressed by individual members to myself; but especially as speaker in the important debate originated in the session of 1866 by Mr. Buxton: and the speech I then delivered is that which I should probably select as the best of my speeches in Parliament.* For more than

---

Vol. 190, cols. 1288–1314 (10 Mar., 1868), and Mill's speech, cols. 1516–32 (12 Mar., 1868).]

*Among the most active members of the Committee were Mr. P. A. Taylor, M.P., always faithful and energetic in every assertion of the principles of liberty; Mr. Goldwin

two years we carried on the combat, trying every avenue legally open to us, to the courts of criminal justice. A bench of magistrates in one of the most Tory counties in England dismissed our case: we were more successful before the magistrates at Bow Street; which gave an opportunity to the Lord Chief Justice of the Queen's Bench, Sir Alexander Cockburn, for delivering his celebrated charge, which settled the law of the question in favour of liberty, as far as it is in the power of a judge's charge to settle it.[*] There, however, our success ended, for the Old Bailey Grand Jury by throwing out our bill prevented the case from coming to trial. It was clear that to bring English functionaries to the bar of a criminal court for abuses of power committed against negroes and mulattoes, was not a popular proceeding with the English middle classes. We had however redeemed, so far as lay in us, the character of our country, by shewing that there was at any rate a body of persons determined to use all the means which the law afforded to obtain justice for the injured. We had elicited from the highest criminal judge in the nation an authoritative declaration that the law was what we maintained it to be; and we had given an emphatic warning to those who might be tempted to similar guilt hereafter, that though they might escape the actual sentence of a criminal tribunal, they were not safe against being put to some trouble and expense in order to avoid it. Colonial Governors and other persons in authority will have a considerable motive to stop short of such extremities in future.

As a matter of curiosity I kept some specimens of the abusive letters, almost all of them anonymous, which I received while these proceedings were going on. They are evidence of the sympathy felt with the brutalities in Jamaica by the brutal part of the population at home. They graduated from coarse jokes, verbal and pictorial, up to threats of assassination.[†]

Among other matters of importance in which I took an active part, but which excited little interest in the public, two deserve particular mention. I joined with

---

Smith, Mr. Frederic Harrison, Mr. Slack, Mr. Chamerovzow, Mr. Shaen, and Mr. Chesson, the Honorary Secretary of the Association. [See Charles Buxton's motion on the Disturbances in Jamaica, *Parliamentary Debates*, 3rd ser., Vol. 184, cols. 1763–85 (31 July, 1866), and, for Mill's speeches and questions, *ibid.*, cols. 1064–6 (19 July, 1866); cols. 1797–1806 (31 July, 1866)—the one he would select as his best; col. 2160 (10 Aug., 1866); and Vol. 189, cols. 598–9 (1 Aug., 1867).]

[*See Alexander James Edmund Cockburn, *Charge of the Lord Chief Justice of England to the Grand Jury at the Central Criminal Courts, in the Case of the Queen against Nelson and Brand*, ed. Frederick Cockburn (London: Ridgway, 1867).]

[†A note by Helen Taylor in the Columbia MS reads: "At one time I reckoned that threats of Assassination were received at least once a week: and I remarked that threatening letters were always especially numerous by Tuesday morning's post. I inferred that they were meditated during the Sunday's leisure and posted on the Mondays. It might be worth while to collect evidence as to the proportions of Crime Committed on the different days of the week. It may be observed however that in England Sunday is generally used for all kinds of letter-writing, innocent as well as guilty."]

several other independent Liberals in defeating an Extradition Bill, introduced at the very end of the session of 1866 and by which, though surrender avowedly for political offences was not authorised, political refugees, if charged by a foreign government with acts which are necessarily incident to all attempts at insurrection, would have been surrendered to be dealt with by the criminal courts of the government against which they had rebelled: thus making the British Government an accomplice in the vengeance of foreign despotisms.[*] The defeat of this proposal led to the appointment of a Select Committee (in which I was included) to examine and report on the whole subject of Extradition Treaties;[†] and the result was that in the Extradition Act, which passed through Parliament after I had ceased to be a member, opportunity is given to any one whose extradition is demanded, of being heard before an English Court of justice to prove that the offence with which he is charged is really political.[‡] The cause of European freedom has thus been saved from a serious misfortune, and our own country from a great iniquity. The other subject to be mentioned is the fight kept up by a body of advanced Liberals in the session of 1868, on the Bribery Bill of Mr. Disraeli's Government,[§] in which I took a very active part. I had taken council with several of those who had applied their minds most carefully to the details of the subject—Mr. W. D. Christie, Serjeant Pulling, Mr. Chadwick—as well as bestowed much thought of my own, for the purpose of framing such amendments and additional clauses as might make the Bill really effective against the numerous modes of corruption, direct and indirect, which might otherwise, as there was much reason to fear, be increased instead of diminished by the Reform Act. We also aimed at engrafting on the Bill, measures for diminishing the mischievous burthen of what are called the legitimate expenses of elections. Among our many amendments was that of Mr. Fawcett for making the returning officer's expenses a charge on the rates instead of on the candidates;[¶] another was the prohibition of paid canvassers, and the limitation of paid agents to one for each candidate; a third was the extension of the precautions and penalties against bribery, to municipal elections, which are well known to be not only a preparatory school for bribery at parliamentary elections, but an habitual cover for it. The Conservative Government, however, when once they had carried the leading provision of their Bill (for which I voted and spoke),[‖] the transfer of the jurisdiction in elections from the House of Commons to the Judges, made a

[*"A Bill for the Amendment of the Law Relating to Extradition," 29 & 30 Victoria (26 July, 1866), *Parliamentary Papers*, 1866, III, 39–42.]

[†See "Report from the Select Committee on Extradition," *ibid.*, 1867–68, VII, 129–336.]

[‡See 33 & 34 Victoria, c. 52 (9 Aug., 1870).]

[§31 & 32 Victoria, c. 125 (31 July, 1868).]

[¶See Henry Fawcett's motion, *Parliamentary Debates*, 3rd ser., Vol. 193, cols. 1443–4 (18 July, 1868). The two amendments next referred to were made by Mill himself: see *ibid.*, cols. 1640–1 (22 July, 1868), and cols. 1166–8 (14 July, 1868).]

[‖*Ibid.*, Vol. 191, cols. 308–11 (26 Mar., 1868).]

determined resistance to all other improvements: and after one of our most important proposals, that of Mr. Fawcett, had actually obtained a majority, they summoned the strength of their party and threw out the clause in a subsequent stage. The Liberal party in the House was greatly dishonoured by the conduct of many of its members in giving no help whatever to this attempt to secure the necessary conditions of an honest representation of the people. With their large majority in the House they could have carried all the amendments, or better ones if they had better to propose. But it was late in the Session; members were eager to set about their preparations for the impending General Election: and while some (such as Sir Robert Anstruther) honourably remained at their post, though rival candidates were already canvassing their constituency, a much greater number placed their electioneering interests before their public duty. Many Liberals also looked with indifference on legislation against bribery, thinking that it merely diverted public interest from the Ballot, which they considered, very mistakenly as I expect it will turn out, to be a sufficient, and the only, remedy. From these causes our fight, though kept up with great vigour for several nights, was wholly unsuccessful, and the practices which we sought to render more difficult, prevailed more widely than ever in the first General Election held under the new electoral law.

In the general debates on Mr. Disraeli's Reform Bill, my participation was limited to the one speech already mentioned; but I made the Bill an occasion for bringing the two greatest improvements which remain to be made in representative government formally before the House and the nation. One of them was Personal, or as it is called with equal propriety, Proportional Representation. I brought this under the consideration of the House, by an expository and argumentative speech on Mr. Hare's plan;[*] and subsequently I was active in support of the very imperfect substitute for that plan, which, in a small number of constituencies, Parliament was induced to adopt.[†] This poor makeshift had scarcely any recommendation, except that it was a partial recognition of the evil which it did so little to remedy: as such however it was attacked by the same fallacies, and required to be defended on the same principles, as a really good measure; and its adoption in a few parliamentary elections, as well as the subsequent introduction of what is called the Cumulative Vote in the elections for the London School Board,[‡] have had the good effect of converting the equal claim of all electors to a proportional share in the representation, from a subject of merely speculative discussion, into a question of practical politics, much sooner than would otherwise have been the case.

This assertion of my opinions on Personal Representation cannot be credited

[*See p. 276 above.]

[†See Mill's speech on the Representation of the People Bill, *Parliamentary Debates*, 3rd ser., Vol. 188, cols. 1102–7 (5 July, 1867).]

[‡See Clause 37 of "An Act to Provide for Public Elementary Education in England and Wales," 33 & 34 Victoria, c. 75 (9 Aug., 1870).]

with any considerable or visible amount of practical result. It was otherwise with the other motion which I made in the form of an amendment to the Reform Bill, and which was by far the most important, perhaps the only really important public service I performed in the capacity of a Member of Parliament: a motion to strike out the words which were understood to limit the electoral franchise to males, thereby admitting to the suffrage all women who as householders or otherwise possess the qualification required of male electors.[*] For women not to make their claim to the suffrage at the time when the elective franchise was being largely extended, would have been to abjure the claim altogether; and a movement on the subject was begun in 1866, when I presented a petition for the suffrage signed by a considerable number of distinguished women.[†] But it was as yet uncertain whether the proposal would obtain more than a few stray votes in the House: and when, after a debate in which the speakers on the contrary side were conspicuous by their feebleness, the votes recorded in favour of the motion amounted to 73—made up by pairs and tellers to above 80—the surprise was general and the encouragement great: the greater too because one of those who voted for the motion was Mr. Bright, a fact which could only be attributed to the impression made on him by the debate, as he had previously made no secret of his non-concurrence in the proposal. The time appeared to my daughter, Miss Helen Taylor, to have come for forming a Society for the extension of the suffrage to women. The existence of the Society is due to my daughter's initiative; its constitution was planned entirely by her, and she was the soul of the movement during its first years, though delicate health and superabundant occupation made her decline to be a member of the Executive Committee. Many distinguished members of parliament, professors, and others, and some of the most eminent women of whom the country can boast, became members of the Society, a large proportion either directly or indirectly through my daughter's influence, she having written the greater number, and all the best, of the letters by which adhesion was obtained, even when those letters bore my signature. In two remarkable instances, those of Miss Nightingale and Miss Mary Carpenter, the reluctance those ladies had at first felt to come forward (for it was not on their part difference of opinion) was overcome by appeals written by my daughter though signed by me. Associations for the same object were formed in various local centres, Manchester, Edinburgh, Birmingham, Bristol, Glasgow, and others which have done much valuable work for the cause. All the Societies take the title of branches of the National Society for Women's Suffrage; but each has its own governing body, and acts in complete independence of the others.

[*See pp. 275–6 above.]

[†See Public Petition no. 8501 (7 July, 1866), "For Extension of the Elective Franchise to All Householders without Distinction of Sex," *Reports of Select Committee on Public Petitions,* 1866, p. 697 and (for the text of the Petition) Appendix, p. 305. The petition had 1,521 signatures, headed by those of Barbara Bodichon, Mentia Taylor, and Emily Davies.]

I believe I have mentioned all that is worth remembering of my proceedings in the House. But their enumeration, even if complete, would give but an inadequate idea of my occupations during that period, and especially of the time taken up by correspondence. For many years before my election to Parliament I had been continually receiving letters from strangers, mostly addressed to me as a writer on philosophy, and either propounding difficulties or communicating thoughts on subjects connected with logic or political economy. In common, I suppose, with all who are known as political economists, I was a recipient of all the shallow theories and absurd proposals by which people are perpetually endeavouring to shew the way to universal wealth and happiness by some artful reorganisation of the currency. When there were signs of sufficient intelligence in the writers to make it worth while attempting to put them right, I took the trouble to point out their errors, until the growth of my correspondence made it necessary to dismiss such persons with very brief answers. Many, however, of the communications I received were more worthy of attention than these, and in some, oversights of detail were pointed out in my writings, which I was thus enabled to correct. Correspondence of this sort naturally multiplied with the multiplication of the subjects on which I wrote, especially those of a metaphysical character. But when I became a member of parliament I began to receive letters on private grievances and on every imaginable subject that related to any kind of public affairs, however remote from my knowledge or pursuits. It was not my constituents in Westminster who laid this burthen on me: they kept with remarkable fidelity the understanding on which I had consented to serve. I received indeed now and then an application from some ingenuous youth to procure for him a small government appointment: but these were few, and how simple and ignorant the writers were, was shewn by the fact that the applications came in about equally whichever party was in power. My invariable answer was, that it was contrary to the principles on which I was elected to ask favours of any Government. But on the whole hardly any part of the country gave me less trouble than my own constituents. The general mass of correspondence, however, swelled into an oppressive burthen. At this time, and thenceforth, a great proportion of all my letters (including many which found their way into the newspapers)* were not written by me but by my daughter; at first merely from her willingness to help in disposing of a mass of letters greater than I could get through without assistance, but afterwards because I thought the letters she wrote superior to mine, and more so in proportion to the difficulty and

*One which deserves particular mention is a letter respecting the Habitual Criminals Act [32 & 33 Victoria, c. 99 (11 Aug., 1869)] and the functions of a police generally, written in answer to a private application for my opinion, but which got into the newspapers and excited some notice. [See *LL, CW,* Vol. XVI, pp. 1523–6 (to James Beal, 14 Dec., 1868); printed in the *Morning Star,* 23 Dec., 1868, p. 6.] This letter which was full of original and valuable thoughts was entirely my daughter's. The fertility and aptness which distinguishes her practical conceptions of the adaptation of means to ends is such as I can never hope to rival.

importance of the occasion. Even those which I wrote myself were generally much improved by her, as is also the case with all the more recent of my prepared speeches, of which, and of some of my published writings, not a few passages, and those the most successful, were hers. [b]

While I remained in Parliament my work as an author was unavoidably limited to the recess. During that time I wrote (besides the pamphlet on Ireland already mentioned) the Essay on Plato published in the *Edinburgh Review* and reprinted in the third volume of *Dissertations and Discussions*;[*] and the Address which conformably to custom I delivered to the University of St. Andrews, whose students had done me the honour of electing me to the office of Rector.[†] In this Discourse I gave expression to many thoughts and opinions which had been accumulating in me through life respecting the various studies which belong to a liberal education, their uses and influences, and the mode in which they should be pursued to render those influences most beneficial. The position I took up, vindicating the high educational value alike of the old classic and the new scientific studies, on even stronger grounds than are urged by most of their advocates, and insisting that it is only the stupid inefficiency of the usual teaching which makes those studies be regarded as competitors instead of allies, was, I think, calculated, not only to aid and stimulate the improvement which has happily commenced in the national institutions for higher education, but to diffuse juster ideas than we often find even in highly educated men on the conditions of the highest mental cultivation.

During this period also I commenced (and completed soon after I had left Parliament) the performance of a duty to philosophy and to the memory of my father, by preparing and publishing an edition of the *Analysis of the Phenomena of the Human Mind* with notes bringing up the doctrines of that admirable book to the latest improvements in science and in speculation.[‡] This was a joint undertaking: the psychological notes being furnished in about equal proportions by Mr. Bain and myself, while Mr. Grote supplied some valuable contributions on points in the history of philosophy incidentally raised, and Dr. Andrew Findlater supplied the deficiencies in the book which had been occasioned by the imperfect philological knowledge of the time when it was written. Having been originally published at a

---

[*"Grote's *Plato*," *Edinburgh Review*, CXXIII (Apr., 1866), 297–364; reprinted in *D&D*, Vol. III, pp. 275–379; in *CW*, Vol. XI, pp. 375–440.]

[†*Inaugural Address Delivered to the University of St. Andrews* (London: Longmans, Green, Reader, and Dyer, 1867).]

[‡2nd ed., 2 vols., ed. J. S. Mill (London: Longmans, Green, Reader, and Dyer, 1869).]

[b][*Cancelled text (a passage added on the opposite verso):*] I must add that whatever has been done by us for the diffusion of our opinions and of our principles of action by private intercourse and the direct influence of mind over mind, has been almost wholly her work, my own capacities of the kind being almost confined to my writings: and no one but myself knows at how great a sacrifice both of her personal tastes and inclinations and of her health that function was performed by her.

time when the current of metaphysical speculation ran in a quite opposite direction to the psychology of Experience and Association, the *Analysis* had not obtained the amount of immediate success which it deserved, though it had made a deep impression on many individual minds, and had largely contributed, through those minds, to create that more favourable atmosphere for the Association Psychology of which we now have the benefit. Admirably adapted for a class-book of the Experience Metaphysics, it only required to be enriched, and in some cases corrected, by the results of more recent labours in the same school of thought, to stand, as it now does, in company with Mr. Bain's treatises, at the head of the systematic works on Analytic psychology.

In the autumn of 1868 the Parliament which passed the Reform Act was dissolved, and at the new election for Westminster I was thrown out; not to my surprise, nor, I believe, to that of my principal supporters, though in the few days preceding the election they had become more sanguine than before. That I should not have been elected at all would not have required any explanation; what excites curiosity is that I should have been elected the first time, or, having been elected then, should have been defeated afterwards. But the efforts made to defeat me were far greater on the second occasion than on the first. For one thing, the Tory Government was now struggling for existence, and success in any contest was of more importance to them. Then, too, all persons of Tory feelings were far more embittered against me individually than on the previous occasion; many who had at first been either favourable or indifferent, were vehemently opposed to my reelection. As I had shewn in my political writings that I was aware of the weak points in democratic opinions, some Conservatives, it seems, had not been without hopes of finding me an opponent of democracy: as I was able to see the Conservative side of the question, they presumed that, like them, I could not see any other side. Yet if they had really read my writings they would have known that after giving full weight to all that appeared to me well grounded in the arguments against democracy, I unhesitatingly decided in its favour, while recommending that it should be accompanied by such institutions as were consistent with its principle and calculated to ward off its inconveniences: one of the chief of these remedies being Proportional Representation, on which scarcely any of the Conservatives gave me any support. Some Tory expectations appear to have been founded on the approbation I had expressed of plural voting, under certain conditions: and it has been surmised that the suggestion of this sort made in one of the Resolutions[*] which Mr. Disraeli introduced into the House preparatory to his Reform Bill (a suggestion which meeting with no favour he did not press) may have been occasioned by what I had written on the point: but if so, it was forgotten that I had made it an express condition that the privilege of a plurality of votes should be annexed to

[*The fifth of Disraeli's "Resolutions on the Representation of the People," *Parliamentary Debates*, 3rd ser., Vol. 185, cols. 214–43 (11 Feb., 1867).]

education, not to property, and even so, had approved of it only on the supposition of universal suffrage.[*] How utterly inadmissible such plural voting would be under the suffrage given by the present Reform Act, is proved, to any who could otherwise doubt it, by the very small weight which the working classes are found to possess in elections even under the law which gives no more votes to any one elector than to any other.

While I thus was far more obnoxious to the Tory interest, and to many Conservative Liberals than I had formerly been, the course I pursued in Parliament had by no means been such as to make Liberals generally at all enthusiastic in my support. It has already been mentioned, how large a proportion of my prominent appearances had been on questions on which I differed from most of the Liberal party or about which they cared little, and how few occasions there had been on which the line I took was such as could lead them to attach any great value to me as an organ of their opinions. I had moreover done things which had excited, in many minds, a personal prejudice against me. Many were offended by what they called the persecution of Mr. Eyre: and still greater offence was taken at my sending a subscription to the election expenses of Mr. Bradlaugh. Having refused to be at any expense for my own election, and having had all its expenses defrayed by others, I felt under a peculiar obligation to subscribe in my turn where funds were deficient for candidates whose election was desirable. I accordingly sent subscriptions to nearly all the working class candidates, and among others to Mr. Bradlaugh. He had the support of the working classes; having heard him speak I knew him to be a man of ability, and he had proved that he was the reverse of a demagogue by placing himself in strong opposition to the prevailing opinion of the democratic party on two such important subjects as Malthusianism and Personal Representation. Men of this sort, who while sharing the democratic feelings of the working classes, judged political questions for themselves and had courage to assert their individual convictions against popular opposition, were needed, as it seemed to me, in Parliament, and I did not think that Mr. Bradlaugh's anti-religious opinions (even though he had been intemperate in the expression of them) ought to exclude him. In subscribing, however, to his election, I did what would have been highly imprudent if I had been at liberty to consider only the interests of my own reelection; and, as might be expected, the utmost possible use, both fair and unfair, was made of this act of mine, to stir up the electors of Westminster against me. To these various causes, combined with an unscrupulous use of the usual pecuniary and other influences on the side of my Tory competitor[†] while none were used on my side, it is to be ascribed that I failed at my second election after having succeeded at the first. No sooner was the result of the election known

[*See, e.g., in *CW*, Vol. XIX, *Thoughts on Parliamentary Reform*, pp. 324–5; "Recent Writers on Reform," pp. 353–7; and *Considerations on Representative Government*, pp. 474–9.]

[†Again, W. H. Smith; see p. 275 above.]

than I received three or four invitations to become a candidate for other constituencies, chiefly counties; but even if success could have been expected, and this without expense, I was not disposed to deny myself the relief of returning to private life. I had no cause to feel humiliated at my rejection by the electors; and if I had, the feeling would have been far outweighed by the numerous expressions of regret which I received from all sorts of persons and places, and in a most marked degree from those members of the liberal party in Parliament with whom I had been accustomed to act.

Since that time little has occurred which there is need to commemorate in this place. I returned to my old pursuits and to the enjoyment of a country life in the South of Europe; alternating twice a year with a residence of some weeks or months in the neighbourhood of London. I have written various articles in periodicals (chiefly in my friend Mr. Morley's *Fortnightly Review*),[*] have made a small number of speeches on public occasions, especially at the meetings of the Women's Suffrage Society,[†] have published *The Subjection of Women*, written some years before, with some additions by my daughter and myself, and have commenced the preparation of matter for future books, of which it will be time to speak more particularly if I live to finish them.[‡] Here, therefore, for the present, this Memoir may close.

[*In the period implied (if one interprets the text literally) Mill in fact published only two articles, both in the *Fortnightly Review*: "Endowments," n.s. V (Apr., 1869), 377–90 (in *D&D*, Vol. IV, pp. 1–24, and *CW*, Vol. V, pp. 613–29); and (in two instalments) "Thornton on Labour and Its Claims," n.s. V (May and June, 1869), 505–18, and 680–700 (in *D&D*, Vol. IV, pp. 25–85, and *CW*, Vol. V, pp. 631–68).]

[†Again, if the text is interpreted literally (see the preceding note), in this period only one speech appears to have been delivered, at a meeting of the National Society for Women's Suffrage, in the Architectural Gallery, Conduit St., Regent St., on 17 July, 1869 (see the *Daily News*, 19 July, p. 2, and a leading article in *The Times*, 20 July, p. 9). Mill may also have had in mind his speech at a meeting of the Education League (MS, Harvard University), in St. James's Hall, on 25 Mar., 1870 (see the reports on 26 Mar. in *The Times*, p. 5, the *Daily News*, p. 3, and the *Daily Telegraph*, p. 3), though it was delivered only one day before that reported in Helen Taylor's continuation of the *Autobiography* (see App. H, p. 625 below).]

[‡After Mill's death (7 May, 1873), Helen Taylor prepared for publication the *Autobiography* (London: Longmans, Green, Reader, and Dyer, 1873); *Three Essays on Religion* (London: Longmans, Green, Reader, and Dyer, 1874), in *CW*, Vol. X, pp. 369–489; and "Chapters on Socialism," *Fortnightly Review*, n.s. XXV (Feb., Mar., Apr., 1879), 217–37, 373–82, 513–30, in *CW*, Vol. V, pp. 703–53.]

PERIODICAL LITERATURE: EDINBURGH REVIEW

1824

EDITORS' NOTE

Westminster Review, I (Apr., 1824), 505–41. Unsigned. Headed: "ART. X. Periodical Literature. / *Edinburgh Review.*" Running titles: "Periodical Literature / Edinburgh Review." Not republished. Identified in Mill's bibliography as "An article on the Edinburgh Review, in the second number of the Westminster Review" (MacMinn, p. 5). There are no corrections or emendations in the Somerville College copies. For comment, see the Introduction, p. xxxi above.

Periodical Literature: Edinburgh Review

IN A FORMER ARTICLE,[*] we analysed the various misleading interests under the influence of which the *Edinburgh* and *Quarterly* Reviews are placed; both as periodical publications, and as the organs of the two great parties into which the British aristocracy is divided. We then proceeded to criticize the *Edinburgh Review* in detail; and we began to prove, by quotations from the work itself, that it has really exhibited the vices, which we described as likely to characterize a periodical publication attached to the Opposition party.

The most prominent feature in its character—its disposition to compromise—to say a little for the aristocracy and a little for the people alternately, and always to give up so much of every important question, as to avoid an irreparable breach either with the one side or with the other; this characteristic quality of the Review we illustrated by numerous quotations, selected from the volumes preceding the year 1812. We shall now prove, by further citations, that it has since persevered, and does still persevere, in the self-same course.

The first passage which we shall extract is from an article on Spain, in the twenty-third volume. The conduct of Ferdinand in re-establishing the old despotism, contrary to the expectations which had been held out to the Spaniards, in order to stimulate their exertions for the expulsion of the French, is here spoken of with that abhorrence which it so justly deserves.[†] The writer appears, however, to have trembled lest he should have gone too far; lest the aristocracy should take the alarm at so severe a censure on an established government; on one, too, which it was the fashion of the day to call legitimate: and he continues,

We have but a word or two to add on the moral of this strange drama. We subscribe unreservedly to the doctrine of Mr. Hume, that every people, not absolutely subdued by foreign force, must be governed by opinion;[‡] or, if the admirers of Mr. Paine object to that word, by prejudice. Government is founded—not on divine right—not on a social contract, but on the general consent and tacit agreement of the people, as at the moment subsisting.

[*James Mill, "Periodical Literature: *Edinburgh Review*," *Westminster Review*, I (Jan., 1824), 206–49.]

[†John Allen, "Cortes of Spain," *Edinburgh Review*, XXIII (Sept., 1814), 379–80.]

[‡See David Hume, "Of the First Principles of Government," in *Essays and Treatises on Several Subjects*, 2 vols. (London: Cadell; Edinburgh: Bell and Bradfute, *et al.*, 1793), Vol. I, pp. 39–40.]

But we are not to conclude, because power is derived from the people, that all governments in which they do not reserve a portion for themselves are illegitimate. For it is very clear (notwithstanding what has been written), that the people can as easily give the right of raising taxes on themselves to one hereditary officer, as to five hundred, renewed every seven years. (P. 380.)

This passage is a specimen of the vague language, so convenient for the purpose of compromise, which the Opposition party makes use of when it takes the popular side of any question.

"All power is derived from the people;" "government is founded on the general consent and tacit agreement of the people:" and the like. It is obvious that the people are not in any respect benefitted by this verbal recognition of their sovereignty. It does not bring them one particle nearer to obtaining good government. This they can obtain, only by providing real and efficient *securities* for it. But these vague phrases, though of no service to the people, are admirably suited to the purpose of the Whigs; which is, to please the people, just as far as is consistent with not alarming the aristocracy. A well-turned rhetorical sentence asserting popular supremacy, is expected to be grateful to the ears of many among the people, who not having a clear conception of what constitutes efficient securities for good government, are incapable of discerning that mere declamation gives no security whatever. The aristocracy, on their side, risk nothing by conceding to their adversaries a general maxim which leads to no consequences. Their power and emolument remain untouched. The only thing which they have any reason to dread—the establishment of efficient securities against misrule—the *Edinburgh Review*, from the first, has strenuously opposed. If the people will be cajoled with fine language concerning their sovereignty, they may have as much of it as they please from the *Edinburgh Review*. But, if they require any thing tangible—if they ask *what they are to get* by this boasted sovereignty, it calls them radicals and democrats, who wish for the annihilation of property, and the subversion of the social order.

We may explain on the same principles, the warmth which the *Edinburgh Review* has constantly shown, in defence of the people's right to resist oppression by rising against the government. The following passage is extracted from an article in the twenty-seventh volume,[*] on the dangers of the Constitution:

What is it that secures the system against such attacks as we have alluded to, and in like manner against more direct and open invasions of power?—It is unquestionably the influence of public opinion, and the apprehension of resistance, intimately connected with it. As long as the proceedings of parliament occupy the attention of the people, an effectual control is exerted over them; and the discussions in the two houses, how little soever they may seem to influence the votes, are engines of the highest power in controlling the executive through the public. As long as judges sit in the face of the country, and, above all, in the face of an enlightened and jealous bar, the most scrutinizing and unsparing of all

[*Henry Peter Brougham, "Dangers of the Constitution," *Edinburgh Review*, XXVII (Sept., 1816), 245–63.]

auditories,—the Crown can neither fill the bench with its tools, nor can better instruments degenerate into that occupation. As long as all the proceedings of government are public,—canvassed freely by the press, and made known through that and other channels of information; and as long as there is reason to believe that gross mis-rule will engender resistance,—a corrupt judicature and a venal parliament may in vain combine with a despotic court, in defiance of public opinion. Tyranny will dread going beyond a certain length, and this fear will supersede the necessity of applying the ultimate check. This sacred principle of resistance is the very foundation of all our liberties; it is the cause to which we owe them:—Let it only be destroyed, and they are gone. (P. 249.)

To suppose resistance necessary, is to suppose the existence of bad government; and to speak of it as a security, is only calculated to make the people contented with a bad government, by looking to resistance as a remedy for its evils. The fact is, that resistance is any thing but a remedy: and this for two reasons. One reason is, that from the aversion which all men feel to commit their persons and their property to the hazards of a civil war, they are willing to submit to a great degree of mis-government before they will resist. But, besides, a revolution, even when it does happen, is not, in itself, productive of any good. It is useful, only in so far as it contributes to establish permanent securities for good government. Take away this effect, and the whole cost of the revolution is unmixed evil. Yet the *Edinburgh Review*, which has always earnestly deprecated the establishment of securities for good government, holds up the principle of resistance as our only safeguard against oppression. Why? Because this principle, like all other principles which appear to be, without really being a security, is calculated to catch the favour of the less clear-sighted part of the people; while it does not alarm any but the more timid portion of the aristocracy. All among them whose fears do not entirely overcome their reason, are aware that a successful insurrection, the only kind of resistance which they have any reason to dread, rarely happens under a regular government; and that an ordinary share of prudence on their part, might, in most cases, prevent it from happening at all. They are, therefore, well contented that the people should be hindered from turning their attention to the remedies which are effectual, by having it fixed upon remedies which are not.

The whole language of the *Edinburgh* Reviewers, on the subject of government, proves their wish to prevent the people from looking out for securities against misrule. They do not approve of a law or of an institution, because it is conducive to good government, but because it is favourable to liberty. They do not disapprove of a ministerial measure, because it opens a door to oppression, but because it is unconstitutional. These phrases, as we shall presently show, are extremely convenient to those who wish to compromise the question of good government.

"The constitution" either means nothing at all, or it means the aggregate of the securities, such as they are, which our present form of government affords us, against misrule. These securities are either adequate to their purpose, or they are inadequate to it. The doctrine of the *Edinburgh Review* is, that they are not adequate. For it is continually asserting, in the most unqualified terms, that parliament, instead of being, as by the constitution it ought to be, an efficient check upon the conduct of ministers—is, on the contrary, a ready tool in their hands. We shall only quote one passage among many, in which this charge of inefficacy is brought against the constitution:

> After all that we have seen of parliaments, it would be a vain fancy to imagine that the representation of the people is of itself a security for their rights. Even if that representation were much more perfect than it is, it would be liable to the influence of the Crown, and might be intimidated by violence. In fact, to what baseness has not the parliament, at one time or another, made itself a party? (*Ibid.*, p. 247.)

If the securities provided by the constitution are inefficient, so inefficient as not to prevent the government from being party to any act of baseness whatever; most men will probably conclude, that it is time to think of providing more perfect securities. Not so the *Edinburgh* reviewers: their ideas of amelioration go no farther than to bid us cling more closely to the imperfect securities which we have. To improve the constitution, is with them a very secondary object. To preserve it is the one thing needful. The necessity of guarding it against the encroachments of ministers, is the burden of their song, even in the very article from which the above extract was taken. They admit that misgovernment may be carried very far, with the concurrence of parliament, and therefore without violating the constitution. To this kind of misgovernment, however, it appears, we are to submit. If ministers will compound not to violate the constitution, they may oppress, as much as they please, in any other way. Is this not compromise? If not, the word is without a meaning.

We are aware that, on other occasions, the *Edinburgh Review* has represented the constitution as standing in need of improvement, and even of considerable improvement. But this, far from invalidating the truth of our observations, is only another instance of the habitual see-saw. When the tide ran high for reform, the *Edinburgh Review* was compelled, to a certain extent, to go with the tide. It is enough, that it has never proposed any plan of reform which would, to any practical purpose, diminish the power of the aristocracy, or add to the people's securities for good government. To do so would have been to renounce the compromise, to break with the aristocracy, and to adhere to the people. This did not suit the Opposition party; nor, consequently, did it suit their faithful and devoted organ.

Liberty, another favourite word with the *Edinburgh Review*, is equally suited with the word "constitution," to the ends of compromise. Liberty, in its original sense, means freedom from restraint. In this sense, every law, and every rule of morals, is contrary to liberty. A despot, who is entirely emancipated from both, is the only person whose freedom of action is complete. A measure of government, therefore, is not necessarily bad, because it is contrary to liberty; and to blame it for that reason, leads to confusion of ideas. But to create confusion of ideas, is essential to the purpose of those who have to persuade the people, that small abuses should be reformed, while great ones should remain untouched. The true reason for reform is evidently much stronger in the case of a great abuse than of a small one. They cannot therefore put forward the true reason; they must put forward something, which shall have the semblance of a reason, but which they can explain away when they please, and which, therefore, cannot be turned against themselves.

Liberty is the word which they make use of for this purpose. Small abuses are to be reformed, because they are contrary to liberty. There are minor reasons, as, that they hurt the prosperity of the country, and so forth, but this is the main argument. On the other hand, when a great abuse is to be upheld, these gentlemen proceed to explain away their own doctrine: they tell us that freedom may be carried to a dangerous excess; that it is apt to degenerate into licentiousness; and they coin certain convenient phrases, "rational liberty," "constitutional liberty," "liberty rightly understood," and the like: with which elegant kinds of liberty they declare the great abuses to be consistent.

The above remarks afford a key to much of the language which the *Edinburgh Review* has held, and still holds, concerning government. Whatever it may be necessary to say concerning their plans of reform in the detail, will be said hereafter in a separate article.[*]

Among the instruments of misgovernment which the rulers of this country have at their command, the law of libel is justly considered one of the most dangerous: as it enables them to free themselves from that which is in itself a considerable check upon them, and without which all other checks are ineffectual, free discussion. There is no legal definition of libel: there can be no definition, so long as libel law continues in its present state, that of common, or unwritten law. A judge, dependant upon the government, is left with full power to decide any publication libellous, or not, as he pleases: whatever disposition the jury might have to set aside his opinion, being got rid of by the practice of packing special juries.* As might have been expected under such circumstances, the judges have allowed themselves no small latitude in declaring publications to be libellous. Lord Ellen-

[*James Mill, "Periodical Literature: *Edinburgh Review* on Parliamentary Reform," *Westminster Review*, IV (July, 1825), 194–233.]

*The special jury system is one of those abuses which the *Edinburgh Review* has uniformly slurred over. In an article in the thirteenth volume, it professes not to believe that any evil arises from the practice of packing juries. ([Thomas Moore Musgrave (or James Musgrave), "Sir R. Phillips on the Office of Sheriff," *Edinburgh Review*, XIII (Oct., 1808),] 172.) More recently it declares that the principal part of the evil has been corrected in recent practice. ([Henry Cockburn, "Nomination of Scottish Juries (Part I)," *ibid.*,] XXXVI [(Oct., 1821)], 174.) It remains, however, uncorrected to this day; and yet the *Edinburgh Review*, which professes so much regard for free discussion, and for trial by jury, has never dropped one word in reprobation of it.

borough once said from the Bench, that a libel was *any thing which hurt the feelings of any body.*[*] The common judge-made definition of a public libel, is, *any thing which tends to bring the constituted authorities into hatred and contempt.*[†] But all censure of their conduct must, *pro tanto*, have this tendency; and most so, when their misconduct is most glaring, and the censure which is bestowed on it most urgently required. With the help, therefore, of so convenient a definition of libel, and of such convenient instruments as English judges, government have it in their power to suppress all censure whatever.

The twenty-seventh volume of the *Edinburgh Review* contains an article on Holt's *Law of Libel*, in which this subject is canvassed at considerable length.[‡] For the people, there is abundance of general remarks on the importance of free discussion; remarks such as we hear from no one more frequently than from Lord Eldon himself. But when the reviewer comes to something specific; when he undertakes "to find the quantity of liberty, and the species of restraint, which will secure to the press the greatest amount of free discussion consistent with the tranquillity of the community, and the safety of private character;"[§] he proceeds in the most deliberate manner to surrender up all the essential points to the aristocracy.

The undefined nature of the offence of libel; that which is really at the root of the mischief; that which enables the government to punish as libellous any publication containing sentiments unpleasing to themselves; this enormous evil, the *Edinburgh Review* not only does not suggest the means of *correcting*, but expressly declares not to be an evil.

One charge which has been urged against the system, we are inclined to dismiss at once, as founded in an extremely superficial view of the matter. It has been stated as a great defect, that there is no law defining a libel; or expounding what shall be considered libellous. In no code, either formed by successive acts of legislation, or composed at once by speculative lawgivers, was ever such a definition attempted. The attempt would in truth be vain. The nature of the thing precludes all minute definition; and a general description is useless for the end in view. (P. 108.)

In the next page, however, we are told that "means may be found of limiting the sense of the word in practice as effectually as is desirable, and preventing the prosecution of *any thing that at any time displeases any body*, as the modern practice has been alleged to have described the offence."[¶]

[*For the statement, see Thomas Bayly Howell, *A Complete Collection of State Trials*, 34 vols. (London: Longman, *et al.*, 1809–28), Vol. XXIX, col. 49.]

[†Cf. Peregrine Bingham (probably), "M. Cottu and Special Juries," and "Periodical Literature: *Quarterly Review*," *Westminster Review*, I (Jan., 1824), 158, and 258.]

[‡Brougham, "Liberty of the Press and Its Abuses," *Edinburgh Review*, XXVII (Sept., 1816), 102–44, reviewing Francis Ludlow Holt, *The Law of Libel* (London: Reed; Dublin: Phelan, 1812).]

[§*Ibid.*, p. 104.]

[¶Brougham is quoting Bentham; cf. Bentham, *The Elements of the Art of Packing* (London: Wilson, 1821), p. 94.]

The inconsistency of this doctrine with itself is remarkable. We are to limit the meaning of the word: if we do not, all kinds of mischief will ensue. But we are not to limit it in the only mode in which any man in his senses ever thought of limiting the meaning of a word; namely, by a definition. What is the tendency of this doctrine is evident. It is to give us something which should *appear* to limit the meaning of the word, without *really* limiting it: to deceive the people into a belief that freedom of discussion exists by law, when in fact so much of it only exists as public opinion renders it unsafe to destroy.

The two following passages form an appropriate comment upon the preceding:

> It is manifest, that a statement, either against the government, or an individual, may be libellous; or, to use a phrase which no one can object to, may be criminal, although founded in truth. Undoubted facts may be involved in furious or inflammatory invective. Some cases may be conceived (though they are exceedingly rare) in which a simple statement of facts respecting the government would be an offence against the public tranquillity; but innumerable cases may be put, in which the publication of the truth, without any comment, would be an offence against private individuals. (P. 109.)

And further on,

> That there are public libels, properly so called, which may be criminal, though true, is easily shown. The instances are no doubt rare, but they exist. It may be libellous to state in an inflammatory way, that which, if plainly stated, would be innocent; as, to address the passions of the multitude about scarcity of provisions, or of soldiers about pay. It may be libellous to address to particular classes a plain statement of that which, published generally, would be innocent, as to disperse it among a mob or an army. It may be libellous to state, even plainly, truths of a delicate nature at a peculiar crisis—as, during an invasion, a rebellion, or a mutiny. Finally, there are certain truths (but the number is extremely small), of so peculiarly delicate a nature, that the plainest statement of them at any time would be libellous; as, the legitimacy of the reigning sovereign;—his right to the crown generally;—his political conduct, for which he is not responsible;—his private conduct, of which the law takes no notice. (P. 126.)

Mark the concessions which are here made to the aristocracy. "It may be libellous to state in an inflammatory way, that which, if plainly stated, would be innocent." We are sorry the reviewer did not teach us how to draw a precise line between two modes of stating the same fact, one of them an inflammatory mode, the other not. Only entrust a judge dependant on the aristocracy, and a packed special jury, with the power of punishing all statements conveyed in what they may call inflammatory language; and nothing more is wanting to enable them to punish any statements whatever.

The other passage, however, goes even beyond this in open and undisguised enmity to free discussion. In some cases "a simple statement of facts respecting the government would be an offence against the public tranquillity:" much more, a statement accompanied by a comment, however calm and dispassionate. This gives a degree of latitude to the government, which is scarcely claimed even by the Tories themselves. Moderate Tories usually admit that calm and dispassionate discussion on the conduct of the government should be allowed. The *Edinburgh Review*, however, tells us, that in some cases, which it is impossible to define by law, not merely all discussion, however cool and unimpassioned, but a bare statement of facts, ought to be punished. It tells us, indeed, that these cases are rare. Happily it would not be safe, in this age and country, to say that they are *not rare*. But, rare as they are, it tells us that they cannot be defined: and as there must be somebody to judge, and as the *Edinburgh Review* has not told us who this somebody shall be, we are left to conclude that it means the government to judge: and to judge what? To judge what shall, and shall not be spoken of itself!

In return for all these concessions to the aristocracy, what is to be done for the people? Truth should be permitted to be given in evidence on the trial, and should have some weight in determining the verdict of the jury: although it would rest with the judge and packed jury to decide what degree of weight it should have. The greatest benefit of a free press is, the discussion which it calls forth concerning the conduct of the government. This discussion consists in the statement of facts and expression of opinions. We have seen how the *Edinburgh Review* disposes of the statement of facts; and as for the expression of opinions, how would freedom in this respect be increased by the adoption of the only remedy which the *Edinburgh Review* proposes for the defects of the law of libel?

Within the last six or seven years, when the desire of efficient securities for good government has become much more general than it has been at any previous period of history, the interest of all other political questions has been to a considerable degree swallowed up by that of parliamentary reform. It was to be expected, therefore, that this subject should occupy a more conspicuous place than before in the pages of the *Edinburgh Review*. And in the tone which the Review has adopted on this most momentous of all topics, there appears not less of the disposition to compromise than on every other subject of importance. Its ordinary course has been to speak loudly of reform in general, but specifically to approve only such plans as, if adopted, would leave the means of misgovernment with unimpaired strength in the hands of the aristocracy; and to impute either the grossest folly, or the most detestable wickedness, to those who desire a more extensive reform, as well as to those who would have no reform at all. In conformity to the habitual see-saw, they have occasionally deviated from this course.

Thus an article on America, in the thirty-first volume, contains an unusual proportion of democratic sentiments.[*] The same observation applies to another article on the same subject, in the thirty-third volume,[†] where a charge which had been brought against the Review of illiberality towards America, seems to have extorted from it sundry expressions in favour of popular governments, exceeding

[*Sydney Smith, "Travellers in America," *Edinburgh Review*, XXXI (Dec., 1818), 132–50.]

[†Francis Jeffrey, "Dispositions of England and America," *ibid.*, XXXIII (May, 1820), 395–431.]

perhaps, in boldness, any which had yet appeared in its pages. America is quoted as an instance to show "within what limits popular institutions are safe and practicable, and what a large infusion of democracy is consistent with the authority of government and the good order of society." (P. 405.) Then follows a prediction that, ere long, a struggle will take place in all the countries of Europe, for the amelioration of their political institutions; "even in England," says the reviewer, "the more modified elements of the same principles are stirring and heaving around, above, and beneath us, with unprecedented agitation and terror" [p. 403]; and he observes that the assistance of America may be needed to give preponderance to the good cause.

In the very next number we find an article on France,[*] which almost returns to the anti-jacobin tone of the early numbers. In direct opposition to the doctrines of the article to which we just referred; it repeats the wretched aristocratic fallacy, of which too many well-meaning persons are even now the dupes, that "wherever universal suffrage is actually established, Agrarian law may be expected to follow." (Pp. 27–8.) It laments bitterly over the decay and discredit into which, fortunately for France, the old feudal nobility have fallen [pp. 14–16]. It says as much as it can venture to say in palliation of the vices of the old French despotism: thus, it doubts whether the abolition of the *jurandes*, the *maîtrises*, and similar commercial restrictions, was a benefit [p. 3]. It lauds the *parlemens* for the purity of their administration of justice [p. 17], as if it had forgotten the fate of Calas, and other transactions of a similar stamp.* When at last it is compelled to admit that great evils existed, it tells us that "France had never been in so fair a way to see the defects of its old institutions corrected, and civil liberty introduced with success, as it was just before the Revolution. But the restless impatience of reformers could brook no delay." [P. 18.] And then it goes on imputing all the evils of the revolution to the impatience of the reformers, and none of them to the opposition of the court. It accuses the French government, subsequent to the restoration of the Bourbons, of too great a tendency to liberalism! and vindicates Louis XVIII from the accusation of mistrusting the people, and of being insincere in his professions of a desire to establish a constitutional government in France! [P. 30.] Be it observed, also, that this article was written, not immediately after the return of the Bourbons, when it could only as yet be surmised what course they would pursue; but after the passing of the election law of 1820,[†] by which a permanent majority in the Chamber of Deputies was secured to the Court, and but for which, neither the

---

[*Louis Simond, "France," *ibid.*, XXXIV (Aug., 1820), 1–39.]

*In an article as early as the 10th volume (a review of Capmany's *Questiones Criticas*); we are told distinctly that in France, under the Bourbons, the administration of justice was not only bad, but nearly as bad as in Spain. ([John Allen, "Capmany's *Questiones Criticas*," *ibid.*,] X [(July, 1807)], 425.)

[†Loi sur les élections, Bulletin 379, No. 8910 (29 juin, 1820), *Bulletin des lois du royaume de France*, 7ième sér., X, 1001–6.]

Spanish war, nor any of the other iniquitous measures of the French government would probably ever have taken place.* On this law the *Edinburgh Review* bestows unqualified praise; because, forsooth, "the republican principle predominates in the French monarchy" [p. 28]; a defect which, it seems, is to be remedied by giving preponderance to a very different principle—the despotic. After this we need not feel surprise on being told that our own complaints against our government, including, of course, those of the *Edinburgh Review*, are unfounded.

> Foreigners are apt to be misled by what they read in our newspapers, or hear from their own travellers. Complaints against the government, and dismal forebodings about the loss of liberty, are nowhere so frequent and so loud as in those countries where there is, on the whole, the least reason for such apprehensions. [P. 33.]

We know not whether the following sentence is more remarkable for the boldness with which it begs the question, or for the unintelligible jargon in which the assumption is wrapt up, to conceal its utter falsehood:

> We think ourselves warranted in saying, that most of the abuses and troublesome results of our institutions may be traced directly to some principle of exuberant vigour shooting beyond the mark; they are the price we pay for overbalancing advantages; the wrong side of a good government, and the reasoning of those who condemn them on that account, would prove, if admitted, that a bad government is the best. [P. 34.]

From the length to which our remarks upon the see-saw have already extended, we have only room for one additional instance. This we shall select from an article in the thirty-seventh volume, on the Liberty of the Press and the Constitutional Association;[*] in which, by the way, a defect in the law which, in a former article, was affirmed to be irremediable—the absence of all definition of libel—is acknowledged and complained of (p. 116). The frequent use which government has sometimes made of the privilege of *ex-officio* informations is here spoken of as meriting the severest censure. But the reader will judge how much value is to be attached to those declarations, when we tell him that it complains as loudly of the "culpable indifference" with which, at other times, government has abstained from prosecuting certain periodical works; although "every one else," says the Review, "was daily sickened at the audacity and activity of their authors" (p. 112); an assertion which, if true, proves, conclusively, that the publications in question cannot have done any mischief, and, consequently, that it would have been altogether unjustifiable, upon all principles, to punish the authors.

That the spirit of compromise has been a marked characteristic of the *Edinburgh*

---

*This is a remarkable instance of see-saw. Five years before, when the Bourbons had not yet done half so much to re-establish despotism as they had in 1820, the *Edinburgh Review* itself charged them with all those iniquitous designs, from which it afterwards endeavoured to exculpate them. See a long article on France, in the twenty-fifth volume. [Jeffrey, "France," *Edinburgh Review*, XXV (Dec., 1815), 501–26.]

[*Brougham, "Constitutional Association," *ibid.*, XXXVII (June, 1822), 110–21.]

Review, from its commencement to the present day, insomuch that there is scarcely a question of any importance, of which it has not either given up half, or preached alternately, first on the one side and then on the other, is now, we hope, sufficiently clear to all our readers.

It shall next be our business to prove that it has been equally distinguished by the other vices to which we have shown periodical literature to be liable. And first, we shall examine how far it has made a practice of chiming in with existing prejudices.

Of its sacrifices at the altar of aristocratic prejudice, two remarkable instances occur in the first number; the one in a review of Southey's *Thalaba*, the other in an article on the sugar colonies.[*]

To most of our readers Mr. Southey is probably known only as the warm advocate of every existing abuse, and the reviler of all who think that governments were made for the people, and not the people for governments. He, and the other Lake poets, however, commenced writing with higher objects. They saw that the aristocracy, while they profess a whining sympathy with the poor as individuals, inflict the most tremendous evils, without compunction, upon the poor, *en masse*; and they resolved to set the example of condemning murder and robbery on a large as well as on a small scale. They saw that the aristocracy, as a class, claim merit for every crime which they do not commit; while it is urged as a reproach against the poor, that they are not always proof against temptations, which nothing less than heroic virtue could withstand. They saw this, and were indignant: they contrasted the vices of the people with the vices of the aristocracy, and bestowed the severest condemnation, where every candid mind will admit that the severest condemnation was due. In such a cause, even some exaggeration would have been excusable; there is certainly no want of exaggeration on the other side. Hear, however, the *Edinburgh Review*:

A splenetic and idle discontent with the existing institutions of society, seems to be at the bottom of all their serious and peculiar sentiments. Instead of contemplating the wonders and the pleasures which civilization has created for mankind, they are perpetually brooding over the disorders by which its progress has been attended. They are filled with horror and compassion at the sight of poor men spending their blood in the quarrels of princes, and brutifying their sublime capabilities in the drudgery of unremitting labour. For all sorts of vice and profligacy in the lower orders of society, they have the same virtuous horror, and the same tender compassion. While the existence of these offences overpowers them with grief and confusion, they never permit themselves to feel the smallest indignation or dislike towards the offenders. The present vicious constitution of society alone is responsible for all these enormities: the poor sinners are but the helpless victims or instruments of its disorders, and could not possibly have avoided the errors into which they have been betrayed. Though they can bear with crimes, therefore, they cannot reconcile themselves to punishments; and have an unconquerable antipathy to prisons, gibbets, and houses of correction, as engines of oppression, and instruments of atrocious injustice. While the plea of moral necessity is thus

[*Jeffrey, "Southey's *Thalaba*," *ibid.*, I (Oct., 1802), 63–83, reviewing Robert Southey, *Thalaba the Destroyer*, 2 vols. (London: Longman and Rees, 1801); Brougham, "The Crisis of the Sugar Colonies," *ibid.*, I, 216–37.]

artfully brought forward to convert all the excesses of the poor into innocent misfortunes, no sort of indulgence is shown to the offences of the powerful and rich. Their oppressions, and seductions, and debaucheries, are the theme of many an angry verse; and the indignation and abhorrence of the reader is relentlessly conjured up against those perturbators of society and scourges of mankind.

It is not easy to say, whether the fundamental absurdity of this doctrine, or the partiality of its application, be entitled to the severest reprehension. If men are driven to commit crimes through a certain moral necessity; other men are compelled, by a similar necessity, to hate and despise them for their commission. The indignation of the sufferer is at least as natural as the guilt of him who makes him suffer; and the good order of society would probably be as well preserved, if our sympathies were sometimes called forth in behalf of the former. At all events, the same apology ought certainly to be admitted for the wealthy, as for the needy offender. They are subject alike to the over-ruling influence of necessity, and equally affected by the miserable condition of society. If it be natural for a poor man to murder and rob, in order to make himself comfortable, it is no less natural for a rich man to gormandize and domineer, in order to have the full use of his riches. Wealth is just as valid an excuse for the one class of vices, as indigence is for the other.[*]

To blame a man for being "filled with horror and compassion at the sight of poor men shedding their blood in the quarrels of princes;" and to accuse him, on that account, of a "splenetic and idle discontent with the existing institutions of society," is to put forth a doctrine which we could not characterise in adequate terms, and on which, therefore, we shall abstain from offering any remark. Nor will we refute the assertion, that the vices of the poor are not more excusable than those of the rich: it would be an insult both to the understanding and to the feelings of our readers. But do the rich try themselves even by *the same* standard as the poor? We give them full credit for their virtuous horror of poachers and of sabbath-breaking orange-women; but we submit that if vices are to be weighed by their tendency to deprave and corrupt the character, gambling, the vice of the rich, is entitled to rank somewhat above even sabbath-breaking and poaching: yet those very gentlemen who habitually enforce against poachers the utmost penalties of an atrocious law, daily receive into their houses persons notorious for gambling at Newmarket, if not in Pall Mall; but who are not, on that account, less "moral men" in the eyes of their vice-suppressing friends. While these are the habitual feelings of the higher classes—feelings which ninety-nine out of every hundred poets foster, and will continue to foster, so long as the aristocracy shall continue, as at present, to lead public opinion; what are we to think of a writer who, like the *Edinburgh* Reviewer, blames the hundredth for bestowing "exclusive sympathy" upon the poor?

The other article to which we alluded presents a remarkable contrast with the tone which the *Edinburgh Review* afterwards assumed, on the subject of negro slavery. Its object is, to prove that we ought to wish success to an armament which the French government was then fitting out against Hayti; and that we ought even, if necessary, to assist the French in their enterprise. When we consider what that

[*Jeffrey, "Southey's *Thalaba*," pp. 71–2.]

enterprise was—an enterprise for the purpose of reducing a whole nation of negroes to the alternative of death, or of the most horrible slavery; and when we consider upon what ground we are directed to co-operate in it, namely, the danger to which our colonies would be exposed, by the existence of an independent negro commonwealth, we can have no difficulty in appreciating such language as the following:

> We have the greatest sympathy for the unmerited sufferings of the unhappy negroes; we detest the odious traffic which has poured their myriads into the Antilles; but we must be permitted to feel some tenderness for our European brethren, although they are white and civilized, and to deprecate that inconsistent spirit of canting philanthropy which, in Europe, is only excited by the wrongs or miseries of the poor and the profligate, and, on the other side of the Atlantic, is never warmed but towards the savage, the mulatto, and the slave.*

To couple together "the poor" and "the profligate," as if they were two names for the same thing, is a piece of complaisance to aristocratic morality which requires no comment. Then all who venture to doubt whether it is perfectly just and humane to aid in reducing one half of the people of Hayti to slavery, and exterminating the other half, are accused of sympathizing exclusively with the blacks. We wonder what the writer would call sympathizing exclusively with the whites. We should have thought that the lives and liberties of a whole nation, were an ample sacrifice, for the sake of a slight, or rather, as the event has proved, an imaginary addition to the security of the property of a few West-India planters. This is, indeed, to abjure "canting philanthropy." What it is that the reviewer gives us in the place of it we leave to the reader to judge.

In the third volume there is a passage, in an article[*] on Millar's *View of the English Government*, where the writer, attempting to draw a character of Millar, thus expresses himself:

> There never was any mind, perhaps, less accessible to the illusions of that sentimental and ridiculous philanthropy which has led so many to the adoption of popular principles. He took a very cool and practical view of the condition of society, and neither wept over the imaginary miseries of the lower orders, nor shuddered at the imputed vices of the higher. (P. 158.)

By all in whom aristocratic bigotry has not extinguished every spark of candour or honesty, but one judgment can be passed upon a writer who can apply to the unmerited sufferings of the poor the appellation of "imaginary miseries," and who can insinuate that the "imputed vices" of the higher orders are imputed to them without foundation.

He continues, "While no man could be more convinced of the *incapacity and worthlessness of the clamorous multitude*, he thought that the indirect influence of

*[Brougham, "The Crisis of the Sugar Colonies,"] p. 227.

[*Jeffrey, "Millar's *View of the English Government*," *Edinburgh Review*, III (Oct., 1803), 154–81, reviewing John Millar, *An Historical View of the English Government*, 4 vols. (London: Mawman, 1803).]

public opinion was the only safeguard of our liberties."[*] Can Toryism go beyond this? The passage is, besides, an amusing specimen of see-saw. The attempt to unite contradictory opinions is more undisguised, less carefully wrapped up in vague and obscure language, than is usual with the *Edinburgh Review*. For the aristocracy, abuse is heaped upon the people, under the name of the "clamorous multitude;" for the people, the influence of public opinion is described as the only safeguard of our liberties: the opinion of that public which, in the preceding part of the very same sentence, is accused of incapacity and worthlessness.

The *Edinburgh Review* could have hoped for no success with the aristocracy, had it let slip any opportunity of possessing them with high ideas of their own importance to the community. We need not wonder, therefore, to find it describing a resident gentry as one of the greatest of all blessings; and one, of which the infallible consequence would be, "the improvement of their lands, and the improvement of their tenantry in morals, in comfort, and in industry." (Vol. V, p. 302; see also Vol. XXIV, p. 523; Vol. XXXIV, p. 326, *et passim*.)[†] There is only one thing of which the writer has neglected to inform us: how these most desirable effects are brought about. The tenants, at least, are not impressed with a due sense of them; for in Scotland (and the same, we suppose, would be found to be the case in England), a higher rent is commonly paid for a farm, when it is known that the proprietor is not to reside in the neighbourhood. It is a pity that so flattering a picture as the reviewer holds up to us, should differ so widely from the real state of the facts.*

The only remaining instance which space will permit us to notice, of the obloquy thrown upon the people by the *Edinburgh Review*, shall be selected from a very recent article on the Westminster Infant School.[‡]

The reviewer mentions with regret, that this establishment, though well attended so long as it continued a free school, had fallen off considerably when the payment of three pence a week was required. This he ascribes to "that vulgar feeling which makes the poor too often greedy at once, and ungrateful; expecting as a kind of right, what their richer neighbours give in charity, and almost thinking that whoever volunteers his services in their behalf, has a personal interest in their good, and should pay for his fancy." (P. 445.) We do not precisely see what the writer means. If he is finding fault with the poor, for not liking better to pay for what they want than to receive it gratis, we suspect it is a fault to which all men, not excepting even the reviewer himself, must plead guilty. But if he means to

[*Jeffrey, "Millar's *View*," p. 159.]

[†Anon., "Observations on the Residence of the Clergy," *Edinburgh Review*, V (Jan., 1805), 301–17; James Mackintosh, "France," *ibid.*, XXIV (Nov., 1814), 505–37; and Sydney Smith, "Ireland," *ibid.*, XXXIV (Nov., 1820), 320–38.]

*It is the less excusable in the *Edinburgh Review* to flatter this aristocratic prejudice, as from the general goodness of its political economy, it cannot be the dupe of the vulgar error that landlords benefit their estates by spending their money there.

[‡Brougham, "Early Moral Education," *ibid.*, XXXVIII (May, 1823), 437–53.]

insinuate, that they refrain from sending their children to the school, because they suspect the motives of the gentlemen who set it on foot, the absurdity is so palpable as scarcely to need a refutation. The idea that any one, in determining whether he will avail himself of a proffered benefit, is influenced by any other considerations than, first, whether it is really a benefit, and secondly, whether the cost does not exceed the advantage, almost provokes a laugh. In this instance, there can be no doubt as to the cause of the falling-off of the school. The parents uniformly evinced the acutest sensibility to the benefits they derived from it. But a great proportion of them were from the very poorest of the people, and really could not spare threepence a week, much less fourpence or sixpence. Mark, however, the uncandidness of the reviewer; he knew that some parents chose rather to withdraw their children, than to pay threepence a week. He knew also, that some parents formerly paid fourpence or sixpence a week to the dame schools. He immediately lays it down as certain, that these two classes of persons are the same; and on these premises he accuses the poor in general of giving a preference to the dame schools!

That the poor, in all countries, instead of erring on the side of distrust, have uniformly erred on the side of confidence, is proved by their habitual submission to misgovernment. Perhaps, if it were admitted that they are habitually suspicious of the rich, the influence would be more unfavourable to their superiors than to themselves. To borrow an illustration from another branch of morality; the veracity of that man must be more than suspected, whose word is disbelieved even when he speaks the truth. By the same rule, then, if the poor habitually suspect that the rich, when they profess to serve them, are really serving their own sinister purposes, the fair inference would be, not that these suspicious habits had grown up, as suspicious habits never were known to grow up, of themselves; but that, from the frequency with which the poor have seen their interests disregarded by the rich, they cannot bring themselves to repose any confidence in the professions which they hear from those rich, of a desire to serve them.*

The *Edinburgh Review* has pandered with as much perseverance to national as to aristocratic prejudices. English and excellent it employs as synonymous terms; that a foreigner admires England, is a sure passport to its praise; that he does not, is of itself sufficient to draw down upon him its censure. The habits and institutions of other nations are praised exactly in proportion as they approach to the English standard; blamed in proportion as they depart from it. On the other hand, the prejudices which prevail in this country against the French, are carefully nourished and fostered. Every opportunity is taken of showing how much the character and

*In another place, the reviewer quotes with approbation a passage from Pole, on Infant Schools, in which an attempt is made to account for this imputed suspiciousness, by a supposition of which it is difficult to say whether the candour or the liberality be most remarkable—"The poor scarcely know how to believe others can be actuated by dispositions so superior to what they have been accustomed to cherish in themselves." [Brougham, p. 453, quoting Thomas Pole, *Observations Relative to Infant Schools* (Bristol: Macdowall, 1823), p. 72.]

habits of that nation differ from excellence; meaning, of course, by excellence, the English habits and character. Sometimes, indeed, a torrent of mere abuse is poured out against the French, for the sole purpose of gratifying national antipathy.

We could fill a whole article with instances of these practices; but the few which we shall select are so flagrant, that any one who peruses them, will readily dispense with the remainder.

In an article in the second volume, on Dallas's *History of the Maroons*,[*] the writer, after very properly deprecating the use of bloodhounds in hunting down the insurgent slaves, adds the following note:

> If common fame may be credited, the French are at present engaged in a campaign against the St. Domingo rebels, with the aid of blood-hounds. Considering the nature of the consular government, and the wretched people over whom it is stretched, we cannot avoid being astonished at this measure having only now been adopted. [P. 384n.]

The consular government was not worse than any other despotism. Nevertheless, we should not object to the censure, were it levelled against the government alone. But why are the people held responsible for the cruelties of the government? For this reason, that when the above passage was written, the English aristocracy abhorred every thing French—the government as well as the people; but the people most: because they had incurred the guilt of throwing off despotism; the government only that of substituting one despotism for another. On any of the occasions on which the *Edinburgh Review* has declared the English ministers worthy of impeachment; on the occasion, for instance, of the Walcheren expedition—would they have dared to lay the guilt of the ministers at the door of the English people?[†] Yet the English people had as great a hand in the Walcheren expedition, as the French people had in the employment of blood-hounds in St. Domingo—a reflection which the reviewer probably thought not likely to occur to his anti-gallican readers.

An article on Dr. Black's *Lectures*, in the following Number,[‡] is remarkable for its offerings both to national antipathies and to national vanity. Upon the French men of science, the writer is peculiarly severe. He who could ascribe the invention of the most beautiful system of weights and measures ever yet known, to a combination of "innovating phrenzy and puerile vanity" [p. 22], must have sat down with a predetermination to find matter for censure. In his next charge he is almost equally unfortunate. Some French *savans*, it seems, in the warmth of their self-congratulation upon a most important discovery, had indulged in certain

[*Brougham, "Dallas's *History of the Maroons*," *Edinburgh Review*, II (July, 1803), 376–91, reviewing Robert Charles Dallas, *History of the Maroons*, 2 vols. (London: Longman and Rees, 1803).]

[†See Sydney Smith, "Walcheren Expedition," *Edinburgh Review*, XVII (Feb., 1811), 330–9.]

[‡Brougham, "Dr. Black's *Lectures*," *ibid.*, III (Oct., 1803), 1–26, reviewing Joseph Black, *Lectures on the Elements of Chemistry*, 2 vols. (London: Longman and Rees; Edinburgh: Creech, 1803).]

ludicrous ceremonies, repugnant indeed to English gravity, but of which the worst that can be said is, that they were a harmless piece of child's play:

When the Parisian chemists, it seems, had finished their grand experiment on the composition of water, they held a sort of festival, at which Madame Lavoisier, in the habit of a priestess, burnt Stahl's *Fundamenta* on an altar, while solemn music played a *requiem* to the departed system.*

We confess we do not see any thing very atrocious in this; and we suspect no one but an *Edinburgh* or a *Quarterly* reviewer would have thought of magnifying it into a proof of "that universal *charlatanerie* (the word cannot be translated by a people so destitute of the thing) which renders the French national character the least *respectable* of any in the civilized world." [P. 22.] John Bull, whose gullibility has been the subject of so many sarcasms, would no doubt feel agreeably surprised at being told that no such thing as *charlatanerie* is known in England. If he reflected, however, that this very England is the only country where a quack doctor ever succeeded, we fear he would feel inclined to doubt the sincerity of his panegyrist.

In another article in the same Number,[*] "a vicious and perverted love of obscenity" is described as "peculiarly and characteristically the disgrace of French literature." (P. 125.) In a subsequent article[†] this charge is repeated, and directed more peculiarly against Diderot, whose works are affirmed to be characterized by a peculiar and revolting kind of indecency. (P. 283.) We think it sufficient to appeal to the knowledge of any one who is well versed in French literature, whether there is as much indecency in any French writer of reputation—probably in any two French writers of reputation—as there is in Shakspeare alone; Shakspeare, whom the *Edinburgh Review* holds up as the *ne plus ultra* of literary excellence.[‡]

For some years, when the cry of the *Edinburgh Review* was for peace; to continue reviling the French, would have been to fight against its own object. In the more recent volumes, however, it has returned to its former practice, which it had never more than partially intermitted.

The charge of indecency against the French is one which it has thought proper frequently to repeat. At the end of an article in the thirty-first volume, on Madame d'Epinay's *Correspondence*, the writer observes—"But if all the decencies and delicacies of life were in one scale, and five francs in the other, what French bookseller would feel a single moment of doubt in making his election?"[§] Now, we take the case to be, that in this, as in most other respects, a French bookseller is

*Pp. 22–3. [The reference is to Georg Ernst Stahl, *Fundamenta chymiae dogmaticae et experimentalis*, 3 pts. (Nuremberg: Endter, 1723–32).]

[*Walter Scott, "*Amadis de Gaul*, [translations] by Southey and by Rose," *Edinburgh Review*, III (Oct., 1803), 109–36.]

[†Jeffrey, "Correspondance littéraire et philosophique de Grimm," *ibid.*, XXI (July, 1813), 263–99.]

[‡See, e.g., Jeffrey, "Hazlitt on Shakespeare," *ibid.*, XXVIII (Aug., 1817), 472–88.]

[§Sydney Smith, "Madame d'Epinay," *ibid.*, XXXI (Dec., 1818), 53, reviewing Louise Florence d'Epinay, *Mémoires et correspondance*, 3 vols. (Paris: Brunet, 1818).]

very like any other bookseller. The love of gain, we are apt to think, is not peculiar to the French people: and when a writer inveighs against a particular nation, for being acted upon by the same inducements which influence men all over the world, we are at no loss in what terms to characterize his conduct.

Three recent articles, one in the thirty-fourth, one in the thirty-fifth, and another in the thirty-seventh volume,[*] are devoted to the express purpose of extolling all English, and depreciating all French books and authors;* of extolling the morality, taste, and knowledge of the English public, and depreciating that of the French. The writer appears not to be aware, that there are two sides to a question. In as far as he is concerned, there is only one. On the English side he enumerates nothing but excellencies; on the French side, nothing but defects. As if this were not enough, he draws largely upon his imagination for fresh excellencies to be ascribed to the English, and fresh defects to the French. Not content with pronouncing in favour of the English national taste, on every point on which it differs from the French; he traces up all such differences to the superiority of the English over the French public—first in good sense, and next in morality. A detailed analysis of these articles would not convey an adequate conception of their spirit to those who have not read them, and would be superfluous to those who have. Our limits will admit only of one specimen. Flagrant as that specimen is, it is not the worst. He presents us with what is meant to be a parallel between the eminent men of the last half-century in England and France. With this view he makes a pompous display of all the English authors who have attained, during that period, any, even the smallest, share of celebrity; down to the merest party scribblers, or vulgar versifiers, and including many whose names we never heard before.[†] On the other hand, he sets up on the French side a sort of *index expurgatorius*, and instead of a page and a half of names pronounced worthy of immortality, he furnishes us with a list of authors whom he, by his fiat, consigns to oblivion [p. 180]. Among these are not only Jouy, Millevoye, and Raynouard, poets, to say the least, not inferior to many who are enumerated in the same article among the ornaments of the British nation; not only Ségur, Thouret, and Boissy d'Anglas, authors unquestionably far superior, both in liberality, in talents, and in style, to average English historians; but Say,—one of the few French writers who never sacrifices truth to display,—

[*Richard Chenevix, "State of Science in England and France," *Edinburgh Review*, XXXIV (Nov., 1820), 383–422; Chenevix, "English and French Literature," *ibid.*, XXXV (Mar., 1821), 158–90; and Chenevix and Jeffrey, "French Poetry," *ibid.*, XXXVII (Nov., 1822), 407–32.]

*It is not strictly correct to say that the *Edinburgh Review* depreciates *all* the French writers. Upon one of them—upon Montesquieu, it bestows even more than the due praise: but why? It almost confesses the reason—Montesquieu admired England. The English institutions were the standard by which Montesquieu judged of all other institutions. To eulogize Montesquieu, therefore, was one way of eulogizing England. [See Chenevix. "English and French Literature," pp. 169–70.]

†[Chenevix, "English and French Literature,"] pp. 184–5.

who is never led astray from the path of reason, by sentimentality, or by a taste for floridity and declamation,—Say, who first introduced the French nation to the true principles of political economy, and whose name will be mentioned with honour among the philosophers who have raised that important branch of knowledge to the rank of a science; he, too, is ranked among those "revolutionary worthies," who will be utterly forgotten in half a century, and the very ablest of whom "would find in this country, and at this moment, at the least ten persons of more ability than himself, yet whose names are absolutely unknown." (*Ibid.*)

If there is a fault with which French authors, collectively, can be charged (though even to this rule there are exceptions), it is declamation and sentimentality. And when we consider what has been the character of English literature since Johnson and Burke wrote,—when we see that, in this country, the meanest creature who can hold a pen aims at being eloquent, we cannot pronounce even declamation and sentimentality, though the common faults of French writers, to be characteristic of French literature. Observe that these, the only faults which can be justly ascribed to the French authors generally, are almost the only faults which have not been ascribed to them by the *Edinburgh Review*. This is not wonderful, considering of what stamp some of the works have been upon which the *Edinburgh Review* has been the most prodigal of its praise;* and considering also the examples of declamation and sentimentality with which its pages abound.

The sentiments which the *Edinburgh Review* has put forth concerning female character, are as little creditable to itself, and exemplify as completely the characteristic malady of periodical literature, as any which we have yet quoted.

He who is restrained by indolence from improving himself, has a direct interest in preventing the improvement of others; since, if others improve, and he does not keep pace with them, he must necessarily lose his rank in their estimation. But he is most of all interested in the non-improvement of his wife. For he thinks, and he believes that others think, that he ought to be her guardian and protector: to rely, therefore, upon her for protection and guidance, instead of extending it to her, is more than usually humiliating. There is another and a very powerful motive, which renders ordinary men averse to instructed women. Every man desires that his wife should prefer him, and prefer him beyond comparison, to all other men. But if she is capable of discriminating between merit and no merit, she will not reserve for her husband alone that admiration which ought to be given wherever it is deserved;

*For instance, Alison's *Sermons*; Hazlitt's Lectures on the Drama; Madame De Staël's Work on Germany, &c. [See Jeffrey, "Alison's *Sermons*," *Edinburgh Review*, XXIII (Sept., 1814), 424–40, reviewing Archibald Alison, *Sermons* (Edinburgh: Constable; London: Longman, *et al.*, 1814); Thomas Noon Talfourd, "Hazlitt's Lectures on the Drama," *Edinburgh Review*, XXXIV (Nov., 1820), 438–49, reviewing William Hazlitt, *Lectures Chiefly on the Dramatic Literature of the Age of Elizabeth* (London: Stodart and Steuart, 1820); and James Mackintosh, "*De l'Allemagne*, par Madame de Staël," *Edinburgh Review*, XXII (Oct., 1813), 198–238, reviewing *De l'Allemagne*, 3 vols. (Paris: Nicolle, 1810).]

and if he is neither wiser nor better than others, he will not, by her, be rated higher, or valued more.

To these causes must be ascribed the morality which is usually chalked out for women. It is a sort of morality, the prevalence of which it would be difficult to account for in any other way. The qualities which are said to constitute excellence in a woman, are very different from those which constitute excellence in a man. It is considered meritorious in a man to be independent: to be sufficient to himself; not to be in a constant state of pupillage. In a woman, helplessness, both of mind and of body, is the most admired of attributes. A man is despised, if he be not courageous. In a woman, it is esteemed amiable to be a coward. To be entirely dependant upon her husband for every pleasure, and for exemption from every pain; to feel secure, only when under his protection; to be incapable of forming any opinion, or of taking any resolution without his advice and aid; this is amiable, this is delicate, this is feminine: while all who infringe on any of the prerogatives which man thinks proper to reserve for himself; all who can or will be of any use, either to themselves or to the world, otherwise than as the slaves and drudges of their husbands, are called masculine, and other names intended to convey disapprobation. Even they who profess admiration for instructed women, not unfrequently select their own wives from among the ignorant and helpless.

That the *Edinburgh Review* has never stood up manfully to resist this prejudice, is in itself no trifling charge. But it has done more: it has repeatedly given a direct sanction to it. Madame De Staël, Miss Edgeworth, and other eminent women, were to be praised; it could not, therefore, in distinct terms, number incapacity among female virtues. But it could say, "Shakspeare has expressed the very perfection of the feminine character, existing only for others, and leaning for support on the strength of its affections."* A character which has nothing to lean upon but the strength of its affections, must be a helpless character indeed. This is vague enough; and, like almost every thing which the *Edinburgh Review* says in defence of prejudices, admits of being explained away. The tendency of it, however, is manifest; and it is equally evident, that the vague language in which it is wrapped up, only serves to render it the more pernicious, by inveigling many into assent, who would shrink from the proposition, if presented to them in its naked deformity.

Such additional remarks as our limits will admit of shall be devoted to illustrate the morality of the *Edinburgh Review*.

This, it might be thought, is a labour which, after the specimens already exhibited, might be spared. What can be more immoral than the see-saw? a practice which is, throughout, a mere sacrifice of truth to convenience: a practice which habituates its votaries to play fast and loose with opinions—to lay down

*[William Hazlitt, "Schlegel on the Drama," *Edinburgh Review*,] XXVI [(Feb., 1816)], 103.

one, and take up another, with every change of audience? Can there be a spectacle more repugnant to that candour and sincerity which are so essential a part of morality, than a continual attempt to varnish over inconsistencies, and to reconcile in appearance doctrines which are really irreconcileable? What immorality, again, can exceed that of pandering to those prejudices which render one nation the enemy of another, or one portion of the people the enemy of the mass?

In the Whig morality, however, as delivered in the *Edinburgh Review*, there are some features which call for a more detailed examination.

In the following passage, extracted from an article in the twentieth volume on Leckie's View of the English Government,[*] we have a tolerable specimen of the sort of conduct which answers to the Whig ideas of public virtue:

Parties are necessary in all free governments—and are indeed the characteristics by which such governments may be known. One party, that of the rulers of the court, is necessarily formed and disciplined from the permanence of its chief, and the uniformity of the interests it has to maintain—the party in opposition, therefore, must be marshalled in the same way. When bad men combine, good men must unite—and it would not be less hopeless for a crowd of worthy citizens to take the field without leaders or discipline, against a regular army, than for individual patriots to think of opposing the influence of the sovereign by their separate and uncombined exertions. As to the lengths which they should be permitted to go in support of the common cause, or the extent to which each ought to submit his private opinion to the general sense of his associates, it does not appear to us—though casuists may mask dishonour, and purists startle at shadows—either that any man of upright feelings can be at a loss for a rule of conduct, or that, in point of fact, there has ever been any blameable excess in the maxims upon which our parties in this country have been generally conducted. The leading principle is, that a man should satisfy himself that the party to which he attaches himself means well to the country, and that more substantial good will accrue to the nation from its coming into power, than from the success of any other body of men whose success is at all within the limits of probability.—Upon this principle, therefore, he will support that party in all things which he approves—in all things that are indifferent—and even in some things which he partly disapproves, provided they neither touch the honour and vital interests of the country, nor imply any breach of the ordinary rules of morality.—Upon the same principle he will attack not only all that he individually disapproves in the conduct of the adversary, but all that might appear indifferent and tolerable enough to a neutral spectator, if it afford an opportunity to weaken him in the public opinion, and to increase the chance of bringing that party into power from which alone he sincerely believes that any sure or systematic good is to be expected. Farther than this we do not believe that the leaders or respectable followers of any considerable party, intentionally allow themselves to go. (Pp. 343–4.)

Observe the course which is here chalked out for a public man. The first thing he has to do is to choose a party. As he is to fix his choice upon the party of whose measures he approves, one would think he ought to stand by it so long as he approves of its measures, and no longer. Such would be the dictate of honesty; but

[*Jeffrey, "Leckie on the British Government," *ibid.*, XX (Nov., 1812), 315–46, reviewing Gould Francis Leckie, *Essay on the Practice of the British Government* (London: Valpy, 1812).]

such is not the dictate of the *Edinburgh Review*. To stand by it in all things which he approves, in all things which are indifferent, and in some things which he disapproves: this is the Whig morality. By supporting it in things which he approves, he is only doing what he might have done, and kept, notwithstanding, perfectly clear from the trammels of party. The only thing peculiar to the party system, is the obligation to stand by his party in things which are indifferent, and in things which he disapproves. Observe, now, what this implies. To support the party in things which are indifferent, he must profess to believe them not to be indifferent. To support the party in things which he disapproves, he must, where he really disapproves, profess to approve. He must pretend to hold, and act as if he held, opinions directly contrary to his real opinions.

Another rule of party morality is pretty clearly expressed in the foregoing passage—"He will attack not only all that he individually disapproves in the conduct of the adversary, but all that might appear indifferent and tolerable enough to a neutral spectator, if it afford an opportunity to weaken him in the public opinion." For the sake of weakening the minister in the public opinion, a deception is to be practised upon the public: means are to be used for misleading them, by instilling into them a false opinion, by persuading them that the minister has acted wrong, when in truth he has acted right. We presume it would be meritorious to invent any convenient sophism which should have the effect of furthering so laudable an object.

The reader will do well to peruse, as a specimen of the Whig style of argument, an elaborate article on the state of parties in the thirtieth volume, in which all this jesuitry is vindicated under the name of concert and co-operation.[*] The ministry—such is the language—have an organized and well-disciplined body of adherents constantly at their devotion: when bad men combine, good men must unite; and in this, as in every thing else, small things must be yielded for the sake of great ones.

Let us bear in mind what sort of "concert" it is, which is here recommended: a concert which consists in opposing the ministry when they are right, supporting the opposition when they are wrong: a concert of which the fundamental principle is, that every thing to which the majority of the party is favourable, shall be supported by the whole; every thing to which the majority is adverse, opposed by the whole. To call this "yielding in small things for the sake of great ones,"[†] is to beg the question. There are sufficient reasons to make it certain that the yielding will be precisely in those things which are the most important of all.

While public men continue to be, what public men, with few exceptions, are at present, so little versed in the science of human nature, so little skilled in predicting effects from their causes; excessive timidity must be, in the great majority of cases, the governing principle of their conduct. A short-sighted man is ever timid. He

[*Brougham, "State of Parties," *Edinburgh Review*, XXX (June, 1818), 181–206.]
[†*Ibid.*, p. 187.]

sees that, under the present system, person and property are to a certain degree secure. Change the system, and he knows not what will happen. Not knowing what will happen, he fears the worst. And though he dreads great changes most, his opposition extends even to the smallest. Innovation once begun, though it be but in a trifle, he knows not when or where it will end.

In the present situation of Great Britain, and of all countries in Europe, extensive and searching reforms are imperatively required. All half measures are useless, with reference to the production of any great or permanent good. To effect extensive and searching reforms, boldness and decision are absolutely necessary. Boldness and decision, however, are qualities, in which, for the reasons which we have stated, the public men of the present day, at least the great majority of them, are, of necessity, and to a lamentable degree, deficient. All decisive measures, therefore, are sure to meet with opposition at their hands. They never venture to strike at the root of the evil. Some miserable palliative is all they dare to apply. It is to the more manly and clear-sighted alone, that the advocate of effectual improvement must look for support. Here, however, the evils of the party system are most clearly shown. The clear-sighted and manly, who would have been instruments of good, become instruments of mischief. Instead of aiding effectual improvement, they are compelled to oppose it. They are dragged down to the level of the meanest animal who can give a vote; they dare not advance a step without *his* previous sanction; they are pressed into the service of every abuse which he in his wisdom may consider it unsafe to remove.

This is to "yield in small things for the sake of great ones." But what are the great ones? What is the end, for which every thing which is of most importance, and almost every thing which is of any importance, is to be sacrificed? Simply the displacement of the ministry: an important object, we admit, to those who hope to succeed them; but would it be of any benefit to the people? Even on the principles of the *Edinburgh Review* it would not. For if the removal of a particular set of ministers is of so much importance, that ministry must have been guilty of immense mischief: of what sort then must be the constitution which permitted them to do so? And if the constitution be such as not to prevent an abuse of trust, by what right does the opposition lay claim to more confidence than the ministry?

When such is the state of the question; to talk of the necessity of concert, is to talk in the air. No one is more sensible of the necessity of concert than ourselves. Not that sort of concert which consists in speaking and voting on one side, thinking and feeling on the other—but a concert which involves no sacrifice of principle—a concert for mutual aid among those who agree, without imposing fetters upon those who differ; a concert, in short, not for men, but for measures. All would then co-operate, where all were agreed; and the advocate of bold and decisive measures—of the only measures which in the present state of the world can be of great or permanent utility; would have the support of every sincere man whom he could convince.

Even though it had not been in our power to quote, as we have done, from the pages of the *Edinburgh Review*, explicit declarations in favour of bad morality—the morality of party—that Review would still have been far from blameless on the moral score. There is such a thing as negative immorality—there is the immoral by omission; and of this it stands convicted out of its own mouth. Witness the following extracts from an article in the twenty-first volume.[*] In what respect does a moral work differ from one which is not moral? In aiming at rendering mankind wiser and better. What, then are we to think of a publication which declares all improvement in wisdom and in virtue, to be hopeless?

All knowledge which admits of demonstration will advance, we have no doubt, and extend itself; and all processes will be improved, that do not interfere with the passions of human nature, or the apparent interest of its ruling classes. But with regard to every thing depending on probable reasoning, or susceptible of debate, and especially with regard to every thing touching morality and enjoyment, we really are not sanguine enough to reckon on any considerable improvement; and suspect that men will go on blundering in speculation and transgressing in practice, pretty nearly as they do at present, to the latest period of their history. (P. 12.)

Then follows a series of paragraphs to corroborate this assertion. We copy one or two of them. They throw some light upon the logic as well as upon the morality of the *Edinburgh Review*.

Take the case, for example, of war—by far the most prolific and extensive pest of the human race, whether we consider the sufferings it inflicts, or the happiness it prevents—and see whether it is likely to be arrested by the progress of intelligence and civilization. In the first place, it is manifest, that instead of becoming less frequent or destructive, in proportion to the rapidity of that progress, our European wars have been incomparably more constant, and more sanguinary, since Europe became signally enlightened and humanized,—and that they have uniformly been most obstinate and most popular in its most polished countries. The brutish Laplanders, and bigotted and profligate Italians, have had long intervals of repose; but France and England are now pretty regularly at war for about fourscore years out of every century. In the second place, the lovers and conductors of war are by no means the most ferocious or stupid of their species,—but for the most part the very contrary;—and their delight in it, notwithstanding their compassion for human suffering, and their complete knowledge of its tendency to produce suffering, seems to us sufficient almost of itself to discredit the confident prediction of those who assure us, that when men have attained to a certain degree of intelligence, war must necessarily cease among all the nations of the earth. There can be no better illustration indeed, than this, of the utter futility of all those dreams of perfectibility, which are founded on a radical ignorance of what it is that constitutes the real enjoyment of human nature, and upon the play of how many principles and opposite *stimuli* that happiness depends, which, it is absurdly imagined, would be found in the mere negation of suffering, or in a state of Quakerish placidity, dulness, and uniformity. Men delight in war, in spite of the pains and miseries which it entails upon them and their fellows, because it exercises all the talents, and calls out all the energies of their nature—because it holds

[*Jeffrey, "Madame de Staël—sur la littérature," *Edinburgh Review*, XXI (Feb., 1813), 1–50, reviewing Anne Louise Germaine de Staël-Holstein, *De la littérature considérée dans ses rapports avec les institutions sociales*, 2nd ed., 2 vols. (Paris and London: Colburn, 1812).]

them out conspicuously as the objects of public sentiment and general sympathy—because it gratifies their pride of art, and gives them a lofty sentiment of their own power, worth, and courage,—but principally because it sets the game of existence upon a higher stake, and dispels, by its powerful interest, those feelings of *ennui* which steal upon every condition from which hazard and anxiety are excluded, and drive us into danger and suffering as a relief. While human nature continues to be distinguished by those attributes, we do not see any chance of war being superseded by the increase of wisdom and morality. We should be pretty well advanced in the career of perfectibility if all the inhabitants of Europe were as intelligent, and upright, and considerate, as sir John Moore, or lord Nelson, or lord Wellington,—but we should not have the less war, we take it, with all its attendant miseries. The more wealth, and intelligence, and liberty, there is in a country, indeed, the greater love there will be for war;—for a gentleman is uniformly a more pugnacious animal than a plebeian, and a free man than a slave. The case is the same with the minor contentions that agitate civil life, and shed abroad the bitter waters of political animosity, and grow up into the rancours and atrocities of faction and cabal. The actors in these scenes are not the lowest or most debased characters in the country,—but, almost without exception, of the very opposite description. It would be too romantic to suppose that the whole population of any country should ever be raised to the level of Fox and Pitt, Burke, Windham, or Grattan; and yet, if that miraculous improvement were to take place, we know that they would be at least as far from agreeing, as they are at present; and may fairly conclude, that they would contend with far greater warmth and animosity.

For that great class of evils, therefore, which arise from contention, emulation, and diversity of opinion upon points which admit of no solution, it is evident that the general increase of intelligence would afford no remedy; and there even seems to be reason for thinking, that it would increase their amount. If we turn to the other great source of human suffering, the abuse of power and wealth, and the other means of enjoyment, we suspect we shall not find any ground for indulging in more sanguine expectations. Take the common case of youthful excess and imprudence, for example, in which the evil commonly rests on the head of the transgressor,—the injury done to fortune, by thoughtless expense—to health and character, by sensual indulgence, and to the whole felicity of after-life, by rash and unsorted marriages. The whole mischief and hazard of such practices, we are per-suaded, is just as thoroughly known and understood at present, as it will be when the world is five thousand years older; and as much pains are taken to impress the ardent spirits of youth with the belief of those hazards, as can well be taken by the monitors who may discharge that office in the most remote futurity. The truth is, that the offenders do not offend so much in ignorance, as in presumption. They know very well, that men are oftener ruined than enriched at the gaming table; and that love marriages, clapt up under age, are frequently followed by divorces: But they know, too, that this is not always the case; and they flatter themselves that their good luck, and good judgment, will class them among the exceptions, and not among the ordinary examples of the rule. They are told well enough, for the most part, of the excessive folly of acting upon such a presumption in matters of serious importance:—But it is the nature of youth to despise much of the wisdom that is pressed upon them, and to think well of their fortune and sagacity, till they have actually had experience of their slipperiness. We really have no idea that their future teachers will be able to change this nature; or to destroy the eternal distinction between the character of early and mature life; and therefore it is that we despair of the cure of the manifold evils that spring from this source; and remain persuaded, that young men will be nearly as foolish, and as incapable of profiting by the experience of their seniors, ten thousand years hence, as they are at this moment.

With regard to the other glittering curses of life—the heartless dissipations—the cruel seductions—the selfish extravagance—the rejection of all interesting occupation or serious affection, which blast the splendid summit of human fortune with perpetual barrenness and discomfort—we can only say, that as they are miseries which exist almost exclusively among the most polished and intelligent of the species, we do not think it very probable, at least, that they will be eradicated by rendering the species more polished and intelligent. They are not occasioned, we think, by ignorance or improper education; but by that eagerness for strong emotion and engrossing occupation, which still proclaim it to be the genuine and irreversible destiny of man to earn his bread by the sweat of his brows. It is a fact indeed rather perplexing and humiliating to the advocates of perfectibility, that as soon as a man is delivered from the necessity of subsisting himself, and providing for his family, he generally falls into a state of considerable unhappiness; and, if some fortunate anxiety, or necessity for exertion, does not come to his relief, is generally obliged to seek for a slight and precarious distraction in vicious and unsatisfactory pursuits. It is not for want of knowing that they are unsatisfactory that he persists in them, nor for want of being told of their folly and criminality;—for moralists and divines have been occupied with little else for the best part of a century; and writers of all descriptions, indeed, have charitably expended a good part of their own *ennui* in copious directions for the innocent and effectual reduction of that common enemy. In spite of all this, however, the malady has increased with our wealth and refinement, and has brought along with it the increase of all those vices and follies in which its victims still find themselves constrained to seek a temporary relief. The truth is, that military and senatorial glory is neither within the reach, nor suited to the taste, of any very great proportion of the sufferers; and that the cultivation of waste lands, and the superintendence of tippling-houses and charity-schools, have not always been found such effectual and delightful remedies as the inditers of godly romances have sometimes represented. So that those whom fortune has cruelly exempted from the necessity of doing any thing, have been led very generally to do evil of their own accord, and have fancied that they rather diminished than added to the sum of human misery, by engaging in intrigues and gaming-clubs, and establishing coteries for detraction or sensuality. (Pp. 14–17.)

We must call the attention of our readers to one short passage more.

There will be improvements, we make no doubt, in all the mechanical and domestic arts;—better methods of working metal, and preparing cloth;—more commodious vehicles, and more efficient implements of war. Geography will be made more complete, and astronomy more precise;—natural history will be enlarged and digested;—and perhaps some little improvement suggested in the forms of administering law. But as to any general enlargement of the understanding, or more prevailing vigour of judgment, we will own, that the tendency seems to be all the other way; and that we think strong sense, and extended views of human affairs, are more likely to be found, and to be listened to at this moment, than two or three hundred years hereafter. (P. 21.)

We are here told, not obscurely, but distinctly—not indirectly, but in as many words—that morality will never be better understood than at present; that morality will never be better practised than at present; that mankind will never be more prudent than they now are; that vigour of intellect and sound views of human affairs are oftener found and better listened to at this moment, than they are likely to be at any future period.

This is a bold attempt to catch the favour of aristocracy, by affording a new pretext for checking the diffusion of knowledge. In the mean time, how gross is the hypocrisy of which, by its own confession, the *Edinburgh Review* must have been guilty, as often as it has cried out, and it has cried out often, for the instruction, and, above all, for the moral instruction of the people! We think also, that it may fairly be asked, by what title a work which sets out by assuming the impossibility of human improvement, can be supposed to have human improvement at heart, or to have any object whatever in view, beyond the mere temporary amusement of its readers?

And, indeed, if the value which a writer sets upon morality can be gathered from the judgments which he passes upon other writers, the *Edinburgh Review* has not traced its own portrait with too severe a pencil.

The examples which we shall adduce of this part of its character are not to be viewed as isolated instances, but as illustrative of its general practice. To be over-partial to this or that writer is a trifling offence. But habitually to bestow praise, not upon one production only, but upon many, without for a moment adverting to their moral tendency, implies a state of mind on which we shall leave the reader to his own reflections.

We shall select, as our first instance, the tenor of its criticism upon Shakspeare: if that can be called criticism, where all is unmingled admiration.

No one, we suppose, will dispute to Johnson the title of an admirer of Shakspeare, though not, perhaps, an admirer to the taste of the *Edinburgh Review*: for he contented himself with being the ablest and most successful of the eulogists of Shakspeare as a poet; and did not, as some have done, hold him up as a perfect teacher of morality also.

His first defect, [says Johnson,] is that to which may be imputed most of the evil in books or in men. He sacrifices virtue to convenience, and is so much more careful to please than to instruct, that he seems to write without any moral purpose. From his writings, indeed, a system of social duty may be selected, for he that thinks reasonably must think morally; but his precepts and axioms drop casually from him; he makes no just distribution of good or evil, nor is always careful to show in the virtuous a disapprobation of the wicked: he carries his persons indifferently through right and wrong, and at the close dismisses them without further care, and leaves their examples to operate by chance. This fault the barbarity of his age cannot extenuate; for it is always a writer's duty to make the world better, and justice is a virtue independent on time and place.*

We should be sorry to be suspected of affecting prudery. It is one thing to be a moralist, another thing to be a poet; and a high degree of excellence in the one capacity is not incompatible with great deficiency in the other. But we assert that in a species of writing which admits so easily of being made subservient to morality, to be without a moral object is one of the greatest of defects; and we do say, that amid all the praises which the *Edinburgh Review* has lavished upon Shakspeare, its never having uttered even a wish that the moral tendency of his plays had been more decided, gives the lie direct to all its professions of zeal for morality. But the *Edinburgh Review* is written for Englishmen: Shakspeare is the idol of English-

---

*[Samuel] Johnson's "Preface to Shakspeare," in his *Works*. Ed. 1806 [12 vols. (London: Johnson, *et al.*)], Vol. II, pp. 146–7.

men: Shakspeare, therefore, must be praised, and for the more complete satisfaction of his admirers, all his merits must be exaggerated, and all his demerits must be sunk. To render men wiser or better is but a secondary concern: to please the public taste, is the first.

If to write without a moral purpose be a fault which the barbarity even of Shakspeare's age cannot extenuate, we presume it will be held to be still less excusable in Sir Walter Scott. He too shows no decided leaning between virtue and vice. There is no one of his productions from which, unless it be by chance, any one useful lesson can be derived. It is impossible to peruse them without being convinced that amusement, and amusement only, is there studied. This highly-gifted author, is, like Shakspeare, an object of admiration to the *Edinburgh Review*;[*] but not, like Shakspeare, of unqualified admiration. It has not judged him faultless; it has found defects; other defects, but never that of wanting a moral purpose; never has it abated, on this account, one iota of its praise; never for a moment has it lamented that his productions were not useful, as well as agreeable.

This indifference to the moral tendency of a work is perfectly consistent with the declaration of the *Edinburgh Review*, that the human race is without the capacity of moral improvement. But it forms a notable contrast with the scrupulosity which the same Review has assumed, when opprobrium is to be heaped upon an unpopular writer: upon Voltaire, for example: towards whom it seems to think that it is scarcely possible to be too foul-mouthed. "To him, more than to any other individual, the eighteenth century owes, we fear, its crimes."* Such is its ordinary language. Yet it cannot be said of Voltaire as it can of Shakspeare, that virtue and vice appear to be nearly indifferent in his eyes. He was even remarkable for the contrary quality. With Voltaire, even in his lighter pieces, to make the reader wiser and better is the consideration to which all others are subordinate. It is the part, not of moralists, but of bigots, to be blinded by the irreligious tendency of some of his writings, to the transcendant importance of the services which he rendered to mankind. It is the characteristic of fanaticism to find nothing which is not odious in the objects of its pious abhorrence. As to the hackneyed charge of licentiousness, we do not hesitate to meet it with a direct contradiction. Excepting, perhaps, the *Pucelle d'Orleans*,[†] one of his earlier productions, and published, as is well known, not only without his consent, but against his will—bring together all the licentious passages in all his voluminous works—set them against the indecencies of a single play of Shakspeare—and let any man of common candor and honesty be judge between them. But the besetting sin of Voltaire was, that he waged war against aristocratic prejudices. This it is which has drawn upon him the hatred of

[*See, e.g., Jeffrey, "Scott's *Marmion: A Poem*," *Edinburgh Review*, XII (Apr., 1808), 1–35; and Jeffrey, "*Ivanhoe*," *ibid.*, XXXIII (Jan., 1820), 1–54.]

*[Chenevix, "English and French Literature,"] p. 171.

[†In *Oeuvres complètes*, 66 vols. (Paris: Renouard, 1817–25), Vol. IX.]

the aristocracy; this it is, which constitutes his title to the reproaches of the *Edinburgh Review.*

There is one part of the language of the *Edinburgh Review* concerning morals, on which it is necessary to offer a few remarks: as it might otherwise lead to the supposition, that we have been guilty of misrepresentation; that our accusation against it, of a disregard for morality, is untrue; that far from showing disregard, it has gone into the opposite extreme. This might be said, and, at first sight, with some appearance of truth. It is no doubt true, that there is one branch of morals on which it has affected even prudery. Of this we gave some instances in our former number.[*] We could point out many articles, which, as examples of what is termed cant, have, we think, rarely been surpassed. Of such a kind are the various articles on Moore's amatory poetry. Even the ancients are considered very immoral, if their ideas, on this branch of morality, do not precisely correspond with those of the *Edinburgh Review.** In the second volume, there is a long *tirade* against the morality of Anacreon;[†] and at a later period Plato is represented as exceedingly wicked, for having expounded, in his *Republic*, the footing upon which he thought that the marriage contract could most advantageously be placed.[‡] Still more recently Mr. Edgeworth is blamed for having informed the world, in his posthumous memoirs, of his successive marriage of two sisters, that is, for not having made himself appear to the world other than what he really was.[§]

That one offence is at all palliated by committing another, is what we cannot admit. Among all conceivable methods of atoning for the offence of leaving all other virtues to shift for themselves—to lay an excessive and disproportionate stress upon those which are of least importance to society, is surely the most extraordinary. Why this class of acts is thus exalted above all others, one obvious consideration will go far to explain. This is a branch of morality of which the priests have been suffered, for their own purposes, to assume the regulation: and they have accordingly laid down, not that system of rules which is most conducive to the well-being of the two sexes, or of society at large; but that which is best calculated to promote *their* ascendancy. To these virtues, therefore—the virtues of

[*See James Mill, "Periodical Literature: *Edinburgh Review*," pp. 230–1.]

*[Jeffrey, "Moore's *Poems*," *Edinburgh Review*,] VIII [(July, 1806)], 456–63, *et passim.*

†[John Eyre, "Moore's Translation of Anacreon," *ibid.*, II (July, 1803),] 463–4.

‡[Anon., "Memoirs, etc. of Sir Thomas More," *ibid.*,] XIV [(July, 1809)], 367, *et passim.* [See Plato, *Republic* (Greek and English), trans. Paul Shorey, 2 vols. (London: Heinemann; Cambridge, Mass.: Harvard University Press, 1946), Vol. I, pp. 448–68 (Bk. V, 456–61).]

§[Jeffrey, "Edgeworth's *Memoirs*," *Edinburgh Review*,] XXXIV [(Aug., 1820)], 122 [reviewing Richard Lovell Edgeworth, *Memoirs*, 2 vols. (London: Hunter, and Baldwin, Cradock, and Joy, 1820); the two sisters were Honora and Elizabeth Sneyd].

priestcraft—the aristocracy clings, as the firmest support of the consecrated prop: and that the *Edinburgh Review*, habituated as it is to disregard inconsistencies, should, notwithstanding its declaration that mankind can never be made better, have gone to the full length of the prevailing cant on these subjects, can to us, after what we have seen of that Review, be matter of no surprise.

On the only remaining feature of its morality upon which we shall at present insist—its sentimentality—our limits necessarily compel us to be brief. All, however, which it is absolutely necessary to say, may, we think, be said in few words.

There is a class of persons who rest their claims to admiration, not upon any thing which they have done to benefit mankind, or even that portion of mankind with whom they are immediately in contact, but upon the possession of fine feelings and acute sensibility. They would have us believe them emancipated from all the chains which attach other mortals to the earth. To the acquisition of wealth and power, they would willingly persuade us that they are indifferent; and the pleasures of sense have no charms for them. Not satisfied with this, they insist that all others shall feel exactly as they profess to feel. Gross, sordid, grovelling, are the mildest of the epithets which they deal out against all who set any value upon the ordinary objects of human desire. To think of himself, is an offence which they can pardon in no man. Virtuous creatures! In their minds, all sordid and selfish considerations are swallowed up in the intensity of their tenderness for their fellow-men. So strong are their sympathies, so distressing their sensibility, that their reason is completely mastered, and it would be as impossible for them to withstand the irresistible strength of their emotions, as to resist the action of the elements, or to overcome the force of gravitation. It may be very fine, they admit, to be able to sit down coolly and weigh the consequences to ourselves and to others, of every thing that we do: for their parts, they never could bring themselves to endure so cold and calculating a process. What they regard with the greatest horror of all, is to look after our own interest. Many of them go so far as to stigmatise the virtue of prudence by name. But to reflect, though it be only on the best mode of serving others, though not altogether so heinous, is still considered very unfeeling; and unfeeling, with them, is synonymous with wicked. Their hearts revolt at the idea of subjecting all the refined feelings of our nature to a heartless calculation of public utility, and restraining the indulgence of every generous emotion, until every item of good and evil which can result from it, is weighed and appreciated. Does a fellow-creature in distress stand before them? The frigid systems of philosophers may teach that, in giving alms, they are encouraging idleness and improvidence, and inevitably creating more distress than they relieve. This may be very true, they allow; but heartless indeed must be the man whose hand would be stayed by such considerations! When a crime has been committed, they regulate the quantum of punishment, not according as more or less is necessary for the future prevention of the offence, but according as they do or do not sympathise with the offender. In the former case, they can scarcely endure that any punishment should be inflicted at all. They complain bitterly of the cruelty of the law, and sometimes even of law in general: they are continually placing justice and humanity in opposition, and lauding to the skies injustice under the name of mercy. On the other hand, is the offence of a sort with which they do not sympathise (and both their sympathies and antipathies are in the highest degree capricious and unreasonable), then no infliction appears too severe. Their virtuous horror of crime cannot descend to compute the exact amount of punishment which the nature of the case requires: of what consequence to them are a few degrees more or less of suffering endured by a criminal? They have another curious method of showing the intensity of their sympathies. This is, to make violent demonstrations of feeling on occasions on which practical good sense would tell them that there is no demand for more than ordinary emotion. They will not indeed submit to more labours and privations than other people, for the relief of distressed fellow-creatures: but they make amends by whining over them more.

It is not difficult to trace this sort of affectation to its cause. It originates in the common practice of bestowing upon *feelings* that praise which actions alone can deserve. By properly regulating his actions, a man becomes a blessing to his species. His mere feelings are a matter of consummate indifference to them. And who will say that praise is well bestowed on that which by no possibility can be of any use whatever? Not to mention that nothing is so easily counterfeited as feeling, and that the most intense demonstrations of it are not inconsistent with the total absence of the reality; what can be more absurd than to praise a man because he has a feeling; to praise him because he has something which he can no more help having, than he can help having ten fingers, or two feet, and which, for any good which it does, he might as well not have at all. The effect is, to create fictitious virtues, and thus to hold out the means of atonement for the absence of real ones; to render it possible, nay easy, to obtain a reputation for virtue, without the trouble of deserving it. Whether this is likely to give any great encouragement to real virtue, is a question which we may fairly leave it to the reader to determine.

There is a class of moralists, however, and this class unhappily includes almost all who have written on the subject of morals, who, instead of correcting, make it their business to find excuses for, the sort of persons whom we have described. To benefit mankind is, in their eyes, a secondary merit; since it is possible to benefit mankind without having fine feelings. So far do they carry this perversion of the moral sanction, that even when they bestow praise upon actions, it is not according as those actions are useful, but according to the motives which they conjecture to have influenced the actors. Another inference from their doctrine is, that to think of consequences, instead of being essential to virtue, is inconsistent with it: a man of fine feelings ought to take those feelings exclusively for his guide: and there is no one so virtuous as he who disregards consequences altogether.

That this is altogether a false doctrine, and that it is, moreover, an exceedingly pernicious doctrine, must be apparent to every one who thinks that the happiness of mankind is at least deserving of some little regard, and is not altogether to be left out of the consideration, when the fine feelings of sentimentalists are in question.

The above description may perhaps appear exaggerated, as applied to the *Edinburgh Review*. But it must be remembered that we have been describing an extreme case. There is probably no one who carries the sentimental principle to its full extent, but some carry it further than others. There is a certain average rate of sentimentality, which may be considered habitual among ordinarily educated English gentlemen. A periodical publication is interested in going to the full length of the existing prejudices; but it lies under no inducement to go beyond them. Whenever any one carries sentimentality beyond the average rate, he is assailed by the *Edinburgh Review* with the double weapon of argument and ridicule. Witness its articles on the poets of the Wordsworth school, on Karamsin's *Travels*, Kotzebue's *Travels*, Montgomery's *Poems*, Goethe's *Life*, and many other works.* But this is only when it has the reader on its side. It will never do any thing to set the reader right—to correct his errors—to overcome his prejudices. When he is right already, it will be right along with him: a poor merit!

In a very early article, which we have already had occasion to quote, we find the following explicit declaration in favour of the *principle* of sentimentality:

Is it by such a reference, made by cautious deductions in every situation of public feeling, that generosity, patriotism, and all the devotions of benevolence, are to be fostered into habits? We blame the system of those calculators of the general good, who prohibit the indulgence of any sentiment of affection, until we have compared it, as to its result, with every other feeling.†

*We quote the following passage to show the light in which the *Edinburgh Review* regards all *unusual* affectation of strong and fine feelings:

"Mr. [James] Montgomery is one of the most musical and melancholy fine gentlemen we have lately descried on the lower slopes of Parnassus. He is very weakly, very finical, and very affected. His affectations, too, are the most usual, and the most offensive, of those that are commonly met with in the species to which he belongs; they are affectations of extreme tenderness and delicacy, and of great energy and enthusiasm. Whenever he does not whine, he must rant. The scanty stream of his genius is never allowed to steal quietly along its channel, but is either poured out in melodious tears, or thrown up to heaven in all the frothy magnificence of tiny jets and artificial commotions." ([Jeffrey, "Montgomery's *Poems*," *Edinburgh Review*,] IX [(Jan., 1807)], 348–9.) [The other articles referred to by Mill include Jeffrey, "*Poems* by W. Wordsworth," *ibid.*, XI (Oct., 1807), 214–31; Jeffrey, "Wordsworth's *White Doe*," *ibid.*, XXV (Oct., 1815), 355–63; Brougham, "Karamsin's *Travels in Europe*," *ibid.*, III (Jan., 1804), 321–8; Brougham, "Kotzebue's *Travels to Paris, etc.*," *ibid.*, V (Oct., 1804), 78–91; Brougham, "Kotzebue's *Travels in Italy*," *ibid.*, VII (Jan., 1806), 456–70; and Francis Palgrave, "Goethe's *Life of Himself* (Part I)," *ibid.*, XXVI (June, 1816), 304–37.]

†[Thomas Brown, "Belshaw's *Philosophy of the Mind, etc.*," *Edinburgh Review*,] I [(Jan., 1803)], 483. [The article had been quoted by James Mill in his "Periodical Literature: *Edinburgh Review*," pp. 228–30, for which J. S. Mill had done the research.]

But it is in a review of Mr. Bentham's *Traités de Législation* (Vol. IV), that the most elaborate attempt is made to erect sentimentality into a system, to clothe it in the garb of philosophy, and to support it by arguments having the semblance of being drawn from the principles of human nature.[*] Utility is here declared to be a very unsafe standard, whether in morals or in legislation; and feeling to be the only secure guide, even in making laws between man and man. This article will bear a comparison with the most barefaced specimen of *petitio principii*, which ever proceeded from the pen of man. To dissect its sophistry in detail would require more space than we can at present devote to the task.

[*Jeffrey, "Bentham, *Principes de législation* par Dumont," *Edinburgh Review*, IV (Apr., 1804), 1–26.]

ON GENIUS

1832

EDITORS' NOTE

Monthly Repository, n.s. VI (Oct., 1832), 649–59. Signed: "Antiquus." Headed: "On Genius"; running title: "On Genius." Not republished. Identified in Mill's bibliography as "An article in the 70th number of the New Series of the Monthly Repository (for October 1832) headed (by the Editor) 'On Genius' and signed 'Antiquus'" (MacMinn, p. 22). In the Somerville College copy Mill made two corrections, changing "an inferiority" to "our inferiority" (334.39), and "as, a preparation for" to "as a preparation for," (336.15–16). For comment on the essay, see the Introduction, pp. xxxi–xxxii above.

On Genius

Addressed to the Author of an Article, entitled "Some Considerations respecting the Comparative Influence of Ancient and Modern Times on the Development of Genius;" and of its continuation, headed, "On the Intellectual Influences of Christianity."[*]

SIR,—You have turned your attention, and that of the readers of the *Monthly Repository*, to a question, with which, if we well consider its significance, none of the controversies which fill the present age with flame and fury is comparable in interest. You have shown that, without being indifferent to politics, you can see a deeper problem in the existing aspect of human affairs, than the adjustment of a ten-pound franchise; and that with no inclination to undervalue the intellect of these "latter days,"[†] you do not write it down transcendant because steam-carriages can run twenty-five miles an hour on an iron railway; because little children are taught to march round a room and sing psalms, or because mechanics can read the *Penny Magazine*. You do not look upon man as having attained the perfection of his nature, when he attains the perfection of a wheel's or a pulley's nature, to go well as a part of some vast machine, being in himself nothing. You do not esteem the higher endowments of the intellect and heart to be given by God, or valuable to man, chiefly as means to his obtaining, first, bread; next, beef to his bread; and, as the last felicitous consummation, wine and fine linen. Rather, you seem to consider the wants which point to these bodily necessaries or indulgences, as having for their chief use that they call into existence and into exercise those loftier qualities. You judge of man, not by what he does, but by what he is. For, though man is formed for action, and is of no worth further than by virtue of the work which he does; yet (as has been often said, by one of the noblest spirits of our time) the works which most of us are appointed to do on this earth are in themselves little better than trivial and contemptible: the sole thing which is indeed valuable in them, is the *spirit* in which they are done.[‡] Nor is this mere mysticism; the most

[*Anon., *Monthly Repository*, n.s. VI (Aug., 1832), 556–64, and *ibid.*, n.s. VI (Sept., 1832), 627–34.]

[†See Deuteronomy, 31:29.]

[‡Mill is referring to Thomas Carlyle. See, for example, "Characteristics," *Edinburgh Review*, LIV (Dec., 1831), 351–83, *passim*, but especially pp. 357–63, 367–8, and 372–3.]

absolute utilitarianism must come to the same conclusion. If life were aught but a struggle to overcome difficulties; if the multifarious labours of the *durum genus hominum* were performed for us by supernatural agency, and there were no demand for either wisdom or virtue, but barely for stretching out our hands and enjoying, small would be our enjoyment, for there would be nothing which man could any longer prize in man. Even men of pleasure know that the means are often more than the end: the delight of fox-hunting does not consist in catching a fox. Whether, according to the ethical theory we adopt, wisdom and virtue be precious in themselves, or there be nothing precious save happiness, it matters little; while we know that where these higher endowments are not, happiness can never be, even although the purposes for which they might seem to have been given, could, through any mechanical contrivance, be accomplished without them.

To one who believes these truths, and has obtained thus much of insight into what the writer to whom I have already alluded would call "the significance of man's life,"[*] it was a fitting inquiry what are really the intellectual characteristics of this age; whether our mental light—let us account for the fact as we may—has not lost in intensity, at least a part of what it has gained in diffusion; whether our "march of intellect" be not rather a march towards doing without intellect, and supplying our deficiency of giants by the united efforts of a constantly increasing multitude of dwarfs. Such, too, is actually the problem which you have proposed. Suffer, then, one who has also much meditated thereon, to represent to you in what points he considers you to have failed in completely solving, and even in adequately conceiving the question.

Have you not misplaced the gist of the inquiry, and confined the discussion within too narrow bounds, by countenancing the opinion which limits the province of genius to the discovery of truths never before known, or the formation of combinations never before imagined? Is not this confounding the mere *accidents* of Genius with its essentials, and determining the order of precedence among minds, not by their powers, but by their opportunities and chances? Is genius any distinct faculty? Is it not rather the very faculty of thought itself? And is not the act of *knowing* anything not directly within the cognizance of our senses (provided we really *know* it, and do not take it upon trust), as truly an exertion of genius, though of a less *degree* of genius, as if the thing had never been known by any one else?

Philosophic genius is said to be the discovery of new truth. But what is new truth? That which has been known a thousand years may be new truth to you or me. There are born into the world every day several hundred thousand human beings, to whom all truth whatever is new truth. What is it to him who was born yesterday, that somebody who was born fifty years ago knew something? The question is, how *he* is to know it. There is one way; and nobody has ever hit upon more than one—by *discovery*.

[*Carlyle, "Biography," *Fraser's Magazine*, V (Apr., 1832), 255.]

There is a language very generally current in the world, which implies that knowledge can be *vicarious*; that when a truth has become known to *any one*, all who follow have nothing to do but passively to receive it; as if one man, by reading or listening, could transport another man's knowledge ready manufactured into his own skull. As well might he try the experiment upon another man's eyesight. Those who have no eyesight of their own, or who are so placed that they cannot conveniently use it, must believe upon trust; they cannot *know*. A man who knows may tell me what he knows, as far as words go, and I may learn to parrot it after him; but if I would *know* it, I must place my mind in the same state in which he has placed his; I must make the thought my own thought; I must verify the fact by my own observation, or by interrogating my own consciousness.

The exceptions and qualifications with which this doctrine must be taken, and which are more apparent than real, will readily present themselves. For example, it will suggest itself at once that the truth of which I am now speaking is *general* truth. To know an *individual* fact may be no exercise of mind at all; merely an exercise of the senses. The sole exercise of mind may have been in bringing the fact sufficiently close for the senses to judge of it; and *that* merit may be peculiar to the first discoverer: there may be talent in finding where the thief is hid, but none at all in being able to see him when found. The same observation applies in a less degree to some *general* truths. To know a general truth is, indeed, always an operation of the *mind*: but some physical truths may be brought to the test of sensation by an experiment so simple, and the conclusiveness of which is so immediately apparent, that the trifling degree of mental power implied in drawing the proper inference from it, is altogether eclipsed by the ingenuity which contrived the experiment, and the sagacious forecast of an undiscovered truth which set that ingenuity to work: qualities, the place of which may now be supplied by mere imitation.

So, again, in a case of mere *reasoning* from assumed premises, as, for instance, in mathematics, the process bears so strong an analogy to a merely mechanical operation, that the first discoverer alone has any real difficulty to contend against; the second may follow the first with very little besides patience and continued attention. But these seeming exceptions do not trench in the least upon the principle which I have ventured to lay down. If the first discovery alone requires genius, it is because the first discovery alone requires any but the simplest and most commonplace exercise of thought. Though genius be no peculiar mental power, but only mental power possessed in a peculiar degree, what implies no mental power at all, requires to be sure no genius.

But can this be said of the conviction which comes by the comparison and appreciation of numerous and scattered proofs? Can it, above all, be said of the knowledge of supersensual things, of man's mental and moral nature, where the appeal is to internal consciousness and self-observation, or to the experience of our common life interpreted by means of the key which self-knowledge alone can supply? The most important phenomena of human nature cannot even be conceived, except by a mind which has actively studied itself. Believed they may be, but as a blind man believes the existence and properties of colour. To *know* these truths is always to *discover* them. Every one, I suppose, of adult years, who has any capacity of knowledge, can remember the impression which he experienced when he *discovered* some truths which he thought he had known for years before. He had only believed them; they were not the fruits of his own consciousness, or of his own observation; he had taken them upon trust, or he had taken upon trust the premises from which they were inferred. If he had happened to forget them, they had been lost altogether; whereas the truths which we *know* we can discover again and again *ad libitum*.

It is with truths of this order as with the ascent of a mountain. Every person who climbs Mont Blanc exerts the same identical muscles as the first man who reached the summit; all that the first climber can do is to encourage the others and lend them a helping hand. What he has partly saved them the necessity of, is *courage*: it requires less hardihood to attempt to do what somebody has done before. It is an advantage also to have some one to point out the way and stop us when we are going wrong. Though one man cannot *teach* another, one man may *suggest* to another. I may be indebted to my predecessor for setting my own faculties to work; for hinting to me what questions to ask myself, and in what order; but it is not given to one man to *answer* those questions for another. Each person's own reason must work upon the materials afforded by that same person's own experience. Knowledge comes only from within; all that comes from without is but *questioning*, or else it is mere *authority*.

Now, the capacity of extracting the knowledge of general truth from our own consciousness, whether it be by simple *observation*, by that kind of self-observation which is called *imagination*, or by a more complicated process of analysis and induction, is *originality*; and where truth is the result, whoever says Originality says Genius. The man of the greatest philosophic genius does no more than this, evinces no higher faculty; whoever thinks at all, thinks to that extent, originally. Whoever knows anything of his own knowledge, not immediately obvious to the senses, manifests more or less of the same faculty which made a Newton or a Locke. Whosoever does this same thing systematically—whosoever, to the extent of his opportunity, gets at his convictions by his own faculties, and not by reliance on any other person whatever—that man, in proportion as his conclusions have truth in them, is an *original thinker*, and is, as much as anybody ever was, a *man* of *genius*; nor matters it though he should never chance to find out anything which somebody had not found out before him. There may be no hidden truths left for him to find, or he may accidentally miss them; but if he have courage and opportunity he *can* find hidden truths; for he has found all those which he knows, many of which were as hidden to *him* as those which are still unknown.

If the genius which *discovers* is no peculiar faculty, neither is the genius which *creates.* It was genius which produced the *Prometheus Vinctus*, the *Oration on the Crown*, the *Minerva*, or the *Transfiguration*;[*] and is it not genius which *comprehends* them? Without genius, a work of genius may be *felt*, but it cannot possibly be understood.

The property which distinguishes every work of genius in poetry and art from incoherency and vain caprice is, that it is *one, harmonious*, and a *whole*: that its parts are connected together as standing in a common relation to some leading and central idea or purpose. This idea or purpose it is not possible to extract from the work by any mechanical rules. To transport ourselves from the point of view of a spectator or reader, to that of the poet or artist himself, and from that central point to look round and see how the details of the work all conspire to the same end, all contribute to body forth the same general conception, is an exercise of the same powers of imagination, abstraction, and discrimination (though in an inferior degree) which would have enabled ourselves to produce the selfsame work. Do we not accordingly see that as much genius is often displayed in explaining the design and bringing out the hidden significance of a work of art, as in creating it? I have sometimes thought that *conceptive* genius is, in certain cases, even a higher faculty than *creative*. From the data afforded by a person's conversation and life, to frame a connected outline of the inward structure of that person's mind, so as to know and feel what the man is, and how life and the world paint themselves to his conceptions; still more to decipher in that same manner the mind of an age or a nation, and gain from history or travelling a vivid conception of the mind of a Greek or Roman, a Spanish peasant, an American, or a Hindu, is an effort of genius, superior, I must needs believe, to any which was ever shown in the creation of a fictitious character, inasmuch as the imagination is limited by a particular set of conditions, instead of ranging at pleasure within the bounds of human nature.

If there be truth in the principle which the foregoing remarks are intended to illustrate, there is ground for considerable objection to the course of argument which you have adopted in the article which gave occasion to the present letter. You argue, throughout, on the obstacles which oppose the growth and manifestation of genius, as if the future discoverer had to travel to the extreme verge of the ground already rescued from the dominion of doubt and mystery, before he can find any scope for the faculty thereafter to be developed in him,—as if he had first to learn all that has already been known, and then to commence an entirely new series of intellectual operations in order to enlarge the field of human knowledge. Now I conceive, on the contrary, that the career of the discoverer is only the career of the learner, carried on into untrodden ground; and that he has only to continue to do exactly what he ought to have been doing from the first, what he *has* been doing if he be really qualified to be a discoverer. You might, therefore, have spared

[*The references are, respectively, to Aeschylus' *Prometheus vinctus*, Demosthenes' *De corona*, the statue of Minerva called the *Palladium* (or to Phidias' *Athena Parthenos*), and Raphael's *Transfiguration*.]

yourself the inquiry, whether new truths, in as great abundance as ever, are within reach, and whether the approach to them is longer and more difficult than heretofore. According to my view, genius stands not in need of access to new truths, but is always where knowledge is, being itself nothing but a mind with capacity to know. There will be as much room and as much necessity for genius when mankind shall have found out everything attainable by their faculties, as there is now; it will still remain to distinguish the man who knows from the man who takes upon trust—the man who can feel and understand truth, from the man who merely assents to it, the active from the merely passive mind. Nor needs genius be a rare gift bestowed on few. By the aid of suitable culture all might possess it, although in unequal degrees.

The question, then, of "the comparative influence of ancient and modern times on the development of genius," is a simpler, yet a larger and more commanding question, than you seem to have supposed. It is no other than this: have the moderns, or the ancients, made most use of the faculty of thought, and which of the two have cultivated it the most highly? Did the ancients *think* and find out for themselves what they ought to believe and to do, taking nothing for granted?—and do the moderns, in comparison, merely *remember* and *imitate*, believing either nothing, or what is told them, and doing either nothing, or what is set down for them?

To this great question I am hardly able to determine whether you have said aye or no. You are pleading for the moderns against those who place the ancients above them, for civilization and refinement against the charge of being impediments to genius; yet you seem incidentally to admit that inferiority in the higher endowments, which it appeared to be your object to disprove. Your only salvo for the admission is, that, if the fact be so, it must be our own fault. Assuredly it is always our own fault. It is just as possible to be a great man now as it ever was, would but any one try. But that does not explain why we do not try, and why others, mere men like ourselves, *did*; any more than we can explain why the Turks are not as good sailors as the English, by saying that it is all their own fault.

I cannot say that I think you have much advanced the question by terminating where you do. If you were writing to Pagans, it might have been to the purpose to tell them that they would find in Christianity a corrective to their faults and ills; or if we had been superior to the ancients instead of inferior, as in numerous other respects we really are, Christianity might have been assigned as the cause. But to refer us to Christianity as the fountain of intellectual vigour, in explanation of our having fallen off in intellectual vigour since we embraced Christianity, will scarcely be satisfactory. In proportion as our religion gives us an advantage over our predecessors, must our inferiority to them be the more manifest if we have fallen below them after all. If genius, as well as other blessings, be among the natural fruits of Christianity, there must be some reason why Christianity has been our faith for 1500 years, without our having yet begun to reap this benefit. The important question to have resolved would have been, what is the obstacle? The solution of this difficulty I have sought in vain from your two articles—permit me now to seek it from yourself.

I complain of what you have omitted, rather than of what you have said. I have found in your general observations much that is *true*, much that is wise, and eternally profitable to myself and to all men. The fact which you announce, of the intimate connexion of intellectual with moral greatness, of all soundness and comprehensiveness of intellect with the sublime impartiality resulting from an ever-present and overruling attachment to duty and to truth, is deeply momentous; and, though many have known it heretofore, you also speak as one who knows it,—who therefore has discovered it in himself. It is as true now as it was of yore, that "the righteousness of the righteous man guideth his steps."[*] But Christianity, since it first visited the earth, has made many righteous men according to their lights, many in whom the spiritual part prevailed as far as is given to man over the animal and worldly, yet we have not proportionally abounded in men of genius.

There must, then, be some defect in our mental training, which has prevented us from turning either Christianity or our other opportunities to the account we might. Christianity, and much else, cannot have been so taught or so learnt as to make us thinking beings. Is it not that these things have *only* been taught and learnt, but have *not* been *known*?—that the truths which we have inherited still remain traditional, and no one among us, except here and there a man of genius, has made them truly his own?

The ancients, in this particular, were very differently circumstanced. When the range of human experience was still narrow—when, as yet, few facts had been observed and recorded, and there was nothing or but little to learn by rote, those who had curiosity to gratify, or who desired to acquaint themselves with nature and life, were fain to look into things, and not pay themselves with opinions; to see the objects themselves, and not their mere images reflected from the minds of those who had formerly seen them. Education *then* consisted not in giving what is called knowledge, that is, grinding down other men's ideas to a convenient size, and administering them in the form of *cram*—it was a series of exercises to form the thinking faculty itself, that the mind, being active and vigorous, might go forth and know.

Such was the education of Greece and Rome, especially Greece. Her philosophers were not formed, nor did they form their scholars, by placing a suit of ready-made truths before them, and helping them to put it on. They helped the disciple to form to himself an intellect fitted to seek truth for itself and to find it. No Greek or Roman schoolboy learnt anything by rote, unless it were verses of Homer or songs in honour of the gods. Modern superciliousness and superficiality have treated the disputations of the sophists as they have those of the schoolmen, with

[*Cf. Proverbs, 11:5, and 13:6.]

unbounded contempt: the contempt would be better bestowed on the tuition of Eton or Westminster. Those disputations were a kind of mental gymnastics, eminently conducive to acuteness in detecting fallacies; consistency and circumspection in tracing a principle to its consequences; and a faculty of penetrating and searching analysis. They became ridiculous only when, like all other successful systems, they were imitated by persons incapable of entering into their spirit, and degenerated into foppery and *charlatanerie*. With powers thus formed, and no possibility of parroting where there was scarcely anything to parrot, what a man knew was his own, got at by using his own senses or his own reason; and every new acquisition strengthened the powers, by the exercise of which it had been gained.

Nor must we forget to notice the fact to which you have yourself alluded, that the life of a Greek was a perpetual conflict of adverse intellects, struggling with each other, or struggling with difficulty and necessity. Every man had to play his part upon a stage where *cram* was of no use—nothing but genuine *power* would serve his turn. The studies of the closet were combined with, and were intended as a preparation for, the pursuits of active life. There was no *littérature des salons*, no dilettantism in ancient Greece: wisdom was not something to be prattled about, but something to be done. It was this which, during the bright days of Greece, prevented theory from degenerating into vain and idle refinements, and produced that rare combination which distinguishes the great minds of that glorious people,—of profound speculation, and business-like matter-of-fact common sense. It was not the least of the effects of this union of theory and practice, that in the good times of Greece there is no vestige of anything like sentimentality. Bred to action, and passing their lives in the midst of it, all the speculations of the Greeks were for the sake of action, all their conceptions of excellence had a direct reference to it.

This was the education to form great statesmen, great orators, great warriors, great poets, great architects, great sculptors, great philosophers; because, once for all, it formed *men*, and not mere knowledge-boxes; and the men, being men, had minds, and could apply them to the work, whatever it might be, which circumstances had given them to perform. But this lasted not long: demolishing the comparatively weak attempts of their predecessors, two vast intellects arose, the one the greatest observer of his own or any age, the other the greatest dialectician, and both almost unrivalled in their powers of metaphysical analysis,—Aristotle and Plato. No sooner, by the exertions of these gigantic minds, and of others their disciples or rivals, was a considerable body of truth, or at least of opinion, got together—no sooner did it become *possible* by mere memory to seem to know something, and to be able for some purposes even to use that knowledge, as men use the rules of arithmetic who have not the slightest notion of the grounds of them, than men found out how much easier it is to remember than to think, and abandoned the pursuit of intellectual power itself for the attempt, without possessing it, to appropriate its results. Even the reverence which mankind had for these great men became a hinderance to following their example. Nature was studied not in nature, but in Plato or Aristotle, in Zeno or Epicurus. Discussion became the mere rehearsal of a lesson got by rote. The attempt to think for oneself fell into disuse; and, by ceasing to exercise the power, mankind ceased to possess it.

It was in this spirit that, on the rise of Christianity, the doctrines and precepts of Scripture began to be studied. For this there was somewhat greater excuse, as, where the authority was that of the Omniscient, the confirmation of fallible reason might appear less necessary. Yet the effect was fatal. The interpretation of the Gospel was handed over to grammarians and language-grinders. The words of him whose speech was in figures and parables were iron-bound and petrified into inanimate and inflexible *formulæ*. Jesus was likened to a logician, framing a rule to meet all cases, and provide against all possible evasions, instead of a poet, orator, and *vates*, whose object was to purify and spiritualize the mind, so that, under the guidance of its purity, its own lights might suffice to find the law of which he only supplied the spirit, and suggested the general scope. Hence, out of the least dogmatical of books, have been generated so many dogmatical religions—each claiming to be found in the book, and none in the mind of man; they are above thought, and thought is to have nothing to do with them; until religion, instead of a spirit pervading the mind, becomes a crust encircling it, nowise penetrating the obdurate mass within, but only keeping out such rays of precious light or genial heat as might haply have come from elsewhere.

And after all which has been done to break down these vitiating, soul-debasing prejudices, against which every great mind of the last two centuries has protested, where are we now? Are not the very first general propositions that are presented for a child's acceptance, theological dogmas, presented not as truths believed by others, and which the child will hereafter be encouraged to know for itself, but as doctrines which it is to believe before it can attach any meaning to them, or be chargeable with the greatest guilt? At school, what is the child taught, except to repeat by rote, or at most to apply technical rules, which are lodged, not in his reason, but in his memory? When he leaves school, does not everything which a young person sees and hears conspire to tell him, that it is not expected he shall think, but only that he shall profess no opinion on any subject different from that professed by other people? Is there anything a man can do, short of swindling or forgery, (*à fortiori* a woman,) which will so surely gain him the reputation of a dangerous, or, at least, an unaccountable person, as daring, without either rank or reputation as a warrant for the eccentricity, to make a practice of forming his opinions for himself?

Modern education is all *cram*—Latin cram, mathematical cram, literary cram, political cram, theological cram, moral cram. The world already knows everything, and has only to tell it to its children, who, on their part, have only to hear, and lay it to rote (not to *heart*). Any purpose, any idea of training the mind itself, has gone out of the world. Nor can I yet perceive many symptoms of amendment.

Those who dislike what is taught, mostly—if I may trust my own experience— dislike it not for being *cram*, but for being other people's cram, and not theirs. Were they the teachers, they would teach different doctrines, but they would teach them *as* doctrines, not as subjects for impartial inquiry. Those studies which only train the faculties, and produce no fruits obvious to the sense, are fallen into neglect. The most valuable kind of mental gymnastics, logic and metaphysics, have been more neglected and undervalued for the last thirty years, than at any time since the revival of letters. Even the ancient languages, which, when rationally taught, are, from their regular and complicated structure, to a certain extent a lesson of logical classification and analysis, and which give access to a literature more rich than any other, in all that forms a vigorous intellect and a manly character, are insensibly falling into disrepute as a branch of liberal education. Instead of them, we are getting the ready current coin of modern languages, and physical science taught empirically, by committing to memory its results. Whatever assists in feeding the body, we can see the use of; not so if it serves the body only by forming the mind.

Is it any wonder that, thus educated, we should decline in genius? That the ten centuries of England or France cannot produce as many illustrious names as the hundred and fifty years of little Greece? The wonder is, that we should have produced so many as we have, amidst such adverse circumstances. We have had some true philosophers, and a few genuine poets; two or three great intellects have revolutionized physical science; but in almost every branch of literature and art we are deplorably behind the earlier ages of the world. In art, we hardly attempt anything except spoiled copies of antiquity and the middle ages. We are content to copy them, because that requires less trouble and less cultivated faculties than to comprehend them. If we had genius to enter into the *spirit* of ancient art, the same genius would enable us to clothe that spirit in ever-new forms.

Where, then, is the remedy? It is in the knowledge and clear comprehension of the evil. It is in the distinct recognition, that the end of education is not to *teach*, but to fit the mind for learning from its own consciousness and observation; that we have occasion for this power under ever-varying circumstances, for which no routine or rule of thumb can possibly make provision. As the memory is trained by remembering, so is the reasoning power by reasoning; the imaginative by imagining; the analytic by analysing; the inventive by finding out. Let the education of the mind consist in calling out and exercising these faculties: never trouble yourself about giving knowledge—train the *mind*—keep it supplied with materials, and knowledge will come of itself. Let all *cram* be ruthlessly discarded. Let each person be made to feel that in other things he may believe upon trust—if he find a trustworthy authority—but that in the line of his peculiar duty, and in the line of the duties common to all men, it is his business to *know*. Let the feelings of society cease to stigmatize independent thinking, and divide its censure between a lazy dereliction of the duty and privilege of thought, and the overweening self-conceit of a half-thinker, who rushes to his conclusions without taking the trouble to understand the thoughts of other men. Were all this done, there would be no complaint of any want of genius in modern times. But when will that hour come? Though it come not at all, yet is it not less your duty and mine to strive for it,—and first to do what is certainly and absolutely in our power, to realize it in our own persons.

I am, Sir, yours respectfully,
ANTIQUUS.

THOUGHTS ON POETRY AND ITS VARIETIES

1833

EDITORS' NOTE

Dissertations and Discussions, 2nd ed. (1867), Vol. I, pp. 63–94, where the title is footnoted, "*Monthly Repository*, January and October 1833." Running title: "Poetry and Its Varieties." Republished from "What Is Poetry?" *MR*, n.s. VII (Jan., 1833), 60–70; and "The Two Kinds of Poetry," *ibid.*, n.s. VII (Oct., 1833), 714–24. Both signed: "Antiquus." Running titles as titles. Identified in Mill's bibliography as "An article headed 'What is Poetry' and signed Antiquus in the 73d numb. of the Monthly Repository. (In Jan. 1833)" (MacMinn, p. 24), and "An article headed 'The two kinds of Poetry' and signed 'Antiquus' in the same number of the Monthly Repository"—i.e., the number for Oct., 1833, in which his "Blakey's History of Moral Science" appeared (MacMinn, p. 34). In the copy in Somerville College of the first of these, "paga pii" is corrected to "paga fui" (351.11); this correction was made in *D&D*. Also, in a passage not reprinted in *D&D*, Mill indicated that each "a" should read "or" in "a loveliness, a cheerfulness, a wildness, a melancholy, a terror" (353^{s-s}). (This is a frequent confusion in Mill's hand.) In the Somerville College copy of the second, the dubious grammar at 364.29 is called into question by a pencilled underlining, possibly by Mill's wife, of "impressions, is proportional", and by a "?" in the margin; the passage, however, was unaltered in *D&D*, and is left unaltered here.

For comment on the essay, see the Introduction, pp. xxxii–xxxvi and xliii–xliv above.

The following text, taken from the 2nd ed. of *D&D* (the last in Mill's lifetime), is collated with that in *D&D*, 1st ed. (1859), and those in *MR*. In the footnoted variants, "33" indicates *MR*; "59" indicates *D&D*, 1st ed. (1859); and "67" indicates *D&D*, 2nd ed. (1867).

Thoughts on Poetry and Its Varieties

I

IT HAS OFTEN BEEN ASKED, What is Poetry? And many and various are the answers which have been returned. The vulgarest of all—one with which no person possessed of the faculties to which poetry addresses itself can ever have been satisfied—is that which confounds poetry with metrical composition: yet to this wretched mockery of a definition, many *had* been led back, by the failure of all their attempts to find any other that would distinguish what they have been accustomed to call poetry, from much which they have known only under other names.

That, however, the word *poetry imports* something quite peculiar in its nature, something which may exist in what is called prose as well as in verse, something which does not even require the instrument of words,[*] but can speak through *the* other audible symbols called musical sounds, and even through the visible ones which are the language of sculpture, painting, and architecture; all this, *d* we believe, is and must be felt, though perhaps indistinctly, by all upon whom poetry in any of its shapes produces any impression beyond that of tickling the ear. *The* distinction between poetry and what is not poetry, whether explained or not, is felt to be *fundamental: and where* every one feels a difference, a difference there must be. All other appearances may be fallacious, but the appearance of a difference is *g* a real difference. Appearances too, like other things, must have a cause, and that which can *cause* anything, even an illusion, must be a reality. And hence, while a half-philosophy disdains the classifications and distinctions

[*Wordsworth, "To B. R. Haydon, Esq.," in *Poetical Works* (1827), Vol. II, p. 296 (l. 2).]

*a–a*33, 59   have
*b–b*33   "poetry" *does* import]   59   "poetry" imports
*c–c*33   those
*d*33   as
*e–e*33   To the mind, poetry is either nothing, or it is the better part of all art whatever, and of real life too; and the
*f–f*33   fundamental. [*paragraph*] Where
*g*33   itself
*h–h*33   *cause*

indicated by popular language, philosophy carried to its highest point *frames* new ones, but *rarely* sets aside the old, content with correcting and regularizing them. It cuts fresh channels for thought, but *k* does not fill up such as it finds ready-made *l*; it *traces, on the contrary, more deeply, broadly, and distinctly, those into which the current has spontaneously flowed.

Let us then attempt, in the way of modest inquiry, not to coerce and confine nature within the bounds of an arbitrary definition, but rather to find the boundaries which she herself has set, and erect a barrier round them; not calling mankind to account for having misapplied the word *"poetry,"* but attempting to clear up *n* the conception which they already attach to it, and to bring *forward* as a distinct *principle* that which, as a vague *feeling*, has really guided them in their *r* employment of the term.

The object of poetry is confessedly to act upon the emotions; and therein is poetry sufficiently distinguished from what Wordsworth affirms to be its logical opposite, namely, not prose, but matter of fact or science.[*] The one addresses itself to the belief, the other to the feelings. The one does its work by convincing or persuading, the other by moving. The one acts by presenting a proposition to the understanding, the other by offering interesting objects of contemplation to the sensibilities.

This, however, leaves us very far from a definition of poetry. *This distinguishes* it from one thing, but we are bound to distinguish it from everything. To *bring* thoughts or images *before* the mind for the purpose of acting upon the emotions, does not belong to poetry alone. It is equally the province (for example) of the novelist: and yet the faculty of the poet and *that* of the novelist are as distinct as any other two faculties; as the *faculties* of the novelist and of the orator, or of the poet and the metaphysician. The two characters may be united, as characters the most disparate may; but they have no natural connexion.

Many of the *greatest* poems are in the form of *fictitious narratives*, and in almost all good *serious fictions* there is true poetry. But there is a radical distinction between the interest felt in a *story* as such, and the interest excited by poetry; for the one is derived from *incident*, the other from the representation of *feeling*. In one, the source of the emotion excited is the exhibition of a state or

[*"Preface to the Second Edition of Lyrical Ballads," *ibid.*, Vol. IV, p. 368n (note to para. 12).]

*i–i*33	may frame	*t–t*33	present
*j–j*33	never	*u–u*33	to
*k*33	it	*v–v*33	the faculty
*l–l*33	, but	*w–w*33	faculty
*m–m*33, 59	"poetry,"	*x–x*33	finest
*n*33	to them	*y–y*33	novels
*o–o*33	before their minds	*z–z*33	novels
*p–p*33	*principle*	*a–a*33	novel
*q–q*33	*feeling*	*b–b*33	*incident*
*r*33	actual	*c–c*33	*feeling*
*s–s*33	We have distinguished		

states of human sensibility; in the other, of a series of states of mere outward circumstances. Now, all minds are capable of being affected more or less by representations of the latter kind, and all, or almost all, by those of the former; yet the two sources of interest correspond to two distinct, and (as respects their greatest development) mutually exclusive, characters of mind. [d]

At what age is the passion for a story, for almost any kind of story, merely as a story, the most intense? In childhood. But that also is the age at which poetry, even of the simplest description, is least relished and least understood; because the feelings with which it is especially conversant are yet undeveloped, and not having been even in the slightest degree experienced, cannot be sympathized with. In what stage of the progress of society, again, is story-telling most valued, and the story-teller in greatest request and honour?—In a rude state, like that of the Tartars and Arabs at this day, and of almost all nations in the earliest ages. But in this state of society there is little poetry except ballads, which are mostly narrative, that is, essentially [e]stories[e], and derive their principal interest from the [f]incidents[f]. Considered as poetry, they are of the lowest and most elementary kind: the feelings depicted, or rather indicated, are the simplest our nature has; such joys and griefs as the immediate pressure of some outward event excites in rude minds, which live wholly immersed in outward things, and have never, either from choice or a force they could not resist, turned themselves to the contemplation of the world within. Passing now from childhood, and from the childhood of society, to the grown-up men and women of this most grown-up and unchildlike age—the minds and hearts of greatest depth and elevation are commonly those which take greatest delight in poetry; the shallowest and emptiest, on the contrary, are, [g]at all events, not those least[g] addicted to novel-reading. This accords, too, with all analogous experience of human nature. The sort of persons whom not merely in books, but in their lives, we find perpetually engaged in hunting for excitement from without, are invariably those who do not possess, either in the vigour of their intellectual powers or in the depth of their sensibilities, that which would enable them to find ample excitement nearer [h] home. The [i]most idle and frivolous persons[i] take a natural delight in fictitious narrative; the excitement it affords is of the kind which comes from without. Such persons are rarely lovers of poetry, though they may fancy themselves so, because they relish novels in verse. But poetry, which is the delineation of the deeper and more secret workings of [j]human emotion[j], is interesting only to those to whom it recals what they have felt, or whose imagination it stirs up to

[d]33 So much is the nature of poetry dissimilar to the nature of fictitious narrative, that to have a really strong passion for either of the two, seems to presuppose or to superinduce a comparative indifference to the other.
    [e-e]33 *stories*
    [f-f]33 *incidents*
    [g-g]33 by universal remark, the most
    [h]33 at
    [i-i]33 same persons whose time is divided between sight-seeing, gossip, and fashionable dissipation,
    [j-j]33 the human heart

conceive what they could feel, or what they might have been able to feel had their outward circumstances been different.

Poetry, when it is really such, is truth; and fiction also, if it is good for anything, is truth: but they are different truths. The truth of poetry is to paint the human soul truly: the truth of fiction is to give a true picture of ^{k}life^k. The two kinds of knowledge are different, and come by different ways, come mostly to different persons. Great poets are often proverbially ignorant of life. What they know has come by observation of themselves; they have found ^{l}within them^l one highly delicate and sensitive ^{m} specimen of human nature, on which the laws of ^{n} emotion are written in large characters, such as can be read off without much study ^{o}. Other^o knowledge of mankind, such as comes to men of the world by outward experience, is not indispensable to them as poets: but to the novelist such knowledge is all in all; he has to describe outward things, not the inward man; actions and events, not feelings; and it will not do for him to be numbered among those who, as Madame Roland said of Brissot, know man but not ^{p}men^p.$^{[*]}$

All this is no bar to the possibility of combining both elements, poetry and narrative or incident, in the same work, and calling it either a novel or a poem; but so may red and white combine on the same human features, or on the same canvas ^{q}. There is one order of composition which requires the union of poetry and incident, each in its highest kind—the dramatic. Even there the two elements are perfectly distinguishable, and may exist of unequal quality, and in the most various proportion. The incidents of a dramatic poem may be scanty and ineffective, though the delineation of passion and character may be of the highest order; as in Goethe's ^{r}admirable^r ^{s}Torquato Tasso^s:$^{[†]}$ or again, the story as a mere story may be well got up for effect, as is the case with some of the most trashy productions of the Minerva press: it may even be, what those are not, a coherent and probable series of events, though there be scarcely a feeling exhibited which is not ^{t}represented^t falsely, or in a manner absolutely commonplace. The combination of the two excellencies is what renders Shakespeare so generally acceptable, each sort of

[*Marie Jeanne Phlipon Roland de la Platière, *Appel à l'impartiale postérité*, ed. Louis Augustin Guillaume Bosc, 4 pts. (Paris: Louvet, 1795), Pt. I, p. 36.]

[†In *Werke*, 55 vols. (Stuttgart and Tübingen: Cotta'schen Buchhandlung, 1828–33), Vol. IX, pp. 99–245.]

$^{k-k}$33   *life*
$^{l-l}$33   *there*
^{m}33   and refined
^{n}33   human
$^{o-o}$33   : and other
$^{p-p}$33, 59   *men*
^{q}33   ; and so may oil and vinegar, though opposite natures, blend together in the same composite taste
$^{r-r}$33   glorious
$^{s-s}$33   "Torquato Tasso" [*italics added to the present text*]
$^{t-t}$33   exhibited

readers finding in him what is suitable to their faculties. To the many he is great as a story-teller, to the few as a poet.

In limiting poetry to the delineation of states of feeling, and denying the name where nothing is delineated but outward objects, we may be thought to have done what we promised to avoid—to have not ^{u}found^u, but ^{v}made^v a definition, in opposition to the usage of ^{w} language, since it is established by common consent that there is a poetry called ^{x}descriptive^x. We deny the charge. Description is not poetry because there is descriptive poetry, no more than science is poetry because there is such a thing as a didactic poem ^{y}. But an object which admits of being described, or a truth which may fill a place in a scientific treatise, may ^{z}also^z furnish an occasion for the generation of poetry, which we thereupon choose to call descriptive or didactic. The poetry is not in the object itself, nor in the scientific truth itself, but in the state of mind in which the one and the other may be contemplated. The mere delineation of the dimensions and colours of external objects is not poetry, no more than a geometrical ground-plan of St. Peter's or Westminster Abbey is painting. Descriptive poetry consists, no doubt, in description, but in description of things as they appear, not as they ^{a}are^a; and it paints them not in their bare and natural lineaments, but ^{b}seen through the medium and arrayed in the colours^b of the imagination set in action by the feelings. If a poet ^{c}describes^c a lion, he ^{d}does not describe^d him as a naturalist would, nor even as a traveller would, who was intent upon stating the truth, the whole truth, and nothing but the truth. He ^{e}describes^e him by ^{f}imagery^f, that is, by suggesting the most striking likenesses and contrasts which might occur to a mind contemplating the lion, in the state of awe, wonder, or terror, which the spectacle naturally excites, or is, on the occasion, supposed to excite. Now this is describing the lion professedly, but the state of excitement of the spectator really. The lion may be described falsely or ^{g}with exaggeration^g, and the poetry be all the better; but if the human emotion be not painted with ^{h} scrupulous truth, the poetry is bad poetry, *i.e.* is not poetry at all, but a failure.

Thus far our progress towards a clear view of the essentials of poetry has brought

$^{u-u}$33   *found*
$^{v-v}$33   *made*
^{w}33   the English
$^{x-x}$33   *descriptive*
^{y}33   ; no more, we might almost say, than Greek or Latin is poetry because there are Greek and Latin poems
$^{z-z}$33   *also*
$^{a-a}$33   *are*
$^{b-b}$33   arranged in the colours and seen through the medium
$^{c-c}$33   is to describe
$^{d-d}$33   will not set about describing
$^{e-e}$33   will describe
$^{f-f}$33   *imagery*
$^{g-g}$33   in exaggerated colours
^{h}33   the most

us very close to the last two attempts at a definition of poetry which we happen to have seen in print, both of them by poets and men of genius. The one is by Ebenezer Elliott, the author of *Corn-Law Rhymes*, and other poems of still greater merit. "Poetry," says he, "is impassioned truth."[*] The other is by a writer in *Blackwood's Magazine*, and comes, we think, still nearer the mark. *'He defines'* poetry, "man's thoughts tinged by his feelings."[†] There is in either definition a near approximation to what we are in search of. Every truth which *'a* human being can enunciate*'*, every thought, even every outward impression, which can enter into his consciousness, may become poetry when shown through any impassioned medium, when invested with the colouring of joy, or grief, or pity, or affection, or admiration, or reverence, or awe, or even hatred or terror: and, unless so coloured, nothing, be it as interesting as it may, is poetry. But both these definitions fail to discriminate between poetry and eloquence. Eloquence, as well as poetry, is impassioned truth; eloquence, as well as poetry, is thoughts coloured by the feelings. Yet common apprehension and philosophic criticism alike recognise a distinction between the two: there is much that every one would call eloquence, which no one would think of classing as poetry. A question will sometimes arise, whether some particular author is a poet; and those who maintain the negative commonly allow, that though not a poet, he is a highly *^keloquent^k* writer. *^l* The distinction between poetry and eloquence appears to us to be equally fundamental with the distinction between poetry and narrative, or between poetry and description *^m*, while it*^m* is still farther from having been satisfactorily cleared up than either of the others *ⁿ* .

Poetry and eloquence are both alike the expression or *^outterance^o* of feeling. But if we may be excused the *^p* antithesis, we should say that eloquence is *heard*, poetry is *over*heard. Eloquence supposes an audience; the peculiarity of poetry appears to us to lie in the poet's utter unconsciousness of a listener. Poetry is feeling, confessing itself to itself in moments of solitude, and *^qembodying itself^q* in symbols, which are the nearest possible representations of the feeling in the exact shape in which it exists in the poet's mind. Eloquence is feeling pouring itself *^rout^r*

[*Ebenezer Elliott, Preface to 3rd ed., *Corn Law Rhymes* (London: Steill, 1831), p. v.]
[†Mill almost certainly has John Wilson in mind, but these exact words have not been located.]

*ⁱ⁻ⁱ*33   We forget his exact words, but in substance he defined
*^{j-j}*33   man can announce
*^{k-k}*33   *eloquent*
*^l*33   [*paragraph*]
*^{m-m}*33   . It
*ⁿ*33   , unless, which is highly probable, the German artists and critics have thrown some light upon it which has not yet reached us. Without a perfect knowledge of what they have written, it is something like presumption to write upon such subjects at all, and we shall be the foremost to urge that, whatever we may be about to submit, may be received, subject to correction from *them*
*^{o-o}*33   uttering forth   *^{q-q}*33   bodying itself forth
*^p*33   seeming affectation of the   *^{r-r}*33   forth

to other minds, courting their sympathy, or endeavouring to influence their belief, or move them to passion or to action.

All poetry is of the nature of soliloquy. It may be said that poetry which is printed on hot-pressed paper and sold at a bookseller's shop, is a soliloquy in full dress, and on the stage. *It is so; but* there is nothing absurd in the idea of such a mode of soliloquizing. What we have said to ourselves, we may tell to others afterwards; what we have said or done in solitude, we may voluntarily reproduce when we know that other eyes are upon us. But no trace of consciousness that any eyes are upon us must be visible in the work itself. The actor knows that there is an audience present; but if he act as though he knew it, he acts ill. A poet may write poetry *not only* with the intention of "printing" it *v*, but* for the express purpose of being paid for it; that it should *be* poetry, being written under *w* such influences, is *x* less probable; not, however, impossible; but no otherwise possible than if he can succeed in excluding from his work every vestige of such lookings-forth into the outward and every-day world, and can express his *y*emotions* exactly as he has felt them in solitude, or as he *z*is conscious* that he should feel them though they were to remain for ever unuttered *a*, or (at the lowest) as he knows that others feel them in similar circumstances of solitude*a*. But when he turns round and addresses himself to another person; when the act of utterance is not itself the end, but a means to an end—viz. by the feelings he himself expresses, to work upon the feelings, or upon the belief, or the will, of another,—when the expression of his emotions, or of his thoughts tinged by his emotions, is tinged also by that purpose, by that desire of making an impression upon another mind, then it ceases to be poetry, and becomes eloquence.

Poetry, accordingly, is the natural fruit of solitude and meditation; eloquence, of intercourse with the world. The persons who have most feeling of their own, if intellectual culture *b*has*b* given them a language in which to express it, have the highest faculty of poetry; those who best understand the feelings of others, are the most eloquent. The persons, and the nations, who commonly excel in poetry, are those whose character and tastes render them least dependent *c* upon the applause, or sympathy, or concurrence of the world in general. Those to whom that applause, that sympathy, that concurrence are most necessary, generally excel most in eloquence. And hence, perhaps, the French, who are the *d*least*d* poetical of all great and *e*intellectual*e* nations, are among the *f*most*f* eloquent: the French, also, being the most sociable, the vainest, and the least self-dependent.

*s–s*33 But
t–t+59, 67
*u–u*33 publishing
*v–v*33 ; he may write it even
*w*33 any
*x*33 far
*y–y*33 feelings

*z–z*33 feels
a–a+59, 67
*b–b*33 have
*c*33 for their happiness
*d–d*33 *least*
*e–e*33 refined
*f–f*33 *most*

If the above be, as we believe, the true theory of the distinction commonly admitted between eloquence and poetry; or [g]even[g] though it be not [h]so[h], yet if, as we cannot doubt, the distinction above stated be a real *bonâ fide* distinction, it will be found to hold, not merely in the language of words, but in all other language, and to intersect the whole domain of art.

Take, for example, music: we shall find in that art, so peculiarly the expression of passion, two perfectly distinct styles; one of which may be called the poetry, the other the oratory of music. This difference, being seized, would put an end to much musical sectarianism. There has been much contention whether the [i]music of the modern Italian school, that of Rossini and his successors, be impassioned or not[i]. Without doubt, the passion it expresses is not the musing, meditative tenderness, or pathos, or grief of Mozart [j]or Beethoven[j]. Yet it is passion, but [k]garrulous[k] passion—the passion which pours itself into other ears; and therein the better calculated for [l]dramatic[l] effect, having a natural adaptation for dialogue. Mozart also is great in musical oratory; but his most touching compositions are in the opposite style—that of soliloquy. Who can imagine "Dove sono"[*] *heard*? We imagine it *over*heard. [m]

Purely pathetic music commonly partakes of soliloquy. The soul is absorbed in its distress, and though there may be bystanders, it is not thinking of them. When the mind is looking within, and not without, its state does not often or rapidly vary; and hence the even, uninterrupted flow, approaching almost to monotony, which a good reader, or a good singer, will give to words or music of a pensive or melancholy cast. But grief taking the form of a prayer, or of a complaint, becomes oratorical; no longer low, and even, and subdued, it assumes a more emphatic rhythm, a more rapidly returning accent; instead of a few slow equal notes,

[*Wolfgang Amadeus Mozart, *Le nozze di Figaro*, Act III, Scene viii (first London performance, King's Theatre, Haymarket, 18 June, 1812).]

[g-g]+59, 67
[h-h]33   *that*
[i-i]33   character of Rossini's music—the music, we mean, which is characteristic of that composer—is compatible with the expression of passion
[j-j]33   , the great poet of his art
[k-k]33   *garrulous*
[l-l]33   *dramatic*
[m]33   The same is the case with many of the finest national airs. Who can hear those words, which speak so touchingly the sorrows of a mountaineer in exile:

> My heart's in the Highlands—my heart is not here;
> My heart's in the Highlands, a-chasing the deer.
> A-chasing the wild-deer, and following the roe—
> My heart's in the Highlands, wherever I go.

Who can hear those affecting words, married to as affecting an air, and fancy that he *sees* the singer? That song has always seemed to us like the lament of a prisoner in a solitary cell, ourselves listening, unseen, in the next. As the direct opposite of this, take "Scots wha hae wi' Wallace bled," where the music is as oratorical as the poetry. [The two songs are by Robert Burns.]

following one after another at regular intervals, it crowds note upon note, and *"*often*"* assumes a hurry and bustle like joy. Those who are familiar with some of the best of Rossini's serious compositions, such as the air "Tu che i miseri conforti," in the opera of *Tancredi*, or the duet "Ebben per mia memoria," in *La Gazza Ladra*,[*] will at once understand and feel our meaning. Both are highly tragic and passionate; the passion of both is that of oratory, not poetry. The like may be said of that most moving *"*invocation*"* in Beethoven's *Fidelio*—

> Komm, Hoffnung, lass das letzte Stern
> Der Müde nicht erbleichen;

in which Madame *"*Schröder*"* Devrient *9* exhibited such consummate powers of pathetic expression.[†] How different from Winter's beautiful "Paga fui,"[‡] the very soul of melancholy exhaling itself in solitude; fuller of meaning, and, therefore, more profoundly poetical than the words for which it was composed— for it seems to express not simple melancholy, but the melancholy of remorse.

If, from vocal music, we now pass to instrumental, we may have a specimen of musical oratory in any fine military symphony or march: while the poetry of music seems to have attained its consummation in Beethoven's Overture to *Egmont* *r*, so wonderful in its mixed expression of grandeur and melancholy*r*.

In the arts which speak to the eye, the same distinctions will be found to hold, not only between poetry and oratory, but between poetry, oratory, narrative, and simple imitation or description.

Pure *s*description*s* is exemplified in a *'*mere*'* portrait or a *"*mere*"* landscape— productions of art, it is true, but of the mechanical rather than of the fine arts, being works of simple imitation, not *v*creation*v*. We say, a *w*mere*w* portrait, or a *x*mere*x* landscape, because it is possible for a portrait or a landscape, without ceasing to be

[*Gioacchino Antonio Rossini, *Tancredi*, Act II, Scene i (first London performance, King's Theatre, Haymarket, 4 May, 1820), and *La gazza ladra*, Act II, Scene vi (first London performance, King's Theatre, Haymarket, 10 Mar., 1821).]

[†Ludwig van Beethoven, *Fidelio*, Act I; she appeared in the first London performance, King's Theatre, Haymarket, 18 May, 1832.]

[‡Peter von Winter, *Il ratto di Proserpina*, Act II, Scene i (first London performance, King's Theatre, Haymarket, 3 May, 1804).]

*n-n*33   ofttimes
*o-o*33   prayer
p-p+59, 67
*q*33   , last summer,
*r-r*33   . We question whether so deep an expression of mixed grandeur and melancholy was ever in any other instance produced by mere sounds
*s-s*33   *description*
*t-t*33   *mere*
*u-u*33   *mere*
*v-v*33   *creation*
*w-w*33   *mere*
*x-x*33   *mere*

such, to be also a *y*picture; like Turner's landscapes, and the great portraits by Titian or Vandyke.*y*

Whatever in painting or sculpture expresses human feeling—or *z*character*z*, which is only a certain state of feeling grown habitual—may be called, according to circumstances, the poetry, or the eloquence, of the painter's or the sculptor's art: the poetry, if the feeling declares itself by such signs as escape from us when we are unconscious of being seen; the oratory, if the signs are those we use for the purpose of voluntary communication. *a*

The narrative style answers to what is called historical painting, which it is the fashion among connoisseurs to treat as the climax of the pictorial art. That it is the most difficult branch of the art we do not doubt, because, in its perfection, it includes *b* the perfection of all the other branches *c*: as in like manner*c* an epic poem, though in so far as it is epic (*i.e.* narrative) it is not poetry at all, is yet esteemed the greatest effort of poetic genius, because there is no kind whatever of poetry which may not appropriately find a place in it. But an historical picture as such, that is, as the representation of an incident, must necessarily, as it seems to us, be poor and ineffective. The narrative powers of painting are extremely limited. Scarcely any picture, scarcely *d*even any series*d* of pictures, *e* tells its own story without the aid of an interpreter *f*. But it is the single figures which, to us, are the great charm even of an historical picture. It is in these that the power of the art is really seen *g*. In*g* the attempt to *h*narrate*h*, visible and permanent signs are *i*too*i* far behind the fugitive audible ones, which follow so fast one after another, while the faces and figures in a narrative picture, even though they be Titian's, stand still. Who would not prefer one Virgin and Child of Raphael, to all the pictures which

---

*y-y*33 *picture.* A portrait by Lawrence, or one of Turner's views, is not a mere copy from nature: the one combines with the given features that particular expression (among all good and pleasing ones) which those features are most capable of wearing, and which, therefore, in combination with them, is capable of producing the greatest positive beauty. Turner, again, unites the objects of the given landscape with whatever sky, and whatever light and shade, enable those particular objects to impress the imagination most strongly. In both, there is *creative* art—not working after an actual model, but realizing an idea.

*z-z*33 *character*

*a*33 [*paragraph*] The poetry of painting seems to be carried to its highest perfection in the *Peasant Girl* of Rembrandt, or in any Madonna or Magdalen of Guido; that of sculpture, in almost any of the Greek statues of the gods; not considering these in respect to the mere physical beauty, of which they are such perfect models, nor undertaking either to vindicate or to contest the opinion of philosophers, that even physical beauty is ultimately resolvable into expression; we may safely affirm, that in no other of man's works did so much of soul ever shine through mere inanimate matter.

*b*33 , in a manner,

*c-c*33 . As

*d-d*33 any series even

*e*33 which we know of,

*f*33 ; you must know the story beforehand; *then*, indeed, you may see great beauty and appropriateness in the painting

*g-g*33 : in

*h-h*33 *narrate*

i-i+59, 67

Rubens, with his fat, frouzy Dutch Venuses, ever painted? Though Rubens, besides excelling almost every one in his mastery over ^{j} the mechanical parts of his art, often shows real genius in ^{k}grouping^k his figures, the peculiar problem of historical painting. But then, who, except a mere student of drawing and colouring, ever cared to look twice at any of the figures themselves? The power of painting lies in poetry, of which Rubens had not the slightest tincture—not in narrative, ^{l}wherein^l he might have excelled.

The single figures, however, in an historical picture, are rather the ^{m}eloquence^m of painting than the poetry: they mostly (unless they are quite out of place in the picture) express the feelings of one person as modified by the presence of others. Accordingly the minds whose bent leads them rather to eloquence than to poetry, rush to historical painting. The French painters, for instance, seldom attempt, because they could make nothing of, single heads, like those glorious ones of the Italian masters, with which they might ^{n}feed^n themselves day after day in their own Louvre. They must all be ^{o}historical^o; and they are, almost to a man, attitudinizers. If we wished to give ^{p} any young artist the most impressive warning our ^{q}imagination^q could devise against that kind of vice in the pictorial, which corresponds to rant in the histrionic art, we would advise him to walk once up and once down the gallery of the Luxembourg ^{r}. Every figure in French painting or statuary seems to be showing itself off before spectators: they are ^{s}not poetical, but in the worst style of corrupted eloquence.^{s}

^{j}33   all
$^{k-k}$33, 59   *grouping*
$^{l-l}$33   where
$^{m-m}$33   *eloquence*
$^{n-n}$33   glut
$^{o-o}$33   *historical*
^{p}33   to
$^{q-q}$33   imaginations
^{r}33   ; even now when David, the great corrupter of taste, has been translated from this world to the next, and from the Luxembourg, consequently, into the more elevated sphere of the Louvre
$^{s-s}$33   in the worst style of corrupted eloquence, but in no style of poetry at all. The best are stiff and unnatural; the worst resemble figures of cataleptic patients. The French artists fancy themselves imitators of the classics, yet they seem to have no understanding and no feeling of that *repose* which was the peculiar and pervading character of Grecian art, until it began to decline: a repose tenfold more indicative of strength than all their stretching and straining; for strength, as Thomas Carlyle says, does not manifest itself in spasms. [See "Corn Law Rhymes," *Edinburgh Review*, LV (July, 1832), 351.]

There are some productions of art which it seems at first difficult to arrange in any of the classes above illustrated. The direct aim of art as such, is the production of the *beautiful*; and as there are other things beautiful besides states of mind, there is much of art which may seem to have nothing to do with either poetry or eloquence as we have defined them. Take for instance a composition of Claude, or Salvator Rosa. There is here *creation* of new beauty: by the grouping of natural scenery, conformably indeed to the laws of outward nature, but not after any actual model; the result being a beauty more perfect and faultless than is perhaps to be found in any actual landscape. Yet there is a character of poetry even in these, without which they could not be so beautiful. The unity, and wholeness, and æsthetic congruity of the picture still lies in singleness of expression; but it is expression in a different sense from that in which we have hitherto employed the term. The objects in an imaginary landscape cannot be said, like the words of a poem or the notes of a melody, to be the actual utterance of a feeling; but there must be

II

'NASCITUR POËTA' is a maxim of classical antiquity, which has passed to these latter days with less questioning than most of the doctrines of that early age. When it originated, the human faculties were occupied, fortunately for posterity, less in examining how the works of genius are created, than in creating them: and the adage, probably, had no higher source than the tendency common among mankind to consider all power which is not visibly the effect of practice, all skill which is not capable of being reduced to mechanical rules, as the result of a peculiar gift. Yet this aphorism, born in the infancy of psychology, will perhaps be found, now when that science is in its adolescence, to be as true as an epigram ever is, that is, to

---

some feeling with which they harmonize, and which they have a tendency to raise up in the spectator's mind. They must inspire a feeling of grandeur, or loveliness, or cheerfulness, or wildness, or melancholy, or terror. The painter must surround his principal objects with such imagery as would spontaneously arise in a highly imaginative mind, when contemplating those objects under the impression of the feelings which they are intended to inspire. This, if it be not poetry, is so nearly allied to it, as scarcely to require being distinguished.

In this sense we may speak of the poetry of architecture. All architecture, to be impressive, must be the expression or symbol of some interesting idea; some thought, which has power over the emotions. The reason why modern architecture is so paltry, is simply that it is not the expression of any idea; it is a mere parroting of the architectural tongue of the Greeks, or of our Teutonic ancestors, without any conception of a meaning.

To confine ourselves, for the present, to religious edifices: these partake of poetry, in proportion as they express, or harmonize with, the feelings of devotion. But those feelings are different according to the conception entertained of the beings, by whose supposed nature they are called forth. To the Greek, these beings were incarnations of the greatest conceivable physical beauty, combined with supernatural power: and the Greek temples express this, their predominant character being graceful strength; in other words, solidity, which is power, and lightness which is also power, accomplishing with small means what seemed to require great; to combine all in one word, *majesty*. To the Catholic, again, the Deity was something far less clear and definite; a being of still more resistless power than the heathen divinities; greatly to be loved; still more greatly to be feared; and wrapped up in vagueness, mystery, and incomprehensibility. A certain solemnity, a feeling of doubting and trembling hope, like that of one lost in a boundless forest who thinks he knows his way but is not sure, mixes itself in all the genuine expressions of Catholic devotion. This is eminently the expression of the pure Gothic cathedral; conspicuous equally in the mingled majesty and gloom of its vaulted roofs and stately aisles, and in the "dim religious light" which steals through its painted windows. [Milton, "Il Penseroso," in *The Poetical Works* (London: Tonson, 1695), p. 6 (l. 160).]

There is no generic distinction between the imagery which is the *expression* of feeling and the imagery which is felt to *harmonize* with feeling. They are identical. The imagery in which feeling utters itself forth from within, is also that in which it delights when presented to it from without. All art, therefore, in proportion as it produces its effects by an appeal to the emotions partakes of poetry, unless it partakes of oratory, or of narrative. And the distinction which these three words indicate, runs through the whole field of the fine arts.

The above hints have no pretension to the character of a theory. They are merely thrown out for the consideration of thinkers, in the hope that if they do not contain the truth, they may do somewhat to suggest it. Nor would they, crude as they are, have been deemed worthy of publication, in any country but one in which the philosophy of art is so completely neglected, that whatever may serve to put any inquiring mind upon this kind of investigation, cannot well, however imperfect in itself, fail altogether to be of use. [*signed:*] ANTIQUUS.

ᶦ⁻ᶦ33 *Nascitur poëta*

contain some truth: truth, however, which has been so compressed and bent out of shape, in order to tie it up into so small a knot of only two words, that it requires an almost infinite amount of unrolling and laying straight, before it will resume its just proportions.

We are not now intending to remark upon the grosser misapplications of this ancient maxim, which have engendered so many races of poetasters. The days are gone by, when every raw youth whose borrowed phantasies have set themselves to a borrowed tune, mistaking, as Coleridge says, an ardent desire of poetic reputation for poetic genius,[*] while unable to disguise from himself that he had taken no means whereby he might "become" a poet, could fancy himself a born one. Those who would reap without sowing, and gain the victory without fighting the battle, are ambitious now of another sort of distinction, and are born novelists, or public speakers, not poets. And the wiser thinkers ᵛ understand and acknowledge that poetic excellence is subject to the same necessary conditions with any other mental endowment; and that to no one of the spiritual benefactors of mankind is a higher or a more assiduous intellectual culture needful than to the poet. It is true, he possesses this advantage over others who use the "instrument of words,"[†] that, of the truths which he utters, a larger proportion are derived from personal consciousness, and a smaller from philosophic investigation. But the power itself of discriminating between what really is consciousness, and what is only a process of inference completed in a single instant—and the capacity of distinguishing whether that of which the mind is conscious be an eternal truth, or but a dream—are among the last results of the most matured and "perfect" intellect. Not to mention that the poet, no more than any other person who writes, confines himself altogether to intuitive truths, nor has any means of communicating even these but by words, every one of which derives all its power of conveying a meaning, from a whole host of acquired notions, and facts learnt by study and experience.

Nevertheless, it seems undeniable in point of fact, and consistent with the principles of a sound metaphysics, that there are poetic *natures*. There is a mental and physical constitution or temperament, peculiarly fitted for poetry. This temperament will not of itself make a poet, no more than the soil will the fruit; and as good fruit may be raised by culture from indifferent soils, so may good poetry from naturally unpoetical minds. But the poetry of one who is a poet by nature, will be clearly and broadly distinguishable from the poetry of mere culture. It may not be truer; it may not be more useful; but it will be different: fewer will appreciate it, even though many should affect to do so; but in those few it will find a keener sympathy, and will yield them a deeper enjoyment.

[*Biographia Literaria, Vol. I, p. 37, and Vol. II, p. 14 (Chaps. ii and xv).]
[†See p. 343 above.]

ᵘ⁻ᵘ33, 59 *become*
ᵛ33 begin to
ʷ⁻ʷ33 perfected

One may write genuine poetry, and not be a poet; for whosoever writes out truly any [x] human feeling, writes poetry. All persons, even the most unimaginative, in moments of strong emotion, speak poetry; and hence the drama is poetry, which else were always prose, except when a poet is one of the characters. What [y]is[y] poetry, but the thoughts and words in which emotion spontaneously embodies itself? As there are few who are not, at least for [z]some moments and in some situations, capable of some[z] strong feeling, poetry is natural to most persons at some period of their lives. And any one whose feelings are genuine, though but of the average strength,—if he be not diverted by uncongenial thoughts or occupations from the indulgence of them, and if he acquire by culture, as all persons may, the faculty of delineating them correctly,—has it in his power to be a poet, so far as a life passed in writing unquestionable poetry may be considered to confer that title. But [a]ought[a] it to do so? Yes, perhaps, in [b] a collection of "British Poets." But "poet" is the name also of a variety of [c]man[c], not solely of the author of a particular variety of [d]book[d]: now, to have written whole volumes of real poetry, is possible to almost all kinds of characters, and implies no greater peculiarity of mental construction than to be the author of a history or a novel.

Whom, then, shall we call poets? Those who are so constituted, that emotions are the links of association by which their ideas, both sensuous and spiritual, are connected together. This constitution belongs (within certain limits) to all in whom poetry is a pervading principle. In all others, poetry is something extraneous and superinduced: something out of themselves, foreign to the habitual course of their every-day lives and characters; a [e] world to which they may make occasional visits, but where they are sojourners, not dwellers, and which, when out of it, or even when in it, they think of, peradventure, but as a phantom-world, a place of *ignes fatui* and spectral illusions. Those only who have the peculiarity of association which we have mentioned, and which is [f]a natural though not an universal consequence[f] of intense sensibility, instead of seeming not themselves when they are uttering poetry, scarcely seem themselves when uttering anything to which poetry is foreign. Whatever be the thing which they are contemplating, [g]if it be capable of connecting itself with their emotions,[g] the aspect under which it first and most naturally paints itself to them, is its poetic aspect. The poet of culture sees his object in prose, and describes it in poetry; the poet of nature actually sees it in poetry.

This point is perhaps worth some little illustration; the rather, as metaphysicians (the ultimate arbiters of all philosophical criticism), while they have busied themselves for two thousand years, more or less, about the few [h]universal[h] laws of

[x]33 one
[y-y]33, 59 *is*
[z-z]33 *some . . . some . . . some*
[a-a]33, 59 *ought*
[b]33 the table of contents of
[c-c]33 *man*

[d-d]33 *book*
[e]33 quite other
[f-f]33 one of the natural consequences
[g-g]+59, 67
[h-h]33, 59 *universal*

human nature, have strangely neglected the analysis of its *i*diversities*i*. Of these, none lie deeper or reach further than the varieties which difference of nature and of education makes in what may be termed the habitual bond of association. In a mind entirely uncultivated, which is also without any strong feelings, objects, whether of sense or of intellect, arrange themselves in the mere casual order in which they have been seen, heard, or otherwise perceived. Persons of this sort may be said to think chronologically. If they remember a fact, it is by reason of a fortuitous coincidence with some trifling incident or circumstance which took place at the very time. If they have a story to tell, or testimony to deliver in a witness-box, their narrative must follow the exact order in which the events took place: *dodge* them, and the thread of association is broken; they cannot go on. Their associations, to use the language of philosophers, are chiefly of the successive, not the synchronous kind, and whether successive or synchronous, are mostly *j*casual*j*.

To the man of science, again, or of business, objects group themselves according to the artificial classifications which the understanding has voluntarily made for the convenience of thought or of practice. But where any of the impressions are vivid and intense, the associations into which these enter are the ruling ones: it being a well-known law of association, that the stronger a feeling is, the more *k*quickly*k* and strongly it associates itself with any other object or feeling. Where, therefore, nature has given strong feelings, and education has not created factitious tendencies stronger than the natural ones, the prevailing associations will be those which connect objects and ideas with emotions, and with each other through the intervention of emotions. Thoughts and images will be linked together, according to the similarity of the feelings which cling to them. A thought will introduce a thought by first introducing a feeling which is allied with it. At the centre of each group of thoughts or images will be found a feeling; and the thoughts or images *l*will be there only*l* because the feeling was there. *m*The*m* combinations which the mind puts together, *n* the pictures which it paints, *o* the wholes which imagination constructs out of the materials supplied by fancy, will be indebted to some dominant *p*feeling*p*, not as in other natures to a dominant *q*thought*q*, for their unity and consistency of character—for what distinguishes them from incoherencies.

The difference, then, between the poetry of a poet, and the poetry of a cultivated but not naturally *r*poetic*r* mind, is, that in the latter, with however bright a halo of feeling the thought may be surrounded and glorified, the thought itself is *s*always*s* the conspicuous object; while the poetry of a poet is feeling itself, employing thought only as the medium of its *t*expression*t*. In the one, feeling waits upon thought; in the other, thought upon feeling. The one writer has a distinct aim,

*i–i*33, 59 *diversities*
*j–j*33 casual
*k–k*33 rapidly
*l–l*33 are only there
*m–m*33 All the
*n*33 all

*o*33 all
*p–p*33, 59 *feeling*
*q–q*33, 59 *thought*
*r–r*33 poetical
*s–s*33 still
*t–t*33 utterance

common to him with any other didactic author; he desires to convey the thought, and he conveys it clothed in the feelings which it excites in himself, or which he deems most appropriate to it. The other merely pours forth the overflowing of his feelings; and all the thoughts which those feelings suggest are floated promiscuously along the stream.

It may assist in rendering our meaning intelligible, if we illustrate it by a parallel between the two English authors of our own day who have produced the greatest quantity of true and enduring poetry, Wordsworth and Shelley. Apter instances could not be wished for; the one might be cited as the type, the *exemplar*, of what the poetry of culture may accomplish; the other as perhaps the most striking example ever known of the poetic temperament. How different, accordingly, is the poetry of these two great "writers." In Wordsworth, the poetry is almost always the mere setting of a thought. The thought may be more valuable than the setting, or it may be less valuable, but there can be no question as to which was first in his mind: what he is impressed with, and what he is anxious to impress, is some proposition, more or less distinctly conceived; some truth, or something which he deems such. He lets the thought dwell in his mind, till it excites, as is the nature of thought, other thoughts, and also such feelings as the measure of his sensibility is adequate to supply. Among these thoughts and feelings, had he chosen a different walk of authorship (and there are many in which he might equally have excelled), he would probably have made a different selection of media for enforcing the parent thought: his habits, however, being those of poetic composition, he selects in preference the strongest feelings, and the thoughts with which most of feeling is naturally or habitually connected. His poetry, therefore, may be defined to be, his thoughts, coloured by, and impressing themselves by means of, emotions.[*] Such poetry, Wordsworth has occupied a long life in producing. And well and wisely has he so done. Criticisms, no doubt, may be made occasionally both upon the thoughts themselves, and upon the skill he has demonstrated in the choice of his *v*media*v*: for, an affair of skill and study, in the most rigorous sense, it evidently was. But he has not laboured in vain: he has exercised, and continues to exercise, a powerful, and mostly a highly beneficial influence over the formation and growth of not a few of the most cultivated and vigorous of the youthful minds of our time, over whose heads poetry of the opposite description would have flown, for want of an original organization, physical *w*or*w* mental, in sympathy with it.

On the other hand, Wordsworth's poetry is never bounding, never ebullient; has little even of the appearance of spontaneousness: the well is never so full that it overflows. There is an air of calm deliberateness about all he writes, which is not

[*Cf. Wordsworth, "Preface to the Second Edition of Lyrical Ballads," in *Poetical Works* (1827), Vol. IV, pp. 361–2 (paras. 6–7).]

*u–u*33, 59   writers!
*v–v*33   *media*
*w–w*33   and

characteristic of the poetic temperament: his poetry seems one thing, himself another; he seems to be poetical because he wills to be so, not because he cannot help it: did he will to dismiss poetry, he need never again, it might almost seem, have a poetical thought. He never seems *possessed* by *any* feeling; no emotion seems ever so strong as to have entire sway, for the time being, over the current of his thoughts. He never, even for the space of a few stanzas, appears entirely *given up* to exultation, or grief, or pity, or love, or admiration, or devotion, or even animal spirits. He now and then, though seldom, *attempts* to write as if he were; and never, we think, without leaving an impression of poverty: as the brook which on nearly level ground quite fills its banks, appears but a thread when running rapidly down a precipitous declivity. He has feeling enough to form a decent, graceful, even beautiful decoration to a thought which is in itself interesting and moving; but not so much as suffices to stir up the soul by mere sympathy with itself in its simplest manifestation, nor enough to summon up that array of "thoughts of power" which in a richly stored mind always attends the call of really intense feeling. It is for this reason, doubtless, that the genius of Wordsworth is essentially unlyrical. Lyric poetry, as it was the earliest kind, is also, if the view we are now taking of poetry be correct, more eminently and peculiarly poetry than any other: it is the poetry most natural to a really poetic temperament, and least capable of being successfully imitated by one not so endowed by nature. *a*

Shelley is the very reverse of all this. Where Wordsworth is strong, he is weak; where Wordsworth is weak, he is strong. Culture, that culture by which Wordsworth has reared from his own inward nature the richest harvest ever brought forth by a soil of so little depth, is precisely what was wanting to Shelley: or let us rather say, he had not, at the period of his deplorably early death, reached sufficiently far in that intellectual progression of which he was capable, and which, if it has done so much for *greatly* inferior natures, might have made of him the *most perfect, as he was already the most gifted,* of our poets. For him, *voluntary* mental discipline had done little: the vividness of his emotions and of his sensations had done all. He seldom follows up an idea; it starts into life, summons from the fairy-land of his inexhaustible fancy some three or four bold images, then vanishes, and straight he is off on the wings of some casual association into quite another sphere. He had *scarcely* yet acquired the consecutiveness of thought necessary for a long poem; his more ambitious compositions too often resemble the

---

*x–x*33 a
*y–y*33 *given up*
*z–z*33 *attempts*
*a*33 All Wordsworth's attempts in that strain, if we may venture to say so much of a man whom we so exceedingly admire, appear to us cold and spiritless.
*b–b*33 far
*c–c*33 greatest
*d–d*33 intentional
*e–e*33 not

scattered fragments of a mirror; colours brilliant as life, single images without end, but no picture. It is only when under the overruling influence of some one state of feeling, either actually experienced, or summoned up in ^{f} the vividness of reality by a fervid imagination, that he writes as a great poet; unity of feeling being to him the harmonizing principle which a central idea is to minds of another class, and supplying the coherency and consistency which would else have been wanting. Thus it is in many of his smaller, and especially his lyrical poems. They are obviously written to exhale, perhaps to relieve, a state of feeling, or of conception of feeling, almost oppressive from its vividness. The thoughts and imagery are suggested by the feeling, and are such as it finds unsought. The state of feeling may be either of soul or of sense, or oftener (might we not say invariably?) of both: for the poetic temperament is usually, perhaps always, accompanied by exquisite senses. The exciting cause may be either an object or an idea. But whatever of sensation enters into the feeling, must not be local, or consciously ^{g}organic^g; it is a ^{h}condition^h of the whole frame, not of a part only ^{i}. Like^i the state of sensation produced by a fine climate, or indeed like all strongly pleasurable or painful sensations in an impassioned nature, it pervades the entire nervous system. States of feeling, whether sensuous or spiritual, which thus possess the whole being, are the fountains of that ^{j} which we have called the poetry of poets; and which is little else than ^{k}a pouring forth^k of the thoughts and images that pass across the mind while some permanent state of feeling is occupying it.

To the same original fineness of organization, Shelley was doubtless indebted for another of his rarest gifts, that exuberance of imagery, which when un-repressed, as in many of his poems it is, amounts ^{l} to a ^{m}fault^m. The susceptibility of his nervous system, which made his emotions intense, made also the impressions of his external senses deep and clear: and agreeably to the law of association by which, as already remarked, the strongest impressions are those which associate themselves the most easily and strongly, these vivid sensations were readily recalled to mind by all objects or thoughts which had coexisted with them, ^{n}and^n by all feelings which in any degree resembled them. Never did a fancy so teem with sensuous imagery as Shelley's. Wordsworth economizes an image, and detains it until he has distilled all the poetry out of it, and it will not yield a drop more: Shelley lavishes his with a profusion which is unconscious because it is inexhaustible. ^{o}

^{f}33   almost
$^{g-g}$33   bodily
$^{h-h}$33   state
$^{i-i}$33   ; like
^{j}33   poetry
$^{k-k}$33   the utterance
^{l}33   even
$^{m-m}$33   vice
$^{n-n}$+59, 67
^{o}33   The one, like a thrifty housewife, uses all his materials and wastes none: the other scatters them with a reckless prodigality of wealth of which there is perhaps no similar instance.

If, then, the maxim *Nascitur poëta*, mean, either that the power of producing poetical compositions is a peculiar faculty which the poet brings into the world with him, which grows with his growth like any of his bodily powers, and is as independent of culture as his height, and his complexion; or that *P*any*P* natural peculiarity *q*whatever*q* is implied in producing poetry, real poetry, and in any quantity—such poetry too, as, to the majority of educated and intelligent readers, shall appear quite as good as, or even better than, any other; in either sense the doctrine is false. And nevertheless, there *is* poetry which could not emanate but from a mental and physical constitution peculiar, not in the *r*kind,*r* but in the *s*degree*s* of its susceptibility: a constitution which makes its possessor capable of greater happiness than mankind in general, and also of greater unhappiness; and because greater, so also more various. And such poetry, to all who know enough of nature to own it as being *t*in*t* nature, is much *u*more*u* poetry, is poetry in a far higher sense, than any other; since the common element of all poetry, that which constitutes poetry, human feeling, enters far more largely into this than into the poetry of culture. Not only because the natures which we have called poetical, really feel more, and consequently have more feeling to express; but because, the capacity of feeling being so great, feeling, when excited and not voluntarily resisted, seizes the helm of their thoughts, and the succession of ideas and images becomes the mere utterance of an emotion; not, as in other natures, the emotion a mere ornamental colouring of the thought.

Ordinary education and the ordinary course of life are constantly at work counteracting this quality of mind, and substituting habits more suitable to their own ends: if instead of *v*substituting,*v* they were content to *w*superadd, there would be*w* nothing to complain of. But when will education consist, not in repressing any mental faculty or power, from the uncontrolled action of which danger is apprehended, but in training up to its proper strength the corrective and antagonist power?

In whomsoever the quality which we have described exists, and is not stifled, that person is a poet. Doubtless he is a *x*greater*x* poet in proportion as the fineness of his perceptions, whether of sense or of internal consciousness, furnishes him with an ampler supply of lovely images—the vigour and richness of his intellect with a greater abundance of moving thoughts. For it is through these thoughts and images that the feeling speaks, and through their impressiveness that it impresses itself, and finds response in other hearts; and from these media of transmitting it (contrary to the laws of physical nature) increase of intensity is reflected back upon the feeling itself. But all these it is possible to have, and not be a poet; they are mere materials, which the poet shares in common with other people. What constitutes

---

*p–p*33   *any*
*q–q*33   *whatever*
*r–r*33   *kind*
*s–s*33   *degree*
*t–t*33   *in*

*u–u*33   *more*
*v–v*33   *substituting*
*w–w*33   *superadd*, then there were
*x–x*33   *greater*

the poet is not the imagery nor the thoughts, nor even the feelings, but the law according to which they are called up. He is a poet, not because he has ideas of any particular kind, but because the succession of his ideas is subordinate to the course of his emotions.

Many who have never acknowledged this in theory, bear testimony to it in their particular judgments. In listening to an oration, or reading a written discourse not professedly poetical, when do we begin to feel that the speaker or author is putting off the character of the orator or the prose writer, and is passing into the poet? Not when he begins to show strong feeling; *then* we merely say, he *is in earnest, he feels* what he says; still less when he expresses himself in imagery; *then*, unless illustration be manifestly his sole object, we are apt to say, This is affectation. It is when the feeling (instead of passing away, or, if it continue, letting the train of thoughts run on exactly as they would have done if there were no influence at work but the mere intellect) becomes itself the originator of another train of association, which expels, or blends, with the former; *when (for example) either his words, or the mode of their arrangement, are such as* we spontaneously use only when in a state of excitement, *proving* that the mind is at least as much occupied by a passive state of its own feelings, as by the desire of attaining the premeditated end which the discourse has in view.*

Our judgments of authors who lay actual claim to the title of poets, follow the same principle. *Whenever*, after a writer's meaning is fully understood, it is still matter of reasoning and discussion whether he is a poet or not, he will be found to be wanting in the characteristic peculiarity of association *k* so often adverted to. When, on the contrary, after reading or hearing one or two passages, *we* instinctively and without hesitation *cry* out, This is a poet, the probability is,

*And this, we may remark by the way, seems to point to the true theory of poetic diction; and to suggest the true answer to as much as is erroneous of *d* Wordsworth's celebrated doctrine on that subject. [See "Preface to the Second Edition of Lyrical Ballads," in *Poetical Works* (1827), Vol. IV, pp. 360–1 and 365ff. (paras. 5, 9ff.).] For on the one hand, *all* language which is the natural expression of feeling, is really poetical, and will *f* be felt as such, apart from conventional associations; but on the other, whenever intellectual culture has afforded a choice between several modes of expressing the same emotion, the stronger the feeling is, the more naturally and certainly will it prefer *the* language which is most peculiarly appropriated to itself, and kept sacred from the contact of *h* more vulgar *i* objects of contemplation.

$^{y-y}$33, 59   *then*
$^{z-z}$33   seems to feel
$^{a-a}$33   *then*
$^{b-b}$33   as when (to take a simple example) the ideas or objects generally, of which the person has occasion to speak for the purposes of his discourse, are spoken of in words which
$^{c-c}$33   and which prove
^{d}33   Mr.
$^{e-e}$33, 59   *all*
^{f}33   always
$^{g-g}$33   that
^{h}33   all

^{i}33   and familiar
$^{j-j}$33   We believe that whenever
^{k}33   which we have
$^{l-l}$33   the mind
$^{m-m}$33   cries

that the passages are strongly marked with this peculiar quality. And we may add that in such case, a critic who, not having sufficient feeling to respond to the poetry, is also without sufficient philosophy to understand it though he feel it not, will be apt to pronounce, not "this is prose," but "this is exaggeration," "this is mysticism," or, "this is nonsense."

Although a philosopher cannot, by culture, make himself, in the peculiar sense in which we now use the term, a poet, unless at least he have that peculiarity of nature which would probably have made poetry his earliest pursuit; a poet may always, by culture, make himself a philosopher. The poetic laws of association are by no means incompatible with the more ordinary laws; are by no means such as "must" have their course, even though a deliberate purpose require their suspension. If the peculiarities of the poetic temperament were uncontrollable in any poet, they might be supposed so in Shelley; yet how powerfully, in _The Cenci_,[*] does he coerce and restrain all the characteristic qualities of his "genius; what severe simplicity, in place of his usual barbaric splendour; how rigidly does he keep the feelings and the imagery in subordination to the thought."

The investigation of nature requires no habits or qualities of mind, but such as may always be acquired by industry and mental activity. Because "at one time" the mind may be so given up to a state of feeling, that the succession of its ideas is determined by the present enjoyment or suffering which pervades it, "this" is no reason but that in the calm retirement of study, when under no peculiar excitement either of the outward or of the inward sense, it may form any combinations, or pursue any trains of ideas, which are most conducive to the purposes of philosophic inquiry; and may, while in that state, form deliberate convictions, from which no excitement will afterwards make it swerve. Might we not go even further than this? We shall not pause to ask whether it be not a misunderstanding of the nature of passionate feeling to imagine that it is inconsistent with "calmness;" whether they who so deem of it, do not "mistake passion in the militant or antagonistic state, for the type of passion universally; do not confound passion struggling towards an outward object, with passion brooding over itself". But without entering into this deeper investigation; that capacity of strong feeling, which is supposed necessarily to disturb the judgment, is also the material out of which all _motives_ are made; the motives, consequently, which lead human beings to the pursuit of truth. The greater the individual's capability of happiness and of misery, the stronger interest has that individual in arriving at truth; and when once that interest is felt, an impassioned nature is sure to pursue this, as to pursue any

[*_The Cenci, a Tragedy_ (London: Ollier, 1819).]

_n-n_33, 59   _must_
_o-o_33   genius! . . . splendour! . . . thought!
_p-p_33   in one state
_q-q_33   that
_r-r_33   calmness, and
_s-s_33   confound the state of _desire_ which unfortunately is possible to all, with the state of _fruition_ which is granted only to the few

other object, with greater ardour; for energy of character is ᶠcommonlyᶠ the offspring of strong feeling. If, therefore, the most impassioned natures do not ripen into the most powerful intellects, it is always from defect of culture, or something wrong in the circumstances by which the being has originally or successively been surrounded. Undoubtedly strong feelings ᵘrequireᵘ a strong intellect to carry them, as more sail requires more ballast: and when, from neglect, or bad education, that strength is wanting, no wonder if the grandest and swiftest vessels make the most utter wreck.

Where, as in ᵛsome of our older poetsᵛ, a poetic nature has been united with logical and scientific culture, the peculiarity of association arising from the finer nature so perpetually alternates with the associations attainable by commoner natures trained to high perfection, that its own particular law is not so conspicuously characteristic of the result produced, as in a poet like Shelley, to whom systematic intellectual culture, in a measure proportioned to the intensity of his own nature, has been wanting. Whether the superiority will naturally be on the side of the ᵂphilosopher-poetᵂ or of the mere poet—whether the writings of the one ought, as a whole, to be truer, and their influence more beneficent, than those of the other—is too obvious in principle to need statement: it would be absurd to doubt whether two endowments are better than one; whether truth is more certainly arrived at by two processes, verifying and correcting each other, than by one alone. Unfortunately, in practice the matter is not quite so simple; there the question often is, which is least prejudicial to the intellect, uncultivation or malcultivation. For, as long as ˣeducationˣ consists chiefly of the mere inculcation of traditional opinions, many of which, from the mere fact that the human intellect has not yet reached perfection, must necessarily be false; ʸso long as even those who are best taught, are rather taught to know the thoughts of others than to think,ʸ it is not always clear that the poet of acquired ideas has the advantage over him whose feeling has been his sole teacher. For, the depth and durability of wrong as well as of right impressions, is proportional to the fineness of the material; and they who have the greatest capacity of natural feeling are generally those whose artificial feelings are the strongest. Hence, doubtless, among other reasons, it is, that in an age of revolutions in opinion, the ᶻcotemporaryᶻ poets, those at least who deserve the name, those who have any individuality of character, if they are not before their age, are almost sure to be behind it. An observation curiously verified all over Europe in the present century. Nor let it be thought disparaging. However urgent

ᶠ⁻ᶠ33   always
ᵘ⁻ᵘ33   *require*
ᵛ⁻ᵛ33   Milton, or, to descend to our own times, in Coleridge
ᵂ⁻ᵂ33   logician-poet
ˣ⁻ˣ33   so much of education is made up of artificialities and conventionalisms, and the so-called training of the intellect
ʸ⁻ʸ+59, 67
ᶻ⁻ᶻ33   contemporary

may be the necessity for a breaking up of old modes of belief, the most strong-minded and discerning, next to those who head the movement, are generally those who bring up the rear of it. *a*

*a*33   A text on which to dilate would lead us too far from the present subject. [*signed:*] ANTIQUUS.*
[*footnote:*] *This signature is only used to identify the authorship of the present article with that of a paper headed, "What is Poetry?" in a former number of the *Repository*. The writer had a reason for the title, when he first adopted it; but he has discarded it in his later articles, as giving a partial, and so far a false, notion of the spirit by which he would wish his thoughts and writings to be characterised. As Wordsworth says,

> *Past* and *future* are the wings
> On whose support, harmoniously conjoined,
> Moves the great spirit of human knowledge;

and though the present as often goes amiss for lack of what time and change have deprived us of, as of what they have yet to bring, a title which points only one way is unsuitable to a writer who attempts to look both ways. [Wordsworth, "Essay, Supplementary to the Preface," in *Poetical Works* (1827), Vol. II, p. 390; later published in *The Prelude*, Bk. VI, ll. 448–50.] In future, when a signature is employed, it will be the single letter A.

WRITINGS OF JUNIUS REDIVIVUS [I]

1833

EDITORS' NOTE

Monthly Repository, n.s. VII (Apr., 1833), 262–70. Headed: "Writings of Junius Redivivus"; running title as title. Title footnoted: "*The Producing Man's Companion; an Essay on the Present State of Society, Moral, Political, and Physical, in England.* Second Edition, with additions. [London: Wilson, 1833.] / *A Tale of Tucuman, with Digressions, English and American, &c. &c.* [London: Wilson, 1831.]" The first edition of Junius Redivivus' (William Bridges Adams's) *Producing Man's Companion* was entitled *The Rights of Morality* (London: Wilson, 1832). The review is unsigned. Not republished. Identified in Mill's bibliography as "A review of the writings of Junius Redivivus in the 76th number of the Monthly Repository (for April 1833.)" (MacMinn, p. 25). The Somerville College copy (tear sheets) is headed in Mill's hand: "From the Monthly Repository for April 1833", and four corrections in his hand are made by cancellation and marginal addition: at 370.4 "some" is altered to "sore"; at 371.1 "with" is altered to "worth"; at 371.38 "fame" is altered to "frame"; and at 374.34 "openly" is replaced by "clearly".

For comment on the essay, see the Introduction, pp. xxxvi–xxxviii above.

Writings of Junius Redivivus [I]

THE PROLIFIC AND POPULAR WRITER who has stumbled upon this pseudonyme, literally, as we surmise, "in default of a better," (for a title less indicative of his individualizing peculiarities could not well have been chosen,) has recently made himself known through our pages to as many of the readers of the *Repository* as had not made his acquaintance previously through some other medium.[*] By including *us* among the many organs of utterance through which he speaks forth the truths which are in him, to a world which never stood more in need of truths so profitable, he has afforded to us a testimonial of his good wishes and good opinion, which we prize highly, but which would be somewhat less precious to us, if it carried with it any obligation to be silent concerning the good we think of him. We know to what constructions we expose ourselves in praising an avowed contributor to our work; but no person shall be a contributor to any work of ours whom we cannot conscientiously praise. As of all other friends, so of literary auxiliaries, we hold nothing unfit to be spoken which is fit to be thought. And they who, in all cases without exception, regulate their speech by no other rule than that of sincerity and simplicity, are indeed more liable to misconstruction on any single occasion than those who are studious of appearances, but less so in their total career: on that security we rely.

On the present occasion our remarks will relate, not so much to the two books of which we have transcribed the titles, or any of the other writings of the same author, but rather to the qualities of the author himself as therein exhibited. Nor is this, when rightly considered, the least important of the aspects under which a book, be it ever so valuable, (unless it be a book of pure science,) can be looked at. Let the word be what it may, so it be but spoken with a truthful intent, this one thing *must* be interesting in it, that it has been spoken by man—that it is the authentic record of something which has actually been thought or felt by a human being. Let that be sure, and even though in every other sense the word be false, there is a truth in it greater than that which it affects to communicate: we learn from it to know one

[*Adams, in addition to three poems, had contributed four other items to the *Monthly Repository*: in n.s. VI, "Junius Redivivus on the Conduct of the Monthly Repository" (Dec., 1832), 793–7 (with reply); and in n.s. VII, "On the State of the Fine Arts in England" (Jan., 1833), 1–33, "Beauty" (Feb., 1833), 89–96, and "On the Condition of Women in England" (Apr., 1833—i.e., the same number as this review of his work by Mill), 217–31.]

human soul. "Man is infinitely precious to man,"[*] not only because where sympathy is not, what we term *to live* is but to *get through* life, but because in all of us, except here and there a star-like, self-poised nature, which seems to have attained without a struggle the heights to which others must clamber in sore travail and distress, the beginning of all nobleness and strength is the faith that such nobleness and such strength have existed and do exist in others, how few soever and how scattered. A book which gives evidence of any rare kind of moral qualities in its author is a treasure to which all the contents of all other books are as dross. What is there in the writings even of Plato or of Milton so eternally valuable to us as the assurance they give that a Plato and a Milton have been? been in this very world of ours, where, therefore, we also, according to the measure of our opportunities, may, if we will, be the like. The gospel itself is not more a gospel (εὐαγγελίον) by the doctrines it teaches, than because it is the record of the *life* of Christ.

It is one of the evils of modern periodical writings, that we rarely learn from them to know their author. In those sibylline leaves wherein men scatter abroad their thoughts, or what seem their thoughts, we have little means of identifying the productions of the same sibyl; and no one particular oracle affords by itself sufficient materials for judging whether the prophet be a real *soothsayer*. It is so easy in a single article to pass off *adopted* ideas and feelings for the genuine produce of the writer's mind; it is so difficult on one trial to detect him who, aiming only at the plausible, finds and converts to that meaner purpose the same arguments which occur to him who is earnestly seeking for the true. Would but every person who writes anonymously adopt, like Junius Redivivus, a uniform signature, whereby all the emanations of one individual mind might have their common origin attested, great would be the advantage to upright and truthful writing, and great the increase of difficulties to imposture in all its kinds and degrees. A periodical writer would then have a character to lose or to gain; the unfairness, or ignorance, or presumption which he might manifest in one production, would have their due influence in diminishing the credit of another; a comparison between different writings of the same author would disclose whether his opinions varied according to the point he had to carry, or wavered from the absence of any fixed principles of judgment. A man who pretends to the intellect or the virtue which he has not, may deceive once, but he will betray himself somewhere: it is easy to keep up a false seeming for the space of an article, but difficult for a whole literary life. If the writer, on the contrary, be wise and honest, the more we read of his writings, knowing them to be his, the more thoroughly we shall trust him, and the better we shall learn to comprehend him. Every one of his opinions or sentiments which comes to our knowledge helps us to a more perfect understanding of all the rest; and the light they reflect on each other is a protection to the author against having

[*Thomas Carlyle, letter to Mill, 12 Jan., 1833, in *The Collected Letters of Thomas and Jane Welsh Carlyle*, Vol. VII, p. 300.]

his meaning mistaken, worth all precautions taken together. He may then write with directness and freedom, not timidly guarding himself by a running comment of deprecatory explanation, nor encumbering his argument or interrupting the flow of his feelings by qualifications or reserves which may better be supplied from the reader's previous acquaintance with the writer. The importance of this considera- tion will be most apparent to those who are most sensible how intimately all truths are connected: to those who know, that only by the general cast of an author's opinions and sentiments, and not by any sufficient explanation which he usually has it in his power to give on that particular occasion, can we with certainty determine the sense in which he understands, and means us to understand, his own propositions.

The foregoing remarks cannot be better illustrated than by the example of the writer who furnished the occasion on which they are made. We prize the writings of Junius Redivivus for the many valuable truths which are embodied and diffused in them, truths often, as we cheerfully acknowledge, new to us, almost always newly illustrated, and to have arrived at which required, if not a subtle and profound, a penetrating, sagacious, and enlarged understanding. But this, which is so much, is the least part of what we owe to Junius Redivivus, nor are his writings chiefly precious for what *they* are, but for what they show *him* to be: in so far as is possible for inanimate letter-press, they give to the world, once more, assurance of a *man*. It is *men* the world lacks now, much more than books; or if it wants books, wants them principally for lack of men: of old mankind were often so far superior to their ideas; *now* their ideas are so far superior to *them*. There are truths spread abroad in the world in ample measure, were there but the intellect to grasp them, and the strength to act up to them. But how often does it happen that when he is most wanted, we know where to look for the man who is *possessed* by the truth—whose mind has *absorbed* it, and, better still, of whose desires and affections it has become the paramount ruler! We do not mean by the truth, this or that little bit of truth here and there, but the *all* of truth which a conscientious man *needs* in order to shape his path through the world, much more to be a light and a protection to others:—the *all*, or but barely so *much* of it as is necessary for doing any *one* important thing well and thoroughly.

We are grateful, then, to Junius Redivivus, that he has put the mark of common parentage upon his mind's offspring,—that he has not cut up his literary identity into separate and small fragments, each of which might have belonged to an entire being so far inferior to what (it is impossible not to believe) HE is. For if any writings of the present age bespeak a strong, healthy, and well-proportioned mental frame, his do. If he had told us his name, his birth, parentage, station, profession, all these particulars the knowledge of which is usually termed know- ledge of the man, *that* were probably nothing: of all that in any way concerns us, his moral and intellectual being, we have assurance sufficient. With all the freshness of youthful feelings, he unites an extent of practical experience and knowledge of life, impossible in one very young, and affording the happiest earnest that the fountains of emotion at which others drink and pass on, will flow beside his path, refreshing and inspiring the whole of his earthly journey. One-sided men commonly enforce their partial views with a vehemence and an air of strong conviction which persons of more comprehensive minds are often without, being unable to throw their whole souls into a part only of the truth which lies before them: but the advantage for which others are indebted to their narrowness, Junius Redivivus derives from the excitability and ardour of his temperament: the idea or feeling required by the immediate purpose, seems to possess him as entirely as if that were the only purpose he had in life: but the other idea or feeling which ought to accompany and qualify the first, is there in reality, though appearing not, unless called for: look somewhere else and you will find the remainder of the truth supplied, and what seemed partial in the feeling, corrected by tokens that all other feelings proper to the occasion, are equally strong and equally habitual. There is an evidence of hearty conviction and energetic will in all the writings of this author which compels the persuasion that he would be as ready to act upon all he professes as to profess it: being, as we may gather from the particulars he lets fall of his own life, inured to self-reliance, and not unaccustomed to difficulties or even to emergencies. He writes as one in whom there still survived something of the spirit of the ancient heroes, along with the superior humanity and the superior refinement of modern times.

It is seldom, indeed, that a wise man's praise can be unqualified; yet of the *man* Junius Redivivus, as shown in his writings, there is little or nothing to be said on the disparaging side; of the works themselves somewhat. He is *not* a *great* writer: will he ever be? Possibly not: yet only perhaps because he does not desire it: he has never shown the capacity, but then he has never shown the wish, to produce a *finished* performance. Is this to be regretted? we hesitate to answer yes: great writers write for posterity, but *frequent* writers are those who do good in their generation; and no great writer, whom we remember, was a frequent writer, except Voltaire. Junius Redivivus writes far more powerfully than could be expected, from one who has written in two years as much as would amount to many volumes, and every word of it with thought. Writing of a very high order is thrown away when it is buried in periodicals, which are mostly read but once, and that hastily: yet the only access now to the general public, is through periodicals. An article in a newspaper or a magazine, is to the public mind no more than a drop of water on a stone; and like that, it produces its effect by *repetition*.

The peculiar "mission" of this age, (if we may be allowed to borrow from the new French school of philosophers a term which they have abused,)[*] is to popularize among the many, the more immediately practical results of the thought

[*For the term, see Claude Henri de Saint-Simon, *Nouveau christianisme* (Paris: Bossange père, *et al.*, 1825), pp. 76 and 87–8. Mill comments on the issue in a review in the *Examiner*, 2 Feb., 1834, pp. 68–9.]

and experience of the few. This is marked out as the fittest employment for the present epoch, partly because now for the first time it *can* be done, partly because anything of a still higher description *cannot*; unless writers are willing to forego immediate usefulness, and take their chance, that what is neglected by their own age will reach posterity. In this, then, which is the great intellectual business of our time, Junius Redivivus is better qualified to render eminent service, than a more eminent writer. It is true, that all he has written, perhaps all he will ever have the inclination or the patience to write, will be ephemeral: but if each production only lasts its day or year, each new day or year produces a successor: and though his works shall perish, it will not be until they have planted in many minds, truths which shall survive them, and awakened in many hearts a spirit which will not die.

The staple of all popular writing in the present crumbling condition of the social fabric, must be politics: and politics predominate in the writings of Junius Redivivus. But he writes not as one to whom politics are all in all: he knows the limits of what laws and institutions can do: he never expresses himself, as if any form of polity could give to mankind even the outward requisites of happiness, much less render them actually happy, in spite of themselves, or as if a people individually ignorant and selfish, could as a community by any legerdemain of checks and balances conjure up a government better than the men by whom it is carried on. Politics with our author are important, but not all-important. The great concern with him is, the improvement of the human beings themselves: of which the improvement of their institutions will be a certain *effect*, may be in some degree a *cause*, and is so far even a necessary condition, that until it is accomplished, none of the other causes of improvement can have fair play. The individual man must after all work out his own destiny, not have it worked out for him by a king, or a House of Commons; but he can hardly be in a suitable frame of mind for seeing and feeling this, while he is smarting under the sense of hardship and wrong from other men. Nor is this the worst; for the laws of a country, to a great degree, make its morals. Power, and whatever confers power, have been in all ages the great objects of the admiration of mankind: the most obvious kind of power to common apprehension, is power in the state; and according as that is obtained by rank, court favour, riches, talents, or virtues, the favourable sentiments of mankind will attach themselves, and their ambition will be directed to one or another of these attributes. Plato expected no great improvement in the lot of humanity, until philosophers were kings, or kings philosophers:[*] without indulging so romantic a wish, we believe that in the many there will be little of the requisite culture of the internal nature, and therefore little increase even of outward enjoyments, until institutions are so framed, that the ascendency over the minds of men, which naturally accompanies the supreme direction of their worldly affairs, shall be exercised, we do not say by philosophers, but at the least by honest men, and men

[*_Republic_, Vol. I, p. 508 (Bk. V, 473^d).]

who with adequate practical talents combine the highest appreciation of speculative wisdom.

In politics, Junius Redivivus is a radical. But since there are various kinds of radicals, it is fitting to state to which variety of the species our author belongs. Some men (it has been well said) are radicals, only because they are not lords: this will not suit our author; who, it is evident, would scorn equally to accept or to submit to, irresponsible or unearned superiority. Others are radicals, because they are of a fretful and complaining disposition, and accustomed to think present evils worse than any future contingent ones: such men in the United States would be aristocrats: be the order of things what it may, it must have some faults peculiarly its own, and those faults in the estimation of such people ensure its condemnation: neither is our author one of these. He is full of that spirit of love, which suffers little besides loveliness to be visible where loveliness *is*, and which boils up, and explodes in indignation only when heated by the contact of evil unmixed or predominant. Even in a semi-barbarous people, like those of Spanish America, he finds ample food for admiration and sympathy; in the *Tale of Tucuman*, and elsewhere, he dwells with peculiar complacency upon whatever those nations afford of beautiful or noble. Others again are radicals, merely because the taxes are too high: they can conceive of no evil except poverty, and finding themselves poor, or seeing that their neighbours are so, think it is the fault of the Government for hindering them from being rich; not so our author: *he* sees that there is a cause independent of Government, which makes the majority poor, and keeps them so, where it is not counteracted either by natural or artificial checks; this is, the tendency of population to a more rapid increase than is compatible with high wages. No person has inculcated this truth with greater earnestness and perseverance, or in a manner more likely to impress it upon the minds of those who are most directly interested in it, than Junius Redivivus. And there is nothing by which he is more honourably distinguished, both from the demagogue, and from the more ignorant or narrow-minded of the radicals. This is one of the most striking instances of the remark we made, that his truths are seldom half-truths. A perception of the abuses of existing Governments without a sense of the dependence of wages on a limitation of the number of labourers, has led many into grievous errors: so has a perception of the latter half-truth without the former: but let a man once clearly perceive and understand *both*, and his aberrations in political opinion are by that sole fact restrained within comparatively narrow limits.

Our author is a radical, because he is convinced both from principle and from history, that is both from the experience of men and of nations, that power, without accountability to those over whom, and for whose benefit it is to be exercised, is for the most part a source of oppression to them, and of moral corruption to those in whom the power resides. On the same principle *we* are radicals also: not that we consider the above proposition to be true without exception: nor do we in any case look upon it as embracing the *whole* of what ought to be taken into consideration in forming our practical conclusions: but we hold it to contain as much of the truth, as is amply sufficient to prove all institutions worthless, which like most of those which now exist, are constructed in utter defiance, or entire negligence of it.

For the details of our author's political opinions, and his applications of them to the existing state of society in England, we refer our readers to *The Producing Man's Companion*, which has been revised and greatly enlarged in this second edition. We shall make no extracts, because, to convey any but a most partial view of the contents of the volume, would require more copious citations than our space admits of, and because so interesting, and so cheap, and portable a work, should be in the hands of every one whom words of ours can influence. A connected or systematic treatise we cannot call it: the wonder is, how with so little apparent order or concatenation in his ideas, the author has contrived always to think consistently with himself. The book is like those kinds of living creatures which have joints, but no limbs: no reason can be given why the animals, or why the book, should not be twice as long; why the writer stopped when he did, or why he did not stop sooner. But all his opinions are so nicely adjusted to one another; they seem mutually to receive and give so exactly the proper, and none but the proper modifications; that in his own mind it is clear his ideas are in their right places, though when poured out upon paper they defy the very notion of arrangement, and lie one upon another in a kind of heap. This would be disagreeable if the book were very long, but being short, and made up of parts so good in themselves, it scarcely needs that they should be more artfully put together.

Our author is a most minute observer, both of things and men; the extent of his miscellaneous information is truly surprising: and most of it has evidently been acquired by himself, not derived from books. He appears to be well versed in experimental physics, and familiar with the processes of very many branches of practical industry. His sagacity and ingenuity display themselves here also in numerous contrivances, and a still greater number of prophecies of contrivances, which will probably some time or other be fulfilled. But these belong neither to the works we are reviewing, nor to the general scope of this article.

One of the most delightful qualities of this author, his lively admiration and keen enjoyment of the beautiful in all its kinds, both spiritual and physical, has been nowhere more exemplified than in his contributions to our work; and our readers do not require from us any assurance of it. Besides the value of this quality in itself, it has saved him from an error which many, and they not the most narrow-minded of our social reformers, habitually fall into; the error of expecting that the regeneration of mankind, if practicable at all, is to be brought about exclusively by the cultivation of what they somewhat loosely term the *reasoning* faculty; forgetting that reasoning must be supplied with *premises*, complete as well as correct, if it is to arrive at any conclusions, and that it cannot furnish any test of the principles or facts from which it sets out; forgetting too that, even supposing perfect knowledge to be attained, no good will come of it, unless the *ends*, to which the means have been pointed out, are first *desired*. But of this, perhaps, on another occasion, and at greater length. Our object in introducing the topic was to observe, that this error demonstrates of those who hold it either a deficiency in themselves, of all mental faculties, except the calculating understanding, or else that the other powers are so uncultivated, or so ill-cultivated, as to be at habitual variance with that faculty. It is otherwise with Junius Redivivus: his sensibility to beauty has contributed largely to quicken his intellect and expand his views; and in nothing more so than in opening his eyes to the importance of poetry and art, as instruments of human improvement on the largest scale. Where the sense of beauty is wanting, or but faint, the understanding must be contracted: there is so much which a person, unfurnished with that sense, will never have observed, to which he will never have had his attention awakened: there is so much, of the value of which to the human mind he will be an incompetent and will be apt to be a prejudiced judge; so many of the most important means of human culture which he will not know the use of, which he is almost sure to undervalue, and of which he is at least unable to avail himself in his own efforts, whether for his own good or for that of the world. It is true of this as of all the other sensibilities, that without intellect they run wild; but without them, intellect is stunted. A time will come, when the education of both will proceed hand in hand; let us rather say, when the aid of culture will be more particularly invoked to strengthen the part which is relatively deficient: or at lowest, to bestow the power of *appreciation*, when the quality to be appreciated is one which only nature can give.

Our author is as much of a poet as intense sensibility and vigorous intellect can make him, with the assistance of a memory richly stored with accurate pictures of things seen, and *well* seen, and keenly enjoyed, by himself. We do not think he has much fancy: his descriptions are extremely literal, and indeed profess to be so. The *Tale of Tucuman*, his longest poem, was avowedly composed, not to body forth the ideal, but to delineate the actual: "To convey," he says in the preface, "in as agreeable a form as may be, a knowledge of the manners and customs of the Southern Americans: the descriptions," he adds, "of scenery, costume, manners, and customs, are as accurate as though it were a prose work. Most of the incidents are of actual occurrence; and living beings have sat for the portraits of the actors."[*] Having thus an object in view, altogether distinct from that of the poet and artist, the wonder is not great if he have not succeeded equally well in both. He had in reality a third purpose in addition; the inculcation of his opinions, concerning things in general, not excepting persons, in digressions, after the manner of *Don Juan*,[†] of which he has likewise imitated the versification. The work is interesting, though most readers will, we are afraid, skip a great part of the descriptive passages, for the sake of which all the rest would appear to have been

[*A *Tale of Tucuman*, pp. 5 and 9.]
[†Byron, *Don Juan, a Poem*, 2 vols. (Edinburgh: Kay, 1825).]

written. The claim of this publication to the character of poetry rests, we think, upon the strong human sympathies which unfold themselves in some passages of the rather meagre story. In several of our author's shorter poems, we think there is more poetry; though still of the same grade of excellence: no high order of imagination; little beyond memory and strong feeling; both of these, however, of the best kind, and quite sufficient to ensure his being always read with pleasure. The versification is often rugged, evidently from haste: when our author writes in verse, he should write more carefully, and alter more freely; otherwise it is not worth while: the only reason for preferring verse to prose, being the music of its sound.

WRITINGS OF JUNIUS REDIVIVUS [II]

1833

EDITORS' NOTE

Tait's Edinburgh Magazine, III (June, 1833), 347–54. Headed: "Writings of Junius Redivivus. / The Producing Man's Companion." Title footnoted: "*The Producing Man's Companion; an Essay on the Present State of Society, Moral, Political, and Physical, in England. By Junius Redivivus* [William Bridges Adams]. *Addressed to the productive classes of the community.* Second edition, with additions. [London:] 1833. Effingham Wilson." Running titles: "Writings of Junius Redivivus" (to the equivalent of 384.26) and then "The Producing Man's Companion." The first edition of Adams's work was entitled *The Rights of Morality* (London: Wilson, 1832). The review is unsigned. Not republished. Identified in Mill's bibliography as "A review of 'The Producing Man's Companion' by Junius Redivivus in the 15th number of Tait's magazine (June 1833.)" (MacMinn, p. 32). The Somerville College copy (tear sheets) is headed in Mill's hand: "From Tait's Magazine for June 1833"; there are no corrections or emendations.

For comment on the essay, see the Introduction, pp. xxxvi–xxxvii above.

Writings of Junius Redivivus [II]

THE ANONYMOUS, AND UNKNOWN AUTHOR of this work, made, we believe, his first appearance in the world of letters as a writer in the *Tatler*, about two years ago; since which time he has published, in quantity alone, almost as much as has been written in the same time by any editor of any daily newspaper; and even his hastiest productions so abound in ideas, are so replete with various information, and expatiate over so wide a range of subjects, in all of which he seems equally at home, that he has been suspected of being not *one* writer, but a literary partnership, or *coterie*,—a society of friends agreeing to use a common signature. But the perfect unity of spirit and tone which pervades these writings, the distinctness with which the individuality of the writer preserves and paints itself in all that issues from his pen, and the identity of the style, both in its merits and in its defects, are, to our judgment, conclusive indications that *Junius Redivivus* is the (somewhat inappropriate) pseudonyme of a writer who is one and indivisible. The wonder, that a single mind, and one which, by its own confession, has not numbered many years, should be capable of producing, with such rapidity, works, mostly indeed of a fugitive kind, yet of so varied a cast, and requiring attainments so multifarious and diversified,—quite accounts for the doubt whether the unity of authorship be other than fictitious.

To a large class of readers Junius Redivivus is probably best known by the letters which have appeared from time to time under his signature in the *Examiner* newspaper. These, however, though far from being without merit, are, in our opinion, his least valuable productions. He seems to have selected that journal as an organ chiefly for personal attacks on public characters; and it is not there that we consider his strength to lie. In the bitterness and unsparingness of his invective, he resembles his namesake, but not prototype, the elder Junius; here, however, the resemblance ceases. His vituperation is as inferior to that of *Junius's Letters*,[*] in potency, as it is superior to those mere party productions in sincerity and purity of purpose. Personalities, to be effective, must be condensed; and our author's style is diffuse. Personalities require the most minute nicety in the adaptation of the words to the slightest shade of the thought; and our author never takes time to

[*See *Junius: Including Letters by the Same Writer, under Other Signatures*, 3 vols. (London: Rivington, *et al.*, 1812).]

weigh his words. Personalities never *tell* with so much force as when they are indirect, containing more by implication than they proclaim by assertion; and our author always blurts out, in the plainest and straightest terms, the whole of what he has to say. Personalities are pungent nearly in proportion to the studied polish and elegance of the style in which they are conveyed; and our author is hasty and careless in the minutiæ of composition. He frequently, also, exhibits a tendency (excusable enough in any one who is writing of modern English statesmen) to put the very worst possible interpretation upon any fault, whether of act or omission, and therefore to carry his censure to a pitch of severity often greater than the facts, in the estimation of any one who is disposed to put a more charitable construction upon them, appear to justify. This greatly impairs the efficiency of his personal attacks; for readers always incline to sympathize with any one who is assailed with greater appearance of animosity than seems warranted by the grounds laid for it by the assailant himself. In this, as in many things besides, to attempt more than you have the means of succeeding in, is to accomplish less.

But no one who is conversant with the writings of Junius Redivivus, can mistake the nature or the source of this seeming bitterness of spirit. It springs from no personal ill-will towards the individuals or the classes attacked;—it is the offspring neither of an intolerant intellect nor a malignant temper, but of an intense and impatient sympathy with all who are oppressed or in bondage. It is the remark of one of the wisest of women, that they who love ardently, hate bitterly; but, if they live long enough, outgrow their hate;—and so will Junius Redivivus. He always will, he always ought to condemn all he now condemns; but in a somewhat calmer tone, and a mitigated spirit.

With this exception, we know not of a single fault to charge him with. In the work before us, and in his almost innumerable contributions (the best of which we should much like to see collected into a volume) to the *Mechanics' Magazine*,* the *Tatler*, the *True Sun*, the *New Monthly Magazine*, Mr. Fox's excellent *Monthly Repository*, and we know not how many other works, he has attempted various kinds of composition, from the tale, poem, or descriptive sketch, to the philosophical essay. He has travelled over innumerable topics, from the humblest questions of practical mechanics, through the whole range of the applications of physical knowledge to the arts of life, up to some of the highest practical problems of moral and social science; and if we may be permitted (as every writer must, in fact, whether he avow it or not) to erect our own judgment into the standard of

---

*One of his most valuable papers in the *Mechanics' Magazine*—a statement of a plan for the better training of the working classes, by the partial introduction (he purposes of domestic economy only) of Mr. Owen's co-operative principle, is, we are happy to see, reprinted as part of the additional matter inserted in the present edition of the work which has given occasion to this article. ["Plan for the Better Housing of the Working Classes," *Mechanics' Magazine*, No. 434 (3 Dec., 1831), 165–71; reprinted in *The Producing Man's Companion*, pp. 204–23.]

comparison, he has scarcely touched upon a single subject on which he has not rendered important service to the cause of truth.

Professing to be a self-educated man, our author has the merit, so much oftener found in the self-taught than in the regularly educated, viz. that his opinions are, in the only valuable sense of the word, original—that is, are his own, and not adopted from others: while great natural powers, and a wide and varied intercourse with mankind, turned to the best account by a most inquisitive and searching disposition, have supplied the place of a more extensive book-knowledge, and have saved him from the narrowness and self-conceit which are the counterbalancing failings of the self-instructed. Our author appears to us to possess, in a degree rare among minds of any class, the faculty of going straight into the very pith and marrow of a subject, and fixing at once upon the great and governing elements of a question. In a few sentences or pages, he will dispose, clearly and decisively, of topics on which many, who pass for deep thinkers, are not even able to understand the truth when it is pointed out and explained to them. Were he a profounder metaphysician, or more conversant with, and more accustomed to analyze the thoughts of those who have examined his subjects before him, or who look at them from different points of view, he would, it is true, be a more skilful controversialist;—he would dig closer to the foundations of error and fallacies, and would often root out an objection, when he now only mows it down; but in the attainment of positive and practical truth, such additional acquirements could do little more for him than he has had strength to do for himself without that assistance.

The work before us is not systematic, but desultory; it has no particular plan, scarcely even a beginning, middle, or end; but seems to consist of the results of years of thought, allowed to accumulate, and poured out altogether in a confused stream. The present is the second edition; the first was published about a year ago, under the loose and inaccurate title—*The Rights of Morality*.[*] The renunciation of this and similar incorrect expressions, not only in the title-page, but throughout the work, is one of the numerous improvements, we are happy to observe, in the new edition, which is also enriched with seventy additional pages, under the name of a supplement.

As our object is to induce our readers to resort to the work itself for the stores of intellectual aliment which it contains, we shall not attempt any abstract of its contents, but shall rather select such passages as may serve for a sample of the author's speculations, and of the general character of his mind.

Our author is a radical in the best sense of the term, that is, he is an enemy to all institutions and all usages which deliver over any portion of the species, unprotected, to the tender mercies of any other portion; whether the sacrifice be of blacks to whites, of Catholics to Protestants, of the community at large to lords and boroughmongers, of the middle and working classes to the higher, of the working

[*London: Wilson, 1832.]

classes to the middle, or (a surer test of genuine high-minded radicalism than all the rest) of women to men. Irresponsible power, by whomsoever held, or over whomsoever exercised, our author abhors. He abhors it as intensely as if he thought with the more narrow-minded and exclusive of the lovers of liberty, that nothing is necessary but knocking off the fetters of the serf, to make him fit for the proper exercise of freedom. From this mistake, however, no Tory is more perfectly exempt than Junius Redivivus; and what might otherwise be the inflammatory tendency of his vehement invectives against those whom he calls, with a slight taint of exaggeration, the "tyrannical taskmasters" of the people,[*] receives a salutary correction from the force with which, in his appeals to the most numerous and most oppressed class, he insists upon the brutalized and degraded state of their own minds. Wretched as is the operation of bad social institutions upon the merely physical and worldly interests of mankind, in our author's eyes, their most lamentable and most detestable property, is their depraving influence upon the human character. He regards oligarchies of all sorts with aversion, less for the wealth which they misappropriate, or the actual tyranny which they perpetrate, than because it is at once their interest and their instinct to subdue the spirit of the people, and keep them in intellectual and moral darkness. The cultivation of the minds of the people is the source to which he looks exclusively for any sensible improvement in their well-being. But he is convinced that any thing deserving the name of universal cultivation will never be had until our social institutions are purified from the infection of jobbery and lying, which poisons all that would otherwise be good in them; not until they are so re-modelled, that every vestige of irresponsible power shall disappear, and high mental faculties assiduously devoted to the disinterested pursuit of the public good, shall be the only passport to a share in the government of the nation: and, therefore, as well as for the inherent vileness of the abuses themselves does he urge war upon them with so much acrimony.

There is nothing upon which our author insists more earnestly and more frequently than this, that government is a work of nicety and difficulty, the subject of a peculiar science, requiring long study and appropriate intellectual culture.[†] This is one of the marks by which our author's radicalism stands most strikingly distinguished from the radicalism of a vulgar demagogue, who may generally be known by his appeals to "plain understanding" and "commonsense," and attempts to persuade the ignorant that ignorance is no disqualification for judging of politics, and knowledge no advantage. Being convinced that few persons are capable of being good legislators, and that these few are more likely to be found among those who are compelled to be industrious, than among those who are at liberty to be idle, our author contends strongly for reducing the number of the House of Commons, and allowing salaries to the members.

[*The Producing Man's Companion, p. 11.]
[†See, e.g., pp. 37, 95–9, 103–6, 189–92, 201–2.]

The number of persons at present before the public, and possessing the requisite qualifications for legislators, is few, and it is only by degrees that they can expect to find them. The qualifications which fit a man for a legislator are precisely those which will prevent him from thrusting himself before the public, to squabble with brawling dema-gogues and designing knaves. Men fitted for legislators are few and valuable; they must be sought ere they can be found. Until a sufficient number shall appear, the people must continue strictly to cross-examine all claimants; more especially until a sufficient salary shall be attached to the office, to support the incumbent, while he is giving his services to those who employ him. So long as a man shall be expected to transact a painful duty gratis, so long will he, if not honest, contrive the means of remunerating himself in an indirect manner, to a far greater amount than he would receive if directly paid. One of the honestest men upon record—Andrew Marvell—received public pay as a member of Parliament until the day of his death. The absurdity of not paying legislators, of not supporting them while engaged in the public service, is monstrous. The highest possible talent is required, together with the severest study, to make them fit for the office. They are the most important class in the community, for on them the welfare of the community, to a great extent, depends. Judges are paid, and they are mostly the mere executors of what the intellect of legislators has prepared for them in the shape of laws. Magistrates are paid; lawyers are paid,—as well as all those engaged in every branch of executive justice, yet the highest of all, the law-makers, are in many cases left to want. Can it enter into the imagination of any one that the science of law-making is indigenous to peculiar breeds of men? Do they conceive that the possession of "property" is sufficient to confer moral and political knowledge in its highest grade? Do they imagine that the most wealthy men are likely to pursue the business of legislation as an amusing study? If not, would they wish to exclude a man of high intellect, merely because he happens to be poor and industrious; for the exclusion of all such men is the inevitable consequence of the present absurd arrangement? The proper payment of members should be amongst the first things for the community at large to insist upon, as a great security for the honesty of their representatives. It should, in fact, form one of the pledges required from candidates. The Scot, when about to hire himself as a servant, was asked what wages he required. Understanding well his own pecuniary interests, he would not state any sum, which would have fixed the amount, but replied in a general manner, "I'll just pick up the wee things aboot the hoose; sae I carena muckle for the pennie fee." The "wee things," of course, he contrived to make available to three times the amount he would have received in hard cash; and just so has been the case with the unpaid members of Parliament. [Pp. 185–7.]

Our author's sense of the unspeakable value of intellect and knowledge, evinces itself in his proposition that men of letters, and inventors in science and art, should be pensioned at the expense of the state; patent rights and copyrights being abolished, as injurious monopolies, and not an effectual nor a skilful mode of rewarding the labour and merit of the writer or the inventor. We are the more desirous to attract notice to this feature in our author's speculations, as the enemy are fond of imputing to persons of strong democratic opinions, a disdain of literary attainments, and of all intellectual pre-eminence.

There are two classes of persons, who probably contribute more to the general welfare of the community than any others. I allude to literary authors, and mechanical and other inventors. It is clearly most desirable that the comfortable maintenance of these persons should be provided for, in a mode which might afford the best possible security against their falling into want, and which, at the same time, might leave them the fullest leisure for prosecuting their valuable labours, without being under the necessity of occupying their time with painful exertions in the pursuit of money, to yield them a subsistence; or of petty details, which more ordinary men would perhaps plod through to greater advantage. The power of invention is, unfortunately for the possessors, though perhaps under present arrangements, advantageously for the public at large, rarely accompanied by prudence; but when it is, the condition of the inventor is improved at the cost of the public. He who invents one thing by a process of induction, as is the case with the higher class of inventors, could, and probably would invent more; but if he be a prudent man, so soon as he has secured one valuable scheme, he sets to work to perfect it, and then becomes a manufacturer, realizing in that mode an infinitely larger pecuniary recompense, than he could possibly attain were he to content himself with following the bent of his genius. It is understood, that the valuable results of the powers of the late Dr. Wollaston were much cramped in this way. It was also the case with Mr. Heathcote, the inventor of the bobbinet machine, which has been of such immense service to trade. Had a trustworthy and responsible government existed, means would long since have been devised to reward inventive talent, in such a mode as would insure the development of the largest possible amount. But until such a government shall exist, the present imperfect mode must continue; which, after all, is, in its actual operation, more of a boon to speculative capitalists, than a recompense to the efforts of genius.

Even in the case of really valuable inventions, useful to the whole community, how rarely do the inventors permanently benefit by them! The speculator, the dealer, is constantly on the watch, to appropriate them, and realizes a large fortune, while the inventor is usually left to starve, till he has struck out some fresh plan, whereby to procure another small supply of means. How then can the patent-right be said to encourage invention? Thus it is with the inventive writers of books. With years of labour and study, they accomplish new discoveries in the regions of thought. The copyright is secured to them: but what avails it? The booksellers see a chance of profit, and the market is deluged with compilations; using the same matter and ideas, couched in varied language. The author angrily complains: but he might as well talk to the winds. The fact is, that the patent-right of the inventor, and the copy-right of the author are injudicious modes of remunerating public services, and do not accomplish the desired object. In a more healthy state of the public mind, better means will be resorted to. At present they are a necessary evil.

It has been shewn, that the profiters by inventions are not usually the inventors themselves, but mercantile speculators. Would it not, then, be better to make the pecuniary reward hereafter an inalienable annual pension, paid by the public, the amount of which might be regulated by the importance of the invention, the number of people by whom it was used, and the national saving or advantage accruing therefrom? The pension should also terminate with the life of the inventor. Such a method would clearly be to the advantage of the whole body of inventors; for they would thus be saved from the miseries of want which many of them undergo. Should any inventors object to such a mode of remuneration, and, vain of their own abilities, think that they ought still to be allowed to dictate to the public, by means of a monopoly, it would be well to remind them, that there is no obligation on them to make known, any more than there is on the public to use their inventions. It is a matter of mutual bargain. The skill of the workman who executes is as needful for the perfection of the invention as is the genius of the discoverer who devises it; and neither of them would be one whit benefited, were it not for the public, who purchase and use it. Let not the inventor, then, arrogate too much to himself, because those happen to be few who pursue his vocation; but let him remember the fable of the belly and the members![*] Many varieties of talent are requisite to accomplish the perfection of a machine.

[*See Plutarch, *Caius Marcius Coriolanus*, in *Lives* (Greek and English), trans. Berna-dotte Perrin, 11 vols. (London: Heinemann; Cambridge, Mass.: Harvard University Press,

Authors, also, who have written works containing new matter beneficial to the community, are entitled to a recompense from the public, as much as other inventors, perhaps more so, because their discoveries are more valuable, as the happiness of man is at the present period more contingent on moral discovery than it is on physical. To degrade the profession of a teacher of morality, to a mere matter of trade and barter, is injurious to the community. Philosophers can rarely gain a living by their works; the public will not buy enough of copies to leave a profit on their publication. To live by trade, a man must manufacture an article which will ensure a sale. The public prefer books which administer to their passions and amusement. The philosopher would not write the first, even if he could; and it is rarely that he possesses the faculty of writing the latter. Therefore, there can be few writing philosophers, capable of teaching a nation, under the present system; and, unfortunately, men born to wealth, seldom get the necessary mental training to form philosophers. The only good public act of George IV—perhaps the only good one public or private—was the establishment of a literary fund of one thousand pounds per annum, to be divided among ten literary men of reputation in decayed circumstances. It will be a lasting reproach to the Whig Government, that they deprived these men of their living, in their rage for economy, and at the same time kept up the numberless extravagant pensions of harlots, panders, and sycophants. [Pp. 115–16, 118–19, 123–5.]

It is one of our author's leading doctrines, that "the whole raw material of the whole globe is the property of the whole human race, as tenants in common;" that private property in land will one day cease to exist, a reasonable compensation being made to *bonâ fide* possessors; and that the land will then be administered (as it is in India, and other countries of the East) for the benefit of the community generally; that, in the meantime, every human being who is born into the world, "has a moral right to live in the world, and, consequently, has a right to his share of those things, as raw materials, without which he cannot live." [P. 13.] This, without further explanation, is somewhat vague, and susceptible of being practically misapplied; but from any such danger it is secure, if viewed in conjunction with our author's other opinions. What is meant is this, that as nobody is to blame for being born, nobody ought to be allowed to starve while there is food in the world to feed him, when others who preceded him have engrossed, by mere occupancy, those lands and raw materials, which are no more of their making than of his; to which he has as fair a claim as they had originally; and of which, if not previously monopolized, his fractional share might have been sufficient to enable him to live.

This doctrine, the developments of which, though highly interesting we have not space to quote, might easily have misled a less expanded mind than our author's into the vagaries of Spenceanism or Owenism. Holding, as he does, that the original appropriation of the raw material of the globe was wrongful, and the result of force or fraud, he might easily have been led, like so many well-meaning persons before him, into the notion that it is proper to redress this wrong by some of the innumerable modes, direct or indirect, of taking from those who have, to give to those who have not. From all such errors he has been kept clear, by a strong

---

1914–16), Vol. IV, p. 130 (para. VI, §§2–4), the source for Shakespeare, in *Coriolanus*, I, i, 96–163; see also Aesop, "The Belly and the Members," in *Aesop's Fables*, trans. Vernon Stanley Jones (London: Heinemann; New York: Doubleday, Page, 1912), p. 128.]

conviction of the tendency of population to tread upon the verge of subsistence; and, consequently, to render all additions to the fund for the maintenance of the labourers ineffectual for the improvement of their condition, except in so far as accompanied by increased habits of prudence. Our author has placed this subject in a light which may be new to some of our readers; and we cannot refrain from quoting him at some length.

The notion which is commonly entertained, that because a man has a large annual income, he therefore consumes more than his neighbour, is absurd. For example: A man has an estate producing him in rent a thousand pounds per annum. He cannot have this rent till the farmers and labourers who cultivate the land have been fed and clothed sufficiently to keep them, at any rate, in a state of working health. If they were kept lower than this, they either could not work, or they would perish, or break out into riot. I may therefore assume that they are fed and clothed. The rent and tithes, therefore, are the surplus or profit of the estate. The rent goes to the squire, the tithes to the parson, and we will suppose them one thousand pounds per annum each. What purpose do they turn it to? The squire has a house in which are maintained five of his own family, and three servants; and he must moreover pay his proportion towards the poor rates. The poor he thus maintains yield him no service whatever; and his servants are not exclusively his. One makes his bed, but she also makes her own: another cooks the dinner, but it is for her own benefit as well as his: another washes his clothes, but she washes her own also. The real personal service which falls to his individual share will be a very small proportion of the whole labour which is performed in the household; and his personal consumption of food and clothing will be the same, because all must be provided for out of the income. He may, if he chooses, have expensive food and clothes, but it must be only out of the surplus, after all the household are provided; and he cannot eat two dinners, or wear two coats, at a time. If one coat per annum is the amount of actual wear, and he has fifty made annually, he can only consume the fiftieth part of each; they will then go to the community to be worn out. And all the time he must have his share of labour, in purchasing provisions, and giving directions for the joint benefit of the household. He must see that the house is repaired, and that the garden produces its crop: and, in short, perform all the business of an overlooker. In fact, he is only a distributor, and were his income doubled, trebled, quadrupled, he would still be only a distributor. Were he to keep six servants, or fifty, he would not consume one jot more. He could eat but one dinner, and sleep in but one bed, and wear but the same quantity of clothing, unless indeed he were wantonly to destroy it, which no man does, any more than he burns his house down. And his personal labour would be increased, because he would become a distributor to fifty instead of three. If he turned the matter over to a steward, then the steward would become the distributor instead, and the squire would be merely the receiver of what he needed for his own personal accommodation. The power would pass into the hands of the steward. The parson does all this the same as the squire.

The parson, the stockholder, the merchant, the manufacturer, the aristocrat, the place-man, the pensioner, the soldier, the judge, all, up to the king, are in the same precise condition—they are only distributors. Whatever may be the amount of their income, be it hundreds or millions, still they can only individually consume their maintenance, which differs little in quantity, whether for king or peasant. The surplus must be distributed, and the reason is plain. There is a certain amount of food and necessaries annually produced, and a certain quantity imported. They are jointly, rather under than over the demand, and therefore they are sure not to be wasted. By the process called trade, the whole of the provisions are divided amongst the whole of the population. The most energetic amongst the people are sure to be the distributors, just as the foreman of a manufactory is usually the cleverest man in it. It is true that the custom of hereditary succession has placed many dolts in the office of distributors, but they are only apparently so—they are mere tools in the hands of ministers, stewards, &c., who hold the real power. The first class of distributors, of course, help themselves first, and plentifully, to the choicest of food, just as the foreman gets the largest wages. Thus game and rich wines, &c., being comparatively scarce articles, fall to their share. Coarser meats fall to the share of the next class of distributors, and so on downwards, till the poor operatives have nothing left but salt provisions and vegetable substances, as is the case with weavers. Below them again, there are a portion of people dwelling, as it were, on the outskirts of society, who do not get, upon an average, more than two-thirds of the food necessary to keep them in health, and a part of these die off from time to time, when a temporary scarcity occurs. These are principally composed of persons who are, from want of skill, unfit to work, but are too proud, or possess too little energy, to scramble for their share of parochial assistance. They are like the little boys at school, who are pushed away from the fire by the great ones, because it is not sufficiently warm to heat all round. In the parish workhouses, and receiving weekly assistance from the parishes, are comprised a large number of operatives of robust habits, many willing to work, and many lazy, but none of whom would suffer the distributors to go on quietly, if their wants were not tolerably well attended to. From this feeling of self-preservation, the distributors have established poor-laws, *i.e.* the wealthier distributors; for it must be borne in mind, that the poor weaver, who receives his weekly stipend, is a distributor, when he feeds his wife and children with the provisions his earnings have purchased.

Thus, it is clear, that the immediate cause of the misery which the people endure is the fact, that their numbers are beyond the proportion of the supply of food and necessaries. Were the food and necessaries in greater proportion than the number of the people, there would be no misery arising from that source. A large number of the people who are well fed would possibly remain in perfect health, were they to cede one-fourth of their food, to be divided amongst the ill-fed; but this would, in a short time, be productive of still more extensive misery. They have possibly a claim to an equal share all round, because, although food is produced by labour, and not one in ten actually gives any labour to that object, still we may suppose that all would be equally willing to labour, and the land, as before stated, is the joint property of all. In their half-fed state, the surplus population are incapable of procreation; or, if they have children, they are weakly and die off. But were their food increased to a sufficient quantity, by an equal division, they would breed very rapidly, and the consequence would be, that unless the supply of food and necessaries could be artificially increased, the whole population would soon be reduced to a half allowance. And if the supply of food were again artificially increased to full allowance, they would again breed beyond it. The struggle might thus go on, if science and industry were successful, till every square yard of land held a human being, and then, in case of a famine, having nothing to fall back upon, they would eat one another. [Pp. 24–9.]

Our author, therefore, relies for the improvement of the physical condition of the people upon that increase of prudence and self-control, as to the multiplication of their numbers, which he believes to be the natural result of even such increase of intelligence as is now actually taking place.

We must here close our extracts. We might have found numerous passages superior, as mere pieces of writing, to those we have quoted. The energy, and strong feeling with which Junius Redivivus almost always writes, occasionally rise into something deserving the name of eloquence. But we preferred to give specimens of his argumentative powers. We have quoted enough to convince, we trust, almost all our readers, that few among the writers for the day are either so bold and independent in thought, or so manly and pure in purpose, as Junius Redivivus; and we shall rejoice if such praise as ours can do any thing to spread the reputation, or (what we are sure he regards much more,) to extend the usefulness of his writings.

VIEWS OF THE PYRENEES

1833

EDITORS' NOTE

Monthly Repository, n.s. VII (Sept., 1833), 660. This brief notice appeared in the "New Publications" section of the *MR*, where, along with a list of new works, there appeared notes appended to some of the titles. Here the entry reads: "Views of the Pyrenees, with Descriptions, by the Author of the Sketches. Part I. Bagnères de Bigorre, and the Valley of Campan. Part II. The Pass of the Tourmalet and Barège. (9)." The note (the item here reprinted) begins: "(9). Exactly . . . ." Unsigned. Not republished. Identified in Mill's bibliography as "A note at the end of the Monthly Repository for September 1833, being a notice of 'Views from the Pyrenees' " (MacMinn, p. 33). No copy in the Somerville College library.

The work, actually entitled neither "Views of . . ." nor "Views from . . . ," but "Views in . . . ," has a text by Mrs. R. E. Young, with ten plates based on her sketches. It was published in London by the author, and Leggatt, Colnaghi and Son, Moon, Boys, and Graves, and Walther, in 1831. For comment, see the Introduction, p. xxxviii above.

Views of the Pyrenees

EXACTLY THIRTEEN YEARS AGO, when the continent had been but a few years open to the annual influx from England, of those who travel either to refresh themselves after the toils of business, or because they have no business to toil at, we, who belong to the former class, visited the lovely and majestic scenery delineated in these sketches; and we have often wondered since, that so few persons among the crowds of pleasure-hunters have diverged from the beaten track of the Rhine, Switzerland, and Italy, to visit a region equally accessible, and quite equally worthy to be sought. Of late years we have reason to believe, that the scenery of the Pyrenees has been treated with less negligence, and that our tourists having grown familiar with the more celebrated regions to which they at first flocked, are resorting in considerable numbers to this comparatively untrodden soil. The beautiful sketches which we have now the pleasure of noticing, and which, we understand, are the production of a lady, will, we think, send many visitants to these glorious mountains, in whom the desire was not yet awakened, and will be a beautiful and interesting ornament of a drawing-room table for the still larger class who remain at home.

TENNYSON'S POEMS

1835

EDITORS' NOTE

London Review, I (equivalent to *Westminster Review*, XXX) (July, 1835), 402–24. Headed: "(ART. VII.) / Tennyson's Poems. / 1. *Poems, chiefly Lyrical, by Alfred Tennyson.* [London:] Effingham Wilson. 1830. / 2. *Poems. By Alfred Tennyson.* [London:] Moxon. 1833." Running title: "Tennyson's Poems." Signed: "A." Not republished. Identified in Mill's bibliography as "A review of Tennyson's Poems in the same number of the same work"—i.e., the *London Review* for July, 1835, in which his "Rationale of Political Representation" appeared (MacMinn, p. 45). In the Somerville College copy (tear sheets), at 399.21 "pots" has been corrected by pencilled interlineation to "plots".

For comment, see the Introduction, pp. xxxix and xliv–xlv above.

Tennyson's Poems

TOWARDS THE CLOSE OF THE YEAR 1830 appeared a small volume of poems, the work of a young and unknown author, and which, with considerable faults (some of them of a bad kind), gave evidence of powers such as had not for many years been displayed by any new aspirant to the character of a poet. This first publication was followed in due time by a second, in which the faults of its predecessor were still visible, but were evidently on the point of disappearing; while the positive excellence was not only greater and more uniformly sustained, but of a higher order. The imagination of the poet, and his reason, had alike advanced: the one had become more teeming and vigorous, while its resources had been brought more habitually and completely under the command of the other.

The notice which these poems have hitherto received from the more widely-circulated and influential organs of criticism consists, so far as we are aware, of two articles—a review of the first publication, in *Blackwood's Magazine*, and of the second, in the *Quarterly Review*.[*] The article in *Blackwood*, along with the usual flippancy and levity of that journal, evinced one of its better characteristics— a genuine appreciation and willing recognition of genius. It was not to be expected that a writer in *Blackwood* could accomplish a criticism on a volume of poetry, without cutting capers and exhibiting himself in postures, as Drawcansir says, "because he dare."[†] The article on Mr. Tennyson is throughout in a strain of mocking exaggeration. Some reviewers write to extol their author, others to laugh at him; this writer was desirous to do both—first to make the book appear beyond all measure contemptible, next in the highest degree admirable—putting the whole force of his mind alternately into these two purposes. If we can forgive this audacious sporting with his reader and his subjects, the critique is otherwise not without merit. The praise and blame, though shovelled out rather than measured, are thrown into the right places; the real merits and defects of the poems are pointed out with discrimination, and a fair enough impression left of the proportion between the two; and it is evident that if the same writer were to review Mr.

[*John Wilson, "Tennyson's *Poems*," *Blackwood's Magazine*, XXXI (May, 1832), 721–41; and John Wilson Croker, "*Poems* by Alfred Tennyson," *Quarterly Review*, XLIX (Apr., 1833), 81–96.
[†George Villiers, *The Rehearsal* (London: Dring, 1672), p. 38 (IV, i).]

Tennyson's second publication, his praise, instead of being about equally balanced by his censure, would be but slightly qualified by it.

Of Mr. Tennyson's two volumes, the second was the only one which fell into the hands of the *Quarterly* Reviewer; and his treatment of it, compared with the notice taken by *Blackwood* of its more juvenile predecessor, forms a contrast, character-istic of the two journals. Whatever may be in other respects our opinion of *Blackwood's Magazine*, it is impossible to deny to its principal writers (or writer) a certain susceptibility of sense, a geniality of temperament. Their mode of writing about works of genius is that of a person who derives much enjoyment from them, and is grateful for it. Genuine powers of mind, with whatever opinions connected, seldom fail to meet with response and recognition from these writers. The *Quarterly Review*, on the other hand, both under its original and under its present management, has been no less characterised by qualities directly the reverse of these. Every new claim upon its admiration, unless forced upon it by the public voice, or recommended by some party interest, it welcomes, not with a friendly extension of the hand, but with a curl of the lip: the critic (as we figure him to ourselves) taking up the book, in trusting anticipation of pleasure, not from the book, but from the contemplation of his own cleverness in making it contemptible. He has not missed the opportunity of admiring himself at the expense of Mr. Tennyson: although, as we have not heard that these poems have yet, like those of Mr. Robert Montgomery, reached the eleventh edition,[*] nor that any apprehension is entertained of danger to the public taste from their extravagant popularity, we may well be astonished that performances so utterly worthless as this critic considers them, should have appeared to him deserving of so much attention from so superior a mind. The plan he adopts is no new one, but abundantly hacknied: he selects the few bad passages (not amounting to three pages in the whole), and such others as, by being separated from the context, may be made to look ridiculous; and, in a strain of dull irony, of which all the point consists in the ill-nature, he holds forth these as a specimen of the work. A piece of criticism, resembling, in all but their wit, the disgraceful articles in the early Numbers of the *Edinburgh Review*, on Wordsworth and Coleridge.[†]

Meanwhile, these poems have been winning their way, by slow approaches, to a reputation, the exact limits and measure of which it would be hazardous at present to predict, but which, we believe, will not ultimately be inconsiderable. Desiring, so far as may depend upon us, to accelerate this progress, and also not without a desire to exhibit, to any who still have faith in the *Quarterly Review*, the value of its critical judgments, we propose to lay before those of our readers who are still

[*Presumably a reference to Robert Montgomery, *The Omnipresence of the Deity. A Poem*, 11th ed. (London: Maunder, 1830), which contains, as well as the title poem, a section entitled "Poems."]

[†See, e.g., Francis Jeffrey, "Poems by W. Wordsworth," *Edinburgh Review*, XI (Oct., 1807), 214–31, and anon. (Thomas Moore or William Hazlitt?), "Coleridge's *Christabel*," *ibid.*, XXVII (Sept., 1816), 58–67.]

unacquainted with the poems, such specimens as may justify the terms in which we have spoken of them—interspersing or subjoining a few remarks on the character and the present state of developement of Mr. Tennyson's poetic endowment.

Of all the capacities of a poet, that which seems to have arisen earliest in Mr. Tennyson, and in which he most excels, is that of scene-painting, in the higher sense of the term: not the mere power of producing that rather vapid species of composition usually termed descriptive poetry—for there is not in these volumes one passage of pure description: but the power of *creating* scenery, in keeping with some state of human feeling; so fitted to it as to be the embodied symbol of it, and to summon up the state of feeling itself, with a force not to be surpassed by anything but reality. Our first specimen, selected from the earlier of the two volumes, will illustrate chiefly this quality of Mr. Tennyson's productions. We do not anticipate that this little poem will be equally relished at first by all lovers of poetry: and indeed if it were, its merit could be but of the humblest kind; for sentiments and imagery which can be received at once, and with equal ease, into every mind, must necessarily be trite. Nevertheless, we do not hesitate to quote it at full length. The subject is Mariana, the Mariana of *Measure for Measure*, living deserted and in solitude in the "moated grange."[*] The ideas which these two words suggest, impregnated with the feelings of the supposed inhabitant, have given rise to the following picture:

With blackest moss the flower-plots
    Were thickly crusted, one and all,
The rusted nails fell from the knots
    That held the peach to the garden-wall.
The broken sheds looked sad and strange,
    Unlifted was the clinking latch,
    Weeded and worn the ancient thatch
Upon the lonely moated grange.
        She only said, "My life is dreary,
            He cometh not," she said;
        She said, "I am aweary, aweary;
            I would that I were dead!"

Her tears fell with the dews at even,
    Her tears fell ere the dews were dried,
She could not look on the sweet heaven,
    Either at morn or eventide.
After the flitting of the bats,
    When thickest dark did trance the sky,
    She drew her casement-curtain by,
And glanced athwart the glooming flats.
        She only said, "The night is dreary,
            He cometh not," she said:
        She said, "I am aweary, aweary,
            I would that I were dead!"

[*See Shakespeare, *Measure for Measure*, III, i.]

Upon the middle of the night,
  Waking she heard the night-fowl crow:
The cock sung out an hour ere light:
  From the dark fen the oxen's low
Came to her: without hope of change,
  In sleep she seemed to walk forlorn,
  Till cold winds woke the grey-eyed morn
About the lonely moated grange.
      She only said, "The day is dreary,
        He cometh not," she said;
      She said, "I am aweary, aweary,
        I would that I were dead!"

About a stone-cast from the wall,
  A sluice with blackened waters slept,
And o'er it many, round and small,
  The clustered marishmosses crept.
Hard by a poplar shook alway,
  All silver-green with gnarled bark,
  For leagues no other tree did dark
The level waste, the rounding grey.
      She only said, "My life is dreary,
        He cometh not," she said;
      She said, "I am aweary, aweary,
        I would that I were dead!"

And ever when the moon was low,
  And the shrill winds were up an' away,
In the white curtain, to and fro,
  She saw the gusty shadow sway.
But when the moon was very low,
  And wild winds bound within their cell,
  The shadow of the poplar fell
Upon her bed, across her brow.
      She only said, "The night is dreary,
        He cometh not," she said;
      She said, "I am aweary, aweary,
        I would that I were dead!"

All day within the dreamy house,
  The doors upon their hinges creaked,
The blue-fly sung i' the pane; the mouse
  Behind the mouldering wainscot shrieked,
Or from the crevice peered about.
  Old faces glimmered through the doors,
  Old footsteps trod the upper floors,
Old voices called her from without.
      She only said, "My life is dreary,
        He cometh not," she said;
      She said, "I am aweary, aweary,
        I would that I were dead!"

> The sparrow's chirrup on the roof,
>   The slow clock ticking, and the sound
> Which to the wooing wind aloof
>   The poplar made, did all confound
> Her sense; but most she loathed the hour
>   When the thickmoted sunbeam lay
>   Athwart the chambers, and the day
> Downsloped was westering in his bower.
>   Then, said she, "I am very dreary,
>   He will not come," she said;
>   She wept, "I am aweary, aweary,
>   Oh God, that I were dead!"[*]

In the one peculiar and rare quality which we intended to illustrate by it, this poem appears to us to be pre-eminent. We do not, indeed, defend all the expressions in it, some of which seem to have been extorted from the author by the tyranny of rhyme; and we might find much more to say against the poem, if we insisted upon judging of it by a wrong standard. The nominal subject excites anticipations which the poem does not even attempt to fulfil. The humblest poet, who is a poet at all, could make more than is here made of the situation of a maiden abandoned by her lover. But that was not Mr. Tennyson's idea. The love-story is secondary in his mind. The words "he cometh not" are almost the only words which allude to it at all. To place ourselves at the right point of view, we must drop the conception of Shakspeare's Mariana, and retain only that of a "moated grange," and a solitary dweller within it, forgotten by mankind. And now see whether poetic imagery ever conveyed a more intense conception of such a place, or of the feelings of such an inmate. From the very first line, the rust of age and the solitude of desertion are, on the whole, picture. Words surely never excited a more vivid feeling of physical and spiritual dreariness: and not dreariness alone—for that might be felt under many other circumstances of solitude—but the dreariness which speaks not merely of being far from human converse and sympathy, but of being *deserted* by it.

Our next specimen shall be of a character remote from this. It is the second of two poems, "The May Queen" and "New Year's Eve"[†]—the one expressing the wild, overflowing spirits of a light-hearted girl, just chosen Queen of the May; the latter, the feelings of the same girl some months afterwards, when dying by a gradual decay. We regret that the opening of the latter poem must lose in our pages the effect of contrast produced by its immediately succeeding the former:

> If you're waking, call me early, call me early, mother dear,
> For I would see the sun rise upon the glad Newyear.
> It is the last Newyear that I shall ever see,
> Then ye may lay me low i' the mould, and think no more o' me.

[*"Mariana," in *Poems, Chiefly Lyrical*, pp. 14–18.]
[†In *Poems*, pp. 90–4, 95–100.]

To-night I saw the sun set: he set and left behind
The good old year, the dear old time, and all my peace of mind;
And the Newyear's coming up, mother, but I shall never see
The may upon the blackthorn, the leaf upon the tree.

Last May we made a crown of flowers: we had a merry day;
Beneath the hawthorn on the green they made me Queen of May;
And we danced about the maypole and in the hazel-copse,
Till Charles's wain came out above the tall white chimney-tops.

There's not a flower on all the hills: the frost is on the pane:
I only wish to live till the snow-drops come again:
I wish the snow would melt and the sun come out on high—
I long to see a flower so before the day I die.

The building rook will caw from the windy tall elmtree
And the tufted plover pipe along the fallow lea,
And the swallow will come back again with summer o'er the wave,
But I shall lie alone, mother, within the mouldering grave.

Upon the chancel-casement, and upon that grave o' mine,
In the early early morning the summer sun will shine,
Before the red cock crows from the farm upon the hill,
When you are warm-asleep, mother, and all the world is still.

When the flowers come again, mother, beneath the waning light,
Ye'll never see me more in the long gray fields at night;
When from the dry dark wold the summer airs blow cool,
On the oat-grass and the sword-grass, and the bulrush in the pool.

Ye'll bury me, my mother, just beneath the hawthorn shade,
And ye'll come sometimes and see me where I am lowly laid.
I shall not forget ye, mother, I shall hear ye when ye pass,
With your feet above my head in the long and pleasant grass.

I have been wild and wayward, but ye'll forgive me now;
Ye'll kiss me, my own mother, upon my cheek and brow;
Nay—nay, ye must not weep, nor let your grief be wild,
Ye should not fret for me, mother, ye have another child.

If I can I'll come again, mother, from out my resting place;
Though ye'll not see me, mother, I shall look upon your face;
Though I cannot speak a word, I shall hearken what ye say,
And be often—often with ye when ye think I'm far away.

Goodnight, goodnight, when I have said goodnight for evermore,
And ye see me carried out from the threshold of the door;
Don't let Effie come to see me till my grave be growing green:
She'll be a better child to you than ever I have been.

She'll find my garden tools upon the granary floor:
Let her take 'em: they are hers: I shall never garden more:
But tell her, when I'm gone, to train the rosebush that I set,
About the parlour-window and the box of mignonette.

Good-night, sweet mother: call me when it begins to dawn.
All night I lie awake, but I fall asleep at morn;
But I would see the sun rise upon the glad Newyear,
So, if you're waking, call me, call me early, mother dear.

This poem is fitted for a more extensive popularity than any other in the two volumes. Simple, genuine pathos, arising out of the situations and feelings common to mankind generally, is of all kinds of poetic beauty that which can be most universally appreciated; and the genius implied in it is, in consequence, apt to be overrated, for it is also of all kinds that which can be most easily produced. In this poem there is not only the truest pathos, but (except in one passage)* perfect harmony and keeping.

The next poem which we shall quote is one of higher pretensions. Its length exceeds the usual dimensions of an extract. But the idea which would be given of the more perfect of Mr. Tennyson's poems, by detached passages, would be not merely an incomplete but a false idea. There is not a stanza in the following poem which can be felt or even understood as the poet intended, unless the reader's imagination and feelings are already in the state which results from the passage next preceding, or rather from all which precedes. The very breaks, which divide the story into parts, all tell.

If every one approached poetry in the spirit in which it ought to be approached, willing to feel it first and examine it afterwards, we should not premise another word. But there is a class of readers, (a class, too, on whose verdict the early success of a young poet mainly depends,) who dare not enjoy until they have first satisfied themselves that they have a warrant for enjoying; who read a poem with the critical understanding first, and only when they are convinced that it is right to be delighted, are willing to give their spontaneous feelings fair play. The consequence is, that they lose the general effect, while they higgle about the details, and never place themselves in the position in which, even with their mere understandings, they can estimate the poem as a whole. For the benefit of such readers, we tell them beforehand, that this is a tale of enchantment; and that they will never enter into the spirit of it unless they surrender their imagination to the guidance of the poet, with the same easy credulity with which they would read the *Arabian Nights*, or, what this story more resembles, the tales of magic of the middle ages.

Though the agency is supernatural, the scenery, as will be perceived, belongs to the actual world. No reader of any imagination will complain, that the precise nature of the enchantment is left in mystery.

---

*We allude to the second line of the second stanza. The concluding words of the line appear to us altogether out of keeping with the rest of the poem.

THE LEGEND OF
THE LADY OF SHALOTT

Part the First

On either side the river lie
Long fields of barley and of rye,
That clothe the wold, and meet the sky;
And thro' the field the road runs by
        To manytower'd Camelot.
The yellowleavèd waterlily,
The green-sheathèd daffodilly,
Tremble in the water chilly,
        Round about Shalott.

Willows whiten, aspens shiver,
The sunbeam-showers break and quiver
In the stream that runneth ever
By the island in the river,
        Flowing down to Camelot.
Four grey walls and four grey towers
Overlook a space of flowers,
And the silent isle imbowers
        The Lady of Shalott.

Underneath the bearded barley,
The reaper, reaping late and early,
Hears her ever chanting cheerly,
Like an angel, singing clearly,
        O'er the stream of Camelot.
Piling the sheaves in furrows airy,
Beneath the moon, the reaper weary
Listening whispers, " 'Tis the fairy
        Lady of Shalott."

The little isle is all inrailed
With a rose-fence, and overtrailed
With roses: by the marge unhailed
The shallop flitteth silken-sailed,
        Skimming down to Camelot.
A pearl garland winds her head:
She leaneth on a velvet bed,
Full royally apparellèd,
        The Lady of Shalott.

Part the Second

No time has she to sport and play:
A charmèd web she weaves alway,
A curse is on her, if she stay
Her weaving, either night or day,
        To look down to Camelot.

She knows not what the curse may be;
Therefore she weaveth steadily,
Therefore no other care hath she,
      The Lady of Shalott.

She lives with little joy or fear.
Over the water, running near,
The sheepbell tinkles in her ear.
Before her hangs a mirror clear,
      Reflecting towered Camelot.
And, as the mazy web she whirls,
She sees the surly village-churls,
And the red-cloaks of market-girls,
      Pass onward from Shalott.

Sometimes a troop of damsels glad,
An abbot or an ambling pad,
Sometimes a curly shepherd lad,
Or longhaired page, in crimson clad,
      Goes by to towered Camelot.
And sometimes thro' the mirror blue,
The knights come riding, two and two.
She hath no loyal knight and true,
      The Lady of Shalott.

But in her web she still delights
To weave the mirror's magic sights:
For often thro' the silent nights,
A funeral, with plumes and lights
      And music, came from Camelot.
Or, when the moon was overhead,
Came two young lovers, lately wed:
"I am half-sick of shadows," said
      The Lady of Shalott.

Part the Third

A bow-shot from her bower-eaves
He rode between the barley-sheaves:
The sun came dazzling thro' the leaves,
And flamed upon the brazen greaves
      Of bold Sir Launcelot.
A redcross knight for ever kneeled
To a lady in his shield,
That sparkled on the yellow field,
      Beside remote Shalott.

The gemmy bridle glittered free,
Like to some branch of stars we see
Hung in the golden galaxy.
The bridle-bells rang merrily
      As he rode down from Camelot.

And, from his blazoned baldric slung,
A mighty silver bugle hung,
And, as he rode, his armour rung,
    Beside remote Shalott.

All in the blue unclouded weather,
Thickjewelled shone the saddle-leather.
The helmet, and the helmet-feather,
Burned like one burning flame together,
    As he rode down from Camelot.
As often thro' the purple night,
Below the starry clusters bright,
Some bearded meteor, trailing light,
    Moves over green Shalott.

His broad clear brow in sunlight glowed.
On burnished hooves his war-horse trode.
From underneath his helmet flowed
His coalblack curls, as on he rode,
    As he rode down from Camelot.
From the bank, and from the river,
He flashed into the crystal mirror,
"Tirra lirra, tirra lirra,"
    Sang Sir Launcelot.*

She left the web: she left the loom:
She made three paces thro' the room:
She saw the waterflower bloom:
She saw the helmet and the plume:
    She looked down to Camelot.
Out flew the web, and floated wide,
The mirror cracked from side to side,
"The curse is come upon me," cried
    The Lady of Shalott.

Part the Fourth

In the stormy eastwind straining,
The pale-yellow woods were waning,
The broad stream in his banks complaining,
Heavily the low sky raining
    Over towered Camelot:
Outside the isle a shallow boat
Beneath a willow lay afloat,
Below the carven stern she wrote,
    THE LADY OF SHALOTT.

---

*In this most striking passage, which we should have thought would have commanded admiration from every one who can read, all that the *Quarterly* Reviewer could see is, that the rhymes are incorrect! [See Croker, "*Poems* by Alfred Tennyson," p. 86.]

A cloudwhite crown of pearl she dight.
All raimented in snowy white
That loosely flew, (her zone in sight,
Clasped with one blinding diamond bright,)
    Her wide eyes fixed on Camelot,
Though the squally eastwind keenly
Blew, with folded arms serenely
By the water stood the queenly
    Lady of Shalott.

With a steady, stony glance—
Like some bold seer in a trance,
Beholding all his own mischance,
Mute, with a glassy countenance—
    She looked down to Camelot.
It was the closing of the day,
She loosed the chain, and down she lay,
The broad stream bore her far away,
    The Lady of Shalott.

As when to sailors while they roam,
By creeks and outfalls far from home,
Rising and dropping with the foam,
From dying swans wild warblings come,
    Blown shoreward; so to Camelot
Still as the boathead wound along,
The willowy hills and fields among,
They heard her chanting her deathsong,
    The Lady of Shalott.

A longdrawn carol, mournful, holy,
She chanted loudly, chanted lowly,
Till her eyes were darkened wholly,
And her smooth face sharpened slowly*
    Turned to towered Camelot:
For ere she reached upon the tide
The first house by the waterside,
Singing in her song she died,
    The Lady of Shalott.

Under tower and balcony,
By gardenwall and gallery,
A pale, pale corpse she floated by,
Deadcold, between the houses high,
    Dead into towered Camelot.

*This exquisite line, the egregious critic of the *Quarterly* distinguishes by italics as specially absurd! proving thereby what is his test of the truth of a description, even of a physical fact. He does not ask himself, Is the fact so? but, Have I ever seen the expression in the verses of any former poet of celebrity? [See Croker, p. 86.]

> Knight and burgher, lord and dame,
> To the plankèd wharfage came,
> Below the stern they read her name,
> "The Lady of Shalott."*

In powers of narrative and scene-painting combined, this poem must be ranked among the very first of its class. The delineation of outward objects, as in the greater number of Mr. Tennyson's poems, is, not picturesque, but (if we may use the term) statuesque; with brilliancy of colour superadded. The forms are not, as in painting, of unequal degrees of definiteness; the tints do not melt gradually into each other, but each individual object stands out in bold relief, with a clear decided outline. This statue-like precision and distinctness, few artists have been able to give to so essentially vague a language as that of words: but if once this difficulty be got over, scene-painting by words has a wider range than either painting or sculpture; for it can represent (as the reader must have seen in the foregoing poem), not only with the vividness and strength of the one, but with the clearness and definiteness of the other, objects in motion. Along with all this, there is in the poem all that power of making a few touches do the whole work, which excites our admiration in Coleridge. Every line suggests so much more than it says, that much may be left unsaid: the concentration, which is the soul of narrative, is obtained, without the sacrifice of reality and life. Where the march of the story requires that the mind should pause, details are specified; where rapidity is necessary, they are all brought before us at a flash. Except that the versification is less exquisite, the "Lady of Shalott" is entitled to a place by the side of the "Ancient Mariner," and "Christabel."[*]

Mr. Tennyson's two volumes contain a whole picture-gallery of lovely women: but we are drawing near to the limits of allowable quotation. The imagery of the following passage from the poem of "Isabel," in the first volume, is beautifully typical of the nobler and gentler of two beings, upholding, purifying, and, as far as possible, assimilating to itself the grosser and ruder:

> A clear stream flowing with a muddy one,
>   Till in its onward current it absorbs
>   With swifter movement and in purer light
>   The vexed eddies of its wayward brother—
>   A leaning and upbearing parasite,
>   Clothing the stem, which else had fallen quite,

*[*Poems*, pp. 8–19.] We omit the remaining stanza, which seems to us a "lame and impotent conclusion," where no conclusion was required. [See Shakespeare, *Othello*, II, i, 161.]

[*Coleridge, "The Rime of the Ancyent Marinere," in Wordsworth and Coleridge, *Lyrical Ballads with Other Poems* (London: Arch, 1798), pp. 1–51; and Coleridge, "Christabel," in *Christabel; Kubla Khan, a Vision; The Pains of Sleep* (London: Murray, 1816), pp. 3–48.]

With clustered flowerbells and ambrosial orbs
Of rich fruitbunches leaning on each other.[*]

We venture upon a long extract from what we consider the finest of these ideal portraits, the "Eleänore." The reader must not, in this case, look for the definiteness of the "Lady of Shalott;" there is nothing statuesque here. The object to be represented being more vague, there is greater vagueness and dimness in the expression. The loveliness of a graceful woman, words cannot make us see, but only feel. The individual expressions in the poem, from which the following is an extract, may not always bear a minute analysis; but ought they to be subjected to it? They are mere colours in a picture; nothing in themselves, but everything as they conduce to the general result.

> How may fullsailed verse express,
> How may measured words adore
> The fullflowing harmony
> Of thy swanlike stateliness,
> Eleänore?
> The luxuriant symmetry
> Of thy floating gracefulness,
> Eleänore?
> Every turn and glance of thine,
> Every lineament divine,
> Eleänore,
> And the steady sunset glow
> That stays upon thee? For in thee
> Is nothing sudden, nothing single;
> Like two streams of incense free
> From one censer, in one shrine,
> Thought and motion mingle,
> Mingle ever. Motions flow
> To one another, even as tho'
> They were modulated so
> To an unheard melody,
> Which lives about thee, and a sweep
> Of richest pauses, evermore
> Drawn from each other mellowdeep—
> Who may express thee, Eleänore?
>
> I stand before thee, Eleänore;
> I see thy beauty gradually unfold,
> Daily and hourly, more and more.
> I muse, as in a trance, the while
> Slowly, as from a cloud of gold,
> Comes out thy deep ambrosial smile.

[*Poems, Chiefly Lyrical, p. 8.]

I muse, as in a trance, whene'er
The languors of thy lovedeep eyes
Float on to me. I would I were
    So tranced, so rapt in ecstacies,
To stand apart, and to adore,
Gazing on thee for evermore,
Serene, imperial Eleänore!

Sometimes, with most intensity
Gazing, I seem to see
Thought folded over thought, smiling asleep,
Slowly awakened, grow so full and deep
In thy large eyes, that, overpowered quite,
I cannot veil, or droop my sight,
But am as nothing in its light.
As though a star, in inmost heaven set,
Ev'n while we gaze on it,
Should slowly round its orb, and slowly grow
    To a full face, there like a sun remain
    Fixed—then as slowly fade again,
        And draw itself to what it was before,
            So full, so deep, so slow
            Thought seems to come and go
        In thy large eyes, imperial Eleänore.

As thunderclouds that, hung on high
    Did roof noonday with doubt and fear,
    Floating through an evening atmosphere
Grow golden all about the sky;
In thee all passion becomes passionless,
Touched by thy spirit's mellowness,
Losing his fire and active might
    In a silent meditation,
Falling into a still delight
    And luxury of contemplation:
As waves that from the outer deep
    Roll into a quiet cove,
        There fall away, and lying still,
Having glorious dreams in sleep,
        Shadow forth the banks at will;
    Or sometimes they swell and move,
        Pressing up against the land,
            With motions of the outer sea:
            And the selfsame influence
            Controlleth all the soul and sense
        Of Passion gazing upon thee.
His bowstring slackened, languid Love,
    Leaning his cheek upon his hand,
        Droops both his wings, regarding thee,
            And so would languish evermore,
            Serene, imperial Eleänore.[*]

[*Poems, pp. 27–31.]

It has for some time been the fashion, though a fashion now happily on the decline, to consider a poet as a poet, only so far as he is supposed capable of delineating the more violent passions; meaning by violent passions, states of excitement approaching to monomania, and characters predisposed to such states. The poem which follows will show how powerfully, without the slightest straining, by a few touches which do not seem to cost him an effort, Mr. Tennyson can depict such a state and such a character.

THE SISTERS

We were two daughters of one race:
She was the fairest in the face:
    The wind is blowing in turret an' tree.
They were together, and she fell;
Therefore revenge became me well.
    O the Earl was fair to see!

She died: she went to burning flame:
She mixed her ancient blood with shame.
    The wind is howling in turret an' tree.
Whole weeks and months, and early and late,
To win his love I lay in wait:
    O the Earl was fair to see!

I made a feast; I bad him come;
I won his love, I brought him home.
    The wind is roaring in turret an' tree.
And after supper, on a bed,
Upon my lap he laid his head:
    O the Earl was fair to see!

I kissed his eyelids into rest;
His ruddy cheek upon my breast.
    The wind is raging in turret an' tree.
I hated him with the hate of hell,
But I loved his beauty passing well.
    O the Earl was fair to see!

I rose up in the silent night:
I made my dagger sharp and bright.
    The wind is raving in turret an' tree.
As half-asleep his breath he drew,
Three times I stabbed him through and through.
    O the Earl was fair to see!

I curled and combed his comely head,
He looked so grand when he was dead.
    The wind is blowing in turret an' tree.
I wrapped his body in the sheet
And laid him at his mother's feet.
    O the Earl was fair to see![*]

[*Ibid., pp. 65–7.]

The second publication contains several classical subjects treated with more or less felicity. The story of the Judgment of Paris, recited by Œnone, his deserted love, is introduced in the following stately manner:

> There is a dale in Ida, lovelier
> Than any in old Ionia, beautiful
> With emerald slopes of sunny sward, that lean
> Above the loud glenriver, which hath worn
> A path through steepdown granite walls below,
> Mantled with flowering tendriltwine. In front
> The cedarshadowy valleys open wide.
> Far-seen, high over all the Godbuilt wall
> And many a snowycolumned range divine,
> Mounted with awful sculptures—men and Gods,
> The work of Gods—bright on the dark blue sky
> The windy citadel of Ilion
> Shone, like the crown of Troas. Hither came
> Mournful Œnone, wandering forlorn
> Of Paris, once her playmate. Round her neck,
> Her neck all marblewhite and marblecold,
> Floated her hair or seemed to float in rest;
> She, leaning on a vine-entwinèd stone,
> Sang to the stillness, till the mountain-shadow
> Sloped downward to her seat from the upper cliff.*

The length to which our quotations have extended, and the unsatisfactoriness of short extracts, prevent us from giving any specimen of one of the finest of Mr. Tennyson's poems, the "Lotos-eaters." The subject is familiar to every reader of the *Odyssey*.[*] The poem is not of such sustained merit in the execution as some of the others; but the general impression resembles an effect of climate in a landscape: we see the objects through a drowsy, relaxing, but dreamy atmosphere, and the

---

*[*Ibid.*, pp. 51–2.] The small critic of the *Quarterly* finds fault [see Croker, p. 89,] with the frequent repetition, in Œnone's recital, of the following two verses:

> O mother Ida, many-fountained Ida,
> Dear mother Ida, hearken ere I die.

To return continually to the same *refrain* is, as the reader must have observed even in our extracts, a frequent practice of Mr. Tennyson, and one which, though occasionally productive of great beauty, he carries to a faulty excess. But on this occasion, if ever, it was allowable. A subject from Greek poetry surely justifies imitation of the Greek poets. Repetitions similar to this are, as everybody knows, universal among the pastoral and elegiac poets of Greece, and their Roman imitators: and this poem is both pastoral and elegiac.

[*Homer, *The Odyssey* (Greek and English), trans. Augustus Taber Murray, 2 vols. (London: Heinemann; New York: Putnam's Sons, 1919), Vol. I, p. 308 (Bk. IX, ll. 82–104).]

inhabitants seem to have inhaled the like. Two lines near the commencement touch the key-note of the poem:

> In the afternoon they came unto a land
> Wherein it seemèd always afternoon.

The above extracts by no means afford an idea of all the variety of beauty to be found in these volumes. But the specimens we have given may, we hope, satisfy the reader, that if he explore further for himself, his search will be rewarded. We shall only subjoin a few remarks, tending to an estimation of Mr. Tennyson's general character as a writer and as a poet.

There are in the character of every true poet, two elements, for one of which he is indebted to nature, for the other to cultivation. What he derives from nature, is fine senses: a nervous organization, not only adapted to make his outward impressions vivid and distinct (in which, however, practice does even more than nature), but so constituted, as to be, more easily than common organizations, thrown, either by physical or moral causes, into *states* of enjoyment or suffering, especially of enjoyment: states of a certain duration; often lasting long after the removal of the cause which produced them; and not local, nor consciously physical, but, in so far as organic, pervading the entire nervous system. This peculiar kind of nervous susceptibility seems to be the distinctive character of the poetic temperament. It constitutes the capacity for poetry; and not only produces, as has been shown from the known laws of the human mind, a predisposition to the poetic associations, but supplies the very materials out of which many of them are formed.* What the poet will afterwards construct out of these materials, or whether he will construct anything of value to any one but himself, depends upon the direction given, either by accident or design, to his habitual associations. Here, therefore, begins the province of culture; and, from this point upwards, we may lay it down as a principle, that the achievements of any poet in his art will be in proportion to the growth and perfection of his thinking faculty.

Every great poet, every poet who has extensively or permanently influenced mankind, has been a great thinker;—has had a philosophy, though perhaps he did not call it by that name;—has had his mind full of thoughts, derived not merely from passive sensibility, but from trains of reflection, from observation, analysis, and generalization; however remote the sphere of his observation and meditation may have lain from the studies of the schools. Where the poetic temperament exists in its greatest degree, while the systematic culture of the intellect has been neglected, we may expect to find, what we do find in the best poems of Shelley—

*It may be thought, perhaps, that among the gifts of nature to a poet, ought also to be included a vivid and exuberant imagination. We believe, however, that vividness of imagination is no further a gift of nature, than in so far as it is a natural consequence of vivid sensations. All besides this, we incline to think, depends on habit and cultivation.

vivid representations of states of passive and dreamy emotion, fitted to give extreme pleasure to persons of similar organization to the poet, but not likely to be sympathized in, because not understood, by any other persons; and scarcely conducing at all to the noblest end of poetry as an intellectual pursuit, that of acting upon the desires and characters of mankind through their emotions, to raise them towards the perfection of their nature. This, like every other adaptation of means to ends, is the work of cultivated reason; and the poet's success in it will be in proportion to the intrinsic value of his thoughts, and to the command which he has acquired over the materials of his imagination, for placing those thoughts in a strong light before the intellect, and impressing them on the feelings.

The poems which we have quoted from Mr. Tennyson prove incontestably that he possesses, in an eminent degree, the natural endowment of a poet—the poetic temperament. And it appears clearly, not only from a comparison of the two volumes, but of different poems in the same volume, that, with him, the other element of poetic excellence—intellectual culture—is advancing both steadily and rapidly; that he is not destined, like so many others, to be remembered for what he might have done, rather than for what he did; that he will not remain a poet of mere temperament, but is ripening into a true artist. Mr. Tennyson may not be conscious of the wide difference in maturity of intellect, which is apparent in his various poems. Though he now writes from greater fulness and clearness of thought, it by no means follows that he has learnt to detect the absence of those qualities in some of his earlier effusions. Indeed, he himself, in one of the most beautiful poems of his first volume (though, as a work of art, very imperfect), the "Ode to Memory," confesses a parental predilection for the "first-born" of his genius.[*] But to us it is evident, not only that his second volume differs from his first as early manhood from youth, but that the various poems in the first volume belong to different, and even distant stages of intellectual development;—distant, not perhaps in years—for a mind like Mr. Tennyson's advances rapidly—but corresponding to very different states of the intellectual powers, both in respect of their strength and of their proportions.

From the very first, like all writers of his natural gifts, he luxuriates in sensuous* imagery; his nominal subject sometimes lies buried in a heap of it. From the first, too, we see his intellect, with every successive degree of strength, struggling

[*See *Poems, Chiefly Lyrical*, p. 63.]

Sensuous, a word revived by Coleridge, as he himself states, "from our elder classics." [*Biographia Literaria*, Vol. I, p. 159.] It is used by Milton, who, in his little tract on Education, says of poetry, as compared with rhetoric, that it is "less subtile and fine, but more simple, *sensuous*, and passionate." [Milton, "Of Education," in *Prose Works*, ed. Charles Symmons, 7 vols. (London: Johnson, *et al.*, 1812), Vol. I, p. 281.] The word *sensual* is irretrievably diverted to another meaning; and a term seems to be required, which (without exciting any ethical associations) shall denote all things pertaining to the bodily senses, in contradistinction to things pertaining to the intellect and the mental feelings. To this use, the word *sensuous* seems as well adapted as any other which could be chosen.

upwards to shape this sensuous imagery to a spiritual meaning;* to bring the materials which sense supplies, and fancy summons up, under the command of a central and controlling thought or feeling. We have seen, by the poem of "Mariana," with what success he could occasionally do this, even in the period which answers to his first volume; but that volume contains various instances in which he has attempted the same thing, and failed. Such, for example, are, in our opinion, the opening poem, "Claribel," and the verses headed "Elegiacs."[*] In both, there is what is commonly called imagination—namely, fancy: the imagery and the melody actually haunt us; but there is no harmonizing principle in either;—no appropriateness to the spiritual elements of the scene. If the one poem had been called "A solitary Place in a Wood," and the other, "An Evening Landscape," they would not have lost, but gained. In another poem, in the same volume, called "A Dirge," and intended for a person who, when alive, had suffered from calumny—a subject which a poet of maturer powers would have made so much of, Mr. Tennyson merely glances at the topics of thought and emotion which his subject suggested, and expatiates in the mere scenery about the grave.[†]

Some of the smaller poems have a fault which in any but a very juvenile production would be the worst fault of all: they are altogether without meaning: none at least can be discerned in them by persons otherwise competent judges of poetry; if the author had any meaning, he has not been able to express it. Such, for instance, are the two songs on the Owl; such, also, are the verses headed "The How

*We conceive ourselves warranted, both by usage and the necessity of the case, in using the word *spiritual* as the converse of *sensuous*. It is scarcely necessary to say that we do not mean *religious*.

[*Poems, Chiefly Lyrical, pp. 1–2, 9–10.]

†[Ibid., pp. 104–7.] There are instances in the volume, of far worse failures than these. Such are the two poems "The Merman" and "The Mermaid." [Pp. 24–6, 27–30.] When a poet attempts to represent to us any of the beings either of religious or of popular mythology, we expect from him, that, under the conditions prescribed by the received notion of those beings, some mode of spiritual existence will be figured, which we shall recognise as in harmony with the general laws of spirit, but exhibiting those laws in action among a new set of elements. The faculty of thus bringing home to us a coherent conception of beings unknown to our experience, not by logically *characterizing* them, but by a living *representation* of them, such as they would, in fact, *be*, if the hypothesis of their possibility could be realized—is what is meant, when anything is meant, by the words creative imagination. Mr. Tennyson not only fails in this, but makes nothing even of the sensuous elements of the scene: he does not even produce, what he in no other instance misses—a suitable representation of outward scenery. He is actually puerile.

Of the two productions (the most juvenile, we should think, of the set)—"An English War Song," and "National Song," [ibid., pp. 138–40, 141–2,] we can only say, that unless they are meant for bitter ridicule of vulgar nationality, and of the poverty of intellect which usually accompanies it, their appearance here is unaccountable. The sonnet, "Buonaparte," in the second volume [Poems, p. 5], though not so childish in manner, has still something of the same spirit which was manifested in the two just cited (if they are to be taken as serious).

and the Why," in the first volume, and the lines on To-day and Yesterday, in the second.[*] If in the former of these productions Mr. Tennyson aimed at shadowing forth the vague aspirations to a knowledge beyond the reach of man—the yearnings for a solution of all questions, soluble or insoluble, which concern our nature and destiny—the impatience under the insufficiency of the human faculties to penetrate the secret of our being here, and being what we are—which are natural in a certain state of the human mind; if this was what he sought to typify, he has only proved that he knows not the feeling—that he has neither experienced it, nor realized it in imagination. The questions which a Faust calls upon earth and heaven, and all powers supernal and infernal, to resolve for him, are not the ridiculous ones which Mr. Tennyson asks himself in these verses.

But enough of faults which the poet has almost entirely thrown off merely by the natural expansion of his intellect. We have alluded to them chiefly to show how rapidly progressive that intellect has been.* There are traces, we think, of a continuance of the same progression, throughout the second as well as the first volume.

In the art of painting a picture to the inward eye, the improvement is not so conspicuous as in other qualities; so high a degree of excellence having been already attained in the first volume. Besides the poems which we have quoted, we may refer, in that volume, to those entitled, "Recollections of the Arabian Nights," "The Dying Swan," "The Kraken," and "The Sleeping Beauty."[†] The beautiful poems (songs they are called, but are not) "In the glooming light," and "A spirit haunts the year's last hours," are (like the "Mariana") not mere pictures, but states of emotion, embodied in sensuous imagery.[‡] From these, however, to the command over the materials of outward sense for the purpose of bodying forth states of feeling, evinced by some of the poems in the second volume, especially "The Lady of Shalott" and "The Lotos-eaters," there is a considerable distance; and Mr. Tennyson seems, as he proceeded, to have raised his aims still higher—to

[*"Song.—The Owl," "Second Song.—To the Same," and "The 'How' and the 'Why,' " Poems, Chiefly Lyrical, pp. 46, 47, 11–13; and "Song," Poems, p. 142.]

*With the trifling exceptions already mentioned, the only pieces in the second volume which we could have wished omitted are, the little piece of childishness beginning "O darling room," and the verses to Christopher North, which express, in rather a commonplace way, the author's resentment against a critique, which merited no resentment from him, but rather (all things considered) a directly contrary feeling. [Poems, pp. 152–3, 153. "Christopher North" is John Wilson, whose review of Tennyson's Poems, Chiefly Lyrical is cited at p. 397n above.]

One or two poems, of greater pretension than the above, may be considered not indeed as absolute, but as comparative failures. Among these we must place the second poem in the volume (which affords to the Quarterly critic the opportunities for almost his only just criticisms [see Croker, pp. 83–5]); and even, notwithstanding its fine sonorous opening, the "Hesperides." ["To ——," and "The Hesperides," Poems, pp. 2–4, 101–7.]

[†Poems, Chiefly Lyrical, pp. 48–57, 101–3, 130, 143–6.]

[‡Ibid., pp. 65–6, 67–8. Both entitled "Song."]

have aspired to render his poems not only vivid representations of spiritual states, but symbolical of spiritual truths. His longest poem, "The Palace of Art," is an attempt of this sort.[*] As such, we do not think it wholly successful, though rich in beauties of detail; but we deem it of the most favourable augury for Mr. Tennyson's future achievements, since it proves a continually increasing endeavour towards the highest excellence, and a constantly rising standard of it.

We predict, that, as Mr. Tennyson advances in general spiritual culture, these higher aims will become more and more predominant in his writings; that he will strive more and more diligently, and, even without striving, will be more and more impelled by the natural tendencies of an expanding character, towards what has been described as the highest object of poetry, "to incorporate the everlasting reason of man in forms visible to his sense, and suitable to it."[†] For the fulfilment of this exalted purpose, what we have already seen of him authorizes us to foretell with confidence, that powers of execution will not fail him; it rests with himself to see that his powers of thought may keep pace with them. To render his poetic endowment the means of giving impressiveness to important truths, he must, by continual study and meditation, strengthen his intellect for the discrimination of such truths; he must see that his theory of life and the world be no chimera of the brain, but the well-grounded result of solid and mature thinking;—he must cultivate, and with no half devotion, philosophy as well as poetry.

It may not be superfluous to add, that he should guard himself against an error, to which the philosophical speculations of poets are peculiarly liable—that of embracing as truth, not the conclusions which are recommended by the strongest evidence, but those which have the most poetical appearance;—not those which arise from the deductions of impartial reason, but those which are most captivating to an imagination, biassed perhaps by education and conventional associations. That whatever philosophy he adopts will leave ample materials for poetry, he may be well assured. Whatever is comprehensive, whatever is commanding, whatever is on a great scale, is poetical. Let our philosophical system be what it may, human feelings exist: human nature, with all its enjoyments and sufferings, its strugglings, its victories and defeats, still remain to us; and these are the materials of all poetry. Whoever, in the greatest concerns of human life, pursues truth with unbiassed feelings, and an intellect adequate to discern it, will not find that the resources of poetry are lost to him because he has learnt to use, and not abuse them. They are as open to him as they are to the sentimental weakling, who has no test of the true but the ornamental. And when he once has them under his command, he can wield them for purposes, and with a power, of which neither the dilettante nor the visionary have the slightest conception.

We will not conclude without reminding Mr. Tennyson, that if he wishes his

[*Poems, pp. 69–89.]
[†For the sense, but not the exact words, see Wordsworth, "Preface to the Second Edition of Lyrical Ballads," in Poetical Works (1827), Vol. IV, p. 360 (para. 5).]

poems to live, he has still much to do in order to perfect himself in the merely mechanical parts of his craft. In a prose-writer, great beauties bespeak forgiveness for innumerable negligences; but poems, especially short poems, attain permanent fame only by the most finished perfection in the details. In some of the most beautiful of Mr. Tennyson's productions there are awkwardnesses and feeblenesses of expression, occasionally even absurdities, to be corrected; and which generally might be corrected without impairing a single beauty. His powers of versification are not yet of the highest order. In one great secret of his art, the adaptation of the music of his verse to the character of his subject, he is far from being a master: he often seems to take his metres almost at random. But this is little to set in the balance against so much excellence; and needed not have been mentioned, except to indicate to Mr. Tennyson the points on which some of his warmest admirers see most room and most necessity for further effort on his part, if he would secure to himself the high place in our poetic literature for which so many of the qualifications are already his own.

APHORISMS: THOUGHTS IN THE CLOISTER AND THE CROWD

1837

EDITORS' NOTE

London and Westminster Review, IV & XXVI (Jan., 1837), 348–57. Headed: "ART. III. / [Arthur Helps,] *Thoughts in the Cloister and the Crowd.* [London:] Wix, New Bridge Street, Blackfriars. 1835. 12mo. pp.111." Running titles: "Aphorisms. / Thoughts in the Cloister and the Crowd." Signed: "A." Part republished as "Aphorisms. A Fragment" in *D&D*, Vol. I, pp. 206–10, where the title is footnoted: "*London and Westminster Review,* January 1837," and the running title is "Aphorisms." Identified in Mill's bibliography as "A review of a book entitled 'Thoughts in the Cloister and the Crowd'—running title: 'Aphorisms.' In the London and Westminster Review for January 1837 (No. 8 and 51)" (MacMinn, p. 48). There are no corrections or emendations in the Somerville College copy (tear sheets) of the *L&WR* version.

For comment, see the Introduction, pp. xxxix–xl above.

Because only part of the text was republished, the copy-text is the *L&WR* article, which has been collated with the extract in *D&D*, 1st and 2nd eds. In the footnoted variants, "59" indicates *D&D*, 1st ed. (1859); "67" indicates *D&D*, 2nd ed. (1867).

Aphorisms:
Thoughts in the Cloister and the Crowd

[a]THERE ARE TWO KINDS OF WISDOM: in the one, every age in which science flourishes, surpasses, or ought to surpass, its predecessors; of the other, there is nearly an equal amount in all ages. The first is the wisdom which depends upon long chains of reasoning, a comprehensive survey of the whole of a great subject at once, or complicated and subtle processes of metaphysical analysis: this is properly philosophy [b]: the[b] other is that acquired by [c] experience of life, and a good use of the opportunities possessed by all who have mingled much with the world, or who have a large share of human nature in their own breasts. This unsystematic wisdom, drawn by acute minds in all periods of history from their personal experience, is properly termed the wisdom of ages; and every lettered age has left a portion of it upon record. It is nowhere more genuine than in the old fabulists, Æsop and others. The speeches in Thucydides are among the most remarkable specimens of it.[*] Aristotle and Quintilian have worked up rich stores of it into their systematic writings; nor ought Horace's *Satires*, and especially his *Epistles*,[†] to be forgotten. But the form in which this kind of wisdom most naturally embodies itself is that of aphorisms; and such, from the Proverbs of Solomon to our own day, is the shape it has oftenest assumed.

Some persons, who cannot be satisfied unless they have the forms of accurate knowledge as well as the substance, object to aphorisms because they are unsystematic. These objectors forget that to be unsystematic is of the essence of all truths which rest on specific experiment. A systematic treatise is the most natural form for delivering truths which grow out of one another; but truths, each of which rests upon its own independent evidence, may [d], we venture to think,[d] be exhibited in the same unconnected state in which they were discovered. Philosophy may

[*See, e.g., *Thucydides* (Greek and English), trans. Charles Forster Smith, 4 vols. (London: Heinemann; Cambridge, Mass.: Harvard University Press, 1969), Vol. I, pp. 238–52 (Bk. I, §§cxl–cxliv), pp. 360–72 (Bk. II, §§lx–lxiv), and Vol. II, pp. 224–8 (Bk. IV, §x).]

[†See *Satires, Epistles, and Ars poetica* (Latin and English), trans. H. Rushton Fairclough (London: Heinemann; New York: Putnam's Sons, 1926).]

[a–a]424 [*reprinted in* D&D *as* "Aphorisms. A Fragment"]
[b–b]59, 67   The
[c]67   the
[d–d]59, 67   surely

afterwards trace the connection among these truths, detect the more general principles of which they are manifestations, and so systematize the whole. But we need not wait till this is done before we record them and act upon them. On the contrary, these detached truths are at once the materials and the tests of philosophy itself; since philosophy is not called in to prove them, but may very justly be required to account for them.

A more valid objection to aphorisms, as far as it goes, is, that they are very seldom exactly true; but then this, unfortunately, is an objection to all human knowledge. A proverb or an apophthegm—any proposition epigrammatically expressed—almost always goes more or less beyond the strict truth: the fact which it states is *stated* in a more unqualified manner than the truth warrants. But, when logicians have done their best to correct the proposition by just modifications and limitations, is the case much mended? Very little. Every really existing Thing is a compound of such innumerable properties, and has such an infinity of relations with all other things in the universe, that almost every law to which it appears *to us* to be subject is liable to be set aside, or frustrated, either by some other law of the same object or by the laws of some other object which interferes with it: and as no one can possibly foresee or grasp all these contingencies, much less express them in such an imperfect language as that of words, no one *need* flatter himself that he can lay down propositions sufficiently specific to be available for practice, which he may afterwards apply mechanically without any exercise of thought. It is given to no human being to stereotype a set of truths, and walk safely by their guidance with his mind's eye closed. Let us envelop our proposition with what exceptions and qualifications we may, fresh exceptions will turn up, and fresh qualifications be found necessary, the moment any one attempts to act upon it. Not aphorisms, therefore, alone, but all general propositions whatever, require to be taken with a large allowance for inaccuracy; and, we may venture to add, this allowance is much more likely to be made when, the proposition being avowedly presented without any limitations, every one must see that he is left to make the limitations for himself.

If aphorisms were less likely than systems to have truth in them, it would be difficult to account for the fact that almost all books of aphorisms, which have ever acquired a reputation, have retained *it*; and, we apprehend, have generally* deserved to retain it; while, how wofully the reverse is the case with systems of philosophy no student is ignorant. One reason for this difference may be, that books of aphorisms are seldom written but by persons of genius. There are, indeed, to be found books like Mr. Colton's *Lacon*[*]—centos of trite truisms and trite

[*Charles Caleb Colton, *Lacon: or, Many Things in Few Words*, 2 vols. (London: Longman, *et al.*, 1820, 1822).]

*e-e*59, 67   enunciated
f-f—59, 67
*g-g*59, 67   needs
*h-h*59, 67   , and

falsisms pinched into epigrams. But, on the whole, he who draws his thoughts (as Coleridge says) from a cistern, and not from a spring,[*] will generally be more sparing of them than to give ten ideas in a page instead of ten pages to an idea. And where there is originality in aphorisms there is generally truth, or a bold approach to some truth which really lies beneath. A scientific system is often spun out of a few original assumptions, without any intercourse with nature at all; but he who has generalized copiously and variously from actual experience, must have thrown aside so many of his first *observations* as he went on, that the residuum can hardly be altogether worthless.

Of books of aphorisms, written by men of genius, the *Pensées* of Pascal is, perhaps, the least valuable in comparison with its reputation; but even this, in so far as it is aphoristic, is acute and profound: it fails *j*, where*j* it is perverted by the author's *systematic* views on religion.[†] La Rochefoucault, again, has been inveighed against as a "libeller of human nature," &c. *k*, merely*k* from not understanding his drift. His *Maxims* are a series of delineations, by a most penetrating observer, of the workings of habitual selfishness in the human breast; and they are true to the letter, of all thoroughly selfish persons, and of all *persons whatever* in proportion as they are selfish.[‡] A man of a warmer sympathy with mankind would, indeed, have enunciated his propositions in less sweeping terms; not that there was any fear of leading the world into the mistake that there was neither virtue nor feeling in it; but because a generous spirit could not have borne to chain itself down to the contemplation of littleness and meanness, unless for the express purpose of showing to others against what degrading influences, and in what an ungenial atmosphere, it was possible to maintain elevation of feeling and nobleness of conduct. The error of La Rochefoucault has been avoided by Chamfort, the more high-minded and more philosophic La Rochefoucault of the eighteenth century. In his posthumous work, *"the" Pensées, Maximes, Caractères, et Anecdotes* (a book which, to its other merits, adds that of being one of the best collections of *bons mots* in existence),[§] he lays open the basest parts of vulgar human nature, with as keen an instrument and as unshrinking a hand as his precursor; but not with that cool indifference of manner, like a man who is only

[*Cf. "Preface to Christabel," in *Christabel; Kubla Khan, a Vision; The Pains of Sleep*, p. vi.]

[†Blaise Pascal, *Pensées de Mr. Pascal sur la religion et sur quelques autres sujets*, ed. Etienne Périer (Paris: Desprez, 1670).]

[‡François de La Rochefoucauld, *Réflexions; ou, Sentences et maximes morales* (Paris: Barbin, 1665 [1664]).]

[§Sébastien Roch Nicolas Chamfort, *Maximes, pensées, caractères et anecdotes*, ed. Pierre Louis de Ginguené (Paris: printed London, Baylis, 1796).]

*i-i*59, 67   generalizations
*j-j*59, 67   when
*k-k*59, 67   chiefly
*l-l*59, 67   other persons
m-m—67

thinking of saying clever things; he does it with the concentrated bitterness of one whose own life has been made valueless to him by having his lot cast among these basenesses, and whose sole consolation is in the thought that human nature is not the wretched thing it appears, and that, in better circumstances, it will produce better things. Nor does he ever leave his reader, for long together, without being reminded, that he is speaking, not of what might be, but of what now is.[a]

Much might here be said of Burke, whose γνῶμαι are the best, if not the only valuable, part of his writings; of Goethe, and Bacon, the greatest masters, perhaps, of aphoristic wisdom upon record. But we must abridge. Let us turn rather to the fact that our own age and nation have given birth to some not contemptible productions of the same kind,[*] and that one of these lies before us, some specimens of which will be interesting to our readers.

This little volume, entitled *Thoughts in the Cloister and the Crowd*, is a work

---

[*]Among the best of them is a book in two small volumes, intituled *Guesses at Truth, by Two Brothers*, one of the brothers being understood to be the Rev. Julius Hare. [(London: Taylor, 1827.) The second brother was Augustus William Hare.] The book is strongly religious, and in its views of religion there is much that seems to us questionable, but much also that is admirable, while it abounds with thoughts which could have proceeded from no ordinary mind. *The Statesman* [(London: Longman, Rees, Orme, Brown, Green, and Longman, 1836)], by Mr. Henry Taylor, the author of *Philip Van Artevelde* [(London: Moxon, 1834)], may also be classed among books of aphorisms. Accident alone prevented us from reviewing this work immediately on its appearance; and although it will have lost somewhat of the gloss of novelty before we can now fulfil our intention, it contains so many just and profound observations applicable to all times, and so many important criticisms and suggestions peculiarly deserving the attention of practical reformers at the present time, that we shall return to it at the very earliest opportunity. [See George Grote and J. S. Mill, "Taylor's Statesman," *London and Westminster Review*, V & XXVII (Apr., 1837), 1–32; reprinted in *CW*, Vol. XIX, pp. 617–47.] The unpublished writings of Mr. Coleridge must contain much valuable matter of an aphoristic kind. The two volumes published by his nephew, as specimens of his "Table-talk," excited our expectations highly, and disappointed them utterly. [*Specimens of the Table Talk of Samuel Taylor Coleridge*, ed. Henry Nelson Coleridge, 2 vols. (London: Murray, 1835).] It is the first thoroughly bad book which ever appeared under Mr. Coleridge's name. In the whole two volumes there are not more than two or three thoughts above common-place, and many which are greatly below it: he dogmatises with the most unbounded confidence on subjects which it is evident that he never took the trouble to study; and his blunders are not only such as would have been impossible with the most ordinary knowledge of what had previously been thought and written, but are often such as, if they had come from any but one of the subtlest intellects of this or of any age, would have appeared conclusive proofs of positive obtuseness of understanding. It is pitiable to find a man of Mr. Coleridge's genius uttering on population, taxes, and many other topics, stuff which was barely pardonable in any thinking person forty years ago, and which is now below the average knowledge and intellect of the commonest hacks of the press. The two volumes of *Letters and Recollections*, published by Moxon, are much better. [*Letters, Conversations, and Recollections*, ed. Thomas Allsop, 2 vols. (London: Moxon, 1836).] The *Literary Remains*, which are now in course of publication, we have not yet seen. [Published as *The Literary Remains of Samuel Taylor Coleridge*, ed. Henry Nelson Coleridge, 4 vols. (London: Pickering, 1836–39).]

of extraordinary promise, if, as we have heard, and as there is some internal evidence, it is the production of a young man who has just left the university. All the indications of a thoughtful, and, on every matter to which it has yet turned its attention, really original mind are here. The "Thoughts" are really thoughts: that is, they are drawn from things, and not from books or tradition; and this is no less evident in the author's failures than in his successes. Whether he shoots over the heads of his predecessors, or timidly throws out some small fragment of a truth which others before him have seen in all its plenitude, in either case it is because he speaks what he himself has felt or observed, and stops where that stops. We have spoken of failures; but these are far from numerous. The book contains one hundred and sixty-four maxims; among which are five or six decidedly false, or questionable, and fifty or sixty truths which have been as well or better said before. The remainder are a real addition to the world's stock of just thoughts happily expressed; and some of these may be ranked with the best things of the best satirists, while others give evidence of a soul far above that of any satirist—far too habitually intent upon its own ideal standard to bestow any other than an incidental notice upon the shortcomings of others.

We cannot better commence our quotations than with one which is in the very spirit of La Rochefoucault, and might be prefixed as a motto to every book containing novelties in thought:

Few will at first be pleased with those thoughts which are entirely new to them, and which, if true, they feel to be truths which they should never have discovered for themselves.

Perhaps if the power of becoming beautiful were granted to the ugliest of mankind, he would only wish to be so changed, that when changed he might be considered a very handsome likeness of his former self. (P. 110.)

We quote those which follow, not as the best, but as being in a similar vein:

It is an error to suppose that no man understands his own character. Most persons know even their failings very well, only they persist in giving them names different from those usually assigned by the rest of the world; and they compensate for this mistake by naming, at first sight, with singular accuracy, these very same failings in others. (P. 48.)

You cannot insure the gratitude of others for a favour conferred on them in the way which is most agreeable to yourself. (P. 77.)

Some are contented to wear the mask of foolishness in order to carry on their vicious schemes; and not a few are willing to shelter their folly behind the respectability of downright vice. (P. 69.)

You may be forgiven for an injury which, when made known to the world, will render you alone the object of its ridicule. (P. 99.)

The world will tolerate many vices, but not their diminutives. (P. 62.)

Men love to contradict their general character. Thus a man is of a gloomy and suspicious temperament, is deemed by all morose, and ere long finds out the general opinion. He then suddenly deviates into some occasional acts of courtesy. Why? Not because he ought, not because his nature is changed; but because he dislikes being thoroughly understood. He will not be the thing whose behaviour on any occasion the most careless prophet can with certainty foretell.* (P. 49.)

The following is an observation of very great reach and importance:

It would often be as well to condemn a man unheard, as to condemn him upon the reasons which he openly avows for any course of action. (P. 9.)

The explanation of this is to be found in another maxim of our author:

The reasons which any man offers to you for his own conduct betray his opinion of *your* character. (P. 75.)

How true! how obvious! yet how seldom adverted to, and, we think, never written before. The reason which a man gives for his conduct is not that which he feels, but that which he thinks you are most likely to feel. It often requires less moral courage to do a noble action than to avow that it proceeds from a noble motive. They who act on higher motives than the multitude suffer their conduct to be imputed to their personal position, to their friends, to their humour, even to some object of personal advancement—to anything, in short, which will not involve a reproach to others for not doing the like. They would rather the mean should think them as mean as themselves than incur the odium of setting up to be better than their neighbours, or the danger of giving others any cause to infer that they despise them.

The two which follow are in a vein of thought somewhat similar:

If you are very often deceived by those around you, you may be sure that you deserve to be deceived; and that, instead of railing at the general falseness of mankind, you have first to pronounce judgment on your own jealous tyranny, or on your own weak credulity. *Those only who can bear the truth will hear it.* (P. 76.)

And again:

We often err by contemplating an individual solely in his relation and behaviour to us, and generalizing from that with more rapidity than wisdom. We might as well argue that the moon has no rotation about her axis, because the same hemisphere is always presented to our view. (Pp. 26–7.)

There is nothing which persons oftener overlook, in judging of the characters of

*Mr. Taylor, in his *Statesman,* notes the same fact, and accounts for it differently; both explanations being correct. "In our judgment of men, we are to beware of giving any great importance to occasional acts. By acts of occasional virtue, weak men endeavour to redeem themselves in their own estimation, vain men to exalt themselves in that of mankind. It may be observed that there are no men more worthless and selfish in the general tenor of their lives than some who from time to time perform feats of generosity. Sentimental selfishness will commonly vary its indulgences in this way, and vainglorious selfishness will break out with acts of munificence. But self-government and self-denial are not to be relied upon for any real strength, except in so far as they are found to be exercised in detail." (*The Statesman,* p. 20.)

others, than that there are portions of those characters which possibly would never be shown to *them*. They think they know a person thoroughly, because they have seen and conversed with him under all varieties of circumstances. They *have* seen him under all circumstances, except that of their own absence.

The maxims we have hitherto quoted relate chiefly to our judgments of others; the following are to aid our self-judgment:

> The world will find out that part of your character which concerns it: that which especially concerns yourself it will leave for you to discover. (P. 4.)

> We talk of early prejudices, of the prejudices of religion, of position, of education; but in truth we only mean the prejudices of others. . . . In a quarrel between two friends, if one of them, even the injured one, were, in the retirement of his chamber, to consider himself as the hired advocate of the other at the court of wronged friendship; and were to omit all the facts which told in his own favour, to exaggerate all that could possibly be said against himself, and to conjure up from his imagination a few circumstances of the same tendency, he might with little effort make a good case for his former friend. Let him be assured that, whatever the most skilful advocate could say, his poor friend really believes and feels; and then, instead of wondering at the insolence of such a traitor walking about in open day, he will pity his friend's delusion, have some gentle misgivings as to the exact propriety of his own conduct, and perhaps sue for an immediate reconciliation. (Pp. 23–5.)

The following is true, and ingeniously expressed:

> It must be a very weary day to the youth when he first discovers that after all he will only become a man. (P. 78.)

The next is one which many will not understand, but which all who do understand will recognise the truth of: we have never met with it before:

> We have some respect for one who, if he tramples on the feelings of others, tramples on his own with equal apparent indifference. (P. 50.)

We know not if the state of mind of the common herd, on subjects of speculation, was ever more happily characterized than in the following observation:

> The unfortunate Ladurlad did not desire the sleep that for ever fled his weary eyelids with more earnestness than most people seek *the deep slumber of a decided opinion.* (P. 2.)[*]

It is, too truly, so: the motive which induces most people to wish for certainty is the uneasiness of doubt; that uneasiness removed, they turn on their pillow and go to sleep: as if truths were meant to be assented to, but not acted upon. We think the having attained a truth should be the signal for rousing oneself, and not for sleeping; unless it be a reason for renouncing your voyage that you have just acquired a compass to steer by. Nor is the fact of having arrived at a "decided opinion," even though it be a true one, any reason for not thinking more on the subject; otherwise the time will soon come when, instead of knowing the truth, you

[*Ladurlad is a character in Robert Southey's *The Curse of Kehama* (London: Longman, Hurst, Rees, Orme, and Brown, 1810).]

will only remember that you have known it, and continue believing it on your own authority: which is nearly as pernicious a form of taking upon trust as if you believed it on the authority of popes or councils.

The next, though stated too universally, is both ingenious and just:

When your friend is suffering under great affliction, either be entirely silent, or offer none but the most common topics of consolation: for, in the first place, they are the best; and also from their commonness they are easily understood. Extreme grief will not pay attention to any new thing. (P. 34.)

The following is a genuinely poetical thought expressed in fine prose:

The Pyramids!—what a lesson to those who desire a name in the world does the fate of these restless, brick-piling monarchs afford! Their names are not known, and the only hope for them is, that, by the labours of some cruelly-industrious antiquarian, they may at last become more *definite* objects of contempt. (P. 22.)

The following are not new, but they are truths which cannot be too often repeated:

The business of the head is to form a good heart, and not merely to rule an evil one, as is generally imagined. (P. 2.)

The noblest works, like the temple of Solomon, are brought to perfection in silence. (Pp. 45–6.)

This is especially true of ideas. A great idea always dawns upon the intellect by degrees, and is seen confusedly for a long period, during which the attempt to seize it and fix it in words would merely disturb the process by which the different rays of light are gradually made to converge, until at last the truth flashes upon the mind's eye a completed image. But if there be one thing, more than another, which is brought to perfection in silence, it is, a fine character: for first, no one who talks much, has time, or is likely to have a taste, for solitary reflection; and next, it is impossible that those who habitually give out their most cherished feelings to all comers, can permanently maintain a tone of feeling much above what is prevalent among those by whom they are surrounded.

There are some books which we at first reject, because we have neither felt, nor seen, nor thought, nor suffered enough to understand and appreciate them. Perhaps *The Excursion*[*] is one of these. (P. 69.)

When our author has lived longer, he will be able to give still more pregnant instances than that of *The Excursion*. His remark is true of all books, whether of poetry, philosophy, or fictitious narrative, the matter of which is drawn from the personal experiences of the finer natures or the profounder intellects.

There are occasional lapses in this volume, obviously the effect of inexperience. Thus the author has persuaded himself, Heaven knows how, that "the love of being considered well-read is one of the most fatal of all the follies which subdue the

[*I.e., Wordsworth's poem.]

present generation" (p. 51); and thereupon he says, very truly and profitably, that what we are the better for is not what we have read, but what we have assimilated; and that "those who are much engaged in acquiring knowledge, will not always have time for deep thought or intense feeling." (P. 49.) For our part, we are heartily glad to hear that there are some circles in which "the love of being considered well-read" is still the besetting sin: we, unless to run through newspapers and Guides to Knowledge and magazines and novels is to be well-read, have not happened to fall in with many such people. There are so few well-read persons in this generation (in this country we mean) that any charlatan who sets up for the character can get his pretensions admitted without question, no one having depth enough of his own to fathom another person's shallowness. We are, thanks to our Church and our Universities, a most unlearned nation. Those "venerable institutions" have nearly rooted out learning from among us.

Besides these errors of inexperience, our author sometimes stops curiously short of some obvious inference from his own observations. Thus he notices, what has so often been noticed, the superiority of women over men in patient endurance, and dismisses the subject with an expression of idle wonder. The power of endurance in women is the faithful measure of how much they have to endure. If all dark-haired men were condemned by their organization to incessantly recurring physical suffering—and if, in addition to this, their very minutest act, and their very smallest enjoyment, required the consent, either express or tacit, of another, he on his part being under no reciprocity of that obligation—dark-haired men would soon be distinguished for the virtue of endurance: and doubtless it would, ere long, be regarded as one of their natural gifts, as the virtue appropriate to their kind; and their capacity of patience would be thought ample justification for giving them much to be patient of.

We take leave of *Thoughts in the Cloister and the Crowd* with a feeling towards the author which we seldom entertain towards any of the young writers of this writing generation—namely, a full determination to read his next production, whatever it may be.

WARE'S LETTERS FROM PALMYRA

1838

EDITORS' NOTE

London and Westminster Review, VI & XXVIII (Jan., 1838), 436–70. Headed: "ART. V.—[William Ware,] *Letters of Lucius Manlius Piso, from Palmyra, to his Friend, Marcus Curtius, at Rome. Now first translated and published.* 2 vols. 12mo. New York: [Francis,] 1837." Running title: "Letters from Palmyra." Signed: "S." The concluding two paragraphs republished as "A Prophecy. / (From a Review of 'Letters from Palmyra.')" in *D&D*, Vol. I, pp. 284–6, where the title is footnoted: "*London and Westminster Review*, January 1838" and the running title is "A Prophecy." Identified in Mill's bibliography as "A review of a book entitled 'Letters of Lucius Piso from Palmyra' in the London and Westminster Review for January 1838. (No. 12 and 55.)" (MacMinn, p. 50). There are no corrections or emendations in the Somerville College copy (tear sheets) of the *L&WR* version.

For comment, see the Introduction, p. xl above.

Because only part of the text was republished, the copy-text is the *L&WR* article, which has been collated with the extract in *D&D*, 1st and 2nd eds. In the footnoted variants, "59" indicates *D&D*, 1st ed. (1859); "67" indicates *D&D*, 2nd ed. (1867).

Ware's Letters from Palmyra

SPEAKING OF THE DIFFICULTIES which in America retard the formation of a vigorous and original National Literature, and of the copies and imitations, mere echoes of the inspired voices of the Old World, which must in the mean time be accepted as great things, until a greater appear, Miss Martineau says:

> I met with one gem in American literature where I should have least expected it—in the *Knickerbocker*, a New York Monthly Magazine. Last spring a set of papers began to appear, called *Letters from Palmyra*, six numbers of which had been issued when I left the country. I have been hitherto unable to obtain the rest; but if they answer to the early portions, there can be no doubt of their being shortly in everybody's hands, in both countries. These letters remain in my mind, after repeated readings, as a fragment of lofty and tender beauty. Zenobia, Longinus, and a long perspective of characters, live and move in natural majesty; and the beauties of description and sentiment appear to me as remarkable as the strong conception of character and of the age. If this anonymous fragment be not the work of a true artist—if the work, when entire, do not prove to be of a far higher order than anything which has issued from the American press,—its early admirers will feel yet more surprise than regret.*

Such testimony from one who has so clearly discerned, and so forcibly drawn, the characteristic deficiencies of American literature (which, as we have observed in a former article,† are no other than the deficiencies of *provincial* literature in general) excited a natural desire for a nearer acquaintance with the production so highly commended. We have read the *Letters from Palmyra* (which are now complete), and can vouch that the sequel not only "answers to the early portions," but is executed with a more vigorous hand, and adds to every good characteristic which the work possessed from its commencement, an animation of style and a dramatic talent which we did not equally recognize in the introductory letters. As this interesting work is still unknown in England, except to the few into whose hands a stray copy of the American edition has chanced to fall, we will lay a short account of it before our readers; rather desirous of making its contents known, than

---

*[Harriet Martineau,] *Society in America*, [3 vols. (London: Saunders and Otley, 1837),] Vol. III, pp. 216–17.

†[J. S. Mill, "State of Society in America,"] *London Review*, no. 4 [Jan., 1836].— Review of "Travels in America." [I.e., *London Review*, II (*Westminster Review*, XXXI), 365–89; in *CW*, Vol. XVIII, pp. 91–115. The reference will be found in the latter at pp. 100–1.]

of subjecting them to a rigid critical examination. The young literature of a great people in a state of adolescence, who have not yet found leisure for much other employment of their activity than "felling the largest tree in four minutes," and carrying bags of cotton from the great experimental farm of the world to the great workshop of it, must not be tried by the standard of what has been accomplished during three thousand years, with all appliances and means,[*] by the labours and inspirations of a select literary class writing for a numerous leisured one. Without making any lofty pretensions for this little book, or challenging in its behalf any comparisons with the great works of art which ennoble an age, we have found as much in it, both to love and to admire, as may well justify us in claiming for it a few moments of that attention which is bestowed so readily upon the merely passing productions of the time, to compare almost any of which with this would be nearly as absurd as it would be to place this on a level with the noblest and most enduring monuments of the present age.

We must premise a few words to prevent disappointment. The reader need expect nothing highly wrought, nothing stimulating in this book. It is not of the passionate school. It will be more to the taste of the admirers of Fenelon or Barthelemy than of Byron; indeed, it reminds us forcibly of the first of these writers, by its union of a gentle and peace-loving spirit with the warmest sympathy for the active and energetic virtues, and a facility of kindling, with the imagination merely, at the conception of scenes of bloodshed and mortal struggle; a combination which, like almost all blending of qualities superficially incompatible, is both evidence and cause of a general healthiness of intellect and feeling. But if, from Miss Martineau's high estimate of this book in comparison with American literature generally, any one should expect to find in it, as a work of fiction, the stirring action on the imagination and breathless excitement with which we read the novels of Brockden Brown* (a man of true genius, little estimated by his cotemporaries, and whom Miss Martineau has unaccountably over-looked), or even the less deeply-seated but almost equally enchaining interest of the best productions of Cooper—or (we will venture to add) the wild flashes of truth and reality, the actual observation of human nature and personal experience of feeling, which we occasionally find, amidst much extravagance and absurdity, in the eccentric writings of

---

[*See Shakespeare, *The Second Part of Henry the Fourth*, III, i, 29.]

*Author of *Wieland, Edgar Huntly, Ormond, Arthur Mervyn*, &c., and one of the rare instances of an imitator who surpasses his original: a more gifted man than Godwin, yet whose novels all bear the strongest family likeness to *Caleb Williams*, the only novel of Godwin which is worthy of being compared with them. [See Charles Brockden Brown, *Wieland* (New York: Caritat, 1798); *Edgar Huntly*, 3 vols. (Philadelphia: Maxwell, 1799); *Ormond* (New York: Caritat, 1799); *Arthur Mervyn*, 2 vols. (Philadelphia: Maxwell, 1799); and William Godwin, *Things As They Are; or, The Adventures of Caleb Williams* (1794), 3 vols., 4th ed. (London: Simpkin and Marshal, 1816).]

John Neal;* whoever takes up this book with any such hope will soon lay it down. It is another kind of work altogether. It belongs to a class of fictitious writings, which bears to an ordinary or even a historical novel or romance, the relation which Shakspeare's historical plays bear to his tragedies. If *King John*, or *King Henry the Fourth*, were altogether fictitious stories, they would be very poor ones. In them the author does not invent the incidents and characters which suit him best, but takes those which a certain period of history presents him with, and gives life and reality to those: he tells, not *a* story, but *the* story, as it may have occurred, and did, for aught we know, actually occur. We should read those plays not certainly without pleasure, but with far less of it, if that portion of the interest were cut off which is derived from the fact that the events which are described and the characters which are drawn did actually exist.

The *Letters from Palmyra* are written with a similar aim. Not that they are a mere delineation of historical events and personages. Many of the characters, and their personal adventures and actions, are fictitious; and among these is the hero (as we suppose we must call him) the imaginary writer of the letters, who—though a spectator and not an actor in the great drama of the book, the greatness and fall of Palmyra—excites a personal interest in us by the sentiments which, like the chorus of a Greek tragedy, he is made the organ of—and, for his own part, fulfils with propriety the essential functions of a novel-hero, by saving the Queen's life, and by duly falling in love and being married. But though, as our extracts will show, the book, in its merely fictitious parts, displays much of the talent of the novel-writer, it could not afford to dispense with the interest derived from its relation to the history of the period; to Zenobia, Longinus, and the other real characters, who, as Miss Martineau says, "live and move in natural majesty" in its pages; and to that curious, eminently interesting, and yet, we may almost say, neglected period in the progress of the world and of mankind, of which it is the great merit of these letters that they really, and so far as we know for the very first time, present us with a living picture.

The author has been peculiarly happy in the choice of his historical period: From the time of Nero or Vespasian to that of Constantine, there is a space of about three

---

*Author of *Brother Jonathan*, a novel, published about a dozen years ago by Blackwood; and of *Randolph*, by far his best work, though in this country utterly unknown. [*Brother Jonathan*, 3 vols. (Edinburgh: Blackwood, 1825); and *Randolph*, 2 vols. ([Baltimore?], 1823).] *Logan*, and *Seventy-six*, two of his novels which have been reprinted in England, have little if any portion of the merits of the two we have mentioned. [*Logan*, 4 vols. (London: Newman, 1823); and *Seventy-Six*, 3 vols. (London: Whittaker, 1823).] Neal appears to be little thought of in his own country, the natural fate of an original writer in a literature of imitation and convention. But we will hazard a prediction, that when a great and original novelist or poet shall arise in America, he will be found to be more like what John Neal is, with all his frothiness and rant, than what any of the American writers are, whose productions have been most blazoned by the critics either of their own country, or of ours.

hundred years, during which some of the greatest things were transacted which ever were transacted upon this earth, and the least like any other known series of events. Nor were these transactions performed in some little corner of the globe, but over the whole civilized world at once. During those centuries Christianity was working itself upwards, from the poorest and most despised classes and races of mankind, through the whole body of civilized society to the highest summits— from whence, mingled with the polluted streams which in such a state of society emanate from such places, it again flowed forth, and overspread barbarous countries and unknown races of men with its fructifying and wholesome waters, and with the foulness that was mixed therewith. During the same three centuries, military despotism was working in the opposite direction, from those high places *downwards*, into the very vitals of the people: sucking up and consuming their substance, to the extent of actual depopulation; allowing no one to live who was strong enough or good enough to be conspicuous and an object of jealousy; preying upon mankind and letting them prey upon one another, until no law remained but that of the strongest, and no refuge from tyranny but in the cunning and treachery of the slave; killing by inanition whatever of liberal pursuits or intellectual culture could be so killed; and in fine, trampling down the most advanced nations of the earth into a state of moral imbecility and corruption, from which one-half of the enervated Roman Empire has never since recovered itself:—nor could anything have recovered the other half, but being conquered and overrun by a hardy race of primitive barbarians; who, bringing again into the civilized world what had so long been wanting—their rude energy, and ardent love of personal freedom—found and yielded to the tempering and soul-awakening influence of the gentlest and at the same time the most powerful of religions: and by this intermixture produced the modern European character.

This double movement, of Christianity mounting up from the low places, and of tyranny descending from the heights, composes the history of the first three centuries of our era: and this history, do we find it in the books? Until the present generation it may safely be said, that no historian had seen more than a glimpse of it. M. Guizot first, in his "Essay on the Municipal Institutions of the Romans," showed us despotism in the concrete, coming home to every peasant's hearth.[*] As for Christianity, historians and martyrologists have shown us the sufferings of the Christian Church and its triumph; Nero's pitch-jackets and Constantine's *labarum*. But where do we see, and who has mentally depicted to himself, that irresistible under-current of Christianity, which must have been flowing with ever-increasing rapidity in the silent depths; when nothing was visible on the surface of society but a philosophically incredulous Few, and a populace ever gaping for new and more barbarous superstitions, for a "Syrian Goddess," an Isis,

---

[*See "Du régime municipal dans l'empire romain," in *Essais sur l'histoire de France*, 2nd ed. (Paris: Brière, 1824), pp. 1–51.]

or a Cybele? The period in which the power of Christianity had begun to be felt, without being publicly recognized, has never, we believe, been chosen for illustration, even by any writer of fiction, previous to these letters.

In this great portion of the world's history, the mind dwells with peculiar interest upon the episode of Palmyra; which, though little connected with the main plot, commands attention, both for its own surprising nature, and for the interesting characters which figure in it. An insignificant town, in the very centre of a vast desert ("Tadmor in the wilderness," recorded to have been among the towns built by Solomon),[*] with no agricultural resources, no advantages over the burning sands around, except copious springs—a place, says Pliny the naturalist, *velut terris exempta a rerum naturâ*[†]—starts up almost at the first moment when it is heard of in civilized literature, into an imperial city able to dispute the empire of the East with Rome herself; and of a magnificence, the remains of which, sixteen hundred years later, are still the admiration of the world:* then, crushed as suddenly by the terrible vengeance of a despotic conqueror, it sinks at once into oblivion and is heard of no more. The ignorant and uninquiring historians of the later Roman Empire have told us nothing which can satisfactorily account for this meteor-like apparition of a great and flourishing capital in a dreary wilderness. Doubtless the true origin of the wealth of Palmyra, as shown by Gibbon,[‡]and by a recent traveller (Mr. Addison),[†] was her geographical position, directly on the main track which is even now followed by the caravans passing between the Persian Gulph and the Mediterranean: then the great line of commercial communication, and likely again to become that of commercial intelligence, between the east and the west. Palmyra was the emporium of the commerce of India—the Venice of the desert. But if these advantages of situation, which rendered her

[*See II Chronicles, 8:4.]

[†Pliny, *Natural History* (Latin and English), trans. Harris Rackham, *et al.*, 10 vols. (London: Heinemann; Cambridge, Mass.: Harvard University Press, 1938–62), Vol. II, p. 288.]

*Bruce, the celebrated traveller, calls the first view of the ruins of Palmyra "the most astonishing, stupendous sight that perhaps ever appeared to mortal eyes. The whole plain below, which was very extensive, was covered so thick with magnificent buildings as that the one seemed to touch the other, all of fine proportions, all of agreeable forms, all composed of white stones, which at that distance appeared like marble. At the end of it stood the Palace of the Sun, a building worthy to close so magnificent a scene." The mud cottages of the present inhabitants are all comprised within the court of *one* of these great buildings. [James Bruce, *Travels to Discover the Source of the Nile*, 5 vols. (London: Robinson, 1790), Vol. I, p. lvii.]

[‡See Edward Gibbon, *The History of the Decline and Fall of the Roman Empire*, 6 vols. (London: Strahan and Cadell, 1776–88), Vol. I, pp. 310–11; in "A New Edition," 6 vols. (London: Strahan and Cadell, 1782), Vol. I, pp. 370–1. Mill's quotations correspond to the latter version, and so in subsequent footnotes it is cited first.]

†*Damascus and Palmyra* [2 vols. (London: Bentley, 1838)], by Charles G. Addison, Esq.

greatness possible, had been of themselves sufficient to produce it, Palmyra would have revived after her destruction by Aurelian. The greatest natural advantages suffice not without wise guidance. The glories of Palmyra were the creation of Odenatus and Zenobia; and fell when they fell. Of the latter and more illustrious of these personages, the heroine of the *Letters*, we shall now speak in the words of Gibbon, who, in his description of her, translates almost literally from her biography in the *Augustan History*, by Trebellius Pollio.[*]

Modern Europe has produced several illustrious women who have sustained with glory the weight of empire; nor is our own age destitute of such distinguished characters. But if we except the doubtful achievements of Semiramis, Zenobia is perhaps the only female whose superior genius broke through the servile indolence imposed on her sex by the climate and manners of Asia. She claimed her descent from the Macedonian kings of Egypt, equalled in beauty her ancestor Cleopatra, and far surpassed that princess in chastity and valour. Zenobia was esteemed the most lovely as well as the most heroic of her sex. She was of a dark complexion; her teeth were of a pearly whiteness [*ut margaritas eam plerique putarent habere, non dentes*], and her large black eyes [*oculis supra modum ingentibus, nigris, spiritus divini, venustatis incredibilis*, are the enthusiastic words of Pollio] sparkled with uncommon fire, tempered by the most attractive sweetness. Her voice was strong and harmonious [*vox clara et virilis*]. She was not ignorant of the Latin tongue, but possessed in equal perfection the Greek, the Syriac, and the Egyptian languages. She had drawn up for her own use an epitome of Oriental history, and familiarly compared the beauties of Homer and Plato, under the tuition of the sublime Longinus.

This accomplished woman gave her hand to Odenatus, who, from a private station, raised himself to the dominion of the East. She soon became the friend and companion of a hero. In the intervals of war Odenatus passionately delighted in the exercise of hunting: he pursued with ardour the wild beasts of the desert, lions, panthers, and bears; and the ardour of Zenobia in that dangerous amusement was not inferior to his own. She had inured her constitution to fatigue, disdained the use of a covered carriage, generally appeared on horseback in a military habit, and sometimes marched several miles on foot at the head of the troops. The success of Odenatus was in a great measure ascribed to her incomparable prudence and fortitude. Their splendid victories over the Great King, whom they twice pursued as far as the gates of Ctesiphon, laid the foundations of their united fame and power.[†]

Odenatus having been cut off by private revenge, Zenobia punished his murderer, and,

with the assistance of his most faithful friends, she immediately filled the vacant throne, and governed with manly counsels Palmyra, Syria, and the East, above five years. . . . Disdaining both the senate and Gallienus, she obliged one of the Roman generals, who was sent against her, to retreat into Europe, with the loss of his army and his reputation. . . . To the dominions of Odenatus, which extended from the Euphrates to the frontiers of Bithynia,

[*See Trebellius Pollio, *The Thirty Pretenders*, in *Scriptores historiae augustae* (Latin and English), trans. David Magie, 3 vols. (London: Heinemann; New York: Putnam's Sons, 1922–32), Vol. III, pp. 134–43 (Cap. xxx).]

[†*Decline and Fall*, 1782 ed., Vol. I, pp. 365–7; 1st ed., Vol. I, pp. 306–7. Mill has inserted the bracketed Latin wordings; cf. Pollio, *The Thirty Pretenders*, Vol. III, p. 138.]

his widow added the inheritance of her ancestors, the populous and fertile kingdom of Egypt.[*]

Her administration was at once firm and gentle: "the severity," says Pollio, "of a tyrant when necessity demanded it; the clemency of good princes when that was required by piety."[†] She had the rarest of virtues in a despotic ruler, strict economy; yet she was "larga prudenter,"[‡] judiciously liberal. "She blended," continues Gibbon, "with the popular manners of Roman princes, the stately pomp of the courts of Asia, and exacted from her subjects the same adoration that was paid to the successors of Cyrus."[§]

To have such a character to depict, in a period of history so barren (at least in the high places) of individual goodness or greatness, is a *bonne fortune* to a writer of fiction. And the moment of the greatest splendour of Palmyra and of Zenobia, that immediately preceding the war by which they were ruined, has been chosen by the author of the *Letters* for the commencement of his tale.

The supposed writer of the letters is a young and high-born Roman, Lucius Piso, who, having received intelligence that his brother Calpurnius (supposed to have perished after the memorable overthrow of the Emperor Valerian by Sapor, King of Persia) was still alive and in captivity, sets out for Palmyra on an attempt to effect his liberation. The first hope of attaining it, rested upon the intercession of the powerful Zenobia, whose good offices Piso hoped to ensure through the influence of one of her chief counsellors, Gracchus, a noble Roman, and an early friend of his house. This Gracchus, and his daughter Fausta, are two of the principal characters of the book: the former a personification of a bland and affectionate old man and a prudent counsellor; the latter, a young and beautiful heroine, worshipping Zenobia, and an imitator and emulator of her splendid qualities.

The first letter describes the voyage from Rome to Berytus in Syria, during which Piso forms an acquaintance with two persons, a Jew and a Christian, who re-appear at intervals throughout the narrative. This is followed by the journey across the Desert, and the first aspect of the magnificent Eastern capital. It is described in accordance with the evidence of its existing remains: and what had hitherto been, in our imagination, merely a picture like that in Byron's "Dream,"[¶] of fallen columns and among them camels grazing, is very successfully peopled and vivified with the hum and stir of a busy commercial city and the splendour of an Eastern throne.

[*Decline and Fall, 1782 ed., Vol. I, pp. 367–8; 1st ed., Vol. I, pp. 308–9; the general was Heraclianus.]
[†Pollio, Vol. III, p. 138.]
[‡Ibid.]
[§Decline and Fall, 1782 ed., Vol. I, p. 368; 1st ed., Vol. I, p. 309.]
[¶"The Dream," in The Prisoner of Chillon, and Other Poems (London: Murray, 1816), pp. 35–45.]

The city filled the whole plain as far as the eye could reach, both toward the North and toward the South. It seemed to me to be larger than Rome. . . . The city proper is so studded with groups of lofty palm-trees, shooting up among its temples and palaces; and, on the other hand, the plain in its immediate vicinity is so thickly adorned with magnificent structures, of the purest marble, that it is not easy, nay, it is impossible, at the distance at which I contemplated the whole, to distinguish the line which divided the one from the other. It was all city and all country—all country and all city. I imagined that I saw under my feet the dwellings of purified men and of gods. They were too glorious for the mere earthborn. The vast Temple of the Sun stretched upward its thousand columns of polished marble to the heavens, in its matchless beauty, casting into the shade every other work of art of which the world can boast. On each side of this, the central point, there rose upward slender pyramids, pointed obelisks, domes of the most graceful proportions, columns, arches, and lofty towers, for number and for form beyond my power to describe—all, as well as the walls of the city, either of white marble, or of some stone as white, and everywhere in their whole extent interspersed with multitudes of overshadowing palm-trees. A flood of golden light, of a richer hue, it seemed to me, than our sun ever sheds upon Rome, rolled over the city and plain, and distant mountains, giving to the whole a gorgeousness agreeing well with all my impressions of oriental magnificence. . . . Not one expectation was disappointed, but rather exceeded, as we came in sight of the vast walls of the city, and of the Roman gate—so it is called—through which we were to make our entrance. It was all upon the grandest scale. The walls were higher, and more frequently defended by square massy towers springing out of them, than those of Rome. The towers, which on either side flanked the gateway, and which were connected by an immense arch, flung from one to the other, were magnificent. No sooner had we passed through it than we found ourselves in a street lined as it were with palaces. It was of great width—we have no street like it in this respect—of an exact level, and stretched onward farther than the eye could distinctly reach, till, as I was told, it was terminated by another gate, similar to that by which we had entered. . . . (Vol. I, pp. 21–4.)

Everything bears a newer, fresher look than in Rome. The buildings of the republic, which many are so desirous to preserve, and whole streets even, of ante-Augustan architecture, tend to spread around, here and there in Rome, a gloom—to me full of beauty and poetry—but still gloom. Here all is bright and gay: the buildings of marble—the streets paved and clean—frequent fountains of water throwing up their foaming jets, and shedding around a delicious coolness,—temples, and palaces of the nobles or of wealthy Palmyrene merchants. Then conceive, poured through these long lines of beautiful edifices, among these temples and fountains, a population drawn from every country of the far East, arrayed in every variety of the most showy and fanciful costume, with the singular animals, rarely seen in our streets, but here met at every turn—elephants, camels, and dromedaries, to say nothing of the Arabian horses with their jewelled housings, with every now and then a troop of the Queen's cavalry, moving along to the sound of their clanging trumpets—conceive this ceaseless tide of various animal life poured along among the proud piles, and choking the ways, and you will have some faint glimpses of the strange and imposing reality. (*Ibid.*, p. 53.)

On turning a corner the chariot comes suddenly in sight of the world-famous Temple of the Sun:

Upon a vast platform of marble, itself decorated with endless lines of columns—elsewhere of beauty and size sufficient for the principal building, but here a mere appendage—stood in solitary magnificence this peerless work of art. All I could do was, and the act was involuntary, to call upon the charioteer to rein up his horses and let me quietly gaze. In this Fausta, nothing unwilling, indulged me. Then, when satisfied with this, the first point of view, we wound slowly around the spacious square upon which it stands, observing it well in all directions, and taking my fill of that exalted but nameless pleasure which flows in upon the soul from the contemplation of perfect excellence.

"This is, if I err not, Fausta, the work of a Greek artist."

"It is," said she; "here both Romans and Palmyrenes must acknowledge their inferiority; and, indeed, all other people. In every city of the world, I believe, all the great works of art are the offspring of Grecian genius and Grecian taste. Truly, a wonderful people! In this very city, our artists, our men of letters, even the first minister of state, all are Greeks. But come, let us move on to the Long Portico, an edifice which will astonish you yet more than even the Temple of the Sun, through your having heard of it so much less. We shall reach it in about half a Roman mile."

This space was soon passed, and the Portico stood revealed, with its interminable ranges of Corinthian columns, and the busy multitudes winding among them. Here the merchants assemble and meet each other. Here various articles of more than common rarity are brought and exhibited for sale. Here the mountebanks resort, and entertain the idle and lovers of amusement with their fantastic tricks. And here strangers from all parts of the world may be seen walking to and fro, observing the customs of the place, and regaling themselves at the brilliant rooms, furnished with every luxury, which are opened for their use, or else at the public baths, which are found in the immediate neighbourhood. The Portico does not, like the Temple, stand upon an elevated platform, but more upon a level with the streets. Its greatness is derived from its extreme length, and its exquisitely perfect designs and workmanship, as seen in the graceful fluted columns and the rich entablature running round the whole. The life and achievements of Alexander are sculptured upon the frieze; the artist, a Greek also, having been allowed to choose his own theme.

"Fausta," said I, "my soul is steeped in beauty. It will be to no purpose to show me more now." (*Ibid.*, pp. 54–5.)

Into the scene thus prepared, the author at once introduces Zenobia and all the historical characters of the book:

As we were thus idly discoursing, we became suddenly conscious of an unusual commotion in the street. The populace began to move quickly by in crowds, and vehicles of all sorts came pouring along as if in expectation of something they were eager to see.

"What's all this? What's all this?" said Demetrius, leaving his work, which he had resumed, and running to the door of his shop: "What's the matter, friend?" addressing a citizen hurrying by; "is Aurelian at the gates, that you are posting along in such confusion?"

"Not Aurelian," replied the other, "but Aurelian's mistress. The Queen is coming. Clouds of dust on the skirts of the plain show that she is advancing toward the city."

"Now, Roman, if thou wouldst see a sight, be advised and follow me. We will mount the roof of yonder market, whence we shall win a prospect such as no eye can have seen that has not gazed from the same point. It is where I go to refresh my dulled senses, after the day's hard toil. . . .

"We are here just at the right moment," said he; "come quickly to this corner and secure a seat, for you see the people are already thronging after us. There! can Elysium offer a more perfect scene? And look, how inspiring is the view of these two multitudes, moving toward each other in the spirit of friendship! How the city opens her arms to embrace her Queen!"

At the distance of about a mile from the walls we now saw the party of the Queen, escorted by a large body of horse; and, approaching them from the city, apparently its whole population, some on foot, some on horse, some in carriages of every description. The plain was filled with life. The sun shooting his beams over the whole, and reflected from the spears and corslets of the cavalry, and the gilding and polished work of chariots and harness, caused the scene to sparkle as if strewed with diamonds. As soon as the near approach of Zenobia to the walls began to conceal her and her escort, we returned to the steps of the shop of Demetrius, as the Queen would pass directly by them on her way to the palace.

We had been here not many minutes before the shouts of the people, and the braying of martial music, and the confused sound of an approaching multitude, showed that the Queen was near. Troops of horse, variously caparisoned, each more brilliantly, as it seemed, than another, preceded a train of sumptuary elephants and camels, these too richly dressed, but heavily loaded. Then came the body guard of the Queen, in armour of complete steel, and then the chariot of Zenobia, drawn by milk-white Arabians. So soon as she appeared the air resounded with the acclamations of the countless multitudes. Every cry of loyalty and affection was heard from ten thousand mouths, making a music such as filled the heart almost to breaking. "Long live the great Zenobia!" went up to the heavens. "The blessings of all the Gods on our good Queen!"—"Health and happiness to the mother of her people!"— "Death and destruction to her enemies!"—these and cries of the same kind came from the people, not as a mere lip-service, but evidently, from the tone in which they were uttered, prompted by real sentiments of love, such as it seems to me never before can have existed towards a supreme and absolute prince.

It was to me a moment inexpressibly interesting. I could not have asked for more than, for the first time, to see this great woman just as I now saw her. I cannot, even at this time, speak of her beauty, and the imposing, yet sweet dignity of her manners; for it was with me, as I suppose it was with all—the diviner beauty of the emotions and sentiments which were working at her heart and shone out in the expressive language of her countenance, took away all power of narrowly scanning complexion, feature and form. Her look was full of love for her people. She regarded them as if they were her children. She bent herself fondly toward them, as if nothing but the restraints of form withheld her from throwing herself into their arms. This was the beauty which filled and agitated me. I was more than satisfied.

"And who," said I to Demetrius, "is that beautiful being, but of a sad and thoughtful countenance, who sits at the side of the Queen?"

"That," he replied, "is the Princess Julia; a true descendant of her great mother; and the Gods grant that she, rather than either of her brothers, may succeed to the sovereign power."

"She looks indeed," said I, "worthy to reign—over hearts at least, if not over nations. Those in the next chariot are, I suppose, the young Cæsars, as I hear they are called—about as promising, to judge by the form and face, as some of our Roman brood of the same name. I need not ask whose head that is in the carriage next succeeding; it can belong to no other in Palmyra than the great Longinus. What a divine repose breathes over that noble countenance! But—Gods of Rome and of the world!—who sits beside him? Whose dark soul is lodged in that fearful tenement? fearful and yet beautiful, as would be a statue of ebony?"

"Know you not him? Know you not the Egyptian Zabdas? the mirror of accomplished knighthood, the pillar of the state, the Aurelian of the East? Ah! far may you go to find two such men as those—of gifts so diverse, and power so great—sitting together like brothers. It all shows the greater power of Zenobia, who can tame the roughest and most ambitious spirits to her uses. Who is like Zenobia?"

"So ends, it seems to me," I replied, "every sentence of every Palmyrene,—'Who is like Zenobia?'" (*Ibid.*, pp. 59–62.)

With these personages, all of whom except the Princess Julia are historical, we are made intimately acquainted in the scenes and conversations, which, alternately with the progress of Piso's attempt to recover his brother, occupy the whole of the first volume. Our author has not escaped the danger to which writers of his class are most liable. Very few writers can maintain sufficient discrimination between one of their good characters and another: and his are too much alike; they are all heroes or heroines, and all, with some slight exceptions, heroes and heroines of the same sort. Longinus, the great philosophical ornament of his age, one of the latest authors who, in the decline of letters, maintained their place among the great writers of antiquity, is not sufficiently distinguished from Gracchus, who is also a philosopher—an Epicurean indeed, while the other is a Platonist, but in the main he philosophizes in much the same way, and, to our thinking, full as wisely. Fausta is but a lesser Zenobia; and the Princess Julia differs from them both, only by having somewhat less strength and somewhat more gentleness, and by being a semi-convert to Christianity. This last is hardly a distinction, as the author (we fear without historical authority) represents most of his good characters (except Zenobia herself, whose partialities are rather towards Judaism) as either entertaining from the beginning of the book, or acquiring in the course of it, sentiments which must very soon have ended in their complete adoption of Christianity. The effect of this uniformity of character is, that the reader is not strongly interested in any of the personages, considered as an individual. But, all things duly weighed, we question whether this is a defect. In the first place, that there would really have been among the intimate companions and chosen advisers of so remarkable a person as Zenobia as much resemblance (either original or caught from her) to the great features of her own character as is here assigned to them, is in itself highly probable. And what spoils the personages as individual figures, improves the effect of the entire picture. We see what we wish to see, Zenobia as the centre of the whole, with a small band of devoted friends forming an inner circle round her, and an enthusiastic and worshipping people for the framework beyond. The effect, in this view of the design, is completely what it was intended to be. Zenobia alone stands out as an individual character. We see in her all the natural qualities of a great and good despot: the lofty and almost godlike feelings derived from the consciousness of vast power won by wisdom and energy and exercised with virtue; the passion for excitement, to which not to reign were not to live; the unbending pride which cannot brook a diminution of importance, and the self-confidence which feels assured of victory when rushing into the most hopeless enterprises. The author has very skilfully and naturally bespoken our indulgence for these pardonable weaknesses, by depicting them as, what they most probably were, the weaknesses not more of Zenobia herself than of her people, intoxicated with their own greatness, and fondly believing that the world in arms must give way before the irresistible genius of their queen. Even with this rash confidence the author makes us sympathize; the reader becomes a Palmyrene, and feels with the Palmyrenes their enthusiasm. His management of the character of Zenobia herself is in this respect extremely skilful. After the scene in the amphitheatre, in which her sons appear with the imperial purple of the Cæsars, a presumption which is the immediate cause of the rupture with Rome—being asked "Why put at hazard the peace and prosperity of this fair realm for a shadow—a name? What is it to you or to me that Timolaus, Herennianus, and Vabalathus, be hailed by the pretty style of Cæsar?" [*Ibid.*, p. 93.] The Queen replies,

"Julia, as the world deems—and we are in the world and of it—honour and greatness lie not in those things which are truly honourable and great; not in learning or genius, else were Longinus on this throne, and I his waiting woman; not in action, else were the great Zabdas king; not in merit, else were many a dame of Palmyra where I am, and I a patient household drudge. Birth, and station and power are before these. Men bow before names and sceptres and robes of office, lower than before the gods themselves. Nay, here in the East, power itself were a shadow without its tinsel trappings. 'Tis vain to stand against the world. I am one of the general herd. What they honour, I crave. This coronet of pearl, this gorgeous robe, this golden chair, this human footstool, in the eye of a severe judgment may signify but little. Zeno or Diogenes might smile upon them with contempt. But so thinks not the world. It is no secret that in Timolaus, Herennianus and Vabalathus dwells not the wisdom of Longinus, nor the virtue of Valerian. What then so crazed the assembled people of Palmyra, but the purple-coloured mantle of the Roman Cæsar? I am, for that, fathoms deeper in the great heart of my people." (*Ibid.*, pp. 93–4.)

The author has managed well the only weakness of his greatest character. He has so well seized the light in which the unmeasured love of power and of its trappings represents itself to itself in a mind fit for better things; he has blended so much of greatness with its littleness, that in her it scarcely appears to be a fault. Hear her afterwards, at the deliberation in council upon Aurelian's warlike message, thus avow and justify, on the noblest grounds, her love of dominion:

"I am charged with pride and ambition. The charge is true, and I glory in its truth. Who ever achieved anything great in letters, arts, or arms, who was not ambitious? Cæsar was not more ambitious than Cicero. Let the ambition be a noble one, and who shall blame it? I confess I did once aspire to be Queen, not only of Palmyra, but of the East. That I am. I now aspire to remain so. Is it not an honourable ambition? Does it not become a descendant of the Ptolemys and of Cleopatra? I am applauded by you all for what I have already done. You would not it should have been less. But why pause here? Is so much ambition praiseworthy, and more criminal? Is it fixed in nature that the limits of this empire should be Egypt on the one hand, the Hellespont and the Euxine on the other? Were not Suez and Armenia more natural limits? Or hath empire no natural limits, but is broad as the genius that can devise, and the power than can win. Rome has the West. Let Palmyra possess the East. Not that nature prescribes this and no more. The Gods prospering, and I swear not that the Mediterranean shall hem me in upon the West, or Persia on the East. Longinus is right—I would that the world were mine. I feel within the will and the power to bless it, were it so.

"Are not my people happy? I look upon the past and the present, upon my nearer and my remoter subjects, and ask, nor fear the answer—Whom have I wronged? what province have I oppressed? what city pillaged? what region drained with taxes? whose life have I unjustly taken, or estates coveted or robbed? whose honour have I wantonly assailed? whose rights, though of the weakest and poorest, have I trenched upon? I dwell where I would ever dwell, in the hearts of my people. It is writ in your faces, that I reign not more over you than within you. The foundation of my throne is not more power than love. Suppose now, my ambition add another province to our realm? Is it an evil? The kingdoms already bound to us by the joint acts of ourself and the late royal Odenatus, we found discordant and at war. They are now united and at peace. One harmonious whole has grown out of hostile and sundered parts. At my hands they receive a common justice and equal benefits. The channels of their commerce have I opened, and dug them deep and sure. Prosperity and plenty are in all their borders. The streets of our capital bear testimony to the distant and various industry which here seeks its market. This is no vain boasting—receive it not so, good friends—it is but truth. He who traduces himself sins with him who traduces another. He who is unjust to himself, or less than just, breaks a law as well as he who hurts his neighbour. I tell you what I am and what I have done, that your trust for the future may not rest upon ignorant grounds. If I am more than just to myself, rebuke me. If I have overstepped the modesty that became me, I am open to your censure, and will bear it. But I have spoken that you may know your Queen—not only by her acts, but by her admitted principles. I tell you, then, that I am ambitious; that I crave dominion; and while I live, will reign. Sprung from a line of kings, a throne is my natural seat—I love it. But I strive, too—you can bear me witness that I do—that it shall be, while I sit upon it, an honoured, unpolluted seat. If I can, I will hang a yet brighter glory around it." (*Ibid.*, Vol. II, pp. 26–8.)

We pass over the letters in which we are introduced to the private life, the social intercourse and amusements, the conversations and speculations of Zenobia and her friends. In these, the first philosopher of his age being one of the interlocutors, and some of the others being persons who had listened approvingly to the teachers of Christianity, the subjects touched are naturally those of the highest and most solemn nature; but there is nothing controversial in the tone, and the dialogue exhibits fairly enough what may be conceived to have been in that age the feelings of persons like those represented, in regard to the great problem of human existence, in this life and in a life to come. Piso's thoughts incline him more and more towards the Christian faith, of which the sincere and pure-minded votaries are typified in Probus (the Christian with whom Piso became acquainted on his voyage from Rome), and the more vain-glorious and worldly-minded in Paul of Samosata, Bishop of Antioch, whom it is historically true that Zenobia protected and countenanced.

We quote a passage of another kind: the *tableau de mœurs* which concludes the description of a trial of strength and skill in martial exercises. The trial was "to throw the lance with such unerring aim and force, as to pass through an aperture in a shield of fourfold ox-hide, of a size but slightly larger than the beam of the lance, so as not so much as to graze the sides of the perforated place." (*Ibid.*, Vol. I, p. 138.) The incapable sons of Zenobia, genuine samples of hereditary oriental princes, try their skill, and fail with different degrees of disgrace. Zabdas, the stern and swarthy warrior already mentioned,

now, suddenly springing from his seat, which he had taken among those who apparently declined to join in the sport, seized a lance from the hands of the slave who bore them, and hurling it with the force of a tempest, the weapon, hissing along the air, struck the butt near the centre; but the wood of which it was made, unused to such violence, shivered and crumbled under the blow. Without a word, and without an emotion, so far as the face was its index, the Egyptian returned to his seat. It seemed as if he had done the whole in his sleep. It is actual war alone that can rouse the energies of Zabdas. (*Ibid.*, p. 139.)

Zenobia herself next makes the attempt, and succeeds, but

in passing through the aperture the weapon, not having been driven with quite sufficient force, did not preserve its level, so that the end grazed the shield, and the lance then consequently taking an oblique direction, plunged downward, and buried its head in the turf. (*Ibid.*)

Fausta follows, and her success is perfect. There remains the Princess Julia; the gentle and sensitive character of the story, and the one with whom, of course, Piso is to fall in love.

With a form of so much less apparent vigour than either Zenobia or Fausta, so truly Syrian in a certain soft languor that spreads itself over her, whether at rest or in motion, it was amazing to see with what easy strength she held and balanced the heavy weapon. Every movement showed that there lay concealed within her ample power for this and every manly exercise, should she please to put it forth.

"At the schools," said the princess, "Fausta and I went on ever with equal steps. Her advantage lies in being at all times mistress of her power. My arm is often treacherous through failure of the heart."

It was not difficult to see the truth of what she said, in her varying colour, and the slightly agitated lance.

But addressing herself to the sport, and with but one instant's pause, the lance flew toward the shield, and entering the opening, but not with a perfect direction, it passed not through, but hung there by the head.

"Princess," said Zabdas, springing from his repose with more than wonted energy, "that lance was chosen, as I saw, by a Roman. Try once more with one that I shall choose, and see what the issue will be."

"Truly," said Julia, "I am ready to seize any plea under which to redeem my fame. But first give me yourself a lesson, will you not?"

The Egyptian was not deaf to the invitation, and once more essaying the feat, and with his whole soul bent to the work, the lance, quicker than sight, darted from his hand, and following in the wake of Fausta's, lighted farther than hers—being driven with more force—upon the lawn.

The princess now, with more of confidence in her air, again balanced and threw the lance which Zabdas had chosen—this time with success, for passing through the shield it fell side by side with Fausta's.

"Fortune still unites us," said Julia; "if for a time she leaves me a little in the rear, yet she soon repents of the wrong, and brings me up." Saying which she placed herself at Fausta's side.

The villain of the tale now makes his appearance.

"But come, our worthy cousin," said the Queen, now turning and addressing Antiochus, who stood with folded arms, dully surveying the scene, "will you not try a lance?"

"'Tis hardly worth our while," said he, "for the gods seem to have delivered all the honour and power of the East into the hands of women."

"Yet it may not be past redemption," said Julia, "and who more likely than Hercules to achieve so great a work? Pray begin."

That mass of a man, hardly knowing whether the princess was jesting or in earnest—for to the usual cloud that rested on his intellect there was now added the stupidity arising from free indulgence at the tables—slowly moved toward the lances, and selecting the longest and heaviest, took his station at the proper place. Raising then his arm, which was like a weaver's beam, and throwing his enormous body into attitudes which showed that no child's play was going on, he let drive the lance, which, shooting with more force than exactness of aim, struck upon the outer rim of the shield, and then glancing sideways was near spearing a poor slave, whose pleasure it was, with others, to stand in the neighbourhood of the butt, to pick up and return the weapons thrown, or withdraw them from the shield, where they might have fastened themselves.

Involuntary laughter broke forth upon this unwonted performance of the lance; upon which it was easy to see, by the mounting colour of Antiochus, that his passions were inflamed. Especially—did we afterwards suppose—was he enraged at the exclamation of one of the slaves near the shield, who was heard to say to his fellow, "now is the reign of women at an end." Seizing, however, on the instant, another lance, he was known to exclaim by a few who stood near him, but who did not take the meaning of his words: "with a better mark, there may be a better aim." Then resuming his position, he made at first, by a long and steady aim, as if he were going with certainty now to hit the shield; but, changing suddenly the direction of his lance, he launched it with fatal aim, and a giant's force, at the slave who had uttered those words. It went through him, as he had been but a sheet of papyrus, and then sung along the plain. The poor wretch gave one convulsive leap into the air, and dropped dead.

"Zenobia!" exclaimed Julia.

"Great queen!" said Fausta.

"Shameful!"—"dastardly!"—"cowardly!"—broke from one and another of the company.

"That's the mark I never miss," observed Antiochus; and at the same time regaled his nose from a box of perfume.

"'Tis his own chattel," said the Queen; "he may do with it as he lists. He has trenched upon no law of the realm, but only upon those of breeding and humanity. Our presence, and that of this company, might, we think, have claimed a more gentle observance."

"Dogs!" fiercely shouted Antiochus—who, as the Queen said these words, her eyes fastened indignantly upon him, had slunk skulking to his seat—"dogs!" said he, aiming suddenly to brave the matter, "off with yonder carrion!—it offends the queen."

"Would our cousin," said Zenobia, "win the hearts of Palmyra, this surely is a mistaken way. Come, let us to the palace. This spot is tainted. But that it may be sweetened, as far as may be, slaves!" she cried, "bring to the gates the chariot and other remaining chattels of Antiochus!"

Antiochus, at these words, pale with the apprehension of a cowardly spirit, rose and strode toward the palace, from which, in a few moments, he was seen on his way to the city. (*Ibid.*, pp. 140–3.)

The sports are interrupted by the arrival of an embassy from Aurelian, demanding from Zenobia the renunciation of all those provinces of the Roman empire which, during the anarchy of the "Thirty Tyrants," she and her husband had severed from it. The penalty of refusal is war. A large and interesting portion of the book is occupied by the reception of the ambassadors, their several audiences, the deliberations of the queen and her counsellors on the propositions they bring, and their dismissal with a dignified refusal.

The underplot of the drama meanwhile proceeds; and Piso's brother is rescued from his Persian captivity through the instrumentality of Isaac the Jew; a personage who stands among the sceptics and half-believers of the story, a complete picture of a man who is wholly a believer, and whose life is devoted to the cause in which he has faith, that of his lost Jerusalem. He alone, of all the characters in the book, hates Christianity; and though full of the kindly feelings which our author, to the credit of his own, liberally bestows upon almost all his personages, he undertakes the rescue of Calpurnius in no spirit of love and charity, but in consideration of "one talent" if he lives, and two talents if he dies, to be bestowed upon his sacred cause. Calpurnius proves to have been, by Rome's long neglect of him in his captivity, exasperated into the bitterest hatred of the Roman name: he repairs to Palmyra, distinguishes himself in Zenobia's army, survives her defeat, and ends by marrying Fausta. We can only quote, from the well-told tale of Isaac's perils and adventures in the desert and in the Persian capital, the story of his encounter with Manes, the great heresiarch, founder of the Manichean religion:

"Ye have heard, doubtless, [says Isaac,] of Manes the Persian, who deems himself some great one, and sent of God. It was noised about ere I left Palmyra, that, for failing in a much boasted attempt to work a cure by miracle upon the Prince Hormisdas, he had been strangled by order of Sapor. Had he done so, his love of death-doing had at length fallen upon a proper object, a true child of Satan. But, as I can testify, his end was not such, and is not yet. He still walks the earth, poisoning the air he breathes, and deluding the souls of men. Him I encountered one day, the very day I had despatched thy letter, in the streets of Ecbatana, dogged at the heels by his twelve ragged apostles, dragging along their thin and bloodless limbs, that seemed each step ready to give way beneath the weight—little as it was—they had to bear. Their master, puffed up with the pride of a reformer—as forsooth he holds himself—stalked by at their head, drawing the admiration of the besotted people by his great show of sanctity, and the wise saws which every now and then he let drop, for the edification of such as heard. Some of these sayings fell upon my ear, and who was I to hear them and not speak? Ye may know that this false prophet has made it his aim to bring into one the Magian and Christian superstitions, so that, by such incongruous and deadly mixture, he might feed the disciples of those two widely sundered religions, retaining—as he foolishly hoped— enough of the faith of each to satisfy all who should receive the compound. In doing this he hath cast dirt upon the religion of the Jew, blasphemously teaching that our sacred books are the work of the author of evil, while those of Christ are by the author of good. With more zeal it must be confessed than wisdom, seeing where I was, and why I was there, I resisted this father of lies, and withstood him to his face. 'Who art thou, bold blasphemer,' I said, 'that takest away the God-head? breaking into twain that which is infinite and indivisible? Who art thou, to tread into dust the faith of Abraham, and Moses, and the prophets, imputing their words, uttered by the spirit of Jehovah, to the great enemy of mankind? I wonder, people of Ecbatana, that the thunders of God sleep and strike him not to the earth as a rebel—nay, that the earth cleaveth not beneath him and swalloweth him not up, as once before the rebels Korah, Dathan, and Abiram,'[*] and much more in the same mad way, till, while I was yet speaking, those lean and hungry followers of his set upon me with violence, crying out against me as a Jew, and stirring up the people, who were nothing unwilling, but fell upon me, and throwing me down, dragged me to a gate of the city, and casting me out as I had been a dead dog, returned themselves, like dogs to their vomit[†]—that accursed dish of Manichean garbage. I believed myself for a long while surely dead; and in my half-conscious state took to myself, as I was bound to do, shame for meddling in the affairs of

[*See Numbers, 16:1.]
[†See II Peter, 2:22.]

Pagan misbelievers—putting thy safety at risk. Through the compassion of an Arab woman, dwelling without the walls, I was restored and healed—for whose sake I shall ever bless the Ishmaelite." (*Ibid.*, Vol. II, pp. 45–6.)

Piso in the meantime has ventured to ask Julia in marriage from the queen, and been refused. In consistency with what history records of her, Zenobia is sceptical and even scornful on the subject of love—of all at least in love which distinguishes it from friendship; declares her daughter and herself wedded irrevocably and exclusively to the interests of Palmyra, and Julia the destined bride of the Persian prince, Hormisdas:

"Roman, [says she,] I live for Palmyra. I have asked of the Gods my children, not for my own pleasure, but for Palmyra's sake. I should give the lie to my whole life, to every sentiment I have harboured since the day I gave myself to the royal Odenatus, were I now to bestow upon a private citizen, her, through whom we have so long looked to ally ourselves by a new and stronger bond to some neighbouring kingdom. . . . How many of our brave soldiers—how many of our great officers, with devoted patriotism, throw away their lives for the country. You will not say that this is done for the paltry recompense which at best scarce shields the body from the icy winds of winter, or the scorching rays of summer. And shall not a daughter of the royal house stand steady to encounter the hardships of a throne—the dangers of a Persian court, and the terrors of a royal husband, especially when, by doing so, fierce and bloody wars may be staid, and nations brought into closer unity? . . . The world envies the lot of those who sit upon thrones. It seems all summer with them. But upon whom burst more storms, or with redder fury? They seem to the unreflecting mind to be the only independent—while they are the slaves of all. The prosperous citizen may link himself and his children when and with whom he likes, and none may gainsay him. He has but to look to himself, and his merest whim. The royal family must go and ask his leave. My children are more his than mine. And if it be his pleasure and preference that my daughters ally themselves to an Indian or a Roman prince, their will is done, not mine—theirs is the gain, mine the loss." (*Ibid.*, pp. 32–3, 32.)

We now arrive at a scene of peril.

I am just returned, [says Piso to his correspondent,] from a singular adventure. My hand trembles as I write. I had laid down my pen and gone forth upon my Arab, accompanied by Milo, to refresh and invigorate my frame after our late carousal—shall I term it?—at the palace. I took my way, as I often do, to the Long Portico, that I might again look upon its faultless beauty, and watch the changing crowds. Turning from that, I then amused my vacant mind by posting myself where I could overlook, as if I were indeed the builder or superintendent, the labourers upon the column of Aurelian. I became at length particularly interested in the efforts of a huge elephant, who was employed in dragging up to the foundations of the column, so that they might be fastened to machines to be then hoisted to their place, enormous blocks of marble. He was a noble animal, and, as it seemed to me, of far more than common size and strength. Yet did not his utmost endeavours appear to satisfy the demands of those who drove him, and who plied, without mercy, the barbed scourges which they bore. His temper at length gave way. He was chained to a mass of rock, which it was evidently beyond his power to move. It required the united strength of two at least. But this was nothing to his inhuman masters. They ceased not to urge him with cries and blows. One of them, at length, transported by that insane fury which seizes the vulgar when their will is not done by the brute creation, laid hold upon a long lance, terminated with a sharp iron goad long as my sword, and rushing upon the beast, drove it into his hinder part. At that very moment the chariot of the Queen, containing Zenobia herself, Julia and the other Princesses, came suddenly against the column, on its way to the palace. I made every possible sign to the charioteer to turn and fly. But it was too late. The infuriated monster snapped the chains that held him to the stone, at a single bound, as the iron entered him, and trampling to death one of his drivers, dashed forward to wreak his vengeance upon the first object that should come in his way. That, to the universal terror and distraction of the gathered but now scattered and flying crowds, was the chariot of the Queen. Her mounted guards, at the first onset of the maddened animal, put spurs to their horses, and by quick leaps escaped. The horses attached to the chariot, springing forward to do the same, urged by the lash of the charioteer, were met by the elephant, with straightened trunk and tail, who, in the twinkling of an eye, wreathed his proboscis around the neck of the first he encountered, and wrenching him from his harness, whirled him aloft, and dashed him to the ground. This I saw was the moment to save the life of the Queen, if, indeed, it was to be saved. Snatching from a flying soldier his long spear, and knowing well the temper of my horse, I put him to his speed, and running upon the monster, as he disengaged his trunk from the crushed and dying Arabian for a new assault, I drove it with unerring aim into his eye, and through that opening into the brain. He fell as if a bolt from heaven had struck him. The terrified and struggling horses of the chariot were secured by the now returning crowds, and the Queen with the Princesses relieved from the peril which was so imminent, and had blanched with terror every cheek but Zenobia's. She had stood the while, I was told—there being no exertion which she could make—watching with eager and intense gaze my movements, upon which she felt that their safety, perhaps their lives, depended.

It all passed in a moment. Soon as I drew out my spear from the dying animal, the air was rent with the shouts of the surrounding populace. Surely, at that moment, I was the greatest—at least the most fortunate man in Palmyra. (*Ibid.*, pp. 39–42.)

Notwithstanding this great service, the Queen's inflexibility does not give way. "Palmyra married to Persia, through Julia married to Hormisdas," [*ibid.*, p. 33,] is the irrevocable decree; nor is it reversed while Palmyra remains a kingdom.

Piso's brother joins the Palmyrene host: Piso himself cannot fight against Rome, but accepts the commission to keep a watchful eye upon Antiochus and his profligate followers in the city. The Queen marches out to encounter Aurelian: her appearance on the day of departure is thus described:

The city was all pouring forth upon the plains in its vicinity. The crowds choked the streets as they passed out, so that our progress was slow. Arriving, at length, we turned toward the pavilion of the Queen, pitched over against the centre of the army. . . . The braying of trumpets and other warlike instruments announced her approach. We turned, and looking toward the gate of the city, through which we had but now passed, saw Zenobia, having on either side Longinus and Zabdas, and preceded and followed by a select troop of horse. She was mounted upon her far-famed white Numidian—for power an elephant, for endurance a dromedary, for fleetness a very Nicœan, and who had been her companion in all the battles by which she had gained her renown and her empire. . . .

The object that approached us truly seemed rather a moving blaze of light than an armed woman, which the eye and reason declared it to be, with such gorgeous magnificence was she arrayed. The whole art of the armourer had been exhausted in her appointments. The caparison of her steed, sheathed with burnished gold, and thick studded with precious stones of every various hue, reflected an almost intolerable splendour as the rays of a hot morning sun fell upon it. She, too, herself being clothed in armour of polished steel, whose own fiery brightness was doubled by the diamonds—that was the only jewel she wore—sown with profusion over all its more prominent parts, could be gazed upon scarcely with more ease than the sun himself, whose beams were given back from it with undiminished glory. In her right hand she held the long slender lance of the cavalry; over her shoulders hung a quiver, well loaded with arrows, while at her side depended a heavy Damascus blade. Her head was surmounted by a steel helmet, which left her face wholly uncovered, and showed her forehead, like Fausta's, shaded by the dark hair, which, while it was the only circumstance that revealed the woman, added to the effect of a countenance unequalled for a marvellous union of feminine beauty, queenly dignity, and masculine power. Sometimes it has been her usage, upon such occasions, to appear with arms bare and gloved hands; they were now cased, like the rest of the body, in plates of steel. . . .

No sooner was the Queen arrived where we stood, and the whole extended lines became aware of her presence, than the air was filled with the clang of trumpets and the enthusiastic cries of the soldiery, who waved aloft their arms, and made a thousand expressive signs of most joyful greeting. When this hearty salutation, commencing at the centre, had died away along the wings, stretching one way to the walls of the city, and the other toward the desert, Zenobia rode up nearer the lines, and being there surrounded by the ranks which were in front, and by a crowd of the great officers of the army, spoke to them in accordance with her custom. Stretching out her hand, as if she would ask the attention of the multitude—a deep silence ensued, and in a voice clear and strong, she thus addressed them.

Her address, which we cannot venture to quote, being concluded—

Shouts long and loud, mingled with the clash of arms, followed these few words of the Queen. Her own name was heard above all: "Long live the great Zenobia," ran along the ranks from the centre to the extremes, and from the extremes back again to the centre. It seemed as if, when her name had once been uttered, they could not cease—through the operation of some charm—to repeat it again and again, coupled, too, with a thousand phrases of loyalty and affection. (*Ibid.*, pp. 75–8.)

The campaign is related with great spirit and fidelity to history. After the loss of two battles the Queen shuts herself up in Palmyra, whither she is followed by Aurelian, and closely besieged. The various incidents of the siege, the treachery of the base Antiochus, Zenobia's escape to seek for assistance at the Persian court, and her capture by Aurelian's troops, are told with much vigour and animation. But we hurry to a scene which far surpasses any of our other quotations in dramatic interest, the first interview of the Emperor Aurelian with the captive Queen.

"As we entered the tent [it is Zenobia's secretary who speaks] the Emperor stood at its upper end, surrounded by the chief persons of the army. He advanced to meet the Queen, and in his changing countenance and disturbed manner might it be plainly seen how even an Emperor, and he the Emperor of the world, felt the presence of a majesty such as Zenobia's. And never did our great mistress seem more a Queen than now—not through that commanding pride, which, when upon her throne, has impressed all who have approached her with a feeling of inferiority, but through a certain dark and solemn grandeur, that struck with awe, as of some superior being, those who looked upon her. There was no sign of grief upon her countenance, but many of a deep and rooted sadness, such as might never pass away. No one could behold her and not lament the fortune that had brought her to such a pass. Whoever had thought to enjoy the triumph of exulting over the royal captive, was rebuked by that air of calm dignity and profound melancholy, which, even against the will, touched the hearts of all, and forced their homage.

"'It is a happy day for Rome,' said Aurelian, approaching and saluting her, 'that sees you, lately Queen of Palmyra and of the East, a captive in the tent of Aurelian.'

"'And a dark one for my afflicted country,' replied the Queen.

"'It might have been darker,' rejoined the Emperor, 'had not the good providence of the Gods delivered you into my hands.'

"'The Gods preside not over treachery. And it must have been by treason among those in whom I have placed my most familiar trust, that I am now where and what I am. I can but darkly surmise by whose baseness the act has been committed. It had been a nobler triumph to you, Roman, and a lighter fall to me, had the field of battle decided the fate of my kingdom, and led me a prisoner to your tent.'

"'Doubtless it had been so,' replied Aurelian; 'yet, was it for me to cast away what chance threw into my power? A war is now happily ended, which, had your boat reached the further bank of the Euphrates, might yet have raged—and but to the mutual harm of two great nations. Yet it was both a bold and sagacious device, and agrees well with what was done by you at Antioch, Emesa, and now in the defence of your city. A more determined, a better appointed, or more desperate foe, I never yet have contended with.'

"'It were strange, indeed,' replied the Queen, 'if you met not with a determined foe, when life and liberty were to be defended. Had not treason, base and accursed treason, given me up like a chained slave to your power, yonder walls must have first been beaten piece-meal down by your engines, and buried me beneath their ruins, and famine clutched all whom the sword had spared, ere we had owned you master. What is life, when liberty and independence are gone?'

"'But why, let me ask,' said Aurelian, 'were you moved to assert an independency of Rome? How many peaceful and prosperous years have rolled on since Trajan and the Antonines, while you and Rome were at harmony—a part of us, and yet independent—allies rather than a subject province—using our power for your defence, yet owning no allegiance. Why was this order disturbed? What madness ruled, to turn you against the power of Rome?'

"'The same madness,' replied Zenobia, 'that tells Aurelian he may yet possess the whole world, and sends him here into the far East to wage needless war with a woman—Ambition! Yet, had Aurelian always been upon the Roman throne, or one resembling him, it had perhaps been different. Then there could have been nought but honour in any alliance that had bound together Rome and Palmyra. But was I—was the late renowned Odenatus, to confess allegiance to base souls, such as Aureolus, Gallienus, and Balista? While the thirty tyrants were fighting for the Roman crown, was I to sit still, waiting humbly to become the passive prey of whosoever might please to call me his? By the immortal Gods, not so! I asserted my supremacy, and made it felt; and in times of tumult and confusion to Rome, while her Eastern provinces were one scene of discord and civil broil, I came in, and reduced the jarring elements; and out of parts broken and sundered, and hostile, I constructed a fair and well-proportioned whole. And when once created, and I had tasted the sweets of sovereign and despotic power—what they are, thou knowest—was I tamely to yield the whole at the word or threat even of Aurelian? It could not be. So many years as had passed, and seen me Queen, not only of Palmyra, but of the East—a sovereign honoured and courted at Rome, feared by Persia, my alliance sought by all the neighbouring dominions of Asia,—had served but to foster in me that love of rule which descended to me from a long line of kings. Sprung from a royal line, and so long upon a throne, it was superior force alone, divine or human, that should drag me from my right. Thou hast been but four years King, Aurelian, monarch of the great Roman world, yet wouldst thou not, but with painful unwillingness, descend and mix with the common herd. For me, ceasing to reign, I would cease to live.'

" 'Thy speech,' said Aurelian, 'shows thee well worthy to reign. It is no treason to Rome, Carus, to lament that the fates have cast down from a throne one who filled its seat so well. Hadst thou hearkened to the message of Petronius, thou mightest still, lady, have sat upon thy native seat. The crown of Palmyra might still have girt thy brow.'

" 'But not of the East,' rejoined the Queen.

" 'Fight against ambition, Carus; thou seest how, by aiming at too much, it loses all: it is the bane of humanity. When I am dead, may ambition then die, nor rise again.'

" 'May it be so,' replied his general: 'it has greatly cursed the world. It were better perhaps that it died now.'

" 'It cannot,' replied Aurelian, 'its life is too strong. I lament too, great Queen, for so I may well call thee, that upon an ancient defender of our Roman honour, upon her who revenged Rome upon the insolent Persian, this heavy fate should fall. I would willingly have met for the first time, in a different way, the brave conqueror of Sapor, the avenger of the wrongs and insults of the virtuous Valerian. The debt of Rome to Zenobia is great, and shall yet, in some sort at least, be paid. Curses upon those who moved thee to this war. They have brought this calamity upon thee, Queen, not I, nor thou. What ill-designing aspirants have urged thee on? This is not a woman's war.'

" 'Was not that a woman's war,' replied the Queen, 'that drove the Goths from Upper Asia? Was not that a woman's war that hemmed Sapor in his capital, and seized his camp—and that beat Heraclianus, and gained thereby Syria and Mesopotamia, and that which worsted Probus, and so won the crown of Egypt? Does it ask for more, to be beaten by Romans, than to conquer these? Rest assured, great Prince, that the war was mine. My people were indeed with me, but it was I who roused, fired, and led them on. I had indeed great advisers. Their names are known through the whole world. Why should I name the renowned Longinus, the princely Gracchus, the invincible Zabdas, the honest Otho. Their names are honoured in Rome as well as here. They have been with me; but without lying or vanity, I may say I have been their head.'

" 'Be it so, nevertheless, thy services shall be remembered. But let us now to the affairs before us. The city has not surrendered—though thy captivity is known, the gates are still shut. A word from thee would open them.'

" 'It is a word I cannot speak,' replied the Queen, her countenance expressing now, instead of sorrow, indignation—'wouldst thou that I too should turn traitor?'

" 'It surely would not be that,' replied the Emperor. 'It can avail naught to contend further—it can but end in a wider destruction, both of your people and my soldiers.'

" 'Longinus, I may suppose,' said Zenobia, 'is now supreme. Let the Emperor address him, and what is right will be done.'

"Aurelian turned and held a brief conversation with some of his officers.

" 'Within the walls,' said the Emperor, again addressing the Queen, 'thou hast sons. Is it not so?'

" 'It is not they,' said the Queen quickly, her countenance growing pale, 'it is not they, or either of them, who have conspired against me?'

" 'No—not quite so. Yet he who betrayed thee calls himself of thy family. Thy sons surely were not in league with him. Soldiers,' cried the Emperor, 'lead forth the great Antiochus, and his slave.'

"At his name the Queen started—the Princess uttered a faint cry, and seemed as if she would have fallen.

"A fold of the tent was drawn aside, and the huge form of Antiochus appeared, followed by the Queen's slave, her head bent down and eyes cast upon the ground. If a look could have killed, the first glance of Zenobia, so full of a withering contempt, would have destroyed her base kinsman. He heeded it but so much as to blush, and turn away his face from her. Upon Sindarina the Queen gazed with a look of deepest sorrow. The beautiful slave stood there where she entered, not lifting her head, but her bosom rising and falling with some great emotion—conscious, as it seemed, that the Queen's look was fastened upon her, and fearing to meet it. But it was so only for a moment, when, raising her head and revealing a countenance swollen with grief, she rushed towards the Queen and threw herself at her feet, embracing them and covering them with kisses. Her deep sobs took away all power of speech. The Queen only said, 'My poor Sindarina.'

"The stern voice of Aurelian was first heard, 'Bear her away—bear her from the tent.'

"A guard seized her, and forcibly separating her from Zenobia, bore her weeping away.

" 'This,' said Aurelian, turning now to Zenobia, 'this is thy kinsman, as he tells me—the Prince Antiochus.'

"The Queen replied not.

" 'He has done Rome a great service.' Antiochus raised his head, and strained his stooping shoulders. 'He has the merit of ending a weary and disastrous war. It is a rare fortune to fall to any one. 'Tis a work to grow great upon. Yet Prince,' turning to Antiochus, 'the work is not complete. The city yet holds out. If I am to reward thee with the sovereign power, as thou sayest, thou must open the gates. Can'st thou do it?'

" 'Great Prince,' replied the base spirit, eagerly, 'it is provided for. Allow me but a few moments, and a place proper for it, and the gates, I warrant, shall quickly swing upon their hinges.'

" 'Ah! do you say so? That is well. What, I pray, is the process?'

" 'At a signal, which I shall make, noble Prince, and which has been agreed upon, every head of every one of the Queen's party rolls in the dust—Longinus, Gracchus, and his daughter, Seleucus, Gabrayas, and a host more—their heads fall. The gates are then to be thrown open.'

" 'Noble Palmyrene, you have the thanks of all. Of the city then we are at length secure. For this, thou wouldst have the rule of it under Rome; wielding a sceptre in the name of the Roman Senate, and paying a tribute as a subject province. Is it not so?'

" 'It is. That is what I would have and would do, most excellent Aurelian.'

" 'Who are thy associates in this? Are the Queen's sons, Herennianus, Timolaus, Vabalathus, of thy side, and partners in this enterprise?'

" 'They are not knowing of the design to deliver up to thy great power the Queen, their mother; but they are my friends, and most surely do I count upon their support. As I shall return King of Palmyra, they will gladly share my power.'

" 'But if friends of thine, they are enemies of mine,' rejoined Aurelian, in terrific tones, 'they are seeds of future trouble; they may sprout up into kings also, to Rome's annoyance. They must be crushed. Dost thou understand me?'

" 'I do, great Prince. Leave them to me; I will do for them. But, to say the truth, they are too weak to disturb any—friends or enemies.'

" 'Escape not so. They must die,' roared Aurelian.

" 'They shall, they shall,' ejaculated the alarmed Antiochus; 'soon as I am within the walls their heads shall be sent to thee.'

" 'That now is as I would have it. One thing more thou hast asked—that the fair slave, who accompanies thee, be spared to thee, to be thy Queen.'

" 'It was her desire; hers, noble Aurelian, not mine.'

" 'But didst thou not engage to her as much?'

" 'Truly, I did. But among princes such words are but politic ones. That is well understood. Kings marry for the state. I would be higher matched,' and the sensual demon cast his eyes significantly towards the Princess Julia.

" 'Am I understood?' continued Antiochus, Aurelian making no response; 'the Princess Julia I would raise to the throne.' The monster seemed to swell to twice his common size, as his mind fed upon the opening glories.

"Aurelian had turned from him, looking first at his Roman attendants, then at the Queen and Julia—his countenance kindling with some swelling passion.

" 'Do I understand thee?' he then said. 'I understand thee to say, that for the bestowment of the favours and honours thou hast named, thou wilt do the things thou hast now specifically promised. Is it not so?'

" 'It is, gracious King.'

" 'Dost thou swear it?'

" 'I swear it by the great God of Light.'

"The countenance of the Emperor now grew black with, as it seemed, mingled fury and contempt. Antiochus started, and his cheek paled. A little light reached his thick brain.

" 'Romans,' cried Aurelian, 'pardon me for so abusing your ears; and you, our royal captives. I knew not that such baseness lived—still less that it was here. Thou foul stigma upon humanity! Why opens not the earth under thee, but that it loathes and rejects thee! Is a Roman like thee, dost thou think, to reward thy unheard-of treacheries? Thou knowest no more what a Roman is, than what truth and honour are. Soldiers! seize yonder miscreant, write traitor on his back, and spurn him forth the camp. His form and his soul both offend alike. Hence, monster!'

"Antiochus was like one thunderstruck. Trembling in every joint, he sought to appeal to the Emperor's mercy, but the guard stopped his mouth, and dragged him from the tent. His shrieks pierced the air as the soldiers scourged him beyond the encampment.

" 'It was not for me,' said Aurelian, as these ceased to be heard, 'to refuse what fate threw into my hands. Though I despised the traitorous informer, I could not shut my ears to the facts he revealed without myself betraying the interests of Rome. But, believe me, it was information I would willingly have spared. My infamy were as his to have rewarded the traitor. Fear not, Queen; I pledge the word of a Roman and an emperor for thy safety. Thou art safe both from Roman and Palmyrene.'

" 'What I have but now been witness of,' replied the Queen, 'assures me that in the magnanimity of Aurelian I may securely rest.'

"As the Queen uttered these words a sound, as of a distant tumult, and the uproar of a multitude, caught the ears of all within the tent.

" 'What mean these tumultuous cries?' inquired Aurelian of his attending guard. 'They increase and approach!'

" 'It may be but the soldiers at their game with Antiochus,' replied Probus.

"But it was not so. At the moment a centurion, breathless, and with his head bare, rushed madly into the tent.

" 'Speak,' said the Emperor, 'what is it?'

" 'The legions,' said the centurion, as soon as he could command his words, 'are advancing, crying out for the Queen of Palmyra. They have broken from their camp and their leaders, and in one mixed body come to surround the Emperor's tent.'

"As he ended the fierce cries of the enraged soldiery were distinctly heard, like the roaring of a forest torn by a tempest. Aurelian, baring his sword, and calling upon his friends to do the same, sprung toward the entrance of the tent. They were met by the dense throng of the soldiers, who now pressed against the tent, and whose savage yells now could be heard.

" 'The head of Zenobia!' 'Deliver the Queen to our will!' 'Throw out the head of Zenobia, and we will return to our quarters!' 'She belongs to us.'

"At the same moment the sides of the tent were thrown up, showing the whole plain filled with the heaving multitude, and being itself instantly crowded with the ringleaders, and their more desperate associates. Zenobia, supporting the Princess, who clung to her, and pale through a just apprehension of every horror, but otherwise firm and undaunted, cried out to Aurelian, 'Save us, O Emperor, from this foul butchery.'

" 'We will die else,' replied the Emperor, who, with the word, sprung upon a soldier making toward the Queen, and with a blow clove him to the earth. Then swinging around him that sword which had drunk the blood of thousands, and followed by the gigantic Sandarion, by Probus, and Carus, a space around the Queen was soon cleared. 'Back, ruffians,' cried Aurelian, in a voice of thunder, 'for you are no longer Romans; back to the borders of the tent. There I will hear your complaints.' The soldiers fell back, and their ferocious cries ceased.

" 'Now,' cried the Emperor, addressing them, 'what is your will, that thus in wild disorder you throng my tent?'

"One from the crowd replied—'Our will is that the Queen of Palmyra be delivered to us, as our right, instantly. Thousands and thousands of our bold companions lie buried upon these accursed plains, slain by her and her fiery engines. We demand her life. It is but justice, and faint justice too.'

" 'Her life!'—'Her life!'—arose in one shout from the innumerable throng.

"The Emperor raised his hand, waving his sword, dripping with the blood of the slain soldier; the noise subsided;—and his voice, clear and loud, like the tone of a trumpet, went to the farthest bounds of the multitude.

" 'Soldiers,' he cried, 'you ask for justice—and justice you shall have.'—'Aurelian is ever just,' cried many voices.—'But you shall not have the life of the Queen of Palmyra.'— He paused—a low murmur went through the crowd—'or you must first take the life of your Emperor, and of these that stand with me.' The soldiers were silent. 'In asking the life of Zenobia,' he continued, 'you know not what you ask. Are any here who went with Valerian to the Persian war?' A few voices responded, 'I was there'—'and I,' 'and I.'—'Are there any here whose parents, or brothers, or friends, fell into the tiger clutches of the barbarian Sapor, and died miserably in hopeless captivity?'—Many voices everywhere throughout the crowd were heard in reply—'Yes, yes'—'Mine were there, and mine.'—'Did you ever hear it said,' continued Aurelian, 'that Rome lifted a finger for their rescue, or for that of the good Valerian?'—They were silent; some crying, 'No, no.'—'Know then, that when Rome forgot her brave soldiers and her Emperor, Zenobia remembered and avenged them, and Rome, fallen into contempt with the Persian, was raised to her ancient renown by the arms of her ally, the brave Zenobia, and her dominions throughout the East saved from the grasp of Sapor only by her valour. While Gallienus wallowed in sensuality and forgot Rome, and even his own great father, the Queen of Palmyra stood forth, and with her royal husband, the noble Odenatus, was in truth the saviour of the empire. And is it her life you would have? Were that a just return? Were that Roman magnanimity? And grant that thousands of your brave companions lie buried upon these plains—it is but the fortune of war. Were they not slain in honourable fight, in the siege of a city, for its defence unequalled in all the annals of war? Cannot Romans honour courage and military skill, though in an enemy? But you ask for justice. I have said you shall have justice. You shall. It is right that the heads and advisers of this revolt, for such the senate deems it, should be cut off. It is the ministers of princes who are the true devisers of a nation's acts. These, when in our power, shall be yours. And now, who, soldiers! stirred up this mutiny; bringing inexpiable shame upon our brave legions? Who were the leaders of the tumult?' Enough were found to name them.—'Firmus,' 'Carinus,' 'The centurions, Plancus, Tatius, Burrhus, Valens, Crispinus.'

" 'Guards, seize them and hew them down! Soldiers, to your tents!' The legions fell back as tumultuously as they had come together,—the faster, as the dying groans of the slaughtered ringleaders fell upon their ears.

"The tent of the Emperor was once more restored to order. After a brief conversation, in which Aurelian expressed his shame for the occurrence of such disorders in the presence of the Queen, the guard were commanded to convey back to the Palace of Seleucus, whence they had been taken, Zenobia and the Princess." (*Ibid.*, pp. 165–78.)

The character of Aurelian is finely drawn. The rude soldier, risen from the ranks to the empire—the stern disciplinarian, known to the army by the nickname of "Hand to his Sword"—the sovereign whose "love of justice," says Gibbon, "often became a blind and furious passion," who "disdained to hold his power by any other title than that of the sword, and governed by right of conquest an empire which he had saved and subdued,"[*] is painted as he was, with his scorn of all low and treacherous vice, his strong and savage passions and generous impulses, and that magnanimity and clemency so characteristic of kings, which after having humbled consents to spare the crowned heads with whom it sympathizes, but makes its vengeance fall with tenfold weight upon their comparatively unoffending subjects with whom it does not sympathize. The generous hero who heaped benefits and honours upon Zenobia, and admitted Tetricus, the abdicated Emperor of Gaul, to his friendship and intimacy (not, however, until he had led them both, Zenobia almost weighed down to the earth with gems and gold, after his car of triumph)—this chivalrous conqueror could not satiate his rage with less than the blood of the illustrious Longinus, and the other friends and counsellors of the Queen: and as for the city of Palmyra (not indeed till after one more attempt to assert its independence), he burnt it to the ground, and put all the inhabitants, old men, women, and children, indiscriminately to the sword. The last hours of Longinus are portrayed by our author in the very spirit in which, in two sentences, they are delineated by Gibbon: "Genius and learning were incapable of moving a fierce, unlettered soldier, but they had served to elevate and harmonise the soul of Longinus. Without uttering a complaint, he calmly followed the executioner, pitying his unhappy mistress, and bestowing comfort on his afflicted friends."[†]

We must give the reader one more glimpse of Zenobia, a captive and at Rome. It is from the description of Aurelian's triumph—that triumph which was opened, says Gibbon,[‡] by twenty elephants, four royal tigers, and above two hundred of the living wonders of every climate in the empire; in which the triumphal car of the Emperor was drawn by four stags; and "the pomp was so long and so various that, although it opened with the dawn of day, the slow majesty of the procession ascended not the Capitol before the ninth hour from sunrise."[§] After a lively description of the show, Piso continues:

But why do I detain you with these things, when it is of one only that you wish to hear. I cannot tell you with what impatience I waited for that part of the procession to approach

[*Decline and Fall, 1782 ed., Vol. I, p. 381; 1st ed., Vol. I, p. 320.]
[†Ibid., 1782 ed., pp. 373–4; 1st ed., p. 313.]
[‡Ibid., 1782 ed., p. 375; 1st ed., p. 315.]
[§Ibid., 1782 ed., pp. 377–8; 1st ed., p. 317.]

where were Zenobia and Julia. I thought its line would stretch on for ever. And it was the ninth hour before the alternate shouts and deep silence of the multitudes announced that the Emperor was drawing near the Capitol. As the first shout arose, I turned towards the quarter whence it came, and beheld, not Aurelian, as I expected, but the Gallic Emperor Tetricus— yet slave of his army and of Victoria—accompanied by the Prince his son, and followed by other illustrious captives from Gaul. All eyes were turned in pity upon him, and with indignation too that Aurelian should thus treat a Roman, and once—a senator. But sympathy for him was instantly lost in a stronger feeling of the same kind for Zenobia, who came immediately after. You can imagine, Fausta, better than I can describe them, my sensations when I saw our beloved friend—her whom I had seen treated never otherwise than as a sovereign queen, and with all the imposing pomp of the Persian ceremonial—now on foot, and exposed to the rude gaze of the Roman populace—toiling beneath the rays of a hot sun, and the weight of jewels, such as both for richness and beauty were never before seen in Rome; and of chains of gold, which first passing around her neck and arms, were then borne up by attendant slaves. I could have wept to see her so—yes, and did. My impulse was to break through the crowd, and support her almost fainting form—but I well knew that my life would answer for the rashness on the spot. I could only, therefore, like the rest, wonder and gaze. And never did she seem to me, not even in the midst of her own court, to blaze forth with such transcendent beauty—yet touched with grief. Her look was not that of dejection—of one who was broken and crushed by misfortune—there was no blush of shame. It was rather one of profound heart-breaking melancholy. Her full eyes looked as if privacy only was wanted for them to overflow with floods of tears. But they fell not. Her gaze was fixed on vacancy, or else cast toward the ground. She seemed like one unobservant of all around her, and buried in thoughts to which all else were strangers, and had nothing in common with. They were in Palmyra, and with her slaughtered multitudes. Yet though she wept not, others did; and one could see all along, wherever she moved, the Roman hardness yielding to pity, and melting down before the all-subduing presence of this wonderful woman. The most touching phrases of compassion fell constantly upon my ear. And ever and anon, as in the road there would happen some rough or damp place, the kind souls would throw down upon it whatever of their garments they could quickest divest themselves of, that those feet, little used to such encounters, might receive no harm. And as, when other parts of the procession were passing by, shouts of triumph and vulgar joy frequently arose from the motley crowds, yet, when Zenobia appeared, a death-like silence prevailed, or it was interrupted only by exclamations of admiration or pity, or of indignation at Aurelian for so using her. But this happened not long. For when the Emperor's pride had been sufficiently gratified, and just there where he came over against the steps of the Capitol, he himself, crowned as he was with the diadem of universal empire, descended from his chariot, and unlocking the chains of gold that bound the limbs of the Queen, led and placed her in her own chariot—that chariot in which she had hoped herself to enter Rome in triumph—between Julia and Livia. Upon this the air was rent with the grateful acclamations of the countless multitudes. The Queen's countenance brightened for a moment as if with the expressive sentiment, "The Gods bless you," and was then buried in the folds of her robe. And when, after the lapse of many minutes, it was again raised and turned toward the people, every one might see that tears burning hot had crossed her cheeks, and relieved a heart which else might well have burst with its restrained emotion. Soon as the chariot which held her had disappeared upon the other side of the Capitol, I extricated myself from the crowd and returned home. It was not till the shades of evening had fallen that the last of the procession had passed the front of the Capitol, and the Emperor reposed within the walls of his palace. (*Ibid.*, pp. 246–8.)

The Emperor presents Zenobia (conformably to history) with a villa at Tibur;

treats her with distinguished honour, and her daughter Livia becomes the Roman Empress. Relieved now from the burthens, as well as defeated in the ambitious aspirations, of the Queen of Palmyra, she is no longer deaf to the entreaties of Julia and of Piso: and at the conclusion we are allowed to believe that in the splendour of one of her children, and the domestic felicity of another, she found, if not happiness, consolation for her own downfall.

A few words remain to be added, by way of a general estimate of the merits of the work.

Doubtless this writer is not the great artist whom Miss Martineau tells us[*] that the American people are looking for—a Messiah who will one day arise, but probably (as Messiahs are wont) in such a shape that those who were the first to prophesy his coming will be the last to recognise him when come. This author has no claims to so great an honour. He has made no new revelations to us out of the depths of human feeling, has conceived no new and interesting varieties of spiritual nature, nor announced any original and pregnant views of human affairs. But there is that in him which, in the present state of literature, deserves to be prized most highly, and which entitles him to a most honourable place among the writers not only of his own country, but of ours at the present time. We do not refer to his power of throwing his own mind, and of making his readers throw theirs, into the minds and into the circumstances of persons who lived far off and long ago; of making us see things as those persons saw, or might have seen them; of making us feel with them, and, in some measure, understand them. We give him a higher praise; he is one of the few (and among writers of fiction they never were so few as in this age) who can conceive, with sufficient strength and reality to be able to represent, genuine unforced nobleness of character.

*a*The time was, when it was thought that the best and most appropriate office of fictitious narrative was to awaken high aspirations, by the representation, in interesting circumstances, of characters conformable indeed to human nature, but whose actions and sentiments were of a more generous and loftier *b*order*b* than are ordinarily to be met with by everybody in every-day life. But now-a-days nature and probability are thought to be violated, if there be shown to the reader, in the personages with whom he is called upon to sympathize, characters on a larger scale than himself, or *c* the persons he is accustomed to meet *d*with*d* at a dinner or a quadrille party. Yet, from such representations, familiar from early youth, have not only the noblest minds in modern Europe derived *e* what made them noble, but even the commoner spirits what made them understand and respond to nobleness. And *this* is Education. It would be well if the more narrow-minded portion, both of

[*Society in America, Vol. III, p. 208.]

*a–a*461 [*reprinted in* D&D *as* "A Prophecy. (From a Review of 'Letters from Palmyra.')"]
*b–b*59, 67   cast
*c*59, 67   than
d–d–59, 67
*e*59, 67   much of

the religious and of the scientific education-mongers, would consider whether the books which they are banishing from the hands of youth, were not instruments of national education to the full as powerful as the catalogues of physical facts and theological dogmas which they have substituted—as if science and religion were to be taught, not by imbuing the mind with their spirit, but by cramming the memory with summaries of their conclusions. Not what a boy or a girl can repeat by rote, but what they have learnt to love and admire, is what forms their character. The chivalrous spirit has almost disappeared from books of education; the popular novels of the day teach nothing but (what is already too soon learnt from actual life) lessons of worldliness, with at most the huckstering virtues which conduce to getting on in the world; and, for the first time perhaps in history, the youth of both sexes of the educated classes are universally growing up unromantic. What will come in mature age from such a youth, the world has not yet had time to see. But the world may rely upon it, that Catechisms, whether Pinnock's[*] or the Church of England's,[†] will be found a poor substitute for those old romances, whether of chivalry or of faery, which, if they did not give a true picture of actual life, did not give a false one, since they did not profess to give any, but (what was much better) filled the youthful imagination with pictures of heroic men, and of what are at least as much wanted, heroic women. The book before us does this *f*. And*f* greatly is any book to be valued, which in this age, and in a form suited to it, *g*and not only unexceptionable but fitted to be most acceptable to the religious reader,*g* does its part towards keeping alive the chivalrous spirit, which was the best part of the old romances; towards giving to the aspirations of the young and susceptible a noble direction, and keeping present to the mind an exalted standard of worth, by placing before it heroes and heroines worthy of the name.

It is an additional title to praise in this author, that his great women are imagined in the very contrary spirit to the modern cant, according to which a heroic woman is supposed to be something intrinsically different from the best sort of heroic men. It was not *h*thought so*h* in the days of Artemisia or Zenobia, or in that era of great statesmen and stateswomen, the fifteenth and sixteenth centuries, when the daughters of royal houses were governors of provinces, and displayed, as such, talents for command equal to any of their husbands or brothers—and when negociations which had baffled the first diplomatists of Francis and of Charles V, were brought to a successful issue by the wisdom and dexterity of two princesses.[‡] The book before us is in every line a virtual protest against the narrow and degrading doctrine

[*See, *inter alia*, William Pinnock, *A Catechism of Sacred Geography* (London: Whittaker, 1823); *Pinnock's Catechism of Drawing* (London: Whittaker, 1828).]
[†See *The Book of Common Prayer*.]
[‡Louise of Savoy, and Margaret of the Netherlands.]

*f-f*59, 67 : and
g-g—59, 67
*h-h*59, 67   so thought

which has grown out of the false refinement of later times. And it is the author's avowed belief, that one of the innumerable great purposes of Christianity was to abolish the distinction between the two characters, by teaching that neither of them can be really admirable without the qualities supposed to be distinctive of the other, and by exhibiting, in the person of its Divine Founder, an equally perfect model of both.[a]

WRITINGS OF ALFRED DE VIGNY

1838

EDITORS' NOTE

Dissertations and Discussions, 2nd ed. (1867), Vol. I, pp. 287–329. Title footnoted: "Consisting of—1. Souvenirs de Servitude et de Grandeur Militaires. 2. Cinq-Mars; ou, une Conjuration sous Louis XIII. 3. Stello; ou, les Consultations du Docteur Noir. 4. Poëmes. 5. Le More de Venise, tragédie traduite de Shakespeare en Vers Français. 6. La Maréchale d'Ancre, drame. 7. Chatterton, drame.—*London and Westminster Review*, April 1838." Running title: "Alfred de Vigny." Republished from *L&WR*, VII & XXIX (Apr., 1838), 1–44, where it is headed: "ART. I.—*Œuvres de Alfred de Vigny*. Bruxelles [and Leipzig: Hochhausen and Fournes], 1837. Consisting of [the same list as above]." Running titles: left-hand, "Poems and Romances of Alfred de Vigny"; right-hand, "Royalist Poetry" (the equivalent of pp. 466.28–471.26), "Cinq-Mars" (pp. 472.26–475.7), "Military Recollections" (pp. 487.28–492.17), "Stello" (pp. 493.16–496.11), and "Moïse, Eloa, etc." (pp. 497.13–500.9). Signed: "A." Identified in Mill's bibliography as "An article on the 'Poems and Romances of Alfred de Vigny' in the same number of the same review"—i.e., as that (Jan., 1838) in which "Ware's Letters from Palmyra" appeared, but in fact the article was in the next number (Apr., 1838); the copyist who transcribed the bibliography may have allowed her eye to jump back to the preceding entry, for "Radical Party and Canada," which properly concludes "in the same number of the same review" (MacMinn, p. 50). The copy (tear sheets) of the *L&WR* version in Somerville College has no corrections or emendations.

For comment, see the Introduction, pp. xl–xli above.

The following text, taken from the 2nd ed. of *D&D* (the last in Mill's lifetime) is collated with that in *D&D*, 1st ed., and that in *L&WR*. In the footnoted variants, "38" indicates *L&WR*; "59" indicates *D&D*, 1st ed. (1859); and "67" indicates *D&D*, 2nd ed. (1867).

Writings of Alfred de Vigny

IN THE FRENCH MIND (the most active national mind in Europe at the present moment) one of the most *a* stirring elements, and among the fullest of promise for the futurity of France and of the world, is the Royalist, or Carlist, ingredient. We are not now alluding to the attempts of M. de Genoude, and that portion of the Carlist party of which the *Gazette de France* is the organ, to effect an alliance between legitimacy and universal suffrage; nor to the eloquent anathemas hurled against *b*the existing*b* institutions of society *c* by a man of a far superior order, the Abbé de la Mennais, whose original fervour of Roman Catholic absolutism has given place to a no less fervour of Roman Catholic ultra-Radicalism. These things too have their importance as symptoms, and even intrinsically are not altogether without their value. But we would speak rather of the somewhat less obvious inward working, which (ever since the Revolution of 1830 annihilated the Carlist party as a power in the State) has been going on in the minds of that accomplished and *d* numerous portion of the educated youth of France, whose family connexions or early mental impressions ranked them with the defeated party; who had been brought up, as far as the age permitted, in the old ideas of monarchical and Catholic France; were allied by their feelings or imaginations with whatever of great and heroic those old ideas had produced in the past; had not been sullied by participation in the selfish struggles for Court favour and power, of which the same ideas were the pretext in the present—and to whom the Three Days were really the destruction of something which they had loved and revered, if not for itself, at least for the reminiscences associated with it.

These reflections present themselves naturally when we are about to speak of the writings of Alfred de Vigny, one of the earliest in date, and one of the most genuine, true-hearted, and irreproachable in tendency and spirit, of the new school of French literature, termed the romantic. It would, in fact, be impossible to understand M. de Vigny's writings, especially the later and better portion, or to enter sympathizingly into the peculiar feelings which pervade them, without this clue. M. de Vigny is, in poetry and art, as a *e*still more eminent*e* man, M. de Tocqueville, is in philosophy, a result of the influences of the age upon a mind and

*a*38 active and
*b-b*38 all the
*c*38 taken together,

*d*38 even
*e-e*38 greater

character trained up in opinions and feelings opposed to those of the age. Both these writers, educated in one set of views of life and society, found, when they attained manhood, another set predominant in the world they lived in, and, at length, after 1830, enthroned in its high places. The contradictions they had thus to reconcile—the doubts and perplexities and misgivings which they had to find the means of overcoming before they could see clearly between these cross-lights— were to them that, for want of which so many otherwise well-educated and naturally-gifted persons grow up hopelessly commonplace. To go through life with a set of opinions ready-made and provided for saving them the trouble of thought, was a destiny that could not be theirs. Unable to satisfy themselves with either of the conflicting formulas which were given them for the interpretation of what lay in the world before them, they learnt to take formulas for what they were worth, and ^{f}to^f look into the world itself for the philosophy of it. They looked with both their eyes, and saw much there, which was neither in the creed they had been taught, nor in that which they found prevailing around them: much that the prejudices, either of Liberalism or of Royalism, amounted to a disqualification for the perception of, and which would have been hid from themselves if the atmosphere of either had surrounded them both in their youth and in their maturer years.

That this conflict between a Royalist education, and the spirit of the modern world, triumphant in July 1830, must have gone for something in giving to the speculations of a philosopher like M. de Tocqueville the catholic spirit and comprehensive range which distinguish them, most people will readily admit. But, that the same causes must have exerted an analogous influence over a poet and artist, such as Alfred de Vigny is in his degree; that a political revolution can have given to the genius of a poet what principally distinguishes it—may not appear so obvious, at least to those who, like most Englishmen, rarely enter into either politics or poetry with their whole soul. Worldly advancement, or religion, are an Englishman's real interests: for Politics, except in connexion with one of those two objects, and for Art, he keeps only bye-corners of his mind, which naturally are far apart from each other: and it is but a ^{g}small^g minority among Englishmen who can comprehend, that there are nations among whom Politics, or the pursuit of social well-being, and Poetry, or the love of ^{h}beauty^h and of imaginative emotion, are passions as intense, as absorbing—influencing as much the whole tendencies of the character, and constituting as large a part of the objects in life of a considerable portion of the cultivated classes, as either the religious feelings, or those of worldly interest. Where both politics and poetry, instead of being either a trade or a pastime, are taken ^{i} completely *au sérieux*, each will be more or less coloured by the other; and that close relation between an author's politics and his poetry, which

$^{f-f}$+59, 67
$^{g-g}$+59, 67
$^{h-h}$38   the Beautiful
^{i}38   so

with us is only seen ^{j} in the great poetic figures of their age, ^{k} a Shelley, a Byron, or a Wordsworth, is broadly conspicuous in France (for example), through the whole range of her literature.

It may be worth while to employ a moment in considering what are the general features which, in an age of revolutions, may be expected to distinguish a Royalist or Conservative from a Liberal or Radical poet or imaginative writer. We are not speaking of political poetry, of Tyrtæus[*] or Körner,[†] of Corn-Law Rhymes,[‡] or sonnets on the Vaudois or on Zaragoza;[§] ^{l}these^l are rather oratory than poetry. We have nothing to do with the Radical poet as the scourge of the oppressor, or with the Tory one as the ^{m}denouncer of^m infidelity or jacobinism. They are not poets by virtue of what is negative or combative in their feelings, but by what is positive and sympathizing ^{n}. The pervading spirit, then, of the one, will be love of the Past; of the other, faith in the Future. The partialities of the one will be towards things established, settled, regulated; of the other, towards human free-will, cramped and fettered in all directions, both for good and ill, by those establishments and regulations. Both ^{o}, being poets,^{o} will have a heroic sympathy with heroism ^{p} ; but the one will respond most readily to the heroism of endurance and self-control, the other to that of ^{q}action^q and struggle. Of the virtues and beauties of our common humanity, the one will view with most affection those which have their natural growth under the shelter of fixed habits and firmly settled opinions: local and family attachments, tranquil tastes and pleasures, those gentle and placid feelings towards man and nature, ever most easy to those upon whom is not imposed the burthen of being their own protectors and their own guides. ^{r}Greater^r reverence, deeper humility, the virtues of abnegation and forbearance carried to a higher degree, will distinguish his favourite personages: while, as subjection to a common faith and law brings the most diverse characters to the same standard, and

---

[*See, e.g., The War-Songs of Tyrtaeus, trans. Richard Polwhele, in The Idylls of Theocritus, Bion, and Moschus, and the War-Songs of Tyrtaeus (London: Bohn, 1853), pp. 337–43.]

[†See Karl Theodor Körner, Leyer und Schwerdt (Berlin: Nicolaischen Buchhandlung, 1814).]

[‡A reference to works such as that, with this title, by Ebenezer Elliott. See p. 348 above.]

[§Wordsworth, "The Vaudois," in Yarrow Revisited, and Other Poems (London: Longman, Rees, Orme, Brown, Green, and Longman, et al., 1835), p. 282; and "Hail, Zaragoza," in Poetical Works (1827), Vol. III, p. 174.]

^{j}38   , and that but faintly,
^{k}38   in
$^{l-l}$38   those
$^{m-m}$38   inveigher against
^{n}38   ; it is in that aspect only that we would speak of them
$^{o-o}$+59, 67
^{p}38   , for both are poets
$^{q-q}$38.   strength
$^{r-r}$38   A greater spirit of

tends more or less to efface their differences, a certain monotony of goodness will be apparent, and a degree of distaste for *prononcé* characters, as being ^snearly^s allied to ill-regulated ones. The sympathies of the Radical or Movement poet will take the opposite direction. Active qualities are what he will demand, rather than passive; those which fit ^tpersons^t for making changes in the circumstances which surround them, rather than for accommodating themselves to those circumstances. Sensible he must of course be of the necessity of restraints, but ^usince he is^u dissatisfied with those which exist, his dislike of established opinions and institutions turns naturally into sympathy with all things, not in themselves bad, which those opinions and institutions restrain, that is, ^vwith^v all natural human feelings. Free and vigorous developments of human nature, even when he cannot refuse them his disapprobation, will command his sympathy: a more marked individuality will usually be conspicuous in his creations; his heroic characters will be all armed for conflict, full of energy and strong self-will, of grand conceptions and brilliant virtues, but, in habits of virtue, often below those of the Conservative school: there will not be so broad and black a line between his good and bad personages; his characters of principle will be more tolerant of his characters of mere passion. Among human affections, the Conservative poet will give the preference to those which can be invested with the character of duties; to those of which the objects are as it were marked out by the arrangements ^weither^w of nature ^xor of society^x, we ourselves exercising no choice: as the parental—the filial—the conjugal ^yafter^y the irrevocable union, or a solemn betrothment equivalent to it, and with due observance of all decencies, both real and conventional. The other will delight in painting the affections which choose their own objects, especially the most powerful of these, passionate love; and of that, the more vehement oftener than the more graceful aspects; will select by preference its subtlest workings, and its most unusual and unconventional forms; will show it at war with the forms and customs of society, nay even with its laws and its religion, if the laws and tenets which regulate that branch of human relations are among those which have begun to be murmured against. By the Conservative, feelings and states of mind which he disapproves will be indicated rather than painted; to lay open the morbid anatomy of human nature will appear to him contrary to good taste always, and often to morality: and inasmuch as feelings intense enough to threaten established decorums with any danger of violation will most frequently have the character of morbidness in his eyes, the representation of passion in the colours of reality will commonly be left to the Movement poet. To him, whatever exists will appear, from that alone, fit to be represented: to probe the wounds of society and humanity

^{s-s}38   near
^{t-t}38   men
^{u-u}38   being
^{v-v}38   for

^{w-w}+59, 67
^{x-x}+59, 67
^{y-y}38   *after*

is part of his business, and he will neither shrink from exhibiting what is in nature, because it is morally culpable, nor because it is physically revolting. Even in their representations of inanimate nature there will be a difference. The pictures most grateful and most familiar to the one will be those of a universe at peace within itself—of stability and duration—of irresistible power serenely at rest, or moving in fulfilment of the established arrangements of the universe: whatever suggests unity of design, and the harmonious co-operation of all the forces of nature towards ^{z}ends^z intended by a Being in whom there is no variableness nor shadow of change. In the creations of the other, nature will oftener appear in the relations which it bears to the individual, rather than to the scheme of the universe; there will be a larger place assigned to those of its aspects which reflect back the troubles of an unquiet soul, the impulses of a passionate, or the enjoyments of a voluptuous one; and on the whole, here too the Movement poet will extend so much more widely the bounds of the permitted, that his sources both of effect and of permanent interest will have a far larger range; and he will generally be more admired than the other, by all those by whom he is not actually condemned.

There is room in the world for poets of both these kinds; and the greatest will always partake of the nature of both. A comprehensive and catholic mind and heart will doubtless feel and exhibit all these different sympathies, each in its due proportion and degree; but what that due proportion may happen to be, is part of the larger question which every one has to ask of himself at such periods, viz., whether it were for the good of humanity at the particular era, that Conservative or Radical feeling should most predominate? For there is a perpetual antagonism between these two; and until ^{a}human affairs^a are ^{b}much better^b ordered ^{c}than they are likely to be for some time to come^c, each will require to be, in a greater or less degree, tempered by the other: nor until the ordinances of law and of opinion are so framed as to give full scope to all individuality not positively noxious, and to restrain all that is noxious, will the two classes of sympathies ever be entirely reconciled.

Suppose, now, a poet of conservative sympathies, surprised by the shock of a revolution, which sweeps away the surviving symbols of what was great in the Past, and decides irrevocably the triumph of new things over the old: what will be the influence of this event on his imagination and feelings? To us it seems that they will become both sadder and wiser. He will lose that blind faith in the Past, which previously might have tempted him to fight for it with a mistaken ardour, against what is generous and worthy in the new doctrines. The fall of the objects of his reverence, will naturally, if he has ^{d}any discernment^d, open ^{e}his mind^e to the perception of that in them whereby they deserved to fall. But while he is thus

---

$^{z-z}$38 the end
$^{a-a}$38 all things
$^{b-b}$38 as well

$^{c-c}$38 as they can ever be
$^{d-d}$38 an eye
$^{e-e}$38 it

disenchanted of the old things, he will not have acquired that faith in the new, which ᶠanimatesᶠ the Radical poet. Having it not before, there is nothing in the triumph of those new things which can inspire him with it: institutions and creeds fall by their own badness, not by the goodness of that which strikes the actual blow. The destiny of mankind, therefore, will naturally appear to him in rather sombre colours; gloomy he may not be, ᵍbut he will everywhere tendᵍ to the elegiac, to the contemplative and melancholy rather than to the epic and active; his song will be a subdued and plaintive symphony, more or less melodious according to the measure of his genius, on the old theme of blasted hopes and defeated aspirations. Yet there will now be nothing partial or one-sided in his sympathies: no sense of a conflict to be maintained, of a position to be defended against assailants, will warp the impartiality of his pity—will make him feel that there are wrongs and sufferings which must be dissembled, inconsistencies which must be patched up, vanities which he must attempt to consider serious, false pretences which he must try to mistake for truths, lest he should be too little satisfied with his own cause to do his duty as a combatant for it: he will no longer feel obliged to treat all that part of human nature which rebelled against the old ideas, as if it were accursed—all those human joys and sufferings, hopes and fears, which ʰareʰ the strength of the new doctrines, and which the old ones did not take sufficient account of, as if they were unworthy of his sympathy. His heart will open itself freely and largely to the love of all that is loveable, to pity of all that is pitiable: every cry of suffering humanity will strike a responsive chord in his breast; whoever carries nobly his own share of the general burthen of human life, or generously helps to lighten that of ⁱothersⁱ, is sure of his homage; while he has a deep fraternal charity for the erring and disappointed—for those who have aspired and fallen—who have fallen because they have aspired, because they too have felt those infinite longings for something greater than merely to live and die, which he as a poet has felt—which, as a poet, he cannot but have been conscious that he would have purchased the realization of by an even greater measure of error and suffering—and which, as a poet disenchanted, he knows too well the pain of renouncing, not to feel a deep indulgence for those who are victims of their inability to make the sacrifice.

In this ideal portraiture may be seen the genuine lineaments of Alfred de Vigny. The same features may, indeed, be traced more or less, in the greater part of the Royalist literature of young France; even in Balzac all these characteristics are distinctly visible, blended of course with his individual peculiarities, and modified by them. But M. de Vigny is ʲa moreʲ perfect type, because he, more entirely than most others, writes from his real feelings, and not from mere play of fancy. Many a

---

ᶠ⁻ᶠ38, 59   animated
ᵍ⁻ᵍ38   for to be gloomy is to be morbid, but there will be everywhere a tendency
ʰ⁻ʰ38, 59   were
ⁱ⁻ⁱ38   another
ʲ⁻ʲ38   the most

writer in France, of no creed at all, and who therefore gives himself all the latitude of a Movement poet, is a Royalist with his imagination merely, for the sake of the picturesque effect of donjons and cloisters, crusaders and troubadours. And in retaliation many a Liberal or Republican critic will stand up stiffly for the old school in literature, for the *grand siècle*, because, like him, it *takes* its models from Greece or Rome; and will keep no terms with the innovators who find anything grand and poetical in the middle ages, or who fancy that barons or priests may look well in rhyme. But this is accident; an exception to the ordinary relation between political opinions and poetic tendencies. A Radical who finds his political *beau idéal* still *farther* back in the Past than the Royalist finds his, is not the type of a Radical poet; he will more resemble the Conservative poet of ages back: less of the Movement spirit may be found in him, than in many a nominal Royalist whose Royalist convictions have no very deep root. But when we would see the true character of a Royalist poet, we must seek for it in one like M. de Vigny, a conservative in feeling, and not in mere fancy, and a man (*if we may judge from his writings*) of *rare simplicity of heart, and freedom from egotism and self-display. The most complete exemplification of the feelings and views of things which we have described as naturally belonging to the Royalist poet of young France, will be found in his *productions*, subsequent to the Revolution of 1830. But we must first see him as he was before 1830, and in writings in which the qualities we have enumerated had as yet manifested themselves only in a small degree.

Count Alfred de Vigny was born on the 27th *of* March 1799, at Loches in Touraine, that province which has given birth to so many of the literary celebrities of France. His father was an old cavalry officer of ancient lineage, who had served in the Seven Years War, and whose stories of his illustrious friends Chevert and d'Assas, and of the great Frederic (who was not a little indebted even for his victories, to the *prestige* he exercised over the enthusiastic imaginations of the French officers who fought against him), were the earliest nourishment of the son's childish aspirations. In the latter years of Napoleon our author was a youth at college; and he has *described*, in the first chapter of his *Souvenirs de Servitude Militaire*, the restless and roving spirit, the ardour for military glory and military adventure, the contempt of all pursuits and wishes not terminating in a Marshal's bâton, which were the epidemic diseases of every French schoolboy during those years when "the beat of drum," to use his own expression, "drowned the voice of the teacher,"[*] and of which M. de Vigny confesses, in all humility, that the traces

[*Translated from *Souvenirs*, in *Oeuvres*, p. 9.]

*k-k*38 fetches	*o-o*38 writings
*l-l*38 further	*p-p*+59, 67
*m-m*38 as it seems to us	*q-q*38 held up to us
*n*38 a	

in himself are not entirely effaced. On the fall of Napoleon, he entered, at sixteen, into the royal guard; accompanied the Bourbons to Ghent during the Hundred Days, and remained in the army up to 1828. Fourteen years a soldier without seeing any service (for he was not even in the ^{r}brief^r Spanish campaign)—the alternation of routine duties and enforced idleness, the *ennui* of an active profession without one opportunity for action except in obscure and painful civil broils, would have driven many to find relief in dissipation; M. de Vigny found it in contemplation and solitary thought.

Those years of my life, [he says,] would have been ^{s} wasted, if I had not employed them in attentive and persevering observation, storing up the results for future years. I owe to my military life views of human nature which could never have reached me but under a soldier's uniform. There are scenes which one can only arrive at through disgusts, which, to one not forced to endure them, would be unendurable. . . . Overcome by an *ennui* which I had little expected in that life so ardently desired, it became a necessity for me to rescue at least my nights from the empty and tiresome bustle of a soldier's days. In those nights I enlarged in silence what knowledge I had received from our tumultuous ^{t} public studies; and thence ^{u}"the origin of my writings^u.[*]

M. de Vigny's first publications were poems, of which we shall say a few words presently, and which, whatever be the opinion formed of their absolute merit, are considered by a sober and impartial critic, M. Sainte-Beuve, as of a more completely original character than those of either Lamartine or Victor Hugo.[†] It is ^{v}, therefore, ^{w}"only in the common course of things,"^{w} that they were ^{x}at the time^x but moderately successful. The first of his works which attained popularity was *Cinq-Mars, or a Conspiracy under Louis XIII*, an historical romance of the school of Sir Walter Scott, then at the height of his popularity in France, and who was breathing the breath of life into the historical literature of France, and, through France, of all Europe. ^{y}

M. de Vigny has chosen his scene at that passage of French history, which completed the transformation of the feudal monarchy of the middle ages into the despotic and courtly monarchy of Louis XIV. The iron hand of Richelieu, reigning

---

[*]*Ibid.*, pp. 8, 10.]
[†See Charles Augustin Sainte-Beuve, "M. de Vigny," *Revue des Deux Mondes*, ser. 4, IV (Oct., 1835), 216–17.]

$^{r-r}$+59, 67
^{s}38   years
^{t}Source [in French], 38   and
$^{u-u}$Source [in French], 38   my poems and my books
^{v}38   no wonder
$^{w-w}$+59, 67
$^{x-x}$+59, 67
^{y}38   The reputation of this work in its native country has survived the vogue of the moment, and, as it is entirely unknown in England, we will offer to our readers a brief sketch of it.

in the name of a master who both feared and hated him, but whom habit and conscious incapacity rendered his slave, had broken the remaining strength of those great lords, once powerful enough to cope single-handed with their sovereign, and several of whom, by confederating, could, to a very late period, dictate for themselves terms of capitulation. The crafty and cruel policy of the minister had mowed down all of *these* who, by position and personal qualities, stood pre-eminent above the rest. As for those whom, because they could not be dangerous to him, he spared, their restlessness and turbulence, surviving their power, might, during a royal minority, break out once more into impotent and passing tumults, but the next generation of them were and could be nothing but courtiers; an aristocracy still for purposes of rapine and oppression, for resistance to the despotism of the monarch they were as the feeblest of the multitude. A most necessary and salutary transformation in European society, and which, whether completed by the hands of a Richelieu or a Henry the Seventh, was, as M. de Vigny clearly sees (and perhaps no longer laments), the destined and inevitable preparation for the era of modern liberty and democracy. But the age was one of those (there are several of them in history) in which the greatest and most beneficial ends were accomplished by the basest means. It was the age of struggle between unscrupulous intellect and brute force; intellect not yet in a condition to assert its inherent right of supremacy by pure means, and no longer wielding, as in the great era of the Reformation, the noble weapon of an honest popular enthusiasm. Iago prime minister, is the type of the men who crumbled into dust the feudal aristo-cracies of Europe. In no period were the unseen springs both of the good and the evil that was done, so exclusively the viler passions of humanity: what little of honourable or virtuous feeling might exist in high places during that era, *was* probably *oftenest* found in the aristocratic faction so justly and beneficially extirpated; for in the rule of lawless force, some noble impulses are possible in the rulers at least—in that of cunning and fraud, none.

Towards the close of Richelieu's career, when the most difficult part of his task was done, but his sinking health, and the growing jealousy and fear of that master, one word of whom would even then have dismissed him into private life, made the cares of his station press heavier on him, and required a more constant and anxious watchfulness than ever; it was his practice to amuse the frivolous monarch with a perpetual succession of new favourites, who served his purpose till Louis was tired of them, or whom, if any of them proved capable of acquiring a permanent tenure of the royal favour, and of promoting other designs than his own, he well knew how to remove. The last, the most accomplished, and the most unfortunate of these

---

*z-z*59   those [*printer's error?*]
*a-a*38   were
*b-b*38   easiest

was Henri d'Effiat, Marquis de Cinq-Mars, and of him our author has made the hero of his tale. ᶜ *

*   *   *   *   *

Such is *Cinq-Mars, or a Conspiracy under Louis XIII*—a work not free from the fault, so far as it is a fault, most common in the romantic literature of young

*[59] Here followed originally a sketch of the plot of the romance, now omitted as unnecessary. [See ᶜ below.]

ᶜ[*paragraph*] The story opens in this Byron-like, or Goethe-like manner: "Know you that region which has been surnamed the Garden of France? that country of pure air and verdant plains, watered by a mighty river"—followed by a tasteful description of Touraine, and, in Touraine, of the château of Chaumont, where, "in a morning of June 1639, the bell having, at the usual hour of noon, called the family to their repast, there passed in that old dwelling things which were not usual." [Translated from *Cinq-Mars*, in *Oeuvres*, pp. 77, 78.] The household of the widowed Maréchale d'Effiat was in the commotion of preparation for the departure of her second son, Henri de Cinq-Mars, to the royal camp before Perpignan; the minister's all-seeing eye having singled him out, unknown to himself, as a fit person to fill during his employer's pleasure the dangerous and now vacant post of favourite. To share the solemnities of his leave-taking there were assembled at table, besides the family, some nobles of the suite of a young princess of Mantua, whom family circumstances had caused to remain for some time under the protection of Madame d'Effiat before joining the French court; two illustrious friends of the family, M. de Puy-Laurens and the celebrated Maréchal de Bassompierre; and a deaf abbé, advanced in years, who turns out to be a spy of Richelieu. Bassompierre, the old companion in arms of Henri Quatre, the very soul of honour and of *bonhomie*, represents the chivalrous hero of the preceding generation. While he, with natural open-heartedness, artfully drawn out by M. de Launay (one of the attendant noblemen), utters his affectionate regret for the days of the great and good Henry, and his lamentations and forebodings over the jealous and artful rule of the cardinal-minister, the young Cinq-Mars is casting a last melancholy look upon the tranquil splendour of the magnificent landscape, with its azure sky, its bright green isles, its waves of limpid gold, and the white sails of the barks descending the Loire, and sighs a last farewell to quiet joys and youthful remembrances—"O Nature, beautiful Nature, adieu! Ere long my heart will not be simple enough to feel thee, and thou wilt no longer be grateful to my eyes; already consumed by a profound passion, the sound of worldly interests fills me with an unknown trouble; I must enter into this labyrinth, perhaps to perish; but for Marie's sake—" [*Ibid.*, p. 81.] And stifling his feelings, he takes a rapid leave, and gallops off for Tours.

"The day was *triste* and the supper silent at the château of Chaumont. At ten in the evening the old Marshal retired to the north tower, near the gate of the castle, and on the contrary side to the river. The air was sultry; he opened the casement, and, wrapping himself in an ample robe of silk, placed a heavy lamp upon the table, and dismissed his attendant. The window looked out upon the plain, which the waning moon lighted with but an uncertain glimmer; the sky was becoming overcast, and the scene was tinged with melancholy. Reverie was no part of Bassompierre's character, yet the turn which the conversation had taken came back upon his mind, and he recalled in memory the events of his previous life; the sad changes brought by the new reign, which seemed to have breathed upon him the breath of calamity; the death of a cherished sister; the disorders of the heir of his name; the loss of his estates and favour; the recent end of his friend, the Maréchal d'Effiat, whose chamber he occupied; all these thoughts drew from him an involuntary sigh: he placed himself at the window for breath.

"At this moment he seemed to hear, in the direction of the wood, the sound of a troop of horse, but the wind rising at the same moment, made him think himself mistaken, and all sound suddenly ceasing, it passed from his memory. He watched for some time the various lights of the castle as they were successively extinguished, after winding among the embrasured windows of the staircases and flitting about the court-yards and stables; then reposing on his vast tapestry-covered fauteuil, his arm leaning on the table, he sunk into reflection, and presently taking from his bosom a medallion, suspended by a black ribbon, 'Come,' said he, 'my kind old master, converse with me as thou didst so often; forget thy court in the joyous laugh of a true friend; consult me once again on Austria and her ambition; tell me

France; it partakes somewhat of the "Literature of Despair;"[*] it too much resembles M. Eugène Sue's *d*early *d* novels,[†] in which every villain dies honoured and prosperous at a good old age, after every innocent person in the tale has been crushed and exterminated by him without pity or remorse—through which the mocking laugh of a chorus of demons seems to ring in our ears that the world is delivered over to *e*an*e* evil spirit, and that man is his creature and his prey. But such is not the character of M. de Vigny's writings, and the resemblance in this single

[*See Sarah Austin, *Characteristics of Goethe*, Vol. II, pp. 318–19, where she is translating from Theodor Adam Heinrich Friedrich von Müller, *Goethe in seiner practischen Wirksamkeit* (Weimar: Hoffmann, 1832), p. 45, in which the key phrase (applied to modern French literature) is "Literatur der Verzweiflung."]

[†E.g., *Kernock le pirate* (1830), *Atar-Gull* (1831), *La salamandre* (1832), and *La coucaratcha* (1832–34).]

d-d+59, 67
*e-e*38   the

---

once more, inconstant knight, of the *bonhomie* of thy loves and the frankness of thy inconstancies; reproach me again, heroic soldier, with outshining thee in combat—ah! why did I not so at Paris—why received I not thy fatal wound! The blessings thy reign brought to the world have perished with thee.'

"His tears dimmed the glass of the medallion, and he was effacing them by respectful kisses, when his door hastily opened, made him start, and lay his hand on his sword. *Qui va là?* he cried in a tone of surprise. His surprise was greater on recognizing M. De Launay, who advanced to him hat in hand, and said with some embarrassment, 'M. le Maréchal, it is with a heart full of grief that I am forced to inform you that the King has commanded me to arrest you. A coach awaits you at the gate, with thirty *mousquetaires* of M. the Cardinal-Duke.'

"Bassompierre was still seated, and had the medallion in his left hand, his sword in the right. He extended it disdainfully to the man, and said, 'Monsieur, I know that I have lived too long, and it was of that I was thinking. It is in the name of the great Henry that I peaceably surrender my sword to his son. Follow me.' He said this with a look of so much firmness that De Launay could not meet it, and followed him with downcast looks as if he himself had just been arrested by the noble old man." [*Ibid.*, pp. 83–4.]

As De Launay and his prisoner passed through a defile in a wood, the carriage was stopped by an attempt at rescue; the young Cinq-Mars, returning secretly to the château for a parting interview with the lady of his love, would have liberated the Marshal, had not his submissive loyalty rejected the offer of escape. They part, the one to his twelve years' captivity in the Bastille, where our history leaves him; the other to the chamber-window of the Princess Marie de Gonzague.

"It was past midnight, and the roofs and turrets of the castle formed a black mass, but just distinguishable in the extreme darkness from the clouded sky. Without dismounting, he lifted the *jalousie* of the window, and was answered by a soft low voice from behind the casement, 'Is it you, M. de Cinq-Mars?'—'Alas! who else should it be, that returns like a malefactor to his paternal home, without visiting his mother and bidding her again adieu? who, but I, would return to bewail the present, expecting nothing from the future?'

"The soft voice faltered, and tears accompanied the answer. 'Alas! Henri, of what do you complain? Have I not done more, far more than I ought? Is it my fault if my ill-fate has willed that a sovereign prince should be my father? Can we choose our parents, and say, I will be born a shepherdess? For two years I have warred in vain against my ill-fortune which separates us, and against you who turn me from my duty. You know it, I have wished to be thought dead—I have almost prayed for revolutions! I could have blest the blow which should have taken away my rank; I thanked God when my father was deprived of his throne. But the Court wonders, the Queen demands me, our dreams must take flight. Henri, our slumber has been too long; let us awake with courage. Think no more of these two cherished

instance is only casual. Still, as a mere work of art, if the end of art be, as conceived by the ancients and by the great German writers, the production of the intrinsically beautiful, *Cinq-Mars* cannot be commended. A story in which the odious and the contemptible in man and life act so predominant a part, which excites our scorn or our hatred so much more than our pity—comes within a far other category than that of the Beautiful, and can be justified on no canons of taste of which that is the end. But it is not possible for the present generation of France to

years: forget all, remember only our great resolution—have but one thought; be ambitious from—ambitious for me . . . .

"'And must *all* be forgotten, Marie?' said Cinq-Mars, in a gentle tone.

"She hesitated. 'Yes—all that I have myself forgotten,' she replied. An instant after, she resumed with vivacity—

"'Yes; forget our happy days, our long evenings, and even our walks in the wood and on the lake; but remember the future; go: your father was a Marshal, be more, be Constable; Prince. Go; you are young, noble, rich, brave, beloved—'

"'For ever?' asked Henri.

"'For life and eternity.'

"Cinq-Mars started with emotion, and extending his hand, cried, 'I swear then, by the Virgin whose name you bear, that you shall be mine, Marie, or my head shall fall on the scaffold.'

"'Heavens! what say you?' cried she, as her white hand, stretched from the casement, joined his. 'No, swear to me that your efforts shall never be criminal; that you will never forget that the King of France is your master—love him more than all, yet after her who will sacrifice everything to you, and will wait for you in suffering.' 'Adieu,' said he; 'I go to accomplish my destiny,' and the casement closed slowly on their two hands still joined." [*Ibid.*, pp. 84–5.]

The light of this honest and genuine passion, illuminating the narrow and slippery paths through which the hero of the tale is conducted by his ambitious projects, bespeaks for him the truest human interest which he excites, and along with the disinterested attachment of his simple and upright friend De Thou, constitutes the romance of the book.

The reader, having been already brought into the midst of the age by these opening passages, is now at once introduced into its darkest recesses, by a transfer of the scene to the little town of Loudun in Poitou, during the perpetration of a tragedy, familiar to readers of the *Causes Célèbres*, and which will be found recorded by our author with perfect fidelity; the trial and burning of Urbain Grandier, curé of Loudun, accused of having, by magical arts, caused devils to take possession of certain Ursuline nuns of that place. [See François Gayot de Pitaval, "Urbain Grandier," *Causes célèbres et intéressantes*, 6 vols. (The Hague: Neaulme, 1735), Vol. II, pp. 247–397.] The characters, and almost the minutest incidents, in this part of our author's narrative, are historical: the extraordinary beauty of this young priest; his talents and fervid eloquence, which excited the jealousy and hatred of rival ecclesiastics; his unfortunate, and so far as is known, chaste attachment to the beautiful Madeleine de Brou, and the manuscript treatise against the celibacy of the clergy, written to calm her scruples, which was found among his papers; the tutoring of the nuns by Urbain's enemies, the juggleries in simulation of supernatural agency, the detection of some of these, and the failure, for a long time, of all attempts to procure a condemnation; the disgrace of imposture which fell upon the accusers, and in which Jeanne de Belfiel, the young and beautiful superior of the convent, being implicated, her uncle Laubardemont, the well-known instrument of Richelieu's judicial enormities, obtained a commission for himself to try the cause, by working upon the Cardinal's resentment for a trifling affront received from Grandier some years before, and for a lampoon of which he was led to believe him the author. No less true to history are the horrid iniquities of this final trial; the peculiarly atrocious mode in which the torture was administered to the prisoner; the appearance in court of two of the accusing nuns, smitten by remorse, to declare the whole mystery of their subornation and of their feigned convulsions; but our author has heightened this last trait by making Jeanne de Belfiel herself one of these repentant false witnesses, incited originally by the jealousy of slighted love, and driven to insanity by the unexpected result of the

restrict the purposes of art within this limit. They are too much in earnest. They take life too much *au sérieux*. It may be possible (what some of his *ᶠmoreᶠ* enthusiastic admirers say of Goethe) that a thoroughly earnest mind may struggle upwards through the region of clouds and storms to an untroubled summit, where all other good sympathies and aspirations confound themselves in a serene love and culture of the calmly beautiful—looking down upon the woes and struggles of perplexed humanity with as calm a gaze (though with a more helping arm) as that

*ᶠ-ᶠ*38   most

machinations she had been a tool of. One other incident is of our author's invention, at least we find no traces of it in the history of the transaction. As the procession advanced towards the fatal pile, amidst a storm of lightning and rain, four priests exorcising the air which the magician breathed, the earth which he touched, and the wood with which he was to be burnt, the *lieutenant criminel* meanwhile reading aloud in a hurried manner the condemnation and sentence; Cinq-Mars, who was among the crowd under the portico of the church from which the procession issued, was struck by the words, "The magician cannot utter the name of the Saviour, and rejects his image." [*Ibid.*, p. 101.] Lactance, one of his persecutors, at this moment came forth from among the *Grey Penitents*, holding, with great apparent precaution and respect, an immense iron crucifix.

"He made it approach the lips of the sufferer, who did certainly shrink backward, and rallying his remaining strength, made a gesture with his arm which made the crucifix fall from the hands of the capuchin. 'See,' exclaimed the monk, 'he has flung down the crucifix.' A'murmur of doubtful import arose. 'Profanation!' cried the priests. The procession advanced towards the pile. Meanwhile Cinq-Mars, who, from behind one of the columns, had been an eager looker-on, perceived that the crucifix, falling on the steps of the portico, which were moistened by the rain, smoked and made a hissing sound. While the crowd were looking another way he rushed forward, laid his hand on it, and felt it burning hot. In a transport of indignation he seized the crucifix in the folds of his mantle, advanced to Laubardemont, and striking him on the forehead, 'Villain,' cried he, 'bear the brand of this burning iron.' The multitude heard and rushed forward. 'Arrest the madman,' exclaimed in vain the unworthy magistrate. He was himself seized by men crying, 'Justice, Justice, in the King's name.' 'We are lost,' said Lactance, 'quick to the pile.' " [*Ibid.*]

The monks dragged their victim to the place of torment, while the mounted gendarmerie made head against the crowd, who pressed against them with passionate strength, drove them inch by inch into a closer circle round the pile, and at last, by one violent effort, broke and scattered them, but too late: the sacrifice was accomplished, and all that remained of Urbain was "a blackened hand, preserved from the flames by an enormous iron bracelet and chain; the fingers still grasped a small ivory cross, and an image of St. Mary Magdalen," the patron saint of his beloved. [*Ibid.*, pp. 101-2.]

Under these sinister auspices does Cinq-Mars enter into life. His coming fate, as was doubtless intended, casts its shadow by anticipation over the very commencement of the story; we feel from the first that we are about to witness the progressive development of a dark tragedy. The author crowds with gloomy presages the outset of his hero; ominous accidents accompany his leaving the paternal home; on the night of the catastrophe of Grandier he sees, in a dream, Marie de Gonzague leading him by the hand, but pale and sad of mien, amidst the strange shouts of a mysterious multitude, up the steps of a throne, and when he reached it and turned to kiss her hand, it was the hand of the executioner. He awoke shuddering, and found the maniac Jeanne de Belfiel by his bedside, chanting over him the service for the dead, and reading in his face that he is destined to a violent death: *l'homme que tu as frappé te tuera.* [*Ibid.*, p. 104.] As the mere machinery of a story all this would be childish, but it is not without its worth, even for the truth of the performance viewed as a poem or work of art; it puts the reader into the desired frame of mind, into that which is suitable to the story and to the times, and does for the scene what is done by *atmosphere* for a picture on canvas.

We are now conducted to Narbonne on the Mediterranean, and to the cabinet of an old man, who, seated in an immense and luxurious fauteuil, surrounded by attendants busy in arranging papers but

of him who is most placidly indifferent to human weal. But however this may be the great majority of persons in earnest will remain always in the intermediate region; will feel themselves more or less militant in this world—having something to pursue in it, different from the Beautiful, different from their own mental tranquillity and health, and which they will pursue, if they have the gifts of an artist, by all the resources of art, whatever becomes of canons of criticism, and

---

noiseless as the grave, is engaged alternately in dictating to four pages (who pass what they write to eight secretaries employed in copying round a large table) and in writing on his knee private memoranda to be slipped into the packets before sealing them with his own hand. This old man, with "an expanded forehead and a few exceedingly white hairs, large mild eyes, a pale wiry face, to which a short white beard, terminating in a point, gave that air of subtlety noticeable in all the portraits of that age; a mouth compressed, and with scarcely any lips, bordered by two grey *moustaches*, and a *royale* (a sort of ornament then fashionable, and in shape somewhat like a comma); on his head a red *calotte* or cardinal's hat; on his feet, hose of purple silk; his form enveloped in a vast *robe de chambre*," was Armand Duplessis, Cardinal de Richelieu. [*Ibid.*, p. 106.]

A mirror suddenly betrays to this personage that his youngest page is writing a few hurried words on a slip of paper, and then hiding it under the sheet of a larger size, which the Cardinal has ordered him to fill. "Come here, Monsieur Olivier."

"These words were a thunder-bolt to the poor boy, who seemed not more than sixteen years of age. He, however, stood up immediately, and placed himself before the minister, with downcast looks and dependant arms. The other pages and the secretaries took no more notice than soldiers do when one of them is struck dead by a cannon-shot.

"'What is that you are writing?' 'Monseigneur, what your Eminence is dictating to me.' 'What!' 'Monseigneur, the letter to Don Juan de Braganza.' 'No evasions, Sir, you are doing something else.' 'Monseigneur,' said the page, with tears in his eyes, 'it was a note to one of my cousins.' 'Let me see it.'

"The page trembled all over, and was forced to lean on the chimneypiece, while he said, in a low voice, 'It is impossible.'

"'M. le Vicomte Olivier d'Entraigues,' said the minister, without showing the least emotion, 'you are no longer in my service.'

"The page withdrew; he knew there was nothing more to be said; he slipped his billet into his pocket and opening the folding-door just wide enough to make room to pass, slid through it like a bird escaping from his cage. The minister continued the memoranda which he was writing on his knee." [*Ibid.*]

A man of sinister aspect, in the most austere dress of the Franciscan order, appeared at the door: the attendants instantly withdrew, and left Richelieu alone with his celebrated secret agent, known by the soubriquet of *l'Eminence grise*—Father Joseph, the capuchin friar. The conversation which follows, like all those in which the character of Richelieu is unfolded to us, is full of dramatic power, and admirably true to the age. The mixture of hypocrisy and frankness in the communications between these two; the employer canting to his tool, yet opening to him his real feelings also; trusting him with all his secrets, except one, his detestation of the confident himself, and intention to break his promises with him; while the friar, no less treacherous to his employer, makes himself necessary to him by playing upon his jealousies and apprehensions and his colossal *amour propre*—are finely true to nature; and no less so are the workings of such a mind as the Cardinal's, when, after jesting with the lives of all the great men of the court, he sheds tears for the fate of Strafford, a minister abandoned by his master—when being told that the King has "ideas which he never had before," "that he thinks of recalling the Queen-mother from exile," he exclaims—"Recal my enemy, recal his mother, what perfidy! That thought never came from himself—he dared not—but what said he? tell me his exact words."

"'He said, publicly, and in the presence of his brother, the Duke of Orleans, "I know that one of the first duties of a christian is to be a good son, and I shall not much longer resist the murmurs of my conscience."'

"'Christian? Conscience? those are no words of his; it is Father Caussin, it is his confessor, who betrays me. Perfidious jesuit! I must turn off that confessor, Joseph; he is an enemy of the state, I see

beauty in the abstract. The writers and readers of works of imagination in France have the desire of amusement as much as English readers, the sense of ᵍbeautyᵍ generally much more; but they have also, very generally, a thirst for something which shall address itself to their real-life feelings, and not to those of imagination merely—which shall give them an idea or a sentiment connected with the actual world. And if a story or a poem is ʰpossessedʰ by an idea—if it powerfully exhibits

ᵍ⁻ᵍ38   the beautiful   ʰ⁻ʰ38   *possessed*

clearly. I have been negligent these last days: I have not hastened sufficiently the arrival of this little D'Effiat, who will succeed, no doubt; he is handsome and *spirituel*, they say. What a blunder! I deserve to be turned out for it. To leave this old fox of a jesuit near the King without secret instructions, without any hostage, any pledge of his fidelity! Take a pen, Joseph, and write this for the next confessor—Father Sirmond, I think, will do.' " [*Ibid.*, pp. 107–8.]

And when he had done dictating his instructions to the royal confessor—

" 'What tiresomeness, what interminable *ennui*! If an ambitious man saw me, he would fly to a desert. What is my dominion! A miserable reflexion of the royal power; and what toils eternally renewed, to keep that flickering light steadily upon me! For twenty years I try it in vain. There is no comprehending that man! He dares not fly me, but they steal him away from me, he slips through my fingers! *What things could I not have done with his hereditary rights, if I had had them?* But such a world of combinations expended only to keep my balance—what faculties have I left for my undertakings! I hold all Europe in my hand, and my destiny hangs by a hair. His cabinet of six feet square gives me more trouble to govern than the whole earth. What it is to be a prime minister! Envy me my guards, now, if you can!' " [*Ibid.*, p. 108.]

From this time the story is full of movement and bustle: the Cardinal's levee, with all the illustrious personages of the period; then the King's camp before Perpignan, where we come into the midst of Richelieu's enemies, and the Abbé de Gondi, afterwards so well known as Cardinal de Retz, begins to flit about the scene, laughing, chattering, fighting, conspiring, the most busy and restless political intriguer of his time, having nothing ecclesiastical about him but his priest's habit, which he took by compulsion, and desires to get rid of: the first adventure of Cinq-Mars on his arrival in the camp is to be engaged as one of his seconds, in a duel after the fashion of the time (the seconds as well as the principals fighting) with our former acquaintance De Launay. The King is then introduced; in the midst of his nobles, all disaffected to Richelieu (at least in his absence), and endeavouring, but without committing themselves, to strengthen the feeble-minded monarch in his timid half-purposes of breaking with the terrible Cardinal. The King, talking quick and excitedly, and venturing an occasional jest to the nobles around him at the Cardinal's expense, tries to screw up his courage to speak the decisive word. Richelieu's enemies are in joyful expectation, and when the Cardinal enters, he sees in the face and demeanour of every courtier the forecast of his downfal: all shun him save Fabert, the commander of the troops, who with military frankness advances and addresses him—and Mazarin, the supple insinuating man of the world, who gives him a look unseen by all other eyes, expressive of the deepest respect and affliction. Richelieu takes his resolution instantly; he approaches the King, and begs permission to restore into the hands of his sovereign a power of which he had long been weary, and prepare in retirement, by prayer and meditation, for his approaching end. The King, though taken by surprise, yet shocked by some haughty expressions, and feeling that the eyes of all his court are upon him, gives none of his usual signs of weakness and indecision, but coldly, and with a look of dignity, accepts the resignation. Nothing embarrassed by this unexpected stroke, the Cardinal proceeded:

" 'The only recompense I ask for my services is, that your Majesty will deign to accept as a gift from me the Palais Cardinal' (now Palais Royal), 'erected in Paris at my expense.'

"The King, astonished, gave a nod of consent; a murmur of surprise went through the assembled court.

" 'I also implore your Majesty to grant me the revocation of a severity of which I was the adviser, and which I, perhaps mistakenly, deemed needful for the repose of the state. There is a personage, Sire,

some form of real life, or some conception respecting human nature or society which may tend to consequences, not only is it not necessarily expected to represent abstract beauty, but it is pardoned for exhibiting even hideousness. These considerations should enable us to understand and tolerate such works as *Le Père Goriot*, of Balzac, or *Leoni*, of George Sand, and to understand, *'if'* we do not tolerate, such as the *Antony*, or *Richard Darlington*, of Alexandre Dumas.[*]

Now, among the ideas with which French literature has been *'possessed'* for the last ten years, is that of realizing, and bringing home to the imagination, the history

[*Honoré de Balzac, *Le père Goriot*, 2 vols. (Paris: Werdet, 1835); Amandine Aurore Dupin ("George Sand"), *Leone Leoni* (Paris: Bonnaire, 1835); Alexandre Dumas, *Antony* (Paris: Auffray, 1831), and (with Jacques Félix Beudin and Prosper Parfait Goubaux), *Richard Darlington* (Paris: Barba, 1832).]

*i-i*38 though   *j-j*38 *possessed*

whom, in spite of her faults towards your Majesty, and although for the good of the state I forgot too much my oldest feelings of respect and attachment, I have always loved; one who, notwithstanding her armed enterprises against your person, cannot but be dear to you; to whom, now that I am detached from the world and its interests, I feel that I owe reparation, and whom it is my parting entreaty that you will recall from her exile—Queen Mary de' Medici, your royal mother.' " [*Ibid.*, p. 118.]

The King, who little expected this name, uttered an involuntary cry. The whole fabric of his resolution was overset; his heart was touched, he held out his hand to the Cardinal, and this moment decided the destiny of France. Soon after a courier enters with a packet, sealed with black, to be delivered into the King's own hand; it is the news of his mother's death, known to Richelieu the day before.

A duel follows, under the walls of the besieged town, ending in the storm of an outwork by Cinq-Mars, Gondi, and others; and a battle arranged by Richelieu to amuse the King, without the intention of its leading to any result—an artifice in some danger of being disconcerted by the impetuous valour of Louis himself, whose feebleness (conformably to history) vanishes in the presence of the enemy; and who returns, flushed with victory, to resume his pale and melancholy look under the cold shadow of his minister. Cinq-Mars is presented to the King, taken at once into favour, and accompanies him to Paris; while the Cardinal, now apprised of his attempt to rescue Bassompierre, and of his escapade at Loudun, and discovering that he may be dangerous, lays his plans to ruin him by sending his agent Joseph (already the enemy of Cinq-Mars) to Paris, as a spy upon him. Richelieu himself remains at a distance, that his enemies may be encouraged to put themselves in his power by another, which he knows will be the last, conspiracy. "Wretches," says he, as his tools, Joseph and Laubardemont, each the other's bitter enemy, leave his tent—"wretches—go, accomplish a few more of my secret designs, and then be crushed yourselves, impure instruments of my power. Soon the King will sink under the slow malady which consumes him; I shall be Regent—King—I shall have no longer to fear the caprices of his feebleness; I will destroy, without redemption, all those arrogant houses; I will pass the scythe of Tarquin over them. I will be alone above them all, Europe shall tremble—I . . ." he is interrupted by a gush of blood from his mouth, himself a prey to an incurable disease. [*Ibid.*, p. 134.]

The story here passes over two years, and carries us to the Louvre, where Cinq-Mars is now Grand-Ecuyer, and the soul of a conspiracy, of which the King was tacitly the chief, to which the Queen was privy, to which the King's only brother, Gaston, Duke of Orleans, lent his name, and the Duke de Bouillon, the most powerful of the nobles, and commander of the army in Italy, his counsels. For ten days Cinq-Mars has been, not married, but affianced (by his worthy old preceptor, the Abbé Quillet, the defender of Grandier) to the Princess of Mantua, whom, constantly in attendance on the Queen, he but rarely sees in private, and that in a church and in the presence of the good Abbé, but the love of whom is the sole animating principle of his designs. The Queen, Anne of Austria, in whom our author shows us a pleasing picture of dignity and gentleness in misfortune, is not in the secret of the lovers, but, suspecting it, looks on with a melancholy interest. After an *émeute*, in which the populace heap execrations on

and spirit of past ages. Sir Walter Scott, having no object but to please, and having readers who only sought to be pleased, would not have told the story of Richelieu and [k] Cinq-Mars without greatly softening the colouring; and the picture would have been more agreeable than M. de Vigny's, but it would not have been so true to the age. M. de Vigny preferred the truer to the more pleasing, and *his* readers have sanctioned the preference.

Even according to this view of its object, the work has obvious defects. The

[k]38 of

Richelieu, and shout for the King and Cinq-Mars, but which, like all the other proceedings of this unfortunate cabal, ends in nothing—the Princess speaking hopefully to the Queen of the Cardinal's loss of favour, and the King's attachment to *another*—

"The Queen smiled; she contemplated for awhile in silence the innocent and open countenance of the beautiful Marie, and the look full of ingenuousness which was raised languidly towards her: she parted the dark locks which veiled that fair forehead—kissed her cheek, and said: 'Thou suspectest not, poor child, the sad truth, that the King loves no one, and that those who seem most in his favour are nearest to being abandoned, and flung to the man who swallows up and devours everything.'

" 'Ah! good heavens, what is it you tell me!'

" 'Know'st thou how many he has destroyed?' continued the Queen, in a lower voice; 'know'st thou the end of his favourites? have they told thee of the exile of Baradas, that of Saint Simon, the shame of D'Hautefort, the convent of La Fayette, the death of Chalais? All have fallen before an order from Richelieu to his master; and but for that favour, which thou mistakest for attachment, their lives would have been peaceful; his affection is deadly; they perish like the Semele on that tapestry; it dazzles while it consumes them.'

"But the young Princess was no longer in a condition to listen; her large dark eyes, veiled by tears, remained fixed on the Queen, who held her trembling hands, while her lips quivered convulsively.

" 'I am very cruel, am I not, Marie?' continued the Queen, in the gentlest voice, caressing her like a child who is to be coaxed into confession, 'your heart is full, my child; come, tell me what has passed between you and Cinq-Mars?'

"At these words grief forced itself a way, and, still kneeling at the Queen's feet, Marie hid her face and broke out into a deluge of tears, with infantine sobs, and violent convulsive emotions of her head and neck, as if her heart would burst. The Queen waited long for the end of this first gush of emotion, lulling her in her arms to appease her grief, and soothing her with kind expressions.

" 'Ah, Madame,' cried she, 'I am very culpable towards you, but I did not think to find such a heart; I have been very wrong, I shall, perhaps, be cruelly punished for it. But alas! Madame, how could I have dared speak to you? It was not opening my heart that would have been difficult; but confessing to you that I needed that you should read in it.' " [*Ibid.*, p. 152.]

The Queen receives her full confidence, and after some gentle reproaches, continues, as if soliloquizing:

" 'But the mischief is done, let us think of the future. Cinq-Mars is well in himself, he is brave, accomplished, profound even in his conceptions; I have observed him, he has made much way in two years, and I see that it was for Marie. He conducts himself well; he is worthy, yes, he is worthy of her in my eyes; but in the eyes of Europe, not. He must rise still higher; the Princess of Mantua must not have married less than a Prince. He must become one. As for me, I can do nothing: I am not the Queen—I am the neglected wife of the King. There is only the Cardinal, the eternal Cardinal, and he is his enemy, and perhaps this *émeute*—'

" 'Alas! it is the beginning of war between them, I saw it too plainly this moment.'

" 'He is lost, then!' cried the Queen, embracing Marie. 'Forgive me, my child; I am tearing your heart, but we must see all and say all now; he is lost unless he can himself overthrow that wicked man; for the King will not renounce him; force alone—'

" 'He *will* overthrow him, Madame; he will if you assist him. You are the providence of France. Oh! I

characters of some of the subordinate personages, Friar Joseph for instance, are even more revolting than the truth of history requires. De Thou, the pious and studious man of retirement, cast out into storms for which he was never meant—the only character of principle in the tale, yet who sacrifices principle as well as life to romantic friendship—is but coldly represented; his goodness is too simple, his attachment too instinctive, too dog-like, and so much intensity of friendship is not sufficiently accounted for; Balzac would have managed these things better. The

---

conjure you, protect the angel against the demon; it is your cause, that of your royal family, of your nation—'

"The Queen smiled. 'It is thy cause above all, is it not, my child; and as such will I embrace it with all my power; that power is but small, as I have told thee, but the whole of it shall be given to thee; provided, however, that this *angel* do not stoop to mortal sins,' said she, with a look full of acuteness; 'I heard his name shouted this night by voices very unworthy of him.' " [*Ibid.*, p. 154.]

The story develops itself in a narrative rapid and enchaining, crowded with incidents, and with *tableaux* full of life and character. But we see that the enterprise is not fated to succeed. Of the conspirators, Cinq-Mars alone shows any spirit or conduct; and with him it is a desperate throw for Marie or a scaffold: he knows that the poor-spirited chiefs of the conspiracy "tremble while they threaten, and are ready at the first word to make their peace by the sacrifice of him." [*Ibid.*, p. 164.] He does what man can do, but an unseen hand plays with him from two hundred leagues off, like a cat with a mouse: the contest is with a mightier than he, and we see that he is doomed.

One scene, that of the evening rendezvous of Cinq-Mars and Marie in the church of St. Eustache, tells the story both of what precedes and of what follows.

"The young and trembling Marie pushed with a timid hand the heavy door of the church; she found there Cinq-Mars, in his accustomed disguise, anxiously waiting for her. Scarcely had she recognized him, when, with a hurried step, she rushed across the church, her velvet mask over her face, and took refuge in a confessional, while Henri carefully closed the door by which she entered. Having made sure that it could not be opened from without, he followed her, to kneel, according to their custom, in the place of penitence. Arrived an hour before her, he had found the door open, the usual sign that the Abbé Quillet, his preceptor, was waiting in the accustomed place; and joyful at the good abbé's punctuality, without going to thank him, he, in his anxiety to prevent surprise, remained at the entrance till Marie's arrival.

"The old parish church of St. Eustache would have been in total darkness, but for the lamp which was always burning, and four flambeaux of yellow wax, attached to as many principal columns, over the *bénitiers*, throwing a ruddy light across the grey and black marbles of the deserted temple. This glimmering light scarcely penetrated into the more distant niches in the aisles of the sacred edifice. In one of the most sombre of these was the confessional, all of which, except the little dome and the wooden cross, was masked by a high iron grating, lined with thick planks. Cinq-Mars and Mary of Mantua knelt down on the two sides; they could but just see each other, and they found that, as usual, the abbé, seated between them, had been long waiting. They could see through the little grating the shadow of his *camail*. Henri d'Effiat had approached slowly; this hour was to fix the remainder of his destiny. He was about to appear, not now before his King, but before a more powerful sovereign, her for whom he had undertaken his immense enterprise. He was about to try her faith, and he trembled.

"He shook still more when his young betrothed knelt face to face with him; the sight of her recalled to him all the happiness he was perhaps about to lose; he dared not be the first to speak, but remained gazing, in the dim light, at that young head, on which rested all his hopes. In spite of all his love, whenever he saw her he could not help feeling a sort of terror at having undertaken so much for a girl whose passion was but a feeble reflection of his, and who, perhaps, had not appreciated all his sacrifices—his character bent, for her sake, to the compliances of a courtier; condemned to the intrigues and sufferings of ambition, to the anxious combinations, the criminal meditations, the dark and violent labours of a conspirator. Hitherto, in their secret and chaste interviews, she had heard every new step in his progress with a child-like joy, asking him with *naïveté* how soon he should be Constable, and when

author also crowds his story too much with characters; he cannot bear that any celebrated personage whom the age affords should be passed over, and consequently introduces many who ought not to *have been* drawn at all unless they could be drawn truly, and on whom he has not been able to employ the same accurate study as he has on his principal characters. *"* Richelieu and *"* Louis *°XIII°* are *P* historical figures *qof q* which he has taken the trouble to *rform* a well-digested conception *r*; but he can know *slittle s* of Milton, whom he introduces, on his way from Italy, reading his *Paradise Lost*, not written till twenty years after, to

*l–l*38	be	*P*38	admirable, for these are
*m*38	His	*q–q*+59, 67	
*n*38	his	*r–r*38	understand
*o–o*38	the XIIIth	*s–s*38, 59	nothing

---

they should be married, as she might have asked when he would come to the tilt, and if it was fine weather. Till now he had smiled at this inexperience, so pardonable at eighteen, in a child born on a throne and bred in an atmosphere of grandeur; but he now reflected more seriously, and when, after the voices of the conspirators swearing to commence a vast war had scarcely done sounding in his ears, he heard the first words of her for whom that war had been undertaken, he feared, for the first time, that this innocence might be levity, and the childishness might extend to the heart: he resolved to penetrate it.

"'O heavens!' said she, 'how afraid I am, Henri! you make me come without carriage or guards; I tremble lest my people should see me as I leave the palace. Shall I have to hide myself much longer like a guilty person? The Queen was not pleased when I made my confession to her; if she speaks about it to me again, it will be with that severe look which you know, and which always makes me weep—I am terrified.'

"She was silent, and Cinq-Mars only answered by a deep sigh.

"'What! do you not speak to me?' said she.

"'Are those all your terrors?' answered he, bitterly.

"'Ought I to have greater ones? Oh my beloved,' said she, 'in what a tone, in what a voice you speak to me! Are you displeased because I have arrived too late?'

"'Too soon, Madame, much too soon, for the things you have to hear—for you are far, very far from them.'

"Marie wept. 'Alas! what have I done, that you should call me *Madame*, and speak so harshly to me?'

"'Ah! take courage,' replied Cinq-Mars, ironically. '*You* have done nothing; I alone am guilty, not against you, but for your sake.'

"'Have you done any wrong then? have you ordered the death of any one? O no, I am sure of it; you are so gentle!'

"'What!' said Cinq-Mars, 'have *you* then no part in my projects? did I misunderstand that look which you gave me in the presence of the Queen? can I no longer read in your eyes? the admiration you promised to him who should dare tell all to the King, where is it gone? Was it all falsehood?'

"Her tears burst out afresh. 'I do not deserve this; if I speak not to you of this dreadful conspiracy, think you I have forgotten it? am I not unhappy enough? if you wish to see my tears, behold them. Believe me, if in our late meetings I have avoided the terrible subject, it was for fear of learning too much—have I one thought but that of your dangers? Alas, if you combat for me, have I not to maintain as cruel a struggle for you? Happier than I, you have only to contend against hatred, I against affection—the Cardinal will send armed men against you; but the Queen, the gentle Anne of Austria, employs only tenderness, caresses, and tears.'

"'Touching and invincible constraint!' said Cinq-Mars with bitterness, 'to make you accept a throne' [she was asked in marriage by the King of Poland]. 'I acknowledge, some efforts are required to resist such seductions: but first, Madame, it is necessary to release you from your vows.'

"'Alas! great God, what is there then against us?'

"'God is over us, and against us,' said Henri in a severe voice. 'The King has deceived me.'

Corneille, Descartes, and a crowd of other poets, wits, and philosophers, in the ^{t}*salon*^{t} of the celebrated courtezan, Marion ^{u}"Delorme."^{u} But these are minor blemishes. As a specimen of art employed in embodying the character of an age, ^{v}the merit of *Cinq-Mars* is very great. The^v spirit of the age penetrates every nook and corner of it; the same atmosphere which hangs over the personages of the story hangs over us; we feel the eye of the omnipresent Richelieu upon us, and the influences of France in its Catholic and aristocratic days, of ardent, pleasure-

---

${}^{t-t}$38   salon
${}^{u-u}$38   Delorme!
${}^{v-v}$38   there are few works superior to *Cinq-Mars*: the

---

"The Abbé stirred in the confessional.

" 'I had a presentiment of it,' exclaimed Marie; 'that was the misfortune I dreaded. Am I the cause of it?'

" 'He deceived me while he grasped my hand,' continued Cinq-Mars; 'he has betrayed me by means of the wretch Joseph, whom they have offered me to poignard.'

"The Abbé made a gesture of horror, which half opened the door of the confessional.

" 'Ah, fear nothing, Father,' said Henri, 'your pupil will never strike such blows. Those I prepare will be heard afar off, and seen in broad daylight: but I have first a duty to perform: your child is about to immolate himself before you. Alas! I have not lived long for happiness. Your hand, which gave it to me, is now perhaps about to take it back.'

"While he said this he opened the little grating which separated him from his old preceptor, who, still silent, lowered his *camail* over his forehead.

" 'Restore,' said Cinq-Mars in a less firm voice; 'restore this nuptial ring to the Duchess of Mantua; I cannot keep it, unless she gives it to me a second time, for I am no longer the same man of whom she promised to be the wife.'

"The priest took the ring hastily, and passed it through the bars of the grating on the other side; this mark of indifference surprised Cinq-Mars. 'What! Father,' said he, 'are you too changed!'

"Marie's tears had ceased, and lifting up her angelic voice, which awakened a gentle echo along the vaulted building, like the softest note of an organ, she said,

" 'O my beloved! be no more angry with me; I understand you not; can we break what God has but just joined, and can I quit you when I know you are unhappy? If the King loves you no longer, be sure he will do you no ill, as he has done none to the Cardinal, whom he never loved. Do you think all lost because he was perhaps unwilling to discard his old servant? Well, then, let us wait the return of his friendship; forget those conspirators, who terrify me. If they have no hope, I thank God for it; I shall no longer have to tremble for you. Why afflict ourselves needlessly? The Queen loves us, we are both very young, let us wait. We are united and sure of each other; the future is ours. Tell me what the King said to you at Chambord; how I followed you with my eyes! how sad, to me, was that hunting party!'

" 'He has betrayed me, I repeat,' answered Cinq-Mars: 'and who would have thought it, when you saw him pressing our hands, passing from his brother to me, from me to the Duke of Bouillon—when he made us inform him of the minutest particulars of the plot, inquired the very day when Richelieu was to be arrested at Lyons, fixed the place of his exile (*they* wished for his death, but I thought of my father, and begged his life)! The King said he would himself direct everything at Perpignan; and at that very time Joseph, that foul spy, was coming out of his secret cabinet! O Marie! when I learnt this I was at first stupified. I doubted every thing, the universe seemed to totter from its foundations, when truth quitted the heart of a King. Our whole edifice was blown up; one hour longer, the conspiracy was scattered, and I lost you for ever; one resource was left me, I have used it.'

" 'What?' said Marie.

" 'The treaty with Spain was in my hands, I have signed it.'

" 'O heavens! destroy it!'

" 'It is sent.'

" 'Who bears it?'

loving, laughter-loving, and danger-loving France, all ᵂ"around"ᵂ us. To this merit is to be added, ˣ that the representations of feeling are always simple and graceful; the author has not, like so many inferior writers, supplied by the easy resource of mere exaggeration of colouring, the incapacity to show us anything subtle or profound, any trait we knew not before, in the workings of passion in the human heart. On the whole, *Cinq-Mars* is admirable as a first production of its kind,

ᵂ⁻ᵂ59   round
ˣ38   what our extracts sufficiently testify,

" 'Fontrailles.'
" 'Recal him!'
" 'He must by this time have got beyond Oléron, in passing the Pyrenees,' said Cinq-Mars, rising. 'All is ready at Madrid, at Sédan; armies are waiting me, Marie; armies! and Richelieu is in the midst of them. He totters, there needs but one blow to overthrow him, and you are united to me for ever, to Cinq-Mars triumphant!'
" 'To Cinq-Mars a rebel!' said she, with a groan.
" 'A rebel, then, but at least no longer a favourite. A rebel, a criminal, worthy of the scaffold, I know it,' cried the impassioned young man, falling again on his knees—'but a rebel for love, a rebel for you, whom my sword shall make mine for ever!'
" 'Alas!' said she, 'a sword dipped in your country's blood, is it not a poignard?'
" 'For pity's sake, Marie! let kings desert me, let warriors abandon me, I shall but stand the firmer; but one word from you would fling me prostrate. Besides, the time for reflection is past for me; yes, I am a criminal, and therefore do I hesitate to think myself still worthy of you. Renounce me, Marie, take back this ring.'
" 'I cannot,' said she: 'whatever you are, I am your wife.'
" 'You hear, Father,' said Cinq-Mars, transported with happiness: 'your blessing on this second union, it is that of sacrifice, more glorious still than that of love. Make her mine, mine till death!'
"Without answering, the Abbé opened the door of the confessional, ran hastily out, and had left the church before Cinq-Mars could rise and follow.
" 'Whither go you? what mean you?' he cried. But no one answered, nor came.
" 'In heaven's name do not cry out,' said Marie, 'or I am lost; he must have heard some one move in the church.'
"But D'Effiat, in alarm, rushed, without answering, across the church, to a door which he found closed. Drawing his sword he made the tour of the building, and arriving at the entrance, supposed to be guarded by Grandchamp [his servant], called to him, and listened." [*Ibid.*, pp. 183–8. The square brackets indicate Mill's additions.]

They found the old Abbé, his preceptor, alone in the snow, his head uncovered, himself bound and gagged. The man who had taken his place in the confessional was Father Joseph. " 'Fly,' exclaimed Marie, 'or you are lost!' " [*Ibid.*, p. 188.]

The sequel may be abridged. Marie de Gonzague verifies too well the misgivings of Cinq-Mars. The Queen, who was interested for her, not for him, and to whom Cinq-Mars is now nothing but "un petit ambitieux qui s'est perdu," [*ibid.*, p. 194,] uses all her efforts, not in vain, to turn the thoughts of the weak-minded girl into another channel; and at the moment when Cinq-Mars, at the camp at Perpignan, is about to fire the pistol-shot which is the signal of the insurrection, he receives the following letter:

" 'Monsieur le Marquis de Cinq-Mars,
" 'I write this to conjure you to restore to her duty our beloved adopted daughter, the Princess Marie de Gonzague, whom your affection alone withholds from the throne of Poland, which is offered to her. I have sounded her soul; she is very young as yet, and I have reason to believe that she would accept the crown with less of effort and of grief than you perhaps believe.
" 'It is for her that you have undertaken a war which will fill with fire and slaughter my dear and noble kingdom of France; I implore you to act with the honour of a nobleman, and generously release the

but altogether of an inferior order to its successors, the *Grandeur et Servitude Militaires*, and *Stello*; to which we proceed.

Of M. de Vigny's prose works, *Cinq-Mars* alone was written previous to the revolution of 1830; and though the ^yroyalist^y tendency of the author's political opinions is manifest throughout—indeed the book is one long protest against the levelling of the feudal aristocracy—it does not, nor does any part of the ^zroyalist^z

^{y–y}38　Carlist
^{z–z}38　Carlist

Duchess of Mantua from the promises she may have made you, thus restoring peace to her heart and tranquillity to our dear country.

" 'The Queen, who throws herself at your feet if it be necessary—

" 'ANNE OF AUSTRIA.'

"Cinq-Mars replaced calmly the pistol on the table; his first movement had been to turn it against himself; but he laid it down, and seizing a pencil wrote on the back of the same letter:

" 'Madame,

" 'Marie de Gonzague, being my wife, can only be Queen of Poland after my death; I am dying.

" 'CINQ-MARS.'

"And as if not to give himself a moment of reflexion, thrusting it into the hand of the messenger, 'To horse, to horse,' he cried, in a furious voice: 'if thou remainest an instant longer thou art dead.'

"The messenger gone, he re-entered. Alone with his friend, he stood still for an instant, but pale, his eyes fixed, and gazing on the earth like a madman. He felt himself tottering.

" 'De Thou!' cried he.

" 'What would you have, friend, dear friend! I am near you; you have been grand, noble, sublime!'

" 'De Thou!' he cried again in a terrible voice; and fell with his face to the ground like a tree uprooted by the tempest." [*Ibid.*, p. 198.]

He countermands the insurrection, sends passports to all the conspirators, and goes to deliver himself up, with his faithful and innocent friend De Thou, who, disapproving the conspiracy, had entered into it from love of him, and to watch over his safety; and now joins him in surrendering himself, resolved to die with him. Had the insurrection proceeded he would have found, instead of the whole army, a few companies only faithful to him; the rest had Richelieu's permission to give a simulated obedience: the Duke of Bouillon had already been arrested at the head of his troops, the King's brother had made his peace by abject submission, and the intercepted treaty was in Richelieu's hands, to be shown to the King, to extort from him the death of Cinq-Mars. An admirable scene follows. Louis holds out long. At length Richelieu leaves him, among masses of papers, and secretaries of state in attendance, to try his hand at governing. The first half hour's difficulties throw the unfortunate monarch into despair. He recals the Cardinal; says to him "*Reign*," and almost dead with suffering, signs the death-warrant of Cinq-Mars and De Thou. [*Ibid.*, p. 206.]

The friar Joseph visits them in their prison, the castle of Pierre-Encise near Lyons—offers them escape and to poison the Cardinal, if Cinq-Mars will promise him protection and promotion when restored to the King's favour; the offer is heroically refused. They are tried in prison by Laubardemont, that the prophecy may be fulfilled, *l'homme que tu as frappé te tuera*. [See above, p. 477.] In fulfilment of Grandier's dying curse, Laubardemont himself perishes the same day, being employed first to try his accomplices in that catastrophe, whose time like his own is now come, and immediately after precipitated along with them through a trap-door into the Saone. Cinq-Mars and De Thou are led out for execution. The conspirators from the camp at Perpignan, instead of making their escape, had come in disguise to Lyons, to rescue their two friends by a *coup de main*; all is arranged, they have contrived to inform the prisoners, near every soldier there is a conspirator prepared to cut him down at the expected signal; when Cinq-Mars, in passing to the scaffold, gives the sign by putting his hat on his head, he is to be free. But he no longer desires to live: he passes, flings his hat away from him, and his head falls.

literature of the last twenty years, entirely answer to our description of the Conservative school of poetry and romance. To find a real Conservative literature in France one must look earlier than the first Revolution, as, to study the final transformation of that literature, one must descend below the last. One must distinguish three periods; Conservatism triumphant, Conservatism militant, Conservatism vanquished. The first is represented by Racine, Fénélon, and Voltaire in his tragedies, before he quitted the paths of his predecessors. Jean Jacques Rousseau is the father and founder of the Movement literature of France, and Madame de Staël its second great apostle: in them first the revolt of the modern mind against the social arrangements and doctrines which had descended from of old, spoke with the inspired voice of genius. [a] At the head of the literature of Conservatism in its second or militant period, stands Chateaubriand: a man whose name marks one of the turning points in the literary history of his country: [b]poetically a Conservative[b] to the inmost core—rootedly feudal and Catholic— whose genius burst into life during the tempest of a revolution which hurled down from their pedestals all his objects of reverence; which saddened his imagination, modified (without impairing) his Conservatism by the addition of its [c]multiform[c] experiences, and made the world to him too full of disorder and gloom, too much a world without harmony, and ill at ease, to allow of his exhibiting the pure untroubled spirit of Conservative poetry as [d] exemplified in Southey, or still more in Wordsworth. To this literature, of Conservatism discouraged but not yet disenchanted, still hopeful and striving to set up again its old idols, *Cinq-Mars* belongs. From the final and hopeless overthrow of the old order of society in July 1830, begins the era of Conservatism disenchanted—Conservatism which is already in the past tense—which for practical purposes is abandoned, and only contributes its share, as all past associations and experiences do, towards shaping and colouring the individual's impressions of the present.

This is the character which pervades the two principal of M. de Vigny's more recent works, the *Servitude et Grandeur Militaires*, and *Stello*. He has lost his faith in Royalism, and in the system of opinions connected with it. His eyes are opened to all the iniquities and hypocrisies of the state of society which is passing away. But he cannot take up with any of the systems of politics, and of either irreligious or religious philosophy, which profess to lay open the mystery of what is to follow, and to guarantee that the new order of society will not have its own iniquities and hypocrisies of as dark a kind. He has no faith in any systems, [e]or[e] in man's power of prophecy; nor is he sure that the new tendencies of society, take them for all in all, have more to satisfy the wants of a thoughtful and loving spirit, than the old

[a]38   What Voltaire did, with all his infidelity, was but child's play compared with these two.
[b-b]38   a Conservative poet
[c-c]38   multiplex
[d]38   we see it
[e-e]38   none

had; at all events not so much more, as to make the condition of human nature a cheerful subject to him. He looks upon life, and sees most things crooked, and (saving whatever assurance his religious impressions may *afford* to him that in some unknown way all things must be working for good) sees not how they shall be made straight. This is not a happy state of mind, but it is not an unfavourable one to poetry. If the *worse* forms of it produce a "Literature of Despair," the better are seen in a writer like M. de Vigny—who having now no *theories of his own or of his teachers* to save the credit of, looks life steadily in the face—applies himself to understanding whatever of evil, and of heroic struggle with evil, it presents to his individual experience—and gives forth his pictures of both, with deep feeling, but with the calmness of one who has no point to carry, no quarrel to maintain, over and above "the general one of every son of Adam with his lot here below."

M. de Vigny has been a soldier, and he has been, and is, a poet: the situation and feelings of a soldier (especially a soldier not in active service), and, so far as the measure of his genius admits, those of a poet, are what he is best acquainted with, and what, therefore, as a man of earnest mind, not now taking anything on trust, it was most natural he should attempt to delineate. The *Souvenirs Militaires* are the embodiment of the author's experiences in the one capacity, *Stello*, in the other. Each consists of three touching and beautifully told stories, founded on fact, in which the life and position of a soldier in modern times, and of a poet at all times, in their relation to society, are shadowed out. In relation to society chiefly; for that is the prominent feature in all the speculations of the French mind; and thence it is that their poetry is so much shallower than ours, and their works of fiction so much deeper; that, of the metaphysics of every mode of feeling and thinking, so little is to be learnt from them, and of its social influences so much.

The soldier, and the poet, appear to M. de Vigny alike misplaced, alike ill at ease, in the present condition of human life. In the soldier he sees a human being set apart for a profession doomed to extinction, and doomed consequently, in the interval, to a continual decrease of dignity and of the sympathies of mankind. War he sees drawing to a close; compromises and diplomatic arrangements now terminate the differences among civilized nations; the army is reduced more and more to mere parade, or the functions of a police; called out from time to time, to shed its own blood and that of malcontent fellow-citizens in tumults where much popular hatred is to be earned, but no glory; disliked by taxpayers for its burthensomeness; looked down upon by the industrious for its enforced idleness: its employers themselves always in dread of its numbers, and jealous of its restlessness, which, in a soldier, is but the impatience of a man who is useless and nobody, for a chance of being useful and *of being* something. The soldier thus remains with all the burthens, all the irksome restraints of his condition, aggravated, but

*f–f*38   yield   *h–h*38   formulas
*g–g*38   worst   *i–i*+59, 67

without the hopes which lighted it up, the excitements which gave it zest. Those alone, says M. de Vigny, who have been soldiers, know what servitude is. To the soldier alone is obedience, passive and active, the law of his life, the law of every day and of every moment; obedience not stopping at sacrifice, nor even at crime. In him alone is the abnegation of his self-will, of his liberty of independent action, absolute and unreserved; the grand distinction of humanity, the responsibility of the individual as a moral agent, being made over, once for all, to superior authority. The type of human nature which these circumstances create, well deserves the study of the artist and the philosopher. M. de Vigny has deeply meditated on it. He has drawn with delicacy and profundity that mixture of Spartan and stoical impassibility with child-like *insouciance* and *bonhomie*, which is the result, on the one hand, of a life of painful and difficult obedience to discipline— on the other, of a conscience freed from concern or accountability for the quality of the actions of which that life is made up. On the means by which the moral position of the soldier might be raised, and his hardships alleviated, M. de Vigny has ^jideas^j worthy of the consideration of him who is yet to come—the statesman who has care and leisure for plans of social amelioration unconnected with party contests and the cry of the hour. His stories, full of melancholy beauty, will carry into thousands of minds and hearts which would otherwise have been unvisited by it, a conception of a soldier's trials and a soldier's virtues in times which, like ours, are not those of martial glory.

The first of these tales at least, if not all the three, if the author's words are to be taken literally, is unvarnished fact. But familiar as the modern French romance-writers have made us with the artifice of assimilating their fictions, for the sake of ^kartistic^k reality, to actual recollections, we dare not trust these appearances; and we must needs suppose that, though suggested by facts, the stories are indebted to M. de Vigny's invention not only for their details, but for some of their main circumstances. If he ^lhad been^l so fortunate as to meet with facts which, related as they actually occurred, served so perfectly as these do his purposes of illustration, he would hardly have left any possibility of doubt as to their authenticity. He must know the infinite distance, as to power of influencing the mind, between the best contrived and most probable fiction, and the smallest fact.

The first tale, "Laurette, ou Le Cachet Rouge,"[*] is the story of an old *chef de bataillon* (an intermediate grade between captain and major), whom the author, when following Louis XVIII in the retreat to Ghent, overtook on his march. This old man was leading along the miry road, on a day of pelting rain, a shabby mule drawing "a little wooden cart covered over with three hoops and a piece of black oilcloth, and resembling a cradle on a pair of wheels."[†] On duty he was

[*In *Souvenirs de servitude militaire, Oeuvres*, pp. 13–24.]
[†*Ibid.*, p. 14.]

^{j–j}38   views   ^{l–l}38   was
^{k–k}38   artistical

[m]escorting[m] the King as far as the frontier, and on duty he was about to return from thence to his regiment, to fight [n]against[n] the King at Waterloo. He had begun life at sea, and had been taken from the merchant service to command a brig of war, when the navy, like the army, was left without officers by the emigration. In 1797, under the government of the Directory, he weighed anchor for Cayenne, with sixty soldiers and a prisoner, one of those whom the *coup d'état* of the 18th [o]of[o] Fructidor had consigned to deportation. Along with this prisoner, whom he was ordered to treat with respect, he received a packet "with three red seals, the middle one of enormous size,"[*] not to be opened till the vessel reached one degree north of the Line. As he was nailing-up this packet, the possession of which made him [p]feel[p] uncomfortable, in a nook of his cabin, safe and in sight, his prisoner, a mere youth, entered, holding by the hand a beautiful girl of seventeen. His offence, it appeared, was a newspaper article: he had "trusted in their liberty of the press,"[†] had stung the Directory, and, only four days after his marriage, he was seized, tried, and received sentence of death, commuted for deportation to Cayenne, whither his young wife determined on accompanying him. We will not trust ourselves to translate any of the scenes which exhibit these two: a Marryat would be required to find a style for rendering the sailor-like *naïveté* of the honest officer's recital. A more exquisite picture we have never seen of innocence and ingenuousness, true warm-hearted affection, and youthful buoyancy of spirits breaking out from under the load of care and sorrow which had been laid so early and so suddenly on their young heads. They won the good-natured captain's heart: he had no family and no ties; he offered, on arriving at Cayenne, to settle there with his little savings, and adopt them as his children. On reaching the prescribed latitude he broke the fatal seal, and shuddered at beholding the sentence of death, and an order for immediate execution. After a terrible internal struggle, military discipline prevailed: he did as was commanded him, and "that moment," says he, "has lasted for me to the present time; as long as I live I shall drag it after me as a galley-slave drags his chain." Laurette became an incurable idiot. "I felt something in me which said—remain with her to the end of thy days and protect her." Her mother was dead; her relations wished to put her into a madhouse; "I turned my back upon them, and kept her with me."[‡] Taking a disgust to the sea, he exchanged into the army; the unhappy girl was with him in all Napoleon's campaigns, even in the retreat from Russia, tended by him like a daughter, and when the author overtook him he was conducting her in the cart with its three hoops and its canvas cover. The author shows her to us—a picture not inferior to Sterne's

[*]*Ibid.*, p. 16.]
[†]*Ibid.*, p. 19.]
[‡]*Ibid.*, pp. 21–2.]

[m-m]38   following
[n-n]38   *against*

[o-o]+59, 67
[p-p]+59, 67

Maria,[*] and which ^qdeserves to^q live as long: to detach it from the rest of the story would be unjust to the author. M. de Vigny parted from the old ^rofficer^r at the frontier, and learnt, long after, that he perished at Waterloo; she, left alone, and consigned to a madhouse, died in three days.

"La Veillée de Vincennes"[†] is a less tragical story: the life and destiny of an old adjutant of artillery, with whom the author, an officer in the guards, then in garrison at Vincennes, made acquaintance in the court-yard of the fortress, the evening previous to a general review and inspection. The old adjutant, who was in charge of the powder, was anxiously casting up long columns of figures, feeling himself eternally disgraced if there should be found on the morrow the most trifling inaccuracy in his books; and regretting the impossibility, from the late hour, of giving another glance that night at the contents of the powder magazine. The soldiers of the guard, who were not merely the *élite* of the army, but the *élite* of the *élite*, "thought themselves," says our author,

dishonoured by the most insignificant fault. "Go, you are puritans of honour, all of you," said I, tapping him on the shoulder. He bowed, and withdrew towards the barrack where he was quartered; then, with an innocence of manners peculiar to the honest race of soldiers, he returned with a handful of hempseed for a hen who was bringing up her twelve chickens under the old bronze cannon on which we were seated.[‡]

This hen, the delight of her master and the pet of the soldiers, could not endure any person not in uniform. At a late hour that night the author caught the sound of music from an open window: he approached; the voices were those of the old adjutant, his daughter, and a young non-commissioned officer of artillery, her intended husband; they saw him, invited him in, and we owe to this evening a charming description of the simple, innocent interior of this little family, and their simple history. The old soldier was the orphan child of a villager of Montreuil, near Versailles; brought up, and taught music and gardening, by the curé of his village. At sixteen, a word sportively dropped by Marie Antoinette when, alone with the Princess de Lamballe, she met him and his pretty playmate Pierrette in the park of Montreuil, made him enlist ^sas^s a soldier, hoping to be made a serjeant and to marry Pierrette. The latter wish was in time accomplished through the benevolence of Marie Antoinette, who, finding him resolute not to owe the attainment of his wishes to the bounty of a patron, herself taught Pierrette to sing and act in the opera of *Rose et Colas*,[§] and through her protection the *début* of the unknown actress

---

[*]In Laurence Sterne, *A Sentimental Journey through France and Italy*, 2 vols. (London: Becket and De Honat, 1768).]

[†]In *Souvenirs*, pp. 27–43.]

[‡]*Ibid.*, p. 28.]

[§]Pierre Alexandre Monsigny, *Rose et Colas* (first London performance, Covent Garden, 18 Sept., 1778).]

^{q-q}38   will
^{r-r}38   *chef de bataillon*   ^{s-s}38   for

was so successful that in one representation she earned a suitable portion for a soldier's wife. The merit of this little anecdote of course lies in the management of the details, which, for nature and gracefulness, would do credit to the first names in French literature. Pierrette died young, leaving her husband with two treasures, an only daughter, and a miniature of herself, painted by the Princess de Lamballe. Since then he had lived a life of obscure integrity, and had received all the military honours attainable by a private soldier, but no promotion, which, indeed, he had never much sought, thinking it a greater honour to be a serjeant in the guard than a captain in the line. "How poor," thought M. de Vigny,

are the mad ambitions and discontents of us young officers, compared with the soul of a soldier like this, scrupulous of his honour, and thinking it sullied by the most trifling negligence or breach of discipline; without ambition, vanity, or luxury, always a slave, and always content and proud of his servitude; his dearest recollection being one of gratitude; and believing his destiny to be regulated for his good by an overruling Providence![*]

An hour or two after this time the author was awakened from sleep by something like the shock of an earthquake: part of one of the powder magazines had exploded. With difficulty and peril the garrison stopped the spread of mischief. On reaching the seat of the catastrophe, they found the fragments of the body of the old adjutant, who [t], apparently having[t] risen at early dawn for one more examination of the powder, had, by some accident, set it on fire. The King presently arrived to return thanks and distribute rewards: he came, and departed. "I thought," says M. de Vigny, "of the family of the poor adjutant: but I was alone in thinking of them. In general, when princes pass anywhere they pass too quickly."[†]

"La Vie et la Mort du Capitaine Renaud, ou La Canne de Jonc,"[‡] is a picture of a more elevated description than either of these two, delineating a character of greater intellectual power and a loftier moral greatness. "Captain[u] Renaud is a philosopher; one like those of old, who has learnt the wisdom of life from its experiences; has weighed in the balance the greatnesses and littlenesses of the world, and has carried with him from every situation in which he has been placed, and every trial and temptation to which he has been subject, the impressions it was fitted to leave on a thoughtful and sensitive mind. There is no story, no incident, in this life; there is but a noble character, unfolding to us the process of its own formation; not [v]so much telling[v] us, [w]as[w] making us [x]see[x], how one circumstance disabused it of false objects of esteem and admiration, how another revealed to it the true. We feel with the young soldier his youthful enthusiasm for Napoleon, and for all of which that name is a symbol; we see this enthusiasm die within him as the

[*Souvenirs, p. 40.]
[†Ibid., p. 41.]
[‡Ibid., pp. 45–71.]

[t-t]38   having apparently
[u-u]38   The Capitaine
[v-v]38   telling

[w-w]38   but
[x-x]38   see

truth dawns upon him that this great man is an actor, that the *prestige* with which he overawed the world is in much, if not in the largest portion of it, the effect of stage-trick, and that a life built upon deception, and directed to essentially selfish ends, is not the ideal he had worshipped. He learns to know a real hero in Collingwood, whose prisoner he is for five years; and never was that most beautiful of military and naval characters drawn in a more loving spirit, or with a nobler appreciation, than in this book. From Collingwood, all his life a martyr to duty—the benignant father and guardian angel of all under his command—who pining for an English home, his children growing up to womanhood without having seen him, lived and died at sea, because his country or his country's institutions could not furnish him a successor;—from him the hero of our author's tale learnt to exchange the paltry admiration of mere power and success, the worship of the vulgar objects of ambition and vanity, for a heartfelt recognition of the greatness of devotion and self-sacrifice. A spirit like that of Collingwood governed and pervaded the remainder of his life. One bitter remembrance he had: it was of a night attack upon a Russian outpost, in which, hardly awakened from sleep, an innocent and beautiful youth, one of the boys of fourteen who sometimes held officers' commissions in the Russian army, fell dead in his gray-haired father's sight, by the unconscious hand of Renaud. He never used sabre more, and was known to the soldiers by carrying ever after a *canne de jonc*, which dropped from the dying hand of the poor boy. Many and solemn were the thoughts on war and the destiny of a soldier, which grew ^y in him from this passage in his life—nor did it ever cease to haunt his remembrance, and, at times, vex his conscience with misgivings. Unambitious, unostentatious, and therefore unnoticed, he did his duty always and everywhere without reward or distinction, until, in the Three Days of July 1830, a military point of honour retaining him with his corps on the Royalist side, he received his death-wound by a shot from a poor street-boy—who tended him in tears and remorse in his last moments, and to whom he left by will a provision for his education and maintenance, on condition that he should not become a soldier.

Such is a brief outline of this remarkable book: to which we have felt throughout, and feel still more on looking back, what scanty justice we have done. Among the writings of our day we know not one which breathes a nobler spirit, or in which every detail is conceived and wrought out in a manner more worthy of that spirit. But whoever would know what it is, must read the book itself. No *résumé* can convey any idea of it; the impression it makes is not the sum of the impressions of particular incidents or particular sayings, it is the effect of the tone and colouring of the whole. We do not seem to be listening to the author, to be receiving a "moral" from any of his stories, or from his characters an "example" prepense; the poem of human life is opened before us, and M. de Vigny does but chaunt from it, in a voice

^y38 up

of subdued sadness, a few strains telling of obscure wisdom and unrewarded virtue; of those antique characters which, without self-glorification or hope of being appreciated, "carry out," as he expresses it, "the sentiment of duty to its extremest consequences,"[*] and whom he avers, as a matter of personal experience, that he has never met with in any walk of life but the profession of arms.

Stello[†] is a work of similar merit to the *Military Recollections*, though, we think, somewhat inferior. The poet, and his condition—the function he has to perform in the world, and its treatment of him—are the subject of the book. Stello, a young poet, having, it would appear, no personal cause of complaint against the world, but subject to fits of nervous despondency, seeks relief under one of these attacks from a mysterious personage, the *docteur noir*; and discloses to him that in his *ennui* and his thirst for activity and excitement, he has almost determined to fling himself into politics, and sacrifice himself for some one of the parties or forms of government which are struggling with one another in the world. The doctor prescribes to him three stories, exhibiting the fate of the poet under every form of government, and the fruitlessness of his expecting from the world, or from men of the world, aught but negligence or contempt. The stories are of three poets, all of whom the *docteur noir* has seen die, as, in fact, the same person might have been present at all their deaths: under three different governments—in an absolute monarchy, a constitutional government, and a democratic revolution. Gilbert, the poet and satirist, called from his poverty Gilbert *sans-culotte*, who died mad in a hospital at Paris, he who wrote in the last days of his life the verses beginning

> Au banquet de la vie infortuné convive
> J'apparus un jour, et je meurs[‡]—

Chatterton—

> the marvellous boy,
> The sleepless soul, who perished in his pride[§]—

driven to suicide at eighteen by the anguish of disappointment and neglect; and André Chénier, the elder brother of Chénier the revolutionary poet—whose own poems, published not till many years after his death,[¶] were at once hailed by the new school of poetry in France as having anticipated what they ᶻhadᶻ since done,

[*Ibid., p. 24.]

[†*Stello, ou les diables bleus (blue devils)*, in *Oeuvres*, pp. 225–303.]

[‡Nicolas Joseph Laurent Gilbert, "Ode imitée de plusieurs pseaumes," in *Oeuvres complètes* (Paris: Le Jay, 1788), p. 81; Vigny quotes the first of these verses, p. 238.]

[§Wordsworth, "Resolution and Independence," in *Poetical Works* (1827), Vol. II, p. 127 (ll. 44–5).]

[¶André Marie Chénier, *Oeuvres posthumes* (1819), 2nd ed., ed. D. C. Robert, intro. H. J. de Latouche (Paris: Guillaume, 1826).]

ᶻ⁻ᶻ38 have

and given the real commencement to the new era: he perished by the guillotine only two days before the fall of Robespierre; on the scaffold he exclaimed, striking his forehead, "*Il y avait pourtant quelque chose là!*"[*] The stories adhere strictly to the spirit of history, though not to the literal facts, and are, as usual, beautifully told, especially the last and most elaborate of them, "André Chénier."[†] In this tale we are shown the prison of Saint-Lazare during the reign of terror, and the courtesies and gallantries of polished life still blossoming in the foulness of the dungeon and on the brink of the tomb. Madame de St. Aignan, with her reserved and delicate passion for André Chénier, is one of the most graceful of M. de Vigny's creations. We are brought into the presence of Robespierre and Saint-Just—who are drawn, not indeed like Catoes and Brutuses, though there have been found in our time Frenchmen not indisposed to take that view of them. But the hatred of exaggeration *a* which always characterizes M. de Vigny, does not desert him here: the terrorist chiefs do not figure in his pages as monsters thirsting for blood, nor as hypocrites and impostors with merely the low aims of selfish ambition: either of these representations would have been false to history. He shows us these men as they were, as such men could not but have been; men distinguished, morally, chiefly by two qualities, entire hardness of heart, and the most overweening and bloated self-conceit: for nothing less, assuredly, could lead any man to believe that his individual judgment respecting the public good is a warrant to him for exterminating all who are suspected of forming any other judgment, and for setting up a machine to cut off heads, *b* sixty or seventy every day, till some unknown futurity be accomplished, some Utopia realized.

The lesson which the *docteur noir* finds in these tragical histories, for the edification of poets, is still that of abnegation: to expect nothing *c*for themselves*c* from changes in society or in political institutions; to renounce for ever the idea that the world will, or can be expected to fall at their feet and worship them; to consider themselves, once for all, as martyrs, if they are so, and instead of complaining, to take up their cross and bear it.

This counsel is so essentially wise, and *d* so much required everywhere, but above all in France—where the idea that intellect ought to rule the world, an idea in itself true and just, has taken such root that every youth who fancies himself a thinker or an artist thinks *e*that*e* he has a right to everything society has to give, and *f*deems himself*f* the victim of ingratitude because he is not loaded with its riches and honours; M. de Vigny has so genuine a feeling of the true greatness of a poet, of the spirit which has dwelt in all poets deserving the name of great—that he may be pardoned for what there is in his picture of a poet's position and destiny in the

[*Ibid., Intro., p. xix.]
[†See Vigny, *Stello, Oeuvres*, pp. 255–95.]

*a*38 (that vice of the day)   *d*38 of such deep import, and is
*b*38 at   *e-e*+59, 67
c-c+59, 67   *f-f*38 is

actual world, somewhat morbid and overcharged, though with a ^{g} foundation of universal truth. It is most true that, whether in poetry or in philosophy, a person endowed in any eminent degree with genius—originality—the gift of seeing truths at a greater depth than the world can penetrate, or of feeling deeply and justly things which the world has not yet learnt to feel—that such a person ^{h}needs^h not hope to be appreciated, to be otherwise than made light of and evil entreated, in virtue of what is greatest in him, his genius. For (except in things which can be reduced to mathematical demonstration, or made obvious to sense) that which all mankind ^{i}will be^i prepared to see ^{j}and understand to-morrow^j, it cannot require much genius to perceive ^{k}to-day^k; and all persons of distinguished originality, whether thinkers or artists, are subject to the eternal law, that they must themselves create the tastes or the habits of thought by ^{l}means of^l which they will afterwards be appreciated.[*] No great poet or philosopher ^{m}since the Christian era^m (apart from the accident of a rich patron) could have ^{n}gained either rank^n or subsistence ^{o}as^o a poet or a philosopher; but things are not, and have seldom been, so badly ordered in the world, as that he could not get it in any other way. Chatterton, and probably Gilbert, could have earned an honest livelihood, if their inordinate pride would have accepted ^{p} it in the common paths of obscure industry. And much as it is to be lamented, for the world's sake more than that of the individual, that they who are equal to the noblest things are not reserved for such,—it is nevertheless true that persons of genius, persons whose superiority is that they can do what others cannot do, can generally also, if they choose, do better than others that which others do, and which others are willing to honour and reward. If they cannot, it is usually from something ill regulated in themselves, something to be cured of which would be for the health even of their own minds; perhaps oftenest because they will not take the pains which less gifted persons are willing to take, though less than half as much would suffice; because the habit of doing with ease things on a large scale, makes them impatient of slow and unattractive toil. It is their own choice, then. If they wish for worldly honour and profit, let them seek it in the way others do; the struggle indeed is hard, and the attainment uncertain, but not specially so to them; on the contrary, they have advantages over most of their competitors. If they prefer their nobler vocation, they have no cause of quarrel with the world because they follow that vocation under the conditions necessarily implied in it. If it were possible that they should ^{q}from the first^q have the

[*Cf. Wordsworth, "Essay, Supplementary to the Preface," in *Poems* (1815), Vol. I, p. 368.]

^{g}38   large
$^{h-h}$38   need
$^{i-i}$38   are
$^{j-j}$38   the *next* minute
$^{k-k}$38   in *this*
$^{l-l}$+59, 67

$^{m-m}$38   that ever lived
$^{n-n}$38   got either honour
$^{o-o}$38, 59   *as*
^{p}38   of
$^{q-q}$+59, 67

acclamations of the world, they could not be deserving of them; all they could be doing for the world must be comparatively little: they could not be the great men they fancy themselves.

A story, or a poem, might nevertheless be conceived, which would throw tenfold more light upon the poetic character, and upon the condition of a poet in the world, than any instance, either historical or fictitious, of the world's undervaluing of him. It would exhibit the sufferings of a poet, not from mortified vanity, but from the poetic temperament itself—under arrangements of society made by and for harder natures, and in a world which *r*, for any but the unsensitive, is not a place of contentment ever, nor of peace *s*until*s* after many a hard-fought battle*r*. That M. de Vigny could conceive such a subject in the spirit in which it should be conceived, is clear from the signs by which his Stello recognises himself as a poet.

Because there is in nature no beauty, nor grandeur, nor harmony, which does not cause in me a prophetic thrill—which does not fill me with a deep emotion, and swell my eyelids with tears divine and inexplicable. Because of the infinite pity I feel for mankind, my companions in suffering, and the eager desire I feel to hold out my hand to them, and raise them incessantly by words of commiseration and of love. Because I feel in my inmost being an invisible and undefinable power which resembles a presentiment of the future, and a revelation of the mysterious causes of the present:[*]

a presentiment which is not always imaginary, but often the instinctive insight of a sensitive nature, which from its finer texture vibrates to impressions so evanescent as to be unfelt by others, and, by that faculty as by an additional sense, is apprised, it cannot tell how, of things without, which escape the cognizance of the less delicately organized.

These *are* the tests, or some of the tests, of a poetic nature; and it must be evident that to such, even when supported by a positive religious faith, and that a cheerful one, this life is naturally, or at least may easily be, a vale of tears; a place in which there is no rest. The poet who would speak of such, must do it in the spirit of those beautiful lines of Shelley—himself the most perfect type of that which he described:

> High, spirit-winged heart, who dost for ever
> Beat thine unfeeling bars with vain endeavour,
> Till those bright plumes of thought, in which arrayed
> It over-soared this low and worldly shade,
> Lie shattered, and thy panting wounded breast
> Stains with dear blood its unmaternal nest!
> I weep vain tears: blood would less bitter be,
> Yet poured forth gladlier, could it profit thee.[†]

[*Stello, p. 232.]
[†Percy Bysshe Shelley, *Epipsychidion* (London: Ollier, 1821), pp. 7–8 (ll. 13–20).]

*r–r*38 its Creator himself did not intend to be a place of contentment or peace for any but the unsensitive
*s–s*59 till

The remainder of M. de Vigny's works are plays and poems. The plays are *Le More de Venise*, a well-executed and very close translation of *Othello*; *La Maréchale d'Ancre*, from the same period of history as *Cinq-Mars*; and *Chatterton*, the story in *Stello*, with the characters more developed, the outline more filled up.[*] Without disparagement to these works, we think the narrative style more suitable than the dramatic to the quality of M. de Vigny's genius. If we had not read these plays, we should not have known how much of the impressiveness of his other writings comes from his own 'presence' in them (if the expression may be allowed), animating and harmonizing the picture, by blending with its natural tints the colouring of his own feelings and character.

Of the poems[†] much were to be said, if a foreigner could be considered altogether a competent judge of them. For our own part we confess that, of the admirable poetry "to be found" in French literature, that part is most poetry to us, which is written in prose. In regard to verse-writing, we would even exceed the severity of Horace's precept against mediocrity;[‡] we hold, that nothing should be written in verse which is not exquisite. In prose, anything may be said which is worth saying at all; in verse, only what is worth saying better than prose can say it. The gems alone of thought and fancy, are worth setting with so finished and elaborate a workmanship; and even of them, those only whose effect is heightened by it: which takes place under two conditions; and in one or other of these two, if we are not mistaken, must be found the origin and justification of all composition in verse. A thought or feeling requires verse for its adequate expression, when in order that it may dart into the soul with the speed of a lightning-flash, the ideas or images that are to convey it require to be pressed closer together than is compatible with the rigid grammatical construction of ʰthe prose sentenceʰ. One recommendation of verse, therefore, is, that it affords a language more *condensed* than prose. The other is derived from one of the natural laws of the human mind, in the utterance of its thoughts impregnated with its feelings. All emotion which has taken possession of the whole being—which flows unresistedly, and therefore equably—instinctively seeks a language that flows equably like itself; and must either find it, or be conscious of an unsatisfied want, which even impedes and prematurely stops the flow of the feeling. Hence, ever since man has been man, all deep and sustained feeling has tended to express itself in rhythmical language; and the deeper the feeling, the more characteristic and decided the rhythm; provided always the feeling be sustained as well as deep; for a *fit* of passion has no natural connexion with verse or music, a *mood* of passion has the strongest. No one, who

[*In *Oeuvres*, pp. 355–407, 413–64, and 465–504, respectively.]
[†*Ibid.*, pp. 305–53.]
[‡*Ars poetica*, in *Satires, Epistles, and Ars poetica*, p. 480 (ll. 372–3).]

ᶦ⁻ᶦ38   *presence*
ᵘ⁻ᵘ38   which abounds
ᵛ⁻ᵛ38   prose: this, the inversions and elisions of verse, afford the means of accomplishing

does not hold this distinction in view, will comprehend the importance which the Greek lawgivers and philosophers attached to music, and which appears inexplicable till we understand how perpetual an aim of their polity it was to subdue *fits* of passion, and to sustain and reinforce *moods* of it.* This view of the origin of rhythmic utterance in general, and verse in particular, naturally demands *short* poems, it being impossible that a feeling so intense as to require a more rhythmical cadence than that of eloquent prose, should sustain itself at its highest elevation for long together; and we *ᵡthink (heretical as the opinion may be)ᵡ* that, except in the ages when the absence of written books occasioned all things to be thrown into verse for facility of memory, or in those other ages in which writing in verse may happen to be a *ʸfashionʸ*, a long poem will always be felt *ᶻ(though perhaps unconsciously)ᶻ* to be something unnatural and hollow; something which it requires the genius of a Homer, a Dante, or a Milton, to induce posterity to read, or at least to read through.

Verse, then, being only allowable where prose would be inadequate; and the inadequacy of prose arising either from its not being sufficiently condensed, or from its not having cadence enough to express sustained passion, which is never long-winded—it follows, that if prolix writing is vulgarly called *prosy* writing, a very true feeling of the distinction between verse and prose shows itself in the vulgarism; and that the one unpardonable sin in a versified composition, next to the absence of meaning, and of true meaning, is diffuseness. From this sin it will be impossible to exculpate M. Alfred de Vigny. His poems, graceful and often fanciful though they be, are, to us, marred by their diffuseness.

Of the more considerable among them, that which most resembles what, in our conception, a poem *ᵃ* ought to be, is "Moïse."[*] The theme is still the sufferings of the man of genius, the inspired man, the intellectual ruler and seer: not however, this time, the great man persecuted by the world, but the great man honoured by it, and in his natural place at the helm of it, *ᵇheᵇ* on whom all rely, whom all

---

* *ʷ* The Dorian mood
Of flutes and soft recorders; such as raised
To height of noblest temper heroes old
Arming to battle; and, *instead of rage,*
Deliberate valour breathed, firm and unmoved
With dread of death, to flight or foul retreat:
Nor wanting power to mitigate and swage,
With solemn touches, troubled thoughts, and chase
Anguish, and doubt, and fear, and sorrow and pain,
From mortal or immortal minds. [Milton, *Paradise Lost,* in
    The Poetical Works (London: Tonson, 1695), p. 18 (Bk. I, ll. 550–9).]
[*Oeuvres, pp. 311–12.]

*ʷ*38	Milton understood this:	*ᶻ⁻ᶻ*+59, 67
*ᵡ⁻ᵡ*38	are persuaded	*ᵃ*38 in verse
*ʸ⁻ʸ*38	*fashion*	*ᵇ⁻ᵇ*38 the man

reverence—Moses on Pisgah, Moses the appointed of God, the judge, captain and hierarch of the chosen race—crying to God in anguish of spirit for deliverance and rest; that the cares and toils, the weariness and solitariness of heart, of him who is lifted altogether above his brethren, be no longer imposed upon him—that the Almighty may withdraw his gifts, and suffer him to sleep the sleep of common humanity. His cry is heard; when the clouds disperse, which veiled the summit of the mountain from the Israelites waiting in prayer and prostration at its foot, Moses is no more seen: and now, "marching towards the promised land, Joshua advanced, pale and pensive of mien; for he was already the chosen of the Omnipotent."[*]

The longest of the poems is "Eloa; or, the Sister of the Angels;"[†] a story of a bright being, created from a tear of the Redeemer, and who falls, tempted by pity for the Spirit of Darkness. The idea is fine, and the details graceful, a word we have often occasion to use in speaking of M. de Vigny: but this and most of his other poems are written in the heroic verse, that is to say, he has aggravated the imperfections, for his purpose, of the most prosaic language in Europe, by choosing to write in its most prosaic metre. The absence of prosody, of long and short or accented and unaccented syllables, renders the French language essentially unmusical; while—the unbending structure of its sentence, of which there is essentially but one type for verse and prose, almost precluding inversions and elisions—all the screws and pegs of the prose sentence are retained to encumber the verse. If it is to be raised at all above prose, variety of rhythm must be sought in variety of versification; there is no room for it in the monotonous structure of the heroic metre. Where is it that Racine, always an admirable writer, appears to us more than an admirable *prose* writer? In his irregular metres—in the choruses of *Esther* and of *Athalie*.[‡] It is not wonderful then if the same may be said of M. de Vigny. We shall conclude with the following beautiful little poem, one of the few which he has produced in the style and measure of lyric verse:

> Viens sur la mer, jeune fille,
>   Sois sans effroi;
> Viens sans trésor, sans famille,
>   Seule avec moi.
> Mon bateau sur les eaux brille,
>   Voi ses mâts, voi
> Ses pavillons et sa quille.
> Ce n'est rien qu'une coquille,
>   Mais j'y suis roi.

[*Translated from "Moïse," p. 312.]
[†*Oeuvres*, pp. 323–30.]
[‡Jean Racine, *Esther* (Paris: Thierry, 1689), and *Athalie* (Paris: Thierry, 1691).]

Pour l'esclave on fit la terre,
  O ma beauté!
Mais pour l'homme libre, austère,
  L'immensité.
Les flots savent un mystère
  De volupté;
Leur soupir involontaire
Veut dire: amour solitaire,
  Et liberté.[*]

[*Vigny, "Le bateau," *Oeuvres*, p. 352.]

MILNES'S POEMS

1838

EDITORS' NOTE

London and Westminster Review, VII & XXIX (Aug., 1838), 308–20. Headed: "ART. III.—1. *Poems of Many Years.* By Richard Monckton Milnes. [London: Moxon,] 1838. (For private circulation.) / 2. *Memorials of a Residence on the Continent, and Historical Poems.* By Richard Monckton Milnes. [London:] Moxon. 1838." (The two volumes also appeared with title pages identifying them as Vols. I and II of *The Poems of Richard Monckton Milnes* [London: Moxon, 1838].) Running titles: left-hand, "Milnes' Poems of Many Years"; right-hand, "The Lay of the Humble" (the equivalent of pp. 505.9–506.18, 507.17–508.12), "Coleridgian Toryism" (pp. 509.9–510.4, 510.41–511.35, 512.38–513.27), and "Departure of St. Patrick" (pp. 514.27–515.22). Signed: "S." Not republished. Identified in Mill's bibliography as "A review of Milnes' Poems in the same number of the same review"—i.e., as "Bentham" (MacMinn, p. 50). The Somerville College copy (tear sheets) has no corrections or emendations.

For comment, see the Introduction, pp. xli–xlii above.

Milnes's Poems

THESE TWO VOLUMES OF POEMS, although the one was not designed for publication, and the other is not yet published, are not entirely unknown even to the general reader—some beautiful extracts from the earlier volume, and some just praises of both, having appeared in an article, from a pen not to be mistaken, in one of our monthly periodicals.[*] This first draught from the well leaves it, however, still fresh and full, and we too having been admitted to it, need not fear to exercise the privilege of dispensing its waters. We regard Mr. Milnes' poems as of singular merit in their kind, and the kind as one possessing strong claims upon the notice of a student of the age. They are representative of a whole order of thoughts and feelings; they are a voice from one corner of the mind and heart of this age, which had not found fitting poetical utterance till now; and there are many who will recognise in it the voice of their own soul, the language of their daily consciousness.

But we prefer beginning our selection by something not characteristic; and showing that the author is a poet, before we detain the reader with any remarks on the particular character of his poetry. We begin, therefore, unhesitatingly with

THE LAY OF THE HUMBLE

> I have no comeliness of frame,
>   No pleasant range of feature;
> I'm feeble, as when first I came
>   To earth, a weeping creature;
> My voice is low whene'er I speak
>   And singing faint my song;
> But though thus cast among the weak,
>   I envy not the strong.
>
> The trivial part in life I play
>   Can have so light a bearing
> On other men, who, night or day,
>   For me are never caring;
> That, though I find not much to bless,
>   Nor food for exaltation,
> I know that I am tempted less,
>   And that is consolation.

[*See John Wilson, "Christopher in His Cave," *Blackwood's Magazine*, XLIV (Aug., 1838), 268–84.]

The beautiful! the noble blood!
  I shrink as they pass by,
Such power for evil or for good,
  Is flashing from each eye;
They are indeed the stewards of Heaven,
  High-headed and strong-handed:
From those, to whom so much is given,
  How much may be demanded!

'Tis true, I am hard buffeted,
  Though few can be my foes,
Harsh words fall heavy on my head,
  And unresisted blows;
But then I think—"Had I been born—
  Hot spirit—sturdy frame—
And passion prompt to follow scorn—
  I might have done the same."

To me men are for what they are,
  They wear no masks with me;
I never sicken'd at the jar
  Of ill-tuned flattery;
I never mourned affections lent
  In folly or in blindness;—
The kindness that on me is spent
  Is pure, unasking kindness.

And, most of all, I never felt
  The agonizing sense
Of seeing love from passion melt
  Into indifference:
The fearful shame that, day by day,
  Burns onward, still to burn,
To have thrown your precious heart away,
  And met this black return.

I almost fancy that the more
  I am cast out from men,
Nature has made me of her store
  A worthier denizen;
As if it pleased her to caress
  A plant grown up so wild,
As if the being parentless
  Made me the more *her* child.

Athwart my face when blushes pass
  To be so poor and weak,
I fall unto the dewy grass,
  And cool my fevered cheek;
And hear a music strangely made,
  That you have never heard,
A sprite in every rustling blade,
  That sings like any bird.

My dreams are dreams of pleasantness,
    But yet I always run,
As to a father's morning kiss,
    When rises the round sun;
I see the flowers on stalk and stem,
    Light shrubs, and poplars tall,
Enjoy the breeze,—I rock with them,
    We are merry brothers all.

I do remember well, when first
    I saw the great blue sea,—
It was no stranger-face, that burst
    In terror upon me;
My heart began, from the first glance,
    His solemn pulse to follow,
I danced with every billow's dance,
    And shouted to their hollo.

The lamb, that at its mother's side
    Reclines, a tremulous thing,
The robin in cold winter-tide,
    The linnet in the spring,
All seem to be of kin to me,
    And love my slender hand,—
For we are bound, by God's decree,
    In one defensive band.

And children, who the worldly mind
    And ways have not put on,
Are ever glad in me to find
    A blithe companion:
And when for play they leave their homes,
    Left to their own sweet glee,
They hear my step, and cry—"He comes,
    Our little friend—'tis he."

Have you been out some starry night,
    And found it joy to bend
Your eyes to one particular light,
    Till it became a friend?
And then, so loved that glistening spot,
    That, whether it were far,
Or more or less, it mattered not,—
    It still was your own star.

Thus, and thus only, can you know,
    How I, even scorned I,
Can live in love, tho' set so low,
    And my ladie-love so high;
Thus learn, that on this varied ball,
    Whate'er can breathe and move,
The meanest, lornest thing of all
    Still owns its right to love.

With no fair round of household cares
   Will my lone hearth be blest,
Nor can the snow of my old hairs
   Fall on a loving breast;
No darling pledge of spousal faith
   Shall I be found possessing,
To whom a blessing with my breath
   Would be a double blessing;

But yet my love with sweets is rife,
   With happiness it teems;
It beautifies my waking life,
   And waits upon my dreams;
A shape that floats upon the night,
   Like foam upon the sea,—
A voice of seraphim,—a light
   Of present Deity!

I hide me in the dark arcade,
   When she walks forth alone,—
I feast upon her hair's rich braid,—
   Her half-unclasped zone;
I watch the flittings of her dress,
   The bending boughs between,—
I trace her footstep's faery press
   On the scarcely ruffled green.

Oh deep delight! the frail guitar
   Trembles beneath her hand;
She sings a song she brought from far,
   I cannot understand;
Her voice is *always* as from heaven,
   But yet I seem to hear
Its music best, when thus 'tis given
   All music to my ear.

She has turned her tender eyes around,
   And seen me crouching there,
And smiles, just as that last full sound
   Is fainting on the air;
And now, I can go forth so proud,
   And raise my head so tall,—
My heart within me beats so loud,
   And musical withal—

And there is summer all the while,
   Mid-winter tho' it be,—
How should the universe not smile,
   When she has smiled on me?
For tho' that smile can nothing more
   Than merest pity prove,
Yet pity, it was sung of yore,
   Is not *so* far from love.

From what a crowd of lover's woes
   My weakness is exempt!
How far more fortunate than those
   Who mark me for contempt!
No fear of rival happiness
   My fervent glory smothers,
The zephyr fans me none the less
   That it is bland to others.

Thus without share in coin or land,
   But well content to hold
The wealth of nature in my hand,
   One flail of virgin gold,—
My love above me like a sun—
   My own bright thoughts my wings,
Thro' life I trust to flutter on,
   As gay as aught that sings.

One hour I own I dread,—to die
   Alone and unbefriended,—
No soothing voice, no tearful eye,
   But that must soon be ended;
And then I shall receive my part
   Of everlasting treasure,
In that just world where each man's heart
   Will be his only measure.[*]

This poem requires no commentator; it goes straight to the common heart of humanity; and we shall be surprised if it do not become widely known, and find its way into collections. The man who can thus write, is entitled to write in verse; a privilege which we would confine to a very small proportion indeed of those who usurp it. Let such a man speak from the fulness of his own heart—give him thoughts and feelings to express which are deeply interesting to him—and it will be a little your own fault if he does not make them interesting to you. Now these poems, as a whole, if there be faith in internal evidence, do come from the heart of the writer; what they express, he feels, or has felt; they are the deepest and most earnest part of himself, thrown into melodious language; there is as much sincerity in them as there can be in words; for, properly speaking, it is only a man's whole life which is sincere—*that* alone is the utterance of the whole man, contemplative and active taken together.

Of Mr. Milnes, personally, we know little or nothing, save that he is a young and active member of the House of Commons, who generally votes with the Tories; but if he be like his poems—and the man who could write them cannot be altogether unlike them—he is one of the representatives of a school which has grown up within a few years, is spreading rapidly among the refined and cultivated youth, and deserves to be much honoured, and, above all, to be understood. This school is

[*Poems of Many Years, pp. 28–36.]

one of the products of what may be termed the Coleridgian reaction. In politics, its aim is, to save the Church and the Aristocracy, by making them really what they pretend to be. With Conservatives of this description, however we may doubt the practicability of their objects, we feel, and have always professed, the most entire sympathy; and no one can more heartily rejoice at any accession to their numbers or influence. Mr. Milnes' poems, however, do not show them in their character as politicians, but as men; and as such they are in some measure a class apart.

They are, in general, earnest men, with a deep sense of duty towards God and man, and of responsibility to an Eternal Judge. With this they seem not unusually to combine a degree of distrust of their own spiritual strength, very becoming in most persons, but which certainly is not usually found in those destined to accomplish great things, even in the cause of religion; for, however innocent of any vain-glorious trust in his own unassisted power or goodness, the Christian hero has generally a sure faith that upon certain simple conditions, which in his healthier moods he feels confident that he can and will fulfil, strength will be lent him from God, to perform all that God requires of him. But these men (at least in one stage of their growth) seem as though weighed down by the immensity of God's requirements. To be a spiritual being, and to have an account to render as such, of the employment of powers and opportunities, appears to them not only an awful, but almost a fearful destiny; its dangers alarm them much more than its privileges excite; and the period of infancy, when they were alike strangers to both, is looked back to, with manly endurance no doubt, but with the fondest regret. It is astonishing how large a portion of Mr. Milnes' poems are impregnated with this feeling; it can scarcely be more finely expressed than in the following lines:

> Youth, that pursuest with such eager pace
>   Thy even way,
> Thou pantest on to win a mournful race;
>   Then stay! oh, stay!
>
> Pause and luxuriate in thy sunny plain;
>   Loiter,—enjoy:
> Once past, Thou never wilt come back again
>   A second Boy.
>
> The hills of Manhood wear a noble face,
>   When seen from far;
> The mist of light from which they take their grace
>   Hides what they are.
>
> The dark and weary path those cliffs between
>   Thou canst not know,
> And how it leads to regions never green,
>   Dead fields of snow.
>
> Pause, while thou may'st, nor deem that fate thy gain,
>   Which, all too fast,
> Will drive thee forth from this delicious plain,
>   A Man at last.[*]

[*Untitled poem, *ibid.*, pp. 7–8.]

And again in the following, to a child five years old:

> Delighted soul! that in thy new abode
>   Dwellest contentedly, and knowest not
> What men can mean who faint beneath the load
>   Of mortal life, and mourn an earthly lot:
>
> Who would believe thou wert so far from home?
>   Who could suppose thee exiled or astray?
> This world of twilight whither thou art come
>   Seems just as welcome as thy native day.
>
> That comely form, wherein thy thoughts are pent,
>   Hiding its rebel nature, serves thee still,
> A pliable and pleasant instrument,
>   Harmonious to thy impulses and will.
>
> Thou hast not spent as yet thy little store
>   Of happy instincts:—Thou canst still beguile
> Painful reflection and ungrateful lore
>   With many a placid dream and causeless smile.
>
> And when the awful stranger Evil bends
>   His eye upon thee, Thou wilt first essay
> To turn him from his dark pursuits and ends
>   By gracious dalliance and familiar play.
>
> As well might kindly words arrest the roll
>   Of billows raging o'er a wintry sea.
> O Providence! remit to this one soul
>   Its destined years, and take it back to Thee.[*]

Such feelings as these occur as moods, in the life probably of every person who has a conscience; but wherever they fill a large place, they point to something unhealthful either in the individual mind or in the times.

Whether as cause or consequence, these feelings are not unnaturally connected with a rather melancholy view of life. For the duty of a good man is not to these minds the simple thing it was to the religious minds of former ages. Their morality does not say only, Thou shalt abstain,—thou shalt keep thy thoughts and actions pure; it says, Thou shalt *do*; not to thee alone, O pastor, or to thee O missionary, but even to thee O meanest of mankind, is the boundless mass of evil which surrounds thee on every side, delivered as thy task; of which mass unless thou remove all that thou canst, the whole shall be imputed to thee.

> We have come out upon the field of Life
>   To war with Evil—

says Mr. Milnes; and if the Boy, resolute and confiding in his resolve, dares hope for victory, Mr. Milnes tells him—

> Poor youthful Heart! poor noble Self-deceit!
> Weak-winged Aspirant!—Step with me aside,

[*"To——, Five Years Old," *ibid.*, pp. 3–4.]

Tis for a moment,—mount this little hill,—
Tell me, and tell thyself, what see'st Thou now.
Look East and West, and mark how far extends
This vainly mockt, this haughtily defied,
This Might so easily to be laid low!
There is no eminence on this wide space,
So high that thou from it canst e'er behold
A clear horizon: dark is all the space,
Black with the masses of thine Enemy;
There is no point where Light can penetrate
Those densely-banded Legions,—the green plain
Shines through no interval. Brave though thou art,
My Boy, where is thy trust in Victory now?
Now gaze below, gaze on that waving crowd,
The marshalled army of Humanity,
From which thou art come out,—Loyal thou art,
My Boy; but what avails thy feeble Truth,
When, as thou seest, of the huge multitude,
The still succeeding myriads there arrayed
For fight, how few, how miserably few,
Not only do not fervently work out
Their Soldier-duty, but whose craven souls
Do not pass over to the very Foe,
And, mingling with his numbers numberless,
Against their brethren turn unnatural arms—
Or else of honest wills at first, like thine,
After the faint resistance of an hour,
Yield themselves up half-willing prisoners,
Soon to be won by golden-guileful tongues,
To do blithe service in the cause of Sin!

* * * * *

Yet there are some to whom a strength is given,
A will, a self-constraining energy,
A Faith which feeds upon no earthly hope,
Which never thinks of Victory, but content
In its own consummation, combatting
Because it ought to combat (even as Love
Is its own cause, and cannot have another),
And conscious that to find in martyrdom
The stamp and signet of most perfect life
Is all the science that mankind can reach,
Rejoicing fights, and still rejoicing falls.
It may be that to Spirits high-toned as these
A revelation of the end of Time
Is also granted; that they feel a sense
Giving them firm assurance that the foe
By which they must be crusht (in Death well-won
Alone to find their freedom) in his turn
Will be subdued, though not by such as They.[*]

[*"The Combat of Life," *ibid.*, pp. 147, 148–9, 150–1.]

This is nobly expressed, and the views of life such as are natural to a clear-headed and pure-minded Conservative. Of all persons living, such a man has the fewest illusions left as to the amount of evil in the world. When times are quiet, and men's minds settled, the unbroken respect for rules and ordinances (seldom questioned even when transgressed), and the reverence still ostensibly maintained towards those superiors, who are the representatives (however unfaithful) of all that is most venerable to man, keep the worst parts of human nature under a veil; mankind in such times seem better than they are, and *are* somewhat better than their genuine dispositions would prompt. In proportion as this respect wears off, and the actions of mankind become the expression of their real feelings, the veil is gone, and they appear as they are: to a Conservative, worse than they are; for to him the sham which they have discarded is still a holy truth. *He* has not the consolation of thinking that the old Formulas are gone because the time has come for something better; no hope and faith in a greater good beyond, tempers to him the sense of present evil.

For a good man to live healthy and happy in a world which presents to him so dreary a prospect, he requires to have a clear view at least of his own path in it; but few of the men whom we speak of seem yet to have attained this; they *believe*, doubtless, that they are in the right road, but we question whether most of them feel quite *sure* of it—as indeed in these days it is not easy that any open-minded Conservative should. In proportion as they shall arrive at full unclouded certainty respecting the course which duty marks out for themselves, a vigorous and healthful development of their active faculties will correct what may now be unduly preponderant in the merely passive part of their moral sensibility; and, whether they are destined to aid in infusing another spirit into old beliefs and institutions, or in calmly substituting others, we shall be disappointed if some of them do not play a noble part in that "combat of life"[*] which one of them has so feelingly described. We cannot better close these remarks than by extracting a poem, in which Mr. Milnes has painted with great truth the feelings of a deeply religious mind—not lamenting to itself its own insufficiency, and the vastness of what it has to do—but, while it feels all this, still pressing on to do what it can, with that strong and living faith in its own impulses, the almost necessary condition of high and heroic deeds.

THE DEPARTURE OF ST. PATRICK FROM SCOTLAND
(From his own "Confessions")

Twice to your son already has the hand of God been shown,
Restoring him from alien bonds to be once more your own,
And now it is the self-same hand, dear kinsmen, that to-day
Shall take me for the third time from all I love away.

While I look into your eyes, while I hold your hands in mine,
What force could tear me from you, if it were not all divine!

[*I.e., the title of the poem quoted above.]

Has my love ever faltered? Have I ever doubted yours?
And think you I could yield me now to any earthly lures?

I go not to some balmier land in pleasant ease to rest,—
I go not to content the pride that swells a mortal breast,
I go about a work my God has chosen me to do;
Surely the soul which is his child must be his servant too.

I seek not the great city where our sacred father dwells,—
I seek not the blest eremites within their sandy cells,—
I seek not our Redeemer's grave in distant Palestine,—
Another, shorter pilgrimage, a lonelier path is mine.

When sunset clears and opens out the breadth of western sky,
To those who in yon mountain isles protect their flocks on high
Loom the dark outlines of a land, whose nature and whose name
Some have by harsh experience learnt, and all by evil fame.

Oh, they are wild and wanton men, such as the best will be,
Who know no other gifts of God but to be bold and free,
Who never saw how states are bound in golden bonds of law,
Who never knew how strongest hearts are bent by holy awe.

When first into their pirate hands I fell, a very boy,
Skirting the shore from rock to rock in unsuspecting joy,
I had been taught to pray, and thus those slavish days were few,
A wondrous hazard brought me back to liberty and you.

But when again they met me on the open ocean field,
And might of numbers prest me round and forced my arm to yield,
I had become a man like them, a selfish man of pride,
I could have curst the will of God, for shame I had not died.

And still this torment haunted me three weary years, until
That summer night,—among the sheep,—upon the seaward hill,
When God of his miraculous grace, of his own saving thought,
Came down upon my lonely heart and rested unbesought!

That night of light! I cared not that the day-star glimmered soon,
For in my new-begotten soul it was already noon;
I knew before what Christ had done, but never felt till then
A shadow of the love for him that he had felt for men!

Strong faith was in me—on the shore there lay a stranded boat,
I hasted down, I thrust it out, I felt it rock afloat;
With nervous arm and sturdy oar I sped my watery way,
The wind and tide were trusty guides,—one God had I and they.

As one from out the dead I stood among you free and whole,
My body Christ could well redeem, when he had saved my soul;
And perfect peace embraced the life that had been only pain,
For Love was shed upon my head from everything, like rain.

Then on so sweetly flowed the time, I almost thought to sail
Even to the shores of Paradise in that unwavering gale,

When something rose and nightly stood between me and my rest,
Most like some one, besides myself, reflecting in my breast.

I cannot put it into words, I only know it came,
A sense of self-abasing weight, intolerable shame,
"That I should be *so* vile that not one tittle could be paid
Of that enormous debt which Christ upon my soul had laid!"

This yielded to another mood, strange objects gathered near,
Phantoms that entered not by eye, and voices not by ear,
The land of my injurious thrall a gracious aspect wore,
I yearned the most toward the forms I hated most before.

I seemed again upon that hill, as on that blissful night,
Encompast with celestial air and deep retiring light,
But sight and thought were fettered down, where glimmering lay below
A plain of gasping, struggling, men in every shape of woe.

Faint solemn whispers gathered round, "Christ suffered to redeem,
Not you alone, but such as these, from this their savage dream,—
Lo, here are souls enough for you to bring to him, and say,
These are the earnest of the debt I am too poor to pay."

A cloud of children freshly born, innumerable bands,
Past by me with imploring eyes and little lifted hands,
And all the Nature, I believed so blank and waste and dumb,
Became instinct with life and love, and echoed clearly "Come!"

"Amen!" said I; with eager steps a rude descent I tried,
And all the glory followed me like an on-coming tide,
With trails of light about my feet, I crost the darkling wild,
And as I toucht each sufferer's hand, he rose and gently smiled.

Thus night on night the vision came, and left me not alone,
Until I swore that in that land should Christ be preacht and known,
And then at once strange coolness past on my long fevered brow,
As from the flutter of light wings; I feel, I feel it now!

And from that moment unto this, this last and proving one,
I have been calm and light at heart as if the deed were done;
I never thought how hard it was our earthly loves to lay
Upon the altar of the Lord, and watch them melt away!

Speak, friends! speak what you will—but change those asking looks forlorn,
Sustain me with reproachful words—uphold me with your scorn;
I know God's heart is in me, but my human bosom fears
Those drops that pierce it as they fall, those full and silent tears.

These comrades of my earliest youth have pledged their pious care
To bear me to the fronting coast, and gently leave me there:
It may be I shall fall at once, with little toil or need,—
Heaven often takes the simple will for the most perfect deed:

Or, it may be that from that hour beneath my hand may spring
A line of glories unachieved by hero, sage, or king,—

That Christ may glorify himself in this ignoble name,
And shadow forth my endless life in my enduring fame.

All as He wills! now bless me, mother,—your cheek is almost dry:—
Farewell, kind brothers!—only pray ye may be blest as I;
Smile on me, sisters,—when death comes near each of you, still smile,
And we shall meet again somewhere, within a little while![*]

[*Memorials of a Residence on the Continent, and Historical Poems, pp. 143–51.]

MILNES'S POETRY FOR THE PEOPLE

1840

EDITORS' NOTE

Westminster Review, XXXIV (Sept., 1840), 511–13. This notice appeared in the Poetry section of the Miscellaneous Notices part of the *WR*, with the heading: *"Poetry for the People, and other Poems.* By Richard Monckton Milnes. [London:] Moxon. 1840." Running titles: "Miscellaneous Notices. / Poetry." Signed: "A." Not republished. Identified in Mill's bibliography as "A short notice of Milnes' Poetry for the people, in the same number of the same review"—i.e., as his notice of two publications on Plato (MacMinn, p. 52). No copy in the Somerville College library.

For comment, see the Introduction, p. xlii above.

Milnes's Poetry for the People

MOST OF THESE POEMS have already appeared in periodicals; and although they bear marks of the same hand as the two volumes already published by Mr. Milnes,[*] there are indications of haste, and a want of finish in their composition, such as we are too apt to see in the contributions even of real poets to those fugitive pages. It is the besetting sin of the poets of our age that they write too much: even of Wordsworth, his most sincere admirers could spare nearly all which he has written in the last twenty years: and Ebenezer Elliott is wasting his great powers and noble feelings in careless, empty productions of no permanent value. It would be well for them to consider how few are the voluminous poets who have descended to posterity. Mr. Milnes has, we think, need of the same lesson; not that these poems are not good, but that he might so easily have made them better; or have written, in lieu of them, a much smaller number of far superior performances.

The "Specimens of Poetry for the People"[†] are, for the most part, excellent in sentiment and purpose; some of them are warnings to the poor, others are rather pleadings *for* the poor to the rich, and therefore hardly merit their title. But neither the warnings nor the pleadings are so impressive as they would have been, had Mr. Milnes taken half the pains with them which he must have employed upon some of his earlier productions. Some of the very short poems are far more perfect; such as the following, one of several entitled "Love-Thoughts."

> Think not, because I walk in power,
>   While thou art by my side,
> That I could keep the path one hour
>   Without my guard and guide.
>
> The keeper left me once alone
>   Within a mad-house hall,
> With gibber, shriek, and fixed smile
>   About me,—madmen all!
>
> The horrid sense which then I felt
>   Is what my life would be,

[* *Poems of Many Years*, and *Memorials of a Residence on the Continent, and Historical Poems* (both London: Moxon, 1838); reviewed by Mill in "Milnes's Poems," above, pp. 503–16.]
[† A section of *Poetry for the People*, pp. 37–59.]

> If in this world of pain and guilt
>   I once lost sight of Thee.[*]

Or this:

> Beneath an Indian palm a girl
>   Of other blood reposes;
> Her cheek is clear and pale as pearl,
>   Amid that wild of roses.
>
> Beside a northern pine a boy
>   Is leaning, fancy-bound,
> Nor listens where with noisy joy
>   Awaits the impatient hound.
>
> Cool grows the sick and feverish calm
>   Relaxt the frosty twine,—
> The pine-tree dreameth of the palm,
>   The palm-tree of the pine.
>
> As soon shall nature interlace
>   Those dimly-visioned boughs,
> As these young lovers face to face
>   Renew their early vows![†]

The following is of a higher character, as suggestive to the inward imagination as it is picturesque to the outward and visual one:

> She had left all on earth for him,
>   Her home of wealth, her name of pride,
> And now his lamp of love was dim,
>   And, sad to tell, she had not died.
>
> She watcht the crimson sun's decline
>   From some lone rock that fronts the sea—
> "I would, O burning heart of mine,
>   There were an ocean-rest for thee.
>
> "The thoughtful moon awaits her turn,
>   The stars compose their choral crown,
> But those soft lights can never burn
>   Till once the fiery sun is down."[‡]

Our last quotation shall be a legendary tale:

> A gentle household spirit, unchallenged and unpaid,
> Attended with his service a lonely servant-maid.
>
> She seemed a weary woman, who had found life unkind,
> Whose youth had left her early, and little left behind.

[*Poetry for the People, p. 162.]
[†Poem V of "Shadows," ibid., p. 173.]
[‡Poem VI of "Shadows," ibid., p. 174.]

Most desolate and dreary her days went on until
Arose this unseen stranger her labours to fulfil.

But now she walkt at leisure, secure of blame she slept,
The meal was always ready, the room was always swept.

And by the cheerful fire-light, the winter evenings long,
He gave her words of kindness and snatches of sweet song;—

With useful housewife secrets and tales of faeries fair,
From times when gaunt magicians and dwarfs and giants were.

Thus, habit closing round her, by slow degrees she nurst
A sense of trust and pleasure, where she had feared at first.

When strange desire came on her, and shook her like a storm,
To see this faithful being distinct in outward form.

He was so pure a nature, of so benign a will,
It could be nothing fearful, it could be nothing ill.

At first with grave denial her prayer he laid aside,
Then warning and entreaty, but all in vain, he tried.

The wish upgrew to passion,—she urged him more and more—
Until, as one outwearied, but still lamenting sore,—

He promist in her chamber he would attend her call,
When from the small high window the full-moonlight should fall.

Most proud and glad that evening she entered to behold
How there her phantom-lover his presence would unfold;

When lo! in bloody pallor lay, on the moonlit-floor,
The babe she bore and murdered some thirteen years before.[*]

[*"The Brownie. A Legend," *ibid.*, pp. 75–6.]

MACAULAY'S LAYS OF ANCIENT ROME

1843

EDITORS' NOTE

Westminster Review, XXXIX (Feb., 1843), 105–13. Headed: "ART. V.—*Lays of Ancient Rome*. By Thomas Babington Macaulay. [London:] Longman. 1842." Running title: "Macaulay's Lays of Ancient Rome." Signed: "A." Not republished. Identified in Mill's bibliography as "A review of Macaulay's 'Lays of Ancient Rome' in the Westminster Review for Febry. 1843 (No. 76.)" (MacMinn, p. 55). The Somerville College copy (tear sheets) is headed in Mill's hand: "(Westminster Review, February 1843)" and two corrections are made: at 525.31 "no" is altered to "on", and at 527n.6 "ylaeddfed" is changed to "deadly feud"; there was a second issue of this number (a tear-sheet copy of Mill's article in this version is also in Somerville College, with no corrections or emendations), in which the first correction was made, and part of the second (the reading became "deadly fed").

For comment, see the Introduction, p. xlii above.

Macaulay's Lays of Ancient Rome

THE GENERAL READER, even if he be so much an exception among general readers as to have remained personally ignorant of this volume, must be sufficiently cognizant of its contents from criticisms and extracts, not to require either outline or additional specimens on the present occasion; but he must not suppose that specimens, however well selected, can give a sufficiently favourable idea of such a work. No one can judge of a tragedy, from seeing only its fifth act, or of a novel from having read its most highly-wrought scenes; and the more perfect and harmonious the composition may be as a work of art, the less can those portions of it be properly estimated by themselves, because they pre-suppose in the reader or spectator a state of excitement as well as a mental preparation which can only be the effect of the previous portions. A reviewer, fresh from reading these poems, quotes the passage by which he has been most strongly moved, expecting that it will move his own reader as strongly; but it is nothing to be in at the death when you have not followed the hounds: and we ourselves at first read in the newspapers with a certain sensation of flatness, the very incidents and descriptions which afterwards, when read in their proper place, acted upon us like the most stirring strains of Campbell or Scott.

For it is with those two great masters of modern ballad poetry that Mr. Macaulay's performances are really to be compared, and not with the real ballads or epics of an early age. The *Lays*, in point of form, are not in the least like the genuine productions of a primitive age or people, and it is no blame to Mr. Macaulay that they are not. He professes imitation of Homer, but we really see no resemblance, except in the nature of some of the incidents, and the animation and vigour of the narrative; and the *Iliad*, after all, is not the original ballads of the Trojan war, but those ballads moulded together, and wrought into the forms of a more civilized and cultivated age. It is difficult to conjecture what the forms of the old Roman ballad may have been, and certain, that whatever they were, they could no more satisfy the æsthetic requirements of modern culture, than an ear accustomed to the great organ of Freyburg or Harlem could relish Orpheus's hurdy-gurdy; although the airs which Orpheus played, if they could be recovered, might perhaps be executed with great effect on the more perfect instrument.

The forms of Mr. Macaulay's ballad poetry are essentially modern; they are those of the romantic and chivalrous, not the classical ages, and even in those they are a reproduction, not of the originals, but of the imitations of Scott. In this we think he has done well, for Scott's style is as near to that of the ancient ballad as we conceive to be at all compatible with real popular effect on the modern mind. The difference between the two may be seen by the most cursory comparison of any real old ballad, "Chevy Chase"[*] for instance, with the last canto of *Marmion*,[†] or with any of these Lays. Conciseness is the characteristic of the real ballad— diffuseness, of the modern adaptation. The old bard did everything by single touches; Scott and Mr. Macaulay by repetition and accumulation of particulars. They produce all their effect by what they *say*; he by what he *suggested*; by what he stimulated the imagination to paint for itself. But then the old ballads were not written for the light reading of tired readers. To do the work in *their* way, they required to be brooded over, or had at least the aid of tune and of impassioned recitation. Stories which are to be told to children in the age of eagerness and excitability, or sung in banquet halls to assembled warriors, whose daily ideas and feelings supply a flood of comment ready to gush forth on the slightest hint of the poet, cannot fly too swift and straight to the mark. But Mr. Macaulay wrote to be only read, and by readers for whom it was necessary to do all.

These poems, therefore, are not the worse for being un-Roman in their form; and in their substance they are Roman to a degree which deserves great admiration. Mr. Macaulay's prose writings had not prepared us for the power which he has here manifested of identifying himself easily and completely with states of feeling and modes of life alien to modern experience. Nobody could have previously doubted that he possessed fancy, but he has here added to it the higher faculty of Imagination. We have not been able to detect, in the four poems, one idea or feeling which was not, or might not have been, Roman; while the externals of Roman life, and the feelings characteristic of Rome and of that particular age, are reproduced with great felicity, and without being made unduly predominant over the universal features of human nature and human life.

Independently, therefore, of their value as poems, these compositions are a real service rendered to historical literature: and the author has made this service greater by his prefaces, which will do more than the work of a hundred dissertations in rendering that true conception of early Roman history, the irrefragable establishment of which has made Niebuhr[‡] illustrious, familiar to the minds of general readers. This is no trifling matter even in relation to present interests, for there is no estimating the injury which the cause of popular institutions has suffered, and still suffers, from misrepresentations of the early condition of the Roman Plebs, and its noble struggles against its taskmasters. And the study of the manner in which the heroic legends of early Rome grew up as poetry and gradually

[*"The Ancient Ballad of Chevy-Chase," in Thomas Percy, *Reliques of Ancient English Poetry*, 3 vols. (London: Dodsley, 1765), Vol. I, pp. 1–17.]
[†Walter Scott, *Marmion* (Edinburgh: Constable, 1808).]
[‡In his *History of Rome*.]

became history, has important bearings on the general laws of historical evidence, and on the many things which, as philosophy advances, are more and more seen to be therewith connected. On this subject Mr. Macaulay has not only presented, in an agreeable form, the results of previous speculation, but has, though in an entirely unpretending manner, thrown additional light upon it by his own remarks: as where he shows, by incontestable instances, that a similar transformation of poetic fiction into history has taken place on various occasions in modern and sceptical times.

"History," says Hume, with the utmost gravity, "has preserved some instances of Edgar's amours, from which, as from a specimen, we may form a conjecture of the rest."[*] He then tells, very agreeably, the stories of Elfleda and Elfrida; two stories which have a most suspicious air of romance, and which, indeed, greatly resemble in their general character, some of the legends of early Rome. He cites, as his authority for these two tales, the chronicle of William of Malmesbury, who lived in the time of King Stephen. The great majority of readers suppose that the device by which Elfleda was substituted for her young mistress, the artifice by which Athelwold obtained the hand of Elfrida, the detection of that artifice, the hunting party, and the vengeance of the amorous king, are things about which there is no more doubt than about the execution of Anne Boleyn, or the slitting of Sir John Coventry's nose. But when we turn to William of Malmesbury, we find that Hume, in his eagerness to relate these pleasant fables, has overlooked one very important circumstance. William does, indeed, tell both the stories; but he gives us distinct notice that he does not warrant their truth, and that they rest on no better authority than that of ballads.*

Such is the way in which these two well-known tales have been handed down. They originally appeared in a poetical form. They found their way from ballads into an old chronicle. The ballads perished; the chronicle remained. A great historian, some centuries after the ballads had been altogether forgotten, consulted the chronicle. He was struck by the lively colouring of these ancient fictions: he transferred them to his pages; and thus we find inserted, as unquestionable facts, in a narrative which is likely to last as long as the English tongue, the inventions of some minstrel whose works were probably never committed to writing, whose name is buried in oblivion, and whose dialect has become obsolete. It must, then, be admitted to be possible, or, rather, highly probable, that the stories of Romulus and Remus, and of the Horatii and Curiatii, may have had a similar origin. (Pp. 31–3.)

And again, on the legend of the appearance of the Dioscuri actively aiding the Roman host in the battle of the Lake Regillus, and afterwards personally announcing at Rome that the republic had been victorious:

How the legend originated, cannot now be ascertained: but we may easily imagine several ways in which it might have originated; nor is it at all necessary to suppose, with Julius

[*David Hume, *History of England*, 8 vols. (Oxford: Talboys and Wheeler; London: Pickering, 1826), Vol. I, p. 108; the stories, with the references to William of Malmesbury, are on pp. 109–12.]

*" 'Infamias quas post dicam magis resperserunt cantilenæ.' Edgar appears to have been most mercilessly treated in the Anglo-Saxon ballads. He was the favourite of the monks; and the monks and minstrels were at deadly feud." [For Macaulay's quotation, see William of Malmesbury, *Gesta regum anglorum*, ed. Thomas Duffus Hardy, 2 vols. (London: English Historical Society, 1840), Vol. II, p. 236 (Bk. II, §148).]

Frontinus, that two young men were dressed up by the Dictator to personate the sons of Leda.[*] It is probable that Livy is correct when he says that the Roman general, in the hour of peril, vowed a temple to Castor.[†] If so, nothing could be more natural than that the multitude should ascribe the victory to the favour of the Twin Gods. When such was the prevailing sentiment, any man who chose to declare that, in the midst of the confusion and slaughter, he had seen two god-like forms on white horses scattering the Latines, would find ready credence. We know, indeed, that in modern times, a similar story actually found credence among a people much more civilised than the Romans of the fifth century before Christ. A chaplain of Cortes, writing about thirty years after the conquest of Mexico, in an age of printing-presses, libraries, universities, scholars, logicians, jurists, and statesmen, had the face to assert that, in one engagement against the Indians, St. James had appeared on a grey horse at the head of the Castilian adventurers.[‡] Many of those adventurers were living when this lie was printed. One of them, honest Bernal Diaz, wrote an account of the expedition. He had the evidence of his own senses against the chaplain's legend; but he seems to have distrusted even the evidence of his own senses. He says that he was in the battle, and that he saw a grey horse with a man on his back, but that the man was, to his thinking, Francesco de Morla, and not the ever-blessed apostle St. James. "Nevertheless," he adds, "it may be that the person on the grey horse was the glorious apostle St. James, and that I, sinner that I am, was unworthy to see him."[§] The Romans of the age of Cincinnatus were probably quite as credulous as the Spanish subjects of Charles the Fifth. It is therefore conceivable that the appearance of Castor and Pollux may have become an article of faith before the generation which had fought at Regillus had passed away. Nor could anything be more natural than that the poets of the next age should embellish this story, and make the celestial horsemen bear the tidings of the victory to Rome. (Pp. 85–7.)

There is no greater triumph of skill and taste in these poems than the manner in which Mr. Macaulay has treated this very incident. The supernatural is always a touchstone of an author's genius and tact, and it was here necessary that the supernatural should be pure ancient-Roman, and yet so presented as to act with overawing effect upon modern imaginations. We are almost reluctant to quote passages which have so often been quoted before, but we think that, viewed in this particular light, they deserve a more critical attention than has perhaps been paid to them.

> And Aulus the Dictator
> Stroked Auster's raven mane,
> With heed he looked unto the girths,
> With heed unto the rein;

[*Sextus Julius Frontinus, *The Stratagems*, in *The Stratagems, and The Aqueducts of Rome* (Latin and English), trans. Charles E. Bennett (London: Heinemann; New York: Putnam's Sons, 1925), p. 75 (Bk. I, Chap. xi, §8).]

[†*Livy* (Latin and English), 14 vols., trans. B. O. Foster, *et al.* (London: Heinemann; New York: Putnam's Sons; Cambridge, Mass.: Harvard University Press, 1919–59), Vol. I, p. 285 (Bk. II, Chap. xx).]

[‡Francisco Lopez de Gómara, *The Pleasant Historie of the Conquest of the Weast India*, trans. Thomas Nicholas (London: Bynnemann, 1578), pp. 44–5.]

[§Bernal Díaz del Castillo, *The True History of the Conquest of Mexico*, trans. Maurice Keatinge (London: Wright, 1800), p. 48.]

"Now bear me well, black Auster,
 Into yon thick array;
And thou and I will have revenge
 For thy good lord this day."

So spake he; and was buckling
 Tighter black Auster's band,
When he was aware of a princely pair
 That rode at his right hand.
So like they were, no mortal
 Might one from other know;
White as snow their armour was,
 Their steeds were white as snow:
Never on earthly anvil
 Did such rare armour gleam;
And never did such gallant steeds
 Drink of an earthly stream.

And all who saw them trembled,
 And pale grew every cheek;
And Aulus the Dictator
 Scarce gathered voice to speak.
"Say by what name men call you?
 What city is your home?
And wherefore ride you in such guise
 Before the ranks of Rome?"*

             *   *   *   *   *

So answered those strange horsemen,
 And each couched low his spear;
And forthwith all the ranks of Rome
 Were bold and of good cheer.
And on the thirty armies
 Came wonder and affright;
And Ardea wavered on the left
 And Cora on the right.
"Rome, to the charge!" cried Aulus;
 "The foe begins to yield!
Charge for the hearth of Vesta,
 Charge for the golden shield!"

Then the fierce trumpet-flourish,
 From earth to heaven arose,
The kites know well the long stern swell
 That bids the Roman close.

*We notice here what seems to us the single blemish in this fine poem. The twin-gods should not have made a speech in reply to Aulus. Their divinity should have been felt, without being told. The Homeric gods mixed openly as gods, in the battles as in the banquets of men; but the type of the Etrusco-Roman supernatural legend (also not without its Greek prototype in the Arcadian Pan and elsewhere) was the voice which, in the dead of the night following the conflict in which the first Brutus was slain, announced that one fewer had fallen of the Romans than of the enemy. [See *Livy*, Vol. I, p. 239 (Bk. II, Chap. vii).]

Then the good sword of Aulus
   Was lifted up to slay:
Then, like a crag down Apennine,
   Rushed Auster through the fray:
But under those strange horsemen
   Still thicker lay the slain;
And after those strange horses
   Black Auster toiled in vain.
Behind them Rome's long battle
   Came rolling on the foe,
Ensigns dancing wild above,
   Blades all in line below.
So comes the Po in flood-time
   Upon the Celtic plain,
So comes the squall, blacker than night,
   Upon the Adrian main.

       *   *   *   *   *

Sempronius Atratinus
   Sate in the eastern gate;
Beside him were three fathers,
   Each in his chair of state:
Fabius, whose nine stout grandsons
   That day were in the field,
And Manlius, eldest of the twelve
   Who keep the golden shield;
And Sergius, the high pontiff,
   For wisdom far renown'd;
In all Etruria's colleges
   Was no such pontiff found.
And all around the portal,
   And high above the wall,
Stood a great throng of people,
   But sad and silent all;
Young lads and stooping elders,
   That might not bear the mail,
Matrons with lips that quivered,
   And maids with faces pale.
Since the first gleam of daylight
   Sempronius had not ceased
To listen for the rushing
   Of horse-hoofs from the east.
The mist of eve was rising,
   The sun was hastening down,
When he was aware of a princely pair
   Fast pricking towards the town.
So like they were, man never
   Saw twins so like before;
Red with gore their armour was,
   Their steeds were red with gore.

"Hail to the great asylum!
     Hail to the hill tops seven!
Hail to the fire that burns for aye,
     And the shield that fell from heaven!
This day, by Lake Regillus,
     Under the Porcian height,
All in the lands of Tusculum
     Was fought a glorious fight.
To-morrow your Dictator
     Shall bring in triumph home
The spoils of thirty cities,
     To deck the shrines of Rome!"

Then burst from that great concourse
     A shout that shook the towers,
And some ran north, and some ran south,
     Crying, "The day is ours!"
But on rode those strange horsemen,
     With slow and lordly pace,
And none who saw their bearing
     Durst ask their name or race.
On rode they to the Forum,
     While laurel boughs and flowers,
From house-tops and from windows,
     Fell on their crests in showers.
When they drew nigh to Vesta
     They vaulted down amain,
And washed their horses in the well
     That springs by Vesta's fane;
And straight again they mounted,
     And rode to Vesta's door;
Then, like a blast, away they passed,
     And no man saw them more.[*]

Mr. Macaulay shows himself so well acquainted with the best modern views of Roman history, that we presume it is purposely, and from conviction, that he adheres to Livy's story of the five years' anarchy which preceded the passing of the Licinian laws;[†] although Niebuhr and Arnold have, as it seems to us, shown sufficient reason to believe that it was an inference, grounded on the absence of the names of consuls or military tribunes from the Fasti during an apparent interval of five years, produced solely by an error of chronology.[‡]

We are more disposed to break a lance with our author on the general merits of Roman literature, which, by a heresy not new with him, he sacrifices, in what

[*"The Battle of Lake Regillus," *Lays*, pp. 121–9.]
[†*Livy*, Vol. III, pp. 315–19 (Bk. VI, Chap. xxxv); Macaulay, *Lays*, pp. 39–41.]
[‡Niebuhr, *History of Rome*, Vol. II, pp. 557–9, and Vol. III, p. 24n; and Thomas Arnold, *History of Rome*, 3 vols. (London: Fellowes; Oxford: Parker; Cambridge: Deighton, 1838–43), Vol. II, p. 40n.]

appears to us a most unfair degree, on the score of its inferior originality, to the Grecian. It is true the Romans had no Æschylus nor Sophocles, and but a second-hand Homer, though this last was not only the most finished but even the most original of imitators. But where was the Greek model of the noble poem of Lucretius?[*] What, except the mere idea, did the *Georgics*[†] borrow from Hesiod? and who ever thinks of comparing the two poems? Where, in Homer or in Euripides, will be found the original of the tender and pathetic passages in the *Æneid*, especially the exquisitely-told story of Dido? There is no extraordinary merit in the *Carmen Sæculare* as we have it, the only production of Horace which challenges comparison with Pindar;[‡] although we are not among those who deem Pindar one of the brightest stars in the Greek heaven. But from whom are the greater part of Horace's *Carmina*[§] borrowed, (they should never be termed Odes), any more than those of Burns or Bérenger, the analogous authors in modern times? and by what Greek minor poems are they surpassed? We say nothing of Catullus, whom some competent judges prefer to Horace. Does the lyric, then, or even the epic poetry of the Romans, deserve no better title than that of "a hot-house plant, which, in return for assiduous and skilful culture, yielded only scanty and sickly fruits?"[¶] The complete originality and eminent merit of their satiric poetry, Mr. Macaulay himself acknowledges. As for prose, we give up Cicero as compared with Demosthenes, but with no one else; and is Livy less original, or less admirable, than Herodotus? Tacitus may have imitated, even to affectation, the condensation of Thucydides, as Milton imitated the Greek and Hebrew poets; but was not the mind of the one as essentially original as that of the other? Is the Roman less an unapproachable master, in his peculiar line, that of sentimental history, than the Grecian in his? and what Greek historian has written anything similar or comparable to the sublime peroration of the *Life of Agricola*?[||] The Latin genius lay not in speculation, and the Romans did undoubtedly borrow all their philosophical principles from the Greeks. Their originality *there*, as is well said by a remarkable writer in the most remarkable of his works,* consisted in taking those principles *au sérieux*. They *did* what the others talked about. Zeno, indeed, was not a Roman; but Pætus Thrasea and Marcus Antoninus were.

[*I.e., *De rerum natura*.]
[†Virgil, *Georgics*, in *Virgil*, Vol. I, pp. 80–236.]
[‡Horace, *Carmen saeculare*, in *The Odes and Epodes* (Latin and English), trans. C. E. Bennett (London: Heinemann; New York: Macmillan, 1914), pp. 350–6; Pindar, *Carmina* (Glasgow: Foulis, 1744).]
[§In *The Odes and Epodes*, pp. 2–346.]
[¶Macaulay, *Lays*, p. 143.]
[||In Tacitus, *Dialogus, Agricola, Germania* (Latin and English), trans. William Peterson (London: Heinemann; New York: Macmillan, 1914), pp. 168–252.]
*Mr. Maurice, in the essay on the history of moral speculation and culture, which forms the article "Moral and Metaphysical Philosophy" in the *Encyclopædia Metropolitana*. [See Vol. II, pp. 626–9.]

LETTER TO THE EDITOR OF THE EDINBURGH REVIEW, ON JAMES MILL

1844

EDITORS' NOTE

Edinburgh Review, LXXIX (Jan., 1844), 267–71. Headed: "Letter from John S. Mill, Esq., to the Editor," with an introductory paragraph (given as a footnote to the title in the present text) by the editor, Macvey Napier. Running title: "Letter to the Editor." Signed: "J. S. Mill." Not republished. Identified in Mill's bibliography as "A Letter to the Editor in vindication of my father, in the same number of the same review"—i.e., as his "Michelet's History of France" (MacMinn, p. 56). No copy in Somerville College.

For comment, see the Introduction, p. xlii above.

Letter to the Editor of the Edinburgh Review, on James Mill[*]

sir—In an Article on Dr. Bowring's "Life of Bentham," published in the last Number of the *Edinburgh Review*,[†] statements are made, on the authority of that work, tending to give a most false impression of the character of one who, by his writings and personal influence, has done more for philosophy and good government than almost any man of his generation, and who has peculiar claims upon the justice of the *Edinburgh Review*, to which he was for many years an important contributor—I mean the late Mr. James Mill, my father.

That those whose lives are devoted to the service of mankind should meet with inadequate appreciation from their contemporaries can surprise no one; but when their motives and moral character are misrepresented, not only justice, but the public interest requires that the misrepresentation should be corrected; and I trust you will not refuse the necessary opportunity to the person on whom that duty is, in the present case, peculiarly incumbent.

The Reviewer, quoting from the "Memoirs," says, "Bentham said of Mill, that his willingness to do good to others depended too much on his power of making the good done to them subservient to good done to himself. His creed of politics results less from love for the many than from hatred of the few. It is too much under the influence of social and dissocial affection."[‡]

What is here promulgated as Bentham's deliberate judgment, was never, I will venture to affirm, believed by any human being who had the smallest knowledge of Mr. Mill.

[*Though it is not the practice to insert in this Journal any controversial statements respecting the Articles contained in it, the Editor's great respect for the memory of the Father defended in the following Letter, and for the Son who writes it, induces him to comply with that claim "for justice" which it urges, by giving it all the publicity which its appearance here can insure. He leaves all comment or observation upon its contents to others; feeling, that if there is any case in which, independently of any opinion as to the justness of the complaint, such a claim ought to be complied with, it must be that where a son craves the opportunity of vindicating, in the same work where he thinks it was injured, the character of a Father of whose name and services to the cause of liberal knowledge he is justly proud.]

[†William Empson, "Jeremy Bentham," *Edinburgh Review*, LXXVIII (Oct., 1843), 460–516, reviewing John Bowring, "Memoirs of Bentham," Parts 19, 20, 21 (later Vols. X and XI) of Bentham's *Works* (Edinburgh: Tait, 1842 [Parts], 1843 [Vols.]).]

[‡Empson, p. 461n, quoting Bowring, "Memoirs," *Works of Bentham*, Vol. X, p. 450.]

I know not how a biographer is to be justified in giving publicity and permanence to every idle word which may have been said to the prejudice of others, under some passing impression or momentary irritation. It would, besides, be easy to show, that the reports of Bentham's conversations contained in the Biography, abound in the inaccuracies which are to be expected when things carelessly stated by one person, are afterwards noted down from memory by another. But whatever Bentham may really have said, when a statement so injurious to another is made on his authority, justice to that other imposes the necessity of declaring what the "Memoirs" amply confirm, that among Mr. Bentham's eminent intellectual endowments, capacity for judging of character was not one. The manner of his intercourse with others was not favourable to his acquiring a real knowledge of them; and his warmest friends and admirers often lamented that his opinion of men depended less on their merits than on accidental circumstances, and on the state of his personal relations with them at the time. On no other principle can I account for his expressing any opinion of Mr. Mill bearing the complexion of that quoted in the Article.

It imputes to Mr. Mill, as the source of his democratic opinions, the vulgarest motives of an unprincipled demagogue; namely, selfish ambition, and a malignant hatred of the ruling classes. Now, there was perhaps no one man among Mr. Mill's contemporaries, holding similar opinions to his, who stood more manifestly clear from even the suspicion of these motives.

He could in no way hope for "good to himself" from the opinions he professed. In many respects they stood in the way of his personal interest. They deprived his writings of the countenance of either of the great parties in the state, in times when that countenance was much more important than it now is, and when he might have obtained it as easily as many others did, who had not a tithe of his talents. Even had his opinions become predominant, which he never expected would be the case during his life, he would, as he well knew, have reaped no personal benefit from them; and assuredly, the time when he embraced democratic doctrines, was a time when no person in his senses could have entertained the smallest hope of gaining any thing by their profession.

As for "hatred of the few," the phrase seems introduced solely to round an antithesis. There never was a man more free from any feelings of hatred. His hostility was to institutions and principles, not to persons. It was his invariable doctrine that the ruling individuals were not intentionally bad, nor in any way worse than other men. Towards some of them he entertained strong feelings of personal friendship. A certain asperity, no doubt, appears occasionally in his controversial writings; but it proceeded from no private motives:—the individuals against whom it showed itself never injured him, never wounded his vanity, or interfered with his interests; his path and theirs never crossed. It has been shown in the highly honourable acknowledgment recently made by Mr. Macaulay, how far Mr. Mill was from retaining any grudge, even when he *had* been personally attacked, and with a severity which the assailant himself cannot now approve.[*] Mr. Mill never wrote severe things of any one but from honest conviction, and in the exercise, as he believed, of a duty; and the fault, if fault it be, is one which we of this age may view with leniency, when we see how often the absence of it has no better source than incapacity of earnest feeling on any subject not personal.

The Reviewer, still following the "Memoirs," enters into some points of private history, of so personal a nature, and so little interesting to the public, that it is unpleasant to feel called upon to speak of them; but since the impression conveyed is, that Mr. Mill received obligations from Bentham, such as one man rarely receives from another, and that for these obligations he made but an ungrateful return, it is necessary to show how incorrectly the facts are stated, and how false a colouring is put upon such of them as are true.

The statements in the "Memoirs" are, that Bentham "found Mill in great distress, about to emigrate to Caen; that he put him into a house, and took him and his family to live with him for the half of every year, for ten years together."[†]

At the time when Bentham is said to have "*found* Mill about to emigrate," they had already been intimate for many years, as the dates prove; since the "emigration" spoken of could not have been projected until after the Continent was open. Like many others, Mr. Mill had thoughts of removing to a country where a small income would go further in supporting and educating a family; but a person is not usually said to be "in great distress" who never in his life was in debt, and whose income, whatever it might be, always covered his expenses.

Secondly, that Bentham "put him into a house." If this means that he occupied any house of Bentham's, free of rent, the assertion is contrary to fact. He paid to Mr. Bentham between £50 and £60 a-year rent, which was as high a rent as he had been accustomed to pay.

Thirdly, that Mr. Mill and his family lived with Mr. Bentham for half of ten years. They did so for half of *four* years, at Ford Abbey; and they passed small portions of several previous summers with him at Barrow Green. His last visit to Barrow Green, I know, was of not more than a month's duration, and the previous ones all together, did not, as I am informed, (for my own memory does not reach so far back,) extend to more than six months, or seven at most. Bentham himself, in a letter published in the "Life," says, the half of *five* years:[‡] which is not far from the mark.

The pecuniary benefit, therefore, which Mr. Mill derived from his intimacy with

---

[*See Macaulay, "Preface," *Critical and Historical Essays*, Vol. I, p. viii.]
[†Empson, p. 467n, based on Bowring, "Memoirs," *Works of Bentham*, Vol. X, p. 483.]
[‡Mill may be referring to the passage in "Memoirs," p. 480, where Bentham mentions his renting Ford Abbey for "nearly five years" (cf. *ibid.*, p. 25), though, if so, Mill's interpretation is strained. Empson's comment is based on Bentham's reported remark that James Mill and his family "lived with [him] a half of every year, from 1808 to 1817 inclusive" (*ibid.*, p. 483).]

Bentham consisted in this, that he and his family lived with him as his guests, while he was in the country, periods amounting in all to about two years and a half. I have no reason to think that this hospitality was either given, or accepted, as pecuniary assistance; and I will add, that the obligation was not exclusively on one side. Bentham was not then, as he was afterwards, surrounded by persons who courted his society, and were ever ready to volunteer their services; and to a man of his secluded habits, it was no little advantage to have near him such a man as Mr. Mill, to whose advice and aid he habitually had recourse in all business transactions with the outward world, of a troublesome or irksome nature. Such as the connexion was, that it was not of Mr. Mill's seeking, is shown by a remarkable letter from him to Mr. Bentham, which is to be found in the "Life," and which was written, as its date proves, during the first visit to Ford Abbey.[*]

Lastly, the Reviewer, on his own authority, asserts, that Mr. Mill became estranged from Bentham, and, in after years, "so far withdrew his allegiance from the dead lion as to deny that he had ever called him master."[†] There was, during the last few years of Bentham's life, less frequency and cordiality of intercourse than in former years, chiefly because Bentham had acquired newer, and to him, more agreeable intimacies; but Mr. Mill's feeling never altered towards him, nor did he ever fail, publicly or privately, in giving due honour to Bentham's name, and acknowledgment of the intellectual debt he owed to him. The "allegiance" which he disclaimed was only that which no man, who thinks for himself, will own to another. He was no otherwise a disciple of Bentham, than of Hobbes, Hartley, or Ricardo.

These are small matters in themselves—quite unworthy to be brought before the public; but if the things are trivial, the inferences drawn from them are not so, and nothing is small which involves injustice to the memory, and a total misconception of the character, of an eminent man. Reluctant, therefore, as I am so to occupy your space; yet as the extensive circulation of the *Edinburgh Review* has been given to these misstatements, I do not feel that I am unreasonable in soliciting a place, in the next Number, for this contradiction of them.

I am, Sir, your obedient servant,

J. S. MILL.

[*See James Mill to Jeremy Bentham, 19 Sept., 1814, *ibid.*, pp. 481–2.]
[†Empson, p. 516.]

APPENDICES

Appendix A

Juvenilia

OF MILL'S CHILDHOOD COMPOSITIONS (see App. C below) only the opening pages of his first "History of Rome" and his "Ode to Diana" have survived. Both are in BL Add. MS 33230, c.1 and c.2, presented by Mill's sister Harriet on 29 April, 1887.

The "History" is written on sheets cut, folded, and sewn to make a little booklet of ten leaves: the title and name (with the information that the author was $6\frac{1}{2}$ years old when he wrote—or began?—it) are on 1r; the text is recto, with the facing versos used for notes and the lists of consuls in office during the events described in the latter part of the text (a common device in Roman histories of the period). In the text below, the notes are given as footnotes and the lists as marginal notes. As the text breaks off in·mid-sentence, and the list of consuls on 10v implies a facing text, it may be inferred that the "History" continued into another booklet, and probably into more than one. The paper is watermarked "G Pike" but there is no date on any of these sheets. The hand is not that of the young Mill; Alexander Bain, who saw this version of the "History" before it was given to the British Museum, says "a lady friend of the family copied and preserved it" (*John Stuart Mill* [London: Longmans, Green, 1882], p. 3).

In editing this fragment, the great temptation (one that some will think we should have succumbed to) was to print a diplomatic text, preserving all the idiosyncrasies of the original. But several problems militate against this single happy solution: first, since the manuscript is not in Mill's hand, we would be preserving someone else's version, as we are not able to determine which of the many errors of various kinds are Mill's responsibility; second, we do not know exactly on which source he was drawing for particular bits of information, so we cannot tell when an "error" is in his source or is the result of carelessness or failure of comprehension on his part; third, there are different renderings (both Greek and Latin) of various proper names, so there is no one contemporary correct form; fourth, while with juvenilia of this kind it is important to preserve the flavour of the original, one should not leave the reader puzzled and unable to solve small mysteries.

Our attempt to balance these considerations has resulted in the following decisions:

1. The text follows the manuscript in substantives and accidentals except (a) when the reading of a proper name is uncertain, in which case an accepted version is used, (b) when different erroneous versions of a proper name occur, in which case the version that dominates in the "History" is used, even though it is mistaken, (c) in the few places where aberrant accidentals might impede the reader's understanding, in which case normal forms are used, and (d) where there is a manifest though minor error in syntax, likely to be the copyist's responsibility, in which case a correction is made. A list of these corrections is given at the end. Also listed are places where, though no correction has been made, the reader may be given pause (for example, "Aborian" [542.3 (of the text)], which must be wrong, is not altered, but in this list "Aborigian [Aboriginal]" is suggested as the intended word).

2. The marginal list of Consuls, like the text relating specifically to the Consuls and their succession, is left unamended, except that—as in (a) and (b) above—names are adjusted to the dominant (even if erroneous) form. There are misidentifications, misorderings, and gaps, but to have altered and corrected these would have involved a major distortion of the manuscript's text; the reader interested in comparing this version with the modern one should consult T. Robert S. Broughton, *The Magistrates of the Roman Republic*, Vol. I (New York: American Philological Association, 1951).

3. The references in the manuscript's notes are rudimentary, and so have been expanded and the accidentals altered to make comprehension easier. The individual changes are not listed, but are summarized. Some notes have been expanded and some added by the editors; square brackets signal these changes.

4. As elsewhere in this volume, we have changed "&" to "and" and have lowered superscripts to the line. In the manuscript there are inked lines drawn across the page to separate the "chapters"; these have been omitted here. Normal footnote indicators, in sequence, have replaced the superscript "(a)" that appears in each case in the manuscript.

The History of Rome
by
John Stuart Mill
aged 6½ yrs

First Alban Government
Roman Conquest in Italy

We know not well any part, says Dionysius of Halicarnassus, of the History of Rome till the Sicilian invasion.[*] Before that time, the country had not been visited by any foreign invader. After the expulsion of the Sicilians, Aborian Kings reigned for several years: but in the time of Latinus, Aneas, son of Venus and Anchises came to Italy, and established a kingdom there called Albania. He then succeeded Latinus in the government, and engaged in the wars of Italy. The Rutuli, a people living near the sea, and extending along the Numicus up to Lavinium opposed him. However Turnus their King was defeated and killed by Aneas. Aneas was killed soon after this. The war continued to be carried on chiefly against the Rutuli, to the time of Romulus, the first king of Rome. By him it was, that Rome was built.

Latin Government Regal State

Romulus, then conquered the Lavinienses, and defeated the Veians. He established a Senate. The Romans seized the Sabine women and on account of this the

---

[*The reference would appear to be to Διονυσίου ‘Αλικαρνασέως τὰ εὑρισκόμενα, ἱστορικά τε καὶ ῥητορικά, συγγράμματα (Greek and Latin), 2 vols. (Frankfurt: Weschel Heirs, 1586), which (as Mill says at p. 544n below) is in folio. In this edition (as in others of similar format) *The Roman Antiquities* occupies Vol. I. Specifically indicated is Vol. I, p. 7 (I, 9, 1–2), where, however, the "Sicels" are identified as a native race.]

Sabines made war with them. *Romulus took Canina, Crustiminium, and Antemna.

He also took Cures and died.

Numa Pompilius chosen King

Numa Pompilius a Sabine was chosen king in the room of Romulus. He thoroughly restored his People to the exercise of peace. He died however soon.

Taking of Alba, Death of Hostilius

Tullus Hostilius, a very warlike prince, succeeded him. He took the cities of Alba, Fidæna and died. Ancus Marcius succeeded him. He took Politorium, Tellena and Ficcana, Latin cities[†] and also Fidæna and Velitræ and died.

Tarquinius Evergetes chosen King
Origin of Collatinus and death of the King

Tarquinius Priscus, his successor, took Apiolæ, Crustiminium and Collatia. He gave to his brother Arynx the government of Collatia, with the name of Collatinus. Collatinus defeated the Tuscans at Veii and Cera. Tarquin himself defeated them near Eratum, a city of Sabinia. He died and was succeeded by Servius Tullius.

This Prince defeated the Sabines and Tuscans and died.

Tarquinius Superbus, his Successor took Suessa, a city of the Volsci. He finally reduced the Sabines.

Government of Rome after the deposition of Kings

Tarquin at the time was banished from Rome, at the instigation of one Junius Brutus.

A new form of government was appointed, a consular[‡] government. The first Consuls were L. Junius Brutus, and L. Tarquinius Collatinus, whom I have formerly mentioned as governor of Collatia, in the reign of the elder Tarquin. Collatinus had been also a

Consuls
L. Junius Brutus
L. Tarquinius
Collatinus

*Hooke's *History of Rome*, *vide* remarks in the History of the Seven Roman Kings on the reign of Romulus, p. xxxi. That same Author also says that it was he who called the rich, Patricians, the poor, Plebeians. *Ibid.*, Regal state of Rome in full account of the reign of Romulus. [Presumably the first reference is to the "Preface," which appeared in the 2nd and subsequent editions of Hooke; however the information and the page reference do not match any edition examined. Bk. I, entitled "The Regal State of Rome," covers the reigns of the seven Kings of Rome. The second reference is to Chap. ii ("Romulus"), §4.]

†Hooke, *ut supra*, Ancus Marcius, p. 187, in regal state of Rome. [The reference is to Bk. I, Chap. v ("Ancus Marcius"), §1.]

‡Consuls were only annual magistrates.

principal instrument for the banishment of Tarquin. There existed too a Valerius Poplicola. This Poplicola had been another instrument for the banishment of Tarquin.

Behaviour of Collatinus and Poplicola

A conspiracy, formed in favor of Tarquin, was quelled. It had been carried on by near relations of the Consuls. Collatinus retired from Rome to Lavinium, where he lived and died in peace. *Poplicola was appointed Consul in his stead. Brutus (though the Romans gained the victory) was slain in a battle against Tarquin. Sp. Lucretius was appointed Colleague of Poplicola.

Tuscan war

P. Valerius
Poplicola
M. Horatius
Pulvillus

P. Valerius
Poplicola
Sp. Largius
Rufus

He died in a few days, T. Lucretius Tricipitinus was appointed and Poplicola resigned. It was not however long before he (Poplicola) was elected 2nd time Consul in conjunction with M. Horatius Pulvillus. Tarquin in conjunction with Porsenna, King of Tuscany, besieged Rome, where Poplicola (for no example has been given us of his 2d Consulship) was now Consul the 3rd time, in conjunction with Sp. Largius Rufus, successor of Pulvillus.[†] He laid close siege to the city, and nothing

---

*Plutarch (vide p. 273, 301) calls this man Publicola. But Hooke (vide p. 255) and Dionysius Halicarnassus (Chronology of the Consuls, pp. 766–7) call him Poplicola. It is always spelt Ποπλικολας (Poplicola) in Greek not Πυβλικολας (Publicola). Therefore that is the reason of its being Poplicola in Dionysius not Publicola, as in Plutarch. Livy also calls him Poplicola. I know not the reason of its being Poplicola in Hooke and Livy. It is also spelt Ποπλιος (Poplius) in Greek, not Πυβλιος (Publius). It must doubtless be a mistake in Langhorne's Plutarch. [This learned footnote is not without its difficulties. In *Plutarch's Lives*, trans. John and William Langhorne, 6 vols. (London: Dilly, 1770). "Publicola" is indeed used, but the references do not match this or any other edition examined (in this, the 1st edition, the relevant passages are Vol. I, pp. 243–73, and 274–9). Once again the Hooke reference does not correspond to any edition examined, but is presumably to Bk. II, Chap. i, §6, where the conferring of the name is explained; in §5 of that chapter, he is referred to as "Publius." The reference to the "Chronology of the Consuls" in the edition of Dionysius cited above is correct. The Livy reference is probably to Bk. II, Chap. viii, §2; however (and we do not know what edition is in the mind of the young Mill, who is not thought to have yet begun to learn Latin), various versions of the name appear in different editions, including "Publicola" and "Poblicola." Of course no "mistake" is involved, but merely different versions of the actual and honorific names.]

†Dionysius of Halicarnassus, Chronology, *ut supra*, p. 767. Dionysius's book is written one Volume in folio. [The reference is correct.]

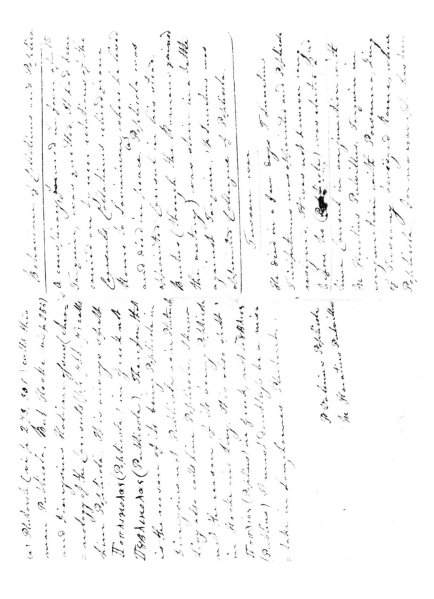

Folio 6r of the "History of Rome" MS
British Library

but the bravery of Mucius, a Youth of the Roman army made him agree to a peace.*

Sabine war. Disorder of the government

M. Valerius Poplicola brother of Publius Poplicola and P. Posthumias Tubertas, now Consuls twice defeated the Sabines. Publius Poplicola defeated the Sabines near Fidæna and died. P. Posthumias Tubertas, and Agrippa Menenius Lanatus were chosen Consuls.

M. Valerius Poplicola
P. Posthumias Tubertas
P. Posthumias Tubertas
Agrippa Menenius Lanatus

Latin War

The Consuls defeated the Sabines at Eratum. Sp. Cassius Vicelinus and Opiter Tricostus Virginius were elected consuls in their room. Cassius defeated the Sabines a second time. Virginius took Camerium. Posthumus Cominius and T. Largius Flaccus were made Consuls. They performed no important action. Next Servius Sulpicius Camerinus and Man. Tullius Longus were made Consuls. Manius infested Fidæna. The siege of that city continued through the following Consulship of P. Veturius Geminus and T. Abutius Elva. But at length it was taken in the next, that of T. Largius Flaccus and Q. Clœlius Siculus. Largius abdicated the Consulship, and was made Dictator. †A. Sempronius Atratinus and M. Minucius Augurinus were chosen Consuls. They performed no memorable action. A. Posthumius and T. Virginius succeeded them. The former was appointed Dictator. He defeated the Latins. Tarquin died, and all the rest of his family with him.

Sp. Cassius Vicelinus
Opiter Tricostus Virginius

Posthumius Cominius
T. Largius Flaccus
Serv. Sulp. Cam.
Man. Tull. Long.

P. Vetur. Gemin.
T. Abutius Elva

T. Larg. Flaccus
Q. Clœl. Siculus

A. Semp. Atrat.
M. Min. Augu.

A. Posthumius
T. Virginius

Aquian and Volscian wars

Ap. Claudius Sabinus and P. Servilius Priscus were appointed Consuls. Servilius twice defeated the

Ap. Claudius Sabinus
P. Servilius Priscus

---

*In this case it seems that Q. Mucius Cordus had been the ancestor of this Mucius, who himself was the 1st of his family who ever obtained the Surname of Scævola. It seems also that Sp. Largius and T. Herminius were Consuls before Valerius and Posthumias.

†Aulus Sem. Atratinus was descended from a Plebeian family, called the Sempronii. Of this family was the Consul Albinus who lived in the time of Jugurtha the Numidian.

A. Verginius
Montanus
T. Vetasius Gemini

Posthumius
Cominius
Sp. Cassius
Vessilinus

T. Geganius
P. Minucius

A. Sempronius
Atrat. II
M. Minucius
Augur. II

Q. Sulpicius
Camer. II
Sp. Largius
Flaccus III

C. Julius Tullus
P. Pinarius Rufus

Sp. Nautius
Sext. Furius

C. Aquilius Tuscus
T. Sicinnius
Sabinus

Sp. Cassius III
Pr. Virginius

Q. Fab. Vibulanus
Serv. Corn.

Cæso Fabius
L. Æmil. Mamer.

M. Fabius Vibul.
L. Valerius

C. Julius Tullus
Q. Fabius Vibul. II

Sp. Furius Med.
Cæso Fabius

M. Fab. Vibul. II
Cn. Man. Cincin.

Volsci. That people gave him 300 hostages. He took Suessa. Appius beheaded the hostages. Servilius defeated the Aurunci. Virginius Montanus and T. Vetasius Gemini were elected Consuls.* They performed no important action. Posthumias Cominius and Spurias Cassius were elected Consuls.† Cominius took Longula, Polusca and Corioli. T. Geganius and P. Minucius were elected Consuls. L. Junius Brutus and P. Sicinnius Bellutus were made Ædiles. A. Sempronius Atratinus and M. Minucius Augurinus were elected Consuls. Caius Marcius Coriolanus was banished from Rome. No remarkable action was performed in the next Consulship, that of Q. Sulpicius Camerinus and Sp. Largius Flaccus, nor in that of C. Julius and P. Pinarius Rufus. But in the next of Sp. Nautius and Sext. Furius, Coriolanus besieged Rome, at the head of a Volscian army. Three deputations were sent to him without success. A 4th moved him from Rome. He returned, and, was soon after stoned by the Volsci. Two Victories were gained over the Volsci. C. Aquilius Tuscus and T. Sicinnius Sabinus were made Consuls. Aquilius defeated the Hernici and Sicinnius the Volsci. Veian war did not succeed. Sp. Cassius and Proculus Virginius

---

*Vide Hooke, *ut supra*, p. 327. [The reference, which again does not match the pages of any edition examined, is to Bk. II, Chap. vi. §1.]

†Dionysius, *ut supra*, *ibid*. [The reference is correct.]

Alterations in the text (the original version is given first, with the altered one in square brackets).

542.1 (of text)   or Rome [of Rome]
542.9   cheifly [chiefly]
542.13   Lavneiaii [Lavinienses] [*the reading is quite uncertain, but certainly wrong—cf.* Lavinium *correctly given above*]
543.3   died, [died.]
543.9   Fidæne [Fidæna] [*as in following line, and* 545.7; 545.17 *may read* Fidænæ, *but should be* Fidenæ]
543.9   Politorium [Politorium,]
543.10   Ficcana [Ficcana,]
543.13   Apiolæ [Apiolæ,]
543.13   Crastiminium [Crustiminium] [*to correspond to* 543.1; *should read* Crustumerium *(or* Crustumium *or* Crustumesia*)—but certainly does not anywhere*]
543.18, 546.19   Volci [Volsci] [*as elsewhere and correct*]
545.3   war disorder [war. Disorder]
545.7   Tubertus [Tubertas] [*see* 545.5, list.3–6, n.3 *in "Not altered" list*]
545 list.5–8   [*moved slightly up page to proper place*]
545.13   to Camerium [took Camerium] [*he did*]
545.21, and list.22   Clodius [Clœlius] [*copyist's error?*]
546 list.9   Minucias [Minucius]
546 list.18   Junius [Julius] [*as in text and* 546 list.33; *but see "Not altered" list for* ibid.]

Alterations in the footnotes (the notes being hurried and rudimentary, the punctuation has been silently altered; also italics have been added to titles and foreign words, and some short forms have been expanded ["Hist" becomes "*History*"; "vid" and "vi" become "*vide*"; "Atrat" becomes "Atratinus"; and "Dionys Halic" becomes "Dionysius of Halicarnassus"]).

543n.1   on the [in the] [*for sense*]
543n.8, 544n.19   at [*ut*]
544n.2   chronology [Chronology]
544n.2   (pp [pp] [*i.e., there was an extra parenthesis*]
544n.2   calls [call]
545n.1   Cordun [Cordus]
545n.4   Sempronii of [Sempronii. Of]

Not altered (possible corrections and explanations are given in square brackets after the reading in the text).

542.2,3 (of text)   Sicilians [*the invasion was by the Siculi,* Σικελοι, *or Sicels*]
542.3   Aborian [*intended* Aborigian?*/* Aboriginal?; *the word is underlined in pencil in the MS, but no correction is offered*]
542.4, 8, 9   Aneas [Aeneas]
542.5   kingdom . . . Albania [city . . . Alba]
542.7   Numicus [*in MS the word is underlined in pencil and* "i" *interlined; Livy gives* Numicus; *Dionysius,* Numicius]
543.1   Crustiminium [Crustumerium? *(see "Altered" list,* 543.13*)*]
543.10   Ficcana [Ficana; *the* "i" *could also be an* "e"]
543.15   Cera [Caere]
543.16, 545.10   Eratum [Eretum]
545.5, list.3–6, n.3   Posthumias Tubertas [Posthum(i)us Tubertus]
545.11, list.10   Vicelinus [Viscellinus; Vecellinus *in Dionysius*]
545 list.13   Posthumius [Posthumus *in text, but a variant*]
545 list.20   Elva [Helva]
545.14   Flaccus [Flavus; *there is what may be an intended correction here, in ink; elsewhere the reading is unmistakably* Flaccus]
545.29   *Aquian [Aequian]*

546.3, list.3   Vetasius [Vetusius *in Livy;* Veturius *in Hooke and Dionysius*]

546.5   Posthumias Cominius [Posthumius Cominius]

546.8–9   P. Sicinnius [L. Sicinnius]

546 list.18, 33   Tullus [Iulus; *but see "Altered" list,* ibid.]

546.21, list.23   Sicinnius [Sicinius *in Hooke and Livy;* Siccius *in Dionysius*]

546 list.35   Med. [*should be* Fusus. *There was a Sp. Furius Medullinus Fusus as Quaestor in the 34th Consulship; probably Mill made a slip.*]

The "Ode to Diana," written recto and verso on a single sheet (watermarked "R Lomas" but lacking a date), is probably in Mill's hand, and likely was written slightly later than the "History" (see App. C, nos. 2 and 6). The manuscript, a fair copy, presents no textual problems, except that wear and folding make the reading of stanza 5, line 1 ("Th'unhappy") and line 4 ("sweet") just less than certain.

Ode to Diana

1

Sol's virgin sister, young and fair,
Let me to tell thy actions dare,
If I may thus presume;
And lay before the sight of all,
Thy hapless nymph Calisto's fall,
And young Actæon's doom.

2

Over the mountains when you go,
The mountains, crown'd with trackless snow,
Your virgin looks are sweet:
You bound along the highest mounts,
O'er meadows, groves, and crystal founts,
With safe and wary feet.

3

The wildest beasts in ev'ry wood,
To which all others serve as food,
You strike, and quickly kill:
All o'er the groves and waters wide,
In ev'ry place, on ev'ry side,
And by each murm'ring rill.

4

Thy quiver, and thy golden bow,
With which thou shootest hart or roe,
Are certain signs of thee:
And by thy face, (divinely fair,)
By thy loose robe, and flowing hair,
Well who thou art we see.

5

Th'unhappy maid, Calisto fair,
Adorn'd with splendid golden hair,
Far from your woods you drove:
Because th'Arcadian virgin sweet,
On issuing from thy retreat,
Had chanc'd to meet with Jove!

6

The young Actæon didst thou slay,
(So do thy vot'ries youthful say)
For looking upon thee,
When bathing in the crystal stream,
Hid from gay Phœbus' sunny beam,
Under a shady tree.

Adieu, sweet Phœbus' sister fair,
Thou goddess, deck'd with beauties rare.

Appendix B

Mill's Early Reading, 1809–22

MILL's "unusual and remarkable" education, as he himself calls it,* is best revealed in the record of his early reading. In fact, accounts of his precocity and high intelligence are based on that record, drawn from the opening pages of the *Autobiography*. Other sources, however, give some information, and while his references to works studied and read for pleasure are often sufficient for easy identification (admittedly some of the Classics are now much better known by their names than their contents), frequently his mention of them is allusive, and there are some puzzles. We have, therefore, brought together here all the references from the major sources: the *Autobiography* (supplemented by its Early Draft), the letter to Samuel Bentham of 30 July, 1819 (when Mill was thirteen years old), outlining his studies from 1814 to 1819,[†] and the Journal and Notebook of his sojourn in France in 1820–21, with a few amplifying and corroborating references from other sources.

The list begins in the year when Mill says he started to learn Greek (he can hardly have begun to read English much earlier), and ends in the year indicated when he says, "I have now, I believe, mentioned all the books which had any considerable effect on my early mental developement" (*Autobiography*, p. 73). As that remark itself indicates, he read other works during those years, many of which could now be identified only tentatively, and many more, one must assume, not at all. We have erred on the side of caution: for example, it might seem reasonable to include Clarendon's *History*, of which James Mill borrowed six volumes from Bentham on 1 September, 1812, and five volumes on 25 June, 1815,[‡] during the period when his son was reading history avidly; however, there is no contemporary evidence that J. S. Mill read Clarendon at this time (he had read it by 1824, as is shown in his review of Brodie's *History*).

Autobiography, p. 5 above.
[†]The text of this letter comes from Alexander Bain, *John Stuart Mill* (London: Longmans, Green, 1882), who says he was given a copy by one of Jeremy Bentham's amanuenses. The wording being, therefore, several times removed from its original, we have made three emendations, in nos. 81, 113, and 152.
[‡]BL Add. MS 33564 (2), ff. 42v, and 32v.

The works are here listed in the chronological order one can derive from Mill's accounts (which probably were based on a running record), but as will be seen, the exact order is uncertain, except for the entries from the French Journal and Notebook, which are precisely dated. The list gives the year (and month when possible) in which Mill read the work, his age at that time, the author, title,* the date of the first edition, evidence for the dating of his reading, evidence (when possible) concerning the edition he was using (including information about the collection in his library, Somerville College, Oxford),† any information about Mill's reaction to the work, and the sources of the evidence and information. For this last purpose we have used these abbreviations: *A* = *Autobiography*; ED = Early Draft of the *Autobiography* (page references given in italics, and when the information merely duplicates that in *A*, also in parentheses without "ED"); *EL* = the letter to Samuel Bentham of 30 July, 1819 (page references to *Earlier Letters*, *CW*, Vol. XII, where the letter appears on pp. 6–10); and *J* = Anna Jean Mill, ed., *John Mill's Boyhood Visit to France: A Journal and Notebook* (Toronto: University of Toronto Press, 1960).

Though the authors and works are listed in the Bibliographic Index below, to make reference easier we have supplied a separate index of authors at the end of this list. Compilations, anonymous works, and periodicals are given under their titles. The references are to the item numbers within the appendix.

1809. *Aet.* 3–4.

1. Aesop, *Fables*. Mill mentions this as the first Greek work he read ("I faintly remember"), but the context suggests only that he did so not long after he began to learn Greek when he was three years old. He read the fables in *Aesopi Phrygis fabulae graece et latine, cum aliis opusculis* (Pladunes Collection) (Basel: Heruagius, 1544), which is in SC, with the first twenty pages and the last page missing. There are some interesting marginalia in Mill's childish hand: at 31.18 and 19 he twice altered "Xāthus" (in the Latin version) to "Xanthus" (both versions appear throughout the text), and at p. 64 he underlined the Greek in the text three lines before the last line on the page and wrote in the margin: "See page 1 Rolin hist of Greece." There are other marginalia probably in his later, more mature hand, and several in another hand, probably that of a previous owner (1736) of the book, Matthew Mallioch. See also no. 27. *A9 (8)*

2. Xenophon, *The Anabasis of Cyrus*. The second Greek work read by Mill, presumably as soon as he finished Aesop, and which, he says, "I remember better." It seems unlikely that

---

*To avoid duplication, we give here only (in most cases) the short title; fuller information is given in the Bibliographic Index, App. I below.

†This collection is indicated in the entries by "SC." Formed from the books placed in storage by Mill's step-daughter and heir, Helen Taylor, when she moved to France, and then given to Somerville in 1906 after her return to England, the collection has suffered depredations over the years. Also, very few of the books that Mill had in his second home in Avignon can now be traced. Consequently the record of books actually owned and used is less complete than one would wish.

he read the whole work at this age. He probably used the ed. of Xenophon's works, ed. Thomas Hutchinson, 9 vols. (Glasgow: Foulis, 1768), which was formerly in SC (it is on a list prepared by the librarian in the 1930s). *A9 (8)*

Before May, 1813. *Aet.* up to 7.

3. Herodotus, *History*. This he says he read "the whole of," sometime before he began Latin in his "eighth year" (which we interpret as *aet.* 7). He may have read other Greek prose; he lists only what he explicitly remembers, nos. 3–10 in this appendix. He probably read one of the two Greek and Latin eds. formerly in SC: ʽΗ τοῦ ʽΗροδότου ʽΑλικαρνασσέως ἱστορία. *Herodoti Halicarnassensis historia*, 9 vols. (Glasgow: Foulis, 1761), and *Herodotus graece et latine*, 7 vols. (Edinburgh: Laing, 1806). *A9 (8)*

4. Xenophon, *Cyropaedia*. The implication is that he read the whole of this extensive work. For the ed., see no. 2. *A9 (8)*

5. Xenophon, *Memorabilia (Memorials of Socrates)*. Again the whole of the work would appear to have been read. For the ed., see no. 2. At *A49 (48)* Mill emphasizes the significance of the work for him: "Even at the very early age at which I read with him [James Mill] the *Memorabilia* of Xenophon, I imbibed from that work and from his comments a deep respect for the character of Socrates; who stood in my mind as a model of ideal excellence: and I well remember how my father at that time impressed upon me the lesson of the 'Choice of Hercules' [Bk. II, Chap. i, ll. 21–34]." *A9 (8)*, 49 *(24n, 48)*

6. Diogenes Laertius, *Lives of the Philosophers*. He says only that he read "some of the lives," probably in Vol. I of *De vitis, dogmatibus et apophthegmatibus clarorum philosophorum libri x. Graece et latine*, 2 vols. (Amsterdam: Wetstenius, 1692), which is in SC. *A9 (8)*

7. Lucian. In *A*, Mill says only that he read "part of Lucian," probably in Λουκιανοῦ Σαμοσατέως ἅπαντα. *Luciani Somosatensis opera*, 4 vols. (Amsterdam: Wetstenius, 1743–46), which is in SC. (See also no. 160, and the references there given.) *A9 (8)*

8. Isocrates, *Ad Demonicum*. He probably read the oration in *Opera omnia graece et latine*, ed. Athanasius Auger, 3 vols. (Paris: Didot l'aîné, 1782), which is in SC (*Ad Demonicum* is the first oration). In ED, he says merely that he read "a little of Isocrates." *A9 (8)*

9. Isocrates, *Ad Nicoclem*. (This is the second oration in *Opera*.) *A9 (8)*

10. Thucydides. In a clause omitted from *A*, Mill says in ED that he thinks he read "part of Thucydides" before learning Latin; he later says he read "all Thucydides" in the period from his "eighth to [his] twelfth year," and in *EL* he indicates that in 1814 he read, and in 1817 reread, Thucydides. In a letter of 7 Dec., 1814 (abstract by Francis Place, Jr.), to Francis Place from Ford Abbey, James Mill mentions the studies of John and Wilhelmina, and says John has just read "the last half of Thucydides." There were formerly two complete Greek and Latin eds. in SC: 8 vols. (Glasgow: Foulis, 1759), and 2 vols. (Leipzig: Schwickert, 1790, 1804). Cf. App. C, no. 16. ED8, A15 *(14)*; *EL* 7, 8; BL Add. MS 35152, f. 119

1813. *Aet.* 6–7.

11. Plato, *Euthyphron*. Mill explicitly dates his reading of "the first six" of Plato's dialogues "in the common arrangement" (nos. 11–16) to 1813. It is not known what ed. he read; the only one now in SC is *Platonis et quae vel Platonis esse feruntur vel Platonica*

solent comitari scripta graece omnia, ed. Immanuel Bekker, 11 vols. (London: Priestley, 1826), which postdates these references. Mill later translated this dialogue: *CW*, Vol. XI, pp. 187–96. *A9 (8)*

12. Plato, *Apology*. In "the common arrangement" of Plato's dialogues, this comes second. Later translated by Mill: *CW*, Vol. XI, pp. 151–74. *A9 (8)*

13. Plato, *Crito*. The third in the common arrangement. *A9 (8)*

14. Plato, *Phaedo*. The fourth in the common arrangement. *A9 (8)*

15. Plato, *Cratylus*. The fifth in the common arrangement. *A9 (8)*

16. Plato, *Theaetetus*. Mill notes that this dialogue was totally beyond his comprehension at that age, thereby implying that the previous five were not. *A9 (8)*

1810–13. Aet. 4–7.

17. William Robertson, *The History of America* (1777). It may be inferred that this work (along with nos. 18–45) was read in the years when they lived in Newington Green. The reference is simply to "Robertson's histories." The only ed. now in SC long postdates the reference: *Works*, 6 vols. (London: Longman, Brown, Green, and Longmans, 1851). *A11 (10)*

18. Robertson, *The History of the Reign of the Emperor Charles V* (1769). See no. 17. *A11 (10)*

19. Robertson, *The History of Scotland under Mary and James VI* (1759). See no. 17. *A11 (10)*

20. David Hume, *The History of England* (1754–62). *A11 (10)*

21. Edward Gibbon, *The History of the Decline and Fall of the Roman Empire* (1776–88). *A11 (10)*

22. Robert Watson, *The History of the Reign of Philip II, King of Spain* (1777). This work and the next were, Mill says, "my greatest delight, then and for long afterwards." Along with an anonymous work (no. 58), he used this "favorite" work to compose a history of Holland (*A17*). BL Add. MS 33564 (2), in part a list by Bentham of books borrowed from him, cites "Watson's Philip II & III" as borrowed by James Mill on 31 Mar., 1816 (f. 43r); there can be little doubt that the young Mill read them before that date, but it seems likely that the books were borrowed for him from Bentham. See also App. C, no. 4. *A11 (10)*, *17 (16)*

23. Robert Watson and William Thomson, *The History of the Reign of Philip III, King of Spain* (1783). Mill likely read Bentham's copy (see no. 22), but the 2nd ed., 2 vols. (London: Robinson, *et al.*, 1786), is in SC. *A11 (10)*

July, 1812. Aet. 6.

24. Nathaniel Hooke, *The Roman History, from the Building of Rome to the Ruin of the Commonwealth* (1738–71). Mill's earliest extant letter is concerned with his "recapitulating" Hooke, which he borrowed from Bentham. This, after Watson (nos. 22 and 23), was his "favorite historical reading." (See also no. 57.) The "History of Rome" (see App. A above), partly based on Hooke, written by Mill at this time, indicates in its footnotes that he also then used nos. 25, 26, and 72. Cf. App. C, no. 2. *A11 (10)*, 15; *EL*, *CW*, Vol. XII, pp. 3–4.

25. Dionysius of Halicarnassus, *The Roman Antiquities*. In *A*, Mill first refers to his having read "a little" of Dionysius (and he later helped his sisters through it: see no. 152). He also used the work in his "History of Rome"; in the extant fragment (see App. A above), his references (which are all to the "Chronology of the Consuls") correspond to the text of Διονυσίου Ἁλικαρνασέως τὰ εὑρισκόμενα, ἱστορικά τε καὶ ῥητορικά, συγγράμματα. *Dionysii Halicarnassei scripta quae extant, omnia, et historica, et rhetorica* (Greek and Latin), 2 vols. (Frankfurt: Weschel Heirs, 1586), which is, as Mill says his text was, in folio, and in which *The Roman Antiquities* occupies Vol. I. (This ed. is not unique in these features, however.) *A*15 (*14*), 17 (*16*); *EL* 10; App. A, pp. 542, 544n, 546n

26. Plutarch, *Lives*, trans. and ed. John and William Langhorne (1770). *A*11 (*10*); App. A, p. 544n

1810–13. *Aet.* 4–7.

27. Charles Rollin, *The Ancient History of the Egyptians, Carthaginians, Assyrians, Babylonians, Medes and Persians, Macedonians, and Grecians* (in French, 1730–38). Mill implies that he read only the later volumes, beginning with Philip of Macedon (i.e., Vols. V–VIII in 8-vol. eds.). See also no. 1 above. *A*11 (*10*)

28. Gilbert Burnet, *Bishop Burnet's History of His Own Time* (1724–34). *A*11 (*10*)

29. *The Annual Register of World Events: A Review of the Year* (1758ff.). Mill remarks that he read "the historical part" of the volumes from 1758 to "about" 1788, where Bentham's set, which the Mills borrowed, ended. Bentham lists (see no. 22) James Mill as borrowing Vols. XXIX and XXX on 28 Apr., 1810 (f. 41r), and Vols. VII–X on 8 Mar., 1823 (f. 44v): this list is certainly not complete, but verifies Mill's memory that the books were borrowed from Bentham. *A*11 (*10*)

30. John Millar, *An Historical View of the English Government* (1787). A work "highly valued" by James Mill, formerly in SC. *A*11 (*10*)

31. Johann Lorenz von Mosheim, *An Ecclesiastical History* (in Latin, 1755). *A*11 (*10*)

32. Thomas McCrie, *The Life of John Knox* (1812). *A*11 (*10*)

33. Willem Sewel, *The History of the Rise, Increase, and Progress of the Christian People Called Quakers* (1722). *A*11 (*10*)

34. Thomas Wight and John Rutty, *A History of the Rise and Progress of the People Called Quakers in Ireland* (1751). *A*11 (*10*)

35. Philip Beaver, *African Memoranda* (1805). One of the books Mill says his father "was fond of putting" into his hands because they "exhibited men of energy and resource in unusual circumstances, struggling against difficulties and overcoming them." *A*11

36. David Collins, *An Account of the English Colony in New South Wales* (1798–1802). See no. 35. *A*11

37. George Anson, *A Voyage round the World* (1748). A book, says Mill, that he "never wearied of reading." *A*11 (*10*)

38. David Henry, *An Historical Account of All the Voyages round the World* (1774). Like no. 37, a work Mill "never wearied of reading." This work fits Mill's description of a 4-vol. collection beginning with Drake and ending with Cook and Bougainville; he says, "Hawkesworth's, I believe," but John Hawkesworth, *An Account of the Voyages Undertaken by the Order of His Present Majesty for Making Discoveries in the Southern*

Hemisphere (London: Strahan, Cadell, 1773; and other eds.), is normally in three vols., and does not include either Drake or Bougainville. *A*11–13 (*10–12*)

39. John Hamilton Moore, *A New and Complete Collection of Voyages and Travels* (1780?). In a cancelled passage in ED, Mill says he has a faint recollection of "some folio collection" in which he read "an account of the first circumnavigation of the globe, by Magellan." Moore's collection, which is in folio, includes "The Voyage of Ferdinand Maghellan" (Vol. I, pp. 13–15); another possibility, though less likely, is Samuel Purchas, *Purchas His Pilgrimes* (1625), also in folio, which includes "Of Fernandes Magalianes" (Vol. I, pp. 33–46). No other folio collection in English containing Magellan's voyage has been located. ED *12n*

40. Daniel Defoe, *The Life and Strange Surprizing Adventures of Robinson Crusoe* (1719). SC formerly contained an ed. (London: Daly, 1837) that long postdates the reference, though Mill says he possessed the work as a child. *A*13 (*12*)

41. *The Arabian Nights* (in English, 1706). Mill says his father borrowed several works, of which this was one, but the 5-vol. trans. by Edward Forster (London: Miller, 1802) is in SC (Vol. IV now missing). *A*13 (*12*)

42. *Arabian Tales; or, A Continuation of the Arabian Nights Entertainments* (in English, 1794). Another work Mill says his father borrowed. *A*13 (*12*)

43. Miguel de Cervantes, *The History and Adventures of the Renowned Don Quixote* (in English, 1612), trans. Tobias Smollett (1755), 6th ed., 4 vols. (London: Rivington, *et al.*, 1792). This is another of the books Mill says his father borrowed; probably this ed., which is in SC, was obtained later. *A*13 (*12*)

44. Maria Edgeworth, *Popular Tales* (1804). It is not known which ed. of this work Mill read; again a book he recalls his father's having borrowed. *A*13

45. Henry Brooke, *The Fool of Quality; or, The History of Henry Earl of Moreland* (1766–70). It is not known which ed. of this popular work Mill read; this is the last of the list of books he recalls his father's having borrowed for him at this time. *A*13 (*12*)

1813–14. *Aet.* 7.

46. Latin grammar. It is not known which grammar Mill used; a representative work is the so-called "Eton" or "Royal" grammar, e.g., *An Introduction to the Latin Tongue, for the Use of Youth*, new ed., rev. (Eton: Pote and Williams, 1806). "In my eighth year," Mill says, "I commenced learning Latin, in conjunction with a younger sister [Wilhelmina], to whom I taught it as I went on, and who afterwards repeated the lessons to my father: and from this time, other sisters and brothers being successively added as pupils, a considerable part of my day's work consisted of this preparatory teaching." (The comment continues; see *A*13.) For other references to Mill's teaching his sisters, see nos. 47, 48, 51, 52, 53, 73, 74, 101, 102, 152, 153; see also no. 111. George Bentham records in his MS Autobiography (Royal Botanical Gardens, Kew, f. 11) that the young Mill ("in a scarlet jacket with nankeen trousers buttoned over it") accompanied the Samuel Benthams on a visit to Lady Spencer; Bentham says: "At this time at the age of six he was a Greek and Latin scholar and a logician and fond of shewing off his proficiency without the slightest reserve." But the entry is for 1814, and in any case Bentham may have written "Greek and Latin" without really knowing exactly what the boy's accomplishments were. *A*13 (*12*)

47. Cornelius Nepos, *Excellentium imperatorum vitae*. (Other titles often used.) This is one of the works Mill used to teach Latin to his sisters Wilhelmina and Clara. In his letter to

Francis Place of 7 Dec., 1814 (see no. 10), James Mill says: "Willie has read along with [John] several lines in Cornelius Nepos and has got over the most difficult part of the task of learning Latin, while John wants little of being able to read Latin with ease." By 30 July, 1819, Wilhelmina had read all, and Clara, some, of Cornelius Nepos. Mill says (*A*13) that he went through "a considerable part" of Cornelius Nepos with Wilhelmina, but afterwards "added to the superintendance of these lessons, much longer ones" of his own. *A*13 (*12*); *EL* 10; BL Add. MS 35152, f. 119

48. Julius Caesar, *Commentaries*. Like no. 47, this was used by Mill to teach his sisters, both of whom had read "some of Cæsar" by 30 July, 1819. Having superintended Wilhelmina's study (presumably as early as 1813), he went on to longer lessons of his own. They probably used one of the two eds. formerly in SC: *C. Iulii Caesaris quae exstant, cum selectis variorum commentariis* (Amsterdam: Elzevir, 1661); and *C. Julii Caesaris quae exstant opera*, 2 vols. (Paris: Barbou, 1755). *A*13 (*12*); *EL* 10

49. Homer, *Iliad*. He likely read this in Ἰλιὰς καὶ Ὀδύσσεια, 4 vols. (in 2) (Oxford: Typographicus Academicus, 1800), which is in SC. He made his "first commencement in the Greek poets with the *Iliad*," in the same year that he began Latin (see no. 46). At *A*15, Mill says, of the period 1813–17 generally, that he read in Greek the *Iliad* "through." *A*13 (*12*), 15 (*14*)

50. Homer, *Iliad*, trans. Alexander Pope. He probably read *Homer's Iliad*, trans. Pope (1715), 6 vols. (London: Lintot, 1720), which is in SC. "It was the first English verse I had cared to read," says Mill, "and it became one of the books in which for many years I most delighted: I think I must have read it from twenty to thirty times through." See also App. C, no. 5. *A*13 (*12*)

1813–17. *Aet.* 7–11.

51. Phaedrus. Mill probably read *Fabularum Aesopiarum libri v*, ed. Peter Burmannus (Utrecht: van de Water, 1718), which is in SC. This is one of the works mentioned in *A* as having been read between his eighth and twelfth years that is not mentioned in *EL* as part of his own study from 1814 to July, 1819. As it seems likely that some (though probably not all) such works were in fact read in 1813, they (nos. 51–8) are given here before the works mentioned in *EL* for 1814. He used Phaedrus as a teaching text, his sister Wilhelmina having read "almost all" before 30 July, 1819. *A*15 (*14*); *EL* 10

52. Sallust. Mill probably read *Opera omnia*, ed. H. Homer (London: Payne, 1789), which is in SC. In *A*, Mill says he read "all Sallust." Another teaching text: by the end of July, 1819, Wilhelmina had read all *Cataline* and part of *Jugurtha*; Clara almost as much as her sister. Cf. App. C, no. 24. *A*15 (*14*); *EL* 10

53. Terence. Mill says in *A* merely that he read "some plays of Terence," and does not mention him in *EL*. But he does there indicate that by 30 July, 1819, Wilhelmina had, under his direction, read two of Terence's plays. They probably used *Publii Terentii Afri comoediae* (Birmingham: Baskerville, 1772), which is in SC. *A*15 (*14*); *EL* 10

54. Lysias. Mill says merely that he read "a great part" of Lysias. It is not known which ed. of the orations he used; a 2-vol. ed. of *Oratores Attici* was formerly in SC. *A*15 (*14*); *EL* 10

55. William Mitford, *The History of Greece* (1784–1818). Mill mentions the work in *EL*, but without giving a date. In *A*, he says: "History continued [in my private reading] to be my strongest predilection, and most of all ancient history. Mitford's *Greece* I read continually. My father had put me on guard against the Tory prejudices of this writer . . . with such effect

that in reading Mitford, my sympathies were always on the contrary side to those of the author, and I could, to some extent, have argued the point against him: yet this did not diminish the ever new pleasure with which I read the book." Formerly in SC was the 10-vol. ed. (London: Cadell and Davies, 1818–20), which postdates the references. *A*15 (*14*); *EL*9

56. Adam Ferguson, *The History of the Progress and Termination of the Roman Republic* (1783). It is not known which ed. Mill used. See no. 57. *A*15 (*14–16*); *EL*9

57. *An Universal History, from the Earliest Account of Time to the Present*, 7 vols. (London: Batley, *et al.*, 1736–44). This is the "Ancient Part"; the work was completed by the *Modern Part of the Universal History*, 16 vols., plus a vol. of maps and charts (London: Osborne, *et al.*, 1759–66). Mill refers to his reading "the Ancient Universal History," a "book which, in spite of what is called the dryness of its stile," he "took great pleasure in." He attempted (*A*17) "an abridgment" of it (see App. C, no. 3). "Roman history," Mill says, "both in my old favorite, Hooke, and in Ferguson, continued to delight me." *A*17 (*16*)

58. Anon., *The History of the Republick of Holland, from Its First Foundation to the Death of King William*, 2 vols. (London: Bell, *et al.*, 1705). Probably read at this time, but the reference does not come in a strictly sequential listing, and it may well be that Mill read it at or about the time he read the two works of Watson (see nos. 22 and 23). Mill does not give a title, but this would appear to be the work intended (no appropriate rival has been located) when he refers in *A* to "an anonymous compilation," and in ED to "an anonymous history which somebody who knew my liking for the subject, picked up at a book stall and gave to me." He used it, along with his "favorite Watson," to write a history of Holland. See App. C, no. 4. *A*17 (*16*)

1814. *Aet.* 7–8.

59. Cicero, *Pro A. Licinio archia poëta*. In *A*, Mill refers to his reading "several [ED "some"] of the Orations of Cicero"; this one (with no. 60) is specifically mentioned in *EL* for 1814. Mill probably read this in *Opera*, 10 vols. (in 8) (Leyden: Elzevir, 1642), Vol. III, pp. 369–82, which is in SC. Again in *EL* he reports reading "part of Cicero's Orations" in 1815. *A*15 (*14*); *EL*7

60. Cicero, *In C. Verrem invective septem*. In *EL*, Mill says, curiously, "the (first or last) part of [Cicero's] pleading against Verres" (there are seven parts). He probably read this in *Opera*, Vol. II, pp. 112–556 (first part, pp. 112–35; last part, pp. 476–556). *A*15 (*14*); *EL*7

61. Anacreon. In both *A* and *EL*, Mill says merely that he read Anacreon. He probably used *Anacreon Teius, poeta lyricus . . .* (Greek and Latin), ed. Joshua Barnes (Cambridge: Jeffery, 1705), which is in SC. *A*15 (*14*); *EL*7

62. Sophocles, *Electra*. In *A*, Mill says he read "one or two plays of Sophocles, Euripides, and Aristophanes, though by these I profited little"; in *EL*, he specifically mentions this play (and nos. 63–5). It is not known which ed. he used. *A*15 (*14*); *EL*7

63. Euripides, *Phoenissae*. See no. 62. Mill probably read this in Αἱ τοῦ Εὐριπίδου τραγῳδίαι σωζόμεναι. *Euripidis tragoediae quae supersunt* (Greek and Latin), ed. Samuel Musgrave, 10 vols. (Glasgow: Foulis; Edinburgh: Laing; London: Bremner, 1797), which was formerly in SC; the play is in Vol. II, pp. 1–88. *A*15 (*14*); *EL*7

64. Aristophanes, *Plutus*. See no. 62. In his letter to Francis Place of 7 Dec., 1814 (see no. 10), James Mill reports that John has recently read one (undesignated) play by Aristophanes. It is not known which ed. Mill used. *A*15 (*14*); *EL*7; BL Add. MS 35152, f. 119

65. Aristophanes, *Clouds*. See nos. 62 and 64. *A*15 (*14*); *EL*7

66. Demosthenes. In *A*, Mill says that in the period between his eighth and twelfth years he read "a great part of Demosthenes" (*A*15); later he refers to reading "some" of Demosthenes' orations "several times over," and writing "a full analysis of them" (*A*23; cf. App. C, no. 11); he also mentions reading Demosthenes (and Plato) in Greek aloud to his father (*A*25). In *EL*, he specifically refers to reading the *Philipics* in 1814, and says he read "a great many Orations of Demosthenes" in 1817. He reports also that he read "some more of Demosthenes" in 1818. See also no. 80. It is not known what ed. he used; *Demosthenis et Aeschinis quae exstant omnia* (Greek and Latin), 10 vols. (London: Priestley, 1827), which postdates the references, is in SC. *A*15 (*14*), 23 (*22*), 25 (*24*); *EL*7, 8

Dec., 1814. *Aet.* 8.

67. Plutarch, Περὶ παίδων ἀγωγῆς ("On the Education of Children"). In his letter to Francis Place of 7 Dec., 1814 (see no. 10), James Mill refers to John's having just read (in Greek) "the treatise of Plutarch on education." It is not mentioned in *A* or *EL*. BL Add. MS 35152, f. 119

1814. *Aet.* 7–8.

68. Euclid, *Elements of Geometry*. In *A*, Mill says he began Euclid, "still under" his father's tuition, "soon after" the works listed in nos. 46–50; in *EL*, he says that in 1814 he was reading Euclid, and that in 1815, "after finishing the first six books, with the eleventh and twelfth" (the ones usually studied), he went on to the works mentioned in nos. 71 and 81–3. In his letter to Francis Place of 7 Dec., 1814 (see no. 10), James Mill says: "John is now an adept in the first 6 books of Euclid." See also no. 101. It is not known which ed. of Euclid Mill used, but in *EL* he indicates that he later read "Playfair's Trigonometry at the end of his Euclid"; i.e., John Playfair, *Elements of Geometry: Containing the First Six Books of Euclid, with Two Books on the Geometry of Solids. To Which Are Added, Elements of Plane and Spherical Trigonometry* (Edinburgh: Bell and Bradfute; London: Robinson, 1795). (The "two books on the geometry of solids" are equivalent to Books XI and XII of Euclid.) *A*15 (*14*); *EL*7–8; BL Add. MS 35152, f. 119

69. Leonhard Euler, *Elements of Algebra* (in English, 1797). In *A*, Mill refers only to the beginning of his study of algebra; the title is given in *EL*. In his letter to Francis Place of 7 Dec., 1814 (see no. 10), James Mill says that John "in algebra performs simple equations with great ease." It is not known which ed. Mill used, although a likely one is the anonymous translation, 2 vols. (London: Johnson, 1797). *A*15 (*14*); *EL*7; BL Add. MS 35152, f. 119

70. John Bonnycastle, *An Introduction to Algebra* (1782). See no. 69. In *EL*, Mill says he used Bonnycastle "principally for the sake of the examples to perform." It is not known which ed. he used. *A*15 (*14*); *EL*7

71. John West, *Elements of Mathematics. Comprehending Geometry, Conic Sections, Mensuration, Spherics* (1784). Writing of the period from his eighth to his twelfth year, Mill merely refers to his learning "elementary geometry and algebra thoroughly, the differential calculus and other portions of the higher mathematics far from thoroughly" (*A*15; ED*14* has "not thoroughly" for "far from thoroughly"); in *EL*, he says he read "some of West's Geometry" in 1814, and, having finished it in 1815, then went on to West's "Conic Sections, Mensuration and Spherics." He continued to work on West, taking it with him to France in 1820, where, on 27 June, he reports: "tried two propositions in West's App'x.

Solved one of them, which I have tried over for several years and have never been able to solve: found the other too difficult, but hope to solve it to-morrow." On the 29th he tried some more "problems and theorems," resolving three, including the recalcitrant one of the 27th. Two more that he had frequently tried before were resolved on 5 July, and he attempted more on the 6th. On the 13th he resolved two more (and George Bentham resolved "several"); on the 14th Mill worked out three more. On the 19th he reports that he "tried ineffectually some problems and theorems in West's Appx." A15 (*14*); *EL*7; *J*29, 35, 45, 46, 50

1815. *Aet*. 8–9.

72. Livy. Mill probably read *Historiarum ab urbe condita*, ed. Johannes Fredericus Gronovius, 3 vols. (Amsterdam: Elzevir, 1665, 1664), which (with James Mill's bookplate) is in SC. Formerly in SC was the 10-vol. ed., ed. Joannes Clericus (Amsterdam: Wetstenius; Utrecht: van de Water, 1710). In *A*, covering 1813–17 generally, Mill mentions "the first five books of Livy (to which from my love of the subject I voluntarily added, in my hours of leisure, the remainder of the first decad)"; in *EL*, he lists the first five books for 1815, and later says, without specific date, "I have also read a great deal of Livy by myself." But see no. 24; the "History of Rome" there cited implies that he was using Livy in 1812, though he says (see no. 46) he began to learn Latin only in his eighth year. A15 (*14*); *EL*7, 9

73. Ovid, *Metamorphoses*. In *A*, covering 1813–17 generally, Mill says he read "a considerable part" of the *Metamorphoses*; in *EL*, he writes, of 1815, "I read the first six books, I believe." He also says that, as of 30 July, 1819, his sister Clara was reading Ovid (he does not mention Ovid in connection with Wilhelmina, who was more advanced). They probably used *Opera omnia*, 3 vols. (Amsterdam: Blaviana, 1683), which is in SC (the *Metamorphoses* is in Vol. II). A15 (*14*); *EL*7, 10

74. Virgil, *Eclogues* (*Bucolics*). At the time of the letter to Bentham (30 July, 1819), his sister Wilhelmina was, under Mill's direction, reading the *Eclogues*. He continued on his own in France in the next year, reading "some" Virgil on the 10th and the 16th of June, two eclogues on each of the 26th and 28th, one on the 29th, and two more on the 30th. A15 (*14*); *EL*7, 10; *J*13, 15, 28, 29, 30

75. Virgil, *Aeneid*. In *A*, Mill refers to his reading the first six books in the period 1813–17; the specific year is given in *EL*. Cf. App. C, no. 24. A15 (*14*); *EL*7

76. Homer, *Odyssey*. In *A*, Mill says he read in Greek the *Odyssey* "through" in the period 1813–17; in *EL* (with an "I think" that may refer to the accuracy of the Greek list for 1815 as a whole), he says he read it in 1815. For the ed., see no. 49. A15 (*14*); *EL*7

77. Theocritus. Mill probably read him in Θεοκρίτου, Μόσχου, Βίωνος, Σιμμίου τὰ εὑρισκόμενα. *Theocriti, Moschi, Bionis, Simmii quae extant* (Greek and Latin), ed. D. Heincius (Heidelberg: Commelinian, 1604), or in *Idyllia* (Greek), ed. F. C. W. Jacobs (Gotha: Ettinger, 1789), both of which were formerly in SC. A15 (*14*); *EL*7

78. Pindar. Pindar is the only Classical author known to have been read by Mill in his formative years who is not mentioned by name in *A*; in *EL*, he says he read "some of Pindar" in 1815. He probably read him in Πάντα τὰ Πινδάρου σωζόμενα. *Omnia Pindari quae extant. Cum interpretatione latina* (Greek and Latin), 2 vols. (in 1) (Glasgow: Foulis, 1744), which is in SC. *EL*7

79. Aeschines. In *A*, covering 1813–17, Mill says he read "a great part" of Aeschines; in *EL*, he specifies for 1815 "the two Orations" of Aeschines (*Contra Timarchum*, and *De*

male gesta legatione). It is not known what ed. he used; *Demosthenis et Aeschinis quae exstant omnia* (Greek and Latin), 10 vols. (London: Priestley, 1827), which postdates the references, is in SC. *A*15 (*14*); *EL*7

80. Demosthenes, *De corona* (*On the Crown*). Specifically mentioned and dated in *EL*. See no. 66. *EL*7

81. Robert Simson, *Sectionum conicarum libri v* (1735). See no. 71. Title given in *EL*, which reads "Simpson's Conic Sections." Mill, who normally read mathematical texts in Latin, probably used this rather than the English translation (which included only the first three of the five books), *Elements of the Conic Sections* (Edinburgh: Elliot; London: Cadell, *et al.*, 1775). *A*15 (*14*); *EL*7

82. John Kersey, *The Elements of That Mathematical Art Commonly Called Algebra* (1673–74). See no. 71. *A*15 (*14*); *EL*7

83. Isaac Newton, *Arithmetica universalis; sive de compositione et resolutione arithmetica liber* (1707). It is not known which ed. Mill used. See no. 71. *A*15 (*14*); *EL*7

1816. *Aet.* 9–10.

84. Horace, *Ars poetica*. Mill may have read it in *Opera*, ed. William Baxter, new ed. (Glasgow and Edinburgh: Mundell; London: Robinson, *et al.*; Cambridge: Lunn, 1796), which is in SC. Dated in *EL* to 1816; in *A*, to the period between his eighth and twelfth years. Though in ED he says he read "all Horace" at this time, in both *A* and *EL* he says all except the *Epodes* (which he presumably read later). See also App. C, no. 7. *A*15 (*14*); *EL*7

85. Horace, *Carmen saeculare*. See no. 84. *A*15 (*14*); *EL*7

86. Horace, *Carmina* (*Odes*). See no. 84. Four years later, while in France, Mill translated into French the first and third odes (see App. C, no. 24). *A*15 (*14*); *EL*7; *J*40, 48

87. Horace, *Epistles*. See no. 84. *A*15 (*14*); *EL*7

88. Horace, *Satires*. See no. 84. In 1820, when in France, Mill reports reading a Satire on 22 Dec. *A*15 (*14*); *EL*7; *J*89

89. Polybius, *Histories*. In *A*, Mill says he read in this period "several books of Polybius" (there are five); in ED, "the first two or three"; in *EL*, merely "Part of Polybius." *A*15 (*14*); *EL*7

90. Xenophon, *Hellenics*. In *EL*, he says he read "all" of the work at this time. For the ed., see no. 2. *A*15 (*14*); *EL*7

91. Sophocles, *Ajax*. See no. 62. *A*15 (*14*); *EL*7

92. Sophocles, *Philoctetes*. See no. 62. *A*15 (*14*); *EL*7

93. Euripides, *Medea*. See no. 62. See also no. 63; *Medea* appears in the ed. there cited, Vol. II, pp. 90–155. *A*15 (*14*); *EL*7

94. Aristophanes, *Frogs*. See no. 62. See also no. 64. *A*15 (*14*); *EL*7

95. *Anthologia graeca*. In *A*, Mill says he read "part of the *Anthology*"; in *EL*, a "great part"; one may assume he read it all eventually. See also no. 152. He probably read it in *Anthologia graeca sive poetarum graecorum lusus*, ed. Friedrich Jacob, 13 vols. (Leipzig: Dyck, 1794–1814), which is in SC. *A*15 (*14*); *EL*7

96. Matthew Stewart, *Propositiones geometricae, more veterum demonstratae, ad geometricum antiquam illustrandam et promovendam idoneae* (1763). For comment, see no. 71. A15 (*14*); EL7

97. John Playfair, *Elements of Geometry; . . . Elements of Plane and Spherical Trigonometry* (1795). See nos. 68 and 71. A15 (*14*); EL7–8

98. William Wallace, "Geometry," *Edinburgh Encyclopaedia* (1830), Vol. X, Pt. 1, pp. 185–240. The author is identified in Vol. I, Pt. 1; though the completed encyclopaedia was published in 1830, it had been issued in parts over a twenty-year period by David Brewster, its main mover and editor (the work is often called *Brewster's Edinburgh Encyclopaedia*). See no. 71. A15 (*14*); EL8

99. Thomas Simpson, *A Treatise of Algebra* (1745). See no. 71. It is not known which ed. Mill used. A15 (*14*); EL8

1816. Aet. 10.

100. Thomas Thomson, *A System of Chemistry*, 4 vols. (Edinburgh: Bell and Bradfute, *et al.*; London: Robinson; Dublin: Gilbert and Hodges, 1802). Mill says: "I devoured treatises on Chemistry, especially that of my father's early friend and schoolfellow Dr. Thomson, for years before I attended a lecture or saw an experiment" (A21). That he first read the work (presumably in the first ed., cited above) "years before" his visit to the Royal Military College, Bagshot, in Oct., 1818, when he saw experiments, is borne out by a letter to Thomson from James Mill, who reports that John, at age ten, "read your *System of Chemistry* with vast ardour"; again, at twelve, he "fastened with great greediness upon your book" (Alexander Bain, *James Mill* [London: Longmans, Green, 1882], pp. 157, 168). In *EL*, discussing his reading in 1819, Mill says he has read "the last edition" of Thomson's work, that is, the 5th ed., 4 vols. (London: Baldwin, Cradock, and Joy; Edinburgh: Blackwood, *et al.*; Dublin: Hodges and MacArthur, 1817), which was much revised. In 1820 he was again studying Thomson, while in France. (It is possible that he was then reading Thomson's *Elements of Chemistry* [Edinburgh: Blackwood; London: Longman, Hurst, Rees, and Orme, 1810], which is in one vol., rather than the 4-vol. *System*.) The same enthusiasm is evident in his Journal, as he records reading Thomson on 25 and 30 June, 1, 2, 5, 6, 7, and 9 July, sometimes as often as three times a day, and on two occasions making "out various chemical tables &c." See App. C, no. 23. A21 (*20*); EL9; J28, 30, 35, 36, 39

1817. Aet. 10–11.

101. James Mill, *The History of British India*, 3 vols. (London: Baldwin, Cradock, and Joy, 1817 [1818]). Mill's reading of his father's *History* might be dated much earlier; in a passage not used in *A*, he says in ED: "my father . . . used to give me the manuscript of part of his history of India to read. Almost as soon as I could hold a pen I must needs write a history of India too . . ." (ED*16*; cf. App. C, no. 1); this he soon abandoned for his "Roman history," which dates from 1812 (printed above, pp. 541–8). (James Mill began his *History* in 1806.) In *A*, Mill says he read the completed manuscript aloud to his father while the latter corrected the proofs; in a letter of 7 Aug., 1817, from Ford Abbey, Francis Place wrote to his wife: "Mill is up between 5 and 6, he and John compare his proofs—Jn. reading the copy and his father the proof—Willie and Clara are in the Saloon before 7—and as soon as the proofs are done with Jn goes to the further end of the room to teach his sisters—when this has been done—and part of the time while it is doing he learns Geometry." He adds that John "teaches the children" and does his own work also in the afternoon; John Flowerdew

Colls, Bentham's amanuensis at the time, was teaching the younger children writing. Mill indicates in his account how important the reading of his father's *History* was to his education. The only ed. now in SC is the 3rd., 6 vols. (London: Baldwin, Cradock, and Joy, 1826). ED*16*, A27 (*26*); BL Add. MS 35143, f. 285

102. Lucretius, *De rerum natura*. Mentioned in *A* as part of his reading between his eighth and his twelfth year; dated in *EL* to 1817. In *A*, Mill says he read then "two or three books of Lucretius" (there are six); in *EL*, he says "all Lucretius, except the last book." By 30 July, 1819, his sister Wilhelmina, under his direction, had read the first and part of the second book. They probably read *De rerum natura libri sex*, ed. Gilbert Wakefield, 4 vols. (Edinburgh: Bell and Bradfute, *et al.*; Glasgow: Duncan, 1813), which is in SC. A15 (*14*); *EL*8, 10

103. Cicero, *Letters to Atticus* (*Epistolarum ad T. Pomponium Atticum*). Mill read this in Latin; it appears in *Opera*, Vol. VI, pp. 1–517 (see no. 59); his father (see *A*) translated the French notes from the Latin and French version, *Lettres de Cicéron à Atticus*, ed. Nicolas Hubert Mongault, 6 vols. (Paris: Delaulne, 1738), which is also in SC, and which Mill probably used as well (though he could not at the time read French). The French version is not mentioned in *EL*. A15 (*14*); *EL*8

104. Cicero, *Topica*, in *Opera*, Vol. I, pp. 694–722 (see no. 59). In *A*, Mill says he read "several" (ED, "some") of Cicero's "writings on oratory"; in *EL*, this title is given. A15 (*14*); *EL*8

105. Cicero, *De partitione oratoria*, in *Opera*, Vol. I, pp. 722–62 (see no. 59). This title given in *EL*. See no. 104. A15 (*14*); *EL*8

106. Aristotle, *Rhetoric*. In *A*, Mill says: "as the first expressly scientific treatise on any moral or psychological subject which I had read, and containing many of the best observations of the ancients on human nature and life, my father made me study [it] with peculiar care, and throw the matter of it into synoptic tables." In *EL*, he says: "I read . . . all Aristotle's Rhetoric, of which I made a synoptic table." See App. C, no. 10. Mill may have read Ἀριστοτέλους τέχνης ῥητορικῆς βιβλία τρία. *Aristotelis de rhetorica seu arte dicendi libri tres* (Greek and Latin), ed. Theodore Goulston (London: Griffin, 1619), two copies of which are in SC. A15 (*14*); *EL*8

107. William Wallace, "Conic Sections," *Encyclopaedia Britannica*, 4th ed. (1810), Vol. VI, pp. 519–48 (+ 92 figures). See no. 71. It is much more likely that Mill refers to this rather than the very slight article in the 3rd ed. (1797), Vol. V, pp. 329–32. Cf. no. 109. He says: "I read in Conic Sections an article in the *Encyclopædia Britannica*." The author is identified in the Preface to Vol. I of the 4th ed., pp. xvi–xvii. A15 (*14*); *EL*8

108. Leonhard Euler, *Introductio in analysiu infinitorum* (1748). Title given in *EL*. See no. 71. It is not known which ed. Mill studied. A15 (*14*); *EL*8

109. "Fluxions," *Encyclopaedia Britannica*, 4th ed. (1810), Vol. VIII, pp. 697–778 (+ 39 figures). It is much more likely that Mill refers to this rather than the less detailed article in the 3rd ed. (1797), Vol. VII, pp. 311–16. Cf. no. 107. See also no. 71. In 1817 Mill says: "I . . . began Fluxions, on which I read an article in the *Encyclopædia Britannica*" (*EL*8). This article is not specifically assigned to any author in the Preface to Vol. I of the 4th ed., where, however, it is said that "the articles Algebra, Conic Sections, Trigonometry, and several others in the mathematical and physical sciences were furnished by Mr. William Wallace of the Royal Military College, Great Marlow" (pp. xvi–xvii), and no mathematical articles are assigned to anyone else. But see also no. 135: has Mill confused the two articles? A15 (*14*); *EL*8

110. Thomas Simpson, *The Doctrine and Application of Fluxions* (1750). See no. 71. It is not known which ed. Mill read. *A*15 (*14*); *EL*8

Oct., 1817. Aet. 11.

111. Isaac Newton, *Philosophiae naturalis principia mathematica* (1686). Ann, Lady Romilly, in a letter to Maria Edgeworth (6 Oct., 1817), commenting on life at Ford Abbey, where the Mills were living with Bentham, says that the young Mill was "observed twice when he came out of a room where he had been shut up with Newton's principia before him, that he was but just awake." She mentions also that "he has the care of the learned part of the education of his two eldest sisters who are making great progress in Latin and Greek under his tuition" (Samuel Henry Romilly, ed., *Romilly-Edgeworth Letters, 1813–1818* [London: Murray, 1936], p. 177).

1817. Aet. 10–11.

112. John Keill, *Introductiones ad veram physicam et veram astronomiam* (1702, 1718). See no. 71. In *EL*, Mill refers to this as part of his study of "the application of mathematics"; there is no reference in *A* or ED to this study. It is not known which ed. Mill used. *A*15 (*14*); *EL*8

113. John Robison, *Elements of Mechanical Philosophy* (1804). See no. 112. *EL* reads "Robinson's Mechanical Philosophy." *A*15 (*14*); *EL*8

1813–17. Aet. 7–11.

114. James Thomson, "Winter" (1744). This is referred to (with all the items through no. 128) in *A* after Mill's mention of his reading between his eighth and twelfth years (*A*15), and before his saying "From about the age of twelve" (*A*21), but the text is very vague as to date. "I also remember," says Mill, "[my father's] giving me Thomson's 'Winter' to read, and afterwards making me attempt (without book) to write something myself on the same subject. The verses I wrote were of course the merest rubbish, nor did I ever attain any facility of versification, but the practice may have been useful in making it easier for me, at a later period, to acquire readiness of expression." Cf. App. C, no. 8. *A*19 (*18*)

115. Joanna Baillie, *Constantine Paleologus* (1804). The date is not clear from Mill's account; he says, "In a subsequent stage of boyhood" to that (itself vague) implied in no. 114, he wrote tragedies inspired by Baillie, but he probably read her at about this time. His comment suggests that he read other of Baillie's plays, most likely in *Miscellaneous Plays*, 2nd ed. (London: Longman, Hurst, Rees, and Orme; Edinburgh: Constable, 1805), which is in SC. He says that it was her inspiration rather than Shakespeare's that led him to write tragedies in his youth; *Constantine Paleologus* then appeared to him "one of the most glorious of human compositions," and when he wrote *A* he still thought it (after rereading) "one of the best dramas of the last two centuries." Cf. App. C, no. 13. *A*19n (*26*)

116. Shakespeare, plays. "Shakespeare my father had put into my hands," Mill says, "chiefly for the sake of the historical plays, from which however I went on to the others." *A*19 (*18*)

117. John Milton, poetry. Mill says his father admired Milton's poetry; it may be inferred that he introduced him to it at an early age, though he says in a cancelled passage in ED: "Milton's poetry he did admire but did not think me of an age to comprehend" (ED *18n*). *A*19 (*18*)

118. Oliver Goldsmith, poetry. Mill indicates his father's partiality for Goldsmith's poetry; it may be inferred that he introduced him to it at an early age. *A*19 (*18*)

119. Robert Burns, poetry. James Mill was also partial to Burns, though he was at pains to dissociate himself from his Scottish background; it may be noted that the younger Mill here includes Burns in a list of "English" poets. *A*19 (*18*)

120. Thomas Gray, "The Bard" (1757). His father, Mill says, preferred "The Bard" to *An Elegy Wrote in a Country Church Yard*; it may be inferred that he introduced him to them at an early age. He probably used *The Works of Thomas Gray, with Memoirs of His Life and Writings by William Mason*, ed. Thomas James Mathias, 2 vols. (London: Porter, 1814), which is in SC; in that ed. "The Bard" appears in Vol. I, pp. 25–32, and the *Elegy* in Vol. I, pp. 57–63. *A*19 (*18*)

121. Thomas Gray, *An Elegy Wrote in a Country Church Yard* (1751). See no. 120. *A*19 (*18*)

122. William Cowper, poetry. At *A*19, Mill refers to his father's partiality for Cowper's poetry (again probably introduced to the boy at an early age); at *A*21, he gives his own reaction to Cowper's shorter poems, which he read in a 2-vol. ed. (the first 2-vol. ed. was *Poems*, 2nd ed. [London: Johnson, 1786], called the 2nd ed. because both its vols. had been published separately in 1782). See also no. 123. *A*19, 21 (*20*)

123. William Cowper, "Account of the Author's Treatment of Hares." It is not known which version Mill read: it is not in the ed. cited in no. 122, but appears in *Works*, 10 vols. (London: Baldwin, Cradock, and Joy, 1817), Vol. II, pp. 363–8; it first was published as "Unnoticed Properties of That Little Animal the Hare," *Gentleman's Magazine*, LIV (1784), 412–14. Nothing, says Mill, in Cowper's poetry interested him as did "the prose account of his three hares." *A*21 (*20*)

124. James Beattie, poetry. Mill refers to his father's probable partiality for Beattie's poetry; it may be inferred that he introduced him to it at an early age. *A*19 (*18*)

125. Edmund Spenser, *The Faerie Queene* (1590–96). The reference initially is to James Mill's valuing Spenser: "I remember his reading to me (unlike his usual practice of making me read to him) the first book of the *Fairie Queene*; but I took little pleasure in it." He probably read it in *Works*, ed. Henry John Todd, 8 vols. (London: Rivington, *et al.*, 1805), which is in SC. *A*19 (*18*)

126. Walter Scott, metrical romances. One may infer that Mill read ("at [James Mill's] recommendation and was intensely delighted with") several of *The Lay of the Last Minstrel* (1805), *Marmion* (1808), *The Lady of the Lake* (1810), etc. See also the comment quoted in no. 127. *A*19 (*18*)

127. John Dryden, poetry. Mill says Dryden's poems were among his father's books, but there is now no ed. in SC. James Mill had him read many of the poems, but, he says, "I never cared for any of them except *Alexander's Feast*, which, as well as many of the songs in Walter Scott, I used to sing internally, to a music of my own: to some of the latter indeed I went so far as to compose airs, which I still remember." See no. 126. *A*19 (*18*)

128. John Dryden, *Alexander's Feast* (1697). See no. 127. *A*19 (*18*)

1818. *Aet.* 11–12.

129. Aristotle, *Organon.* "From about the age of twelve," Mill says in *A*, he entered a "more advanced stage" of his "course of instruction; in which the main object was no longer

the aids and appliances of thought, but the thoughts themselves. This commenced with Logic," in which he "began at once with the *Organon*, and read it to the Analytics inclusive, but profited little by the Posterior Analytics, which belong to a branch of speculation" he was "not yet ripe for." In *EL*, he indicates that in 1818 he read the first four books of the *Organon*, "all of which [he] tabulated in the same manner as [Aristotle's] Rhetoric" (see no. 106); he notes that in 1819 he had carried his logical studies in Latin texts "as far as" he had gone in Aristotle. He probably used one or both of 'Αριστοτέλους ὄργανον. *Aristotelis stagiritae peripateticorum principis organum* (Greek and Latin), 2nd ed. (Frankfurt: Weschel Heirs, *et al.*, 1597), and *ibid.*, 3rd ed. (Geneva: ex typis Vignonianis, 1605), which are in SC. See also App. C, no. 12. *A*21 *(20)*; *EL8*

130. Tacitus. Mill comments in ED that he does not think he "meddled" with Tacitus until his thirteenth year (ED*14*); he later says in *A*, of the period "from about the age of twelve" (*A*21), he read "the whole of Tacitus." In *EL*, he says he read all of Tacitus, "except the dialogue concerning oratory," in 1818. He also mentions writing two tragedies based on Tacitus (ED*26*); see App. C, nos. 13 and 15. ED*14*, *A*25 *(24)*; *EL8*

131. Juvenal, *Satires*. In a cancelled passage of ED *(14n)*, Mill indicates that some time in the period between his eighth and twelfth years he read "part of Juvenal"; in *A*, writing of the period "from about the age of twelve" (*A*21), he says he read "the whole" of Juvenal (*A*25). In *EL*, he says (of 1818) he read a "great part" of Juvenal. He probably read it in *Decii Junii Juvenalis et A*. *Persii Flacci satyrae* (London: Brindley, 1744), pp. 1–98, which is in SC (and which is, incidentally, one of the very few books small in format that he seems to have read). ED*14n*, *A*25; *EL8*

132. Quintilian, *De institutione oratoria libri duodecim*. In *EL*, Mill says he "began Quintilian" in 1818, and adds, in his account of 1819, "I am still reading Quintilian." In a cancelled passage of ED *(14n)*, he indicates that some time in the period between his eighth and twelfth years he read "a great part" of Quintilian; in *A*, writing of the period "from about the age of twelve" (*A*21), he says he read "the whole" of Quintilian, who, he adds, "owing to his obscure stile and to the scholastic details of which many parts of his treatise are made up, is little read and seldom sufficiently appreciated. His book is a kind of encyclopædia of the thoughts of the ancients on the whole field of education and culture; and I have retained through life many valuable ideas which I can distinctly trace to my reading of him, even at that early age." (*A*25.) ED*14n*, *A*25 *(24)*; *EL8*

133. William Emerson, *The Elements of Optics* (1768). Title given in *EL*; not mentioned in *A*. *EL8*

134. William Wallace, a treatise on trigonometry. Mill says the work, which we have not identified, was "intended for the use of cadets" at the Military College near Bagshot, which he visited during the year. Wallace was a friend of James Mill's. It is possible, though not likely, that Mill is referring to Wallace's "Trigonometry," *Encyclopaedia Britannica*, 4th ed. (1810), Vol. XX, pp. 477–88 (+ 28 figures); he had read Wallace's "Conic Sections," and "Fluxions" (which may be by Wallace) in that ed.: see nos. 107 and 109 (and also nos. 98 and 135). Title given in *EL*; not mentioned in *A*. *EL8*

135. William Wallace, "Fluxions," *Edinburgh Encyclopaedia* (1830), Vol. IX, Pt. 2, pp. 382–467. Mill says he began the article in 1818; in 1819 he was "still reading" it. See no. 98. See also no. 109: has Mill confused the two articles? Title given in *EL*; not mentioned in *A*. *EL8*

1818–19. Aet. 12.

136. Thomas Campbell, "Lochiel's Warning." "In my thirteenth year," says Mill, "I met

with Campbell's Poems, among which 'Lochiel,' 'Hohenlinden,' 'The Exile of Erin,' and some others, gave me sensations I had never before experienced from poetry. Here, too, I made nothing of the longer poems, except the striking opening of 'Gertrude of Wyoming,' which long kept its place in my feelings as the perfection of pathos." It is not known which ed. of Campbell Mill read, but *Gertrude of Wyoming, and Other Poems*, 3rd ed. (London: Longman, Hurst, Rees, Orme, and Brown, *et al.*, 1810), is the first that contains all the poems Mill mentions. *A*21 (*20*)

137. Thomas Campbell, "Gertrude of Wyoming." See no. 136. *A*21 (*20*)

138. Thomas Campbell, "Hohenlinden." See no. 136. *A*21 (*20*)

139. Thomas Campbell, "The Exile of Erin." See no. 136. *A*21 (*20*)

140. Jeremiah Joyce, *Scientific Dialogues, Intended for the Instruction and Entertainment of Young People* (1800ff.). It is difficult to date with confidence Mill's reading of this work. "During this part of my childhood," he says (his last reference having been to "my thirteenth year"), "one of my greatest amusements was experimental science; in the theoretical, however, not the practical sense of the word; not trying experiments, . . . nor even seeing, but merely reading about them. I never remember being so wrapt up in any book, as I was in Joyce's *Scientific Dialogues*. . . ." However, he next mentions having "devoured treatises on Chemistry," especially Thomson's, which we know he read at age ten (see no. 100). It is not known which ed. of Joyce's 6-vol. work Mill read. The subjects covered are Mechanics, Astronomy, Hydrostatics, Pneumatics, Optics and Magnetism, and Electricity and Galvanism. He comments: ". . . I was rather recalcitrant to my father's criticism of the bad reasoning respecting the first principles of physics which abounds in the early part of that work." *A*21 (*20*)

1819. *Aet.* 12–13.

141. Samuel Smith, *Aditus ad logicam* (1613). Contemporaneously with Aristotle's *Organon* (see no. 129), Mill says in *A*, he read "Latin treatises on the scholastic logic; giving each day to [my father], in our walks, a minute account of what I had read, and answering his numerous and searching questions." This title is given in *EL*, where it is clear that he began Aristotle in the preceding year, and is continuing with him. For other such texts, see nos. 142–4, and 179. Mill presumably read Smith in the 7th ed. (Oxford: Hall, 1656), a copy of which (bound with no. 142) is in the London Library, autographed "J. Mill," being part of Mill's gift of his father's books. *A*21 (*20*); *EL*8

142. Edward Brerewood, *Elementa logicae* (Oxford: Hall, 1657). See no. 141. *A*21 (*20*); *EL*8

143. Phillipus Du Trieu, *Manuductio ad logicam* (1618). See no. 141. Mill probably first used the 1662 ed. (Oxford: Oxlad and Pocock), which was formerly in SC. As he indicates later (*A*125), he and his friends had the work reprinted (London: printed McMillan, 1826) for their private study; this ed. too was formerly in SC. *A*21 (*20*); *EL*8

144. Franco Petri Burgersdijk, *Institutionum logicarum libri duo* (1637). The edition published in Cambridge by Field, 1660, is in SC. See no. 141. *A*21 (*20*); *EL*8

145. Thomas Hobbes, "Computatio sive logica" (1668). In *A*, after mentioning the way he had studied the previous items with his father, Mill says: "After this, I went, in a similar manner, through the 'Computatio sive Logica' of Hobbes, a work of a much higher order of thought than the books of the school logicians, and which [my father] estimated very highly; in my own opinion beyond its merits, great as these are." In *EL*, Mill says: "I have also read

Hobbes' Logic." The only ed. now in SC is that in *Opera philosophica quae latine scripsit omnia*, ed. William Molesworth, 5 vols. (London: Bohn, 1839–54), which long postdates the reference. *A*21 (*20*); *EL*8

146. Plato, *Gorgias*. In *A*, Mill says (vaguely as to time): "It was at this period that I read, for the first time, some of the most important dialogues of Plato, in particular the *Gorgias*, the *Protagoras*, and the *Republic*." (He goes on to mention his father's and his own indebtedness to Plato.) For the ed., see no. 11. Mill (and his father) later translated this dialogue: see *CW*, Vol. XI, pp. 97–150. *A*25 (*24*); *EL*8

147. Plato, *Protagoras*. See no. 146. Later translated by Mill: see *CW*, Vol. XI, pp. 39–61. *A*25 (*24*); *EL*8

148. Plato, *Republic*. See no. 146. In *EL*, Mill says in addition that he "made an abstract" of the *Republic* at this time (see App. C, no. 17). *A*25 (*24*); *EL*8

July, 1819. *Aet.* 13.

149. John Simpson, *Select Exercises for Young Proficients in the Mathematicks* (1752). In *EL*, Mill says he is, at the time of writing the letter (30 July, 1819), "performing without book the problems in Simpson's Select Exercises." *EL*8

1819. *Aet.* 12–13.

150. James Mill, *Elements of Political Economy* (1821). In 1819 James Mill took John "through a complete course of political economy." It seems proper at this point to mention the work (not published until two years later), because in their walks at this time James Mill "expounded each day a portion" of economic theory, of which his son "gave him next day a written account," which he insisted be rewritten "over and over again until it was clear, precise, and tolerably complete. In this manner," Mill continues, "I went through the whole extent of the science; and the written outline of it which resulted from my daily *compte rendu*, served him afterwards as notes from which to write his *Elements of Political Economy*." (See App. C, no. 18.) In *EL*, he says: "I am now [as of 30 July, 1819] learning political economy. I have made a kind of treatise from what my father has explained to me on that subject, and I am now reading Mr. Ricardo's work and writing an abstract of it." In *A*, he says that after his return from France, when the *Elements* was ready for printing, James Mill made him "perform an exercise on the manuscript, which Mr. Bentham practised on all his own writings—making what he called 'marginal contents'; a short abstract of every paragraph, to enable the writer more easily to judge of, and improve, the order of the ideas, and the general character of the exposition" (*A*65). *A*31 (*30*), 65 (*64*); *EL*8

151. David Ricardo, *On the Principles of Political Economy and Taxation* (1817). In *A*, he continues the account cited in no. 150: "After this I read Ricardo, giving an account daily of what I read, and discussing, in the best manner I could, the collateral points which offered themselves in our progress." See also no. 156, and App. C, no. 19. *A*31 (*30*); *EL*8

152. "The Greek Mythology." In *EL*, discussing his teaching of his sisters Wilhelmina and Clara, Mill says they were, at the time of the letter, reading "the Roman Antiquities and the Greek Mythology." The former is undoubtedly Dionysius of Halicarnassus (see no. 25), which they would be reading in Greek; the latter may be an unidentified compendium of myths in Greek, but it seems more likely to have been the *Greek Anthology* (see no. 95), the text of *EL* being based on a misreading. *EL*10

153. John Mair, *An Introduction to Latin Syntax* (1750). The sentence in *EL* quoted in no.

152 continues: "[Willie and Clara] are translating into English from Mair's *Introduction to Latin Syntax*"—one may assume their teacher also learned from this popular eighteenth-century text, which was still much used in Mill's time (e.g., 15th ed. [Edinburgh: Bell and Bradfute, *et al.*, 1811]). It presents parallel columns in English and Latin. *EL*10

Latter half of 1819. *Aet.* 13.

154. David Ricardo, *The High Price of Bullion* (1810). Not given in *EL* (which concludes on 30 July, 1819). See nos. 150–1. In *A*, continuing his account of his father's instructing him in political economy, Mill says: "On Money, as the most intricate part of the subject, he made me read in the same manner Ricardo's admirable pamphlets, written during what was called the Bullion controversy." *A*31 (*30*)

155. David Ricardo, *Reply to Mr. Bosanquet's Practical Observations on the Report of the Bullion Committee* (1811). See no. 154. *A*31 (*30*)

156. Adam Smith, *An Inquiry into the Nature and Causes of the Wealth of Nations* (1776). To the study of Ricardo (see nos. 151, 154–5) "succeeded Adam Smith; and in this reading it was one of my father's main objects," Mill says in *A*, "to make me apply to Smith's more superficial view of political economy, the superior lights of Ricardo, and detect what was fallacious in Smith's arguments, or erroneous in any of his conclusions." In SC is the 3-vol. 8th ed. (1796), which Mill may have first used, as well as a gift copy of McCulloch's ed. (4 vols. [1828]), and Rogers' 2-vol. ed. (1869). When he concludes his discussion of the method his father used to teach him political economy, Mill goes on to say: "At this point concluded what can properly be called my lessons. When I was about fourteen I left England for more than a year" (*A*33); see the comment in no. 157 and in no. 213 (where the account in *A* resumes). *A*31 (*30*)

Before May, 1820. *Aet.* 13–14.

157. François Marie Arouet Voltaire, *Essai sur les moeurs* (1756). In his entry for 29 June, Mill noted that his lack of "any regular French book to read" would be remedied by loans of Voltaire's works from Dr. Russell. On 4 July he borrowed the *Essai*, and read six chapters, beginning where he had "left off in England." As he had begun French only shortly before his departure for France, he almost certainly was reading Voltaire in late winter or early spring, 1820. On each of 5, 6, 7, and 8 July he read five further chapters, and one on the 10th (there are 197 chapters). In SC is *Oeuvres complètes*, 66 vols. (Paris: Renouard, 1817–25), in which the *Essai* is in Vols. XIII–XVI. From here to no. 212, names and dates derive from Mill's Journal and Notebook of his visit to France. It should be noted (see *J*21–2) that Mill took some books with him, though most of what he read in France he must have borrowed or (in some cases, probably) bought. *J*29, 34–7, 39

June, 1820. *Aet.* 14.

158. Claude François Xavier Millot, *Elémens de l'histoire de France, depuis Clovis jusqu'à Louis XV* (1768). Mill says, 5 June: "Began, by [George Bentham's] advice, to read Millot"; 6 June: "read some . . . of Millot." *J*12

159. Jean de La Fontaine, *Fables* (1668). Some, if not all, of the fables read by Mill in French were La Fontaine's. He says, 11 July: "I have learned fables by Lady Bentham's advice, for besides that the pronunciation is much improved by repeating them aloud, the fables of Lafontain[e] and some others are expressed in language so remarkably pure and appropriate that nothing can more contrib[ute to] fix in my memory the rules of construction

as [well as] the French words in their proper acceptation" (*J*42). In all, Mill refers to his memorizing nine or ten (a few of them "extremely long") between 6 June and 1 Aug., 1820. *J*12, 13, 14, 28, 29, 32, 59

160. Lucian. Mill, who began to read Lucian when very young (see no. 7), read or reread many of his dialogues when in France. Most of the references are to specific dialogues, and these are given as separate items below (see nos. 165, 170, 173, 176, 178, 180, 182, 183, 188, 192, and 193); the non-specific ones are on 6, 14, 17, and 22 June ("several dialogues" read on the last date), 20 July ("some of Lucian's short dialogues"), 1 Oct., 6 Dec., 1820, and 13 Jan., 1821 ("un morceau"). On 19 July, 1820, he summarizes his recent reading of Lucian, saying that he has read many of his dialogues "with great attention, and with extreme admiration: in particular the Hermotimus [no. 165], which is a masterpiece of ingenious reasoning, and two or three exquisitely witty dialogues, in the Vitarum Auctio [no. 170], the Cataplus [no. 178], Jupiter Tragoedus [no. 192], three which can scarcely be equalled, and, though in a less degree, the Necyomantia [no. 180], the Vocalium Judicium [no. 176], and some others. The four first mentioned, it is impossible not to admire."

It has not been determined what ed. Mill was using in France, though it could hardly have been that in SC (see no. 7); the titles he uses give little clue. Though he was almost certainly reading them in Greek, he uses (as was common) Latin titles (when only a proper name is used, of course, one cannot tell which language lies behind the citation), except for those cited in nos. 170 (he twice gives the Greek title, and then, once, the Latin), and 173 (he uses the Greek subtitle); in no. 180, he uses the subtitle that appears in both Greek and Latin. In our listing we give the title Mill uses, with (where necessary) the Latin version, and (again where necessary) the English title used in the Loeb ed. (8 vols., trans. A. M. Harmon, *et al.* [London: Heinemann; New York: Macmillan, 1913ff.]). *J*12, 14, 19, 23, 50, 52, 75, 88, 92

161. Jean Racine, three plays. Mill comments: "I read plays chiefly by the advice of Mr. George and of Lady Bentham, who say that dialogues are better to be read, on account of their giving the 1st and 2nd person of the verbs, and for many other reasons" (*J*14). On 9 June he "took a volume of Racine" in his pocket and "read two plays"; on the 12th he read "another tragedy of Racine." In SC is one ed. he can hardly have carried in his pockets: *Oeuvres*, ed. I. L. Geoffroy, 7 vols. (Paris: Le Normant, 1808). *J*13, 14

162. Voltaire, eight plays. See no. 161. Between 9 and 24 June Mill mentions reading eight plays (the number is inferential), twice specifying "a comedy," and five times "a tragedy." He can hardly have been using the 66-vol. set in SC (see no. 157). *J*13, 14, 15, 19, 21, 25

163. Pierre Corneille, two tragedies. See no. 161. On 10 June Mill says he read a tragedy by Corneille, and says the same on the 17th. Formerly there were in SC a 4-vol. ed. (1818), and one other volume. *J*13, 19

164. Jean Baptiste Poquelin Molière, two plays. See no. 161. Mill mentions reading a comedy by Molière on 11 June, and says on the 13th he was again reading Molière. *J*13, 14

165. Lucian, "Hermotimus." See no. 160. Mill says that on 12 June he read part of the dialogue; he probably refers to it when he says he read some of Lucian on the 14th and 17th; he finished it on the 19th. *J*13, 14, 19, 21, 50

166. *Le code Napoléon* (1804). "In consequence of a conversation with Lady B.," writes Mill on 15 June, "she recommended to me to read such parts as she should point out of the Code Napoleon. Accordingly I read some part, taking notes carefully"; on the 16th he says: "read something more of the Code Napoleon." It is not known which ed. he used; a useful

contemporary edition is that published in Paris by the Imprimerie impériale in 1807. *J*15

167. Adrien Marie Legendre, *Eléments de géométrie* (1794). A standard text, containing, as usual, eight books. On 17 June Mill says: "Madame de Chesnel [daughter of the Benthams] had shewn me last night Legendre's Geometry: I began this morning to read a portion with the intention of learning the French mathematical terms." He worked on it on the 27th and 28th (finding much to praise and a little to criticize), and finished the first book on 1 July. He read the definitions and five propositions of the second book on the 4th, five more propositions on the 5th, seven on the 7th, ten on the 8th, and eight more on the 12th, finishing the second book. *J*19, 28, 29, 30, 34, 35, 36, 37, 44

168. An unidentified article in the *Annales de Chimie; ou, Recueil de Mémoires Concernant la Chimie et les Arts Qui en Dépendent* (1789–1815). Mill says only, on 19 June, "I read part of an article in the Annales de Chimie." *J*21

169. Jean François Regnard, a comedy. See no. 161. On 21 June Mill writes: "Read a comedy by Regnard, and several other things—indeed I was reading French almost all day, as it was raining most of the time, and my books were all packed up." *J*22

170. Lucian, "Βιῶν πρᾶσις" ("Vitarum auctio"; "Philosophies for Sale"). See no. 160. Mill says that on 22 June, after reading "several dialogues of Lucian," he began this, which he finished on the 25th. *J*23, 28, 50

171. Arthur Young, *Travels during the Years 1787, 1788, and 1789* (1792, 1794). On 23 June Mill mentions "the plain of the Garonne, which Arthur Young thought, in point of cultivation, the finest in the world." Mill (who may be reporting the judgment at second hand, but who certainly read the work at some time and very likely before this date) exaggerates somewhat: in his discussion of the "Plain of the Garonne" (Vol. I, pp. 348–51), Young refers to "this rich plain" with its soil of "capital fertility," "a soil, and even . . . a husbandry . . . amongst the best in Europe," and says that the cultivation is more like that of "gardens than farms"; a more limited but parallel judgment is found at Vol. II, p. 66: "This noble vale of the Garonne, which is one of the richest districts of France, is also one of the most productive in hemp that is to be found in the kingdom." *J*24

172. Charles Pierre Girault-Duvivier, *Grammaire des grammaires* (1812). Mill studied French grammar mainly from this work, both on his own and under the supervision of M. Sauvage, who had been hired to tutor him. Apart from the subtitle (where "traités" appears), the parts of the work are not identified as "treatises," the word Mill repeatedly uses; however, he twice refers to the *Grammaire des grammaires* by title, and links other references by saying he has previously mentioned the work. In one case he refers to the *Dictionnaire des difficultés* (no. 195) almost certainly by mistake, as there is no "treatise on Construction" in that work, and there is in this. He refers (26 June) to reading "a treatise on the use of the Subjunctive Mood, in a very elaborate grammar" (Pt. II, Chap. v, Art. xx, §iii; Vol. I, pp. 506–17); on 28 June he read part, and on 1 July the remainder, of a "Treatise on Indefinite Pronouns" (Pt. II, Chap. iv, Art. v [which is divided into four subordinate chapters]; Vol. I, pp. 274–325); on 4 July he began, and continued on the 7th and 8th, "a treatise on the Use of various Adverbs" (Pt. II, Chap. vii, Art. vi; Vol. II, pp. 58–98); from this point on, under Sauvage's guidance, he worked on "a treatise on Pronunciation" (Pt. I, Chaps. i–iii; Vol. I, pp. 5–76 [or perhaps only Chaps. ii–iii; pp. 21–76]) on 14, 23, 25, and 26 July, 1 and 2 Aug.; and on "a treatise on Construction" (Pt. II, Chap. xi; Vol. II, pp. 136–88 [and possibly Chap. xii; pp. 188–203]) on 14 and 26 July (on the latter date Mill gives the reference to the *Dictionnaire des difficultés*), and 1 Aug. Also, on 10 July, he worked on "some passages which [Sauvage] had marked out . . . in a French Grammar"

(probably the same work, though it is just possible that he here meant the *Dictionnaire des difficultés*, in which passages could easily be marked out for study). *J*28, 29, 30, 34, 36, 37, 40, 45, 53, 54, 55, 59

173. Lucian, "Alectryon" ("Somnium, seu gallus"; "The Dream; or, The Cock"). See no. 160. Read, Mill says, on 26 June. *J*28

174. Silvestre François Lacroix, *Traité du calcul différentiel et du calcul intégral* (1798). Mill obviously does not record all his work on Lacroix, saying only, on 27 June: "Had not time to read to day any of Lacroix," and on the 29th: "I have performed over and over all the problems in Lacroix's Differential Calculus." Though the size of the volumes makes the assumption unlikely, he may have been using the 2nd ed., 3 vols. (Paris: Courcier, 1810, 1814, 1819), which is in SC. *J*29

175. Jeremy Bentham, *Chrestomathia* (1816). On 28 June Mill says: "Studied Mr. Bentham's Chrestomatic [*sic*] Tables, including the great Table of the division of human knowledge, or of Eudaemonics [Table V]." *J*29

176. Lucian, "Vocalium judicium" ("Judicium vocalium"; "The Consonants at Law"). See no. 160. Having begun this on 28 June, Mill says that he finished it on the 29th. *J*29, 50

177. Nicolas Boileau-Despréaux, "some . . . little pieces." Mill gives no further identification in his entry for 29 June. It is extremely improbable that he was using the large folio volumes of *Oeuvres*, new ed., 2 vols. (The Hague: Gosse and Neaulme, 1729), which are in SC. *J*29

178. Lucian, "Cataplus" ("Cataplus, sive tyrannus"; "The Downward Journey; or, The Tyrant"). See no. 160. Late in the day on 29 June, having finished Lucian's "Vocalium judicium" (no. 176) in the morning, Mill began the "Cataplus," and finished it on the 30th. He reread it on 20 July (calling it "one of my favourite dialogues"), and again on 26 Nov. *J*29, 30, 50, 52, 86

179. Robert Sanderson, *Logicae artis compendium* (1615). Mill comments, on 30 June: "read some of Sanderson's Logic"; on 1 July: "read also some of Sanderson"; and on the 3rd: "read Sanderson." He may well have been using the 2nd ed. (Oxford: Lichfield and Short, 1618), which is in SC. For similar texts, see nos. 141–4. *J*30, 32

July, 1820. *Aet.* 14.

180. Lucian, "Necyomantia" ("Menippus, sive necyomantia"; "Menippus; or, The Descent into Hades"). See no. 160. Mill began this dialogue on 1 July, continued with it on the 2nd, and finished it on the 5th. *J*30, 35, 50

181. Virgil, *Georgics*. While it seems unlikely that Mill had not begun the *Georgics* earlier, the first reference comes in France on 2 July, 1820, when he reports reading "99 lines of the Georgics of Virgil"; he mentions reading another forty-seven lines on the 4th, and forty-six more on the 7th. *J*30, 34, 36

182. Lucian, "Jupiter confutatus" ("Zeus Catechized"). See no. 160. In three separate stints during the morning of 7 July, Mill read this dialogue. *J*36

183. Lucian, "Prometheus." See no. 160. Mill says that he began, and later continued reading, this dialogue on 8 July; there can be little doubt that he finished it before beginning another (see no. 188) on the 12th. *J*37

184. Jules Mascaron, *Oraison funèbre de très-haut et très-puissant Prince Henri de la*

Tour-d'Auvergne, vicomte de Turenne (1676). A commonly reprinted item. On 10 July Mill says: "Wrote a French *critique* on a passage of Mascaron's Oraison Funèbre de Turenne"; on the 11th: "finished my French lesson by learning by heart the remainder of Mascaron's Mort de Turenne, and of Laharpe's Paral[lel] of Corneille and Racine." *J*40, 44

185. Boileau-Despréaux, "Epistre VI, à Lamoignon" (1683). See no. 177. On 10 July Mill says: "Began to learn by heart part of Boileau Despréaux's epistle to Lamoignon but had not time to finish it." *J*40

186. Jean François de Laharpe, "parallel of Corneille and Racine." After the comment on 11 July cited in no. 184, Mill says on the 12th: "wrote a commentary in French on Laharpe's parallel of Corneille and Racine, . . . and turned part of Laharpe's parallel into Lati[n]." He was probably using a text taken from Laharpe's *Cours de littérature* (1799–1805). *J*44

187. Jean de La Bruyère, "parallel" of Corneille and Racine. On 12 July Mill says: "learned by hear[t] half Labruyère's parallel of the same author[s]" (see no. 186); on the 13th he learned the remainder, and then (unusually for him) says, of the 14th, that he learnt "by heart perfectly the whole of Labruyère's parallel." He was probably using a text taken from "Des ouvrages de l'esprit," in *Les caractères; ou, Les moeurs de ce siècle* (1688). *J*44, 45

188. Lucian, "Icaromenippus." See no. 160. Beginning his reading on 12 July, Mill continued it on the 13th, and finished on the 19th. He reread it on 21 Dec. *J*44, 45, 50, 89

189. George Bentham, MS synoptic table of the classes of insects. Though a work of a different kind, this seems worth citing because Mill obviously owed a great deal to George Bentham's introduction to biological sciences. On 12 July Mill says: "Studied a synoptic table (made by Mr. G.) of the classes of insects"; and again, on the 16th: "studied classification of Insects." *J*44, 47

190. Jules de P. . . . , review of *Programme du cours du droit public, positif, et administratif, à la Faculté de Droit de Paris; pour l'année 1819–20, par M. le baron de Gérando* (Paris: Baudoin, 1819), *Revue Encyclopédique*, VI (June, 1820), 496–512. (There is a one-paragraph notice of the same work, *ibid.*, V [Feb., 1820], 347, signed "Ph. Ch.," but Mill surely is referring to the longer review.) On 13 July he says: "Read part of a review of a work called Programme du Cours du Droit public à la faculté de droit à Paris; in a periodical publication entitled Revue Encyclopédique. Of this article, when I have finished it I will render you [James Mill] an account." No such account is extant. *J*45

191. Charles Jean François Hénault, "parallel" of the reigns of Augustus and Louis XIV. Mill was presumably reading a text taken from the concluding three paragraphs of Hénault's *Nouvel abrégé chronologique de l'histoire de France* (1744). On 15 July he began to learn the parallel "by heart," learnt "more" of it on the 17th, "another part" on the 20th, and "the remainder" on the 22nd. *J*46, 48, 52, 53

192. Lucian, "Jupiter tragoedus" ("Zeus Rants"). See no. 160. Read, says Mill, on 17 July. *J*48, 50

193. Lucian, "Deorum concilium" ("The Parliament of the Gods"). See no. 160. Having read part of this on 21 July, Mill finished it on the 29th. *J*53, 57

194. Antoine Léonard Thomas, "character of Bossuet." On 24 July Mill says he "learnt by heart part of Thomas's literary character of Bossuet"; and on the 26th: "learnt by heart another portion of the character of Bossuet but better." He was probably using a text extracted from "De Mascaron et de Bossuet," Chap. xxxi of Thomas's *Essai sur les éloges* (1773). *J*54

195. Pierre Claude Victoire Boiste, *Dictionnaire des difficultés de la langue française*

(1800). On 26 July Mill says: "M. Sauvage . . . read with me another portion of the treatise on pronunciation as also of the treatise on construction in the Dictionaire des Difficultés." There is, however, no such treatise in this small work (which is arranged as an alphabetical dictionary, with only a very few long entries—that on adjectives runs for ten pages, as does that on participles), and the "treatise on pronunciation" is not in this work, but in the *Grammaire des grammaires*, which Mill was studying thoroughly at this time, and which also contains a treatise on construction (see no. 172). It seems probable that Mill simply wrote down the wrong title at this point. However, it does not seem likely that he invented the name, and one may reasonably assume that he was using this handy text; he may even be referring to it on 10 July when he mentions working on passages in an unspecified grammar. (In the *Grammaire des grammaires*, Girault-Duvivier cites, as one of his authorities, Boiste's *Dictionnaire universel, contenant les principales difficultés de la langue françoise*, from which the smaller work is extracted.) *J55*

196. Charles Lebeau, Latin poetry. On 28 July Mill says he "began to translate into French some Latin poetry of Lebeau." He probably is referring to some of the shorter "Carmina" found in, for example, the first volume of *Opera latina d. Caroli Lebeau* (1782–83). See App. C, no. 24. *J56*

Aug., 1820. *Aet.* 14.

197. J. B. Joudu, *Guide des voyageurs à Bagnères-de-Bigorre et dans les environs* (1818). Mill says he finished reading this work on 21 Aug. *J63*

198. Arnaud Abadie, *Itinéraire topographique et historique des Hautes-Pyrénées* (1819). On 21 Aug. Mill begins a *Description des Hautes Pyrénées*; on the 26th he gives as an authority *Itinéraire topographique et descriptif des Hautes-Pyrénées*; and on 18 Oct. he gives the same title as a footnote to his account for 14 and 17 Sept. It would appear that Mill's "Description" and "descriptif" are slips of the mind. See App. C, no. 29. *J63, 65, 73*

199. Jean Jacques Faget de Baure, *Essais historiques sur le Béarn* (1818). Mill says that, on 26 Aug., he used this work (with the previous item) as a source for his "Notes on 'Usages des Béarnais et des Bigorrais.'" See App. C, no. 29. *J65*

Sept., 1820. *Aet.* 14.

200. Philippe Picot de Lapeyrouse, *Histoire abrégée des plantes des Pyrénées, et itinéraire des botanistes dans ces montagnes* (1813). On 18 Oct. Mill gives his father his authorities for statements in his Journal entry for 14 Sept.; one of these is "La Peyrouse, Histoire des Plantes des Pyrénées, Topographie." On 20 Oct. he says: "J'arrangeai mes plantes, je fis une catalogue de celles qui croissent dans les Pyrenées: c'était pris de l'ouvrage de Lapeyrouse sur les plantes de ces montagnes." A "Table Topographique" is found on pp. 661–700 of the ed. cited above. (Another ed. in 2 vols., with a *Supplément à l'histoire abrégée . . . ,* appeared in 1818.) See App. C, no. 29. *J73, 79*

201. *Nouvelles Annales des Voyages, de la Géographie et de l'Histoire.* This periodical, published in Paris, was a continuation (beginning in 1819) of the earlier *Annales des Voyages . . .* (1808–14); though Mill uses the earlier title, his one specific reference, and the first he gives (on 25 Sept.), is to an article in the second series, and it appears likely that he was reading the work as a current periodical. On 25 Sept. he was reading "une description du labyrinthe d'Egypte dans les Annales des voyages": i.e., Jean Antoine Letronne, "Essai sur le plan et la disposition générale du labyrinthe d'Egypte, d'après Hérodote, Diodore de Sicile et Strabon," *Nouvelles Annales*, VI (1820), 133–54. And, without specifying which

articles, he mentions reading in the *Annales* on 26 Sept., 24, 25, 26, 30, and 31 Oct., and 4 Nov. *J*74, 80, 81

Oct., 1820. *Aet.* 14.

202. Jean Marie Joseph Deville, *Annales de la Bigorre* (1818). Mill says that on 1 Oct. he was reading this work. George Bentham had bought it on 28 Aug. (See *J*121, which gives Bentham's diary entry.) *J*75

203. Cicero, *Pro Milone.* Mill began translating this oration into French on 7 Oct. (probably the part recorded in his Notebook, f. 28r&v); on the 16th he says: "Je m'occupai . . . à lire l'oraison Milonienne de Ciceron," and read more on the 17th and 21st; on the 23rd he remarks: "j'achevai lire l'Oraison de Ciceron." In *Opera* (see no. 59), it appears in Vol. IV, pp. 220–62. Cf. App. C, no. 24. *J*76, 78, 79, 80

204. Henry Hunt, *Memoirs* (1820–22). (The work was issued and sold initially in parts.) On 18 Oct. Mill says: "Je m'occupai . . . à lire les Memoires de Hunt." *J*79

Nov., 1820. *Aet.* 14.

205. Joseph Louis de Lagrange, *Théorie des fonctions analytiques* (1797). On 5 Nov., commenting on the "Cahiers" lent him by Jacques Etienne Bérard, Mill says that the one on differential calculus is based on Lagrange's "Théorie des Fonctions"; one may infer at least that he knew of the work, though he may not have used it. *J*82

206. Jean Baptiste Biot, *Traité analytique des courbes et des surfaces du second degré* (1802; 2nd ed., 1805, retitled, *Essai de géométrie analytique*). On 8 Nov., says Mill, M. Lenthéric "me prêta . . . l'ouvrage de Biot sur ce sujet [Analytical Geometry]; je commençai le soir à l'étudier"; he worked on it on the 10th, 11th, 14th, 16th, 18th, and 19th, and then, after a gap, on 7 Jan., 1821. *J*82, 84, 91

207. Sylvestre François Lacroix, *Elémens d'algèbre* (an VIII). On 15 Nov. Mill says: "je lus un morceau de l'Algèbre de Lacroix." *J*84

208. Boileau-Despréaux, "L'art poétique" (1674). On 22 Nov. Mill says: "j'appris par coeur un morceau de l'Art Poétique de Boileau"; on 26 Nov., "un peu"; and on 28 Nov. and 8 Dec., "un morceau." For the ed. in his library, which it is most unlikely he was using in France, see no. 177. *J*85, 86, 88

Dec., 1820. *Aet.* 14.

209. French plays. See no. 161. On 20, 21, and 22 Dec. Mill says he read "une tragedie française"; on the 23rd: "Je lus . . . une pièce de théatre français"; on the 24th and again on the 25th: "Je lus des pièces de théatre." *J*89, 90

210. Jean Baptiste Say, *Traité d'économie politique* (1803). On 22 Dec. Mill says: "je commençai l'étude de l'Economie Politique de Say"; on the 23rd: "je lus un morceau de Say"; on the 27th: "je continuai la lecture de Say, en fesant des notes de ce que je trouvai à remarquer" (e.g., that Say "confond la valeur avec les richesses"); on the 29th: "je lus un morceau de Say"; on the 31st, and again on 1 Jan., 1821: "Je continuai la lecture de Say." It seems likely that he obtained at that time the ed. in SC, 2 vols. (Paris: Deterville, 1819). Cf. App. C, no. 25. *J*89, 90

211. Cicero, *Familiar Letters.* On 23 Dec. Mill says: "Je lus quelques unes des *lettres familières* de Ciceron." "J'achevai le premier livre," he records on the 27th, and says he

began the Second Book on the 28th, adding on the 29th: "Je lus quelques lettres de Cicéron." In *Opera* (see no. 59), they appear in Vol. V. *J*89, 90

Jan., 1821. *Aet.* 14.

212. Pierre Simon de Laplace, *Exposition du système du monde* (1796). On 2 Jan., 1821, Mill says: "Je commençai l'étude du Système du Monde de Laplace"; his reading continued on the 3rd, 5th, 7th, 10th, 11th, 12th, 13th, 15th, 18th, 20th, and 29th. It seems unlikely that he was using the 4th ed. (Paris: Courcier, 1813), which is in SC. *J*90, 91, 92, 93, 96

1821. *Aet.* 14–15.

213. Etienne Bonnot de Condillac, *Traité des sensations* (1754). As noted in no. 156, Mill says in *A*, "what can properly be called my lessons" concluded when he left for France. He continues: "after my return, though my studies went on under my father's general direction, he was no longer my schoolmaster" (*A*33). In his account he then turns to matters "of a more general nature," and does not resume his description of his reading until (at *A*65) he begins Chap. iii by saying: "For the first year or two after my visit to France, I continued my old studies, with the addition of some new ones." He mentions his work on his father's *Elements* (see no. 150), and then says: "Soon after, my father put into my hands Condillac's *Traité des Sensations*, and the logical and metaphysical volumes of his *Cours d'Etudes*; the first (notwithstanding the superficial resemblance between Condillac's psychological system and my father's) quite as much for a warning as for an example." *Oeuvres complètes*, 31 vols. (Paris: Dufart, 1803), is in SC; the *Traité* is Vol. IV in that ed. *A*65 (*64*)

214. Condillac, *Cours d'études*. See no. 213, where Mill is quoted as saying he read the logical and metaphysical volumes of the *Cours*. There are, however, no metaphysical volumes in the work known by that name, and Mill read some logical works also not there included. It seems very probable that at this period, or soon afterwards, he read Condillac's *De l'art de penser* (*Oeuvres complètes*, Vol. IX), *De l'art de raisonner* (*ibid.*, Vol. XI; this is in the *Cours*), *Essai sur l'origine des connoissances humaines* (*ibid.*, Vols. I–II), *La logique; ou, Les premiers developpemens de l'art de penser* (*ibid.*, Vol. XXX; also in *Cours*), and *Traité des systêmes* (*ibid.*, Vol. III), in addition to the *Traité des sensations*, which he specifically cites. *A*65 (*64*)

1821–22, or 1822–23. *Aet.* 15 or 16.

215. François Emmanuel Toulongeon, *Histoire de France, depuis la révolution de 1789* (1801–10). The reference is to "a history of the French Revolution" read by Mill in the winter of 1821–22, or that of 1822–23 ("I am not sure," he says); of relevant works mentioned by him in his letters, only this was available at the time (see *EL*, *CW*, Vol. XII, p. 22). *A*65 (*64*)

Before no. 217. *Aet.* 15?

216. James Mill, "Jurisprudence." Mill says: "To Bentham's general views of the construction of a body of law I was not altogether a stranger, having read [presumably on its first appearance, or in MS] with attention that admirable compendium, my father's article "Jurisprudence": but I had read it with little profit, and scarcely any interest, no doubt from its extremely general and abstract character, and also because it concerned the form more than the substance of the *corpus juris*, the logic rather than the ethics of law." (One may safely assume that Mill had also by this time read his father's other articles for the

Supplement to the *Encyclopaedia Britannica*: "Banks for Saving," "Beggar," "Benefit Societies," "Caste," "Colonies," "Economists," "Education," "Government," "Law of Nations," "Liberty of the Press," and "Prisons and Prison Discipline.") *A*69 (*68*)

1821. *Aet.* 15.

217. Jeremy Bentham, *Traités de législation civile et pénale, précédés de Principes généraux de législation, et d'une Vue d'un corps complet de droit: terminés par un Essai sur l'influence des tems et des lieux relativement aux lois*, ed. Pierre Etienne Louis Dumont (1802). (See no. 218.) Mill says: "at the commencement" of his studies of law under John Austin in 1821–22, James Mill, "as a needful accompaniment to them, put into my hands Bentham's principal speculations, as interpreted to the Continent, and indeed to all the world, by Dumont, in the *Traité de Législation*. The reading of this book was an epoch in my life; one of the turning points in my mental history." *A*67 (*66*)

1821–22? *Aet.* 15–16?

218. Jeremy Bentham, *An Introduction to the Principles of Morals and Legislation* (1789). At this point in *A*, Mill is writing of Dumont's redaction in *Traités* (see no. 217); however, Mill quotes words in English that suggest a reference not to the translation, but to Bentham's original work, which he must have read then or soon after. In his "Historical Preface to the Second Edition" (1828) of his *Fragment on Government*, Bentham says of his *Introduction to the Principles of Morals and Legislation*: "It has not been so [incomprehensible] to babes and sucklings. Two boys of sixteen have been giving a spontaneous reading to it: in the person of a tailor, it has found a spontaneous and unpaid Editor, who, having read it as an amateur, gives himself in this way a second reading of it." (*Works*, Vol. I, p. 252.) The tailor is unquestionably Francis Place; the boys of sixteen very probably John Mill and Richard Doane. See also no. 223. Mill may have read this ed., or the 2-vol. ed. (1823). *A*67 (*66*)

1821–22. *Aet.* 15.

219. Johann Gottlieb Heineccius, *Elementa juris civilis secundum ordinem institutionum* (1726). "During the winter of 1821/2," says Mill, "Mr. John Austin . . . kindly allowed me to read Roman law with him. . . . With Mr. Austin I read Heineccius on the Institutes, his Roman Antiquities, and part of his exposition of the Pandects." In SC are *Operum ad universam juris prudentiam*, 8 vols. (Geneva: Cramer Heirs, *et al.*, 1744–49), in which the *Institutes* is found in Vol. V; and the 1766 ed. (Leipzig: Fritsch). *A*67 (*66*)

220. Heineccius, *Antiquitatum romanarum jurisprudentiam illustrantium syntagma secundum ordinem institutionum Justiniani digestum* (1719). See no. 219; in the first ed. there cited, the *Roman Antiquities* is in Vol. IV. *A*67 (*66*)

221. Heineccius, *Elementa juris civilis, secundum ordinem pandectarum* (1731). See no. 219; in the first of the two eds. there cited, the *Pandects* is in Vol. V. *A*67 (*66*)

222. William Blackstone, *Commentaries on the Laws of England* (1765–69). To Mill's reading of Heineccius (see nos. 219–21), Austin added "a considerable portion of Blackstone." The 5th ed., 4 vols. (Oxford: Clarendon Press, 1773), is in SC. *A*67 (*66*)

After the Winter of 1821–22. *Aet.* 15+.

223. Jeremy Bentham, *A Fragment on Government* (1776). At the conclusion of his account of his legal studies in 1821–22, Mill says: "After this I read, from time to time, the

most important of the other works of Bentham which had then seen the light, either as written by himself or as edited by Dumont." See nos. 224–8 and 238, and also nos. 175, 217, and 218. *A*71 (*70*)

224. Bentham, *Panopticon* (1791). See no. 223. *A*71 (*70*)

225. Bentham, *A Table of the Springs of Action* (1817). See no. 223. *A*71 (*70*)

226. Bentham, *Tactique des assemblées législatives, suivie d'un Traité des sophismes politiques*, ed. Dumont (1816). See no. 223. *A*71 (*70*)

227. Bentham, *Théorie des peines et des récompenses*, ed. Dumont (1811). See no. 223. *A*71 (*70*)

228. Bentham, *Traité des preuves judiciaires*, ed. Dumont (1823). See no. 223; although this appeared slightly later than the period Mill is writing of, he almost certainly had it in mind. *A*71 (*70*)

1822. Aet. 15–16.

229. John Locke, *Essay Concerning Human Understanding* (1689). Having digressed to mention his reading, "from time to time," Bentham's works, Mill presumably returns to the period immediately following his study of Roman law with Austin in 1821–22, saying: "under my father's direction, my studies were carried into the higher branches of analytic psychology. I now read Locke's *Essay*, and wrote out an account of it, consisting of a complete abstract of every chapter, with such remarks as occurred to me: which was read by, or (I think) to, my father, and discussed throughout." (*A*71.) He indicates here that he read all of nos. 229–31 and 233–8 in the course of this year. He probably read Locke's *Essay* in an ed. earlier than the only one now in SC, *Works*, new ed., 10 vols. (London: Tegg, *et al.*, 1823), Vols. I–III. Cf. App. C, no. 32. *A*71 (*70*)

230. Claude Adrien Helvétius, *De l'esprit* (1758). See no. 229. Mill says he "performed the same process" with Helvétius as with Locke, having read Helvétius of his "own choice." Cf. App. C, no. 33. *A*71 (*70*)

231. David Hartley, *Observations on Man, His Frame, His Duty, and His Expectations* (1749). See no. 229. "After Helvetius," says Mill, "my father made me study what he deemed the really master-production in the philosophy of mind, Hartley's *Observations on Man*. This book, though it did not, like the *Traité de Législation*, give a new colour to my existence, made a very similar impression on me in regard to its immediate subject." *A*71 (*70*)

Summer, 1822ff. Aet. 16+.

232. James Mill, *Analysis of the Phenomena of the Human Mind* (1829). James Mill began the work in the summer of 1822, and "allowed" John to read "the manuscript, portion by portion, as it advanced." *A*71 (*70*)

1822. Aet. 15–16.

233. George Berkeley. See no. 229. Mill says simply that he read, as he "felt inclined," Berkeley among the "other principal English writers on mental philosophy." *A*71 (*70*)

234. David Hume, *Essays and Treatises on Several Subjects* (1750–53). See no. 229. Mill simply mentions reading "Hume's *Essays*." (Cf. no. 233.) A 2-vol. ed. (London: Cadell;

Edinburgh: Bell and Bradfute, *et al.*, 1793) is in SC, but he more likely used the un-identified annotated ed. sold in Avignon to T. N. Page in 1906 (see App. I below). *A*71 (*70*)

235. Thomas Reid. See no. 229. Mill simply says he read "Reid." (Cf. nos. 233–4.) *A*71 (*70*)

236. Dugald Stewart. See no. 229. Mill simply says he read "Dugald Stewart." (Cf. nos. 233–5.) *A*71 (*70*)

237. Thomas Brown, *Observations on . . . the Doctrine of Mr. Hume, Concerning . . . Cause and Effect* (1805; 3rd ed., 1818, retitled, *Inquiry into the Relation of Cause and Effect*). See no. 229. Mill simply says he read "Brown on Cause and Effect." Mill probably read the work in the 3rd ed. (Edinburgh: Constable, 1818), which is in SC, with "Brown on Cause & Effect" on the spine. *A*71 (*70*)

238. George Grote ("Philip Beauchamp"), *Analysis of the Influence of Natural Religion* (1822). Edited from Bentham's MSS. See no. 229. A work "which contributed materially to my development," says Mill, remarking that it had been given to his father in MS, and consequently shown to him. "I made a marginal analysis of it as I had done of the *Elements of Political Economy* [no. 150]. Next to the *Traité de Législation* [no. 217], it was one of the books which by the searching character of its analysis produced the greatest effect upon me." His judgment, on rereading it many years later, was still enthusiastic, though less committed. *A*73 (*72*)

239. William Paley, *Natural Theology* (1802). Though Mill does not mention reading this work, he must have done so to write the reply to it he describes in ED (not in *A*). That reply may be referred to in a letter to the Grotes of 14 Nov., 1822. See App. C, no. 36. ED*74*; *EL*, Vol. XII, p. 15

* * * * *

INDEX TO APPENDIX B

Appendix C

Mill's Early Writing, 1811?–22

MILL'S REFERENCES to the writing he did in childhood and youth are less detailed and circumstantial, in the main, than his references to his early reading (which is outlined in Appendix B, above). Nonetheless, the account is of considerable interest as indicating both what was required of him and what he undertook on his own, and as a rare indication of the childish and youthful aspirations and achievements of one later to achieve fame largely through his pen. Unfortunately, almost nothing of what he actually wrote has survived; we have only the beginning of one history ("The History of Rome") and one poem ("Ode to Diana"), both printed above in Appendix A, a very considerable document, his "Traité de logique," and the MS of an essay of 1822 (see nos. 2, 6, 20, 31 and 34 below).

The following list gives the approximate date of composition, with Mill's age (in years) at the time (in most cases the date cannot be accurately fixed), and a few comments. A date such as that for no. 3—1813–16?—does not imply that the item was probably being written during that whole period, but that it was written some time during that period, though the terminal dates cannot be certainly established. The evidence is drawn from the *Autobiography* (*A*), the Early Draft (ED, with the page numbers in italics), the Journal and Notebook of his visit to France in 1820–21 (*J*), with some information from the *Earlier Letters*, Vol. XII of the *Collected Works* (*EL*), and elsewhere. Set exercises and notebooks are not included in the list, except analytical abstracts (see nos. 10–12, 17–19, and 32–3) and translations (see nos. 7 and 24). It should not be inferred that this list is complete, for Mill's comments were usually written long after the event, except for those from the Journal and Notebook, which are much more dense. The account terminates in 1822; Mill's first published writings, two letters on exchangeable value, appeared in the *Traveller* on 6 and 13 Dec., 1822.

1811. *Aet.* 5–6.

1. A "history of India." In *A*, Mill mentions a "voluntary exercise" to which throughout his boyhood he "was much addicted," the writing of histories. In ED, giving details not in *A*, he says this was "of course in imitation" of his father, and adds: "Almost as soon as I could hold

a pen I must needs write a history of India too: this was soon abandoned. . . ." Cf. App. B, no. 101. *A17 (16)*

1812. *Aet.* 6.

2. A "Roman history." This he began after abandoning his history of India, and continued with for a long time. The opening pages of this history are printed above, in App. A, as "The History of Rome." His narrative, he tells us, was "picked out of Hooke," and his earliest extant letter, to Jeremy Bentham, dated July, 1812, asking for Vols. III and IV of Hooke (he has been "recapitulating" Vols. I and II), enables us to give the *terminus a quo* as 1812, which the notation on the manuscript, "by John Stuart Mill aged 6½ yrs," confirms. Cf. App. B, no. 24. *A17 (16); EL3*

1813–16? *Aet.* 7–10?

3. An "abridgment of the *Ancient Universal History.*" (For the work abridged, see App. B, no. 57.) This is merely mentioned as written after his first Roman history. It and the next item are listed by Mill, it should be noted, just after his account (see *A15*) of his "private" historical reading between his eighth and twelfth years. See App. B, no. 51, for dating. *A17 (16)*

4. A "History of Holland." This was based on his "favorite Watson" and "an anonymous compilation" (see App. B, nos. 22, 23, and 58). In his letter to Samuel Bentham summarizing his education up to 30 July, 1819 (the date of the letter), he says, without giving any indication of the year meant: "I had carried a history of the United Provinces from their revolt from Spain, in the reign of Phillip II, to the accession of the Stadtholder, William III, to the throne of England." For dating, see App. B, no. 51; see also no. 3 above. *A17 (16); EL9*

1813–14. *Aet.* 7.

5. In English verse, "as much as one book of a continuation of the *Iliad.*" This he undertook when he "first read Pope's Homer," as a voluntary exercise, under "the spontaneous promptings" of his "poetical ambition." See App. B, no. 50. *A19 (18)*

1813–17? *Aet.* 7–11?

6. English poetry, "mostly addresses to some mythological personage or allegorical abstraction." These were written at his father's command, following on his beginning poetical composition with no. 5 above. The "Ode to Diana" printed above in App. A is undoubtedly one of these "addresses." *A19 (18)*

1816? *Aet.* 9–10?

7. Translations of "Horace's shorter poems." This too was an exercise set by his father, and one can safely assume that there were similar ones later (see also no. 24 below). Since normally boys of the aspiring middle class were required at the time to concentrate on composition in the Classical languages, it should be noted that Mill says he was not required to compose at all in Greek, and only a little in Latin. Cf. App. B, nos. 84–8. *A19 (18)*

1813–17? *Aet.* 7–11?

8. A poem modelled on Thomson's "Winter." Again a set exercise. At this point, though probably not with reference solely to this composition, Mill says: "The verses I wrote were

of course the merest rubbish, nor did I ever attain any facility of versification, but the practice may have been useful in making it easier for me, at a later period, to acquire readiness of expression." Cf. App. B, no. 114. *A*19 (*18*)

1816–17. *Aet.* 10–11.

9. A "history of the Roman Government." This more "serious" work was undertaken in his "eleventh and twelfth year," Mill says in *A*; in his letter to Samuel Bentham he says merely that he had "begun to write a history of the Roman Government, . . . carried down to the Licinian Laws." The account in *A* justifies the description of this history as more serious than his earlier attempts: it was "compiled (with the assistance of Hooke) from Livy and Dionysius: of which I wrote as much as would have made an octavo volume, extending to the epoch of the Licinian Laws. It was, in fact, an account of the struggles between the patricians and plebeians, which now engrossed all the interest in my mind which I had previously felt in the mere wars and conquests of the Romans. I discussed all the constitutional points as they arose: though quite ignorant of Niebuhr's researches, I, by such lights as my father had given me, vindicated the Agrarian Laws on the evidence of Livy, and upheld to the best of my ability the Roman democratic party." He then comments with reference to all his writings to that date: "A few years later, in my contempt of my childish efforts, I destroyed all these papers, not then anticipating that I could ever feel any curiosity about my first attempts at writing and reasoning." And he concludes this section of his commentary by saying: "My father encouraged me in this useful amusement, though, as I think judiciously, he never asked to see what I wrote; so that I did not feel that in writing it I was accountable to any one, nor had the chilling sensation of being under a critical eye." *A*17 (*16*); *EL*9

1817. *Aet.* 10–11.

10. A "synoptic table" of Aristotle's *Rhetoric*. Not mentioned in *A* or ED, this exercise (probably voluntary) is given in Mill's letter to Samuel Bentham as part of his work in 1817. Cf. App. B, no. 106. *EL*8

1817? *Aet.* 10–11?

11. A "full analysis" of Demosthenes' principal orations. Again probably voluntary. Cf. App. B, no. 66. *A*23 (*22*)

1818. *Aet.* 11–12.

12. A synoptic table of the first four books of Aristotle's *Organon*. See App. B, no. 129, and no. 10 above. *EL*8

1818? *Aet.* 11–12?

13. A tragedy, probably in verse, "on the Roman emperor Otho," based on Tacitus. (Cf. App. B, no. 130.) At *A*19n, just after mentioning the worthlessness of his poetical compositions (see no. 8 above), Mill says: "In a subsequent stage of boyhood, when these exercises had ceased to be compulsory, like most youthful writers I wrote tragedies; under the inspiration not so much of Shakespeare as of Joanna Baillie, whose *Constantine Paleologus* in particular appeared to me one of the most glorious of human compositions." (Cf. App. B, no. 115.) In ED, the account is more detailed, and the tragedy on Otho, as well as the next three items, is mentioned. Probably the last two of these are referred to in his letter to Samuel Bentham, where he says: "I have now and then attempted to write Poetry.

The last production of that kind at which I tried my hand was a tragedy. I have now another in view in which I hope to correct the fault of this." (No date is given for the earlier one; the latter is dated by the letter itself, 30 July, 1819.) *A*19n (*26*); *EL*10

14. A verse tragedy "on the story of the Danaides." For comment, see no. 13 above. ED*26*

1818–19? *Aet.* 12–13?

15. A verse tragedy "on a subject from Tacitus." For comment, see no. 13 above. ED*26*

1819? *Aet.* 13?

16. A verse tragedy "on a subject . . . from Thucydides." For comment, see no. 13 above. Cf. App. B, no. 10. ED*26*

1819. *Aet.* 12–13.

17. An "abstract" of Plato's *Republic.* Mentioned only in Mill's letter to Samuel Bentham. See App. B, no. 148. *EL*8

18. An "outline" of the "science" of political economy, based on his father's oral expositions during their walks. His "written account" of each day's discussions was rewritten "over and over again until it was clear, precise, and tolerably complete," and was then used by James Mill as the basis of his *Elements of Political Economy.* Cf. App. B, no. 150. *A*31 (*30*); *EL*8

19. An "abstract" of Ricardo's *Principles of Political Economy.* The study of Ricardo's work is mentioned in *A* and ED, but the "abstract" is listed only in the letter to Samuel Bentham. Cf. App. B, no. 151. *A*31 (*30*); *EL*8

May, 1820–Feb., 1821. *Aet.* 14–15.

20. A journal and a notebook. These were kept "according to [his father's] injunctions" (*J*3) during his visit to France, recording his activities, reading, and observations on various aspects of the country. Excerpts from the journal were used by Alexander Bain in his biography of Mill. The journal MS was presented by Mill's sister Clara to the British Museum (BL Add. MS 31909). The notebook, discovered in 1956, is in the possession of Professor Anna Jean Mill; see her ed., *John Mill's Boyhood Visit to France: A Journal and Notebook* (Toronto: University of Toronto Press, 1960). The following items (nos. 21–31), dating from 15 May, 1820, to 6 Feb., 1821 (though Mill did not return to England until July, 1821), derive from these sources; they are not mentioned in *A* or ED.

May–June, 1820. *Aet.* 14.

21. A "dialogue in continuation" of his father's "dialogue on government" (the latter not to be confused with the famous essay by James Mill, "Government," which, as is indicated at *J*42, the young Mill had not seen at the time). The dialogue having been begun on 24 May, its outline was complete on the 25th; Mill mentions working on it on 7, 8, and 10 June, finishing it on the 11th, and revising it on the 12th. On 6 July, in two sessions, he began to copy and "correct" his dialogue, and on the 11th he writes to his father: "I have taken great pains with the expression as well as with the reasoning, and I hope you will be pleased with it." And he promises to send it soon; however, on 20 Nov. he reread and started to correct it. On f. 49v of his Notebook there is what appears to be the beginning of the dialogue. *J*8–13, 35–6, 42, 85, 103

June–Aug., 1820. *Aet.* 14.

22. A "Livre Statistique [et Géographique], consisting of the Departments of France with their chefs lieux, the rivers, . . . population, . . . &c. &c." This he worked on steadily through June, July, and August. Presumably it included his "table of 58 rivers, the principal in France, classified and arranged; with the whole of their course, that is to say, what departments each passes through and what are the chief towns on their banks," on which he was working on 5 July (*J*35). A *cahier* was bought at the end of July so that he could copy his *livre* into it. *J*15–59, 62

July, 1820. *Aet.* 14.

23. "Chemical classification tables" (*J*53). The preparation of these was a constant preoccupation during July, when more than once he returned, late in the day, after completing his lessons, to what was clearly an exciting pleasure. Cf. App. B, no. 100. *J*36–56

July–Oct.?, 1820. *Aet.* 14.

24. Translations from Latin into French (set exercises by his French teacher, Sauvage). These included, as well as unspecified works, the first ode of Horace (with some observations on it), the monologue of Juno in Book I of the *Aeneid* and an "*Analyse*" of it (*J*45), Sallust's speech of Cataline to his accomplices (*J*46), Horace's third ode with "an Analyse" (*J*48, 50), some of the poetry of Lebeau (*J*56), and part of Cicero's *Pro Milone* (portions of the last appear in Mill's Notebook, f. 28). Cf. App. B, nos. 86, 75, 52, 196, 203. *J*40–59, 76

July, 1820. *Aet.* 14.

25. A "small portion of a Treatise on Value in French." (He may well have worked further on this; he mentions that Samuel Bentham had said that Say's book would be borrowed if possible for the purpose; it was obtained by 22 Dec., and he was reading it during the next two weeks at least [*J*89–90].) This task would appear to have been undertaken as a consequence of conversations with Lady Bentham; Mill had commented just two days before his mention of this composition: "The best exercise in both these branches of knowledge [Political Economy and Logic] would perhaps be to write treatises on particular subjects appertaining to both. This I have not yet commenced doing, but I shall certainly do so." Cf. nos. 26–8, 31 below and App. B, no. 210. *J*43, 45

26. A "rough sketch of a dialogue on a subject proposed to me by Lady Bentham, namely, the question whether great landed estates and great establishments in commerce and manufactures, or small ones, are the most conducive to the general happiness?" (This question was at issue between Say and Sismondi.) It is not known whether or not he finished this dialogue. *J*52–3

27. A "treatise on the definition of political economy," on Lady Bentham's advice. He only mentions beginning this work (on a subject of which he later made much). *J*53

Aug., 1820. *Aet.* 14.

28. Logical tables. "Je commençai," he says, "à me faire des tables Logiques." See no. 31 below. *J*64

29. Notes on "Usages des Béarnais et des Bigorrais." These were drawn "from *Essais historiques sur le Béarn* and *Itinéraire topographique et descriptif des Hautes-Pyrénées*" (see App. B, nos. 198 and 199), and included also his personal observations. *J*65

Oct., 1820. *Aet.* 14.

30. A "catalogue de celles [plantes] qui croissent dans les Pyrenées." This was based on Lapeyrouse; but it should be mentioned that George Bentham's *Catalogue des plantes indigènes des Pyrénées et du Bas Languedoc* (1826), in which he notes corrections needed in Lapeyrouse's *Histoire abrégée des plantes des Pyrénées* (see App. B, no. 200), was developed in the first instance from the botanizing he did (while instructing the young Mill) during the summer of 1820. *J*79

31. "Traité de logique." On 24 Oct., Mill says: "Je commençai à écrire un court Traité de Logique." The "Traité" is not mentioned again, but he completed it; the MS is in the Pierpont Morgan Library. It was, to some extent, based on Gergonne's lectures on Logic, which Mill attended (his notes of the latter part of the course are in the Mill-Taylor Collection, British Library of Political and Economic Science), but is not by any means a mere reproduction of those lectures, which did not begin until 16 Nov., nearly a month after Mill began his "Traité." *J*80

1822. *Aet.* 15–16.

32. An "account" of Locke's *Essay*, "consisting of a complete abstract of every chapter, with such remarks as occurred" to him. The reading of Locke, which came after his encounter with Bentham's major writings (see *A*67ff.), was assigned by his father, but it seems likely that the "account" was voluntary. Cf. App. B, no. 229. *A*71 (*70*)

33. A similar account of Helvétius' *De l'esprit*. In *A*, Mill merely mentions reading Helvétius "of [his] own choice"; in ED, he indicates that he next performed, after Locke, the same process on Helvétius, again the account being voluntary. Cf. App. B, no. 230. *A*71 (*70*)

1822. *Aet.* 16.

34. His "first argumentative essay," in the summer of 1822, "an attack on what [he] regarded as the aristocratic prejudice, that the rich were, or were likely to be, superior in moral qualities to the poor." This voluntary exercise was undertaken in "emulation of a little manuscript essay of Mr. Grote." This essay (or a draft of it) is almost certainly that in Mill's hand in his father's "Common-Place Book," Vol. II, ff. 79v–80r, headed by James Mill "Grote on Moral Obligation" (London Library). *A*73 (*72*)

35. Two "speeches, one an accusation, the other a defence of Pericles." The genre was set by the father, but the subjects were chosen by the son. While with the Austins, in the autumn of 1822, Mill wrote to his father to say that he had finished the defence; his father already had the attack in his possession. The defence had been revised by 14 Nov., as he indicated in a letter to the Grotes. *A*75 (*74*); *EL*13, 15

36. A "reply to Paley's *Natural Theology*." Suggested by his father, this may be the work he refers to by the Benthamic name of "Jug True" in the letter to the Grotes cited in no. 35. The suggestion by James Mill may derive from the entry in his "Common-Place Book" immediately following no. 34 above, headed "No. 1 Jug. Util" (Vol. II, ff. 80v). In 1822

Grote (under the pseudonym "Philip Beauchamp") published *Analysis of the Influence of Natural Religion, on the Temporal Happiness of Mankind*, based on Bentham's MSS. Cf. App. B, no. 239. ED*74*; *EL*15

37. Writings "for the Util. Rev." This matter, which is mentioned only in the letter to the Grotes cited in nos. 35 and 36, may actually be a reference to the Utilitarian Society ("Rev." being a misreading of "Soc."), for which plans were already under way (it began to meet in 1823), and for which Richard Doane had written a trial piece which Mill had read. (The *Westminster Review* had not been thought of at this time.) *EL*15

1822? Aet. 16?

38. Papers "on subjects often very much beyond [his] capacity [at the time], but [giving] great benefit both from the exercise itself, and from the discussions which it led to with [his] father." These may be taken to include the essay referred to only in Kate Amberley's record of Harriet Grote's conversations with her: "J. S. Mill wrote an essay (never printed it) when he was young against all sentiment & feeling etc. He was much ashamed of it later in life & got Mrs. Grote's copy fr. her and destroyed it." *A*75 (*74*); *The Amberley Papers*, ed. Bertrand and Patricia Russell, 2 vols. (London: Hogarth Press, 1937), Vol. I, p. 421

Appendix D

A Few Observations on Mr. Mill (1833)

APPENDIX C in Edward Lytton Bulwer, *England and the English* (London: Bentley, 1833), Vol. II, pp. 345–55. Unsigned; not republished; not listed in Mill's bibliography. In a letter to Carlyle (2 Aug., 1833), Mill mentions his contributions on Bentham to *England and the English* (in *CW*, Vol. X, pp. 3–18, and 499–502), saying that he does not intend to acknowledge them as his; he then continues: "I furnished him also at his request with a few yet rougher notes concerning my father, which he has not dealt so fairly by, but has cut and mangled and coxcombified the whole thing till its mother would not know it: there are a few sentences of mine in it, something like what they were when I wrote them; for the sake of artistic congruity I wish there were not. This I still less own, because it is not mine, in any sense." (*EL, CW*, Vol. XII, p. 172.) In the SC copy of *England and the English* there are no emendations or other marks.

At the end of this text we reprint Mill's slight contribution to Andrew Bisset's article, "James Mill," in the *Encyclopaedia Britannica*, 7th ed. (Edinburgh: Black, 1842), Vol. XV, pp. 77–80 (Mill's sentences are on p. 78).

For further comment, see the Introduction, p. xxxiii above.

Mr. Mill has been frequently represented as the disciple of Bentham. With truth has he been so represented in this respect—he was one of the earliest in adopting—he has been one of the most efficient in diffusing—many of the most characteristic of Bentham's opinions. He admits without qualification—he carries into detail with rigid inflexibility, the doctrine that the sole ground of moral obligation is *general utility*. But the same results may be reached by minds the most dissimilar; else why do we hope for agreement amongst impartial inquirers?—else why do we hope to convert one another? why not burn our lucubrations, or wait to establish a principle until we have found an exact resemblance of ourselves?

In some respects Mr. Mill's mind assimilates to Bentham's, in others it differs from it widely. It is true that Mr. Mill's speculations have been influenced by impressions received from Bentham; but they have been equally influenced by those received from the Aristotelian Logicians, from Hartley, and from Hobbes. He almost alone in the present age has revived the study of those writers—he has preserved, perhaps, the most valuable of their doctrines—he is largely indebted to them for the doctrines which compose, for the spirit which pervades his philosophy. The character of his intellect seems to partake as much of that of either of those three types of speculative inquiry, as it does of the likeness of Bentham.

As a searcher into original truths, the principal contribution which Mr. Mill has rendered to philosophy, is to be found in his most recent work, *The Analysis of the Phenomena of the Human Mind.* Nothing more clearly proves what I have before asserted, viz.—our indifference to the higher kind of philosophical investigation, than the fact, that no full account—no *criticism* of this work has appeared in either of our principal Reviews.

The doctrine announced by Hartley, that the ideas furnished by Sense, together with the law of association, are the simple elements of the mind, and sufficient to explain even the most mysterious of its phenomena, is also the doctrine of Mr. Mill. Hartley, upon this principle, had furnished an explanation of *some* of the phenomena. Mr. Mill has carried on the investigation into all those more complex psychological facts which had been the puzzle and despair of previous metaphysicians. Such, for instance, as Time and Space—Belief—the Will—the Affections—the Moral Sentiments. He has attempted to resolve all these into cases of association. I do not pause here to contend with him—to show, or rather endeavour to show, where he has succeeded—where failed. It would be a task far beyond the limits of this Book—it is properly the task of future metaphysicians.

The moment in which this remarkable work appeared is unfortunate for its temporary success. Had it been published sixty years ago—or perhaps sixty years hence, it would perhaps have placed the reputation of its author beyond any of his previous writings.

There is nothing similar to these inquiries in the writings of Mr. Bentham. This indicates one principal difference between the two men. Mr. Mill is eminently a metaphysician; Bentham as little of a metaphysician as any one can be who ever attained to equal success in the science of philosophy. Every moral or political system must be indeed a corollary from some general view of human nature. But Bentham, though punctilious and precise in the premises he advances, confines himself, in that very preciseness, to a few simple and general principles. *He seldom analyses*—he studies the human mind rather after the method of natural history than of philosophy. He enumerates—he classifies the facts—but he does not *account* for them. You read in his works an enumeration of pains and pleasures—an enumeration of motives—an enumeration of the properties which constitute the value of a pleasure or a pain. But Bentham does not even attempt to *explain* any of the feelings or impulses enumerated—he does not attempt to show that they are subject to the laws of any more elementary phenomena of human nature. Of human nature indeed in its rarer or more hidden parts, Bentham knew but little—wherever he attained to valuable results, which his predecessors had missed, it was by estimating more justly than they the action of some outward circumstance upon the more obvious and vulgar elements of our nature—not by understanding better than they, the workings of those elements which are not obvious and not vulgar. Where but a moderate knowledge of these last was necessary to the correctness of his conclusions, he was apt to stray farther from the truth than even the votaries of common place. He often threw aside a trite and unsatisfactory truism, in order to replace it with a paradoxical error.

If, then, the power of analysing a complex combination into its simple elements be in the mental sciences, as in the physical, a leading characteristic of the philosopher, Mr. Mill is thus far considerably nearer to the philosophic ideal than Mr. Bentham. This, however, has not made so great a difference as might have been expected in the practical conclusions at which they have arrived. Those powers of analysis which, by Mr. Bentham, are not brought to bear upon the phenomena of our nature at all, are applied by Mr. Mill almost solely to our *common universal* nature, to the general structure which is the same in all human beings; not to the differences between one human being and another, though the former is little worthy of being studied except as a means to the better understanding of the latter. We seldom learn from Mr. Mill to understand any of the varieties of human nature; and, in truth, they enter very little into his own calculations, except where he takes cognizance of them as aberrations from the standard to which, in his opinion, all should conform. Perhaps there never existed any writer, (except, indeed, the ascetic theologians,) who conceived the excellence of the human being so exclusively under one single type, to a conformity with which he would reduce all mankind. No one ever made fewer allowances for original differences of nature, although the existence of such is not only compatible with, but a necessary consequence of, his view of the human mind, when combined with the extraordinary differences which are known to exist between one individual and another in the kind and in the degree of their nervous sensibility. I cannot but think that the very laws of association, laid down by Mr. Mill, will hereafter, and in other hands, be found (while they explain the diversities of human nature) to show, in the most striking manner, how much of those diversities is inherent and inevitable; neither the effect of, nor capable of being reached by, education or outward circumstances.* I believe the natural and necessary differences among mankind to be so great, that any practical view of human life, which does not take them into the account, must, unless it stop short in generalities, contain at least as much error as truth; and that any system of mental culture, recommended by such imperfect theory in proportion as it is fitted to natures of one class, will be entirely unfitted for all others.

Mr. Mill has given to the world, as yet, on the subject of morals, and on that of education, little besides generalities: not "barren generalities,"[*] but of the most fruitful kind; yet of which the fruit is still to come. When he shall carry his

---

*I venture to recommend to the notice of the Reader an able paper on the character of Dr. Priestley, published in several recent numbers of Mr. Fox's excellent *Monthly Repository*. [James Martineau, "On the Life, Character, and Works of Dr. Priestley," *Monthly Repository*, n.s. VII (Jan., Feb., Apr., 1833), 19–30, 84–8, 231–41.]

[*Cf. Bacon, *Novum Organum*, Bk. I, Aph. xxii, in *Works*, Vol. I, p. 160 (Latin), and Vol. IV, p. 50 (English). See also p. 25 above.]

speculations into the details of these subjects, it is impossible that an intellect like his should not throw a great increase of light upon them: the danger is that the illumination will be partial and narrow; that he will conclude too readily that, whatever is suitable food for one sort of character, or suitable medicine for bringing it back, when it falls from its proper excellence, may be prescribed for *all*, and that what is *not* needful or useful to one of the types of human nature, is worthless altogether. There is yet another danger, that he will fail, not only in conceiving sufficient variety of excellence, but sufficiently *high* excellence; that the type to which he would reduce all natures, is by no means the most perfect type; that he conceives the ideal perfection of a human being, under *some* only of its aspects, not under all; or at least that he would frame his practical rules as if he so conceived it.

The faculty of drawing correct conclusions from evidence, together with the qualities of moral rectitude and earnestness, seem to constitute almost the whole of his idea of the perfection of human nature; or rather, he seems to think, that with all other valuable qualities mankind are already sufficiently provided, or will be so by attending merely to these. We see no provision in his system, so far as it is disclosed to us, for the cultivation of any other qualities; and therefore, (as I hold to be a necessary consequence,) no *sufficient* provision for the cultivation even of these.

Now there are few persons whose notion of the perfection to which a human being may be brought, does not comprehend much more than the qualities enumerated above. Most will be prepared to find the practical views founded upon so narrow a basis of theory, rather fit to be used as part of the materials for a practical system, than fit in themselves to constitute one. From what cause, or combination of causes, the scope of Mr. Mill's philosophy embraces so partial a view only of the ends of human culture and of human life, it belongs rather to Mr. Mill's biographer than to his mere reader, to investigate. Doubtless the views of almost all inquirers into human nature are necessarily confined within certain bounds by the fact, that they can enjoy complete power of studying their subject only as it exists in themselves. No person can thoroughly appreciate that of which he has not had personal consciousness: but powers of metaphysical analysis, such as Mr. Mill possesses, are sufficient for the understanding and appreciation of all characters and all states of mind, as far as is necessary for practical purposes, and amply sufficient to divest our philosophic theories of everything like narrowness. For this, however, it is necessary that those powers of analysis should be applied to the details, not solely to the outlines, of human nature; and one of the most strongly marked of the mental peculiarities of Mr. Mill, is, as it seems to us, impatience of details.

This is another of the most striking differences between him and Mr. Bentham. Mr. Bentham delighted in details, and had a quite extraordinary genius for them: it is remarkable how much of his intellectual superiority was of this kind. He followed out his inquiries into the minutest ramifications; was skilful in the estimation of small circumstances, and most sagacious and inventive in devising small contrivances. He went even to great excess in the time and labour which he was willing to bestow on minutiæ, when more important things remained undone. Mr. Mill, on the contrary, shuns all nice attention to details; he attaches himself exclusively to great and leading points; his views, even when they cannot be said to be enlarged, are always on a large scale. He will often be thought by those who differ from him, to overlook or undervalue great things,—never to exaggerate small ones; and the former, partly from not being attentive *enough* to details, when these, though small, would have suggested principles which are great.

The same undervaluing of details has, I think, caused most of the imperfections, where imperfections there are, in Mr. Mill's speculations generally. His just contempt of those who are incapable of grasping a general truth, and with whom the grand and determining considerations are always outweighed by some petty circumstance, carries him occasionally into an opposite extreme: he so heartily despises those most obtuse persons who call themselves Practical Men, and disavow theory, as not always to recollect that, though the men be purblind, they may yet "look out upon the world with their dim horn eyes"[*] and see something in it, which, lying out of his way, he may not have observed, but which it may be worth while for him, who *can* see clearly, to note and *explain*. Not only a dunce may give instruction to a wise man, but no man is so wise that he can, in all cases, do without a dunce's assistance. But a certain degree of intellectual impatience is almost necessarily connected with fervour of character and strength of conviction. Men much inferior to Mr. Mill are quite capable of setting limitations to his propositions, where any are requisite; few in our own times, we might say in any times, could have accomplished what he has done.

Mr. Mill's principal works besides the *Analysis* already mentioned, are, 1, *The History of British India*, not only the first work which has thrown the light of philosophy upon the people and upon the government of that vast portion of the globe, but the first, and even now the only work which conveys to the general reader even that knowledge of facts, which, with respect to so important a department of his country's affairs, every Englishman should wish to possess. The work is full of instructive comments on the institutions of our own country, and abounds with illustrations of many of the most important principles of government and legislation.

2. *Elements of Political Economy.* Mr. Mill's powers of concatenation and systematic arrangement peculiarly qualified him to place in their proper logical connexion the elementary principles of this science as established by its great masters, and to furnish a compact and clear exposition of them.

3. Essays on Government, Jurisprudence, Education, &c. originally written for

[*Carlyle, "Biography," p. 255.]

the *Supplement to the Encyclopædia Britannica*; the most important of them have been several times reprinted by private subscription.[*]

These little works, most of which are mere outlines to be filled up, though they have been both praised and animadverted upon as if they claimed the character of complete scientific theories, have been, I believe, more read than any other of Mr. Mill's writings, and have contributed more than any publications of our time to generate a taste for systematic thinking on the subject of politics, and to discredit vague and sentimental declamation. The Essay on Government, in particular, has been almost a text-book to many of those who may be termed the Philosophic Radicals. This is not the place to criticise either the treatise itself or the criticisms of others upon it. Any critical estimate of it thoroughly deserving the name, it has not yet been my fortune to meet with; for Mr. Macauley—assuming, I suppose, the divine prerogative of genius—only entered the contest, in order to carry away the argument he protected in a cloud of words.[†]

Mr. Mill's more popular writings are remarkable for a lofty earnestness, more stern than genial, and which rather flagellates or shames men out of wrong, than allures them to the right. Perhaps this is the style most natural to a man of deep moral convictions, writing in an age and in a state of society like that in which we live. But it seems, also, to be congenial to the character of his own mind; for he appears, on most occasions, much more strongly alive to the evil of what is evil in our destiny, than to the good of what is good. He rather warns us against the errors that tend to make us miserable, than affords us the belief that by any means we can attain to much positive happiness. He does not hope enough from human nature— something despondent and unelevating clings round his estimate of its powers. He saddens the Present by a reference to the Past—he does not console it by any alluring anticipations of the Future;—he rather discontents us with vice than kindles our enthusiasm for virtue. He possesses but little of

The vision and the faculty divine;[‡]—

nor is it through his writings, admirable as they are, that we are taught

To feel that we are greater than we know.[§]

*   *   *   *   *

[*The first collection (London: printed Innis, [1825]) included "Government," "Jurisprudence," "Liberty of the Press," "Prisons and Prison Discipline," "Colonies," "Law of Nations," and "Education."]

[†The reference is to T. B. Macaulay's three essays in the *Edinburgh Review* attacking James Mill's "Government"; see p. 165n above.]

[‡Wordsworth, *The Excursion*, in *Poetical Works* (1827), Vol. I, p. 6 (Bk. I, l. 78).]

[§Wordsworth, Sonnet XXXIV, "After-Thought," of *The River Duddon*, *ibid.*, Vol. IV, p. 156 (l. 14).]

[Mill contributed the following paragraph to Andrew Bisset's article on James Mill in the 7th ed. (1842) of the *Encyclopaedia Britannica*:]

Mr. Mill's ingenuity as a very acute and original metaphysician was abundantly displayed in his *Analysis of the Phenomena of the Human Mind*, published in 1829. In this work he evinced analytical powers rarely, if ever, surpassed; and which have placed him high in the list of those subtile inquirers who have attempted to resolve all the powers of the mind into a very small number of simple elements. Mr. Mill took up this analysis where Hartley had left it, and applied the same method to the more complex phenomena, which the latter did not attempt to explain. From the general neglect of metaphysical studies in the present age, this work, which, at some periods of our history, would have placed its author on a level, in point of reputation, with the highest names in the republic of letters, has been less read and appreciated than any of his other writings.

Appendix E

Browning's Pauline (1833)

PENCILLED MS comments in Mill's hand on blank leaves bound into the back of the copy of Browning's *Pauline* (London: Saunders and Otley, 1833) in the Forster Collection, Victoria and Albert Museum (Press mark 48.D.46).
For comment, see the Introduction, pp. xxxiii–xxxiv above.

With considerable poetic powers, this writer seems to me possessed with a more intense and morbid self-consciousness than I ever knew in any sane human being. I should think it a *sincere confession*, though of a most unloveable state, if the "Pauline" were not evidently a mere phantom. All about *her* is full of inconsistency—he neither loves her nor fancies he loves her, yet insists upon *talking* love to her—if she *existed* and loved him, he treats her most ungenerously and unfeelingly. All his aspirings and yearnings and regrets point to other things, never to her—then, he *pays her off* towards the end by a piece of flummery, amounting to the modest request that she will love him and live with him and give herself up to him *without* his *loving her*, *moyennant quoi* he will think her and call her everything that is handsome, and he promises her that she shall find it mighty pleasant. Then he leaves off by saying he knows he shall have changed his mind by tomorrow, and despise "these intents which seem so fair" but that having been "thus visited" once no doubt he will again—and is therefore "in perfect joy"[*]— bad luck to him! as the Irish say.

A cento of most beautiful passages might be made from this poem—and the psychological history of himself is powerful and truthful, *truth-like* certainly, all but the last stage. *That* he evidently has not yet got into. The self-seeking and self-worshipping state is well described—beyond that, I should think the writer had made, as yet, only the next step, viz. into despising his own state. I even question whether part even of that self-disdain is not *assumed*. He is evidently *dissatisfied*, and feels part of the badness of his state, but he does not write as if it were purged out of him—if he once could muster a hearty hatred of his selfishness,

[*The quotations are from passages near the end of *Pauline*, pp. 68–9 (ll. 992, 1008, and 994 or 1007—the line is repeated).]

it would *go*—as it is he feels only the *lack* of *good*, not the positive *evil*. He feels not remorse, but only disappointment. A mind in that state can only be regenerated by some new passion, and I know not what to wish for him but that he may meet with a *real* Pauline.

Meanwhile he should not attempt to shew how a person may be *recovered* from this morbid state—for *he* is hardly convalescent, and "what should we speak of but that which we know?"[*]

[*Cf. Carlyle's letter to Mill of 18 Apr., 1833, in *Collected Letters of Thomas and Jane Welsh Carlyle*, Vol. VI, p. 373.]

Appendix F

Editorial Notes in the London and Westminster Review

MILL WAS THE ACTUAL, though not the nominal, editor of the *London Review*, founded in 1835, and, after its merger with the *Westminster Review* in 1836, of the *London and Westminster Review* until March, 1840. He was also the proprietor during the period when the issues from Jan., 1838, through Mar., 1840, appeared. The nominal editors (in fact sub-editors) were first Thomas Falconer (Apr., 1835, to Apr., 1837), and then John Robertson (July, 1837, to Mar., 1840). Because there is little external evidence as to the authorship of the editorial notes, not all of those here included can with total certainty be attributed to Mill: however, in one case (no. 3) the note is listed in Mill's bibliography of his writings ("The note introductory to the article on Victor Hugo, in the same number of the same work"; i.e., as that for Jan., 1836, in which "Guizot's Lectures on European Civilization" appeared [MacMinn, pp. 46–7]); in another (no. 22), the note is signed "A," Mill's usual indication of authorship; in others (nos. 9, 10, 11, 14, 16, and 18), the likelihood is very great; and in the rest, the probability seems to us to favour Mill's authorship. The accompanying notes to each item give the provenance, and supporting information. The texts are taken verbatim from the indicated issues of the periodical.

For further comment, see the Introduction, pp. xxxviii–xxxix above.

1. *LR*, II (*L&WR*, XXXI), No. 3 (Oct., 1835), 194n.

This signature should also have been appended to the article in the last number of the Review, headed "Government and People of Austria," which was inadvertently published without a signature.

[This note, unsigned, is attached to the signature, "Z." (J. H. Garnier), at the end of the article, "Character and Manners of the German Students" (pp. 159–94). The earlier article by Garnier appeared in *LR*, I (*L&WR*, XXX), No. 2 (July, 1835), 487–512.]

2. *LR*, II (*L&WR*, XXXI), No. 3 (Oct., 1835), 228n.

As this article is not, with respect to the question of ecclesiastical establishments, conceived in exactly the same spirit with the article in the second Number of the *London Review*, entitled "The Church and its Reform," it may be well to remind the reader, that for neither article are the contributors to the Review collectively responsible. Both writers agree in their abhorrence of a dominant and sectarian church; but the one would establish a church non-sectarian, the other would endow impartially all sects. The former remedy may be the most desirable; and yet the latter, under some combinations of circumstances, the most practicable.

[This note, signed "Ed.," and enclosed in square brackets, was appended to the title of "The Irish Church Question" (pp. 228–69), by "C.C." (George Cornewall Lewis). The earlier article, Vol. I, No. 2 (July, 1835), 257–95, was by "P.Q." (James Mill). See also no. 8 below.]

3. *LR*, II (*L&WR*, XXXI), No. 4 (Jan., 1836), 389n–90n.

The following article is the first of a series of papers on contemporary French literature, with which we have been favoured by one of the first writers and critics in France. We state this, partly because the reader may be aided in understanding the article itself, if the fact of its French origin be previously known to him; and partly because, it being one of our objects to place before our readers a true picture of the present state of the French mind, this object is promoted by apprising them that the present article is itself a specimen, as well as in some degree a description, of that state.

One of the most palpable deficiencies in the principal English Reviews (a deficiency by no means supplied by those which call themselves Foreign) is the absence of any systematic attention either to the philosophy, the literature, or the politics of foreign countries—though the two former at least are in a state of far greater activity in several other nations than among ourselves. We intend to deviate from the example of our predecessors, by touching on these subjects, as with greater frequency, so with more modesty; for they, we observe, when, at long intervals, they condescend to bestow some portion of their notice upon the literature of any other country, never for an instant doubt their own perfect capacity to decide *en souverains* upon the merits of it; while we freely confess, that although the *philosophy* of a foreign country may be correctly appreciated by any person capable of estimating that of his own, in characterising the finer parts of its *literature* we often find it indispensable to call in foreign assistance. We have no fear that this admixture should increase the difficulty of maintaining throughout this work as much unity of tone as our plan requires, or as is in fact maintained by any other Review. Co-operation can be carried on between persons of similar principles in different countries, as well as in the same country; and the judgment of the editors will be exercised in all cases equally, to exclude whatever is not in harmony with the general spirit in which this Review is conducted.

We are, in like manner, enabled to promise a succession of articles on Society and Civilization in France, from a hand perhaps the most competent in Europe to the task; which series, together with the present, will, we believe, exhibit a juster and completer view of France as it exists in our times, than the English reader has ever yet had an opportunity of obtaining.

[This note, signed "Ed.," is appended to the bibliographic details of the heading of "Victor Hugo" (pp. 389–417), by "D.N." (Jean Marie Napoléon Désiré Nisard), who contributed two further articles, "Early French Literature," *L&WR*, III & XXV (July, 1836), 514–58 (see no. 9 below), and "Lamartine," *L&WR*, IV & XXVI (Jan., 1837), 501–41. The reference in the concluding paragraph is to Alexis de Tocqueville, who, in the event, contributed only one article; see no. 5 below.]

4. *L&WR*, III & XXV, No. 1 (Apr., 1836), 28n.

It seems desirable, at the beginning of this article, to inform the reader that the plural pronoun is employed in conformity with established custom; and that, as it will be readily perceived, in regard to certain statements, both matters of fact and expressions of sentiment have a direct reference to the personal knowledge and individual feelings of the writer.

[This note, unsigned, is appended to "We", the first word of "Godoy, Prince of Peace" (pp. 28–60), signed "W." (Joseph Blanco White). Since the note bears upon policy (cf. nos. 2, 13, 15, 22), and cannot have been the author's, it seems reasonable to assign it to Mill.]

5. *L&WR*, III & XXV, No. 1 (Apr., 1836), 137n.

See note prefixed to the article on Victor Hugo, in the fourth number of the *London Review*.

[This note, unsigned, is appended to the title, "Political and Social Condition of France: First Article" (pp. 137–69), signed "Δ." (Alexis de Tocqueville). There were no further articles by him. See no. 3 above.]

6. *L&WR*, III & XXV, No. 1 (Apr., 1836), 220n.

Tests, or declarations, as well as oaths, are equally prohibited in the statute which Lord Kenyon was desirous to evade.

[This note, signed "Ed.," is appended to the remark by George Kenyon, 2nd Baron Kenyon, "we decidedly take no oath," in a letter concerning Orange Society ceremonies to Colonel Fairman, given in an appendix (consisting of correspondence pertaining to the article) to "Orange Conspiracy" (pp. 181–201), by "W.M." (William Molesworth). This appendix (pp. 201–23) is unsigned, but was clearly supplied by Molesworth. The footnote may be presumed to be Mill's; Molesworth (who might be considered to be the "editor" of this correspondence) supplied other footnotes, unsigned, and it appears that Mill wished to call attention to what Molesworth had explicitly affirmed in a footnote (pp. 484n–5n) to his earlier article, "Orange Societies," *LR*, II (Jan., 1836), 480–513, that Kenyon was trying to evade 57 Geo. III, c.19, "An Act for the More Effectually Preventing Seditious Meetings and Assemblies" (31 Mar., 1817), §25, which cites 37 Geo. III, c.123, and 52 Geo. III, c.104.]

7. *L&WR*, III & XXV, No. 1 (Apr., 1836), 278n.

In an article on a work of Colonel Charles Napier on the Ionian Islands, in the first volume of the *London Review*, p. 316, it is stated, "that without any personal interest, and with no great similarity of political sentiment, Colonel Napier, at the request of several intended settlers, *applied* for the government of the new colony of South Australia;" and it was added, "that disagreements had subsequently taken place which had prevented Colonel Napier from being intrusted with the task." There are some errors in these passages which may mislead the reader respecting the conduct of Colonel Napier. 1. No application for the office of governor was made by Colonel Napier; he, upon the contrary, having distinctly refused to apply for it. 2. The office was *refused* by Colonel Napier on account of the Government having declined to comply with certain conditions, made by him, upon public grounds, preliminary to the execution of its duties. 3. If Colonel Napier had chosen to have consulted his own private advantage, his interest was sufficiently powerful to have enabled him to have done so. He, however, though most anxious to have accepted the appointment offered to him, never even asked the amount of the salary connected with it. The character of the remarks on Colonel Napier's work on the Ionian Islands will sufficiently show that these errors were perfectly accidental, and their correction, it is to be hoped, will destroy every inference prejudicial to the person whom they may possibly affect.

[This note, headed "Note," and signed "Editor of the L. AND W.R.," appeared at the bottom of the final printed page of the number. The quotations are from the concluding paragraph of "Θ." (Charles Buller), "Napier on the Ionian Islands," *LR*, I (July, 1835), 295–316, reviewing Charles James Napier, *The Colonies: Treating of Their Value Generally—Of the Ionian Islands in Particular* (London: Boone, 1833).]

8. *L&WR*, III & XXV, No. 2 (July, 1836), 333n.

Mr. Lewis has appended to his work a Paper on the Irish Church Question, which was first published in the *London Review*, No. III. It gives us much pleasure to have this opportunity of making our public acknowledgments to him for that valuable contribution to our journal.

[This note, unsigned, is appended to "G." (George John Graham), "Poor-Laws in Ireland" (pp. 332–65), at the place where Graham begins his description of George Cornewall Lewis's *On Local Disturbances in Ireland; and on the Irish Church Question* (London: Fellowes, 1836), which includes Lewis's "The Irish Church Question," reprinted from *LR*, II (Oct., 1835), 228–69. See no. 2 above.]

9. *L&WR*, III & XXV, No. 2 (July, 1836), 514n.

The accomplished author of the article on "Victor Hugo" in the fourth number of the *London Review*, (M. Nisard, well known by his *Etudes sur les Poètes Latins de la Décadence*, and other critical writings of great merit,) has allowed us the privilege of being the first to publish what will hereafter constitute one of the most interesting chapters in a history of French literature, which he is preparing for the *Dictionnaire de la Conversation et de la Lecture*, a popular Encyclopædia greatly esteemed in France, and conducted, as the name imports, on a plan suggested by that of the celebrated German *Conversations-Lexicon*.

[This note, signed "Ed.," is appended to the title of "D.N." (Nisard), "Early French Literature" (pp. 514–58). (For his "Victor Hugo," see no. 3 above.) Nisard, whose *Etudes de moeurs et de critique sur les poètes latins de la décadence* appeared (Paris: Gosselin) in 1834, used "Early French Literature" in his "Histoire de la littérature ancienne et moderne," *s.v.* France, §IV, in *Dictionnaire de la conversation et de la lecture*, 68 vols. (London and Paris: Bossange, 1833–51), Vol. XXVIII, pp. 211–88. It is not clear which of the German encyclopaedias of similar title Mill had in mind as the model for the *Dictionnaire*, but a likely one is the *Allgemeine deutsche Real-Encyclopädie für die gebildeten Stände. (Conversations-Lexicon.)*, 10 vols. (Leipzig: Brockhaus, 1819–20).]

10. *L&WR*, IV & XXVI, No. 1 (Oct., 1836), 205n.

There is greater excuse for the conduct of the members referred to than the writer regards. During the first reformed Parliament the Whigs relied so entirely upon their majorities, that it was most difficult for any of those who opposed them, who were not leaders among the Tories, to gain the slightest attention to any proposition, however sound or excellent it might be.

[This note, signed "Ed. L. AND W.R.," is appended to "D.S." (Thomas Southwood Smith), "The Factories" (pp. 174–215), at the point where Smith is arguing that Members of Parliament were at fault in not taking an active part in forwarding the recommendations of the report of the Central Board to improve the education (as well as the physical condition) of the factory operatives.]

11. *L&WR*, IV & XXVI, No. 2 (Jan., 1837), 390n–1n.

The respect due to the excellent *collaborateur* and expounder of Bentham compels the Editor of this Review not to assist in giving currency to the remarks in the text, without recording his dissent from such portion of them as seems to impute to M. Dumont a conceited assumption of merits not his own. That M. Dumont did not thoroughly comprehend Mirabeau is possible, and, considering the dissimilar characters of the two men, not improbable: but howsoever he may have misjudged him, he would have done just the same if any one else instead of himself had been the party concerned. That he was biassed by vanity will not be the opinion of any one who considers how he comported himself in his relation to Mr. Bentham, a man whom he was far better qualified thoroughly to comprehend; between whom and the public he constituted himself an interpreter, with the completest abnegation of even such claims to originality as he might legitimately have preferred, and of all pretension to praise for himself as distinguished from his author. And after all, the theory respecting Mirabeau, which is held up to well-merited ridicule in the text, was made, as the writer himself admits, not *by* M. Dumont, but *for* him, by foolish reviewers, very partially borne out by the authority of M. Dumont himself.

[This note, signed "Ed.," is appended to this sentence (p. 390): "It is true, the whim he had of looking at the great Mirabeau as a thing set in motion mainly by him (M. Dumont) and such as he, was one of the most wonderful to be met with in psychology." In the article, "Memoirs of Mirabeau" (pp. 382–439), "C." (Carlyle) reviewed *Souvenirs sur Mirabeau* (London: Bell, 1832), by Pierre Etienne Dumont, whose translated editions of Bentham's major works had greatly influenced the young Mill (see pp. 67–9 above). Carlyle, having said that Dumont's book "was hailed by a universal choral blast from all manner of reviewers and periodical literatures" throughout Europe, goes on, as Mill indicates, to say, "M. Dumont was less to blame here than his reviewers were" (pp. 390, 391).]

12. *L&WR*, IV & XXVI, No. 2 (Jan., 1837), 542.

A defence by Colonel Napier of the History of the Peninsular War, in reply to an Article in the last number of the *Quarterly Review*, is advertised to appear in this number of the *London and Westminster Review*; but the non-arrival of part of the MS., in consequence of the severity of the weather, prevents its issue with all the copies of the *Review*; it may, however, be obtained upon application at the Publishers.—*Dec.* 27, 1836.

[This note, which begins, "*Note.*—" and is unsigned, appears on the unnumbered final page of the issue in some copies only; in others William Napier's signed "Reply to the third article in the *Quarterly Review* on Colonel Napier's *History of the Peninsular War*" appeared on pp. 541–81. George Murray (assisted by J. W. Croker) was the author of all three reviews of Napier's *History of the War in the Peninsula and in the South of France*, 6 vols. (London: Murray, 1828–40) in the *Quarterly Review*, LVI (Apr., and July, 1836), 131–219, and 437–89, and LVII (Dec., 1836), 492–542. The publisher of the *L&WR* at this time was John Macrone, St. James's Square.]

13. *L&WR*, V & XXVII, No. 9 & 52 (Apr., 1837), 246n.

The opinions of this review on the French Revolution not having yet been expressed, the conductors feel it incumbent on them to enter a *caveat* against any presumption respecting those opinions which may be founded on the Newgate Calendar character of the above extracts. Some attempt at a judgment of that great historical event, with its good and its evil, will probably be attempted in the next number.

[This note, unsigned and in square brackets, is appended to the antepenultimate paragraph of "C." (Carlyle), "Parliamentary History of the French Revolution" (pp. 233–47). Many "Newgate Calendars" appeared; the best known contemporary one was by Andrew Knapp and William Baldwin, *The Newgate Calendar; Comprising Interesting Memoirs of the Most Notorious Characters Who Have Been Convicted of Outrages on the Laws of England,* 4 vols. (London: Robins, 1824–28). The concluding reference is to the account in Mill's review of Carlyle's *French Revolution,* which appeared in the next number (*L&WR,* V & XXVII, No. 10 & 53 [July, 1837], 17–53).]

14. *L&WR,* VI & XXVIII, No. 11 & 54 (Oct., 1837), 131n.

We cannot omit noticing here how much more truly Mr. Bulwer has drawn the character of Templeton, an Evangelical layman, in *Ernest Maltravers*—a novel of a higher order of art than any he has hitherto attempted, and which will add a still higher kind of applauses to the already extensive and varied reputation of its author throughout Europe:—a reputation which could not have been raised so high by a man still young, without a rare union of the qualities which merit, with the qualities which obtain, success.

[This note, signed "Ed.," is appended to the sentence, "The destruction of slavery is, so far as it has been destroyed, owing to the moral zeal and disinterestedness of the 'saints,' whose representative our authoress would give us in Mr. Stephen Corbold"; the review, by "R.O.D." (Henry Fothergill Chorley), is "Works of Mrs. Trollope" (pp. 112–31). The reference is to Edward George Lytton Bulwer, *Ernest Maltravers,* 3 vols. (London: Saunders and Otley, 1837), esp. Vol. II, pp. 44–9 (Bk. IV, Chap. v).]

15. *L&WR,* VI & XXVIII, No. 12 & 55 (Jan., 1838), 367n.

The following article is, by agreement, to be considered as the expression of the writer's sentiments, without involving the opinions of the Review. Who the writer is, may easily be discovered by the style, the sentiments, and the initials.

[This note, signed "Ed.," is appended to the heading of "W.F.P.N." (William Francis Patrick Napier), "The Duke of Wellington" (pp. 367–436).]

16. *L&WR,* VII & XXIX, No. 2 (Aug., 1838), 507 (512 in 2nd ed. of no.).

Note to Article VI, p. 477, of the Number for January, 1838.

We have had some correspondence with Mr. A. Hayward respecting a passage in this article, in which his name occurs; and therefore take an opportunity here of repeating what we have stated to him—that neither against him nor against any of the other persons named was any distinct and personal charge made, because we were not in possession of proofs on which our charges could have been made distinct and personal.

[This note, unsigned, appears at the end of the number (which was expanded in its 2nd ed. by the addition of Mill's "Lord Durham and His Assailants"). The reference is to "H.W." (John Robertson), "Miss Martineau's Western Travel," *L&WR*, VI & XXVIII (Jan., 1838), 470–502, where the offending passage reads: "To destroy the causes of such things [poverty, hunger, crime] is our radicalism. . . . We would make our constitution loved. The defence of the causes of these things is Conservatism. The state of things which has borne such deadly fruits is that to whose service are devoted the labours of men—none of whom have a legitimate drop of aristocratic blood in them—most of whom have themselves struggled with poverty, and almost all of whom are sprung from the ranks of the oppressed;—men, such as Lockhart, Wilson, Barnes, Jerdan, Maginn, Mahoney, Palgrave, Sulivan, Banks, D'Israeli, Theodore Hook, Crofton Croker, and Abraham Hayward,—several of them Jews, and most of them Irishmen, who, if they were not ashamed of their fathers, would be on the side of the oppressed—the champions of their own order, in their places as sons of the unprivileged classes—instead of exhibiting the melancholy spectacle of the gifted kissing the feet of the dunces; the feet, which were for ages on the necks of their fathers,—instead of doing the base work of the aristocracy, fighting for them, writing for them, joking for them, blackguardising for them, and (it may be said of not a few) lying for them, against men of their own class, of their own schools and colleges, whose only end is to make, without change when possible, but by change when needful, England, Scotland, and Ireland, not what America is, but like America, 'a fine country for poor people.'" (Pp. 477–8.) Abraham Hayward, who had met Mill at the London Debating Society, became an increasingly virulent opponent, finally writing the unfriendly obituary of Mill in *The Times*. For another comment by Mill on this affair, see *EL*, *CW*, Vol. XIII, p. 367, to Robertson.]

17. *L&WR*, VII & XXIX, No. 2 (Aug., 1838), 507 (512 in 2nd ed. of this no.).

Note to Article VII of the Number for April, 1838.

We have been requested to state that Lord Melbourne is not the author of the *Fashionable Friends*, which we mentioned as having been ascribed to him.

[This note, unsigned, appears immediately below the preceding one. The reference is to "P.B." (probably John Robertson), "Poets of the Melbourne Ministry," *L&WR*, VII & XXIX (Apr., 1838), 193–224, where the author says, "*The Fashionable Friends* has always been ascribed to Lord Melbourne, and there is an epilogue by the Hon. William Lamb, which is, from internal evidence, the production of the pen which produced the piece" (p. 216). (On this assumption, the right-hand running head of the article, pp. 217–23, is "Lord Melbourne.") *The Fashionable Friends: A Comedy* (London: Ridgway, 1802) is ascribed in the British Library Catalogue to Mary Berry. *The Wellesley Index*, Vol. III, suggests that, if Robertson wrote the original article, he (being sub-editor at the time) also wrote this note; however it seems equally likely that it is by Mill (to whom *The Wellesley Index* gives the preceding note, also dealing with a misdemeanour of Robertson's).]

18. *L&WR*, XXXII, No. 1 (Dec., 1838), 202n.

The following lines, by a valued contributor, express feelings more congenial to the character of Heloïse than to that which we have been compelled to ascribe to Abelard; but as embodying the sentiments which might be *conceived* to have been interchanged between them at this period of their lives, they may be interesting to our readers:

[This note, unsigned, is appended to the last sentence on this page of "G.F." (George Fletcher), "Heloïse and Abelard" (pp. 146–219, with the exception of p. 203). The note (which concludes with a colon) introduces "Abelard to Heloïse," signed "£." (John Sterling), which fills the whole of p. 203. Sterling, whose "Simonides" appeared in this number (pp. 99–136), had earlier contributed "Montaigne and His Writings," *L&WR*, VII & XXIX (Aug., 1838), 321–52, and was later to contribute "Carlyle's Works" (see no. 22 below).]

19. *L&WR*, XXXII, No. 2 (Apr., 1839), 404n.

But what will the Hanoverians say? Have they no feelings of nationality to be consulted? We have inserted these speculations by a distinguished contributor, who has had better means of gaining information than have fallen to the share of any other man in this country, not because we wished to identify ourselves with them in any way, but because he gives them as dreams—but curious and instructive dreams, which may be fulfilled.

[This note, signed "Ed.," is appended to the concluding paragraph of a discussion by "G.N." (Thomas Colley Grattan), in his "Leopold and the Belgians" (pp. 357–405), in which he is arguing that the territory of Belgium should be enlarged, in part by areas under the rule of Prussia and Holland, and that Hanover should be, as compensation, divided between Prussia and Holland.]

20. *L&WR*, XXXII, No. 2 (Apr., 1839), 416n.

We should feel it our duty to say more concerning the writings of this lady; but that we purpose, ere long, to review them, as well as the productions of several others of the Irish writers mentioned in our catalogue, separately and at length. Her works not only possess merit of a high order, but they are calculated to have a very beneficial effect upon the Irish character.

[This note, signed "Ed.," is appended to the sentence, "Mrs. S.C. Hall has obtained considerable popularity as a depicter of Irish life," in the unsigned article (probably by John Robertson), "Irish Humour and Pathos" (pp. 415–25). Anna Maria Hall's *The Juvenile Budget* (London: Chapman and Hall, and Newman, 1840 [1839]) was mentioned in "F.B." (Mary Margaret Busk), "Literature of Childhood," *L&WR*, XXXIII (Oct., 1839), 137–62 (Mrs. Hall herself contributed the next article in that number, "Heads of the People"); otherwise Mill's promise was not fulfilled during his editorship.]

21. *L&WR*, XXXIII (1839–40), verso of the title page.

It should have been explained in a preceding volume, that to avoid the double numbering of the *London Review* and the *Westminster Review*, the numbers of each Review were added together, whereby Vol. VII and XXIX became Vol. XXXI of the united series.

[This note, in square brackets and unsigned, is a belated explanation of the solution—still plaguing scholars—of the problem caused by the publication independently of two volumes (four numbers) of the *London Review* while the *Westminster Review* continued (also for four numbers), before amalgamation in the *London and Westminster*. For a fuller explanation, with other complications, see pp. xxxviii n–xxxix n above.]

22. *L&WR*, XXXIII, No. 1 (Oct., 1839), 68n.

In giving our readers the benefit of this attempt by one of our most valued contributors (we believe the first attempt yet made) at a calm and comprehensive estimate of a man, for whom our admiration has already been unreservedly expressed, and whose genius and worth have shed some rays of their brightness on our own pages; the occasion peculiarly calls upon us to declare what is already implied in the avowed plan of this Review—that its conductors are in no respect identified with the opinions delivered in the present criticism, either when the writer concurs with, or when he differs from those of Mr. Carlyle.

While we hope never to relax in maintaining that systematic consistency in our own opinions, without which there can be no clear and firmly-grounded judgment and therefore no hearty appreciation of the merits of others; we open our pages without restriction to those who, though differing from us on some fundamental points of philosophy, stand within a certain circle of relationship to the general spirit of our practical views, and in whom we recognize that title to a free stage for the promulgation of what they deem true and useful, which belongs to all who unite noble feelings with great and fruitful thoughts.

[This note, signed "A.," is appended to the conclusion of "£." (John Sterling), "Carlyle's Works" (pp. 1–68). For Sterling's contributions to the *L&WR*, see no. 18 above. Carlyle contributed four articles in all, "Memoirs of Mirabeau" (see no. 11 above), "Parliamentary History of the French Revolution" (see no. 13 above), "Memoirs of the Life of Scott," *L&WR*, VI & XXVIII (Jan., 1838), 293–345, and "Varnhagen von Ense's Memoirs," *L&WR*, XXXII (Dec., 1838), 60–84. For the admiration of Carlyle, "unreservedly expressed," see Mill's article cited in the note to no. 13 above.]

Appendix G

Rejected Leaves of the Early Draft of the Autobiography

THIS APPENDIX presents extracts from the thirty rejected leaves that Mill kept together at the end of the Early Draft MS, with headnotes describing the relationships between these leaves and the text of the draft as printed in this volume on the verso sides of pp. 4–246. A number of shorter readings from these leaves are (as we point out in the individual headnotes) given in notes to the Early Draft text, with source designated as "R23r," "RII.20v," and the like—the folio number appearing on the leaf, preceded by the abbreviation "R" (for rejected folio[s]) or "RII" (rejected folio[s] from the original Part II of the draft). Most of the extracts given in this appendix are earlier readings of the same sort that are simply too long to print as notes to the main text. The accompanying apparatus provides, in the same manner as for the Early Draft text itself (the methodology is described on p. 2), a selection of cancellations and alterations by Mill and pencilled changes and other markings by his wife. For more specific details concerning the original connections between these leaves and the rest of the MS, see *The Early Draft of John Stuart Mill's "Autobiography,"* ed. Jack Stillinger (Urbana: University of Illinois Press, 1961), pp. 178–200.

R23–5, 24^2–25^2, 19/20

R23–5 contain the first version of the present Early Draft text at 36.14–40.12 ("and that many people . . . as he said, a"). In an intermediate stage of revision Mill rewrote R24 and part of R25 on two new leaves, $R24^2$ and 25^2, and finally reduced the entire sequence (R23, 24^2–25^2, and part of R25v) to a single new leaf, the final text of the span referred to above. The two paragraphs given here, from R23v–25v, originally followed the paragraph ending at 36.31. In addition to the usual information concerning deleted text and HTM's alterations, four of the notes to this extract provide variants from the leaves of the intermediate version, $R24^2$–25^2 (see notes *e–e, k–k, l–l, p–p* below). Variants from the paragraphs preceding and following the extract are given in textual notes on pp. 36, 37, and 40.

My father thus took effectual precautions against some, and those very serious dangers, to which his plan of education was liable. There were others to which he was either not so much alive, or against which he did not guard with equal success.

Not, I am persuaded, by any *ª*necessity inherent*ª* in my education, but *ᵇ*certainly by some omission in it*ᵇ*, I grew up with *ᶜ*great inaptness in*ᶜ* the common

ª–ª[*Earlier version:*] inherent defect [*marked with an exclamation mark in the margin by HTM*]
ᵇ–ᵇ[*Earlier version:*] by some effect resulting jointly from my education and circumstances
ᶜ–ᶜ[*Earlier version:*] extraordinary inaptness and even incapacity in all [*altered to final form (except for the deletion of "all") first by HTM, who marked the next seven sentences (through "personal contact.") for deletion and rewrote Mill's text to read:* I grew up with great inaptness for everything

Folio R24r (see p. 609) of the Early Draft MS
University of Illinois

affairs of every day life. [d] I was far longer than children generally are before I could put on my clothes. I know not how many years passed before I could tie a knot. My articulation was long imperfect; one letter, *r*, I could not pronounce until I was nearly sixteen. [e]I never could, nor can I now, do anything requiring the smallest manual dexterity, but [f]I never put even a common share of the exercise of understanding into practical things[f]. I was continually acquiring odd [g]or disagreeable[g] tricks which I very slowly and imperfectly got rid of. I was, besides, [h]utterly[h] inobservant: I was, as my father continually told me, like a person who had not the organs of sense: my eyes and ears seemed of no use to me, so little did I see or hear what was before me, and so little, even of what I did see or hear, did I observe and remember[e]. My father was the extreme opposite in all these particulars: his senses and his mental faculties were always on the alert; he carried decision and energy of character in his whole manner and into every action of life: and this, as much as his talents, contributed to the great impression which he always made upon those with whom he came in personal contact. The education he gave me was, however, considered in itself, much more fitted for training me to *know* than to *do*. Not that he was unaware of my defects; both as a boy and as a youth I was incessantly smarting under his severe admonitions on the subject. He could not endure stupidity, nor feeble and lax habits, in whatever manner displayed, and I was perpetually exciting his anger by manifestations of them. From the earliest time I can remember he used to reproach me, and most truly, with a general habit of inattention; owing to which, he said, I was constantly acquiring bad habits, and never breaking myself of them; was constantly forgetting what I ought to remember, and judging and acting like a person devoid of common sense; and which would make me, he said, grow up [i]a mere[i] oddity, looked down upon by everybody, and unfit for all the common purposes of life. It was not, therefore, from any insensibility or tolerance on his part towards such faults, that my education, considered in this particular, must be regarded as a failure. [j]Neither do I see any necessary tendency in his plan of education to produce those defects.[j] No

---

requiring manual dexterity. The education he gave me . . . . *Subsequently she cancelled the rest of the paragraph as well.*]

[d][*Cancelled text:*] I had hardly any use of my hands.

[e-e][*Intermediate version in R24²r:*] I continued long, and in some degree always, inexpert in anything which required the smallest manual dexterity; and not only my hands, but my mind never did its work properly when it was applied, or rather when it ought to have been applied, to the practical details which, though singly unimportant, are in the aggregate essential to the conduct of daily life. I was, as my father continually told me, as inobservant as if I had no organs of sight or hearing, or no capacity of remembering what I saw and heard

[f-f][*Earlier version:*] all the common things which everybody does, I did not only in an ungainly and awkward but in a thoroughly ineffective and bungling manner like a person without the most ordinary share of understanding

[g-g][*Deleted by HTM*]

[h-h][*Altered by HTM to read:* very]

[i-i][*Altered by HTM to read:* an]

[j-j][*Marked for deletion by HTM, who pencilled at left: "To escape the contagion of boys society Probably he purposely prevented the intercourse with other boys wh wd have prevented this defect and he was too much occupied himself to share a boys healthful exercises"*]

doubt, they may have had some connexion with the fact, ^{k}otherwise most salutary, of my being educated at home, and not in a school, among other boys, and having no encouragement to practise bodily exercises, from which boys in general derive their earliest lessons of practical skill and contrivance.^{k} It must not however be supposed that play, or time for it, was refused me. Though no holidays were allowed, lest the habit of work should be broken, and taste for idleness acquired, I had abundant leisure in every day to amuse myself: but ^{l}my amusements being solitary or with children younger than myself, gave ^{m}little^m stimulus to either bodily or mental activity. ^{n}There^n were wanting, in addition to the book-lessons which were the staple of my instruction, well devised practical lessons, exercising the hands, and the head in directing the hands, and necessitating careful observation, and adaptation of means to ends^l. ^{o}I had also^o the great misfortune of having, in domestic matters, everything done for me. Circumstanced as I was, nothing but being thrown as much as possible, in daily matters, upon my own powers of contriving and of executing could have given ^{p}me the proper use of my faculties for the occasions of life. This discipline, I presume my father did not see the necessity of; and it would never have occurred to my mother, who without misgivings of any sort worked from morning till night for her children^p.

R19/20, a leaf headed "between 19 and 20," is a rewritten, expanded version of the present Early Draft text at 32.19–32 ("The experiment . . . good it effected."). After Mill drafted the

$^{k-k}$[*Earlier version:*] which was partly intentional on his part, of my having no playfellows or associates among other boys; since if I had, the bodily exercises I should have been led to cultivate and the activity of some sort, and adaptation of means to ends which might have been called forth, would probably have made a difference for the better. [*In the intermediate version (R24^{2}v, in which HTM interlined "dexterity and agility" above "practical skill and contrivance") Mill added at this point:* Some sacrifice in this respect he was no doubt willing to make, as the price of my escaping the contagion of boys' society. But while he saved me from the demoralizing effects of school life, he made no effort to provide me with any substitute for its practicalizing influences. Whatever qualities he, probably, had acquired without difficulty or special instruction, he seems to have supposed that I ought to acquire as easily: and bitter reproaches for being deficient in them, were nearly all the help he ever gave me towards acquiring them. *In the present extract HTM changed "otherwise" (the first word of the passage to which this note is appended) to "morally".*]

$^{l-l}$[*Intermediate version in R25^{2}r:*] as I had no boy companions, and the animal need of physical activity being satisfied by walking, my amusements, which were mostly solitary, were almost all of a quiet, if not a bookish turn, and gave little stimulus to any kind of even mental activity other than that which was already called forth by my studies

$^{m-m}$[*Earlier version:*] no [*At left, opposite the last clause of this sentence, HTM pencilled an exclamation mark and a question mark, and commented:* "It is always *the eldest son of a large family who is* especially *the active and acting spirit".*]

$^{n-n}$[*Earlier version:*] The deficiency in my education as regards this most vital point consisted I think in two things, first; that there

$^{o-o}$[*Earlier version:*] This requisite my father did not provide. And, what was still more fatal, I had

$^{p-p}$[*Intermediate version in R25^{2}r:*] my practical faculties their fair share of developement. Along with this, I required, in addition to the book-lessons which were the staple of my instruction, well devised practical lessons, exercising the hands, and the head in directing the hands, and necessitating careful observation, and adaptation of means to ends. But my father had not bestowed the same amount of thought and attention on this, as on most other branches of education; and (as in some other points of my tuition) he seems to have expected effects without causes

passage on manual dexterity in R23–5, revised and condensed it in R24^2–25^2, and finally omitted it altogether in the Early Draft text at 36.14–40.12 (see the preceding headnote), he inserted parts of it into an earlier summary paragraph by rewriting the present 32.19–32 as R19/20. Possibly the new version did not meet HTM's approval, for Mill set it aside and returned to the text that he had had in the first place. (After her death he introduced into his later draft in the Columbia MS the passage ending Chapter i—37.36–39.39 in the present volume—which, of the three versions in the rejected leaves, is closest in wording to that of R24^2–25^2.) The extract included here represents text that was to have been inserted after the sentence ending at 32.27. Two other variants from R19/20 are given in textual notes on pp. 32–3.

Indeed, my deficiency in these qualities caused the results of my education to appear, in some respects, less advantageous than they really were, since it made my acquisition of those active and practical capacities which my father's discipline did not in the same degree provide for, slow and imperfect. The education he gave me was, considered in itself, much more fitted for training me to *know* than to *do*. Most boys acquire whatever they do acquire of bodily dexterity or practical skill and contrivance, by their own spontaneous activity when left to themselves, or by competition and conflict with other boys. It was a main point with my father to save me from the contagion of boys' society; and though I had ample leisure in every day to amuse myself, my voluntary amusements were almost all of a quiet, and generally of a bookish turn, and gave little stimulus to any kind of even mental activity other than that which was already called forth by my studies. Whatever deficiencies these causes had a tendency to produce, would in the case of a naturally quick, or a naturally energetic youth, have rapidly disappeared on the first contact with the world. But with me, the discipline of life in this respect was long and severe, and even at last, was but imperfectly effectual. This, however, was not owing to the mode of my education but to natural slowness and to a certain mental and moral indolence which, but for the immense amount of mental cultivation which my father gave me, would probably have prevented me from either being or doing anything worthy of note.

R31–7

R31–7 contain the first version of the present Early Draft text at 50.22–58.15 ("as if the agents . . . by the beautiful"). Of the extract given here, from R31v–34r, the first three paragraphs were condensed into the single paragraph beginning at 52.14, and the remaining sentences (which do not constitute a complete paragraph) were replaced by the first two sentences of the paragraph beginning at 54.11. Following the extract, the text of R34r continues as at 54.20, "I was a more frequent visitor . . . ." Other variants from R31, 34–7 are given in textual notes on pp. 50–2 and 54–8.

Personally I believe my father to have had much greater capacities of feeling than were ever developed in him. He resembled almost all Englishmen in being ashamed of the signs of feeling, and by the absence of demonstration, starving the feelings themselves. In an atmosphere of tenderness and affection he would have been tender and affectionate; but his ill assorted marriage and his asperities of temper disabled him from making such an atmosphere. I once heard him say, that there was always the greatest sympathy between him and his children until the time of lessons began, but that the lessons always destroyed it. Certainly his children till six or seven years old always liked him and were happy in his presence, and he liked them and had pleasure in talking to them and in interesting and amusing them; and it is equally true that after the lessons began, *[a]*fear of his severity sooner or later swallowed up all other feelings towards him.*[a]* This is true only of the elder children: with the *[b]*younger*[b]* he followed an entirely different system, to the great comfort of the later years of his life. But in respect to what I am here concerned with, the moral agencies which acted on myself, it must be mentioned as a most baneful one, that my father's *[c]*children neither loved him, nor, with any warmth of affection, any one else.*[c]* I do not mean that things were worse in this respect than they are in most English families; in which genuine affection is altogether exceptional; what is usually found being more or less of an attachment of mere habit, like that to inanimate objects, and a few conventional proprieties of phrase and demonstration. I believe there *[d]*is less personal affection in England than in any other country of which I know anything, and I give my father's family not as peculiar in this respect but only as a too faithful exemplification of the ordinary fact. That rarity in England, a really warm hearted mother, would in the first place have made my father a totally different being, and in the second would have made the children grow up loving and being loved. But my mother, with the very best intentions, only knew how to pass her life in drudging for them. Whatever she could do for them she did, and they liked her, because she was kind to them, but to make herself loved, looked up to, or even obeyed, required qualities which she unfortunately did not possess.

I thus grew up in the absence of love and in the presence of fear: and many and indelible are the effects of this bringing-up, in the stunting of my moral growth.*[d]* One of these, which it would have required a quick sensibility and impulsiveness of natural temperament to counteract, was habitual reserve. Without knowing or believing that I was reserved, I grew up with an instinct of closeness. *[e]*I had no one

---

[a-a][*At left, opposite this passage and the next two sentences, HTM commented:* "*I do not believe it is possible for a parent to teach their own children effectually without the exercise of a degree of severity and authority which will make it impossible that the children should love them. It is easier for a young person to like a schoolmaster—partly because many other youths go thro the same discipline, the severity therefore does not seem so personal besides however some youth may respect and even like a schoolmaster they do not tenderly love him the personal suffering voluntarily inflicted is probably incompatible with tender love on either side*".]

[b-b][*Earlier version:*] three youngest

[c-c][*Altered by HTM to read:* elder children neither loved him, nor any one else. *At this point Mill originally continued (but did not complete the sentence before deleting):* Things would have been very different if under the influence of a mother of strong good sense and]

[d-d][*Marked (beginning at the top of a new page) with a line in the margin by HTM*]

*[e-e]*613[*Deleted by HTM*]

to whom I desired to express everything which I felt; and^e the only person I was in communication with, to whom I looked up, I had too much fear of, to make the communication to him of any act or feeling ever a matter of frank impulse or spontaneous inclination. Instead of a character whose instinct and habit are openness, but who can command reserve when duty or prudence require it, my circumstances tended to form a character, close and reserved from habit and want of impulse, not from will, and therefore, while destitute of the frank communicativeness which wins and deserves sympathy, yet continually failing in retinence where it is suitable and desirable.

Another evil I shared with many of the sons of energetic fathers. ^{f}To have been, through childhood, under the constant rule of a strong will, certainly is not favourable to strength of will.^{f} I was so much accustomed to expect to be told what to do, either in the form of direct command or of rebuke for not doing it, that I acquired a habit of leaving my responsibility as a moral agent to rest on my father, my conscience never speaking to me except by his voice. The things I ought *not* to do were mostly provided for by his precepts, rigorously enforced whenever violated, but the ^{g}things which I *ought* to do I hardly ever did of my own mere motion, but waited till he told me to do them; and if he forbore or forgot to tell me, they were generally left undone. I thus acquired a habit of backwardness, of waiting to follow the lead of others, an absence of moral spontaneity, an inactivity of the moral sense and even to a large extent, of the intellect, unless roused by the appeal of some one else,—for which a ^{h}large^h abatement must be made from the benefits, either moral or intellectual, which flowed from any other part of my education.^{g}

Before taking leave of this first period of my life it may seem that something ought to be said of the persons with whom my father habitually associated and to some of whom, it may be supposed, I was not a stranger. ^{i}But I cannot trace to them any other influence on my development,^{i} than what was due to such of my father's conversations with them as I had an opportunity of listening to. ^{j}My father's narrow income, previous to his appointment from the East India Company, and his unwillingness to invite any persons to his house whom he could not, as he said, make as comfortable as they were at home, caused the habitual

---

$^{f-f}$[*Marked with a line in the margin by HTM; at left, opposite the last eight words of the sentence, she pencilled two X's and a question mark.*]

$^{g-g}$[*Marked (beginning at the top of a new page) with a line in the margin by HTM*]

$^{h-h}$[*Earlier version:*] terrible

$^{i-i}$[*At left HTM pencilled a question mark and queried: "how* shd *you?" In revising this paragraph in the final Early Draft text Mill copied the opening sentence verbatim, and for the whole of the second wrote:* But I cannot trace to any of them, considered individually, any influence on my developement. *After HTM marked the two sentences there, he reduced them to the seven-word prepositional phrase that appears above at* 54.11.]

$^{j-j614}$[*All but the last eight words are deleted by HTM, who underscored and pencilled a question mark opposite "narrow", pencilled* "revisal", *"mesquin", a large X, and "omit or remark upon" at various places opposite the next several lines, and then rewrote the sentence to read, up to this point:* The habitual frequenters of my father's house were]

frequenters of his house to be^j limited to a very few persons, mostly little known, but whom personal worth, and more or less of congeniality with his opinions (then not so frequently to be met with as since) disposed him to cultivate. ^{k}His other friends he saw at their own houses; saving an occasional call which as they knew how important his time was to him they rarely made^k except for some special purpose. ^{l} Such occasional calls (from my being a habitual inmate of my father's study) made me acquainted with the most intimate and congenial of his friends, David Ricardo, who by his benevolent countenance and kindliness of manner was very attractive to ^{m}young persons^m, and who after I became a student of political economy sometimes had me to breakfast and walk with him in order to discuss ^{n}or (as a more correct description of the relation which could exist between him and me) to examine me in^n political economy.

R105–6

R105-6 contain the first version of the present Early Draft text at 170.13–174.24 ("length; but I . . . progress in my"), which, with text given and described in the note on p. 168, originally followed the paragraph ending at 168.5. In expanding and rearranging the materials of these two leaves, Mill first inserted additional leaves before and after them, and then discarded R105–6 altogether, rewriting what remained of their text in a new leaf containing the present 172.10–30 ("the theological . . . replaced by others."). The extract given here, all but the first word ("length.") and the last five lines of R105–6, is a continuation of the new paragraph described at p. 168n. The cancelled last five lines of R106v contain most of the first sentence of the paragraph beginning at 174.22.

But I was struck with the ability, knowledge and large views of the men. I was kept *au courant* of their progress by one of their most enthusiastic disciples, Gustave d'Eichthal, who about that time passed a considerable period in England: and from this time forward I read nearly everything they wrote. The scheme gradually unfolded by them, the management of the labour and capital of the community for the national account, classing all persons according to their capacity and rewarding them according to their works, appeared to me a far superior kind of Socialism to Owen's: their aim seemed to me perfectly rational, and though the machinery for attaining it could not possibly be worked, the proclamation (I thought) of such an ideal of human society could not but be calculated to give a very beneficial direction to the efforts of others for the improvement of society as already constituted. I honoured them above all for the boldness and freedom from prejudice with which they proclaimed the perfect equality of men and women and ^{a}an entirely new order of things^a in regard to the relations between the sexes: a merit which the other great French socialist Fourier possesses in a still greater degree.

$^{k-k}$[*Altered by HTM to read:* His other friends he saw occasionally but as they knew how important his time was to him they rarely came *(she then apparently marked the entire sentence for deletion)*]
^{l}[*Cancelled text:*] I therefore saw little of most of them, and some not at all.
$^{m-m}$[*Earlier version:*] me
$^{n-n}$[*Altered by HTM to read:* questions of]
$^{a-a}$[*Earlier version:*] a regime of freedom

This however is an anticipation. At the time of which I am now speaking, the only very strong impression which I received from anything connected with St. Simonism was derived from an early writing of Auguste Comte, who then called himself in the title page an élève of Saint Simon. In this tract M. Comte announced the doctrine which he has since so copiously illustrated of the natural succession of three states in every branch of knowledge, first, the theological, second, the metaphysical, and third, the positive stage; and contended that social science must be subject to the same law; that the feudal and Catholic system was the last phasis of the theological state of the social science, Protestantism the commencement and the doctrines of the French Revolution the consummation of its metaphysical, and that its positive state was yet to come. This doctrine harmonized very well with my existing notions; I already regarded the methods of physical science as the proper models for political: but one important point in the parallelism much insisted on by M. Comte, had not before occurred to me. In mathematics and physics what is called the liberty of conscience, or the right of private judgment, is merely nominal: though in no way restrained by law, the liberty is not exercised: those who have studied the subject are all of the same opinion; if any one rejected what has been proved by demonstration or experiment, he would be thought to be asserting no right but the right of being a fool: those who have not studied these sciences take their conclusions on trust from those who have, and the practical world goes on incessantly applying laws of nature and conclusions of reasoning which it receives on the faith not of its own reason but of the authority of the instructed. Hitherto it had not occurred to me that the case would be the same in the moral, social, and political branches of speculation if they were equally advanced with the physical. [b]I had always identified deference to authority with mental slavery and the repression of individual thought. I now perceived that these indeed are the means by which adherence is enforced to opinions from which at least a minority of thinking and instructed persons dissent; but that when all such persons are as nearly unanimous, as they are in the more advanced of the physical Sciences, their authority will have an ascendancy which will be increased, not diminished, by the intellectual and scientific cultivation of the multitude, who, after learning all which their circumstances permit, can do nothing wiser than rely for all beyond on the knowledge of the more highly instructed. I did not become one atom less zealous for increasing the knowledge and improving the understanding of the

[b]-[b]616[*Earlier version:*] My hopes of improvement in these respects had hitherto rested upon the reason of the multitude, improved as I hoped it might be by education. I henceforth saw that this was not the best, and not even a reasonable, hope. Without becoming in the smallest degree less zealous for every practicable increase of the knowledge and improvement of the understanding of the many, I saw that they were never likely to be qualified for judges in the last resort of political any more than of physical truths; that what was wanted was such an improvement in the methods of political and social philosophy, as should enable all thinking and instructed persons, who have no sinister interest, to be of one mind on these subjects, as they are on subjects of physical science: after which the more the intelligence of the general multitude became improved, the more they would appreciate the greater knowledge and more exercised judgment of the instructed and the more disposed they would be to defer to their opinion

mass; but I no longer believed that the fate of mankind depended on the possibility of making all of them competent judges of questions of government and legislation. From this time my hopes of improvement rested less on the reason of the multitude, than on the possibility of effecting such an improvement in the methods of political and social philosophy, as should enable all thinking and instructed persons who have no sinister interest to be so nearly of one mind on these subjects, as to carry the multitude with them by their united authority[b]. This was a view of matters which, as it seemed to me, had been overlooked, or its importance not seen, by my first instructors: and it served still further to widen the distance between my present mode of thinking, and that which I had learnt from Bentham and my father.

R113, 109

R113 contains the first version of the present Early Draft text at 182.7–29 ("the manuscript . . . infinitely more."), and originally provided the text between 182.7 and the new paragraph beginning at 188.1. In a subsequent rearrangement of materials, in which the paragraph on doctrinal differences with his father (p. 188) was moved from its original position before the two paragraphs on the Austins (pp. 184, 186) to its present position after them, Mill rewrote only this one leaf—in R109 (a fair copy that he then further revised and recopied as the present 182.7ff.)—making the rest of the alteration by reordering leaves and deleting parts of the text on some pages and recopying them at left on others. Variants from R113, 109 are given in textual notes on pp. 182–3.

R119–21

After the paragraph ending at 190.28, Mill wrote, mainly in R119–21, what were originally the last three paragraphs of Part I of the draft. In rearranging the materials of Part II (see the next headnote), he moved the first two of these paragraphs and part of the third to a later position in the text, and recopied them as the present 202.1–206.25. Variants from R119–20 are given in textual notes on pp. 202, 204, and 206. The original conclusion of Part I, which followed the sentence ending at 206.25, is transcribed here.

From this time to 1840, first in association with Molesworth, afterwards by myself, I was the conductor of a political review. But this new phasis in my literary existence belongs to a different period in my personal history, for which all that preceded was of no value except as a preparation—that in which I enjoyed the friendship and was under the ennobling influence of one to whom I owe all that is best, either in me or in what I have written, and compared with whom I am in myself scarcely worthy of a passing thought.

RII.1–8, 20, 24

"Part II" originally consisted of twenty-four separately numbered leaves—the present RII.1–8, the eleven Early Draft leaves containing the text of 206.28–234.3 (plus text now deleted), RII.20, the three Early Draft leaves containing 236.36–242.29, and RII.24. In revising (to an extent following HTM's directions), Mill compressed RII.1–8—sixteen MS pages on his relationship with his wife—into the seven MS pages containing the present

192.1–198.14, rewrote and repositioned some of the remaining material, including the paragraphs from R119–21 mentioned in the preceding headnote, and wrote three new leaves (the text of 242.29–246.25) to replace the original abrupt conclusion on RII.24. Even though about a third of it is repeated verbatim in the final version of the Early Draft, we print here the complete text of RII.1–8 (all but the last eight lines, which begin a new paragraph substantially the same as the present text at 206.25, "In the years between 1834 and 1840 . . ."). Variants from RII.20, 24 are given in textual notes on pp. 234–7 and 242.

Part II

My first introduction to the lady whose *a*friendship has been the honour and blessing of my existence, and who after many years of confidential intimacy, deigned to be*a* my wife, dates from *b*as early as 1830*b*. *c*Its origin or rather occasion was the accident of a common acquaintance; but I have always been convinced that sooner or later, and rather sooner than later, we should have found each other out: for*c* both of us were at this time ardent seekers for persons of similar opinions and of any intellectual gifts. Had our acquaintance commenced later; had her judgment of me been first formed in maturer years, it would, probably, have been far less favourable; but I, at whatever period of life I had known her, must always have felt her to be the most admirable person I had ever known, *d*and must have made her approbation the guiding light and her sympathy the chief object of my life, though to appreciate the greatness*d* and variety of her preeminence could only have been possible after long and intimate knowledge, *e*to any one not on the same exalted level as herself. To me, so inferior in nature and so widely different in all previous discipline, a complete or adequate appreciation of her is impossible, and such approach to it as I have made has only been the effect of the long course of education derived from the knowledge and contemplation of her.*e*

It is not to be supposed that she was, or that any one, at the age at which I first saw her, could be all that she afterwards became. Least of all could this be true of her, with whom self-improvement, progress in the highest and in all senses, was a law of her nature; a necessity equally from the ardour with which she sought it, and from the spontaneous tendency of faculties which could not receive an impression or an experience without making it the source or the occasion of an accession of wisdom. Up to the time when I knew her, her rich and powerful nature had chiefly unfolded itself according to the received type of feminine genius. To her outer circle she was a beauty, and a wit, *f*with an air of natural distinction, felt by all who approached her*f*: to the inner, a woman of deep and strong feeling, of penetrating

---

a–a[*HTM underscored "existence" and "many years of confidential intimacy", and wrote at left:* and who after twenty years of the most valuable friendship of my life became]

b–b[*HTM deleted "as early as" and added at left:* when I was in my 25th she in her 23d year]

c–c[*Deleted by HTM, who wrote at left three sentences that Mill copied into the revised Early Draft text almost verbatim:* With her husband's family . . . lasting impression. *(See* 192.6–11 *above.)*]

d–d[*Deleted (at the bottom of a page) by HTM*]

e–e[*Marked with a line in the margin by HTM*]

f–f[*Earlier version (one of several attempts):*] and a most distinguée woman [*deleted by HTM*] and intuitive intelligence, and of a most meditative and poetic nature. *g*Morally she was already so perfect that even she could not add anything to her type of perfection in after life.*g* Every noble and beautiful quality seemed in its turn to be her leading characteristic so long as only that side of her character was looked at. The passion of justice might have been thought to be her strongest feeling, but for her boundless generosity and a lovingness ever ready to pour itself forth upon any or all human beings however unlike herself, if they did but shew a capacity of making the smallest return of feeling or even a wish to have feeling bestowed on them. Her unselfishness was not that of a taught system of duties, but of a heart which thoroughly identified itself with the feelings of others, and even, imaginatively investing others with an intensity of feeling equal to its own, often took great suffering upon itself to save others from pain which would have been comparatively small. She was by nature one of those who would have had most excuse for thinking first of themselves, for her impulses were tenfold stronger, her pleasures and pains tenfold more intense than those of common persons: yet to receive all pleasure and all good from the love of others would to her have been the only congenial state, and when she took concern for herself or asserted any claims of her own, *h*every one*h* felt that the impersonal love of justice was speaking, in her neither more nor less than it would have spoken in behalf of a stranger or an enemy. All the rest of her moral characteristics were those which naturally accompany these qualities of mind and heart. The most genuine modesty combined with the loftiest pride; a simplicity and sincerity which was absolute, towards all who were fit to receive it; the utmost scorn of everything mean or cowardly, and indignation at everything brutal or tyrannical, faithless or dishonourable in conduct or character; while making the broadest distinction between *mala in se* and mere *mala prohibita*, between acts giving evidence of intrinsic badness of feeling and character, and those which are mere violations of conventions either good *or* bad, and which whether in themselves right or wrong, may be done by persons otherwise loveable or admirable.

Such a woman could not, except by the rarest destiny, be otherwise than alone in the world, especially in a world like England. Married at *i*a very*i* early age, to a most upright, brave, and honorable man, of liberal opinions *j*and good education, but not of the intellectual or artistic tastes which would have made him*j* a companion for her, though a steady and affectionate friend, for whom she had true esteem and *k*the strongest*k* affection through life and whom she most deeply lamented when dead; shut out by the social disabilities of women from any adequate exercise of her higher faculties in action on the world without, her life

---

g-g[*Marked with a line in the margin by HTM*]
h-h[*Altered by HTM to read:* every good observer must have]
i-i[*Earlier version:*] an [*altered to final reading first by HTM*]
j-j[*Earlier version:*] but of no intellectual or artistic tastes, nowise [*altered to final reading first by HTM*]
k-k[*Interlined in pencil by HTM, then written over in ink by Mill*]

was one of inward meditation varied by familiar intercourse with a small circle of friends, of whom one only ^{l}(a woman)^l was a person of genius, or of capacities of feeling or intellect kindred with her own, but all had more or less of alliance with her in sentiments and opinions. Into this circle I had the good fortune to be admitted, though it was ^{m}many^m years before I could be said to be at all intimate with her. ^{n}But from the time when I could really call her my friend I wished for no other.^{n} All other persons whom I had known either had not the opinions or had not the feelings which were necessary to make them permanently valuable to me. In her ^{o} complete emancipation from every kind of superstition, and an earnest protest both against society as at present constituted, and against the pretended perfection of the order of nature and the universe, resulted not from the hard intellect but from strength of noble and elevated feeling, and coexisted with ^{p}a^p reverential nature. In general spiritual characteristics as well as in temperament and organization I have often compared her, as she was at this time, to Shelley: but in thought and intellect Shelley, so far as his powers were developed in his short life, was but a child to her. I have never known any intellect in man or woman which, taken for all in all, could be compared to hers. ^{q}All other intellects when looked at beside hers^q seem to be but special talents,—a peculiar knack acquired by study and practice of dealing with some one particular thing. On all subjects on which she thinks, that is, on all great subjects of speculation and on all near subjects of important practice, she goes quite down to the very heart and marrow of the matter, severing and putting aside all irrelevancies and non-essentials, cleaving through at one stroke all entanglements of verbal sophistry and haze of confused conceptions. Alike in the highest regions of philosophy and in the smallest practical concerns of daily life, her mind is always the same perfect instrument; always seizing the essential idea or principle, the cause on which the effect depends, the precise end, and the precise obstacle to its attainment. The same exactness and rapidity of operation pervading all her senses as well as her mental faculties, would with her gifts of feeling and imagination have made her a consummate artist ^{r}in any department in which she had had the requisite mechanical instruction^r; as her fiery and tender soul and her vigorous eloquence ^{s}would have made her a great orator, and her coup d'œil and power of practical combination might have made her a great general, if either *carrière*^{s} had been accessible to women. But if I were to say in what above all she is preeminent, it is in her

---

$^{l-l}$[*Deleted by HTM*]

$^{m-m}$[*Interlined in pencil by HTM, then written over in ink by Mill*]

$^{n-n}$[*Deleted by HTM*]

^{o}[*Cancelled text:*] alone [*deleted first by HTM*]

$^{p-p}$[*Earlier version:*] an originally [*altered to final reading first by HTM*]

$^{q-q}$[*Altered by HTM to read:* Most intellects]

$^{r-r}$[*Deleted by HTM*]

$^{s-s}$[*Altered by HTM to read:* might have made an orator if any such *carrières (for "a great orator"* Mill first wrote *"one of the greatest of orators"*)]

profound knowledge of human nature. To know all its depths and all its elevations she had only to study herself: her knowledge of its varieties she owes to an observation which overlooks nothing, and an activity of mind which converts everything into knowledge. Hence while she sees farther ^{t}than, as it appears to me, any one else has done into the possibilities and capabilities of the future^{t}, the thoroughness of her insight into and comprehension of human beings as they are preserves her from all miscalculations or illusions. Those who are dissatisfied with human life as it is and whose feelings are wholly identified with its radical amendment (as all the wisest and best of mankind are) have two main regions of thought, ^{u}in both of which her intellect is supreme and her judgment infallible:^{u} One is the region of ultimate aims, the constituents of the highest realizable ideal of human life; the other is that of the immediately useful and practically attainable. ^{v}In both of these ever since I knew her well, I have been entirely and in the fullest sense her pupil. ^{v} And to say truth, it is in these two extremes that the only real certainty resides. My own strength, ^{w}such as it was (apart from the capacity of appreciating and partly understanding things better and greater than myself, by which alone I was or am in any degree worthy of her), ^{w} lay wholly in the uncertain and slippery intermediate region, that of theory, or so-called moral and political science: respecting the conclusions of which in any of the forms in which I have received or originated them, whether as political economy, analytic psychology, logic, philosophy of history, or anything else, it is not the least of my intellectual obligations to her that I have derived from her a wise scepticism; which, while it has not prevented me from following out the honest exercise of my thinking faculties to whatever conclusions might result from it, has prevented me, I hope, from holding or announcing those conclusions with a confidence which the nature of such speculations does not warrant, and has kept my mind always open to admit clearer perceptions and better evidence. ^{x}Everything in my later writings to which any serious value can be attached, everything either far reaching in speculation or genial in tone and feeling and sympathetic with humanity, everything to which the *Political Economy* in particular owes its reputation and which is thought to distinguish it ^{y}to its advantage^{y} from other treatises under the same name, is in all

---

$^{t-t}$[*Earlier version:*] into the possibilities and capabilities of the future than those who are reputed the most dreamy enthusiasts [*altered several times by both Mill and HTM, the latter first writing the version that Mill accepted as final. She also marked the entire sentence with a line in the margin.*]

$^{u-u}$[*Deleted by HTM, who also underscored "infallible" and pencilled "unerring?" at left*]

$^{v-v}$[*Marked with a large X and a line in the margin by HTM, who also deleted the last eight or nine words of the sentence and interlined "derived &c" above "been"*]

$^{w-w}$[*Deleted by HTM*]

$^{x-x}$^{621}[*Marked with a line in the margin by HTM, who pencilled some forty or fifty words at left, now erased and largely illegible, beginning: "It is a subject on which we have often united as shewing [?] . . ."*]

$^{y-y}$[*Earlier version:*] radically

essentials not my writing but hers: and still more will this be the case with what remains to be written in order to bring our opinions fully before the world.[x]

It is [z] less obvious what even in the immaturity of her powers and of her experience, could attract her to me, than me to her; or what, peculiarly valuable to her, she could find in such a type of character as mine [a]: but a thorough agreement in opinion is to any one, especially to a young person opposed to the reigning opinions,[a] always a support, especially when the concurring minds have been very differently formed and trained and have arrived at their conclusions by very different paths. To her who had reached her opinions by the moral intuition of a character of strong feeling, there was doubtless help as well as encouragement to be derived from one who had arrived at many of the same results by study and reasoning. It was also a strong link between us that we felt alike on that most vital question, the social position of women: whose subordination, by law and custom, to men, we regarded as the last remaining form of primeval tyranny and serfage, and whose equal admissibility to all occupations and equal participation in all rights, we deemed not only to be the clear dictate of justice, but to be an essential condition of any great improvement in mankind either individually or socially. It would give a totally false idea of her character if I were not to say, that her strong feeling on this [b] point was the effect of principle, and not of any desire on her own part to mingle in the turmoil and strife of the occupations which the dominant sex has hitherto reserved to itself. [c]Though her education had been masculine, her personal habits and tastes were all[c] peculiarly feminine; her feelings and inclinations all pointed to a life not of self-help or self-assertion but of loving reliance on the love and care of others. [d]The importance she attached to the social independence and equal rights of women, arose from two of the principal features of her character, her love of justice and her sense of dignity. How indeed can either of these feelings, when a genuine outgrowth of the individual nature, and not a matter of arbitrary convention as much as any of the rules of deportment, tolerate that a human being should be marked out from birth to be the mere appendage of some other? Those most capable of the abnegation of any separate self, and merging of the entire being with that of another, which is the characteristic of strong passion [e]or rather, which strong passion in its most passionate moments strives to realize[e],

[z][*Cancelled text:*] much [*deleted first by HTM, who marked the entire sentence with a line in the margin and pencilled several words at left, now erased and (except for "I mention" [?] and "attainments") illegible*]

[a–a][*Earlier version:*] . My principal recommendation, besides that of strong admiration and desire for sympathy with her, was our thorough agreement in opinion, which to any one, especially to a young person opposed to the reigning opinions, is [*altered to final reading first by HTM*]

[b][*Cancelled text:*] most essential

[c–c][*Earlier version:*] Her education, her personal habits and tastes were all [*HTM deleted "Her education" and "all", and wrote several words, now erased and illegible, at left.*]

[d–d622][*Marked with a line in the margin by HTM*]

[e–e][*Deleted by HTM*]

are precisely those who would disdain to be the objects of this self-annihilating feeling unless ^{f}the renunciation of any separate existence is equally complete on both sides^f and unless it comes from the spontaneous impulse of individual feeling and not from social ordinances prescribing that one half of all human character shall develope itself in this way or have no developement at all. But men have first decreed that women shall have no passions except personal passions, and have then erected one of the natural promptings of strong personal passion into the ideal standard of womanly perfection, from which they endeavour to reap a double advantage: first, the pleasure, the convenience and the vanity of being all in all to their nearest companion without her being all in all to them; and next that in the pursuit of their other objects they not only have not to contend with women as competitors but can *exploiter* their enthusiasm and their quick practical sagacity for the interests of their own success. And then because the feelings of women being denied any other outlet, flow into the channel dug for them with a force proportioned to the capacity of strong feeling with which they are naturally endowed, the inference is drawn that this is the channel demanded by their own nature and that a woman who claims admission to any other, does so because she has not the feelings which, by this kind of practical *petitio principii*, have been decided to be womanly. ^{d} If the commonest laws of human nature did not prove it, my wife is a sufficient proof by example that whoever has the greatest and fullest measure of the feelings that produce self devotion to another or others, is also the best qualified for any other field of action, great or small, and must ever protest inwardly (unless her nature itself is bowed to the yoke of her circumstances) against the stupid and selfish social arrangements which compel her, if she acts at all, however the planning and originating mind and the commanding faculties may be on her side, to act solely through another.

The influence of this most precious friendship upon my own mental developement was of a twofold nature. The first, ^{g}and that of which I earliest reaped the full benefit,^{g} was her effect on my ideal standard of character. My conception of the highest worth of a human being, was immeasurably enlarged and exalted, ^{h}while at the same time this larger ideal was filled and satisfied by her ^{i} in a manner in which no one had ever before satisfied even the far inferior ideal which I had conceived previously. This first kind of influence was not so properly her influence, as^h the effect on my own thoughts and feelings of new experience and new ^{j}subjects of contemplation^j. The second was the direct operation of her

---

$^{f-f}$[*Earlier version:*] they give it in as full measure as they receive it

$^{g-g}$[*Deleted by HTM, who marked the rest of this sentence and the next five sentences (through "now found one.") with a line in the margin*]

$^{h-h}$[*Altered by HTM to read:* This was]

^{i}[*Cancelled text:*] as a really existing character

$^{j-j}$[*Earlier version:*] objects of contemplation which she afforded to me [*HTM underscored "objects" and wrote "Subjects" at left.*]

intellect and character upon mine, and this ^{k} came to its full height only gradually, with the increasing maturity of her own thoughts and powers ^{l}. But at a very early period of my knowledge of her she became to me a living type of the most admirable kind of human being. I had always wished for a friend whom I could admire wholly, without reservation and restriction, and I had now found one. To render this possible, it was necessary that the ^{m}object of my admiration^m should be of a type very different from my own; should be a character preeminently of feeling, combined however as I had not in any other instance known it to be, with a vigorous and bold speculative intellect. Hers was not only ^{n}all this but the perfection of^n a poetic and artistic nature. ^{o}With how eminent a practical capacity these endowments were combined, I only understood by degrees; but the rest was enough without this to make me feel that in any true classification of human beings, such as I are only fit to be the ^{p}subjects^p and ^{q}ministers^q of such as her; and that the best thing I, in particular, could do for the world, would be to serve as a sort of prose interpreter of her poetry, giving a logical exposition to those who have more understanding than feeling, of the reasonableness of that which she either knew by the experience or divined by the intuition of ^{r}one of the richest and strongest of natures guided by the most unselfish and highminded of characters^r.^{o}

Accordingly the first years of ^{s}my friendship with her^s were, in respect of my own development, mainly years of poetic culture. It is hardly necessary to say that I am not now speaking of *written* poetry, either metrical or otherwise; though I did cultivate this taste as well as a taste for paintings and sculptures, and did read with enthusiasm her favorite poets, especially the one whom she ^{t}placed far above^t all others, Shelley. But this was merely accessary. The real poetic culture was, that my faculties, ^{u}such as they were,^{u} became more and more attuned to the beautiful and elevated, in all kinds, and especially in human feeling and character ^{v}and more capable of vibrating in unison with it^v. ^{w}In the same proportion, and by a natural consequence, I became less excitable by anything else. All^w society and personal intercourse became burthensome to me except with those in whom I recognized,

^{k}[*Cancelled text:*] though considerable from the first [*deleted first by HTM, who wrote several words, now erased and illegible, at left*]

^{l}[*Cancelled text:*] : as will be abundantly shewn in the sequel

$^{m-m}$[*Underscored and marked with a question mark by HTM*]

$^{n-n}$[*Altered by HTM to read:* this but in a high degree]

$^{o-o}$[*Marked with a line in the margin by HTM*]

$^{p-p}$[*Altered by HTM to read:* followers]

$^{q-q}$[*Earlier version:*] servants

$^{r-r}$[*Altered by HTM to read:* a rich and strong nature]

$^{s-s}$[*Altered by HTM to read:* our acquaintance]

$^{t-t}$[*Altered by HTM to read:* preferred to]

$^{u-u}$[*Deleted by HTM*]

$^{v-v}$[*Deleted by HTM*]

$^{w-w}$[*Deleted by HTM, who wrote at left:* "explain how what is called society always becomes burthensome to persons of any capacity and therefore especially to those who require a real inter-change of ideas to make a change from solitude refreshing—not wearysome"]

along with more or less sympathy of opinion, at least a strong taste for elevated and poetic feeling, if not the feeling itself. [x]I gradually withdrew myself from much of the society which I had frequented;[x] though I [y]still retained unabated[y] interest in radical politics and kept up my connexion with such of the rising or promising politicians on the radical side, as I had ever been intimate with. I even became more involved in political and literary relations than I had ever been before, through the foundation, as I have already mentioned, by Sir William Molesworth of a new radical review, to be entirely under my direction.

[x-x]*[Deleted by HTM]*
[y-y]*[Altered by HTM to read:* acquired increased]

Appendix H

Helen Taylor's Continuation of the Autobiography

AMONG THE MSS in the Mill-Taylor Collection, British Library of Political and Economic Science, is a two-page draft continuation of the *Autobiography* by Helen Taylor, relating events of Mill's life in 1870 (the year in which he left off writing the work) and the two following years. No doubt originally intended as an end-note or appendix, the draft appears unfinished, possibly because the writer could not bring herself to describe Mill's final illness and death, perhaps merely because she did not complete the account before the work was transcribed and ready for the press. The text given here ignores cancellations, false starts, and other evidences that the MS is a first draft.

The last portion of this memoir was written, at Avignon, in the winter of 1869–1870. The works mentioned in the concluding paragraph are two—one on Socialism upon which the author was still occupied to the last, and which therefore is in an incomplete state; and one on Theism which he had finished, but kept by him, as was his custom with most of his works, for further consideration and retouching. The last three years of his life were fully occupied with literary work in addition to these more important productions; and he himself was of opinion that if his life were prolonged to complete it, his work on Socialism would rank as, at the least, on a level with that on Representative Government. Of his work on Theism the world will be able to judge.

Early in the year 1870 he was in England and delivered a speech at a meeting held at the Hanover Square Rooms in favour of women's suffrage.[*] This was the last speech he spoke on that subject with the exception of one at Edinburgh in January 1871.[†] During the year 1870 he wrote three articles for the *Fortnightly*

[*Speech to the National Society for Women's Suffrage, in the Hanover Square Rooms, on 26 Mar., 1870 (see the reports on 28 Mar. in *The Times*, p. 5, the *Daily News*, p. 2, and the *Daily Telegraph*, p. 3). The speech was printed in *Report of a Meeting of the London National Society for Women's Suffrage, . . . March 26th, 1870* (London: n.p., 1870), pp. 4–9.]

[†Speech in the Music Hall, Edinburgh, on 12 Jan., 1871 (see the report in *The Times*, 13 Jan., p. 3, and a leading article in the *Daily Telegraph*, 14 Jan., p. 5). The speech was printed in *Women's Suffrage. Great Meeting in Edinburgh . . . on 12th January 1871* (Edinburgh: printed Greig, 1871), pp. 7–12.]

Review; one on Professor Cliffe Leslie's work on the Land Systems of different countries; one on Taine's work *De l'Intelligence* and one on "Treaty Obligations":[*] he also wrote two letters to the *Times* in the month of November 1870 on the same topic.[†] They were called forth by a cry, that arose at that time in a portion of the English press, for plunging England into a war with Russia. They were the first protest that appeared in any well known name against such a war; they called forth others and helped to calm down the warlike excitement that was being aroused.

In 1871 he spoke at a public meeting called by the Land Tenure Reform Association, a speech which was afterwards published by the Association.[‡] During that year he was much occupied with the subject of Land Tenure. He wrote for the Land Tenure Association a programme or Expository Statement,[§] setting forth his scheme of reform, and explaining his idea of the equitable claim of the State, as representing the Community, to the increase in the value of land that may arise from the labour of the community as a whole, and at the same time, suggesting the appropriation of this increased value by means of a land tax. Sir Henry Maine's work on Village Communities interested him greatly at this time, bearing as it does on the question of the tenure of land, and he wrote a review of it for the *Fortnightly Review*, published in May 1871.[¶] The illness and death of his old friend Mr. Grote; the threatening illness of a younger but not less valued friend to whom he looked as the man best qualified to carry on his own work;[||] and the failing health of a member of his own family,[**] combined to depress his spirits

[*Professor Leslie on the Land Question," *Fortnightly Review*, n.s. VII (June, 1870), 641–54, reviewing T. E. C. Leslie, *Land Systems and Industrial Economy of Ireland, England, and Continental Countries* (London: Longmans, Green, 1870); "Taine's *De l'intelligence*," n.s. VIII (July, 1870), 121–4, reviewing Hippolyte Taine, *De l'intelligence*, 2 vols. (Paris: Hachette, 1870); and "Treaty Obligations," n.s. VIII (Dec., 1870), 715–20. The three articles were reprinted (posthumously) in *D&D*, Vol. IV, pp. 86–110, 111–18, and 119–29, respectively; the first two in *CW*, Vol. V, pp. 669–85, and Vol. XI, pp. 441–7.]

[†"Mr. Mill on the Treaty of 1856," *The Times*, 19 Nov., 1870, p. 5; "The Treaty of 1856," *ibid.*, 24 Nov., 1870, p. 3.]

[‡Speech in the Freemasons' Hall, Great Queen St., on 15 May, 1871 (see the reports on 16 May in the *Daily News*, p. 2, and the *Daily Telegraph*, p. 2, and on 17 May in *The Times*, p. 7). Printed in *Land Tenure Reform Association. Report of the Inaugural Public Meeting, . . . 15th May, 1871* (London: Land Tenure Reform Association, 1871); reprinted (posthumously) in *D&D*, Vol. IV, pp. 251–65.]

[§*Programme of the Land Tenure Reform Association, with an Explanatory Statement by John Stuart Mill* (London: Longmans, Green, Reader, and Dyer, 1871); reprinted (posthumously) in *D&D*, Vol. IV, pp. 239–50, and in *CW*, Vol. V, pp. 687–95.]

[¶"Maine on Village Communities," *Fortnightly Review*, n.s. IX (May, 1871), 543–56 (reprinted, posthumously, in *D&D*, Vol. IV, pp. 130–53), reviewing Henry James Sumner Maine, *Village-Communities in the East and West* (London: Murray, 1871).]

[||John Elliot Cairnes.]

[**I.e., Helen Taylor herself.]

during the spring and summer of this year and he derived so little benefit from several botanizing excursions he took with an old friend[*] in Cornwall, Yorkshire and Scotland, that there seemed danger of his own health giving way. A few weeks in Switzerland and a residence at Avignon however produced the effect that mountain air and a southern climate seldom failed to produce on him, and he seemed to have recovered his usual health. In November 1871 he published, in the *Fortnightly Review*, an article on Berkeley's Life and Writings, suggested by Professor Fraser's new edition of Berkeley's *Works*.[†]

In the first half of 1872 he was chiefly occupied with the preparation of a new edition of his *System of Logic*,[‡] upon which he bestowed more than usual time and labour. The summer of that year was spent in the Alps of Tyrol, Styria, Carinthia, Carniola, Friuli and Venetia, and it was his invariable custom to do no literary work during the excursions he took for health. In the autumn and winter he wrote a review of Grote's *Aristotle*, published in the *Fortnightly Review* for January 1873, and two articles for the *Examiner* (published January 4th and 11th, 1873) on Land Reform.[§]

[*Alexander Irvine.]

[†"Berkeley's Life and Writings," *Fortnightly Review*, n.s. X (Nov., 1871), 505–24 (reprinted, posthumously, in *D&D*, Vol. IV, pp. 154–87, and in *CW*, Vol. XI, pp. 449–71), reviewing Alexander Campbell Fraser, ed., *The Works of George Berkeley*, 4 vols. (Oxford: Clarendon Press, 1871).]

[‡The 8th ed. (London: Longmans, Green, Reader, and Dyer, 1872).]

[§"Grote's *Aristotle*," *Fortnightly Review*, n.s. XIII (Jan., 1873), 27–50 (reprinted, posthumously, in *D&D*, Vol. IV, pp. 188–230, and in *CW*, Vol. XI, pp. 473–510), reviewing George Grote, *Aristotle*, ed. Alexander Bain and George Croom Robertson, 2 vols. (London: Murray, 1872); and "Advice to Land Reformers," *Examiner*, 4 Jan., 1873, pp. 1–2, and "Should Public Bodies Be Required to Sell Their Lands?" *ibid.*, 11 Jan., 1873, pp. 29–30 (both reprinted, posthumously, under the title "Advice to Land Reformers," in *D&D*, Vol. IV, pp. 266–77).]

Appendix I

Bibliographic Index of Persons and Works Cited, with Variants and Notes

LIKE MOST NINETEENTH-CENTURY AUTHORS, Mill is somewhat cavalier in his attitude to sources, seldom identifying them with sufficient care, and frequently quoting them inaccurately. This appendix is intended to help correct these deficiencies, and to serve as an index of names and titles (which are consequently omitted in the analytic Index). Included here also are (at the end of the appendix) references to parliamentary bills, petitions, reports, and evidence, which are entered in order of date under the heading "Parliamentary Papers and Petitions," and references to British and (one instance) French statute law, which are entered in order of date under the heading "Statutes." The material otherwise is arranged in alphabetical order, with an entry for each person or work reviewed, quoted, or referred to in the text proper and in Appendices A–H (those in the appendices are given in italic type). References to mythical and fictional characters are excluded, as are references to real people that occur in quotations from, or derive from, poems and fictional works, unless Mill comments on them as historical figures. Citations to Appendix A include the works Mill used in writing "The History of Rome," but not the people, real or mythical, in that history. In the footnotes to the text, references to musical works give names and dates; here that information is supplemented with details of their first publication in England. References to the Early Draft of the *Autobiography* are given in italic type; if the reference merely duplicates that in the final version of the *Autobiography*, the reference to the Early Draft is given in parentheses following that to the final version (as the texts are printed on facing pages, with the final version on the right hand, the lower number in these cases follows the higher). Such double references end with p. *246*, where the Early Draft terminates. The same procedure is followed for references within the "Yale Fragment" on Harriet Taylor Mill, printed on pp. *250–8*.

The entries take the following form:
1. Identification: author, title, etc., in the usual bibliographic form.
2. Notes (if required) giving information about Mill's use of the source, indication if the work is in his library, Somerville College, Oxford (referred to simply as SC), and any other relevant information.
3. Lists of the pages where works are reviewed, quoted, and referred to.
4. In the case of quotations, a list of substantive variants between Mill's text and his source, in this form: Page and line reference to the present text. Reading in the present text] Reading in the source (page reference in the source).

The list of substantive variants also attempts to place quoted passages in their contexts by giving the beginnings and endings of sentences. The original wording is supplied where Mill has omitted two sentences or less; only the length of other omissions is given. There being uncertainty about the actual Classical texts used by Mill, the Loeb editions are cited when possible.

ABADIE, ARNAUD. *Itinéraire topographique et historique des Hautes-Pyrénées.* Paris: de Pelafol, 1819.
REFERRED TO: *574, 586*

ABELARD, PETER.
NOTE: the reference derives from John Sterling's poem, "Abelard to Heloïse," *q.v.*
REFERRED TO: *606*

ADAMS, WILLIAM BRIDGES ("Junius Redivivus"). "Beauty," *Monthly Repository*, n.s. VII (Feb., 1833), 89–96.
REFERRED TO: 369

———— "Junius Redivivus on the Conduct of the *Monthly Repository*," *Monthly Repository*, n.s. VI (Dec., 1832), 793–4.
REFERRED TO: 369

———— "On the Condition of Women in England," *Monthly Repository*, n.s. VII (Apr., 1833), 217–31.
REFERRED TO: 369

———— "On the State of the Fine Arts in England," *Monthly Repository*, n.s. VII (Jan., 1833), 1–33.
REFERRED TO: 369

———— "Plan for the Better Housing of the Working Classes," *Mechanics' Magazine, Museum, Register, Journal, and Gazette*, No. 434 (3 Dec., 1831), 165–71.
NOTE: the reference is also to the reprinting of this letter to the editor in Adams's *The Producing Man's Companion*, pp. 204–23 (it is not in the 1st ed. of that work, *The Rights of Morality*). Adams contributed two other letters on the subject to the *Mechanics' Magazine*, No. 432 (19 Nov., 1831), 117–18, and No. 446 (25 Feb., 1832), 371–2.
REFERRED TO: 382n

———— *The Producing Man's Companion: An Essay on the Present State of Society, Moral, Political, and Physical, in England.* 2nd ed., with additions. London: Wilson, 1833.
NOTE: the 1st ed. was entitled *The Rights of Morality, q.v.*
REVIEWED: 367–77, 379–90
QUOTED: 384, 385, 385–7, 387, 388–9
384.9   "tyrannical taskmasters"] The people at large were brutalised by their tyrannical taskmasters, from the fear that they might discover an opening for escape; and that very brutality has produced an opposite effect. (11)
386.19–20   genius. [*paragraph*] Even] genius. [*2-page omission*] [*paragraph*] Even (116, 118)
386.32–3   evil. [*paragraph*] It] evil. [*4-page omission*] [*paragraph*] It (119, 123)
387.6   enough of copies] enough copies (124)
387.18   sycophants.] sycophants.* [*footnote omitted*] (125)
387.20–1   "the whole . . . in common"] There is a principle of sound and enlarged morality, "*that the whole . . . in common, and of this* RIGHT* *no individual can be divested, notwithstanding the actual possession may be taken from him or her, either by force or chicanery.*" [*footnote omitted*] (13)
387.25–6   "has . . . things, as . . . live] This principle was acknowledged by the Jews, by whose laws an equal division of the natal soil took place every fifty years: but if the Jews had not acknowledged it, the principle would have existed just the same, because it is self-evident, that a human being born into the world has . . . things or . . . live, whatever Mr. Malthus may say to the contrary; and

moreover, it is at the discretion of each individual to beget as many children as he chooses, though of course, it is a matter of prudence to consider the evil he may produce to himself or his fellow-creatures, by the injudicious exercise of this discretion. (13–14)

388.7   The notion] But the notion (24)

389.14   assistance.] assistance.* [*footnote omitted*] (28)

389.30   labour,] labour,* [*footnote omitted*] (29)

———— *The Rights of Morality: An Essay on the Present State of Society, Moral, Political, and Physical, in England: with the Best Means of Providing for the Poor and Those Classes of Operatives Who May Be Suddenly Thrown Out of Their Regular Employment by the Substitution of New Inventions.* London: Wilson, 1832.

NOTE: the 2nd ed. (which Mill twice reviewed) was retitled *The Producing Man's Companion, q.v.*

REFERRED TO: 383

———— *A Tale of Tucuman, with Digressions, English and American.* London: Wilson, 1831.

REVIEWED: 367–77

QUOTED: 376

376.28   "To convey," . . . "in] The object of this Poem is to convey, in (5)

376.30   Americans: the descriptions," . . . "of] Americans, who, notwithstanding the many books which have been written about them of late, have been less understood by modern travellers than by those of a century back; because, the ancient travellers were mostly men of education and science, and the moderns, with few exceptions, have been mere soldiers, or buyers and sellers therefore their sphere of observation has generally been as limited as their powers. [$3\frac{1}{2}$-*page omission*] The descriptions of (5, 9)

ADDISON, CHARLES GREENSTREET. *Damascus and Palmyra.* 2 vols. London: Bentley, 1838.

REFERRED TO: 437

AESCHINES.

NOTE: *Demosthenis et Aeschinis quae exstant omnia* (Greek and Latin), 10 vols. (London: Priestley, 1827), is in SC.

REFERRED TO: 15 (*14*), 560–1

AESCHYLUS. Referred to: 532

———— *Prometheus vinctus.*

NOTE: as the reference is general, no ed. is cited. *Tragoediae*, 3 vols. (London: Whittaker, 1823), is in SC.

REFERRED TO: 333

AESOP. *Aesopi Phrygis fabulae graece et latine, cum aliis opusculis* (Pladunes Collection). Basel: Heruagius, 1544.

NOTE: this ed. (or one with identical type, contents, and paging) in SC, with all up to p. 20 (including the title page), and p. 367 (the end of the index and the colophon) missing. At pp. 386 and 421, for ease of reference, *Aesop's Fables*, trans. Vernon Stanley Jones (London: Heinemann; New York: Doubleday, Page, 1912), is cited. The reference to the fable of "The Belly and the Members" is in a quotation from Adams. See also Plutarch, *Lives.*

REFERRED TO: 9 (*8*), 386, 421, *552*

ALDRICH, HENRY. *Artis logicae compendium.* Oxford: Sheldonian Theatre, 1691.

REFERRED TO: 125 (*124*)

ALISON, ARCHIBALD. *Sermons, Chiefly on Particular Occasions.* Edinburgh: Constable; London: Longman, Hurst, Rees, Orme, and Brown, 1814.

REFERRED TO: 311n

ANON. Leading article on Mill's defeat, *The Times*, 23 Dec., 1868, p. 9.
REFERRED TO: 278–9

ANON. "Lord Durham and His Assailants," *Examiner*, 26 Aug., 1838, pp. 529–30.
NOTE: see Anon., Leading article on Lord Durham, *Morning Chronicle*, 20 Aug., 1838, p. 2. The article shows every sign (except a signature) of being by Albany Fonblanque.
REFERRED TO: 223

ANON. "Memoirs, etc. of Sir Thomas More," *Edinburgh Review*, XIV (July, 1809) 360–75.
REFERRED TO: 321

ANON. "Observations on the Residence of the Clergy," *Edinburgh Review*, V (Jan., 1805) 301–17.
QUOTED: 306
306.13 "the improvement] They [members of parliament] cannot doubt the beneficial tendency c such an enactment ["obliging country gentlemen to live upon their estates"]: the improvemer (302)
306.13 lands, and the] lands, the (302)
306.14 industry."] industry, would be its natural result. (302)

ANON. "On the Intellectual Influences of Christianity," *Monthly Repository*, n.s. VI (Sept. 1832), 627–34.
NOTE: Mill addresses "On Genius" to the author of this article and of "Some Considerations," *q.v.*
REFERRED TO: 329

ANON. "Some Considerations Respecting the Comparative Influences of Ancient and Modern Times on the Development of Genius," *Monthly Repository*, n.s. VI (Aug. 1832), 556–64.
NOTE: Mill addresses "On Genius" to the author of this article and of "On the Intellectual Influence of Christianity," *q.v.*
REFERRED TO: 329, 333–4

ANON. *An Universal History, from the Earliest Account of Time to the Present: Compile from Original Authors; and Illustrated with Maps, Cuts, Notes, Chronological an Other Tables.* 7 vols. London: Batley, *et al.*, 1736–44.
NOTE: Vols. I and VII are both in two parts. Mill refers to this as "the Ancient Universal History" (se have, on their spines, "Universal History/Ancient Part"); it was completed by *The Modern Part the Universal History, Compiled from Original Writers; by the Authors of the Antient. Which W Perfect the Work, and Render It a Complete Body of History, from the Earliest Account of Time, the Present*, 16 vols. (London: Osborne, *et al.*, 1759–65) (plus an unnumbered vol., *The Map and Charts to the Modern Part of the Universal History*, 1766) (sets have, on their spine "Universal History/Modern Part").
REFERRED TO: 17 (*16*), *558, 583*

ANSON, GEORGE. *A Voyage round the World, in the Years MDCCXL, I, II, III, IV* Compiled by Richard Walter. London: the Author, 1748.
REFERRED TO: 11 (*10*), *555*

ANSTRUTHER, ROBERT. Referred to: 284

Anthologia graeca sive poetarum graecorum lusus. Ed. Friedrich Jacob. 13 vols. Leipzi Dyck, 1794–1814.
NOTE: this ed. in SC. The anthology itself occupies only Vols. I–IV; Vol. V is an index vol.; ar Vols. VI–XIII are commentary.
REFERRED TO: 15 (*14*), *561, 568*

ANTONINUS, MARCUS AURELIUS. Referred to: 532

634 APPENDIX I

AUSTIN, CHARLES.
NOTE: the reference at p. 77 (76) is to all the sons of Jonathan Austin, of whom Charles was one; tha at p. 99 (98) is to Austin's early articles in the *Westminster Review* (for a list, see *The Wellesle Index*, Vol. III); those at p. 121 (120) are to his editorship of, and authorship of (unidentifie articles in, the *Parliamentary History and Review*.
REFERRED TO: 77 (76), 79–81 (78–80), 97 (96), 99 (98), 101 (100), 105 (104), 110, 121 (120), 12 (126), 129 (128), 131 (130)

——— "Corn Laws," *Parliamentary History and Review; . . . Session of 1825 (q.v.)*, Vol II, pp. 690–705.
NOTE: this identification is based on the sparse annotations in George Grote's copy, University o London Library. Mill says Austin "wrote much" in the *Parliamentary History and Review*, but th is the only article identified as his.
REFERRED TO: 121 (120)

AUSTIN, JOHN.
NOTE: the quotations at 185 (184) and 223 (222) are of remarks made by Austin in conversation.
QUOTED: 185 (184), 223 (222)
REFERRED TO: 67 (66), 75–9 (74–8), 81 (80), 97 (96), 101 (100), 185–7 (184–6)

——— "Disposition of Property by Will—Primogeniture," *Westminster Review*, II (Oct. 1824), 503–53.
REFERRED TO: 99 (98)

——— "Joint Stock Companies," *Parliamentary History and Review; . . . Session of 182. (q.v.)*, Vol. II, pp. 709–27.
NOTE: this identification is based on annotations in George Grote's copy, University of Londo Library.
REFERRED TO: 121 (120)

——— *Lectures on Jurisprudence; or, The Philosophy of Law*. 3rd ed. Ed. Robe Campbell. 2 vols. London: Murray, 1869.
NOTE: in SC. First ed. (1832) entitled *The Province of Jurisprudence Determined, q.v.* The referenc at p. 185 (184) is to Austin's preparation of his lectures for delivery; that at p. 268 is to Mill "Austin on Jurisprudence," *q.v.* The quotation is probably not from the *Lectures*, but fro conversation; however, the references are given for comparison.
QUOTED: 187 (186)
REFERRED TO: 185 (184), 268

——— *A Plea for the Constitution*. London: Murray, 1859.
NOTE: the reference at p. 187 is to Austin's "last publication"; for Mill's review of the 2nd ed. (als 1859), see "Recent Writers on Reform."
REFERRED TO: 187, 263

——— *The Province of Jurisprudence Determined*. London: Murray, 1832.
NOTE: the reference is to Austin's preparation of his lectures, published under this title. Reissued a *Lectures on Jurisprudence, q.v.* Reviewed by Mill, "Austin's Lectures on Jurisprudence," *q.v.*
REFERRED TO: 185 (184)

AUSTIN, JONATHAN.
NOTE: the reference is to "a retired miller in Suffolk," father of John Austin (*q.v.*) and his brother Alfred, Charles (*q.v.*), and George.
REFERRED TO: 75–7 (74–6)

AUSTIN, SARAH. Referred to: 186

——— *Characteristics of Goethe. From the German of Falk, Müller, etc.* 3 vols. Londo Wilson, 1833.

REFERRED TO: *591*

25.14   intellectus sibi permissus] Quod vero attinet ad notiones primas intellectus; nihil est eorum quae intellectus sibi permissus congessit, quin nobis pro suspecto sit, nec ullo modo ratum, nis novo judicio se stiterit et secundum illud pronuntiatum fuerit. (137–8)

BAILEY, SAMUEL. *A Critical Dissertation on the Nature, Measures, and Causes of Value. Chiefly in Reference to the Writings of Mr. Ricardo and His Followers.* London. Hunter, 1825.
REFERRED TO: 123 (*122*)

BAILLIE, JOANNA. *Constantine Paleologus; or, The Last of the Caesars: A Tragedy in Five Acts* (1804). In *Miscellaneous Plays.* 2nd ed. London: Longman, Hurst, Rees, and Orme; Edinburgh: Constable, 1805, pp. 279–438.
NOTE: this ed. in SC.
REFERRED TO: 19n, *26, 564, 584*

BAIN, ALEXANDER.
NOTE: the reference at p. 255n is to Bain's contributions to Mill's *System of Logic*, *q.v.*; that at p. 287 is to Bain's contributions to Mill's ed. of his father's *Analysis* (1869), *q.v.*
REFERRED TO: 255n, 287

———— *The Emotions and the Will.* London: Parker, 1859.
NOTE: reviewed by Mill in "Bain's Psychology," *q.v.* Mill habitually refers to this work and Bain's *The Senses and the Intellect* as one treatise.
REFERRED TO: 263, 270, 288

———— *The Senses and the Intellect.* London: Parker, 1855.
NOTE: reviewed by Mill in "Bain's Psychology," *q.v.* Mill habitually refers to this and Bain's *The Emotions and the Will* as one treatise. The 3rd ed. (London: Longmans, Green, 1868) is in SC.
REFERRED TO: 263, 270, 288

BALDWIN, ROBERT. Referred to: 97 (*96*)

BALDWIN, WILLIAM. See Andrew Knapp.

BALZAC, HONORÉ DE. Referred to: 470, 482

———— *Le père Goriot.* 2 vols. Paris: Werdet, 1835.
REFERRED TO: 480

BARING, ALEXANDER. Referred to: 101–3 (*100–2*)

BARTHÉLEMY, AUGUSTE MARSEILLE. Referred to: 434

BAZARD, AMAND. Referred to: 173 (*172*)

BEALES, EDMOND. Referred to: 278

BEATTIE, JAMES. Referred to: 19 (*18*), 565

"BEAUCHAMP, PHILIP." See George Grote, *Analysis.*

"BEAUMONT, HARRY." See Joseph Spence.

BEAVER, PHILIP. *African Memoranda: Relative to an Attempt to Establish a British Settlement on the Island of Bulama, on the Western Coast of Africa, in the Year 1792.* London: Baldwin, 1805.
REFERRED TO: 11, *555*

BEETHOVEN, LUDWIG VAN. Referred to: 350

――― *The Elements of the Art of Packing, as Applied to Special Juries, Particularly i* *Cases of Libel Law*. London: Wilson, 1821.
NOTE: in *Works*, Vol. V, pp. 61–186. The reference is inferential, deriving from Brougham, wh says merely that he is quoting Bentham. In the passage referred to, Bentham says: "On puttin together these passages [from Ellenborough], all out of the same speech—out of the same *charge* and that not a very long one—it seems evident enough that if they mean any thing, they mea this—*viz.* that it is a *crime* for *any man* to write any thing which it happens to *any other man* not t *like*: or more shortly, that if a man publishes what he writes, under Lord Ellenborough at least, *it* a *crime to write*." (94)
REFERRED TO: 298

――― *A Fragment on Government: Being an Examination of What Is Delivered on th* *Subject of Government in General in the Introduction to Sir William Blackstone'* *Commentaries; with a Preface, in Which Is Given a Critique of the Work at Large* London: Payne, 1776.
NOTE: in *Works*, Vol. I, pp. 221–95. The references at pp. 71 (*70*) and *577–8* are to Mill's reading in the early 1820s, "the most important" of Bentham's then published works.
REFERRED TO: 71 (*70*), 119 (*118*), *577–8*

――― *An Introduction to the Principles of Morals and Legislation*. London: Payne, 1789.
NOTE: in *Works*, Vol. I, pp. 1–154. The ed. of 1789 is in SC, as is the 2-vol. ed. (London: Wilson 1823). The quoted phrases at p. 67 (*66*) reflect the wording of the English ed. (Chap. ii, §xivn) rather than, as the context would suggest, the French version in Dumont's redaction, *Traités d* *législation* (Chap. iii). The reference at pp. 67–9 (*66–8*) is to Chap. xvi; that at p. 71 (*70*) is t Mill's reading, in the early 1820s, "the most important" of Bentham's then published works.
QUOTED: 67 (*66*)
REFERRED TO: 67–9 (*66–8*), 71 (*70*), 577

――― *Panopticon; or, The Inspection House: Containing the Idea of a New Principle o* *Construction Applicable to Any Sort of Establishment, in Which Persons of Any* *Description Are to Be Kept under Inspection: and in Particular to Penitentiary-houses* *Prisons, Houses of Industry, Work-houses, Poor-houses, Manufactories, Mad-houses* *Lazarettos, Hospitals, and Schools: with a Plan of Management Adapted to the* *Principle: in a Series of Letters, Written in the Year 1787, from Crecheff in White* *Russia, to a Friend in England*. 2 vols. London: Payne, 1791.
NOTE: in *Works*, Vol. IV, pp. 37–172. The references are to Mill's reading, in the early 1820s, "the most important" of Bentham's then published works.
REFERRED TO: 71 (*70*), 578

――― *Plan of Parliamentary Reform, in the Form of a Catechism, with Reasons for Eac* *Article: with an Introduction, Showing the Necessity of Radical, and the Inadequacy o* *Moderate, Reform*. London: Hunter, 1817.
NOTE: in *Works*, Vol. III, pp. 433–557.
QUOTED: 109 (*108*)
109.23–4 "corrupter-general,"] [*paragraph*] Yes: in this country—under this Constitution—may be seen an official person, who by his station is, for ever, *ex officio* C――r* [*footnote:* *Whatsoever blanks may eventually be observable in the remainder of this work, the prudence o the printer is the virtue to which the honour of them will be due. In the present instance, for filling up the *deficit* between the *C* and the *r*, the candour and sagacity of the Reader may employ the letters *onservato*, or any others, if any others there be, which in his view may be more apposite [*text:*] General: it is his *situation* makes him so: it suffices for the purpose: *to produce the effect,* (and let this be well observed), *no overt act—no, nor so much as a thought—is on his par necessary:*—were it possible for him to have the *will*, scarcely in his *situation* would it be in his *power* to avoid being so. (Intro., xxii–xxiii)

———— *Rationale of Judicial Evidence, Specially Applied to English Practice.* Ed. J. S. Mill. 5 vols. London: Hunt and Clarke, 1827.
NOTE: in SC. In *Works*, Vols. VI, pp. 188–585, and VII.
REFERRED TO: 117–19 (*116–18*)

———— *The Rationale of Reward.* London: Hunt, 1825.
NOTE: in *Works*, Vol. II, pp. 189–266. One may reasonably infer that Mill did not have a specific work in mind when he observed that Bentham "used to say that 'all poetry is misrepresentation' "; in *The Rationale of Reward*, however, Bentham writes: "Indeed, between poetry and truth there is a natural opposition: false morals, fictitious nature. The poet always stands in need of something else. When he pretends to lay his foundations in truth, the ornaments of his superstructure are fictions; his business consists in stimulating our passions, and exciting our prejudices. Truth, exactitude of every kind, is fatal to poetry. The poet must see everything through coloured media, and strive to make every one else to do the same." (206; III, i)
REFERRED TO: 115 (*114*)

———— *A Table of the Springs of Action: Shewing the Several Species of Pleasures and Pains, of Which Man's Nature Is Susceptible: together with the Several Species of Interests, Desires, and Motives, Respectively Corresponding to Them: and the Several Sets of Appellatives, Neutral, Eulogistic and Dyslogistic, by Which Each Species of Motive Is Wont to Be Designated: to Which Are Added Explanatory Notes and Observations.* London: Hunter, 1817.
NOTE: in *Works*, Vol. I, pp. 195–219. The references are to Mill's reading, in the early 1820s, "the most important" of Bentham's then published works.
REFERRED TO: 71 (*70*), 578

———— *Tactique des assemblées législatives, suivie d'un Traité des sophismes politiques.* Ed. Pierre Etienne Louis Dumont. 2 vols. Geneva: Paschoud, 1816.
NOTE: English version, *An Essay on Political Tactics*, in *Works*, Vol. II, pp. 299–373. The references are to Mill's reading, in the early 1820s, "the most important" of Bentham's works, in Dumont's versions.
REFERRED TO: 71 (*70*), 578

———— *Théorie des peines et des récompenses.* Ed. Pierre Etienne Louis Dumont. 2 vols. London: Dulau, 1811.
NOTE: in *Works* as "Rationale of Punishments," Part II of *Principles of Penal Law*, Vol. I, pp. 388–532. The references are to Mill's reading, in the early 1820s, "the most important" of Bentham's works, in Dumont's versions.
REFERRED TO: 71 (*70*), 578

———— *Traité des preuves judiciaires.* Ed. Pierre Etienne Louis Dumont. 2 vols. Paris: Bossange, 1823.
NOTE: the references at pp. 71 (*70*) and *578* are to Mill's reading, in the early 1820s, "the most important" of Bentham's writings, in Dumont's versions; though this work appeared slightly later than the period Mill is speaking of, he almost certainly had it also in mind at the time of writing the *Autobiography*.
REFERRED TO: 71 (*70*), 117 (*116*), 578

———— *Traités de législation civile et pénale, précédés de Principes généraux de législation, et d'une Vue d'un corps complet de droit: terminés par un Essai sur l'influence des tems et des lieux relativement aux lois.* Ed. Pierre Etienne Louis Dumont. 3 vols. Paris: Bossange, et al., 1802.
NOTE: the quoted words on p. 67 (*66*) are in English; Mill is undoubtedly thinking of the version in Bentham's *An Introduction to the Principles of Morals and Legislation*, xiiin–xviin (Chap. ii, p. xivn); for an approximation in French, see *Traités*, Vol. I, pp. 10–21 (Chap. iii of *Principes*

généraux de législation). The reference at pp. 67–9 *(66–8)* to the work of Bentham on whic
Dumont's redaction is based is also to *An Introduction*; that at p. 69 *(68)* is to *De l'influence de
tems et des lieux.*
QUOTED: 67 *(66)*, *577*
REFERRED TO: 65–73 *(64–70)*, 325

BENTHAM, MARIA SOPHIA (née Fordyce). Referred to: 57–9 *(56–8)*, *58n*

BENTHAM, MARY LOUISE (Madame de Chesnel).
NOTE: the reference is to Samuel Bentham's three daughters, of whom Mary Louise was one.
REFERRED TO: 59 *(58)*

BENTHAM, SAMUEL. Referred to: 57–9 *(56–8)*, *57n*, *58n*, 62

BENTHAM, SARAH.
NOTE: the reference is to Samuel Bentham's three daughters, of whom Sarah was one.
REFERRED TO: 59 *(58)*

BENTINCK, WILLIAM. Referred to: 77 *(76)*

BÉRANGER, PIERRE JEAN DE.
NOTE: Mill uses the spelling Bérenger.
REFERRED TO: 532

BERKELEY, GEORGE.
NOTE: the reference at p. 71 *(70)* is to Mill's general, that at p. *578* is to his early, reading of Berkeley
REFERRED TO: 71 *(70)*, *578*

———— *The Works of George Berkeley*. Ed. Alexander Campbell Fraser. 4 vols. Oxford
Clarendon Press, 1871.
NOTE: the reference, in Helen Taylor's "continuation" of the *Autobiography*, is in relation to Mill'
"Berkeley's Life and Writings," *q.v.*
REFERRED TO: *627*

BERRY, MARY. *The Fashionable Friends: A Comedy, in Five Acts.* London: Ridgway
1802.
REFERRED TO: *605*

BERTHOLLET, CLAUDE LOUIS. Referred to: 62

BEUDIN, JACQUES FÉLIX. See Alexandre Dumas, *Richard Darlington.*

BIBLE. Referred to: 337

———— New Testament. Referred to: 41 *(40)*, 337, 370

———— Old Testament. Referred to: 41 *(40)*

———— II Chronicles.
QUOTED: 437
437.8   "Tadmor in the wilderness,"] And he [Solomon] built Tadmor in the wilderness, and all th
store cities, which he built in Hamath. (8:4)

———— Deuteronomy.
NOTE: the phrase appears several times in the Bible; cf. Deuteronomy, 4:30.
QUOTED: 329
329.10   "latter days,"] For I [Moses] know that after my death ye will utterly corrupt yourselves, an
turn aside from the way which I have commanded you; and evil will befall you in the latter days
because ye will do evil in the sight of the LORD, to provoke him to anger through the work of you
hands. (31:29)

———— Matthew, 5–7.
NOTE: the reference is to the Sermon on the Mount.
REFERRED TO: 72

———— Numbers.
NOTE: the reference is to Korah, Dathan, and Abiram (see Numbers, 16:1).
REFERRED TO: 448

———— II Peter.
NOTE: the reference is in a quotation from Ware.
REFERRED TO: 448

———— Proverbs.
NOTE: the quotation at p. 335 is not exact; cf. Proverbs, 11:5 and 13:6.
QUOTED: 335
REFERRED TO: 421

BINGHAM, PEREGRINE.
NOTE: the reference at p. 117 (*116*) is to Bingham's editing of Bentham's *Book of Fallacies*, *q.v.*, as is that at p. 121 (*120*), which also refers to his editing the *Parliamentary History and Review*; see also Bingham, "Prefatory Treatise."
REFERRED TO: 97 (*96*), 99 (*98*), 115 (*114*), 117 (*116*), 121 (*120*), *120n*

———— "Combination and Combination Laws," *Parliamentary History and Review;* . . . *Session of 1825* (*q.v.*), Vol. II, pp. 730–5.
NOTE: this identification is based on annotations in George Grote's copy, University of London Library. Mill refers to Bingham's writing "much" in the *Parliamentary History and Review*.
REFERRED TO: 121 (*120*); see also Bingham, "County Courts," and "Licensing System."

———— "County Courts," *Parliamentary History and Review;* . . . *Session of 1826* (*q.v.*), Vol. II, pp. 746–54.
NOTE: see also Bingham, "Combination."
REFERRED TO: 121 (*120*)

———— "Licensing System;—Public Houses," *ibid.*, Vol. II, pp. 726–36.
NOTE: see also Bingham, "Combination."
REFERRED TO: 121 (*120*)

———— (probably). "M. Cottu and Special Juries," *Westminster Review*, I (Jan., 1824), 146–71.
NOTE: for the authorship, see *The Wellesley Index*, Vol. III. The reference at p. 97 (*96*) is to Bingham's five articles in the first number of the *Westminster*; that at p. 298 is inferential, Mill's wording probably being his own, but related to that here cited. See also Bingham, "Periodical Literature." It is possible, though not probable, that Mill also had this article in mind when, at p. *96*, he refers to the two articles in the first number of the *Westminster* that he took "extremely to heart" (see note to W. J. Fox, "Men and Things").
REFERRED TO: 97 (*96*), 298

———— "Moore's *Fables for the Holy Alliance*," *Westminster Review*, I (Jan., 1824), 18–27.
NOTE: the reference is to Bingham's five articles in the first number of the *Westminster*.
QUOTED: 115 (*114*)
REFERRED TO: 97 (*96*)
115.12 "Mr. . . . a poet . . . a reasoner,"] [*paragraph*] However, as to this matter [vague generalities], the fault seems to lie rather in the art of poetry than in the artist; and perhaps all we have said amounts to no more than this, that Mr. . . . a *poet* . . . a *reasoner*." (21)

——— "Periodical Literature: *Quarterly Review*," *Westminster Review*, I (Jan., 1824), 250–68.
NOTE: for the authorship, see *The Wellesley Index*, Vol. III. The reference at p. 97 (*96*) is to Bingham's five articles in the first number of the *Westminster*; that at p. 298 is inferential, Mill's wording probably being his own, but related to that here cited. See also Bingham, "M. Cottu and Special Juries."
REFERRED TO: 97 (*96*), 298

——— "Prefatory Treatise on Political Fallacies," *Parliamentary History and Review; . . . Session of 1825* (*q.v.*), Vol. I, pp. 1–28.
NOTE: this is "a condensation and new arrangement of the matter" of Bentham's *Book of Fallacies*, *q.v.*, and was, it may be inferred, prepared by Peregrine Bingham, who had edited Bentham's work, and edited the *Parliamentary History and Review*. The reference is indirect.
REFERRED TO: 121 (*120*)

——— "Travels of Duncan, Flint and Faux," *Westminster Review*, I (Jan., 1824), 101–20.
NOTE: the reference is to Bingham's five articles in the first number of the *Westminster*.
REFERRED TO: 97 (*96*)

——— "Vocal Music," *Westminster Review*, I (Jan., 1824), 120–41.
NOTE: the reference is to Bingham's five articles in the first number of the *Westminster*.
REFERRED TO: 97 (*96*)

BIOT, JEAN BAPTISTE. *Essai de géométrie analytique*. See *Traité analytique*.

——— *Traité analytique des courbes et des surfaces du second degré* (1802). Retitled *Essai de géométrie analytique, appliqué aux courbes et aux surfaces du second ordre*. 2nd ed. Paris: Bernard, 1805.
REFERRED TO: 575

BLACK, JOHN.
NOTE: the references are to Black's editorship of the *Morning Chronicle*.
REFERRED TO: 91 (*90*), 107 (*106*)

BLACK, JOSEPH. *Lectures on the Elements of Chemistry, Delivered in the University of Edinburgh*. 2 vols. London: Longman and Rees; Edinburgh: Creech, 1803.
NOTE: the reference derives from Brougham's "Dr. Black's Lectures," *q.v.*
REFERRED TO: 308

BLACKSTONE, WILLIAM. *Commentaries on the Laws of England*. 4 vols. Oxford: Clarendon Press, 1765–69.
NOTE: the 5th ed., 4 vols. (Oxford: Clarendon Press, 1773), is in SC.
REFERRED TO: 67 (*66*), 577

Blackwood's Magazine.
NOTE: the quotation at p. 348 has not been identified, though it seems likely that it originates with John Wilson.
QUOTED: 348
REFERRED TO: 397, 398

BODICHON, BARBARA. Referred to: 285

BOILEAU-DESPRÉAUX, NICOLAS.
NOTE: the reference is to some of his "little pieces."
REFERRED TO: 572

——— *L'art poétique* (1674). In *Œuvres de Nicolas Boileau Despréaux. Avec des éclaircissemens historiques, donnez par lui-même*. New ed. 2 vols. The Hague: Gosse and Neaulme, 1729, Vol. II, pp. 1–104.
REFERRED TO: 575

———— "Epistre VI, à Lamoignon" (1683). *Ibid.*, Vol. I, pp. 357–70.
REFERRED TO: *573*

BOISSY D'ANGLAS, FRANÇOIS ANTOINE.
NOTE: the reference derives from Chenevix, "English and French Literature," *q.v.*
REFERRED TO: 310

BOISTE, PIERRE CLAUDE VICTOIRE. *Dictionnaire des difficultés de la langue française, résolues par les plus célèbres grammairiens; extrait du Dictionnaire universel par P. C. V. Boiste*. Paris: Boiste, 1800.
REFERRED TO: *573–4*

BOLEYN, ANNE.
NOTE: the reference is in a quotation from Macaulay.
REFERRED TO: 527

BONAPARTE. See Napoleon I.

BONNYCASTLE, JOHN. *An Introduction to Algebra; with Notes and Observations: Designed for the Use of Schools, and Places of Public Education*. London: Johnson, 1782.
REFERRED TO: *559*

The Book of Common Prayer.
NOTE: the reference at p. 161 (*160*) is to the Thirty-Nine Articles; that at p. 460 is to the Church of England Catechism, both of which are found in *The Book of Common Prayer*. See John Henry Blunt, ed., *The Annotated Book of Common Prayer, Being an Historical, Ritual, and Theological Commentary on the Devotional System of the Church of England* (London: Rivington, 1866).
REFERRED TO: 161 (*160*), 460

BOUGAINVILLE, LOUIS ANTOINE DE. Referred to: 13 (*10–12*)

BOWRING, JOHN.
NOTE: the first four references are to Bowring's editorship of the *Westminster Review*; that at p. 536 is to Bowring's "Memoirs of Bentham," *q.v.*
REFERRED TO: 93 (*92*), 95–7 (*94–6*), 101 (*100*), 135 (*134*), 536

———— "Memoirs of Bentham." In *The Works of Jeremy Bentham*, Vols. X–XI.
NOTE: the "Memoirs" were issued as Parts 19–21 of the *Works* in 1842. Mill refers to the "Memoirs" also as the "Life" and the "Biography." The quotations on pp. 535, 536, 537, are at second-hand from Empson, "Jeremy Bentham," *q.v.*
QUOTED: 535, 536, 537
REFERRED TO: 535–8

BRADLAUGH, CHARLES. Referred to: 289

BREREWOOD, EDWARD. *Elementa logicae*. Oxford: Hall, 1657.
NOTE: the copy in the London Library (bound with Samuel Smith, *Aditus ad logicam*, *q.v.*, which is autographed "J. Mill" on the title page) was presumably part of Mill's donation of some of his father's books to the London Library. The reference is simply to "Latin treatises on the scholastic logic"; this title is given in Mill's letter to Samuel Bentham (*EL, CW*, Vol. XII, p. 8); it is also mentioned as a standard text "at hand" in Mill's *Examination of Sir William Hamilton's Philosophy, CW*, Vol. IX, pp. 412–14.
REFERRED TO: 21 (*20*), 567

BRIGHT, JOHN. Referred to: 276, 279, 285

———— Speech "On America, I" (4 Dec., 1861). In his *Speeches on Questions of Public Policy*. Ed. James Edwin Thorold Rogers. 2 vols. London: Macmillan, 1868, Vol. I, pp. 167–95.
REFERRED TO: 267

—— Speech on the Cattle Diseases Bill (1866), *Parliamentary Debates*, 3rd ser., Vol. 181, cols. 472–80 (14 Feb., 1866).
REFERRED TO: 276n–7n

BRISSOT, JACQUES PIERRE.
NOTE: the reference derives from Roland.
REFERRED TO: 346

BRODIE, GEORGE. *A History of the British Empire, from the Accession of Charles I, to the Restoration; with an Introduction, Tracing the Progress of Society, and the Constitution, from the Feudal Times, to the Opening of the History; and Including a Particular Examination of Mr. Hume's Statements, Relative to the Character of the English Government.* 4 vols. Edinburgh: Bell and Bradfute; London: Longman, Hurst, Rees, Orme, and Brown, 1822.
REFERRED TO: 99n

BROOKE, HENRY. *The Fool of Quality; or, The History of Henry Earl of Moreland.* 4 vols. London: Johnston, 1766–70.
REFERRED TO: 13 (*12*), 556

BROUGHAM, HENRY PETER. Referred to: 93 (*92*), 129 (*128*), 203 (*158*)

—— "Constitutional Association," *Edinburgh Review*, XXXVII (June, 1822), 110–21.
QUOTED: 302
302.30 "culpable indifference"] It was strongly suspected, from circumstances which afterwards came to light, that some of the Government spies were connected with the worst of the publications in question; and certain it is, that a ministry which had, to say the very least, by culpable negligence, allowed so great a scandal to attach upon the press, came forward with a bad grace to profit by their own wrong, and demand new laws for checking what the old, if faithfully executed, would have sufficed to prevent. (112–13)
302.31–2 "every one else," . . . "was . . . authors"] But the Law-officers appeared soon to run into the opposite extreme; and in the discussions which took place after the Manchester Outrage, there were produced the most glaring cases of periodical works, in which rebellion, mutiny, and assassination, were openly recommended, in the plainest language, and in the most minute detail, having been suffered, for many months, to pass wholly unnoticed by the Government, while every one else was . . . authors. (112)

—— "The Crisis of the Sugar Colonies," *Edinburgh Review*, I (Oct., 1802), 216–37.
QUOTED: 305–6
REFERRED TO: 303

—— "Dallas's *History of the Maroons*," *Edinburgh Review*, II (July, 1803), 376–91.
QUOTED: 308

—— "Dangers of the Constitution," *Edinburgh Review*, XXVII (Sept., 1816), 245–63.
QUOTED: 294–5, 296
294.34 [*paragraph*] What is it that] [*no paragraph*] What it is, in short, that (249)
295.7 check. This] check. [*paragraph*] This (249)
296.5 [*paragraph*] After] [*no paragraph*] After (247)
296.6 a security] a sufficient security (247)

—— "Dr. Black's *Lectures*," *Edinburgh Review*, III (Oct., 1803), 1–26.
QUOTED: 308, 309
308.32 "innovating . . . vanity,"] Now, Mr. Robison requires us to go a step farther, and to admit that the motive for changing the nomenclature may be found in the same corporation and national spirit,—in a desire to obliterate the remembrance of every thing which did not owe its origin to the associated academicians of France,—in the same combination of innovating . . . vanity, which produced the new calendar and metrology. (21–2)

309.3 [*paragraph*] When] [*no paragraph*] When (22)

309.9 "that] We give it [an account of the incident concerning Madame Lavoisier, which Mill quotes above] to our readers as an amusing instance of that (22)

———— "Early Moral Education," *Edinburgh Review*, XXXVIII (May, 1823), 437–53.
NOTE: at p. 307n Brougham is quoting Pole, *q.v.*
QUOTED: 306–7, 307n

306.28 "that] It [the inconsistency of the poor in their refusal "to contribute even a penny a week" to the Westminster Infant School "when they used to give fourpence and even sixpence to the most wretched Dame schools"] partly arises from the arts of those old women [the Dames], who, of course, set themselves against the new school, both misrepresenting it and cajoling the parents; but it results chiefly from that (445)

———— "Karamsin's *Travels in Europe*," *Edinburgh Review*, III (Jan., 1804), 321–8.
REFERRED TO: 324

———— "Kotzebue's *Travels in Italy*," *Edinburgh Review*, VII (Jan., 1806), 456–70.
REFERRED TO: 324

———— "Kotzebue's *Travels to Paris, etc.*," *Edinburgh Review*, V (Oct., 1804), 78–91.
REFERRED TO: 324

———— *Letter to the Marquess of Lansdowne, K.G., Lord President of the Council, on the Late Revolution in France*. London: Ridgway, 1848.
NOTE: the reference is to Brougham's attacks on the French Provisional Government of 1848.
REFERRED TO: 264

———— "Liberty of the Press and Its Abuses," *Edinburgh Review*, XXVII (Sept.; 1816), 102–44.
QUOTED: 298, 299

298.14 "to] The problem, then, which they ["enlightened men all over the world"] are seeking to solve, is the one which we are about to investigate, namely, to (104)

298.16 character;"] character. (104)

298.24 [*paragraph*] One] [*no paragraph*] One (108)

298.31 "means] Means (109)

298.33 *any . . . body*,] '*any . . . body*,' (109)

299.18 [*paragraph*] That there] [*no paragraph*] But, that there (126)

———— Motion on the Education of the Poor, *Parliamentary Debates*, n.s., Vol. 2, cols. 49–89 (28 June, 1820).
REFERRED TO: 203 (*158*)

———— "Parliamentary History," *Edinburgh Review*, XLIV (Sept., 1826), 458–90.
NOTE: the reference is to Brougham's praise of Mill's "Ireland" (*q.v.*), in the *Parliamentary History and Review*.
REFERRED TO: *120n*

———— "State of Parties," *Edinburgh Review*, XXX (June, 1818), 181–206.
QUOTED: 314, 315

314.34 "yielding in small things for the sake of great ones,"] But, in ordinary cases, the yielding in small matters for the sake of greater ones, is not only no abandonment of private opinion, but is the only way in which that opinion can be effectually pronounced and pursued. (187)

BROWN, CHARLES BROCKDEN. Referred to: 434

———— *Arthur Mervyn; or, Memoirs of the Year 1793*. 2 vols. Philadelphia: Maxwell, 1799.
REFERRED TO: 434n

—— *Edgar Huntly; or, Memoirs of a Sleep-Walker.* 3 vols. Philadelphia: Maxwell, 1799.
REFERRED TO: 434n

—— *Ormond; or, The Secret Witness.* New York: Caritat, 1799.
REFERRED TO: 434n

—— *Wieland; or, The Transformation.* New York: Caritat, 1798.
REFERRED TO: 434n

BROWN, JOHN. Referred to: 266, 266n

BROWN, THOMAS. "Belshaw's *Philosophy of the Mind*," *Edinburgh Review*, I (Jan., 1803), 475–85.
NOTE: the reference is to the quotation from the article in James Mill's "Periodical Literature: *Edinburgh Review*," *q.v.*
QUOTED: 324
324.20   [*paragraph*] Is] [*no paragraph*] Is (483)
324.20   made by] made with (483)
324.23   until] till (483)

—— *Inquiry into the Relation of Cause and Effect* (1805). 3rd ed. Edinburgh: Constable, 1818.
NOTE: this ed. in SC.
REFERRED TO: 71(70), 579

—— *Lectures on the Philosophy of the Human Mind.* 4 vols. Edinburgh: Tait, 1820.
NOTE: in listing his reading in philosophy in 1822–23, Mill says he read Brown's *Inquiry into the Relation of Cause and Effect*, adding: "Brown's *Lectures* I did not read until two or three years later, nor at that time had my father himself read them."
REFERRED TO: 71 (70)

BROWNING, ROBERT. *Pauline. A Fragment of a Confession.* London: Saunders and Otley, 1833.
NOTE: the "review" is on sheets bound at the back into the copy now in the Forster Collection, Victoria and Albert Museum.
REVIEWED: *596–7*
QUOTED: *596*
596.13   "these . . . fair"] But whate'er come of it—and tho' it fade, / And tho' ere the cold morning all be gone / As it will be;—tho' music wait for me, / And fair eyes and bright wine, laughing like sin. / Which steals back softly on a soul half saved; / And I be first to deny all, and despise / This verse, and these . . . fair; / Still this is all my own, this moment's pride, / No less I make an end in perfect joy. (68; 986–94)
596.14   "thus visited" . . . "in perfect joy"] No less I make an end in perfect joy, / For I, having thus again been visited, / Shall doubt not many other bliss awaits, / And tho' this weak soul sink, and darkness come, / Some little word shall light it up again, / And I shall see all clearer and love better; / I shall again go o'er the tracts of thought, / As one who has a right; and I shall live / With poets—calmer—purer still each time, / And beauteous shapes will come to me again, / And unknown secrets will be trusted me, / Which were not mine when wavering—but now / I shall be priest and lover, as of old. (69–70; 1007–19)

BRUCE, JAMES. *Travels to Discover the Source of the Nile in the Years 1768, 1769, 1770, 1771, 1772, and 1773.* 5 vols. London: Robinson, 1790.
QUOTED: 437n
437n.5   "the] [*paragraph*] Just before we came in sight of the ruins, we ascended a hill of white gritty stone, in a very narrow-winding road, such as we call a pass, and, when arrived at the top, there opened before us the (Intro., I, lvii)

BURNS, ROBERT.
NOTE: the quotation at p. 350n is from "My heart's in the Highlands" (published 1790), and the reference at p. 350n is to "Scots wha hae wi Wallace bled" (published 1794); variously titled in different eds. of Burns's poems as "national airs." (The former is also to be found in Walter Scott's *Waverley*, Chap. xxviii.) SC contains *Works*, new ed., 2 pts. (London: Tegg, *et al.*; Dublin: Milliken, *et al.*; Glasgow: Griffin, 1824), and formerly contained *The Poetical Works*, 2 vols. (London: Pickering, 1830).
QUOTED: 350n
REFERRED TO: 19 (*18*), 350n, 532, *565*

BUSK, MARY MARGARET. "Literature of Childhood," *London and Westminster Review*, XXXIII (Oct., 1839), 137–62.
NOTE: the reference is by inference; Mill promises that works by Anna Maria Hall will be mentioned in the *L&WR*, and in this article her *Juvenile Budget* is reviewed.
REFERRED TO: *606*

BUTLER, JOSEPH. *The Analogy of Religion, Natural and Revealed, to the Constitution and Course of Nature. To Which Are Added Two Brief Dissertations: I. Of Personal Identity. II. Of the Nature of Virtue*. London: Knapton, 1736.
REFERRED TO: 41 (*40*)

BUXTON, CHARLES. Referred to: 281

——— Motion on the Disturbances in Jamaica, *Parliamentary Debates*, 3rd ser., Vol. 184, cols. 1763–85 (31 July, 1866).
REFERRED TO: 282n

BYRON, GEORGE GORDON (Lord).
NOTE: the reference at p. 149 (*148*) is to Mill's having read all of Byron during his depression.
REFERRED TO: 149–51 (*148–50*), 153 (*152*), 163 (*162*), 434, 467, 474n

——— *Childe Harold's Pilgrimage, a Romaunt, in Four Cantos* (1812–18). 2 vols. London: Murray, 1819.
REFERRED TO: 151 (*150*)

——— *Don Juan, a Poem* (1819–24). 2 vols. Edinburgh: Kay, 1825.
REFERRED TO: 376

——— "The Dream." In *The Prisoner of Chillon, and Other Poems*. London: Murray, 1816, pp. 35–45.
REFERRED TO: 439

——— *The Giaour, a Fragment of a Turkish Tale*. London: Murray, 1813.
REFERRED TO: 151 (*150*)

——— *Lara, a Tale*. London: Murray, 1814.
REFERRED TO: 151 (*150*)

——— *Manfred, a Dramatic Poem*. London: Murray, 1817.
REFERRED TO: 151 (*150*)

CAESAR, GAIUS JULIUS. *Commentaries*.
NOTE: two eds. were formerly in SC: *C. Iulii Caesaris quae exstant, cum selectis variorum commentariis, quorum plerique novi, operâ et studio Arnoldi Montani. Accedunt notitia Galliae et notae auctiores ex autographo Iosephi Scaligeri* (Amsterdam: Elzevir, 1661); and *C. Julii Caesaris quae exstant opera*, 2 vols. (Paris: Barbou, 1755).
REFERRED TO: 13 (*12*), *557*

CAIRNES, JOHN ELLIOT.
NOTE: the reference, in Helen Taylor's "continuation" of the *Autobiography*, is to "a younger but not less valued friend."
REFERRED TO: *626*

———— *The Slave Power: Its Character, Career and Probable Designs: Being an Attempt to Explain the Real Issues Involved in the American Contest* (1862). 2nd ed. London and Cambridge: Macmillan, 1863.
NOTE: this ed. in SC, inscribed "With the author's regards." The reference at p. 268 is to Mill's "The Slave Power," *q.v.*, a review of Cairnes' book.
REFERRED TO: 266, 268

CALAS, JEAN. Referred to: 301

CAMPBELL, THOMAS. Referred to: 525

———— "The Exile of Erin" (1801). In *Gertrude of Wyoming, and Other Poems*. 3rd ed. London: Longman, Hurst, Rees, Orme, and Brown, *et al.*, 1810, pp. 182–5.
NOTE: it is not known which ed. (or eds.) of Campbell's poems Mill read, but this is the earliest in which all the poems he mentions appear.
REFERRED TO: 21 (*20*), *567*

———— "Gertrude of Wyoming" (1809). *Ibid.*, pp. 1–131.
NOTE: see the preceding entry.
REFERRED TO: 21 (*20*), *567*

———— "Hohenlinden" (1803). *Ibid.*, pp. 143–6.
NOTE: see Campbell, "The Exile of Erin," above.
REFERRED TO: 21 (*20*), *567*

———— "Lochiel's Warning" (1803). *Ibid.*, pp. 133–42.
NOTE: see Campbell, "The Exile of Erin," above.
REFERRED TO: 21 (*20*), *566–7*

CANNING, GEORGE. Referred to: 103 (*102*), 121 (*120*)

CAPMANY Y DE MONTPALAU, ANTONIO DE. *Qüestiones críticas sobre varios puntos de historia económica, política, y militar*. Madrid: Impr. real, 1807.
REFERRED TO: 301n

CARLILE, JANE.
NOTE: the reference is to the prosecution for blasphemy of Richard Carlile's wife.
REFERRED TO: 89 (*88*)

CARLILE, MARY ANNE.
NOTE: the reference is to the prosecution for blasphemy of Richard Carlile's sister.
REFERRED TO: 89 (*88*)

CARLILE, RICHARD.
NOTE: the reference is to the prosecution for blasphemy of Carlile (a radical republican, freethinking journalist and publisher) and his wife and sister.
REFERRED TO: 89 (*88*)

CARLYLE, THOMAS.
NOTE: the reference at p. 163 is to a letter from Sterling to Carlyle; that at p. 181 (*180*) is to Carlyle's telling Mill that when he first read "The Spirit of the Age" he said, "here is a new Mystic," and consequently sought out Mill in London. (For Carlyle's immediate reaction to the articles [which were anonymous], see his letter to his brother John, 21 Jan., 1831, in *The Collected Letters of Thomas and Jane Welsh Carlyle*, *q.v.*, Vol. V, p. 216; on 17 Feb., John told him that Mill was the

author [*ibid.*, p. 235n], and Carlyle met Mill on 2 Sept., 1831 [*ibid.*, p. 398].) The reference at p. 215 (*214*) is to Carlyle's contributions to the *London and Westminster Review*, all of which are listed below.

REFERRED TO: *154*, 163, 181–3 (*180–2*), 215 (*214*), 253, *607*

———— "Biography," *Fraser's Magazine,* V (Apr., 1832), 253–60.

QUOTED: 330, *593*

330.14–15 "the significance of man's life,"] Attempts, here by an inspired Speaker, there by an uninspired Babbler, to deliver himself, more or less ineffectually, of the grand secret wherewith all hearts labour oppressed: The significance of Man's Life;—which deliverance, even as traced in the unfurnished head, and printed at the Minerva Press, finds readers. (255)

593.19 "look out upon the world with their dim horn eyes"] For, observe, though there is *a* greatest Fool, as a superlative in every kind; and *the* most Foolish man in the Earth is now indubitably living and breathing, and did this morning or lately eat breakfast, and is even now digesting the same; and looks out on the world, with his dim horn-eyes, and inwardly forms some unspeakable theory thereof: yet where shall the authentically Existing be personally met with! (255)

———— "Boswell's *Life of Johnson*," *Fraser's Magazine*, V (May, 1832), 379–413.

REFERRED TO: *182*

———— "Characteristics," *Edinburgh Review*, LIV (Dec., 1831), 351–83.

NOTE: both references are inferential; the opinion in that at p. 329 is typical of Carlyle's attitudes in the period, expressed also in his letters to Mill.

REFERRED TO: 145 (*144*), 329

———— *The Collected Letters of Thomas and Jane Welsh Carlyle*. Ed. Charles Richard Sanders, *et al*. Durham, N.C.: Duke University Press, 1970– (in progress).

NOTE: the quotations are from letters from Carlyle to Mill, that at p. 183 (*182*) dating from 20 Jan., 1834, that at p. 370 from 12 Jan., 1833, and that p. 597 from 18 Apr., 1833.

QUOTED: 183 (*182*), 370, *597*

REFERRED TO: 181n

183.14–15 "was as yet . . . mystic."] As it is, I can say, the Creed you write down is singularly like my own in most points,—with this single difference that you are yet . . . Mystic; your very Mysticism (for there is enough of it in you) you have to translate into Logic before you give it place. (VII, 72–3)

370.1 man,"] man! (VII, 300)

597.6–7 "what should we speak of but that which we know?"] Speak of it what *you* know. (VI, 373)

———— "Corn Law Rhymes," *Edinburgh Review*, LV (July, 1832), 338–62.

NOTE: the quotation is indirect. Carlyle says: "Strength, if that be the thing aimed at, does **not** manifest itself in spasms, but in stout bearing of burdens" (p. 351).

QUOTED: 353n

———— *The French Revolution*. 3 vols. London: Fraser, 1837.

NOTE: formerly in SC.

REFERRED TO: 135 (*134*), 225 (*224*)

———— "Jean Paul Friedrich Richter," *Edinburgh Review*, XLVI (June, 1827), 176–95.

NOTE: the reference is to Carlyle's early articles in the *Edinburgh Review*, of which this is illustrative. Mill probably had in mind such other essays as "State of German Literature," XLVI (June, 1827), 176–95; "Burns," XLVI (Oct., 1827), 304–51; "Signs of the Times," XLIX (June, 1829), 439–59; "Taylor's Historic Survey of German Poetry," LIII (Mar., 1831), 151–80; "Characteristics," *q.v.*; and "Corn-Law Rhymes," *q.v.*

REFERRED TO: 169 (*168*)

———— "Life and Writings of Werner," *Foreign Review and Continental Miscellany*, I (Jan., 1828), 95–141.

NOTE: the reference is to Carlyle's early articles in the *Foreign Review*, of which this is illustrative. Mill probably had in mind such other essays as "Goethe's Helena," I (Apr., 1828), 429–68; "Goethe," II (July, 1828), 80–127; "Life of Heine," II (Oct., 1828), 437–64; "German Playwrights," III (Jan., 1829), 94–125; "Voltaire," III (Apr., 1829), 419–75; "Novalis," IV (July, 1829), 97–141.
REFERRED TO: 169 (*168*)

——— *The Life of John Sterling*. London: Chapman and Hall, 1851.
NOTE: in SC.
REFERRED TO: 159 (*158*)

——— "Memoirs of Mirabeau," *London and Westminster Review*, IV & XXVI (Jan., 1837), 382–439.
NOTE: the reference at p. *214n* is to "an article of Carlyle's" that led to Falconer's resignation; that at p. *607* is to Carlyle's contributions to the *London and Westminster Review*.
REFERRED TO: *214n*, *603*, *607*

——— "Memoirs of the Life of Scott," *London and Westminster Review*, VI & XXVIII (Jan., 1838), 293–345.
NOTE: the reference is to Carlyle's contributions to the *London and Westminster Review*.
REFERRED TO: *607*

——— "Parliamentary History of the French Revolution," *London and Westminster Review*, V & XXVII (Apr., 1837), 233–47.
NOTE: the reference at p. *607* is to Carlyle's contributions to the *London and Westminster Review*.
REFERRED TO: *604*, *607*

——— *Sartor Resartus* (1833–34). 2nd ed. Boston: Munroe, 1837.
NOTE: this ed. in SC. The references at pp. 145 (*144*) and 173 (*170–2*), and the second at p. 183 (*182*), are inferential (in the last, the passage referred to reads: "what you see, yet cannot see over, is as good as infinite" [p. 87]); the first at p. 183 (*182*) is to the manuscript of *Sartor* and to its serial publication in *Fraser's Magazine*, VIII (Nov., and Dec., 1833), 581–92, and 669–84; IX (Feb., Mar., Apr., and June, 1834), 177–95, 301–13, 443–55, and 664–74; and X (July, and Aug., 1834), 77–87, and 182–93.
REFERRED TO: 145 (*144*), 173 (*170–2*), 183 (*182*)

——— "Varnhagen von Ense's Memoirs," *London and Westminster Review*, XXXII (Dec., 1838), 60–84.
NOTE: the reference is to Carlyle's contributions to the *London and Westminster Review*.
REFERRED TO: *607*

CAROLINE (of Britain). Referred to: 101 (*100*)

CARPENTER, MARY. Referred to: 285

CATECHISM. See *The Book of Common Prayer*.

CATO, MARCUS PORCIUS.
NOTE: the reference is to Vigny's characterization of Robespierre and Saint-Just, "who are drawn not . . . like Catoes and Brutuses."
REFERRED TO: 495

CATULLUS, GAIUS VALERIUS. Referred to: 532

Causes célèbres. See François Gayot de Pitaval.

CAZOTTE, JACQUES. See *Arabian Tales*.

CERVANTES SAAVEDRA, MIGUEL DE. *The History and Adventures of the Renowned Don Quixote* (in English, 1612). Trans. Tobias Smollett. 6th ed. 4 vols. London: Rivington, *et al.*, 1792.

NOTE: this ed. in SC.
REFERRED TO: 13 (*12*), *556*

CHADWICK, EDWIN. Referred to: 283

CHAMEROVZOW, LOUIS ALEXIS. Referred to: 282n

CHAMFORT, SÉBASTIEN ROCH NICOLAS. *Maximes, pensées, caractères et anecdotes* (1795). Ed. Pierre Louis de Ginguené. Paris: printed London, Baylis, 1796.
NOTE: in SC.
REFERRED TO: 423–4

CHARLES V (Holy Roman Emperor).
NOTE: the reference at p. 528 is in a quotation from Macaulay.
REFERRED TO: 460, 528

CHATEAUBRIAND, FRANÇOIS RENÉ, VICOMTE DE. Referred to: 487

CHATTERTON, THOMAS.
NOTE: the references derive from Vigny.
REFERRED TO: 494, 496

CHENEVIX, RICHARD. "English and French Literature," *Edinburgh Review*, XXXV (Mar., 1821), 158–90.
QUOTED: 311, 320
REFERRED TO: 310, 310n
311.5–6 "revolutionary worthies" . . . "would] 'They had no poet, and they died!'—for we suspect even M. Chenier will not immortalize them; and we have little doubt that the very ablest of those Revolutionary worthies would (180)

———— "State of Science in England and France," *Edinburgh Review*, XXXIV (Nov., 1820), 383–422.
REFERRED TO: 310

———— and Francis Jeffrey. "French Poetry," *Edinburgh Review*, XXXVII (Nov., 1822), 407–32.
REFERRED TO: 310

CHÉNIER, ANDRÉ MARIE.
NOTE: the reference derives from Vigny's fiction.
REFERRED TO: 494–5

———— *Œuvres posthumes*. 2nd ed. Ed. D. C. Robert. Intro. H. J. de Latouche. Paris: Guillaume, 1826.
NOTE: the quotation is from the introduction. (First published as *Œuvres complètes d'André de Chenier*, 1819.)
QUOTED: 495
REFERRED TO: 494–5
495.3 "*Il y avait pourtant quelque*] "Je n'ai rien fait pour la postérité, répondit Chénier; puis, en se frappant le front, on l'entendit ajouter: *Pourtant, j'avais quelque* (xix)

CHÉNIER, MARIE JOSEPH BLAISE. Referred to: 494

CHESSON, FREDERICK WILLIAM. Referred to: 282n

CHEVERT, FRANÇOIS DE. Referred to: 471

"Chevy Chase." See Thomas Percy, *Reliques*.

CHORLEY, HENRY FOTHERGILL. "Works of Mrs. Trollope," *London and Westminster Review*, VI & XXVIII (Oct., 1837), 112–31.
REFERRED TO: *604*

CHRISTIE, WILLIAM DOUGAL. Referred to: 283

CICERO, MARCUS TULLIUS. Referred to: 532

—— De partitione oratoria. In Opera cum optimis exemplaribus accurate collata. 10 vols. Leyden: Elzevir, 1642, Vol. I, pp. 722–62.
NOTE: this ed. in SC; only Vol. I has a title page for Opera, the other volumes having title pages giving their specific contents (Vols. II–IV are a set, the orations, and Vols. VII and VIII are a set, the philosophical writings).
REFERRED TO: 15 (14), 563

—— Epistolarum ad T. Pomponium Atticum libri xvi. Ibid., Vol. VI, pp. 1–517.
NOTE: see also Lettres de Cicéron à Atticus. The quoted words will be found in the Loeb ed., Letters to Atticus (Latin and English), trans. E. O. Winstedt, 3 vols. (London: Heinemann; New York: Macmillan, 1912), Vol. III, p. 230, where the reading is "O Socrates et Socratici viri! numquam . . . referam." (The version in Lettres, ed. Mongault, is the same.)
QUOTED: 49 (48)
REFERRED TO: 15 (14), 563
49.12 "Socratici viri"] O Socrates, ô Socratici viri! numquam vobis gratiam referam? (VI, 438; xiv, 9)

—— Familiar Letters (Epistolarum ad familiares). Ibid. Vol. V.
REFERRED TO: 575–6

—— In C. Verrem invective septem. Ibid., Vol. II, pp. 112–556.
NOTE: the Orations are in Vols. II–IV.
REFERRED TO: 15 (14), 558

—— Letters to Atticus. See Epistolarum ad T. Pomponium Atticum.

—— Lettres de Cicéron à Atticus (Latin and French). Ed. Nicolas Hubert Mongault. 6 vols. Paris: Delaulne, 1738.
NOTE: this ed. formerly in SC. See also Cicero, Epistolarum ad T. Pomponium Atticum.
REFERRED TO: 15 (14), 563

—— Pro A. Licinio archia poëta. In Opera, Vol. III, pp. 369–82.
NOTE: the Orations are in Vols. II–IV.
REFERRED TO: 15 (14), 558

—— Pro Milone. Ibid., Vol. IV, pp. 220–62.
REFERRED TO: 575

—— Topica. Ibid., Vol. I, pp. 694–722.
REFERRED TO: 15 (14), 563

CINCINNATUS, LUCIUS QUINCTIUS.
NOTE: the reference is in a quotation from Macaulay.
REFERRED TO: 528

CINQ-MARS, HENRI COIFFIER DE RUZÉ D'EFFIAT, MARQUIS DE. Referred to: 474, 481

CLARENDON, LORD. See George William Frederick Villiers.

CLAUDE.
NOTE: born Claude Gelée, called Lorrain.
REFERRED TO: 353n

CLÉMENT-DESORMES, NICOLAS.
NOTE: Mill spells the name Clement-Desormes.
REFERRED TO: 62

CLEOPATRA.
NOTE: the reference is in a quotation of Gibbon's translation of Trebellius Pollio.
REFERRED TO: 438

COBBETT, WILLIAM. Referred to: 101 (*100*)

COCKBURN, ALEXANDER JAMES EDMUND. Referred to: 133 (*132*)

———— *Charge of the Lord Chief Justice of England to the Grand Jury at the Central Criminal Courts, in the Case of the Queen against Nelson and Brand. Taken from the Shorthand Writer's Notes. Revised & Corrected by the Lord Chief Justice with Occasional Notes.* Ed. Frederick Cockburn. London: Ridgway, 1867.
REFERRED TO: 282

COCKBURN, HENRY. "Nomination of Scottish Juries (Part I)," *Edinburgh Review*, XXXVI (Oct., 1821), 174–219.
NOTE: the quotation is indirect.
QUOTED: 297n

Code Napoléon. Paris: Imprimerie impériale, 1807.
REFERRED TO: 570

COLERIDGE, HENRY NELSON.
NOTE: the reference is to H. N. Coleridge as S. T. Coleridge's nephew and editor of his *Table Talk.*
REFERRED TO: 424n

COLERIDGE, SAMUEL TAYLOR.
NOTE: the reference at p. 303 is simply to the "Lake poets"; that at p. 424n is (in 1837) to his "unpublished writings"; that at p. 510 is to the school produced by the "Coleridgean reaction"; that at p. 169 (*168*) is to Mill's reading of Coleridge.
REFERRED TO: 77 (*76*), 161 (*160*), 163 (*162*), 169–71 (*168–70*), 227 (*226*), 303, 364n, 398, 408, 424n, 510

———— *Biographia Literaria; or, Biographical Sketches of My Literary Life and Opinions.* 2 vols. in 1. London: Rest Fenner, 1817.
NOTE: this ed. in SC. The quotation at p. 355 is indirect.
QUOTED: 355, 414n
REFERRED TO: *136n*
414n.2 "sensuous" . . . "from our elder classics"] Thus to express in one word, all that appertains to the perception considered as passive, and merely recipient, I have adopted from our elder classics the word *sensuous*; because *sensual* is not at present used, except in a bad sense, or at least as a *moral* distinction, while *sensitive* and *sensible* would each convey a different meaning. (I, 159–60)

———— "Christabel." In *Christabel; Kubla Khan, a Vision; The Pains of Sleep.* London: Murray, 1816, pp. 3–48.
NOTE: the reference at p. 423 is to the "Preface to Christabel."
REFERRED TO: 408, 423

———— "Dejection, an Ode." In *Sibylline Leaves, a Collection of Poems.* London: Rest Fenner, 1817, pp. 237–44.
NOTE: the quotation is from stanza II.
QUOTED: 139 (*138*)
139.18 drowsy, stifled] stifled, drowsy (238)
139.19 outlet or] outlet, no (238)
139.20 tear.] tear—/ O Lady! in this wan and heartless mood, / To other thoughts by yonder throstle woo'd, / All this long eve, so balmy and serene, / Have I been gazing on the western sky, / And it's [*sic*] peculiar tint of yellow green: / And still I gaze—and with how blank an eye! (238)

—— *Letters, Conversations, and Recollections*. Ed. Thomas Allsop. 2 vols. London: Moxon, 1836.
REFERRED TO: 424n

—— *The Literary Remains of Samuel Taylor Coleridge*. Ed. Henry Nelson Coleridge. 4 vols. London: Pickering, 1836–39.
NOTE: the reference at p. 424n is (in 1837) to the work as "now in course of publication," as yet unseen by Mill.
REFERRED TO: 171 (*170*), 424n

—— "The Rime of the Ancyent Marinere." In William Wordsworth and S. T. Coleridge, *Lyrical Ballads, with a Few Other Poems*. London: Arch, 1798, pp. 1–51.
REFERRED TO: 408

—— *Specimens of the Table Talk of Samuel Taylor Coleridge*. Ed. Henry Nelson Coleridge. 2 vols. London: Murray, 1835.
REFERRED TO: 424n

—— "Work without Hope." In *The Poetical Works of S.T. Coleridge*. 3 vols. London: Pickering, 1828, Vol. II, p. 81.
QUOTED: 143–5 (*142–4*)

COLLINS, DAVID. *An Account of the English Colony in New South Wales*. 2 vols. London: Cadell and Davies, 1798–1802.
REFERRED TO: 11, 555

COLLS, JOHN FLOWERDEW.
NOTE: the reference is to Bentham's amanuensis at the time.
REFERRED TO: 57n

COLTON, CHARLES CALEB. *Lacon; or, Many Things in Few Words; Addressed to Those Who Think*. 2 vols. London: Longman, Hurst, Rees, Orme, and Brown, et al., 1820–22.
REFERRED TO: 422–3

COMTE, AUGUSTE. Referred to: 173 (*172*), 219–21, 231 (*230*), 271

—— *Cours de philosophie positive*. 6 vols. Paris: Bachelier, 1830–42.
NOTE: in SC. Vol. I (*Les préliminaires généraux et la philosophie mathématique*) was published in 1830; Vol. II (*La philosophie astronomique et la philosophie de la physique*) in 1835; Vol. III (*La philosophie chimique et la philosophie biologique*) in 1838; Vol. IV (*La philosophie sociale et les conclusions générales: première partie*) in 1839; Vol. V (*La partie historique de la philosophie sociale, en tout ce qui concerne l'état théologique et l'état métaphysique*) in 1841; and Vol. VI (*Le complément de la philosophie sociale, et les conclusions générales*) in 1842. The first references at pp. 217–19 (*216*) and p. 255n are specifically to Vols. I and II; the next are to the remaining volumes (specifically, in one place, to Vol. IV, Leçon 48).
REFERRED TO: 217–19 (*216*), 231 (*230*), 255n

—— *Système de politique positive*. Paris: Saint-Simon, 1824.
NOTE: this work is Cahier 3 of Henri de Saint-Simon, *Catéchisme des industriels*. Comte published a later work, entirely different, under the same main title; see the next entry.
REFERRED TO: 173 (*172*), 219, *615*

—— *Système de politique positive; ou, Traité de sociologie, instituant la religion de l'humanité*. 4 vols. Paris: Vol. I, Mathias, *et al.*; Vols. II–IV, Comte, *et al.*, 1851–54.
NOTE:.in SC.
REFERRED TO: 221

CONDILLAC, ETIENNE BONNOT DE. Referred to: 71 (*70*)

——— *Cours d'études.* See *De l'art de penser.*

——— *De l'art de penser.* In *Œuvres complètes.* 31 vols. Paris: Dufart, 1803, Vol. IX.
NOTE: this ed. in SC. The reference is to Mill's reading, in addition to Condillac's *Traité des sensations*, the "logical and metaphysical volumes" of his *Cours d'études* (in an earlier version in the Early Draft he had said the "first four" volumes); however, the *Cours* (1775) does not, in its various forms, include metaphysical works, and of the logical works includes only *De l'art de raisonner* and *De l'art de penser* (the other two works in the first four volumes of the *Cours* are *La grammaire* and *Traité de l'art d'écrire*). We have listed, therefore, all the works in the *Œuvres complètes* that it seems very likely Mill read and that are primarily either logical or metaphysical (it will be noted that the first four volumes of the *Œuvres* are metaphysical).
REFERRED TO: 65 (*64*), *64n–5n, 576*

——— *De l'art de raisonner* (1775). *Ibid.*, Vol. XI.
NOTE: see note to Condillac, *De l'art de penser*, above.
REFERRED TO: 65 (*64*), *64n–5n*

——— *Essai sur l'origine des connoissances humaines* (1746). *Ibid.*, Vols. I–II.
NOTE: see note to Condillac, *De l'art de penser*, above.
REFERRED TO: 65 (*64*), *64n–5n*

——— *La logique; ou, Les premiers développemens de l'art de penser* (1780). *Ibid.*, Vol. XXX.
NOTE: see note to Condillac, *De l'art de penser*, above.
REFERRED TO: 65 (*64*), *64n–5n*

——— *Traité des sensations* (1754). *Ibid.*, Vol. IV.
NOTE: see note to Condillac, *De l'art de penser*, above; this title, however, is specifically given by Mill.
REFERRED TO: 65 (*64*), *64n–5n, 576*

——— *Traité des systêmes* (1749). *Ibid.*, Vol. III.
NOTE: see note to Condillac, *De l'art de penser*, above.
REFERRED TO: 65 (*64*), *64n–5n*

CONDORCET, MARIE JEAN ANTOINE NICOLAS CARITAT, MARQUIS DE. *Vie de monsieur Turgot.* London: n.p., 1786.
QUOTED: 117 (*116*)
REFERRED TO: 115–17 (*114–16*)
117.1–2   nuisible,"] nuisible. (28)

CONSTANTINE I. Referred to: 435, 436

Conversations-Lexicon. See *Allgemeine deutsche Real-Encyclopädie.*

COOK, JAMES. Referred to: 11 (*10*)

COOPER, JAMES FENIMORE. Referred to: 434

CORNEILLE, PIERRE.
NOTE: the reference at p. 484 derives from Vigny; that at p. *570* is to two of his tragedies.
REFERRED TO: 484, *570*

CORTES, HERNANDO.
NOTE: the reference is in a quotation from Macaulay.
REFERRED TO: 528

COULSON, WALTER. Referred to: 89 (*88*)

———— "Game Laws," *Parliamentary History and Review;* . . . *Session of 1825* (*q.v.*), Vol. II, pp. 775–82.
NOTE: this identification is based on an annotation in George Grote's copy, University of London Library. Mill says Coulson "wrote one article of great merit" in the *Parliamentary History and Review*; this is presumably the one meant, though "Silk Trade," *q.v.*, is also indicated to be his in Grote's copy.
REFERRED TO: 121 (*120*)

———— "Silk Trade," *Parliamentary History and Review;* . . . *Session of 1826* (*q.v.*), Vol. II, pp. 710–18.
NOTE: see Coulson, "Game Laws."
REFERRED TO: 121 (*120*)

COURIER, PAUL LOUIS. Referred to: 119 (*118*)

COVENTRY, JOHN.
NOTE: the reference is in a quotation from Macaulay.
REFERRED TO: 527

COWPER, WILLIAM. "Account of the Author's Treatment of Hares" (1784). In *Works*. 10 vols. London: Baldwin, Cradock, and Joy, 1817, Vol. II, pp. 363–8.
NOTE: first published as "Unnoticed Properties of That Little Animal the Hare," *Gentleman's Magazine*, LIV, Pt. 1 (June, 1784), 412–14.
REFERRED TO: 21 (*20*), *565*

———— *Poems* (1782). 2nd ed. 2 vols. London: Johnson, 1786.
REFERRED TO: 19, 21 (*20*), *565*

CROKER, JOHN WILSON. "*Poems* by Alfred Tennyson," *Quarterly Review*, XLIX (Apr., 1833), 81–96.
REFERRED TO: 397, 398, 406n, 407n, 412n, 416n

CYRUS (the Great).
NOTE: the reference is in a quotation from Gibbon's translation of Trebellius Pollio.
REFERRED TO: 439

DALLAS, ROBERT CHARLES. *History of the Maroons, from Their Origin to the Establishment of Their Chief Tribe at Sierra Leone*. 2 vols. London: Longman and Rees, 1803.
REFERRED TO: 308

DANTE ALIGHIERI. Referred to: 499

DAVID, JACQUES LOUIS. Referred to: 353n

DAVIES, EMILY. Referred to: 285

DEFOE, DANIEL. *The Life and Strange Surprizing Adventures of Robinson Crusoe*. London: Taylor, 1719.
NOTE: it is not known what ed. was read by Mill; SC formerly contained an ed. (London: Daly, 1837) which long postdates the reference.
REFERRED TO: 13 (*12*), *556*

DELORME, MARION.
NOTE: the reference derives from Vigny.
REFERRED TO: 484

DEMOSTHENES.
NOTE: the reference at p. *584* is to Mill's making a "full analysis" of Demosthenes' principal orations.
REFERRED TO: 532, *584*

—— *De corona*. In *De corona and De false legatione* (Greek and English). Trans. C. A. and J. H. Vince. London: Heinemann; New York: Putnam's Sons, 1926, pp. 18–228.
NOTE: this ed. cited for ease of reference. Mill refers to the speech as "the Oration on the Crown."
REFERRED TO: 333, *561*

—— *Demosthenis et Aeschinis quae exstant omnia* (Greek and Latin). 10 vols. London: Priestley, 1827.
NOTE: this ed. (which postdates the references) in SC.
REFERRED TO: 15 (*14*), *14n*, 23 (*22*), 25 (*24*), *559*

DENMAN, THOMAS. "Law of Evidence: Criminal Procedure: Publicity," *Edinburgh Review*, XL (Mar., 1824), 169–207.
NOTE: though Mill mentions "reviewers" of Dumont's *Traité des preuves*, Denman is the only one he answers in his ed. of Bentham's *Rationale* (see Vol. V, pp. 58n–9n, 313–25, 345–9, and 352n–4n).
REFERRED TO: 117 (*116*)

DERBY, LORD. See Edward George Geoffrey Smith Stanley (14th Earl), and Edward Henry Stanley (15th Earl).

DESCARTES, RENÉ.
NOTE: the reference derives from Vigny.
REFERRED TO: 484

DESTUTT DE TRACY, ANTOINE LOUIS CLAUDE, COMTE DE.
NOTE: Mill refers to him as Destutt-Tracy.
REFERRED TO: *62*

DEVILLE, JEAN MARIE JOSEPH. *Annales de la Bigorre*. Tarbes: Lavigne, 1818.
REFERRED TO: *575*

DÍAZ DEL CASTILLO, BERNAL. *The True History of the Conquest of Mexico, by Captain Bernal Díaz del Castillo, Written in the Year 1568*. Trans. Maurice Keatinge. London: Wright, 1800.
NOTE: the quotation is in a quotation from Macaulay, who may have been using another source. The account of Gomara's vision is on pp. 47–8.
QUOTED: 528
528.18–19 "Nevertheless," he adds, "it may be that the person on the grey horse was the glorious apostle St. James, and that I, sinner that I am, was unworthy to see him."] What Gomara asserts might be the case, and I, sinner as I am, was not worthy to be permitted to see it. (48)

DICKSON, LOTHIAN SHEFFIELD. Referred to: 278

Dictionnaire de la conversation et de la lecture. See Nisard, "Early French Literature."

DIDEROT, DENIS. Referred to: 309

DIOGENES LAERTIUS. *De vitis, dogmatibus et apophthegmatibus clarorum philosophorum libri x. Graece et latine*. 2 vols. Amsterdam: Wetstenius, 1692.
NOTE: this ed. in SC.
REFERRED TO: 9 (*8*), *553*

DIONYSIUS OF HALICARNASSUS. *The Roman Antiquities*. In Διονυσίου Ἁλικαρνασέως τὰ εὑρισκόμενα, ἱστορικά τε καὶ ῥητορικά, συγγράμματα. *Dionysii Halicarnassei scripta quae extant, omnia, et historica, et rhetorica* (Greek and Latin). 2 vols. Frankfurt: Weschel Heirs, 1586, Vol. I.
NOTE: this, or another ed. with the same format, text, and pagination (e.g., Leipzig: Weidmann, 1691), is the one used by Mill in his "History of Rome." The "Chronology of the Consuls" is that of Henricus Loritus Glareanus.
REFERRED TO: 15 (*14*), 17 (*16*), *542*, *544n*, *546n*, *555*, *584*

DISRAELI, BENJAMIN. Referred to: 261, 277, 283, 284, 288

—— Resolutions on the Representation of the People, *Parliamentary Debates*, 3rd ser., Vol. 185 (Resolutions printed in Appendix to volume), cols. 214–43 (11 Feb., 1867).
NOTE: the reference is to the Resolution concerning plural voting, the fifth of the thirteen Resolutions.
REFERRED TO: 288

DOANE, RICHARD.
NOTE: the reference is to Bentham's amanuensis at the time, one of the original members of the Utilitarian Society.
REFERRED TO: 83 (*82*), *588*

DRAKE, FRANCIS. Referred to: 11 (*10*), 13n

"DRAWCANSIR, ALEXANDER." See George Villiers.

DRYDEN, JOHN. *Alexander's Feast; or, The Power of Musique. An Ode, in Honour of St. Cecilia's Day*. London: Tonson, 1697.
REFERRED TO: 19 (*18*), *565*

—— Poems. Referred to: 19 (*18*), *565*

DUFFY, CHARLES GAVAN. Referred to: 272

DULAURE, JACQUES ANTOINE. *Histoire physique, civile et morale de Paris depuis les premiers temps historiques jusqu'à nos jours* (1821–25). 2nd ed. 10 vols. Paris: Guillaume, 1823–24.
REFERRED TO: 99n

DUMAS, ALEXANDRE (the elder). *Antony, drame en cinq actes, en prose*. Paris: Auffray, 1831.
REFERRED TO: 480

——, with Jacques Félix Beudin and Prosper Parfait Goubaux ("MM. Dinaux"). *Richard Darlington, drame en trois actes et en prose*. Paris: Barba, 1832.
REFERRED TO: 480

DUMÉRIL, ANDRÉ MARIE CONSTANT. Referred to: 62

DUMONT, PIERRE ETIENNE LOUIS.
NOTE: see also Jeremy Bentham, *Tactique des assemblées législatives, Théorie des peines et des récompenses, Traité des preuves judiciaires*, and *Traités de législation*.
REFERRED TO: 67–9 (*66–8*), 71 (*70*), 117 (*116*), 325, *602–3*

—— *Souvenirs sur Mirabeau et sur les deux premières assemblées législatives*. London: Bull, 1832.
REFERRED TO: *603*

DUNOYER, BARTHÉLEMY CHARLES PIERRE JOSEPH. Referred to: 62

DUPIN, AMANDINE AURORE LUCIE, BARONNE DUDEVANT ("George Sand"). *Leone Leoni*. Paris: Bonnaire, 1835.
REFERRED TO: 480

DURHAM, LORD. See Lambton.

DURHAM REPORT. See under Parliamentary Papers, "Report on the Affairs of British North America" (1839).

DU TRIEU, PHILLIPUS. *Manuductio ad logicam sive dialectica studiosae juventuti ad logicam praeparandae* (1618). Oxford: Oxlad and Pocock, 1662. Reprinted, London: printed by McMillan, 1826.

NOTE: both these eds. formerly in SC. The reference at p. 21 (*20*) is simply to "Latin treatises on the scholastic logic"; this title is given in Mill's letter to Samuel Bentham (*EL*, *CW*, Vol. XII, p. 8); the reference at p. 125 (*124*) is to the 1826 reprint, which was paid for by Mill and his fellow students of logic.
REFERRED TO: 21 (*20*), 125 (*124*), *567*

EDGAR (of England).
NOTE: the references are in quotations from Macaulay, who describes how Hume, citing the authority of William of Malmesbury, accepted the historicity of various legends, derived from ballads, involving the amours of Edgar, King of England from 959 to 975.
REFERRED TO: 527, 527n

EDGEWORTH, MARIA. Referred to: 312

———— *Moral Tales for Young People*. 5 vols. London: Johnson, 1801.
NOTE: the reference is to characters (such as Lady Bentham) of "the Edgeworth kind" (i.e., those in her fictions); see also Edgeworth, *Popular Tales*.
REFERRED TO: 59 (*58*)

———— *Popular Tales*. 3 vols. London: Johnson, 1804.
NOTE: the reference at p. 59 (*58*) is to characters (such as Lady Bentham) of "the Edgeworth kind" (i.e., those in her fictions); see also Edgeworth, *Moral Tales*.
REFERRED TO: 13, 59 (*58*), 556

EDGEWORTH, RICHARD LOVELL. *Memoirs of R.L.E., Begun by Himself, and Concluded by His Daughter, M. Edgeworth*. 2 vols. London: Hunter, *et al.*, 1820.
NOTE: the reference derives from Jeffrey's "Edgeworth's *Memoirs*," *q.v.*
REFERRED TO: 321

The Edinburgh Review.
NOTE: see also James Mill's "Periodical Literature: *Edinburgh Review*" and J. S. Mill's "Periodical Literature: *Edinburgh Review*." The reference at p. *590* is to "either of our principal Reviews" (in 1833), i.e., the *Edinburgh* and the *Quarterly*.
REVIEWED: 291–325
REFERRED TO: 93 (*92*), 95 (*94*), 97 (*96*), 99 (*98*), 103, 169 (*168*), 215 (*214*), 227 (*226*), 398, 535, 538, *590*

EFFIAT, D'. See Cinq-Mars.

EICHTHAL, GUSTAVE D'. Referred to: 173 (*172*), *614*

ELDON, LORD. See John Scott.

ELFLEDA.
NOTE: the reference is in a quotation from Macaulay, who describes how Hume, citing the authority of William of Malmesbury, accepted the historicity of various legends, derived from ballads, involving King Edgar, one of which concerns Elfleda, who, the story has it, became mistress to King Edgar after serving as a maid in a noble house and being employed by the lady of the house to gratify Edgar's sexual demands in place of the lady's own daughter.
REFERRED TO: 527

ELFRIDA.
NOTE: the reference is in a quotation from Macaulay, who describes how Hume, citing the authority of William of Malmesbury, accepted the historicity of various legends, derived from ballads, involving King Edgar, one of which concerns Elfrida, who, as a result of Athelwold's deception of Edgar (the legend has it), first became the wife of Athelwold, and then of Edgar, who, being informed of the deception, murdered Athelwold.
REFERRED TO: 527

ELLENBOROUGH, LORD. See Edward Law.

ELLIOTT, EBENEZER. Referred to: 519

—— *Corn Law Rhymes* (1828). 3rd ed. London: Steill, 1831.
NOTE: the quoted passage is not in the 1st and 2nd eds.
QUOTED: 348
REFERRED TO: 467
348.4 "Poetry," . . . "is impassioned truth."] What *is* poetry but impassioned truth—philosophy in its *essence*—the *spirit* of that bright consummate flower, whose root is in our bosoms? (Pref., v)

ELLIS, WILLIAM.
NOTE: the references at p. 99 (*98*) are to Ellis's early articles in the *Westminster Review*; for a list, see *The Wellesley Index*, Vol. III.
REFERRED TO: 83 (*82*), 99 (*98*), 125 (*124*), 129 (*128*)

EMERSON, WILLIAM. *The Elements of Optics. In Four Books*. London: Nourse, 1768.
REFERRED TO: 566

EMPSON, WILLIAM. "Jeremy Bentham," *Edinburgh Review*, LXXVIII (Oct., 1843), 460–516.
NOTE: the quotations on pp. 535, 536, 537 are derived from John Bowring's "Memoirs of Bentham," *q.v.*
QUOTED: 535, 536, 537, 538
REFERRED TO: 535–8
535.15–18 "Bentham . . . that his . . . affection."] [*paragraph*] Bentham . . . that 'his . . . affection.' (461n) [*In the* "Memoirs" *the passage reads:* Bentham said of him that his . . . himself. "His . . . influence of selfish and dissocial affection. [*the quotation continues*] (X, 450)]
537.13 "found] He [Bentham] found (467n)
537.14 Caen; that he] Caen. He (467n) [*In the* "Memoirs" *the relevant passage reads in part:* He and his family lived with me a half of every year, from 1808 to 1817 inclusive. When I took up Mill he was in great distress, and on the point of migrating to Caen. (X, 483)]
538.14 "so far withdrew his] Within two or three years of his death, Mr James Mill (who had been a kind of English Dumont to him) had so far withdrawn his (516)
538.15 master."] master.* [*footnote:*] *Compare *Fragment on Mackintosh* (124) with Letter, (482, *Memoir*.) (516)

The Encyclopaedia Metropolitana. Ed. Edward Smedley, Hugh James Rose, and Henry John Rose. 26 vols. London: Fellowes, 1817–45.
REFERRED TO: 125 (*124*)

ENFANTIN, BARTHÉLEMY PROSPER. Referred to: 173 (*172*)

EPICURUS. Referred to: 337

EPINAY, LOUISE FLORENCE PÉTRONILLE TARDIEU D'ESCLAVELLES, MARQUISE D'. *Mémoires et correspondance de madame d'Epinay*. 3 vols. Paris: Brunet, 1818.
REFERRED TO: 309

EUCLID. *Elements of Geometry*.
NOTE: as it is not known which ed. Mill used, none is cited; but see John Playfair, *Elements of Geometry*.
REFERRED TO: 15 (*14*), 559, 562

EULER, LEONHARD. *Elements of Algebra*. Trans. anon. 2 vols. London: Johnson, 1797.
REFERRED TO: 559

—— *Introductio in analysiu infinitorum*. 2 vols. Lausanne: Bousquet, 1748.
REFERRED TO: 563

GALLIENUS (Publius Licinius Egnatius).
NOTE: the reference is in a quotation from Gibbon.
REFERRED TO: 438

GALT, JOHN ("Micah Balwhidder"). *Annals of the Parish; or, The Chronicle of Dalmailing during the Ministry of the Rev. Micah Balwhidder. Written by Himself.* Edinburgh: Blackwood; London: Cadwell, 1821.
NOTE: the passage referred to reads: "I told my people that I thought they had more sense than to secede from Christianity to become Utilitarians, for that it would be a confession of ignorance of the faith they deserted, seeing that it was the main duty inculcated by our religion to do all in morals and manners, to which the new-fangled doctrine of utility pretended" (p. 286).
REFERRED TO: 81 (*80*)

GARNIER, JOSEPH HEINRICH. "Character and Manners of the German Students," *London Review*, II (*L&WR*, XXXI) (Oct., 1835), 159–94.
REFERRED TO: *598*

———— "Government and People of Austria," *London Review*, I (*L&WR*, XXX) (July, 1835), 487–512.
REFERRED TO: *598*

GARRISON, WILLIAM LLOYD. Referred to: 266

GAYOT DE PITAVAL, FRANÇOIS. "Urbain Grandier, condamné comme magicien, et comme auteur de la possession des religieuses de Loudun." In *Causes célèbres et intéressantes, avec les jugemens qui les ont décidées.* 6 vols. The Hague: Neaulme, 1735, Vol. II, pp. 247–397.
NOTE: there were later series of *Causes célèbres*, not all prepared by Gayot de Pitaval.
REFERRED TO: 476n

La Gazette de France. Referred to: 465

GENOUDE, ANTOINE EUGÈNE DE. Referred to: 465

GEORGE IV (of England).
NOTE: the reference is in a quotation from William Bridges Adams.
REFERRED TO: 387

GERGONNE, JOSEPH DIAZ. Referred to: 59 (*58*), *64n*

GIBBON, EDWARD. *The History of the Decline and Fall of the Roman Empire.* 6 vols. London: Strahan and Cadell, 1776–88.
NOTE: it is not known which ed. Mill used; his quotations (all from Chap. xi) do not correspond with the reading of the 1st ed. (cited above) or the 2nd ed., but with the revised reading found, e.g., in Vol. I of "A New Edition," 6 vols. (London: Strahan and Cadell, 1782), with which the collations below have been made.
QUOTED: 438–9, 457
REFERRED TO: 11 (*10*), 437, *554*
438.8   [*paragraph*] Modern] [*no paragraph*] Modern ("New Ed.," I, 365; 1st ed., I, 306)
438.12   Asia.] Asia[54]. [*footnote omitted*] ("New Ed.," I, 366; 1st ed., I, 306)
438.13   chastity and] chastity[55] and [*footnote omitted*] ("New Ed.," I, 366; 1st ed., I, 307)
438.15   complexion; her teeth] complexion (for in speaking of a lady, these trifles become important). Her teeth ("New Ed.," I, 366; 1st ed., I, 307)
438.15–17   whiteness . . . and . . . eyes . . . sparkled] whiteness, and . . . eyes sparkled ("New Ed.," I, 366; 1st ed., I, 307)
438.19   harmonious . . . . She] harmonious. Her manly understanding was strengthened and adorned by study. She ("New Ed.," I, 366; 1st ed., I, 307)
438.36   with] [*paragraph*] With ("New Ed.," I, 367; 1st ed., I, 308)

438.37–8 years. . . . Disdaining both] years. By the death of Odenathus, that authority was at an end which the senate had granted him only as a personal distinction; but his martial widow, disdaining both ("New Ed.," I, 367–8; 1st ed., I, 308)

438.38 Gallienus, she obliged] Gallienus, obliged ("New Ed.," I, 368; 1st ed., I, 308)

438.39 reputation. . . . To] reputation[59]. [*footnote omitted; ellipsis indicates 4-sentence omission*] To ("New Ed.," I, 368; 1st ed., I, 308)

439.6–7 blended," . . . "with] blended with ("New Ed.," I, 368; 1st ed., I, 309)

457.7–10 "love of justice," . . . "often . . . passion," . . . "disdained . . . subdued,"] His love of justice often . . . passion; and whenever he deemed his own or the public safety endangered, he disregarded the rules of evidence, and the proportion of punishments. [*5-sentence omission*] Ignorant or impatient of the restraints of civil institutions, he disdained . . . subdued[94]. [*footnote omitted*] ("New Ed.," I, 381; 1st ed., I, 320)

457.28 friends."] friends[74]. [*footnote omitted*] ("New Ed.," I, 374; 1st ed., I, 313)

457.33–5 "the pomp was so long and so various that . . . hour from sunrise."] [*paragraph*] So long and so various was the pomp of Aurelian's triumph, that . . . hour; and it was already dark when the emperor returned to the palace. ("New Ed.," I, 377–8; 1st ed., I, 317)

GILBERT, NICOLAS JOSEPH LAURENT. Referred to: 494, 496

———"Ode imitée de plusieurs pseaumes." In *Œuvres complètes*. Paris: Le Jay, 1788, pp. 80–1.
NOTE: the poem is also known as "Adieux à la vie."
QUOTED: 494
494.24 meurs—] meurs: / Je meurs, & sur ma tombe, où lentement j'arrive, / Nul ne viendra verser des pleurs. (81)

GIRAULT-DUVIVIER, CHARLES PIERRE. *Grammaire des grammaires; ou, Analyse raisonée des meilleurs traités sur la langue françoise*. 2 vols. Paris: Porthmann, 1812.
REFERRED TO: *571*

GLADSTONE, WILLIAM EWART. Referred to: 103 (*102*), 278, 279, 280

GLANVILLE, JOHN. Speech to Both Houses of Parliament. *Journals of the House of Lords*, Vol. III, pp. 813–18 (22 May, 1628).
REFERRED TO: 197 (*196*)

The Globe. See *The Globe and Traveller*.

The Globe and Traveller.
NOTE: the reference at p. 89 (*88*) is to two letters (both entitled "Exchangeable Value," *q.v.*) written by Mill in 1822 for the *Traveller*, which in 1823 was absorbed by the *Globe*.
REFERRED TO: 89 (*88*), 91 (*90*)

GODWIN, WILLIAM. *Things As They Are; or, The Adventures of Caleb Williams* (1794). 4th ed. 3 vols. London: Simpkin and Marshal, 1816.
NOTE: this ed. in SC.
REFERRED TO: 434n

GOETHE, JOHANN WOLFGANG VON.
NOTE: the references at p. 169 (*168*) and p. 260 are generally to Goethe's writings.
REFERRED TO: 161 (*160*), 163 (*162*), 169 (*168*), 171 (*170*), 260, 424, 474n, 475, 477, 488; see also Sarah Austin, *Characteristics*. . . .

———*Aus meinem Leben. Dichtung und Wahrheit* (1811–14, 1832).
NOTE: no ed. cited, as the reference derives from Palgrave's "Goethe's *Life of Himself*," *q.v.* The work appears in Vols. XXIV–XXVI of Goethe's *Werke*, 55 vols. (Stuttgart and Tübingen: Cotta'schen Buchhandlung, 1828–33), which is in SC.
REFERRED TO: 324

———— *Torquato Tasso* (1790). In *Werke*, Vol. IX, pp. 99–245.
REFERRED TO: 346

GOLDSMITH, OLIVER. Referred to: 19 (*18*), 119 (*118*), 565

GOUBAUX, PROSPER PARFAIT. See Alexandre Dumas, *Richard Darlington*.

GRAHAM, GEORGE JOHN.
NOTE: the reference at p. 99 (*98*) is to Graham's early articles in the *Westminster Review*; for a list, see *The Wellesley Index*, Vol. III.
REFERRED TO: 83 (*82*), 99 (*98*), 125 (*124*), *126n*

———— "Poor-Laws in Ireland," *London and Westminster Review*, III & XXV (July, 1836), 332–65.
REFERRED TO: *601*

GRATTAN, HENRY.
NOTE: the reference is in a quotation from Jeffrey's "Madame de Staël," *q.v.*
REFERRED TO: 317

GRATTAN, THOMAS COLLEY. "Leopold and the Belgians," *London and Westminster Review*, XXXII (Apr., 1839), 357–405.
REFERRED TO: *606*

GRAY, THOMAS. "The Bard" (1757). In *The Works of Thomas Gray, with Memoirs of His Life and Writings by William Mason*. Ed. Thomas James Mathias. 2 vols. London: Porter, 1814, Vol. I, pp. 25–32.
NOTE: this ed. in SC.
REFERRED TO: 19 (*18*), 565

———— *An Elegy Wrote in a Country Church Yard* (1751). *Ibid.*, Vol. I, pp. 57–63.
REFERRED TO: 19 (*18*), 565

THE GREAT KING. See Shapur I.

Greek Anthology. See *Anthologia graeca*.

GREY, CHARLES (Lord Grey). Referred to: 179 (*178*)

GREY, HENRY GEORGE (Lord Howick). Referred to: 131 (*130*)

GREY, LORD. See Charles Grey.

GRIMM, FRIEDRICH MELCHIOR, BARON VON. *Correspondance littéraire, philosophique et critique*. Ed. J. Michaud, *et al.* 17 vols. Paris: Longchamps, *et al.*, 1812–14.
REFERRED TO: *110*

GROTE, GEORGE (the elder).
NOTE: the reference is to Mr. Grote's father, "the banker."
REFERRED TO: 75 (*74*)

GROTE, GEORGE (the younger).
NOTE: the reference at p. 287 is to Grote's contribution to Mill's edition of his father's *Analysis* (1869), *q.v.*; one of the references at p. 72 and that at p. 567 are to Mill's writing an essay in "emulation of a little manuscript essay of Mr. Grote."
REFERRED TO: 72, 75–7 (*74–6*), 91 (*90*), 93 (*92*), 101 (*100*), *110*, 123 (*122*), 125 (*124*), *134*, *166n*, 203 (*202–4*), 287, *567*, 626

———— ("Philip Beauchamp"). *Analysis of the Influence of Natural Religion, on the Temporal Happiness of Mankind*. London: Carlile, 1822.

NOTE: compiled and edited by Grote from Bentham's MSS. A presentation copy to Helen Taylor of the French translation by M. E. Cazelles (Paris: Baillière, 1875) is in SC.
REFERRED TO: 73 (*72*), *579*, *588*

———— *Aristotle*. Ed. Alexander Bain and G. Croom Robertson. 2 vols. London: Murray, 1872.
NOTE: the reference, in Helen Taylor's "continuation" of the *Autobiography*, is to Mill's "Grote's *Aristotle*," *q.v.*
REFERRED TO: *627*

———— *A History of Greece*. 12 vols. London: Murray, 1846–56.
NOTE: in SC; each volume or set inscribed as a presentation copy.
REFERRED TO: 99 (*98*), *202*

———— "Institutions of Ancient Greece," *Westminster Review*, V (Apr., 1826), 269–331.
REFERRED TO: 99 (*98*)

———— Motion on the Ballot, *Parliamentary Debates*, 3rd ser., Vol. 17, cols. 608–29 (25 Apr., 1833).
NOTE: for Grote's other annual ballot motions, see *Parliamentary Debates*, 3rd ser., Vol. 28, cols. 369–95 (2 June, 1835); Vol. 34, cols. 781–807 (23 June, 1836); Vol. 37, cols. 8–33 (7 Mar., 1837); Vol. 40, cols. 1131–55 (15 Feb., 1838); and Vol. 48, cols. 442–50 (18 June, 1839).
REFERRED TO: *202*

———— Speeches on the Affairs of Canada, *Parliamentary Debates*, 3rd ser., Vol. 40, cols. 59–65 (16 Jan., 1838), and cols. 633–7 (29 Jan., 1838).
REFERRED TO: *204*

———— Speech on the Suppression of Disturbances (Ireland), *Parliamentary Debates*, 3rd ser., Vol. 15, cols. 1241–6 (27 Feb., 1833).
REFERRED TO: *202–4*

———— *Statement of the Question of Parliamentary Reform; with a Reply to the Objections of the Edinburgh Review, No. LXI*. London: Baldwin, Cradock, and Joy, 1821.
REFERRED TO: 75 (*74*)

———— and John Stuart Mill. "Taylor's *Statesman*," *London and Westminster Review*, V & XXVII (Apr., 1837), 1–32. In *CW*, Vol. XIX, pp. 617–47.
NOTE: the reference is a promise, in the review of Helps's *Thoughts in the Cloister and the Crowd*, that Taylor's work will be reviewed.
REFERRED TO: 424n

GROTE, MARY SELINA (née Peckwell).
NOTE: the reference is to Grote's "intensely Evangelical" mother.
REFERRED TO: 75 (*74*)

GUIDO (of Siena). Referred to: 352n

GUIZOT, FRANÇOIS PIERRE GUILLAUME. Referred to: *128*

———— "Du régime municipal dans l'empire romain, au cinquième siècle de l'ère chrétienne, lors de la grande invasion des Germains en occident." In *Essais sur l'histoire de France* (1823). 2nd ed. Paris: Brière, 1824, pp. 1–51.
NOTE: this ed. in SC.
REFERRED TO: 436

HADFIELD, GEORGE. Referred to: 276

HALL, ANNA MARIA. *The Juvenile Budget; or, Stories for Little Readers.* London Chapman and Hall, *et al.*, 1840 [1839].
NOTE: see Busk.
REFERRED TO: 606

HAMILTON, JAMES. *History, Principles, Practice and Results of the Hamiltonian System for the Last Twelve Years.* Manchester: Sowler, *et al.*, 1829.
NOTE: the reference is to "the Hamiltonian method."
REFERRED TO: 123 (*126*)

HAMILTON, WILLIAM. Referred to: 268–71

——— *Discussions on Philosophy and Literature, Education and University Reform Chiefly from the Edinburgh Review; Corrected, Vindicated, Enlarged, in Notes and Appendices.* London: Longman, Brown, Green, and Longmans; Edinburgh: Maclach lan and Stewart, 1852.
REFERRED TO: 269

——— "Dissertations on Reid." In *The Works of Thomas Reid.* Ed. William Hamilton Edinburgh: Maclachlan and Stewart; London: Longman, Brown, Green, and Long mans, 1846, pp. 742–914.
NOTE: further "Dissertations" were added in the 6th ed. (1861), ed. H. L. Mansel; Hamilton also supplied footnotes to his edition of Reid, but as these were completed in the 1st ed., Mill canno intend them in this place. Both are treated extensively in his *Examination of Sir William Hamilton's Philosophy, CW,* Vol. IX.
REFERRED TO: 269

——— *Lectures on Metaphysics and Logic.* Ed. H. L. Mansel and J. Veitch. 4 vols Edinburgh: Blackwood, 1859–60.
NOTE: Mill mistakenly dates the work as 1860 and 1861 (the two volumes on Metaphysics appeared in 1859, and the two on Logic in 1860).
REFERRED TO: 268–9

Hansard's Parliamentary Debates. Referred to: 121 (*120*)

HARE, AUGUSTUS WILLIAM. See Julius Charles Hare and Augustus William Hare.

HARE, JULIUS CHARLES. "Memoir of John Sterling." In *Essays and Tales, Collected and Edited with a Memoir by Julius Charles Hare.* By John Sterling. 2 vols. London Parker, 1848.
NOTE: in SC.
REFERRED TO: 159 (*158*)

——— and Augustus William Hare. *Guesses at Truth, by Two Brothers.* London: Taylor, 1827.
REFERRED TO: 424n

HARE, THOMAS. *A Treatise on the Election of Representatives, Parliamentary and Munici-pal.* London: Longman, Brown, Green, Longmans, and Roberts, 1859.
NOTE: reviewed by Mill in "Recent Writers on Reform," *q.v.* The 3rd ed., 1865, inscribed "From the Author," is in SC.
REFERRED TO: 262–3, 284

HARRISON, FREDERIC. Referred to: 282n

HARRISON, SAMUEL BEALEY. *Evidence: Forming a Title of the Code of Legal Proceedings, According to the Plan Proposed by Crofton Uniacke, Esq.* London: Butterworth, 1825.

NOTE: this work, cited by Mill in his additions to Bentham's *Rationale of Judicial Evidence*, must be one of the books other than Starkie and Phillipps which he read at the time.
REFERRED TO: *116*

HARTLEY, DAVID.
NOTE: the references at pp. 107 (*106*), 209 (*208*) are to Hartleianism.
REFERRED TO: *34n, 65n,* 107 (*106*), 209 (*208*), 538, *589–90, 595*

———— *Observations on Man, His Frame, His Duty, and His Expectations.* 2 pts. Bath: Leake and Frederick; London: Hitch and Austen, 1749.
NOTE: see also Joseph Priestley, *Hartley's Theory.*
REFERRED TO: 71 (*70*), 125–7 (*124–6*), 578

HAWKESWORTH, JOHN. *An Account of the Voyages Undertaken by the Order of His Present Majesty for Making Discoveries in the Southern Hemisphere, and Successively Performed by Commodore Byron, Captain Wallis, Captain Carteret, and Captain Cook.* 3 vols. London: Strahan and Cadell, 1773.
NOTE: see David Henry, *An Historical Account.*
REFERRED TO: 11–13 (*10–12*), *555–6*

HAY, GEORGE (Marquis of Tweeddale). Referred to: 7

HAYWARD, ABRAHAM. Referred to: 133 (*132*), *604–5*

HAZLITT, WILLIAM. See also Thomas Moore.

———— *Lectures Chiefly on the Dramatic Literature of the Age of Elizabeth.* London: Stodart and Steuart, 1820.
REFERRED TO: 311n

———— "Schlegel on the Drama," *Edinburgh Review,* XXVI (Feb., 1816), 67–107.
QUOTED: 312
312.24–6 "Shakespeare . . . affections"] [*paragraph*] Who, indeed, in recalling the names of Imogen, of Miranda, of Juliet, of Desdemona, of Ophelia and Perdita, does not feel that Shakespear . . . affections? (103)

HEATHCOAT, JOHN.
NOTE: the reference is in a quotation from William Bridges Adams, whose spelling is Heathcote.
REFERRED TO: 386

HEINECCIUS, JOHANN GOTTLIEB. *Antiquitatum romanarum jurisprudentiam illustrantium syntagma secundum ordinem institutionum Justiniani digestum* (1719). 9th ed. (1747). In *Operum ad universam juris prudentiam.* 8 vols. Geneva: Cramer Heirs and Philibert Bros., 1744–49, Vol. IV, pp. 1–690 (separately paged from the rest of Vol. IV).
NOTE: this ed. in SC.
REFERRED TO: 67 (*66*), *577*

———— *Elementa juris civilis secundum ordinem institutionum* (1726). 6th ed. (1747). *Ibid.,* Vol. V, pp. 1–137 (separately paged from the next item, which is also in Vol. V).
NOTE: in addition to that in *Operum* (see preceding entry), another ed. (Leipzig: Fritsch, 1766) is in SC.
REFERRED TO: 67 (*66*), *577*

———— *Elementa juris civilis, secundum ordinem pandectarum* (1727). 6th ed. (1747). *Ibid.,* Vol. V, pp. 1–812 (separately paged from the preceding item, which is also in Vol. V).
NOTE: this ed. in SC (see Heineccius, *Antiquitatum*).
REFERRED TO: 67 (*66*), *577*

HELOÏSE.
NOTE: the reference derives from John Sterling's poem, "Abelard to Heloïse," *q.v.*
REFERRED TO: *606*

HELPS, ARTHUR. *Thoughts in the Cloister and the Crowd*. London: Wix, 1835.
REVIEWED: 419–29
QUOTED: 425, 425–6, 426, 427, 428, 428–9, 429
426.2   thing] *thing* (49)
426.8   *your*] your (75)
426.24–5   credulity. *Those . . . it*] credulity. [*paragraph*] Those . . . it [*not in italics*] (76)
427.10   others. . . . In] others. It is by the observation of trivial matters that the wise learn the influence of prejudice over their own minds at all times, and the wonderfully moulding power which those minds possess in making all things around conform to the idea of the moment. Let a man but note how often he has seen likenesses where no resemblance exists; admired ordinary pictures, because he thought they were from the hands of celebrated masters; delighted in the commonplace observations of those who had gained a reputation for wisdom; laughed where no wit was; and he will learn with humility to make allowance for the effect of prejudice in others [*paragraph*] In (23–4)
427.30   *the . . . opinion*] [*not in italics*] (2)
428.6   consolation: for] consolation. For (34)
428.10   Pyramids!—what] Pyramids! What (22)
428.11   afford! Their] afford. Their (22)
428.38–429.1   "the . . . generation"] [*paragraph*] The . . . generation. (51)
429.3   "those] [*paragraph*] Those (49)

HELVÉTIUS, CLAUDE ADRIEN. *De l'esprit*. Paris: Durand, 1758.
REFERRED TO: 71 (*70*), *70n*, *578*, *587*

HÉNAULT, CHARLES JEAN FRANÇOIS. Parallel of Augustus and Louis XIV. Concluding three paragraphs of *Nouvel abrégé chronologique de l'histoire de France; contenant les événemens de notre histoire depuis Clovis jusqu'à la mort de Louis XIV*. Paris: Prault père, 1744.
REFERRED TO: *573*

HENRY VII (of England). Referred to: 473

HENRY, DAVID. *An Historical Account of All the Voyages round the World, Performed by English Navigators; Including Those Lately Undertaken by Order of His Present Majesty. The Whole Faithfully Extracted from the Journals of the Voyagers*. 4 vols. London: Newberry, 1774 (Vols. III and IV dated 1773).
NOTE: Mill refers to "a Collection (Hawkesworth's, I believe) of Voyages round the world, in four volumes, beginning with Drake and ending with Cook and Bougainville." Hawkesworth's *Account* (*q.v.*), normally in 3 vols., does not include either Drake or Bougainville; Henry's collection is the only one located that fits Mill's description in all respects (Vol. IV actually concludes with a separately paginated Appendix, "Containing the Journal of a Voyage to the North Pole, by the Hon. Commodore Phipps, and Captain Lutwidge").
REFERRED TO: 13 (*12*), *555*

HERACLIANUS.
NOTE: the reference is in a quotation from Gibbon.
REFERRED TO: 438

HERDER, JOHANN GOTTFRIED VON. *Briefe, das Studium der Theologie betreffend* (1780). 4 vols. Frankfurt and Leipzig: n.p., 1790.
NOTE: this ed. used by Coleridge, from whose *Biographia Literaria* the reference derives. (Vols. I and II, and Vols. III and IV, are continuously paged.) The passage in question begins: "Ein Mensch, der die Bibel nur lieset . . ." (Vol. II, p. 371).
REFERRED TO: *136n*

——— *The Odyssey*. In Ἰλιὰς καὶ Ὀδύσσεια, 1800, Vols. III–IV.
NOTE: this ed. in SC. See also the next entry.
REFERRED TO: 15 (*14*), *560*

——— *The Odyssey* (Greek and English). Trans. Augustus Taber Murray. 2 vols. London: Heinemann; New York: Putnam's Sons, 1919.
NOTE: this ed. cited in this instance for ease of reference.
REFERRED TO: 412

HOOKE, NATHANIEL. *The Roman History, from the Building of Rome to the Ruin of the Commonwealth*. 4 vols. London: Bettenham, 1738–71.
REFERRED TO: 11 (*10*), 15, 17 (*16*), *543n, 544n, 546n, 554, 583, 584*

HORACE (Quintus Horatius Flaccus). *Ars poetica*. In *Satires, Epistles, and Ars poetica* (Latin and English). Trans. H. Rushton Fairclough. London: Heinemann; New York: Putnam's Sons, 1926, pp. 450–88.
NOTE: this ed. cited for ease of reference. In SC is *Opera*, ed. William Baxter, new ed. (Glasgow and Edinburgh: Mundell; London: Robinson and Payne; Cambridge: Lunn, 1796), in which the *Ars poetica* is on pp. 525–55. The reference at p. 15 (*14*) is to Mill's having read all Horace except the *Epodes* in 1816; that at p. 245 is to the precept that one should put one's work in a closet for nine years before publishing it (p. 482 [388–9]); that at p. 498 is to the precept against mediocrity in poetry.
REFERRED TO: 15 (*14*), 245, 498, *561*

——— *Carmen saeculare*. In *The Odes and Epodes* (Latin and English). Trans. C. E. Bennett. London: Heinemann; New York: Macmillan, 1914, pp. 350–6.
NOTE: see the preceding entry (the *Carmen saeculare* is in *Opera*, pp. 265–70). This ed. cited for ease of reference. The reference at p. 19 (*18*) is to Horace's "shorter poems."
REFERRED TO: 15 (*14*), 19 (*18*), 532, *561*

——— *Carmina* (*Odes*). *Ibid.*, pp. 2–346.
NOTE: see Horace, *Ars poetica* (the *Carmina* are in *Opera*, pp. 1–218). This ed. cited for ease of reference. The reference at p. 19 (*18*) is to Horace's "shorter poems"; those at pp. *583, 586* are to Mill's translation of some of Horace's shorter poems.
REFERRED TO: 15 (*14*), 19 (*18*), 532, *561, 583, 586*

——— *Epistles*. In *Satires, Epistles, and Ars poetica*, pp. 248–440.
NOTE: see Horace, *Ars poetica* (the *Epistles* are in *Opera*, pp. 421–524). This ed. cited for ease of reference.
REFERRED TO: 15 (*14*), 421, *561*

——— *Epodes*. In *The Odes and Epodes*, pp. 360–417.
NOTE: see Horace, *Ars poetica* (the *Epodes* are in *Opera*, pp. 219–63). This ed. cited for ease of reference. Mill refers here to his having read all Horace except the *Epodes* between 1813 and 1817; he presumably read them later.
REFERRED TO: 15 (*14*)

——— *Satires*. In *Satires, Epistles, and Ars poetica*, pp. 4–244.
NOTE: see Horace, *Ars poetica* (the *Satires* are in *Opera*, pp. 271–420).
REFERRED TO: 15 (*14*), 421, *561*

HORNER, FRANCIS. Referred to: 129 (*128*)

HOWELL, THOMAS BAYLY, ed. *A Complete Collection of State Trials and Proceedings for High Treason and Other Crimes and Misdemeanors from the Earliest Period to the Year 1783, with Notes and Illustrations: Compiled by T. B. Howell, Esq. F.R.S., F.S.A., and Continued from the Year 1783 to the Present Time by Thomas Jones Howell, Esq.* 34 vols. London: Longman, *et al.*, 1809–28.

NOTE: the reference is to Lord Ellenborough's definition of libel as "*any thing which hurt the feelings of any body.*" Ellenborough's statement formed part of his summing up in the case of the King against Cobbett, 24 May, 1804. On that occasion, Ellenborough stated: "Upon the subject of libel, it may be as well for me to observe, before I enter upon the question, that, by the law of England, there is no impunity to any person publishing any thing injurious to the feelings and happiness of an individual, or prejudicial to the general interests of the state" (Vol. XXIX, col. 49).
QUOTED: 298

HOWICK, LORD. See Henry George Grey.

HUGHES, THOMAS. "Opinion on American Affairs," *Macmillan's Magazine*, IV (Sept., 1861), 414–16.
NOTE: the reference is to Hughes's writing in support of the North at the very beginning of the Civil War.
REFERRED TO: 267

HUGO, VICTOR MARIE, VICOMTE.
NOTE: the reference is to his early poetry. See also Nisard.
REFERRED TO: 472

HUMBOLDT, KARL WILHELM VON. *The Sphere and Duties of Government* (in German, 1851). Trans. Joseph Coulthard. London: Chapman, 1854.
NOTE: the references are indirect. This ed. in SC.
REFERRED TO: 260, 261

HUME, DAVID.
NOTE: the reference is in a quotation from John Allen.
REFERRED TO: 293

——— *Essays and Treatises on Several Subjects* (with this title, 1753). 2 vols. London: Cadell; Edinburgh: Bell and Bradfute, *et al.*, 1793.
NOTE: in SC. Another copy of Hume's *Essays*, annotated by Mill, was bought from the Avignon bookseller Roumanille in March, 1906, by the American novelist Thomas Nelson Page; its present location is unknown. The reference at p. 293 is to "Of the First Principles of Government," in *Essays*, Vol. I, pp. 39–44.
REFERRED TO: 71 (*70*), 293, *578–9*

——— *The History of England* (1754–62). 8 vols. (in 4). Oxford: Talboys and Wheeler; London: Pickering, 1826.
NOTE: this ed. formerly in SC. The references (which antedate this ed.) may be to the 1st ed., 6 vols. (London: Millar, 1754–62). The quotation is in a quotation from Macaulay, who does not indicate which ed. he used.
QUOTED: 527
REFERRED TO: 11 (*10*), *554*
527.9 [*paragraph*] "History," . . . "has] [*no paragraph*] History has (I, 108)
527.9 Edgar's] his (I, 108)

HUME, JOSEPH. Referred to: 55 (*54*), 93 (*92*), 101 (*100*), 203 (*202*)

HUNT, HENRY. *Memoirs of Henry Hunt, Esq., Written by Himself, in His Majesty's Jail at Ilchester, in the County of Somerset.* 3 vols. London: Dolby, 1820–22.
REFERRED TO: *575*

HUSKISSON, WILLIAM. Referred to: 103 (*102*)

An Introduction to the Latin Tongue, for the Use of Youth. New ed., rev. Eton: Pote and Williams, 1806.

NOTE: we do not know which text Mill used, but this one is representative of the grammars of the time.
REFERRED TO: 13 (*12*), *556*

IRVINE, ALEXANDER.
NOTE: the reference, in Helen Taylor's "continuation" of the *Autobiography*, is to "an old friend" with whom Mill botanized in 1871.
REFERRED TO: *627*

ISOCRATES. *Ad Demonicum*. In *Opera omnia graece et latine*. Ed. Athanasius Auger. 3 vols. Paris: Didot l'aîné, 1782, Vol. I, pp. 4–45.
NOTE: this ed. in SC.
REFERRED TO: 9 (*8*), *553*

―――― *Ad Nicoclem*. *Ibid.*, pp. 54–95.
REFERRED TO: 9 (*8*), *553*

JEFFREY, FRANCIS. See also Richard Chenevix and Francis Jeffrey, "French Poetry."

―――― "Alison's *Sermons*," *Edinburgh Review*, XXIII (Sept., 1814), 424–40.
REFERRED TO: 311n

―――― "Bentham, *Principes de législation* par Dumont," *Edinburgh Review*, IV (Apr., 1804), 1–26.
REFERRED TO: 325

―――― "Correspondance littéraire et philosophique de Grimm," *Edinburgh Review*, XXI (July, 1813), 263–99.
REFERRED TO: 309

―――― "Dispositions of England and America," *Edinburgh Review*, XXXIII (May, 1820), 395–431.
QUOTED: 300–1
301.2 "within] It [America] shows within (405)
301.6, 7–8 "even in England," . . . "the . . . terror;"] Even in England, the . . . terror; and every thing betokens an approaching crisis in the great European commonwealth, by the result of which the future character of its governments, and the structure and condition of its society, will in all probability be determined. (403)

―――― "Edgeworth's *Memoirs*," *Edinburgh Review*, XXXIV (Aug., 1820), 121–48.
REFERRED TO: 321

―――― "France," *Edinburgh Review*, XXV (Dec., 1815), 501–26.
REFERRED TO: 302n

―――― "Hazlitt on Shakespeare," *Edinburgh Review*, XXVIII (Aug., 1817), 472–88.
NOTE: Mill's references to the *Edinburgh Review*'s unqualified admiration of Shakespeare are general; this article is cited at p. 309 as illustrative of the point.
REFERRED TO: 309, 319

―――― "*Ivanhoe*," *Edinburgh Review*, XXXIII (Jan., 1820), 1–54.
NOTE: Mill's reference to the *Edinburgh Review*'s appreciation of Scott is general; this article cited as illustrative of the point.
REFERRED TO: 320

―――― "Leckie on the British Government," *Edinburgh Review*, XX (Nov., 1812), 315–46.
QUOTED: 313
313.12 [*paragraph*] Parties] [*no paragraph*] Parties (343)

———— "Madame de Staël—sur la littérature," *Edinburgh Review*, XXI (Feb., 1813), 1–50.
QUOTED: 316, 316–18, 318
316.10   [*paragraph*] All] [*no paragraph*] All (12)
318.30   [*paragraph*] There] [*no paragraph*] There (21)

———— "Millar's View of the English Government," *Edinburgh Review*, III (Oct., 1803), 154–81.
QUOTED: 305–6
305.27   [*paragraph*] There] [*paragraph*] In his politics, Mr Millar was a decided whig, and did not perhaps bear any great antipathy to the name of a republican: yet there (158)
305.37–8   *incapacity . . . multitude*] [*not in italics*] (158)
306.1   liberties."] liberties; and though sincerely attached to the limited form of monarchy established at the Revolution, he seems to have thought that the monarchy itself was the least valuable part of the system, and that most of its advantages might have been secured under another system of administration. (159)

———— "Montgomery's *Poems*," *Edinburgh Review*, IX (Jan., 1807), 347–54.
QUOTED: 324n

———— "Moore's *Poems*," *Edinburgh Review*, VIII (July, 1806), 456–65.
REFERRED TO: 321

———— "*Poems* by W. Wordsworth," *Edinburgh Review*, XI (Oct., 1807), 214–31.
NOTE: the reference at p. 324 is cited as illustrative of the *Edinburgh Review*'s "articles on the poets of the Wordsworth school"; that at p. 398 is to "the disgraceful articles in the early Numbers of the *Edinburgh Review*, on Wordsworth and Coleridge."
REFERRED TO: 324, 398

———— "Scott's *Marmion: A Poem*," *Edinburgh Review*, XII (Apr., 1808), 1–35.
NOTE: Mill's reference to the *Edinburgh Review*'s appreciation of Scott is general; this article is cited as illustrative of the point.
REFERRED TO: 320

———— "Southey's *Thalaba*," *Edinburgh Review*, I (Oct., 1802), 63–83.
QUOTED: 303–4
304.13   over-ruling] over-running (71)

———— "Wordsworth's *White Doe*," *Edinburgh Review*, XXV (Oct., 1815), 355–63.
NOTE: cited as illustrative of the *Edinburgh Review*'s "articles on the poets of the Wordsworth school."
REFERRED TO: 324

JOHNSON, SAMUEL.
NOTE: the reference at p. *182* derives from Mill's reference to Carlyle's "Boswell's *Johnson*," *q.v.*
REFERRED TO: *182*, 311

———— "Preface to Shakespeare" (1765). In *The Works of Samuel Johnson*. New ed. 12 vols. London: Johnson, *et al.*, 1806, Vol. II, pp. 133–96.
QUOTED: 319
319.32   time and place] time or place (147)

JONES, JOHN GALE. Referred to: 129 (*128*)

JOUDOU, J.B. *Guide des voyageurs à Bagnères-de-Bigorre et dans les environs*. Tarbes: the author, 1818.
REFERRED TO: *574*

JOUY, VICTOR JOSEPH ETIENNE DE.
NOTE: the reference derives from Chenevix's "English and French Literature," *q.v.*
REFERRED TO: 310

JOYCE, JEREMIAH. *Scientific Dialogues, Intended for the Instruction and Entertainment of Young People: in Which the First Principles of Natural and Experimental Philosophy Are Fully Explained.* 6 vols. London: Johnson, 1800ff.
REFERRED TO: 21 (*20*), *567*

"JUNIUS." *Junius: Including Letters by the Same Writer, under Other Signatures, (Now First Collected.) To Which Are Added, His Confidential Correspondence with Mr. Wilkes, and His Private Letters Addressed to Mr. H. S. Woodfall. With a Preliminary Essay, Notes, Fac-similes, &c.* 3 vols. London: Rivington, *et al.*, 1812.
NOTE: this ed. in SC.
REFERRED TO: 381

"JUNIUS REDIVIVUS." See Adams.

The Jurist; or, Quarterly Journal of Jurisprudence and Legislation. Referred to: 191 (*190*)

JUVENAL. *Satires.* In *Decii Junii Juvenalis et A. Persii Flacci satyrae.* London: Brindley, 1744, pp. 1–98.
NOTE: this ed. in SC.
REFERRED TO: *14n*, 25, *566*

KARAMZIN, NIKOLAI MIKHAILOVICH. *Travels from Moscow, through Prussia, Germany, Switzerland, France, and England.* Trans. from the German attributed to A. A. Feldborg. 3 vols. London: Badcock, 1803.
NOTE: the reference derives from Brougham's "Karamsin's *Travels in Europe*," *q.v.*
REFERRED TO: 324

KEILL, JOHN. *Introductiones ad veram physicam et veram astronomiam. Quibus accedunt trigonometria. De viribus centralibus. De legibus attractionis* (1702, 1718). New ed. Leyden: Verbeak, 1739.
REFERRED TO: *564*

KENYON, GEORGE (Lord Kenyon). Referred to: *600–1*

KEPLER, JOHANNES. Referred to: 165

KERSEY, JOHN. *The Elements of That Mathematical Art Commonly Called Algebra, Expounded in Four Books.* 2 vols. London: Passinger, and Hurlock, 1673–74.
REFERRED TO: *561*

KNAPP, ANDREW, and WILLIAM BALDWIN. *The Newgate Calendar; Comprising Interesting Memoirs of the Most Notorious Characters Who Have Been Convicted of Outrages on the Laws of England since the Commencement of the Eighteenth Century; with Occasional Anecdotes and Observations, Speeches, Confessions, and Last Exclamations of Sufferers.* 4 vols. London: Robins, 1824–28.
NOTE: it is not clear which of the "Newgate Calendars" Mill has in mind, but this is the best known contemporary one.
REFERRED TO: *604*

The Knickerbocker.
NOTE: the reference is in a quotation from Harriet Martineau.
REFERRED TO: 433

LAPEYROUSE. See Picot de Lapeyrouse.

LAPLACE, PIERRE SIMON, MARQUIS DE. Referred to: 165

―――― *Exposition du système du monde* (1796). 4th ed. Paris: Courcier, 1813.
NOTE: this ed. in SC.
REFERRED TO: *576*

LA ROCHEFOUCAULD, FRANÇOIS, DUC DE. *Réflexions; ou, Sentences et maximes morales.*
Paris: Barbin, 1665 [1664].
NOTE: Mill uses the spelling La Rochefoucault.
REFERRED TO: 423, 425

LATIN GRAMMAR. See *An Introduction to the Latin Tongue.*

LATOUCHE, HYACINTHE JOSEPH ALEXANDRE THABAUDE DE (called Henri). See André
Chénier.

LAVOISIER, ANTOINE LAURENT. Referred to: 65 *(64)*

LAVOISIER, MARIE ANNE PIERRETTE (née Paulze).
NOTE: the reference is in a quotation from Brougham's review of Black's *Lectures* (on chemistry),
q.v.
REFERRED TO: 309

LAW, EDWARD (Lord Ellenborough).
NOTE: the reference concerns Law's definition of libel when acting as Chief Justice of the Court of
King's Bench; for the passage, see Thomas Bayly Howell.
REFERRED TO: 297–8

LAWRENCE, THOMAS. Referred to: 352n

LEBEAU, CHARLES. *Opera latina d. Caroli Lebeau.* 3 vols. Paris: Morin, 1782–83.
REFERRED TO: *574, 586*

LECKIE, GOULD FRANCIS. *Essay on the Practice of the British Government, Distinguished
from the Abstract Theory on Which It Is Supposed to Be Founded.* London: Valpy,
1812.
NOTE: the reference derives from Jeffrey's "Leckie on the British Government," *q.v.*
REFERRED TO: 313

LEGENDRE, ADRIEN MARIE. *Eléments de géométrie, avec des notes.* Paris: Firmin Didot,
1794.
REFERRED TO: *571*

LENTHÉRIC, PIERRE. Referred to: 59 *(58)*, *575*

LETRONNE, JEAN ANTOINE. "Essai sur le plan et la disposition générale du labyrinthe
d'Egypte, d'après Hérodote, Diodore de Sicile et Strabon," *Nouvelles Annales des
Voyages, de la Géographie et de l'Histoire*, VI (1820), 133–54.
NOTE: see also *Nouvelles Annales.*
REFERRED TO: *574*

LEWIS, GEORGE CORNEWALL. "The Irish Church Question," *London Review*, II (*L&WR*,
XXXI) (Oct., 1835), 228–69.
REFERRED TO: *598–9, 601*

―――― *On Local Disturbances in Ireland; and On the Irish Church Question.* London:
Fellowes, 1836.
NOTE: the reference derives from the inclusion in this work of Lewis's "The Irish Church Question,"
q.v.
REFERRED TO: *601*

LOUIS NAPOLEON. See Napoleon III.

LOUISE (of Savoy).
NOTE: the reference is to successful diplomatic negotiations conducted by "two princesses"; they were Louise and Margaret (of the Netherlands), who negotiated the Peace of Cambray (3 Aug., 1529), which terminated hostilities between Francis I of France and Charles V, Holy Roman Emperor.
REFERRED TO: 460

LOWE, JOSEPH.
NOTE: the reference is to "an old friend of my father's."
REFERRED TO: 63 (62)

LOWE, ROBERT. Speech on the Cattle Diseases Bill (1866), *Parliamentary Debates*, 3rd ser., Vol. 181, cols. 483–8 (14 Feb., 1866).
REFERRED TO: 276n–7n

LOYOLA, IGNATIUS. Referred to: 221

LUCAS, FREDERICK. Referred to: 272

LUCIAN. Λουκιανοῦ Σαμοσατέως ἅπαντα. *Luciani Samosatensis opera. Cum nova versione Tiber. Hemsterhusii, & Io. Matthiae Gesneri.* Ed. Johannes Fredericus Reitzius. 4 vols. Amsterdam: Wetstenius, 1743–46.
NOTE: this ed. in SC. The first reference is to his reading "part of Lucian"; he later read a great deal.
REFERRED TO: 9 (8), 553, 570

——— "Alectryon" ("Somnium, seu gallus"; "The Dream; or, The Cock").
REFERRED TO: 572

——— "Βιῶν πρᾶσις" ("Vitarum auctio"; "Philosophies for Sale").
REFERRED TO: 571

——— "Cataplus" ("Cataplus, sive tyrannus"; "The Downward Journey; or, The Tyrant").
REFERRED TO: 572

——— "Deorum concilium" ("The Parliament of the Gods").
REFERRED TO: 573

——— "Hermotimus."
REFERRED TO: 570

——— "Icaromenippus."
REFERRED TO: 573

——— "Jupiter confutatus" ("Zeus Catechized").
REFERRED TO: 572

——— "Jupiter tragoedus" ("Zeus Rants").
REFERRED TO: 573

——— "Necyomantia" ("Menippus, sive necyomantia"; "Menippus; or, The Descent into Hades").
REFERRED TO: 572

——— "Prometheus."
REFERRED TO: 572

——— "Vocalium judicium" ("Judicium vocalium"; "The Consonants at Law").
REFERRED TO: 572

LUCRETIUS CARUS, TITUS. Referred to: 43 (*42*)

—— *De rerum natura libri sex*. Ed. Gilbert Wakefield. 4 vols. Edinburgh: Bell and Bradfute, *et al.*; Glasgow: Duncan, 1813.
NOTE: this ed. in SC. At p. 532 the reference is to Lucretius' "noble poem."
REFERRED TO: 15 (*14*), 532, *563*

LUDLOW, JOHN MALCOLM FORBES. "The American Crisis," *Macmillan's Magazine*, IV (June, 1861), 168–76.
NOTE: the reference is to Ludlow's writing in support of the North at the very beginning of the Civil War.
REFERRED TO: 267

LYSIAS.
NOTE: it is not known which ed. of the orations Mill used; a 2-vol. ed. of *Oratores Attici* was formerly in SC.
REFERRED TO: 15 (*14*), *557*

MACAULAY, THOMAS BABINGTON.
NOTE: the reference at p. 526 is to Macaulay's prose writings prior to 1843.
REFERRED TO: 79 (*78*), 129 (*128*), 131 (*130*), 526

—— "Bentham's Defence of Mill: Utilitarian System of Philosophy," *Edinburgh Review*, XLIX (June, 1829), 273–99.
NOTE: see also Macaulay, "Mill's *Essay on Government*," and "Utilitarian Theory of Government." This article was replied to in the *Westminster Review* by T. P. Thompson, with Bentham's help: "'Greatest Happiness' Principle," *q.v.*, and by Thompson alone, in two articles, both entitled "*Edinburgh Review* and the 'Greatest Happiness Principle,'" *q.v.* In the reference at p. *594* the name is misspelled "Macauley."
REFERRED TO: 165 (*164*), 167 (*166*), *594*

—— *Critical and Historical Essays, Contributed to the Edinburgh Review*. 3 vols. London: Longman, Brown, Green, and Longmans, 1843.
NOTE: the references are to Macaulay's explanation, in his Preface, of his reason for not including his three essays attacking James Mill's "Government" in this collection.
REFERRED TO: 165, 536–7

—— *Lays of Ancient Rome*. London: Longman, Brown, Green, and Longmans, 1842.
NOTE: the 2nd ed. (London: Longman, Brown, Green, and Longmans, 1842) is in SC. Mill, in his quotation from "The Battle of Lake Regillus," omits the stanza numbers.
REVIEWED: 523–32
QUOTED: 527, 527n, 527–8, 528–31, 532
527n.6   fed] feud (32n) [*treated as typographical error in this ed.*]
529.23   you] ye (122)
529.24–5 Rome?"*/ . . . / So] [*ellipsis indicates 1-stanza omission*] (122)
529.36   golden shield!"] Golden Shield! / Let no man stop to plunder, / But slay, and slay, and slay: / The Gods who live for ever / Are on our side to-day." (123)
530.16–17 main. / . . . / Sempronius] [*ellipsis indicates 2-page omission*] (124–6)
530.17   Semponius] Sempronius (126) [*treated as typographical error in this ed.*]
530.38   Semponius] Sempronius (127) [*treated as typographical error in this ed.*]
532.16–18 "A . . . fruits?"] It was not, like their tragedy, their comedy, their epic and lyric poetry, a . . . fruits. (143)

—— "Mill's *Essay on Government*: Utilitarian Logic and Politics," *Edinburgh Review*, XLIX (Mar., 1829), 159–89.
NOTE: see Macaulay, "Bentham's Defence of Mill."
REFERRED TO: 165 (*164*), 167 (*166*), *594*

———— "Utilitarian Theory of Government, and the 'Greatest Happiness Principle,'" *Edinburgh Review*, L (Oct., 1829), 99–125.
NOTE: see Macaulay, "Bentham's Defence of Mill."
REFERRED TO: 165 (*164*), 167 (*166*), *594*

MACCALL, WILLIAM. *The Elements of Individualism: A Series of Lectures.* London: Chapman, 1847.
NOTE: this ed. in SC. The "series of writings" to which Mill refers includes *The Agents of Civilization* (London: Green, 1843), *The Creed of a Man: A Summary of the System of Individualism* (London: Chapman, 1845), *The Doctrine of Individuality* (London: Green, 1843), and *The Individuality of the Individual* (London: Chapman, 1844).
REFERRED TO: 260

McCRIE, THOMAS. *The Life of John Knox.* Edinburgh: Ogle, 1812.
REFERRED TO: 11 (*10*), *555*

McCULLOCH, JOHN RAMSEY.
NOTE: the reference at p. 103 (*102*) is to McCulloch's early articles in the *Edinburgh Review*; for a list, see *The Wellesley Index*, Vol. I.
REFERRED TO: 103 (*102*), 129 (*128*)

———— "Disposal of Property by Will-Entails—French Law of Succession," *Edinburgh Review*, XL (July, 1824), 350–75.
NOTE: the reference is to McCulloch's "then lately published" article, which prompted John Austin's "Disposition of Property," *q.v.*
REFERRED TO: 99 (*98*)

MACKINTOSH, JAMES. "*De l'Allemagne*, par Madame de Staël," *Edinburgh Review*, XXII (Oct., 1813), 198–238.
REFERRED TO: 311n

———— *Dissertation on the Progress of Ethical Philosophy, Chiefly during the Seventeenth and Eighteenth Centuries.* Edinburgh: n.p., 1830.
NOTE: offprinted from the 7th ed. of the *Encyclopaedia Britannica* (complete version, 1842), Vol. I, pp. 290–429, where it appeared as "Dissertation Second, Exhibiting a General View of the Progress of Ethical Philosophy, Chiefly during the Seventeenth and Eighteenth Centuries."
REFERRED TO: 103 (*102*), 211 (*210*)

———— "France," *Edinburgh Review*, XXIV (Nov., 1814), 505–37.
REFERRED TO: 306

———— "Parliamentary Reform," *Edinburgh Review*, XXXIV (Nov., 1820), 461–501.
NOTE: the reference is to George Grote's *Statement*, a response to Mackintosh's "celebrated article" in the *Edinburgh Review*.
REFERRED TO: 75 (*74*)

McLAREN, DUNCAN. Referred to: 276

MACLEAN, DONALD.
NOTE: the reference is to the first President of the London Debating Society.
REFERRED TO: 131 (*130*)

MACRONE, JOHN.
NOTE: the reference is to the publisher of the *London and Westminster Review* in Dec., 1836.
REFERRED TO: *603*

MAGELLAN, FERDINAND. Referred to: *12n*

MAGUIRE, JOHN FRANCIS. Motion for a Committee to Consider the State of Ireland, *Parliamentary Debates*, 3rd ser., Vol. 190, cols. 1288–1314 (10 Mar., 1868).

NOTE: see also J. S. Mill, Speech on the State of Ireland.
REFERRED TO: 280

MAINE, HENRY JAMES SUMNER. *Village-Communities in the East and West. Six Lectures Delivered at Oxford.* London: Murray, 1871.
NOTE: referred to in Helen Taylor's "continuation" of the *Autobiography*, in connection with Mill's "Maine on Village Communities," *q.v.*
REFERRED TO: *626*

MAIR, JOHN. *An Introduction to Latin Syntax; or, An Exemplification of the Rules of Construction, as Delivered in Mr. Ruddiman's Rudiments, without Anticipating Posterior Rules.* Edinburgh: Paton, *et al.*, 1750.
REFERRED TO: *568–9*

MALTHUS, THOMAS ROBERT. *An Essay on the Principle of Population, As It Affects the Future Improvement of Society; with Remarks on the Speculations of W. Godwin, M. Condorcet, and Other Writers.* London: Johnson, 1798.
REFERRED TO: 107 (*106*)

MANES (Mani). Referred to: 448

MANSEL, HENRY LONGUEVILLE. *The Limits of Religious Thought* (1858). 4th ed. London: Murray, 1859.
NOTE: this ed. cited by Mill in his *Examination*. The reference is inferential.
REFERRED TO: 270

MARCUS (AURELIUS) ANTONINUS. See Antoninus.

MARGARET (of the Netherlands).
NOTE: the reference is to successful diplomatic negotiations conducted by "two princesses"; they were Margaret and Louise (of Savoy), who negotiated the Peace of Cambray (3 Aug., 1529), which terminated hostilities between Francis I of France and Charles V, Holy Roman Emperor.
REFERRED TO: 460

MARIE ANTOINETTE (of France). Referred to: 65 (*64*)

MARMONTEL, JEAN FRANÇOIS. *Mémoires d'un père* (1804). 4 vols. London: Peltier, 1805.
NOTE: this ed. in SC.
REFERRED TO: 145 (*144*)

MARRYAT, FREDERICK. Referred to: 490

MARSHALL, JAMES GARTH. *Minorities and Majorities: Their Relative Rights. A Letter to the Lord John Russell, M.P., on Parliamentary Reform.* London: Ridgway, 1853.
REFERRED TO: 261

MARSHALL, JOHN. Referred to: 119–21 (*118–20*)

MARTINEAU, HARRIET. *Society in America.* 3 vols. London: Saunders and Otley, 1837.
NOTE: the quotation at p. 435 is from the passage quoted earlier.
QUOTED: 433, 435
REFERRED TO: 434, 459
433.7   *Palmyra*, six] *Palmyra,** [*footnote omitted*] six (III, 216)

MARTINEAU, JAMES. "On the Life, Character, and Works of Dr. Priestley," *Monthly Repository*, n.s. VII (Jan., Feb., Apr., 1833), 19–30, 84–8, 231–41.
REFERRED TO: *591n*

MARVELL, ANDREW.
NOTE: the reference is in a quotation from William Bridges Adams.
REFERRED TO: 385

MASCARON, JULES. *Oraison funèbre de très-haut et très-puissant Prince Henri de la Tour-d'Auvergne, vicomte de Turenne* (1676). In *Recueil des oraisons funèbres prononcées par Messire Jules Mascaron.* Paris: Du Puis, 1704, pp. 303–412.
REFERRED TO: *572–3*

MASON, JAMES MURRAY.
NOTE: the reference is to the seizure of Confederate envoys, of whom Mason was one.
REFERRED TO: 267–8

MAURICE, FREDERICK DENISON. Referred to: 133, 159–61 (*158–60*), 163 (*162*), *169n*

———— "Moral and Metaphysical Philosophy," *Encyclopaedia Metropolitana,* Vol. II (also identified as "Pure Sciences, Vol. 2"), pp. 545–674.
NOTE: the reference is to Maurice's treatment of the "Roman Period," pp. 626–9 *passim.*
REFERRED TO: 532

The Mechanics' Magazine. Referred to: 382

MELBOURNE, LORD. See Lamb.

MIGNET, FRANÇOIS AUGUSTE MARIE ALEXIS. *Histoire de la révolution française depuis 1789 jusqu'en 1814.* 2 vols. Paris: Didot, 1824.
NOTE: translated as *History of the French Revolution from 1789 to 1814,* 2 vols. (London: Hunt and Clarke, 1826).
REFERRED TO: 99n

MILL, CLARA ESTHER.
NOTE: the reference at p. 7 (*6*) is to James Mill's instruction of his children, one of whom was Clara, during the period in which he was working on his *History of British India;* that at p. *36n* concerns the authority exercised by Mill over his younger sisters; that at p. 53 concerns James Mill's relations with his children; the others are to J. S. Mill's teaching of Clara.
REFERRED TO: 7 (*6*), *36n*, 53, *555, 556, 557, 560, 562, 563, 564, 568, 569*

MILL, GEORGE.
NOTE: the reference concerns James Mill's relations with his children, one of whom was George.
REFERRED TO: 53

MILL, HARRIET (née Burrow) (J. S. Mill's mother).
NOTE: the references at pp. *6* and *52* are indirect.
REFERRED TO: *6, 36n, 52, 57n, 610, 612, 612n*

MILL, HARRIET ISABELLA (J. S. Mill's sister).
NOTE: the reference at p. 7 (*6*) is to James Mill's instruction of his children, one of whom was Harriet, during the period in which he was working on his *History of British India;* that at p. *36n* concerns the authority exercised by Mill over his younger sisters; that at p. 53 concerns James Mill's relations with his children.
REFERRED TO: 7 (*6*), *36n*, 53

MILL, HARRIET TAYLOR (née Hardy) (J. S. Mill's wife). Referred to: 5, 183 (*182*), 193–9 (*192–8*), 213 (*212*), 234n–5n, 237–41 (*236–8*), 240n–1n, 247 (*246*), 249–61 (*250–8*), 263, 264–5, *616, 617–23*

MILL, HENRY.
NOTE: the reference concerns James Mill's relations with his children, one of whom was Henry.
REFERRED TO: 53

MILL, JAMES (J. S. Mill's grandfather). See James Milne.

MILL, JAMES
NOTE: the reference at p. 103 (*102*) is to James Mill's early economic writings; those at p. 537 include his wife and older children.

——— "Jurisprudence" (1821). In *Essays*. London: printed Innes, n.d. [1825].
NOTE: see James Mill, "Education," above. The reference at p. *594* is to the reprintings of James Mill's essays, this one being specifically mentioned.
REFERRED TO: 69 (*68*), *576–7, 594*

——— "Law Reform," *London Review*, II (*L&WR*, XXXI) (Oct., 1835), 1–51.
REFERRED TO: 209 (*208*)

——— "Periodical Literature: *Edinburgh Review*," *Westminster Review*, I (Jan., 1824), 206–49.
NOTE: as J. S. Mill indicates in the *Autobiography*, he did the research for this article, which is continued in his own article of the same title, reprinted above at pp. 291–325.
QUOTED: 95 (*94*)
REFERRED TO: 93–7 (*92–6*), 293, 321, 324
95.27 "seesaw"] In their speeches and writings, therefore, we commonly find them [the aristocratic opposition for the time being—i.e., the Whigs of the *Edinburgh Review*] playing at *seesaw*. (218)

——— "Periodical Literature: *Edinburgh Review* on Parliamentary Reform," *Westminster Review*, IV (July, 1825), 194–233.
NOTE: the reference is prospective.
REFERRED TO: 297

——— "Periodical Literature: *Quarterly Review*," *Westminster Review*, II (Oct., 1824), 463–503.
REFERRED TO: 97 (*96*)

——— "Robert Southey's *Book of the Church*," *Westminster Review*, III (Jan., 1825), 167–212.
REFERRED TO: 99 (*98*)

——— "State of the Nation," *Westminster Review*, VI (Oct., 1826), 249–78.
NOTE: the reference is to "a political article" in the twelfth number of the *Westminster*.
REFERRED TO: 99 (*98*)

——— "State of the Nation," *London Review*, I (*L&WR*, XXX) (Apr., 1835), 1–24.
REFERRED TO: 209 (*208*)

——— "Summary Review of the Conduct and Measures of the Imperial Parliament," *Parliamentary History and Review; . . . Session of 1826* (*q.v.*), Vol. II, pp. 772–802.
NOTE: the reference is to the "one article" written by James Mill for the *PH&R*; the identification is based on an annotation in George Grote's copy, University of London Library.
REFERRED TO: 121 (*120*)

——— "Theory and Practice," *London and Westminster Review*, III & XXV (Apr., 1836), 223–34.
REFERRED TO: 209 (*208*)

——— "Whether Political Economy Is Useful?" *London Review*, II (*L&WR*, XXXI) (Jan., 1836), 553–71.
REFERRED TO: 209 (*208*)

MILL, JAMES BENTHAM.
NOTE: the reference concerns James Mill's relations with his children, one of whom was James Bentham.
REFERRED TO: 53

MILL, JANE.
NOTE: the reference at p. *36n* concerns the authority exercised by Mill over his younger sisters; that at p. 53 concerns James Mill's relations with his children, one of whom was Jane.
REFERRED TO: *36n*, 53

———— "Brodie's *History of the British Empire*," *Westminster Review*, II (Oct., 1824), 346–402.
REFERRED TO: 99 *(98)*

———— "Chapters on Socialism," *Fortnightly Review*, n.s. XXV (Feb., Mar., Apr., 1879), 217–37, 373–82, 513–30. In *CW*, Vol. V, pp. 703–53.
NOTE: the reference at p. 290 is to works not completed when Mill wrote the final section of the *Autobiography*; that at p. *625* is in Helen Taylor's "continuation" of the *Autobiography*.
REFERRED TO: 290, *625*

———— "Civilization," *London and Westminster Review*, III & XXV (Apr., 1836), 1–28. In *CW*, Vol. XVIII, pp. 117–47.
NOTE: reprinted in *D&D*, Vol. I, pp. 160–205. The quotation is inferential, and only the words quoted are relevant to the citation.
QUOTED: 187 *(186)*
REFERRED TO: 211 *(210)*
187.2–3 "extraordinary pliability of human nature"] astonishing pliability of our nature (*CW*, XVIII, 145)

———— "Coleridge," *London and Westminster Review*, XXXIII (Mar., 1840), 257–302. In *CW*, Vol. X, pp. 117–63.
NOTE: reprinted in *D&D*, Vol. I, pp. 393–466.
REFERRED TO: 225–7 *(224–6)*

———— *Considerations on Representative Government*. London: Parker, Son, and Bourn, 1861. In *CW*, Vol. XIX, pp. 371–577.
NOTE: 2nd ed., 1861; 3rd ed., 1865; People's Ed., 1865. The 1st, 2nd, and People's eds. and an American ed. (New York: Harper, 1873) are in SC. The reference at p. 249 is to Chap. xviii; that at p. 272 concerns the People's Ed.; that at p. *625* is in Helen Taylor's "continuation" of the *Autobiography*.
REFERRED TO: 199, 201, 249, 265, 272, 277, 288–9, *625*

———— *A Constitutional View of the India Question*. London: Penny, 1858.
NOTE: one of the series Mill wrote for the East India Company in 1858.
REFERRED TO: 249

———— "The Contest in America," *Fraser's Magazine*, LXV (Feb., 1862), 258–68.
NOTE: reprinted in *D&D*, Vol. III, pp. 179–205.
REFERRED TO: 268

———— "The Corn Laws," *Westminster Review*, III (Apr., 1825), 394–420. In *CW*, Vol. IV, pp. 45–70.
REFERRED TO: 99 *(98)*

———— "Corporation and Church Property," *Jurist*, IV (Feb., 1833), 1–26. In *CW*, Vol. IV, pp. 193–222.
NOTE: reprinted in *D&D*, Vol. I, pp. 1–41.
REFERRED TO: 191 *(190)*

———— "The Currency Juggle," *Tait's Edinburgh Magazine*, II (Jan., 1833), 461–7. In *CW*, Vol. IV, pp. 181–92.
NOTE: reprinted in *D&D*, Vol. I, pp. 42–55.
REFERRED TO: 191 *(190)*

———— "De Tocqueville on Democracy in America [I]," *London Review*, II (*L&WR*, XXXI) (Oct., 1835), 85–129. In *CW*, Vol. XVIII, pp. 47–90.
NOTE: reprinted in part in "Appendix," *D&D*, Vol. I, pp. 470–4.
REFERRED TO: 201

———— "De Tocqueville on Democracy in America [II]," *Edinburgh Review*, LXXII (Oct., 1840), 1–47. In *CW*, Vol. XVIII, pp. 153–204.
NOTE: reprinted in *D&D*, Vol. II, pp. 1–83.
REFERRED TO: 201, 227

———— *Dissertations and Discussions*. 2 vols. London: Parker, 1859; 3 vols. London: Longmans, Green, Reader, and Dyer, 1867; 4 vols. London: Longmans, Green, Reader, and Dyer, 1875.
NOTE: the 3-vol. ed. (1867) is in SC, with the 2nd ed. of Vol. IV (1875), and Vols. I and II of the 3-vol. American ed. (Boston: Spencer, 1864) and Vols. I, III, and IV of the 4-vol. American ed. (New York: Holt, 1873).
REFERRED TO: 191, 201, 205, 211, 221, 225, 227, 263, 264, 287

———— "Endowments," *Fortnightly Review*, n.s. V (Apr., 1869), 377–90. In *CW*, Vol. V, pp. 613–29.
NOTE: reprinted (posthumously) in *D&D*, Vol. IV, pp. 1–24. The reference is to Mill's articles for the *Fortnightly* up to the point where the *Autobiography* breaks off.
REFERRED TO: 290

———— *England and Ireland*. London: Longmans, Green, Reader, and Dyer, 1868.
NOTE: 2nd, 3rd, and 4th eds., 1868; 5th ed., 1869.
REFERRED TO: 280, 287

———— *Essays on Some Unsettled Questions of Political Economy*. London: Parker, 1844. In *CW*, Vol. IV, pp. 229–339.
NOTE: in SC. The reference at pp. 123–5 (*122–4*) is to the genesis of the work, and esp. Essays I and IV; that at p. 189 (*188*) includes a specific reference to Essay V.
REFERRED TO: 123–5 (*122–4*), 189 (*188*), 234n

———— *An Examination of Sir William Hamilton's Philosophy*. London: Longmans, Green, Reader, and Dyer, 1865. *CW*, Vol. IX.
NOTE: in SC. 2nd ed., 1865; 3rd ed., 1867; 4th ed., 1872.
REFERRED TO: 268–71

———— "Exchangeable Value," *Traveller*, 6 Dec., 1822, p. 3; and *ibid.*, 13 Dec., 1822, p. 2.
NOTE: Mill's first letter (signed "S") was in response to Torrens's leader, "Political Economy Club," *ibid.*, 2 Dec., 1822, p. 3; Torrens replied in "Exchangeable Value," *ibid.*, 7 Dec., 1822, p. 3; to this Mill's second letter (also signed "S") was a response. The series was terminated by a reply from Torrens appended to Mill's second letter. These were Mill's first publications.
REFERRED TO: 89 (*88*)

———— "A Few Words on Non-Intervention," *Fraser's Magazine*, LX (Dec., 1859), 766–76.
NOTE: reprinted in *D&D*, Vol. III, pp. 153–78.
REFERRED TO: 263

———— "Foreign Dependencies—Trade with India," *Parliamentary Review. Session of 1826–27 (q.v.)*, pp. 58–68.
REFERRED TO: 121 (*120*)

———— "Free Discussion," *Morning Chronicle*, 28 Jan., 1823, p. 3; 8 Feb., 1823, p. 3; 12 Feb., 1823, p. 3.
NOTE: the letters (signed Wickliff, not Wickliffe) were distinguished as "Letter I," "Letter II," and "Letter III." The two unpublished letters in the series are not known to have survived.
REFERRED TO: 89–91 (*88–90*)

———— "The French Revolution," *Westminster Review*, V (Apr., 1826), 385–98.
NOTE: a review of Mignet's *Histoire de la révolution française*, *q.v.*
REFERRED TO: 99 (*98*)

———— *"The French Revolution,"* London and Westminster Review, V & XXVII (July, 1837), 17–53.
NOTE: a review of Carlyle's *French Revolution*, *q.v.*
REFERRED TO: 225 (*224*), *603–4*

———— "The French Revolution of 1848, and Its Assailants," *Westminster Review*, LI (Apr., 1849), 1–47.
NOTE: reprinted in *D&D*, Vol. II, pp. 335–410.
REFERRED TO: 264

———— "The Game Laws," *Westminster Review*, V (Jan., 1826), 1–22.
REFERRED TO: 99 (*98*)

———— "Grote's *Aristotle*," *Fortnightly Review*, n.s. XIII (Jan., 1873), 27–50. In *CW*, Vol. XI, pp. 473–510.
NOTE: reprinted (posthumously) in *D&D*, Vol. IV, pp. 188–230. A review of George Grote, *Aristotle*, *q.v.* The reference is in Helen Taylor's "continuation" of the *Autobiography*.
REFERRED TO: *627*

———— "Grote's *Plato*," *Edinburgh Review*, CXXIII (Apr., 1866), 297–364. In *CW*, Vol. XI, pp. 375–440.
NOTE: reprinted in *D&D*, Vol. III, pp. 275–379.
REFERRED TO: 287

———— "Herschel's *Discourse*," *Examiner*, 20 Mar., 1831, pp. 179–80.
NOTE: a review of Herschel's *A Preliminary Discourse on the Study of Natural Philosophy*, *q.v.*
REFERRED TO: 217 (*216*)

———— "The History of Rome." BL Add. MS 33230, c.1.
NOTE: printed at pp. *542–6* above.
REFERRED TO: 17 (*16*), *583*

———— *Inaugural Address Delivered to the University of St. Andrews*. London: Longmans, Green, Reader, and Dyer, 1867.
NOTE: in SC, with an American ed. (Boston: Littell and Gay, 1867); 2nd ed., 1867.
REFERRED TO: 287

———— "Intercourse between the United States and the British Colonies in the West Indies," *Parliamentary Review. Session of 1826–27 (q.v.)*, pp. 298–335.
REFERRED TO: 121 (*120*)

———— "Ireland," *Parliamentary History and Review; . . . Session of 1825 (q.v.)*, Vol. II, pp. 603–26.
REFERRED TO: 121 (*120*)

———— Journal and Notebook Written in France, 1820–21. Published as *John Mill's Boyhood Visit to France*. Ed. Anna Jean Mill. Toronto: University of Toronto Press, 1960.
REFERRED TO: 57n, *585*

———— Journal of a Walking Tour of Berkshire, Buckinghamshire, and Surrey, 3–15 July, 1828.
NOTE: MS, Yale. The entry for 3 July is relevant.
REFERRED TO: 87n, *150n*

—————— Journal of a Walking Tour of Cornwall, 3–9 Oct., 1832.
NOTE: MS, Mill-Taylor Collection.
REFERRED TO: 87n

—————— Journal of a Walking Tour of Hampshire, West Sussex, and the Isle of Wight, 19 July–6 Aug., 1832.
NOTE: MS, Mount Holyoke.
REFERRED TO: 87n

—————— Journal of a Walking Tour of Sussex, 20–30 July, 1827.
NOTE: MS, St. Andrews.
REFERRED TO: 87n

—————— Journal of a Walking Tour of Yorkshire and the Lake District, 12 July–8 Aug., 1831.
NOTE: MS, Bodleian.
REFERRED TO: 87n

—————— "Law of Libel and Liberty of the Press," *Westminster Review*, III (Apr., 1825), 285–321.
REFERRED TO: 99 (*98*)

—————— "Letter from the Chairman and Deputy Chairman of the Honourable East India Company to the President of the Board of Trade," *Parliamentary Papers*, 1857–58, XLIII, 41–4.
NOTE: one of the series Mill wrote for the East India Company in 1858.
REFERRED TO: 249

—————— Letter to Carlyle, 12 Jan., 1834. In *CW*, Vol. XII, pp. 204–9.
REFERRED TO: 183 (*182*)

—————— Letter to James Beal, 7 Mar., 1865. In *CW*, Vol. XVI, pp. 1005–7.
NOTE: published, *inter alia*, in *Daily News*, 23 Mar., 1865, p. 5.
REFERRED TO: 273–4

—————— Letter to James Beal, 17 Apr., 1865. In *CW*, Vol. XVI, pp. 1031–5.
NOTE: published, *inter alia*, in *Daily News*, 21 Apr., 1865, p. 4.
REFERRED TO: 273–4

—————— Letter to James Beal, 14 Dec., 1868. In *CW*, Vol. XVI, pp. 1523–6.
NOTE: published in part in *Morning Star*, 23 Dec., 1868, p. 6. Mill says the letter is really Helen Taylor's.
REFERRED TO: 286n

—————— Letters to Auguste Comte. In *CW*, Vol. XIII, pp. 488ff.
NOTE: Comte's letters appear in *Lettres inédites de John Stuart Mill à Auguste Comte, publiées avec les réponses de Comte*, ed. L. Lévy-Bruhl (Paris: Germer Baillière, 1899).
REFERRED TO: 219

—————— "Lord Durham and His Assailants," *London and Westminster Review*, VII & XXIX (Aug., 1838), 507–12.
NOTE: the article appears only in the second ed. of this number (which may have been called for by the popularity of Mill's "Bentham," the immediately preceding article).
REFERRED TO: 223 (*222*)

—————— "Lord Durham and the Canadians." See "Radical Party and Canada."

————— "Lord Durham's Return," *London and Westminster Review*, XXXII (Dec., 1838), 241–60.
REFERRED TO: 223 *(222)*, 225 *(224)*

————— "Maine on Village Communities," *Fortnightly Review*, n.s. IX (May, 1871), 543–56.
NOTE: reprinted (posthumously) in *D&D*, Vol. IV, pp. 130–53. A review of Henry Sumner Maine, *Village-Communities*, *q.v.* The reference is in Helen Taylor's "continuation" of the *Autobiography*.
REFERRED TO: *626*

————— *Memorandum of the Improvements in the Administration of India during the Last Thirty Years, and the Petition of the East-India Company to Parliament*. London: Cox and Wyman, 1858.
NOTE: one of the series Mill wrote for the East India Company in 1858.
REFERRED TO: 249

————— "Mr. Mill on the Treaty of 1856," *The Times*, 19 Nov., 1870, p. 5.
NOTE: the reference is in Helen Taylor's "continuation" of the *Autobiography*.
REFERRED TO: *626*

————— "Modern French Historical Works—Age of Chivalry," *Westminster Review*, VI (July, 1826), 62–103.
REFERRED TO: 99 *(98)*

————— *The Moral of the India Debate*. London: Penny, 1858.
NOTE: one of the series Mill wrote for the East India Company in 1858.
REFERRED TO: 249

————— "New Corn Law," *Westminster Review*, VII (Jan., 1827), 169–86. In *CW*, Vol. IV, pp. 141–59.
REFERRED TO: 99 *(98)*

————— "Notes on Some of the More Popular Dialogues of Plato," *Monthly Repository*, n.s. VIII: No. I, "The Protagoras" (Feb., Mar., 1834), 89–99, 203–11; No. II, "The Phaedrus" (June, Sept., 1834), 404–20, 633–46; No. III, "The Gorgias" (Oct., Nov., Dec., 1834), 691–710, 802–15, 829–42; and n.s. IX: No. IV, "The Apology of Socrates" (Feb., Mar., 1835), 112–21, 169–78. In *CW*, Vol. XI, pp. 37–174.
NOTE: Mill translated five other of Plato's dialogues (*Charmides, Euthyphron, Laches, Lysis*, and *Parmenides*), which remained in manuscript until published in *CW*, Vol. XI, pp. 175–238.
REFERRED TO: 207 *(206)*

————— "Notes on the Newspapers," *Monthly Repository*, n.s. VIII (Mar., 1834), 161–76; (Apr., 1834), 233–48, 309–12; (May, 1834), 354–75; (June, 1834), 435–56; (July, 1834), 521–8; (Aug., 1834), 589–600; (Sept., 1834), 656–65.
REFERRED TO: 205 *(204)*

————— *Observations on the Proposed Council of India*. London: Penny, 1858.
NOTE: one of the series Mill wrote for the East India Company in 1858.
REFERRED TO: 249

————— "Ode to Diana." BL Add. MS 33230, c.2.
NOTE: printed at pp. *549–50* above.
REFERRED TO: 19 *(18)*, 583

————— *On Liberty*. London: Parker, 1859. In *CW*, Vol. XVIII, pp. 213–310.
NOTE: 2nd ed., 1859; 3rd ed., 1864; 4th ed., 1869; People's Ed., 1865. Copies of the 1st, 3rd, and People's eds. are in SC. The reference at p. 245 is inferential; the first reference at p. 261 is to the motto quoted from von Humboldt; the second is to Mill's use of the Warrenites' phrase, "the sovereignty of the individual"; the reference at p. 272 concerns the People's Ed.
REFERRED TO: 245, 249, 257–61 *(256–8)*, 272

—— "Paper Currency and Commercial Distress," *Parliamentary Review; . . . Session of 1826* (*q.v.*), Vol. II, pp. 630–62. In *CW*, Vol. IV, pp. 71–123.
REFERRED TO: 121 (*120*)

—— "Parties and the Ministry," *London and Westminster Review*, VI & XXVIII (Oct., 1837), 1–26.
REFERRED TO: 217 (*216*)

—— "Periodical Literature: *Edinburgh Review*," *Westminster Review*, I (Apr., 1824), 505–41.
NOTE: the essay reprinted at pp. 291–325 above.
REFERRED TO: 95n (*94n*), 96n–7n, 99 (*98*)

—— "Pledges," *Examiner*, 1 July, 1832, pp. 417–18, and 15 July, 1832, pp. 449–51.
NOTE: Mill says he wrote "several" articles on the subject, but these are the only ones listed in his bibliography.
REFERRED TO: *180n*

—— "Poems and Romances of Alfred de Vigny," *London and Westminster Review*, VII & XXIX (Apr., 1838), 1–44.
NOTE: the essay reprinted at pp. 463–501 above. In *D&D*, Vol. I, pp. 287–329.
REFERRED TO: *224*

—— *Practical Observations on the First Two of the Proposed Resolutions on the Government of India*. London: Penny, 1858.
NOTE: one of the series Mill wrote for the East India Company in 1858.
REFERRED TO: 249

—— *A President in Council the Best Government for India*. London: Penny, 1858.
NOTE: one of the series Mill wrote for the East India Company in 1858.
REFERRED TO: 249

—— *Principles of Political Economy, with Some of Their Applications to Social Philosophy*. 2 vols. London: Parker, 1848. *CW*, Vols. II–III.
NOTE: 2nd ed., 1849; 3rd ed., 1852; 4th ed., 1857; 5th ed., 1862; 6th ed., 1865; 7th ed., 1871; People's Ed. (1 vol.), 1865. Copies of the 2nd–6th eds. and the 1st American ed. (Boston: Little and Brown, 1848) are in SC. The reference at p. 255 is to Bk. IV, Chap. vii; that at p. 257n is to the dedication of the *Principles* to Harriet Taylor, on a pasted-in slip in some copies, reading: "To Mrs. John Taylor as the most eminently qualified of all persons known to the author either to originate or to appreciate speculations on social improvement, this attempt to explain and diffuse ideas many of which were first learned from herself, is with the highest respect and regard, dedicated." The reference at p. 272 concerns the People's Ed.
REFERRED TO: *122n, 234n*, 241–5 (*240–4*), 255–7 (*254–6*), 257n, 272, *620–1*

—— "Professor Leslie on the Land Question," *Fortnightly Review*, n.s. VII (June, 1870), 641–54. In *CW*, Vol. V, pp. 669–85.
NOTE: reprinted (posthumously) in *D&D*, Vol. IV, pp. 86–110. The reference is in Helen Taylor's "continuation" of the *Autobiography*.
REFERRED TO: *626*

—— *Programme of the Land Tenure Reform Association, with an Explanatory Statement by John Stuart Mill*. London: Longmans, Green, Reader, and Dyer, 1871. In *CW*, Vol. V, pp. 687–95.
NOTE: reprinted (posthumously) in *D&D*, Vol. IV, pp. 239–50. The reference is in Helen Taylor's "continuation" of the *Autobiography*.
REFERRED TO: *626*

—— "*Quarterly Review* on Political Economy," *Westminster Review*, III (Jan., 1825), 213–32. In *CW*, Vol. IV, pp. 23–43.
REFERRED TO: 99 (*98*)

———— Question on the Recent Court Martial in Jamaica (1867), *Parliamentary Debates*, 3rd ser., Vol. 189, cols. 598–9 (1 Aug., 1867).
NOTE: see also Mill, speech of 31 July, 1866.
REFERRED TO: 281–2

———— Questions on the Outbreak in Jamaica (1866), *Parliamentary Debates*, 3rd ser., Vol. 184, cols. 1064–6 (19 July, 1866); *ibid.*, col. 2160 (10 Aug., 1866).
NOTE: see also Mill, speech of 31 July, 1866.
REFERRED TO: 281–2

———— "Radical Party and Canada: Lord Durham and the Canadians," *London and Westminster Review*, VI & XXVIII (Jan., 1838), 502–33.
NOTE: in some copies of the number, the running title on the first eight pages is "Radical Party in Canada"; in all copies, the running title on the remaining pages and the title in the Table of Contents of the *L&WR* is "Lord Durham and the Canadians."
REFERRED TO: 223 (*222*)

———— "Recent Writers on Reform," *Fraser's Magazine*, LIX (Apr., 1859), 489–508. In *CW*, Vol. XIX, pp. 341–70.
NOTE: reprinted in *D&D*, Vol. III, pp. 47–96.
REFERRED TO: 263, 288–9

———— "Remarks on Bentham's Philosophy." App. B in Edward Lytton Bulwer's *England and the English*. 2 vols. London: Bentley, 1833, Vol. II, pp. 321–44. In *CW*, Vol. X, pp. 3–18.
NOTE: in SC. Mill indicates that he also wrote part of the text concerning Bentham in Bulwer's work (Vol. II, pp. 163–70); this is reprinted in *CW*, Vol. X, pp. 499–502. He also wrote notes, which Bulwer "cut and mangled and coxcombified" (letter to Thomas Carlyle, *CW*, Vol. XII, p. 172 [2 Aug., 1833]) for App. D, "A Few Observations on Mr. Mill" (reprinted at pp. *589–95* above).
REFERRED TO: 207 (*206*)

———— *Report to the General Court of Proprietors*. London: Cox and Wyman, 1858.
NOTE: one of the series Mill wrote for the East India Company in 1858.
REFERRED TO: 249

———— "Scott's *Life of Napoleon*," *Westminster Review*, IX (Apr., 1828), 251–313.
REFERRED TO: 99 (*98*), 135 (*134*)

———— "Sedgwick's *Discourse*," *London Review*, I (*L&WR*, XXX) (Apr., 1835), 94–135. In *CW*, Vol. X, pp. 31–74.
NOTE: the reference at p. 227 is to the reprinting of this article, vindicating Bentham, in *D&D*, Vol. I, pp. 95–159.
REFERRED TO: 209 (*208*), 227

———— "Should Public Bodies Be Required to Sell Their Lands?" *Examiner*, 11 Jan., 1873, pp. 29–30.
NOTE: reprinted (posthumously) in *D&D*, Vol. IV, pp. 266–77. The reference is in Helen Taylor's "continuation" of the *Autobiography*.
REFERRED TO: *627*

———— "The Silk Trade," *Westminster Review*, V (Jan., 1826), 136–49. In *CW*, Vol. IV, pp. 125–39.
NOTE: this is the only one of the thirteen articles Mill contributed from the second to the eighteenth number of the *Westminster* not listed in Mill's own bibliography.
REFERRED TO: 99 (*98*)

———— "The Slave Power," *Westminster Review*, LXXVIII (Oct., 1862), 489–510.
NOTE: reprinted in the American ed. of *D&D*, 3 vols. (Boston: Spencer, 1864), Vol. III, pp. 264–99.
REFERRED TO: 266

—— Speeches. Mill's speeches will be found listed chronologically at the end of this list of his works.

—— "The Spirit of the Age," *Examiner*: No. I, 9 Jan., 1831, pp. 20–1; No. II, 23 Jan., 1831, pp. 50–2; No. III, 6 Feb., 1831, pp. 82–4, and 13 Mar., 1831, pp. 162–3; No. IV, 3 Apr., 1831, pp. 210–11; No. V, 15 May, 1831, p. 307, and 29 May, 1831, pp. 339–41.
REFERRED TO: 181 (*180*)

—— "State of Society in America," *London Review*, II (*L&WR*, XXXI) (Jan., 1836), 365–89. In *CW*, Vol. XVIII, pp. 91–115.
REFERRED TO: 433

—— *The Subjection of Women*. London: Longmans, Green, Reader, and Dyer, 1869.
NOTE: 2nd ed., 1869; 3rd ed., 1870. A copy of the 2nd ed. is in SC.
REFERRED TO: 253n, 265, 290

—— *A System of Logic, Ratiocinative and Inductive, Being a Connected View of the Principles of Evidence and the Methods of Scientific Investigation*. 2 vols. London: Parker, 1843. *CW*, Vols. VII–VIII.
NOTE: 2nd ed., 1846; 3rd ed., 1851; 4th ed., 1856; 5th ed., 1862; 6th ed., 1865; 7th ed., 1868; 8th ed., 1872. The 1st, 2nd, 3rd, 4th, and 6th eds. are in SC. The reference at p. 125 (*124*) is to Bk. I; that at p. 169 (*168*) is to Bk. VI; that at p. 177 (*176*) is to Bk. VI, Chap. ii; that at p. 191 (*190*) is to both Bk. II and Bk. I; that at p. *627*, in Helen Taylor's "continuation" of the *Autobiography*, is to Mill's revisions for the 8th ed.
REFERRED TO: 125 (*124*), 167–9 (*166–8*), 177 (*176*), 189–91 (*188–90*), 215–19 (*214–16*), 229–35 (*228–34*), 234n, 243 (*242*), 246, 255 (*254*), 255n, 259, 270, 271, *627*

—— "Taine's *De l'intelligence*," *Fortnightly Review*, n.s. VIII (July, 1870), 121–4. In *CW*, Vol. XI, pp. 441–7.
NOTE: reprinted (posthumously) in *D&D*, Vol. IV, pp. 111–18. The reference is in Helen Taylor's "continuation" of the *Autobiography*.
REFERRED TO: *626*

—— "Thornton on Labour and Its Claims," *Fortnightly Review*, n.s. V (May, and June, 1869), 505–18, and 680–700. In *CW*, Vol. V, pp. 631–68.
NOTE: reprinted (posthumously) in *D&D*, Vol. IV, pp. 25–85. The reference is to Mill's articles for the *Fortnightly*, up to the point where the *Autobiography* breaks off.
REFERRED TO: 290

—— *Thoughts on Parliamentary Reform*. London: Parker, 1859. In *CW*, Vol. XIX, pp. 311–39.
NOTE: in SC. 2nd ed., 1859; reprinted in *D&D*, Vol. III, pp. 1–46.
REFERRED TO: 261–2, 263, 274, 288–9

—— "Thoughts on Poetry and Its Varieties," *Dissertations and Discussions*, Vol. I, pp. 89–120.
NOTE: the essay (combining "What Is Poetry?" and "The Two Kinds of Poetry") reprinted at pp. 341–65 above. The references are given under "What Is Poetry?" and "The Two Kinds of Poetry," *q.v.*

—— *Three Essays on Religion*. London: Longmans, Green, Reader, and Dyer, 1874. In *CW*, Vol. X, pp. 369–489.
NOTE: in SC. The reference at p. 245 is inferential; that at p. 290 is to works not completed when Mill wrote the final section of the *Autobiography*; that at p. *625*, specifically to "Theism," is in Helen Taylor's "continuation" of the *Autobiography*.
REFERRED TO: 245, 290, *625*

———— "Traité de logique."
NOTE: MS, Pierpont Morgan Library.
REFERRED TO: 59n, *587*

———— "Treaty Obligations," *Fortnightly Review*, n.s. VIII (Dec., 1870), 715–20.
NOTE: reprinted (posthumously) in *D&D*, Vol. IV, pp. 119–29. The reference is in Helen Taylor's "continuation" of the *Autobiography*.
REFERRED TO: *626*

———— "The Treaty of 1856," *The Times*, 24 Nov., 1870, p. 3.
NOTE: the reference is in Helen Taylor's "continuation" of the *Autobiography*.
REFERRED TO: *626*

———— "The Two Kinds of Poetry," *Monthly Repository*, n.s. VII (Nov. 1833), 714–24.
NOTE: see J. S. Mill, "Thoughts on Poetry," above.
REFERRED TO: 205 (*204*)

———— Unheaded leader, *Morning Chronicle*, 9 May, 1823, p. 3.
NOTE: the article concerns the debate in the House of Commons on the petition of Richard Carlile: see *Parliamentary Debates*, n.s., Vol. 9, cols. 114–17 (8 May, 1823).
REFERRED TO: 91 (*90*)

———— *Utilitarianism*. London: Parker, Son, and Bourn, 1863. In *CW*, Vol. X, pp. 203–59.
NOTE: 2nd ed., 1864; 3rd ed., 1867; 4th ed., 1871. First appeared in three instalments in *Fraser's Magazine*, LXIV (Oct., 1861), 391–406 (Chaps. i–ii); (Nov., 1861), 525–34 (Chaps. iii–iv); (Dec., 1861), 658–73 (Chap. v). The reference at p. 245 is inferential.
REFERRED TO: 245, 265–6

———— "War Expenditure," *Westminster Review*, II (July, 1824), 27–48. In *CW*, Vol. IV, pp. 1–22.
REFERRED TO: 99 (*98*)

———— "What Is Poetry?" *Monthly Repository*, n.s. VII (Jan., 1833), 60–70.
NOTE: see J. S. Mill, "Thoughts on Poetry," above.
REFERRED TO: 205 (*204*), 365n

———— "Whately's *Elements of Logic*," *Westminster Review*, IX (Jan., 1828), 137–72. In *CW*, Vol. XI, pp. 1–35.
REFERRED TO: 99 (*98*)

———— "Whewell on Moral Philosophy," *Westminster Review*, LVIII (Oct., 1852), 349–85. In *CW*, Vol. X, pp. 165–201.
NOTE: the reference is to the reprinting of this article, vindicating Bentham, in *D&D*, Vol. II, pp. 450–509.
REFERRED TO: 227

———— "Writings of Junius Redivivus [II]," *Tait's Edinburgh Magazine*, III (June, 1833), 347–54.
NOTE: reprinted at pp. 379–90 above. The reference is to Mill's essays in the first series of *Tait's*.
REFERRED TO: 191 (*190*)

———— See also Jeremy Bentham, *Rationale of Judicial Evidence*, ed. J. S. Mill; George Grote and John Stuart Mill, "Taylor's *Statesman*"; James Mill, *Analysis of the Phenomena of the Human Mind*, 2nd ed., ed. J. S. Mill; and, under Parliamentary Papers, Mill, "Letter . . . ."

SPEECHES (in chronological order)

———— "Population" (1825).
NOTE: known through a typescript in the possession of the Fabian Society.
REFERRED TO: 127 (*126*)

———— "Population. Reply" (1825).
NOTE: known through a typescript in the possession of the Fabian Society.
REFERRED TO: 127 (*126*)

———— "Proaemium of a Speech on Population" (1825).
NOTE: known through a typescript in the possession of the Fabian Society.
REFERRED TO: 127 (*126*)

———— "Second Speech on Population in Answer to Thirlwall" (1825).
NOTE: the MS is in the Mill-Taylor Collection.
REFERRED TO: 127 (*126*)

———— "First Speech on the Cooperative System" (fragment; 1825).
NOTE: the MS is in the Mill-Taylor Collection.
REFERRED TO: 129 (*128*)

———— "Intended Speech at the Cooperation Society, never delivered" (1825).
NOTE: the MS is in Connecticut College.
REFERRED TO: 129 (*128*)

———— "Closing Speech on the Cooperative System" (1825).   .
NOTE: part of the MS is in the Mill-Taylor Collection, and part in Connecticut College.
REFERRED TO: 129 (*128*)

———— "On the Influence of the Aristocracy" (9 Dec., 1825).
NOTE: MS, Mill-Taylor Collection. The reference is to Mill's opening the debate at the second meeting of the London Debating Society. His later speeches at the Society are generally referred to at pp. 131–3 (*130–2*)
REFERRED TO: 131 (*130*)

———— "On Wordsworth" (30 Jan., 1829).
NOTE: MS, Mill-Taylor Collection. Mill must be referring to the debate at the London Debating Society during which he delivered the speech here cited when he mentions his opposition to Roebuck on the relative merits of Wordsworth and Byron; Sterling, who opened this debate on 16 Jan. (when Roebuck also spoke), was not a member two years earlier, on 19 Jan., 1827, when Roebuck and Mill opposed one another on the merits of Byron's poetry.
REFERRED TO: 153 (*152*), 163 (*162*)

———— On the Cattle Diseases Bill, *Parliamentary Debates*, 3rd ser., Vol. 181, cols. 488–92 (14 Feb., 1866).
REFERRED TO: 276n–7n

———— On the Habeas Corpus Suspension (Ireland) Bill, *Parliamentary Debates*, 3rd ser., Vol. 181, cols. 705–6 (17 Feb., 1866).
REFERRED TO: 277

———— On the Representation of the People Bill, *Parliamentary Debates*, 3rd ser., Vol. 182, cols. 1253–63 (13 Apr., 1866); Vol. 183, cols. 1590–2 (31 May, 1866).
NOTE: the references are to Gladstone's Reform Bill.
REFERRED TO: 275, 277, 278

———— On the Malt Duty—Resolution, *Parliamentary Debates*, 3rd ser., Vol. 182, cols. 1524–8 (17 Apr., 1866).

NOTE: the reference is to Mill's speech on the National Debt and coal supplies.
REFERRED TO: 277

——— On the Tenure and Improvement of Land (Ireland) Bill, *Parliamentary Debates*, 3rd ser., Vol. 183, cols. 1087–97 (17 May, 1866).
NOTE: reprinted as "Speech on Mr. Chichester Fortescue's Land Bill," in *Chapters and Speeches on the Irish Land Question* (London: Longmans, Green, Reader, and Dyer, 1870), pp. 97–107. The Bill referred to, "A Bill Further to Amend the Law Relating to the Tenure and Improvement of Land in Ireland" (30 Apr., 1866), *q.v.*, was introduced by Fortescue on behalf of the Russell government, but was not enacted.
REFERRED TO: 279–80

——— On the Reform Meeting in Hyde Park, *Parliamentary Debates*, 3rd ser., Vol. 184, cols. 1410–12 (24 July, 1866).
REFERRED TO: 278

——— On the Proposed Reform Meeting in Hyde Park, *Parliamentary Debates*, 3rd ser., Vol. 184, cols. 1540–1 (26 July, 1866).
NOTE: reported in *The Times*, 27 July, 1866, p. 7. The reference is to Mill's persuading the leading members of the Council of the Reform League to abandon their plan to meet in Hyde Park; the speech cited gives Mill's public statement that the plan had been given up.
REFERRED TO: 278

——— On the Disturbances in Jamaica, *Parliamentary Debates*, 3rd ser., Vol. 184, cols. 1797–1806 (31 July, 1866).
NOTE: see also J. S. Mill, Question, and Questions.
REFERRED TO: 281–2

——— To the Reform League Meeting at the Agricultural Hall, *The Times*, 31 July, 1866, p. 3.
REFERRED TO: 278

——— On Municipal Reform, *Parliamentary Debates*, 3rd ser., Vol. 185, cols. 1608–10 1616 (8 Mar., 1867); cols. 1678–9, 1680, 1685 (11 Mar., 1867); col. 1696 (12 Mar. 1867); cols. 1861–2 (14 Mar., 1867); Vol. 187, cols. 882–5, 891 (21 Apr., 1867); and Vol. 189, cols. 1040–1 (7 Aug., 1867).
REFERRED TO: 276

——— On the Representation of the People Bill, *Parliamentary Debates*, 3rd ser., Vol 187, cols. 280–4 (9 May, 1867); Vol. 188, cols. 1102–7 (5 July, 1867).
NOTE: the references at p. 277 and the first at p. 284 are to Disraeli's Reform Bill; the second at p. 284 is to Mill's support for the proposal for cumulative voting, which he calls a "poor makeshift."
REFERRED TO: 277, 284

——— *Speech of John Stuart Mill, M.P., on the Admission of Women to the Electoral Franchise. Spoken in the House of Commons, May 20, 1867.* London: Trübner, 1867.
NOTE: cf. *Parliamentary Debates*, 3rd ser., Vol. 187, cols. 817–29, 842–3. Copies of the published version are in SC.
REFERRED TO: 276, 285

——— *Personal Representation, Speech of John Stuart Mill, Esq., M.P., Delivered in the House of Commons, May 29 [sic], 1867.* London: Henderson, *et al.*, 1867.
NOTE: cf. *Parliamentary Debates*, 3rd ser., Vol. 187, cols. 1343–56, 1362. The speech was actually delivered on 30 May. A copy of the 2nd ed. (London: Henderson, *et al.*, 1867) is in SC.
REFERRED TO: 276, 285

——— On the Meetings in Royal Parks Bill, *Parliamentary Debates*, 3rd ser., Vol. 188 cols. 1888, 1890–3 (22 July, 1867); Vol. 189, cols. 1482–4 (13 Aug., 1867).
REFERRED TO: 279

—— On the Declaration of Paris, *Parliamentary Debates*, 3rd ser., Vol. 189, cols. 876–84 (5 Aug., 1867).
NOTE: the reference is to Mill's speech on the right of seizing enemies' goods in neutral vessels.
REFERRED TO: 275

—— On the State of Ireland, *Parliamentary Debates*, 3rd ser., Vol. 190, cols. 1516–32 (12 Mar., 1868).
NOTE: reprinted as "Speech on Mr. Maguire's Motion on the State of Ireland," in *Chapters and Speeches on the Irish Land Question* (London: Longmans, Green, Reader, and Dyer, 1870), pp. 108–25. See also Maguire, Motion (10 Mar., 1868).
REFERRED TO: 280

—— On the Election Petitions and Corrupt Practices Bill, *Parliamentary Debates*, 3rd ser., Vol. 191, cols. 308–11 (26 Mar., 1868); Vol. 193, cols. 1166–8 (14 July, 1868); cols. 1640–1 (22 July, 1868).
NOTE: the first reference is to the amendment, moved by Mill (22 July), proposing the prohibition of paid canvassers and the limiting of each candidate to one paid agent; the second reference is to the amendment, also proposed by Mill (14 July), proposing the application of the penal provisions of the Bill to municipal elections; the third is to Mill's speech (26 March) on the principle of Disraeli's Bribery Bill.
REFERRED TO: 283

—— On the Capital Punishment within Prisons Bill, *Parliamentary Debates*, 3rd ser., Vol. 191, cols. 1047–55 (21 Apr., 1868).
REFERRED TO: 275

—— At the Meeting of the National Society for Women's Suffrage in the Architectural Gallery, Conduit St., Regent St., 17 July, 1869.
NOTE: reported in *Daily News*, 19 July, 1869, p. 2.
REFERRED TO: 290

—— At the Meeting of the Education League at St. James's Hall, 25 Mar., 1870.
NOTE: MS, Harvard University. Reported on 26 Mar., 1870, in *The Times*, p. 5, *Daily News*, p. 3, and *Daily Telegraph*, p. 3
REFERRED TO: 290

—— On Women's Suffrage. In *Report of a Meeting of the London National Society for Women's Suffrage, Held at the Hanover Square Rooms, Saturday, March 26th, 1870.* [London: n.p., 1870,] pp. 4–9.
NOTE: reported in *The Times*, 28 Mar., 1870, p. 5. The reference is in Helen Taylor's "continuation" of the *Autobiography*.
REFERRED TO: 625

—— On Women's Suffrage. In *Women's Suffrage. Great Meeting in Edinburgh in the Music Hall, on 12th January 1871, under the Auspices of the Edinburgh Branch of the National Society for Women's Suffrage.* Edinburgh: printed Greig, 1871, pp. 7–12.
NOTE: reported in *The Times*, 13 Jan., 1871, p. 3. Reprinted as a pamphlet, *Speech of the Late John Stuart Mill . . .* (Edinburgh: printed Greig, 1873). The reference is in Helen Taylor's "continuation" of the *Autobiography*.
REFERRED TO: 625

—— At a Meeting of the Land Tenure Reform Association. In *Land Tenure Reform Association. Report of the Inaugural Public Meeting, Held at the Freemason's Hall, London, Monday, 15th May, 1871.* London: Land Tenure Reform Association, 1871.
NOTE: reprinted posthumously in *D&D*, Vol. IV, pp. 251–65. The reference is in Helen Taylor's "continuation" of the *Autobiography*.
REFERRED TO: 626

MILL, MARY ELIABETH.
NOTE: the reference at p. *36n* concerns the authority exercised by Mill over his younger sisters; that at p. 53 concerns James Mill's relations with his children, one of whom was Mary.
REFERRED TO: *36n*, 53

MILL, WILHELMINA FORBES.
NOTE: the reference at p. 7 (*6*) is to James Mill's instruction of his children, one of whom was Wilhelmina, during the period in which he was working on his *History of British India*; that at p. *36n* concerns the authority exercised by Mill over his younger sisters; that at p. 53 concerns James Mill's relations with his children; the others are to J. S. Mill's teaching of Wilhelmina.
REFERRED TO: 7 (*6*), 13 (*12*), *36n*, 53, *555*, *556*, *557*, *560*, *562*, *563*, *564*, *568*, *569*

MILLAR, JOHN. *An Historical View of the English Government, from the Settlement of the Saxons in Britain to the Accession of the House of Stewart.* London: Strahan and Cadell, 1787.
NOTE: this ed. formerly in SC. The reference at p. 305 derives from Jeffrey's review (*q.v.*) of the 4-vol. ed. (London: Mawman, 1803), which has additional matter.
REFERRED TO: 11 (*10*), 305, *555*

MILLEVOYE, CHARLES HUBERT.
NOTE: the reference derives from Chenevix, "English and French Literature," *q.v.*
REFERRED TO: 310

MILLOT, CLAUDE FRANÇOIS XAVIER. *Elémens de l'histoire de France, depuis Clovis jusqu'à Louis XV.* Paris: Durand, 1768.
REFERRED TO: *569*

MILNE, JAMES (J. S. Mill's grandfather).
NOTE: Mill is in Scotland a variant of Milne.
REFERRED TO: 5 (*4*)

MILNES, RICHARD MONCKTON. *Memorials of a Residence on the Continent, and Historical Poems.* London: Moxon, 1838.
NOTE: Mill wrote his review before the actual publication of the volume, which appeared also as Vol. II of *The Poems of Richard Monckton Milnes*, 2 vols. (London: Moxon, 1838), Vol. I being *Poems of Many Years*, *q.v.*
REVIEWED: 503–16
QUOTED: 513–16
REFERRED TO: 519
513.41   divine!] divine? (143)

———— *Poems of Many Years*. London: Moxon, 1838.
NOTE: Mill says, in his review, that this volume was "not designed for publication." He does not give the publisher, and says of it in his heading "(For private circulation.)"; the volume, however, also appeared as Vol. I of *The Poems of Richard Monckton Milnes*, 2 vols. (London: Moxon, 1838), Vol. II being *Memorials of a Residence on the Continent, and Historical Poems*, *q.v.* From this volume Mill quotes "The Lay of the Humble," an untitled poem ("Youth, that pursuest . . ."), "To ———, Five Years Old," and "The Combat of Life."
REVIEWED: 503–16
QUOTED: 505–9, 510, 511, 511–12, 513
REFERRED TO: 519
506.5   They] *They* (29)
509.1   lover's] lovers' (35)
511.38   Evil—] Evil; by some mightier power / Than Memory can embrace, or Reason know, / We were enlisted into this great strife, / And led to meet that unknown Enemy: / Yet not like men brought blinded to a wood, / Who, looking round them, where a hundred paths / All undistinguisht lead a hundred ways, / Tormented by that blank indifference, / Rather sit down and die than wander

———— "Orange Conspiracy," *London and Westminster Review*, III & XXV (Apr., 1836), 181–223.
REFERRED TO: *600–1*

MOLIÈRE, JEAN BAPTISTE POQUELIN.
NOTE: the reference is to two of his plays.
REFERRED TO: *570*

———— *Les femmes savantes*. Paris: Promé, 1672.
QUOTED: *126*
126.13   "des clartés de tout,"] Je consens qu'une Femme ait des clartez de tout, / Mais je ne luy veux point la passion choquante / De se rendre sçavante afin d'estre Sçavante; / Et j'aime que souvent aux questions qu'on fait, / Elle sçache ignorer les choses qu'elle sçait; / De son étude enfin je veux qu'elle se cache, / Et qu'elle ait du sçavoir sans vouloir qu'on le sçache, / Sans citer les Autheurs, sans dire de grands mots / Et cloüer de l'esprit à ses moindres propos. (10; I, iii, 4–12)

MONGAULT, NICOLAS HUBERT. See Cicero, *Lettres de Cicéron*.

MONSIGNY, PIERRE ALEXANDRE. *Rose et Colas*.
NOTE: the opera was first performed in England at Covent Garden, 18 Sept., 1778; published (libretto by M. J. Sedaine, trans. Charles Dibdin) London: Kearsly, 1778.
REFERRED TO: 491

MONTESQUIEU, CHARLES LOUIS DE SECONDAT, BARON DE LA BRÈDE ET DE. Referred to: 310n

MONTGOMERY, JAMES. *The Wanderer of Switzerland, and Other Poems* (1806). 3rd ed. London: Longman, Hurst, Rees, and Orme, 1806.
REFERRED TO: 324

MONTGOMERY, ROBERT. *The Omnipresence of the Deity: A Poem* (1828). 11th ed. London: Maunder, 1830.
NOTE: presumably Mill is referring to this volume (in its 11th ed. not long before he wrote the passage), which contains, despite its title, a section entitled "Poems."
REFERRED TO: 398

The Monthly Repository. Referred to: 205 (*204*), 329, 369, 382

MOORE, JOHN.
NOTE: the reference is in a quotation from Jeffrey's "Madame de Staël," *q.v.*
REFERRED TO: 317

MOORE, JOHN HAMILTON. *A New and Complete Collection of Voyages and Travels*. 2 vols. London: Hogg, [1780?].
NOTE: this collection may be the one Mill so vaguely refers to: it contains "The Voyage of Ferdinand Maghellan" (Vol. I, pp. 13–15), and is in folio. Less likely is Samuel Purchas, *Purchas His Pilgrimes*, 3 vols. (London: Fetherstone, 1625), which includes "Of Fernandus Magalianes" (Pt. I, Bk. II, Chap. ii), Vol. I, pp. 33–46, and is also in folio.
REFERRED TO: *12n, 556*

MOORE, THOMAS. Referred to: 115 (*114*), 321

———— [?] or William Hazlitt [?]. "Coleridge's *Christabel*," *Edinburgh Review*, XXVII (Sept., 1816), 58–67.
NOTE: the reference is to "the disgraceful articles in the early Numbers of the *Edinburgh Review*, on Wordsworth and Coleridge." The tentative identification is in *The Wellesley Index*, Vol. I.
REFERRED TO: 398

MORE, THOMAS. Referred to: 266n–7n. See also Francis Bacon, "Apophthegms New and Old," and William Roper, *The Mirrour of Vertue*.

MORLA, FRANCESCO DE.
NOTE: the reference, which is in a quotation from Macaulay, derives from Díaz.
REFERRED TO: 528

MORLEY, JOHN. Referred to: 290

The Morning Chronicle. Referred to: 89–91 (*88–90*), 243 (*242*)

The Morning Post. Referred to: *130*

MOSES. Referred to: 499–500

MOSHEIM, JOHANN LOREN VON. *An Ecclesiastical History, Antient and Modern, from the Birth of Christ, to the Beginning of the Present Century: in Which the Rise, Progress, and Variations of Church Power Are Considered in Their Connexion with the State of Learning and Philosophy, and the Political History of Europe during That Period* (in Latin, 1755). Trans. Archibald Maclaine. 2 vols. London: Millar, 1765.
REFERRED TO: 11 (*10*), 555

MOZART, WOLFGANG AMADEUS. Referred to: 149 (*148*), 350

―――― *Le nozze de Figaro.*
NOTE: the reference is to the aria "Dove sono" (III, viii). First performed in England at the King's Theatre, Haymarket, 18 June, 1812; published (libretto by Lorenzo da Ponte) London: Winchester, 1816.
REFERRED TO: 350

MÜLLER, THEODOR ADAM HEINRICH FRIEDRICH VON. See Sarah Austin, *Characteristics . . . .*

MURRAY, GEORGE. "Napier's *Peninsular War,*" *Quarterly Review*, LVI (Apr., and July, 1836), 131–219, and 437–89, and LVII (Dec., 1836), 492–542.
NOTE: *The Wellesley Index*, Vol. II, says that Murray was "assisted by J. W. Croker." Napier replied to the third of these articles; see William Napier, "Reply."
REFERRED TO: *603*

MURRAY, JOHN. Referred to: 231 (*230*)

MUSGRAVE, THOMAS MOORE (or James Musgrave). "Sir R. Phillips on the Office of Sheriff," *Edinburgh Review*, XIII (Oct., 1808), 170–86.
NOTE: for the identification of the author, see *The Wellesley Index*, Vol. I.
REFERRED TO: 297n

NAPIER, CHARLES JAMES. *The Colonies: Treating of Their Value Generally—Of the Ionian Islands in Particular; The Importance of the Latter in War and Commerce—As regards Russian Policy—Their Finances—Why an Expense to Great Britain—Detailed Proofs That They Ought Not to Be So—Turkish Government—Battle of Navarino—Ali Pacha—Sir Thomas Maitland—Strictures on the Administration of Sir Frederick Adam.* London: Boone, 1833.
REFERRED TO: *601*

NAPIER, WILLIAM FRANCIS PATRICK. "The Duke of Wellington," *London and Westminster Review*, VI & XXVIII (Jan., 1838), 367–436.
REFERRED TO: *604*

―――― *History of the War in the Peninsula and in the South of France, from the Year 1807 to the Year 1814.* 6 vols. London: Murray, 1828–40.
REFERRED TO: *603*

———— "Reply to the Third Article in the *Quarterly Review* on Colonel Napier's *History of the Peninsular War*," *London and Westminster Review*, IV & XXVI (Jan., 1837), 541–81.
NOTE: this article did not appear in all copies of the issue; see p. *603*.
REFERRED TO: *603*

NAPOLEON I (of France). Referred to: 63 (*62*), 65 (*64*), 471–2, 490

NAPOLEON III (of France). Referred to: 245

NEAL, JOHN. Referred to: 434–5

———— *Brother Jonathan; or, The New Englanders*. 3 vols. Edinburgh: Blackwood, 1825.
REFERRED TO: 435n

———— *Logan, a Family History*. 4 vols. London: Newman, 1823.
NOTE: 1st ed., 2 vols. (Philadelphia: Carey and Lea, 1822).
REFERRED TO: 435n

———— *Randolph*. 2 vols. [Baltimore?], 1823.
REFERRED TO: 435n

———— *Seventy-six*. 3 vols. London: Whittaker, 1823.
NOTE: 1st ed., 2 vols. (Baltimore: Robinson, 1823).
REFERRED TO: 435n

NECKER, JACQUES. Referred to: *62*

NELSON, HORATIO.
NOTE: the reference is in a quotation from Jeffrey's "Madame de Staël," *q.v.*
REFERRED TO: 317

NEPOS, CORNELIUS. *Excellentium imperatorum vitae*.
NOTE: it is not known which of the many eds. (which have differing titles) Mill read.
REFERRED TO: 13 (*12*), *556–7*

NERO. Referred to: 435, 436

The New Monthly Magazine. Referred to: 382

NEWTON, ISAAC. Referred to: 165, 332

———— *Arithmetica universalis; sive de compositione et resolutione arithmetica liber*. London: Tooke, 1707.
NOTE: it is not known which ed. Mill read.
REFERRED TO: *561*

———— *Philosophiae naturalis principia mathematica*. London: Royal Society, 1686.
NOTE: the copy in SC is the so-called "Jesuit's Edition" (Geneva: Barrillot, 1739–42).
REFERRED TO: *564*

NIEBUHR, BARTHOLD GEORG. Referred to: 526

———— *The History of Rome* (in German, 1811–12). 3 vols. Trans. Julius Charles Hare and Connop Thirlwall (Vols. I and II); William Smith and Leonhard Schmitz (Vol. III). London (Vols. I and II printed Cambridge): Taylor, 1828 (Vol. I); 1832 (Vol. II); Taylor and Walton, 1842 (Vol. III).
NOTE: the references are indirect. A German ed., 3 vols. (Berlin: Reimer, 1827–32—Vol. II is of the 1836 ed.), is in SC, as are the two vols. of lectures, ed. Schmitz (London: Taylor and Walton, 1844), that complete Niebuhr's *History*.
REFERRED TO: 17 (*16*), 526, 531, *584*

PAINE, THOMAS.
NOTE: the reference is in a quotation from John Allen.
REFERRED TO: 293

PAKINGTON, JOHN. Speech on the Representation of the People Bill (1866), *Parliamentary Debates*, 3rd ser., Vol. 183, cols. 1572–90 (31 May, 1866).
NOTE: Mill refers to "some of the Tory leaders," but Pakington (col. 1574) made the remark cited by Mill. See Mill, Speech on the Representation of the People Bill (1866).
REFERRED TO: 277n

PALEY, WILLIAM. Referred to: 209 (*208*)

———— *Natural Theology; or, Evidences of the Existence and Attributes of the Deity, Collected from the Appearances of Nature*. London: Faulder, 1802.
REFERRED TO: *74, 579, 587*

PALGRAVE, FRANCIS. "Goethe's *Life of Himself* (Part I)," *Edinburgh Review*, XXVI (June, 1816), 304–37.
REFERRED TO: 324

PALMERSTON, LORD. See Temple.

PAOLI, PASQUALE. Referred to: 11 (*10*)

PARKER, JOHN WILLIAM. Referred to: 231 (*230*)

The Parliamentary History and Review.
NOTE: as Mill says, this annual continued for only three years (actually, three issues, as the first two sets were both published in 1826, and the final volume in 1828); there were five volumes in all, the first two sets each consisting of one volume of *Parliamentary History*, and one of *Parliamentary Review*, and the last being only *Parliamentary Review* (an arrangement having been made with *Hansard's Debates* to use references to it, instead of publishing a "History"). The first issue is entitled *The Parliamentary History and Review; Containing Reports of the Proceedings of the Two Houses of Parliament during the Session of 1825:—6 Geo. IV. With Critical Remarks on the Principal Measures of the Session*, 2 vols. (London: Longman, Rees, Orme, Brown, and Green, 1826). The second issue has the same publishing data, date, and title, except for the identification of the session as that "*of 1826:—7 Geo. IV.*" The third is entitled *The Parliamentary Review. Session of 1826–7:—7 & 8 Geo. IV* (London: Baldwin and Cradock, 1828).
REFERRED TO: 121–3 (*120–2*), *132*; see also Charles Austin, "Corn Laws"; John Austin, "Joint Stock Companies"; Peregrine Bingham, "Combination and Combination Laws," "County Courts," "Licensing System," and "Prefatory Treatise"; Walter Coulson, "Game Laws" and "Silk Trade"; James Mill, "Summary Review"; and J. S. Mill, "Foreign Dependencies," "Intercourse between the United States and the British Colonies in the West Indies," "Ireland," and "Paper Currency."

The Parliamentary Review. See *The Parliamentary History and Review*.

PASCAL, BLAISE. Referred to: 119 (*118*)

———— *Pensées de Mr. Pascal sur la religion et sur quelques autres sujets, qui ont esté trouvées après sa mort parmy ses papiers*. Ed. Etienne Périer. Paris: Desprez, 1670.
NOTE: *Œuvres*, 5 vols. (Paris: Lefèvre, 1819) is in SC.
REFERRED TO: 423

PAUL (of Samosata). Referred to: 445

PEEL, ROBERT. Referred to: 103 (*102*)

The Penny Magazine. Referred to: 329

PERCY, THOMAS. *Reliques of Ancient English Poetry: Consisting of Old Heroic Ballads, Songs, and Other Pieces of Our Earlier Poets, (Chiefly of the Lyric Kind.) Together with Some Few of Later Date.* 3 vols. London: Dodsley, 1765.
NOTE: the reference is to "The Ancient Ballad of Chevy-Chase" (the first ballad in Percy), Vol. I, pp. 1–17. Mill does not indicate that Macaulay (to whose "lays" he compares "Chevy Chase") himself calls attention to, and even quotes from, this ballad (in Percy's version) in his *Lays*, pp. 42–3.
REFERRED TO: 526

PERICLES. Referred to: 75 (*74*), 587

PERRY, JAMES. Referred to: 91 (*90*)

PESTALOZZI, JOHANN HEINRICH. Referred to: 260

PHAEDRUS. *Fabularum Aesopiarum libri v.* Ed. Peter Burmannus. Utrecht: van der Vater, 1718.
NOTE: this ed. in SC.
REFERRED TO: 15 (*14*), 557

PHIDIAS.
NOTE: the reference is inferential.
REFERRED TO: 333

PHILIP II (of Macedonia). Referred to: 11 (*10*)

PHILLIPPS, SAMUEL MARCH. *A Treatise on the Law of Evidence.* London: Butterworth, 1814.
REFERRED TO: *116*

PHILLIPS, WENDELL. Referred to: 266

PICOT DE LAPEYROUSE, PHILIPPE. *Histoire abrégée des plantes des Pyrénées, et itinéraire des botanistes dans ces montagnes.* Toulouse: Bellegarrigue, 1813.
REFERRED TO: *574*, *587*

PINDAR. *Carmina.* In Πάντα τὰ Πινδάρου σωζόμενα. *Omnia Pindari quae extant. Cum interpretatione latina* (Greek and Latin). 2 vols. (in 1). Glasgow: Foulis, 1744.
NOTE: this ed. in SC. The reference at p. *560* is simply to Mill's reading Pindar.
REFERRED TO: 532, *560*

PINNOCK, WILLIAM. *A Catechism of Sacred Geography: Being a Familiar Description of Such Countries, Cities, and Minor Places, As Are Mentioned in the Holy Scriptures; with the Necessary Historical Elucidations.* London: Whittaker, 1823.
NOTE: the reference is to Pinnock's "Catechisms." Pinnock was the author of numerous catechisms, on a wide variety of subjects, the above being one example.
REFERRED TO: 460

———— *Pinnock's Catechism of Drawing in Which the Essential Rules for Acquiring That Accomplished Art Are Given.* London: Whittaker, 1828.
NOTE: see the preceding entry.
REFERRED TO: 460

PITT, WILLIAM (the younger).
NOTE: the reference is in a quotation from Jeffrey's "Madame de Staël," *q.v.*
REFERRED TO: 317

PLATO.
NOTE: *Platonis et quae vel Platonis esse feruntur vel Platonica solent comitari scripta graece omnia ad codices manuscriptos* (Greek and Latin), ed. Immanuel Bekker, 11 vols. (London: Priestley,

1826), is in SC. The reference at p. 49 (*48*) is generally to Plato's writings; that at p. *68* is to the Dialogues in general (in the equivalent passage in the *Autobiography*, p. 69, the reference is to Plato's "dialectics"); that at p. 115 (*114*) is to his pictures of Socrates; that at p. 207 (*206*) is to Mill's abstracts of some of Plato's dialogues; that at p. 438 is in a quotation from Gibbon's rendering of Trebellius Pollio.
REFERRED TO: 25 (*24*), *24n*, 49 (*48*), 67 (*66*), 69 (*68*), 115 (*114*), 153 (*152*), 207 (*206*), 336, 337, 370, 438

——— *Apology*. In Bekker ed., Vol. II, pp. 273–366.
REFERRED TO: 9 (*8*), *554*

——— *Cratylus*. In Bekker ed., Vol. IV, pp. 185–328.
REFERRED TO: 9 (*8*), *554*

——— *Crito*. In Bekker ed., Vol. II, pp. 367–422.
REFERRED TO: 9 (*8*), *554*

——— *Euthyphron*. In Bekker ed., Vol. II, pp. 93–167.
REFERRED TO: 9 (*8*), *553–4*

——— *Gorgias*. In Bekker ed., Vol. III, pp. 127–375.
REFERRED TO: 25 (*24*), *568*

——— *Phaedo*. In Bekker ed., Vol. V, pp. 115–411.
REFERRED TO: 9 (*8*), *554*

——— *Protagoras*. In Bekker ed., Vol. I, pp. 249–372.
REFERRED TO: 25 (*24*), *568*

——— *Republic* (Greek and English). Trans. Paul Shorey. 2 vols. London: Heinemann; Cambridge, Mass.: Harvard University Press, 1946.
NOTE: this ed. cited for ease of reference. In Bekker ed., Vol. VI, p. 251–Vol. VII, p. 229.
REFERRED TO: 25 (*24*), 321, 373, *568, 585*

——— *Theaetetus*. In Bekker ed., Vol. III, pp. 377–568.
REFERRED TO: 9 (*8*), *554*

PLAYFAIR, JOHN. *Elements of Geometry: Containing the First Six Books of Euclid, with Two Books on the Geometry of Solids. To Which Are Added, Elements of Plane and Spherical Trigonometry*. Edinburgh: Bell and Bradfute; London: Robinson, 1795.
REFERRED TO: *559, 562*

PLINY (the Elder). *Natural History* (Latin and English). Trans. Harris Rackham, *et al.* 10 vols. London: Heinemann; Cambridge, Mass.: Harvard University Press, 1938–62.
NOTE: this ed. used for ease of reference.
QUOTED: 437
437.10–11 *velut terris exempta . . . naturâ*] [*paragraph*] Palmyra urbs nobilis situ, divitiis soli et aquis amoenis, vasto undique ambitu harenis includit agros, ac velut terris exempta . . . natura, privata sorte inter duo imperia summa Romanorum Parthorumque, et prima in discordia semper utrimque cura. (II, 286–8; V, xxxi, 88)

PLUTARCH. *Lives* (Greek and English). Trans. Bernadotte Perrin. 11 vols. London: Heinemann; Cambridge, Mass.: Harvard University Press, 1914–26.
NOTE: this ed. cited for ease of reference. The fable of the "belly and the members," which was borrowed from Plutarch by Shakespeare (*Coriolanus*, I, i, 96–163), occurs in the life of Caius Marcius Coriolanus (Vol. IV, pp. 118–218); it is also found in Aesop, *q.v.* The reference at p. 386 is in a quotation from Adams.
REFERRED TO: 115 (*114*), 386

—— *"Περὶ παίδων ἀγωγῆς"* ("On the Education of Children").
NOTE: as it is not known which ed. Mill used, none is cited.
REFERRED TO: *559*

—— *Plutarch's Lives, Translated from the Original Greek, with Notes Critical and Historical, and a New Life of Plutarch*. Trans. and ed. John and William Langhorne. 6 vols. London: Dilly, 1770.
NOTE: see also Plutarch, *Lives*.
REFERRED TO: 11 (*10*), *555*

POLE, THOMAS. *Observations Relative to Infant Schools, Designed to Point Out Their Usefulness to the Children of the Poor, to Their Parents, and to Society at Large. Calculated to Assist Those Who May Benevolently Incline to Establish Such Schools*. Bristol: Macdowall, 1823.
NOTE: the quotation derives from Brougham's quotation of Pole in his "Early Moral Education," *q.v.*
QUOTED: 307n

POLLIO, TREBELLIUS. *The Thirty Pretenders*. In *Scriptores historiae augustae* (Latin and English). Trans. David Magie. 3 vols. London: Heinemann; New York: Putnam's Sons, 1922–32, Vol. III, pp. 64–151.
NOTE: this ed. cited for ease of reference; it is not known which ed. Mill used. The quotations occur in Mill's interpolations in Gibbon's version. Zenobia is described in Cap. xxx (pp. 134–43 in Magie's trans.).
QUOTED: 438, 439
438.14–15   *ut . . . dentes*] tantus candor in dentibus ut . . . dentes. (138)
438.15–16   *oculis . . . ingentibus, . . . incredibilis*] fuit vultu subaquilo, fusci coloris, oculis . . . vigentibus [ingentibus *given as variant*] . . . incredibilis. (138)
439.3–5   "the severity," . . . "of . . . piety."] [*translated from:*] severitas, ubi necessitas postulabat, tyrannorum, bonorum principum clementia, ubi pietas requirebat. (138) [*rendered by Magie,* "Her sternness, when necessity demanded, was that of a tyrant, her clemency, when her sense of right called for it, that of a good emperor." (139)]
439.6   "larga prudenter,"] larga prudenter, conservatrix thesaurorum ultra femineum modum. (138)

POLYBIUS. *Histories* (Greek and English). Trans. W. R. Paton. 6 vols. London: Heinemann; Cambridge, Mass.: Harvard University Press, 1960.
NOTE: this ed. cited for ease of reference; it is not known which ed. Mill read.
REFERRED TO: 15 (*14*), *561*

POMPIGNAN, JEAN JACQUES LEFRANC, MARQUIS DE.
NOTE: the reference is to him as "Voltaire's enemy."
REFERRED TO: 59 (*58*)

POMPIGNAN, JEAN LOUIS GEORGES MARIE LEFRANC, MARQUIS DE.
NOTE: the reference is to "a descendant" (in fact, the son) of Voltaire's enemy.
REFERRED TO: 59 (*58*)

POPE, ALEXANDER. *An Essay on Man* (1733–34). In *The Works of Alexander Pope: with Notes and Illustrations by Joseph Warton and Others*. Ed. Joseph Warton, *et al.* 9 vols. and Supplementary Vol. London: Priestley, 1822 (Supp. Vol., London: Hearne, 1825), Vol. III, pp. 1–160.
NOTE: in SC.
REFERRED TO: 115 (*114*)

—— *The Iliad of Homer*. See Homer, *Homer's Iliad*, trans. Pope.

POTTER, THOMAS BAYLEY. Referred to: 276

PRAED, WINTHROP MACKWORTH. Referred to: 131 (*130*)

PRESCOTT, WILLIAM GEORGE.
NOTE: the reference at p. 81 (*80*) is to one of the original members of the Utilitarian Society; Prescott is so identified at 123 (*122*).
REFERRED TO: 81 (*80*), 123 (*122*), 125 (*124*)

PRIESTLEY, JOSEPH. *Hartley's Theory of the Human Mind, on the Principle of the Association of Ideas; with Essays Relating to the Subject of It*. London: Johnson, 1775.
REFERRED TO: 125–7 (*124–6*)

PROVENÇAL, JEAN MICHEL. Referred to: 59 (*58*)

PULLING, ALEXANDER. Referred to: 283

PURCHAS, SAMUEL. See John Hamilton Moore.

The Quarterly Review.
NOTE: see also James Mill's "*Quarterly Review*" above. The reference at p. *590* is to "either of our principal Reviews" (in 1833), i.e., the *Quarterly* and the *Edinburgh*.
REFERRED TO: 93 (*92*), 97 (*96*), 215 (*214*), 293, 309, 398, *590*

QUINTILIAN (Marcus Fabius Quintilianus). *De institutione oratoria libri duodecim*.
NOTE: as the references are general, and it is not known which ed. Mill used, none is cited.
REFERRED TO: *14n*, 25 (*24*), 421, *566*

RACINE, JEAN.
NOTE: the reference at p. *570* is to Mill's reading three plays by Racine.
REFERRED TO: 487, 500, *570*

———— *Athalie, tragédie tirée de l'écriture sainte*. Paris: Thierry, 1691.
NOTE: *Oeuvres*, ed. I. L. Geoffroy, 7 vols. (Paris: Le Normant, 1808), is in SC; in that ed. *Athalie* appears in Vol. V, pp. 193–389.
REFERRED TO: 500

———— *Esther, tragédie tirée de l'écriture sainte*. Paris: Thierry, 1689.
NOTE: in *Oeuvres* (see preceding entry), Vol. V, pp. 1–169.
REFERRED TO: 500

RAPHAEL.
NOTE: full name Raphael Sanzio. The reference at p. 333 is to Raphael's *Transfiguration*.
REFERRED TO: 333, 352

RAYNOUARD, FRANÇOIS.
NOTE: the reference derives from Chenevix, "English and French Literature," *q.v.*
REFERRED TO: 310

REGNARD, JEAN FRANÇOIS.
NOTE: the reference is to an unidentified comedy by Regnard.
REFERRED TO: *571*

REID, THOMAS.
NOTE: the reference at p. 71 (*70*) is to Mill's general reading; that at p. 269 is to Hamilton's edition of Reid, *q.v.*; that at p. *579* is to Mill's early reading of Reid.
REFERRED TO: 71 (*70*), 269, *579*

REMBRANDT.
NOTE: full name Rembrandt Harmens van Rijn. The reference is to his *Peasant Girl*.
REFERRED TO: 352n

The Retrospective Review. Referred to: *94n*

RICARDO, DAVID.
NOTE: one reference at p. 103 (*102*) is a general one to Ricardo's economic writings; that at p. *128* is to the "Ricardo Lectures" delivered by McCulloch.
REFERRED TO: 31 (*30*), 55 (*54*), 75 (*74*), 89 (*88*), 93 (*92*), 103 (*102*), *128*, 538, *614*

———— *The High Price of Bullion, a Proof of the Depreciation of Bank Notes.* London: Murray, 1810.
REFERRED TO: 31 (*30*), *569*

———— *On the Principles of Political Economy and Taxation.* London: Murray, 1817.
REFERRED TO: 31 (*30*), 123 (*122*), *568*, *585*

———— *Reply to Mr. Bosanquet's Practical Observations on the Report of the Bullion Committee.* London: Murray, 1811.
REFERRED TO: 31 (*30*), *569*

RICHELIEU, ARMAND JEAN DU PLESSIS, CARDINAL DE. Referred to: 472–3, 473, 483, 484

ROBERTSON, JOHN. Referred to: 215 (*214*)

———— "Irish Humour and Pathos," *London and Westminster Review*, XXXII (Apr., 1839), 405–25.
NOTE: *The Wellesley Index*, Vol. III, attributes the article "probably" to Robertson.
REFERRED TO: *606*

———— "Miss Martineau's Western Travel," *London and Westminster Review,* VI & XXVIII (Jan., 1838), 470–502.
NOTE: see the evidence for Robertson's authorship in *The Wellesley Index*, Vol. III, p. 590, where the resultant editorial note (pp. *604–5*) is ascribed to Mill.
REFERRED TO: *605*

ROBERTSON, WILLIAM. *The History of America with a Disquisition on Ancient India* (1777). In *Works.* 6 vols. London: Longman, Brown, Green, and Longmans, 1851, Vols. V–VI.
NOTE: this ed. in SC. The reference is to Mill's early reading of "Robertson's histories"; see also Robertson, *History of the Reign of Charles V*, and *History of Scotland.*
REFERRED TO: 11 (*10*), *554*

———— *The History of Scotland under Mary and James VI* (1759). *Ibid.*, Vols. I–II.
NOTE: see the preceding entry.
REFERRED TO: 11 (*10*), *554*

———— *The History of the Reign of the Emperor Charles V* (1769). *Ibid.*, Vols. III–IV.
NOTE: see William Robertson, *History of America*, above.
REFERRED TO: 11 (*10*), *554*

ROBESPIERRE, MAXIMILIEN FRANÇOIS MARIE ISIDORE DE. Referred to: 495

ROBISON, JOHN. *Elements of Mechanical Philosophy, Being the Substance of a Course of Lectures on That Science.* Vol. I: *Including Dynamics and Astronomy.* [No more published.] Edinburgh: Constable; London: Cadell and Davies, *et al.*, 1804.
REFERRED TO: *564*

ROEBUCK, HENRIETTA (née Falconer).
NOTE: the reference is to Roebuck's having married.
REFERRED TO: *158*

ROEBUCK, JOHN ARTHUR.
NOTE: the reference at p. 99 (*98*) is to Roebuck's early articles in the *Westminster Review*; for a list, see *The Wellesley Index*, Vol. III.
REFERRED TO: 83 (*82*), 99 (*98*), 125 (*124*), 127 (*126*), 129 (*128*), 131 (*130*), 133 (*132*), 153–9 (*152–8*), *178n*, 203 (*202*), 206

———— Resolution on National Education, *Parliamentary Debates*, 3rd ser., Vol. 20, cols. 139–66 (30 July, 1833).
NOTE: Roebuck's motion occurred thirteen years after Brougham's (*q.v.*) not twelve as is indicated by Mill.
REFERRED TO: 203 (*158*)

———— Speech against the Puritanical Observance of Sunday, *Parliamentary Debates*, 3rd ser., Vol. 38, cols. 1229–34 (7 June, 1837).
NOTE: see also "A Bill to Promote the Observance of the Lord's Day" (4 May, 1837).
REFERRED TO: *158*

ROEBUCK, ZIPPORAH (née Tickell). Referred to: *154*

ROLAND DE LA PLATIÈRE, MARIE JEANNE PHLIPON. *Appel à l'impartiale postérité.* Ed. Louis Augustin Guillaume Bosc. 4 pts. Paris: Louvet, 1795.
NOTE: the passage, from "Notices historiques, sur la révolution," was later incorporated in other collections, for example in *Oeuvres*, ed. L. A. Champagneux, 3 vols. (Paris: Bidault, 1800), Vol. II, p. 64. The quotation is indirect.
QUOTED: 346
346.15 know man but not men.] Savant publiciste, livré dès sa jeunesse à l'étude des rapports sociaux et des moyens de bonheur pour l'espèce humaine, il [Brissot] juge bien l'homme et ne connoît pas du tout les hommes. (I, 36)

ROLLIN, CHARLES. *The Ancient History of the Egyptians, Carthaginians, Assyrians, Babylonians, Medes and Persians, Macedonians, and Grecians* (in French, 1730–38). Trans. Francis Roffen. 8 vols. Edinburgh: Fairbairn; Glasgow: Robertson, *et al.*; London: Lackington, *et al.*, 1803.
NOTE: it is not known which ed. Mill used. He says he had read "the last two or three volumes . . . beginning with Philip of Macedon"; it seems more likely, therefore, that he used an 8-vol. ed., in which Vol. V begins with Philip (implying that he read four vols.), than a 10-vol. ed. (such as the 2nd., London: Knapton, 1738–40), where Vol. VI begins with Philip (in which case he would have read five vols.).
REFERRED TO: 11 (*10*), 552, 555

ROMILLY, EDWARD. Referred to: 203 (*202*)

ROMILLY, JOHN.
NOTE: the reference at p. 121 (*120*) is to Romilly's authorship of (unidentified) articles in the *Parliamentary History and Review*.
REFERRED TO: 79, 105 (*104*), 121 (*120*), 131 (*130*), 203 (*202*)

ROMILLY, SAMUEL. Referred to: 105 (*104*)

ROPER, WILLIAM. *The Mirrour of Vertue in Worldly Greatness; or, The Life of Syr Thomas More.* Paris: [St. Omer, English College Press,] 1626.
NOTE: the reference is inferential.
REFERRED TO: 266n–7n

ROSA, SALVATOR. Referred to: 353n

ROSSINI, GIOACCHINO ANTONIO. Referred to: 351

———— *La gazza ladra.*
NOTE: the reference is to the duet "Ebben, per mia memoria" (II, vi; the scene varies in different

SCHILLER, JOHANN CHRISTOPH FRIEDRICH VON. Referred to: 163 (*162*)

SCHRÖDER-DEVRIENT, WILHELMINE. Referred to: 351

SCOTT, JOHN (Lord Eldon). Referred to: 298

SCOTT, WALTER.
NOTE: the reference at p. 19 (*18*) is to James Mill's recommendation of Scott's metrical romances, such as *The Lay of the Last Minstrel* (1805), *Marmion* (1808), *The Lady of the Lake* (1810), etc.; that at pp. 19–21 (*18–20*) is to the "songs" in these romances.
REFERRED TO: 19 (*18*), 19–21 (*18–20*), 151, 320, 472, 481, 525, 526, *565*

———— "*Amadis de Gaul*, [translations] by Southey and by Rose," *Edinburgh Review*, III (Oct., 1803), 109–36.
QUOTED: 309
309.17 "a vicious] Tressan, in particular, whose talents and taste made it totally inexcuseable, dwells with infinitely higher gust upon the gallantries of Don Galaor, than upon the Love of Amadis; and describes them with that vicious (125)
309.18 obscenity" is described as "peculiarly . . . literature."] obscenity, which Mr Southey so justly reprobates, as 'peculiarly . . . Literature.' (125)

———— *The Life of Napoleon Buonaparte, Emperor of the French, with a Preliminary View of the French Revolution.* 9 vols. Edinburgh: Cadell; London: Longman, Rees, Orme, Brown, and Green, 1827.
REFERRED TO: 99n, 135 (*134*)

———— *Marmion, a Tale of Flodden Field.* Edinburgh: Constable, 1808.
REFERRED TO: 526

SEDGWICK, ADAM. *A Discourse on the Studies of the University* (1833). 3rd ed. London: Parker, 1834.
NOTE: the 3rd ed. is reviewed by Mill in "Sedgwick's *Discourse*," *q.v.*
REFERRED TO: 209 (*208*)

SÉGUR, LOUIS PHILIPPE, COMTE DE.
NOTE: the reference derives from Chenevix, "English and French Literature," *q.v.*
REFERRED TO: 310

SEMIRAMIS (of Assyria).
NOTE: the reference is in a quotation from Gibbon.
REFERRED TO: 438

SEWEL, WILLEM. *The History of the Rise, Increase, and Progress of the Christian People Called Quakers, . . . Written Originally in Low-Dutch by W. Sewel, and by Himself Translated into English.* London: Assigns of J. Sowle, 1722.
NOTE: Mill spells the name "Sewell."
REFERRED TO: 11 (*10*), 555

SHAEN, WILLIAM. Referred to: 282n

SHAKESPEARE, WILLIAM.
NOTE: the reference at p. 19 (*18*) is to Mill's early reading of Shakespeare's plays; that at p. 312 is in a quotation from Hazlitt.
REFERRED TO: 19 (*18*), 19n, *26*, 309, 312, 319–20, 346–7, *564*

———— *Coriolanus*.
NOTE: no ed. cited, as the reference (which is in a quotation from Adams) is probably to Plutarch, *Lives, q.v.*, or Aesop, *q.v.*
REFERRED TO: 386

———— *Julius Caesar.*
NOTE: as the reference is inferential, no ed. is cited.
REFERRED TO: 213 (*212*)

———— *King Henry the Fourth.*
NOTE: as the reference is general, no ed. is cited.
REFERRED TO: 435

———— *King John.*
NOTE: as the reference is general, no ed. is cited.
REFERRED TO: 435

———— *Macbeth.*
NOTE: the reference is to Macbeth's plea to the physician (V, iii, 40–5).
REFERRED TO: 139 (*138*)

———— *Measure for Measure.*
NOTE: the reference, which derives from Tennyson's "Mariana," is to III, i, where the Duke says: "I will presently to St. Luke's; there, at the moated grange, resides this dejected Mariana." (Also the opening location, IV, i, reads, "The moated Grange at St. Luke's.")
REFERRED TO: 399, 401

———— *Othello.*
NOTE: the references being general, no ed. is cited. The reference at p. 473 is simply to Iago as a type; that at p. 498 is to Vigny's *Le more de Venise* as a close translation of *Othello*; the quotation is collated with the version in Horace H. Furness's variorum ed. The words are Desdemona's, in reply to Iago.
QUOTED: 408n
REFERRED TO: 473, 498
408n.1–2 "lame and impotent conclusion,"] Oh most lame and impotent conclusion. (II, i, 161)

———— *The Second Part of Henry the Fourth.* In *The Riverside Shakespeare.* Ed. G. Blakemore Evans. Boston: Houghton Mifflin, 1974, pp. 886–923.
NOTE: the quotation is indirect. This ed. cited for ease of reference.
QUOTED: 434
434.6 appliances and means] Canst thou, O partial sleep, give [then] repose / To the wet [sea-boy] in an hour so rude, / And in the calmest and most stillest night, / With all appliances and means to boot, / Deny it to a king? (III, i, 26–30)

SHAPUR (Sapor) I (of Persia).
NOTE: the reference at p. 438 is in a quotation from Gibbon; Shapur, as ruler of Persia, is also referred to in Ware's fiction as "The Great King."
REFERRED TO: 438, 439

SHEE, WILLIAM. Referred to: 133 (*132*)

SHELLEY, PERCY BYSSHE. Referred to: 195 (*194*), 358–60, 363, 364, 413–14, 467, 497, *619*, *623*

———— *The Cenci, a Tragedy.* London: Ollier, 1819.
REFERRED TO: 363

———— *Epipsychidion: Verses Addressed to the Noble and Unfortunate Lady Emilia V——Now Imprisoned in the Convent of ——.* London: Ollier, 1821.
QUOTED: 497

SHERIDAN, ELIABETH ANN (née Linley). Referred to: *154*

SIMOND, LOUIS. "France," *Edinburgh Review*, XXXIV (Aug., 1820), 1–39.
QUOTED: 301, 302

301.14   "wherever] Wherever (27)
301.15   law] laws (28)
301.16   follow."] follow; yet an equal division of the land would be impossible in practice, if it were only from the smallness of the shares into which it would be split: and from this, as well as other causes, the property of the soil will ultimately fall into the hands of a despotic administrator, who distributes the proceeds amongst the needy multitude. (28)
301.23   "France] [*paragraph*] With all this, France (18)
301.25   Revolution. But] Revolution.—A reform of criminal jurisprudence had begun; torture was abolished; the administration of prisons and hospitals was greatly improved; provincial administrations, the most beneficial, perhaps, of any improvement in its consequences, had been tried; *servage* of all kinds, and the *corvées*, were at an end; several of the grievances of the Protestants had been removed, and the exercise of their religion allowed. The scandalous fortunes made by favourite Ministers in former reigns, were unknown under Louis XVI, and the general aspect of the country was that of a progress both towards happiness and freedom: But (18)
302.3–4   "the republican principle predominates in the French monarchy;"] Now it appears to us that the republican principle predominates at present in the French monarchy; and the transition from a republic to an arbitrary government is easier there than anywhere else, from the military bias of the nation—and because their present love for *equality* is not accompanied with an equal attachment to, or any fixed principles of *civil liberty*. (28–9)
302.9   [*paragraph*] Foreigners] [*no paragraph*] Foreigners (33)
302.9   their] our (33)
302.16   [*paragraph*] We] [*no paragraph*] We (34)

SIMPSON, JOHN.
NOTE: the reference is to Roebuck's stepfather.
REFERRED TO: *154*

SIMPSON, JOHN. *Select Exercises for Young Proficients in the Mathematicks*. London: Nourse, 1752.
REFERRED TO: *568*

SIMPSON, THOMAS. *The Doctrine and Applications of Fluxions. Containing (Besides What Is Common on the Subject) a Number of New Improvements in the Theory. And the Solution of a Variety of New, and Very Interesting, Problems in Different Branches of the Mathematicks*. 2pts. London: Nourse, 1750.
REFERRED TO: *564*

———— *A Treatise of Algebra. Wherein the Principles Are Demonstrated, and Applied in Many Useful and Interesting Enquiries, and in the Resolution of a Great Variety of Problems of Different Kinds. To Which Is Added, the Geometrical Construction of a Great Number of Linear and Plane Problems, with the Method of Resolving the Same Numerically*. London: Nourse, 1745.
REFERRED TO: *562*

SIMSON, ROBERT. *Sectionum conicarum libri v*. Edinburgh: Ruddiman, 1735.
REFERRED TO: *561*

SISMONDI, JEAN CHARLES LÉONARD SIMONDE DE. *Histoire des Français*. 31 vols. Paris: Treuttel and Würtz, 1821–44.
REFERRED TO: 99n

SLACK, HENRY JAMES. Referred to: 282n

SLIDELL, JOHN.
NOTE: the reference is to the seizure of Confederate envoys, of whom Slidell was one.
REFERRED TO: 267–8

SOCRATES. Referred to: 49 (*48*), 115 (*114*)

SOLOMON.
NOTE: the reference at p. 421 is to Solomon as the author of Proverbs; that at p. 428 is in a quotation from Helps.
REFERRED TO: 421, 428, 437

SOPHOCLES. Referred to: 532

——— *Ajax.*
REFERRED TO: 15 (*14*), *561*

——— *Electra.*
REFERRED TO: 15 (*14*), *558*

——— *Philoctetes.*
REFERRED TO: 15 (*14*), *561*

SOUTHERN, HENRY.
NOTE: the references are to Southern as one of the two original editors of the *Westminster Review*.
REFERRED TO: 95–7 (*94–6*), 135 (*134*)

SOUTHEY, ROBERT. Referred to: 303, 487

——— *The Book of the Church.* 2 vols. London: Murray, 1824.
NOTE: the reference is to James Mill's "Robert Southey's *Book of the Church*," *q.v.*
REFERRED TO: 99 (*98*)

——— *The Curse of Kehama.* London: Longman, Hurst, Rees, Orme, and Brown, 1810.
NOTE: the reference, in a quotation from Helps, is to Ladurlad, a character in the above.
REFERRED TO: 427

——— *Thalaba the Destroyer.* 2 vols. London: Longman and Rees, 1801.
NOTE: the reference derives from Jeffrey's "Southey's *Thalaba*," *q.v.*
REFERRED TO: 303

SPENCE, JOSEPH ("Sir Harry Beaumont"). *Moralities; or, Essays, Letters, Fables, and Translations.* London: Dodsley, 1753.
NOTE: the reference (to "Fable X. The Party-Colour'd Shield," pp. 99–102) is inferential; this gives the substance of Mill's account, though he has the sides of the shield white and black rather than gold and silver (in the "Fable," however, one knight is in white armour, the other in black). The knights battle to exhaustion because they disagree about the colour of the shield; they are succoured and admonished by a Druid, whose moral closes the fable: "Permit me therefore to entreat you . . . never to enter into any Dispute for the future, till you have fairly consider'd each Side of the Question" (p. 102).
REFERRED TO: 171 (*170*)

SPENCE, THOMAS.
NOTE: the reference is to Spenceanism.
REFERRED TO: 387

SPENCER, LAVINIA (Lady; née Bingham). Referred to: *556*

SPENSER, EDMUND. *The Faerie Queene* (1590–96). In *Works.* Ed. Henry John Todd. 8 vols. London: Rivington, *et al.*, 1805, Vol. II, p. 1–Vol. VII, p. 249.
NOTE: this ed. in SC. The reference is initially to James Mill's valuing Spenser.
REFERRED TO: 19 (*18*), *565*

STAËL-HOLSTEIN, ANNE LOUISE GERMAINE NECKER, BARONNE DE.
REFERRED TO: 312, 487

————— *De l'Allemagne*. 3 vols. Paris: Nicolle, 1810.
REFERRED TO: 311n

————— *De la littérature considérée dans ses rapports avec les institutions sociales* (1800). 2nd ed. 2 vols. Paris and London: Colburn, 1812.
NOTE: the reference derives from Jeffrey's "Madame de Staël—sur la littérature," *q.v.*
REFERRED TO: 316n

STAHL, GEORG ERNST. *Fundamenta chymiae dogmaticae et experimentalis*. 3 pts. Nuremberg: Endter, 1723–32.
NOTE: the reference is in a quotation from Brougham's "Dr. Black's *Lectures*," *q.v.*
REFERRED TO: 309

STANLEY, EDWARD GEORGE GEOFFREY SMITH (14th Earl of Derby). Referred to: 261, 279

STANLEY, EDWARD HENRY (15th Earl of Derby). Referred to: 249

STARKIE, THOMAS. *A Practical Treatise of the Law of Evidence*. 3 vols. London: Clarke, 1824.
REFERRED TO: *116*

STEPHEN (of England).
NOTE: the reference is in a quotation from Macaulay.
REFERRED TO: 527

STERLING, JOHN.
NOTE: the reference at p. 215 (*214*) is to Sterling's contributions to the *London and Westminster Review*, all of which are listed below.
REFERRED TO: 133, 153, 159 (*158*), 161–3 (*160–2*), *169n*, 215 (*214*)

————— "Abelard to Heloïse," *London and Westminster Review*, XXXII (Dec., 1838), 203.
NOTE: the reference is actually a brief introduction to the poem.
REFERRED TO: *605–6*

————— "Carlyle's Works," *London and Westminster Review*, XXXIII (Oct., 1839), 1–68.
REFERRED TO: *607*

————— *Essays and Tales*. See Julius Charles Hare.

————— "Montaigne and His Writings," *London and Westminster Review*, VII & XXIX (Aug, 1838), 321–52.
NOTE: the references are to Sterling as a valued contributor to the *London and Westminster Review*.
REFERRED TO: *606, 607*

————— "Simonides," *London and Westminster Review*, XXXII (Dec., 1838), 99–136.
NOTE: the reference is to Sterling's contributions to the *London and Westminster Review*.
REFERRED TO: *606*

STERNE, LAURENCE. *A Sentimental Journey through France and Italy*. 2 vols. London: Becket and De Hondt, 1768.
NOTE: the reference is to Sterne's character Maria, who appears also in Bk. VII of Sterne's *Tristram Shandy*.
REFERRED TO: 490–1

STEWART, DUGALD.
NOTE: the reference at p. 71 (*70*) is to Mill's reading of Stewart, by which he almost certainly means his *Elements*, *q.v.*; that at p. *579* is to his early reading of Stewart.
REFERRED TO: 71 (*70*), *579*

————— *Elements of the Philosophy of the Human Mind*. 3 vols. Vol. I, London: Strahan and

Cadell; Edinburgh: Creech, 1792. Vol. II, Edinburgh: Constable; London: Cadell and Davies, 1814. Vol. III, London: Murray, 1827.

NOTE: the reference is generally to "the chapters on Reasoning in the second volume"; in fact all the chapters in that volume are on reasoning.

REFERRED TO: 189–91 (*188–90*)

STEWART, MATTHEW. *Propositiones geometricae, more veterum demonstratae, ad geometricum antiquam illustrandam et promovendam idoneae.* London: Millar, *et al.*; Edinburgh: Sands, *et al.*, 1763.

REFERRED TO: 562

STRUTT, EDWARD.

NOTE: the reference at p. 121 (*120*) is to Strutt's (unidentified) articles in the *Parliamentary History and Review*.

REFERRED TO: 79 (*78*), 105 (*104*), 121 (*120*), 203 (*202*)

STUART, JANE. Referred to: 7 (*6*)

STUART, JOHN. Referred to: 5–7 (*4–6*)

SUE, EUGÈNE.

NOTE: the reference is to Sue's early novels, which include *Kernock le pirate* (1830), *Atar-Gull* (1831), *La salamandre* (2 vols., 1832), and *La coucaratcha* (4 vols., 1832–34).

REFERRED TO: 475

SWIFT, JONATHAN. *Gulliver's Travels* (1726). In *The Works of Jonathan Swift, D.D., Dean of St. Patrick's, Dublin: Containing Additional Letters, Tracts, and Poems, Not Hitherto Published; with Notes and a Life of the Author.* Ed. Walter Scott. 19 vols. Edinburgh: Constable; London: White, *et al.*; Dublin: Cumming, 1814, Vol. XII, pp. 1–382.

NOTE: this ed. in SC.

REFERRED TO: 149 (*148*)

SYDENHAM, LORD. See Charles Edward Poulett Thomson.

TACITUS, CORNELIUS.

NOTE: the references at pp. 26, 584, 585 are to Mill's writing two tragedies based on Tacitus.

REFERRED TO: *14*, 25 (*24*), *26*, 532, *566*, *584*, *585*

——— *Agricola.* In *Dialogus, Agricola, Germania* (Latin and English). Trans. William Peterson. London: Heinemann; New York: Macmillan, 1914, pp. 168–252.

NOTE: this ed. cited for ease of reference.

REFERRED TO: 532

Tait's Edinburgh Magazine. Referred to: 191 (*190*)

TALFOURD, THOMAS NOON. "Hazlitt's *Lectures on the Drama*," *Edinburgh Review*, XXXIV (Nov., 1820), 438–49.

REFERRED TO: 311n

The Tatler. Referred to: 381, 382

TAYLOR, DAVID (grandfather of John Taylor). Referred to: 193 (*192*)

TAYLOR, HARRIET. See Harriet Taylor Mill.

TAYLOR, HELEN (daughter of Harriet and John Taylor).

NOTE: the references at pp. 286–7, 286n are to her part in Mill's correspondence; that at p. 290 to her

fairest / Or boldest since, but lightly weighs / With thee unto the love thou bearest / The firstborn of thy genius. ("Ode to Memory," 62–3)

TERENCE (Publius Terentius Afer). *Publii Terentii Afri comoediae*. Birmingham: Baskerville, 1772.
NOTE: this ed. in SC.
REFERRED TO: 15 (*14*), 557

TERNAUX, GUILLAUME LOUIS, BARON. Referred to: 62

TETRICUS I (of Gaul). Referred to: 457

THEOCRITUS. In Θεοκρίτου, Μόσχου, Βίωνος, Σιμμίου τὰ εὑρισκόμενα. *Theocriti, Moschi, Bionis, Simmii quae extant* (Greek and Latin). Ed. D. Heincius. Heidelberg: Commelinian, 1604.
NOTE: this ed. formerly in SC, as was *Idyllia ex recensione Valkenaerii cum scholiis selectis scholarum in usum edita* (Greek), ed. F. C. W. Jacobs (Gotha: Ettinger, 1789).
REFERRED TO: 15 (*14*), 560

THIRLWALL, CONNOP. Referred to: 129 (*128*), 131 (*130*)

THOMAS, ANTOINE LÉONARD. "De Mascaron et de Bossuet." Chap. xxxi of *Essai sur les éloges; ou, Histoire de la littérature et de l'éloquence, appliquées à ce genre d'ouvrage*. In *Oeuvres*. 4 vols. Paris: Moutard, 1773, Vols. I–II.
REFERRED TO: 573

THOMPSON, THOMAS PERRONET. Referred to: 135 (*134*), 207 (*206*)

———— "*Edinburgh Review* and the 'Greatest Happiness Principle,'" *Westminster Review*, XI (Oct., 1829), 526–36.
NOTE: see also Thompson's second article of the same title, and his article with Bentham, "'Greatest Happiness' Principle." Together, these three articles represented the *Westminster*'s contribution to the controversy set off by Macaulay's "Mill's *Essay on Government*," *q.v.*
REFERRED TO: 165 (*164*)

———— "*Edinburgh Review* and the 'Greatest Happiness Principle,'" *Westminster Review*, XII (Jan., 1830), 246–62.
NOTE: see the preceding entry.
REFERRED TO: 165 (*164*)

———— and Jeremy Bentham. "'Greatest Happiness' Principle," *Westminster Review*, XI (July, 1829), 254–68.
NOTE: see the preceding two entries. Macaulay replied to this article in "Utilitarian Theory of Government and the 'Greatest Happiness Principle,'" *q.v.*
REFERRED TO: 165 (*164*)

THOMPSON, WILLIAM. Referred to: 129 (*128*)

———— *Appeal of One Half the Human Race, Women, against the Pretensions of the Other Half, Men, to Retain Them in Political, and Thence in Civil and Domestic Slavery*. London: Longman, Hurst, Rees, Orme, Brown, and Green, 1825.
REFERRED TO: 129 (*128*)

———— *An Inquiry into the Principles of the Distribution of Wealth Most Conducive to Human Happiness*. London: Longman, Hurst, Rees, Orme, Brown, and Green, 1824.
REFERRED TO: 129 (*128*)

THOMSON, CHARLES EDWARD POULETT (Lord Sydenham). Referred to: 131 (*130*)

TOOKE, WILLIAM EYTON.
NOTE: the reference at p. 99 (*98*) is to Tooke's early articles in the *Westminster Review*; for a list, see *The Wellesley Index*, Vol. III.
REFERRED TO: 83 (*82*), 99 (*98*), 105 (*104*), 161 (*160*)

TORRENS, ROBERT. "Exchangeable Value," *Traveller*, 7 Dec., 1822, p. 3.
NOTE: this article is a reply to Mill's first publication, "Exchangeable Value," *q.v.*; Mill responded with a second letter, to which Torrens appended a final reply. See also the next entry.
REFERRED TO: 89 (*88*)

———— "Political Economy Club," *Traveller*, 2 Dec., 1822, p. 3.
NOTE: the reference is to Torrens's article criticizing Ricardo and James Mill, which led to Mill's first publication, "Exchangeable Value," *q.v.*
REFERRED TO: 89 (*88*)

TOULONGEON, FRANÇOIS EMMANUEL. *Histoire de France, depuis la révolution de 1789, écrite d'après les mémoires et manuscrits contemporains, recueillis dans les dépôts civils et militaires*. 4 vols. Paris: Treuttel and Würtz, 1801–10.
NOTE: the reference is to "a history of the French Revolution" read by Mill in the early 1820s; of relevant works mentioned by him in his letters, only this would have been available to him at the time (see *EL, CW*, Vol. XII, p. 22).
REFERRED TO: 65 (*64*), 576

The Traveller. See *The Globe and Traveller*.

The True Sun. Referred to: 382

TURGOT, ANNE ROBERT JACQUES, BARON DE L'AULNE. Referred to: 115 (*114*)

TURNER, JOSEPH MALLORD WILLIAM. Referred to: 352

TWEEDDALE, LORD. See Hay.

TYRTAEUS. *The War-Songs of Tyrtaeus*. Trans. Richard Polwhele. In *The Idylls of Theocritus, Bion, and Moschus, and The War-Songs of Tyrtaeus*. London: Bohn, 1853, pp. 337–43.
NOTE: this ed. cited for ease of reference.
REFERRED TO: 467

VALERIAN (Publius Licinius Valerianus). Referred to: 439

VAN DYCK, ANTHONY.
NOTE: Mill's spelling is Vandyke.
REFERRED TO: 352

VESPASIAN (Titus Flavius Vespasianus). Referred to: 435

VIGNY, LÉON PIERRE, COMTE DE.
NOTE: the reference is to Alfred de Vigny's father.
REFERRED TO: 471

VIGNY, VICTOR ALFRED, COMTE DE. Referred to: 465–501, *passim*.

———— *Œuvres*. Brussels and Leipzig: Hochhausen and Fournes, 1837.
NOTE: the volume contains the works listed by Mill: *Souvenirs de servitude*, *Cinq-Mars*, *Stello*, *Poëmes*, *Le more de Venise*, *La maréchale d'Ancre*, and *Chatterton*. Quotations from and references to individual works are given under their titles, below. The volume is set in double columns: page references in the text are simply to the pages; in the collations, the columns are also indicated.
REVIEWED: 463–501

———— *Chatterton* (1835). In *Œuvres*, pp. 465–504.
NOTE: this work, and not the section of *Stello* devoted to Chatterton, is the drama to which Mill refers.
REFERRED TO: 498

———— *Cinq-Mars, ou une conjuration sous Louis XIII* (1826). *Ibid.*, pp. 75–225.
QUOTED: 474n–86n
REFERRED TO: 472–6, 481–7, 498

474n.3–5 "Know . . . river"] [*translated from:*] [*paragraph*] "Connaissez-vous cette partie de la France que l'on a surnommée son jardin? ce pays où l'on respire un air pur dans les plaines verdoyantes arrosées par un grand fleuve? (77a)

474n.6–7 "in a morning . . . usual."] [*translated from:*] [*paragraph*] Ce fut là que, dans une matinée du mois de juin 1639, la cloche du château ayant sonné à midi, selon l'usage, le dîner de la famille qui l'habitait, il se passa dans cette antique demeure des choses qui n'étaient pas habituelles. (78a)

474n.23–7 "O Nature . . . Marie's sake—"] [*translated from:*] O nature, nature! se disait-il, belle nature, adieu! Bientôt mon cœur ne sera plus assez simple pour te sentir, et tu ne plairas plus qu'à mes yeux; il est déjà brûlé par une passion profonde, et le récit des intérêts des hommes y jette un trouble inconnu; il faut donc entrer dans ce labyrinthe; je m'y perdrai peut-être; mais pour Marie . . . (81a)

474n.29–475n.22 "The day . . . man."] [*translated from:*] [*paragraph*] La journée fut triste et le souper silencieux au château de Chaumont. [*paragraph*] Quand vinrent dix heures du soir, le vieux maréchal, conduit par son valet de chambre, se retira dans la tour du nord, voisine de la porte et opposée à la rivière. La chaleur était extrême, il ouvrit la fenêtre; et s'enveloppant d'une vaste robe de soie, plaça un flambeau pesant sur une table, et voulut rester seul. Sa croisée donnait sur la plaine, que la lune dans son premier quartier n'éclairait que d'une lumière incertaine; le ciel se chargeait de nuages épais, et tout disposait à la mélancolie. Quoique Bassompierre n'eût rien de rêveur dans le caractère, la tournure qu'avait prise la conversation du dîner lui revint à la mémoire, et il se mit à repasser en lui-même toute sa vie; les tristes changements que le nouveau règne y avait apportés, règne qui semblait avoir soufflé sur lui un vent d'infortune; la mort d'une sœur chérie, les désordres de l'héritier de son nom, les pertes de ses terres et de sa faveur, la fin récente de son ami le maréchal d'Effiat dont il occupait la chambre: toutes ces pensées lui arrachèrent un soupir involontaire; il se mit à la fenêtre pour respirer. [*paragraph*] En ce moment, il crut entendre du côté du bois la marche d'une troupe de chevaux; mais le vent qui vint à augmenter le dissuada de cette première pensée, et tout bruit cessant tout à coup, il l'oublia. Il regarda encore quelque temps tous les feux du château s'éteignant successivement, après avoir serpenté dans les ogives des escaliers et rôdé dans les cours et les écuries; retombant ensuite sur son grand fauteuil de tapisserie, le coude appuyé sur la table, il se livra profondément à ses réflexions; et bientôt après, tirant de son sein un médaillon qu'il y cachait suspendu à un ruban noir: Viens, mon bon et vieux maître, dit-il, viens causer avec moi comme tu fis si souvent; viens, grand roi, oublier ta cour pour le rire d'un ami véritable; viens, grand homme, me consulter sur l'ambitieuse Autriche; viens, inconstant chevalier, me parler de la bonhomie de ton amour et de la bonne foi de ton infidélité; viens, héroïque soldat, me crier encore que je t'offusque au combat; ah! que ne l'ai-je fait dans Paris! que n'ai-je reçu ta blessure! Avec ton sang le monde a perdu les bienfaits de ton règne interrompu. [*paragraph*] Les larmes du maréchal troublaient la glace du large médaillon, et il les effaçait par de respectueux baisers, quand sa porte ouverte brusquement le fit sauter sur son épée. [*paragraph*] — Qui va là? cria-t-il dans sa surprise. Elle fut bien plus grande quand il reconnut M. de Launay, qui, le chapeau à la main, s'avança jusqu'à lui, et lui dit avec embarras: [*paragraph*] —Monsieur le maréchal, c'est le cœur navré de douleur que je me vois forcé de vous dire que le roi m'a commandé de vous arrêter. Un carrosse vous attend à la grille, avec trente mousquetaires de M. le cardinal-duc. [*paragraph*] Bassompierre ne s'était point levé et avait encore le médaillon dans sa main gauche et l'épée dans l'autre main; il la tendit dédaigneusement à cet homme et lui dit: [*paragraph*] —Monsieur, je sais que j'ai vécu trop longtemps, et c'est à quoi je pensais; c'est au nom de ce grand Henri que je remets paisiblement cette épée à son fils. Suivez-moi. [*paragraph*] Il accompagna ces mots d'un regard si ferme, que de Launay fut atterré, et le suivit en baissant la tête, comme si lui-même eût été arrêté par le noble vieillard, qui, saisissant un flambeau, sortit de la cour et trouva tout ouvert par des gardes à cheval qui avaient effrayé les gens du château, au nom du roi, et ordonné le silence. (83a–84a)

475n.29–476n.17 "It was . . . joined."] [*translated from:*] [*paragraph*] Il était alors plus de minuit, et la lune s'était cachée. Tout autre que le maître de la maison n'eût jamais su trouver son chemin par une obscurité si grande. Les tours et les toits ne formaient qu'une masse noire qui se détachait à peine sur le ciel un peu plus transparent; aucune lumière ne brillait dans toute la maison rendormie. Cinq-Mars, caché sous un chapeau à larges bords et un grand manteau, attendait avec anxiété. [*paragraph*] Qu'attendait-il? qu'était-il venu chercher? un mot d'une voix qui se fit entendre très bas derrière la croisée: [*paragraph*]—Est-ce vous, monsieur de Cinq-Mars? [*paragraph*]—Hélas! qui serait-ce? qui reviendrait comme un malfaiteur toucher la maison paternelle sans y entrer et sans dire encore adieu à sa mère? qui reviendrait pour se plaindre du présent sans rien attendre de l'avenir, si ce n'était moi? [*paragraph*] La voix douce se troubla, et il fut aisé d'entendre que des pleurs accompagnaient sa réponse: [*paragraph*]—Hélas! Henri, de quoi vous plaignez-vous? n'ai-je pas fait plus, et bien plus que je ne devais? Est-ce ma faute si mon malheur a voulu qu'un prince souverain fût mon père? peut-on choisir son berceau? et dit-on: Je naîtrai bergère? Vous savez bien quelle est toute l'infortune d'une princesse: on lui ôte son cœur en naissant, toute la terre est avertie de son âge, un traité la cède comme une ville, et elle ne peut jamais pleurer. Depuis que je vous connais, que n'ai-je pas fait pour me rapprocher du bonheur et m'éloigner des trônes! Depuis deux ans j'ai lutté en vain contre ma mauvaise fortune qui me sépare de vous, et contre vous qui me détournez de mes devoirs. Vous le savez bien, j'ai désiré que l'on me crût morte; que dis-je? j'ai presque souhaité des révolutions! J'aurais presque béni le coup qui m'eût ôté mon rang, comme j'ai remercié Dieu lorsque mon père fut renversé; mais la cause s'étonne, la reine me demande; nos rêves sont évanouis; Henri, notre sommeil a été trop long; réveillons-nous avec courage. Ne songez plus à ces deux belles années: oubliez tout, pour ne vous souvenir que de notre grande résolution; n'ayez qu'une seule pensée, soyez ambitieux par . . . ambitieux pour moi . . . . [*paragraph*]—Faut-il donc oublier tout, ô Marie? dit Cinq-Mars avec douceur . . . [*paragraph*] Elle hésita . . . . [*paragraph*]—Oui, tout ce que j'ai oublié moi-même, reprit-elle. Puis un instant après elle continua avec vivacité. [*paragraph*]—Oui, oubliez nos jours heureux, nos longues soirées, et même les promenades de l'étang et du bois; mais souvenez-vous de l'avenir; partez. Votre père était maréchal, soyez plus, connétable; prince. Partez, vous êtes jeune, noble, riche, brave, aimé . . . . [*paragraph*]—Pour toujours? dit Henri. [*paragraph*]—Pour la vie et l'éternité. [*paragraph*] Cinq-Mars tressaillit, et tendant la main, s'écria: Eh bien! j'en jure par la Vierge dont vous portez le nom, vous serez à moi, Marie, ou ma tête tombera sur l'échafaud. [*paragraph*]—O ciel, que dites-vous? s'écria-t-elle en prenant sa main avec une main blanche qui sortit de la fenêtre. Non, vos efforts ne seront jamais coupables, jurez-le-moi, vous n'oublierez jamais que le roi de France est votre maître, aimez-le plus que tout, après celle pourtant qui vous sacrifiera tout et vous attendra en souffrant. Prenez cette petite croix d'or; mettez-la sur votre cœur, elle a reçu beaucoup de mes larmes. Songez que si jamais vous étiez coupable envers le roi, j'en verserais de bien plus amères. Donnez-moi cette bague que je vois briller à votre doigt; ô Dieu! ma main et la vôtre sont toutes rouges de sang. [*paragraph*]—Qu'importe! il n'a pas coulé pour vous; n'avez-vous rien entendu il y a une heure? [*paragraph*]—Non; mais à présent n'entendez-vous rien vous-même? [*paragraph*]—Non, Marie, si ce n'est un oiseau de nuit sur la tour. [*paragraph*] —On a parlé de nous, j'en suis sûre; mais d'où vient donc ce sang? dites vite, et partez. [*paragraph*]—Oui, je pars, voici un nuage qui nous rend la nuit; adieu, ange céleste, je vous invoquerai. L'amour a versé l'ambition dans mon cœur comme un poison brûlant; oui, je le sens pour la première fois, l'ambition peut être ennoblie par son but. Adieu, je vais accomplir ma destinée. [*paragraph*] —Adieu! mais songez à la mienne. [*paragraph*]—Peuvent-elles se séparer? [*paragraph*]—Jamais! s'écria Marie, que par la mort. [*paragraph*]—Je crains plus encore l'absence, dit Cinq-Mars. [*paragraph*]—Adieu! je tremble; adieu! dit la voix chérie, et la fenêtre s'abaissa lentement sur les deux mains encore unies. (84b–85b)

477n.6–7 "The magician . . . image."] [*translated from:*] [*paragraph*]—Le magicien n'a jamais pu prononcer le nom du Sauveur et repousse son image. (101a)

477n.10–21 "He . . . to the pile.'"] [*translated from:*] [*paragraph*] Lactance sortit en ce moment du milieu des pénitents, ayant dans sa main un énorme crucifix de fer qu'il semblait tenir avec précaution et respect; il l'approcha des lèvres du patient, qui effectivement se jeta en arrière, et réunissant toutes ses forces, fit un geste du bras qui le fit tomber des mains du capucin. [*paragraph*] —Vous le voyez, s'écria celui-ci, il a renversé le crucifix. [*paragraph*] Un murmure s'éleva dont

le sens était incertain: Profanation! s'ecrièrent les prêtres. [*paragraph*] On s'avança vers le bûcher. [*paragraph*] Cependant Cinq-Mars, se glissant derrière un pilier, avait tout observé d'un œil avide; il vit avec étonnement que le crucifix en tombant sur les degrés, plus exposés à la pluie que la plate-forme, avait fumé et produit le bruit du plomb fondu jeté dans l'eau. Pendant que l'attention publique se portait ailleurs, il s'avança et y porta une main qu'il sentit vivement brûlée. Saisi d'indignation, et de toute la fureur d'un cœur loyal, il prend le crucifix avec les plis de son manteau, s'avance vers Laubardemont, et le frappant au front: [*paragraph*]—Scélérat, s'écrie-t-il, porte la marque de ce fer rougi. [*paragraph*] La foule entend ce mot et se précipite. [*paragraph*]— Arrêtez cet insensé, dit en vain l'indigne magistrat. [*paragraph*] Il était saisi lui-même par des mains d'hommes qui criaient: Justice, justice, au nom du roi! [*paragraph*]—Nous sommes perdus, dit Lactance; au bûcher, au bûcher! (101a–b) [*though Mill did not enclose it in quotation marks, the sentence preceding this quotation is a virtual translation of the first clause in the opening sentence above*]
477n.25–7   "a blackened hand . . . Magdalen,"] [*translated from:*] [*paragraph*] La garde était rompue et renversée de toutes parts, le peuple se jette en hurlant sur le bûcher, mais aucune lumière n'y brillait plus, tout avait disparu, même le bourreau; on arrache, on disperse les planches, l'une d'elles brûlait encore, et sa lueur fit voir, sous un amas de cendre et de boue sanglante, une main noircie, préservée du feu par un énorme bracelet de fer et une chaîne; une femme eut le courage de l'ouvrir; les doigts serraient une petite croix d'ivoire et une image de sainte Madeleine. (101b– 102a)
477n.36   *l'homme . . . tuera.*] L'homme . . . tuera. (104b)
478n.3–8   "an expanded forehead . . . *chambre,*"] [*translated from:*] Il avait le front large et quelques cheveux fort blancs, des yeux grands et doux, une figure pâle et effilée à laquelle une petite barbe blanche et pointue donnait cet air de finesse que l'on remarque dans tous les portraits du siècle de Louis XIII. Une bouche presque sans lèvres, et nous sommes forcés d'avouer que le docteur Lavater regarde ce signe comme indiquant la méchanceté à n'en pouvoir douter; une bouche pincée, disons-nous, était encadrée par deux petites moustaches grises et par une *royale*, ornement alors à la mode, et qui ressemble assez à une virgule par sa forme. Ce vieillard avait sur sa tête une calotte rouge et était enveloppé dans une vaste robe de chambre, portait des bas de soie pourprée, et n'était rien moins qu'Armand Duplessis, cardinal de Richelieu. (106a)
478n.12–26   "Come here . . . knee."] [*translated from:*] Tout à coup Richelieu, lui adressant la parole sèchement, lui dit: Venez ici, monsieur Olivier. [*paragraph*] Ces deux mots furent comme un coup de foudre pour ce pauvre enfant qui paraissait n'avoir pas seize ans. Il se leva pourtant très-vite et vint se placer debout devant le ministre, les bras pendants et la tête baissée. [*paragraph*] Les autres pages et les secrétaires ne remuèrent pas plus que des soldats lorsque l'un d'eux tombe frappé d'une balle, tant ils étaient accoutumés à ces sortes d'appels. Celui-ci pourtant s'annonçait d'une manière plus vive que les autres. [*paragraph*]—Qu'écrivez-vous là? [*paragraph*]—Mon- seigneur . . . ce que Votre Eminence me dicte. [*paragraph*]—Quoi? [*paragraph*]—Monseigneur . . . la lettre à D. Juan de Bragance. [*paragraph*]—Point de détours, monsieur, vous faites autre chose. [*paragraph*]—Monseigneur, dit alors le page, les larmes aux yeux, c'était un billet à une de mes cousines. [*paragraph*]—Voyons-le. [*paragraph*] Alors un tremblement universel l'agita, et il fut obligé de s'appuyer sur la cheminée, en disant à demi voix: C'est impossible. [*paragraph*]— M. le vicomte Olivier d'Entraigues, dit le ministre sans marquer la moindre émotion, vous n'êtes plus à mon service. Et le page sortit; il savait qu'il n'y avait pas à répliquer; il glissa son billet dans sa poche, et ouvrant la porte à deux battants, justement assez pour qu'il y eût place pour lui, il s'y glissa comme un oiseau qui s'échappe de sa cage. [*paragraph*] Le ministre continua les notes qu'il traçait sur son genou. (106b)
478n.38–40   "ideas . . . before," "that . . . exile," . . . "Recal . . . words."] [*translated from:*] [*paragraph*]—Le roi a des idées qu'il n'avait pas eues encore. [*3-paragraph omission*] [*paragraph*]—Il a parlé de rappeler la reine-mère, dit le capucin à voix basse, de la rappeler de Cologne. [*4-sentence omission*] [*paragraph*] Rappeler mon ennemie, rappeler sa mère, quelle perfidie! non, il n'aurait jamais osé y penser . . . . [*paragraph*] Puis après avoir rêvé un instant, il ajouta en fixant un regard pénétrant et encore plein du feu de sa colère, sur le P. Joseph: [*paragraph*]—Mais . . . dans quels termes a-t-il exprimé ce désir? dites-moi les mots précis. (107b–108a)

478n.41–479n.6 "He said . . . will do.'"] [*translated from:*] [*paragraph*]—Il a dit assez publique
ment et en présence de Monsieur: Je sens bien que l'un des premiers devoirs d'un chrétien est d'êtr
bon fils, et je ne résisterai pas longemps aux murmures de ma conscience. [*paragraph*
—Chrétien, conscience! ce ne sont pas ses expressions; c'est le P. Caussin, c'est son confesseu
qui me trahit, s'écria le cardinal. Perfide jésuite! je t'ai pardonné ton intrigue de la Fayette; mais je
ne te passerai pas tes conseils secrets. Je ferai chasser ce confesseur, Joseph; il est l'ennemi de
l'État, je le vois bien. Mais aussi j'ai agi avec négligence depuis quelques jours; je n'ai pas asse
hâté l'arrivée de ce petit d'Effiat, qui réussira sans doute: il est bien fait et spirituel, dit-on. Ah
quelle faute! je mériterais une bonne disgrâce moi-même. Laisser près du roi ce renard de jésuite
sans lui avoir donné mes instructions secrètes, sans avoir un otage, un gage de sa fidélité à me
ordres! quel oubli! Joseph, prenez une plume, et écrivez vite ceci pour l'autre confesseur, que nou
choisirons mieux. Je pense au Père Sirmond . . . . (108a) [*follows immediately the preceding
quotation*]

479n.8–16 "'What tiresomeness . . . if you can!'"] [*translated from:*] [*paragraph*] Quel ennu
profond! quelles interminables inquiétudes! Si l'ambitieux me voyait, il fuirait dans un désert
Qu'est-ce que ma puissance? un misérable reflet du pouvoir royal; et que de travaux pour fixer su
mon étoile ce rayon qui flotte sans cesse! Depuis vingt ans je le tente inutilement. Je ne comprend
rien à cet homme! Il n'ose pas me fuir, mais on me l'enlève, il me glisse entre les doigts. . . . Que de
choses j'aurais pu faire avec ses droits héréditaires, si je les avais eus! Mais employer tant de
calculs à se tenir en équilibre! Que reste-t-il de génie pour les entreprises? J'ai l'Europe dans ma
main, et je suis suspendu à un cheveu qui tremble. Qu'ai-je à faire de porter mes regards sur le
cartes du monde, si tous mes intérêts sont renfermés dans mon étroit cabinet? Ses six pied
d'espace me donnent plus de peine à gouverner que toute la terre. Voilà donc ce qu'est un premie
ministre! Enviez-moi mes gardes, à présent. (108b)

479n.39–480n.10 "'The only . . . mother.'"] [*translated from:*] [*paragraph*]—La seule récom-
pense que je demande de mes services est que Votre Majesté daigne accepter de moi en pur don le
palais-cardinal, élevé de mes deniers dans Paris. [*paragraph*] Le roi étonné fit un signe de tête
consentant: un murmure de surprise agita un moment la cour attentive. [*paragraph*]—Je me jette
aussi aux pieds de Votre Majesté pour qu'elle veuille m'accorder la révocation d'une rigueur que
j'ai provoquée (je l'avoue publiquement), et que je regardai peut-être comme trop utile au repos de
l'Etat. Oui, quand j'étais de ce monde, j'oubliais trop mes plus anciens sentiments de respect e
d'attachement pour le bien général. A présent que je jouis déjà des lumières de la solitude, je voi
que j'ai eu tort et je me repens. [*paragraph*] L'attention redoubla, et l'inquiétude du roi devin
visible. [*paragraph*]—Oui, il est une personne, sire, que j'ai toujours aimée, malgré ses tort
envers vous, et l'éloignement que les affaires du royaume me forcèrent à lui montrer; une personne
à qui j'ai dû beaucoup et qui vous doit être chère, malgré ses entreprises à main armée contre
vous-même; une personne enfin que je vous supplie de rappeler de l'exil, je veux dire la reine Marie
de Médicis, votre mère. (118a)

480n.26–31 "Wretches," . . . "wretches . . . I . . ."] [*translated from:*] [*paragraph*]—Misérables
s'écria-t-il lorsqu'il fut seul, allez encore accomplir quelques œuvres secrètes, et ensuite je vou
briserai vous-mêmes, ressorts impurs de mon pouvoir. Bientôt le roi succombera sous la lente
maladie qui le consume; je serai régent alors, je serai roi de France moi-même, je n'aurai plus à
redouter les caprices de sa faiblesse; je détruirai sans retour les races orgueilleuses de ce pays; j'y
passerai un niveau terrible et la baguette de Tarquin, je serai seul sur eux tous, l'Europe tremblera,
je. . . . (134a–b)

481n.5–29 "The Queen . . . in it.'"] [*translated from:*] [*paragraph*] La reine sourit; elle contempla
quelques temps en silence les traits naïfs et purs de la belle Marie et son regard plein de candeur qui
se levait sur elle languissamment; elle écarta les boucles noires qui voilaient ce beau front, et parut
reposer ses yeux et son âme en voyant cette innocence ravissante, exprimée sur un visage si beau;
elle baisa sa joue, et reprit: [*paragraph*]—Tu ne soupçonnes pas, pauvre ange, une triste vérité;
c'est que le roi n'aime personne, et que ceux qui paraissent le plus en faveur sont les plus près d'être
abandonnés par lui, et jetés à celui qui engloutit et dévore tout. [*paragraph*]—Ah! mon Dieu! que
me dites-vous? [*paragraph*]—Sais-tu combien il en a perdu? poursuivit la reine d'une voix plus
basse, et regardant ses yeux comme pour y lire toute sa pensée et y faire entrer la sienne; sais-tu la
fin de ses favoris? t'a-t-on conté l'exil de Baradas, celui de Saint-Simon, le couvent de la Fayette,

la honte d'Hautefort, la mort de Chalais? Tous ont tombé devant un ordre de Richelieu à son maître, et sans cette faveur que tu prends pour de l'amitié, leur vie eût été paisible; mais elle est mortelle; c'est un poison. Tiens, vois cette tapisserie qui représente Sémélé; les favoris de Louis XIII ressemblent à cette femme; son attachement dévore comme ce feu qui l'éblouit et la brûle. [*paragraph*] Mais la jeune duchesse n'était plus en état d'entendre la reine; elle continuait de fixer sur elle de grands yeux noirs, qu'un voile de larmes obscurcissait; ses mains tremblaient dans celles d'Anne d'Autriche, et une agitation convulsive faisait frémir ses lèvres. [*paragraph*]—Je suis bien cruelle, n'est-ce pas, Marie? poursuivit la reine avec une voix d'une douceur extrême, et en la caressant comme un enfant dont on veut tirer un aveu; oh! oui! sans doute, je suis bien méchante! notre cœur est bien gros! vous n'en pouvez plus, mon enfant; allons, parlez-moi; où en êtes-vous avec Cinq-Mars? [*paragraph*] A ce mot, la douleur se fit un passage, et, toujours à genoux aux pieds de la reine, Marie versa à son tour, sur le sein de cette bonne princesse, un déluge de pleurs, avec des sanglots enfantins et des mouvements si violents dans sa tête et ses belles épaules, qu'il semblait que son cœur dût se briser. La reine attendit longtemps la fin de ce premier mouvement en la berçant dans ses bras comme pour apaiser sa douleur, et répétant souvent: Ma fille! allons, ma fille! ne t'afflige pas ainsi. [*paragraph*]—Ah! madame, s'écria-t-elle, je suis bien coupable envers vous; mais je n'ai pas compté sur ce cœur-là; j'ai eu bien tort, j'en serai peut-être bien punie! Mais hélas! comment aurais-je osé vous parler, madame! Ce n'était pas d'ouvrir mon âme qui m'était difficile; c'était de vous avouer que j'avais besoin d'y faire lire. (152a–b)

481n.32–482n.6   "'But the mischief . . . of him.'"] [*translated from:*] [*paragraph*]—Les reproches sont inutiles et cruels si le mal est fait; le passé n'est plus à nous, pensons au reste du temps. Cinq-Mars est bien par lui-même, brave, spirituel, profond même dans ses idées; je l'ai observé, il a fait en deux ans bien du chemin, et je vois que c'était pour Marie. . . . Il se conduit bien; il est digne, oui, il est digne d'elle à mes yeux; mais à ceux de l'Europe, non. Il faut qu'il s'élève davantage encore; la princesse de Mantoue ne peut pas avoir épousé moins qu'un prince. Il faudrait qu'il le fût. Pour moi, je n'y peux rien; je ne suis point la reine, je suis la femme négligée du roi. Il n'y a que le cardinal, l'éternel cardinal, . . . et il est son ennemi, et peut-être cette émeute . . . . [*paragraph*]—Hélas! c'est le commencement de la guerre entre eux. Je l'ai trop vu tout à l'heure. [*paragraph*]—Il est donc perdu! s'écria la reine en embrassant Marie. Pardon, mon enfant, je te déchire le cœur, mais nous devons tout voir et tout dire aujourd'hui; oui, il est perdu s'il ne renverse lui-même ce méchant homme; car le roi n'y renoncera pas; la force seule. . . . [*paragraph*]—Il le renversera, madame; il le fera si vous l'aidez. Vous êtes comme la divinité de la France; oh! je vous en conjure! protégez l'ange contre le démon; c'est votre cause, celle de votre royale famille, celle de toute votre nation. . . . [*paragraph*] La reine sourit. [*paragraph*]—C'est ta cause surtout, ma fille, n'est-il pas vrai? et c'est comme telle que je l'embrasserai de tout mon pouvoir; il n'est pas grand, je te l'ai dit, mais tel qu'il est, je te le prête tout entier; pourvu cependant que cet *ange* ne descende pas jusqu'à des péchés mortels, ajouta-t-elle avec un regard plein de finesse; j'ai entendu prononcer son nom cette nuit par des voix bien indignes de lui. (154a)

482n.10–11   "tremble . . . him."] [*translated from:*] [*paragraph*]—Je les connais toutes; j'ai lu leur espérance à travers leur feinte colère; je sais qu'ils tremblent en menaçant; je sais qu'ils sont déjà prêts à faire leur paix en me donnant comme gage; mais c'est à moi de les soutenir et de décider le roi: il le faut, car Marie est ma fiancée, et ma mort est écrite à Narbonne. (164b)

482n.16–485n.28   "The young . . . listened."] [*translated from:*] [*paragraph*] Mais pendant que sa femme de chambre était allée trouver Grandchamp, la jeune et tremblante Marie avait poussé d'une main timide la porte battante de l'église; elle avait rencontré là Cinq-Mars, debout, déguise, et attendant avec inquiétude. A peine l'eut-elle reconnu, qu'elle marcha d'un pas précipité dans le temple, tenant son masque de velours sur son visage, et courut se réfugier dans un confessionnal, tandis que Henri refermait avec soin la porte de l'église qu'elle avait franchie. Il s'assura qu'on ne pouvait l'ouvrir du dehors, et vint après elle s'agenouiller, comme d'habitude, dans le lieu de la pénitence. Arrivé une heure avant elle avec son vieux valet, il avait trouvé cette porte ouverte, signe certain et convenu que l'abbé Quillet, son gouverneur, l'attendait à sa place accoutumée. Le soin qu'il avait d'empêcher toute surprise le fit rester lui-même à garder cette entrée jusqu'à l'arrivée de Marie: heureux de voir l'exactitude du bon abbé, il ne voulut pourtant pas quitter son poste pour l'en aller remercier. C'était un second père pour lui, à cela près de l'autorité, et il agissait avec ce bon prêtre sans beaucoup de cérémonie. [*paragraph*] La vieille paroisse de Saint-Eustache était obscure; seulement, avec la lampe perpétuelle, brûlaient quatre flambeaux de cire jaune, qui, attachés au-dessus des bénitiers, contre les principaux piliers, jetaient une lueur rouge sur les marbres bleus et noirs de la basilique déserte. La lumière pénétrait à peine dans les niches enfoncées des ailes du pieux bâtiment. Dans l'une de ces chapelles, et la plus sombre, était ce confessionnal dont une grille de fer assez élevée, et doublée de planches épaisses, ne laissait apercevoir que le petit dôme et la croix de bois. Là, s'agenouillèrent de chaque côté Cinq-Mars et Marie de Mantoue; ils ne se voyaient qu'à peine, et trouvèrent que, selon son usage, l'abbé Quillet, assis entre eux, les avait attendus depuis longtemps. Ils pouvaient entrevoir à travers les petits grillages l'ombre de son camail. Henri d'Effiat s'était approché lentement; il venait arrêter et régler, pour ainsi dire, le reste de sa destinée. Ce n'était plus devant son roi qu'il allait paraître, mais devant une souveraine plus puissante, devant celle pour laquelle il avait entrepris son immense ouvrage. Il allait éprouver sa foi, et tremblait. [paragraph] Il frémit surtout lorsque sa jeune fiancée fut agenouillée en face de lui; il frémit parce qu'il ne put s'empêcher, à l'aspect de cet ange, de sentir tout le bonheur qu'il pourrait perdre; il n'osa parler le premier, et demeura encore un instant à contempler sa tête dans l'ombre, cette jeune tête sur laquelle reposaient toutes ses espérances. Malgré son amour, toutes les fois qu'il la voyait, il ne pouvait se garantir de quelque effroi d'avoir tant entrepris pour une enfant dont la passion n'était qu'un faible reflet de la sienne, et qui n'avait peut-être pas apprécié tous les sacrifices qu'il avait faits; son caractère ployé pour elle aux complaisances d'un courtisan; condamné aux intrigues et aux souffrances de l'ambition; livré aux combinaisons profondes, aux criminelles méditations, aux sombres et violents travaux d'un conspirateur. Jusque-là, dans leurs secrètes et chastes entrevues, elle avait toujours reçu chaque nouvelle de ses progrès dans sa carrière avec les transports de plaisir d'un enfant, mais sans apprécier la fatigue de chacun de ces pas si pesants que l'on fait vers les honneurs, et lui demandant toujours avec naïveté quand il serait connétable enfin, et quand ils se marieraient, comme si elle eût demandé quand il viendrait au carousel, et si le temps était serein. Jusque-là il avait souri de ces questions et de cette ignorance pardonnable à dix-huit ans, dans une jeune fille née sur un trône et accoutumée à des grandeurs, pour ainsi dire, naturelles et trouvées autour d'elle en venant à la vie; mais à cette heure il fit de plus sérieuses réflexions sur ce caractère, et lorsque, sortant presque de l'assemblée imposante des conspirateurs représentants de tous les ordres du royaume, son oreille, où résonnaient encore les voix mâles qui avaient juré d'entreprendre une vaste guerre, fut frappée des premières paroles de celle pour qui elle était commencée, il craignit, pour la première fois, que cette sorte d'innocence ne fût de la légèreté et ne s'étendît jusqu'au cœur: il résolut de l'approfondir. [paragraph]—Dieu! que j'ai peur, Henri! dit-elle en entrant dans le confessionnal; vous me faites venir, sans gardes, sans carrosse; je tremble toujours d'être vue de mes gens, en sortant de l'hôtel de Nevers. Faudra-t-il donc me cacher encore longtemps comme une coupable? La reine n'a pas été contente lorsque je le lui ai avoué; si elle m'en parle encore, ce sera avec son air sévère que vous connaissez, et qui me fait toujours pleurer: j'ai bien peur. [paragraph] Elle se tut, et Cinq-Mars ne répondit que par un profond soupir. [paragraph]—Quoi? vous ne me parlez pas? dit-elle. [paragraph]—Sont-ce bien là toutes vos terreurs? dit Cinq-Mars avec amertume. [paragraph]—Dois-je en avoir de plus grandes? O mon ami! de quel ton, avec quelle voix me parlez-vous? êtes-vous fâché parce que je suis venue trop tard? [paragraph]—Trop tôt, madame, beaucoup trop tôt, pour les choses que vous devez entendre, car je vous en vois bien éloignée. [paragraph] Marie, affligée de l'accent sombre et amer de sa voix, se prit à pleurer. [paragraph] —Hélas! mon Dieu! qu'ai-je donc fait, dit-elle, pour que vous m'appeliez madame, et me traitiez si durement? [paragraph]—Ah! rassurez-vous, reprit Cinq-Mars, mais toujours avec ironie. En effet, vous n'êtes pas coupable; mais je le suis, je suis seul à l'être; ce n'est pas envers vous, mais pour vous. [paragraph]—Avez-vous donc fait du mal? avez-vous ordonné la mort de quelqu'un? Oh! non, j'en suis bien sûre, vous êtes si bon! [paragraph]—Eh quoi! dit Cinq-Mars, n'êtes-vous pour rien dans mes projets? ai-je mal compris votre pensée lorsque vous me regardiez chez la reine? ne sais-je plus lire dans vos yeux? le feu qui les animait était-ce un grand amour pour Richelieu? cette admiration que vous promettiez à celui qui oserait tout dire au roi, qu'est-elle devenue? Est-ce un mensonge que tout cela? [paragraph] Marie fondait en larmes. [paragraph]—Vous me parlez toujours d'un air contraint, dit-elle, et je ne l'ai pas mérité. Si je ne vous dis rien de cette conjuration effrayante, croyez-vous que je l'oublie? ne me trouvez-vous pas assez malheureuse? avez-vous besoin de voir mes pleurs? les voilà. J'en verse assez en secret, Henri; croyez que si j'ai évité, dans nos dernières entrevues, ce terrible sujet, c'était de crainte d'en trop apprendre: ai-je une autre pensée que celle de vos dangers? ne sais-je pas bien que c'est pour moi que vous les courez? Hélas! si vous combattez pour moi, n'ai-je pas aussi à soutenir des attaques non moins cruelles? Plus heureux que moi, vous n'avez à combattre que la haine, tandis que je lutte contre l'amitié: le cardinal vous opposera des hommes et des armes; mais la reine, la douce Anne d'Autriche n'emploie que de tendres conseils, des caresses et quelquefois des larmes. [*paragraph*] —Touchante et invincible contrainte, dit Cinq-Mars avec amertume, pour vous faire accepter un trône. Je conçois que vous ayez besoin de quelques efforts contre de telles séductions! mais avant, madame, il importe de vous délier de vos serments. [*paragraph*]—Hélas! grand Dieu! qu'y a-t-il donc contre nous? [*paragraph*]—Il y a Dieu sur nous et contre nous, reprit Henri d'une voix sévère; le roi m'a trompé. [*paragraph*] L'abbé s'agita dans le confessionnal. [*paragraph*] Marie s'écria: [*paragraph*]—Voilà ce que je pressentais; voilà le malheur que j'entrevoyais. Est-ce moi qui l'ai causé? [*paragraph*]—Il m'a trompé en me serrant la main, poursuivit Cinq-Mars, il m'a trahi par le vil Joseph qu'on m'offre de poignarder. [*paragraph*] L'abbé fit un mouvement d'horreur qui ouvrit à demi la porte du confessionnal. [*paragraph*]—Ah mon père! ne craignez rien, continua Henri d'Effiat, votre élève ne frappera jamais de tels coups. Ils s'entendront de loin, ceux que je prépare, et le grand jour les éclairera; mais il me reste un devoir à remplir, un devoir sacré: voyez votre enfant s'immoler devant vous. Hélas! je n'ai pas vécu longtemps pour le bonheur, je viens le détruire peut-être, par votre main, la même qui l'avait consacré. [*paragraph*] Il ouvrit en parlant ainsi le léger grillage qui le séparait de son vieux gouverneur; celui-ci gardant toujours un silence surprenant avança le camail sur son front. [*paragraph*]—Rendez, dit Cinq-Mars d'une voix moins ferme, rendez cet anneau nuptial à la duchesse de Mantoue, je ne puis le garder qu'elle ne me le donne une seconde fois; car je ne suis plus le même qu'elle promit d'épouser. [*paragraph*] Le prêtre saisit brusquement la bague et la passa au travers des losanges du grillage opposé; cette marque d'indifférence étonna Cinq-Mars. [*paragraph*]—Eh! quoi, mon père, dit-il, êtes-vous aussi changé? [*paragraph*] Cependant Marie ne pleurait plus; mais élevant sa voix angélique qui éveilla un faible écho le long des ogives du temple comme le plus doux soupir de l'orgue, elle dit: [*paragraph*]—O mon ami! ne soyez plus en colère; je ne vous comprends pas, pouvons-nous rompre ce que Dieu vient d'unir, et pourrais-je vous quitter quand je vous sais malheureux? Si le roi ne vous aime plus, du moins vous êtes assuré qu'il ne voudra pas vous faire du mal, puisqu'il n'en a pas fait au cardinal qu'il n'a jamais aimé. Vous croyez-vous perdu parce qu'il n'aura pas voulu peut-être se séparer de son vieux serviteur? Eh bien! attendons le retour de son amitié; oubliez ces conspirateurs qui m'effrayent. S'ils n'ont plus d'espoir, j'en remercie Dieu; je ne tremblerai plus pour vous. Qu'avez-vous donc, mon ami? et pourquoi nous affliger inutilement? La reine nous aime, et nous sommes tous deux bien jeunes; attendons. L'avenir est beau, puisque nous sommes unis et sûrs de nous-mêmes. Racontez-moi ce que le roi vous disait à Chambord? Je vous ai suivi longtemps des yeux. Dieu! que cette partie de chasse fut triste pour moi! [*paragraph*]—Il m'a trahi! vous dis-je, répondit Cinq-Mars; et qui l'aurait pu croire, lorsque vous l'avez vu nous serrant la main, passant de son frère à moi et au duc de Bouillon, qu'il se faisait instruire des moindres détails de la conjuration, du jour même où l'on arrêterait Richelieu à Lyon, fixait le lieu de son exil (car ils voulaient sa mort; mais le souvenir de mon père me fit demander sa vie)! Le roi disait que lui-même dirigerait tout à Perpignan, et cependant Joseph, cet impur espion, sortait du cabinet des Lys! O Marie, vous l'avouerai-je? au moment où je l'ai appris, mon âme a été bouleversée; j'ai douté de tout, et il m'a semblé que le centre du monde chancelait en voyant la vérité quitter le cœur d'un roi. Je voyais s'écrouler tout notre édifice; une heure encore, et la conjuration s'évanouissait (vous perdais pour toujours; un moyen me restait, je l'ai employé. [*paragraph*]—Lequel? dit Marie. [*paragraph*]—Le traité d'Espagne était dans ma main, je l'ai signé. [*paragraph*]—O ciel! déchirez-le. [*paragraph*]—Il est parti. [*paragraph*]—Qui le porte? [*paragraph*]—Fontrailles. [*paragraph*]—Rappelez-le. [*paragraph*]—Il doit avoir déjà dépassé les défilés d'Oloron, dit Cinq-Mars, se levant debout. Tout est prêt à Madrid, tout à Sedan; des armées m'attendent, Marie; des armées! et Richelieu est au milieu d'elles! Il chancelle, il ne faut plus qu'un seul coup pour le renverser, et vous êtes à moi pour toujours, à Cinq-Mars triomphant! [*paragraph*]—A Cinq-Mars rebelle! dit-elle en gémissant. [*paragraph*]—Eh bien! oui! rebelle, mais non plus favori. Rebelle, criminel, digne de l'échafaud, je le sais, s'écria ce jeune homme passionné en retombant à genoux: mais rebelle par amour, rebelle pour vous que mon épée va conquérir enfin tout entière. [*paragraph*]—Hélas! l'épée que l'on trempe dans le sang des siens n'est-elle pas un poignard? [*paragraph*]—Arrêtez, par pitié, Marie! Que des rois m'abandonnent, que des guerriers me délaissent, j'en serai plus ferme encore; mais je serais vaincu par un mot de vous, et encore une fois le temps de réfléchir est passé pour moi; oui, je suis criminel; et c'est pourquoi j'hésite à me croire encore digne de vous. Abandonnez-moi, Marie, reprenez cet anneau. [*paragraph*]—Je ne le puis, dit-elle, car je suis votre femme, quel que vous soyez. [*paragraph*]— Vous l'entendez, mon père, dit Cinq-Mars, transporté de bonheur; bénissez cette seconde union, c'est celle du dévouement, plus belle encore que celle de l'amour. Qu'elle soit à moi tant que je vivrai! [*paragraph*] Sans répondre, l'abbé ouvrit la porte du confessionnal, sortit brusquement, et fut hors de l'église avant que Cinq-Mars eût le temps de se lever pour le suivre. [*paragraph*]—Où allez-vous? qu'avez-vous? s'écria-t-il. [*paragraph*] Mais personne ne paraissait et ne se faisait entendre. [*paragraph*]—Ne criez pas, au nom du ciel! dit Marie, ou je suis perdue, il a sans doute entendu quelqu'un dans l'église. [*paragraph*] Mais troublé et sans lui répondre, d'Effiat, s'élançant sous les arcades et cherchant en vain son gouverneur, courut à une porte qu'il trouva fermée, tirant son épée, il fit le tour du temple, et arrivant à l'entrée que devait garder Grandchamp, il appela et écouta. (183a–188a)

485n.31–2 "Fly, . . . lost!"] [*translated from:*] [*paragraph*]—Fuyez! vous êtes perdu! s'écria Marie. (188a)

485n.34–5 "un . . . perdu,"] Ton Cinq-Mars est un . . . perdu. (194b)

485n.38–486n.19 "'Monsieur . . . tempest."] [*translated from:*] [*centred heading*] "Monsieur le marquis de Cinq-Mars, [*paragraph*] Je vous fais cette lettre pour vous conjurer et prier de rendre à ses devoirs notre bien-aimée fille adoptive et amie, la princesse Marie de Gonzague, que votre affection détourne seule du trône de Pologne à elle offert. J'ai sondé son âme; elle est bien jeune encore, et *j'ai lieu de croire* qu'elle accepterait la couronne avec *moins d'effort et de douleur que vous ne le pensez peut-être*. [*paragraph*] C'est pour elle que vous avez entrepris une guerre qui va mettre à feu et à sang mon beau et cher royaume de France; je vous conjure et supplie d'agir en gentilhomme, et de délier noblement la duchesse de Mantoue des promesses qu'elle aura pu vous faire. Rendez aussi le repos à son âme et la paix à notre cher pays. [*paragraph*] La reine, qui se jette à vos pieds s'il le faut. [*in right margin*] Anne d'Autriche." [*paragraph*] Cinq-Mars remit avec calme le pistolet sur la table; son premier mouvement avait fait tourner le canon contre lui-même; cependant il le remit, et, saisissant vite un crayon, écrivit sur le revers de la même lettre. [*centred heading*] "Madame, [*paragraph*] Marie de Gonzague étant ma femme, ne peut être reine de Pologne qu'après ma mort; je meurs. [*in right margin*] Cinq-Mars." [*paragraph*] Et comme s'il n'eût pas voulu se donner un instant de réflexion, la mettant de force dans la main du courrier: [*paragraph*]—A cheval! à cheval! lui dit-il d'un ton furieux: si tu demeures un instant de plus, tu es mort. [*paragraph*] Il le vit partir et rentra. [*paragraph*] Seul avec son ami, il resta un instant debout, mais pâle, mais l'œil fixe et regardant la terre comme un insensé. Il se sentit chanceler. [*paragraph*]—De Thou! cria-t-il. [*paragraph*]—Que voulez-vous, ami, cher ami? je suis près de vous; vous venez d'être grand, bien grand! sublime! [*paragraph*]—De Thou! cria-t-il encore d'une voix horrible, et il tomba la face contre terre, comme tombe un arbre déraciné. (198a–b)

486n.30 "Reign,"] [*translated from:*]—Régnez, dit-il d'une voix faible. (206b)

——— *La maréchale d'Ancre* (1831). *Ibid.*, pp. 413–64.
REFERRED TO: 498

——— *Le more de Venise, Othello. Tragédie traduite de Shakespeare en vers français* (1829). *Ibid.*, pp. 355–407.
REFERRED TO: 498

——— *Poëmes. Ibid.*, pp. 305–53.
NOTE: "Moïse" (1826) is referred to, pp. 499–500, and quoted, p. 500; "Eloa; ou, La sœur des anges. Mystère" (1824), is referred to, p. 500; and "Le bateau" (first published as "Barcarolle," 1831) is quoted, pp. 500–1.
QUOTED: 500, 500–1
REFERRED TO: 498–500

500.8–10 "marching . . . Omnipotent."] [*translated from:*] Marchant vers la terre promise, / Josué s'avançait pensif, et pâlissant, / Car il était déjà l'élu du Tout-Puissant. ("Moïse," 312b)

—— *Souvenirs de servitude militaire et de grandeur militaire* (1835). *Ibid.*, pp. 5–74.
NOTE: the title page reads: *Servitude et grandeur militaires*; Bks. I and II are "Souvenirs de servitude militaire," and Bk. III is "Souvenirs de grandeur militaire." Bk. I contains within it the tale, "Laurette; ou, Le cachet rouge," which is referred to and quoted, pp. 489–91 and 494; Bk. II contains "La veillée de Vincennes," which is referred to and quoted, pp. 491–2; Bk. III contains "La vie et la mort du capitaine Renaud; ou, La canne de jonc," which is referred to pp. 492–3.
QUOTED: 471, 472, 489, 490, 491, 492, 494
REFERRED TO: 486, 487, 488–94
471.35–6   "the . . . drum," . . . . "drowned . . . teacher,"] [*translated from:*] La guerre était debout dans le lycée, le tambour étouffait à mes oreilles la voix des maîtres, et la voix mystérieuse des livres ne nous parlait qu'un langage froid et pédantesque. (9b)
472.9–13   Those . . . life, [he says,] would . . . unendurable. . . .] [*translated from:*] C'eût été là assurément quatorze ans perdus, si je n'y eusse exercé une observation attentive et persévérante, qui faisait son profit de tout pour l'avenir. Je dois même à la vie de l'armée des vues de la nature humaine que jamais je n'eusse pu rechercher autrement que sous l'habit militaire. Il y a des scènes que l'on ne trouve qu'à travers des dégoûts qui seraient vraiment intolérables, si on n'était forcé de les tolérer. (8a–10a) [*ellipsis indicates 2-page omission*]
472.13–16   Overcome . . . writings.] [*translated from:*] [*paragraph*] Accablé d'un ennui que je n'attendais pas dans cette vie si vivement désirée, ce fut alors pour moi une nécessité que de me dérober, dans les nuits, au tumulte fatigant et vain des journées militaires: de ces nuits, où j'agrandis en silence ce que j'avais reçu de savoir de nos études tumultueuses et publiques, sortirent mes poëmes et mes livres; de ces journées, il me reste ces souvenirs dont je rassemble ici, autour d'une idée, les traits principaux. (10a)
489.37–8   "a little . . . wheels."] [*translated from:*] [*paragraph*] A une centaine de pas, je vins à distinguer clairement une petite charrette de bois blanc, couverte de trois cercles et d'une toile cirée noire. Cela ressemblait à un petit berceau posé sur deux roues. (14b)
490.8–9   "with . . . size,"] [*translated from:*] J'avais ordre de traiter cet individu avec ménagement; et la première lettre du Directoire en renfermait une seconde, scellée de trois cachets rouges, au milieu desquels il y en avait un démesuré. (16a)
490.13   "trusted . . . press,"] [*translated from:*] J'ai cru à leur liberté de la presse! (19a)
490.27–9   "that moment," . . . "has . . . chain."] [*translated from:*] Mais ce moment a duré pour moi jusqu'au jour où nous sommes, et je le traînerai toute ma vie comme un boulet. (21a)
490.29–30   "I felt . . . her."] [*translated from:*] [*paragraph*] De ce moment-là je devins aussi triste qu'elle, et je sentis quelque chose en moi, qui me disait: *Reste devant elle jusqu'à la fin de tes jours, et garde-la*: je l'ai fait. (22b)
490.31–2   "I turned . . . me."] [*translated from:*] Je leur tournai le dos, et je la gardai avec moi. (22b)
491.14–19   "thought themselves," . . . dishonoured . . . seated.] [*translated from:*] [*paragraph*] Il est vrai que ces braves soldats, pris dans l'armée parmi l'élite de l'élite, se croyaient déshonorés pour la plus légère faute. [*paragraph*]—Allez, vous êtes tous des puritains de l'honneur, lui dis-je en lui frappant sur l'épaule. [*paragraph*] Il salua et se retira vers la caserne où était son logement; puis, avec une innocence de mœurs particulière à l'honnête race des soldats, il revint apportant du chenevis, dans le creux de ses mains, à une poule qui élevait ses douze poussins sous le vieux canon de bronze où nous étions assis. (28a–b)
492.9–14   "How poor," . . . are . . . Providence!] [*translated from:*] [*paragraph*]—Combien de fois, dis-je, ce vieux soldat vaut-il mieux, avec sa résignation, que nous autres, jeunes officiers, avec nos ambitions folles! Cela nous donna à penser. [*paragraph*]—Oui, je crois bien, continuai-je, en passant le petit pont qui fut levé après nous; je crois que ce qu'il y a de plus pur dans nos temps c'est l'âme d'un soldat pareil, scrupuleux sur son honneur et le croyant souillé par la moindre tache d'indiscipline ou de négligence; sans ambition, sans vanité, sans luxe, toujours esclave et toujours fier et content de sa Servitude, n'ayant de cher dans sa vie qu'un souvenir de reconnaissance. [*paragraph*]—Et croyant que la Providence a les yeux sur lui! me dit Timoléon, d'un air profondément frappé et me quittant pour se retirer chez lui. (40b)
492.21–3   "I thought," . . . "of . . . quickly."] [*translated from:*] [*paragraph*] Je pensai à la famille du pauvre adjudant. Mais j'y pensais seul. En général, quand les princes passent quelque part, ils passent trop vite. (43b)
494.3–4   "carry out," . . . "the . . . consequences,"] [*translated from:*] Or, durant quatorze années

que j'ai vécu dans l'armée, ce n'est qu'en elle, et surtout dans les rangs dédaignés et pauvres de l'infanterie, que j'ai retrouvé ces hommes de caractère antique, poussant le sentiment du devoir jusqu'à ses dernières conséquences, n'ayant ni remords de l'obéissance ni honte de la pauvreté, simples de mœurs et de langage, fiers de la gloire du pays et insouciants de la leur propre, s'enfermant avec plaisir dans leur obscurité, et partageant avec les malheureux le pain noir qu'ils payent de leur sang. (24b)

────── *Stello; ou, Les diables bleus (blue devils)* (1831). *Ibid.*, pp. 225–303.
NOTE: on the title page, above *Stello*, appears "Les consultations du Docteur-Noir."
QUOTED: 497
REFERRED TO: 486, 487, 488, 494–7, 498
497.13–19　Because . . . present:] [*translated from:*] [*paragraph*]—Je crois en moi, parce que je sens au fond de mon cœur une puissance secrète, invisible et indéfinissable, toute pareille à un pressentiment de l'avenir et à une révélation des causes mystérieuses du temps présent. Je crois en moi, parce qu'il n'est dans la nature aucune beauté, aucune grandeur, aucune harmonie qui ne me cause un frisson prophétique, qui ne porte l'émotion profonde dans mes entrailles, et ne gonfle mes paupières par des larmes toutes divines et inexplicables. Je crois fermement en une vocation ineffable qui m'est donnée, et j'y crois, à cause de la pitié sans bornes que m'inspirent les hommes, mes compagnons en misère, et aussi à cause du désir que je me sens de leur tendre la main et de les élever sans cesse par des paroles de commisération et d'amour. (232b) [*Mill moves Vigny's first sentence to third place in his translation*]

VILLIERS, CHARLES PELHAM. Referred to: 79 (*78*), 129 (*128*), 131 (*130*), *132*

VILLIERS, GEORGE. *The Rehearsal*. London: Dring, 1672.
QUOTED: 397
397.9　"because he dare."] I drink, I huff, I strut, look big and stare; / And all this I can do, because I dare. (38)

VILLIERS, GEORGE WILLIAM FREDERICK (4th Earl of Clarendon). Referred to: 131 (*130*), *132*

VILLIERS, THOMAS HYDE. Referred to: 79 (*78*), 131 (*130*), *132*

VIRGIL (Publius Virgilius Maro).
NOTE: the reference is to Virgil as "a second-hand Homer."
REFERRED TO: 532

────── *Aeneid*. In *Virgil* (Latin and English). Trans. H. Rushton Fairclough. 2 vols. London: Heinemann; New York: Putnam's Sons, 1922, Vol. I, pp. 240–570 (Bks. I–VI), and Vol. II, pp. 2–364 (Bks. VII–XII).
NOTE: this ed. cited for ease of reference. The reference at p. 532 is to the story of Dido.
QUOTED: 81 (*80*), 103 (*102*)
REFERRED TO: 15 (*14*), 532, *560, 586*
81.20　*haud passibus æquis*] haec fatus latos umeros subiectaque colla / veste super fulvique insternor pelle leonis, / succedoque oneri; dextrae se parvus Iulus / implicuit sequiturque patrem non passibus aequis; / pone subit coniunx. (I, 342; II, 721–5)
103.29　*quorum pars magna fui*] "Infandum, regina, iubes renovare dolorem, / Troianas ut opes et lamentabile regnum / eruerint Danai, quaeque ipse miserrima vidi / et quorum pars magna fui. (I, 294; II, 3–6)

────── *Bucolics*. See *Eclogues*.

────── *Eclogues*. In *Virgil* (Latin and English). Trans. H. Rushton Fairclough. 2 vols. London: Heinemann; New York: Putnam's Sons, 1922, Vol. I, pp. 2–76.
NOTE: this ed. cited for ease of reference. Mill refers to the *Eclogues* under their other title, *Bucolics*.
REFERRED TO: 15 (*14*), *560*

——— *Georgics. Ibid.*, Vol. I, pp. 80–236.
NOTE: this ed. cited for ease of reference.
REFERRED TO: 532, *572*

VOLTAIRE, FRANÇOIS MARIE AROUET.
NOTE: the reference at p. *487* is to Voltaire's tragedies; that at p. *570* is to his dramas.
REFERRED TO: 59 (*58*), 119 (*118*), 213 (*212*), 320–1, 372, 487, 487n, *570*

——— *Dictionnaire philosophique* (1764).
NOTE: the reference being general, no ed. is cited; it appears as Vols. XXXIII–XXXVIII in *Œuvres complètes*, 66 vols. (Paris: Renouard, 1817–25), which is in SC.
REFERRED TO: *110*

——— *Essais sur les mœurs et l'esprit des nations, et sur les principaux faits de l'histoire, depuis Charlemagne jusqu'à Louis XIII* (1756). In *Œuvres complètes*, Vols. XIII–XVI.
REFERRED TO: *569*

——— *La pucelle d'Orléans* (1755). *Ibid.*, Vol. IX.
REFERRED TO: 320

WAKEFIELD, EDWARD GIBBON. Referred to: 225 (*224*)

WALLACE, WILLIAM.
NOTE: the reference at p. *566* is to an unidentified treatise on trigonometry.
REFERRED TO: 21, *566*

——— "Conic Sections," *Encyclopaedia Britannica*, 4th ed. (1810), Vol. VI, pp. 519–48 (+ 92 figures).
REFERRED TO: *563, 566*

——— "Fluxions," *Edinburgh Encyclopaedia*, Vol. IX, Pt. 2, pp. 382–467.
REFERRED TO: *566*

——— "Geometry," *ibid.*, Vol. X, Pt. 1, pp. 185–240.
REFERRED TO: *562*

WALPOLE, SPENCER HORATIO. Referred to: 278

WARBURTON, HENRY. Referred to: 203

WARE, WILLIAM. *Letters of Lucius Manlius Piso from Palmyra, to His Friend, Marcus Curtius, at Rome. Now First Translated and Published.* 2 vols. New York and Boston: Francis, 1837.
REVIEWED: 431–61
QUOTED: 440, 440–1, 441–2, 444, 444–5, 445, 446, 446–7, 448–9, 449, 449–50, 450, 450–1, 451, 451–7, 457–8
440.1 The city] [*no paragraph*] Flanked by hills of considerable elevation on the East, the city (I, 21)
440.1 plain as] plain below as (I, 21)
440.2 South. It] South. This immense plain was all one vast and boundless city. It (I, 21)
440.2 Rome. . . . The] Rome. Yet I knew very well that it could not be—that it was not. And it was some time before I understood the true character of the scene before me, so as to separate the city from the country, and the country from the city, which here wonderfully interpenetrate each other, and so confound and deceive the observer. For the (I, 21–2)
440.7 city. I] city. Those which lay before me I was ready to believe were the Elysian Fields. I (I, 22)
440.8 gods. They] gods. Certainly they (I, 22)
440.9 earthborn. The] earth-born. There was a central point, however, which chiefly fixed my attention, where the (I, 22)

440.11   boast. On] boast. [*3-sentence omission*] On (I, 22)
440.13   describe—all, as] describe. These buildings, as (I, 22)
440.14   city, either] city, being all either (I, 22)
440.14–15   and everywhere] and being every where (I, 23)
440.15   interspersed with] interspersed, as I have already said, with (I, 23)
440.15–16   palm-trees. A flood] palm trees, perfectly filled and satisfied my sense of beauty, and made me feel for the moment, as if in such a scene I should love to dwell, and there end my days. [*1-page omission*] This rendered every object so much the more beautiful; for a flood (I, 23, 24)
440.18   gorgeousness agreeing] gorgeousness altogether beyond any thing I ever saw before, and agreeing (I, 24)
440.18   magnificence. . . . Not] magnificence. It was seen under the right aspect. Not (I, 24)
440.24   were magnificent] were particularly magnificent (I, 24)
440.28–9   entered. . . . [*paragraph*] [*line space added in this edition*] Everything] entered. [*ellipsis indicates 29-page omission*] [*no paragraph*] Then every thing (I, 24, 53)
440.29   Everything bears a] [*no paragraph*] Then every thing wears a (I, 53)
440.32   gay: the] gay. The (I, 53)
440.35   merchants. Then] merchants—altogether present a more brilliant assemblage of objects than I suppose any other city can boast. Then (I, 53)
440.40–1   conceive this] conceive, I say, this (I, 53)
440.46   Upon] [*no paragraph*] Upon (I, 54)
441.16   them. Here] them, and pursuing their various avocations, for which this building offers a common and convenient ground. Here (I, 55)
441.42   lulled] dulled (I, 59) [*treated as typographical error in this ed.*]
441.43–4   toil. . . . [*paragraph*] "We] toil.' [*paragraph*] So saying, and pausing a moment only to give some necessary directions to the pupils, who were stationed at their tasks throughout the long apartment, telling them to wait for the show till it should pass by the shop, and not think to imitate their master in all his ways—saying these things in a half earnest and half playful manner—we crossed the street, and soon reached the level roof, well protected by a marble breastwork, of the building he had pointed out. [*paragraph*] 'We (I, 59)
442.5   diamonds. As] diamonds. [*3-sentence omission*] As (I, 60)
442.6   escort, we returned] escort, then we again changed our position, and returned (I, 60)
442.21   towards] toward (I, 61)
442.23   cannot, even at this time, speak] cannot, at this time, even speak (I, 61)
442.24   manners] manner (I, 61)
442.39–40   countenance! But] countenance! What a clear and far-sighted spirit looks out of those eyes! But (I, 62)
444.1–2   "Why . . . hazard . . . for] [*paragraph*] 'But,' said Julia, in her soft persuasive voice whose very tones were enough to change the harshest sentiment to music, 'why . . . hazard the certain good we now enjoy, . . . for what at best is but (I, 93)
444.5   "Julia, as] "Julia,' replied the queen, 'as (I, 93)
444.27   Cicero. Let] Cicero. It was but in another way. All greatness is born of ambition. Let (II, 26)
444.32   limits] limit (II, 27)
444.39–40   and my remoter] and remoter (II, 27)
445.5   friends—it] friends. It (II, 28)
445.13   seat—I] seat. I (II, 28)
445.31   "to] It was to (I, 138)
445.38   now,] Zabdas now (I, 139)
446.1   in] For, in (I, 139)
446.28   hers] her's (I, 141)
446.43   was] were (I, 142)
447.8   afterwards] afterward (I, 142)
447.28   skulking] sulkily (I, 143)
447.34   apprehension] apprehensions (I, 143)
448.12   "Ye . . . doubtless, [says Isaac,] of] [*no paragraph*] Ye . . . doubtless, of (II, 45)
448.34   into dust] into the dust (II, 46)
449.10   "Roman, [says she,] I] [*no paragraph*] Roman, I (II, 32)

449.12   since the day] since that day (II, 32)
449.14   kingdom . . . . How] kingdom. [*ellipsis indicates 7-sentence omission*] How (II, 32–3)
449.16   for the country] for their country (II, 33)
449.18   steady] ready (II, 33)
449.20–1 unity? . . . The] unity? [*Mill moves back 1 page, continuing with material that precedes the beginning of this quotation, and omitting one intervening sentence*] The (II, 33, 32)
449.21   thrones. It] thrones. But the seat is not without its thorns. It (II, 32)
449.22   or with] or charged with (II, 32)
449.30   returned, [says Piso to his correspondent,] from] returned from (II, 39)
450.14   if, indeed, it was to] if it was indeed to (II, 41)
450.18   opening into] opening on into (II, 41)
450.28   Hormisdas,"] Hormisdas, is that upon which I and my people dwell.' (II, 33)
450.34   city was] city itself was (II, 75)
450.36   army. . . . The] army. There we stood, joined by others, awaiting her arrival—for she had not yet left the palace. We had not stood long, before the (II, 75)
450.40   horse. She] horse, advancing at her usual speed toward the pavilion. She (II, 75)
450.42–3 empire. . . . [*paragraph*] The] empire. [*ellipsis indicates 5-sentence omission (including a full paragraph)*] The (II, 75)
450.43   [*paragraph*] The object] [*no paragraph*] The object (II, 75)
451.3   profusion over all its] profusion all over its (II, 76)
451.12–13 steel. . . . [*paragraph*] No] steel. [*ellipsis indicates 2-paragraph omission*] [*paragraph*] No (II, 76–7)
451.24   all: "Long] all. 'Long (II, 78)
451.36   entered the tent [it is Zenobia's secretary who speaks] the] entered, the (II, 165)
451.37   of the army] of his army (II, 165–6)
451.43   of] if (II, 166)
452.34   different. Then there could] different. There then could (II, 168)
452.36   Gallienus and Balista] Gallienus, Balista (II, 168)
452.45   not only of Palmyra, but] not of Palmyra only, but (II, 168)
453.8   all: it] all. It (II, 169)
453.22   that beat] that which beat (II, 169)
453.26   known through the whole world] known throughout the world (II, 170)
454.40   me; I] me. I (II, 172)
454.47   her's] hers (II, 173) [*treated as typographical error in this ed.*]
455.2   swell] dilate (II, 173)
455.14   ears; and] ears. And (II, 174)
455.25   ears] ear (II, 174)
456.23   that] who (II, 176)
456.38   plains—it] plains. It (II, 177)
456.45   were] are (II, 177)
458.3   Emperor] conqueror (II, 246)
458.6   in] with (II, 246)
458.44   crossed] coursed (II, 248)

WARREN, JOSIAH. *Equitable Commerce: A New Development of Principles, as Substitutes for Laws and Governments, for the Harmonious Adjustment and Regulation of the Pecuniary, Intellectual, and Moral Intercourse of Mankind. Proposed as Elements of New Society*. Ed. Stephen Pearl Andrews. New York: Fowlers and Wells, 1852.
NOTE: this is an expanded version of a work first issued in 1846; the page reference given is illustrative, the phrase appearing frequently in the Warrenites' publications. It also appears, for example, in a paper that Mill likely read, William Pare, "On 'Equitable Villages' in America"; see *Report of the Twenty-fifth Meeting of the British Association for the Advancement of Science* (London: Murray, 1856), p. 184 (Statistical Section).
QUOTED: 260
REFERRED TO: 261

260.31–2 "the Sovereignty of the Individual,"] It [the true basis for society] is FREEDOM to differ in all things, or the SOVEREIGNTY OF EVERY INDIVIDUAL. (26)

WATSON, ROBERT. *The History of the Reign of Philip II, King of Spain.* 2 vols. London: Strahan and Cadell; Edinburgh: Balfour and Creech, 1777.
NOTE: at p. 11 (*10*) Mill refers specifically to the defence of the Knights of Malta (Vol. I, pp. 127–60; Bk. VI), and to the defence of the revolted provinces of the Netherlands (see esp. Vol. I, p. 271–Vol. II, p. 72; Bks. X–XIV).
REFERRED TO: 11 (*10*), 17 (*16*), *554, 583*

———— and WILLIAM THOMSON. *The History of the Reign of Philip III, King of Spain.* London: Robinson, *et al.*, 1783.
NOTE: the first four books are by Watson; the final two by Thomson. The 2nd ed., 2 vols. (London: Robinson, *et al.*, 1786), is in SC.
REFERRED TO: 11 (*10*), 17 (*16*), *554, 583*

WEBER, KARL MARIA VON. Referred to: 149 (*148*)

———— *Oberon; or, The Elf-King's Oath.*
NOTE: the opera, first performed in England at Covent Garden on 12 Apr., 1826, was published (libretto by James Robinson Planché) London: Hunt and Clarke, 1826.
REFERRED TO: 149 (*148*)

WELLESLEY, ARTHUR (Duke of Wellington).
NOTE: the reference is in a quotation from Jeffrey's "Madame de Staël," *q.v.*
REFERRED TO: 317

WELLINGTON, DUKE OF. See Wellesley.

WEST, JOHN. *Elements of Mathematics. Comprehending Geometry, Conic Sections, Mensuration, Spherics. Illustrated with 30 copper-plates. For the Use of Schools.* Edinburgh: Creech; London: Longman, *et al.*, 1784.
REFERRED TO: *559–60*

The Westminster Review. Referred to: 93–103 (*92–102*), *110*, 115 (*114*), 121 (*120*), 123 (*122*), *132*, 135 (*134*), 137 (*136*), 207 (*206*), 209 (*208*), 227 (*226*), *234n, 264, 268, 271, 588*; see also *London Review.*

WHATELY, RICHARD. *Elements of Logic. Comprising the Substance of the Article in the Encyclopaedia Metropolitana: with Additions, etc.* London: Mawman, 1826.
NOTE: in SC. First appeared in the *Encyclopaedia Metropolitana* (complete version, 1845), Vol. I (also identified as "Pure Sciences, Vol. 1"), pp. 193–240.
REFERRED TO: 99n, 125 (*124*), 189 (*188*), 231

WHEWELL, WILLIAM.
NOTE: the references are generally to Whewell's writings up to 1843.
REFERRED TO: 231 (*230*)

———— *History of the Inductive Sciences.* 3 vols. London: Parker, 1837.
NOTE: the 3rd ed., 3 vols. (London: Parker and Son, 1857), formerly in SC.
REFERRED TO: 215–17 (*214–16*)

———— *Of Induction, with Especial Reference to Mr. J. Stuart Mill's System of Logic.* London: Parker, 1849.
NOTE: Mill gives the date of publication as 1850.
REFERRED TO: 231 (*230*)

———— *The Philosophy of the Inductive Sciences, Founded upon Their History.* 2 vols. London: Parker, 1840.
REFERRED TO: 231 (*230*)

365n.7   *Past* and *future*] "—Past and future, (II, 390) [*Wordsworth is quoting himself from a then unpublished MS*]
365n.9   knowledge;] knowledge—" (I, 374)

———— *The Excursion, Being a Portion of The Recluse, a Poem*. London: Longman, Hurst, Rees, Orme, and Brown, 1814.

NOTE: though the reference at p. 151 (*150*) is almost certainly to this (first) ed., specific citation is of the version in *Poetical Works* (*q.v.*), for consistency of reference. The first reference at p. 428 is in a quotation from Helps.

QUOTED: *594*

REFERRED TO: 151 (*150*), 428

594.28 "The . . . divine;"] Oh! many are the Poets that are sown / By Nature; Men endowd with highest gifts, / The . . . divine, / Yet wanting the accomplishment of Verse / (Which, in the docile season of their youth, / It was denied them to acquire, through lack / Of culture and the inspiring aid of books, / Or haply by a temper too severe, / Or a nice backwardness afraid of shame); / Nor having e'er, as life advanced, been led / By circumstance to take unto the height / The measure of themselves, these favour'd Beings, / All but a scattered few, live out their time, / Husbanding that which they possess within, / And go to the grave, unthought of. (V, 6–7; I, 76–90)

———— "Hail, Zaragoza." In *Poetical Works* (*q.v.*), Vol. III, p. 174.

NOTE: this sonnet, in this ed., is no. XVI of "Sonnets Dedicated to Liberty, Second Part"; in *Poems* (1815), it is no. XIV (Vol. II, p. 240).

REFERRED TO: 467

———— "Ode. Intimations of Immortality from Recollections of Early Childhood." *Ibid.*, Vol. IV, pp. 346–55.

REFERRED TO: 153 (*152*)

———— *Poems by William Wordsworth, Including Lyrical Ballads, and the Miscellaneous Pieces by the Author. With Additional Poems, a New Preface, and a Supplementary Essay*. 2 vols. London: Longman, Hurst, Rees, Orme, and Brown, 1815.

NOTE: another vol., *Poems by William Wordsworth: Including The River Duddon; Vaudracour and Julia; Peter Bell; The Waggoner; A Thanksgiving Ode; and Miscellaneous Pieces*, was added, as Vol. III, in 1820.

REFERRED TO: 151–3 (*150–2*)

———— *The Poetical Works of William Wordsworth*. 5 vols. London: Longman, Rees, Orme, Brown, and Green, 1827.

NOTE: this ed., which is in SC, is used for consistency of reference wherever possible. All references to these volumes are given under the poems or essays specifically cited. For other volumes referred to by Mill, see *Poems* (1815), *The Excursion*, and "The Vaudois."

———— "Preface to the Second Edition of the Lyrical Ballads." In *Poetical Works* (*q.v.*), Vol. IV, pp. 357–89.

NOTE: this ed. used for consistency of reference. The Preface first appeared in the 2nd ed. of *Lyrical Ballads*, 2 vols. (London: Longman and Rees, 1800), but Mill's wording at p. 344 indicates that he is using a later version. The quotation at p. 417 gives the sense but not the exact language of the passage cited.

QUOTED: 417

REFERRED TO: 151 (*150*), 344, 358, 362n

———— "Resolution and Independence." *Ibid.*, Vol. II, pp. 125–31.

QUOTED: 494

494.26–7 the . . . soul, who . . . pride] I thought of Chatterton, the . . . Soul that . . . Pride; / Of Him who walked in glory and in joy / Following his plough, along the mountain-side: / By our own spirits are we deified: / We Poets in our youth begin in gladness; / But thereof comes in the end despondency and madness. (II, 127; 44–50)

—— Sonnet XXXIV, "After Thought," *The River Duddon. Ibid.*, Vol. IV, p. 156.
NOTE: Sonnet XXXIII, "Conclusion," in *Poems (q.v.)*, Vol. III, p. 35. In *Poetical Works* the whole sonnet is in italics.
QUOTED: *594*
594.30 "To feel . . . know."] *Enough, if something from our hands have power / To live, and act, and serve the future hour; / And if, as tow'rd the silent tomb we go, / Through love, through hope, and faith's transcendent dower, / We feel . . . know.* (IV, 156; 10–14)

—— "To B. R. Haydon, Esq." ("Miscellaneous Sonnets, Part First," Sonnet XLII). *Ibid.*, Vol. II, p. 296.
NOTE: the same words are quoted in both places, the first time without quotation marks.
QUOTED: 343, 355
343.11 the instrument of words] High is our calling, Friend!—Creative Art / (Whether the instrument of words she use; / Or pencil pregnant with ethereal hues,) / Demands the service of a mind and heart, / Though sensitive, yet, in their weakest part, / Heroically fashioned—to infuse / Faith in the whispers of the lonely Muse, / While the whole world seems adverse to desert. (II, 296; 1–8)

—— "The Vaudois." In *Yarrow Revisited, and Other Poems*. London: Longman, Rees, Orme, Brown, Green, and Longman, and Moxon, 1835.
NOTE: in SC. The sonnet (which is not in *Poetical Works*, 1827) was later included in collections of Wordsworth's *Ecclesiastical Sonnets*.
REFERRED TO: 467

XENOPHON. *The Anabasis of Cyrus*. In *Hellenica, Anabasis, Symposium, and Apology*. Trans. Carleton L. Brownson and O. J. Todd. 3 vols. London: Heinemann; New York: Putnam's Sons, 1918, 1921, 1922, Vol. II, pp. 229–493, and Vol. III, pp. 1–371.
NOTE: a 9-vol. ed. of Xenophon's works, ed. Thomas Hutchinson (Glasgow: Foulis, 1768), was formerly in SC.
REFERRED TO: 9 (*8*), *552–3*

—— *Cyropaedia*. Trans. Walter Miller. 2 vols. London: Heinemann; New York: Macmillan, 1914.
NOTE: see Xenophon, *Anabasis*, above.
REFERRED TO: 9 (*8*), *553*

—— *Hellenics*. In *Hellenica, Anabasis, Symposium, and Apology*, Vol. I and Vol. II, pp. 1–227.
NOTE: see Xenophon, *Anabasis*, above.
REFERRED TO: 15 (*14*), *561*

—— *Memorabilia*. In *Memorabilia and Oeconomicus*. Trans. E. C. Marchant. London: Heinemann; New York: Putnam's Sons, 1923, pp. 1–525.
NOTE: also referred to as *Memorials of Socrates*. See Xenophon, *Anabasis*, above. The reference at p. 49 (*48*) is to the "Choice of Hercules" (Prodicus' essay, "On Heracles," as given by Xenophon, Bk. II, chap. i, ll. 21–34).
REFERRED TO: 9 (*8*), 24n, 49 (*48*), *553*

—— *Memorials of Socrates*. See the preceding entry.

YORK, DUKE OF. See Frederick Augustus.

YOUNG, ARTHUR. *Travels during the Years 1787, 1788, and 1789. Undertaken More Particularly with a View of Ascertaining the Cultivation, Wealth, Resources, and Natural Prosperity, of the Kingdom of France*. 2 vols. Bury St. Edmunds: Richardson, 1792, 1794.
REFERRED TO: *571*

YOUNG, R. E. (Mrs.). *Views in the Pyrenees: with Descriptions by the Author of the Sketches*. London: the author, *et al.*, 1831.

NOTE: the work, dedicated to the Duchess of Kent, contains thirty-two pages of text and ten plates engraved by Edward Finden, drawn by Henry Gastineau (nos. I, III, IV, VI, IX, and X), David Cox (II), Young herself (V and VII), and P. H. Rogers (VIII), from sketches by Young (actually no sketch is mentioned on plate VI). The text is divided into two "numbers" (though the pagination is continuous), in the first of which are included "General Survey of the Pyrenees," and "Bagnères de Bigorre, and the Valley of Campan," and in the second, "The Pass of Tourmalet; with Barèges and Its Environs."

REVIEWED: 393

ZENO. Referred to: 337, 532

ZENOBIA.

NOTE: some references at pp. 438–9 are in quotations from Gibbon and Pollio; one at p. 457 is also in a quotation from Gibbon.

REFERRED TO: 435, 438–9, 445, 457, 458–9, 460

PARLIAMENTARY PAPERS AND PETITIONS

"Petition of the Merchants of London," *Journals of the House of Commons*, LXXV, 410 (6 July, 1820).

NOTE: presented on 6 July, the petition was referred to the Select Committee on Foreign Trade on 10 July, 1820 (see *ibid.*, p. 435).

REFERRED TO: 101–3 (*100–2*)

"A Bill to Promote the Observance of the Lord's Day," 7 William IV (4 May, 1837), *Parliamentary Papers*, 1837, III, 351–60.

NOTE: the reference is to Roebuck's losing his parliamentary seat for Bath in 1837 because of his opposition to Sabbatarian bills, of which the one cited was the most recent. He spoke against this bill on its Second Reading (moved by Sir Andrew Agnew) on 7 June, 1837 (see *Parliamentary Debates*, 3rd ser., Vol. 38, cols. 1229–34). Similar bills had been presented on 20 Mar., 1833 (see *Parliamentary Papers*, 1833, III, 561–72), 11 Apr. and 8 May, 1834 (*ibid.*, 1834, Vol. IV, pp. 1–11, and 13–20), and 21 Apr., 1836 (*ibid.*, 1836, Vol. IV, pp. 405–14).

REFERRED TO: *158*

"Report on the Affairs of British North America, from the Earl of Durham," *Parliamentary Papers*, 1839, XVII, 1–690.

NOTE: better known as the Durham Report. See also Lambton, Buller, and Wakefield.

REFERRED TO: 223–5 (*224*)

"A Bill Further to Amend the Laws Relating to the Representation of the People in England and Wales," 17 Victoria (16 Feb., 1854), *Parliamentary Papers*, 1854, V, 375–418.

NOTE: the Bill was not enacted. The reference is to Mill's having first drafted *Thoughts on Parliamentary Reform* "on the occasion of one of the abortive Reform Bills."

REFERRED TO: 261

"A Bill to Amend the Laws Relating to the Representation of the People in England and Wales, and to Facilitate the Registration and Voting of Electors," 22 Victoria (28 Feb., 1859), *Parliamentary Papers*, 1859 (Session 1), II, 649–715.

NOTE: the Bill was not enacted.

REFERRED TO: 261

"A Bill to Extend the Right of Voting at Elections of Members of Parliament in England and Wales," 29 Victoria (13 Mar., 1866), *Parliamentary Papers*, 1866, V, 87–100.
NOTE: the Bill ("Gladstone's Reform Bill") was not enacted.
REFERRED TO: 275, 278

"A Bill Further to Amend the Law Relating to the Tenure and Improvement of Land in Ireland," 29 Victoria (30 Apr., 1866), *Parliamentary Papers*, 1866, V, 353–64.
NOTE: the Bill, to which Mill refers at p. 280 as Fortescue's Bill, was not enacted. See also J. S. Mill, Speech on the Tenure and Improvement of Land (Ireland) Bill.
REFERRED TO: 279, 280

"Petition for Extension [of the Elective Franchise] to All Householders without Distinction of Sex" (Public Petition no. 8501, presented 7 July, 1866), *Reports of Select Committee on Public Petitions*, 1866, p. 697, and Appendix, p. 305.
NOTE: presented by Mill to the House of Commons.
REFERRED TO: 285

"A Bill for the Amendment of the Law Relating to Extradition," 29 & 30 Victoria (26 July, 1866), *Parliamentary Papers*, 1866, III, 39–42.
NOTE: the Bill was not enacted.
REFERRED TO: 283

"First Report from the Select Committee on Metropolitan Local Government, etc.," *Parliamentary Papers*, 1866, XIII, 171–315. "Second Report," *ibid.*, XIII, 317–713.
REFERRED TO: 276

"A Bill to Promote the Improvement of Land by Occupying Tenants in Ireland," 30 Victoria (18 Feb., 1867), *Parliamentary Papers*, 1867, VI, 385–98.
NOTE: the Bill was not enacted.
REFERRED TO: 279

"A Bill for the Better and More Effectually Securing the Use of Certain Royal Parks and Gardens for the Enjoyment and Recreation of Her Majesty's Subjects," 30 Victoria (3 May, 1867), *Parliamentary Papers*, 1867, IV, 63–6.
NOTE: the Bill was not enacted.
REFERRED TO: 279

"Report from the Select Committee on Extradition; together with the Proceedings of the Committee, Minutes of Evidence, and Appendix," *Parliamentary Papers*, 1867–68, VII, 129–336.
REFERRED TO: 283

STATUTES

BRITISH

37 Geo. III, c. 123. See 57 Geo. III, c. 19.

52 Geo. III, c. 104. See 57 Geo. III, c. 19.

57 Geo. III, c. 19. An Act for the More Effectually Preventing Seditious Meetings and Assemblies (31 Mar., 1817).
NOTE: the reference is specifically to §25, concerning unlawful oaths and engagements, which cites 37 Geo. III, c. 123, An Act for More Effectually Preventing the Administering or Taking of

Unlawful Oaths (19 July, 1797), and 52 Geo. III, c. 104, An Act to Render More Effectual an Act, Passed in the Thirty Seventh Year of His Present Majesty, for Preventing the Administering or Taking Unlawful Oaths (9 July, 1812).
REFERRED TO: *600–1*

60 George III & 1 George IV, c. 1. An Act to Prevent the Training of Persons to the Use of Arms, and to the Practice of Military Evolutions and Exercise (11 Dec., 1819).
NOTE: the reference is to the "Six Acts," of which the above was the first.
REFERRED TO: 101 (*100*)

60 George III & 1 George IV, c. 2. An Act to Authorise Justices of the Peace, in Certain Disturbed Counties, to Seize and Detain Arms Collected or Kept for Purposes Dangerous to the Public Peace; to Continue in Force until the Twenty Fifth Day of March 1822 (18 Dec., 1819).
NOTE: the reference is to the "Six Acts," of which the above was the second.
REFERRED TO: 101 (*100*)

60 George III & 1 George IV, c. 4. An Act to Prevent Delay in the Administration of Justice in Cases of Misdemeanor (23 Dec., 1819).
NOTE: the reference is to the "Six Acts," of which the above was the third.
REFERRED TO: 101 (*100*)

60 George III & 1 George IV, c. 6. An Act for More Effectually Preventing Seditious Meetings and Assemblies; to Continue in Force until the End of the Session of Parliament Next after Five Years from the Passing of the Act (24 Dec., 1819).
NOTE: the reference is to the "Six Acts," of which the above was the fourth.
REFERRED TO: 101 (*100*)

60 George III & 1 George IV, c. 8. An Act for the More Effectual Prevention and Punishment of Blasphemous and Seditious Libels (30 Dec., 1819).
NOTE: the reference is to the "Six Acts," of which the above was the fifth.
REFERRED TO: 101 (*100*)

60 George III & 1 George IV, c. 9. An Act to Subject Certain Publications to the Duties of Stamps upon Newspapers, and to Make Other Regulations for Restraining the Abuses Arising from the Publication of Blasphemous and Seditious Libels (30 Dec., 1819).
NOTE: the reference is to the "Six Acts," of which the above was the sixth.
REFERRED TO: 101 (*100*)

1 & 2 George IV, c. 47. An Act to Exclude the Borough of Grampound, in the County of Cornwall, from Sending Burgesses to Serve in Parliament; and to Enable the County of York to Send Two Additional Knights to Serve in Parliament, in Lieu Thereof (8 June, 1821).
REFERRED TO: 119

2 & 3 William IV, c. 45. An Act to Amend the Representation of the People in England and Wales (7 June, 1832).
NOTE: the First Reform Act.
REFERRED TO: 179 (*178*), *180*, 185 (*184*), *202*

3 William IV, c. 4. An Act for the More Effectual Suppression of Local Disturbances and Dangerous Associations in Ireland (2 Apr., 1833).
REFERRED TO: 203 (*202*)

4 & 5 William IV, c. 76. An Act for the Amendment and Better Administration of the Laws Relating to the Poor in England and Wales (14 Aug., 1834).
REFERRED TO: 203

1 Victoria, c. 9. An Act to Make Temporary Provision for the Government of Lower Canada (10 Feb., 1838).
REFERRED TO: 203 (*202*)

10 Victoria, c. 31. An Act to Make Further Provision for the Relief of the Destitute Poor in Ireland (8 June, 1847).
REFERRED TO: 243 (*242*)

29 Victoria, c. 1. An Act to Empower the Lord Lieutenant or Other Chief Governor or Governors of Ireland to Apprehend, and Detain for a Limited Time, Such Persons as He or They Shall Suspect of Conspiring against Her Majesty's Person and Government (17 Feb., 1866).
REFERRED TO: 277

29 Victoria, c. 2. An Act to Amend the Law Relating to Contagious or Infectious Diseases in Cattle and Other Animals (20 Feb., 1866).
REFERRED TO: 276n–7n

30 & 31 Victoria, c. 102. An Act Further to Amend the Laws Relating to the Representation of the People in England and Wales (15 Aug., 1867).
NOTE: the Second Reform Act. The references at pp. 284–5 are to Mill's participation in the Reform Bill debates. The first concerns his proposed amendment and speech for personal representation (*Parliamentary Debates*, 3rd ser., Vol. 187, cols. 1343–56, 1362 [29 May, 1867]), which he did not bring to a division; the second concerns his speech in support of Robert Lowe's amendment for cumulative voting (*ibid.*, Vol. 188, cols. 1102–7 [5 July, 1867]); the third refers to his amendment for the enfranchisement of women on the same basis as men (*ibid.*, Vol. 187, cols. 817–29 [20 May, 1867]), which was defeated by a vote of 196 to 73.
REFERRED TO: 275, 277, 278, 283, 284–5, 288–9

31 & 32 Victoria, c. 125. An Act for Amending the Laws Relating to Election Petitions, and Providing More Effectually for the Prevention of Corrupt Practices at Parliamentary Elections (31 July, 1868).
REFERRED TO: 283

32 & 33 Victoria, c. 99. An Act for the More Effectual Prevention of Crime (11 Aug., 1869).
REFERRED TO: 286n

33 & 34 Victoria, c. 46. An Act to Amend the Law Relating to the Occupation and Ownership of Land in Ireland (1 Aug., 1870).
REFERRED TO: 280

33 & 34 Victoria, c. 52. An Act for Amending the Law Relating to the Extradition of Criminals (9 Aug., 1870).
REFERRED TO: 283

33 & 34 Victoria, c. 75. An Act to Provide for Public Elementary Education in England and Wales (9 Aug., 1870).
NOTE: the reference is to clause 37 of the Act.
REFERRED TO: 284

FRENCH

Loi sur les élections. Bulletin 379, No. 8910 (29 juin, 1820), *Bulletin des lois du royaume de France*, 7 sér., X, 1001–6.
NOTE: Mill was in France, living with the Samuel Benthams, when this law was passed, and commented in his letters to his father on the excitement it caused.
REFERRED TO: 301

Index

life, 489; worst parts of, 513; and moral and
political systems, *590*; Bentham's limited
understanding of, *590*; JM's view of, *591*,
592, *594*; sexual equality and laws of, *622*
Hundred Days, Napoleon's, 472
Hyde Park, 37 (*36*), 278
Hypotheses, Comte's influence on JSM's treatment of, 255n

IMAGERY, poetic: description and, 347; in painting and architecture, 354n; and definition of
poet, 361–2; Shelley's, 360, 363; Tennyson's, 399–401, 408, 414–15, 416
Imagination: and idea of wickedness, 42n;
physical relation between sexes and perversion of, 109 (*108*); Benthamites undervalue,
115 (*114*); cultivation of feelings through,
157 (*156*); HTM's, 195 (*194*, *619*); and discrimination of truths, 332, 417; genius and,
332, 333; training of, 338; poetry and, 345–
6, 347, 414; association and, 357; Shelley's,
360; Junius Redivivus lacks high order of,
376, 377; Tennyson's, 397, 415; source of
vivid, 413n; meaning of creative, 415n;
Ware's application of, 434; old romances and
youthful, 460; works of, 479; French historical literature and, 480–1; Macaulay's faculty
of, 526
Impossibility, rules of evidence and Bentham's
theory of, 117 (*116*)
Improbability, rules of evidence and Bentham's
theory of, 117 (*116*)
Improvement: Bentham's doctrines and, 69–71
(*68–70*), 227 (*226*); John Austin's concern
for, 77 (*76*), 185 (*184*); *Morning Chronicle*'s
service to, 91 (*90*); JM's confidence in progress of, 105 (*104*); and doctrine of association, 111 (*110*); and effect of educated intellect, 113–15 (*112–14*); JSM and promotion
of, 137 (*136*), 193 (*192*), *615n*; and sources
of happiness, 145 (*144*); analysis as condition
of, 147 (*146*); and sympathetic and imaginative pleasure, 151 (*150*); old political economy and conditions of, *168n*, 175 (*174*), 239
(*238*); Saint-Simonians and, 175 (*174*, *614*);
and political institutions, 177 (*176*); 373; English aristocracy and, 179 (*178*); in Prussia
and England, 185 (*184*); doctrine of intuition
impedes, 233 (*232*); lack of in England, 237
(*236*), 245 (*244*), 267; ideal of ultimate, 239–
41 (*238–40*); question of prospects of, 247;
and position of women, 253n (*252*), *621*;
economic generalizations and progress of,
257; HTM and speculations on, 257n; great
stumbling block to, 270; party system and,

315; *ER* on prospects of, 316, 318; *ER* on war
and, 316–17; *ER* and, 319, 320; concern of
Junius Redivivus for, 373; poetry and art as
instruments of, 376; and limitation of population, 388, 389. *See also* Progress
India: JM's history of, 7 (*6*), 9 (*8*), *10n*, *16*, 27–9
(*26–8*), 213, *593*; and JM as employee of
East India Company, 29 (*28*); Joseph Hume's
return from, 55 (*54*); JSM's responsibilities
respecting, 83–5 (*82–4*), 87, 247–9; and
JSM's view of international morality, 263;
administration of land in, 387; Palmyra and,
437. *See also* East India Company
India House. *See* East India Company
Individuality: consequences of losing sight of
value of, 221; doctrine of rights of, 260; in
creations of Radical poet, 468; and ordinances of law and opinion, 469
Induction: method of alien to Roebuck's intellect,
154; nature of process of, 167 (*166*); JSM's
problem with, 191 (*190*); JSM and theory of,
215–17 (*214–16*); Whewell's writings excite
interest in theory of, 231; originality as process of analysis and, 332; Junius Redivivus
on invention and, 386
Infant Schools, 307n
Inference, process of, 355
Inns of Court, 127 (*126*), 129 (*128*)
Institutions: Mitford and popular, 15 (*14*); Demosthenes and Athenian, 23 (*22*); *HBI* and
English, 27–9 (*26–8*), *593*; Bentham's conception of, 69 (*68*); reform of, 87, 103 (*102*),
139 (*138*), *180n*, 245 (*244*); English legal, 91
(*90*); defence in London Debating Society of
existing, *132*; relative nature of questions of,
169 (*168*); choosing political, 177 (*176*);
source of political power under English, 179
(*178*); pledges and democratic, *180n*; good
government and popular, 185 (*184*); doctrine
of intuition and bad, 233 (*232*); cooperative
socialism and form of, 239; selfishness fostered by existing, 241 (*240*); and determination of wages, profits, rent, 255–7; and development of new opinions, 259; organization of and threat to liberty, 260; personal
representation and democratic, 262; discussion in *Representative Government* of organic, 265; American, 267; and inconveniences
of democracy, 288; *ER*'s judgment of
foreign, 307; Montesquieu's admiration of
English, 310n; Junius Redivivus' treatment
of, 373, 383, 384; and political accountability, 375; Abbé de la Mennais and French,
465; Radical poet and established, 468; fall of
bad, 470; Collingwood and English, 493;

election expenses, 273; service in as public duty, 273; JSM's 1865 candidacy for, 273–5; JSM as member of, 275–86; membership of limits JSM's work as author, 287; 1868 dissolution of, 288; Liberals and course pursued by JSM in, 289; need for men such as Bradlaugh in, 289; Liberals in express regret at JSM's defeat, 290; *ER* on public opinion and proceedings of, 294–5; *ER* on executive and, 296; and misgovernment, 296; reforms concerning proposed by Junius Redivivus, 384; Junius Redivivus on payment of members of, 385; Milnes's membership of, 509; conduct of Whigs during first reformed, *602. See also* Parliamentary Reform

Parliamentary Reform: Grote's pamphlet in defence of Radical, 75 (*74*); demand for, 103 (*102*); Marshall as supporter of, 119 (*118*); JM's "Government" as argument for, 165 (*164*); JSM's pamphlet on, 261–2; and personal representation, 262–3, 276, 284, 288, 289; John Austin opposes, 263; JSM speaks in House on, 277–8, 284–5; House of Commons engrossed in subject of, 279. *See also* Parliament, Representation

Party: characteristics of aristocratic opposition, 293, 294; *ER*'s treatment of question of, 313–16; *Junius's Letters* as product of, 381; *Quarterly Review* and, 398; social amelioration and contests of, 489. *See also* Conservative party, Liberal party, Radical party, Whigs, Tories

Passion: and analytic habits, 143 (*142*); music and, 350, 499; motives and, 363; poetry and, 411, 468, 498, 499; characteristic of strong, *621–2*

Patent rights, 385, 386

Patricians, 17 (*16*), *543n*

Patriotism, *ER* on fostering of, 324

Pau, 59 (*58*)

Peasant proprietors, JSM's articles in *Morning Chronicle* on, 243 (*242*)

Peninsular War, *603*

People's Editions of JSM's works, 272

Periodicals: JM's dependence on writing for, 7 (*6*); JM's analysis of, 95 (*94*); problem of anonymous authorship in, 370; provide writers with access to public, 372; treatment of foreign countries in English, *599. See also* Newspapers, Press

Persia, 439, 447, 448, 449, 451

Phenomena: analysis of mental, *64n–5n*, 71 (*70*), *590, 595*; modes of treating political, 165 (*164*); chemical and mechanical, 167 (*166*)

Philanthropy, *ER* on, 305

Philology, 287

Philosophers: Greek, 49 (*48*), 335–6, 499; questions of moral and intellectual ascendancy of, 219; *Logic* as challenge to intuition school of, 233 (*232*); some true modern, 338; language of respecting association, 357; and poets, 363–4; Saint-Simonians as, 372; Plato wants kings to be, 373; Junius Redivivus on payment of, 387

Philosophes, 111 (*110*), 213 (*212*)

Philosophic Radicalism: character of group first propagating, 103–11 (*102–10*); in politics and literature, *132*; Roebuck and, *154*; JSM's scheme of conciliating old and new, 209 (*208*); *L&WR* and, 221–3 (*220–2*). *See also* Benthamism, Philosophic Radicals, Utilitarianism

Philosophic Radicals: in London Debating Society, 133 (*132*); in parliament, 203–5 (*202–4*); JSM edits periodical organ of, 207–9 (*206–8*); JM's "Government" as text-book of, *594. See also* Benthamites, Philosophic Radicalism, Utilitarians

Philosophy: study of logic and education of students in, 23 (*22*); Grote's studying of, 75 (*74*); feeling and, 113 (*112*); JSM's reverence for heroes of, 115 (*114*); reaction against 18th-century, 133 (*160*), 227 (*226*); HTM and highest regions of, 195 (*194, 619*); trespassing of Sedgwick into, 209; as instrument to combat prejudice, 233–5 (*232–4*); application of to exigencies of society and progress, 257 (*256*); correspondence addressed to JSM as writer on, 286; JM's contributions to, 287, 535, *590*; *ER* clothes sentimentality in garb of, 325; and framing of new classifications and distinctions, 343–4; poetry and, 363–4; Tennyson must cultivate, 417; wisdom and, 421; and unsystematic truths, 421–2; truth and systems of, 422–3; understanding books of, 428; Vigny and Tocqueville look into world for, 466; Vigny rejects systems of, 487; society's treatment of genius in, 496; and laws of historical evidence, 527; pursuit of in foreign countries, *599. See also* Logic, Metaphysics, Psychology

Physical science: and Macaulay's notion of philosophizing, 165; mode of tracing causes and effects in, 167 (*166*); political science and methods of, 173 (*172, 615*); and theory of induction, 215 (*214*); nature of evidence of, 233 (*232*); teaching of, 338; revolutionized, 338; Junius Redivivus considers applications of, 382; and analysis of complex combina-